5th World Congress on DISASTER MANAGEMENT

5th World Congress on DISASTER MANAGEMENT

Volume 1
DISASTER RISK MANAGEMENT

Edited by

Dr. S. Ananda Babu
President and Convenor
DMICS-WCDM

Routledge
Taylor & Francis Group

LONDON AND NEW YORK

DMICS
Disaster Management, Initiatives and Convergence Society
Envisioning a Disaster Resilient Future

WORLD
CONGRESS ON
DISASTER
MANAGEMENT

First published 2023
by Routledge
4 Park Square, Milton Park, Abingdon, Oxon OX14 4RN

and by Routledge
605 Third Avenue, New York, NY 10158

Routledge is an imprint of the Taylor & Francis Group, an informa business

British Library Cataloguing-in-Publication Data
A catalogue record for this book is available from the British Library

Library of Congress Cataloging-in-Publication Data
A catalog record has been requested for this book

ISBN: 9781032355429 (hbk)
ISBN: 9781003341956 (ebk)

Table of Contents

List of Figures — *ix*

List of Tables — *xv*

Preface — *xvii*

Acknowledgement — *ix*

Part 1: Harnessing Science and Technology for Building Resilience to Disasters

1. **"Information Technology": The Utopian Solution to Achieving Disaster Resilience & Ensuring Disaster Management** — **3**
   Col. Gaurav Bhatia, Arundhati Bhatia, Ranju Bhatia and Abhimanyu Bhatia

2. **Female Frontline Health Workers' and ICT in the COVID-19 Response in India** — **9**
   Krishnan Sneha and Purwar Deepshikha

3. **Co-creating Climate Resilience Technological Solutions for Poor** — **18**
   Siraz Hirani

4. **Exploring the Potential of Solar Energy in Disaster Management and Rescue Operations** — **28**
   Pooja Punetha, Sukriti Sharma and Asad H. Sahir

5. **Harnessing Technology for Disaster Risk Management** — **36**
   Usman, A. Kibon, Bulus, A. Sawa and Ibrahim M. Bako

6. **Technological Advances in the Development of Disaster Response Management Systems and Applications** — **47**
   Amritanjali and Geetanjali Kumari

7. **Reaching Beyond Low Hanging Apelles to Technological Convergence to Combat Disasters Like Desertification** — **53**
   Kavya Kamepalli

8. **Technological Preparedness for Fire Disasters** — **61**
   K. C. Wadhwa

Part 2: Innovations in Construction Technology

9. **A New Fire Safe Design Solution for Reinforced Concrete Beams at Catastrophic Fire Conditions** — **73**
   Banti A. Gedam

10. **Seismic Evaluation of Frictional Damper Developed Using Waste Rubber Tires** — **90**
    Bharati, Amit Goyal and R. Siva Chidambram

11. **Flexural Behaviour of Masonry Wall Strengthened with Waste PET Grid** — **96**
    Dinesh Chandra Pandey, Amit Goyal and R. Siva Chidambram

12. **Numerical Approximation of 3D Heat Conduction in Early Age Mass Concrete Using Crank Nicholson Implicit Finite Difference Method** — **104**
    Ugwuanyi Donald Chidiebere and Okafor Fidelis Onyebuchi

13. **A Study on the Economic Perspective of Utilizing Liquid Tanks as Dynamic Vibration Absorbers in Building Structures** — **115**
    Tanmoy Konar and Aparna (Dey) Ghosh

14. **Smart Shelters for Multi Disasters—A Framework with Cloud Technology and Measurement Devices** — **123**
    K. Sasikala, P. Harikrishna, S. Thamarai Selvi and N. Lakshmanan

15. **A Critical Analysis of Building Codes of Pakistan; Fire Safety Provision 2016** — **138**
    Ahmed Faraz Khan and Ijaz Ahmad

Part 3: Using Artificial Intelligence and Internet of Things for Managing Risks of Disasters

16. **IoT Enabled Manufacturing and Health Care Services: Potentialities and Prospects in India** 147
    Ashok G. Matani and Shamal. K. Doifode

17. **Disasters—A New Setback to be Prepared vis-à-vis Artificial Intelligence** 152
    Nikhil Kaushal and Prerna Prajapati

18. **Application of Artificial Intelligence for Managing Risks of Disasters** 159
    Akanksha Jain and Mudit Saxena

19. **Scalable IOT solutions with the Amazon Echo Flex Model for 3P integrations** 168
    Anil Kumar Bheemaiah

20. **Harnessing Technology for Disaster Risk Management: Internet of Things Applications Towards Mapping of Technologies in Areas of Diagnostics, Testing, Healthcare Delivery Solutions and Equipment Supplies: Challenges and Opportunities in India** 173
    Ashok G. Matani

21. **Latest Advancements in IoT and Sensors Applications in Renewable Energy Systems Optimization** 176
    Ashok G. Matani

Part 4: Application of Remote Sensing, GIS, Drone and UAV for Disaster Risk Management

22. **GIS, Remote Sensing and Drones for Disaster Risk Management** 183
    Venkata Rajgopala Gunturu

23. **Integrating Weather Model & Remote Sensing Indices for Wheat Yield Prediction in Haryana, India** 195
    Manjeet, Anurag, Ram Niwas, Rajeev, Dinesh Tomar, Ram Niwas and S. K. Bansal

24. **Floods, Sandbar Dynamics, and its Impact on Communities: GIS Based Case Studies from Assam, India** 201
    Pulak Das

25. **GIS Based Hazard Mapping and Vulnerability Assessment of Natural Hazards: A Case Study of Rudraprayag, Uttarakhand** 212
    Vaibhav Pundir

26. **Preparedness and Damage Assessment using UAVs for Management of Flood in India** 223
    Rudrashis Majumder, Shuvrangshu Jana, Prathyush P. Menon, Debasish Ghose, N. M. Prusty, Bipasha Mukherjee and Aditi Ghosh

27. **Cyclone Preparedness, Rescue Operations and Damage Assessment using UAVs** 235
    Rudrashis Majumder, Shuvrangshu Jana, Prathyush P. Menon, Debasish Ghose, N. M. Prusty, Bipasha Mukherjee and Aditi Ghosh

Part 5: Application of Remote Sensing, GIS, Drone and UAV for Disaster Risk Management

28. **Analysis of Compensatory Citizen Services from the Disaster Management Institutional Set Up in India** 247
    Devashish De

29. **Assessment for Efficient Achievement of Disaster Resilience in India** 254
    Gargaei M. Chakravarthy

30. **Multi-player Game-based Algorithm Using Set Partitioning for Resource Allocation During Natural Disaster Response** 271
    Rudrashis Majumder and Debasish Ghose

31. **Comparing priorities of Providers and Users with Respect to Disaster Management Strategies** 279
    Rajat Agrawal and Div Jyot Singh

32. **Law and Disaster Management: A Critical Understanding** 285
    Awekta Verma

33. **Governance of Disaster Management: Lessons Learnt and a Roadmap to Avert a Future Chamoli Like Disaster** 292
    Gopal Vasudeo Wamane

34. **Disaster Risks and Management In India: A Critical Analysis of the Disaster Management Act** 300
    Akash Kumar Patel and Divya Jain

35. **Democratizing Disaster Risk Reduction: A Local Governance Approach to Contextual Knowledge Production for Flood Planning in Kuttanad, India** 311
    Kaniska Singh, Fathima Nidha, Rohit Joseph and N. C. Narayanan

36. **Sustainable Operation & Maintenance (O&M) of Multi-purpose Disaster Shelters (MPDS) in Bangladesh** 322
    Mohammad Shariful Islam, Samira Tasnim Progga and Tahsin Reza Hossain

37. **Disaster Management in India: A Systematic Approach** 332
    Sunil Kumar Chaudhary

Part 6: Risk Governance in the Age of Pandemics

38. **Existing Resilience Framework for Disaster Risk Management in India** 341
    Manish Sharma, Nand Kumar and Ashwani Kumar

39. **System Dynamics Approach for COVID-19 Disaster Management** 355
    Anjali Saraswat and Satish Pipralia

40. **Global Pandemic: Need for a Legal Framework** 365
    N. Nabila Hoque

41. **Governance for COVID-19 in Bangladesh** 374
    Nasim Banu

42. ***Atmanirbharta*—The Journey from Disaster to Human Resilience** 385
    Falguni Garg and Lakhan Dhameja

43. **Development of Decision Support System for Effective COVID-19 Management** 399
    Shuvrangshu Jana, Rudrashis Majumder, Aashay Bhise, Nobin Paul, Stuti Garg and Debasish Ghose

44. **Disaster Management Law in the Context of Covid 19** 408
    Priya A Sondhi

45. **Accelerating Action on SFDRR Targets D, E and G and Related SDGs in this Decade of Implementation** 415
    Aloysius Rego

List of Figures

1.1	*Types of Disaster*	4
1.2	*Interdisciplinary Nature of DM*	4
1.3	*India: Disaster Prone*	5
1.4	*India: Ranking on the INFORM 2019*	5
1.5	*India and Neighbours – Comparative Score on the INFORM Index 2019*	6
1.6	*Satellite Sensing the Globe Through Its On-Board Sensors*	6
2.1	*Study area map of FFHWs interviewed across India*	10
3.1	*Project Theory of Change*	19
3.2	*Realization: Principles of evaluation of Technology by Poor*	24
3.3	*Barriers to Climate Resilience*	25
4.1	*(a) Survey results for power failure problem [7][18], (b) possible use of solar energy in disaster management operations [7][18] and (c) power failure during disaster [7][18].*	31
4.2	*Devices working during a disaster (a) No power failures (b) Complete shutdown including damage to all kinds of grids including damage to solar panels (c) roads blocked, no food supply [7][18]*	32
4.3	*Types of disasters (including more than one disaster experienced in one or different time) [7][18]*	32
4.4	*Modern technologies that can help ordinary citizens and disaster personnel in increasing risk-mitigation efforts [7][18]*	33
5.1	*The Study Area.*	37
5.2	*Seasonal Rainfall Anomalies for Lake Chad Region (Maidment, Ross, Black, Emily, & Matthew, 2017)*	38
5.3	*Monthly Rainfall for Lake Chad Region (Maidment, Ross, Black, Emily, & Matthew, 2017)*	38
5.4	*Total Rainfall in (mm) for Study Area*	39
5.5	*Land Cover 2000*	40
5.6	*Land Cover 2020*	40
5.7	*Land Cover Transition 2000 to 2020*	41
5.8	*Change in size of Lake Chad water bodies*	42
5.9	*Rate of Evapotranspiration 2000*	42
5.10	*Rate of Evapotranspiration 2020*	43
5.11	*Average Annual NDVI for Study Area*	44
5.12	*2000 NDVI for Study Area*	44
5.13	*2020 NDVI for Study Area*	45
6.1	*Types of disaster data based temporal characteristics*	48
7.1	*Contributing Factors of Desertification in India (area in Mha)*	54
7.2	*Rapid Advances in Space Sector by India*	56
7.3	*Confluence of Space Technologies with Soil Health Card to Combat Desertification*	57
7.4	*(a) Downscaling and Categorising, (b) Case study in the village Retur, Andhra Pradesh*	58
7.5	*The Process of Amalgamation of Space Technologies and Soil Health Cards*	59
9.1	*(a) 24-storey residential Grenfell Tower block in Latimer Road, London, (b) 17-storey oldest high-rise iconic landmark building in Tehran, (c) Fire breaks out at CSIR-National Chemical Laboratory in Pune (India), and (d) Fire Incident at AMRI Hospital in Kolkata (India) [1-3].*	74
9.2	*A standard time-temperature heating condition for RC beams of the horizontal furnace during testing.*	74

9.3   A cross-sectional schematic view and the RC beams installation details at the horizontal furnace for fire resistance testing.   75

9.4   Cross-sectional details of RC beams (all dimensions are in mm): (a) surface exposure conditions and (b) nomenclature of boundary conditions.   75

9.5   Nomenclature for the numerical solution as a two-dimensional unsteady-state heat: (a) internal elements, (b) outer boundary elements and (c) corner boundary elements.   77

9.6   Temperature-dependent stress-strain relationship variation with safety factor: (a) for concrete and (b) for steel.   79

9.7   RC beam strain and stress variation across the section: (a) cross-section details, (b) strain diagram and (c) stress block diagram.   81

9.8   FDM heat transfer model prediction with the test result of the RC beams for NSC at locations T1 (75, 75) and T3 (75, 175).   84

9.9   FDM heat transfer model prediction with the test result of the RC beams for HSC at locations T1 (75, 75), T2 (75, 125), and T3 (75, 175).   85

9.10   Flexural behaviour of RC beams exposed to the external fire load.   86

9.11   Flexural behaviour of RC beams exposed to standard ASTM E119 fire load.   86

9.12   Effects of fire scenarios on the flexural carrying capacity for RC beams using siliceous aggregate.   87

10.1   (a) Vehicle rubber tires (b) strip of a tire (c) rubber pads joined with SR glue (d) hole drilled in rubber pads (e) Damper installed at Beam-column joint   91

10.2   (a) Setup of Damper test, (b) Torque Wrench   92

10.3   Force vs displacement curve of proposed friction damper at (a) 50 N-m (b) 100N-m (c) 200N-m (d) 300 N-m (e) Cumulative energy dissipation curve   93

10.4   Rubber on steel friction test at (a) 50N-m Torque (b) 100N-m Torque (c) 200N-m Torque (d) 300N-m Torque (e) Non-Dimensional force (F_0) versus Cycle number for Rubber tire on steel friction interface   94

10.5   (a) Proposed friction damper installed at beam-column joint (b) Cyclic behavior of beam-column assemblage test without damper (c) with damper (d) Cumulative energy dissipation curve   95

11.1   Manufacturing process of PET grid.   97

11.2   Schematic representation for flexure test for both normal to and parallel to bed joints   98

11.3   Load vs. deflection curve for bending tension (a) normal to bed joint (b) parallel to bed joints.   99

11.4   Failures patterns of masonry wallets in OOP flexure test (a) brittle failure of UN (b) brittle failure of PN(c) brittle failure of UP(d) failure of PET strengthened sample PP   99

11.5   Grid failure ruptures in PET grid   100

11.6   Comparative graph of samples used for flexure test showing(a)Peak deflection at maximum load (b) Energy dissipation   100

11.7   Schematic representation of diagonal tension test set up.   100

11.8   Shear Stress-Strain curve for diagonal tension.   101

11.9   Crack patterns of diagonal test on brick wallets (a) crack initiation in UD (b) failure of UD sample (c) crack initiation in PD (d) interaction of plaster to the PD even after test completion   101

11.10   Comparative graph of samples used for diagonal test showing (a) Peak load at maximum load (b) ductility.   102

12.1   Mass concrete block showing the layout of the thermocouples. (dimensions in mm)   105

12.2   Digital thermometer and Type-K thermocouple.   105

12.3   Cast mass concrete showing the thermocouples.   105

12.4   Graphical user interface (GUI) for the MATLAB programe.   107

12.5   (a) Plot of temperature against time for thermocouple locations (TC1 to TC7), (b) Plot of temperature against time for thermocouple locations (TC4, TC8, TC9 and TC10)   108

12.6   Temperature time relationship for Observed and model temperatures.   109

12.7   Coefficient of determination for model verification.   109

12.8	*3D plot of temperature profile at initial time of concrete placement.*	**109**
12.9	*3D plot of temperature profile at 24 hours of concrete placement.*	**110**
12.10	*3D plot of temperature profile at 48 hours of concrete placement.*	**110**
12.11	*3D plot of temperature profile at 72 hours of concrete placement.*	**110**
12.12	*3D plot of temperature profile at 96 hours of concrete placement.*	**110**
12.13	*Temperature time relationship for Observed and model temperatures*	**111**
12.14	*Coefficient of determination for model validation.*	**111**
12.15	*3D plot of temperatures in block at 0hr*	**112**
12.16	*3D plot of temperatures in block at 24hr*	**112**
12.17	*3D plot of temperatures in block at 48hr*	**112**
12.18	*3D plot of temperatures in block at 72hr*	**113**
12.19	*3D plot of temperatures in block at 96hr*	**113**
12.20	*3D plot of temperatures in block at 120hr*	**113**
13.1	*Simplified model of building structure with two basic configurations of dynamic vibration absorber (DVA) (a) tuned mass damper (TMD), (b) tuned liquid damper (TLD).*	**116**
13.2	*Crystal Tower, Osaka, Japan (a) View of the completed building (https://fr.m.wikipedia.org/wiki/Fichier: Crystal_Tower_Osaka_20060321-001.jpg), (b) one of the tanks of icy water used as auxiliary mass of TMD system (Nagase & Hisatoku, 1992).*	**117**
13.3	*One Bloor Street East, Toronto, Canada (a) View of the completed building (https://commons.wikimedia.org/wiki/File:OneBloorEastToronto2018.jpg), (b) TLD used in the building (Lago et al., 2019).*	**117**
13.4	*Schematic drawing of example building frame (a) typical floor plan and (b) elevation.*	**119**
14.1	*Covid-19 Care Centre*	**125**
14.2	*Covid-19 Care Centre*	**125**
14.3	*Covid-19 Care Centre*	**126**
14.4	*Covid-19 Care Centre*	**126**
14.5	*Covid-19 Care Centre*	**127**
14.6	*Covid-19 Care Centre*	**127**
14.7	*Covid-19 Care Centre*	**128**
14.8	*Covid-19 Care Centre*	**128**
14.9	*Covid-19 Care Ambulance*	**129**
14.10	*Covid-19: Open Ground-converted for Cremation (This is to be addressed, since every Disaster is crossing this phase)*	**129**
14.11(a)	*View of cyclone shelter (Model 1)*	**130**
14.11(b)	*View of cyclone shelter (Model 2)*	**130**
14.12	*View of Earthquake Bamboo Frame Shelter (Ref: Disaster Relief Shelter; Walta Asfaw, David Headley, Nick Liza, Dan Nederhoed, Engr,339/340 Senior Design Project, Calvin College Engineering, 6 May 2013)*	**131**
14.13	*View of Tsunami Steel Frame Shelter (Ref: Disaster Relief Shelter; Walta Asfaw, David Headley, Nick Liza, Dan Nederhoed, Engr,339/340 Senior Design Project, Calvin College Engineering, 6 May 2013)*	**132**
14.14	*View of Flood-Triangular Timber shelter (Ref: Disaster Relief Shelter; Walta Asfaw, David Headley, Nick Liza, Dan Nederhoed, Engr,339/340 Senior Design Project, Calvin College Engineering, 6 May 2013)*	**132**
14.15	*View of 'Smart Building Architecture' (Ref: https://internetofthingsagenda.techtarget.com/definition/smart-home-or-building)*	**133**
14.16	*Automation and DOMOTICS (Ref: https://www.thoughtco.com/what-is-a-smart-house-domotics-177572; Photo by Javier Pierini/The Image Bank Collection/Getty Images)*	**134**
14.17	*Smart Shelter-Automation and DOMOTICS (Ref: https://internetofthingsagenda.techtarget.com/definition/smart-home-or-building)*	**134**

14.18	*Disaster Risk Management Cycle*	
	(Ref: https://reliefweb.int/sites/reliefweb.int/files/resources/Dominica%20ESM%2 0Manual%20%28v9%29.pdf)	135
16.1	*Global IoT in healthcare market (2014–2025)*	148
18.1	*Disaster Management*	161
19.1	*The Echo Flex from Amazon, an e-literacy solution and a new era in alternative computing models?*	
	(im-tomu n.d.; Krol 2019)	168
19.2	*I Am Tomu, the New Open Source Arm M3 Based Iot Architecture For Alexa Integration. (im-tomu n.d.)*	169
19.3	*The Circuit Diagram for the Tomu. ("Tomu - A ARM Microprocessor Which Fits in Your USB Port" n.d.)*	169
20.1	*Split of doctors and population*	174
22.2	*GIS in Disaster Management Indian context*	187
22.3	*General picture of Disaster Recovery*	188
22.6	*Location map*	192
22.7	*Google earth image of the study area*	192
22.8	*Aerial view of the location*	192
22.10	*Valley on the return path side*	193
23.1	*Wheat growing sites for NDVI image interpretation in Karnal and Hisar district*	197
24.1	*Study sites in Chirang and Sonitpur district, Assam, India*	203
24.2	*Schematic diagram of the geospatial approach.*	204
24.3	*Planform geometry of uninhabited and inhabited sandbars in study site 1.*	205
24.4	*Changes in area of uninhabited and inhabited sandbars.*	205
24.5	*Socioeconomic variables in study site 1.*	206
24.6	*Planform geometry of sandbars in study site 2*	207
24.7	*Socioeconomic variables in study site 2*	208
25.1	*Steps in Hazard Assessment*	213
M25.1	*Location map of Study Area - Rudraprayag District in Uttarakhand State, India*	214
25.2	*Methodology for Hazard Vulnerability Mapping*	215
M25.2	*Administrative Map of Rudraprayag District using ArcGIS*	216
M25.3	*Elevation Map of Study Area from DEM-SRTM*	216
M25.4	*Aspect map of Study Area using DEM-SRTM*	217
M25.5	*Slope Map of Study Area using DEM-SRTM*	217
M25.6	*Landslide Susceptibility Map of Study Area using Frequency Ratio*	218
M25.7	*Water Basin Map of Study Area using DEM-SRTM*	218
M25.8	*Flood Zonation Map of Study Area classifying flood zones*	219
M25.9	*Earthquake Zonation Map of Study Area for Earthquake hit on December 6, 2017*	219
25.3	*Methodology for Social Vulnerability Assessment*	220
25.10	*Vulnerability Map of Rudraprayag District*	220
26.1	*Digital elevation map (DEM) in Dihapal, Odisha, India*	229
26.2	*Indication of structural damages from UAV images*	229
26.3	*Submerged agricultural land captured from UAVs*	230
26.4	*Crop damage analysis in Dihapal, Odisha, India*	230
26.5	*Submerged roads in Dihapal, Odisha, India*	231
27.1	*Application of UAV in cyclone management*	237
27.2	*Damages captured by UAVs in West Bengal: damaged building, damaged Jetty, uprooted trees, damaged*	
	embankment (anti-clockwise from top corner)	241
27.3	*Sagar Island, West Bengal*	242

27.4	*Analysis of crop damage at Ganga Sagar in West Bengal*	242
28.1	*Representational image of Earthquake Prone regions in India*	250
29.1	*World Risk Index-Indicators of India*	255
29.2	*Total disaster events by type: 1980–1999 vs. 2000–2019*	256
29.3	*Total numbers of deaths compared to the average number of deaths per disaster by income group (2000–2019)*	256
29.4	*(a) Global population distribution by income group (millions), (b) Population various types of impacts on countries/territories by income group (2000-2019)*	256
29.5	*Recorded climate-related disaster losses per income group compared to GDP losses 1998–2017*	257
29.6	*% of population below poverty lie in Indian states*	258
29.7	*Action plan*	258
29.8	*Goal-wise performance*	259
29.9	*Development of the Public Private Partnership landscape in India through different phases*	260
29.10	*SPI of India 2016–2019*	261
29.11	*Contingency Fund of all States*	263
29.12	*India GDP Growth Rate 2005–2020, Macrotrends*	263
29.13	*State wise releases of SDRF from 2014–15 to 2017–18 from MHA*	264
29.14	*Revenue Expenditure on Natural disaster relief of India's Central and state Governments FY 1991–2018 (in Billion INR)*	264
29.15	*State wise and EWE wise distribution of morality rates (Deaths/year/million population) during 2000–2019 with state more than 15 million population*	265
29.16	*SDG Data Index, performance of Indian States*	265
29.17	*Expenditure on Operations and maintenance of states, 2002–2020*	266
29.18	*Development Expenditure of the states*	266
29.19	*Development Expenditure of states with % of GSDP, 2017–2020*	267
29.20	*Non-Development Expenditure of State, 2017–2020*	267
29.21	*Development expenditure-Social Sector Expenditure with % of GSDP*	268
29.22	*Development Expenditure-Capital Outlay with % of GSDP*	268
30.1	*Flowchart for multi-player game*	275
31.1	*Steps for comparing priorities of providers and users*	282
31.2	*Average score for the strategies for both groups*	282
34.1	*Major Disasters in India Source: Wikimedia Commons*	301
34.2	*Institutional Framework for DM*	303
34.3	*Comparison of Impact of Disasters Before and After 2005*	307
35.1	*Ward Map of Kainakary (Kainakary Gram Panchayat, 2021)*	314
35.2	*Methodological Choices And Disaster Risk Components.*	316
35.3	*Class Distribution Within Different Land Typologies, Compiled From The Survey.*	318
36.1	*Different level of risk zone of Bangladesh*	323
36.2	*Condition of the existing MPDS in different location (Care Bangladesh and C3ER, n.d.)*	325
36.3	*Vulnerability (%) of existing MPDS against different disaster (Mahmood, Dhakal and Kamruzzaman, 2013)*	325
36.4	*Different constructing authorities of MPDS in Bangladesh (Care Bangladesh and C3ER, n.d.)*	327
36.5	*Different management authorities of MPDS (Care Bangladesh and C3ER, n.d.)*	328
36.6	*No of occurrence of cyclone on different months from 1960-2010 (https://en.banglapedia.org).*	328
36.7	*Flowchart showing the steps of survey*	329
37.1	*Mortality due to natural hazards (1990-2000)*	332

37.2	*Tsunami of 2004*	**333**
37.3	*Bhuj(2001) earthquake*	**333**
37.4	*Orissa super cyclone*	**333**
37.5	*Bihar Flood 2009*	**333**
38.1	*No. of deaths due to various natural disasters in India.*	**345**
38.2	*No. of people deaths due to various technological disasters in India.*	**345**
38.3	*Comparison of Health infrastructure in various countries of the world.*	**348**
38.4	*Mid and high rise development are on the rise in the current developmental scenario.*	**352**
38.5	*(a). (b) and (c) Old city cores, characterized by narrow, congested streets, have some old inhabited buildings in dilapidated conditions,*	**352**
39.1	*Rinsing Covid cases in India; Rapid antigen covid tests; Increasing mortality rate; Vaccination against coronavirus*	**356**
39.2	*Red, orange and green zones classification in Indian districts*	**357**
39.3	*Total covid cases in Indian states*	**358**
39.4	*Distribution and share of covid cases in Indian states*	**359**
39.5	*Causal loop diagram for Covid-19 assessment*	**361**
39.6	*Recommendations for Covid-19 management*	**362**
42.1	*Diagram depicting natural surveillance*	**386**
42.2	*Venn diagram showing the concept of a self-sustained model*	**388**
42.3	*Satellite image of the site*	**389**
42.4	*Different stages of form evolution*	**391**
42.5	*Bird's eye view of the site highlighting various regions*	**392**
42.6	*Site plan indicating area coverage*	**392**
42.7	*Site plan*	**393**
42.8	*Bar chart showing the savings obtained per dwelling unit by using RESCO*	**394**
42.9	*Floor plans of cluster type 1 (Area – 60 sq.m.)*	**395**
42.10	*Cluster plan showing the unit connectivity with the courtyard and roads*	**395**
42.11	*Section across the cluster*	**396**
42.12	*Diagram showing various disaster resilient features*	**396**
42.13	*Diagram showing the various construction materials used*	**397**
43.1	*COVID management at different level*	**401**
43.2	*Input-output block diagram of GUI*	**402**
43.3	*Prediction Tab (a)*	**403**
43.4	*Prediction Tab (b)*	**403**
43.5	*Prediction Tab (c)*	**404**
43.6	*Allocation Tab (a)*	**404**
43.7	*Allocation Tab (b)*	**405**
43.8	*Lockdown Tab*	**405**
45.1	*Reducing direct damage to critical infrastructure and basic services disruption*	**418**

List of Tables

2.1	*Respondents categories and state for the study on FFHWs in India's COVID-19 response*	**11**
3.1	*Treatment Type and Sample Slums, by City Baseline*	**20**
3.2	*No. of Sampled HHs by City, Slum type and Treatment Type for Baseline and Endline survey*	**20**
3.3	*Vulnerability proportion, by Baseline, Endline*	**21**
3.4	*Percentage households with decrease of respective risks and susceptibility by more than 20%*	**21**
5.1	*Rainfall for Years 2000, 2005, 2010, 2015 and 2020*	**39**
5.2	*Change in LULC from 2000 to 2020*	**41**
5.3	*Water Bodies in Sq Km*	**41**
5.4	*Average Annual NDVI value of the Lake Chad from year 2001 to 2019 (19yrs)*	**43**
7.1	*Status of Desertification in India*	**55**
9.1	*Summary of the stress-strain relationships for NSC and HSC at elevated temperatures*	**80**
9.2	*Optimized thermal material properties for heat transfer analysis*	**83**
9.3	*The fire-resistance rating for RC beams at different fire scenario*	**88**
11.1	*Material properties of constituent materials*	**97**
11.2	*Specimen dimensions and strengthening details*	**97**
13.1	*Damper cost as percentage of total building construction cost (P_d) for DVAs in the form of water tanks.*	**118**
13.2	*Damper cost as percentage of total building construction cost (P_d) for other conventional dampers.*	**119**
13.3	*Salient parameters of example building structure.*	**120**
21.1	*Renewable energy capacity (GW) – for the year 2018*	**177**
22.1	*Methods and List of Data Aqusitions*	**186**
23.1	*Weather and spectral indices used in models using composite weather variables*	**197**
23.2	*Effective weather parameters for Hisar and Karnal district (Sum products-correlation)*	**198**
23.3	*Agromet regression model equation for Hisar and Karnal districts*	**198**
23.4	*Validation of Agromet models*	**199**
23.5	*Regression yield model equation developed with addition of NDVI (MODIS) for Hisar and Karnal district*	**199**
23.6	*Validation of Agromet-spectral (MODIS-NDVI) Yield models for wheat yield estimation for districts Hisar and Karnal during 2015-16 & 2016-17*	**199**
25.1	*Details of Data Source*	**215**
25.2	*Secondary Data for Social Vulnerability Assessment*	**219**
25.3	*Social Vulnerability of Study Area*	**221**
28.1	*Reference to select projects and missions that are integrated in Disaster Management*	**248**
28.2	*India Disaster Vulnerability in %ages[8]-Rough Estimates.*	**250**
28.3	*Compensation/ Insurance package[9]*	**251**
30.1	*Resource allocation using set partitioning*	**275**
31.1	*Identified disaster management strategies*	**281**
31.2	*Average ranking for disaster management strategies*	**282**
34.1	*NDMA and Important Sections*	**302**
34.2	*Comparative Analysis of DM Act of India, South Africa, Philippines, and Australia*	**305**
34.3	*Strengths and Weaknesses of DM Act*	**308**

35.1	*Mean Flood Level In Different Land Typologies, Compiled From The Survey And Spatial Mapping.*	317
36.1	*Basic details of the 3 standard designs of cyclone shelters (Cyclone Shelter Policy, 2011)*	324
36.2	*Responsible authority for MPDS management in different situation (Cyclone Shelter Policy, 2011)*	327
38.1	*Disaster Management Action Priorities in developed and developing regions*	342
38.2	*Countries with highest numbers of deaths due to natural disasters during the period 1997-2017 and their respective populations for 2017.*	342
38.3	*Some of the major the disaster events in India during the period 1999-2014.*	343
38.4	*Damage due to natural disasters in India.*	344
38.5	*Supporting ministries for different disasters in India.*	346
38.6	*Status of Health Centres in India in 2005 and 2012.*	349
38.7	*Healthcare staff status in India.*	350
41.1	*The Shortage of Bangladesh Health Care Personnel in March 2020*	376
42.1	*Risk Assessment Matrix (From TARU Leading Edge, 2020)*	386
42.2	*Risk assessment matrix for Bhoi nagar, Bayababa slum site in Bhubaneswar, Odisha*	390
42.3	*Area Statement*	393
45.1	*Selected achievements and challenges of international DRR Governance under HFA.*	417
45.2	*Ministerial Distribution of Official Sendai Focal Points in OECD Countries.*	419
45.4	*Progress on National DRR Strategies by region*	420
45.5	*Progress on 'Local' DRR Strategies by region*	421
45.6	*Similarities and differences between Chile and Ecuador*	421
45.7	*Disasters and losses, by African Regional Economic Community (REC), 2015–2018 (Van Niekerk, 2019)*	422
45.8	*African member states' progress: Sendai Framework Target (E)*	422
45.9	*Similarities n differences between global input indicator G from Chile and Ecuador*	425
45.10	*Sections and Information in the Gap Reports*	427
45.11	*Data disaggregation and statistical processing - SDG 11.5.2 and SFDRR Target(d)*	428
45.12	*Number of countries at a specific stage of reporting SFDRR indicators for year 2018 as of Oct 2020. (UNDRR,)*	428

Preface

The Fifth World Congress on Disaster Management (WCDM) was organised in Delhi from 24th to 27th November 2021 jointly by the Government of Delhi, the Indian Institute of Technology Delhi, and the Disaster Management Initiative and Convergence Society which created the platform of WCDM. Over the years, WCDM has emerged as the largest conference on disaster management in the developing world.

The theme of the Fifth WCDM was *Technology, Finance and Capacity.* 7 Plenary Sessions, 50 Technical Sessions and Special Technical Sessions were organised around this overarching theme. While eminent thought leaders and experts delivered keynote addresses and participated in the panel discussions of the Plenary Sessions. It is the Technical Sessions that received the longest traction as Call for Papers was issued for these sessions months in advance and more than 600 researchers, practitioners and policy makers responded with abstracts of their ideas. These were reviewed by experts and subsequently, 250 of these abstracts were developed as full papers. This is the first of five-volume series of compendium of these papers.

The papers have been published in the same form these were received without any peer review to provide a flavour of the raw ideas that emerged from the Technical Sessions of the conference. Some of these papers presented by the young researchers and practitioners may not have the rigours of academic disciplines, but these do reflect the cross current of thoughts that went around in these sessions of the Conference. These provide new ideas and insights that provide value to the current discourses on the subject.

These papers have been arranged under five broad themes—first: Disaster Risk Management, second: Nature and Human Induced Disasters, third: Coronavirus Pandemic, fourth: Disaster Response and fifth: Challenges and Opportunities of Disaster Management. Understandably the papers do not cover every aspect of the themes, these discuss only those aspects that the authors have chosen to highlight. The present volume is a compilation of 45 papers on the theme of Disaster Risk Management, which is further divided into six sub-themes, first: Harnessing Science and Technology for Building Resilience to Disasters, second: Innovations in Construction Technology, third: Using Artificial Intelligence and Internet of Things for Managing Risks of Disasters, fourth: Application of Remote Sensing, GIS, Drone and UAV for Disaster Risk Management, fifth: Disaster Management Laws and Governance and, sixth: Risk Governance in the Age of Pandemics.

The Conference secretariat has brought the papers together, but his credit lies solely and exclusively on the authors.

Dr S. Ananda Babu
Convener
Fifth World Conference on Disaster Management

Acknowledgement

DMICS, the organizer of the 5th World Congress on Disaster Management (WCDM), expresses its deep appreciation to Government of Delhi (GNCTD), NDMA, NIDM, DRDO, UNICEF, ICMR, GSI, and Knowledge Partners, delegates who have supported the 2021 World Congress on Disaster Management with either earmarked or unearmarked contributions. A special acknowledgement goes to Indian Institute of Technology, Delhi for hosting the 5th WCDM for its strong support.

DMICS would like to express our deepest appreciation to Hon'ble Union Minister of Defence, Shri Rajnath Singh for inaugurating the 5th WCDM and delivering the inaugural address; Mami Mizutori, UN-DRR Chief and Special Representative of the UN Secretary General for her special message and Dr Balram Bhargava, Secretary, DHR and Director General, ICMR for his key note address. We would also like to convey our heartfelt appreciation and gratitude to Prof. V. Ramgopal Rao, Director of IIT Delhi, Dr. Parvez Hyatt, for their strategic support and guidance. Our indefatigable team members, Col. Sanjay Srivastava Dr. Chandrappa, Dr. A. Kishan, Prof. B. Gopal Rao, Mr. Bhaskar Rao Volam, Dr. B. Ram, Prof. V. Prakasam, Dr. A. Gayathri Devi, Dr. R.K. Srivastava, Mr. Amit Kumar, Mr. Mohan Kasthala, Mr. Pavan Parlapalli, Mr. Manish Vishnoi, Ms. Suparna Dutta, Ms. Parul Sharma, Ms. Megha B Bhati, M. Zoya Khan, Ms. Areeba Naaz, Mr. Rohit Kumar Azad and Ms. Shweta Zanjrukia, deserve a huge appreciation for working tirelessly for the last one year in ensuring that 5th WCDM reaches new horizons in bringing together the Government Duty bearers, Policy makers, Planners, Researchers, Academicians, Practitioners and other key stakeholders.

DMICS extends its sincere gratitude to the large number of organisations, individuals and volunteers who have contributed to the 5th WCDM, through technical support and in numerous other ways. DMICS would like to express its deepest appreciation also to the members of the Scientific and Technical Committee (S&TC) along with its Chair, technical leads and collaborative organisations of Pre-Conference Webinars, Plenaries, Special Feature Events, Special Technical Sessions and Exhibitiors.

Part 1

HARNESSING SCIENCE AND TECHNOLOGY FOR BUILDING RESILIENCE TO DISASTERS

Chapter 1 "Information Technology": The Utopian Solution to Achieving Disaster Resilience & Ensuring Disaster Management

Chapter 2 Female frontline health workers' and ICT in the COVID-19 response in India

Chapter 3 Co-creating Climate Resilience Technological Solutions for Poor

Chapter 4 Exploring the Potential of Solar Energy in Disaster Management and Rescue Operations

Chapter 5 Centre for Disaster Risk Management and Development Studies, Ahmadu Bello University, Zaria

Chapter 6 Technological Advances in the Development of Disaster Response Management Systems and Applications

Chapter 7 Reaching beyond Low Hanging Apelles to technological convergence to combat disasters like Desertification

Chapter 8 Technological Preparedness for Fire Disasters

"Information Technology": The Utopian Solution to Achieving Disaster Resilience & Ensuring Disaster Management

Col. Gaurav Bhatia
Corresponding Author: fear_naught@hotmail.com

Arundhati Bhatia
arundhati0104@gmail.com

Ranju Bhatia
ranjubhatia13@gmail.com

Abhimanyu Bhatia
abhimanyu.bhatia05@gmail.com

Abstract

India's geo-climatic conditions as well as its high degree of socio-economic vulnerability, make it one of the most disaster-prone countries in the world. Disaster risks in India are further compounded by increasing vulnerabilities related to changing demographics and socio-economic conditions, unplanned urbanization, development within high-risk zones, environmental degradation, climate change, geological hazards, epidemics and pandemics. All these contribute to a situation where disasters seriously threaten India's economy, its population and sustainable development. The fact that India exists in the High-Risk category as evaluated by the INFORM Global Risk Index which measures the risk of humanitarian crises and disasters in 191 countries, must propel us to, not only be aware of this Risk but also to attempt to combat it at all levels of human endeavour.

Though it is not possible to completely avoid natural disasters, the sufferings can be minimized by creating proper awareness of the likely disasters and its impact by developing a suitable warning system, disaster preparedness and management of disasters through the application of Information Technology tools. The changing trends have opened a large number of scientific and technological resources and skills to reduce disaster risk. There are mainly applications we can use to manage disasters - GIS and Remote Sensing; Internet; Warning and Forecasting System. The paper delves into the three aspects and how they aid in utilisation of IT tools for DM.

Key Words: Disaster Resilience, Disaster Management, Utopia, Information Technology, GIS and Remote Sensing; Internet; Warning and Forecasting System, Awareness

1. Etymology: Disaster

The word 'Disaster' originates from Middle French désastre and Old Italian disastro, which in turn comes from the Greek pejorative prefix δυσ-,(dus) "bad"+ αστήρ (aster), "star". The root of the word disaster ("bad star" in Greek and Latin) comes from an astrological theme which in ancient times referred to the destruction or deconstruction of a star as a disaster' (Government of India, 2011).

2. What is a Disaster?

A disaster is an extreme disruption of the functioning of a society that causes widespread human, material, or environmental losses that exceed the ability of the affected society to cope with its own resources. Disasters, both natural and man-induced are not new to mankind. They have been the constant, though inconvenient, companions of human beings since time immemorial. The High Power Committee on Disaster Management, constituted in 1999, has identified 31 types of disasters categorized into five major sub-groups (Government of India, 2011).

i.	Water and climate related disasters	a)	Floods and drainage management
		b)	Cyclones
		c)	Tornadoes and hurricanes
		d)	Hailstorm
		e)	Cloud burst
		f)	Heat wave and cold wave
		g)	Snow avalanches
		h)	Droughts
		i)	Sea erosion
		j)	Thunder and lightening
		k)	Tsunami
ii.	Geological related disasters	a)	Landslides and mudflows
		b)	Earthquakes
		c)	Dam failures/ Dam bursts
		d)	Minor fires
iii.	Chemical, industrial and nuclear related disasters	a)	Chemical and industrial disasters
		b)	Nuclear disasters
iv.	Accident related disasters	a)	Forest fires
		b)	Urban fires
		c)	Mine flooding
		d)	Oil spills
		e)	Major building collapse
		f)	Serial bomb blasts
		g)	Festival related disasters
		h)	Electrical disasters and fires
		i)	Air, road and rail accidents
		j)	Boat capsizing
		k)	Village fire
v.	Biological related disasters	a)	Biological disasters and epidemics
		b)	Pest attacks
		c)	Cattle epidemics
		d)	Food poisoning

Fig. 1.1 Types of Disaster

Source: http://www.preventionweb.net/english/professional/publications

Not many scholars realise that Disaster Management (DM) is an interdisciplinary subject - as is amply borne out by the Fig. 1.2.

The awareness and knowledge about this realm are as important (if not more) to the Management students, Managers and Leaders – who are currently largely focused on their traditional duties bouquet of planning, organizing, staffing, leading, and controlling.

3. India's Vulnerability

India's geo-climatic conditions as well as its high degree of socio-economic vulnerability, make it one of the most disaster-prone countries in the world. (Atmanand, 2003; Madan, 2006; Government of India, 2011; National Disaster Management Authority, 2012; National Disaster Management Authority, 2013)

Natural hazards have always attracted greater attention and focus from the government authorities and NGO's - with scant attention being given to the management of man-induced disasters. This fact is amply borne out by the fact that in common parlance whenever the term "disaster management" is used it is usually expected to deal with one or the other type of natural disaster e.g. Floods, Earthquake, Landslide etc.

Disciplines	Subjects
Earth sciences	Geography, Geology, Seismology, Hydrology, Oceanography, Glaciology
Atmospheric sciences	Meteorology, Climatology
Environmental sciences	Climate Change
Agriculture sciences	Agriculture, Horticulture, Fisheries
Engineering sciences	Civil Engineering, Structural Engineering, Earthquake Engineering, Architecture, Town and Country Planning
Information & Communication sciences	Remote Sensing, Information Technology, Telecommunication
Social sciences	Economics, Sociology, Anthropology, Social Work, Political Science, Psychology, Behavioral Science
Medical sciences	Emergency Health Management, Trauma and Stress Management,
Management and Business Studies	Public Administration and Management, Supply Chain Management, Risk Finance & Insurance, Business Continuity Studies
Security related studies	Disaster and National Security, Role of Armed and Para-Military Forces in Disaster Response, Nuclear-Chemical-Biological Warfare.
Diplomatic studies	International Conventions on Humanitarian Aids and Disaster Risk reduction., Regional Cooperation on Disaster Risk Reduction and Management

Fig. 1.2 Interdisciplinary Nature of DM

Source: First India DM Congress, Nov 2006 http://nidm.gov.in/idmc/Discipline_subjects.htm

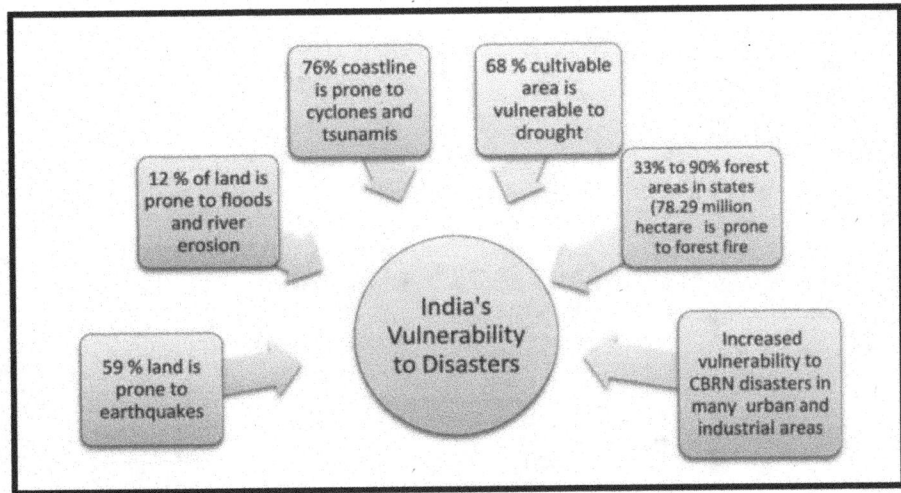

Fig. 1.3   India: Disaster Prone

Source: CAG REPORT 2013 – PG 3 (Ministry of Home Affairs, 2013)

Disaster risks in India are further compounded by increasing vulnerabilities related to changing demographics and socio-economic conditions, unplanned urbanization, development within high-risk zones, environmental degradation, climate change, geological hazards, epidemics and pandemics. All these contribute to a situation where disasters seriously threaten India's economy, its population and sustainable development.

4. INFORM 2019 Risk Index

	Value	Rank	Trend
INFORM	5.50	30	EQUAL
Hazard	7.00	21	EQUAL
Vulnerability	5.20	44	EQUAL
Coping Capacity	4.50	94	EQUAL

Fig. 1.4   India: Ranking on the INFORM 2019

Source: Index for Risk Management 2019 (INFORM 2019) - http://www.inform-index.org

The INFORM model adopts the three aspects of vulnerability reflected in the United Nations International Strategy for Disaster Reduction (UNISDR) definition. The aspects of physical exposure and physical vulnerability are integrated into the hazard & exposure dimension, the aspect of the fragility of the socio-economic system becomes INFORM's vulnerability dimension while lack of resilience to cope and recover is treated under the lack of coping capacity dimension (Fig. 1.5).

The fact that India exists in the High-Risk category as evaluated by the INFORM Global Risk Index which measures the risk of humanitarian crises and disasters in 191 countries, must propel us to, not only be aware of this Risk but also to endeavour to combat it at all levels of human endeavour.

5. Disaster Management Act - 2005

Post the DM Act 2005, there has been a paradigm shift from a response and relief-centric approach to a proactive, and comprehensive mindset towards DM covering all aspects from prevention, mitigation, preparedness to rehabilitation, reconstruction and recovery.

It is hence, imperative for Management students, Managers and Leaders to be able to comprehend the nuances of this paradigm shift and expeditiously reorient themselves and their organisations to implement concrete measures – so that no disaster is required to be "managed" instead all prospective disasters are minimized by proactive steps being taken towards ensuring Disaster Resilience and Disaster Risk Reduction (DRR).

6. Application of Information Technology in Disaster Management

Though it is not possible to completely avoid natural disasters, the sufferings can be minimized by creating proper awareness of the likely disasters and its impact by developing a suitable warning system, disaster preparedness and management of disasters through the application of Information Technology tools. The changing trends have opened a large number of scientific and technological resources and skills to reduce disaster risk.

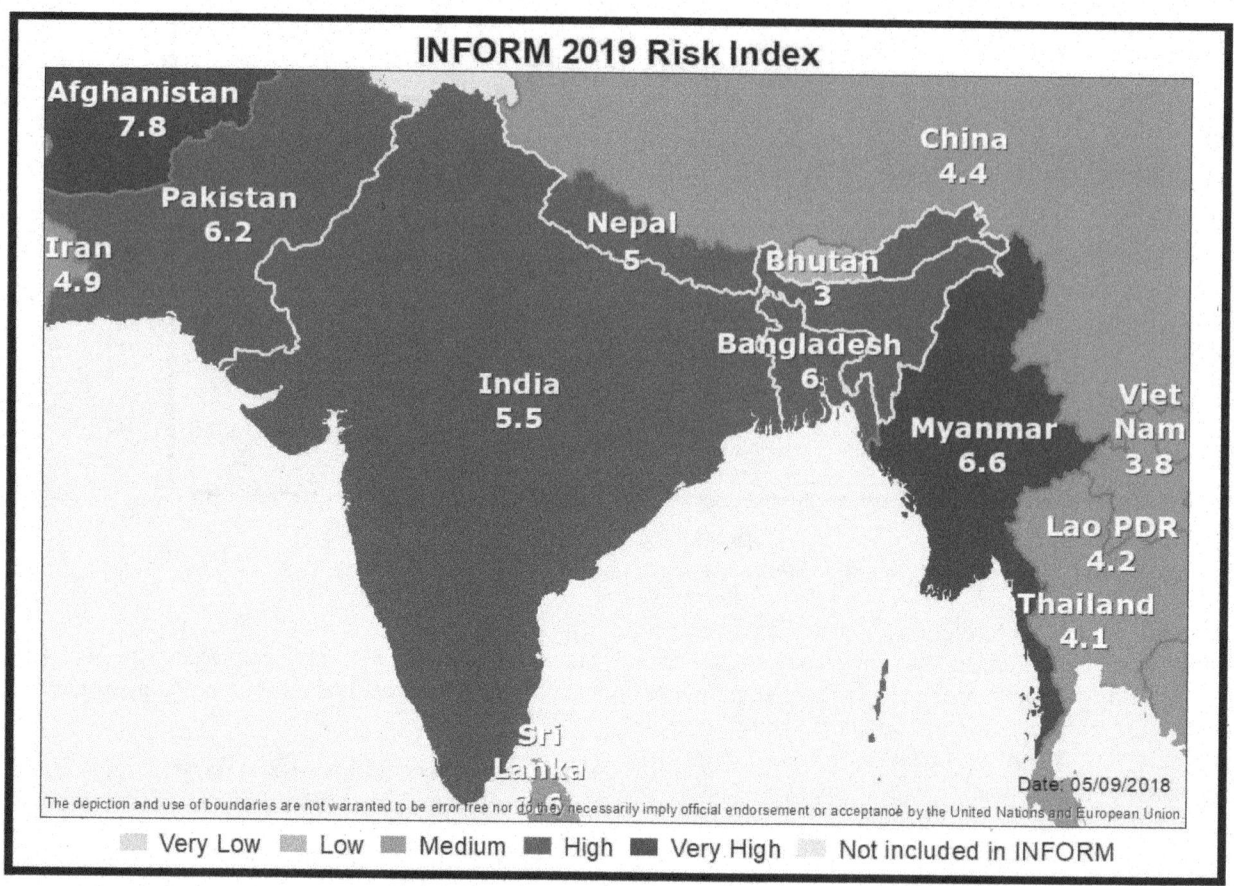

Fig. 1.5   India and Neighbours – Comparative Score on the INFORM Index 2019

Source: Index for Risk Management 2019 (INFORM 2019) - http://www.inform-index.org

There are mainly applications we can use to manage disasters:

- GIS and Remote Sensing
- Internet
- Warning and Forecasting System

6.1 GIS and Remote Sensing

GIS provides a tool for effective and efficient storage and manipulation of remotely sensed data and other spatial and non-spatial data types for both scientific management and policy-oriented information. This can be used to facilitate measurement, mapping, monitoring and modelling of a variety of data types related to natural phenomenon. The specific GIS application in the field of Risk Assessment is for Hazard Mapping to show earthquake, landslides, floods or fire hazards.

Theses map could be created for cities, districts or even for the entire country and tropical cyclone Threat Maps are used by meteorological departments to improve the quality of the tropical storm warning services and quickly communicate the risk to the people likely to get affected by the cyclone.

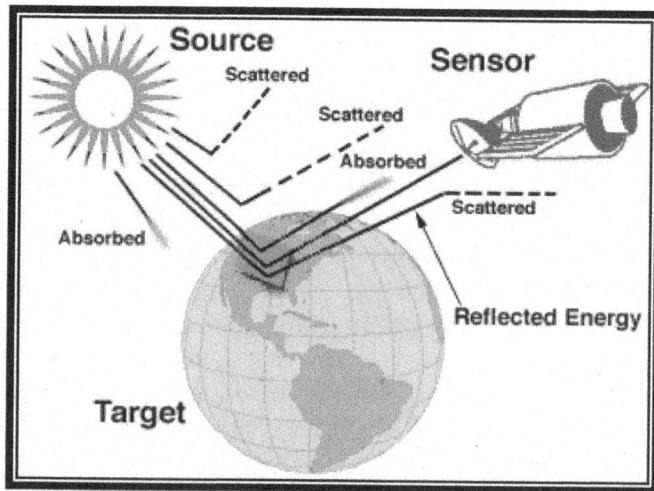

Fig. 1.6   Satellite Sensing the Globe Through Its On-Board Sensors

Source: (Nirupama and Simonovic 2002)

Remote sensing makes observation of any object from a distance and without coming into actual contact. Remote sensing can gather data much faster than ground-based observation, can cover a large area at one time to give a synoptic view. Remote sensing comprises Aerial Remote Sensing which is the process of recording information, such as photographs and images from the sensor on aircraft and Satellite Remote Sensing which consists of several satellites remote sensing system which can be used to integrate natural hazard assessments into development planning studies. These are: Land sat, SPOT Satellite, Satellite Radar System, Advanced Very High-Resolution Radio. Some applications of GIS and Remote Sensing in various disasters are as follows: -

Drought

GIS and Remote Sensing can be used in drought relief management such as early warnings of drought conditions will help to plan out the strategies to organize relief work. Satellite data may be used to target potential groundwater sites for taking up well-digging programmers. Satellite data provides valuable tools for evaluating areas subject to desertification. Film transparencies, photographs and digital data can be used for locating, assessing and monitoring deterioration of natural conditions in a given area.

Earthquake

GIS and Remote Sensing can be used for preparing seismic hazards maps to assess the exact nature of risks.

Floods

Satellite data can be effectively used for mapping and monitoring the flood inundated areas, flood damage assessment, flood hazard zoning and post-flood-survey of rivers configuration and protection works.

Landslides

Landslide zonation map comprises a map demarcating the stretches or area of varying degree of anticipated slope stability or instability. The map has an inbuilt element of forecasting and is hence probabilistic. Depending upon the methodology adopted and the comprehensiveness of the input data used, a landslide hazard zonation map, able to provide help to the concerning location, the extent of the slope area likely to be affected, and the rate of mass movement of the slope mass.

Search and Rescue

GIS can be used in carrying out search and rescue operations in a more effective manner by identifying areas that are disasters prone and zoning them accordingly to risk magnitudes.

6.2 Internet

In the present era of electronic communication, the internet provides a useful platform for disaster mitigation communications. Launching of a well-defined web site is a very cost-effective means of making an intra-national and international presence felt. It provides a new and potentially revolutionary option for the rapid, automatic, and global dissemination of disaster information. Many individuals and groups, including several national meteorological services, are experimenting with the Internet for real-time dissemination of weather observation, forecasts, satellite and other data. In the most critical phase of natural disasters, electronic communication has provided the most effective and, in some instances, perhaps the only means of communication with the outside world.

6.3 Warning and Forecasting System

An advance system of forecasting, monitoring and issuing early warnings plays the most significant role in determining whether a natural hazard will assume disastrous proportions or not. The country has the following forecasting systems:

Indian Meteorological Department (IMD)

IMD provides cyclone warnings from the Area Cyclone Warning Centers (ACWCs) It has developed the necessary infrastructure to originate and disseminate the cyclone warnings at appropriate levels. It has made operational a satellite-based communication system called Cyclone Warning Dissemination System for direct dissemination of cyclone warnings to the cyclone-prone coastal areas. IMD runs operationally a Limited-area Analysis and Forecast System (LAFS), based on an Optimal Interpretation (OI) analysis and a limited area Primitive Equation (PE) model, to provide numerical guidance.

National Remote Sensing Agency (NRSA)

Long term drought-proofing programmes on the natural resources of the district have been greatly helped using satellite data obtained by NRSA. Satellite data can be used very effectively for mapping and monitoring the flood inundated areas, flood damage assessment, flood hazard zoning and past flood-survey of river configuration and protection works.

Seismological Observations

Seismological observations in the country are made through the national network of 36 seismic stations operated by the IMD, which is the nodal agency. These stations have collected data over long periods.

Warning System for Drought

The National Agricultural Drought Assessment and Management System (NADAMS) has been developed by the Department of Space for the Department of Agriculture and Cooperation and is primarily based on monitoring of vegetation status through National Oceanic and Atmospheric Administration (NOAA), Advanced Very High Resolution (AVHR) data. The drought assessment is based on a comparative evaluation of satellite observed green vegetation cover (both area and greenness) of a district in any specific period, with that of any similar period in previous years.

Flood Forecasting

Flood forecasts and warnings are issued by the Central Water Commission (CWC), Ministry of Water Resources. These are used for alerting the public and for taking appropriate measures by concerned administrative and state engineering agencies in the flood hazard mitigation. Information is gathered from the CWC's vast network of Forecasting Stations on various rivers in the country.

Cyclone Tracking

Information on cyclone warnings is furnished on a real-time basis to the control room set up in the Ministry of Agriculture, Government of India. High-power Cyclone Detection Radars (CDRs) that are installed along the coastal belt of India have proved to be a very useful tool for the cyclone warning work. These radars can locate and track approaching Tropical Cyclones within a range of 400 km. Satellite imagery received from weather satellite is extensively used in detecting the development and movement of Tropical Cyclones over oceanic regions, particularly when they are beyond the range of the coastal radars. The existing model of dissemination of cyclone warnings to various government officials is through high priority telegrams, telephones, telex and fax.

7. Conclusion

It may be observed that advancement in Information Technology in the form of Internet, GIS, Remote Sensing, Satellite communication, etc. can help a great deal in planning and implementation of hazards reduction. For maximum benefit, new technologies for public communication should be made use and natural disaster mitigation messages should be conveyed through these measures. GIS can improve the quality and power of analysis of natural hazards assessments, guide development activities and assist planners in the selection of mitigation measures and the implementation of emergency preparedness and response action. Remote Sensing, on the other hand, as a tool can very effectively contribute towards identification of hazardous areas, monitor the planet for its changes on a real-time basis and give early warning to many impending disasters. Communication

satellites have become vital for providing emergency communication and timely relief measures. Integration of space technology inputs into natural disaster monitoring and mitigation mechanisms are critical for hazard reduction. It is necessary to create awareness amongst the public as well as decision-makers for allocating resources for appropriate investments in information technology. Awareness and training in Information technology in a much greater measure are required to develop human resources, particularly in developing countries, who are chronically suffering from natural disasters. The disasters usually occur in the well-defined areas, even though the community does not know the coping mechanism for the disaster. The disaster mitigation programmes must be extensively taken up covering various aspects at the national level to minimise the disaster damages. There should be a greater emphasis on the development of new technologies in disaster mitigation. Disaster preparedness and awareness is the only effective way of mitigating the impact of future disasters.

REFERENCES

1. Atmanand (2003). Insurance and Disaster Management: the Indian Context. Disaster Prevention and Management, 12(4), 286–304. https://doi.org/10.1108/09653560310493105
2. Government of India. (2011). Disaster Management in India. In Management. Retrieved from http://www.preventionweb.net/english/professional/publications/v.php?id=31020
3. Kaul, D., Ayaz, M., & Lohitkumar, S. (2005). Disaster Management in India. Catastrophic Risks and Insurance, 381–392. https://doi.org/http://dx.doi.org/10.1787/9789264009950-22-en
4. Mandal, G. S. (1999), Forecasting and Warning Systems for Cyclones in India, Shelter, October 1999, pp. 24–26.
5. Ministry of Home Affairs. (2013). Comptroller and Auditor General (CAG) Report: Disaster Preparedness of India. Report Number 5 of 2013 (Vol. 1). https://doi.org/10.1017/CBO9781107415324.004
6. National Disaster Management Authority. (2012). National Disaster Management Information and Communication System. https://doi.org/110029/9789380440125
7. National Disaster Management Authority. (2013). National Disaster Management Guidelines (Draft) -Community Based Disaster Management.
8. Sinha, Anil & Sharma, Vinod K., (1999), Culture of Prevention, Government of India, Ministry of Agriculture, Natural Disaster Management Division, New Delhi.
9. Sinha, Anil (1999), Relief Administration and Capacity Building for Coping Mechanism towards Disaster Reduction, Shelter, October 1999, pp. 9–12

CHAPTER 2

Female Frontline Health Workers' and ICT in the COVID-19 Response in India

Krishnan Sneha

Jindal Global University, Jindal School of Environment and Sustainability,
Sonepat, Haryana and
Environment, Technology and Community Health Consultancy Services
Corresponding author: skrishnan@jgu.edu.in

Purwar Deepshikha

ITC, University of Twente, Netherlands
deepshikhapurwar@gmail.com

Abstract

Community health workers play a critical role as intermediaries between communities and public health systems, for delivering key maternal and child health and nutrition interventions in low and middle-income countries. Female frontline health workers (FFHWs) led India's COVID-19 response in 2020. A capabilities approach emphasising on their digital and health literacy helped unpack systemic inequalities that women suffer, inequalities in resources and opportunities, educational deprivations, the failure of work to be recognized as work, and insults to bodily integrity. We studied FFHWs' role in sub national and local health response to the COVID-19 pandemic in six states in India—Odisha, Bihar, Madhya Pradesh, Uttarakhand, Kerala and Maharashtra – using interviews and policy analysis. The data was thematically analysed, and studied within the government policies and guidelines to combat the emerging concerns in COVID-19. It is essential to recognise FFHWs' role inside the health system, improving their working conditions and enabling enhanced usage of information, communication and technology. Concerted efforts by policy-makers are required to recalibrate how FFHWs are empowered as leaders of change with systems-level change and impetus through recognition and rewards. This alone will address issues of parity, equity, participation, and representation in a gender-responsive health system.

Keywords: Health response, Frontline female health workers, Digital-Health literacy, Equity Justice, Covid-19, Community Health Workers

1. Introduction

Resilience of health systems is a key objective for global health studies, particularly to withstand shocks and emergencies, and avoid disruptions of routine service delivery (Durski, 2020). Community health workers play a critical role as intermediaries between communities and public health systems, for delivering key maternal and child health and nutrition interventions in low and middle-income countries (John et al., 2020).

The objective of this paper is to understand how information and communications technology (ICT) innovations could better support local action for health emergencies, by exploring the role of female, community-level health workers in the COVID-19 response. This paper asks, ""*To what extent are female frontline health workers (FFHWs) capable to manage the COVID-19 pandemic in rural India?*" We review their preparedness and capacities in using various digital and smart-phone applications to coordinate the response.

In India, the task for managing the health response at community level fell on the shoulders of female frontline health workers (FFHWs), namely the voluntary community health worker (CHW), christened as ASHA (Accredited Social Health Activists), the Anganwadi Workers (AWWs) and Auxiliary Nurse Midwives (ANMs). In 2015, the ASHA programme matured as the National Health Mission, focussing on both rural and urban areas.

Several studies have highlighted the plight of the FFHWs: Scott et al (2019) suggested further research should investigate programme financing and reporting, ASHA grievance redressal or peer communications. Sreerekha (2016) extensively studied political economy of AWW's work in India and found that the status of women workers in state-sponsored social welfare schemes was poor in India. Bhatia (2014) urged that an institutionalised response is warranted to meet the aspirations and the vulnerabilities of these women. These studies draw attention to the concerns and questions about the expectations of FFHWs from the public health system ranging from how they are recruited from marginalised social groups, and further exploited within a system that exploits their vulnerability without building their capacities and offering them just and decent working conditions (Kedia et al, 2020).

2. Methods

We studied FFHWs' role in sub-national and local health response to the COVID-19 pandemic in six states in India – Odisha, Bihar, Madhya Pradesh, Uttarakhand, Kerala and Maharashtra. Our objective is to develop a qualitative analysis to explain the engagement between the FFHWs' and the communities, especially in the context of a pandemic like Covid19. In this paper, we interacted with CHWs and FFHWs, within the context of pandemic and health systems in India to understand how supportive is the public health system in India for FFHWs', especially the Asha workers and Anganawadi workers. Through semi-structured phone-based interviews and policy analysis– with the help of partner organizations and networks for recruitment, data collection and facilitation as shown in Fig. 2.1.

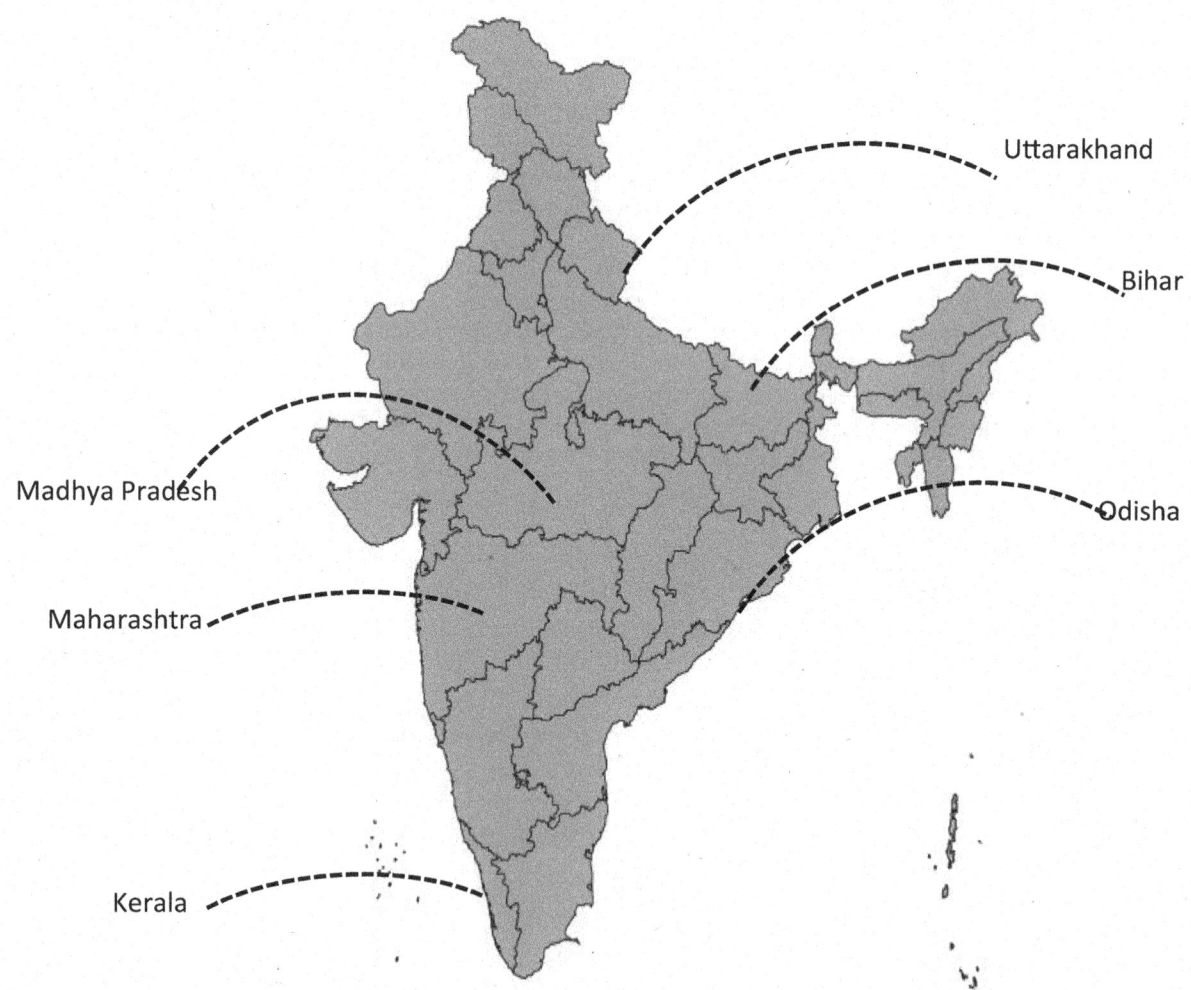

Fig. 2.1 Study area map of FFHWs interviewed across India

3. Data Collection

Five teams of local, trained interviewers interviewed the respondents using a topic guide developed in English and translated into Odia, Marathi, Malayalam and Hindi languages. We interviewed 35 frontline workers in six states in India between March – July 2020. The interviewers made a call with the respondents and set up a suitable time for the interview. The respondents provided informed consent before the interview began, and these phone conversations were recorded during the call. We substantiated these findings with participant quotes in a descriptive report, and contrasted the emerging themes with an analysis of developed guidelines and recommendations at the national level.

4. Results

Respondent characteristics

We interviewed 35 FFHWs and 10 other stakeholders as part of the survey. Their details are provided in Table 2.1.

Table 2.1 Respondents categories and state for the study on FFHWs in India's COVID-19 response

No	Position of Stakeholders interviewed	State	Number
1	ASHA Supervisors	Maharashtra	5
2	ASHA Supervisors	Bihar	4
3	Anganwadi workers	Odisha	7
4	ASHA workers	Odisha	5
5	ASHA workers	Uttarakhand	5
6	ASHA workers	Madhya Pradesh	4
7	ASHA workers	Kerala	3
8	Other stakeholders (NGO staff, Government officers, Academics)	Mumbai, Delhi, Bhubaneshwar	7
	TOTAL		40

The exploratory approach of the study highlights the various issues and challenges faced by FFHWs in COVID-19 response in India.

(a) Disruption of essential services delivery due to COVID-19:

Prior to the pandemic the burden of the healthcare system fell upon ASHAs, who assisted Auxiliary Nurse Midwives to carry out essential health service delivery: maternal and newborn care, child care and nutrition, infectious and non-infectious diseases and social mobilization. When the pandemic erupted, AWWs, ASHAs and ASHA supervisors were tasked with additional responsibilities to trace and isolate people coming to villages from outside. AWWs, who fall under the Ministry of Women & Child Development, undertake implementation of Integrated Child Development Services (ICDS) in the states. An AWW respondent summarised her routine tasks as follows:

"We do surveys of households, provide egg and malt powder to pregnant women and lactating women, take pregnant women to the village health nutrition day (VHND). We provide rations (Dry foods) to pregnant and lactating women of (children) up to 6 months. We are providing cooked food to the Anganwadi children. We organize VHND and Immunization and provide knowledge regarding health and food" (AWW 1, Odisha)

As a routine activity, Village Health and Nutrition Days is a community-based health service package – includes early registration of pregnancy, regular antenatal care and postnatal care, growth monitoring and referral of sick children, discussion of health topics to generate awareness, and convergence between health and nutrition – delivered on a fixed day approach, usually once or twice every month at the Anganwadi Centre. AWW were asked to describe protocols maintained for these meetings:

"VHND and Immunization Day is organised following social distancing protocol to disseminate knowledge regarding health and food during pregnancy." (ASHA 1, Uttarakhand)

"There have been some disruptions. ASHA has to go to each household in her village for these activities, people are scared so they ask her to leave afraid that she will spread the disease to them" (ASHA Supervisor 1, Maharashtra).

Despite the lockdown restrictions ASHA workers across the six states reported carrying out antenatal check-ups, and supporting Auxiliary Nurse Midwives (ANM) in immunization and institutional delivery, health awareness, and regularly meeting pregnant women and mothers.

"ASHAs have been monitoring more than 25 homes on a daily basis, to check for symptoms related to fever, cough, or if people have returned from cities. Make a note of them and share with the GP. To check for symptoms of corona"

AWWs in Odisha, Bihar and Maharashtra reported that despite lockdown measures, their work has increased:

"We have declared a holiday for the anganwadi, so I am (supposed to be) at home. Yet, I have to go for Corona duty, monitor people coming from outside the village. We have to stay alert due to Corona. We have to take dry food to homes of children registered at Anganwadi, and also

provide awareness on Corona. There's too much pressure on us". (AWW 2, Odisha)

(b) COVID-19 health literacy: information on finger-tips

FFHWs received information on COVID-19 and prevention through different channels and modes: majority of them reported TV channels, news coverage, and videos sent on Whatsapp groups. Others received training from health officials, which were considered to be more authoritative and valid:

> *"There was a meeting on 26th March in the PHC [Primary Health Centre], the Medical officer gave us all the information on Corona for both us and ASHAs. We have compulsory monthly meetings"*. (ASHA Supervisor 2, Maharashtra).

ANM and doctors at the Primary Health Centre were considered reliable for accurate and valid information. ASHA undertook dissemination activities – distributing pamphlets provided by PHC, or show videos received via Whatsapp to pregnant women, elderly members, putting up posters of community walls or slogans – to generate awareness of proper preventive measures for COVID-19.

FFHW respondents articulated a range of protective measures they took to prevent getting affected themselves while undertaking their responsibilities. *"I cover my face and stand at distance from others, wash hands when come from outside" (ASHA 3, Madhya Pradesh),* while another respondent from same state mentioned:

> *"I use gloves, mask, rub my hands with sanitizer frequently; I talk from a distance of 1m from everybody, and do not sit in anybody's home while on visit. Once I come back home, I take a bath and change clothes" (ASHA 1, Madhya Pradesh).*

Another respondent described her knowledge and practice to prevent Corona as follows:

> *"Use mask while going out, keep sanitizer, don't shake hands, if someone is coughing then tell them to use mask and maintain distance, inform PHC to check them, if necessary then quarantine them, using mask and gloves and sanitizer for ourselves while going to the field."* (ASHA supervisor 2, Bihar)

> *"These three measures (wearing masks, washing hands and social distancing) are elementary and complementary to each other. But we should provide good awareness too. Because we have experience that even very after of such awareness's people don't actually care about the aforementioned measures. During the initial days people were vigilant, but now they seriously don't care about all these."* (ASHA 1, Kerala)

When probed to mention how they know if a patient would require testing for Corona, FFHWs generally looked for symptoms for people who came from outside their village in the last two weeks, and then referred them to the nearest health centre.

> *"We just ask if someone has any fever, or cough or cold for body pain; has anybody come from outside like Delhi or Bombay, if yes, we tell them to go to health centre for check-up" (ASHA 1, Uttarakhand)*

(c) Mobile ownership, use of apps and digital literacy for FFHWs

In Osmanabad, Maharashtra, online training on COVID-19 was provided in the Zoom app.

> *"Once the Corona started, Zoom meetings were conducted, where we received online training. From Playstore we downloaded this zoom app. We got the zoom id and password, from which attended the meeting. The training was given in Marathi. This was organized by officers at district level." (ASHA Supervisor 2, Maharashtra).*

Some respondents were part of Facebook and Whatsapp groups to immediately share information, reporting to the PHC on a daily basis. Although respondents had a mobile phone, not all of them owned smartphones, they relied on family members – son or husband – who owned a smartphone to send photographs of daily reports to PHC, or to download apps for training, or for monitoring. In Maharashtra, ANMs used the Reproductive and Child Health (RCH) portal for maintaining records of pregnant women and mothers of young children in the villages. ASHA assisted in this record-keeping by transferring these records from paper registry to app. One respondent mentions:

> *"All ASHAs and Supervisors have been asked to download the Aarogya Setu app. Not everyone has a smartphone; more than 6 ASHAs under me do not own a smartphone. 25 ASHAs have a phone. They can watch videos as well on the phone. ANM has an RCH portal. ASHA five registers with her – RCH (reproductive child health) register, ANC (antenatal check-ups) monitoring register. Child immunization register, and Births-deaths register. These are reported to ANM and are reported twice monthly"* (ASHA Supervisor 1, Maharashtra)

> *"We were added to a whatsapp group for ASHA workers in our Panchayat. It was primarily created to share the numbers of people who are in quarantine, also for the community kitchen arrangements, and to know about the movement of labourers from our states returning from outside" (ASHA 2, Kerala)*

Aarogya Setu was launched by the Government of India as a contract tracing app that could provide detailed information of people who have been in contact with Corona-positive patients. The Centre sent directives for the mandatory use of its contact tracing app, Aarogya Setu by all government staff. Some FFHWs were asked to use the Aarogya Setu app by their supervisors, but they were not able to articulate how it will help them. In Kodungallur, Kerala, one of our respondents said, "Yes, our majority tasks are offline duties. We don't have too much online work or tasks." (ASHA 3, Kerala)

In Bihar, ASHA supervisors reported using Diksha app for training. FFHWs relied on phones to receive messages from their colleagues, peers and community members, as well as disseminate urgent warnings or reports to their community members. They communicate with their supervisors, access health services such as ambulances, and communicate with peers using phones. *"In case of emergency, an ambulance is available on call, if we can communicate on phone, otherwise we arrange private vehicles. We also talk to pregnant women over phone and give them essential information for diets"* (ASHA Supervisor 2, Madhya Pradesh).

(d) Lack of Personal Protective Equipment (PPE) for FFHWs

PPE is a protective gear – goggles, face-shield, mask, gloves, coverall/gowns (with or without aprons), head cover and shoe cover – designed to safeguard the health of workers by minimizing the exposure to a biological agent. These are to be used based on the risk settings where the health staff work. The Ministry of Home and Family Welfare provides guidelines on PPE use for ASHA workers, who conduct surveillance in low risk settings. Despite the sensitivity of the nature of their work, ASHAs are recommended to wear a triple-layered mask and gloves, while maintaining a distance of one meter. The other stakeholders interviewed here observed that, *"PPE provided to ASHA workers are basic, inadequate and inappropriate. We are putting their lives at risk just because their work is of voluntary nature"* (Academic 1, New Delhi).

The provision of PPE has also not been uniform across the states. In some districts in Uttarakhand, and Maharashtra they received gloves, caps and sanitizers, elsewhere they received cloth masks and sanitizers. In Madhya Pradesh, Odisha and Bihar, ASHA workers bought masks and gloves from their own money as nobody provided these. These were neither cheap, not easily available, given their low earnings. In Kerala, one participant mentioned,

> *"We didn't get access to Aprons and gloves yet, but masks yes. We participated in a campaign recently and we got gloves from there, and occasionally from the side of panchayat. Most of the time we purchase masks for ourselves."* (ASHA 1, Kerala)

The lack of safety equipment and infrastructure for frontline workers has been one of the reasons for high numbers of positive cases amongst healthcare workers. Triple layered masks and gloves are not adequate protection while FFHWs go door-to-door in containment zones to identify infected persons, thereby putting themselves at risk. The chances of ASHA workers contracting the infection are very high, because of their interaction with a large population (Jain, 2020). The out-of-pocket expenditures incurred by ASHAs actually added to their economic burden in light of non-payments and inappropriate or lack of remunerations.

(e) Lack of appropriate financial remunerations and systemic irregularities in recruitment and payment of ASHAs

There was a huge disparity in financial remuneration provided for FFHWs in each state for undertaking COVID-19 work. In Maharashtra, ASHAs received additional Rs 1000 per month (for 2 months) by the Gram Panchayat, while ASHA supervisors were assured but yet to receive Rs 500. In Odisha and Uttarakhand, Anganwadi workers did not receive any compensation. While in Bihar and Madhya Pradesh they reported hearing about getting additional payment but not receiving it yet. An elderly FFHW from Uttarakhand notes, *"I am not doing this for money, people respect me where I go, come to me with their problems< I do this for the community"* (ASHA 2, Uttarakhand). In Odisha AWW commented, *"People know me, that Didi (sister) will definitely come; it's her duty. We also give information on the phone. They respect us."*(AWW 2, Odisha). This shows that most FFHWs are doing it as a community service and are motivated by taking on leadership roles in their village.

ASHA workers from Kerala reported getting timely payments:

> *"Yes, we receive them properly, even if it is less. It was 4500 earlier and from last April they have increased it to 5000.we did have a lot of conditions earlier for that, like participation in campaigns regularly and all, but now , due to the situation, we get the salary without any condition. For the last four months, we have been getting an additional 1000 pay."* (ASHA 2, Kerala)

(f) Other concerns

During the lockdown ASHAs are limited in their movements: either they rely on personal transport, or walk several kilometres daily. Some reported having family support, when a male family member – son or husband – accompanied them to the PHC. There have been some disruptions for providing routine services:

> *"ASHA has to go to most households for these activities, but people are scared so they ask her to leave afraid that she will spread the disease to them".* (NGO official, Maharashtra)

While ASHA workers also expressed their concerns and challenges of working in the COVID-19 response,

"I'm scared from the news of affected ANM and doctors, don't know if someday I come home infected by corona. I'm concerned for my family as they can get infected because of me" (ASHA supervisor 3, Bihar)

"Transport is a challenge, I have to request my husband to ferry me on his motorcycle, since everything is closed now. In this lockdown, our troubles have only doubled." (ASHA Supervisor 2, Maharashtra)

The COVID-19 lockdown measures complicated not only their routine activities, but also their personal situation as families struggle to access basic amenities:

I am not able to take pregnant women for checkups, due to unavailability of vehicles; I am not able to visit kids who used to come to anganwadi (ASHA 2, Madhya Pradesh)

"My family is suffering too, we cannot go out, there is a shortage of food, the supervisor is not doing visits and meetings so we are facing problems in providing information, anddistributing dry food packets from anganwadi, even though cooking in anganwadi has stopped". (ASHA 1, Madhya Pradesh)

ASHAs faced stigma from community members, because people are apprehensive that she will spread the disease while doing household surveys. This occurred despite taking precautionary measures: wearing masks or gloves, washing hands with soap. Most respondents perceived that the threat of COVID-19 will persist, and social distancing measures will have to continue at least for 2 more months. Moreover, workers in Maharashtra expressed concerns that despite taking precautionary measures, in the summer and monsoons there will be an increase in other infectious diseases and hence measures should be in place to mitigate these.

"Dehydration and other waterborne diseases will increase. We provide awareness on keeping water clean, boiling water for consumption." (ASHA 2, Odisha)

"We are demonstrating people how to wash their hands with proper techniques" (ASHA 5, Madhya Pradesh)

"Immunizations are still taking place; we maintain distance (of 1ms) and continue with these efforts. Pregnant woman's 3 antenatal check-ups are also continued: some are asked to come in next month. We are doing these in 2 batches." (ASHA Supervisor 4, Maharashtra)

When probed further on what preparedness was required to tackle the oncoming monsoon season, ASHA across the states reported the necessity to reach out to pregnant women, young mothers and children during floods and cyclones.

"There are certain minor issues to be corrected. Mainly the environment. I think once we start discussing it with people, we will be able to overcome it soon. As the land is a bit prone to floods and all, we have to be a bit conscious especially in the time of a pandemic like COVID-19". (ASHA 3, Kerala)

There were several situational and context-specific challenges which posed challenges to adoption of preventive measures:

"My field is based on a colony space which is a colony of Tsunami rehabilitated people. It consists of 185 rehabilitation homes where around 120 homes are occupied. Even the households have basic facilities and all they have very little space for day to day things, like the sanitation and toilet facilities are not proper, and the space is very congested and badly engineered to take care of the hygiene.The drainage and waste disposal system is also weak there. The spaces between the rehabilitation homes are very less and unhygienic. I strived to the maximum of my capacity for their betterment but the situations are still bad and invited less attention from the superior authorities." (ASHA 1, Kerala)

5. Discussion

To our knowledge, this is the first study to understand the role and participation of women in the frontline of India's COVID-19 response. Drawing upon gendered implications of health system resilience, we explored the influence of broader contextual barriers on the forms of agency that women are able to exercise: access to information, resources and technologies to reduce their workload, improvements in service delivery and supporting the communities affected by an health emergency. These include an understanding of gender and institutional factors that shape FFHWs' experiences, their capabilities in health and digital literacy and resources available to strengthen their work in preventive health and management.

We find that the response to pandemic relies heavily on the shoulders of FFHWs to prevent community transmission, managing quarantine centres and generate awareness by quelling misinformation at the community level. In order to improve their capabilities an approach that enhances their health and digital literacy is key, which can be leveraged through web-based or app-based learning. The study highlighted disparities across states, in how these approaches strengthened FFHWs' digital and health literacy: by using apps for surveillance, training and contact tracing. There were disparities across states in how each state relied upon ICT for disseminating and training the FFHWs. Telephone emerged as a primary mode of communication, along with digital whatsapp and facebook groups to view content and awareness videos on Corona. The findings show that for optimal use of technologies by FFHWs, a thorough analysis of gendered mechanisms at household and community level is necessary for engagement, along with ongoing training and on-field support.

Central Government declared insurance cover of INR 50 lakhs for COVID-19 responders for 90 days, including community health workers; while Maharashtra has announced a INR 25 lakh insurance cover for AWWs (Sundar, 2020). Before the outbreak, ASHA workers were promised a base salary of approximately 2000/-per month varying across states. On 20th April 2020, NHM Director notified that ASHA workers should get INR 2000 for their work, over their regular incentives under Janani Suraksha Yojana and other schemes. Academics have criticised the honorarium system for few years now, because their consolidated pay includes neither cost-of-living allowance nor ensure structured guidelines for their periodic revision as would be the case in any kind of state employment (Sundar, 2020). There are concerns that the FFHWs are undertaking additional responsibilities for COVID-19, which could result in disruption of essential health services, despite the Union health ministry's March 25, 2020 guidelines to ensure routine immunisation activities and antenatal check-ups for at-risk mothers. The ministry recommended more immunisation sessions with smaller groups mobilised over the phones by ASHA (Salve, 2020).

Findings show that FFHWs depended on local resource persons and social networks to undertake their tasks efficiently in their communities. Therefore, developing similar cadre of workers at the frontline is strongly encouraged. In Odisha, the Odisha Livelihoods Mission has been active in leveraging nutrition and livelihoods, where *Poshan sakhis* (part of the National Rural Livelihoods Mission) are employed to work with ASHAs and ANMs delivering Take Home Ration (THR) (Salve, 2020). Odisha also relies on multipurpose workers, traditionally male volunteers who support development activities at the village level. However, these workforces require security and financial support, alongside technical and training support.

This study also highlights financial remuneration as the most pressing concern for FFHWs like ASHAs. ASHAs have been demanding to be included within the cadre of permanent healthcare staff with a fixed pay of 18,000 per month along with social security and maternity benefits, fixed tasks and work hours (Rao and Tewari 2020). FFHWs have to balance not only personal safety and family responsibilities but also undertake tasks for routine health service delivery, alongside COVID-19 prevention and management measures. The financial compensation for such overwhelming work burden puts an unequal burden on women, and is a determining

factor of their bargaining power with the institutional set up. This is line with Bhatia (2014), who found linkages between absenteeism/attrition and remuneration. There were discrepancies in what they were promised for undertaking additional COVID-19 work and whether they received the payments, lesser pay and remuneration standards also varied across states. When their work is not recognised and appropriately remunerated with possibilities of a secure job, this overwhelming burden on ASHAs becomes inconvenient as they are expected to do several other non-compensatory activities to engage with communities and build rapport to achieve increasingly difficult goals of improving institutional delivery, reducing infant mortality, controlling spread of infection (Swaminathan, 2015).

The policymakers argue that a fixed salary could lead to complacency, as well as entitle ASHA workers to national government pensions, among other benefits (Jain, 2020). Hence, in several regions, their honoraria are less than the minimum wages of unskilled workers. Sundar (2020) notes that ASHA's compensation system is rather complex, comprising variable components that are linked to defined tasks (e.g. INR 100 for full immunisation; INR 50 for reporting child death; INR 1,000 for 42 contacts over 6-7 months of TB treatment). ASHAs have also been demanding testing for themselves for the fear of infecting their families. They are also demanding separate quarantine facilities. (Rao and Tewari 2020)

ASHAs are facing threats and abuse, and exploitation not only in the hands of the communities they serve but also by an exploitative employer. Most of these women look for encouragement as they belong to low-income families and contribute to society from altruistic attitudes. A just remuneration and provision of other benefits to the health warriors is important for empowering FFHWs and their families and enhancing gender justice and bargaining power within community and institutional set up. Women's active participation in community health stems from conducive factors such as personal motivation, service and altruistic attitudes, being part of a community tackling an unseen danger, and being part of a wider network of health workers. For women to engage in this sphere, a supporting family is key – perhaps indicating social capital and extra-household support leaving women with time to undertake more work – are all important over and above their household duties as mother, wife and daughter-in-law.

This study benefits from a wide range of respondents to capture plurality of approaches in supporting the female workforce. There are some important limitations. The sample size is small, restricted by the limitations of movement. It is also unfair to compare and contrast examples from these six states with a heterogenous sample. Since these interviews were conducted over phone, we were not able to observe and note their non-verbal reactions and responses. Further areas of research identified in this study include – analysing the trade-offs between online training or face-to-face training and support on the job to promote changes in behaviour.

6. Conclusions

The gendered experiences of the FFHWs in COVID-19 response in India has emphasised FFHW's role and importance of their workplace dignity. Using a capability approach, this study illustrates that digital and health literacy of FFHWs for COVID-19 is a growing area of application and requires further scaffolding to sustain their ongoing operations. Using ICT in an equitable and just manner provides an opportunity to support local action for health resilience swiftly and promptly by building capacities and increasing representation of the frontline workers. This understanding can be further grounded around issues of equity, participation, representation in a gender-responsive health system. This study demonstrates that gender differences may be accommodated in crises through changes to local policies and practices that enable women to access resources.

It is essential to recognise FFHWs' role inside of the health system, improving their working conditions and enabling enhanced usage of information, communication and technology. Concerted efforts by policy-makers are required to recalibrate how FFHWs are empowered as leaders of change with systems-level change and impetus through recognition and rewards. This alone will address issues of parity, equity, participation, and representation in a gender-responsive health system.

REFERENCES

1. Ballard, M; Bancroft, E; Nesbit, J; Johnson, A, & Holeman, I, 2020, *Prioritising the role of community health workers in the COVID-19 response.* BMJ Global Health 2020, 7 April, pp. 6.

2. Bhatia, K, 2014, *Performance-Based Incentives of the ASHA Scheme Stakeholders' Perspectives*, Economic Political Weekly, Vol. XLIX, No. 22, 31 May, pp. 145–151.

3. Choudhury, N, 2009, T*he Question of Empowerment: Women's Perspective on Their Internet Use*, Gender, Technology and Development, Vol 13, Issue 3, https://doi.org/10.1177/097185241001300302

4. Chew, H E; Ilavarasan, P V & Levy, M R, 2015, *Mattering Matters: Agency, Empowerment, and Mobile Phone Use by Female Microentrepreneurs*, Information Technology for Development Vol.21, 4 Pgs 523-542 https://doi.org/10.1080/02681102.2013.839437

5. Durski KN, Osterholm M, Majumdar SS, et al., 2020, *Shifting the paradigm: using disease outbreaks to build resilient health systems.* BMJ Global Health. doi:10.1136/bmjgh-2020-002499

6. Gigler, B S, 2006, *Experiences of Indigenous Peoples with ICTs* in Enacting and Interpreting Technology-From Usage to Well-Being, Ch 6.

7. Masika, R; Bailur, S (2015), *Negotiating Women's Agency through ICTs: A Comparative Study of Uganda and India*, Gender, Technology and Development 19(1) 43–69 DOI: 10.1177/0971852414561615

8. Nussbaum, M 2003: *Capabilities as Fundamental Entitlements: Sen And Social Justice*, Feminist Economics, 9:2-3, pp 33–59

9. Jain, D, 2020, *Time to bring some hope to ASHA workers fighting Coronavirus at frontline*, Outlook India, 2 April 2020, https://www.outlookindia.com/website/story/opinion-time-to-bring-some-hope-to-asha-workers-fighting-coronavirus-at-frontline/349914 (Accessed 29 May 2020)

10. Jones A, Howard N, Legido-Quigley H. 2015, *Feasibility of health systems strengthening in South Sudan: a qualitative study of international practitioner perspectives.* BMJ Open; 5. doi:10.1136/bmjopen-2015-009296

11. Kabeer 2000, *The power to choose: Bangladeshi women and labour market decisions in London & Dhaka,* Verso, London and New York, 2000, ISBN: 1 85984 804 4

12. Rushton, A, Phibbs, S, Kenney, C, Anderson, C; 2020, *The gendered body politic in disaster policy and practice*, International Journal of Disaster Risk Reduction, pp. 47. https://doi.org/10.1016/j.ijdrr.2020.101648

13. Kandiyoti, D, 1988, *Bargaining with Patriarchy*, Gender and Society, Vol. 2, No. 3, Special Issue to Honor Jessie Bernard, pp. 274-290.

14. Mabsout, R and van Staveren, I 2010, *Disentangling Bargaining Power from Individual and Household Level to Institutions: Evidence on Women's Position in Ethiopia*, World Development 38: 5, pp. 783 – 796.

15. Salve, P, 2020, *Essential Outreach Services Hit In States With Worst Health Indicators* 20 April, 2020 IndiaSpend https://www.indiaspend.com/essential-outreach-services-hit-in-states-with-worst-health-indicators/ (Accessed 29 May 2020)

16. Schaaf, M., Warthin, C., Freedman, L., & Topp, S. M. 2020, *The community health worker as service extender, cultural broker and social change agent: a critical interpretive synthesis of roles, intent and accountability.* BMJ Global Health 2020, 22 April, pp. 8.

17. Sen, A, 1990., *''Gender and Cooperative Conflicts''* in Irene Tinker (ed.) Persistent Inequalities, pp. 123 – 49. New York: Oxford University Press.

18. Sreerekha, MS, 2016, *State without Honour: Women Workers in India's Anganwadis*, Oxford University Press; pp 348.

19. Sundar, KR Shyam, 2020, *ASHA, Anganwadi workers deserve pay, social security, not just applause*, Deccan Herald, 22 April 2020, https://www.deccanherald.com/opinion/panorama/asha-anganwadi-workers-deserve-pay-social-security-not-just-applause-828665.html (Accessed 29 May 2020)

20. Swaminathan, P; 2015, *The formal creation of informality, and therefore, gender injustice: illustrations from India's*

social sector, Indian Journal of Labour Economics 58:23-42, DOI 10.1007/s41027-015-0006-z

21. Rao, B and Tewari, S 2020, Article 14 https://www.article-14. com/post/anger-distress-among-india-s-frontline-workers-in-fight-against-covid-19 (Accessed 29 November 2020)

22. Warrier, A, 2020, *The Women Warriors Fighting COVID-19 at the Frontline, ASHA Workers Left Without Hope, An Amnesty India report,* Amnesty India, May 2020, pp.1-4.

CHAPTER 3

Co-creating Climate Resilience Technological Solutions for Poor

Siraz Hirani

M.Sc. (Disaster Mitigation), MBA (Finance) Senior Program Management Specialist
Mahila Housing Trust (MHT) Mobile: +91-9833122355
siraz@mahilahsg.org; hiranisiraz@gmail.com

Abstract

The "Women-led Resilience Building of Urban Poor in South Asia" project was developed by Mahila Housing SEWA Trust (MHT) and its partners as a part of the Global Resilience Partnership (GRP) challenge. The project aimed to build the resilience capacities of 25000 low income families living in slums/informal settlements in seven cities of South Asia, to take the lead in action against four climate risks. These four climate stressors (a) heat waves; (b) flooding and inundation; (c) water scarcity; and (d) increased climate change-related incidence of water and vector borne diseases; are slower-onset and less apparent, often impacting the poor most but attract less attention compared to disasters and extreme events. The project worked to create an integrated model wherein women take a lead through collective action and technology incubation, to devise locally relevant pro-poor and gender sensitive climate resilient solutions and promote a culture of sustainable development and resilience among the urban poor in South Asia.

One of the key components of the project was use of technologies to promote resilience among poor communities. An innovative approach for technology transfer/adaptation was developed in this project wherein the implementing organisation (Mahila Housing Trust), poor communities, private sector technology partners and financial institutions worked in a collaborative way leading to acceptance and replication of new technological solutions by poor.

Mahila Housing Trust facilitated demonstration of product/service of innovative entrepreneurs and businesses in the slums. As a result, entrepreneurs and business got an entry into the communities and a space to show case their product. Various technologies were tested in slums areas where in slum dwellers can see, feel and experience the benefit of the technology over a duration of 6 months to 1 years. Based on their experience, slum dwellers provided feedback to MHT regarding what needs to be improved in a particular technology to make it more acceptable for poor. MHT shared those feedbacks with entrepreneurs who then made agreed upon modifications and made renewed technological product available for poor community. MHT's interest was mainly to explore multiple solutions to the various problems to be able to support the communities to select the most efficient and cost-effective solution. The idea was to create a basket of choices for the community to choose from based on their needs, aspirations and financial status. During the project a range of such partners dealing with improved roofing solutions, water purification products, composting technologies, building technologies, etc. was explored. Key to success was facilitating interactions between communities and technical experts so that both parties communicate clearly and develop mutually agreeable solutions to resilience problems.

The paper presentation will cover the technology transfer mechanism and key learning emerging from the mix method (quantitative & qualitative) study that was conducted on completion of this project. The findings will highlight key barrier to adaptation of technological solutions by poor and mechanism to address it.

Keywords: Climate change, Climate stresses, Resilience, Urban Poor, Technology, Co-creation

Key Theme – Harnessing Technology for Disaster Risk Management
Technical Session – Technology Transfer & Technology Facilitation Mechanism

1. Introduction

The project aimed to create and implement resilience plans to address four major climate risks - heat stress, flash floods, acute water shortages and vector borne diseases - in 100 slum communities in 7 cities of South Asia. These include Ahmedabad, Jaipur, Bhopal, Ranchi, Bhubaneshwar (India), Kathmandu (Nepal) and Dhaka (Bangladesh). The key strategy was to tackle the institutional, information and knowledge barriers in building capacities of slum communities and city governments for assessing vulnerabilities and risks of Climate Change on poor populations. The project addressed this by building the social capital of slum communities by organising them into Community-Based Organisations (CBOs); promoting critical partnerships between technical experts, local governments and low-income communities;

developing tools and process for transfer of scientific knowledge and participatory risk assessments; and working with communities and partners jointly towards designing and implementing resilience technical solutions. The project has directly impacted the lives of more than 25,000 poor families living in urban slums in the 7 cities by creating their capacities to deal with climate risks and vulnerability.

Project's Theory of Change has been that "If the urban poor are provided with the requisite knowledge to undertake vulnerability and risk assessments and equipped with available resilient-technologies, they will be able to devise and implement locally relevant and pro-poor climate resilient solutions. If the poor are empowered to implement their own resilience plans, they will be able to better influence climate resilient city planning and ensure that effective urban adaptation practices are in place."

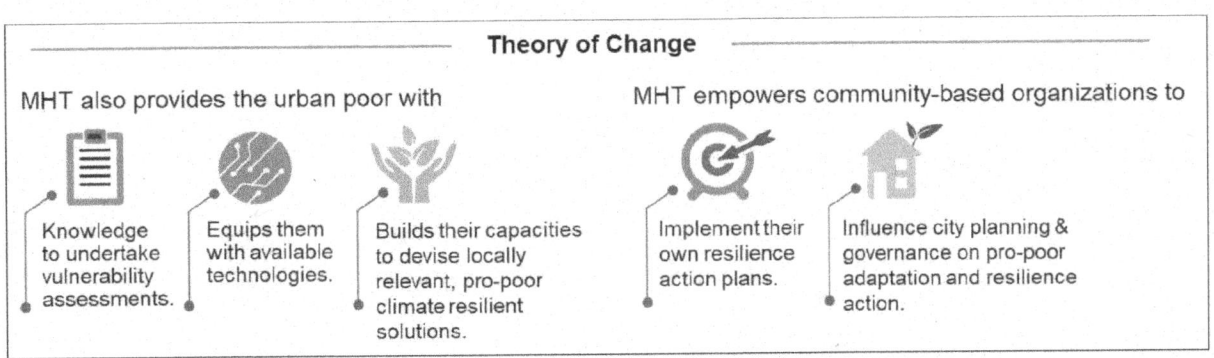

Fig. 3.1   Project Theory of Change

2. Methods

Key questions that study attempted to answer are as follows:

(a) Does the model of change and corresponding interventions improve resiliency in slums with existing internal and citywide social networks?

(b) Can the model be used to simultaneously build such networks and to improve resilience within the slum communities that currently lack internal and citywide social networks?

(c) Can the model be transferred to other NGOs for implementation in cities where MHT does not work?

Study used mix of both quantitative and qualitative methods. The baseline-end line study was designed to asses if the theory of change was effective in bringing expected outcomes across project geography. Stratified sampling technique was used for the research study. The baseline survey was designed to provide baseline data from which post-intervention changes could be compared. While baseline conditions are measured at the household level, interventions occur primarily at the

slum-level. The household to be interviewed were therefore selected using a stratified random sample method, with slums randomly selected for inclusion, then individual households within each slum randomly sampled from the households living in each slum.

The study was undertaken to evaluate the effect of the intervention on climate vulnerability. The same HHs that were surveyed during the baseline were re-surveyed for the End line survey. 19.7% of the sample pre-intervention survey could not be found or declined to participate in the post-intervention survey. No pattern to the missing households could be identified, and the number of slums which were included in the baseline remained unchanged. The detailed account of sampled HHs in Baseline and End line by City, Slum type and Treatment type is given in Table 3.2.

Sixty informal settlement communities from the four cities were included in the study. The intervention slums were categorized into two types; 1. Established slum and 2. Emerging slum. Established slums are the slums where MHT is working for more than 10 years and Emergent slums are

Table 3.1   Treatment Type and Sample Slums, by City Baseline

City	Slum Type	Treatment Slums in Sample				Control Slums in Sample	
		Number of Slums	No. of CAG Households per Slum	No. of Non-CAG Households per Slum	Total No. of Households	No. of Slums	No. of Households
Ahmedabad	Established	10	10	15	250	10	150
	Emergent	10	10	15	250		
Jaipur	Emergent	5	10	15	125	5	75
Bhopal	Emergent	5	10	15	125	5	75
Ranchi	Emergent	5	10	15	125	5	75
					875		375

Table 3.2   No. of Sampled HHs by City, Slum type and Treatment Type for Baseline and Endline survey

City	Slum Type	Baseline (Count)			Endline (Count)		
		Treatment HHs		Control HHs	Treatment HHs		Control HHs
		CAG HHs	Non-CAG HHs		CAG HHs	Non-CAG HHs	
Ahmedabad	Established	94	150	150	83	108	125
	Emergent	98	150		86	92	
Jaipur	Emergent	49	75	75	43	57	60
Bhopal	Emergent	50	75	75	48	54	69
Ranchi	Emergent	50	75	75	46	69	56
Total		341	525	375	306	380	310

ones where MHT had either recently began work or became operational as a result of this project.

The missing 19.7% of HHs in the end line survey are a result of one of four conditions:

1. The same respondent was not available, *
2. Relocation of family – (Within slum/city/to other city),
3. Challenges in relocating the same Household, or
4. Woman head of household declined to participate in the survey.

(*The House was visited several to survey the same respondent before dropping that HHs from the sample)

In addition to demographic data, the questionnaires included variables to calculate scores for household climate vulnerability. These vulnerability scores are based on risk (potential exposure to climate change hazard) and susceptibility (incapacity to access financial and social capital resources needed to cope with hazards either by preventative investments or coping strategies).

Five risk and two susceptibility scores have been constructed for each of the surveyed households.

The risk scores included:

1. Heat stress
2. Water adequacy/quantity,
3. Water quality,
4. Flooding and
5. Vector-borne disease risks.

The susceptibility scores included:

1. Financial capital** and
2. Social capital.

(**Financial capital was not calculated for the End line, considering that there will not be significant change in financial status in a year)

The risks and susceptibility scores were developed from the household survey data, and standardized to a 0 to 10 scale. Each scale indicates the household's liability to be adversely affected by the climate risk or their precariousness due to socio economic conditions. Scale value of "0" indicates lower risk/susceptibility, a "5" indicates average risk/susceptibility, and "10" indicates higher risk/susceptibility. The level of risk or susceptibility indicated by these scores are relative measures, measured along the lines of typical risks and susceptibilities faced by urban poor in South Asia. Even slum dwellers with "lower" risk or vulnerability remain at significant risk compared to wealthier South Asia residents, and especially compared to most residents of more developed nations located in more temperate climates. We used these Risks and Susceptibility scores to classify households into low, moderate and severely vulnerable. Ninety-four percent of our sample was susceptible in terms of financial or social capital or both, and was also exposed to one or more climate risks of heat stress, water scarcity, poor water quality, flooding and vector-borne diseases. We therefore set a higher threshold to be considered moderately and highly vulnerable. Those households which were socially and/or financially susceptible and were exposed to (i) no or one risk, (ii) two risks or (iii) three and more climate risks were classified as low, moderate and highly vulnerable households.

Case Analysis qualitative method/approach was also used because the model of change being tested in this project is fundamentally a process-driven model. The case analysis thus focuses on process tracing to examine interaction amongst the three major spheres of action – the slum dwellers, the technical support systems, and citywide networks – and intervention strategies that best explain the intervening process dynamics and outcomes, as well as eventual impacts at household, slum and city levels of intervention.

3. Results

Quantitate:

- Based on thresholds (refer methodology section), 33% of the Baseline survey households are least vulnerable, 36% of the households (455) were moderately vulnerable and 30% (375) were highly vulnerable.
- The End line survey reveals large shifts in the vulnerability levels of the sampled households. The proportion of less vulnerable has increased by 15%, while moderately and highly vulnerable have decreased by 4% and 11% respectively.
- Majority of the Baseline Low vulnerable remained the same, 17% shifted to Moderate and 7% into High vulnerability group. From the baseline Moderate and High vulnerability households, 46% and 30% respectively shifted into the low vulnerability group.
- Only 29% of the baseline high vulnerability group remained highly vulnerable, 1/3 of which became low vulnerable and 2/5 became moderately vulnerable.
- Out of the total moderately vulnerable households in the pre-intervention period, 46% became low vulnerable, 38% remained moderately vulnerable and 15% have increased vulnerability level to high.

- As shown in the table and figure below, decreases in vulnerability are not uniform across all groups. In particular, the most significant improvements occur in CAG and non-CAG treatment groups (as compared to controls). We also note that vulnerability is lowest in Ahmedabad, where MHT has worked the longest.

Table 3.3 Vulnerability proportion, by Baseline, Endline

	Baseline			Endline		
	Low	Moder-ate	High	Low	Moder-ate	High
CAG	36.60%	29.70%	31.70%	52.30%	29.70%	18.00%
NON CAG	42.40%	36.60%	21.10%	61.30%	29.70%	8.90%
Control	36.80%	37.70%	25.50%	45.80%	32.90%	21.30%
Ahmedabad	56.70%	30.00%	13.40%	73.30%	21.70%	5.10%
Bhopal	18.70%	35.70%	45.60%	37.40%	45.60%	17.00%
Jaipur	21.30%	35.00%	41.90%	30.60%	40.00%	29.40%
Ranchi	25.70%	48.00%	26.30%	35.10%	33.30%	31.60%

A significant number of households with decreases of respective risks and susceptibility by more than 20 % (relative to baseline condition)

Table 3.4 Percentage households with decrease of respective risks and susceptibility by more than 20%

	Water Quantity	Water Quality	Flood-ing	Health	Heat Stress	Social Capital
% of households in which risk has decreased by 20% or more	61.8%	49.4%	23.6%	32.7%	36.9%	32.7%

Qualitative:

- Entry into new communities requires perceptions of legitimacy, trust and incentives on the part of community women to partner, which can only be built over time with multiple engagements

  In an established city like Ahmedabad, where MHT has been working on slum improvement for the last 20 years, the organization enjoys credibility and trust amongst poor communities, sometimes even amongst 'emerging communities' where it has not worked directly. The Vikasini network and elected councillors play a crucial role in upholding this reputation of the organization by connecting communities in need to MHT. For example, in Silver Park, an emerging slum identified for intervention under the GRP program, Nafisaben, the elected councillor of the ward (and ex Vikasini member) played a key role in initiating the partnership between MHT and the community. In such instances, MHT has to build on the existing relationships; some level of trust already exists.

In communities where MHT's work is 'unknown', trust building is a long drawn process. MHT's field coordinators and spearhead teams conduct multiple visits in the area to meet with individuals and groups to start talking to them about MHT, and how it can support them in bringing improvements into their area. Initially MHT's field team is often met with scepticism. To gain the community's trust, MHT's spearhead teams often emphasize their own poor backgrounds. They can empathize with the communities and are able to relate with the communities' experiences.

- Continued participation by highly disenfranchised women in marginalised communities requires strategies to promote individual and community empowerment, solve tangible problems, and build recognition/identify within community

Most grassroots programs and initiatives in India by NGOs as well as the government emphasize involvement of communities in planning, implementing and monitoring specific development programs. However, the 'participation' of communities in decision-making is often limited to the duration of the 'externally funded' program. Once the program ends, the framework for participation also ends. Continued participation of communities in decisions concerning their lives and well-being requires development of empowered change agents within the community. MHT's experience in Ahmedabad offers strong evidence to support this claim. Some of the earliest intervention communities where MHT worked more than 15 years back continue to show leadership. CBO leaders in several of these early intervention communities have remained actively engaged in development activities in their slum (without active support from MHT). MHT's role for these communities has changed from a facilitator/ service provider to that of an advisor.

- Leadership works best when it is developed and interacts at and promotes coordinated action at the slum, community and city level

MHT organizes sensitization campaigns, hosts area meetings with CBO members to identify needs and aspirations of the community. CBO members are then encouraged to identify women leaders among themselves as members of the Community Action Group (CAG). The CAG, comprising 10-12 women leaders acts as the executive committee of the CBO members and leads action on their behalf. This is the second step. MHT builds and nurtures this leadership in slums by involving them in implementation of programs. Over years the

CAG members become highly knowledgeable about their communities, as well as their rights as citizens. They are able to independently work with government and service providers to bring improvements in their communities. MHT's leadership development model further offers these community leaders opportunity to move beyond driving change in their own communities to strengthening their influence on urban development plans and policies as part of the Vikasini forum. This is the final step in the process. Vikasini members represent the collective voices of poor and women in multi-stakeholder dialogues and workshops. They also work with MHT as part of the spearhead team to lead the mobilization process in new communities. They train and mentor CAG members in these communities and ensure that the community level institutions created in slums remain engaged and active.

This ladder of leadership offers opportunities to engage with the government at different levels. At each level in the leadership process, the women see a role for themselves.

Collectivising all slum families into a CBO allows MHT to engage with the community as a whole and inform the residents about their rights and how to exercise the. From time to time CBO members come together for campaigns. This is a strategy for 'show of strength' helps them rally support for their cause. The CAG members have a more defined role. They engage with area councillors to implement local improvements. The Vikasini leaders operate at the city level to engage with and influence decision-making. In Ahmedabad, where the Vikasini is well established, Vikasini members are often invited to be part of working groups and committees constituted by the government.

- Empowering women to advocate in a non-confrontational and collaborative manner increases municipal support to address these needs.

MHT has been working with communities to improve sanitation conditions and living environments in slums for more than 20 years. This requires significant investment in public infrastructure, and hence government support for such initiatives is vital.

In Ahmedabad, AMC has a history of extending basic infrastructure in slums. Though in some areas it takes much longer (up to 8 to 10 years) to reach services for multiple reasons. Sometimes the lands are under dispute or the communities are located on difficult terrain, which poses technical challenges to lay infrastructure. Communities located in the periphery or communally sensitive areas also find it difficult to access services. Even in these areas, MHT's core strategy is not to promote insurgent activism, but to empower women from these underserved communities to collaborate with the institutional powers, so that a two-way collaboration can be facilitated. MHT trains and mentors' women to patiently and persistently work with elected representatives and technical staff of AMC, to influence budgets, to collaboratively find solutions to difficult problems.

- Systematic, repeated and innovative communication tools are necessary to enable scientific and futuristic thinking in communities whose members are used to thinking short term.

MHT's work before the GRP program has largely focused on delivering tangible change in the short-term (2-3 years). This included enabling access to water and sanitation infrastructure, legal electricity connections, loans for incremental home improvements etc. Mobilizing communities around their immediate needs and requirements largely entails communicating information (either on accessing government scheme and processes, or specifics of loan products etc.) There already is an evident demand so there is often no need to create 'community interest'. Hence MHT has primarily relied on area meetings and classroom style trainings to deliver these messages. However, to trigger and sustain communities' interest in macro level concepts of 'global warming' and 'climate change' MHT had to get creative.

The first sets of communication tools were developed to educate the community on climate change, its reasons and its impacts. MHT conducted video shows in local languages and engaged women in interactive games that helped women understand and register long-term impacts of climate change, and understand concepts of vulnerability and resilience.

- Community's continued interest in resilience planning requires delivery of more immediate tangible action or benefits.

MHT recognizes that to increase resilience, it is important to have a long-term approach that incorporates strategies for knowledge generation, triggering behaviour change, and promoting community led action. MHT's experience suggests that to mobilize communities around climate change and sustain their interest in long term resilient planning, it is often essential to serve their immediate interest.

In Ahmedabad, MHT has ensured sustained progress over the last two decades by adopting an incremental and phased approach in its work. It directs public (and sometimes private) funds into a community to improve their current living conditions, and then building on its credibility and ability to deliver results, expands across

the 'share of people's day to day' pain through multiple initiatives.

- Community-led data collection leads to an increased understanding within the communities on their own vulnerabilities and issues affecting them, thereby leading to more resilient actions.

Instituting community based surveillance, especially in communities that have a high level of organization and leadership has proved to be a very effective strategy in Ahmedabad. There is evidence that real time collection and monitoring of climate data has triggered a behaviour change in communities towards making more informed decisions, and empowered them with knowledge to demand improved government services. Bhanuben, A Viksaini member had a weather monitoring station installed in her house in Rajiv Nagar. She used to note the temperature and humidity every day and share with community. The community also got into a habit of checking weather forecasts in newspapers or their mobile phones.

Evidence from Bhopal also points to the importance of community-led data collection in triggering behaviour change. In communities like BagSewaniya, Rahul Nagar, and Jatkhedi, regular water quality and vector surveillance drives have led to visible changes. Women leaders from Rahul Nagar rallied municipal support to get the area cleaned. Jatkhedi had faced regular quality issues and had complained about the same from time to time. The water testing drive in the community yielded results showing very poor water quality. Now the community had scientific evidence to back their claim. They showed the test results in their Ward Office and submitted an application to resolve the issue. The Ward Councillor soon visited the community (for the first time ever) address community level issues. The CAG members got him to fix the defunct hand-pump. The CAG is continuing to work together with the ward councillor on water quality and other community improvement initiatives in Jaatkhedi.

- Demonstration of technology solutions, coupled with facilitated engagement between communities and technical expert enhances the development of mutually agreeable solution to resilience.

Facilitating co-creation of technology was central to the GRP program. Field demonstrations of relevant technologies and solutions help build the confidence of the communities regarding the solutions and induce behaviour changes thereby increasing adoption rates, Ground-level technical support will further increase the possibility of adoption. During the course of the program, MHT demonstrated 21 types of climate resilient solutions at the household-level reaching out to 2,453 families across the cities. Further, 5 community-level resilient solutions were implemented reaching out to 4,425 individuals. MHT realised that in addition to demonstration projects, it is important to facilitate interactions between technical experts and communities. For example, MHT facilitated the field visit of Dr. Kohli, an epidemiologist to Bhopal, to speak to community leaders about larvae breeding and the science behind vector-borne diseases. MHT facilitated his visit to slum communities for him to view the living environment in slums and develop appropriate content for the trainings. MHT team also worked with him to develop simplified messages that the community is able to understand. At the end of the training, most women reported gaining new knowledge (that Dengue is also caused by mosquitos, that mosquitos can only breed in water etc.) and an increased interest in dealing with vector borne diseases in their slum.

MHT had a similar experience during the water management training that was facilitated by Theresa Formmen from FUB, where MHT also worked with Theresa to translate the training material in Hindi. Theresa also worked independently with the communities in Jaipur on an action research project to develop water management solutions. In a project reflection meeting Theresa shared how sometimes it was challenging to work with the communities because they often had different expectations from her. As a technical researcher, she adopted a more scientific approach to her work, where her first task was to get enough evidence to articulate the problem. This meant a lot of time spent on data collection from the field. But the communities didn't fully understand this approach. They would often get impatient and demand immediate solutions to their problems. This points to MHT's crucial role in such programs that bring together a diverse range of stakeholders; that of clearly communicating the processes, managing expectations and helping them understand each other's perspective.

• Successful pro-poor technologies should be cost-effective, commercially available, culturally appealing, with proper services provided along with the purchase.

In the last few years, MHT has piloted and tested a range of technologies and innovations, especially in the energy sector. These include building innovations and products that reduce heat stress, bring in natural light and ventilation, and help reduce energy consumption, thereby making dwellings more energy efficient. Under the GRP program, MHT widened this portfolio to include products and systems that promote more judicious use of water, reduce flooding and inundation, and safeguard food security and health. The types of technologies demonstrated could be categorized in three categories: innovations (by MHT or product innovators), market-based, and community-emerged/ home grown solutions.

Both in Ahmedabad and Bhopal, market-based, commercially available, low cost solutions such as tap water filters, purification liquids, and sprinkler taps saw a higher rate of adoption. In Bhopal, the community showed a lot of interest in water purification liquids, especially after the water drives. More than 300 households purchased these purification liquids. Similarly, 235+ families in Bhopal, and 396 families in Ahmedabad invested in the sprinkler taps. However, while investing in products with a cost higher than a couple of thousand rupees, 'perceived value' became a critical factor. For example, one of the solutions that MHT demonstrated was a Carbon based water filter. However, most families perceived it as inferior to the RO systems that require electricity (popular amongst middle-higher income households). MHT found it difficult to promote it at Market prices. The solution was more acceptable at a subsidized rate.

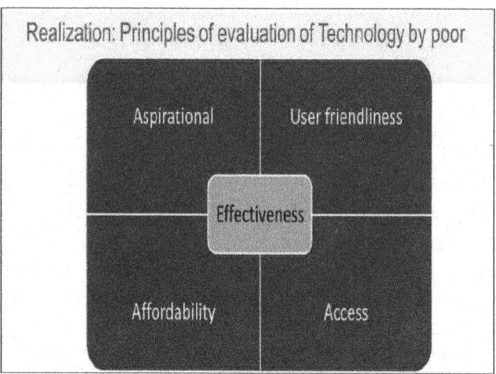

Fig. 3.2   Realization: Principles of evaluation of Technology by Poor

Other than making market-based technologies available, MHT also worked with product innovators to validate new technologies and make these available to the poor. However, MHT has met with limited success in terms of reaching scale. MHT has met with moderate success with the mod-roof system developed by Re-Materials in Ahmedabad. Currently, since the company is in its incubation phase, it is offering the roof system at a subsidized rate. MHT also offers loans to help poor households make this investment.

The community-emerged/home-grown solutions that were demonstrated included terrace gardening, landscaping with native plants, mosquito traps etc. Some families in both Ahmadabad and Bhopal adopted these solutions. Solutions like rainwater harvesting, community based water supply systems, and vermicomposting that require a higher amount of investment were also demonstrated on a pilot basis. These solutions/ services require specialized knowledge. MHT linked communities with these experts to roll out the solutions. Whether communities continue using/ maintaining these solutions is yet to be seen. MHT believes scaling these will require first a market to be developed for these services. A policy push from Government might enable that.

Another important aspect of demonstrating pro-poor solutions was to link communities to available government subsidies for infrastructure. In several slums in Ahmedabad MHT facilitated government supported infrastructure improvements and interventions such as toilets and improved water supply and drainage connections.

- Transfer of resilience-building processes is more effective if 'staff training' and 'application of learning in communities' runs in parallel and reinforces each other.

Another learning from the project has also been that while one does need to train organization staff on the issue, the "learning by doing" approach works much faster with staff too. Staffs particularly of grassroots organisations are able to learn much faster if they are simultaneously involved in project implementation.

4. Discussions

Theory of change being tested in this project is fundamentally a process-based model. The case analysis thus focuses on process tracing to examine interaction amongst the three major spheres of action – the slum dwellers, the technical support systems, and citywide networks – and intervention strategies that best explain the intervening process dynamics and outcomes, as well as eventual impacts at household, slum and city levels of intervention.

The model envisions climate change resilience as not a problem of "knowledge" but as one of barriers for translation of the knowledge into "action", the most critical being the lack of platforms and communication channels which can enable knowledge generators and communities to learn from each other and "co-create solutions". The study examines whether this critical partnership gap can be closed by creating systems for mutual learning, while ensuring that the interests of the primary audience "the communities whose resilience is at stake" is paramount.

Project also identified four key barrier in building climate resilience of poor communities as stated in Fig. 3.3 given below.

Based on the evidence generated from the study, below given factors has been identified as key success factor for co-creating climate resilience solutions for the poor.

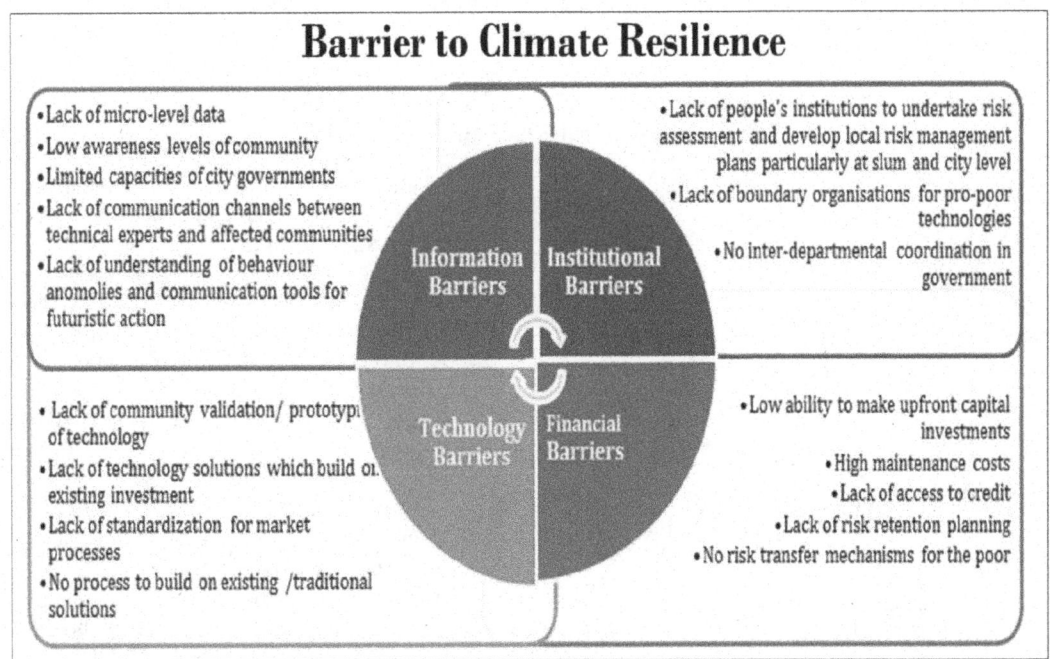

Fig. 3.3 Barriers to Climate Resilience

(a) The creation of strong institutional partnerships for joint action between all knowledge stakeholders: community members, government officials, service providers, technical experts, and other local institutions.

(b) Targeted and localized communication strategies and educational workshops that provide the most relevant information and create incentives for communities to seek technical knowledge and adopt futuristic thinking.

(c) Piloting and community validation of technical solutions to meet the needs of the poor, especially women.

(d) Designing and incubating financial products to support the poor to make investments in resilience solutions.

5. Conclusions

The report gathers evidence towards demonstrating the effectiveness of a community-based, women-led model for building resilience to climate change. It captures the underlying qualitative information and tests the theory of change of the project. However, the key purpose of the study is not only to establish the effectiveness of the model, but to bring out the key learnings emerging from the process which can be useful for other resilience building initiatives.

Key learnings from the study are as follows:

- Entry into new communities requires perceptions of legitimacy, trust, and incentives on the part of community women to partner, which can only be built over time with multiple engagements.

- Continued participation by highly disenfranchised women in marginalized communities requires strategies to promote individual and community empowerment, solve tangible problems, and build recognition/ identity within community

- Leadership works best when it is developed and interacts at and promotes coordinated action at the slum, community & city level

- Empowering women to advocate in a non-confrontational/ collaborative manner increases municipal support to address these needs

- Resilience in informal settlements requires coordinated action amongst many local actors over time, with leadership that is not too concentrated amongst a few members of the slum community and which is maintained over time.

- Systematic, repeated, and innovative communication tools are necessary to enable scientific and futuristic thinking in communities whose members are used to thinking short-term

- Community's continued interest in resilience planning requires delivery of more immediate tangible actions or benefits

- Community-led data collection leads to an increased understanding within the communities on their own vulnerabilities and issues affecting them, thereby leading to more resilient actions

- Successful pro-poor technologies should be cost-effective: commercially available, culturally appealing, with proper services provided along with the purchase

- Facilitating interactions between communities and technical experts enhances the capacity of both to communicate clearly and develop mutually agreeable solutions to resilience problems

6. Acknowledgement

The completion of this study could not have been possible without the consistent guidance of Prof. Michael Elliott, Georgia Institute of Technology. I am also grateful to GRP project team members Bijal Brahmbhatt, Bhavna Maheriya, Dharmistha Chauhan, Vanishree Herelkar, Srishti Singh, Parth Tailor, V. Selvakumar and Women Leaders of Community Action Groups whose contribution to the project has helped to create new knowledge in terms of findings presented in this paper. I am also thankful to the representative of local government bodies and private sector players who have taken out their time and provided their insight which has been pivotal for completing this study.

REFERENCES

1. Pervin, M., Sultana, S., Phirum, A., Camara, I., Nzau, V., Phonnasane, V., . . . Anderson, S. (2013). (Rep.). International Institute for Environment and Development. Retrieved August 23, 2021, from http://www.jstor.org/stable/resrep01244

2. Alam, S., Alam, A., Rahman, M., Rahman, S., & Rahman, N. (2016). *Building Climate Resilience to Noapara Town: A Coastal Urban Centre of Bangladesh* (pp. 24-30, Rep.). International Institute for Environment and Development. Retrieved August 23, 2021, from http://www.jstor.org/stable/resrep28984.12

3. Hughes, S. (2013). Justice in Urban Climate Change Adaptation: Criteria and Application to Delhi. *Ecology and Society*, *18*(4). Retrieved August 23, 2021, from http://www.jstor.org/stable/26269417

4. Kumar, C. (2013). Climate Change and Asian Cities: So Near Yet So Far. *Urban Studies*, *50*(7), 1456-1468. Retrieved August 23, 2021, from http://www.jstor.org/stable/26144301

5. Steele, P., Rai, N., & Nhantumbo, I. (2015). (Rep.). International Institute for Environment and Development. Retrieved August 23, 2021, from http://www.jstor.org/stable/resrep17969

6. SMITH, E. (2020). (Rep.). Stockholm International Peace Research Institute. Retrieved August 23, 2021, from http://www.jstor.org/stable/resrep25311

7. Reid, H., Swiderska, K., King-Okumu, C., & Archer, D. (2015). (Rep.). International Institute for Environment and Development. Retrieved August 23, 2021, from http://www.jstor.org/stable/resrep17971

8. Moser, C., & Satterthwaite, D. (2008). *Towards pro-poor adaptation to climate change in the urban centres of low- and middle-income countries* (pp. 16-27, Rep.). International Institute for Environment and Development. Retrieved August 23, 2021, from http://www.jstor.org/stable/resrep01260.9

9. Schultz, D., & Janković, V. (2014). Climate Change and Resilience to Weather Events. *Weather, Climate, and Society*, 6(2), 157-159. Retrieved August 23, 2021, from http://www.jstor.org/stable/24907322

Exploring the Potential of Solar Energy in Disaster Management and Rescue Operations

Pooja Punetha

Department of Nanotechnology, Centre for Advanced Studies,
Dr. A.P.J. Abdul Kalam Technical University, Lucknow, India
punetha1@gmail.com,

Sukriti Sharma

Indian Institute of Technology Ropar, Rupnagar, Punjab, India
sukriti.20chz0001@iitrpr.ac.in

Asad H. Sahir

Indian Institute of Technology Ropar, Rupnagar, Punjab, India
asad.sahir@iitrpr.ac.in

Abstract

Human society has recently not only coped with the challenge associated with COVID-19 pandemic but also seen disasters like monsoon floods, forest fires, hurricanes, cloud burst incidents, including devastating winter storms. In addition, disasters like the chemical plant explosion in Vizag, the Beirut explosion, boiler explosions, oil spill incidents and the gas leakage incidents, have left different parts of the world in shock. Dealing with pandemic and different kinds of natural and man-made disasters together, has been a challenging task, not only for different governments of the world, but also for personnel involved in rescue operations.

In this paper, a survey of personnel involved in rescue operations, people who had experienced a disaster, or are in contact with someone who is affected by disaster, is included. Reports available in public domain were analysed. Five case studies and 3 interviews were conducted to better understand the real time situation. The focus of paper largely remained on Indian context. India, being in a tropical region has an added advantage of 4-7 kWh/m2 insolation per day, which comes with another advantage that in most remote corners of the country, continuous power for potable water, medical equipment, food, and safety, can be ensured, using solar energy, especially during rescue and risk-mitigation operations. This paper is an attempt to understand what greater potential solar energy holds in intensifying risk mitigation and disaster management activities, along with limitations, for a secure 'disaster-ready' future which is likely to be more 'disaster-prone' in present context.

Keywords: Disaster Management, Solar Energy, Photovoltaics, Risk mitigation, Engineering and Public Policy

1. Introduction

Disasters are unpredictable-emergencies having potential to cause large damage to life and property, and they can always 'reoccur'. According to World Risk Index (WRI), India ranks 89th out of 181 countries, with a score of 52.94 on vulnerability criteria (which means highly vulnerable) but on the contrary the adaptive facilitates are very low (the lack of adaptive capacities criteria is 78.15) which means India lacks ability to cope with the consequences of climate change, but at the same time is highly vulnerable to climate change and its subsequent consequences [1], which is a high-risk situation.

National Institute of Disaster Management (NIDM) in 2014 reported 27 out of 36 states and union territories are disaster prone in India [2]. Around 59% of the landmass is prone to earthquakes with moderate to very high intensity, 12% of its land is at risk of river erosion and floods, long coastlines of

India are prone to cyclones and tsunamis, 68% of cultivable land is susceptible to droughts and hilly areas are prone to landslides and avalanches [7]. In addition to it, India is also vulnerable to chemical, biological, radiological, nuclear, man-made disasters. Disaster risks in India are further intensified by changing demographics, high population, climate change, unplanned urbanization, and recently the pandemic that shook the whole population, economy, and sustainable development.

Whenever a disaster hits, the foremost service that is lost is electricity and its effects can be catastrophic. Without electricity the conventional communication systems are disrupted, many of the fundamental needs inside hospitals, homes, and basic municipal services are badly affected. For a nation, the effect of losing a national network can be immense so it is critically important for the emergency relief agencies to provide safe, efficient, and clean power, and solar solutions are gradually becoming the preferable option over non-renewable services like gasoline or diesel-powered generators that are fraught with inefficiency and unsustainability [8]. Sunlight is free, renewable and solar based devices are remotely deployable that makes solar energy and solar based devices a viable emergency-solution.

Renewable sources such as photovoltaic (PV) cells can increase resilience and meet emergency power needs during critical rescue operations. If integrated with certain more technological solutions solar PV cells can provide clean, reliable, and flexible power as off-grid systems during emergencies. Electricity from photovoltaic cells can be used in medical equipment, lighting, water purification, power communications during disasters. Moreover, cost-effective photovoltaic cells can also reduce dependency on conventional portable diesel, gasoline generators, and fuel sources which can be scarce or expensive during disasters. Various practical standalone systems integrated and mobilized with the technology of photovoltaic cells such as solar generator cart, solar suitcase, and solar micro-grids are emerging solutions in recent times which not only are resilient but are also a viable alternate to conventional methods [9].

2. Case Studies

Understanding disasters is tough, different terrains, different climate conditions, and different risk zones, there is no one solution to all the disaster problems. Thus, disaster solutions have to be very specific to the region, very specific to the kind of disaster, but things common in all the disasters are, they are sudden emergencies, require immediate attention and are capable of damaging livestock, economy and affecting lives of people severely in a very short period of time. This section includes, study of Chennai Floods, 2015, Cold-Waves of 2019 in J & K and Vizag Gas Leak, incident Visakhapatnam, 2020, Cyclone Tauktae and Cyclone Yaas, 2021, Kinnaur Landslides, 2021.

2.1 Chennai (Floods, Nov. 2015–Dec. 2015)

In September 2017, National Disaster Management Authority (NDMA) of India, published a report on Tamil Nadu Floods with special focus upon Chennai, Thiruvallur and Kancheepuram districts. An interesting part of the report covers how during November to December rainfall in Chennai district increased by 883%, including 1254% increase in Kancheepuram [12], this resulted in devastating floods in these districts. More than 300 people were killed and a population of 15 Lakh people were affected in Chennai alone [11].

Due to the scale of damage, a report on these floods was prepared by Citizen Consumer and Civic Action Group (CAG). It was observed, closed drainage systems, insufficient preparedness and waterways improper management together piled up the damage done by floods [3]. In 2016, when a tropical cyclone *Vardah* hit Chennai, the scale of damage according to National Disaster Management Authority (NDMA) was minimized, due to following reasons, (a) proper maintenance of drainage channels, (b) timely evacuation, (c), shifting of diesel generators to elevated levels, to help operate mobile units, (d) ensuring sufficient stock for diesel/power/oil in safe places to run proper telecom services (e) training volunteers beforehand in flood-prone/disaster-prone areas, and (f) priority power restoration in critical units, including government hospitals [10].

2.2 Jammu and Kashmir (Cold-Waves, Nov. 2019–Feb. 2019)

In October 2020, NDMA published a proceedings of a national webinar on Cold-waves, with a part of proceedings especially focused upon Jammu and Kashmir [4]. Cold-waves, not only are capable of severely affecting crops and livestock, but it can also cause widespread damage to life and property. Major challenges are, due to cold-waves power supply fails, leaving people with almost no power for many days, not even a little power to charge mobile devices. Roads, tunnels are completely or partially blocked, halting the supply of essential necessities, including food, fuel and medicines. Crops are damaged, leaving livestock in a dangerous situation of starvation and death.

The problem is grave, the generators do not work properly in these extreme conditions and even primary health-care facilities are hard to reach in these areas. For heating indoors people use local heating methods, which often lead to CO poisoning and burns that sometimes even lead to death. The prices of power supply reaches to thousands of rupees for a single mobile charge during these cold-waves, understanding this problem, charging *Kiosks* were installed in major highways, government is still trying to find out ways to stop conversion of snow to ice, which makes rescue operations more difficult, in extreme conditions, creating huge problem in clearing roads and highways [4].

2.3 Visakhapatnam (Vizag Gas Leak, May 2020)

In May 2019, a gas-leak incident happened in Village of Visakhapatnam, leading to death of 12 people and affecting 1000s of people in a matter of few hours [5]. The incident took place in Visakhapatnam Plant of LG Polymers, a leading South Korean Chemical Company, the gas leaked was Styrene, a colourless gas with a floral smell, having potential to affect central nervous system, eyes, respiratory organs, and in higher concentration even leading to death. According to the report submitted to National Green Tribunal in May, 2020, it was observed that improper monitoring facilities, insufficient inhibitor quantity, leaving tanks idle for many days due to lockdown restrictions and negligence at the part of refrigeration were prime reasons behind this gas leakage [5].

2.4 Cyclone Tauktae and Cyclone Yaas (May–June2021)

Cyclone Tauktae classified as an extremely severe cyclone storm by Indian Meteorological Department with a wind speed greater than 150-160km/hrs. that originated in the Arabian Sea hit the country in May 2021 followed by Cyclone Yaas in June 2021 which originated in the Bay of Bengal within a span of 10 days. The **death toll amassed more than 120 despite early warnings** being issued by the meteorological department.

According to the Solar Energy Society of India, a pan-India organization promoting solar energy in day-to-day usage, a solar lantern comes in handy and is accessible when there is no power supply after such disasters. From keeping the mobile charged enough to use in an emergency, to asking and indicating the help needed for relief material, solar lanterns comes up as a good possibility. Such solar lanterns must be ready at the Panchayat level and should be distributed to the residents as soon as the cyclone warning is issued. Solar lanterns are most helpful in remote villages, tribal hamlets, and tourist places. The need of the hour is to strike a balance between environment and development. Humans can't control disasters but the use of intellect minimizes their damage.

2.5 Himachal Pradesh (Kinnaur Landslides, July–August 2021)

Massive landslides took place in Basteria and Nigulsiri, remote areas of the Kinnaur Valley of Himachal Pradesh. The death toll reached 34, in addition to isolating these villages with the major Kinnaur district. The rescue operation was carried out jointly by the National Disaster Response Force (NDRF), Indo Tibetan Border Police (ITBP), and members of the local police and home guards. NDRF was assisting the state agencies in their preparedness for evacuating people from vulnerable locations. According to the district disaster management plan of Kinnaur, under the article of resource mobilization, which is the most crucial activity in responding to disaster, to restore the power, temporary chargeable generators, batteries and solar lights which were used for searchlights, were provided by Him Urja and Himachal Pradesh state electricity board [6].

3. Current Challenges Faced by Rescue Team and People Stuck in a Disaster

It was observed that during a disaster the power supply plays a vital role, not only it helps in communication, fostering rescue operations, but even helps in tackling effects aftermath, including ensuring potable water supply and running basic life-saving machinery. Out of 30 people surveyed 4 shared the incidents of how proper communication has saved life of people affected by or stuck in the disaster, 1 shared the incident where proper communication could have saved life of a personnel. 53.3% experienced power failure. Restoration of grid-based supply takes time and liquid fuels including heavy batteries are hard to carry power sources, especially in remote or cut-off areas. During or after the disaster relief material, medicines, and emergency medical facilities are essential needs that too have to reach in minimum possible time, to save further damage to life and property. Figure 4.1 shows a brief of the responses obtained from the survey for (a) power failure, 'a problem' during disaster (b) possibility of using solar energy as a part of disaster management operations, and (c) instances of power failure during a disaster.

According to survey results, interview with relief personnel, case studies and the reports submitted to government, it was observed that following are the main problems that are faced during a disaster, (a) delayed communication (b) Communication problem thus unable to inform rescue team (c) Stuck with a disaster at a remote place, communication failure and losing the team members (d) choice between carrying food or fuel (e.g., kerosene, gasoline etc.), (e) multitude of disasters together, e.g., out of thirty people surveyed three experienced more than one disaster together, e.g., cyclone with floods and fire-outbreak with cyclones/hurricane or earthquake accompanied by heavy rain and lightning, (g) unawareness of potential disasters, thus unpreparedness (i) unavailability of funds, helicopters, smart equipment (j) no

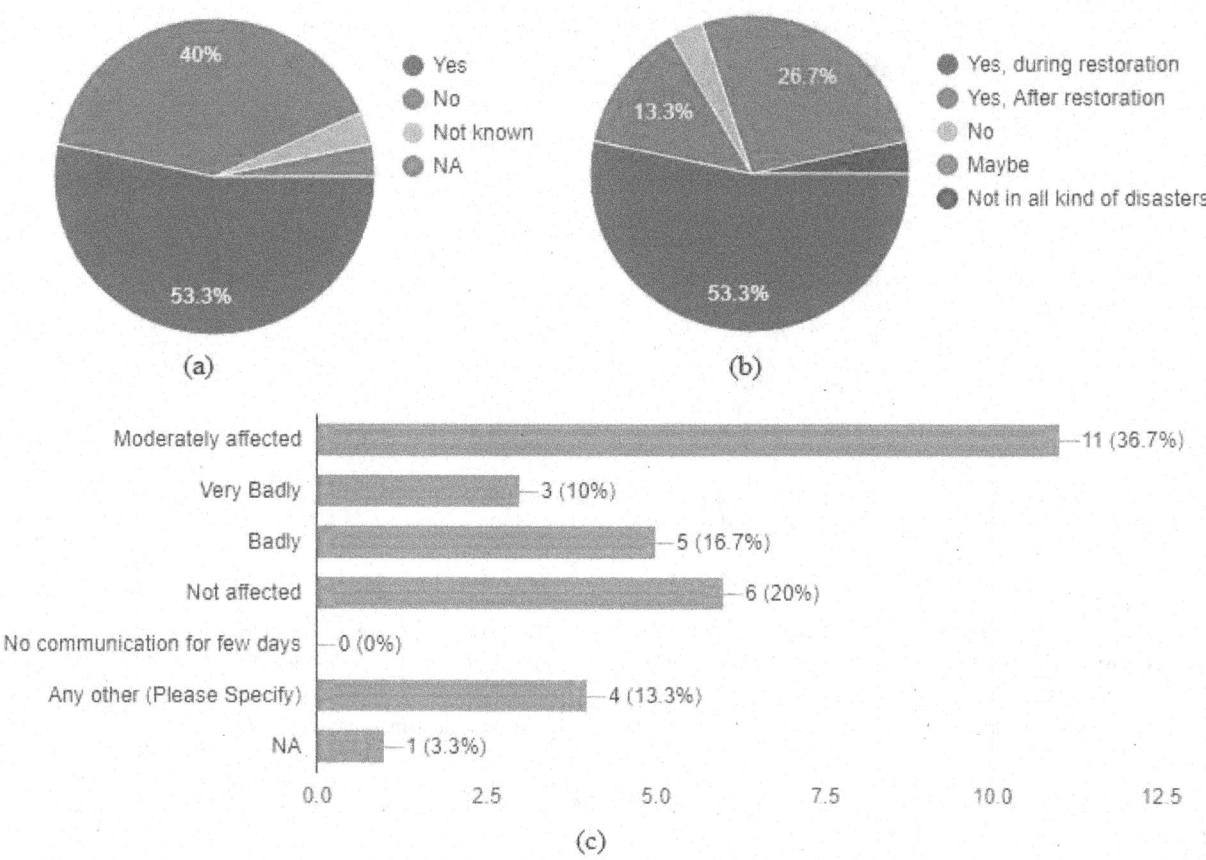

Fig. 4.1 (a) Survey results for power failure problem [7][18], (b) possible use of solar energy in disaster management operations [7][18] and (c) power failure during disaster [7][18].

proper study of terrain, no audit of stakeholders, non-payment of funds for important infrastructure (k) lack of volunteers on highly disaster prone areas.

Some interesting results from survey suggested that most people accepted the primary usage of power is for communication, to understand the situation better, interview were conducted, it was then confirmed that for other purposes, kerosene (majorly), and other such fuels are used they are cheaper and rescue teams bring them for emergency purposes along with medicines, food packets and water. However, personnel accepted the fact that carrying a solid fuel would have been much easier than a liquid fuel and more items for rescue could reach the destination using same amount of energy and personnel capacity. 7 out of 30 people suggested solar devices can help to reduce damage to life and property, 15 out of 30 people agreed solar devices can help in disaster mitigation including by decreasing the time of information received and thus response.

Figure 4.2 shows the devices that were working during the disaster and other inputs about the situation. It is interesting to note that out of 30 responses, 1 response where the member was a part of rescue team, and there was a cyclone, equipment failure and fire outbreak like incident, there was no power failure instead geothermal power was working fine. The person further wrote his rescue team helped him most during the rescue operation. To get a greater dive into 'where in India cyclones and geothermal power can be found together', it was observed that western coast of India is rich in geothermal energy at the same-time prone to cyclones [12].

The case study of cyclone Tauktae, that did a massive damage in west coast of India is another interesting observation, that led large scale damage to livestock, houses, agricultural land and livelihood of people especially fishermen [13]. Indian Navy, Air force, Army, NDRF, SDRF along with local police and other rescue teams, together carried out rapid rescue operations not only to evacuate people from high risk areas, but also to search for people reported missing in oil rigs of Mumbai High. This is **an example of how disasters like cyclones have potential to bring multitude of disasters** along with them including flood like situation due to heavy

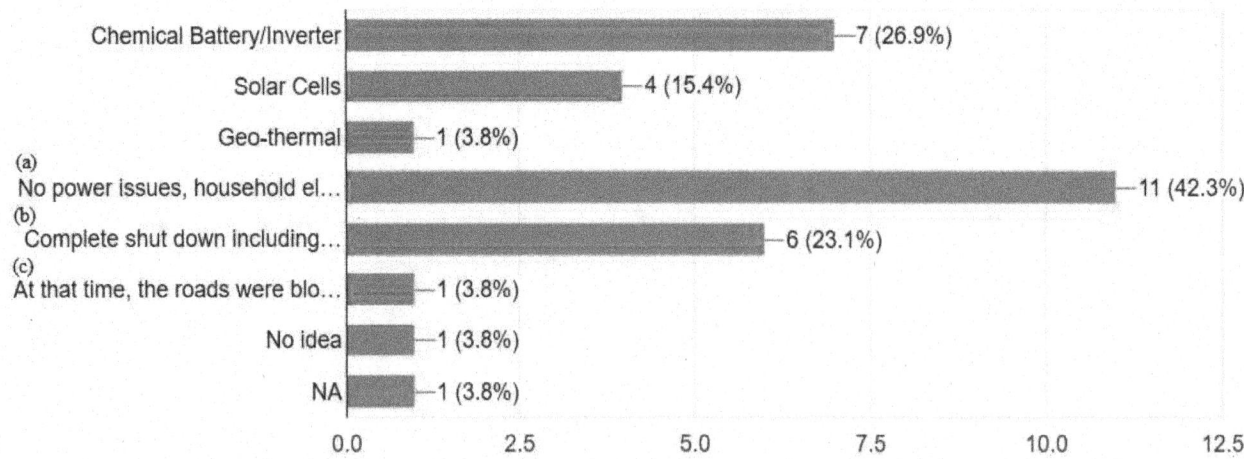

Fig. 4.2 Devices working during a disaster (a) No power failures (b) Complete shutdown including damage to all kinds of grids including damage to solar panels (c) roads blocked, no food supply [7][18]

rain, storm like situation due to high speed of cyclone, and major disasters like oil spills. **In addition, still with advanced predictive technology it is not possible accurately predict exact behaviour of disaster like cyclones.** In such situations advance-rescue is the best option to save life and property.

Other important issues especially faced by ordinary citizens are (a) confusion, (b) no clear information,

(c) no emergency numbers of rescue team, (d) electricity grid failure, (e) no portable water, (f) no food, (g) delay in reaching food, water and medicine facilities, dehydration and starvation, (h) no immediate medical facilities (in 1984 a rescue personnel wrote, if ambulance would be able to reach at that remote place during avalanche, one of the personnel could definitely be saved), (i) no clear mapping of hospitals and other emergency centres in advance, (j) less rescue and self-help resources, (k) improper assessment of impact of

disaster thus no large scale rescue, (l) corruption or improper restoration service distribution, problem related to documents (l) improper communication between different rescue teams during emergency and (m) lack of training to deal with any disastrous situation to an ordinary citizen.

Figure 4.3 provides an analysis of types of disasters, 4 out of 30 people experienced an earthquake of scale greater than 7, but out of 4 only 1 experienced complete shut-down and communication and power failure, for other 2 inverter/ chemical batteries and solar cells were working fine, for another electricity was working fine, this could be probably due to the reason that 3 out of 4 people were in plain region.

Responders have experienced more than one kind of disasters too, thus creating overlapping responses (Fig. 4.3). During pollution and radiation no power failure occurred, but the respondent marked the disaster category as 10 (i.e., having

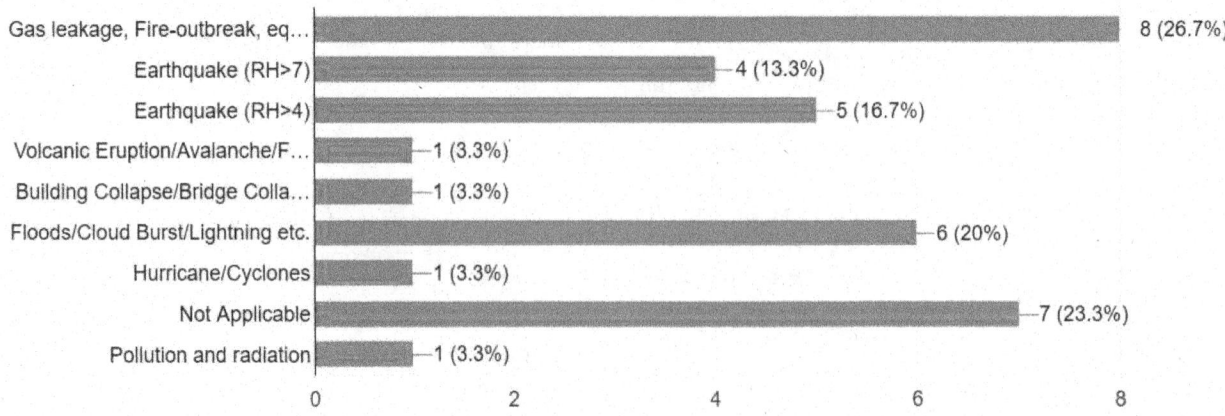

Fig. 4.3 Types of disasters (including more than one disaster experienced in one or different time) [7][18]

high potential to create damage), which is very likely as it directly affects skin, mind and normal health severely. Floods, Cloud burst, lightning and Gas leakage, fire-outbreak, equipment failure incidents are among the common disasters experienced by responders. These incidents largely remained terrain independent, i.e., were likely to occur both in plain and hilly regions, however in plain regions rescue operations are rather easier than hilly regions. Among 7 non applicable responses, one was identified as Avalanche, two responses were discarded and 4 remained unknown.

4. Discussion: Role of Solar Energy in Risk Mitigation During and After a Disaster

The five case studies from three different terrains are included purposefully in the paper, to understand different terrains, situations and impact. It was observed that solar based devices has also been used in past (Case Studies). Flood and cyclone like situations require power for rapid evacuation of water from key areas, for telecommunication, to run necessary life-saving facilities, that too in the situation where power supply has to be switched off to reduce damage or death due to electrocuting (**Case: Assam floods, 2020**). Also, getting clean water to drink during flood situations is a challenge, as per interview results it was found that during Earthquake and even fire-outbreak incidents, the **water supply lines need to be purposefully broken** and **any water stored in the building needs to be completely evacuated,** leaving people to be rescued in a situation of **'no electricity and no water'**. Solar based rapidly deployable distillation units can help solve this problem.

Solar lamps can help solve electricity problems, they are safer and portable, and in addition no grid-lines or bulky set-up is required. Solar concentrators along with traditional solar

cookers can help to solve cooking problems for a while. The stored electricity can be used to dry or vacuum at different instances. These tools are simple and can be used irrespective of other underlying situations.

Cold-waves where require heating households as a primary requirement to survive, Peltier technology integrated with solar power grid can solve problem to a greater extent, the technology is already popular in many parts of world and in hobby projects, there are fundamental limitations for implementation, but again this is the easiest and simplest method to deal with the problem, solar heaters are another viable option, but in cold-wave situations it will be a challenge to trap solar heat.

Solar lamps again can help to solve the problem of electricity, however **solar panels and associated systems are less likely to solve the purpose in floods, cyclones and cold-waves, as saving the batteries and entire system from damage is another big challenge,** here small solar devices including potable distillatory, potable advanced solar cooker, rechargeable solar cooker, rechargeable drier etc. can work miraculously. In situations like Vizag gas leak, power is not a solution, but rapid information transfer is, remote systems with emergency announcements and numbers can be deployed in such areas to help them get better emergency support without much delay, solar panels here can serve a purpose but they are not the only options here.

As per survey (Fig. 4.4) results responders communicated that aerial vehicles, unmanned vehicle, drones, quick prediction technology, quick lifesaving services, devices working in extreme conditions (extreme cold, chemical, nuclear, extreme heat like conditions), remote monitoring technology, improved tunnel rescue methods, including better and modern tools to rescue teams can greatly help them in disaster mitigation, as it was shared that during a communication

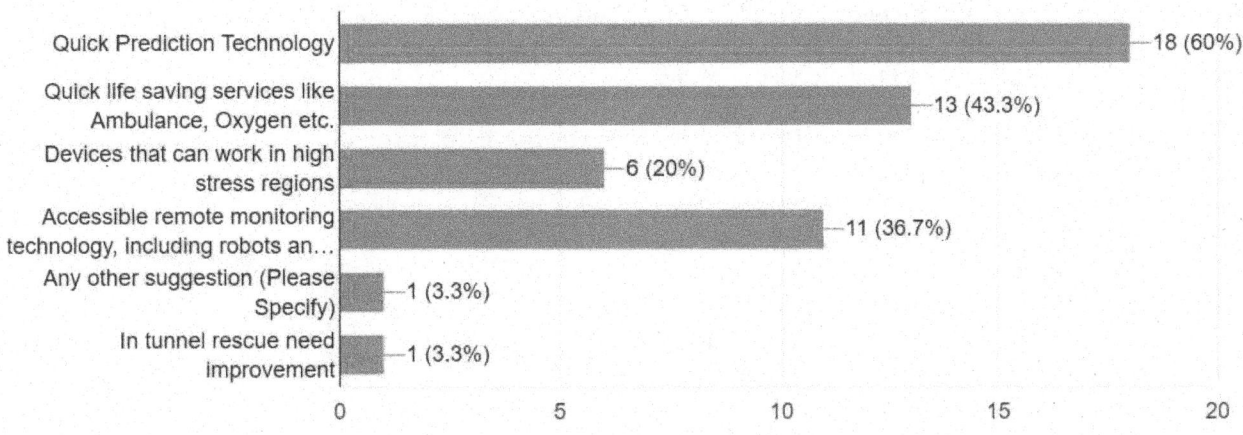

Fig. 4.4   Modern technologies that can help ordinary citizens and disaster personnel in increasing risk-mitigation efforts [7][18]

failure, a satellite phone became life saviour. Personnel often lose their team members not because of disaster, but because of lost communication, delay in reaching ambulance and rescue operations, due to lack of modern tools to search a personnel in different emergency conditions, and sometimes just because they are left with no food and water. Ordinary citizens too remain starved, dehydrated especially during flood, cyclone, hurricane, cloud burst like situations as per information available in news outlets and reports submitted to government (as the time to reach the relief material and time of disaster most of the time remained different).

It was observed that while in many disasters solar based devices can be a boon, but in the situations like flood, cloud burst, lightning, when solar insolation in itself is low, these devices may deem useless, but in the situations like earthquake, fire-break in a residential building, industrial area, oil rig etc., solar powered drones and robots can continue rescue operation until specialised tools and equipment arrive. Solar based heaters and dryers can be used in flood like situations with sufficient insolation, solar cooker and solar distillatory can help to solve problem of cooking food and getting pure water. Solar based torch and mini lightning system can help to provide light until power restoration. In high risk regions grid based electricity system can be replaced by solar based remote systems specially designed to sustain risks, to avoid electrocuting and similar phenomenon that happened in Assam Floods. Solar based devices can again help greatly in restoration purposes, or act as a temporary source of energy, light, disinfection and a tool for pure water.

5. Conclusion, Limitations and Future Scope

Disasters are inevitable, but impact and damage caused by them can always be minimized, as solar as a combination of technology can help in different ways, more products to use solar energy effectively should be encouraged. Solar panels in themselves are bulky and most of the time take a lot of space, thus smaller devices like solar lamps, solar heaters, or simpler devices like solar distillation units, Peltier based cooling and heating systems must be encouraged, while doing so this must be kept in mind that panels are still less bulkier than diesel based generators, safer than chemical based or liquid based lamps. Authors however do not advocate the idea of relying upon just one source of power, and rather would encourage solar energy based devices in disaster rescue operations, as and when required. The problem of fuel can be solved in many cases and basic medical facilities can be restored rapidly even if the power grid is damaged by the disaster.

The first author of the paper observes that questions and responses in the survey are sometimes overlapped, and since user is provided with choice in answers the answers like No, None, Not Applicable, which are likely to have same results were assumed as a single entity. Further, author has tried to remove bias while framing questions, but questions including use of solar power specifically were likely to create a choice based bias. 2 responses were discarded due to insufficient data in most part of the analysis.

With modern technologies and increasing efficiencies authors are hopeful that in near future using cheap, renewable and rapidly deployable technologies like solar devices can greatly help in risk-mitigation and rescue operations.

6. Author Contribution

The survey and most part of the paper is written by first author of the paper, second author has contributed towards exploring the scope and introduction of paper along with two important case studies. The idea and motivation to work upon this field of research was incorporated by third author of the paper, thus contributing towards creating a framework of the study.

7. Acknowledgement

The authors are thankful to the personnel, survivors, saviours and people who know someone stuck by disaster to share their experiences with us, as a part of this study. The author sincerely want to thank those three people who anonymously decided to give us time and shared their experiences from a traumatic incident like disaster. Lastly, first author of paper would like to thank Nalanda E-Consortium for providing with the resources to explore disaster management as a field. Special thanks to Associate Professor Dr. Subhrajit Banerjee, Associate Dean Post Graduate Studies-AKTU, for his valuable time to guide how survey results can be better visualised in terms of research and statistics.

REFERENCES

1. https://reliefweb.int/sites/reliefweb.int/files/resources/WorldRiskReport-2020.pdf
2. https://nidm.gov.in/easindia2014/err/pdf/country_profile/India.pdf
3. https://www.cag.org.in/sites/default/files/database/wfcreport_20160803.pdf
4. https://www.ndma.gov.in/sites/default/files/PDF/Reports/Cold%20Wave%20Risk%20Reduction.pdf
5. https://greentribunal.gov.in/sites/default/files/news_updates/Report%20of%20the%20Joint%20Monitoring%20Committee%20in%20the%20O.%20A.%20No.%2073%20of%202020.pdf

6. https://hpsdma.nic.in/index1.aspx?lsid=70&lev=2&lid=62&langid=1

7. https://nidm.gov.in/easindia2014/err/pdf/country_profile/India.pdf

8. Qazi, S., & Qazi, F. (2014, June), Green Technology for Disaster Relief and Remote Areas Paper presented at 2014 ASEE Annual Conference & Exposition, Indianapolis, Indiana. 10.18260/1-2--20547.

Retrieved from https://peer.asee.org/20547

9. Counting on Solar Power for Disaster Relief: Federal Energy Management Program (FEMP) Technical Assistance Fact Sheet, book, April 1, 1999; Golden, Colorado. Retrieved from https://digital.library.unt.edu/ark:/67531/metadc715033/: accessed August 22, 2021

10. http://www.ndma.gov.in/sites/default/files/PDF/Reports/TAMIL-NADU-FLOODS-english.pdf

11. https://reliefweb.int/sites/reliefweb.int/files/resources/jna-report-tamilnadu-december-2015.pdf

12. Yadav, K., & Sircar, A. (2020). Geothermal energy provinces in India: A renewable heritage. *International Journal of Geoheritage and Parks*.

13. Press Information Bureau of India, written reply to question on Rajya Sabha, published on 28 July, 2021. Retrieved from https://www.pib.gov.in/PressReleseDetail.aspx?PRID=1739933: accessed August 23, 2021.

CHAPTER 5

Harnessing Technology for Disaster Risk Management

Usman, A. Kibon
Department of Geography and Environmental Management,
Ahmadu Bello University, Zaria
Corresponding Author: kibonfaruq@gmail.com

Bulus, A. Sawa
Department of Geography and Environmental Management,
Ahmadu Bello University, Zaria

Ibrahim M. Bako
National Space Research and Development Agency (NASRDA),
Abuja, Nigeria

Abstract

Both natural and human-induced disaster has spatial attribute therefore, application of remotely sensed data is indispensable for disaster risk management. This article focuses on the harnessing/utilization of modern technology in the identification and management of disaster risk in Lake Chad region of North Eastern Nigeria. Lake Chad (French: LacTchad) is a vast land area of fresh water located in the middle of Sand dunes which covers territories in four countries: Nigeria, Chad, Niger and Cameroon. Field survey, satellite images, rainfall from Tropical Applications of Meteorology using Satellite data and ground-based observations (TAMSAT) and Focus Group Discussion (FGD) were the materials and methods used for the study. QGIS, MS Excel and descriptive statistics techniques used for the data analysis. The results of the analysis revealed great reduction in the inflow of water into the lake and heavy accumulation of sediments with increased in vegetation loss. The results further shows that the lake is shrinking (14% in two decades) at a very fast rate and most species of fauna and flora have drastically reduced or completely disappeared along the lake fringes. In view of the growing competition for natural resources from the lake and its environs which gave birth to various forms of disasters such as farmer-herder conflict, communal clashes, migration and now terrorism, there is greater need to employ the use of modern technology that provide visualization of disaster risk zones as well as the impact zones for better management.

Keywords: Technology, Disaster, Risk, Management

1. Introduction

It was widely believed that, Lake Chad used to be one of the most important and largest source of fresh water in the world and source of livelihoods for about 30 million people, the basin is located in central Africa covering some parts of Nigeria, Niger, Chad and Cameroon which has decreased by 90% from 1960s, population growth, climate change and unregulated dam constructions for irrigation and fishing are among the major reasons. The impact of which is already seen in the rise of environmental degradation, migration, population displacement, poverty and food insecurity within the region's communities. This has led heightened competition over resources such as water and land resulting in tension, conflicts and intercommunal violence. Beyond this, terrorist groups, especially Boko Haram and the Islamic State West African Province, are exploiting these fault lines to recruit vulnerable youth and strengthen their insurgencies in communities across the countries of the Lake Chad Basin.

This study focuses on the relevant of technology especially remote sensing and GIS in the disaster risk management in the study area. Application of remotely sensed data is the most reliable means of disaster risk management. QGIS was used to classifying the LULC using satellite (LANSAT 8) images and rainfall data.

In this study, we quantify the variations of freshwater storage over the Lake Chad watershed and analysed the variability of the hydrological cycle over the region during the last two decades using multi-satellite observations from TAMSAT.

2. Study Area and Methodology

The Lake Chad basin covers almost 8% of the African continent. Water from the lake spread to over seven countries: Algeria, Cameroon, Central African Republic, Chad, Libya, Niger and Nigeria.

However, eight countries were selected based on their proximity to the lake including; Cameroon, Chad, Niger, Nigeria, Algeria, the Central African Republic, Libya, and Sudan constitute the Lake Chad Basin Commission.

The commission is an intergovernmental organization that oversees usage of water and natural resources in the basin. Only four of the eight member countries have borders with Lake Chad; Cameroon, Chad Nigeria, and Niger.

2.1 Land Use Land Cover of the Study Area

Satellite images (LANDSAT 8) of 2000 and 2020 were downloaded from the earth explorer: mosaic, run the geometric correction, subset the study area and the later classified the images in other run change detection, so that the change in the LULC of the area examined. The Normalized Vegetation Index (NDVI) was performed in order to determine the health of the plants and vegetations within the study area.

2.2 TAMSAT

Tropical Applications of Meteorology using Satellite data and ground-based observations (TAMSAT) enhances the capacity of African meteorological agencies and other organizations by providing and supporting the use of satellite-based rainfall estimates and related data products. It produces daily rainfall estimates for all of Africa at 4km resolution. The TAMSAT archive spans 1983 to the delayed present. The longevity of the dataset makes it especially suitable for the research purpose. Other applications of the data include famine early warning, drought insurance and agricultural decision support.

2.3 Rainfall Patterns

Rainfall data was used as an indication of rainfall being a key climatic variable in this study area. The rainfall data research covers one climatic period of 30 years that provides a better platform to investigate the variability and changes in the climate systems in the study area. The mean annual rainfall data were used to construct a rainfall chart (Fig. 5.2) of the lake for the climatic period and with the chart, the analysis of the pattern and trends of rainfall in the area was also carried out (Fig. 5.3).

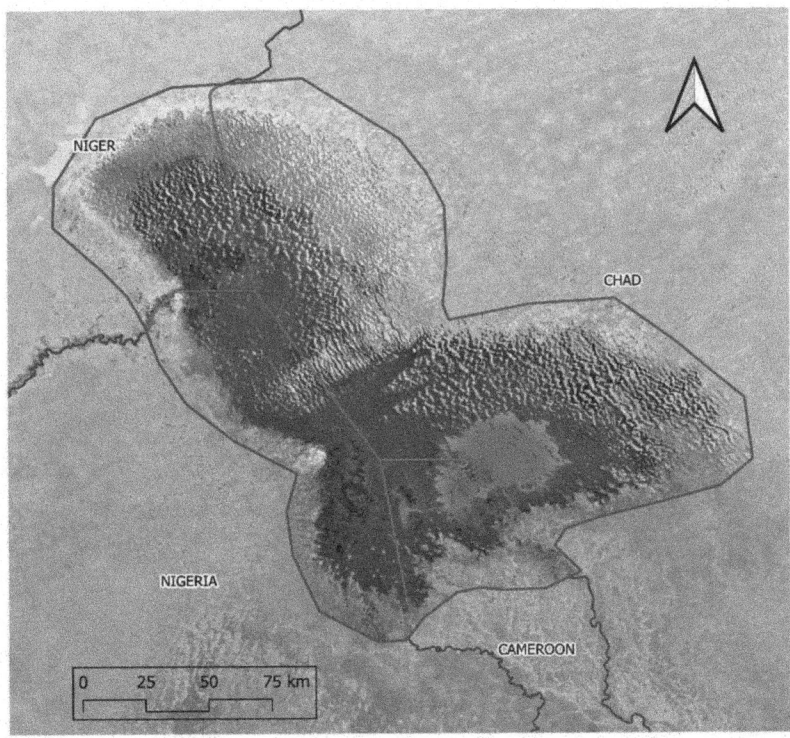

Fig. 5.1 The Study Area.

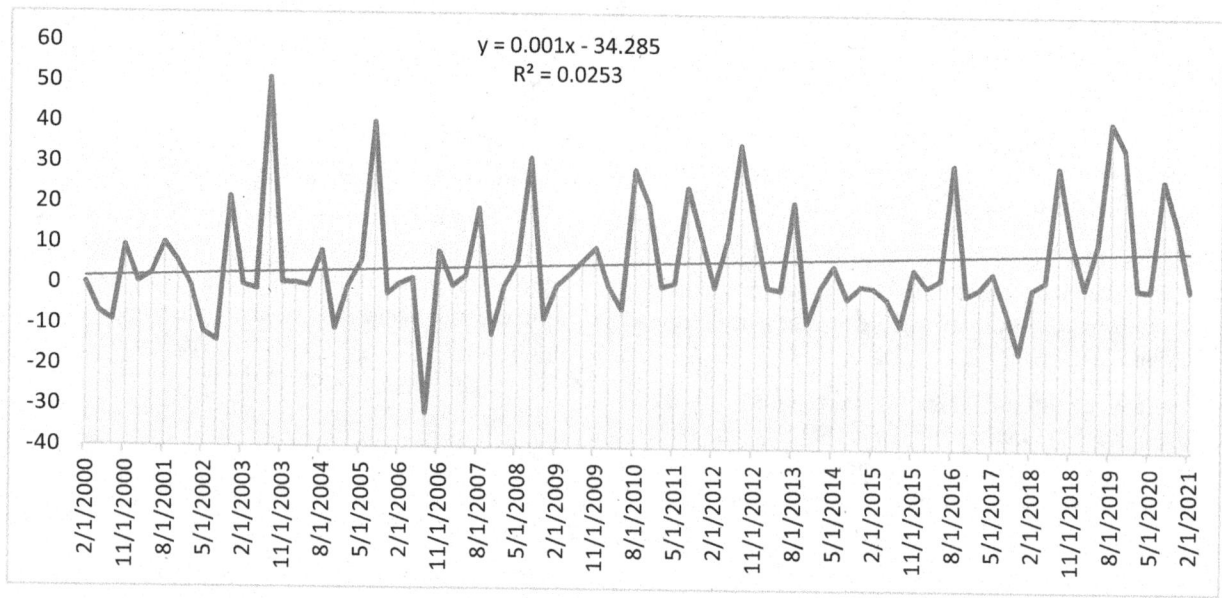

Fig. 5.2 Seasonal Rainfall Anomalies for Lake Chad Region (Maidment, Ross, Black, Emily, & Matthew, 2017)

3. Results and Discussion

3.1 Seasonal Anomalies for Lake Chad

Figure 5.2 shows Seasonal Anomalies for the study area from Feb, 2000 to Feb, 2021. The slope for the period R^2 is 0.0253.

From Fig. 5.1 there seem to be in consistent variation in the annual rain fall pattern of the study area within the period of the study, (2000-2020) where the highest shown in 2003 and the lowest in 2006.

Monthly Rainfall for Lake Chad

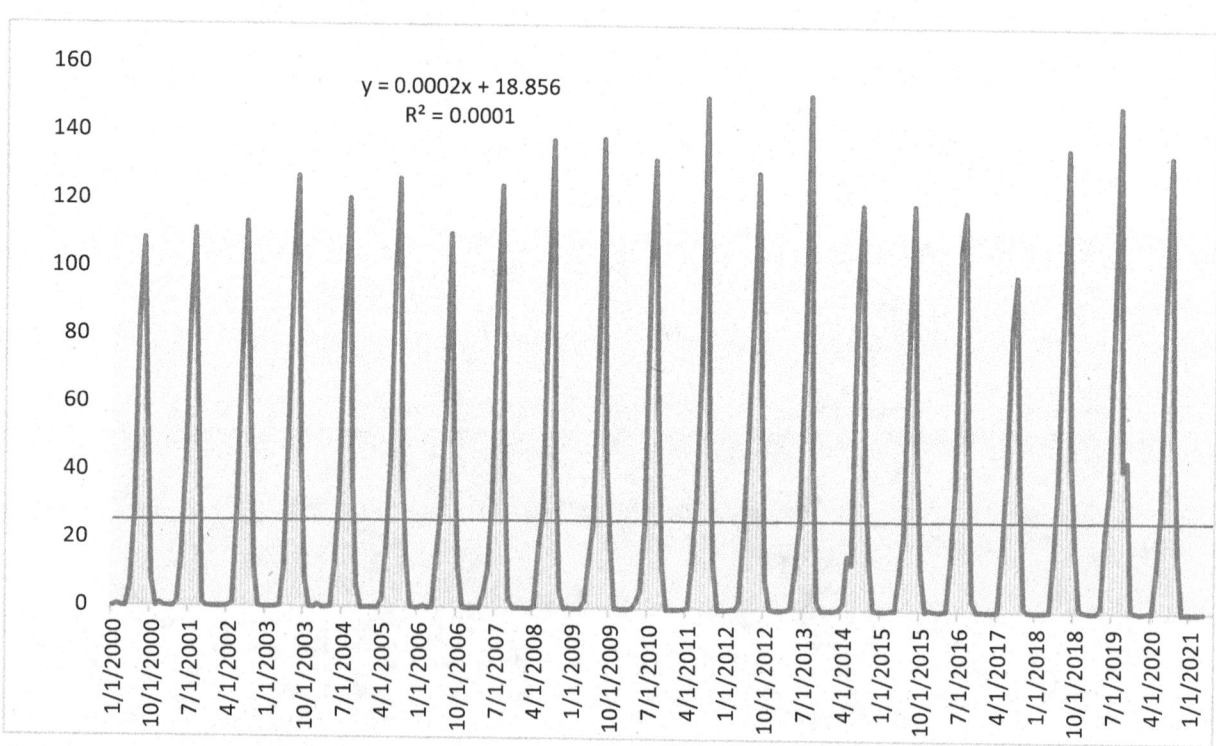

Fig. 5.3 Monthly Rainfall for Lake Chad Region (Maidment, Ross, Black, Emily, & Matthew, 2017)

Table 5.1 Rainfall for Years 2000, 2005, 2010, 2015 and 2020

Year	Total RF (mm)	Monthly Mean (mm)	Mean/30 year Total (%)
2000	289.590	24.1	0.804
2005	338.500	28.2	0.940
2010	338.180	28.2	0.939
2015	287.230	23.9	0.798
2020	337.330	28.1	0.937

Figure 5.3 shows significant variation in the rainfall distribution over the study area from 2000 to 2021, after a consistent decreased of rain fall between 2000 to 2003 which effect can be seen in Fig. 5.7, although there's inconsistent variation from 2003 to 2021 with the highest recorded in 2012 and 2014 which may be the reason for 2012 massive flood in the country published in National Emergency Management Agency annual report 2013. 2019 with the second highest in 2017. This climatic fluctuation has led to further shrinking of the lake which left thousands of households without food.

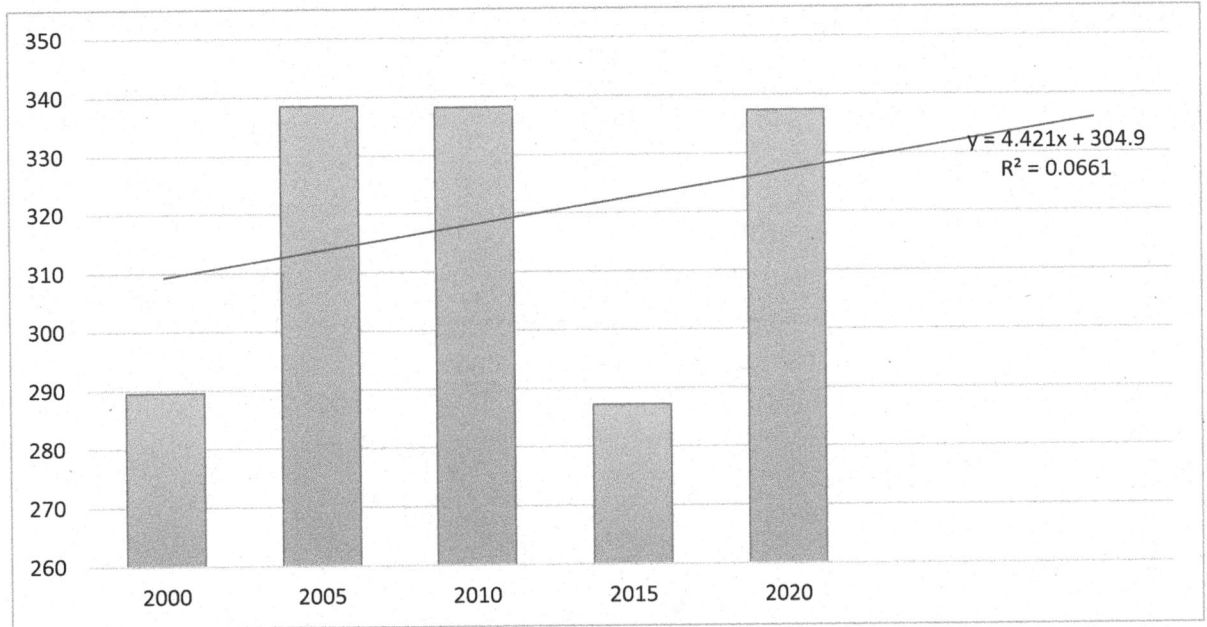

Fig. 5.4 Total Rainfall in (mm) for Study Area

3.2 Land Use/ Land cover Dynamics

As seen from Fig. 5.6, greater part of the study area is been represented by up-white which shows that there's no significant changes in the transition from 2000 to 2020, wetland and grassland, the blue showing the loss of water body which is the second largest land use from Fig. 5.6, which is an indication of the continuous loss of water resources in the lake. Other land use types that seriously affected vegetation cover and grassland a trend that is more pronounce in the northern part of the lake which gives way to dessert encroachment from the border countries.

The results in Table 5.2 shows the estimated dynamism of the land use land cover in the study area over the period of the study (2000-2020). Within the past two decades, there is increased in grasslands area coverage by 15.95% with wetlands increased by 2.06%, grasslands by 0.29% and croplands by 0.88% while on the other hand, water bodies of the lake has drastically reduced by -14.65% and other land use types by -5.66% which can be examined from figure 4 and 5 respectively.

3.3 Change in Size of the Water Bodies

The analysis in Table 5.3: revealed significance changes from the loss of the water bodies of the lake from 2001 to 2018, with the most noticeable changes seen from 2001 to 2006 which could be link with the drastic reduction in annual rain fall from 2000 to 2003 and 2006 see Fig. 5.2.

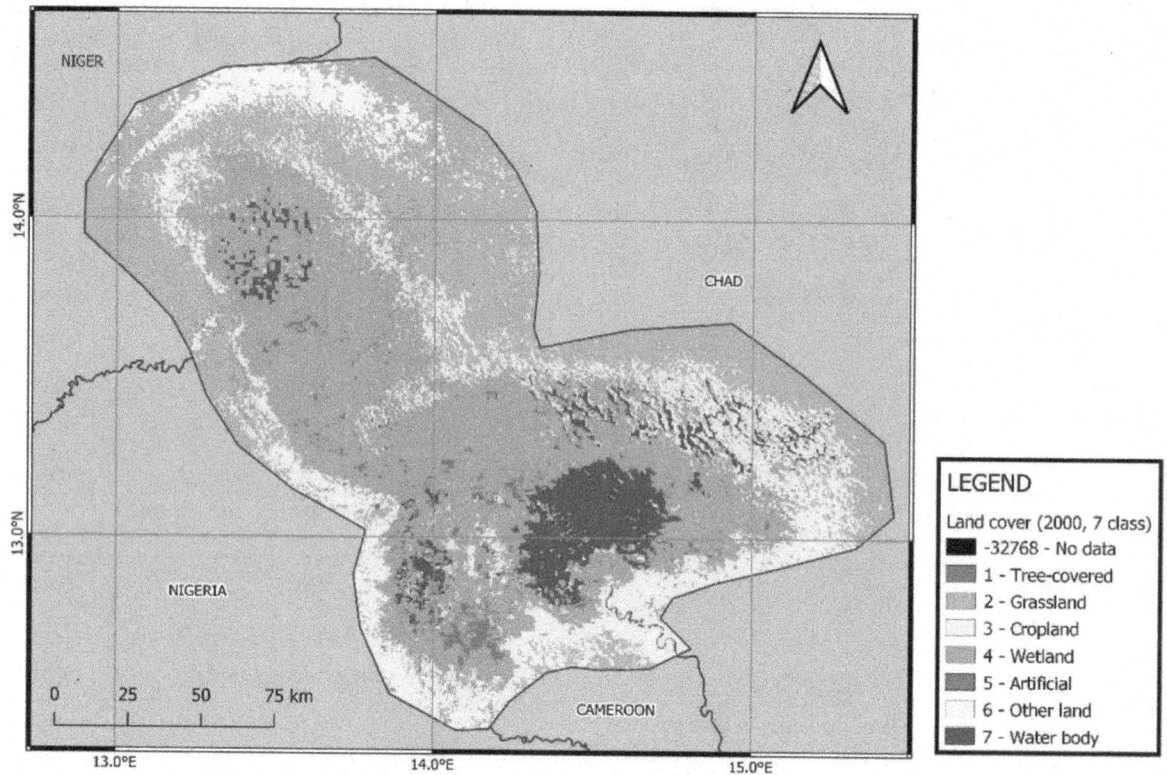

Fig. 5.5   Land Cover 2000

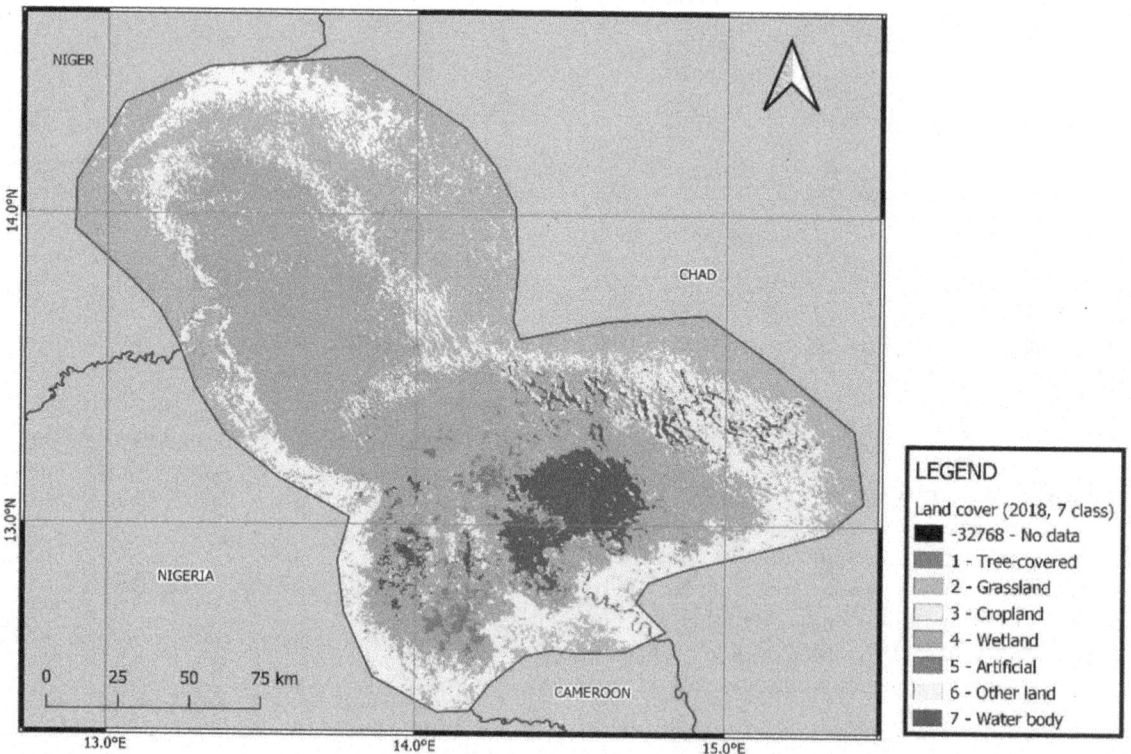

Fig. 5.6   Land Cover 2020

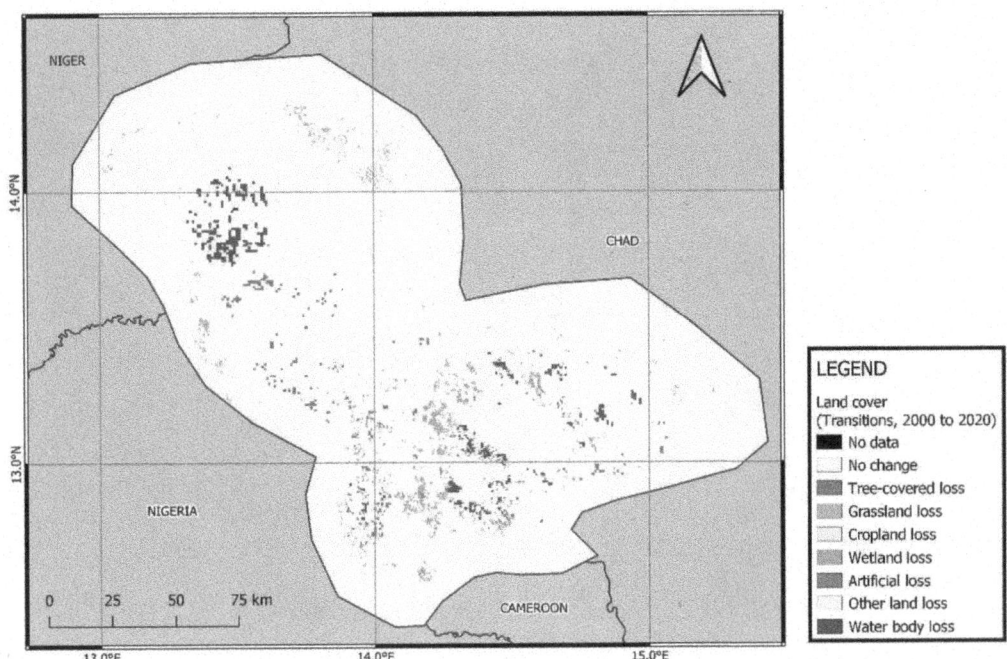

Fig. 5.7 Land Cover Transition 2000 to 2020

Table 5.2 Change in LULC from 2000 to 2020

Land Cover	Baseline Area 2000 (sq. km)	Target area 2020 (sq. km)	Change in area (sq. km)	Change in area (percent)
Tree-covered areas	483.75	560.90	77.16	15.95%
Grasslands	10,190.01	10,219.60	29.59	0.29%
Croplands	7,007.27	7,069.10	61.83	0.88%
Wetlands	11,769.37	12,011.99	242.62	2.06%
Artificial areas	2.84	2.84	0.00	0.00%
Other lands	1,272.70	1,200.65	−72.06	−5.66%
Water bodies	2,314.49	1,975.36	−339.14	−14.65%
Total:	33,040.43	33,040.43	0.00	

Table 5.3 Water Bodies in Sq Km

Year	Water bodies sq. km	Year	Water bodies sq. km
2001	2,314.47	2010	1,980.52
2002	2,272.27	2011	1,960.36
2003	2,063.80	2012	1,954.85
2004	2,060.34	2013	1,957.09
2005	2,066.16	2014	1,962.54
2006	1,999.95	2015	1,962.54
2007	1,992.50	2016	1,981.95
2008	1,988.69	2017	1,985.51
2009	1,989.05	2018	1,975.34

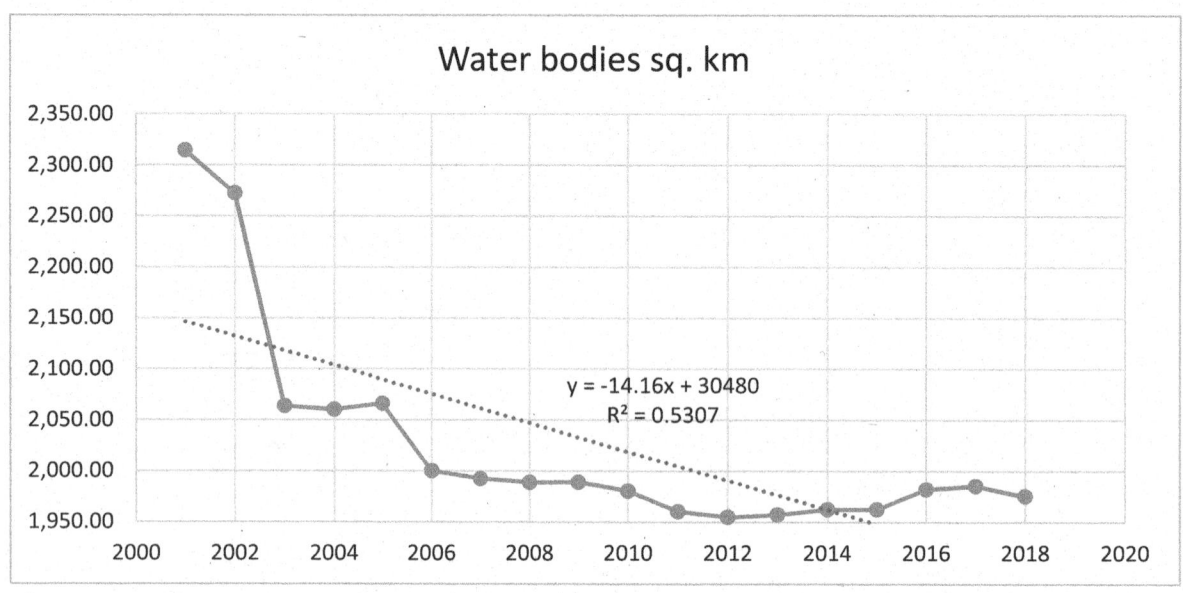

Fig. 5.8 Change in size of Lake Chad water bodies

From foregoing graph, there is significant fall indicating the drastic shrinking in the water bodies from 2,314. 47sq.km in 2001 to 2,060.34sq.km in 2003.

3.4 Evapotranspiration

The results in Fig. 5.8 shows the evapotranspiration pattern in the study area which is represented in green and blue colours ranging from 13-7762mm in 2000. This has raised

to 9223 in 2020 as seen in Fig. 5.9. And even the areas with low evapotranspiration have increased from 12mm to 17 Fig. 5.8 and 5.9.

3.5 Average Annual NDVI *VALUE*

Figure 5.10 shows the graphical representation of the annual NDVI of the study area for a period of nineteen years (19yrs). The graph shows the NDVI annual variation in the study area,

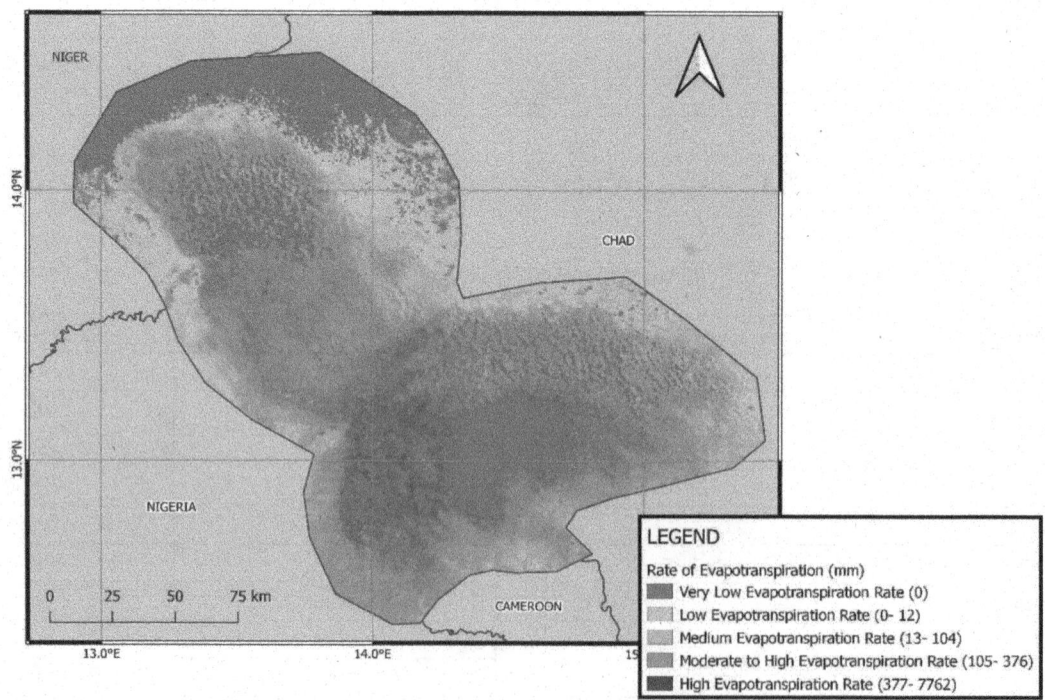

Fig. 5.9 Rate of Evapotranspiration 2000

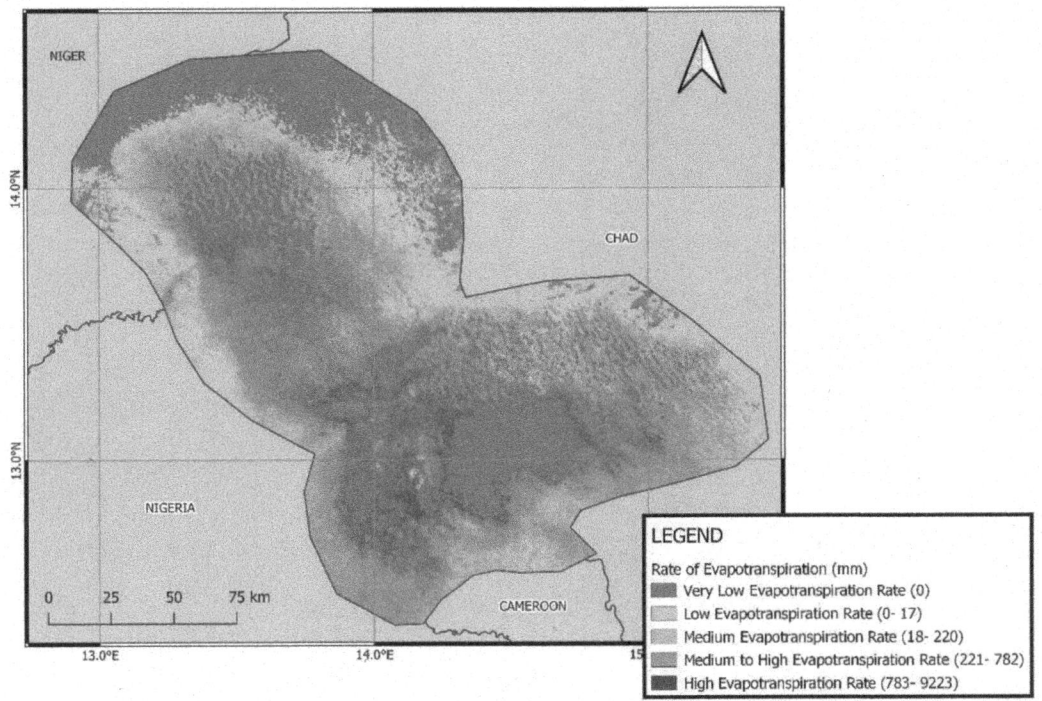

Fig. 5.10　Rate of Evapotranspiration 2020

these variations could be as a result of increase or decrease of water in the lake. The years with high vegetation showed that, there was less water in the lake leading to abundance of wetlands which enabled vegetative growth while the years with low vegetation indicates presence of water in the lake.

Table 5.4　Average Annual NDVI value of the Lake Chad from year 2001 to 2019 (19yrs)

Year	Value
2001	0.193529
2002	0.1807
2003	0.209096
2004	0.186672
2005	0.214004
2006	0.208704
2007	0.207772
2008	0.202127
2009	0.198848
2010	0.214216
2011	0.213192
2012	0.229595
2013	0.197267
2014	0.201967

Year	Value
2015	0.194414
2016	0.206779
2017	0.209161
2018	0.225188
2019	0.214269

Figure 5.11 shows the map of the study area in the year 2000 with an NDVI value of 0.19. The middle part of the map shows rich vegetation which is as a result of drying up of the lake, the north-western part of the map shows presence of water and very low NDVI while the south-eastern part of the map shows what is left of the Lake Chad and so little to no presence of vegetation as a result of the diminishing water in the lake.

There's been significant changes in the space of twenty years in the size of the lake which shows that the lake is continuously shrinking giving rise to wetlands where water existed years before. Fig. 5.12 shows the map of the study area in the year 2020 with an NDVI value of 0.21, the map shows rich vegetation due to the reduced water quantity in the lake. The south-eastern part of the map shows what is left of the Lake Chad with more scattered vegetation and a reduced portion of the waterbody.

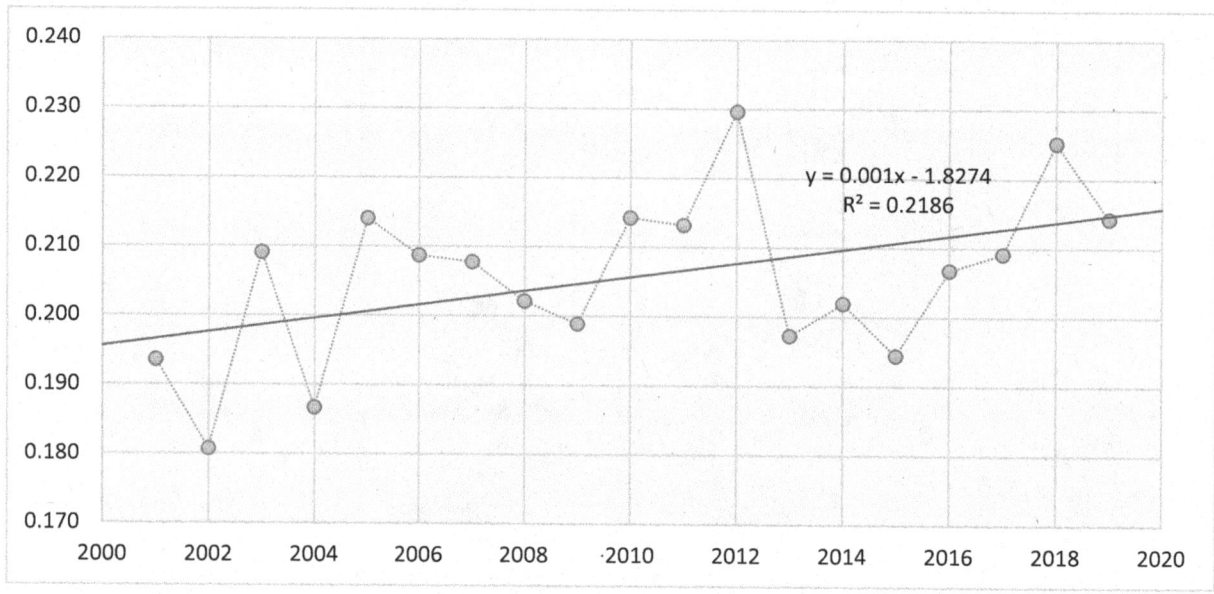

Fig. 5.11 Average Annual NDVI for Study Area

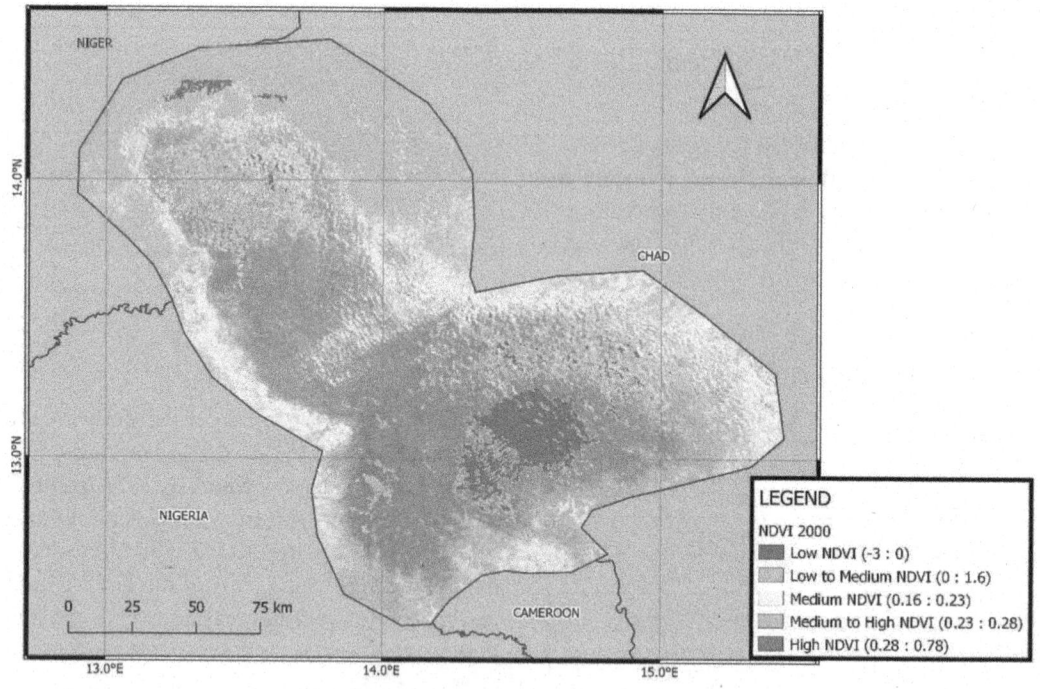

Fig. 5.12 2000 NDVI for Study Area

4. Conclusion and Recommendation

4.1 Conclusion

The research has shown that, there is consistent variation in the annual rain fall pattern (Fig. 5.1) within the period of the study, (2000-2020) where the highest shown in 2003 and the lowest in 2006, with significant variation in the rainfall distribution from 2000 to 2021, after a consistent decreased of rain fall between 2000 to 2003 which effect can be seen in Fig. 5.7, although there's inconsistent variation from 2003 to 2021 with the highest recorded in 2012 and 2014 which is the reason for 2012 massive flood in the country published in National Emergency Management Agency annual report 2013. 2019 with the second highest and 2017

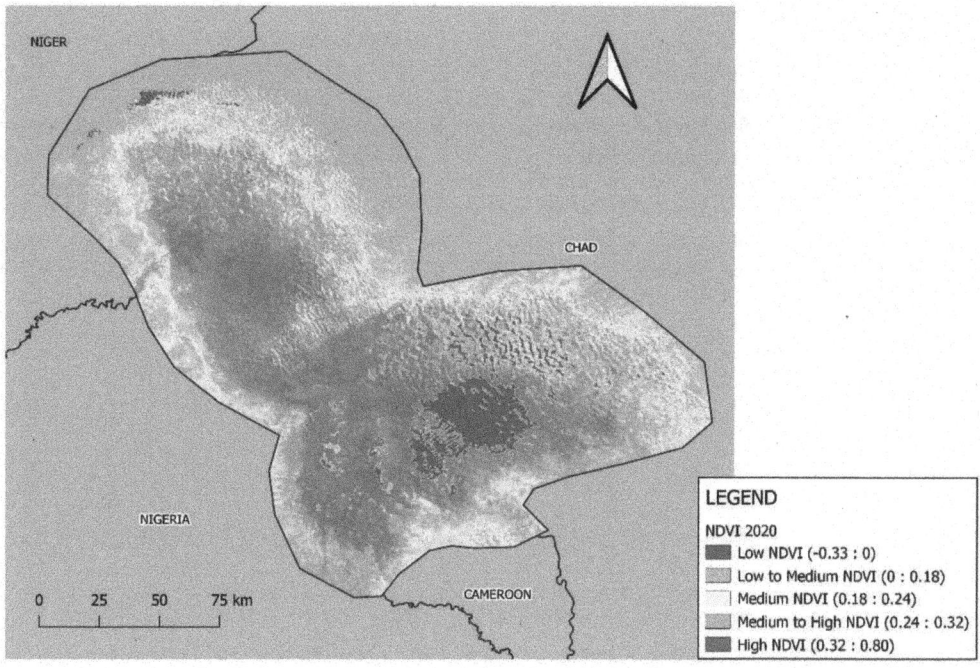

Fig. 5.13   2020 NDVI for Study Area

with the lowest. Theres significant changes in the largest part of the lake which is been covered by wetlands and grasslands (Fig. 5.6) represented as up-white increased by 15.95% and 2.06% respectively, the blue showing the loss of water body which is the second majority from the Fig. 5.6; indication the continuous loss of water in the lake and continuous shrinking by 14.65% in two decades (2000-2020), grasslands increasing by 0.29% (Fig. 5.4 and 5.5) with the continuous loss of tree and grassland in the northern part of the lake which indicate the possibilities of dessert encroachment from the border countries.

There's a significant fall from the graph (Fig. 5.2) indicating the drastic shrinking in the water bodies from 2,314. 47sq.km in 2001 to 2,060.34sq.km in 2003.

From Fig. 5.8 there's evapotranspiration in the majority of the study area represented in green and blue colours ranging from 13-7762 mm in 2000, which has raised to 9223 in 2020 as seen in Fig. 5.9. And even the areas with low evapotranspiration have increased from 12 mm to 17 Fig. 5.8 and 5.9.

Figure 5.11 shows the map of the study area in the year 2000 with an NDVI value of 0.19. The middle part of the map shows rich vegetation which is as a result of drying up of the lake, the north-western part of the map shows presence of water and so low NDVI while the south-eastern part of the map shows what is left of the Lake Chad and so little to no presence of vegetation there as a result of the water

in the lake. There's been significant changes in the space of twenty years in the size of the lake which shows that the lake is continuously shrinking giving rise to wetlands where water existed years before. Figure 5.12 shows the map of the study area in the year 2020 with an NDVI value of 0.21, the map shows rich vegetation due to the reduced water quantity in the lake. The south-eastern part of the map shows what is left of the Lake Chad with more scattered vegetation and a reduced portion of the waterbody.

4.2 Recommendation

Based on the findings of this study the following recommendations are hereby made:

The water resource of the lake is shrinking at a very fast rate giving way to desert encroachment and mass migration which necessitate urgent action by all relevant stakeholders in order to save the teaming population from starvation and total breach of order. There is also greater need for international communities to come to the aid of the countries sharing border with the lake to replenish so safe-guard the number of fauna and flora from total extinction in the already volatile region.

REFERENCE

1. Maidment, R. I., D. Grimes, E. Black, E. Tarnavsky, M. Young, H. Greatrex, R. P. Allan et al. (2017) A new, long-term daily satellite-based rainfall dataset for operational monitoring

in Africa Nature Scientific Data 4: 170063 DOI: 10.1038/sdata.2017.63.

2. Tarnavsky, E., Grimes, D., Maidment, R., Black, E., Allan, R., Stringer, M., Chadwick, R. and Kayitakire, F., (2014). Extension of the TAMSAT Satellite-based Rainfall Monitoring over Africa and from 1983 to present. Journal of Applied Meteorology and Climatology, 53(12): 2805-2822. DOI: 10.1175/JAMC-D-14-0016.1.

3. Maidment, R., Grimes, D., Allan, R., Tarnavsky, E., Stringer, M., Hewison, T., Roebeling, R., and Black, E. (2014). The 30-year TAMSAT African Rainfall Climatology and Time-series (TARCAT) Data Set. Journal of Geophysical Research: Atmospheres, 119: 10,619-10,644. DOI: 10.1002/2014JD021927.

4. Maidment, Ross, Black, Emily and Young, Matthew (2017): TAMSAT Daily Rainfall Estimates (Version 3.0). University of Reading. Dataset. http://dx.doi.org/10.17864/1947.112 Maidment, Ross, Black, Emily and Young, Matthew (2017): TAMSAT Daily Rainfall Estimates (Version 3.0). University of Reading. Dataset. http://dx.doi.org/10.17864/1947.112

Technological Advances in the Development of Disaster Response Management Systems and Applications

Amritanjali

Department of Computer Science and Engineering,
Birla Institute of Technology, Mesra, Ranchi
amritanjali@bitmesra.ac.in

Geetanjali Kumari

Centre of Excellence Disaster Management,
Development Management Institute, Patna
drgeetanjali@dmi.ac.in

Abstract

This paper reviews the technological advances towards application of information management and communication know how for providing timely and effective response during disasters. A variety of system frameworks and applications were studied to investigate the role of state of the art information and communication practices in the domain of disasters response management. Based on the study a comprehensive overview of the objectives, principles and underlying design considerations of the disaster response management systems is presented. The article also examines the recent advancements and future directions towards harnessing the advanced techniques for implementing an integrated and intelligent response management system.

Keywords: Disaster Response Management Systems, Emergency Information Management and Communication, Emergency Decision Making and Collaboration, Intelligent Techniques and Applications, Information and Communication Technologies

1. Introduction

Disaster is a sudden, fatal event that jeopardizes the functioning of a community or a society and poses risks to life, property and environment. According to the UN report released on the International Disaster Risk Reduction Day in 2020, India has been ranked No 3, after China and the USA, in recording the highest number of disasters over the last 20 years (2000-19). Flood is the most frequent disaster in the country causing huge damage to life and property in rural and urban areas. Among the other major hazards disrupting life are the cyclones in the coastline regions and the landslides and the avalanches in the mountainous regions. The country has also seen the devastating impacts of severe earthquakes.

Disaster management is the process of planning and taking actions to minimize the social and physical impact of disasters and reduce the community's vulnerability to the consequences of disasters. Emergency response tasks commence with the onset of the disaster to control its extents and effects. Effective emergency response management requires quick and accurate information gathering from distributed sources, processing, decision making and disseminating to the concerned stakeholders. It include several tasks like allocating and dispatching task force along with required amenities for controlling the disaster, to rescue the victims, providing medical facility to the affected & other relief goods, maintain record of the persons evacuated, missing persons, assessing the damage caused to the life and property and many more. The role played by the information and technology in disaster planning and management has been widely accepted and is being adopted in different regions of the world. Human capabilities augmented with adequate information management and collaboration mechanisms can help to significantly reduce the disaster tolls.

2. Role of Information and Communication Systems in Disaster Response Management

Ideally information management and communication are inseparable parts of every disaster related activities (Sakurai & Murayama, 2019). Several government, private and community level agencies collaborate to work together for preparing, executing response and restoring functioning in the affected region. The disaster response activities include damage, risks and need assessment; mobilizing specialists, response teams and resources; co-ordination of emergency response activities; public and social communication. The disaster related information is needed by the stakeholders ranging from health experts, disaster personnel, primary health care personnel, social service organizations, media, to common man.

Figure 6.1 shows the classification of disaster related data based on temporal characteristics.

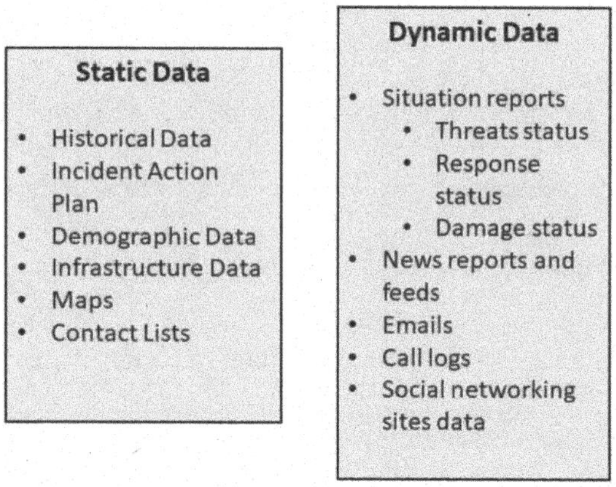

Fig. 6.1 Types of disaster data based temporal characteristics

Distribution and collection of information during emergency is a complicated problem. The information management system provides a computerized database of structured information generated by official agencies in various phases of disaster. The information is used for the development of Vulnerability analysis System (VAS) and Response/Action Plan System (RAS). Some of the key information present in the databases are:

(a) Hazard Assessment Mapping
(b) Vulnerability Assessment
(c) Demographic Distribution
(d) Infrastructure, Lifelines and Critical Facilities
(e) Logistics and Transportation Routes
(f) Human and Material Response Resources
(g) Communication Facilities

Through timely and precise information sharing, agencies can co-ordinate easily and make best utilization of the available resources. The information about disaster impacts also needs to be properly disseminated to the media to depict the disaster situation to the external world and get the required aid from the national/international agencies and humanitarian assistance organizations.

In the following sections we cover different aspects of utilization of the technological advances in the information and communication systems for effective disaster management especially for response management. The last section concludes the paper and present the challenges and gaps in the current time.

3. Advances in Information Management, Analysis and Decision Making System Technologies

A systematic use of information systems for managing response related information is more efficient than the ad hoc mechanisms traditionally used by the controllers and their teams. During disaster new knowledge is generated in the forms of reports, analysis and forecasts. Exchange of information allows making efficient utilization of the resources and provides means for sharing reports on losses and casualties. Information shared can be pertaining to tracing of victims, extent of the affected area, details of damage incurred to the people and property, status of relief assistance, impending threats etc. The Dynamic Emergency Response Information System (DERMIS) by Turoff et al. (2004) is one of the notable development in the early stage of the evolution of disaster information systems.

A number of information systems emerged with the objective of providing humanitarian assistance in the disaster aftermath. Such applications can be used in facilitating the followings:

- confirming the whereabouts and safety of residents
- establishing and operating evacuation centers
- transporting and managing relief goods
- maintaining evacuee records and supporting evacuees

A popular information system Sahana (Careem et al., 2006) is a disaster management application for humanitarian assistance developed in Sri Lanka. The application is open source aiming to assist relief operation, recovery and rehabilitation. Another system designed by Yoshino (2012) is for facilitating operation and evaluation of disaster relief information sharing.

The response management can be made more effective by supporting it with an efficient decision making system. A decision making system make rapid assessments and take informed decisions. Large number of parameters and expertise in different fields are involved in decision making process. Balancing of the information is important in such systems otherwise it could lead to lack of proper information or information overload both of which are undesirable. A task adaptive system called TAID was developed by Netten et al. (2006) to increase the adaptability of the collaborators. Factors like risks, time pressure, limited information, sudden unpredictable change increase the complexities. Leoni et al., (2007) employed layered P2P architecture to develop a software for emergency management decision making.

The objective of any disaster response is to minimize losses and to quickly restore normal life. Several agencies work together to meet these objectives. For effective collaboration both intra-organizational and inter-organizational coordination are important (Kapucu and Garayev, 2011). Due to differences in resources, authorities, operating procedures, and information systems interoperability problems arise. Although both horizontal and vertical communication and coordination are required for effective collaboration, the decision making process involves more of horizontal communication than vertical. Collaborative decision making framework is useful in providing resilient response system (Sakurai et al., 2017). Such frameworks facilitate collaboration of the geographically dispersed communities of experts and decentralized decision making systems. Lessons learnt by the relief agencies from the past disasters are crucial in this regard. Lack of comprehensive intelligence collaboration was the main reason behind failure to prevent the 9/11 attack in the year 2001 (The 9/11 Commission, 2002). Also, in the case of Hurricane Katrina the loss could have been minimized through better collaboration for response and recovery (Chen et al., 2010).

The assessment quality of damage, risks and need determines the degree of situational awareness. The system ADSB (All-hazard Disaster Situation Browser) proposed in Zheng et al. (2011) allows users to get summarized information based on keyword searches and monitor the situation. Dorasamy et al. (2013), researched into challenges and needs experienced by emergency management controllers with specific information technology. Web-based systems are now being employed in most of countries as primary means of communication and incident management. WebEOC is a web-based platform which connect the state EOCs in U.S. User can access the WebEOC through browser or API interface. The database layer has the disaster related information and GIS data. Middle layer has the business logic implemented in the web-server. Both the database server and the web-server are backed up with replication servers.

Among other notable systems, DI-DAP (Li et al., 2016) supports effective information analysis and delivery in disaster management. Based on the experience of 2017 Puebla earthquake Allen et al. (2018) showed the importance of promoting unambiguous simple responses during the onset of emergency and disaster events. Sermit and Demir (2019) presented a method for easy integration of disaster knowledge into expert systems and voice-enabled intelligent applications which can be accessed through wide variety of devices. The recent work of Huggins and Prasanna (2020) elaborates how software can extend and facilitate in processing information for better situational awareness.

4. Advances in Communication System Technologies

When disaster hit any region, the cellular communication usually fails because of partial or total damage to the communication infrastructure. In such a scenario the commanding station maintains communication with the rescue teams with the help of satellite phones. Wi Max technology can be utilized for inter team communication. Wireless mesh networks (WMNs) based on Wi Fi or Wi Max technology has the potential to extend connectivity to isolated areas. The main issue with the satellite communication is the propagation delay. It also suffers from jitters and attenuation problems. Ad hoc network has appeared to be an optional means of connectivity which can be set up instantly without any infrastructure support. Fajardo et al. (2010) developed a mobile disaster management system over Android technology to ease coordination during rescue and relief. Nowadays smartphones are equipped with RFID technology which enables near field communication without the need of any centralized system.

In the disaster aftermath, tackling high volume of data is also a major concern because of bandwidth limitations of the underlying communication systems. Many researchers worked on improving routing protocols and broadcasting mechanisms over mobile ad hoc networks (Onwuka et al., 2011, Raffelsberger and Hellwagner, 2013, Reina et al., 2015, Verma & Chauhan, 2016). Conti et al. (2010) advocated systems using delay tolerant networks for reliable communication. Secure broadcasting schemes over vehicular ad hoc networks have also been explored in various researches.

Wireless sensor networks (WSNs) have applications in situation monitoring and early warning system (Balaji et al, 2017, Thekkil and Prabakaran, 2017, Gan and Jin, 2018) and also in search and rescue activity during emergency response (Shukla & Pandey, 2014, Erdelj, 2017, Wu et al, 2018). More recently routing protocols and information retrieval systems have been developed for enhancing the use of WSN and IoT for disaster management (Grover & Mehta, 2019, Adel et al., 2019).

5. Recent Trend in Data-driven Optimizations

The utility of the information management system can be improved by optimizing its performance through the application of advance technologies for information extraction, retrieval, filtering and data mining. Information extraction is the process of extracting disaster related information from sources like social media or monitoring devices. The information is integrated, organized and stored for further processing. Yang et al. (2012) designed and developed Multimedia Aided Disaster information Integration System (MADIS) which processes each data type independently, then integrates related information according to target topics. Silva et al. (2013) used Linked Open Data (LOD) technology to convert data from diversified sources into a common standard format to allow interoperability. In response to the user queries the information retrieval system extract relevant knowledge from the disaster management repositories. Many a time's information filtering techniques are applied to present precise information to the users. For enhancing strategic decision making data mining techniques are used to extract only relevant information from the collected data. The model proposed by Imran et al. (2013) classify tweets into categories useful for disaster specific information extraction. The vast amount of data collected from social media data makes it difficult to analyze and match the relief request with the specific relief providers. Varga et al. (2013) applied machine learning technique to design SVM classifiers for identifying and matching the request-provider message pairs.

Information retrieval systems searches data relevant to user queries. Using intelligent techniques researchers developed systems to assist in summarizing information relevant to the user needs. The virtual database proposed by Li et al. (2014) facilitates collaborative data sharing among organizations and communities. Song et al. (2014) developed intelligent systems along with models to discover, analyze and simulate evacuation plans during disasters. DI-DAP (Disaster Information Delivery and Information Platform) is an information-centric platform providing convenient, interactive and timely information (Li et al., 2016). It has adopted FIU Miner for data analysis and MapQL for advance query processing. Yang et al., 2017 demonstrates analysis of disaster data stored in cloud by the big data platform. Complete analysis of data was done using relational engine, data mining engine, stream processing engine, search engine, video analysis engine, audio analysis engine and text analysis engine.

The article by Li et al. (2017) presents a comprehensive review of the recent progress along with future directions in the area of data driven disaster management. In more recent developments, Gupta et al. (2018) developed a software system to monitor flood disasters using crowd sourced data. The real-time categorization and classification methods presented by Ragini et al. (2018) works with social media big data to ensure effective disaster response and recovery. Very recently Jung et al. (2020) contributed by developing a conceptual framework for Intelligent Decision Support System (IDSS). The system is designed to analyze big data using open application programming interface (API) and artificial intelligence (AI) algorithms to provide faster and more accurate decision making capabilities.

6. Conclusion

The disaster management systems are continuously evolving. Initially importance was given to the systemic storage of information to support query processing. With the progress in the data-driven technologies a large number of article focused on the management of the dynamics of the operational side. Discovering patterns or trends in the data using data mining techniques enabled decision making in real-time.

The recent trend in the system evolution is integration of wide varieties of communication technologies and inclusion social-media support. Remote sensing applications are being widely adopted for damage assessment and monitoring in disaster aftermath. The communication issues in the regions with disrupted network services are masked through the ad hoc communication mechanisms.

Ideally disaster information management system should have the ability to quickly organize and compile information received from diverse sources and reliably share with the concerned stakeholders for efficient situation assessment, control and recovery. High volume of collected data and heterogeneity in data sources emphasize the importance of having data standards. In the current scenario verification the credibility of data obtained from social media is crucial along with proper authorization and access policies for secure data sharing. This will prevent leakage of private data to public domain and possible misuses.

Recent developments has continued to improve the effectiveness of the disaster response management by augmenting information management, analysis and decision making capabilities. Enhancement in the situational awareness, decision making and relief operation efficiency are some of the key achievements. In summary, the advancements in the information and communication management techniques play a pivotal role towards the development of more efficient and effective systems for supporting disaster response management. Intelligent techniques of information processing present promising approaches for developing systems to facilitate responders in efficiently controlling damages to life and property and managing relief operations in the disaster aftermath.

REFERENCES

1. Turoff, M., Chumer, M., de Walle, B. V., & Yao, X. (2004). The design of a dynamic emergency response management information system (DERMIS). Journal of Information Technology Theory and Application (JITTA), 5(4), 3.

2. Careem, M., De Silva, C., De Silva, R., Raschid, L., & Weerawarana, S. (2006,). Sahana: Overview of a disaster management system. In 2006 International Conference on Information and Automation (pp. 361-366). IEEE

3. Netten, N., Bruinsma, G., Someren, M.V. and Hoog, R.D. (2006), "Task adaptive information distribution for dynamic collaborative emergency response", The International Journal of Intelligent Control and Systems, Vol. 11 No. 4, pp. 238-47.

4. de Leoni, M.; Mecella, M.; de Rosa, F.; Marrella, A.; Poggi, A.; Krek, A.; Manti, F. Emergency management: From user requirements to a flexible P2P architecture. In Proceedings of the 4th International ISCRAM Conference, Delft, The Netherlands, 13–16 May 2007; pp. 271–279.

5. Chen, R., Rao, H. R., Sharman, R., Upadhyaya, S. J., & Kim, J. (2010). An empirical examination of IT-enabled emergency response: the cases of Hurricane Katrina and Hurricane Rita. Communications of the Association for Information Systems, 26(1), 8.

6. Conti, M., & Kumar, M. (2010). Opportunities in opportunistic computing. Computer, 43(01), 42–50.

7. Fajardo, J. T. B., & Oppus, C. M. (2010). A mobile disaster management system using the android technology. WSEAS Transactions on Communications, 9(6), 343-353.

8. Onwuka, E., Folaponmile, A., & Ahmed, M. (2011). Manet: A reliable network in disaster areas. J. Res. Natl. Dev. Transcampus.

9. Kapucu, N., & Garayev, V. (2011). Collaborative decision-making in emergency and disaster management. International Journal of Public Administration, 34(6), 366-375.

10. Zheng, L., Shen, C., Tang, L., Li, T., Luis, S., & Chen, S. C. (2011). Applying data mining techniques to address disaster information management challenges on mobile devices. In Proceedings of the 17th ACM SIGKDD international conference on Knowledge discovery and data mining (pp. 283-291).

11. Yoshino, T. (2012). Fuga: "Operation and evaluation of a disaster relief information sharing system", Sahana at the Great East Japan Earthquake. J Digital Pract, IPSJ, 3(3), 177-183.

12. Yang, Y., Lu, W., Domack, J., Li, T., Chen, S. C., Luis, S., & Navlakha, J. K. (2012, October). MADIS: A multimedia-aided disaster information integration system for emergency management. In 8th International Conference on Collaborative Computing: Networking, Applications and Worksharing (CollaborateCom) (pp. 233-241). IEEE.

13. Imran, M., Elbassuoni, S., Castillo, C., Diaz, F., & Meier, P. (2013, May). Extracting information nuggets from disaster-Related messages in social media. In Iscram.

14. Silva, T., Wuwongse, V., & Sharma, H. N. (2013). Disaster mitigation and preparedness using linked open data. Journal of Ambient Intelligence and Humanized Computing, 4(5), 591-602.

15. Varga, I., Sano, M., Torisawa, K., Hashimoto, C., Ohtake, K., Kawai, T., & De Saeger, S. (2013, August). Aid is out there: Looking for help from tweets during a large scale disaster. In Proceedings of the 51st Annual Meeting of the Association for Computational Linguistics (Volume 1: Long Papers) (pp. 1619-1629).

16. Dorasamy, M.; Raman, M.; Kaliannan, M. Knowledge management systems in support of disasters management: A two-decade review. Technol. Forecast. Soc. Chang. 2013, 80, 1834– 1853.

17. Raffelsberger, C., & Hellwagner, H. (2013, March). A hybrid MANET-DTN routing scheme for emergency response scenarios. In 2013 IEEE international conference on pervasive computing and communications workshops (PERCOM) (pp. 505-510). IEEE.

18. Shukla, S., & Pandey, G. (2014). To design an architectural model for flood monitoring using wireless sensor network system. International Journal of Computer Science and Information Technologies, 5(1), 502-507.

19. Li, J., Li, Q., Liu, C., Khan, S. U., & Ghani, N. (2014). Community-based collaborative information system for emergency management. Computers & operations research, 42, 116-124.

20. Song, X., Zhang, Q., Sekimoto, Y., & Shibasaki, R. (2014, June). Intelligent system for urban emergency management during large-scale disaster. In Proceedings of the AAAI Conference on Artificial Intelligence (Vol. 28, No. 1).

21. Reina, D. G., et al. "A survey on multihop ad hoc networks for disaster response scenarios." International Journal of Distributed Sensor Networks 11.10 (2015): 647037.

22. Reina, D. G., Toral, S. L., Jonhson, P., Barrero, F.A survey on probabilistic broadcast schemes for wireless ad hoc networks, Ad Hoc Networks, 2015

23. Verma, H., and Chauhan N. "MANET based emergency communication system for natural disasters." International Conference on Computing, Communication & Automation. IEEE, 2015.

24. Prasanna, R.; & Huggins, T.J. (2016). Factors affecting the acceptance of information systems supporting emergency operations centers. Comput. Hum. Behav, 57, 168–181.

25. Li, T., Zhou, W., Zeng, C., Wang, Q., Zhou, Q., Wang, D., & Rishe, N. (2016, October). DI-DAP: an efficient disaster information delivery and analysis platform in disaster management. In Proceedings of the 25th ACM international on conference on information and knowledge management (pp. 1593–1602).

26. Li, T., Xie, N., Zeng, C., Zhou, W., Zheng, L., Jiang, Y., & Iyengar, S. S. (2017). Data-driven techniques in disaster information management. ACM Computing Surveys (CSUR), 50(1), 1–45.

27. M. Sakurai, T.A. Majchrzak, V. Latinos Towards a framework for cross-sector collaboration: implementing a Resilience Information Portal. Springer International Publishing, Cham (2017)

28. Yang, C., Su, G., & Chen, J. (2017, March). Using big data to enhance crisis response and disaster resilience for a smart city. In 2017 IEEE 2nd International Conference on Big Data Analysis (ICBDA) (pp. 504-507). IEEE.

29. Balaji, V., et al. "Design of ZigBee based wireless sensor network for early flood monitoring and warning system." 2017 IEEE Technological Innovations in ICT for Agriculture and Rural Development (TIAR). IEEE, 2017.

30. Thekkil, T. M., & Prabakaran, N. (2017, July). Real-time WSN based early flood detection and control monitoring system. In 2017 International Conference on Intelligent Computing, Instrumentation and Control Technologies (ICICICT) (pp. 1709-1713). IEEE.

31. Erdelj, M., Król, M., & Natalizio, E. (2017). Wireless sensor networks and multi-UAV systems for natural disaster management. Computer Networks, 124, 72–86.

32. Gan, B., and Jin, S. "Design of Early Warning System Based on Wireless Sensor Network." International Journal of Online Engineering 14.1 (2018).

33. Wu, H., Mei, X., Chen, X., Li, J., Wang, J., & Mohapatra, P. (2018). A novel cooperative localization algorithm using enhanced particle filter technique in maritime search and rescue wireless sensor network. ISA transactions, 78, 39-46.

34. Allen, R.M.; Cochran, E.S.; Huggins, T.J.; Miles, S.; Otegui, D. Lessons from Mexico's earthquake early warning system. Earth Space Sci. News 2018, 99.

35. Gupta, A. T. (2018). A software system proposing the processing of crowd sourced data to monitor a flood event: an AI approach. Open Water Journal, 5(2), 2.

36. Ragini, J. R., Anand, P. R., & Bhaskar, V. (2018). Big data analytics for disaster response and recovery through sentiment analysis. International Journal of Information Management, 42, 13–24.

37. Sermet, Y., & Demir, I. (2019). Towards an information centric flood ontology for information management and communication. Earth Science Informatics, 12(4), 541–551.

38. Sakurai, M., Murayama Y. (2019). Information technologies and disaster management – Benefits and issues -, Progress in Disaster Science, Volume 2, 2019, 100012, ISSN 2590-0617, https://doi.org/10.1016/j.pdisas.2019.100012.

39. Grover, J. and Mehta A. "On demand multipath routing protocol for emergency ad hoc networks." 2019 Second International Conference on Advanced Computational and Communication Paradigms (ICACCP). IEEE, 2019.

40. Adeel, A., Gogate, M., Farooq, S., Ieracitano, C., Dashtipour, K., Larijani, H., & Hussain, A. (2019). A survey on the role of wireless sensor networks and IoT in disaster management. In Geological disaster monitoring based on sensor networks (pp. 57-66). Springer, Singapore.

41. Al Qundus, J., Dabbour, K., Gupta, S., Meissonier, R., & Paschke, A. (2020). Wireless sensor network for AI-based flood disaster detection. Annals of Operations Research, 1–23.

42. Huggins, T. J., & Prasanna, R. (2020). Information technologies supporting emergency management controllers in New Zealand. Sustainability, 12(9), 3716.

43. Jung, D., Tran Tuan, V., Dai Tran, Q., Park, M. and Park, S., 2020. Conceptual framework of an intelligent decision support system for smart city disaster management. Applied Sciences, 10(2), p.666.

CHAPTER 7

Reaching Beyond Low Hanging Apelles to Technological Convergence to Combat Disasters Like Desertification

Kavya Kamepalli

Student of M.S. (Aerospace Systems Engineering) Department of Aerospace and Geodesy,
Technical University of Munich
Munich, Germany
kavyakamepalli@gmail.com

Abstract

Desertification is a process in which its biological and economic productivity reduced and is a creeping disaster. It is estimated that India could have lost about 30% of land due to desertification in the past three decades and might threaten another 30 million hectares of land. Since the adoption of National Action Plan to Combat Desertification (NAPCD) by Government of India in 2001, concerted efforts are being made to address the desertification problem in India. The strategies adopted were at regional at scale and multi-dimensional in nature with focus on common property resources. On the other hand, reaching out to individuals or to community was not given adequate attention. Involving the individual farmers whose lands are prone to the desertification could be an effective strategy.

Advances in space-based technologies are extensively used in various sectors, but in spite of their potential, they are yet to reach optimal level in the farming sector. Initiatives like spectral reflectance, Soil Health Management, Soil Health Card could be effective tools for enhancing farm productivity. Based on the data from satellites and Soil Health Card initiative for desertification prone soils, a basket of measures, downscaled to an individual farmer level can be developed for drawing effective strategies to combat desertification.

Keywords: Desertification strategies; Satellite Observation Data; Soil Health Card (SHC); Spectral reflectance; Downscaling; Individual Farmers

1. Introduction

Desertification (The term 'Desertification' does not refer to the expansion of existing deserts, but to the degradation of land in arid, semi-arid and dry sub-humid areas as they are extremely vulnerable to overexploitation and inappropriate land use), along with climate change and the loss of biodiversity were identified as the greatest challenges to sustainable development during the 1992 Rio Earth Summit. UNCCD defines desertification as 'land degradation in arid, semiarid and dry sub-humid areas' resulting from various factors including climatic variations and human activities. The word 'land' means the terrestrial bio-productive system' and 'land degradation' means 'reduction or loss of biological or economic productivity' and complexity of rainfed cropland, irrigated cropland, or range, pasture, forest and woodlands resulting from land uses or from a process or combination of processes, including processes arising from human activities and habitation patterns (UNCCD, 1994). Globally, about two billion hectares of land is being degraded due to desertification and land degradation. Health and well-being of about 3.2 billion people is directly or indirectly dependent on it. Various factors catalyze the process of desertification. The seriousness of the situation has ensured that Convention to Combat Desertification (UNCCD) is one of the three Conventions accepted by the world community at Earth Summit in Brazil 1992 along with Convention of Biological Diversity (CBD) and United Nations Framework

Convention on Climate Change (UNFCCC) and UNCCD became a legally binding international agreement and was adopted in 1994. India became a member in 1994 and ratified it in 1996.

2. Drivers of Desertification

- **Water Erosion:** Water is a significant force and through its erosion power, it deteriorates the soil quality by taking away the top soil. About 36.1 Mha of land has become barren because of water erosion.

- **Vegetation degradation:** Vegetation is an important factor in the protection of soil and soil fertility. Soil becomes highly vulnerable to the loss of top soil due to wind and water erosion if it loses its vegetation cover and leads to decrease in soil aggregation and stability, and hence soil fertility. This type of desertification causes about 8.91 per cent of desertification in India.

- **Wind erosion:** Wind can result in removing top soil through Suspension, Saltation and Soil creep and has converted about 18.23 Mha into deserts in the country.

- **Salinity/Alkalinity:** Excessively irrigated areas are prone to this problem as the soil chemistry alters due to presence of water dissolvable salt present in soil, mainly due to excess evapotranspiration, drought, and excess irrigation. The salts increase the toxicity and damage the root growth. About 3.67 Mha of land is affected by this process.

Other factors like frost shattering, settlements, mass movements, water logging and man-made factors like settlements, mining contribute to the process of land degradation (Fig 7.1) (ISRO 2016).

2.1 Extent of Desertification

Based on the extent of land resources under the threat of desertification, States in India can be grouped into three categories for evolving better management practices, viz., states with more than 40 per cent of their total area under desertification, second group with area under 20 to 40 per cent under desertification and third group having less than 20 per cent of its total area under desertification ((MoEF 2001). The state of Jharkhand has higher area (68.98%) under desertification, followed by Rajasthan (62.9%), while the lowest area under desertification was reported from Arunachal Pradesh (1.84%). At all India level, we have about 29.32 per cent of land under desertification and certainly an alarming situation because of its irreversibility (Table 7.1).

2.2 United Nations Convention to Combat Desertification (UNCCD)

Suboptimal performance of measures to control land degradation/desertification in arid, semi-arid and dry sub-humid areas, despite the operationalization of the 'Plan of Action to Combat Desertification (PACD)' from 1977 has made land degradation as a major concern for the United Nations Conference on Environment and Development (UNCED)6 (Earth Summit), held in Rio de Janeiro in 1992. It resulted in establishing an Intergovernmental Negotiating Committee (INCD) to prepare a Convention to Combat Desertification and was adopted in Paris in 17 June 1994 and that 17th June is declared as the **World Day to Combat Desertification and Drought** to raise awareness of the presence of desertification and drought, highlighting methods of preventing desertification and recovering from drought (MoEF 2000).

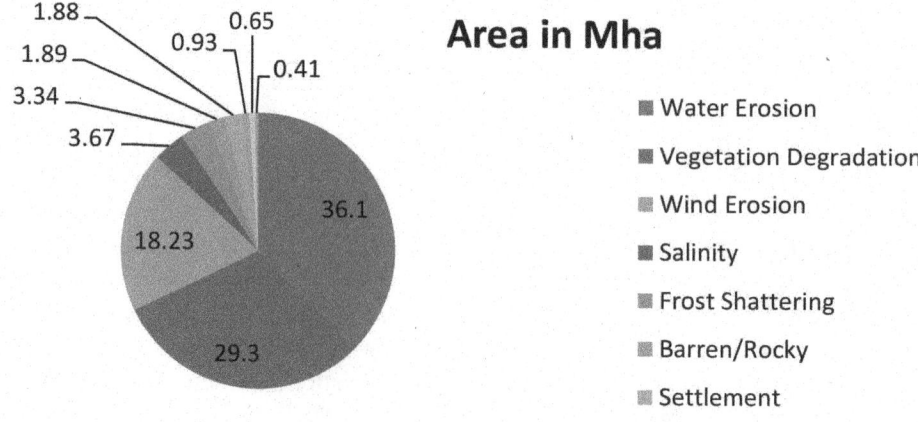

Fig. 7.1 Contributing Factors of Desertification in India (area in Mha)

Source: ISRO 2016

Table 7.1 Status of Desertification in India

State	Total Area under Desertification (ha)	Total Area under Desertification (%)	Change from 2003-05 to 2013-15
States with more than 40% area under desertification			
Jharkhand	5498726	68.98	1.01
Rajasthan	21526512	62.9	−0.29
Delhi	89868	60.6	11.03
Gujarat	10261641	52.29	0.94
Goa	192973	52.13	1.76
Nagaland	786678	47.45	8.71
Maharashtra	13825935	44.93	1.55
Himachal Pradesh	2394240	43.01	4.55
Tripura	437128	41.69	10.48
States with 20 to 40 % area under desertification			
Karnataka	6951000	36.24	0.05
Jammu and Kashmir	7969607	35.86	1.94
Orissa	5304114	34.06	-0.12
Telangana	3598856	31.34	-0.52
Manipur	601959	26.96	0.4
Meghalaya	494880	22.06	0.71
States with less than 20% of area under desertification			
West Bengal	1733931	19.54	0.59
Chhattisgarh	2211153	16.36	0.26
Andhra Pradesh	2298758	14.35	0.19
Madhya Pradesh	3804315	12.34	0.1
Uttarakhand	648253	12.12	1.25
Tamil Nadu	1543898	11.87	0.21
Sikkim	78749	11.1	0.04
Kerala	379587	9.77	0.23
Assam	716596	9.14	1.84
Mizoram	187453	8.89	4.34
Haryana	338964	7.67	0.55
Bihar	694809	7.38	0.38
Uttar Pradesh	1528997	6.35	−1.27
Punjab	144653	2.87	1.02
Arunachal Pradesh	153933	1.84	0.21
Total	96398166	29.32	0.56

Source: Computed from ISRO 2016

In 2008, a 10-year strategic plan and framework to enhance the implementation of the Convention for 2008-2018 was adopted outlined to forge global partnerships to reverse and prevent desertification and land degradation. It was coupled with a mission to provide a worldwide framework to support the development and implementation of national and regional policies that contribute to the reduction of poverty. During the Conference of Parties in 2017 in Ordos, China, a new global roadmap to address land degradation, UNCCD 2018-2030 Strategic Framework was adopted with a sharp focus for a comprehensive global commitment to achieve Land Degradation Neutrality (LDN). UNCCD has five Strategic objective (SO) and several indicators under each Strategic Objective. Among the five SO, the SO 1 – 'To improve the condition of affected ecosystems, combat desertification/ land degradation, promote sustainable land management and contribute to land degradation neutrality', provides ample space for leveraging the space technologies and Soil health cards to make significant contributions in the Indian context.

3. Indian Efforts to Combat Desertification

Very finite nature of land resources underlines the importance of maintaining the health of land resources and ensures that it is used in a sustainable manner for our own survival. Accordingly, India has developed its National Action Plan for Combating Desertification (NAPCD) in 2001 with an integrated approach to tackle desertification (MoEF 2001). It had adopted a multi-sectorial coordinated approach wherein prioritization of preventive and restorative initiatives/ measures based on analysis of the situation, and Water as central to programs for eco-regeneration and for improving the living conditions of the local communities. A Bottom-up approach was adopted for project planning, evaluation and monitoring through Panchayati Raj Institutions. A group of three ministries, viz.,a) inistry of Environment and Forests (MoEF), b) Ministry of Rural Development (MoRD), and

Ministry of Agriculture were entrusted with the formulation and implementation of programs under NAPCD. The Programs for combating desertification can be broadly grouped into;

- Social sector programs based on community and human development and particularly at the local level.
- specifically for poverty eradication.
- for the conservation of natural resources.
- for eco-restoration of degraded lands.
- especially for desert and drought-prone regions.

Despite these efforts, it has been estimated that that about quarter of its area, about 82.64 million hectares (m ha) is under the threat of desertification and in just eight years from 2003-05 and 2011–13, desertification has increased by some

1.16 Mha, whittling away India's gross domestic product by 2.5 per cent every year (ISRO 2016). This situation warrants effective land-use policies that could create a policy environment that also engages with people – local communities, men, women, and youth for protection of land resources and thus safeguard the future of humankind and it is a time to bring in measures to supplement the ongoing programs to ensure that desertification process is halted. One such approach is the amalgamation of space technologies and Soil Health Card initiative.

3.1 Space Technologies for Tackling Climate Change

Commissioning the National Remote Sensing Agency (NRSA) by National Wasteland Development Board (NWDB) way back in the year 1985 to prepare a wasteland map of the country could be called as the first instance of involvement of remote sensing or space-based technologies as a tool for managing soil health. Since then, the Indian Remote Sensing (IRS) satellite services were used extensively in several aspects such as Desertification Monitoring & Assessment, Watershed Management, Drought Early Warning, Preparedness and Management etc. (Fig. 7.2).

- **Desertification:** Using the Spectral Reflectance (SR) technology, the extent of land degradation can be assessed. This technique makes use of the data acquired from different regions of the Electromagnetic Spectra (ES) to

provide non-destructive prediction of soil properties. Soil Moisture (SM) is an important parameter for detection of early drought, flood forecasting, crop productivity etc. Combining these two methods, most vulnerable areas prone to desertification can be identified and classified into desertified, severely degraded, moderately degraded, slightly degraded, depending upon the status of the land. Based on the degree of desertification, prioritization can be made for implementation of remedial measures. ISRO has estimated that in the year 2011-13, about 96.30 Mha area of the country is undergoing the process of desertification while it as only 94.52 Mha in the year 2003-05, an increase of 1.87 Mha (about 0.57 per cent of Total Geographical area of the country) within a decade. Rajasthan, Maharashtra, Gujarat, Jammu& Kashmir, Karnataka, Jharkhand, Odisha, Madhya Pradesh and Telangana were contributing in descending order while rest of the states contributing less than one per cent area under desertification. ISRO has attributed maximum damage from water erosion (10.98%), followed by the vegetation degradation (8.91%) and wind erosion (5.55%) respectively in 2011-13.

3.2 Soil Health Card (SHC)

In order to ensure judicious use of chemical fertilizer and maintaining good soil health in the country, the Government,

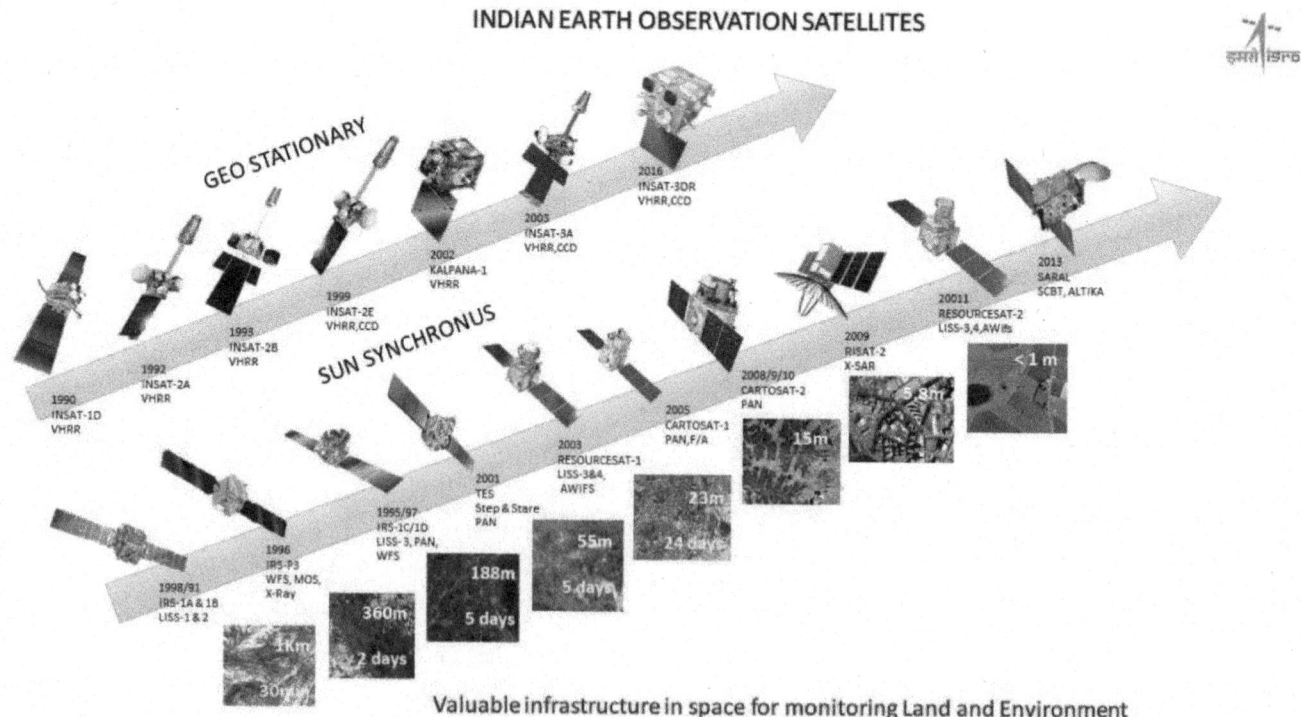

Fig. 7.2 Rapid Advances in Space Sector by India

Source: ISRO

under the component of Soil Health Management of National Mission of Sustainable Agriculture (NMSA), is promoting soil test based balanced and integrated nutrient management. National Mission on Soil Health Card (SHC) has been launched to provide soil test-based fertilizer recommendation to every farmer in the country. Further, to capture the soil fertility changes occurring due to plant uptake or other natural causes, it was envisaged to issue SHC every three years for all landholdings. During its 1st cycle from 2015–2017, 2,53,49,546 soil samples were collected and analyzed. Based on the analytical reports, 10,73,89,421 SHCs were printed and dispatched to respective farmers. During the 2nd cycle from 2017-2019, 2,71,66,065 soil samples were collected and tested for prescribed parameters. Based on the results, 11,51,07,723 SHCs were printed and dispatched (https://www.soilhealth.dac.gov.in/). Thus, SHC offers a huge database of the soil profile and fertility status for the entire country. Confluence of Space technologies with SHC can help devising most appropriate strategy/ approach for individual farmer to adopt to combat desertification effectively (DAC 2015). Convergence of these two different technologies can be effective tool for the protection of the soil resources.

4. Objectives

As can be seen in preceding sections, there has been rapid developments both in space technologies and soil sciences. However, there are hardly any attempts to explore the possibility of convergence of these two disciplines for protection of soil resources from desertification. Hence, this exploratory study is undertaken with following specific research questions;

- Can space technologies help identify the land prone to desertification, downscaled to the individual farmer level,
- With the help of the satellite images of different time periods about degrading soil quality, can farmers be motivated to initiate soil conservation measures,
- Can the information about soil, based on Soil Health Card, help farmer to choose most appropriate cropping pattern and reduce/prevent desertification

4.1 Methodology

Following strategy was adopted for the study (Fig. 7.3)

(a) **Identification of the Problem Area/ downscaling to village and farmer level:** Detecting and identifying the areas prone to desertification/land degradation by using high resolution images through Synthetic Aperture Radar (SAR). Areas with too dry soil or lacking humus content, non-arable, high salinity, wind eroded etc., could be identified and downscaled to at village and individual farmer level.

(b) **Soil Status:** Once the critical area is spotted and marked, using the information available through Soil Health Card, most suitable cropping pattern at individual farmer level is identified with the help of agricultural scientists. Two factors given due importance during the selection of cropping pattern, viz., a) preserving the soil and b) sustaining the farm-based income to the farmer.

(c) **Implementation of the Action Plan:** Inclusion of farmers as primary agents in soil conservation in their own fields would have a very effective impact on the

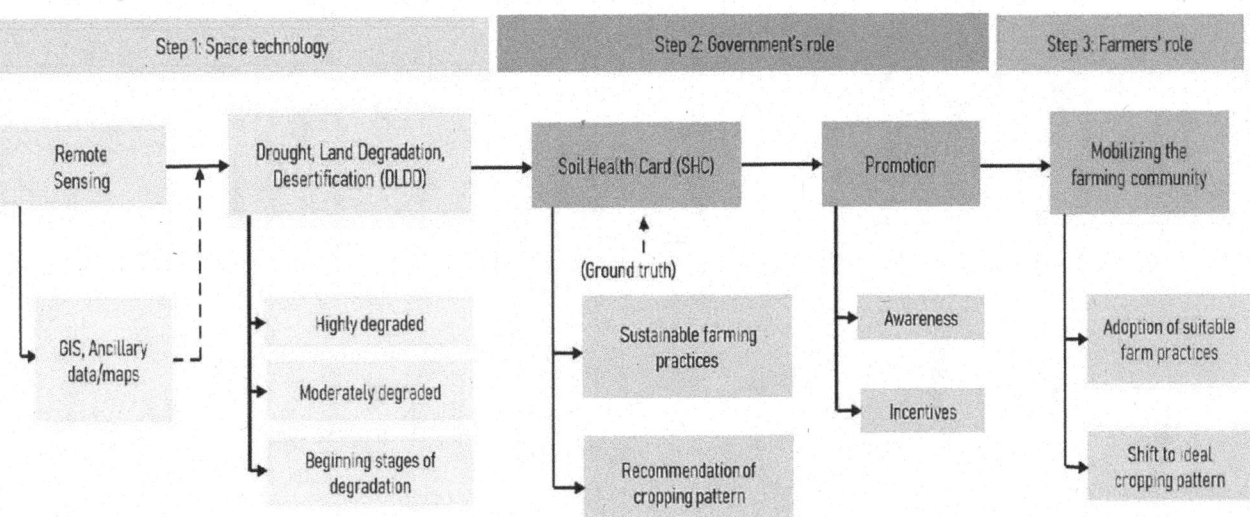

Fig. 7.3 Confluence of Space Technologies with Soil Health Card to Combat Desertification

restoration of soil. Their involvement in soil restoration would prevent further land degradation. With the help of various stakeholders departments like Department of agriculture, rural development, environment & forests, potential adoptions were discussed with farmers to encourage them to adopt the measures in their fields.

(d) **Convergence** with desertification related interventions by the government agencies was made to find possible additional inputs to the farmers

4. Study Area

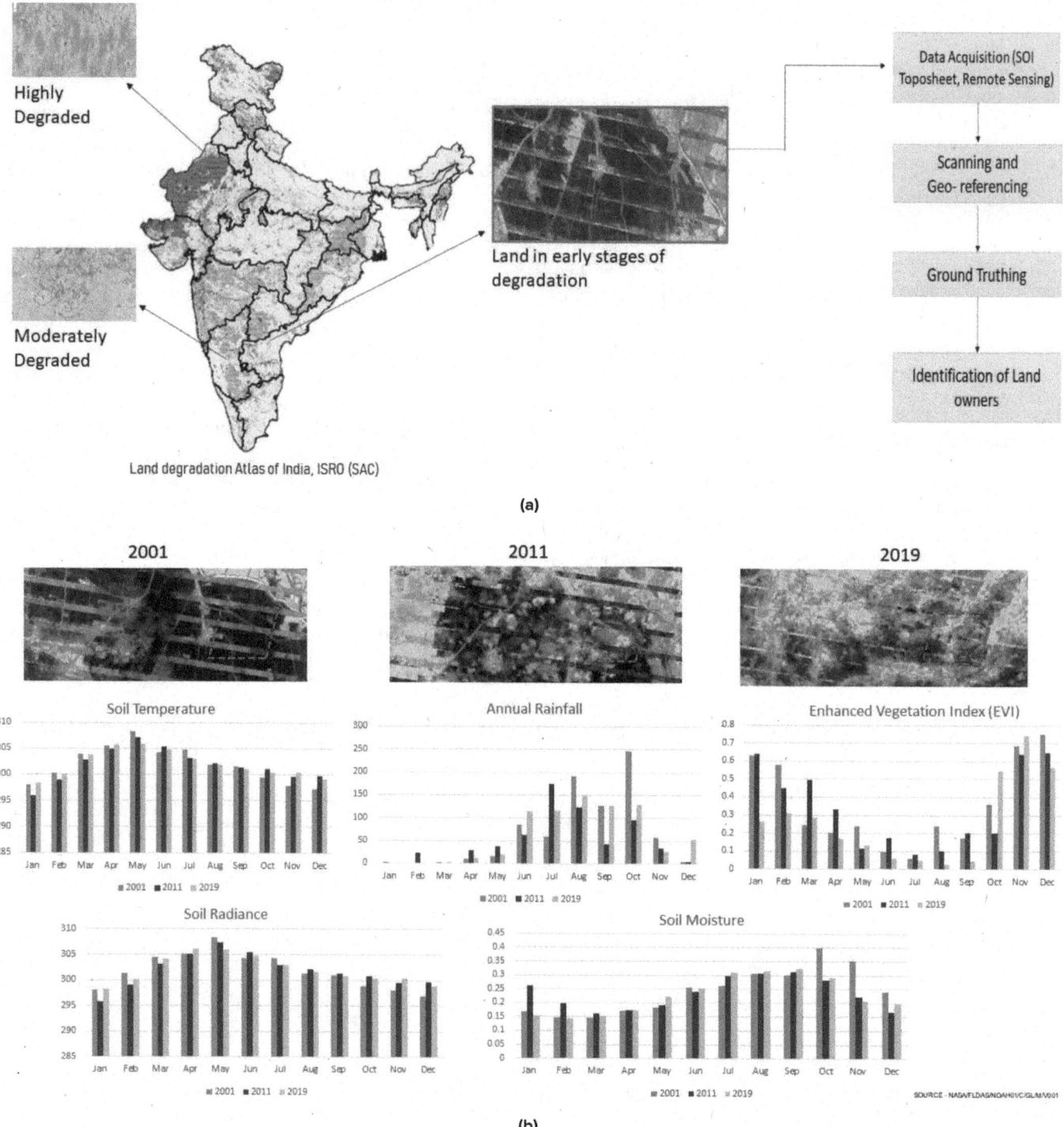

Fig. 7.4 (a) Downscaling and Categorising, (b) Case study in the village Retur, Andhra Pradesh

Sources: (a) ISRO 2016 and (b) Bhuvan Geo Portal

5. Results and Observations

5.1 Use of Space based Technologies

Using the images of different time periods, it is practical to establish the changes in land use and land cover. Further, the downscaling can be carried to the level of individual farmers. With the help of satellite images, soils can be demarcated into different groups based on the level of desertification.

5.2 Soil Health Card (SHC)

Soil cards distributed under Cycle I and II contain information about soil nutrients levels, but lacking in other information, for instance, ideal cropping pattern which could assist farmers to take informed decision.

5.3 Motivating Farmers

With satellite images as proof of changes, there was a significant change in the awareness level of farmers about soil health. With higher awareness, farmers themselves became aware of the need to protect their soil quality.

- Information about various schemes that are being implemented by the government and can be beneficial to the farmer could serve as catalyst to motivate the farmer to adopt measures that could protect his/her soil resources

6. Conclusion

In National Action Plan to Combat desertification, it was government through its various branches has as a primary role and the local community involvement was at peripheral level only. Though the government interventions are effective, their penetration was limited with reference to the farm lands owned by the individuals. This factor could have also contributed to the Therefore sub-optimal performance of preventing land degradation. The suggested model , for a change, puts the farmer, empowered with satellite images and SHC, at the helm of affairs and enables him to make informed decision to protect his/her own land resources. Such a paradigm change is likely to bring effective prevention of desertification and can help in restoring the soil resources as well. By proper scaling up, this strategy could help India tackle the problem of desertification, land degradation .

Way Forward: This exercise was carried out at a single village as a part of graduate engineering student course work, but with excellent results. Similar model with appropriate change to suit local diversities can be adopted in different parts of the country. The model can be scaled up with relative ease (Fig. 7.5)

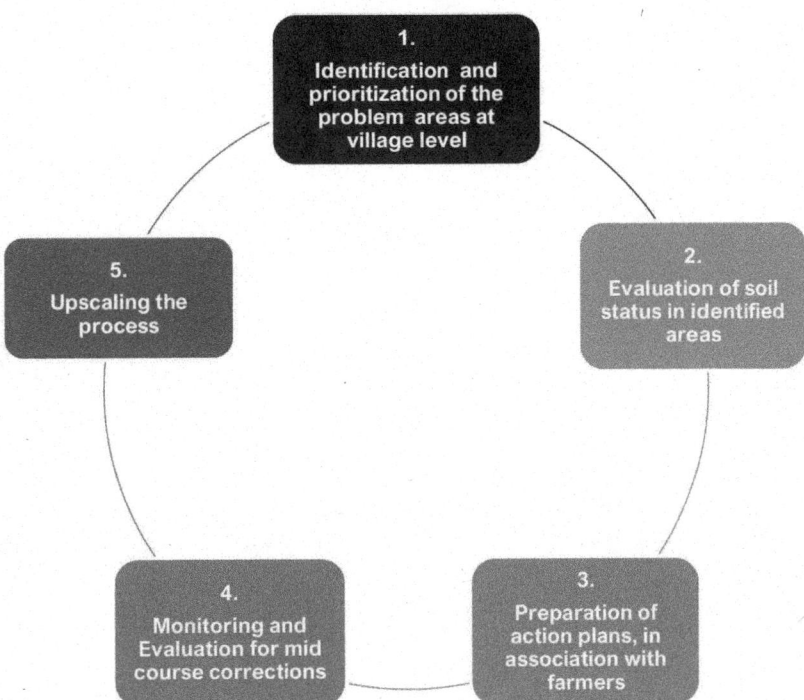

Fig. 7.5　The Process of Amalgamation of Space Technologies and Soil Health Cards

REFERENCES

1. Department of Agriculture and Cooperation, Ministry of Agriculture, 1994. Draft Report on Status of Land Degradation in India, Government of India, New Delhi. 102 pp.
2. United Nations Environment Program (UNEP), 1997: World Atlas of Desertification. Second edition. UNEP, Nairobi.
3. Ministry of Environment & Forests Government of India (MoEF) 2000. Volume I: Status of Desertification submitted to the *United Nations Convention on Combating Desertification* (UNCCD). MoEF, Government of India, New Delhi
4. Ministry of Environment & Forests (MoEF), 2001. *National Action Program to Combat Desertification: In the Context of United Nations Convention to Combat Desertification*
5. Indian Space Research Organization (ISRO) 2016. Desertification and Land Degradation Atlas of India (Based on IRS AWiFS data of 2011-13 and 2003-05), Space Applications Centre, ISRO, Ahmedabad
6. United Nations Convention to Combat Desertification (UNCCD) 2013. *The Economics of Desertification, Land Degradation and Drought: Methodologies and Analysis for Decision-Making.* Background document. UNCCD 2nd Scientific Conference.
7. The Energy and Resource Institute (TERI 2018). Economics of Desertification, Land Degradation and Drought in India, Vol I: *Macroeconomic assessment of the costs of land degradation in India.* New Delhi

DAC 2015: Soil Health Card Scheme. https://www.soilhealth.dac.gov.in/

CHAPTER 8

Technological Preparedness for Fire Disasters

K. C. Wadhwa

OS & Associate Director
Centre for Fire, Explosive and Environment Safety (CFEES),
DRDO, Ministry of Defence

Abstract

Fire disasters are accompanied by devastating impacts affecting both lives and properties. The magnitude of the impacts has been severe in places with low levels of fire disaster preparedness. These hazards threaten millions of lives and cause large scale financial, infrastructure, agriculture and productivity losses that seriously hinder India's overall development. A study was conducted by RMSI Pvt. Ltd. which was engaged by the Ministry of Home Affairs, Govt. of India for the gap analysis in fire services in India in terms of deficiency of fire stations, fire personnel, fire fighting vehicles/appliances and specialized fire fighting equipment to determine the level of fire disaster preparedness considering the availability and condition of firefighting facilities as well as the knowledge on fire safety management among the states and UTs fire services in the country. In addition, the possible impacts of fire disasters in future for forest fires, industrial fires and fires in congested areas in the country were also studied at length and their mitigation measures have been recommended keeping in view the extant rules and regulations and Govt policies on the subject.

Keywords: disaster, mitigation, hazards, risk, fire safety management.

1. Introduction

Centre for Fire, Explosive and Environment Safety (CFEES), a DRDO laboratory, has the unique mandate of providing comprehensive solutions to Ministry of Defence establishments to address Fire Safety issues through R&D, Regulatory, Advisory and Training. It is the nodal agency for implementing HSE (Health, Safety and Environment) in DRDO. CFEES has developed various technologies for fire protection & suppression systems for Defence Platforms and spin-off technologies for civilians use. Products and technologies developed by CFEES are Halon based Systems for Armoured Fighting Vehicles, Water Mist based Systems for Naval Ships & Submarines, Portable Water Mist Gun, Fire Detection & Suppression System for Passenger Buses, Fire Suppression Gel (FSG) for Forest Fires, Aerosols for Fire Suppression, Emergency Escape Chute for rescue from high rise buildings fires and Structural Fire Fighting Suit etc. Many of these products and technologies are very useful for addressing fire disasters viz. forest fire, industrial fire & fire in congested urban areas. This paper discusses the technological preparedness for fire disasters and elaborates the products & technologies developed by CFEES for minimising risk of fire

to a larger extent, thus saving National assets in terms of lives and property.

Fire service is one of the most important emergency response services in the country, which comes under the state subject and has been included as municipal function in the item 7 of Schedule XII under Article 243 W of the Constitution of India. Hence, fire prevention and firefighting services are organised by the concerned States and Union Territories. It may be added here that the fire brigades in India remain heterogeneous in character and majority of them continue to remain ill-equipped and differently organised. The National Building Code (NBC) of India, is the basic model code on matters relating to building construction and fire safety. Since the primary responsibility for fire prevention and fire protection lies with the State Governments, the rules for fire prevention and fire protection are laid in the form of State Regulations or Municipal By-Laws.

The main objective of NBC is to specify measures that will provide that degree of safety from fire, which is practical and can be reasonably achieved. The code insists upon compliance with minimum standards of fire safety necessary for building occupants and users. For ensuring compliance of fire protection equipment / installations to the laid down quality requirements, it is desirable to use such equipment / installation conforming to Bureau of Indian Standards (BIS).

Fire pose a major threat to various occupancies in India. Almost every day some fires are reported by media across the country. These fires not only result into the loss of many precious lives and injuries to many but also inflicted heavy property loss. During the last decade rapid modernisation of Indian Industry have made the scenario more complex. Awareness towards fire safety had not been quite forthcoming. As per the statistical data, about 8004 industrial accidents claimed over 6300 lives between 2014 and 2017 in India. While Delhi, Maharashtra and Rajasthan recorded most such industrial incidents in the period but Rajasthan, Gujarat and Maharashtra witnessed the highest number of deaths.

2. Possible Impact of the Fire Disasters in the Future

2.1 Forest Fires

Forest Fires Impact: It has profound impacts on atmospheric chemistry, biogeochemical cycling and ecosystem structure. Forest fire or wild land fire has become intense and more frequent in the last few decades all over the world and is a critical issue in the biosphere-atmosphere interface. The global carbon and nitrogen emissions from fires have been estimated to be 3.53 trillion Kg / year and 8 billion Kg / year respectively. The number of forest fires shot up to 14,107 from 4,225 between November 2018 and February 2019 according to the Real Time Forest Alert System of the Forest Survey of India (FSI) using near real time data from the SNPP-VIIRS satellite. Between 01 January to 26 February 2019, 209 out of 558 forest fires occurred in the five southern states of India—Andhra Pradesh, Karnataka, Tamil Nadu, Telangana and Kerala, which is 37 per cent of the fires. India loses about Rs 1200 crore a year to forest fires.

Forest fires also pose serious health hazard by creating polluting smoke and noxious gases. The burning of vegetation gives off not only carbon dioxide but also a host of other noxious gases (Green house gases) such as carbon monoxide, methane hydrocarbons, nitric oxide and nitrous oxide, that lead to global warming and ozone layer depletion. So, thousands of people suffer from serious respiratory problems due to these toxic gases. The recent forest fires in Uttarakhand may be only a small part of the overall global problem. But if looked at from the point of view of the fragile Himalayan ecology, they portend a dark future. Already large areas of the Himalayan forests have been cleared indiscriminately for agriculture, making them vulnerable to soil erosion and landslide. The only way to save the fragile Himalayan ecosystem from recurring forest fires is to put in place a viable disaster management action plans.

State forest departments and the MoEF&CC: The parliamentary standing committee on science and technology, environment and forests criticised the forest departments of the five states for ineffective utilisation of the forest fire prevention funds in its report Status of Forests in India during the year 2017-18. While India loses Rs 1,176 crore a year to forest fires, a mere Rs 45-50 crore is allocated per annum under the Forest Fire prevention and Management Fund, which remains unspent. Nearly 24 per cent of the meager forest fire prevention funds were not released and thus, remained unspent in the two financial years, shows the data provided by the Union Ministry of Environment, Forest and Climate Change (MoEF & CC) in January 2019 in the Lok Sabha. Out of Rs 50 crore allocated during each year, 2017-18 and 2018-19, Rs 35 crore and Rs 38 crore were released respectively. While the recent parliamentary standing committee acknowledged the fund constraints faced by the MoEF &CC to prevent and fight forest fires and that the allocated funds need to be utilised effectively and strategically.

Comprehensive policy: The National Green Tribunal has repeatedly asked the MoEF & CC to come out with a national policy on forest fires. In fact, the Draft Forest Policy, 2018, does mention forest fires as a threat and has proposed the mapping of vulnerable areas along with developing and strengthening early warning systems. It has also proposed participation of communities. Uncontrolled fires are a complex problem that require a comprehensive and long term policy. This requires more effective coordination with local communities who are the primary forest users in India. It demands proper co-ordination mechanisms between the state governments forest departments and the MoEF&CC. These fires should be treated as disasters so that disaster management authorities can play a major role in preventing them. The National Forest Commission of 2006 too suggested that all fires that burn an area larger than 20 sq km, should be declared a state disaster.

Causes of Forest Fires: A combination of factors like dry summer, winter rain deficit, low humidity, high temperature and less preparedness lead to the forest fire. It is anthropogenic in nature which gets flamed due to conducive local environment for fire. The possible reasons may be control burning by the locals which go out of hand, casual approach of the locals / visitors while throwing away lighted butts of cigarettes, vested interest group, casual approach of authorities, resource and technology crunch, lack of preparedness for risk reduction etc. Such fires usually start on the ground as the dry litter (senescent leaves and twigs) catches fire easily. Then, flamed by strong winds, the flames soon engulf vast tract forest turning them to ashes and, therefore, cause extensive damage unless controlled in time. Many forest fires start from natural causes such as lightning which sets trees on fire, these type of fires have been recorded periodically in India.

Mitigation Measures: The subject of forests is in the concurrent list of the Constitution of India. The Central Government and State Governments are both competent to legislate on the subject. The issues relating to policy planning and finance are the primary responsibility of the Government of India. The field administration of the forests is the responsibility of the various state governments. The state Government thus has the direct responsibility of the management of forest resources of the country. The state forest departments, therefore, carry out the fire prevention and control measures. Each State and Union Territory has its own separate forest department. At the Government of India level, Director General of Forests & Special Secretary to the Government of India is the head of the professional forest service in the country. The Forest Protection Division in the Ministry, which is headed by an Inspector General of Forests, looks after Forest Fire prevention. The Ministry is implementing a centrally sponsored plan on Intensification of Forest Management Scheme under which the state governments are provided financial assistance for activities including fire prevention and control.

Technological Preparedness: Forest fires are usually seasonal. These usually start in the dry season and can be prevented by adequate precautions. Different State Governments are aware of the severe damage caused by fires to forests and ecology of the area. Traditional methods of fire control are inadequate and limited in India. The modern methods of fire control are yet to be placed on the ground in the required measure. Generally, the fire in the forest is prevented by creating fire lines. This line prevents fire breaking into the forest from one compartment to another. It proves effectively and the collected litter is burnt in isolation. At the same time, the utility of these leaves should be explored. Generally, the fire spreads only if there is continuous supply of fuel (dry vegetation) along its path. The best way to control a forest fire is, therefore, to prevent it from spreading, which can be done by creating Fire Breaks in the shape of small clearings of ditches in the forest as well as using fire suppressing gel. Use of water mixed with 0.6 to 0.8 % (w/v) fire suppressing gel with water holding capacity of 100-200 g water/ g of FSG is usually the last resort, as spraying water on to the fire in dense forests on hill slopes, is usually a tricky job. In severe fire conditions, special aircrafts equipped with water tanks can be used to drop tons of water mixed with FS Gel on the burning trees. More details are covered in the recommendations.

National Forest Policy, 1988: India's National Forest Policy, amended in 1988, presents a visionary strategy for future forest conservation & management laying emphasis on protection of forest against encroachment, fire & grazing. The principle aim of the New National Forest Policy is "to ensure environmental stability and maintenance of ecological balance." The policy addresses the problem of forest fires in the context of forest protection in the specific terms as: "The incidence of the forest fires in the country is high. Standing trees and fodder are destroyed on a large scale and natural regeneration annihilated by such fires. Special precautions should be taken during the fire season. Improved and modern management practices should be adopted to deal with forest fires."

2.2 Industrial Fires

The Industrial core sectors include Energy & Power, Petroleum, Gas and Chemical, Metals, Minerals and Steel, Cement, Coal, Defence Production, Telecom & IT, Automobiles, Textiles etc. Industrial accidents are caused by chemical, mechanical, civil, electrical, or other process failures due to accident, negligence or incompetence, in an industrial plant which may spill over to the areas outside the plant causing damage to life and property. Major Threats may be Fire, Explosion, Toxic release, Poisoning or Combinations of these. These may originate in:

(i) Manufacturing and formulation installations including during commissioning and process operations; maintenance and disposal.

(ii) Material handling and storage in manufacturing facilities, and isolated storages; warehouses and godowns including tank farms in ports and docks and fuel depots.

(iii) Transportation (road, rail, air, water, and pipelines).

Probable causes of accidents:

(i) Process deviations i.e pressure, temperature & flow.

(ii) Parameters with regard to the state of the substance i.e., solid, liquid or gas, proximity to other toxic substances.

(iii) Runaway reaction.

(iv) Hardware failure, resulting in large-scale spills of toxic substances.

(v) Boiling Liquid Expanding Vapour Explosion (BLEVE) on the chemicals during transportation.

(vi) Electrical failure

(vii) Cutting and welding

(viii) Open flame

(ix) Carelessness

(x) Poor housekeeping

(xi) Smoking

(xii) Sabotage

Compounding effects of accidents are due to meteorology of the area, wind speed and direction, rate of precipitation, toxicity/quantity of chemical released, population in the reach of release, probability of formation of lethal mixtures and other industrial activities in vicinity.

Impact of Industrial Accidents: Immediate, Short-term and Long-term Effects which may lead to major consequences such as:

(i) Loss of life / injuries

(ii) Impact on livestock

(iii) Damage to Flora/fauna

(iv) Environmental Impact (air, soil, water)

(v) Financial losses to industry.

2.3 Fires in Congested Areas

Master Plan for Metropolitan cities had been created as an instrument to control the use of land in urban area and protect the welfare of people. The concept of zoning has not yielded desirable results over and above allowing for mixed use and occupancy, authorized as well as unauthorized. Banquet halls in residential areas, cottage industries in congested areas, trade of hazardous chemicals from the highly congested residential/commercial areas, hazardous and non hazardous industries in close vicinity are few to mention which have further deteriorated environmental services. This has certainly added to the fire risk already inherited by a particular occupancy. As a result losses due to fire are increasing to both the life and property. This is developing a dangerous trend. Similar situation has been reported from almost all metropolitan cities in the country. Man-made disasters are likely in these areas.

Trends:

(i) Although the number of calls have only marginally increased, number of deaths have increased potentially. The basic reason is that deaths are not as much due to burning but more because of inhalation of toxic fumes, which get concentrated in high density less open space area. It is the lack of circulation/ventilation within tenements. In industrial areas there is disrespect for the safety measures required and hence large number of deaths or injury due to fires occur.

(ii) Number of fire incidents in jhuggis and jhoparis clusters / high-rise buildings have reduced while fire incidents in industrial and residential areas have increased. One of the reason for such increase is, that industrial areas have started hosting non-confirming

industries and residential areas have become haven for illegal storage's and dangerous commercial activities in pursuit of mixed permitting land and occupancy in these areas. Also, disrespect to circulation space and open space and increase in congestion in these areas have caused poor accessibility to the place of tragic incidence, which takes only records to increase.

(iii) During analysis of the causes of maximum number of fires in such cities it is observed that 70 percent of calls are due to electric short circuiting. This is alarming because a single cause can be disastrous to life and property that major investments are required mitigating these risks. Short-circuiting is often a result of illegal connections, low quality wiring and therefore, even if single major cause is taken, of, not only would it lead to saving innumerable lives and properties but also cut down on expenditure incurred on fire mitigation.

3. Addressing of Issues/Response Mechanism

Policy of Rehabilitation and Response: Every year, about one-third of all forests are damaged or affected by fire. Therefore, an effective policy of forest fire prevention and control is extremely important. It was in this context that the modern forest fire control project was taken up in five districts of Uttarakhand and U.P. viz., Pithoragarh, Nainital, Almora and Rampur & Pilibhit in 1985. The area proposed to be covered was 3,72,693 hectares. The achievements attained through this project included Development and demonstration of modern fire control techniques, Preparation of division wise fire management plans, Estimation of forest fires, Development and application of a forest fire danger rating system, Training of forest personnel, Full fire protection of timber depots and Manufacture of fire finders and hand tools within the country and standardization of fire control equipment.

Risk control measures:

(i) Physical Protection: Strict & rigorous approach in implementing the relevant standards, codes of practice, Built in safety devices and safety system, Venting through tall stacks, Field monitors for different toxic gases and burning waste gases in a flare system, Provision of wind cones, Fire proofing of steel structures, PPEs, Passive protection system and Active protection system.

(ii) Procedural Protection: Fire emergency procedure, Disaster preparedness plan, Mutual aid scheme, No smoking policy, Investigation of all accidents, Hazard identification through safety committee, House keeping committee, Safety audit committee, Conducting plant survey, safety survey, Work permit system, Safety promotional activities, Information notes on unsafe conditions, Material safety data sheet, Annual medical check up of employees, Safe start up & shut down procedure, Regular and preventive maintenance and Periodic testing of fire fighting appliances.

(iii) Educational Protection: Periodic training program on safety, Fire safety and hazardous properties of materials, Mock fire drill, Safety manuals, Health & safety news bulletins & leaflets, Safety motivation schemes, Plant operating manual and Educating the public living nearby about the activities in the industry.

Issues: High population density, crowded streets, un-matching mixed occupancies, inadequate water supply, poor electrical services, unplanned siting of fire stations, encroachment are few examples of ineffective planning in the metropolitan cities which adversely affect the fire response time. Under the present circumstances, a response time of 5-7 minutes in urban areas and 20 minutes in rural areas is very difficult to achieve. Mobilizing a large quantity of water to the fire scene especially in walled city area is more than fire fighting. Fire safety should, therefore, be an integral part of urban planning process rather than an after thought in such cities.

4. Gap Analysis

Fire Stations Gap Analysis: As per detailed analysis carried out in India, there is a requirement of about additional 1,300 Fire Stations in urban areas and about 4,250 Fire Stations in rural areas. Hence this study found an overall gap of about 65% in terms of number of Fire Stations in the entire country. For this analysis, response time of 5-7 minutes in urban area and 20 minutes in rural areas was considered.

Firefighting and Rescue Vehicles and Specialized Equipment Gap Analysis: This, study finds an overall gap of about 83% in the firefighting and rescue vehicles and about 95% in specialized equipment for both operational and new Fire Stations in urban and rural areas.

Fire Personnel Gap Analysis: Administrative Reform Department norms based on duty pattern (double-shift) have been used for optimization of the fire manpower requirements, the duty pattern of fire personnel varies from state to state, i.e., from 8 hours, 12 hours and 24 hours. However, in this study, double shift duty pattern (12 hours) has been followed for optimizing the fire personnel gaps. Thus, as a whole in entire India, this study finds an overall gap of about 91% in fire personnel considering double shift duty pattern.

This gap analysis study indicates that there is lot to be done to upgrade the level of state fire services in the country. As regards the fire incidents in industries and forest areas, respective departments have to take care of any fire emergency within the resources available with them, however state fire service would assist them under mutual-aid-scheme in case of any disaster. It is seen that the situation is better in industries since they have independent fire services set up within their premises. As regards the forest department, it needs to introduce latest fire prevention and fire fighting technologies as recommended in this report.

5. Recommendations

5.1 Forest Fires

The key recommendations to handle forest fire scenarios are summarized as under:

(i) Creation of fire lines and controlled burning of dry leaves/grass under the management of fire fighters.

(ii) Use of operational detection system: Fire towers/watch towers, aerial patrols, electronic lightening detectors and automatic detection system.

(iii) Fire-resistant clothing and other PPEs to be provided to the fire fighters.

(iv) Mobility & Communication:

    (a) The key players who are at the ground confronting the fire (fire watchers, forest guards etc.) have been given large area to monitor but they do not have any facility of mobility and communication. There is a need to strengthen mobility especially during the summer months (February to June).

    (b) Two way radios and mobile phones should be provided to the fire watchers.

(v) Hand Tools:

    (a) Drip torch

    (b) Pulaski

    (c) Chainsaw

    (d) Shovel Fire Beaters/Fire Flappers to be made available.

(vi) Forest Fire Engines: All Terrain Vehicles (ATVs) fitted with special equipment to spray water, foam and fire retardant chemicals / gels should be introduced to handle such fires.

(vii) Forest fire chemicals: Class 'A' fire fighting foam, FS gel (water enhancer).

    (a) Class 'A' foam: Diethylene Glycol Monobutyl Ether based.

    (b) Fire Suppressing Gel / Water Gel / Aqua gel: polyacrylic acid based – developed by CFEES, DRDO should be tried for its effectiveness on forest fires for future applications. Its application results into reduction of water requirement as well as fire extinguishment time upto 50% with shelf life of 5 years.

(viii) Use of Helicopters/UAVs/Aircrafts with water scooping capability: possibility may be explored for its induction as a long term measure to tackle similar incidents.

(ix) Heavy Equipment:

(a) Bulldozers

(b) Tractor ploughs should be made available for creating fire lines.

(x) Training: should be done at regular intervals for Creation of specialized trained manpower / working group/smoke jumpers.

(xi) Development of software for fire behavior modeling, Geographic Information Systems (GIS) for better fire mapping, satellite imagery & automated stations for up-to-the-minute weather forecasts and estimates of fuel and moisture.

(xii) Development of fire shelters.

(xiii) Infrared Wireless Network Sensors for imminent forest fire detection.

(xiv) Extensive use of websites and e-mail, which will allow immediate sending & obtaining information and assets to fire managers, fire fighters and the public alike.

(xv) Development and demonstration of modern fire control techniques.

(xvi) Manufacture of fire finders and hand tools within the country and standardization of fire control equipment.

(xvii) As the subject of forest fire is in the concurrent list and is the responsibility of the National Government for its prevention, mitigation and response, the Ministry of Environment, Forests & Climate Change (MoEF & CC) being the nodal agency may create a Working Group especially to monitor the implementation of the National Forest Policy Resolution (NFPR), 1988.

(xviii) There is a need to create a Corpus Fund for forest fire prevention, rehabilitation and response and the MoEF may work closely with the States in this regard.

(xix) Management of forests has changed over the years and in the present context of some states there are three kinds of forests – Reserve Forests, Civil Forests and Forests controlled by Panchayats. So different strategies have to be adopted for each category of the forests, especially for forests controlled by Panchayats along with other recommendations.

(xx) Community's attachment to the forests has drastically come down as they do not own forests and hence there is apathy for contributing in the management of the fire.

Therefore, it is imperative that community outreach programmes are designed and implemented to have their participation in the forest fire management.

(xxi) As women are working as a support system in providing water, food and other required services to the fire watchers and local villagers so that the fire fighters can continue working for longer periods which is essential at the time of forest fire. Hence, it is recommended that induction of women in the entire fire fighting management be carried out and their distinctive role defined to bring them into the mainstream of fire fighting management.

5.2 Industrial Fires

(i) Provision of Fire safety measures as per the relevant codes.

(ii) Obtaining Fire NOC before commencement of Operations.

(iii) Providing appropriate fire fighting vehicles like Multipurpose fire tenders, DCP tenders, Foam tenders and Industrial fire tower vehicles, fire fighting robots and remotely controlled monitors to the local Fire Brigade with the grants from Govt. of India.

(iv) Fire outpost in every industrial area with minimum no. of fire vehicles and personal protective equipment.

(v) Conducting Onsite and offsite emergency exercises / mock drills once in every 6 months.

(vi) Surprise inspections and classes by the fire authorities to find out emergency preparedness and suggest any additional measures.

(vii) Standardization of SOPs (Standard Operating Procedure) strict compliance.

(viii) Whenever Chemical Factory established in habitation areas the Alarm/Siren to be raised in all times as per National Green Tribunal.

(ix) The Wind action (or) wind direction to be notified and evacuate the people downside.

(x) The Fire fighting/Quick Response Teams to be always alert and available in the Factory premises.

(xi) The Fire fighting Teams shall be fully equipped with modern fire fighting equipment

(xii) Communication and capacity building in industrial fire service.

(xiii) The Chemical Data Sheet of each chemical/ substance made available in Control Room to monitor and take correct preventive steps accordingly.

(xiv) The Firefighting equipment installation shall not be worn out or old age.

(xv) In Industrial Zones, Buffer Zones to be left between factory and village.

(xvi) In light of any accident reported due to failure of safety measures, design fault and lack of training and awareness, immediate action to be taken.

(xvii) The Fire Safety Audit to be conducted periodically.

(xviii) The On-site/Off-site Emergency plans to be updated regularly as per need/change of process of Plant/Industry.

(xix) Hazard (or) Risk Analysis and related Mitigation measures to be Displayed/Practiced.

(xx) The Employee Safety/Good practices to be adopted.

5.3 Fires in Congested Areas

(i) *Strict implementation of laws:* Government of India notified "Unified Building Bye Laws for Delhi" on 2nd March 2016, which shall be applicable to all building activities in urban villages/rural villages, unauthorized regularized colonies and for special areas. But these bye-laws are enforced from the date notified and cannot be enforced on buildings constructed prior to the enactment of these bye-laws. On similar lines, the building by-laws framed for other states for the existing buildings should be uniformly implemented pan India.

(ii) *Awareness about fire safety:* Fire safety awareness programmes should be conducted regularly by fire department across the cities for different occupancies especially in high fire risk prone areas like Jhuggi clusters and un-authorized colonies. Special workshops on fire safety for school teachers, Resident Welfare Organizations (residence and market etc) and hospitals should be conducted.

(iii) *Road network improvement and dedicated lanes for fire tender:* Road network has a direct connection with the response time of fire service in case of an incident. This makes it imperative to devote this infrastructure a special status for fire services. Colonies having limited or narrow approach roads can be identified and fire tenders built on small vehicle chassis can be used.

(iv) *Setting up new sub-fire stations accommodating new infrastructure developments and population distribution:* Considering changes in infrastructure development and population distribution over a period, setting up new sub-fire stations or upgrading the existing sub-fire stations will be required. Such infrastructure could have a direct impact on losses occurring due to fire events. Provision of a Fire Post at every 3 kilometer and a Fire Station at every 7 kilometer distance as per Master Plan should be there in all metropolitan cities. It should also have a provision of Disaster Management Centre and Fire Training Institute.

(v) *Use of latest technology equipment by Fire Department:* Latest technology such as water mist has brought much advantageous equipment for firefighting purposes, where large fires can be extinguished by using limited quantity of extinguishing agent like water and foam. Such equipment can be easily carried by fire fighter as back pack or on the small fire vehicle like motorbike. Similarly, remote-controlled robots equipped with thermal imaging cameras for fire-fighting operations in locations that are dangerous for the fire-fighters can also be used.

(vi) *Use of Geo-spatial Technologies:* Geospatial technologies can contribute in planning for fire services. In addition to giving an idea of land use/land cover in the jurisdiction area, it can help in generating optimum routes, service area as per the time and distance, asset management. Using Global Positioning System (GPS), responders can plan response route in advance as well as get the updates about the live traffic situation. This can drastically cut down the response time and losses. Live Images/Videos from fire fighters cameras and fire fighting vehicles at fire ground connected with fire control room can make a significant difference. Images or videos from Drones or if possible, satellite images in real time, may contribute. These drones fly over the affected area and give an idea of the spread and intensity of the fire and are also useful for search and rescue operations.

(vii) *Fire safety regulations as integral part of urban planning:* With increased population, infrastructure and resulting congestion, modern cities need to prepare for increased fire risks. Delhi Fire Service Rules, 2010 under Delhi Fire Service Act, 2007 have been framed and notified, making mandatory for certain classes of occupancies to incorporate minimum standards for fire prevention/safety such as access to building, arrangement of exits, fire compartmentation, smoke management system and fire protection systems etc. Similarly, the Acts and Rules notified under Maharashtra Fire Prevention and Life Safety Measures Act, 2006 (Amendment 2015) and Rules, 2009, West Bengal Fire Services (Amendment) Act, 1996 and Rules, 2003, Gujarat Fire Prevention and Life Safety Measures Act, 2013 and Regulations, 2016, Odisha Fire Prevention and Fire Safety Act, 1993 and (Amendment) Rules, 2019, Karnataka Fire Force Act, 1964 (as amended by Karnataka Act 40 of 1994) and other States/

UTs which have mandatory fire safety provisions in different type of occupancies should be included in urban planning.

(viii) *Arrangement of Dedicated Underground Water Reservoirs:* In the areas of higher fire risk, it is imperative to have dedicated underground water reservoirs for replenishment of fire tenders in time. Locations for such dedicated reservoirs should be identified based on fire risk analysis. Alternatively, water bowsers/water carriers having large capacity of water shall be provided in adequate numbers in such areas.

(ix) *Human resource development and capacity building:* There is a need to update the fire service personnel with the latest technological development in the field of fire safety and disaster management and accordingly upgrade the existing training infrastructure in all the regional and national level training institutes with more emphasis on hands-on training.

6. Summary of Recommendations

S.No.	Recommendations	Responsible Agency for Implementation
	Forest Fires	
1.	All Terrain Vehicles (ATVs) fitted with special equipment to spray water, foam and fire retardant gels / chemicals should be introduced to handle forest fires.	MoEF & CC should centrally purchase the vehicles and distribute these to States which are vulnerable to forest fires.
2.	Application of UAVs / Aircrafts with water scooping capability to be explored to tackle forest fires.	National Fire Service College / NDRF Academy, Nagpur should take up a Project.
3.	Formation of Consortia regarding application of Satellites for monitoring forest fires on hourly basis.	ISRO and Forest Survey of India.
4.	Development of Software for Fire Behaviour Modelling and use of Geographic Information Systems (GIS) for application in forest fires.	Forest Research Institute in association with Academic Institutes.
	Fire in Congested Areas and Industrial Fires	
5.	Provision of a Fire Post at every 3 kilometer and a Fire Station at every 7 kilometer distance in all metropolitan cities.	State Governments with funding in a phased manner from 15th Finance Commission under allocation of funds for "Expansion and Modernisation of Fire Services".
6.	Small Fire Tenders / Motor bikes with water mist back pack system for colonies having limited or narrow approach roads / congested areas in the city.	State Governments. Manufacturers to be identified by the State Fire Services keeping in view any additional equipment / attachment required to meet local conditions.
7.	Fire Fighting Robots equipped with thermal imaging camera for fire fighting operations in locations that are dangerous to the fire-fighters in Congested Areas and Industries.	Guidelines to be promulgated by MHA for Industrial Establishments and inaccessible areas based on the hazard assessment by the State Fire Services.
8.	Grant-in-Aid to the State Fire Services under 15th Finance Commission for establishment of Fire Stations and procurement of Fire Fighting Equipment.	Ministry of Home Affairs, Govt. of India.
9.	Human resource development and capacity building.	Govt. of India and State Governments.
10.	Promotional avenues and incentives to Fire Service Personnel for their Morale Boosting.	State Governments.

7. Conclusion

Disasters are inevitable. The fact lies in stating "we must all be prepared to try to survive the current and the forthcoming disasters." We cannot rule the nature but we can at least be watchful and vigilant. The structured and preplanned preparedness and the healthy response to the disaster will help save the lives. Our success lies in, as is preached by the great people that existed and exist on earth "unity and unanimity devoid of discords."

Fire is one of the most frequently occurring disasters in India, especially in the hot dry summer months. The country has been a victim of fire incidents numerous times across all states. The urban areas, especially the towns and cities, along with the factories and industries are extremely vulnerable to fire. The highest number of deaths in the country is due to fire hazards. Around 83,872 fire incidents have been recorded in India during the year 2014 to 2018 as per the report released by National Crime Records Bureau.

Recent incidents of wildfires in Australia, the Amazon, California and Uttarakhand in India have lost the world its biodiversity, laying bare huge tracts of land to degradation and causing loss of homes, assets and lives. It is acknowledged that most wild fires have an anthropogenic origin. In densely packed urban areas, devastating fires are the most predominant risks and fire incidents continue to occur with repetitive regularity every year.

With increasing population, rapid urbanization has become a concern for the developing and underdeveloped nations. Rapid and unplanned urbanization, predominant especially in Asia and Africa has resulted in development of poor quality housing, unauthorized and illegal constructions, encroachment, poor wiring, use of old and obsolete machinery, etc. increasing the vulnerabilities to multiple hazards. Concentration of population and activities in urban areas lead to vulnerable conditions and exposure to various hazards, including fire. The high density of urban settlements resulting in narrow and constricted circulation spaces also adds to the urban fire vulnerabilities. Tightly packed dwelling units in slums and squatter settlements are high risk areas in cities. Slums are often made up of flammable materials and cheek-by-jowl tenements, a small fire can become a conflagration in no time. The narrow alleys hinder quick response to the fires. Slum fires are a common occurrence in the hot dry summer months in India every year. The high use of electrical equipment and machinery in urban areas leads to higher chances of faulty electric connections and gadget failures amplifies the risks further. Urban fires, therefore, occur in complex risk settings, with one or more factors coming in to play simultaneously.

Each disaster provides us with lessons to prevent future occurrences. With an aim to identify and record comprehensive insights about the underlying causes of the fire incidents in the country, some fire incidents of different categories have been studied and it has been inferred that preparedness actions can prevent fire hazards from becoming fire disasters.

REFERENCES

1. "Fire Hazard and Risk Analysis for Revamping the Fire Services in the Country"- A Study Report submitted by RMSI, Noida to Director General Fire Services, Home Guards and Civil Defence, Ministry of Home Affairs, Govt of India in December, 2011.
2. The Delhi Fire Service Act (2007) issued as Delhi Act No. 2 of 2009, vide Notification No. F-7(21)/2010/H-III, dated 1-7-2010 and Delhi Fire Service Rules, 2010 vide Notification No. F-7(21)/2010/H-III/962, dated 2-7-2010.
3. National Building Code of India- 2016 (Part IV) on Fire and Life Safety.
4. National Crime Records Bureau, Ministry of Home Affairs, Govt. of India Statistical Report – 2018.
5. The Forest Fire and Disaster Management Wing Report 2021 issued by Uttarakhand Forest Department, Govt. of Uttarakhand.
6. The data submitted by the Union Ministry of Environment, Forest and Climate Change (MoEF & CC) to the Lok Sabha (Parliament House) in January 2019.
7. The Forest Survey of India (FSI) Report – 2020.
8. MoEF (2006) Report of the National Forest Commission, Ministry of Environment and Forests, Government of India, New Delhi.
9. The National Forest Policy, 1988.
10. "Unified Building Bye Laws for Delhi" - Notified by Govt. of India on 2nd March 2016.
11. Expert Committee Report Constituted by Ministry of Home Affairs, Govt. of India "To assess the situation of Forest Fires and suggest remedial measures" in Uttarakhand in April 2016.

Part 2

INNOVATIONS IN CONSTRUCTION TECHNOLOGY

Chapter 9 A new fire safe design solution for reinforced concrete beams at catastrophic fire conditions

Chapter 10 Seismic Evaluation of Frictional Damper Developed Using Waste Rubber Tires

Chapter 11 Flexural Behaviour of Masonry Wall strengthened with Waste PET Grid

Chapter 12 Numerical Approximation of 3D Heat Conduction in Early Age Mass Concrete Using Crank Nicholson Implicit Finite Difference Method.

Chapter 13 A study on the economic perspective of utilizing liquid tanks as dynamic vibration absorbers in building structures

Chapter 14 Smart Shelters For Multi Disasters—A Framework with Cloud Technology and Measurement Devices

Chapter 15 A Critical Analysis of Building Codes of Pakistan; Fire Safety Provision 2016

A New Fire Safe Design Solution for Reinforced Concrete Beams at Catastrophic Fire Conditions

Banti A. Gedam

Scientist in Fire Research Laboratory,
CSIR-Central Building Research Institute, Roorkee (247667),
Uttarakhand, India
bantiagedam@cbri.res.in

Abstract

An accidental fire in buildings is common, which results in an enormous economic loss and face human casualties. For hence, fire prevention and vital installation measures for life safety and evacuation system have been acknowledged in the National Building Code (NBC). However, in the catastrophic fire scenarios, structural stability and integrity is the last option when all safety measure fails and as seen in the NBC, it does not deal with any design safe solution nor IS 456 codes for plain and reinforced concrete (RC) members. Therefore, in this research paper, a performance-based fire safe design solution for RC beams has been proposed for evaluating the ultimate moment carrying capacity at any fire load. The fire safe design solution is considering unsteady-state heat transfer field within RC beam by acknowledging fire exposure condition, and thermal-induced materials and mechanical properties at elevated temperature. The proposed fire safe design solution for RC beams is an essential technique to reduce risks of structural failure and gives pre-information at catastrophic fire scenarios that help planning and design for safe evacuation systems and improve structural fire resistance by the choice of materials and design.

Keywords: performance-based fire resistance design, heat transfer, reinforced concrete beams, experiment, thermal properties

1. Introduction

In the 21st century of India, infrastructure industries have a great interest in the construction of high-rise buildings. Fire disaster in high-rise buildings is one of the major threats that introduces a prominent difficulty for safety and evacuation measures, and in most cases economic and human casualties can be observed due to failure and non-availability of any safety measures. As seen in the past background [1-3], most comprehensive difficulties were faced in hospital, residential, and commercial buildings due to the high use of hazardous material that quickly reacts to fire and resulting vast fire-damaged building structure shown in Fig. 9.1(a-c). In such occupancy, a common measure can be observed as an active and passive fire protection system from the NBC [4]. Nevertheless, once this measure fails then structural stability and integrity is the last option for safe evacuation and rescue operation by firefighters shown in Fig. 9.1(d). As seen in the buildings, reinforced concrete (RC) members are important components that design to carry the desired loads and forces safely to maintain structural stability and integrity against collapse. However, such design provisions specifically focus on earthquake and wind forces and cannot observe for fire load. RC member has its limit of fire resistance, and existing code and standard practices are dealing in terms of fire-resistant rating by acknowledging nominal cover provision of concrete [4, 5], which does not reflect any performance-based approach nor identify any member stability and integrity against collapse.

In the structural application, critical load-bearing RC members are predominantly designed for flexural and when such members come in contact with catastrophic fire may lead to being weaker than the designed flexural carrying capacity [6]. In such a situation, the associate stability and integrity of the RC members are most important to prevent any structural failure. It is a critical issue for firefighters during catastrophic fire events to complete rescue operations before the failure of the structure, which information does not know to firefighters and structural engineers in the form of fire resistance design aspect, and hence many casualties

Fig. 9.1 (a) 24-storey residential Grenfell Tower block in Latimer Road, London, (b) 17-storey oldest high-rise iconic landmark building in Tehran, (c) Fire breaks out at CSIR-National Chemical Laboratory in Pune (India), and (d) Fire Incident at AMRI Hospital in Kolkata (India) [1-3].

can be observed [2]. In this concern, few empirical and partial design concepts can be observed in NBC, EC-II [7] and ACI 216 [8]. Notwithstanding, these codes do not reflect any realistic approach, analysis method and design of fire resistance, and restricted their applicability only on concrete nominal cover provisions. Therefore, a lack of fire resistance design method for evaluating the flexural carrying capacity of RC beam and fire-resistance rating with the type of concrete and thermal-induced properties at different fire scenarios can be observed, which deliberating to develop a performance-based evaluation method. Therefore, considering a realistic performance of structural behaviour at different fire scenarios by experimental studies, this paper is proposed a new fire safe design solution for reinforced concrete beams at catastrophic fire conditions for evaluating flexural carrying capacity of RC beam and fire-resistance rating.

2. Experiment

As seen in the research studies [9,10] that the heat transfer model plays an important role in fire resistance design for RC beams. Therefore, to develop a sophisticated heat transfer model a fire-resistance experimental study on RC beams were performed. The international and national practices, i.e., EC-II, IS 3809, ISO 834, ASTM E119, and ASTM E1529 adopted standard fire load for fire resistance testing

of structural members [9,11-14]. Therefore, in this study standard fire load IS 3809/ISO 834 for the experimental study was adopted, which is a severe condition of any catastrophic fire condition that develop accidentally in residential and commercial buildings. The standard time-temperature heating along with estimated time-temperature using Eq.(1) for the fire resistance test on RC beams are shown in Fig. 9.2. However, this does not reflect any survival time of conventionally designed RC beam at fire load [15], therefore,

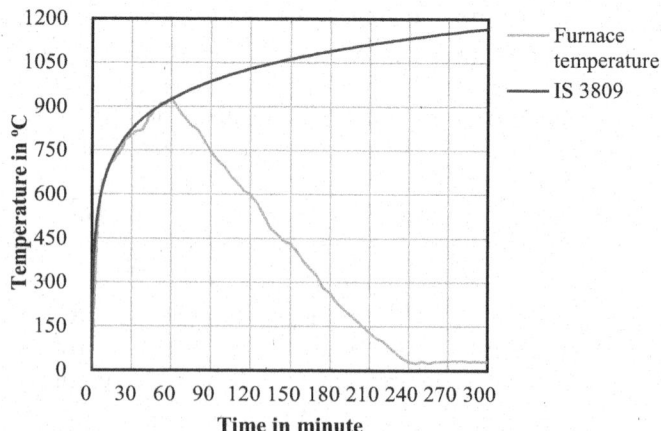

Fig. 9.2 A standard time-temperature heating condition for RC beams of the horizontal furnace during testing.

it is often required to perform a fire resistance test to obtain behaviour and fire-resistance rating at the appropriate time-temperature heating condition, which is a very costly procedure. In real fire scenarios, fire load on RC members is always observed in two-phase, i.e., grown and decay, and to perceive valuable information of RC beam's stability and integrity, these two-phase are essential. In fact, the test results obtained from this experimental study has been used as a benchmark to establish the relevant performance evaluation of the designed RC beams.

$$T = 345 \times \log(8t + 1) + Ti \qquad (1)$$

2.1 Testing Condition

The experimental test was carried out on RC beams to evaluate variable cross-sectional heat transfer fields at standard time-temperature heating conditions. Therefore, well established unique full-scale horizontal furnace facility of the Fire Research Laboratory, CSIR-CBRI Roorkee for fire resistance test was used. In the furnace chamber, the required temperature was maintained with the help of

burners, which creates heat sufficiently using a combination of air and fuel that maintained a standard time-temperature heating curve of IS 3809. The temperature of the furnace chamber at a particular time interval had been measured using K-type thermocouples. Also, 10 ± 5 N/m^2 pressure in the furnace chamber has maintained during the test using the refractory slab and airflow controller damper to avoid a flow of hot gasses from the chamber to the outside. Each burner fire heating was controlled automatization by computerized systems from the control room in such a way that at a time three faces of RC beams were exposed to standard IS 3809 fire loads. All details of the experimental schematic view and unique facility of the horizontal furnace are shown in Fig. 9.3.

2.2 Testing Samples

Four RC beams, two of normal strength concrete (NSC M30) and two of high strength concrete (HSC M60) of size 150 mm in width, 250 mm in depth and 2550 mm in length with 20 mm nominal cover was designed as per IS 456 are shown in Fig. 9.4(a). All RC beams were reinforced with three numbers

Fig. 9.3 A cross-sectional schematic view and the RC beams installation details at the horizontal furnace for fire resistance testing.

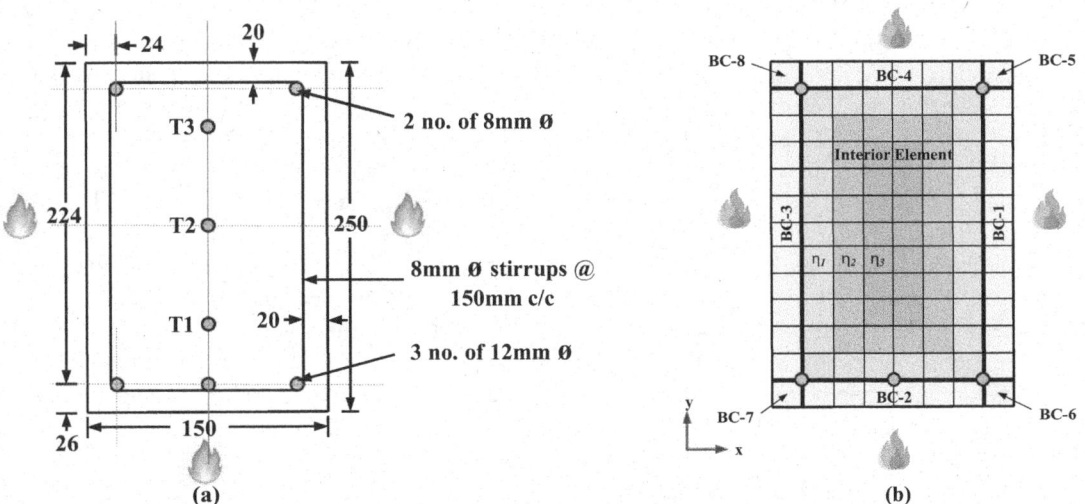

Fig. 9.4 Cross-sectional details of RC beams (all dimensions are in mm): (a) surface exposure conditions and (b) nomenclature of boundary conditions.

of 12 mm diameters as main steel rebars, two numbers of 8 mm diameters as secondary steel rebars and 8 mm diameter stirrups with spacing 150 mm of grade Fe-500 steel that minimum yield stress of steel rebars was observed 598 MPa in tensile testing. The RC beams heat transfer field at specific locations T1, T2 and T3 under the standard time-temperature heating condition were measured and results were considered for validation of the developed heat transfer model [16]. Each RC beam's variable temperature under unsteady-state heat transfer at transient heating boundary conditions was measured using a K-type thermocouple.

2.3 Testing Procedure

For heat transfer evaluation, designed RC beams lengths were limited up to 2550 mm, which gives sufficient valuable information about the heat transfer field within RC beams. The horizontal furnace half portion was used for fire resistance testing with the help of building a vertical shale brick wall that all internal sides were lined with thermal bricks. After then, RC beams were installed on the furnace as simply supported at unloading conditions and the length exposed to the fire was kept at approximately 2500 mm. All RC beams' both two sides and bottom surfaces were exposed to standard fire load IS 3809 (shown in Fig. 9.4) and the top was covered by thermal insulation using the ceramic fibre blanket and refractory material-based slab. All beams were exposed to standard fire load for 60 minutes heating and then cooled down in the same condition as the furnace. The ambient temperature of the furnace before testing was recorded at 30°C. The detail of temperature during test and time-temperature relation up to 60 minutes or more shown in Fig. 9.2.

3. Heat Transfer Model

A general approach to predicting the temperature field within RC members is by the finite-element (FE) or finite difference method (FDM). Various empirical or semi-empirical heat transfer analysis models can also be observed to estimate temperature within RC beams [17-22], but the concept used and limitation of analysis does not satisfy the experimentally measured results. This is because of the variable governing parameters, i.e., geometry, boundary conditions, material properties, exposure conditions and type of fire load. Hence, irrelevant assumptions to satisfy all requirements for heat transfer analysis can be observed, i.e., Kodur and Dwaikat [23] considered conduction with convection heat transfer mechanisms for boundary condition while Lie and Irwin [18] considered conduction and radiation to obtain temperature within RC members. Basically, this is an unsteady-state heat transfer problem that comes under the transient heating boundary condition.

In real practical fire scenarios, RC beam boundaries are exposure to fire through an air gap with heating mechanisms such as convection and radiation. These two mechanisms often need to be incorporated into a numerical procedure of heat transfer analysis. To identify the unsteady-state heat transfer within RC beam at transient heating boundary conditions, both NSC and HSC RC beams were exposed into standard fire load IS 3809 in the enclosed horizontal furnace without any external source of air motion. Inside the furnace, temperature movement was experienced in the form of a density gradient, which directly acting on the exposed surfaces of RC beams. The internal fire exposure phenomenon was subjected to convection and radiation mechanisms, which had been maintained in the furnace chamber throughout the test duration. Now practically, the heat transfers within RC beams is due to the convection by the atmospheric temperature (hot gases) and additional radiation encountered due to the inside larger surface area of the furnace firebrick walls that emits radiation (see in Fig. 9.3). This is a complex phenomenon and hence heat transfer within RC beams were determined experimentally. In these particular situations, the proposed numerical model for heat transfer analysis is confined to a two-dimensional system. It has been assumed that the temperature will be uniform along the length of the RC beam, more specifically this system is easier to simplify when the time-temperature is a function of only two spaces coordinate.

As a numerical model, heat transfer analysis has been proposed to evaluate the variable temperature field within the RC beam using a finite-difference technique. To make the calculation procedure of the proposed numerical model simpler, the derived numerical equations of each boundary condition were implemented in an excel worksheet platform. This simplifies the numerical procedure for predicting the temperature within the RC beam exposed to any standard/non-standard fire load using heat transfer mechanisms. Also, employing numerical equations in excel is simulating (iteration) for any boundary exposure conditions of RC beam and simplifying the heat transfer results by computationally within few seconds at any time-temperature heating intervals. In the numerical simulation, it has assumed that the RC beam body is completely solid, the material is homogenous and there is no damage during exposure to the fire load. Heat flows surround the exposed boundary of the RC beam is caused due to both heating mechanisms, i.e., convection and radiation. Consequently, the energy balance yield Eq.(2) with Fourier law of heat conduction is becoming a two-dimensional analysis equation with no heat generation is shown in Eq.(3).

$$\frac{\partial^2 T}{\partial x^2} + \frac{\partial^2 T}{\partial y^2} = \frac{\rho \cdot C_p}{k} \frac{\partial T_f}{\partial t} \tag{2}$$

$$\underbrace{\left(\frac{\partial^2 T}{\partial x^2} + \frac{\partial^2 T}{\partial y^2}\right)}_{\text{Conduction}} + \underbrace{h\Delta x(T_\infty - T \cdot n)}_{\text{Convection}} + \underbrace{\varepsilon \cdot \sigma \Delta x(T_s^4 - (T_{m \cdot n} + 274)^4)}_{\text{Radiation}}$$

$$= \frac{\rho \cdot C_p}{k}\frac{\partial T_f}{\partial t} \tag{3}$$

3.1 For Internal Nodes FDM

For heat transfer analysis, the RC beam is discretized into the number of elements of an equal size, which physically associates with each other by heat transfer mechanisms. Fig. 9.4(b) shows a two-dimensional heat flow problem for the RC beam, which exhibited a heat transfer scheme for internal elements from the outer boundary elements. Each internal element node for heat transfer depends on the heat flow interface from the outer element node (boundary condition) and this interface has been derived by FDM using a conduction mechanism.

The superscript 'm' denotes the x-coordinate and the superscript 'n' denotes the y-coordinate. The governing equation of unsteady-state heat transfer at transient heating boundary conditions in a two-dimensional, solid homogeneous body, isotropic and constant material properties for physical interface temperature distribution have been elaborated using Eq. (2), which is the Laplace equation and solving by using FDM with pertinent boundary conditions. Numerically, Fig. 9.5(a) shows the RC beam internal nodes temperature distribution scheme as four-node points and that can be expressed as

For x-coordinate

$$\left.\frac{\partial T}{\partial x}\right]_{m+1/2,n} \approx \frac{T_{m+1,n} - T_{m,n}}{\Delta x}$$

$$\left.\frac{\partial T}{\partial x}\right]_{m-1/2,n} \approx \frac{T_{m,n} - T_{m-1,n}}{\Delta x}$$

For y-coordinate

$$\left.\frac{\partial T}{\partial y}\right]_{m,n+1/2} \approx \frac{T_{m,n+1} - T_{m,n}}{\Delta y}$$

$$\left.\frac{\partial T}{\partial y}\right]_{m,n-1/2} \approx \frac{T_{m,n} - T_{m,n-1}}{\Delta y}$$

Second-order partial derivative approximated by

$$\left.\frac{\partial^2 T}{\partial}\right]_{m,n} \approx \frac{\left.\frac{\partial T}{\partial x}\right]_{m+1/2,n} - \left.\frac{\partial T}{\partial x}\right]_{m-1/2,n}}{\Delta x} = \frac{T_{m+1,n} + T_{m-1,n} - 2T_{m,n}}{(\Delta x)^2} \tag{4}$$

$$\left.\frac{\partial^2 T}{\partial y^2}\right]_{m,n} \approx \frac{\left.\frac{\partial T}{\partial y}\right]_{m,n+1/2} - \left.\frac{\partial T}{\partial x}\right]_{m,n-1/2}}{\Delta x} = \frac{T_{m,n+1} + T_{m,n-1} - 2T_{m,n}}{(\Delta y)^2} \tag{5}$$

The time derivative is approximately becoming

$$\frac{\partial T_f}{\partial t} \approx \frac{\Delta T}{\Delta t} - \frac{T_{m,n}^p - T_{m,n}}{\Delta t} \tag{6}$$

In this relation, the superscript designates the time increment. All the relations above give the differential equations equivalent and combined in Eq. (2) and that becomes

$$\frac{T_{m+1,n} + T_{m-1,n} - 2T_{m,n}}{(\Delta x)^2} + \frac{T_{m,n+1} + T_{m,n-1} - 2T_{m,n}}{(\Delta y)^2}$$

$$- \frac{1}{\alpha}\frac{T_{m,n}^p - T_{m,n}}{\Delta T} \tag{7}$$

Thus, if the associated temperatures of four nodes are known at a particular time interval, then the temperature $T_{m,n}^p$ at increment time Δt can be easily calculated by using Eq.(7)

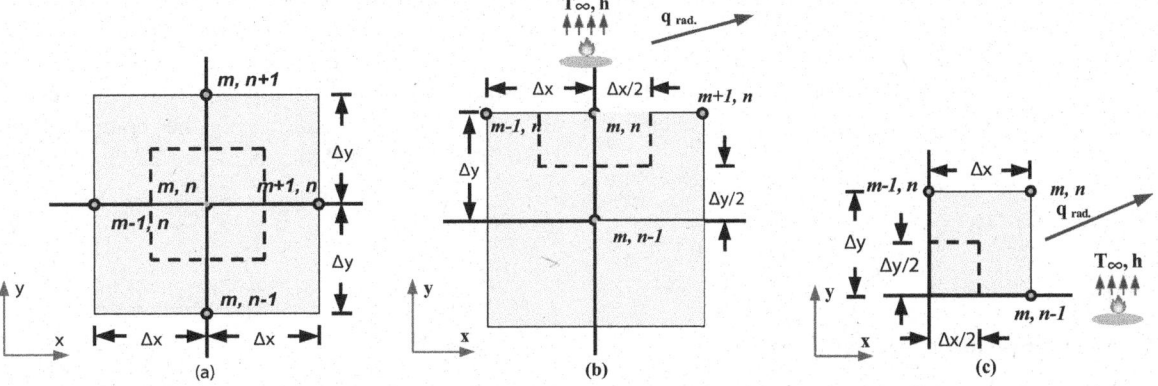

Fig. 9.5 Nomenclature for the numerical solution as a two-dimensional unsteady-state heat: (a) internal elements, (b) outer boundary elements and (c) corner boundary elements.

for each node. It is very simple to calculate net heat flow into any node at optimized thermally induced material properties. This procedure has been repeated to obtain the temperature distribution field within the RC beam at the desired time-step increment with equal space Δx and Δy coordinate. Therefore, for a square grid Eq.(7) becomes

$$T_{m,n}^p = \frac{\alpha \Delta t}{\Delta x^2}[T_{m+1,n} + T_{m-1,n} + T_{m,n+1} + T_{m,n-1} - 4T_{m,n}] + T_{m,n}$$

(8)

Then resulting equation $T_{m,n}^p$ becomes

$$T_{m,n}^p = [\tau T_{m+1,n} + T_{m-1,n} + T_{m,n+1} + T_{m,n-1} - 4T_{m,n}] + T_{m,n} \quad (9)$$

However, in numerical analysis results observed an error between the prediction and experimentally measured results due to the homogeneity of concrete material that is purely considered in the numerical simulation. In real conditions, concrete has been observed highly heterogeneous nature, when it is studied at the microscopic level [24] and this has significantly influenced the temperature distribution field within the RC beam. This knowledge yields reliable information that helps to improve the numerical simulation results. In addition, the distance increments Δx and time increment Δt, the larger values of these two variables gives heat transfer solution more rapidly while the smaller value gives more accurate approximate results but with limitation of Δt. Therefore, a constant value of 0.31 was introduced on a trial-and-error basis to improve the accuracy of temperature prediction into the denominator τ, which makes a two-dimensional numerical simulation easier without compromising with the limitation of Δt. Also, considering the heterogeneous nature of concrete, a θ term has been introduced in Eq.(9), which improves the accuracy of the temperature transmission field within RC beams. This term depends on the type of aggregate used in the RC member due to different specific heat capacity. However, there were no significant differences in temperature field variations using siliceous and calcareous aggregate that has not been observed by experimental studies [18], except for compressive strength. Hence, the θ term is kept constant for both aggregate conditions concerning the optimized specific heat capacity. The modified equation for internal node heat transfer calculation has been obtained from Eq.(9) as below

$$T_{m,n}^p = \tau \cdot \theta \cdot [T_{m-1,n} + T_{m+1,n} + T_{n-1,m} + T_{n+1,m} - 4T_{m,n}] + T_{m,n}$$

(10)

Where, $\tau = \dfrac{k \cdot \Delta t}{0.31 \cdot \rho \cdot C_p \cdot \Delta x^2}$ and $\theta = \dfrac{(\eta_2 \times 0.25 + 0.75)}{10}$

3.2 For External and Corner Nodes FDM

When the RC beam is exposed to convection and radiation heating conditions, the detailed procedures of the evaluation

of temperature by conduction mechanism were followed for external nodes from Eqs. (4-6). Considering external boundary conditions for the numerical solution is shown in Fig. 9.5(b) that the energy balance on a node (m, n) is becoming with complete heat transfer mechanisms given in Eq. (3). If space coordinate Δx and Δy are chosen equally, then the boundary temperature calculation become like the following form

$$h\Delta x(T_\infty - T_{m,n}) + \varepsilon \cdot \sigma \Delta x(T_s^4 - (T_{m,n} + 274)^4)$$
$$+ k\frac{\Delta y}{2}\frac{T_{m-1,n} - T_{m,n}}{\Delta x} + k\frac{\Delta y}{2}\frac{T_{m+1,n} - T_{m,n}}{\Delta x}$$
$$+ k\Delta x\frac{T_{m,n-1} - T_{m,n}}{\Delta y} = \rho\Delta x\frac{\Delta y}{2}C_p\left[\frac{T_{m,n}^p - T_{m,n}}{\Delta t}\right] \quad (11)$$

Simplifying the Eq. (11) by $\Delta x = \Delta y$, thermal diffusivity $\alpha = \dfrac{k}{\rho \cdot C_p}$ and divided $\dfrac{k}{2}$

$$\frac{2h\Delta x}{k}(T_\infty - T_{m,n}) + \frac{2\varepsilon \cdot \sigma \Delta x}{k}(T_s^4 - (T_{m,n} + 274)^4)$$
$$+ T_{m-1,n} - T_{m,n} + T_{m+1,n} + T_{m,n} + 2T_{m,n-1} - 2T_{m,n}$$
$$- \frac{\Delta x^2}{\alpha}\left[\frac{T_{m,n}^p - T_{m,n}}{\Delta t}\right]$$

The corresponding numerical equation $T_{m,n}^p$ becomes

$$T_{m,n}^p = T_{mn}\left[1 - 4\tau - 2\tau\frac{h\Delta x}{k}\right] + \tau\left[T_{mn+1} + T_{m,n-1} + 2T_{m-1,n}\right.$$
$$\left. + \frac{2h\Delta x}{k}T_\infty + 2\cdot\varepsilon\cdot\sigma\frac{\Delta x}{k}(T_s^4 - (T_{m,n} + 274)^4)\right] \quad (12)$$

When a convection and radiation boundary heating condition is present, Eq. (12) must be written for each node along with for the exposed surface shown in Fig. 9.4(b), and for internal nodes, Eq. (10) must be followed. Additionally, Fig. 9.5(c) shown for the corner boundary condition and the heat transfer equation can be solved similarly. If space coordinate is chosen equally $\Delta x = \Delta y$ and element volume affected $\Delta x/2$ and $\Delta y/2$, then the boundary temperature calculation expressed may become like the following form

$$h\left(\frac{\Delta x}{2} + \frac{\Delta y}{2}\right)(T_\infty - T_{m,n}) + \varepsilon \cdot \sigma\left(\frac{\Delta x}{2} + \frac{\Delta y}{2}\right)(T^4 - (T + 274)^4)$$
$$+ k\frac{\Delta y}{2}\frac{T_{m-1,n} - T_{m,n}}{\Delta x} + k\frac{\Delta y}{2}\frac{\Delta y T_{m+1,n} - T_{m,n}}{\Delta x}$$
$$+ k\Delta x\frac{T_{m,n-1} - T_{m,n}}{\Delta y} = \rho\Delta x\frac{\Delta x}{2}\frac{\Delta y}{2}C_p\left[\frac{T_{m,n}^p - T_{m,n}}{\Delta t}\right] \quad (13)$$

Simplifying the Eq.(13) by $\Delta x = \Delta y$, thermal diffusivity $\alpha = \dfrac{k}{\rho \cdot C_p}$ and divided $\dfrac{k}{4}$

$$\frac{4h\Delta x}{k}(T_\infty - T_{m,n}) + \frac{4\varepsilon \cdot \sigma \Delta x}{k}(T_s^4 - (T_{m,n} + 274)^4)$$

$$+ 2(T_{m+1,n} - T_{m,n}) + 2(T_{m,n-1} - T_{m,n})$$

$$= \frac{\Delta x^2}{\alpha}\left[\frac{T_{m,n}^p - T_{m,n}}{\Delta t}\right]$$

The corresponding numerical equation $T_{m,n}^p$ becomes

$$T_{m,n}^p = T_{m,n}\left[1 - 4\tau - 4\tau\frac{h\Delta x}{k}\right] + 2\tau\left[T_{m-1,n} + T_{m,n-1} + \frac{2h\Delta x}{k}T_\infty\right.$$

$$\left. + 2 \cdot \varepsilon \cdot \sigma\frac{\Delta x}{k}(T_s^4 - (T_{m,n} + 274)^4)\right] \qquad (14)$$

The detailed finalized finite difference equations for each boundary condition can also be observed from the literature Gedam [6].

3.3 Stability Criterion

There may exist an error in subsequent calculations for the boundary condition using FDM. Therefore, to eliminate this error in the numerical simulation a stability criterion must be satisfied. It has been observed that the selection of element size, i.e., $\Delta x = \Delta y$ is directly limiting the maximum time step Δt for heat transfer analysis. Hence, this criterion of stability is most restrictive along the boundary between fire and the RC beam exposure surface. Hence, the following condition of Eq.(15) was used for heat transfer analysis to satisfy the stability of the developed numerical heat transfer model. A constant value of 0.31 has been adopted to improve the time domain limitation for heat transfer analysis without compromising the idealized thermally induced concrete

material properties and incremental distance $\Delta x = \Delta y$. This directly dealing with the stability criteria of the proposed heat transfer model that limiting the time domain up to 350 minutes and this appears sufficient for fire resistance design and flexural carrying capacity evaluation of RC beams.

$$\Delta t \leq \frac{0.31\rho c_p \Delta x^2}{k\left(4 + 2\dfrac{h\Delta x}{k}\right)} \qquad (15)$$

4. Fire Resistance Design Method

The existing codes and their standard practices are estimating the ultimate moment carrying capacity of RC beam under normal environmental conditions. Therefore, a simple design solution on the performance-based approach is being proposed, which helps to estimate the flexural carrying capacity of RC beams by taking care of all design features including thermally induced material properties through the heat transfer model. The fire resistance design method is subjecting to the stress-strain compatibility of materials, which is affecting by unsteady-state heat transfer at the transient heating boundary conditions. Also, it is worth notable that the specific permissible stresses development in the RC beam is subjecting to the ultimate strength of the materials at an elevated temperature, and depends on the ratio of yield stress to the corresponding permissible stress.

4.1 Stress-strain Compatibility

The RC beam is a composite member made from different materials. However, when the RC beam is subjected to loading conditions, strain compatibility of both concrete and reinforced steel rebars should be equivalent and that depends on the bonding between bordering concrete for reinforced steel rebar. Consequently, the stress in the reinforced steel rebar becomes linearly that related to the stress developed in

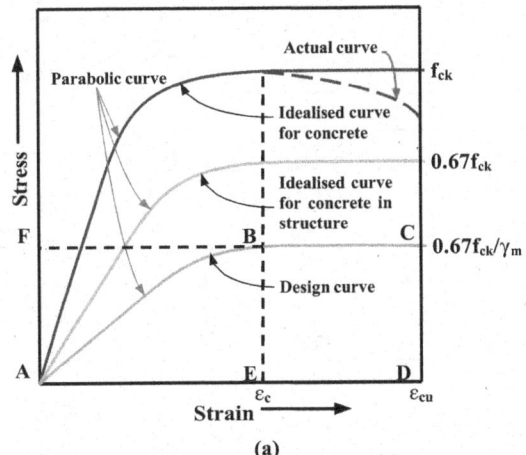
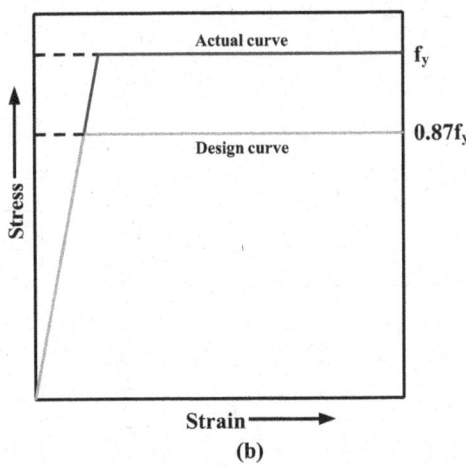

Fig. 9.6 Temperature-dependent stress-strain relationship variation with safety factor: (a) for concrete and (b) for steel.

the bonded concrete. From the fire resistance evaluation point of view, the appropriate temperature dependent stress-strain relationships of concrete and steel have been considered from the research studies [25, 26] and incorporated in the fire resistance design method. The basic concept of the stress-strain relationship for concrete and steel with safety factors at various temperature conditions has been used are shown in Fig. 9.6.

4.2 Stress Block Parameters with Temperature

In India, a common practice for flexural member design follows is cube samples compressive strength. Hence, IS 456 for RC members to obtained structural member strength is recommended equal to 0.67 times of the cube characteristic strength with the respected grade of concrete and for design is considered with the safety factor. As seen in the corresponding stress-strain relationship diagram of concrete and steel from Fig.6, the ultimate flexural carrying capacity of the RC beam depends on a limiting strain in concrete. Therefore, using properties of concrete from Table 9.1, the limiting strain has been extended the same for elevated temperature conditions and it has been used as a critical criterion for concrete crushing in flexural compression for RC beam.

For estimating the flexural carrying capacity of RC beam at elevated temperature conditions, the variation course shown in Fig. 9.7 has been similarly considered concerning the thermal-induced properties of concrete through the heat transfer analysis. It has assumed that the variation of stress

diagram above the neutral axis of RC beam in Fig. 9.7(c) is a parabolic shape from point A to B, which is corresponding to the curve AB of Fig. 9.6(a), and from point B to C is linear as constant stress of $0.67fck$, which is corresponding to line BC of Fig. 9.6(a). A total compressive force Cu at located below the top fibre resulting from stress $ABCDEA$ area and has been expressed in terms of the stress block parameters, which varies concerning temperature.

$k_1 =$ is the stress shape factor defined as the ratio between the stress block area of $ABCD$ and $AFCD$

$$k_1 = \frac{\text{Area}(ABCD)}{\text{Area}(AFCD)} \tag{16}$$

Using strain compatibility from the stress-strain relationship of Fig. 9.6(a), the crushing failure strain $AD = \varepsilon_{cu}$ and ultimate failure strain at loading $AE = \varepsilon_c$ at specific temperature conditions for concrete is considered.

$$\text{Ratio } \frac{AE}{AD} = x_1 = \frac{\varepsilon_c}{\varepsilon_{cu}} \quad \text{and} \quad \frac{ED}{AD} = x_2 = \frac{\varepsilon_{cu} - \varepsilon_c}{\varepsilon_{cu}}$$

$$\text{Area}(ABCD) = \text{Area}(ABE) + \text{Area}(BCDE)$$

$$= \frac{2}{3} AE \cdot EB + ED \cdot DC$$

$$= \frac{2}{3}\left(\frac{\varepsilon_c}{\varepsilon_{cu}}\right) \cdot AD \cdot EB + \left(\frac{\varepsilon_{cu} - \varepsilon_c}{\varepsilon_{cu}}\right) \cdot AD \cdot DC$$

Table 9.1 Summary of the stress-strain relationships for NSC and HSC at elevated temperatures

Concrete temperature °C	Siliceous aggregate	Calcareous aggregate	NSC		HSC/HPC	
	As specified in EN1992-1-2 [7]		Proposed from [25]			
	Normalised strength ratio		Ultimate loading failure strain	Crushing failure strain	Ultimate loading failure strain	Crushing failure strain
20	1.00	1.00	0.0025	0.0200	0.0018	0.0035
100	1.00	1.00	0.0040	0.0225	0.0020	0.0094
200	0.95	0.97	0.0055	0.0250	0.0035	0.0173
300	0.85	0.91	0.0070	0.0275	0.0064	0.0258
400	0.75	0.85	0.0100	0.0300	0.0107	0.0349
500	0.60	0.74	0.0150	0.0325	0.0164	0.0446
600	0.45	0.60	0.0250	0.0350	0.0235	0.0549
700	0.30	0.43	0.0250	0.0375	0.0320	0.0658
800	0.15	0.27	0.0250	0.0400	0.0419	0.0773
900	0.08	0.15	0.0250	0.0425	0.0532	0.0894
1000	0.04	0.06	0.0250	0.0450	0.0659	0.1021
1100	0.01	0.02	0.0250	0.0475	0.0800	0.1154
1200	0.00	0.00	—	—	—	—

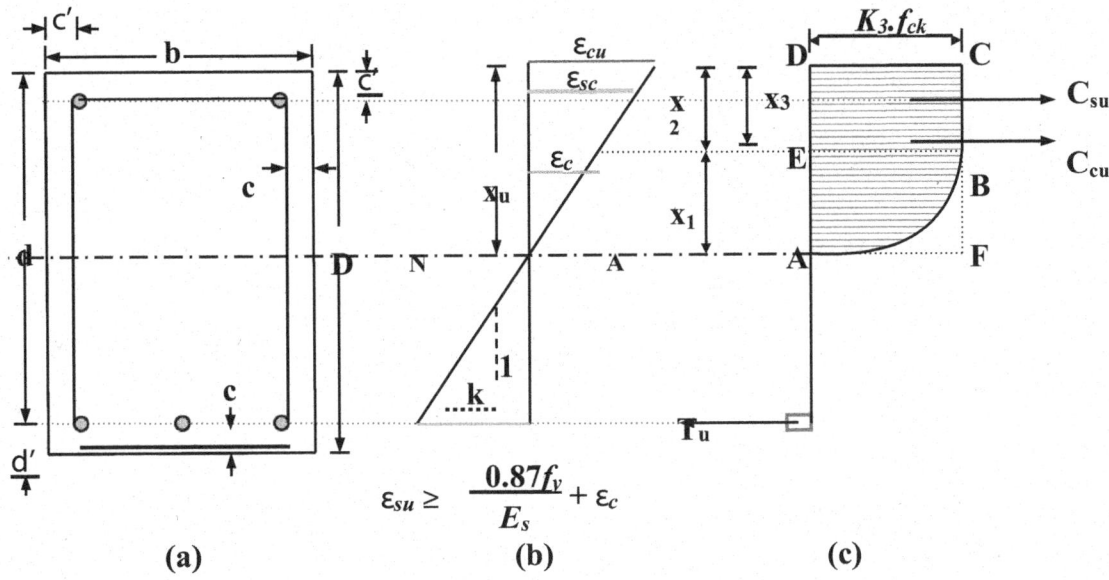

Fig. 9.7 RC beam strain and stress variation across the section: (a) cross-section details, (b) strain diagram and (c) stress block diagram.

Also, $EB = DC$

$$\frac{2}{3}\left(\frac{\varepsilon_c}{\varepsilon_{cu}}\right) \cdot AD \cdot DC + \left(\frac{\varepsilon_{cu} - \varepsilon_c}{\varepsilon_{cu}}\right) \cdot AD \cdot DC$$

$$= \left[\frac{2}{3}\left(\frac{\varepsilon_c}{\varepsilon_{cu}}\right) + \left(\frac{\varepsilon_{cu} - \varepsilon_c}{\varepsilon_{cu}}\right)\right] \cdot AD \cdot DC$$

Also, $AD \cdot DC = AFCD$

$$\text{Area}(ABCD) = \left[\frac{2}{3}\left(\frac{\varepsilon_c}{\varepsilon_{cu}}\right) + \left(\frac{\varepsilon_{cu} - \varepsilon_c}{\varepsilon_{cu}}\right)\right] \cdot AFCD \quad (17)$$

Eq. (17) put in Eq. (16); the stress shape factor become with a temperature condition

$$k_1 = \left[\frac{2}{3}\left(\frac{\varepsilon_c}{\varepsilon_{cu}}\right) + \left(\frac{\varepsilon_{cu} - \varepsilon_c}{\varepsilon_{cu}}\right)\right] \quad (18)$$

As seen in Fig. 9.7(c), the resulting compressive force C_{cu} is located below the top fibre at a distance x_3, where x_u is the neutral axis depth.

$$x_3 = k_2 x_u = k_2 \cdot AD$$

Now,

$$k_2 \cdot AD = \frac{\text{Area}(ABE) \cdot x_1 + \text{Area}(BCDE) \cdot x_2}{\text{Area } ABCD}$$

$$= \frac{\frac{2}{3}\left(\frac{\varepsilon_c}{\varepsilon_{cu}}\right)\left[ED + \frac{3}{8}AE\right] + \left(\frac{\varepsilon_{cu} - \varepsilon_c}{\varepsilon_{cu}}\right)\left(\frac{1}{2}DE\right)}{\frac{2}{3}\left(\frac{\varepsilon_c}{\varepsilon_{cu}}\right) + \left(\frac{\varepsilon_{cu} - \varepsilon_c}{\varepsilon_{cu}}\right)}$$

$$= \frac{\frac{2}{3}\left(\frac{\varepsilon_c}{\varepsilon_{cu}}\right)\left[\left(\frac{\varepsilon_{cu} - \varepsilon_c}{\varepsilon_{cu}}\right) + \frac{3}{8}\left(\frac{\varepsilon_c}{\varepsilon_{cu}}\right)\right]}{\frac{2}{3}\left(\frac{\varepsilon_c}{\varepsilon_{cu}}\right) + \left(\frac{\varepsilon_{cu} - \varepsilon_c}{\varepsilon_{cu}}\right)} \quad (19)$$

Therefore, total compressive force C_{cu} location below the top fibre can be expressed in terms of stress block parameter k_2

$$k_2 = \frac{\frac{2}{3}x_1\left[x_2 + \frac{3}{8}x_1\right] + \frac{1}{2}x_2^2}{\frac{2}{3}x_1 + x_2} \quad (20)$$

and from distance

$$x_3 = \left(\frac{\frac{2}{3}x_1\left[x_2 + \frac{3}{8}x_1\right] + \frac{1}{2}x_2^2}{\frac{2}{3}x_1 + x_2}\right)x_u \quad (21)$$

The maximum flexure compressive stress for the RC beam for ordinate DC at the location x_1 in the relation to the characteristic strength f_{ck}. Therefore, stress block will be $k_3 f_{ck}$ and recommended stress block parameter k_3 as per IS 456 is 0.67 see in Fig. 9.7(c).

4.3 Flexural Carrying Capacity Evaluation of RC Beams

In general, the RC beam is comprising reinforced steel rebars embedded in concrete to avoid any internal tension force at plain concrete. Hence, compressive force C_{cu} and tension force T_u must be evaluated by stress block parameters incorporating the design safety factors for both concrete and steel. The stress-strain relationship with safety factor for concrete and steel have been considered from Table 9.1 to estimate the flexure carrying capacity of RC beam at fire load conditions.

The maximum top fibre compressive stress in the RC beam with the safety factor

$$DC = \frac{k_3 f_{ck}}{\gamma_{mc}}$$

$$= \frac{k_3 f_{ck}}{1.5}$$

The maximum stress in steel with the safety factor

$$Tu = \frac{f_y}{\gamma_{ms}}$$

$$= \frac{f_y}{1.15} \approx 0.87 f_y$$

Therefore, the compressive force C_{cu} in the concrete using stress block parameters is becomes

$$C_{cu} = b \times Area\ (ABCD)$$

$$= b(k_1 \times x_u \times DC)$$

$$= b\left(k_1 x_u \frac{k_3 f_{ck}}{1.5} \right)$$

$$= \left[\frac{2}{3}\left(\frac{\varepsilon_c}{\varepsilon_{cu}} \right) + \left(\frac{\varepsilon_{cu} - \varepsilon_c}{\varepsilon_{cu}} \right) \right] \frac{x_u k_e f_{ck} b}{1.5}$$

$$= 0.446 x_u f_{ck} \left[\frac{2}{3}\left(\frac{\varepsilon_c}{\varepsilon_{cu}} \right) + \left(\frac{\varepsilon_{cu} - \varepsilon_c}{\varepsilon_{cu}} \right) \right] b \quad (22)$$

The ultimate flexural carrying capacity of the RC beam section with respect to temperature ($M_{u,temp}$) in the relation to stressed block is given by

$$M_{u,temp} = C_{cu} \times \text{leverarm}$$

$$M_{u,temp} = C_{cu}\ (d - k_2 x_u)$$

Using Eq. (22), $M_{u,temp}$ becomes

$$M_{u,temp} = 0.446 x_u f_{ck} \left[\frac{2}{3}\left(\frac{\varepsilon_c}{\varepsilon_{cu}} \right) + \left(\frac{\varepsilon_{cu} - \varepsilon_c}{\varepsilon_{cu}} \right) \right] b(d - x)_3$$

Using Eq.(21), $M_{u,temp}$ becomes

$$M_{u,temp} = 0.446 x_u f_{ck} b \left[\frac{2}{3}\left(\frac{\varepsilon_c}{\varepsilon_{cu}} \right) + \left(\frac{\varepsilon_{cu} - \varepsilon_c}{\varepsilon_{cu}} \right) \right]$$

$$\times \left[d - \left(\frac{\frac{2}{3} x_1 \left[x_2 + \frac{3}{8} x_1 \right] + \frac{1}{2} x_2^2}{\frac{2}{3} x_1 + x_2} \right) x_u \right] \quad (23)$$

The proposed Eq. (23) is applicable only for singly RC beams without any consideration of compression reinforcement, even though the nominal reinforcement is provided for stirrups arrangement. Hence, Eq. (23) has limited flexural carrying capacity evaluation corresponding to the arrangement of tension reinforced steel rebars at fire load conditions. Notwithstanding, many practices have been observed that the maximum depth of the RC beam may be limited and restricted by architecture. In such conditions, only alternative provision of reinforcement in compression zone is provided and such section is considered as a doubly reinforced section. Fig. 9.7(a) showing the provision of compression reinforcement at effective depth c' below from top compression fibre. This is a combination of nominal cover and half of the steel rebar diameter at the compression zone of the RC beam. Because steel rebars have embedded in the compression zone of RC beam, hence, there have been considering the loss of concrete area, which were occupied by compression reinforced steel rebars. The final total compressive force C_u has been estimated as follows

$$C_u = C_{cu} + C_{su}$$

Using Eq. (22), C_u becomes

$$= 0.446 x_u f_{ck} \left[\frac{2}{3}\left(\frac{\varepsilon_c}{\varepsilon_{cu}} \right) + \left(\frac{\varepsilon_{cu} - \varepsilon_c}{\varepsilon_{cu}} \right) \right] b + (f_{sc} A_{sc} - 0.446 f_{ck} A_{sc}$$

Therefore, the flexural carrying capacity reaching its limiting value is given by

$$M_{u,temp} = C_u \times \text{leverarm}$$

$$M_{u,limit} = 0.446 x_u f_{ck} \left[\frac{2}{3}\left(\frac{\varepsilon_c}{\varepsilon_{cu}} \right) + \left(\frac{\varepsilon_{cu} - \varepsilon_c}{\varepsilon_{cu}} \right) \right] b(d - x)$$

$$+ (f_{sc} A_{sc} - 0.446 f_{ck} A_{sc} (d - c')$$

Using Eq. (21), $M_{u,temp}$ becomes with respect to temperature

$$M_{u,temp} = 0.446 x_u f_{ck} b \left[\frac{2}{3}\left(\frac{\varepsilon_c}{\varepsilon_{cu}} \right) + \left(\frac{\varepsilon_{cu} - \varepsilon_c}{\varepsilon_{cu}} \right) \right]$$

$$\times \left[d - \left(\frac{\frac{2}{3} x_1 \left[x_2 + \frac{3}{8} x_1 \right] + \frac{1}{2} x_2^2}{\frac{2}{3} x_1 + x_2} \right) x_u \right] \quad (24)$$

$$+ A_{sc}(f_{sc} - 0.446 f_{ck})(d - c')$$

Table 9.2 Optimized thermal material properties for heat transfer analysis

Parameters	Unit	NSC M30	HSC M60
Cross-sectional size for boundary conditions	mm	150 mm × 250 mm	150 mm × 250 mm
Fire heating condition with time (transient)	°C	ISO 834	ISO 834
Heat transfer coefficient in convection; h_c	W/m²K	8	8
Emissivity; ε	—	0.85	0.85
Density of concrete; $\rho(20°C)$	kg/m³	2415	2505
Moisture content; μ	%	0% more than 200°C	0% more than 200°C
Thermal conductivity; k	W/mK	0.6	0.8
Specific heat; C_p	J/kgK	1100	1100
Stefan-Boltzmann Constant; σ	W/m²K⁴	5.67×10^{-8}	5.67×10^{-8}

Note: for calcareous aggregate, C_p = 1500 J/kgK should be considered

5. Results and Discussions

For heat transfer analysis, the required and optimized thermal material properties of NSC and HSC RC beams with siliceous aggregate were considered and incorporated in numerical simulation from Table 9.2. The comparative results of NSC and HSC RC beams with the predicted results by the proposed heat transfer model are shown in Fig. 9.8 and Fig. 9.9. It has been observed that the heat transfer model is predicting temperatures for RC beams at various locations (i.e., T1, T2 and T3) using optimised thermal material properties, and is in good agreement with the experimentally measured database. However, at an initial time experimentally measured results are showing a slightly higher temperature than the predicted results and this discrepancy has been observed relatively in the range 20°C to 200°C due to moisture influence, in this range does not reveal any significant impact on the compressive strength reduction for RC beam under heating [27]. Therefore, it has been considered that the proposed heat transfer model prediction accuracy need not necessarily at this range be highly accurate but in later cases is most important for flexural capacity evaluation and fire-resistance rating.

It is not ensuring, any particular condition a designed RC beam will be sustained fire resistance rating under fire load by using standard provisions of codes [8,11,12]. Therefore, a developed fire resistance design method has been used for evaluating flexural behaviour and fire-resistance rating of RC beam. The fire-resistance rating depends on failure criteria and hence two predominant failure criteria being considered concerning the flexural behaviour of RC beam. The first is the thermal failure criterion at critical temperature 593°C for compression reinforced steel rebars [23] and the second criterion for RC beam is unable to carry 30 per cent of designed flexural capacity as per IS 456 [5]. The fire resistance design method is subjected to the compression zone fibre stress variation and depends on concrete and reinforced steel rebar stresses concerning the heat transfer. The fire resistance design of RC beam is presenting redistribution of flexural carrying capacity in fire load and hence failure criteria are quite acceptable for RC beam exposed to any fire scenario.

The proposed fire resistance design method has been validated and verified by comparing its predictions with experimentally measured database and analytical results available in the research studies. Moetaz et al. [28] performed experimental studies on the flexural behaviour of RC beams at the external fire load. Total four RC beams of 120 mm width, 200 mm depth and 1800 mm length were tested at the standard fire conditions. All beams were reinforced with two number of 10 mm diameter rebars at the top as secondary and bottom as main rebars, which had minimum yield stress 260 MPa and 358.5 MPa. These RC beams were cast with concrete mix had cube crushing strength at 28 days was 25 MPa. Detailed type of aggregate used in concrete mix design was not discussed by Moetaz et al. [28], and hence, the fire resistance has been evaluated by considering for both calcareous and siliceous type aggregate to predict flexural behaviour. It has been observed that the ultimate flexural carrying capacity for each RC beam concerning the control reference beam 16.78 kN-m that for 30-minute was 9.81 kN-m, for 60-minute was 13.54 kN-m and for 120-minute was 10.52 kN-m. These results revealed that a considerable reduction in the flexural carrying capacity of RC beams at external fire load about 11.8%, 19.3% and 38.7% concerning the controlled reference RC beam.

As seen in the experimental results of the flexural behaviour, the provision adopted for RC beams, i.e., small cross-section and nominal top mild steel rebars indicating that the fire resistance analysis for all RC beams would be acceptable to consider as a singly reinforced section. Therefore, a detailed provision adopted for RC beams has been considered for

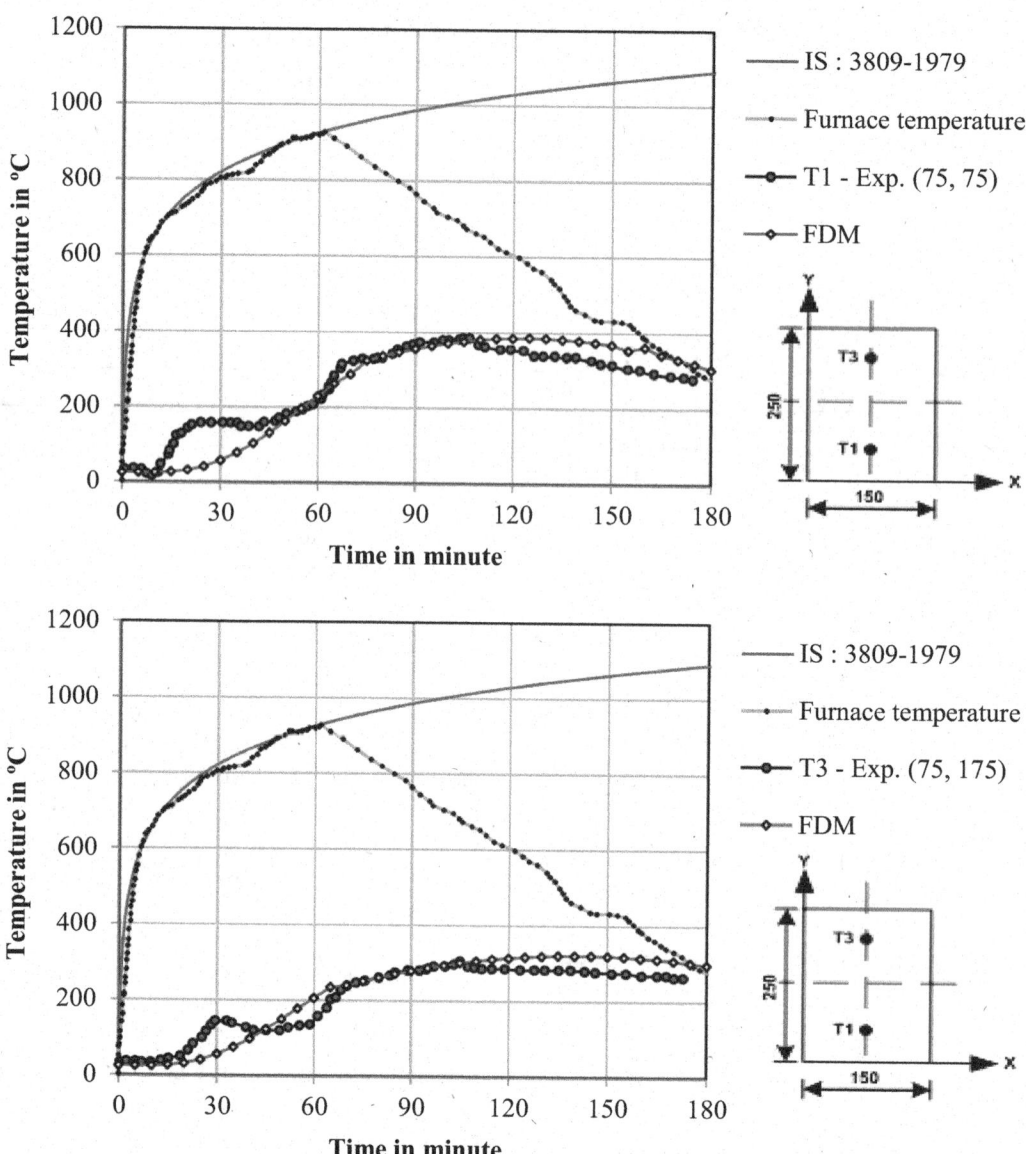

Fig. 9.8 FDM heat transfer model prediction with the test result of the RC beams for NSC at locations T1 (75, 75) and T3 (75, 175).

flexural behaviour evaluation at the external fire load. Fig. 9.10 shows comparative results of predicted and experimentally measured databases that exhibiting good matching of the fire resistance design method results using both types of aggregate.

The proposed fire resistance design method has also been verified by comparing its predictions with the analytical results available from the research studies. Kodur and Dwaikat [23,29] performed parametric studies to find the flexural response of RC beams exposed to ASTM E119 fire load. The RC beams of cross-sectional size 300 mm width and 500 mm depth were analysed at different parameters using the developed microscopic finite element model. The different parameters effect, i.e., fire scenario, load ratio,

concrete cover, aggregate type, failure criteria and span length were considered that had exhibited consequence on the flexural response. In the present study, the fire resistance design method was performed by considering the RC beam as a doubly reinforced section using all parameters at standard fire load (ASTM E119), and predicting flexural behaviour comparatively appraising with analytically available results. Fig. 9.11 shows that the analytically available and fire resistance design method predicted results for both aggregates that follow similar trends and reveals reasonably accurate predictions.

As seen in the validation of the developed models, to investigate the provisions proposed by NBC, IS 456 and IS 1642 [30] for fire-resistance rating, the designed RC beams

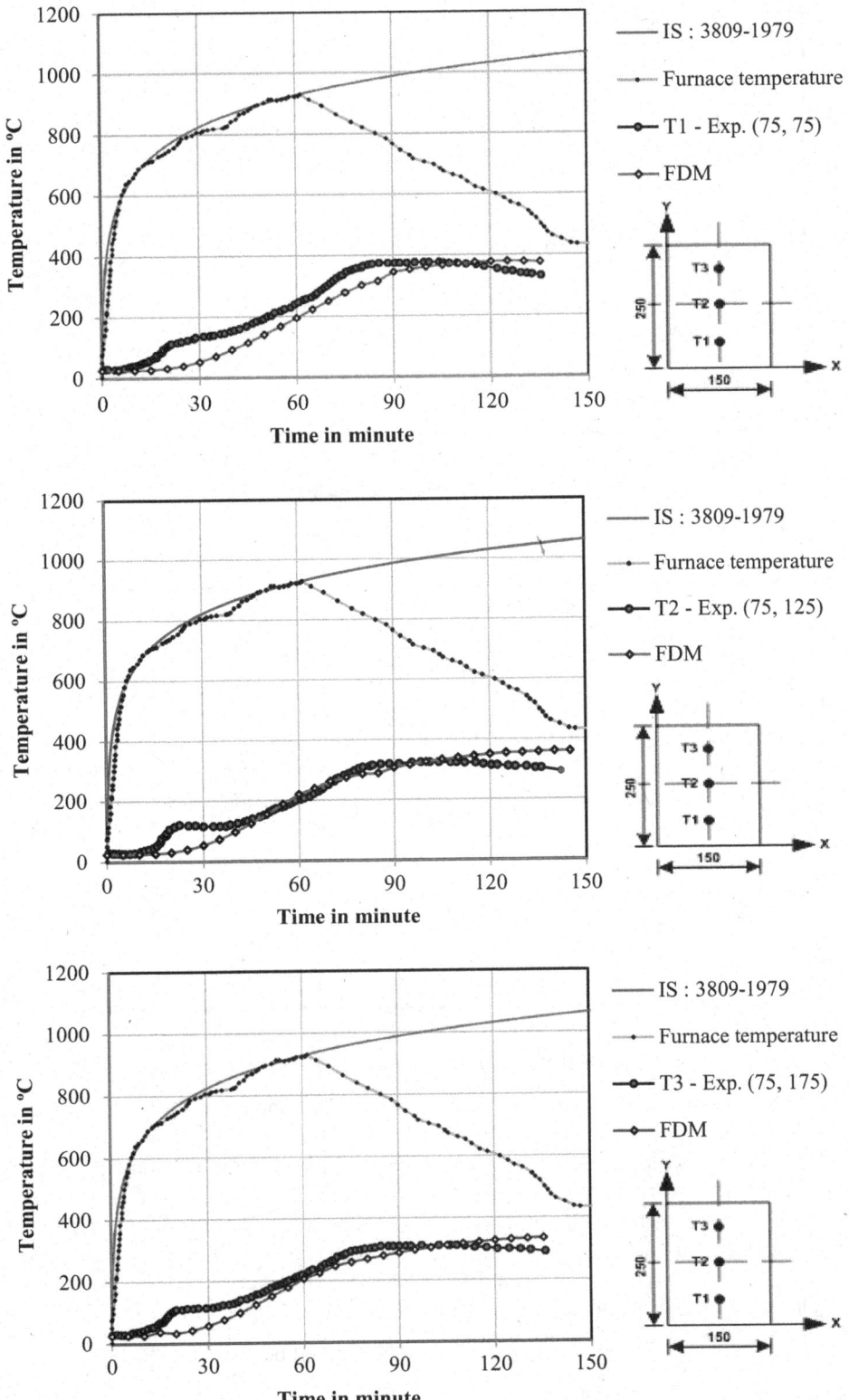

Fig. 9.9 FDM heat transfer model prediction with the test result of the RC beams for HSC at locations T1 (75, 75), T2 (75, 125), and T3 (75, 175).

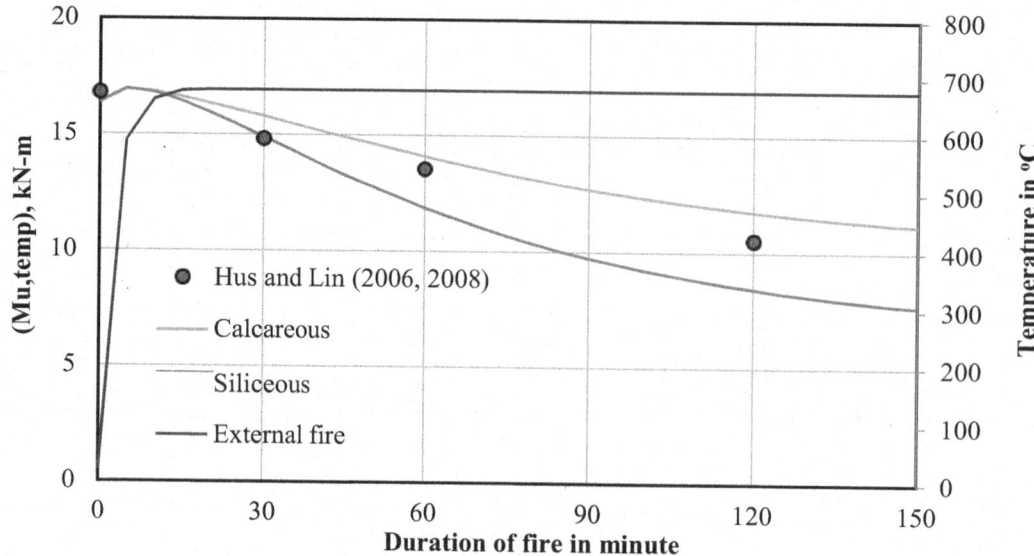

Fig. 9.10 Flexural behaviour of RC beams exposed to the external fire load.

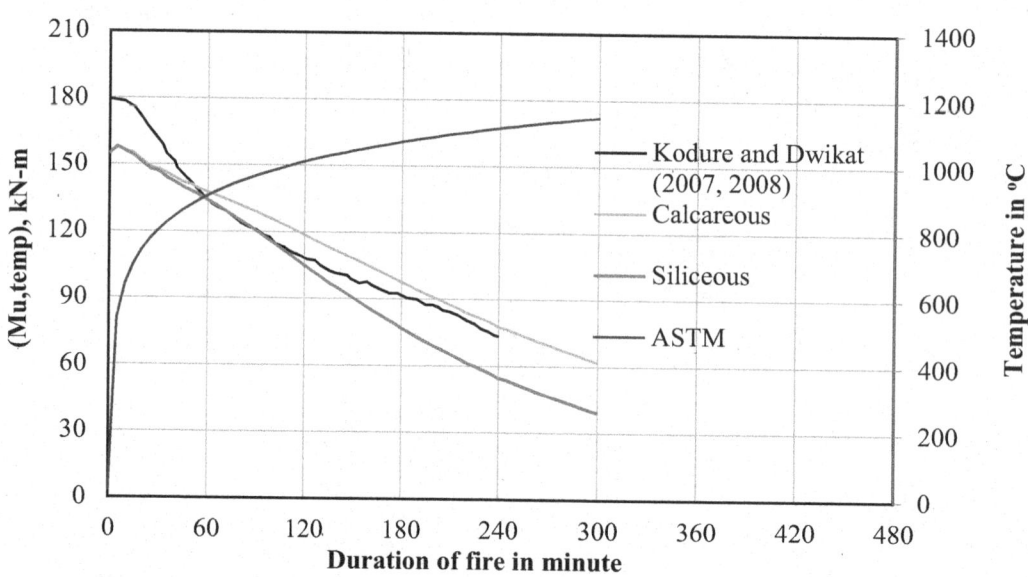

Fig. 9.11 Flexural behaviour of RC beams exposed to standard ASTM E119 fire load.

have been considered for fire resistance evaluation under different fire scenarios. Each RC beam is accommodated by size 200 mm width, 400 mm depth and 6100 mm length with nominal cover provisions 20 mm that designed to carry flexural capacity of 137.96 kN-m at ambient conditions. RC beam is considered to place as a simply supported condition and exposure to any fire scenarios as two sides and one bottom surfaces, and made by using concrete strength of 60 MPa (cylinder) with calcareous and siliceous type aggregates. RC beam is comprised of a 500 MPa yield stress of steel rebars as reinforced with three number of 12 mm diameter rebars in the top compression zone and four number of 16 mm diameter

rebars in the bottom tension zone. The shear reinforcements considered 8 mm diameter about 110 mm centre to centre distance along the length of the RC beam. Each RC beam has been evaluated for fire-resistance rating as a doubly reinforced section based on two failure criteria, i.e., thermal and flexural.

The flexural behaviour of RC beams namely for RC-B1, RC-B2, RC-B3, RC-B4 and RC-B5 have been investigated at different fire scenarios. The first three beams (RC-B1, RC-B2 and RC-B3) have been evaluated under three fire loads namely IS 3809/ISO 834, hydrocarbon fire and external standard fire without any decay phase, which are frequently used for fire resistance evaluation on prescriptive based. The remaining two beams (RC-B4 and RC-B5) are subjected to the compartment properties and have been evaluated under design fire scenarios namely Fire-I and Fire-II [23,29], which are representing realistic scenarios with a decay phase, i.e., growth during the fire and decay in the cooling. The Fire-I represents a severe design fire load that temperature has to exceed 1200°C and Fire-II represents a moderate design fire load that temperature has to exceed 700°C.

The variations of the flexural carrying capacity of each RC beam concerning the fire loads and time are shown in Fig. 9.12. It is observed in the first three fire load conditions that each RC beam flexural carrying capacity is decreasing with exposure time. In the first few minutes for two design fire loads, flexural carrying capacity is decreasing and then increases again. These results were observed due to attribution of the heating and cooling phase of the fire load for RC beams. In the heat transfer simulation, it has been observed that the temperature field variation within the RC beam at high-intensity fire load very rapidly and tries to incorporated from outer exposed elements to inner elements. However, due to the low thermal conductivity of concrete, in the first few minutes, only the outer and associated inner elements of the discretized RC beam have significantly affected. This phenomenon completely slows down in the cooling phase and the RC beam starts its recovery as strength and stiffness. Also, it has been observed that the flexural carrying capacity of the RC beam is not fully recoverable and this is associated due to the stress-strain relationship of concrete concerning the temperature field variation within the RC beam. As seen in Table 1 that the normalised strength ratio has reduced with

temperature and hence the temperature of each discretized element governed the final strength for the RC beam concerning the heat transfer field in the fire resistance design method. Once the strength of concrete for each element has reduced then the combined effect is comprising final thermally induced concrete strength for RC beam, which is not as original strength as observed after fire damage. Hence, the full recovery of flexural carrying capacity, behaviour or other response for RC beam has not been possible.

Results from the evaluation also determined that the type of fire load has significantly affected the fire resistance rating of RC beams. The detailed summary of two failure criteria for each RC beam is shown in Table 9.3 that exhibiting the most conservative fire-resistance rating at different fire scenarios. It has been observed that the RC beam at Fire-I load condition exhibits a fire-resistance rating of 29 minutes at 30 per cent flexural carrying capacity reduction from designed flexural capacity. Also, another severe condition has been observed at hydrocarbon fire load condition that exhibits a fire-resistance rating of about 39 minutes. These results clearly showed that the high-intensity fire load heating in a short duration has significantly influenced the fire-resistance rating of RC beams. However, low-intensity fire load heating in long-duration exposure conditions exhibits a high fire-resistance rating compared to the IS 3809/ISO 834 fire load. For RC-B3 fire-resistance rating has observed about 151 minutes at the external fire load and no failure has been observed for RC-B5 at the designed Fire-II load.

It is also observed from the evaluation results that the fire-resistance rating of RC beams predicted by flexural carrying

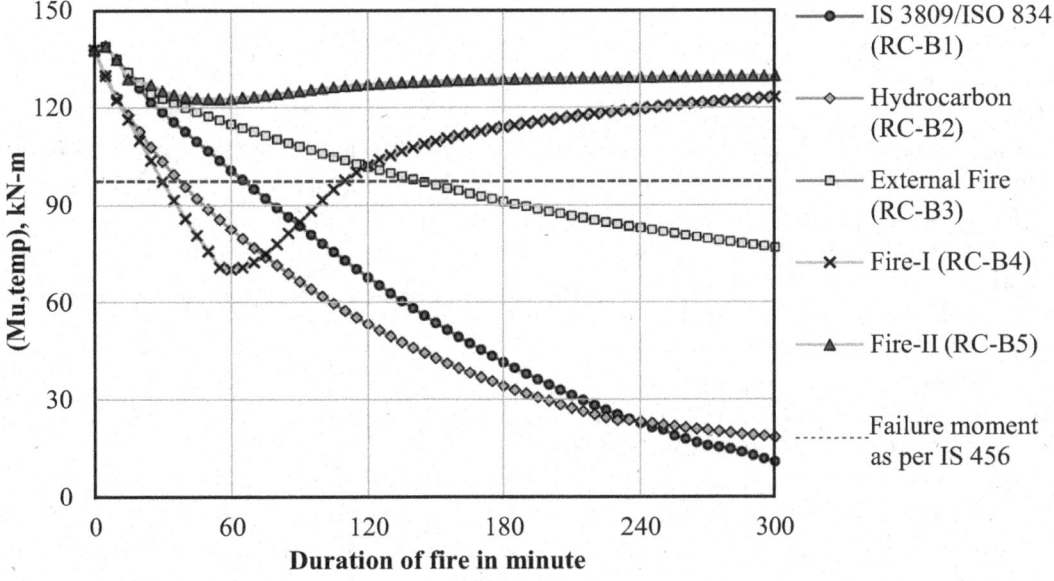

Fig. 9.12 Effects of fire scenarios on the flexural carrying capacity for RC beams using siliceous aggregate.

Table 9.3 The fire-resistance rating for RC beams at different fire scenario

Designation for RC beams	Fire load scenario	Fire-resistance rating based on failure criteria in minute			Fire-resistance rating as per codes in a minute		
		Rebar temperature 593°C	30% flexural carrying capacity reduction		NBC	IS 456	IS 1642
			Calcareous	Siliceous			
RC-B1	ISO 834/ IS 3809	97	84	67	90	90	—
RC-B2	Hydrocarbon	50	52	39	90	90	—
RC-B3	External	NF	235	151	90	90	—
RC-B4	Fire-I	35	39	29	90	90	—
RC-B5	Fire-II	NF	NF	NF	90	90	—

Note: NF is no failure

capacity has provided more conservative results compared to the failure criteria of steel rebar temperature. The fire-resistance rating proposed by NBC, IS 456 and IS 1642 is not found reasonably good at different fire scenarios and does not exhibit any association with the type of fire load and its effect especially for HSC. From the comparative results of the flexural behaviour of RC beams, it can be observed that the designed fire scenario that subjected to the compartment hazarded material properties and its activity that may reflect high-intensity fire load than any standard fire load condition. Therefore, it is most important for the fire resistance evaluation of any RC members to be performed as per compartment material properties, conditions and fire load calculation.

6. Conclusions

1. The proposed fire resistance design method is evaluating the fire resistance of RC beams with governing parameters and thus fire resistance evaluation can be usually integrated into the structural design method.

2. It has revealed a better prediction of fire-resistance rating than those acknowledged by existing code provisions for the specific RC beams and is helpful to evaluate flexural carrying capacity before the damage, during the fire and after damaged of RC beams.

3. The failure criteria for RC beams have significantly influenced the fire resistance rating. The conventional reinforced steel rebar temperature failure criterion at fire scenarios has not reflected any reasonable results of fire-resistance rating. However, the criterion of flexural carrying capacity reduces 30 per cent of designed RC beam has introduced more reasonable and reliable information of fire-resistance rating.

7. Acknowledgement

The author wishes to express their gratitude and sincere appreciation to the authority of the Council of Scientific and Industrial Research (CSIR), India in the FBR of Civil Infrastructure and Engineering at Project No. MLP072002 for financing this research work.

Notation

α = the thermal diffusivity

ε = the emissivity

ε_c = the ultimate load carrying strain in compression concrete

ε_{cu} = the failure strain in compression concrete

ε_{sc} = the strain in compression reinforcement

$\Delta x = \Delta y$ = the size of elements in mm

μ = the moisture content in %

θ = the heat transfer factor for each element

τ = the stability equation

σ = the Stefan-Boltzmann constant in W/m^2K^4

Ast = the total reinforcement in tension side in mm^2

Asc = the total reinforcement in compression side in mm^2

b = the width of reinforced concrete section in mm

C_{cu} = the compressive force in the compression concrete in N

C_{su} = the compressive force in the compression steel in N

C_p = the specific heat in J/kgK

d = the effective depth in mm

d' = the effective cover in mm

f_{sc} = the stress in compression reinforcement in MPa

f_{ck} = the characteristic strength of concrete in MPa

f_y = the characteristic strength of steel in MPa

h_c = the convective heat transfer coefficient in W/m^{2}K

k = the thermal conductivity in W/mK

$M_{u,temp}$ = the moment carrying capacity concerning temperature in kN-m

T_i = the ambient temperature of the horizontal furnace in °C

T_{mn}^p = the temperature in element in °C

t = the time in minutes

x_u = the neutral axis depth in mm

REFERENCES

1. MacLeod, G. (2018). The Grenfell Tower Atrocity: Exposing Urban Worlds of Inequality, Injustice, and an Impaired Democracy, *City*, 22(4), 460–489.

2. Behnam, B. (2019). Fire Structural Response of the Plasco Building: A Preliminary Investigation Report., *International Journal of Civil Engineering*, 17, 563–580.

3. Pal, I., and Ghosh, T. (2014). Fire Incident at AMRI Hospital, Kolkata (India): A Real Time Assessment for Urban Fire., *Journal of Business Management & Social Sciences Research*, 3(1), 9–13.

4. NBC (2016). *National Building Code of India - Volume 1.* New Delhi: Bureau of Indian Standards

5. IS 456 (2000). *Plain and Reinforced Concrete – Code of Practice.* New Delhi: Bureau of India Standards

6. Gedam, B. A. (2021). Fire Resistance Design Method for Reinforced Concrete Beams to Evaluate Fire-Resistance Rating. *Structures*, 33, 855–877.

7. EN 1992-1-2 (2004). *Design of concrete structures – Part 1-2: General Rules – Structural Fire Design.* Brussels: Commission of European Communities

8. ACI 216 (2007). *Code Requirements for Determining Fire Resistance of Concrete and Masonry Construction Assemblies.* Farmington Hills, USA: American Concrete Institute

9. Gao, W.Y., Dai, J.G., Teng, J.G. and Chen, G.M. (2013). Finite Element Modeling of Reinforced Concrete Beams Exposed to Fire. *Engineering Structures*, 52, 488–501.

10. Kumar, P. and Kodur, V.K.R. (2017). Modeling the Behavior of Load Bearing Concrete Walls Under Fire Exposure. *Construction and Building Materials*, 154, 993–1003.

11. IS 3809 (1979). *Fire Resistance Test for Structures.* New Delhi: Bureau of Indian Standards

12. ISO 834 (1999). *Fire Resistance Test Element – Elements of Building Construction – Part 1: General Requirements.* International Standard

13. ASTM E119 (2016). *Standard Test Method for Fire Tests of Building Construction and Materials.* ASTM International

14. ASTM E1529 (1993). *Standard Test Method for Determining Effects of Large Hydrocarbon Pool Fires on Structural Members and Assemblies.* West Conshohocken, Pennsylvania: ASTM International

15. Dwaikat, M. B., and Kodur, V. K. R. (2009). Response of Restrained Concrete Beams Under Design Fire Exposure. *Journal of Structural Engineering*, ASCE, 135(11), 1408-1417.

16. Ahmad M. S. (2013). *Behaviour of Reinforced Concrete Beams Exposed to Fire.* M-Tech Thesis, AcSIR, CSIR-CBRI Roorkee

17. Wickstrom, U. (1986). A Very Simple Method for Estimating Temperatures in Fire Exposed Structures. New Technology to Reduce Fire Losses and Costs. Ed., Grayson. S.J. and Smith, D.A., *Elsevier Applied Science*, London, UK, 186–194.

18. Lie, T.T. and Irwin, R.J. (1993). Method to Calculate the Fire Resistance of Reinforced Concrete Columns with Rectangular Cross Section. *ACI Structural Journal*, 90(1), 52–60.

19. Desai, S.B. (1998). Design of Reinforced Concrete Beams Under Fire Exposure Conditions, *Magazine of Concrete Research*, 50(1), 75–83.

20. Abbasi, A. and Hogg, P.J. (2005). A Model for Predicting the Properties of the Constituents of a Glass Fibre Rebar Reinforced Concrete Beam at Elevated Temperatures Simulating a Fire Test, *Composites Part B: Engineering*, 36(5), 384–389.

21. Kodur, V.K.R., Baolin, Y. and Dwaikat, M.M.S. (2013). A Simplified Approach for Predicting Temperature in Reinforced Concrete Members Exposed to Standard Fire. *Fire Safety Journal*, 56, 39–51.

22. Gao, W.Y., Dai, J.G. and Teng, J.G. (2014). Simple Method for Predicting Temperatures in Reinforced Concrete Beams Exposed to a Standard Fire. *Advances in Structural Engineering*, 17(4), 573–589.

23. Kodur, V. K. R., and Dwaikat, M. (2008). A Numerical Model for Predicting the Fire Resistance of Reinforced Concrete Beams. *Cement and Concrete Composites*, 30, 431–443.

24. Gedam, B. A., Bhandari, N. M., and Upadhyay, A. (2015). Influence of Supplementary Cementitious Materials on Shrinkage, Creep, and Durability of High-Performance Concrete. *Journal of Materials in Civil Engineering*, ASCE, 04015173, 1–11.

25. Diederichs, U., Jumppanen, U., and Penttala, V. (1988). *Material Properties of High Strength Concrete at Elevated Temperatures.* Lisbon, Portugal: IABSE congress report

26. Lie, T. T. (1992). *Fire Protection.* New York: ASCE manual and reports on engineering practice, No.78.

27. Hertz, K. D. (2005). Concrete Strength for Fire Safety Design. *Magazine of Concrete Research*, 57(8), 445–453.

28. Moetaz, M.E., Ahmed, M.R., Ahmed, A.E., and Shadia, E. (1996). Effect of Fire on Flexural Behaviour of RC Beams. *Construction and Building Materials*, 10(2), 147–150.

29. Kodur, V. K. R., and Dwaikat, M. (2007). Performance-based Fire Safety Design of Reinforced Concrete Beams. *Journal of Fire Protection Engineering*, 17, 293–320.

30. IS 1642 (1989). *Code of practice for fire safety of buildings (general) – Details of construction.* New Delhi: Bureau of India Standards

CHAPTER 10

Seismic Evaluation of Frictional Damper Developed Using Waste Rubber Tires

Bharati

Research Scholar, NITTTR, Chandigarh
bharatithakur93@gmail.com
9780417303

Amit Goyal

Assistant Professor, NITTTR, Chandigarh
amitgoyalamit23@gmail.com
9417569559

R. Siva Chidambram

Scientiest, CBRI, Roorkee
krsinelastic@gmail.com
9634430889

Abstract

The past reconnaissance surveys on various earthquake failures show enormous loss of lives and property. A seismic deficient structure lacks the ability to dissipate input energy during the ground motion and fails to offer ductile sway mechanism. Restoration of severely damaged structures may lead to exorbitant cost and some of the damages such as soft storey failure; joint shear failures etc. are not restorable due to the high intensity of damage. In the proposed study an idea of passive damping mechanism has been put forth by developing a new type of affordable friction damping device using Styrene Butadiene Rubber in the form of waste radial rubber tire. Proposed friction damper has been developed to improve the local performance of beam-column joint and tested under cyclic loading. Important parameters such as hysteresis behaviour, energy dissipation, friction coefficient of damper has been evaluated. The response of the beam-column joint specimen installed with damper shows very convincing results in terms of shear resistance and energy dissipation. The rubber-steel friction interface shows increased lateral load resistance and damping behaviour as compared to conventional specimen. Developed friction damper is very robust in nature and can be installed in new as well as old framed structures to improve the seismic resistance.

Keywords: Passive damping, Frictional damper, Beam-Column Joint, Damping, Energy dissipation

1. Introduction

Earthquake is an inevitable natural hazard which is difficult to anticipate. Humans have witnessed massive destruction in terms of life and property due to this natural catastrophe. During a ground motion the structures especially, buildings become the most vulnerable places putting threat to the lives of occupants. However, with the advent of earthquake resistant design codes, engineers have ensured safety to the occupants. Buildings are allowed to undergo inelastic deformation in order to dissipate input seismic energy during an earthquake. The inelastic deformation subsequently leads to the localised damages in the structural components. This give rise to a contradiction that in order to protect buildings from the damages causing due to earthquake the building is allowed to undergo damages [1]. Hence, these structural and non-structural damages lead to exorbitant cost of repair. Moreover, there has been a demand to restore the functionality of a building urgently after an earthquake event [2]. Therefore, the notion of supplemental damping was put forth in order to mitigate the damages so that the cost of repair could be minimised. With the installation of damping devices, the seismic energy gets dissipated resulting lesser damage in the structure during an earthquake. The idea of damping devices can be understood through an equation given by Unang [3] which represents how input seismic energy gets dissipated in various forms during an earthquake.

$$E_i = E_k + E_d + E_s + E_h$$

Here E_i stands for input seismic energy, E_d stands for damping in the structure, E_s represents strain energy and E_h is the hysteresis energy. The above equation can be rearranged as below

$$E_k + E_s = E_i - (E_h + E_d)$$

$(E_k + E_s)$ represents the vibrational energy. It is apparent from the above equation that the vibrational energy can be reduced if damping in the structure increases [4]. However, the inherent damping in the structure is between range of 2-5%. Therefore, if the supplemental damping can be provided the vibrational energy can be substantially abated. Passive damping system is very popular source of energy dissipation and reliable too owing to which numerous applications have been witnessed. Popular passive damping devices are viscoelastic, viscous, friction and yielding dampers [5,6]. In case of high-rise buildings these devices are helpful in reducing wind vibrations as well [7]. Among these devices, friction damper is a good choice for dissipation of energy due to its high energy dissipation per cycle. Unlike yielding damper, friction damper need not to be replaced post-

earthquake. Moreover, friction damper is not influenced by the ambient temperature and there is no issue of fluid leakage as in case of viscous dampers. Therefore, friction dampers exhibit numerous merits over other kinds of dampers. In friction dampers, the friction interfaces slide at a predefined slip load leading to sliding of interfaces thus subsequently dissipating seismic energy in the form of heat [8].

In this paper a new kind of affordable friction damper has been developed. The new friction damper consists of waste rubber tires on steel friction interface. The primary objective of the experiment is to evaluate efficacy of proposed damper in energy dissipation under cyclic loading. Additionally, the influence of damper on seismic performance of beam-column joint has been evaluated too.

2. Damper Specification

Proposed friction damper has been fabricated using styrene butadiene rubber from waste tires of vehicles. Due to easy availability and low-cost of the material, this material has been chosen for fabrication of friction interface. One of the objectives of this experiment is to determine the energy dissipation efficacy of the proposed friction damper. It has been found that metal on metal friction surfaces encounter the problem of corrosion which pose threat on the efficacy and durability of the friction dampers [9]. The proposed damper tends to eliminate this problem too. Rubber tires have been cut into pieces in the form of a friction pad as shown in Fig. 10.1(c). Using a hand grinding tool, the surface of

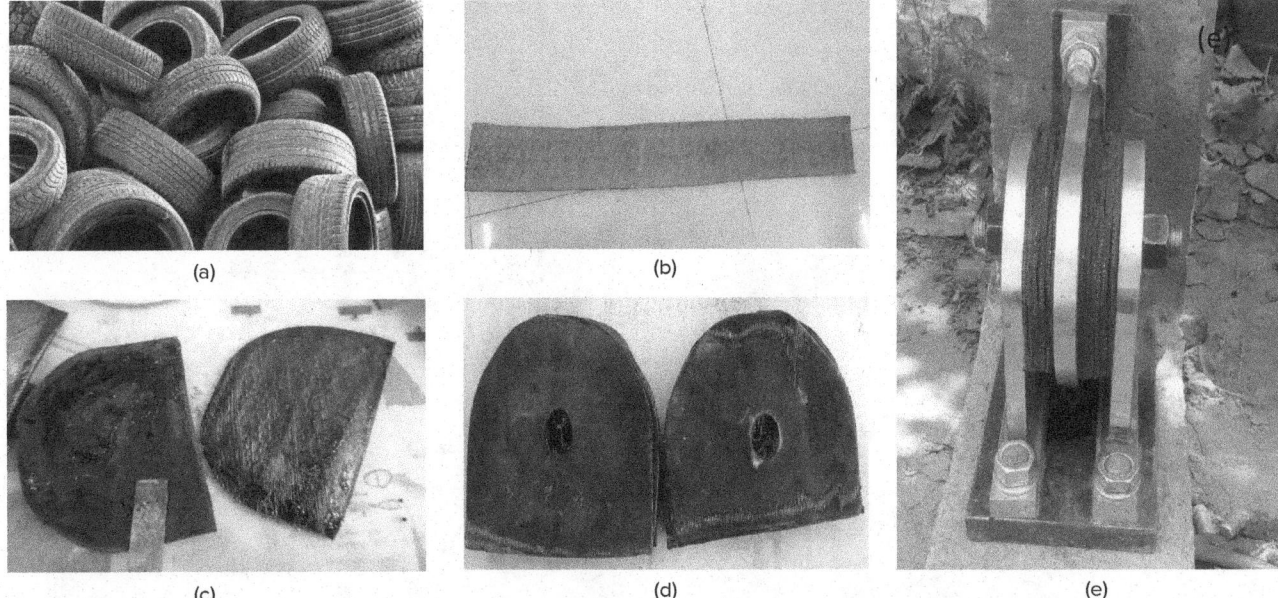

Fig. 10.1 (a) Vehicle rubber tires (b) strip of a tire (c) rubber pads joined with SR glue (d) hole drilled in rubber pads (e) Damper installed at Beam-column joint

these rubber pads has been rubbed well. These pads have been glued using a synthetic resin (SR) glue to form a 25 mm thick friction pad. Two such pads have been made. A 25 mm hole has been drilled in the centre of the pads shown in Fig. 10.1(d). The damper comprises of three mild steel plates, one central and two outer plates. These plates also have a 25 mm diameter hole in the centre. The central damper plate consists of an oversized machine slotted hole to provide free movement. A bolt of 24mm diameter has been inserted through holes of plates and then tightened with nuts. Two damper plates are supposed to be fixed to the column and one central plate must be fixed to the beam. Assembled damper fixed in a beam-column joint is shown in Fig. 10.1(e).

3. Damper Testing

Experimental setup as shown in Fig. 10.2(a) has been prepared in order to determine the energy dissipation efficacy of proposed damper. Coefficient of friction of the proposed damper has also been determined using same setup. Loading frame having capacity of 70T has been used. The center plate has been fixed to the hydraulic jack having 50T capacity. Only the center plate is supposed to move during cyclic loading. In the central hole of the damper, Allen type bolt of 24 mm diameter has been inserted. Tightening torque has been provided at the head of the center bolt using a torque wrench as shown in Fig. 10.2(b). In this experiment, determination of friction coefficient of rubber tire on steel and energy dissipation capacity of the proposed damper at varying torque of 50 N-m, 100 N-m, 200 N-m, 300 N-m has been done. Varying torque value is going to vary the preloading normal force acting on the damper. In order to determine energy dissipation efficiency at varying torque, damper is subjected to cyclic displacement starting from 5 mm up to 20 mm.

3.1 Energy dissipation efficiency of damper

Energy dissipation is represented as the area under hysteresis curve during a cyclic loading. Hysteresis curves for energy dissipation at varying torque is shown in Fig. 10.3(a), (b), (c), (d). From these hysteresis curves it is apparent that energy dissipation is increasing with every successive cycle. For 50 N-m torque the energy dissipation is minimum however highest value is obtained at 300N-m torque. It implies that energy dissipation is higher if the normal force acting on the damper is high. The cumulative energy dissipation curve at varying torque also illustrated same trend as depicted in Fig 10.3(e). It can be observed from this curve that energy dissipation value is increasing with increasing value of torque. At 50 N-m, 100 N-m, 200 N-m, 300 N-m cumulative energy dispelled during the cyclic loading is 1080 kN-mm, 1185 kN-mm, 1392 kN-mm, 1611 kN-mm respectively.

3.2 Coefficient of friction

Coefficient of friction has been determined at varying torque value of 50 N-m, 100 N-m, 200 N-m, 300 N-m. The proposed damper has been subjected to ten cycles of ± 15 mm at four different torque values as shown in Fig. 10.4(a), (b), (c), (d). To evaluate coefficient of friction and effect of normal force on the variation of coefficient of friction with successive cycles, the underlying formulas have been used [10]

$$\mu = \frac{F}{mnN_b} \tag{1}$$

In this equation μ is coefficient of friction, F is the sliding force, m is number of friction interfaces, n is number of bolts used, N_b is preloading bolt force or normal force. To determine N_b another formula has been used as written in equation (2)

$$N_b = \frac{T}{0.2\,d} \tag{2}$$

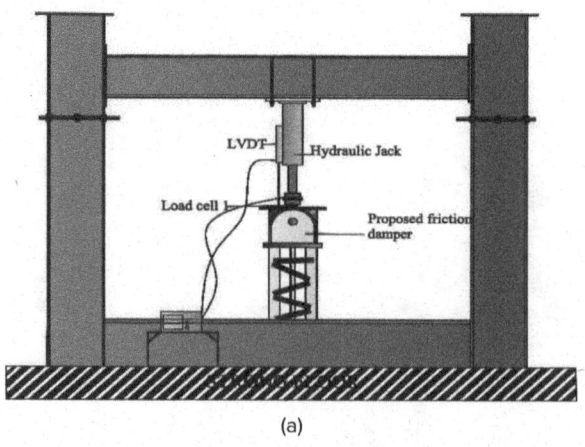

(a)

(b)

Fig. 10.2 (a) Setup of Damper test, (b) Torque Wrench

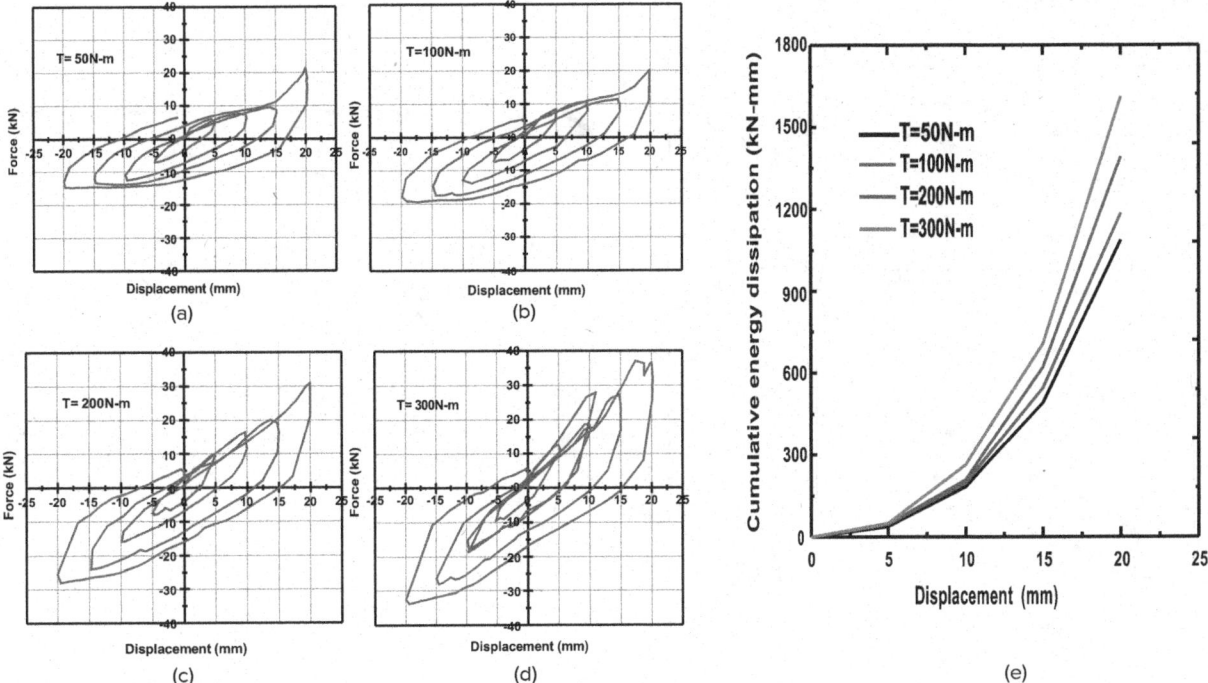

Fig. 10.3   Force vs displacement curve of proposed friction damper at (a) 50 N-m (b) 100N-m (c) 200N-m (d) 300 N-m (e) Cumulative energy dissipation curve

In above equation T stands for tightening torque applied, d stands for nominal diameter of bolt. Coefficient of friction values obtained are .12, .168, .079, .036 at torque value of 50 Nm, 100 Nm, 200 Nm, 300Nm respectively. For 50 N-m, 100 N-m, 200 N-m, 300 N-m torque, value of slip load is 2.55 kN, 7 kN, 5.9 kN, 4.5 kN respectively. Slip load is maximum in case of 100 N-m torque whereas least at 50 N-m torque. At higher torque value of 300 N-m the slip load has been observed to be 4.5 kN. Slip load for 100 N-m torque, 200 N-m torque is higher than 300 N-m torque. Nonetheless slip load for 300 N-m is greater than slip load for 50 N-m. It shows that, slip load first increases with increase in torque and attains maximum value at 100 N-m torque, then decreases with further increase in torque. At very high torque i.e., 200 N-m and 300 N-m torque slip load tend to decrease. However, in friction damper obtaining optimum value of torque is very important to achieve desired results. At very low slip load energy dissipation will be insignificant. On the contrary, at very high slip load the friction surfaces would not slide at all. Hence optimum slip load will result into maximum energy dissipation.

The effect of friction with consecutive number of loading cycles has been evaluated in terms of a non-dimensional force $F_0 = \dfrac{F}{mnN_b}$. This non-dimensional force is equal to the coefficient of friction for first value of slip load. In the following cycles this value is seen varying owing to the loosening of bolt. Also, it is anticipated that the preloading force tend to decrease in consecutive cycles reducing the value of non-dimensional force. Graph for varying non-dimensional force with repeated loading cycles has been given in Fig. 10.4(e). In case of 100 N-m torque, the non-dimensional force initially decreases then maintains almost stable behavior. In case of 50 N-m torque the non-dimensional force is seen increasing initially but reduces to the same initial value at the end of cycle. However, opposite behavior is observed at 200 N-m and 300 N-m torques. The friction coefficient is observed to be small at higher torque than at lower torque value. However, it is apparent that the friction behavior at higher torque values is stable throughout the cycle without much variation.

In friction interfaces due to continuous wear and tear during sliding of the surfaces the friction material is supposed to get damaged. Besides, at higher values of tightening torque, the material can be seriously damaged and the efficiency of friction interface can also reduce. In this rubber tire pads, response of cyclic loading was observed to be stable at higher torque values. It can be attributed to good surface hardness of the tire material. Additionally, there are thin steel wire meshes present inside the rubber tire. Besides, rubber tire exhibits higher non-dimensional force at lower torque values. It is the advantage of the friction material interface that at the low normal force (torque) a higher friction value will be observed and at higher tightening force a stable behavior would be observed without much reduction in energy efficiency.

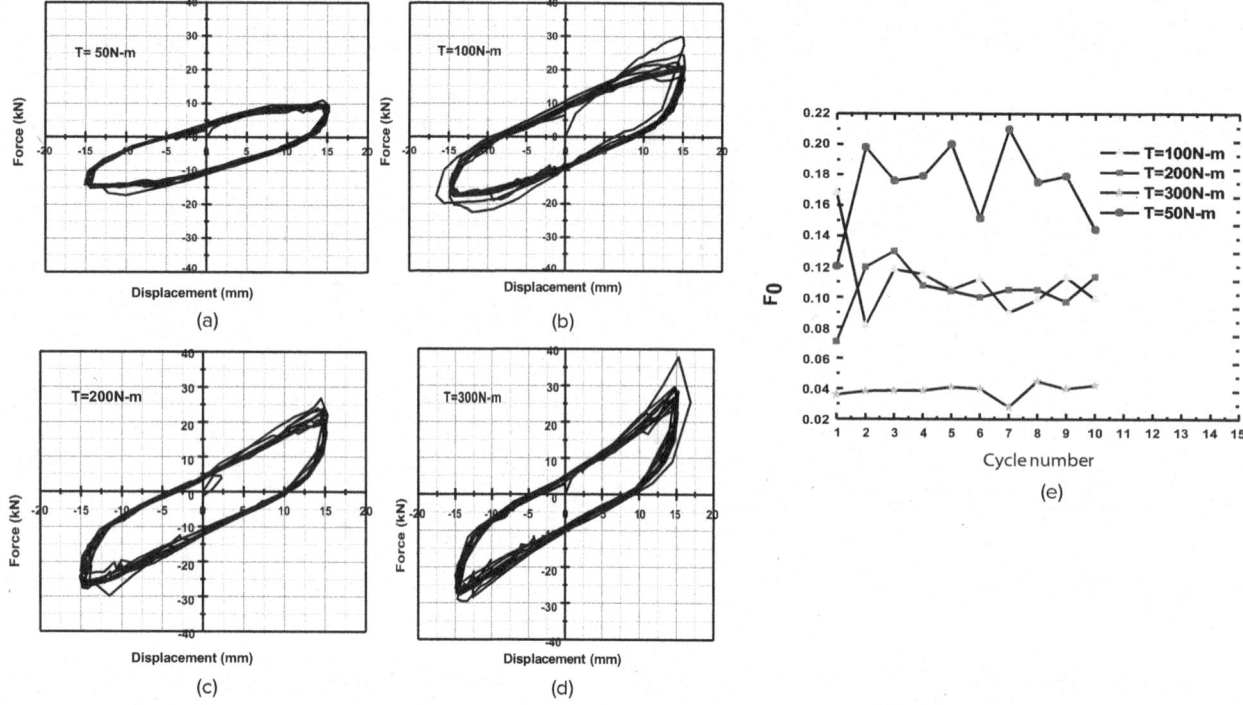

Fig. 10.4 Rubber on steel friction test at (a) 50N-m Torque (b) 100N-m Torque (c) 200N-m Torque (d) 300N-m Torque (e) Non-Dimensional force (F_0) versus Cycle number for Rubber tire on steel friction interface

4. Beam-Column Assemblage Testing

To test the efficacy of the proposed friction damper in ameliorating the cyclic performance of beam-column joint, the damper has been installed at the interface of RC beam-column joint as shown in Fig. 10.5(a). The Beam-column joint is subjected to cyclic loading at the beam end. Static load of 20 kN on the column is placed to imitate gravity load. The cyclic behavior of beam-column joint installed with damper has been compared to the control specimen. The graphs in Fig 10.5(b), (c) illustrates comparison between the cyclic behavior of two specimens. The result of hysteresis has been shown in the form of moment vs rotation curves. The graphs depict that hysteresis curve under specimen with damper is fat as compared to control specimen indicating large amount of energy dissipation in case of damper specimen. Additionally, it is worth to note that the reverse cyclic behavior of specimen with damper is significantly better than the control specimen. The negative moment taken up in damper specimen is five times higher than control specimen. This manifestation is owing to the resistance provided by the rubber pads in reverse cycle. Despite the fact that proposed friction damper was installed at only one side, it was able to dissipate noticeable amount of energy. The curve for cumulative energy dissipation is shown in the Fig. 10.5(d). Cumulative energy dissipation curves exhibit the same trend. Total cumulative energy dissipation in case of specimen with damper (DS) is

9500kN-mm whereas in case of control specimen (CS) it is 5700 kN-mm. The cumulative energy dissipation curve is an indicator that higher energy has been dissipated by the damper when installed at a beam-column joint. This behavior could be improved further if damper had been installed at both sides of the beam-column joint.

5. Conclusion

The proposed damper has been developed as a substitute for steel-on-steel friction interface in which issues of corrosion are countered after a period of time. Hence, the proposed damper is a low-cost as well as efficient alternative to dissipate energy in beam-column joint.

Energy dissipation efficiency of the damper is seen increasing with increasing value of torque. This implies that high energy dissipation can be achieved if high normal force is applied.

From the non-dimensional force vs consecutive number of cycles, it can be concluded that the proposed damper shows a stable behavior in case of higher torque whereas in case of smaller torque high initial coefficient of friction is obtained.

Proposed friction damper illustrates significantly better behavior when installed at beam column-joint relative to the control specimen. Cumulative energy dissipated in case of damper specimen was observed to be 1.67 times more as

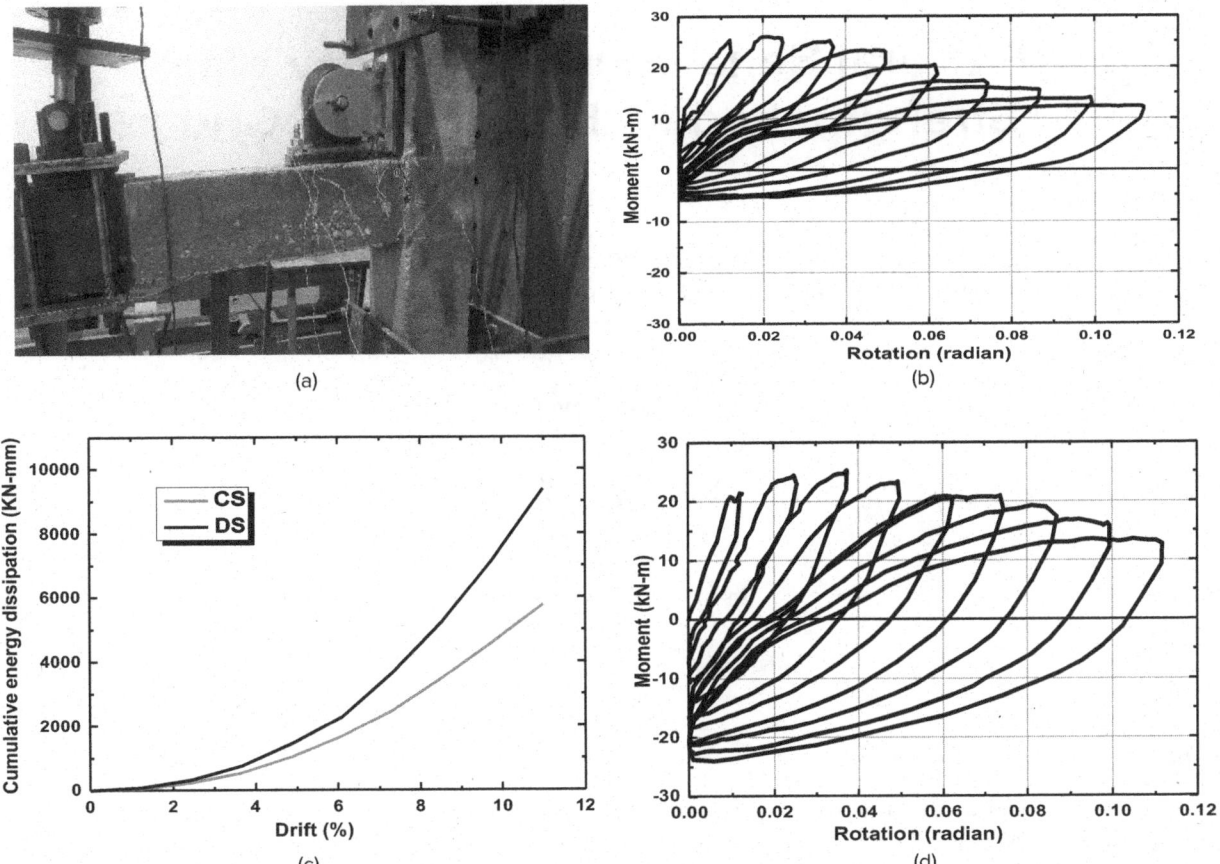

Fig. 10.5 (a) Proposed friction damper installed at beam-column joint (b) Cyclic behavior of beam-column assemblage test without damper (c) with damper (d) Cumulative energy dissipation curve

compared to control specimen. Such noticeable difference in energy dissipation has been attributed to the resistance provided by the rubber material in reverse cycles.

Proposed damper has potential of manifesting better results if installed at both sides of beam-column joint.

REFERENCES

1. Constantinou, M. C., & Symans, M. D. (1993). Seismic response of structures with supplemental damping. *The Structural Design of Tall Buildings*, 2(2), 77–92.
2. Wada, A., Huang, Y. H., & Iwata, M. (2000). Passive damping technology for buildings in Japan. *Progress in structural engineering and materials*, 2(3), 335–350.
3. Uang, C. M., & Bertero, V. V. (1990). Evaluation of seismic energy in structures. *Earthquake Engineering & Structural Dynamics*, 19(1), 77–90.
4. Tirca, L. (2015). Friction dampers for seismic protections of steel buildings subjected to earthquakes: Emphasis on structural design. *Encyclopedia of Earthquake Engineering, Springer, Berlin, 1058*, 1070.
5. Johnson, C. D. (1995). Design of passive damping systems.
6. Symans, M. D., Charney, F. A., Whittaker, A. S., Constantinou, M. C., Kircher, C. A., Johnson, M. W., & McNamara, R. J. (2008). Energy dissipation systems for seismic applications: current practice and recent developments. *Journal of structural engineering*, 134(1), 3–21.
7. Tamura, Y. (1998). Application of damping devices to suppress wind-induced responses of buildings. *Journal of Wind Engineering and Industrial Aerodynamics*, 74, 49–72.
8. Cherry, S., & Filiatrault, A. (1993). Seismic response control of buildings using friction dampers. *Earthquake Spectra*, 9(3), 447–466.
9. Reinhorn, A. M., Constantinou, M. C., & Li, C. (1995). Use of supplemental damping devices for seismic strengthening of lightly reinforced concrete frames. In *Proceedings: Workshop on the Seismic Rehabilitation of Lightly Reinforced Concrete Frames, Gaithersburg, MD, June 12–13, 1995* (p. 129). National Institute of Standards and Technology, Building and Fire Research Laboratory.
10. Latour, M., Piluso, V., & Rizzano, G. (2015). Free from damage beam-to-column joints: Testing and design of DST connections with friction pads. *Engineering Structures*, 85, 219-233.

CHAPTER 11

Flexural Behaviour of Masonry Wall Strengthened with Waste PET Grid

Dinesh Chandra Pandey
Research Scholar, NITTTR, Chandigarh,
dinesh25pandey@gmail.com
9317096219

Amit Goyal
Assistant Professor, NITTTR, Chandigarh,
amitgoyalamit23@gmail.com
9417569559

R. Siva Chidambram
Scientist, CBRI, Roorkee,
krsinelastic@gmail.com
9634430889

Abstract

Masonry is a common and widely used building material in construction field as, it is affordable with various structural and environmental benefits. A masonry structure behaves very efficiently under gravity loading but its performance under horizontal loading is always a matter of great concern for the researchers. In the proposed experimental study, performance of masonry walls strengthened by using a newly developed plastic grid system by waste PET water bottles has been studied. Out of the plane behavior, In-plane behavior of controlled and strengthened samples have been studied and compared for the parameters such as Load-deflection curve, energy dissipation, stiffness and degradation. The failure patterns of all the samples used in the study have been analyzed comparatively. The wall samples strengthened with PET grid inhibits very encouraging results as compare to un-strengthened specimens especially in diagonal compression testing. The energy absorption capacity of the PET sample is much higher than an unreinforced sample. A plastic grid made up of PET water bottles not only provides an effective and affordable retrofitting solution but also saves the environment.

Keywords: Diagonal Tension, PET Water Bottle, Out of plane failure, In-plane failure, Energy Dissipation, Stiffness degradation

1. Introduction

Unreinforced masonry (URM) structures are vulnerable to seismic loading and to protect structural integrity, strengthening of the structure becomes inexorable. The tremendous progress in the field of structural strengthening shifted the curve of conventional strengthening techniques towards modern practices. All the techniques whether old or new have their own pros and cons depending upon their applications. The appliances of these techniques further depend on the structural, economical and technical considerations of the chosen method. Old methods like jacketing can enhance the strength and give the stiffness to the structures but with an expense of increase in the mass of the structures [1]. A combination of Composite materials such as Fiber-reinforced polymer (FRP), Textile reinforced mortar (TRM), etc. can be effective in diminishing the acute failure of URM but the profitable characteristics of these techniques are unlikely to meet the requirements of common people specifically in rural areas. Contemporary methods such as post-tensioning, center core cutting, etc. are favorable in enhancing structural stability but these techniques requires highly skilled and expensive manpower which leads to increase in the cost. As a substitute, there are many new

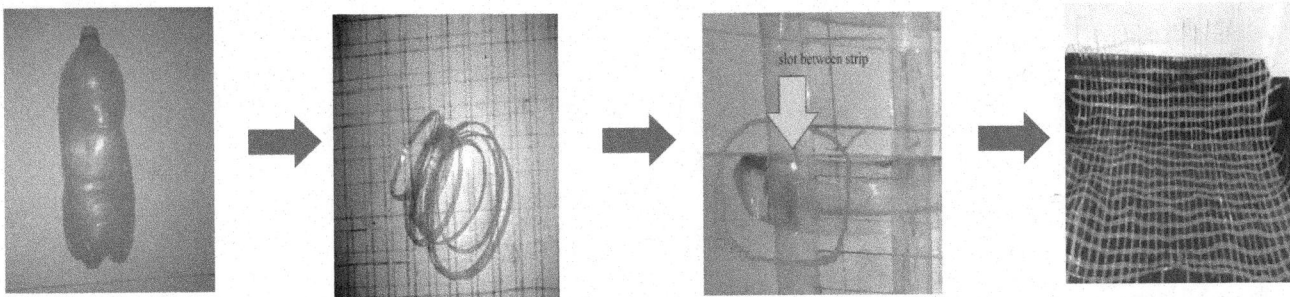

Fig. 11.1 Manufacturing process of PET grid.

environmental friendly materials are also under investigation such as bamboo, Polypropylene bands, etc. which are more economical with sustainable parameters.

Non-biodegradable waste reduction is always a challenge to overcome, especially plastic waste reduction. The only reliable structural solution to reduce this challenge is by re-using it for the strengthening of structures, as its properties can be leveraged to produce a viable solution for strengthening. The use of PET with its high strain value makes it one of the potential materials for the structural strengthening. PET fibers already used in construction shows satisfactory ductile behavior [9].

In this research, tests have been conducted to evaluate out of plane and in-plane behavior of masonry specimen strengthened with a handmade PET grid. The experimental procedure includes a compressive test on elemental materials and a unidirectional tensile test on PET strips. Shear and tensile flexure tests are also performed on unreinforced and strengthened samples. For flexure (OOP) test reinforcement is attached to the whole surface on the tension side of the specimens whereas, for shear test application of grid is carried on three sides (front, back, and top), moreover bottom and two side surfaces are not reinforced. The consequences of loading are studied for both flexure and shear tests. The analysis of this experimental finding includes failure patterns, flexural strength, and energy absorption capacity.

2. Experimental Programs

2.1 Mechanical Characteristics of Constituent Materials

Mechanical properties of the materials used in this program tested with monotonic compressive/tensile tests. Cement sand mortar ratio of 1:4 is used for both plastering and wallet construction. The test specimens built using brick having a nominal size of $230 \times 67 \times 110$mm with single Wythe brick construction for all the samples. Mechanical properties of the

brick, mortar, and PET strip studied as per ASTM standards with coefficient of variation are shown in Table 11.1.

Table 11.1 Material properties of constituent materials

Material	Standard test reference	Average strength (MPa)	COV (%)
Brick	ASTM C-67 20[2]	16.5 (compressive)	17.31
Mortar	ASTM C-109/C109M-20a[3]	7.9 (compressive)	6.32
Prism	ASTM C1314-18[4]	3.4 (compressive)	22.87
PET	ASTM D882-18[5]	138 (tensile)	24.5

2.2 Manufacturing of Pet Grid

Various PET bottles of different companies and sizes are procured from the rag markets. Fine strips having width of 8-10mm are extracted from the waste bottle with a cutting tool. The cutting tools used in the experimental program are made up of wood and steel. Strips having straight portions are preferably selected for the grid and pinned on the cardboard of appropriate size with cardboard pins. The grid is prepared with the help of weaving action and tacking is done by passing the strips from a small slot created in between the strips as shown in the Fig. 11.1.

2.3 Specimen Dimensions and Strengthening Details

Table 11.2 Specimen dimensions and strengthening details

Specimen	Dimension L × B × T	Testing & Retrofitting Details
UD	480 480 140	Plastered URM panel used for Diagonal compression
PD	480 480 140	URM panel retrofitted with PET grid used for Diagonal compression
UN	800 490 140	Plastered URM panel used for bending tension normal to bed joints.
PN	800 490 140	URM panel retrofitted with PET grid used for bending tension normal to bed joints.

Specimen	Dimension L × B × T	Testing & Retrofitting Details
UP	800 490 140	Plastered URM panel used for bending tension parallel to bed joints.
PP	800 490 140	URM panel retrofitted with PET grid used for bending tension parallel to bed joints.

2.4 Oop Flexure Test

The standard recommendation of ASTM E518/518-M15[6] is used for the identification of the OOP flexure behavior of masonry wallets.. The investigational arrangement for the flexure test is shown in Fig. 11.2. Due to the lower tensile strengthening of masonry, ample care is given in the process of conveying the samples to the testing set-up. Deflection of samples is measured with the help of a linear variable differential transducer (LVDT), having the least count of .01mm on the top of the loading cell tied with a hydraulic jack of capacity 30 tons. The Data Acquisition System (DAQ) box is used to record both load cell and LVDT readings.

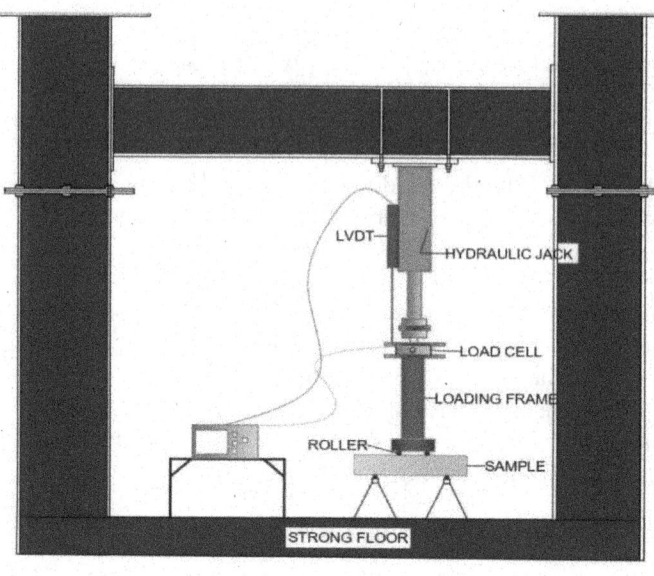

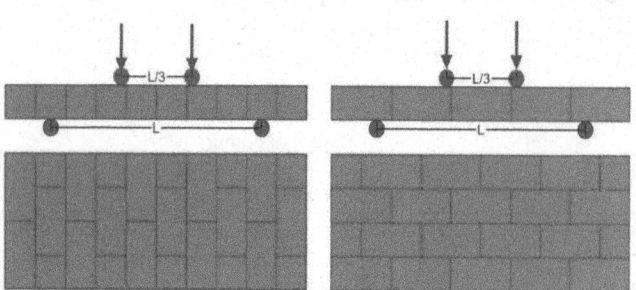

Fig. 11.2 Schematic representation for flexure test for both normal to and parallel to bed joints

Test wallets are tested under four-point loading. Loads are applied in such a manner that bending tension is applied in perpendicular and parallel directions to the test wallets. Initial Controlled loading rate of 0.5mm/min is adopted for all the samples for the test to complete in less than 3 minutes but not before 1 minute.

2.5 Experimental Results

Load-Displacements Curves and Failure Patterns

The failure pattern of unreinforced plastered samples imitates a similar failure pattern as of unreinforced samples without plasters [7]. Propagation of cracks is quick with instant brittle failure. The sample UN manifests no restraint to failure after the first crack and splits in half as shown in Fig. 11.4(a). For the sample UP a little restrain is seen after the first crack but after it reaches the peak value, failure is sudden and brittle in nature as in Fig. 11.4(c). Apex load for sample UN and UP is 4.19 KN and 11.15 KN with maximal peak load-displacement as 1.96 mm and 3.19 mm respectively shown in Fig. 11.3(a), (b). Specimen strengthened with a grid of Polyethylene terephthalate (PET) strips exhibits little augmentation over the non-reinforced sample. For PN and PP Initial fissures are observed at 4.7 KN and 10.9 KN. Maximum displacement at peak load is 7.29 mm and 4.88 mm with summit load as 4.7 KN and 12.9 KN as in Fig. 11.3(a), (b). The load gets dissipated by the grid to some extent but after that, a sudden brittle failure occurs (Fig. 11.4(b), (d)). The brittle failure can be due to the lack of thickness of stripes and bonding between the grids as the failure of the same mainly occurs from the grid joints. The failure arises where the maximum moment is produced (at mid-plane) and causes the collapse of samples. Migration of the forces due to grid did not take place as load intensified on the same line path due to failure of grid joints from maximum loaded point and causes the failure as in Fig 11.5.

Strengthening Influence

The crack formation in case of loading is early through the bed joints and grid action comes into play after the failure of joints. The maximum peak load taken by UN and UP is 1.21 and 1.154 times higher than their counterpart unreinforced samples. Deflection measured for samples with PET grid is 3.72 and 1.53 times higher than that of plastered sample for bending tension normal to and parallel to bed joints respectively. The energy dissipation of the PET is 3.16 times and 1.23 times higher than the unreinforced plastered sample in a direction normal to and parallel to bed joints respectively.

As Unreinforced and PET reinforced sample exhibited brittle failure upon the execution of the

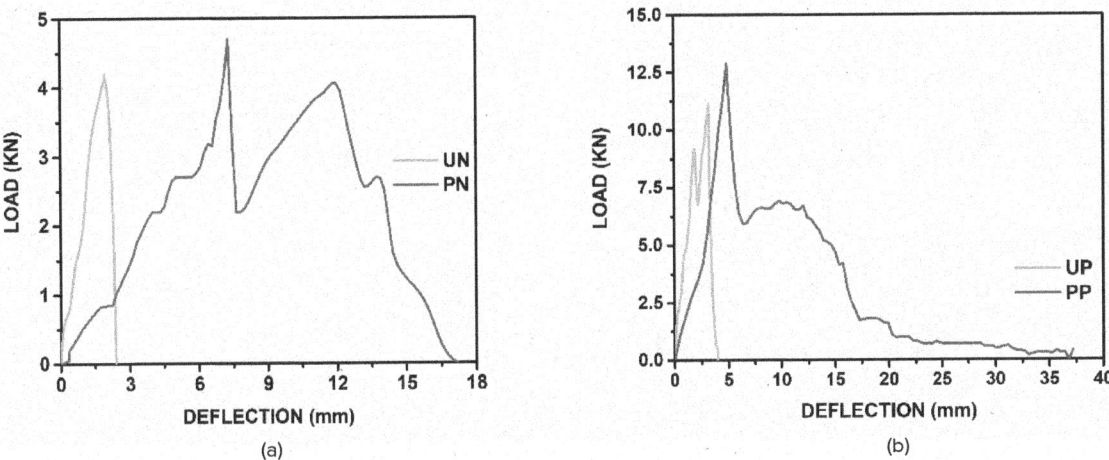

Fig. 11.3 Load vs. deflection curve for bending tension (a) normal to bed joint (b) parallel to bed joints.

(a) UN

(b) PN

(c) UP

(d) PP

Fig. 11.4 Failures patterns of masonry wallets in OOP flexure test (a) brittle failure of UN (b) brittle failure of PN(c) brittle failure of UP(d) failure of PET strengthened sample PP

2.6 Diagonal Tension Test

The standard testing procedure is given by ASTM gives some pre-calculated formulas for easy determination of the stress-strain values directly from load-displacement curves.

The shear stress can be calculated by Eqn. 3.

$$\tau = \frac{707P}{5t(L+H)} \tag{1}$$

where τ = shear stress(MPa); P-load exerted along the compression diagonal(N), An- net area of the compression (mm^2).

Fig. 11.5 Grid failure ruptures in PET grid

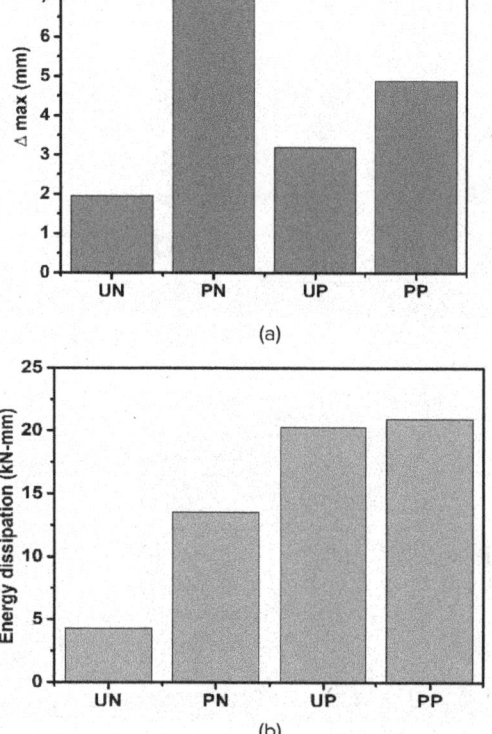

(a)

(b)

Fig. 11.6 Comparative graph of samples used for flexure test showing(a)Peak deflection at maximum load (b) Energy dissipation

Shear strain or drift can be calculated using the Eqn. 4.

$$\gamma = \frac{\Delta x + \Delta y}{g} \qquad (2)$$

Δx = diagonal shortening along the axis of applied force,

Δy = diagonal shortening along the axis perpendicular to the applied force,

g = gauge length, which is normally kept the same for both directions.

Modulus of rigidity (G) is obtained as the Eqn. 5. Shear modulus is calculated using the secant modulus of $0.05\,\tau\mathrm{max}$ and $0.75\,\tau\mathrm{max}$ of the stress-strain curve[8].

$$G = \frac{\tau}{\gamma} \qquad (3)$$

Stiffness of the specimens is quantified by the Modulus of Elasticity (E), by Eqn. 6.

$$E = 2G\,(1 + \nu) \qquad (4)$$

Where $\nu = 0.25$ as adopted by Mustafaraj and Yardim [9].

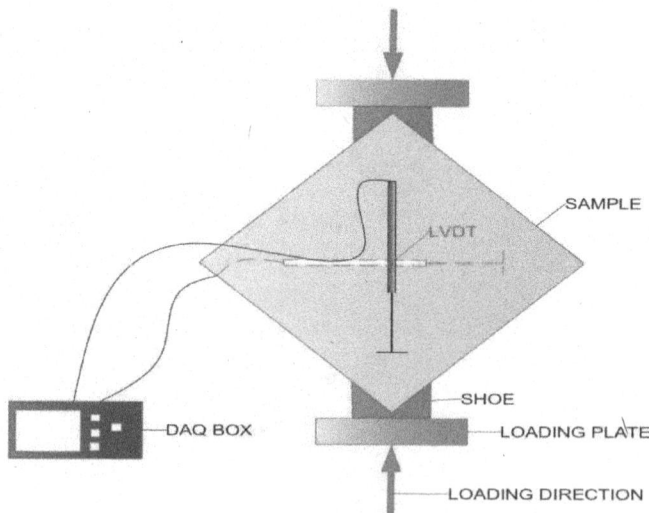

Fig. 11.7 Schematic representation of diagonal tension test set up.

Failure Modes

The unreinforced sample with plaster layer showed a typical brittle failure mode. The initial crack propagated through the loading direction adjacent to the mid-plane of the sample as in Fig. 11.9(a). Sudden brittle failure also occurred at the same place as crack propagation Fig. 11.9(b). The reinforced sample shows ductile failure for both the specimen strengthened with PET grid and geo-grid respectively. The investigational monitoring showed the superiority and effectiveness of the strengthening by PET grid. Failure pattern of strengthened sample initiated from the exact mid-plane through with loading direction is passing Fig. 11.9(c). Failure pattern indicates dissipation of load through the fibers at the stress concentrated region. Propagation of cracks receipts from the top towards the bottom as the load increases. Higher load indicates that fibers help in integrating the structure and facilitate higher energy dissipation. Slippage of the grid wires occurs in the corner with fracture of few wires in the middle of the sample from the slots(provided for weaving action). For

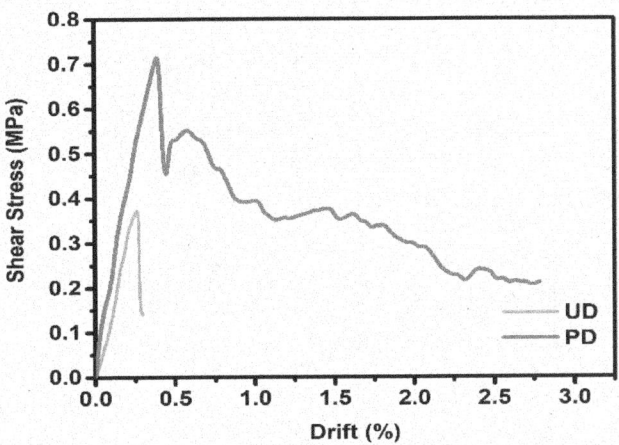

Fig. 11.8 Shear Stress-Strain curve for diagonal tension.

Strengthening influence

The retrofitted specimen shows a significant increase in strength as that of unreinforced plastered Specimen. The strengthened specimen exhibited ductile failure. The load of the strengthened wallets is 1.91 times higher than the controlled sample. The reinforced samples show enhancement over the maximum stress and drift. The ductility of the samples is found out by the ratio of ultimate strain to the yield strain. To find out the yield and ultimate points of masonry, the actual behavior of specimens is idealized with the help of a bilinear curve [10]. Ultimate drift is defined as the drift at which shear strength reduces to 0.8 times the maximum shear strength. Yield drift is calculated from the intersection of an elastic and plastic segment of the equivalent bilinear curve. The bilinear curve is plotted as an area equal to the actual curve up to the ultimate point. A strengthened sample signifies enhancement in ductility to that of the plastered sample.

a large value of deformation, the integrity of PET remained the same as plaster peeled off from the sample surface as in Fig. 11.9(d)

The strengthening procedure helps in increasing the shear modulus and elastic modulus also. The increment in shear modulus is more than UD.

(a) UD

(b) UD

(c) PD

(d) PD

Fig. 11.9 Crack patterns of diagonal test on brick wallets (a) crack initiation in UD (b) failure of UD sample (c) crack initiation in PD (d) interaction of plaster to the PD even after test completion

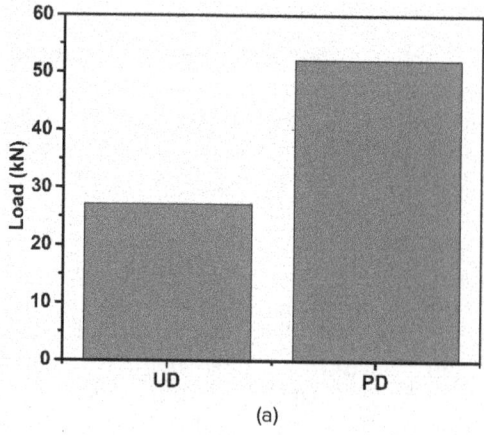 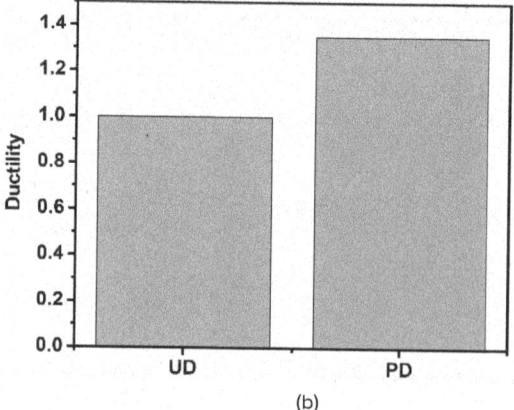

(a)   (b)

Fig. 11.10 Comparative graph of samples used for diagonal test showing (a) Peak load at maximum load (b) ductility.

3. Conclusion

Masonry structures are weak in tension and it is highly susceptible to failure during earthquakes. The main failure caused by any lateral force to masonry is out of plane failure and in pane failure. Depicting a proper method for strengthening is one of the main concerns. The feasibility of the methods depends on certain aspects like cost, user-friendliness, and sustainability, etc. Many researchers had given solutions to strengthen masonry which includes conventional methods to modern techniques. Strengthening with PET bottles and its influence on flexural and shear were experimentally studied. An experimental study is primarily focused on taking a pioneering step towards strengthening masonry by using waste plastic. The load vs. deflection curve for flexure tension is used to estimate energy dissipation. The load vs. deformation curve for diagonal tension help is used to measure the shear stress, shear strain, etc. and the following are the main conclusion drawn from experimental results.

- The tensile test result shows that the PET strand exhibits &strain hardening behavior with noticeable rupture. The tensile behavior shows that the PET samples can be effectively used in various applications due to their strain hardening behavior.

- The flexural behavior under perpendicular and parallel to loading and deflection shows that the strengthened specimens exhibit better elastic and inelastic behavior over control samples. The brittle nature of plastic materials fails to offer better post-peak strain.

- The higher post-peak deletion of PET reinforced sample shows 3 and 1.2 times higher energy absorption capacity than the conventional sample.

- The failure pattern of PET samples shows the rupture of strands at the junction. The brittle failure of PET may

be due to its very less thickness. Failure in strengthened samples is independent of the direction of strengthening.

- For diagonal tension, the maximum load-carrying capacity of the strengthened sample is almost twice with 1.35 times higher ductility than that of conventional specimens.

3.1 Recommendation for Further Study

- Investigation of the effect of strengthening in diagonal tension can be repeated for the standard sample size of 1.2 m by 1.2 m.

- Dimensions of the PET grid can be rearranged for the more promising results.

- The application of the grids can be manipulated by various positional rearrangements over the masonry sample.

- The number of layers can be increased to see the effect of increasing the no of layers in flexure and diagonal tension.

- The finite element method can be performed to validate the experimental results obtained in this research.

REFERENCES

1. Triantafillou, T. C. (1998). Strengthening of masonry structures using epoxy-bonded FRP laminates. Journal of composites for construction, 2(2), 96–104.
2. ASTM Standard test method for sampling and testing brick and structural clay tile. ASTM C67-20.
3. ASTM Standard test method for compressive strength of hydraulic cement mortars (using 2-in. or[50mm] cube specimen). ASTM C 109/ C109-M20a.
4. ASTM Standard test method for compressive strength of masonry prisms. ASTM C1314-18.
5. ASTM Standard test method for tensile properties of thin plastic sheeting. ASTM D882-18

6. ASTM Standard test methods for flexure bond strength of masonry. ASTM E518/518-M15

7. Kadam, S. B., Singh, Y., & Li, B. (2015). Out-of-plane behaviour of unreinforced masonry strengthened using ferrocement overlay. Materials and Structures, 48(10), 3187–3203.

8. Kadam, S. B., Singh, Y., & Li, B. (2014). Strengthening of unreinforced masonry using welded wire mesh and micro-concrete–Behaviour under in-plane action. Construction and Building Materials, 54, 247–257.

9. Mustafaraj, E., & Yardim, Y. (2018). In-plane shear strengthening of unreinforced masonry walls using GFRP jacketing. Periodica Polytechnica Civil Engineering, 62(2), 330–336.

10. Ismail, N., Petersen, R. B., Masia, M. J., & Ingham, J. M. (2011). Diagonal shear behaviour of unreinforced masonry wallettes strengthened using twisted steel bars. Construction and Building Materials, 25(12), 4386–4393.

CHAPTER 12

Numerical Approximation of 3D Heat Conduction in Early Age Mass Concrete Using Crank Nicholson Implicit Finite Difference Method

Ugwuanyi Donald Chidiebere
Department of Civil Engineering,
Enugu State University of Science and Technology, Nigeria
chididonald1981@gmail.com

Okafor Fidelis Onyebuchi
Department of Civil Engineering,
University of Nigeria, Nsukka, Nigeria
fidelis.okafor@unn.edu.ng

Abstract

Heat is always released whenever cement mixes with water. In the case of mass concretes, such heat may not be easily released and could lead to excessive temperature increase internally, depending on the prevailing temperature of the ambient environment, the amount of cement in the concrete mix and the size of the mass concrete. Numerical model using Crank Nicholson implicit finite difference method was developed based on 3D unsteady state heat conduction in mass concretes. Optimized MATLAB based software was developed for simulation and data visualization. A mass concrete block cast with standard mix ration and water cement ratio was used to verify the efficacy of the model. Type-K thermocouples and digital thermometer were used to monitor the temperatures at time intervals. The initial temperature just after placement was found to be uniform at all thermocouple locations. The temperature distribution afterwards exhibited a hotter core and cooler surface within the mass concrete block. The surface of block in contact with the ground recorded lower temperatures than the other surfaces for most of the time intervals. The highest temperatures for all thermocouple locations were recorded within 24 hours after concrete placement with the thermocouples located within the center (core) exhibiting higher temperatures and decreased towards the surface. After 96 hours of concrete placement, the temperature profile of the mass concrete block tends to revert to the prevailing ambient temperature. With the knowledge of the ambient temperature and the size of the mass concrete, the temperature distribution can be reliably predicted from which potential for thermal cracks occurrence can be determined to enable suitable proactive preventive cracks control measures.

Keywords: Temperature, mass concrete, finite difference, MATLAB, software.

1. Introduction

Of utmost concern of the features of mass concretes is its behaviour when subjected to heat. The reactions that herald the formation of cement hydrates is that of exothermic whereby heat is released to the environment. For massive concrete sections as in mass concretes, the issue of heat and its release becomes exacerbated in terms of the extent of behaviour that is expected due to high heat release. The escalation rate of heat in mass concretes stems from the amount of cement in the concrete mixture, its thermo-physical properties, environment conditions, mass concretes geometry and installation conditions. Fresh concretes when utilized during installation of mass concretes namely foundations and dams, priority attention should be paid to the amount of heat release and accompanying volume alterations.

Temperature gradient occurs when the heat of hydration is released to immediate environment resulting in a lower surface temperature when compared to the concrete core. The concrete member will experience contraction at the surface and the interior having higher temperature due to heat being trapped within will offer restraint against the contraction action at the surface, which might result to surface cracks.

Modeling the generation and transfer of heat in early-age concrete is essential to understanding the behaviour of mass concrete [1]. Early-age concrete or young hardening concrete is among the most challenging materials to model. The difficulties are due to a rather complex composite structure which is subject to transient conditions as cement hydration progresses [2]. [3] utilized heat and moisture transport model in hydrating concrete to predict heat generated during concrete hydration. [4] studied thermal crack of massive concrete structures using extended finite element method (XFEM) utilizing thermal fields and creep. [5] estimated cracking risk of concrete at early ages based on thermal stress analysis. [6] modeled early age thermal cracking in hardening concrete based on degree of hydration. [7] developed a model based on hydro-mechanical analysis of hydrating concrete structures which considered hydration heat, concrete composition, reinforcement, shrinkage and creep. [8] applied transient plane source measurement technique to assess the heat capacity and thermal conductivity of hydrating cement. [9] proposed a coupled thermo-chemo-mechanical model to determine the behaviour of early age concrete to simulate cement hydration, aging, damage and creep. [10] applied finite element simulation to predict early age concrete temperature distribution in thick rafts. The objective of the research is to apply Crank Nicholson implicit finite difference method to determine the temperature profile in mass concrete at early ages of cement hydration.

2. Methodology

A mass concrete block of dimension 1.1m x 1.1m x1.1m, mix ratio 1:2:4 and water cement ratio of 0.6 consisting of ordinary Portland cement, river sand and coarse aggregate of maximum size 40mm was used to verify the model. Type-K thermocouples position as shown in Fig. 12.1 and digital thermometer (Fig. 12.2) were used to monitor the temperature within the concrete mass at time intervals of 0, 6, 12, 18, 24, 48, 72, 96, 120 and 144 hours respectively. Plywood formwork of 25mm thickness (Fig. 12.3) internally surrounded by polystyrene sheet as insulation and the top surface of the cast concrete covered with 50mm thick layer of sand.

2.1 Model Development

The governing equation is that of three dimensional unsteady state heat conduction equation based on Fourier law of heat

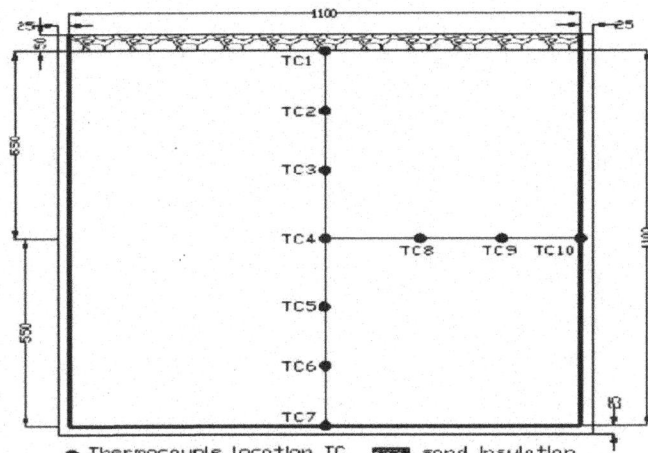

Fig. 12.1 Mass concrete block showing the layout of the thermocouples. (dimensions in mm)

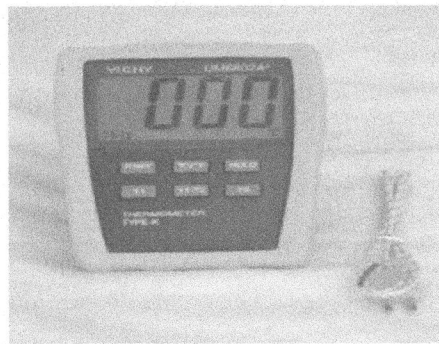

Fig. 12.2 Digital thermometer and Type-K thermocouple.

Fig. 12.3 Cast mass concrete showing the thermocouples.

transfer shown in Equation 1. Finite difference solution of the governing equation using Crank Nicholson implicit finite difference method was determined by applying the boundary and initial conditions.

$$K\left(\frac{\partial^2 T}{\partial x^2} + \frac{\partial^2 T}{\partial y^2} + \frac{\partial^2 T}{\partial z^2}\right) q_H + \rho Cp \frac{\partial T}{\partial t} \tag{1}$$

ρ is density of concrete (kg/m^3), C_P is the specific heat capacity of concrete (J/kg.°C), q is the heat source intensity (KJ/m^3.h), K is the thermal conductivity (KJ/m.h°C), T is transient temperature of concrete (°C) and t is time (hrs).

At the spatial boundaries of the mass concrete, a constant temperature is assumed such that for thermal insulation, there exist the following boundary conditions.

x-direction: $0 \le x \le a$, boundary conditions:

$$T(0, y, z, t) = T(a, y, z, t) = T_a \tag{2}$$

y-direction: $0 \le y \le b$, boundary conditions:

$$T(x, 0, z, t) = T(x, b, z, t) = T_a \tag{3}$$

z-direction: $0 \le z \le c$, boundary conditions:

$$T(x, y, 0, t) = T(x, y, c, t) = T_a \tag{4}$$

T_a is the ambient temperature.

Initial conditions:

At t = 0, there is a uniform temperature such that

$$T(x, y, z, 0) = T_0 \tag{5}$$

T_0 is initial placement temperature.

The general finite difference approximation of Equation (1) starts by forward difference for the time derivative and first forward difference and second central difference for the two spatial derivatives.

$$\rho Cp \frac{(T_{i,j,m}^{k+1} - T_{i,j,m}^k)}{\Delta t} = K \frac{(T_{i+1,j,m} - 2T_{i,j,m} + T_{i,j,-1,m})}{(\Delta x)^2}$$
$$+ K \frac{(T_{i,j+1,m} - 2T_{i,j,m} + T_{i,j-1,m})}{(\Delta y)^2}$$
$$+ K \frac{(T_{i,j,m+1} - 2T_{i,j,m} + T_{i,j,m-1})}{(\Delta x)^2}$$
$$+ q_{i,j,m}^K \tag{6}$$

The subscripts i, j and k signifies the location in space and time steps.

$$T_{i,j,m}^{k+1} - T_{i,j,m}^k = \frac{K\Delta t}{\rho Cp(\Delta x)^2}[T_{i+1,j,m} - 2T_{i,j,m} + T_{i-1,j,m}]$$
$$+ \frac{K\Delta t}{\rho Cp(\Delta y)^2}[T_{i+1,j,m} - 2T_{i,j,m} + T_{i,-1,m}]$$
$$+ \frac{K\Delta t}{\rho Cp(\Delta z)^2}[T_{i,j,m+1} - 2T_{i,j,m} + T_{i,j,m-1}]$$
$$+ \frac{\Delta t}{\rho Cp} q_{i,j,m}^K \tag{7}$$

For purposes of simplification, let the location of the nodes (i, j, m) be indicated as

E ≡ i + 1, j, m; W ≡ i − 1, j, m; N ≡ i, j + 1, m; S ≡ i, j − 1, m; NW ≡ i, j, m + 1; SE ≡ i, j, m − 1; P ≡ i, j , m

Then Equation (7) becomes;

$$T_p^{k+1} - T_p^k = \frac{K\Delta t}{\rho Cp(\Delta x)^2}[T_E - 2T_P + T_W]$$
$$+ \frac{K\Delta t}{\rho Cp(\Delta y)^2}[T_N - 2T_P + T_S]$$
$$\frac{K\Delta t}{\rho Cp(\Delta z)^2}[T_{NW} - 2T_P + T_{SE}]$$
$$+ \frac{\Delta t}{\rho Cp} q_P^k \tag{8}$$

At the right of Equation (7), the temperature values are mean temperatures between time steps so that

$$T_n = f T_n^{k+1} + (1 - f)T_n^k \tag{9}$$

Where f is the weighting factor. Applying Equations (7) and (8), the general finite difference approximation of the three-dimensional unsteady state heat conduction becomes;

$$T_p^{k+1} - T_p^k = \frac{K\Delta t}{\rho Cp(\Delta x)^2}[fT_E^{k+1} + (1 - f)T_E^k + fT_W^{K+1}$$
$$+ (1 - f)T_W^K - 2fT_P^{k+1} - 2(1 - f)T_P^K]$$
$$+ \frac{K\Delta t}{\rho Cp(\Delta y)^2}[fT_N^{k+1} + (1 - f)T_N^k + fT_S^{K+1}$$
$$+ (1 - f)T_S^K - 2fT_P^{K+1} - 2(1 - f)T_P^K]$$
$$+ \frac{K\Delta t}{\rho Cp(\Delta z)^2}[fT_{NW}^{k+1} + (1 - f)T_{NW}^k + fT_{SE}^{K+1}$$
$$+ (1 - f)T_{SE}^K - 2fT_P^{K+1} - 2(1 - f)T_P^K]$$
$$+ \frac{\Delta t}{\rho Cp} q_p^k \tag{10}$$

Taking f as 1/2, Equation (10) reduces to Crank-Nicholson implicit finite difference method.

$$T_p^{k+1} - T_p^k$$
$$= \frac{K\Delta t}{\rho Cp(\Delta x)^2}\left[\frac{1}{2}T_E^{k+1} + \frac{1}{2}T_E^k + \frac{1}{2}T_W^{K+1} + \frac{1}{2}T_W^K - T_P^{k+1} - T_P^K\right]$$
$$+ \frac{K\Delta t}{\rho Cp(\Delta y)^2}\left[\frac{1}{2}T_N^{k+1} + \frac{1}{2}T_N^k + \frac{1}{2}T_S^{K+1} + \frac{1}{2}T_S^K - T_P^{k+1} - T_P^K\right]$$
$$+ \frac{K\Delta t}{\rho Cp(\Delta z)^2}\left[\frac{1}{2}T_{NW}^{k+1} + \frac{1}{2}T_{NW}^k + \frac{1}{2}T_{SE}^{K+1} + \frac{1}{2}T_{SE}^K - T_P^{k+1} - T_P^K\right]$$
$$+ \frac{\Delta t}{\rho Cp} q_P^k \tag{11}$$

$$T_p^{k+1}\left[1+\frac{K\Delta t}{\rho Cp(\Delta x)^2}+\frac{K\Delta t}{\rho Cp(\Delta y)^2}+\frac{K\Delta t}{\rho Cp(\Delta z)^2}\right]$$

$$-\frac{K\Delta t}{2\rho Cp(\Delta x)^2}[T_E^{k+1}+T_W^{k+1}]$$

$$-\frac{K\Delta t}{\rho Cp(\Delta y)^2}[T_N^{k+1}+T_S^{k+1}]$$

$$-\frac{K\Delta t}{\rho Cp(\Delta z)^2}[T_{NW}^{k+1}+T_{SE}^{k+1}]$$

$$=T_p^k\left[1-\frac{K\Delta t}{\rho Cp(\Delta x)^2}-\frac{K\Delta t}{\rho Cp(\Delta y)^2}-\frac{K\Delta t}{\rho Cp(\Delta z)^2}\right]$$

$$+\frac{K\Delta t}{2\rho Cp(\Delta x)^2}[T_E^k+T_W^k]+\frac{K\Delta t}{2\rho Cp(\Delta xy)^2}[T_N^k+T_S^k]$$

$$+\frac{K\Delta t}{2\rho Cp(\Delta xz)^2}[T_{NW}^k+T_{SE}^k]+\frac{\Delta t}{\rho Cp}q_P^K \quad (12)$$

2.2 MATLAB Based Computer Programe

MATLAB based computer programe which is based on the Crank-Nicholson implicit finite difference numerical scheme was written to determine the nodal temperatures at different time steps based on Equation 12. The user interface for the programe is shown in Fig. 12.4. The third dimension dz was constant because the thermocouples were placed at the center of the mass concrete block.

3. Results

The temperature values for the various thermocouple positions within the mass concrete block used for the model verification were recorded for the various time intervals. Figures 5a and 5b shows the graphs of temperature against time for the various thermocouple locations. The zero hour temperature signifies the temperature of the mass concrete block immediately after placement which was found to be uniform throughout the various locations at 28°C.

The thermocouple locations TC1 to TC7 in Fig. 12.5(a) signifies the top to the bottom of the mass concrete while locations TC4, TC8, TC9 and TC10 in Fig. 5(b) are from the center (core) to the right side surface. The temperature profile indicates that the mass concrete exhibited higher temperature values within the core (i.e., TC3, TC4, TC5 and TC8) and the least values at locations close to the surface (ie TC1, TC7 and TC10) for all time intervals. After 120 hours of concrete placement, a constant temperature of 32°C was subsequently recorded for all thermocouple locations. The surface of the mass concrete in contact with the ground exhibited lower temperatures than other surfaces for most of the time intervals. Generally the temperature readings showed a rise from a uniform placement temperature of 28°C to the peak temperature of 51°C at the core after 24 hours and fall afterwards to 32°C at both 120 and 144 hours respectively.

3.1 Calibration

The model parameters were calibrated by adopting definite values based on consideration of the material properties and the local conditions that affect the experimental procedures. Thermal conductivity values for normal weight concrete ranges from 7.1 to 10.6 KJ/mh°C and specific heat capacity ranges from 0.92 to 1.0 KJ/Kg°C according to ACI committee 207, 2005b in [11]. Values of 9 KJ/mh°C and 0.92 KJ/Kg°C were respectively adopted for thermal conductivity and specific heat capacity. The density of fresh normal weight

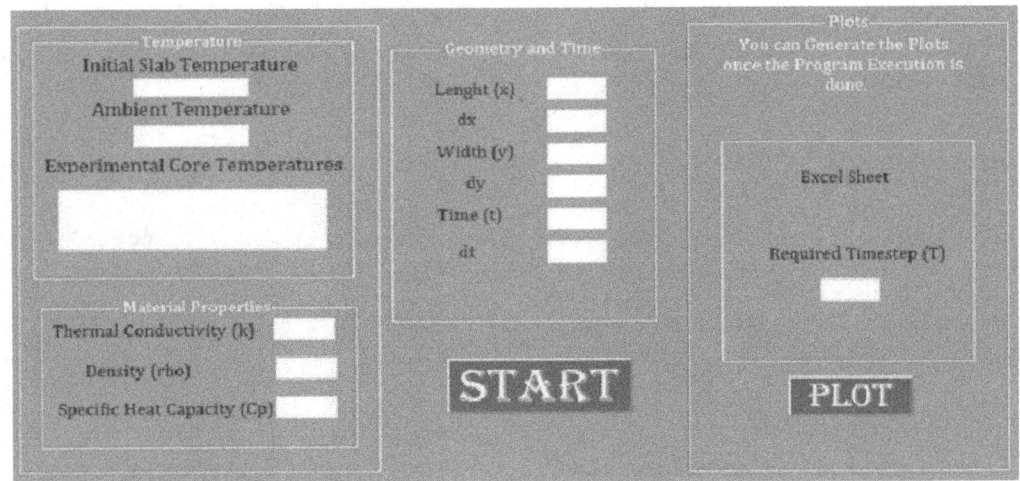

Fig. 12.4 Graphical user interface (GUI) for the MATLAB programe.

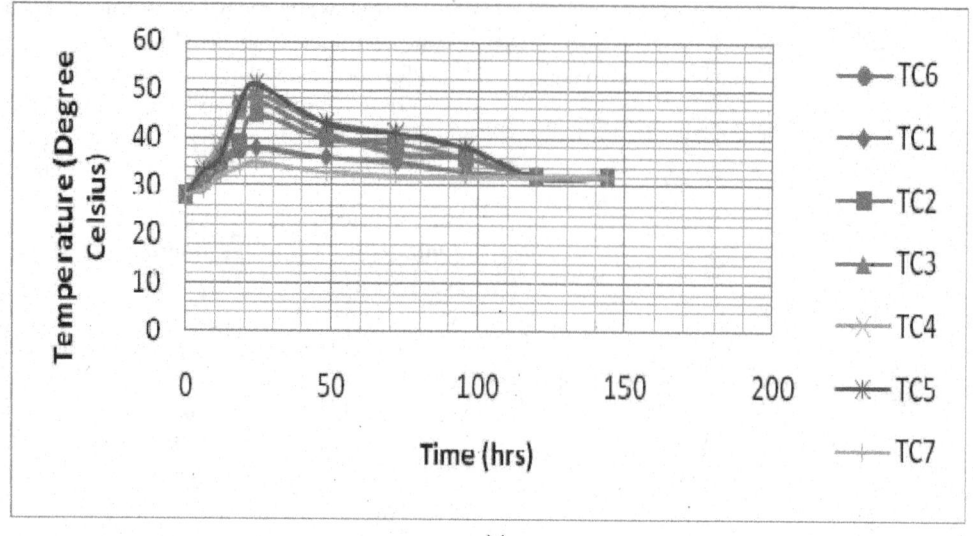

(a)

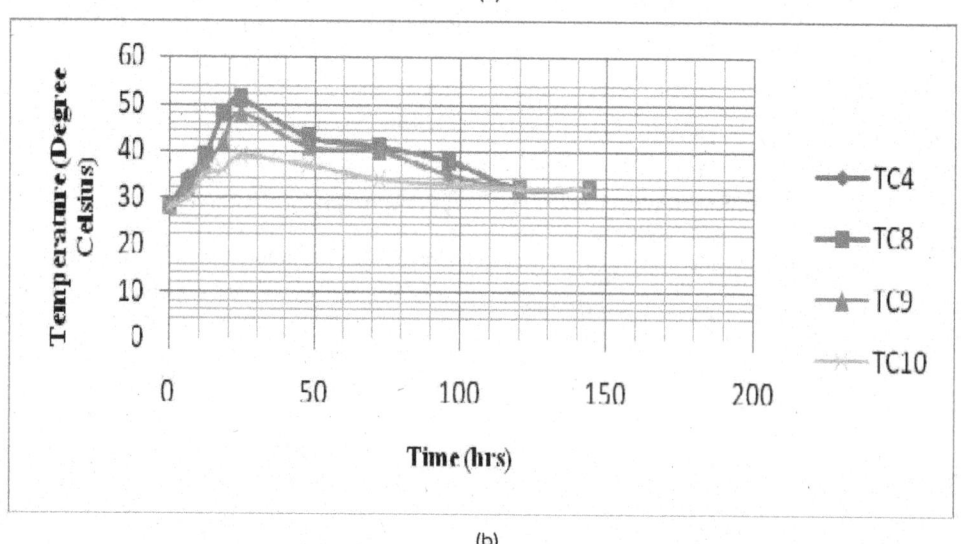

(b)

Fig. 12.5 (a) Plot of temperature against time for thermocouple locations (TC1 to TC7), (b) Plot of temperature against time for thermocouple locations (TC4, TC8, TC9 and TC10)

concrete is 2400Kg/m³. For heat intensity, suzuki's model in [11] was adopted in which

$$q = 20,000\, e^{-0.9398-\frac{t}{24}} \qquad (12)$$

Average ambient temperature (T_a) of 30°C and room temperature value of 26°C were used for the model verification and validation respectively. Initial temperature (T_0) is 28°C.

3.2 Verification

A comparison of the model predicted temperature values and the observed experimental values shows that the model exhibited temperature values higher than the observed up till 48 hours after concrete placement and lower temperature

values afterwards, Fig. 12.6. The temperature values from the model had a constant temperature of 30°C after 72 hours of concrete placement.

A temperature difference of 0.53°C between 18 and 24 hours after concrete placement was recorded for the model. Generally, the model exhibited a steady temperature rise from 28°C at placement to 56.59°C at 24 hours and declined steadily to 32.02°C at 72 hours of placement and remained constant at 30°C afterwards. Both the model data and the experimental data have their highest temperature values of 56.59°C and 51°C at 24 hours of concrete placement respectively. The Figs 12.8 to 12.12 show the 3D plots of temperature profile within the mass concrete at intervals of 0, 24, 48, 72 and 96 hours respectively.

Figure 12.7 shows the core coefficient of determination R^2 for the model verification with value of 0.631 which results to a core correlation coefficient CORR value of 0.79 indicating that it within the acceptable limit for a good correlation.

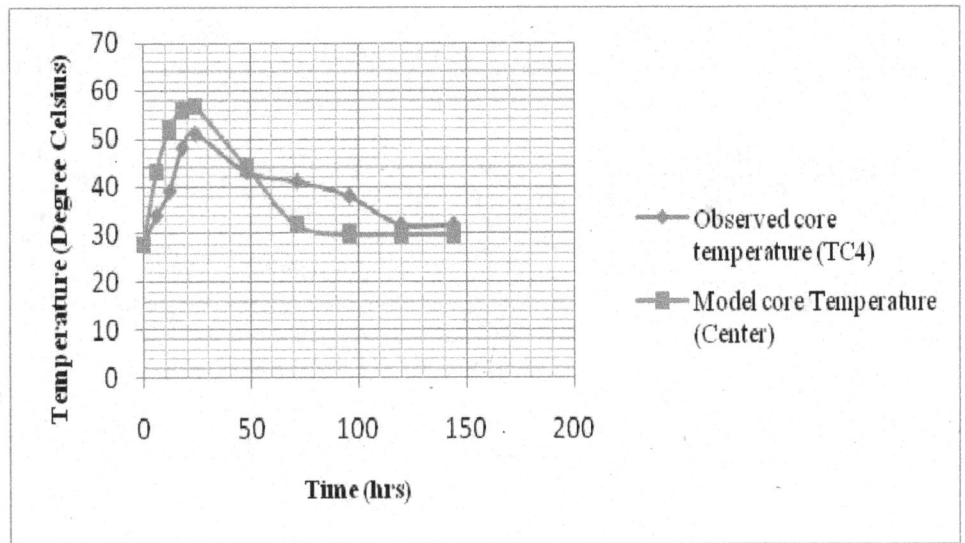

Fig. 12.6 Temperature time relationship for Observed and model temperatures.

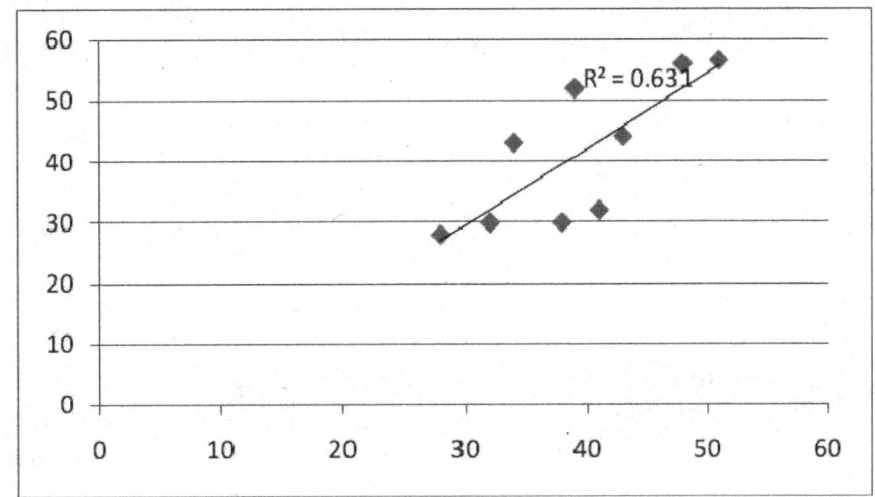

Fig. 12.7 Coefficient of determination for model verification.

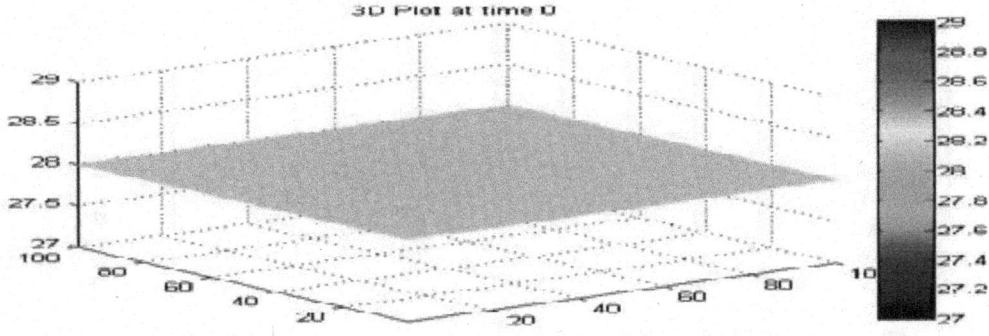

Fig. 12.8 3D plot of temperature profile at initial time of concrete placement.

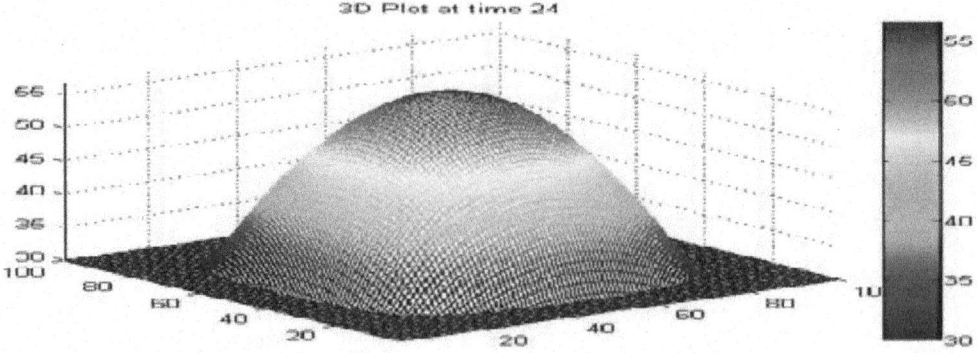

Fig. 12.9   3D plot of temperature profile at 24 hours of concrete placement.

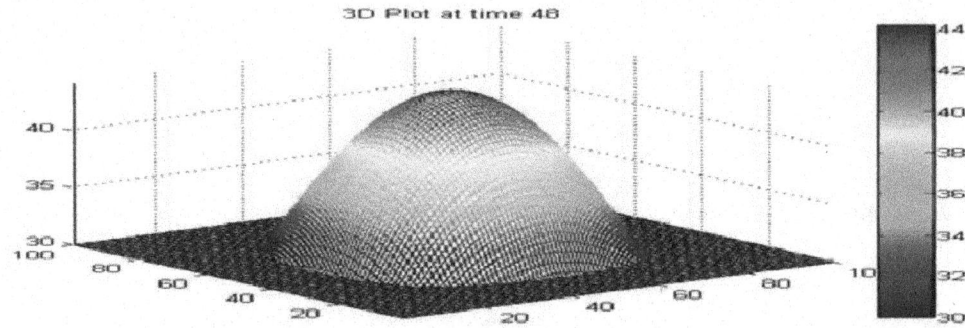

Fig. 12.10   3D plot of temperature profile at 48 hours of concrete placement.

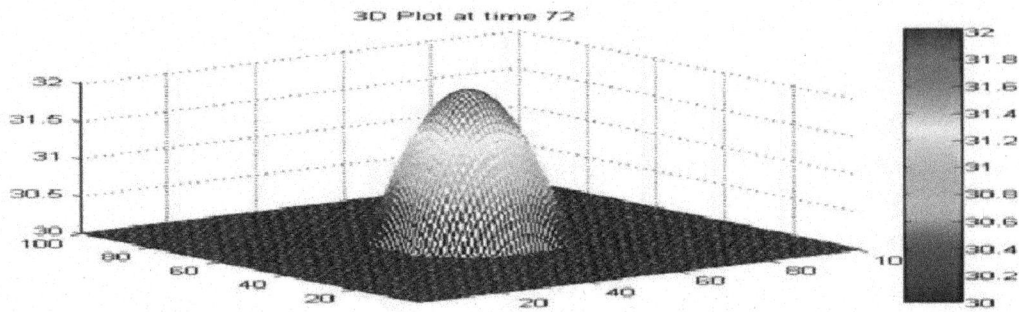

Fig. 12.11   3D plot of temperature profile at 72 hours of concrete placement.

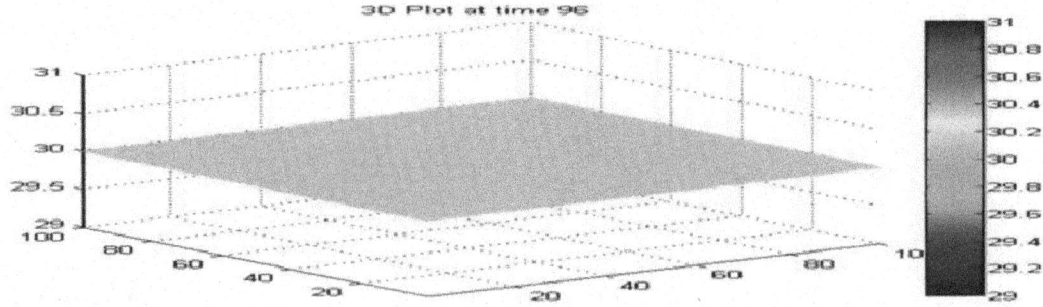

Fig. 12.12   3D plot of temperature profile at 96 hours of concrete placement.

3.3 Validation

The model developed was validated using temperature data from [12]. The boundary temperature is ambient temperature assumed to be room temperature of 26°C. The graphs of the validation temperature data and the model in Fig. 12.13 show fairly identical plots. The peak temperature values for both the validation data and the model occurred at 24 hours of concrete placement of 74.32°C and 73.98°C respectively.

Figure 12.14 shows the coefficient of determination R^2 for the model validation with value of 0.975 which gives a correlation coefficient CORR value of 0.98 representing a very high correlation for the model validation. The Figures 15 to 20 show the 3D plots of temperature profile within the mass concrete at intervals of 0, 24, 48, 72 , 96 and 120 hours respectively.

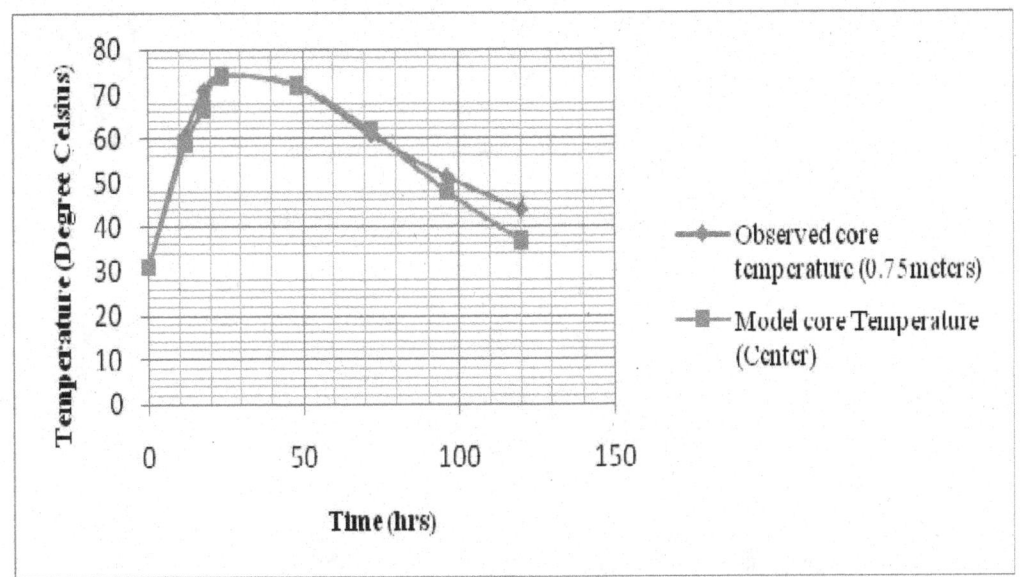

Fig. 12.13   Temperature time relationship for Observed and model temperatures

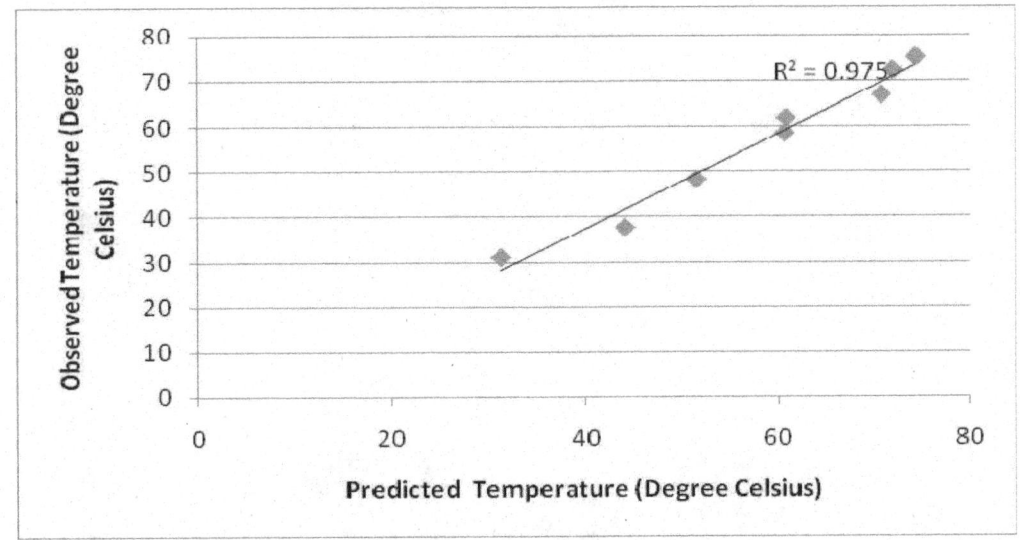

Fig. 12.14   Coefficient of determination for model validation.

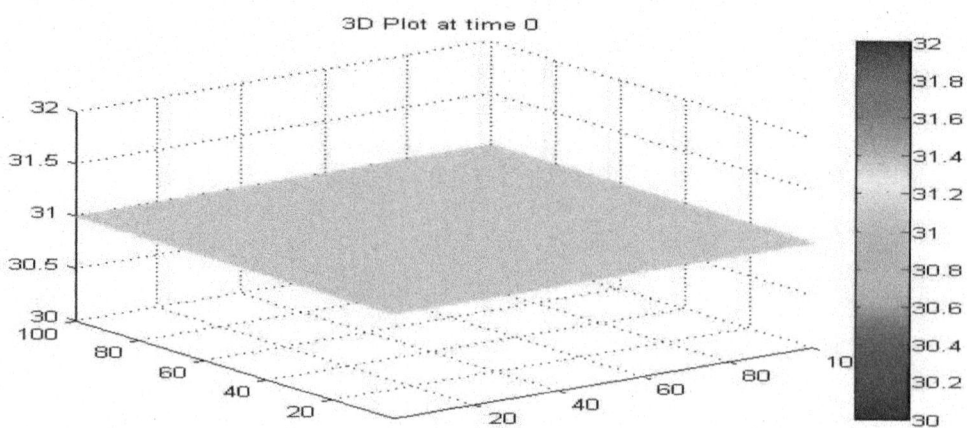

Fig. 12.15 3D plot of temperatures in block at 0hr

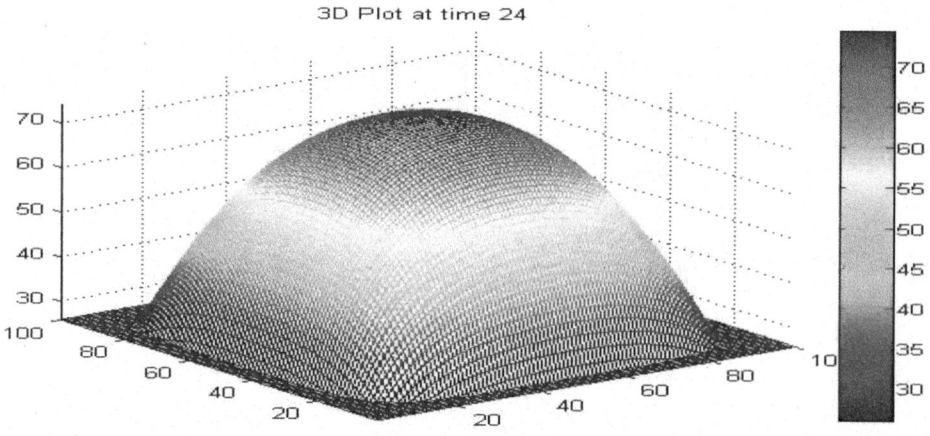

Fig. 12.16 3D plot of temperatures in block at 24hr

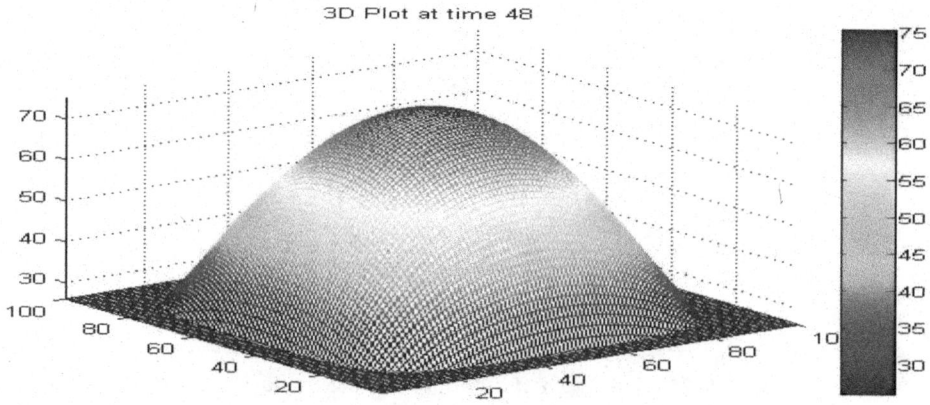

Fig. 12.17 3D plot of temperatures in block at 48hr

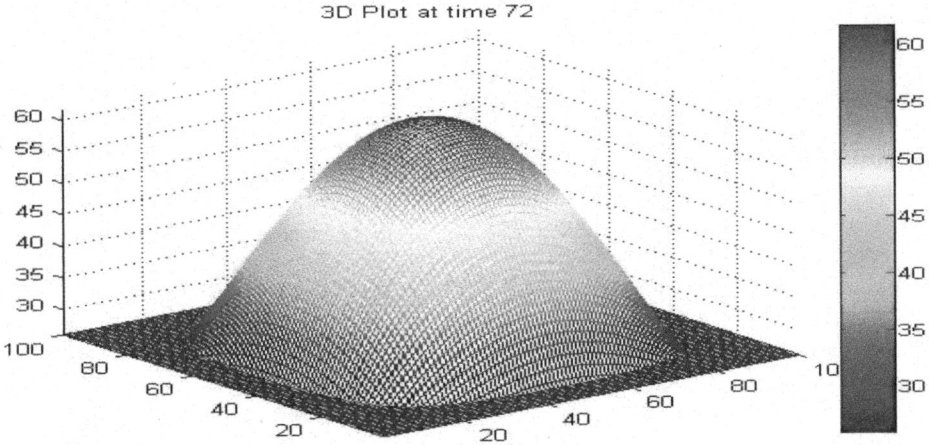

Fig. 12.18   3D plot of temperatures in block at 72hr

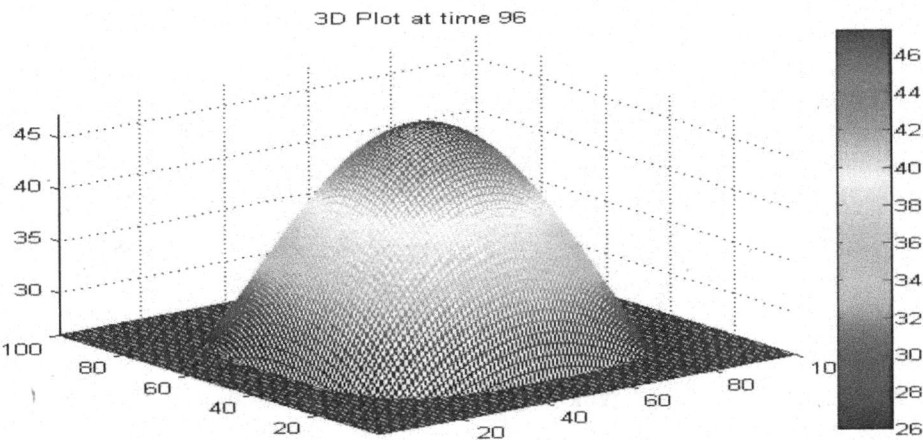

Fig. 12.19   3D plot of temperatures in block at 96hr

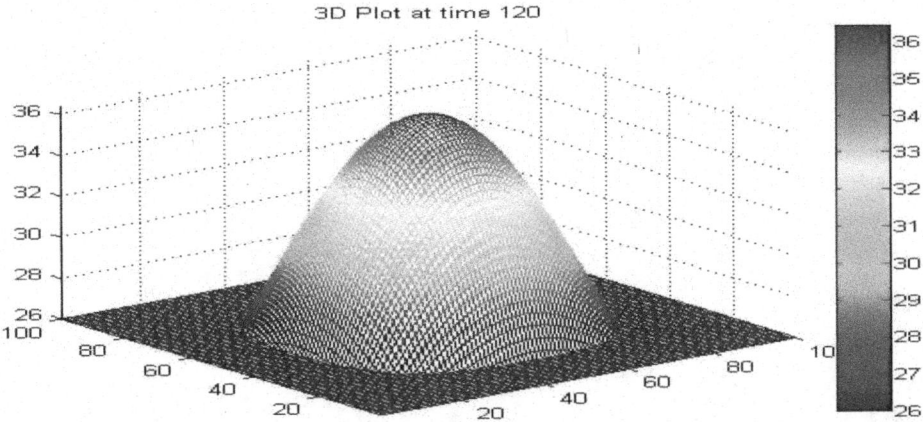

Fig. 12.20   3D plot of temperatures in block at 120hr

4. Conclusion

The thermal behaviour and temperature profile of mass concrete have been determined using a mass concrete block experiment. The initial temperature which is the placement temperature remained constant at all thermocouple locations in the mass concrete. Temperature difference between points in the mass concrete ceased to exit after 120 hours of concrete placement as a uniform temperature was recorded afterwards. The peak temperatures exhibited by the mass concrete occur within 24 hours after concrete placement. Crank Nicholson implicit finite difference method was successfully applied to the two dimensional unsteady state heat conduction within the mass concrete due to cement hydration. An optimized MATLAB based computer program was developed to determine the nodal temperatures at time intervals and for data visualization and simulation. Ease of use, accuracy and applicability are among the major attributes that determine the success of a model. If the temperature arrays in mass concrete members can be estimated, then potentials for thermal cracks occurrence can be determined and appropriate preventive and control measure can be devised. When the environment temperature and the size of the mass concretes are known, the models have the capability of estimating the temperature variance at intervals within the mass concretes. It is therefore suitable for use in the assessment and estimation of thermal cracks in mass concretes.

5. Acknowledgement

The authors appreciate the Department of Civil Engineering, University of Nigeria, Nsukka for their guidance and assistance towards the success of the research.

REFERENCES

1. I. Milovanovic, B. Pecure, I. Gabriel, Measuring thermal properties of hydrating cement pastes, 31st Cement and Concrete Science Conference, Novel Development and Innovation in Cementitious Materials, Imperial College London, United Kingdom, paper number XX (2011).
2. B. Klemczak, A. Knoppik-Wróbel, Reinforced concrete tank walls and bridge abutments: early-age behaviour, Analytic Approaches and Numerical Models, Engineering Structures, 84(2015) 233–251.
3. L. Jendele, V. Smilauer, J. Cervenka, Multi-scale analysis of heat transport in hydrating concrete structures, Proceedings of the Thirteenth International Conference on Civil, Structural and Environmental Engineering Computing, Civil-Comp Press, Stirlingshere, Scotland, paper 124(2011).
4. G. Liu, Y. Hu, Q. Li, Z. Zuo, XFEM for thermal cracks of massive concrete, *Mathematical Problems in Engineering,* http://dx.doi.org/10.1155/2013/343842, (2013).
5. S. Wu, D. Huang, F. B. Liu, H. Zhao, P. Wang, Estimation of cracking risk of concrete at early age based on thermal stress analysis, J.Therm. Anal Calorim, Vol. 105, (2011) 171–186.
6. G. De Schutter, Modeling of early age thermal cracking in hardening concrete including creep and softening behaviour, Concrete Science and Engineering, 3 (2001) 146–150.
7. J. Cervenka, L. Jendel, V. Smilauer, Modeling of crack development in young concrete in young concrete, VIII International Conference on Fracture Mechanics of Concrete and Concrete Structures, FraCos-8, (2017) 1–11.
8. D. P. Bentz, Transient plane source measurement of the thermal properties of hydrating cement pastes, Materials and Structures, 40 (2007) 1073–1080.
9. M. Cervera, J. Oliver, T. Prato, Thermo-chemo-mechanical model for concrete: hydration and aging, Journal of Engineering Mechanics, 125 (9) (1999) 1018–1027.
10. B. Kuriakose, B. N. Rao, G. R. Dodagoudar, Modeling of early age concrete temperature distribution in thick rafts, 5th International Congress on Computational Mechanics and Simulation, (2014) 10–13.
11. H. Abeka, S. Agyeman, M. A. Asamoah, Thermal effect of mass concrete structures in the tropics: experimental, modeling and parametric studies, Cogent Engineering, 4(2017) 1278297.
12. W. G. J. Prasanna, A. P. Subhashini, Cracking due to temperature gradient in concrete, International on Sustainable Built Environment (ICSBE), Kandy, (2010) 496–504.

CHAPTER 13

A Study on the Economic Perspective of Utilizing Liquid Tanks as Dynamic Vibration Absorbers in Building Structures

Tanmoy Konar

Research Scholar, Department of Civil Engineering,
IIEST, Shibpur, Howrah, India,
Corresponding Author: 3tanmoykonar@gmail.com

Aparna (Dey) Ghosh

Professor, Department of Civil Engineering,
IIEST, Shibpur, Howrah, India,
aparna@civil.iiests.ac.in

Abstract

Traditional code-based building designs attempt to ensure non-collapse criteria under disastrous events such as severe earthquakes, strong cyclones, etc. However, the buildings usually become unfit for use after such extreme events. To keep buildings functional post-disaster, dynamic vibration absorbers (DVAs) can be used, which can lower the energy dissipation demand on the building structure and thereby reduce damage. Two basic configurations of the DVA, namely, the tuned mass damper (TMD) and the tuned liquid damper (TLD) are popular for use in buildings. A partially full liquid tank acts as a TLD, while a full liquid tank may be utilized as the auxiliary mass of a TMD. The tuned dampers have several advantages, and the chief amongst them is their cost-effectiveness. When liquid-filled tanks are considered as TLD or TMD, the cost would reduce further. In this paper, cost-related data from practical installations of liquid-filled tanks as DVAs are analyzed. It is observed that the installation of a DVA in the form of a liquid-filled tank with an additional expenditure of only 0.03% to 1.0% can enhance the effective structural damping ratio by 1.5% to 4.5%, which is significant. When compared with other dampers, liquid-filled tanks as tuned dampers are found to be economical in most cases. For further illustration, the cost of installation of a TLD in an example building is calculated and compared with that of a TMD with sold auxiliary mass.

Keywords: dynamic vibration absorber, tuned mass damper, tuned liquid damper, liquid-filled tanks, cost-effectiveness, cost of damper.

1. Introduction

Building structures are vulnerable to lateral dynamic loads that act during disastrous events such as severe earthquakes and strong cyclonic winds. The traditional methods of code-prescribed design provide the provision for combining the effect of these occasional dynamic loads on the structures with that of the dead loads and live loads. The primary focus of these code-based design procedures is to ensure non-collapse conditions under such severe natural calamities. These approaches would certainly reduce the loss of human lives, but the buildings are likely to become unsuitable for use after the disaster has occurred. Only major renovation and rehabilitation could make such buildings usable. In extreme cases, such damaged buildings are required to be demolished. These have a huge economic impact. To avoid the financial burden, structural vibration control measures can be adopted in the buildings. Structural vibration control measures can limit the damage of the buildings by reducing the effect of the dynamic loads. Thus, the buildings can achieve higher performance levels and may require minimal post-disaster repair. It may be noted that the vibration control measures also come with a cost. However, the use of vibration control measures normally reduces the life-cycle cost of a building (Sarkisian et al., 2013).

The first scientific milestone in the field of structural vibration control is the innovation of the base isolation technique for building structures by Touaillon (1870) about one hundred and fifty years ago. Though the base isolation technique is significantly effective for seismic vibration control of structures, it has high cost involvement and is difficult to implement and maintain. Subsequently, several other vibration control techniques for building structures have been developed (Lago, Trabucco, & Wood, 2019). Amongst the available vibration control measures for building structures, the use of the dynamic vibration absorber (DVA) is a popular one. A DVA is an inertia based system comprising an auxiliary mass with some damping mechanism. When the DVA is in the tuned condition, that is, the frequency of the auxiliary mass is close to the frequency of the building structure, the device absorbs vibratory energy from the structure and dissipates the absorbed energy through its own damping mechanism. As a result, the energy dissipation demand on the building structure is reduced, thereby building is protected from excessive vibration. The DVAs used in building structures are broadly divided into two groups. Firstly, the tuned mass dampers (TMDs), in which the auxiliary mass is a solid and requires external stiffness and damping elements (see Fig. 13.1(a)) and secondly, the tuned liquid dampers (TLDs), where the auxiliary mass comprises of liquid, normally water, in a partially filled container. The stiffness and damping of the TLD system are derived from the liquid motion during vibration (see Fig. 13.1(b)). Both forms of tuned dampers are inherently stable and reliable vibration control devices. However, the chief advantage of the DVAs is their relatively low cost as compared to other energy dissipation devices, such as friction dampers, fluid viscous dampers, etc. Sometimes

tanks full of water are also considered as the auxiliary mass of a TMD system. Detailed deliberation on the use of water-filled tanks as tuned dampers can be found in several literature (Konar & Ghosh, 2021b, 2021c; Nagase, 2000). Here it is pertinent to mention that, there are different types of active and semi-active DVAs. However, in this article, the term DVA refers to the passive DVA, which is the most common form of DVA for structural control purposes. As per the 'rule of thumb', the cost of vibration control devices is approximately 2% to 2.5% of the total construction cost for typical buildings (Tse, Kwok, & Tamura, 2012). However, when an active or a semi-active damper system is considered, the cost is likely to increase, and this is why these types of dampers are not so commonly considered for building structures.

As mentioned, the use of water-filled tanks as DVA is expected to reduce the cost further as water is cheaper than any other construction material (Konar & Ghosh, 2021c). However, there is no comprehensive study available on the economic perspective of utilizing liquid tanks as DVAs in building structures. The present work aims to fill this gap. Here, the cost-related data from the prominent real-life applications of DVAs in the form of liquid-filled tanks in buildings are analyzed. The cost of installations of liquid-filled tanks as TLDs as well as TMDs is also compared with the installation cost of other types of passive dampers. Next, to further highlight the economic benefits of DVAs in the form of liquid-filled tanks, the cost of installation of a liquid tank damper and of a TMD with sold auxiliary mass, for an example building structure, are evaluated for comparison.

2. Cost of DVAs in the form of Liquid-Filled Tanks

In this study, the cost and performance related data of significant real-life installations of DVAs in the form of

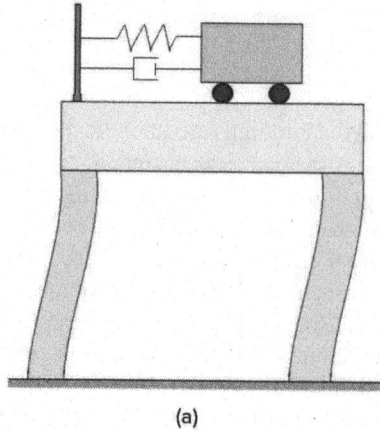

(a)

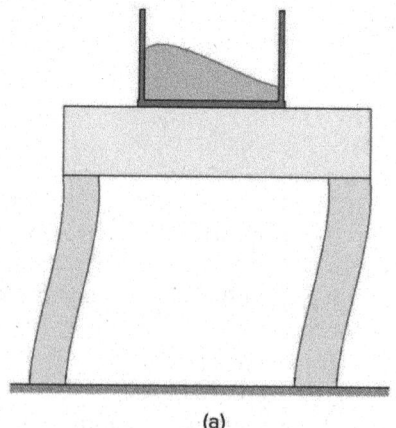

(a)

Fig. 13.1   Simplified model of building structure with two basic configurations of dynamic vibration absorber (DVA) (a) tuned mass damper (TMD), (b) tuned liquid damper (TLD).

liquid-filled tanks are analyzed to have a realistic idea about their cost-effectiveness. To compare the data obtained from various sources, the cost of the damper is expressed as a percentage of the total cost of construction of the building and represented by P_d. Here, P_d for both TMDs and TLDs in the form of liquid-filled tanks are studied. For example, the P_d for the pendulum type TMD system of Crystal Tower of Osaka, Japan (see Fig. 13.2(a)-(b)), the auxiliary mass of which consists of six tanks filled with icy water used for the air conditioning system, is 0.20% and the effectively added damping obtained is 2.5% (Nagase & Hisatoku, 1992). On the other hand, with P_d equal to 0.27%, bi-directional vibration control is achieved in One Bloor Street East, Toronto, Canada using a TLD (see Fig 13.3(a)-(b)) (Lago et al., 2019b; "One Bloor East"). The effective supplemental damping due to the

TLD is 2.5% along both the principal directions. The values of P_d for other significant real-life applications of water-filled tanks as DVA are presented in Table 13.1. The data in Table 1 reflects that P_d for the DVAs in the form of a water-filled tank is in the range of 0.03% to 1.0% and that the dampers provide an effective supplemental damping ratio in the range 1.5% to 4.5%, which is significant.

Here, the authors would like to point out that despite being an integral component of building structures, normally overhead tanks for water supply are not considered as part of the structural vibration control mechanism. This is due to the frequent fluctuation in liquid mass in such tanks, which would lead to fluctuation in damper frequency, ultimately causing detuning of the damper (Konar & Ghosh, 2021a).

(a)

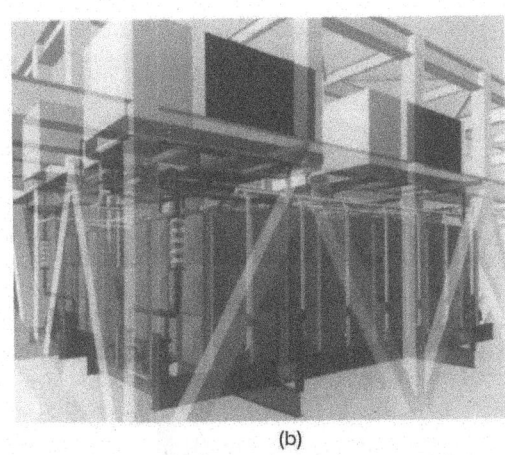
(b)

Fig. 13.2 Crystal Tower, Osaka, Japan (a) View of the completed building (https://fr.m.wikipedia.org/wiki/Fichier:Crystal_Tower_Osaka_20060321-001.jpg), (b) one of the tanks of icy water used as auxiliary mass of TMD system (Nagase & Hisatoku, 1992).

(a)

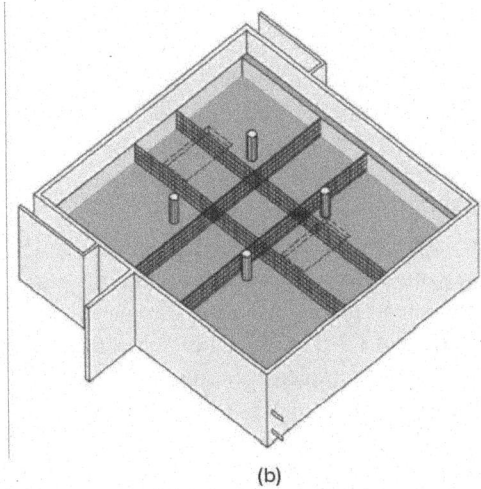
(b)

Fig. 13.3 One Bloor Street East, Toronto, Canada (a) View of the completed building (https://commons.wikimedia.org/wiki/File:OneBloorEastToronto2018.jpg), (b) TLD used in the building (Lago et al., 2019).

Table 13.1 Damper cost as percentage of total building construction cost (P_d) for DVAs in the form of water tanks.

Building	City	Country	Height (m)	Water tank used as	Damping ratio of building without DVA	Effective added damping ratio by DVA	P_d	Reference
Hilton Fukuoka Sea Hawk	Fukuoka	Japan	143	Auxiliary mass of pendulum type TMD	1.1%	3.6%	0.03%	(Nagase, 2000)
Trump International Hotel and Tower	Vancouver	Canada	187	TLD	1.75%	2.0%	0.13%	(Lago et al., 2019; "Trump International Hotel and Tower (Vancouver)," n.d.)
Crystal Tower	Osaka	Japan	157	Auxiliary mass of pendulum type TMD	0.5%	2.5%	0.20%	(Nagase & Hisatoku, 1992)
One Bloor Street East	Toronto	Canada	255	Bi-directional TLD[†]	Data not available	2.5% along both principle directions	0.27%	(Lago et al., 2019; "One Bloor East," n.d.)
L-Tower	Toronto	Canada	234	Bi-directional TLD[†]	1.5%	4.5 % (1st modal direction) 3.5% (2nd modal direction)	0.43%	(Lago et al., 2019; Robinson, 2015)
South tower of One Rincon Hill	San Francisco	USA	188	TLD	1.5%	1.5%	1.00%	(Lago et al., 2019)
Highcliff Apartments	Hong Kong	China	252	TLD	1.5%	1.6%	1.00%	(Lago et al., 2019)

[†] A bi-directional TLD is designed to control structural vibration along two principal axes using a single damper.

Further, deep tanks do not inherently possess high energy dissipation properties as the sloshing mass is much less as compared to the impulsive mass in such tanks. Research to overcome these limitations is being carried out (Konar & Ghosh, 2021a).

3. Cost of Other Popular Passive Dampers

Now, to put the cost of DVAs in the form of liquid-filled tanks into perspective, let us look at the cost of other conventional passive dampers. Table 13.2 presents a list of seven prominent buildings where passive dampers other than DVAs in the form of liquid-filled tanks are used. The other types of passive dampers considered in Table 13.2 are the TMD with solid auxiliary mass, the viscoelastic coupling dampers, the viscous damper, and the fluid viscous dampers. It can be observed from Table 13.2 that the other types of passive dampers provide effective supplemental damping in the range of 1% to 5%, for which P_d lies in the range of 0.9% to 4.0%.

It is clear from Tables 1 and 2 that P_d varies from building to building and there is no direct correlation between effective added damping and P_d. However, DVAs in the form of liquid-filled tanks, in general, are cheaper than other conventional passive dampers. The average P_d for DVAs in the form of water tanks is 0.44%. On the other hand, for other conventional passive dampers, the average P_d is 2.03%. Thus the TLDs or TMDs in the form of water tanks have a clear cost advantage.

4. Cost Comparison between TLD and TMD for Example Building

It is clear from sections 2 and 3 that DVAs in the form of water tanks are, in general, more economical than other conventional passive dampers. However, the data for the DVAs in the form of water tanks and other conventional passive dampers presented in those sections are from different buildings. Now, to make a direct cost comparison, two cases of design of vibration control systems for an example residential building are considered in this section. In 'Case I', a TMD with solid auxiliary mass is designed; whereas, in 'Case II', a TLD in the form of a liquid sloshing tank is designed for the same example building. The building is a 10-story reinforced concrete-framed structure with aerated concrete (AC) block walls. The typical floor plan and

Table 13.2 Damper cost as percentage of total building construction cost (P_d) for other conventional dampers.

Building	City	Country	Height (m)	Type of damper	Damping ratio of building without DVA	Effective added damping ratio by DVA	P_d	Reference
Citicorp Building	New York City	USA	279	TMD (solid auxiliary mass)	1%	4%	0.9%	("Citicorp Center"; Connor, 2003)
454 Yonge	Toronto	Canada	200	Viscoelastic coupling dampers	Data not available	1%	1%	(Lago et al., 2019)
San Diego Central Court-house	San Diego	USA	119	Viscous damper	5%	5%	1.2%	(Barista, 2018; Sarkisian et al., 2013)
Connor Tower,	Manila,	Philippines	174.5	Viscoelastic coupling dampers	Data not available	2%	2%	(Lago et al., 2019)
Wuhan Poly Cultural Plaza	Wuhan	China	212	Viscous damper	Data not available	1%	2.5%	(Lago et al., 2019)
John Hancock Tower	Boston	USA	241	TMD (solid auxiliary mass)	0.9%	2.6%	2.6%	("Hancock Tower Now to Get Dampers," 1975; Lago et al., 2019)
Allianz Tower	Milan	Italy	202	Fluid viscous dampers	1%	4%	4%	(Castellano, Borella, Pigouni, & Infanti, 2017; Lago et al., 2019)

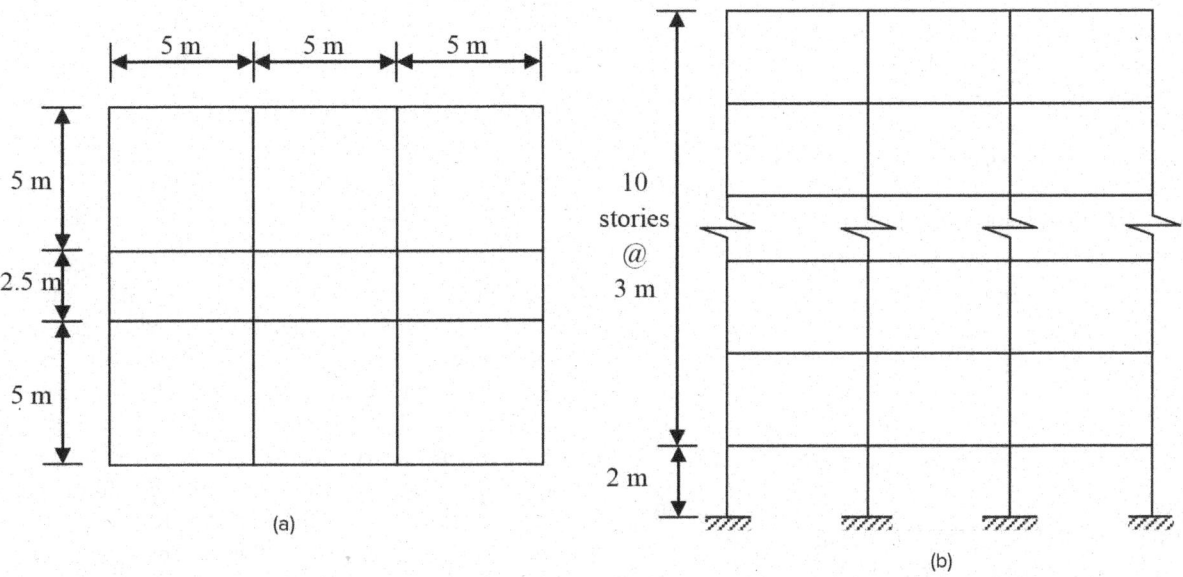

Fig. 13.4 Schematic drawing of example building frame (a) typical floor plan and (b) elevation.

elevation of the example building are shown in Fig. 13.4. The salient parameters of the building structure are presented in Table 13.3. The damping ratio of the building structure is assumed as 2%. The cost of construction of the building is calculated as Rs. 403.2 lakhs based on the CPWD plinth area rates ("Plinth area rates 2019").

Table 13.3 Salient parameters of example building structure.

Parameters of building structure	Value
Characteristic cube compressive strength of concrete	25 MPa
Characteristic yield strength of steel	500 MPa
Size of column	0.350 m × 0.350 m
Size of beam	0.250 m × 0.400 m
Thickness of floor/ roof slab	0.135 m
Thickness of external wall (30% open for doors and windows)	0.250 m
Thickness of internal wall (30% open for doors and windows)	0.100 m
Density of AC block	6.5 kN/m³

The building structure is analyzed using STAAD Pro. V8i software. The frequency and the modal mass corresponding to the first mode of vibration of the building structure are determined as 2.14 s (frequency = 0.47 Hz) and 1279.88 ton respectively. The design of the structural vibration control devices are carried out to control the fundamental mode of vibration of the building structure, which is henceforth denoted as an equivalent single-degree-of-freedom (SDOF) structural system with the natural period (T_s) and mass (M_s), equal to the period and modal mass for the first mode of vibration of the building structure. For both the cases of damper design, a practical value of the mass ratio (μ) equal to 0.5% is considered. For simplicity, the tuning ratio is taken as unity in both cases. Thus, for both cases, the frequency of the damper would be equal to the structural frequency, that is, 0.47 Hz. Again, for the considered mass ratio, the optimum damping ratio for both the dampers, ξ_d, is determined as 3.5% using the following equation (Bakre & Jangid, 2007).

$$\xi_d = \sqrt{\frac{\left(1 - \frac{\mu}{4}\right)\mu}{4\left(1 - \frac{\mu}{2}\right)(1 + \mu)}} \qquad (1)$$

4.1 Case I: TMD with Solid Auxiliary Mass

For the considered mass ratio, the mass of the auxiliary mass of the TMD is 6399 kg. To have the required frequency, the auxiliary mass has to be connected with the building structure with a spring having a stiffness of 55.2 kN/m. Again, to provide the optimum damping ratio, the dashpot system of the TMD should have a damping coefficient equal to 13.3 N-s/m.

In the TMD, the solid auxiliary mass normally consists of blocks of metals, such as steel. In addition to the cost of

the metal block, the spring element, dashpot system, and the preparation of a smooth surface required for the movement of the auxiliary mass during vibration contribute significantly to the overall cost of the TMD. For a conventional TMD with solid auxiliary mass, the cost is approximately Rs. 175 per kg of the mass of the damper (Ruiz, Taflanidis, Lopez-Garcia, & Vetter, 2016) (considering 1 USD = Rs. 70). Thus, the cost of the damping device in 'Case I' is Rs. 11.2 lakhs, which is equal to 2.78% of the cost of construction of the building.

4.2 Case II: TLD

Let us consider that the TLD consists of a cylindrical tank with a circular cross-section. The liquid residing in the damper is water, which experiences sloshing during vibration. Now, in the case of the TLD, all the liquid mass present in the damper does not participate in energy dissipation. In a sloshing type TLD, the energy dissipation is chiefly derived from the portion of liquid mass that participates in the fundamental sloshing mode. Accordingly, the fundamental sloshing frequency of the TLD is tuned to the structural frequency. The liquid mass that participates in the fundamental sloshing mode, M_d, and the fundamental sloshing frequency, f, of the TLD are given by (Abramson, Chu, & Ransleben Jr., 1961),

$$M_d = \frac{\pi \rho d^3}{17.6} \tanh\left(\frac{3.68h}{d}\right) \qquad (2)$$

$$f = \frac{1}{2\pi}\left[\frac{3.682g}{d}\tanh\left(\frac{3.682h}{d}\right)\right]^{1/2} \qquad (3)$$

Here, ρ, d, h, and g respectively represent the mass density of the damper liquid, the diameter of the damper tank, the height of liquid in the tank at rest condition, and the gravitational acceleration.

The mass density of water and the value of the gravitational acceleration are taken as 1000 kg/m³ and 9.81 m/s² respectively. Now, to effectively provide the design mass ratio of 0.5%, M_d should be equal to 0.005 times of M_s, and at the same time, the fundamental liquid sloshing frequency should be equal to the structural frequency. Let us consider the TLD tank has a diameter of 3.5 m. Using Eqs. (2) and (3), the height of liquid in the tank at rest condition is calculated as 1.146 m. Thus, the TLD tank would hold 11026 liters of water. Here, it may be noted that, often, the inherent damping of the TLD is not sufficient to provide required damping for optimum performance of the damper. Thus flow damping devices, such as baffles, screens, etc. are used to enhance the damping of TLD (Konar & Ghosh, 2021b). For the present design, horizontal annular baffles projecting out of the wall of the damper tank are considered as flow damping devices. The energy dissipation by the horizontal annular baffles is given in terms of effective damping ratio as (Langner, 1963),

$$\xi_b = 22.627\left(1 - \frac{w}{d}\right)^{1.5}\left(\frac{w}{d}\right)^{1.5}\left(\frac{h}{dN}\right)^{0.5}\sum_{i=1}^{N} e^{-4.6h(2i-1)/(dN)}$$ (4)

Here, w, and N stand for the width of the baffles, and the number of baffles respectively.

Let us consider that 2 horizontal baffles are fixed at $0.9h$ and $0.8h$ from the bottom of the TLD (Konar & Ghosh, 2021c). Now, using Eq. (4), the value of w/d is calculated as 0.037, for which the damping ratio of the TLD would be equal to the required optimum damping ratio of 3.5%.Thus, the designed TLD requires 2 annular horizontal baffles having an outer diameter of 3.5 m and a width of 0.13 m. Considering that 10 mm thick mild steel plates are used for the baffles, and the mass density of mild steel is equal to 7850 kg/m³, the total steel required for the baffles is 224 kg. From a market survey, the cost of mild steel baffle plates including fixing is about Rs. 500 per kg. Thus, the total cost involvement for the baffles is Rs. 1.12 lakhs. Again, the cost of construction of a TLD tank would be similar to the cost of construction of an overhead water tank which is Rs. 18 per liter of the tank capacity as per the CPWD guidelines ("Plinth area rates 2019"). Here, as already determined, the volume of water to be kept in the TLD is equal to 11026 liters. Thus the cost of construction of the TLD tank is Rs. 1.98 lakhs. Therefore, the total cost of the TLD system with the horizontal baffles is Rs. 3.1 lakhs, which is equal to 0.77% of the total construction cost of the building.

This study clearly highlights that for the vibration control of the considered example building, installation of a TLD is a much cheaper alternative as compared to the installation of a TMD with solid auxiliary mass. Further, the costs of the dampers obtained in this section are in line with the cost of dampers in real-life installations presented in sections 2 and 3.

5. Conclusion

While traditional code-prescribed designs of building primarily focus to ensure non-collapse criteria, vibration control devices can reduce the damage by lowering the energy dissipation demand on building structures. Thus, vibration control devices can be used to help keep buildings functional and reduce repair costs in the post-disaster scenario. However, it is important to look into the economic perspective of using vibration control devices in buildings. The costs of commonly used passive vibration control devices in significant real-life installations in building structures are analyzed. The semi-active and active dampers are kept out of the preview of the present study as they generally have a higher cost than their passive counterparts. It is found that the average cost of DVA in the form of a water-filled tank is 0.44% of the total building construction cost. Here it is pertinent to mention that liquid-filled tanks are used in both the basic forms of DVAs, namely, TLD and TMD. The present study has also considered both types of cases. It is observed that when other popular passive vibration control devices, such as TMD with solid mass, viscous damper, viscoelastic coupling dampers, etc. are used, the average cost of the damping devices is increased to 2.03%. The cost of a TMD with solid auxiliary mass and of a TLD in the form of a liquid sloshing tank having equivalent characteristics are estimated for a 10-story example building and the TLD is found to be more than three-and-half times cheaper. Thus, the DVA in the form of a water-filled tank is one of the most economic options for structural vibration control. Further, the DVAs in the form of liquid tanks can be made more cost-effective by integrating the dampers with the different utility water tanks of the building, such as those for firefighting, etc. Overhead water tanks atop buildings have good potential to act as economically viable vibration control systems, but that has not yet been exploited.

REFERENCES

1. Abramson, H. N., Chu, W.-H., & Ransleben Jr., G. E. (1961). Representation of Fuel Sloshing in Cylindrical Tanks by an Equivalent Mechanical Model. *American Rocket Society Journal*, *31*(12), 1697–1705.

2. Bakre, S. V., & Jangid, R. S. (2007). Optimum parameters of tuned mass damper for damped main system. *Structural Control and Health Monitoring*, *14*(3), 448–470.

3. Barista, D. (2018). High court, big impact: San Diego Central Courthouse. *Building Design & Construction*. Retrieved from https://www.bdcnetwork.com/high-court-big-impact-san-diego-central-courthouse

4. Castellano, M. G., Borella, R., Pigouni, A. E., & Infanti, S. (2017). Wind and Earthquake Damping System for the Isozaki/Allianz Tower in Milan, Italy. *Proceedings of Eurosteel 2017*, *1*(2–3), 1447–1456.

5. Citicorp Center. (n.d.). Retrieved July 25, 2021, from https://www.pbs.org/wgbh/buildingbig/wonder/structure/citicorp.html

6. Connor, J. J. (2003). *Introduction to Structural Motion Control*. Prentice Hall Pearson Education. Hancock Tower Now to Get Dampers. (1975). *Engineering News Record*.

7. Konar, T., & Ghosh, A. D. (2021a). Development of a novel tuned liquid damper with floating base for converting deep tanks into effective vibration control devices. *Advances in Structural Engineering*, *24*(2), 401–407.

8. Konar, T., & Ghosh, A. D. (2021b). Flow Damping Devices in Tuned Liquid Damper for Structural Vibration Control: A Review. *Arch Comput Methods Eng*, *28*(4), 2195–2207.

9. Konar, T., & Ghosh, A. D. (2021c). Use of deep liquid-containing tanks as dynamic vibration absorbers for lateral vibration control of structures: A review. *Iranian Journal of*

Science and Technology, Transactions of Civil Engineering, In Press. https://doi.org/10.1007/s40996-021-00679-8

10. Lago, A., Trabucco, D., & Wood, A. (2019). Damping Technologies for Tall Buildings. In *Elsevier Inc.*

11. Langner, G. (1963). *A preliminary analysis for optimum design of ring and partition antislosh buffles. Southwest Research Institute. Technical Report No. 7 April.*

12. Nagase, T. (2000). Earthquake Records Observed in Tall Buildings With Tuned Pendulum Mass Damper. *12WCEE,* Auckland.

13. Nagase, T., & Hisatoku, T. (1992). Tuned-Pendulum Mass Damper Installed in Crystal Tower. *The Structural Design of Tall Buildings, 1*(1), 35–56.

14. One Bloor East. (n.d.). Retrieved July 25, 2021, from https://urbantoronto.ca/database/projects/one-bloor-east

15. Plinth area rates 2019. (2019). In *Director General, CPWD.*

16. Robinson, M. (2015, November 22). Safety concerns over crane holding up completion of L Tower. *Toronto Star.*

17. Ruiz, R., Taflanidis, A. A., Lopez-Garcia, D., & Vetter, C. R. (2016). Life-cycle based design of mass dampers for the Chilean region and its application for the evaluation of the effectiveness of tuned liquid dampers with floating roof. *Bulletin of Earthquake Engineering, 14*(3), 943–970.

18. Sarkisian, M., Lee, P., Hu, L., Garai, R., Tsui, A., & Reis, E. (2013). Achieving enhanced seismic design using viscous damping device technologies. *Structures Congress 2013: Bridging Your Passion with Your Profession,* 2729–2744.

19. Touaillon, J. (1870). *Patent No. 99973.* USA: United State Patent Office.

20. Trump International Hotel and Tower (Vancouver). (n.d.). Retrieved July 25, 2021, from https://en.wikipedia.org/wiki/Trump_International_Hotel_and_Tower_(Vancouver)

21. Tse, K. T., Kwok, K. C. S., & Tamura, Y. (2012). Performance and Cost Evaluation of a Smart Tuned Mass Damper for Suppressing Wind-Induced Lateral-Torsional Motion of Tall Structures. *Journal of Structural Engineering, 138*(4), 514–525.

CHAPTER 14

Smart Shelters for Multi Disasters—A Framework with Cloud Technology and Measurement Devices

K. Sasikala
Wind Engineering Lab,
CSIR-Structural Engineering Research Centre,
CSIR campus, Taramani, Chennai - 600 113, India.
sasikala@serc.res.in

P. Harikrishna
Wind Engineering Lab,
CSIR-Structural Engineering research Centre,
CSIR campus, Taramani, Chennai - 600 113, India.
hari@serc.res.in

S. Thamarai Selvi
Department of Computer Technology, MIT Campus,
Anna University, Chennai - 600 044, India.
Vice Chancellor at Thiruvalluvar University, Vellore,
Tamil Nadu, India.
thamaraiselvis@gmail.com

N. Lakshmanan
Wind Engineering Lab,
CSIR-Structural Engineering research Centre,
CSIR campus, Taramani, Chennai - 600 113, India.

Abstract

"CSIR-SERC - under Ministry of Science and Technology, Government of India, Chennai unit, Tamil Nadu, India", approached by the 'Indian and German Red Cross' and 'KFW, Germany' to provide an appropriate 'design-solution' for the 'Cyclone Shelters'. CSIR-SERC-Chennai, designed a 'Stilted and Aerodynamically shaped Cyclone-Shelter' for use in 'Orissa coast' with specialized foundation and raised ground level to reduce the effects of storm-surge. All the existing '23 Cyclone-Shelters in Orissa', are based on the 'Design given by CSIR-SERC-Chennai'. The lives of nearly 46,000 people, who took refuge in these shelters, were saved during the Orissa-Super-Cyclone in 1999. At CSIR-SERC, Wind Engineering Lab, Disaster-Mitigation/Management has been one of the thrust areas of R&D over the past two decades and continuing with upgradation of techniques and technology. Recently "Cloud technology/Cloud Environment for Data-Acquisition/DataBase-generation" and "Data-Mining/Data-Mining-Algorithms towards "Data-Fabric/IaaS-Platform/HYBRID-CLOUD" has been proposed/adopted/ tested as a 'FRAMEWORK' for the PhD thesis work, towards 'Cyclone-Disaster Mitigation/Management/DSS', this paper is an extension of PhD thesis work. The Permanent/Emergency/Temporary Shelters for disasters can be converted as 'Smart-Shelters', by 'Measuring-Devices' with Cloud-Computing/ Data-Mining technologies. 'Authenticated Decision-Makers', from village nodal centres/ District headquarters/ state offices can view/ analyse/predict/follow the condition of the shelters and take 'Quick Decisions'.

Keywords: Smart Shelters, Multi Disasters, Measurement Devices, Cloud/Data Mining Technologies

1. Introduction

A "Smart House", is a 'Home' that has highly 'Advanced', 'Automated' systems to control and monitor any function of a house; 'lighting, temperature control, multi-media, security, window and door operations, air quality', or any other task of necessity or comfort performed by a home's resident. Two things are needed to make homes truly "smart," writes 'research journalist Ira Brodsky' in *Computerworld.* "First are sensors, actuators, and appliances that obey commands and provide status information." These digital devices are already omnipresent in our appliances. "Second are protocols and tools that enable all of these devices, regardless of vendor, to communicate with each other," says Brodsky. This is the problem, but Brodsky believes that "smartphone apps, communication hubs, and cloud-based services are enabling practical solutions that can be implemented right now." However, smart home technology is real, and it's becoming increasingly sophisticated. Coded signals are sent through the home's wiring/wirelessly to switches and outlets that are programmed to operate appliances and electronic devices in every part of the house. Home automation can be especially useful for the elderly, people with physical or cognitive impairments, and disabled persons who wish to live independently. Home technology is the toy of the super-wealthy, like Bill and Melinda Gates' home in Washington State. Called Xanadu 2.0, the Gates' house is so high-tech that it allows visitors to choose the mood music for each room they visit. (Ref: https://www.thoughtco.com/what-is-a-smart-house-domotics-177572, "The race to create smart homes is on by Ira Brodsky", Computerworld, May 3, 2016)

As verbs, the difference between 'Housing and Shelter' is that 'housing is house' while 'shelter is, to provide cover from damage, to shield, to protect'. The shelters types are many and few are Air-raid shelter, Animal shelter, Bivouac shelter, Blast shelter, Bus shelter, Emergency shelter, Fallout shelter, Homeless shelter. (Ref: https://wikidiff.com/housing/shelter). Emergency shelters and temporary housing for households who become homeless after disasters or due to economic difficulties. Emergency shelters or transitional shelters are a common issue in the aftermath of disasters. Worldwide, millions of houses are damaged/destroyed by disasters every year. People are forced to leave their homes and seek refuge, sometimes for short time and sometimes for a protracted period based on the nature of the disaster and the extent of the damage done to the housing structures. With the varying levels of affordability of the affected population as well as the external assistance provided, the time for reconstruction of houses might take even months. Such delays sometimes lead to reluctant relocation of the affected communities. Yet, on the issue of livelihoods, some communities cannot avoid living in vulnerable locations, whereas economic constraints do not allow them to invest in stronger housing construction. (Ref:https://www.sciencedirect.com/topics/earth-and-planetary-sciences/emergency-shelter). Municipalities typically use public schools and sports complexes as emergency shelters, but these are often not adequately equipped, and such practices also have side effects. Post-disaster emergency shelter is often provided by organizations or governmental emergency management departments, in response to natural/man-made disasters, such as a cyclone, flood, fire, Epidemic diseases or earthquake. They tend to use tents or other temporary structures, or buildings normally used for another purpose, such as a church or school.

This paper explains the proposal for a framework towards, "Smart Shelters for Multi Disasters—a Framework with Cloud Technology and Measurement Devices". This paper describes the solution framework to connect any kind of 'Emergency/Disaster Shelters' through 'Multi Devices/Sensors and Cloud Computing'. 'Devices/ sensors/ transducers', will measure and acquire the required data in different formats and Cloud

Computing will connect all the 'multi format data' from different devices/ shelters/ villages/ districts/ states/ countries at 'Any time','Any where' and 'Any amount of data'. The data may be cyclone/Fire/Earthquake intensity, flood gauges, patient data or any emergency requirement of the shelters. The permanent shelters for disasters can be converted as 'smart shelters', by measuring devices with cloud computing technologies as per the requirement of the concern authority with in the time limit and also any emergency/temporary shelters also can be converted as 'smart shelters''. The authenticated decision makers from village nodal centres/ District headquarters/ state offices can view/ analyse/predict/ follow the condition of the shelters and take quick decisions.

2. Methods, Results, Discussion

'Covid-19' taught a lesson towards the requirement of disaster shelters for the affected. All the countries converted ship and train also to treat the corona patients along with the regular shelters/ schools/ colleges/ halls/ open grounds. Smart solution needed, to take time bound smart decisions to save the life of the people along with their livelihood from any kind of natural/ un expected disasters like cyclones, earthquakes, floods, fire and recently corona. As India faces, the most dire crisis experienced by any country since the start of the 'Covid-19' pandemic, the media has placed a spotlight on dying people being turned away from hospitals, patients running out of oxygen, and crematoriums on overdrive. In the face of these heart-wrenching reports, healthcare workers and the Indian public have scrambled to mobilise resources to help individuals affected by Covid-19. Most of these efforts have 'understandably focused' on short-term requirements such as 'improving access to make-shift hospital beds' and oxygen tanks. (https://scroll.in/article/993572/covid-19-crisis-india-urgently-needs-a-nationwide-shelter-at-home-directive-but-a-humane-one)

2.1 Different Types of Shelters Used for Covid-19

(Fig. 14.1 to Fig. 14.8); Covid-19 Care Centres, Fig. 14.9; 108-Ambulance used for Covid-19 Emergency as well for Treatment, Fig. 14.10; an Open Ground has been converted for the purpose of Cremation.

2.2 Different Types of Shelters Used for Multi-disaster

Cyclone shelter—CSIR-SERC, CHENNAI, INDIA

[Ref: (1. Journal of Structural Engineering, Vol.34, No.1, April-May 2007 pp. 1–13, "Cyclone and wind disaster mitigation – An overview of R & D contributions of Structural Engineering Research Centre, Dr. N. Lakshmanan...), (2. The Eighth Asia-Pacific Conference on wind Engineering,

Fig. 14.1   Covid-19 Care Centre

Fig. 14.2   Covid-19 Care Centre

Fig. 14.3   Covid-19 Care Centre

Fig. 14.4   Covid-19 Care Centre

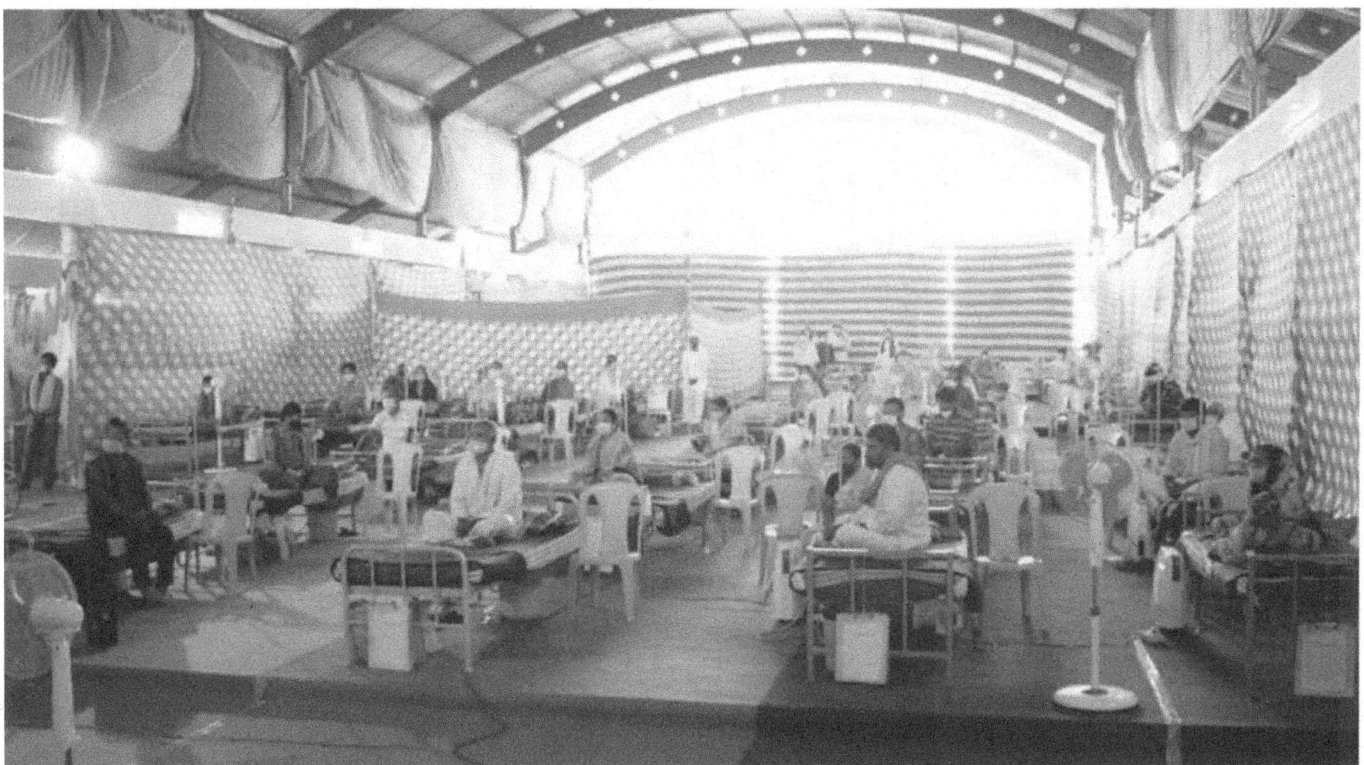

Fig. 14.5 Covid-19 Care Centre

Fig. 14.6 Covid-19 Care Centre

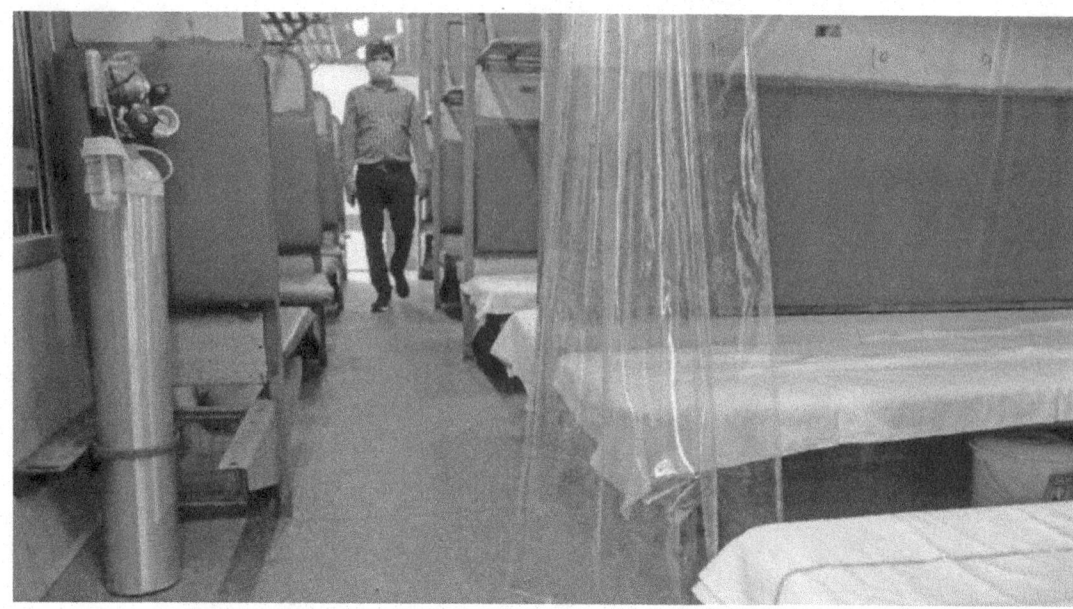

Fig. 14.7 Covid-19 Care Centre

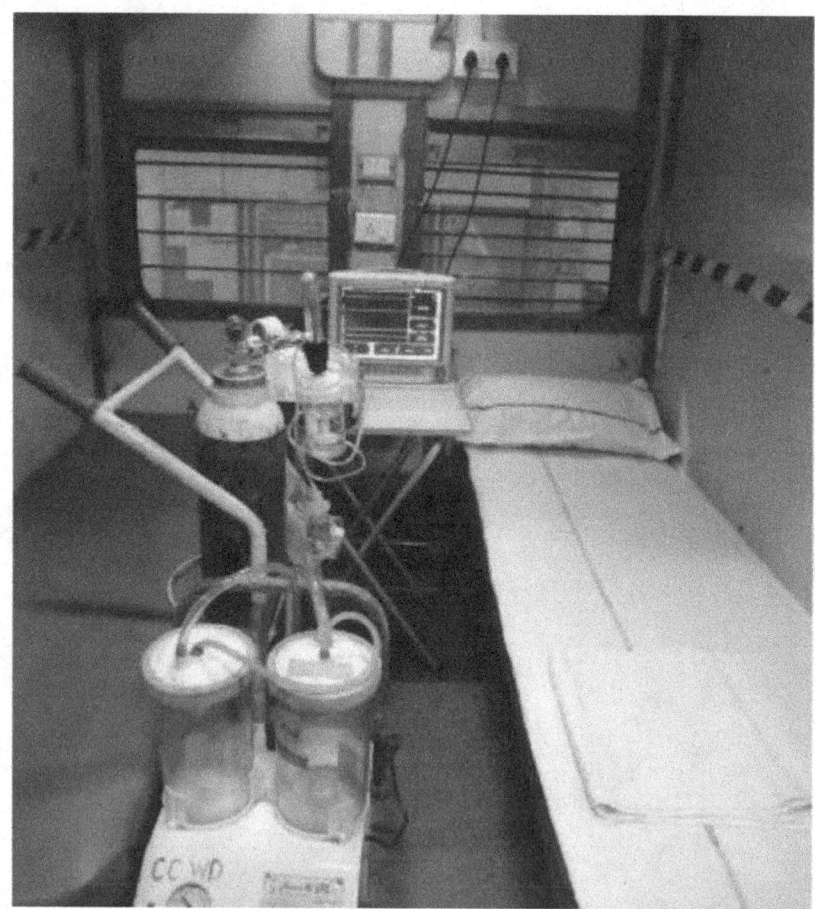

Fig. 14.8 Covid-19 Care Centre

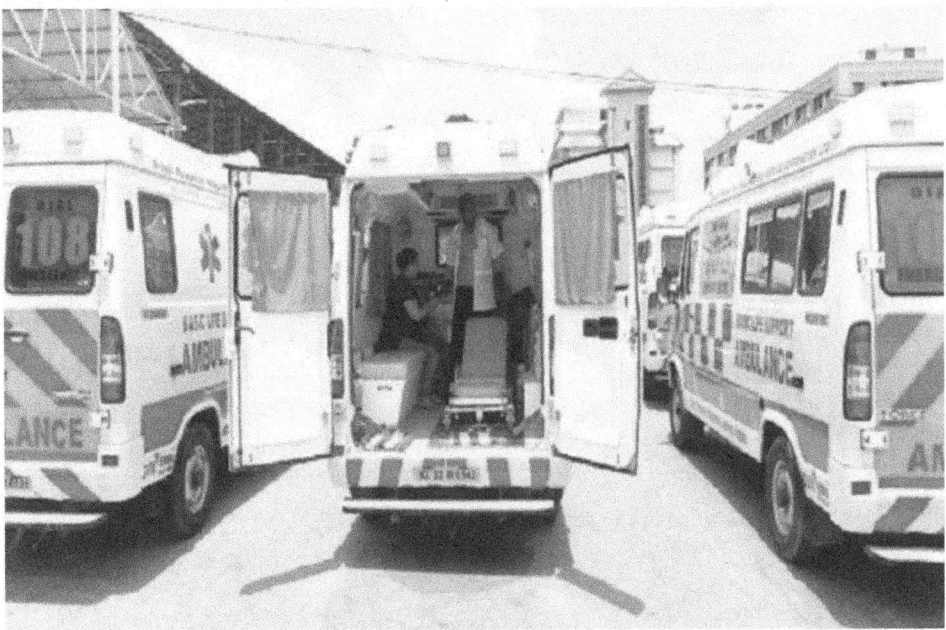

Fig. 14.9   Covid-19 Care Ambulance

Fig. 14.10   Covid-19: Open Ground-converted for Cremation
(This is to be addressed, since every Disaster is crossing this phase)

December 10–14,2013,Chennai, India.,Dr. S. Selvi Rajan)]

Cyclone Shelter Model 1: CSIR-SERC, CHENNAI, INDIA

The 'Cyclone Shelter', of Model 1(Fig. 14.11(a)) is a reinforced concrete framed structure, with rectangular plan shape with chamfered corners and projected head rooms. The overall plan dimensions at the roof level are 8.3 m x 23.0 m (excluding the projecting head rooms). The columns of the frame are circular in shape. The ground floor area is left open excepting for the columns, supporting the super structure to allow storm water to pass through, in case of storm surge. The stilt height is about 3.5 m. The entire structure is on raised platform of height 1.05 m to reduce effects of storm surge. A view of the cyclone shelter in Orissa is shown in Fig. 14.11(a).

Cyclone Shelter Model 2: CSIR-SERC, CHENNAI, INDIA

The cyclone shelter Model 2 has rectangular plan shape with aerodynamically rounded at the four corners to reduce wind load effects. The structure essentially consists of ten reinforced concrete frames. The overall length of the building between the end frames is 21.0 m. The radius of the circular curve at the inner edge has been chosen to be 1.0 m. To reduce the effects of storm surge, the ground level in the area is to be raised by 1.05mm. The building has a corridor of width 1.95 m at first floor level (=4.65 m). A stair case of width 2 m is provided to reach the corridor. The overall dimensions at the roof level are 7.65 m x 23.0 m, which includes an overhang of 1.95 m in front and 0.9 m at the rear of the building. The columns of the frame are circular in shape. The stilt height is about 3.5 m. Since the ground floor is left open,

Fig. 14.11(a)   View of cyclone shelter (Model 1)

Fig. 14.11(b)   View of cyclone shelter (Model 2)

there tends to be additional wind loading on the bottom floor slab, which has been duly considered in the design. A view of the full-scale structure of the cyclone shelter located in Orissa in shown in Fig. 14.11(b)

Earthquake—Bamboo Frame Shelter – West Java, Indonesia

About 430 Bamboo Frame Shelters were built in Indonesia following the earthquake that struck West Java in 2009. The shelter has a life span between 1-5 years, requires 3-4 days to construct, and costs about $350 per shelter. It consists of bamboo frames with woven bamboo matting walls and a length of bamboo cast-in which connects the four main columns. The hipped roof is made from terracotta roof tiles and includes a truss in the center. The floor, made from bamboo joists and panelling, is elevated to create a raised floor away from flooding. A low masonry wall surrounding the floor void creates a confined space which is filled with rubble. Nails are used to fix the floor and roof connections while bamboo pegs and rope are used to pin the frame connections. The structure is supported by five concrete bucket foundations.

Tsunami—Steel Framed shelters – Aceh, Indonesia

In response to the Tsunami that struck Indonesia in 2004 twenty thousand Steel Framed shelters were constructed. The shelter consists of a galvanized steel frame with a 24.3 degree pitched roof with metal sheets screwed to steel purlins. The

structure has six columns fixed to a base plate and an elevated floor made from timber planks connected to steel joists. Each shelter costs more than $5,000 for the material and takes four people three days to construct. The design life span of these shelters is five years.

Flood—Triangular Timber shelters – Pakistan

Flooding in Northern Pakistan caused the displacement of thousands of flood victims resulting in the construction of ten thousand Triangular Timber shelters. The cost for constructing one unit, which takes about one day, is approximately $530. The average life span of these shelters is two years. The shelter consists of 7 triangular frames and a 44 degree pitched roof made of corrugated steel nailed to purlins between the frames. A ridge pole supported by a column at each end is connected to the frame. Plastic sheeting is used to cover the roof and provide insulation inside the shelter. Rafters and columns buried into the ground make up the foundation.

3. Smart Shelters for Multi-Disasters

Human well-being is directly connected to the way we treat our planet's natural resources. Deforestation, pollution, extinction, loss of biodiversity directly impact quality of living. Destroying nature makes life harder for all of us and even more for those who are already vulnerable. (Ref:http://wwf.panda.org/lpr). Efficient design, implies efficient

Fig. 14.12   View of Earthquake Bamboo Frame Shelter (Ref: Disaster Relief Shelter; Walta Asfaw, David Headley, Nick Liza, Dan Nederhoed, Engr,339/340 Senior Design Project, Calvin College Engineering, 6 May 2013)

Fig. 14.13 View of Tsunami Steel Frame Shelter (Ref: Disaster Relief Shelter; Walta Asfaw, David Headley, Nick Liza, Dan Nederhoed, Engr,339/340 Senior Design Project, Calvin College Engineering, 6 May 2013)

Fig. 14.14 View of Flood-Triangular Timber shelter (Ref: Disaster Relief Shelter; Walta Asfaw, David Headley, Nick Liza, Dan Nederhoed, Engr,339/340 Senior Design Project, Calvin College Engineering, 6 May 2013)

utilisation of space by optimising resources. Building design, by way of its siting on the land, orientation to sun and wind, massing of the built and the unbuilt, organisation of activities, size and scale of spaces among other things, can favourably influence not only living comforts, but also resource consumption and energy intake. (Ref:https://www. downtoearth.org.in/blog/living-with-nature-23955).

'Real time Embedded Systems', 'Decision Support Systems', 'Online Data Acquisition Sytems', 'Offline Processing Systems', 'Data Base Generation', 'Artificial Intelligence',

'Artificial Neural Network', 'Machine Learning', 'IOT', 'Cyber Physical System', 'Cloud Computing', 'Big Data', 'Data Mining', 'Data Fabric' and relevant Algorithms/ Models capabilities will finally give the **'Smart Buildings/ shelters/homes'**. Smart TVs connect to the internet to access content through applications, smart lighting systems, such as Hue from Philips Lighting Holding B.V., can detect when occupants are in the room and adjust lighting as needed. Smart lightbulbs can also regulate themselves based on daylight availability. Smart thermostats, such as Nest from Nest Labs

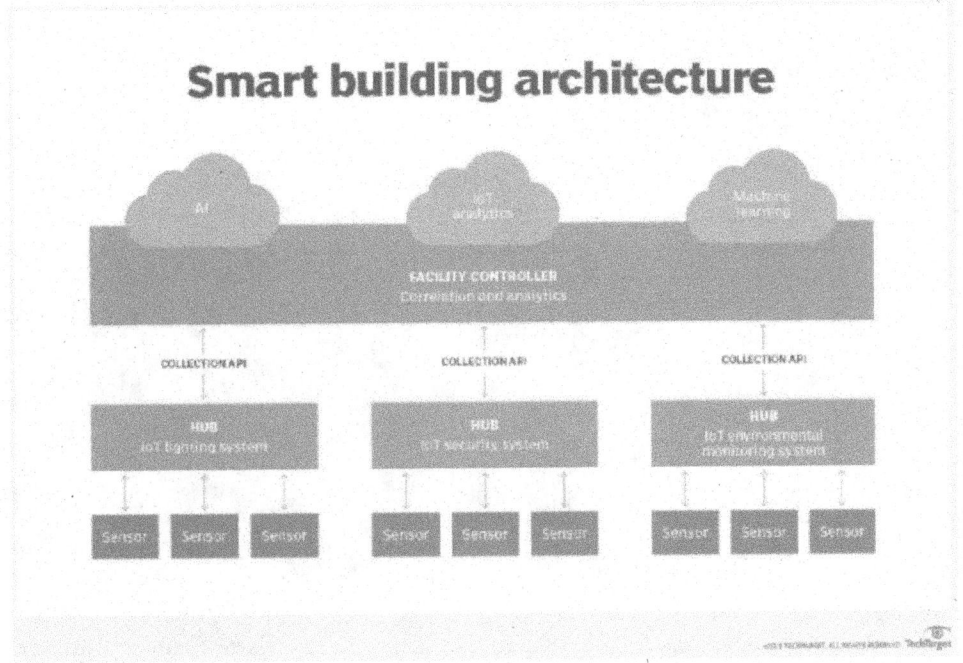

Fig. 14.15 View of 'Smart Building Architecture'
(Ref: https://internetofthingsagenda.techtarget.com/definition/smart-home-or-building)

Inc., come with integrated Wi-Fi, allowing users to schedule, monitor and remotely control home temperatures. These devices also learn homeowners' behaviours and automatically modify settings to provide residents with maximum comfort and efficiency. Smart thermostats can also report energy use and remind users to change filters, among other things. Using smart locks and garage-door openers, users can grant or deny access to visitors. Smart locks can also detect when residents are near and unlock the doors for them. With smart security cameras, residents can monitor their homes when they are away or on vacation. Smart motion sensors are also able to identify the difference between residents, visitors, pets and burglars, and can notify authorities if suspicious behaviour is detected. Pet care can be automated with connected feeders. Houseplants and lawns can be watered by way of connected timers. Kitchen appliances of all sorts are available, including smart coffee makers that can brew a fresh cup automatically at a programmed time; smart refrigerators that keep track of expiration dates, make shopping lists or even create recipes based on ingredients currently on hand; slower cookers and toasters; and, in the laundry room, washing machines and dryers. Household system monitors may, for example, sense an electric surge and turn off appliances or sense water failures or freezing pipes and turn off the water so the basement doesn't flood, for example.

(Ref: https://internetofthingsagenda.techtarget.com/definition/smart-home-or-building)

3.1 Smart Home/Shelters Implementation

Zigbee and Z-Wave are two of the most common home automation communications protocols in use today. Both use mesh network technologies, short-range, low-power radio signals to connect smart home systems. Though both target the same smart home applications, Z-Wave has a range of 30 meters to Zigbee's 10 meters, with Zigbee often perceived as the more complex of the two. Zigbee chips are available from multiple companies, while Z-Wave chips are only available from Sigma Designs. A smart home is not a collection of disparate smart devices and appliances, but ones that work together to create a remotely controllable network. All devices are controlled by a master home automation controller (PRIVATE CLOUD), often called a smart home hub. The smart home hub is a hardware device that acts as the central point of the smart home system and is able to sense, process data and communicate wirelessly. It combines all of the disparate apps into a single smart home app that can be controlled remotely by the Decision makers on the "CLOUD ENVIRONMENT" and the proposed name is **"SHELTERS FOR DISASTERS ON CLOUD"**. Examples of smart home hubs include Amazon Echo, Google Home, Insteon Hub Pro, Samsung SmartThings and Wink Hub. In simple smart home/shelter scenarios, events can be timed or triggered. Timed events are based on a clock, for example, lowering the blinds at 6:00 p.m., while triggered events depend on actions in the

Fig. 14.16 Automation and DOMOTICS (Ref: https://www.thoughtco.com/what-is-a-smart-house-domotics-177572; Photo by Javier Pierini/The Image Bank Collection/Getty Images)

automated system, when the owner's smartphone approaches the door, the smart lock unlocks and the smart lights go on.

Machine learning and artificial intelligence (AI) are becoming increasingly popular in smart home/shelter systems, allowing home automation applications to adapt to their environments. For example, voice-activated systems, such as Amazon Echo or Google Home, contain virtual assistants that learn and personalize the smart home to the residents' preferences and patterns. The smart technologies used in the smart home are deployed in smart buildings, including lighting, energy, heating and air conditioning, and security and building access systems. Smart buildings can also connect to the smart grid. Here, smart building components and the electric grid can "talk" and "listen" to each other. With this technology, energy distribution can be managed efficiently, maintenance can be handled proactively and power outages can be responded to more quickly.

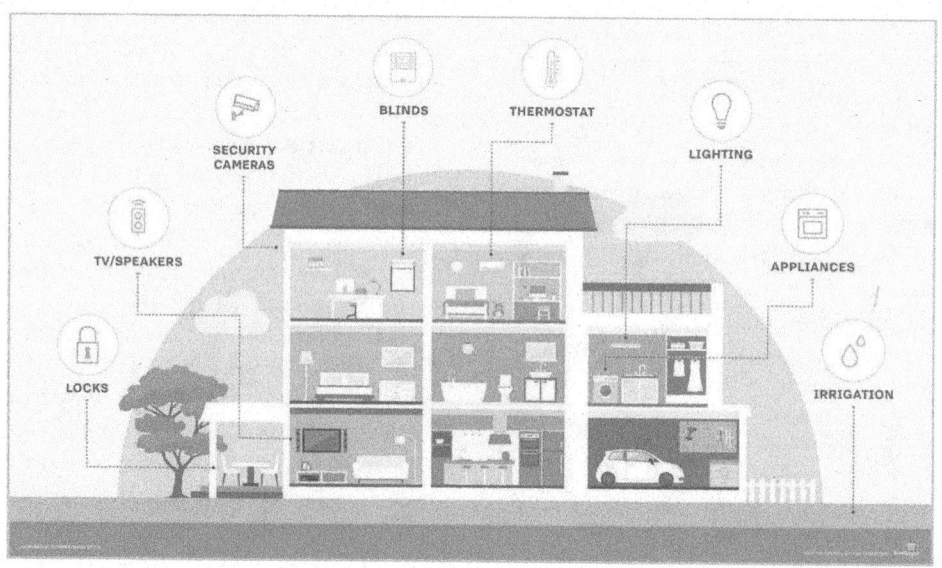

Fig. 14.17 Smart Shelter-Automation and DOMOTICS (Ref: https://internetofthingsagenda.techtarget.com/definition/smart-home-or-building)

With the 1975 release of X10 a communication protocol for home automation sends 120 kHz radio frequency (RF) bursts of digital information onto a home's existing electric wiring to programmable outlets or switches. These signals convey commands to corresponding devices, controlling how and when the devices operate. A transmitter could, for example, send a signal along the house's electric wiring, telling a device to turn on at a specific time.

A Disaster is defined as "an overwhelming ecological or man-caused occurrence that, with or without warning, disrupts the normal pattern of life. It can plunge a country into economic confusion and suffering from the need for food, shelter, clothing, medical attention, and other basic needs, as well as from the burdens of national economic infrastructure rehabilitation, possibly requiring outside assistance". **A good grasp of the phases that comprise the Disaster Risk Management Cycle is essential for understanding Emergency Shelter Management.** (Ref:https://reliefweb. int/sites/reliefweb.int/files/resources/Dominica%20 ESM%20Manual%20%28v9%29.pdf)

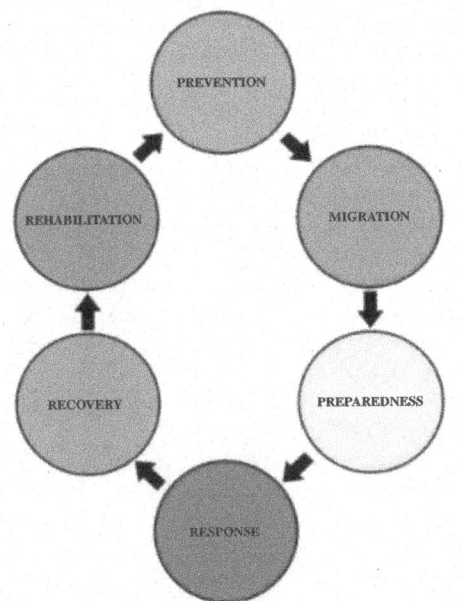

DISASTER RISK MANGEMENT CYCLE

Fig. 14.18 Disaster Risk Management Cycle (Ref: https://reliefweb.int/sites/reliefweb.int/files/resources/Dominica%20ESM%2 0Manual%20%28v9%29.pdf)

PREVENTION refers to the outright avoidance of adverse impacts of hazards and related disasters. Very often though, the complete avoidance of losses is not feasible and the task transforms to that of mitigation. MITIGATION is the lessening, or limiting of the adverse impacts of hazards and related disasters. Mitigation measures encompass

engineering techniques and hazard-resistant construction as well as improved environmental policies and public awareness. PREPAREDNESS pertains to the knowledge and capacities developed by governments, professional response and recovery organizations, communities and individuals to effectively anticipate, respond to, and recover from, the impacts of likely, imminent or current hazard events or conditions. An Early Warning System refers to the set of capacities needed to generate and disseminate timely and meaningful warning information to enable individuals, communities and organizations threatened by a hazard to prepare and to act appropriately and in sufficient time to reduce the possibility of harm or loss. RESPONSE relates to the provision of emergency services and public assistance during or immediately after a disaster in order to save lives, reduce health impacts, ensure public safety and meet the basic subsistence needs of the people affected. RECOVERY deals with the restoration and improvement where appropriate, of facilities, livelihoods and living conditions of disaster-affected communities, including efforts to reduce disaster risk factors. (UNISDR,2009). Shelter Management consists of providing assistance and protection to displaced populations living in shelters, according to the legal protection framework and minimum humanitarian standards, thus ensuring that affected populations participate in shelter daily activities. The Shelter Management House illustrates that Camp Management implies a holistic approach, and a cross-cutting sector response. (Ref:https://reliefweb.int/sites/reliefweb.int/files/resources/Dominica%20ESM%20Manual%20%28v9%29.pdf)

4. Conclusion

The time of the smart home/shelter is now. A staggering 1.15 billion annual shipments of Bluetooth smart home devices are expected by 2023 with connected home devices exceeding home/shelter automation by a ratio of three-to-one, according to a 2019 Bluetooth market update. It's no longer science fiction to control lighting or regulate a home's temperature with a voice command or pressing a button on a smart phone. Smart home technology today has become widely accepted and accessible. The majority of IoT devices are connected wirelessly to the Internet via sources like Wi-Fi, Bluetooth or ZigBee. Wi-Fi is most commonly used for high input applications and streaming data on connected devices and ZigBee is a two-step connection requiring a hub that connects devices to Bluetooth or Wi-Fi. Bluetooth, with advanced BLE or Bluetooth 5, enables long, Wi-Fi-like range in the home and compatibility with smart phones, laptops, earphones and other devices. (Ref: https://internetofthingsagenda.techtarget.com/blog/IoT-Agenda/Battery-free-smart-home-adoption-Its-possible). **Shelter is a process, not just a product.**

It goes beyond simply providing tools and tents to help people cope in the short-term, and involves enabling communities to improve their homes over time so they are better protected should another disaster occur (Ref: https://www.ifrc.org/shelter-and-settlements). Timely Decision making is possible with the information from Smart shelters, which is important at the time of Pre/During/Post Disaster Mitigation and Management.

5. Acknowledgement

I express my gratitude to

Dr.N.Lakshmanan, Former Director, CSIR-SERC, Taramani, Chennai, for the technical guidance for the subject of 'Disaster mitigation and management'.

Dr.Nagesh R Iyer, Former Director, CSIR-SERC, Taramani, Chennai, for the technical guidance for the subject of 'Disaster mitigation and management', 'Cloud Computing' and 'Data Mining'.

Dr.S.Thamarai Selvi, Former Professor & Dean, MIT, Anna University, Chennai & Vice Chancellor, Thiruvalluvar university, Vellore, Phd External Guide, for the technical guidance for the subject of 'Cloud Computing' and 'Data Mining'.

Dr.P,Hari Krishna, Chief Scientist and Head, Wind Engineering Lab, CSIR-SERC, Taramani, Chennai, Phd Internal Guide, for the technical guidance for the subject of 'Disaster mitigation and management', 'Cloud Computing' and 'Data Mining'.

REFERENCES

1. https://www.xfinity.com/hub/smart-home/home-automation
2. https://www.youngwonks.com/blog/What-is-home-automation
3. https://internetofthingsagenda.techtarget.com/definition/smart-home-or-building
4. https://stevessmarthomeguide.com/guide-home-automation/
5. https://www.elprocus.com/understanding-android-based-home-automation-systems/
6. https://www.networx.com/article/intro-to-home-automation
7. https://www.security.org/home-automation/
8. https://www.infineon.com/cms/en/discoveries/smart-home-basics/
9. https://build.com.au/what-smart-home
10. https://en.wikipedia.org/wiki/Home_automation
11. https://home.howstuffworks.com/smart-home.htm
12. https://smartofficesandsmarthomes.com/smarthomes/
13. https://www.constellation.com/energy-101/what-is-a-smart-home.html
14. https://www.androidauthority.com/what-is-a-smart-home-806483/
15. https://www.thoughtco.com/thmb/eXgq3luWUxpA8igilsM3jnIspc0=/768x0/filters:no_upscale():max_bytes(150000):strip_icc():format(webp)/domotics-200365378-011-crop-579c2eba3df78c3276bc7e1f.jpg
16. https://www.thoughtco.com/what-is-a-smart-house-domotics-177572
17. https://cdn.ttgtmedia.com/rms/onlineimages/iota-smart_building_architect_desktop.png
18. https://internetofthingsagenda.techtarget.com/blog/IoT-Agenda/Battery-free-smart-home-adoption-Its-possible
19. https://internetofthingsagenda.techtarget.com/blog/IoT-Agenda/Wireless-power-for-smart-and-secure-homes
20. https://internetofthingsagenda.techtarget.com/blog/IoT-Agenda/The-future-of-the-IoT-enabled-smart-home
21. https://internetofthingsagenda.techtarget.com/definition/smart-home-or-building
22. https://www.investopedia.com/terms/s/smart-home.asp
23. https://towardsdatascience.com/mcculloch-pitts-model-5fdf65ac5dd1
24. https://www.youtube.com/watch?v=TxGupv74KPI&t=26s
25. https://www.downtoearth.org.in/blog/living-with-nature-23955
26. https://www.cdc.gov/coronavirus/2019-ncov/global-covid-19/emergency-shelters-low-resource-global.html
27. https://emergency.unhcr.org/entry/36774/emergency-shelter-standard
28. https://link.springer.com/referenceworkentry/10.1007%2F978-1-4020-4399-4_117
29. https://www.sciencedirect.com/topics/nursing-and-health-professions/emergency-shelter
30. https://www.sciencedirect.com/topics/earth-and-planetary-sciences/emergency-shelter
31. http://www.bollisontarps.com/product/hospital-medical-frame-tent-wedding-party-marquee-tent?gclid=EAIaIQobChMIy9CjkMCX8wIVcJNm Ah01zwNqEAMYAyAAEgJ6_vD_BwE
32. https://www.humanitarianlibrary.org/sites/default/files/2014/02/DRS_FinalReport.pdf
33. https://emergency.cdc.gov/shelterassessment/pdf/315124-A_Health-Assessment-Form-for-Disaster-Shelters_FS-508.pdf
34. https://emergency.cdc.gov/shelterassessment/pdf/Shelter_Assessment_instructions_COVID508.pdf
35. https://emergency.cdc.gov/shelterassessment/pdf/Shelter_Assessment_COVID_508.pdf
36. https://emergency.cdc.gov/shelterassessment/
37. https://www.redcross.org/get-help/disaster-relief-and-recovery-services/find-an-open-shelter.html
38. https://en.wikipedia.org/wiki/Emergency_shelter
39. https://www.smartsshelters.co.nz/
40. https://www.stantec.com/en/ideas/disaster-preparedness-in-the-midst-of-covid-19
41. https://www.researchgate.net/publication/279751488_Smart_shelter_strategies-cost-effective_flood_preparedness
42. https://www.mdpi.com/1660-4601/18/16/8632/htm

43. https://www.wired.com/2013/07/ikeas-innovative-new-refugee-shelter/

44. https://www.iimcal.ac.in/sites/all/files/sirg/4-2-post-disaster-coordinating-disaster.pdf

45. https://www.gsma.com/iot/wp-content/uploads/2013/02/cl_SmartCities_emer_01_131.pdf

46. https://reliefweb.int/sites/reliefweb.int/files/resources/Dominica%20ESM%20Manual%20%28v9%29. pdf

47. https://www.ifrc.org/shelter-and-settlements

48. https://www.preventionweb.net/files/8450_gprch1618.pdf

CHAPTER 15

A Critical Analysis of Building Codes of Pakistan; Fire Safety Provision 2016

Ahmed Faraz Khan
National University of Science and Technology

Ijaz Ahmad
National University of Science and Technology

Abstract

This article presents a critical analysis Building Codes of Pakistan; Fire Safety Provision 2016 which is based on National Fire Protection Association (NFPA-1). Fire hazard is one of the key disasters that can pose significant threat to human life and property. Fire safety is a challenging issue that has taken a kay role in building codes in last several decades. Many countries have adopted the performance-based approaches, are taking over the prescriptive based approaches for fire safety codes in buildings. It is concluded through critical analysis of PBC; FSP-16 that most of the buildings construction, industries and business areas(markets) in Pakistan is vulnerable to fire due to insufficient application of fire safety codes and absence of fire safety authority at National level to have check over. There should be an authority for fire codes enforcement and check and balance of designs, tools and demonstrate codes to enforce, by vesting powers to Authorities Having Jurisdiction cannot only accomplish the goal of FSP-16. A proper mechanism for reviewing an updating these provisions should be adopted. And Fire Safety Codes and Standards should be explained clearly for each facility.

Keywords: Natural hazards, Risk, Fire, Safety Measures and Codes, Authorities, Vulnerable, United States of America (USA), National Fire Protection Association (NFPA), Pakistan Building Codes (PBC), Fire Safety Provision (FSP).

1. Introduction

Fire is good servant but bad master, under control it serves in every possible way in all walks of life, when out of control it causes destruction and devastation beyond imagination (M. Kobes, 2010). To reduce human losses and injuries from fire steps should be taken in the early stages for the adaptation of fire safety measures and codes set by the concern authorities (Tsui & Chow, 2004). If a fire broke into building the people over there are totally dependent on other to be rescued or help by them self (Hazen, 2014).

With rapid unplanned urbanization in developing countries the risk of fire is constantly increasing. The main cause is people residing in multi-story buildings and congested construction without following fire safety codes (Kobes, 2010). Dependency of fossil fuels and electrical appliance has future increased the risk of fire (Andrew and Martin, 2007). Due to short circuit and small ignition can result the complete burning of a building. Lack of awareness and knowledge about fire safety and of precautionary measures can lead to havoc fire incident as may cause by the flammable liquids and chemicals spill (Donaldson, 2005).

From decades the world community had face catastrophic fire incidents resulted in widespread human and economic losses. Despite having latest intelligent technology of fire detection and suppression, fire safety codes and trained rescue personnel's the level of losses from the fire incident has not yet reduced (J. Meacham, 2010). It is universal fact that every country and nation whether developing and developed are equally vulnerable to fire hazard (Helsloot, et al., 2010).

Fire in buildings results in huge losses to lives and assets. Fire is triggered by different factors and developing as well as developed countries are equally affected by fires (Canter, 1980). Each country suffers a lot of monetary and human loses each year from fire related accidents. Most common causes of fire throughout urban settlements of the world are accidental fires, industrial accidents, unlawful acts, and nowadays terrorism. In the United Kingdom, about 800 people lost their lives annually due to fire incidents, beside these human lives fire incidents result in direct damage to materials which exceeds 1200 million UK pounds annually (The News, 2016).

The well-developed country as like United States of America possessed National Fire Protection Association NFPA and set standards according to their needs but still the cases being reported of losses. For example, the 2010 San Bruno explosion in California, USA killed at least 6 people and destroyed several homes. The 2010, Shanghai China fire in high rise apartment building killed 53 people along with physical losses. In 2012, Moscow, Russia a fire broke in market killed about 17 migrant workers (Maqbool and Hussain, 2014).

According to Federal Emergency Management Authority FEMA of USA, 83 percent of deaths are caused by fires ignited in residential buildings, which is estimated as 64 percent of direct financial losses. In Malaysia, about 70,276 fire related events were reported during 2005-2007 which leads to 268 injuries and about 221 deaths (N. H. Salleh, 2009).

In the context of Pakistan as a developing country where till 2016 there were no standard fire safety codes at national level. The cases like in 2012, a fire in Karachi Garment factory and Lahore shoe factory, killed 312 and 25 workers respectively. Nevertheless, the fire disaster in 2018 reported are Tianjin Port fire and explosions killed more than 180 people and damaged about 301 buildings and thousands of vehicles. The fire resulted in to two explosions and other secondary threats. Fire safety measures are always and should be feasible to adopt according to the local circumstances.

Like dealing the other natural disasters by reactive approach, fire is also dealt through reactive approach in Pakistan till now, because no codes were present in the country for fire prevention till 2016. Fire brigade service played active role in controlling fire and other search and rescue agencies played role in evacuation of injured people and recovery of dead bodies. Different provinces have promulgated their emergency services acts after 2000. The Khyber Pakhtunkhwa emergency services act was promulgated in 2012 with the aim to establish rescue 1122 in all districts of the province along with response to fire related incidents by allocating fire brigade vehicles to various districts (KP Emergency services act, 2012). The Punjab emergency services act was promulgated in 2006 which emphasis on the establishment of rescue 1122 service throughout the province and provision of fire brigade service at local level. Sindh and Baluchistan have not yet legally promulgated their emergency services acts and are under process, but fire brigade services are operational in major cities of both provinces along with rescue 1122 service (Dawn, 2015).

At Pakistan's national level in 2002 Emergency Services Ordinance and Fire Code were endorsed. The reason for taking such initiative was the fire ignited in the capital city Islamabad in Shaheed-e-Millat building which affected large number of people and caused extensive economic losses.

The aim of the government was to establish a new federal institution under this ordinance to avoid occurrence of such events in future. This ordinance provided an opportunity to Pakistan fire and emergency council to formulate and implement any code, roles and regulations for making lives and property safe from fires. Ultimately a unit was established by merging the roles of fire brigade and civil defense. This entity was vested with the power to examine any structure which are not according to fire safety regulations (Maqbool and Hussain, 2014).

The need for firm application of fire safety codes in Pakistan can be demonstrated by the recent two events. In Islamabad, the fire submerged Awami Market Building was one incident. It is reveled from the authorities that multistory building was starved from Capital Development Authority completion certificate, the document which verifies obedience with the obligatory fire safety codes. In the interim, around 260 workers lost their lives in Karachi's Baldia factory fire about 6 years ago, it was assumed that the worst industrial coincidence in the antiquity of the state. Protesters and relatives of Karachi's Baldia factory sufferers well thought-out the worst manufacturing fate in the country's past. Although the country has lost a lot of workers in Karachi but still no measures are taken for fire management in large factories, even fire alarm is not yet installed in these factories and this apathy has put lives of skilled workers at high risk. It is observed that in federal capital most of the buildings, malls and offices lack CDA fire requirements, which are designed in 2010 but not yet implemented. The Karachi Baldia factory event should not be ignored, and such type of events can occur in other mega cities of the country. It is evident from the discussion that not only designing fire codes will reduce loses, but the actual challenge is to implement these codes in the existing multi story buildings and incorporate them in design of new mega buildings. (Dawn, 2013)

Recently a survey was conducted of the fire exposed buildings, the survey revealed that apathy, abuse of structure codes, unfamiliarity with safety measures and deficiency of modern fire suppression equipment's are the foremost prompting reasons of fire in Pakistan. Moreover, lack of services and organization for fire-fighting were also keen as life-threatening issues. The system for recording data of fire incidents was also found to be inadequate. (Rafi et al., 2012)

Unfortunately, in Pakistan proper system is not present for recording of fire statistics, but the brief details of some historic fires that occurred in the country are given above. It can be concluded from above discussion and statistics, that it is an urgent need of developing as well as developed countries to design effective fire safety codes and strictly implement and monitor these fire safety codes, because this is the only way to reduce the losses from frequently occurring fires.

3. Literature Review

There is always a need for an authority to inspect the buildings and documents of design for review and reference for future renovation (Hadjisophocleous, 2000). The best fire protection system designs for new buildings are detailed there in National Fire Code 1995 and National Building Code 1995 of Canada, but still the inadequate in implementation (Potworowski, 2010).

The Fire and Rescue Act of 2007 (United Republic of Tanzania) specified that every multistory building, having different floors be about to follow the criteria's as: (1) Satisfactory unrestricted and unhindered means of evacuation from there to the top of the building and to the ground surface contiguous building, (2) other evacuation routes for fire incident should be corporate according to the prescription of Commissioner-General (3) fire safety equipment's for detection should be install according to the standard (Kikwasi, 2015).

The report of design necessity comprises at least of the following material. Satisfactory team design of along with their qualification and experience as criteria. Vivid scope and aim of the design along with objective which is achievable. Construction documents and information of fire protection systems should be mandatory. The design team should define the objectives of fire safety. The equipment's should be inspected regularly to judge performance criteria. The selection of fire scenario should be based to some past incident or indications. The design should be well calculated (Buchanan, 2017). The assumption and engineering measuring should be implemented and well-developed engineering tools for analysis. All maps, drawings, assumptions and analysis should be contained within the design documentation. The document report should be consisting of the following information as fire test results, tools, technical data and literature reports (Hadjisophocleous, 2000).

Fire safety standards varies according to the area of application. As National Fire Protection Association standard NFPA 101, is for life safety codes. Which engrossed on Structure factors important to minimize threat from fire to life along with it also engulfs non-fire incidents. The technical committees of NFPA 101 have manipulated numerous applications that alarms the scope of the document related to hazards other than fire. The NFPA 101 also addresses non-fire related hazards with the main objective to grow a well-ordered catalogue of the life safety provisions (Quintiere, 2006)

In early 1970, in USA trend started moving from prescriptive code to performance bases codes. The new approach was initially implemented in some federal buildings. NFPA and other authorities studied strategies for changing to performance-based codes in early 1990s. They reached the conclusion, that the major problem is that these codes were developed by three private agencies of USA, while in other countries specific ministry or government department perform this task. The names of these private agencies were the building officials and code administrators, the southern building code congress international and international conference of building officials. In order to mix these three types of codes and formulate a new set of codes these three agencies formed a council, which was responsible for forming a new combine set of perspective building codes named international building code (J.Meacham, 2010).

Initially the target year for publishing this new set of code was 2000. The publishing authority was also given the responsibility to design guidelines and requirements for performance based code.in this ra progress was done in designing framework for performance-based design methods. The two major methods were fire risk assessment method and the handbook of fire protection engineering and computer models developed by national fire research foundation and Fitzgerald respectively (Donaldson, 2005). Beside these two publications the SFPE designed user friendly performance-based design in buildings (Meacham, 2013).

Till 1985, the UK buildings regulations were prescriptive and complicated, only lawyers were able to understand these regulations. The size of those provisions was growing with frequent modifications. In view of this complexity, the government in 1980 decided to make changes in these regulations for increasing flexibility in design. Ultimately new revised regulations were published in 1985. These regulations were compiled in 23 pages. Beside this other supporting document was also published in 1994 with the name British Standards Institute (BSI) in 1994. This document helped in clearing ambiguities resulted from the previous document (Robert, 2009).

In 1984, international standard ISO 6241 was issued by international organization of standardization, this document elaborated guidelines for preparation of performance standards in buildings and various methods of assessments. The basic aim of these guidelines was to provide a tool at international level which can help different countries in designing performance standards for buildings. This document clearly explained principles and requirements for to be considered for building performance. It also emphasized on precautionary measures related to spread of fire, physiological impacts, and impact of smoke on occupants (Buchanan, 2017).

Furthermore, in 1990 the TC2 committee which is responsible for fire issues, formed a new committee name SC4 for evaluating and standardizing fire engineering methods. For this purpose, TC4 formed five working groups. The purpose behind this was to design objectives for rescue, detection, activation and suppression. Both the approaches of ISO and BSI are like a larger extent (T.Committee, 2009).

4. Methodology

Methodology includes a critical review of Building Codes of Pakistan (BCP): Fire Safety Provisions (FSP)-2016 by setting NFPA-1 code as a standard.

4.1 BCP(FSP-16) Overview

On directives of government of Pakistan, MOU was signed between Pakistan engineering council and national disaster management authority in 2015 for designing fire safety codes for the country. The aim was to incorporate these fire safety codes with Pakistan building codes to reduce the losses resulting from fire each year. Under technical cooperation of PEC and financial support of NDMA these fire safety provisions were completed and notified in 2016. These fire safety provisions are based on NFPA 1 fire code 2015.

These codes are composed of 15 chapters, 6 appendixes and about 20 tables. Chapter 1 deals with administrative matters having detailed scope, title, purpose and other necessary administrative matters. Beside these roles and responsibilities and powers of authority having jurisdiction, which is an Implementing body for these provisions are elaborated, moreover penalties for violations and procedure for appeal against the penalty imposed by AHJ are explained. Chapter 2 deals with referenced documents used in formulation of these provisions and details of various NFPA standards and other referenced documents are given here. Chapter 3 gives overview of definitions of basic terms and terminologies used in these fire safety provisions, more than 200 definitions related to fire, inflammable liquids, storages and fire extinguishers are defined in this chapter.

Chapter 4 deals with general requirements for these measures, authority having jurisdiction and issuance of fire certificate. Chapter 5 has defined and explained different types of occupancies like residential, non-residential, business, educational, health care, mercantile and industrial. The authority having jurisdiction (AHJ) has been given the authority to put any occupancy in fit category by checking certain requirements given for each occupancy in these provisions. Chapter 6 has elaborated general safety requirements, responsibilities of the owners of buildings,

evacuation mechanisms during fire, specification for fire drills and mechanism for reporting fire incident. Chapter 7 has set up standard and guidelines for electrical equipment's like air conditions, heating systems, elevators, generators, oil stoves, solar systems. Beside these testing mechanism and establishment of emergency coordination room is also discussed here.

Chapter 8 deals with fire safety features and requirements for each type of construction. Total five types of construction are described here and for each type the required strength and measures are explained in detail. Height and other necessities for each type of building are given; moreover, these measures are applicable on old, new, permanent and temporary buildings. Chapter 9 gives general overview of different types of fire protection systems and the areas where each type of system is applicable. The following fire protection systems are explained here; standpipe systems, automatic sprinklers, fire pumps, water supply, portable fire extinguishers and detection alarm and communication systems. Beside these general requirements for each type of fire protection system are given and at the end unapproved fire protection are also defined and explained.

Chapter 10 gives details of standard for exit routes from each type of building like residential, non-residential, industrial and commercial etc. requirement for doors, windows and other fire catching building materials also given here. Size of door and paths in each type of building are also given in this chapter. Chapter 11 deals with designing of fire prevention plan, mechanism for disposal of waste products and mechanism for storing flammable and combustible liquids and gases. Beside these responsibilities of building in charge in case of fire incident are also elaborated here. Chapter 12 gives standards for fire department access and water supplies. Mechanism for access to buildings and roads is given and criteria for water provider is in times of need is explained here.

Chapter 13 deals with responsibilities of building owner, including supervision of his surrounding to remove fire catchable hazardous material, criteria for storage of water material in and outside the buildings are given. Chapter 14 has further elaborated the fire protection requirements for each type of construction against each specific class of fire. Chapter 15 gives requirements and standards for grandstands and bleachers, folding and telescopic seating, tents and membrane structures.

5. Results and Discussion

From a survey it is revealed that most of the buildings in Pakistan is vulnerable to fire due to insufficient application of fire safety codes and absence of fire safety authority at National level. Survey revealed the facts that abuse of structure codes unfamiliarity with safety measures and deficiency of modern fire suppression equipment's are the foremost prompting reason of fire in Pakistan. Moreover, lack of services and organization for fire-fighting and fire safety were also keen as life-threatening issues. The system for recording data of fire incidents was also found to be inadequate.

The adoption and success of performance-based codes depend on the ability to establish performance criteria that will be verifiable and enforceable. The performance criteria should be such that designers can easily demonstrate, using engineering tools, that their designs meet them and that the code authority can enforce them. (Hadjisophocleous, 2000). According to the statement the fire safety provision of any country should be performance based, which can be easily applied or enforced and verified by higher authority. There should be an authority for fire codes enforcement and check and balance of designs, tools and demonstrate codes to enforce.

Although the title of the Building codes of Pakistan, fire safety provision-2016, draws no conclusion on the scope and purpose of the building codes. The purpose of the building codes for fire safety is to provide minimum requirements necessary to establish a reasonable level of fire and life safety and property protection from hazards created by fire. However, the purposed as stated is to provide standards for fire safety and protection all over the country and these provisions cover hazards associated with fire. While the scope of the provision is very broader covering the aspects of fire prevention, life safety, fire safety in buildings and building like structures.

More on the scope continuous with the aim of inspection, investigation, review of construction plans along with assessment of existing occupancies with the recommendations of design, installation, alteration, modification, repair, servicing and testing of fire protection systems and equipment's. These provisions emphasize on proactive approach for fire incidents. For example, the term fire safety defines as the complete measures of managing fire incidents to control losses. The process starts from pre-measures of installing equipment's spreading awareness and testing of fire equipment's to response as early warning systems, firefighting equipment's presence.

In the Chapter 1 of Building Codes of Pakistan; Fire Safety Provision deals with administrative matters having detailed scope, title, purpose and other necessary administrative matters. Beside these roles and responsibilities and powers of authority having jurisdiction, which is an Implementing body for these provisions are elaborated. The implementation and enforcement of building codes vested with the Authority Having Jurisdiction (AHJ) within their respective jurisdiction

and circles rather than the provision should be implemented by specific authority (Pakistan fire and emergency council) having jurisdiction of check and balance and implementation of these codes. moreover, penalties for violations and procedure for appeal against the penalty imposed by AHJ are explained. But if there is no any authority which set standard of penalties then there would be chaos. As CDA will set their own standard and CBP and PDA will follow their own. If there is no authority of specialized personnel of fire equipment's inspection and the application of codes per standards assessment. The application of building codes of Pakistan; Fire safety Provision is impossible.

The fire safety provision 2016 articulates the building codes shall be adopted by all organization (public and privates). As in United States of America the Fire safety codes as NFPA standards are implemented by National Fire Protection Association. The fire safety authority should be established with the powers of carrying out assessments, investigations and inspections all over the country with the collaboration of inline agencies.

All over the world the fire safety codes are based on the specific area of implementation rather than universal code of fire safety. Fire safety standards varies according to the area of application. As National Fire Protection Association standard NFPA 101, is for life safety codes. Which engrossed on Structure factors important to minimize threat from fire to life along with it also engulfs non-fire incidents. The technical committees of NFPA 101 have manipulated numerous applications that alarms the scope of the document related to hazards other than fire. The NFPA 101 also addresses non-fire related hazards with the main objective to grow a well-ordered catalogue of the life safety provisions. In USA the NFPA standards are various, for example the standards for industries differs from the standards for critical facilities as hospital and schools and governmental buildings. While the Building codes of Pakistan Fire safety provision-2016 is based on NFPA-1 and explained as universal standard for Pakistan, which lacks the specific standards for hospitals, chemical facilities and industries. Just focusing on the general criteria of fire safety by installation of fire safety equipment and the incorporation of these codes in new buildings. The area of these codes should be broadened by setting specific standards for each area i.e. industries, hospitals, schools, residential areas and housing, chemical facilities and governmental buildings.

The crux of weaknesses of the provision of fire safety are: they specified the requirements of fire safety, but not defined the standard procedure. The lucrative designs are not encouraged, as it is the requirement of the day. For advanced solution of rare conditions, a very little elasticity as shown in the FSP. They assume the level of safety can be achieved just the setting these codes, but which is not quantified. In FSP of Pakistan no standards or codes are explained for most of today's huge multipart constructions.

6. Conclusion

Unfortunately, in Pakistan proper system is not present for recording of fire statistics, but the brief details of some historic fires that occurred in the country are given above. It can be concluded from above discussion and statistics, that it is an urgent need of developing as well as developed countries to design effective fire safety codes and strictly implement and monitor these fire safety codes, because this is the only way to reduce the losses from frequently occurring fires.

Fire hazard is poorly managed in Pakistan. The country lacks a reliable system for keeping statistics related to fire incidents and losses. The rapid unplanned and poorly designed construction has further increased the risk of damages resulting from fire. There is an urgent need in the country to inspect all the commercial as well as residential buildings to point out their weaknesses in response to fire issncidents. Beside this government needs to rake strict action against those constructors who are violating these safety provisions in construction of new buildings. Fire brigade department has old and obsolete vehicles, they should be provided with latest equipment's to respond effectively to fire incidents. Trainings of international standard should be arranged for fire fighters and relief/ subsidy should be given on fire safety equipment's like fire extinguishers and smoke detectors by government. The development authorities of major cities need to modify their obsolete codes according to Pakistan fire safety provisions 2016. These development authorities should focus on two areas, to construct fire resistant construction and to control fire spread. Introduction of fire safety in education curriculum as a subject will be fruitful in this regard. Trainings and drills of fire-fighting staff should be conducted on regular basis. Pakistan has very well documented plans and policies, but the country has limited capacity and almost failed in implementation of these plans. The government needs to change this trend and take realistic measures for implementation of these newly designed codes throughout the country. A proper mechanism for reviewing an updating these provisions should be adopted.

REFERENCES

1. G. V. Hadjisophocleous, N. Bénichou and A. S. Tamin, "Literature review of performance-based codes and design environment", Journal of Fire Protection Engineering, Vol. 9, No. 1, pp. 12–40 (1998).

2. Brain J. Meacham, J. R. (2013). 20 Years of Performance Based Fire Protection Design. *Fire Protection Engineering, 23.*

3. Dawn. (2013). *No fire safety.* Islamabad: Daily Dawn.

4. Donaldson, I. (2005). *International Engineering Guidlines.* ABCB: Austrialian Governement. G.Ramachandran. (1999). Fire safety management and risk assessment. *Emerald Insight, 17*(9/10), 363–76.

5. Hadjisophocleous, G. (2000). DEVELOPMENT OF PERFORMANCE-BASED CODES, PERFORMANCE. *International Journal on Engineering Performance-Based Fire Codes, 2,* 127–142.

6. J. Meacham, b. (2010). *A Report Of inter jurisdictional Regulatory Collaboration Commite.* Scotland: IRCC.

7. (2012). *Khyber Pakhtunkhwa emergency services act.* Peshawar.

8. Kikwasi, G. J. (2015). A Study on the Awareness of Fire Safety Measures for Users and Staff of Shopping Malls: The Case of Mlimani City and Quality Centre in Dar es Salaam. *Journal of Civil Engineering and Architecture, 9,* 1415–1422.

9. M. Kobes, L. B. (2010). Building Safety and Human Behavior in Fire. *Fire Safety Journal, 45*(1), 1–11.

10. Maqbool, M. Y., & Hussain, D. (2014). Institutionalization of Disaster Risk Management in Pakistan. *ISSRA ppepers,* 47–48.

11. Potworowski, J. (2010). *The Transformation of the National Building Codes Of Canada.* Ottawa: Telfer.

12. Rafi, M. M., Uddin, S. W., & Siddqui, S. H. (2012). Assessment of fire hazard in Pakistan. *Disaster Prevention and Management, 21*(1), 71–84.

13. Robert C.Till, N. G. (2009). Using Desirable System States to Design for a Hypothetical Subway Arson Incident. *Journal of Applied Security Research, 4*(3), 245–247.

14. T. Committee. (2009). *Techincal Information on Methods for Evaluation Behaviour and Movement of People.* Fire Safety Engineering.

15. Dan P., (1978). *Techniques of Safety management*

16. Kobes, M., I. Helsloot, et al. (2010). "Building safety and human behavior in fire: A literature review. "Fire Safety Journal **45**(1): 1–11.

17. Hazen, R. M. and M. H. Hazen (2014). *Keepers of the flame: the role of fire in American culture,* Princeton University Press. 1775–1925,

18. Subramaniam C., (2004) "Human *factors influencing fire safety measures, Disaster Prevention and Management*" Vol.13 Iss. 2, pp.110–116.

19. Fadzil M.M.H., (1998) "*Human Factors in Fire Safety Design, Journal HBP*" Vol.5, pp. 7–17.

20. Helsloot I., Kobes M., B. de Vries, Post J.G., (2010) "*Building Safety and Human Behavior in Fire: A Literature Review*" Fire Safety Journal, Vol. 45, Iss. 1, pp. 1–11.

21. Canter D., (1980) "*Fire and Human Behavior - An Introduction*" pp. 3.

22. Proulx G., Sime J. D., (1991) "*To prevent panic in an underground emergency: why not tell people the truth?*" In: Fire Safety Science-Proceedings of the Third International Symposium. Elsevier Applied Science, New York, pp. 843–852.

23. Andrew F., Martin M., (2007) "*Introduction to Fire Safety Management*".

24. B.de Vries, Post J.G., Kobes M., Helsloot I., (2010) *"Building Safety and Human Behavior in Fire: A Literature Review"*, Fire Safety Journal, Vol. 45, Iss. 1, pp. 1–11.

25. Groner N.E., Williamson R.B., (1997) *"Using A Table of Desirable Systems States to Integrate Models of Fire Development with Active System and Human Responses to A Fire Scenario"*, Proceedings of The Fire Risk and Hazard Assessment Research Application Symposium, San Francisco, CA, pp. 142–151.

26. Tsui S.C., Chow W.K, (2004) *"Legislation Aspects of Fire Safety Management in Hong Kong"*, Facilities, Vol. 22, Iss: 5/6, pp 149–164.

27. Quintiere, J. G. (2006). *"Fundamentals of fire phenomena, John Wiley Chichester"*.

28. V. R. Beck, and D. Yung, (1994) *"The development of a risk-cost assessment model for the evaluation of fire safety in buildings"*, Proceedings of the 4th International Symposium on Fire Safety Science, 13-17 June, Ottawa, Canada, pp. 817–828.

Part 3

USING ARTIFICIAL INTELLIGENCE AND INTERNET OF THINGS FOR MANAGING RISKS OF DISASTERS

Chapter 16 IoT enabled manufacturing and health care services: Potentialities and Propsects in India

Chapter 17 Disasters—A New Setback to be Prepared vis-à-vis Artificial Intelligence

Chapter 18 Abstract: Application of Artificial Intelligence for Managing Risks of Disasters

Chapter 19 Scalable IOT solutions with the Amazon Echo Flex Model for 3P integrations

Chapter 20 Internet of Things Applications Towards Mapping of Technologies in Areas of Diagnostics, Testing, Healthcare Delivery Solutions and Equipment Supplies: Challenges and Opportunities in India

Chapter 21 Latest Advancements in Iot and Sensors Applications in Renewable Energy Systems Optimization

IoT Enabled Manufacturing and Health Care Services: Potentialities and Prospects in India

Ashok G. Matani

Professor- Department of Mechanical Engg,
Government College of Engineering, Jalgaon - 425001[MS] India,l
dragmatani@gmail.com, ashokgm333@rediffmail.com

Abastract

Governments around the world are now relying on ubiquitous instruments, sensors and powerful algorithms. In the war against COVID-19, several governments have implemented these new surveillance tools. Maps of the world show how the decrease in the transportation of people has drastically reduced carbon emissions across different countries, but what's the case for emissions from digital technologies is not estimated till to date. When the volume of people working from home or using digital devices in quarantine cause an increase in emissions from other sources, there is a scope for the large cloud-providers to address the capacity issues.

Keywords: IoT sensors, sensors installed on mobile, health monitors, use of digital and remote technologies, Industry 4.0 drives capabilities.

1. Introduction

The health care sector in India has consistently been flourishing and is one of its fastest-growing sectors. With the amalgamation of automation and healthcare in India, the sector is graced to establish new landmarks. By 2022, the healthcare market might have a worth of $ 370 billion, promising yields up to 35-40 per cent, according to several investors. [2] Health tech is a game- changer, although India has a lengthy way to go in using technology to extend health-related services. It is forecasted to create 40 million jobs by 2030. As per Traxcn data, in 2018, India's investments in health tech amounted to a striking $ 571 million. In April 2019, NASSCOM associated with GE Healthcare to encourage startups in the field to support digital healthcare solutions in the region. Technologies like machine-learning, nanotech, IoT, AI, robotics, 3D printing as just a few illustrations that have functions in the healthcare sector. [1]

2. Factories and Transportation Made Better

Many essential items need to be manufactured and transported as quickly as possible, ranging from masks to ventilators to eventually, large volumes of vaccines. IoT helps factories operate more efficiently and keep costs down. The GPS based systems can alert to issues; if a truck were to go off a set path or if needed, allow the driver to alert if they are feeling threatened or unsafe.[5] Getting the truck safely to its destination is only one part of the issue; the products need to get there in proper condition. IoT sensors can be used to ensure that the vehicle was driven in a safe manner without breaking key vials and that the correct temperature/humidity range was adhered to at all times, ensuring the safety of a vaccine or medicine. [3] This will help us to defeat the world enemy we have faced in our lives. Cities across the world have made infrastructure innovations a priority to safeguard their physical systems so they can stay robust and ant fragile during natural disasters such as earthquakes, tsunami and hurricanes. But pandemics have shown that these methods are not enough when it comes to ensuring connectivity and accessing our society during biological disasters.[4]

3. A boost for Digital and Remote Technologies

In the midst of the current virus outbreak, a dramatic boost in the use of digital and remote technologies is observed.

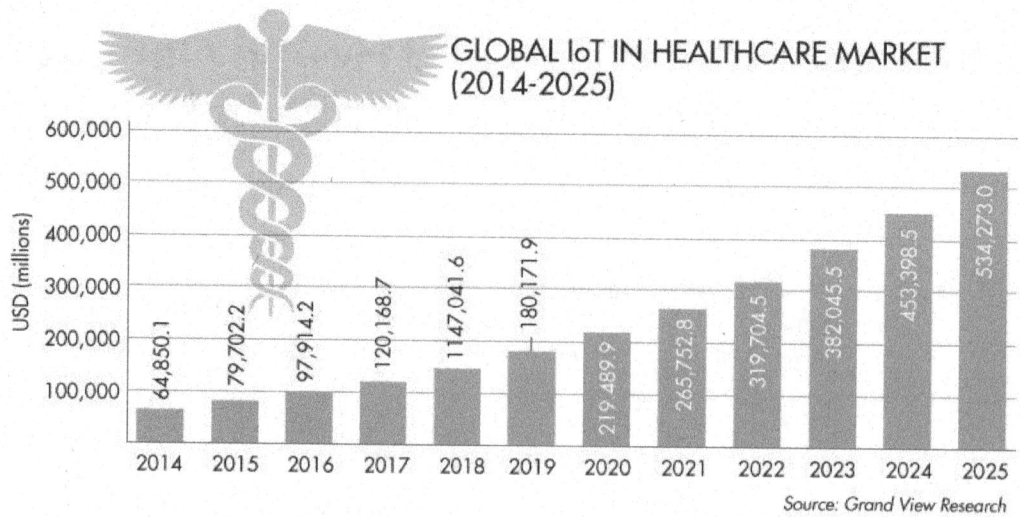

Fig. 16.1 Global IoT in healthcare market (2014–2025)

Source: https://www.digiteum.com/iot-benefits-healthcare-industry/

Videoconferencing is now ubiquitous, which helps with social distancing while keeping businesses running. This has often triggered organizations to adapt new technologies faster than they had planned – schools are changing to video-classes, and even religious gatherings are conducted online. [6] The usage of personal remote monitoring devices or apps – Hong Kong has issued wrist bands for arriving passenger with a high-risk profile, while Singapore has a monitoring app for those on Stay Home Notice. In Singapore, temperature measurements at the entrances of almost all public buildings since weeks – connected and report their data into a central instance for real time analysis. That's a classic IoT scenario. The COVID outbreak have shown the new emerging benefits of smart manufacturing, saying Industry 4.0 drives capabilities for remote operations, monitoring and maintenance of production lines and manufacturing plants. [7]

4. IoT in Hospitals

Connecting health systems together can reduce a huge amount of manual admin tasks by consolidating EMRs (electronic medical records), scheduling systems, and patient monitoring into one place. [8] As all hospital resources are being stretched, having a tool to monitor patients all around the hospital and ensure that medication is delivered effectively will be a massive help. Apart from the many cases of corona virus sectioning off parts of hospitals and taking up a huge proportion of hospital staff's time and attention, other high-risk patients still require the same levels of care. [9] Devices that monitor glucose levels for diabetic patients keep track

of blood pressure and heart rate levels and alert to issues can allow hospital staff to take care of these patients remotely while in another section of the hospital. Devices for patients at home can also connect to EMRs (electronic medical records) so that chronically ill patients do not necessarily have to visit the hospital or medical centre while still being attended by medical staff. [10]

5. Using IoT to Manage Patient Care

The scalability of IoT also comes in handy for monitoring all the patients who are high-risk enough to warrant quarantine but not serious enough to warrant in-hospital care. Right now, the daily check-up of the patients is done manually by healthcare workers who go door-to-door. In one reported instance, a healthcare worker had patients standing in their apartment balconies, so that he could fly a drone up to take their temperatures with an infrared thermometer. [11] With IoT, the patients can have their temperatures taken and upload the data with their mobile devices to the cloud for analysis. This way, healthcare workers can not only collect more data using less time but also reduce the chance for cross-infection with the patients. In addition, IoT can provide relief to the overworked staff at the hospital. IoT has already been used in the remote monitoring of in-home patients with chronic conditions such as hypertension or diabetes. In hospitals, telemetry, the transmission of biometric measurements like heartbeat and blood pressure from wearable, wireless instruments on patients to the central monitoring has been used to monitor a large number of patients with minimal staff.

Here, IoT can be used to reduce the workload and increase the efficiency of the medical staff, all the while reducing the exposure of healthcare workers to infection.[12]

6. The Future of Healthcare with IoT Technology

Applications of IoT in medical and healthcare are abundant and involve a wide range of technologies, from futuristic robots and drones to ML-based data analytics and predictive modeling. [13] Some of the boosters of the medical tech development from the first days of quarantine, for instance, were the growing maturity of UAVs (unmanned aerial vehicles), high demand for telemedicine mobile tools and remote patient tracking technologies, and the increasing role of IoT in healthcare recognized by governments and investors. UAV technologies in the medical supply chain are already getting ubiquitous. Drones are being used to deliver medicines to patients for home treatment. In Rwanda, for example, drones are even used to transport donor blood.[14]

There are many proven benefits of using RFID technology in IoT solutions for healthcare. This is why the development of IoT healthcare solutions comes hand-in-hand with the growing integration of RFID technologies in this niche. This technology paired with other Internet of Things solutions for healthcare is already used in a number of areas, including inventory management in medical institutions as well as patient monitoring and in-hospital tracking.[15]

Other cutting-edge opportunities are:

- **Telemedicine.** Medical Internet of Things paired with mobile apps introduces a whole new model of connectivity and communication between patients and doctors.[16]
- **RFID for patient monitoring.** RFID tags and labels have very broad applicability from people tracking to sanitation control. [17]
- **Wearable devices transmit data directly to doctors.** Most often we will be talking about watches, bands, bracelets and other trackers that collect important information about the patient condition (heart rate, blood pressure, pulse, blood sugar, etc.) and send it to hospitals or directly to doctors for analysis and treatment correction.[18]
- **Diagnosis, preventive medicine.** Patient records, test results, treatment progress and other data that can be collected using IoT are important to improve diagnostic accuracy and drive the development of preventive medicine. [19]

7. Govt. of India Established MHRD's Innovation Cell (MIC) to Work with New Ideas

Ministry of Human Resource Development (MHRD), Govt. of India has established 'MHRD's Innovation Cell (MIC)' to systematically foster the culture of Innovation amongst all Higher Education Institutions (HEIs). The purpose of 'MHRD's Innovation Cell is to encourage, inspire and nurture young students by supporting them to work with new ideas and transform them into prototypes while they are informative years. 'MHRD's Innovation Cell has envisioned encouraging creation of 'Institution's Innovation Council (IICs)' across selected Higher Education Institutions. A network of these Institutions' Innovation Council (IICs)s will be established to promote innovations in the Institutions through multitudinous modes leading to an innovation promotion eco-system in the campuses.[20]

8. IMA Seeks IAS-like All-India Service for Healthcare Administration

The Indian Medical Association (IMA) has requested to the Government of India for setting up of an Indian Medical Service (IMS), on the lines of Indian Administrative Service (IAS), Indian Police Service (IPS) and Indian Foreign Service (IFS) for raising a new cadre of administrators who will be responsible for holding the administrative responsibilities pertaining to the district medical officer, project officers of various disease control programs, and the various ranks of secretaries in the Union health ministry and the state health departments and the heads all other areas in the health sector. The basic qualification to appear for the proposed IMS examination is MBBS. [21]

Considering the urgent need for a new post-COVID healthcare policy providing equal priority to non-COVID care as well. Working closely with the Central and the State Governments during the pandemic, the IMA has been involved in various activities like availing of insurance for healthcare workers, anti-violence ordinance, inclusion of clinics, nursing homes and hospitals in MSME, modifications in testing policy, PPEs in work places, policy for quarantine of caregivers

and plasma therapy among others. Management of COVID pandemic would have been better considering better public infrastructure and the strategies implemented. There is a dire need for the government to increase its GDP allocation to 5 % for the healthcare structure. The IMA also demands for creation of 'One Nation - One set of guidelines for health'. [22]

9. Conclusions

The ascent of healthcare startups in India reveals the benefit of genomics, biotech, and robotics in hospitals and clinics to enhance the efficiency of health-related services. Artificial intelligence can identify diseases with complete certainty while apps that track our vitals and movements can enhance the comprehensive wellbeing of the country. India, despite its infrastructure and immense population, is working its best to fight the ongoing virus through different information campaigns. Clinik Healthcare, one such health-tech startup providing 24/7 primary care through its web of doctors, declared coronavirus care programs including INR 1 lakh insurance cover for families affected with COVID-19 and free tele consultation channels to the society.

Care.fit, a complete healthcare platform, has introduced telemedicine as a solution to increase consumer reach to high-quality doctors across various specialties effortlessly and efficiently during the pandemic in the country. It has also launched Cult.live where they are providing free live classes across fitness formats like strength, cardio, HRX, S&C, dance fitness, and yoga.

Another startup, Bione has identified specific gene groups responsible for an individual's susceptibility to coronavirus. They have also developed a COVID-19 centred Microbiome test, which combined with some AI, predictive analysis tools, can generate tailored recommendations for individuals to strengthen their particular microbiome and thus be more immune to the virus and to fight off. The need of the time is that all citizens of India should accept responsibility to encourage and successfully implement all the efforts taken by Government of India to effectively utilize the IoT and artificial intelligence (AI) in various health care industry and services to offer best services to all citizens towards making India - a healthy India.

REFERENCES

1. B. -W. Chen, M. Imran, N. Nasser and M. Shoaib, "Self-Aware Autonomous City: From Sensing to Planning," in IEEE Communications Magazine, vol. 57, no. 4, pp. 33-39, April 2019, doi: 10.1109/MCOM.2019.1800628.
2. B. Modani, Sagar and C. P. D. Cyril, "IoT based Voice Controlled Smart Health Sensor System," 2021 Fifth International Conference on I-SMAC (IoT in Social, Mobile, Analytics and Cloud) (I-SMAC), 2021, pp. 263-266, doi: 10.1109/I-SMAC52330.2021.9641036.
3. Bikash Pradhan, Saugat Bhattacharyya, Kunal Pal, "IoT-Based Applications in Healthcare Devices", *Journal of Healthcare Engineering*, vol. 2021, Article ID 6632599, 18 pages, 2021. https://doi.org/10.1155/2021/6632599
4. C. Boudagdigue, A. Benslimane, A. Kobbane and J. Liu, "Trust Management in Industrial Internet of Things," in IEEE Transactions on Information Forensics and Security, vol. 15, pp. 3667-3682, 2020, doi: 10.1109/TIFS.2020.2997179.
5. C. -Y. Siao, R. -G. Chang, M. -H. Chen and S. -Y. Wang, "Design of Contact Force for Ultrasonic Scanner," 2021 IEEE 3rd Eurasia Conference on IOT, Communication and Engineering (ECICE), 2021, pp. 614-616, doi: 10.1109/ECICE52819.2021.9645672.
6. D. Liu, J. Ni, C. Huang, X. Lin and X. S. Shen, "Secure and Efficient Distributed Network Provenance for IoT: A Blockchain-Based Approach," in IEEE Internet of Things Journal, vol. 7, no. 8, pp. 7564-7574, Aug. 2020, doi: 10.1109/JIOT.2020.2988481.
7. D. J. Miller, Z. Xiang and G. Kesidis, "Adversarial Learning Targeting Deep Neural Network Classification: A Comprehensive Review of Defenses Against Attacks," in Proceedings of the IEEE, vol. 108, no. 3, pp. 402-433, March 2020, doi: 10.1109/JPROC.2020.2970615.
8. H. -N. Dai, Z. Zheng and Y. Zhang, "Blockchain for Internet of Things: A Survey," in IEEE Internet of Things Journal, vol. 6, no. 5, pp. 8076-8094, Oct. 2019, doi: 10.1109/JIOT.2019.2920987.
9. Herland, M., Khoshgoftaar, T.M. & Bauder, R.A. Big Data fraud detection using multiple medicare data sources. *J Big Data* **5,** 29 (2018). https://doi.org/10.1186/s40537-018-0138-3
10. I. Suhail and S. Pillai, "IoT enabled applications for Healthcare decisions," 2022 International Conference on Decision Aid Sciences and Applications (DASA), 2022, pp. 47-54, doi: 10.1109/DASA54658.2022.9765251.
11. Lennart Ante, Constantin Fischer, Elias Strehle,, A bibliometric review of research on digital identity: Research streams, influential works and future research paths, Journal of Manufacturing Systems, Volume 62, 2022, Pages 523-538, https://doi.org/10.1016/j.jmsy.2022.01.005.
12. M. Shamim Hossain, Ghulam Muhammad, Cloud-assisted Industrial Internet of Things (IIoT) – Enabled framework for health monitoring, Computer Networks, Volume 101, 2016, Pages 192-202, https://doi.org/10.1016/j.comnet.2016.01.009.
13. M. A. Kabir, M. S. A. Khan, K. M. Kadir, C. Y. Choon, F. Jefreen and M. Hasanuzzaman, "Analysis of Different Mobile IoT Models in Smart City Planning: A Technical Investigation of Software & Hardware Architecture," 2021 IEEE 12th Annual Ubiquitous Computing, Electronics & Mobile Communication Conference (UEMCON), 2021, pp. 0290-0297, doi: 10.1109/UEMCON53757.2021.9666688.
14. M. Shen, Y. Deng, L. Zhu, X. Du and N. Guizani, "Privacy-Preserving Image Retrieval for Medical IoT Systems: A Blockchain-Based Approach," in IEEE Network, vol. 33, no. 5, pp. 27-33, Sept.-Oct. 2019, doi: 10.1109/MNET.001.1800503.
15. M. Ahmed and A. -S. K. Pathan, "Blockchain: Can It Be Trusted?," in Computer, vol. 53, no. 4, pp. 31-35, April 2020, doi: 10.1109/MC.2019.2922950.
16. Mohd Javaid, Ibrahim Haleem Khan, Internet of Things (IoT) enabled healthcare helps to take the challenges of COVID-19 Pandemic, Journal of Oral Biology and Craniofacial Research, Volume 11, Issue 2, 2021, Pages 209-214, https://doi.org/10.1016/j.jobcr.2021.01.015.

17. N. Anusha, B. P. Kumar and L. Agarwal, "Study on Recent Trends of Smart Wearable," 2022 2nd International Conference on Artificial Intelligence and Signal Processing (AISP), 2022, pp. 1-5, doi: 10.1109/AISP53593.2022.9760637.

18. N. Spicher, A. Klingenberg, V. Purrucker and T. M. Deserno, "Edge computing in 5G cellular networks for real-time analysis of electrocardiography recorded with wearable textile sensors," 2021 43rd Annual International Conference of the IEEE Engineering in Medicine & Biology Society (EMBC), 2021, pp. 1735-1739, doi: 10.1109/EMBC46164.2021.9630875.

19. N. Choudhury, R. Matam, M. Mukherjee and J. Lloret, "A Beacon and GTS Scheduling Scheme for IEEE 802.15.4 DSME Networks," in IEEE Internet of Things Journal, vol. 9, no. 7, pp. 5162-5172, 1 April1, 2022, doi: 10.1109/JIOT.2021.3110866.

20. Navita and P. Mittal, "Machine Learning (ML) based Human Activity Recognition Model using Smart Sensors in IoT Environment," 2022 12th International Conference on Cloud Computing, Data Science & Engineering (Confluence), 2022, pp. 330-334, doi: 10.1109/Confluence52989.2022.9734152.

21. https://www.startupindia.gov.in/content/sih/en/biomedical-waste-treatment-innovation- challenge.html

22. https://www.digiteum.com/iot-benefits-healthcare-industry

CHAPTER 17

Disasters—A New Setback to be Prepared vis-à-vis Artificial Intelligence

Nikhil Kaushal

Student of B.tech Program,
Vellore Institute of Technology,
nik.kaushal0401@gmail.com, 9997431827

Prerna Prajapati

Student of BBALLB Program,
School of Law, Galgotias University,
prernaprajapati33@gmail.com, 7017119293

Abstract

Today we encounter the application of AI technology in a wide range of different places in our daily life. Artificial intelligence is already starting to play a major role in our society, and with the industry advancing more and more. With all the advantages that could come with the implementation of AI, at least some negative effects are also deemed inevitable. However, this is not an easy task considering the great uncertainty these phenomena present including the multiple numbers of possible scenarios in terms of location, probability of occurrence and impact, the difficulty in estimating the demand and supply. When you feed a machine learning system the right amount of information, it can come back to you with useful insights that may make your disaster recovery strategies more effective. Many of today's businesses are exploring the many benefits that artificial intelligence has to offer when it comes to strengthening various forms of security. AI could use business impact analysis and risk assessment to help you see which parts of your company need better protection, and which you can accord to put less investment into. Similarly, it also concerns the safety of the natural environment or predictions that may be helpful to be known on a prior note which assessed at times can be non-accurate but it's good to be prepared and make oneself prepared to tackle the worst. The increasing number of affected people due to disasters, the complexity, and unpredictability of these phenomena, and the different problems encountered in the planning and response in different scenarios, establish a need to find better measures and practices to reduce the human and economic loss in this kind of events. Artificial intelligence tools use technologies such as deep neural networks to find potential risks and threats that never would have occurred to us, humans. This makes it easier for the AI system to determine what kind of threats you need to protect yourself against, so you can develop a more powerful and robust plan for disaster prevention and recovery. Using predictive analytics, your artificial intelligence system may even be able to determine ahead of time when it's likely that a process or system will fail. It will suggest precautionary measures that you can take to prevent a disaster and so our emphasis lies on the future predictions and ways to protect life and the ecological balance.

Keywords: Disaster Management, Artificial Intelligence, Cyber Security, Natural Disaster, Man-Made Disaster.

1. Introduction

Artificial Intelligence is effectively developing and there are ongoing advancements in AI instruments like machine picking up, thinking, arranging, and thinking capacity. It is generally utilized in different areas like medical services, safeguard, transportation, and other such robotization.

Alongside A.I. utilized in areas, it very well may be a useful device for overseeing both normal and man-made disasters. Natural disasters are out of the reach and influence of human beings. However, a lot can be done to minimize the loss of lives. Artificial intelligence is one viable option that can potentially prevent massive loss of lives while at the same time make rescue efforts easy and efficient. As the realities of climate change take hold across the planet, the risks of natural hazards and disasters are becoming ever more familiar. Meteorologists, aiming to protect increasingly populous countries and communities, are tapping into artificial intelligence (AI) to get them the edge in early detection and disaster relief.

Disaster is any occasion that prompts harm to the climate and society we live in, in this way make colossal sway on human existence. There is a requirement for sure-fire reaction and strategy needed during any sort of disaster. Emergency prompts intricacy of circumstance and requires the board in saving a life, saving foundation and assets. An examination is absent in such regions and the information assembled post the disasters can help in making a data set, which can be of extraordinary assistance for additional arranging of disaster the executives. Man-made brainpower (AI) has acquired tremendous prominence in the present time and the utilization of AI as an apparatus can decrease life hazards, climate harm, affect society, and react to disaster circumstances in a more grounded way.

Different regular and Man-made debacles make an effect each year. There is gigantic actual annihilation and death toll, many individuals who endure the catastrophe experience an extraordinary enthusiastic sway previously, during, and after calamity.

- Natural disaster: The catastrophic events are at an enormous scope and have an incredible capability of misfortune. These calamities are floods, seismic tremors, out of control fires, dry spells, typhoons and tempests, and so on
- Man-made Disasters: The people-caused debacles incorporate mechanical mishaps, dread assaults, and episodes that make viciousness. There is a need for departures and insurance needed for such debacles.
- role of Artificial Intelligence: The job of computerized reasoning in such calamities is required and significant for examining the circumstances and to come out with answers for being ready to confront catastrophes.

Artificial Intelligence advances the progression of innovation and triggers the improvement by diminishing the human existence hazard during emergency circumstances. The above research shows that there is a need of executing AI, which will give the exact yield according to calculations set in the data set of the innovation. The result of the study is that individuals are tolerating the mechanical changes and man-made consciousness will be broadly acknowledged. Assemble

information dependent on the different disasters experienced already so examination is done and a compelling advancement is done to lessen the effect of disasters. Artificial Intelligence can greatly help emergency and disaster management efforts not only in America but also in the rest of the world. Today, Drones, robots, and sensors can provide intelligent and accurate information concerning landscapes and damaged buildings. This allows rescue workers to understand the topography of a landscape and the extent of damage to a building. Drones can be used to find victims trapped in debris allowing rescue workers to get to them quickly.[1] utilizing Artificial Intelligence (AI) in a bid to save lives when catastrophic events happen. Utilizing man-made reasoning has various potential experts making it an appropriate answer for use. Utilizing robots, sensors or robots can help specialists on call and salvage laborers rapidly access the circumstance just as the degree of the harm caused to concoct an appropriate activity plan of saving caught casualties. It additionally puts forth salvage attempts less tedious, safe, and appropriately organized. AI shows extraordinary potential to help information assortment and checking, the reproduction and gauging of outrageous occasions, and powerful and available correspondence previously and during a disaster. This potential was in concentration at a new studio taking care of the main gathering of the new Focus Group on AI for Natural Disaster Management. The gathering is available to all invested individuals, upheld by the International Telecommunication Union (ITU) along with the World Meteorological Organization (WMO) and UN Environment.[2]

2. Artificial Intelligence for Disaster Response (AIDR)[3]

2.1 Qatar Computing Research Institute (QCRI)

Qatar Computing Research Institute (QCRI) is a free online tool developed by the Qatar Foundation for Education, Science, and Community Development. The company is based in Doha, Qatar. QCRI aims to increase the efficiency of agencies and volunteer services during disaster management. The tool utilizes machine learning to automatically identify texts and tweets that relate to particular crises.

2.2 1CONCERN

1CONCERN produces a common and comprehensive picture during emergency operations to be used by emergency operation centers. Its main goal is to assist these centers to allocate resources that are needed for rescue efforts. The tools

---

[1]https://safetymanagement.eku.edu/blog/the-benefits-challenges-of-using-artificial-intelligence-for-emergency-management/
[2]https://www.itu.int/en/myitu/News/2021/03/24/08/49/AI-natural-hazards-disasters
[3]https://safetymanagement.eku.edu/blog/the-benefits-challenges-of-using-artificial-intelligence-for-emergency-management/

also prepare effective planning modules, which stimulate lifelike disasters purely for training purposes. These modules also determine potentially vulnerable areas that would be affected the most during a natural disaster. 1CONCERN has been able to map about 163,696 square miles and has covered over 39 million people so far. In addition, it has analyzed nearly 11 million structures and modeled an impressive 14,967 fault lines. This allows the program to be prepared and stay alert in case a natural disaster occurs.

2.3 BlueLine Grid

BlueLine Grid was created and developed by Bill Braxton, David Riker, and Jack Weiss. Braxton is the current Police Commissioner of the New York Police Department (NYPD). Until 2013, he served as the chief of the Los Angeles Police Department (LAPD). BlueLine Grid is a mobile communications platform developed to assist rescue efforts during disasters. It connects all users to an established network of first responders, security teams, and law enforcement bodies via voice, text, location, and group services. This platform is effective because it allows users to quickly find public employees by geographic proximity, area, or agency. It also fosters efficient connectivity, collaboration, and communication.

2.4 AIDR Around the Globe

Artificial Management for Disaster Response has proven effective in many natural disasters around the world. Technology allows people to quickly and efficiently respond to such cases, and save many lives in the process. However, these systems are not only reactive but also proactive. By predicting earthquakes and quickly warning potential victims about impending disasters, these intelligence systems have proven to be quite useful. Below are two incidents where AIDR averted massive loss of life.

2.5 Nepal Earthquake

In April 2015, an earthquake hit Nepal making enormous harm to property. The 7.8 extent shake happened close to Lamjung. Scarcely 72 hours after the principal wave hit, more than 3,000 volunteers were activated utilizing the Standard Task Force (STF). STF is one of Digital Humanitarian Network's part associations. The volunteers were pooled from more than 90 nations and were soon on the ground prepared to help casualties and survivors. The volunteers had the option to gather rapidly because they were labeled in emergency-related photos and tweets. AIDR utilized every one of the labeled tweets to distinguish and order needs dependent on desperation, foundation harm, and asset organization. This permitted rescuers and volunteers to work proficiently as a unit to help influenced casualties.

2.6 Chile Earthquake

In September 2015, Chile was hit with an enormous seismic earthquake with an extent of 8.3. It happened around 29 miles from the city of Illapel. Speedy response from crisis responders had the option to empty a large number of individuals of the recognized peril zones quickly. This forestalled further death toll. Furthermore, minutes after the shudder, disaster cautioning alarms rang all through the affected regions up to the close by the coast. Cell phones in the space were designated with notice messages of a potential Tsunami following the repercussions of the shudder. Inhabitants in every one of the assigned waterfront regions were approached to empty these risk regions right away.

How might we boost the advantages of AI in catastrophic event situations? There are three freedoms:

- To start with, upgrade coordinated effort between current drives, zeroed in on explicit use cases between a couple of accomplices, into a more effect-centered organization of AI-driven disaster support. The consideration right now committed to creating calculations ought to be adjusted with essentially as much energy and assets to ensure these instruments are broadly accessible and utilized on the bleeding edge of disaster alleviation. As a rule, that implies greater capacity building. We additionally see duplication of endeavors, with the information science local area chipping away at comparative use cases, which could be smoothed out. One alternative may be to build up an area explicit organization or alliance across which industry and worldwide offices would facilitate centered advancement groups, as only one model.

- Second, in the close term, foster more essential information catch and coordination apparatuses across various offices on the ground, as opposed to zeroing in most of the speculation on exceptionally progressed AI. This could give the data "fuel" for new lifesaving calculations in the future. Accordingly, it is valuable to spend an equivalent measure of improvement exertion on these basic apparatuses while more refined calculations are additionally being created.

- At last, there is an earnest requirement for more space explicit concurrences on moral AI standards. Numerous drives have been begun by worldwide offices, including the United Nations and the European Union, to foster standards to direct useful employments of AI for the most part. However, given the expansive extension, this is probably going to set aside time. Meanwhile, it is valuable to adjust partners all the more barely in explicit spaces, like disaster reaction. This may incorporate setting a calculation audit cycle to guarantee

AI arrangements fulfill indicated guidelines before they are generally delivered.

The chance for AI to help in the disaster versatility field is huge – directing aid projects, guaranteeing better departures, dispersing help that could help tens if not a huge number of individuals each year. While there are difficulties to survive, with the right degree of coordination and association, this more promising time to come could be a bit more reachable.

The extensive effect of numerous catastrophic events requires the quick investigation of enormous quantities of pictures, which were customarily done physically by individuals. This includes separating from satellite pictures such data as harmed areas, silt volume, number of casualties, and building destruction, which are essential for post-disaster reaction. Artificial intelligence (AI) is capable of rapidly analyzing large amounts of satellite images in a short period. During the 2018 Hokkaido earthquake in Japan, AI was used for landslide detection. It took about 5 days for skillful engineers to distinguish between damaged places and misleading locations, such as farmlands and roads. Image interpretation by AI takes only 5 minutes to detect damaged places with an accuracy of 93% compared with human visual interpretation. In the 2011 Tohoku earthquake, AI analysis was used to detect damages to houses. The work was carried out to understand the locations of houses that were washed away by the subsequent tsunami. The AI was able to spot the affected houses with an accuracy of 94%.[4]

Natural disasters caused by climate change, extreme weather, and aging, and poorly designed infrastructure, among other risks, represent a significant risk to human life and communities. Globally, $94 trillion in new investment[5] is needed to keep pace with population growth, with a large portion of that going toward repair of the built environment. These projects have long cycles due to government authorization processes, huge financial investments, and multi-year building efforts. We need to think creatively about how to accelerate these processes now. In countries around the world, natural disasters have been much in the news. If you had a hunch such calamities were increasing, you're right. In 2017, hurricanes, earthquakes, and wildfires cost $306 billion worldwide, nearly double 2016's losses of $188 billion.[6]

Artificial intelligence and AI can help public security authorities refine techniques over the long run, getting more intelligent with regards to arranging and reaction. Artificial intelligence can be utilized to dissect occasion information for designs, distinguish current in danger regions and populaces, and model future requirements, given populace development, advancement, and environmental change, among different factors. Government pioneers can utilize these bits of knowledge to create strategies that decrease the effect of disasters on networks, such as arranging new structures in less weak regions. Only one out of every odd emergency is avoidable, however, we currently have the innovation to anticipate and forestall disasters, for example, oil slicks or building breakdowns. At the point when unusual catastrophic events do strike, responders can access continuous information that points to help where it should be quicker, decreasing the extra death toll.

Recently, the regions around the Dead Sea in Jordan were flooded, causing the death of 21 children who were on a school trip, and injuring 35 more. Such disasters affect millions of people every year and cause property damage worth hundreds of billions. In 2017 alone, almost 335 natural disasters have affected more than 95.6 million people, and killed 9,697, costing around the US $335 billion.[7] However, the effect of these marvels can be diminished in case we had the option to anticipate their event. Artificial intelligence-controlled frameworks would already be able to foresee the costs of stocks, which include the examination of various factors. Moreover, scientists are applying man-made reasoning to precisely anticipate catastrophic events. By foreseeing the event of cataclysmic events, we can save a large number of lives and take suitable measures to diminish property harm.

3. Using AI to Predict Natural Disaster

Artificial Intelligence has been helping us in different applications, for example, client care, exchanging, and medical services. Furthermore, presently, scientists have discovered that AI can be utilized to anticipate catastrophic events. With colossal measures of good quality datasets, AI can foresee the event of various cataclysmic events, which can be the distinction among life and passing for a huge number of individuals. A portion of the cataclysmic events that can be anticipated by AI are:

3.1 Earthquake

Specialists are gathering gigantic measures of seismic information for investigation utilizing profound learning frameworks. Computerized reasoning can utilize seismic information to break down the greatness and examples of tremors. Such information can demonstrate helpful to

---

[4]https://development.asia/insight/how-ai-can-boost-disaster-response-and-recovery

[5]https://azure.microsoft.com/es-es/blog/using-ai-and-iot-for-disaster-management/

[6]https://azure.microsoft.com/es-es/blog/using-ai-and-iot-for-disaster-management/

[7]https://www.forbes.com/sites/cognitiveworld/2019/03/15/how-ai-can-and-will-predict-disasters/?sh=259782ba5be2

anticipate the event of quakes. For instance, Google and Harvard are fostering an AI framework that can foresee the post-quake tremors of a quake. Scientists have studied more than 131,000 earthquakes and aftershocks to build a neural network. The researchers tested the neural network on 30,000 events, and the system predicted the aftershock locations more precisely when compared to traditional methods.[8]

Additionally, different analysts are making their applications to anticipate quakes and post-quake tremors. Later on, we might have the option to predict quakes and specialists can begin clearing activities as needs are. As of now, Japan is utilizing satellites to investigate pictures of the earth to anticipate cataclysmic events. Artificial intelligence-based frameworks search for changes in the pictures to foresee the danger of disasters like seismic tremors and tidal waves. Additionally, these frameworks likewise screen maturing foundations. Man-made brainpower frameworks can identify distortions in structures, which can be utilized to lessen the harm brought about by falling structures and extensions, or dying down streets.

3.2 Flood

Google is building an AI stage to foresee floods in India and caution clients through Google Maps and Google Search. The information for preparing the AI framework is gathered with the assistance of precipitation records and flood reproductions. Additionally, scientists are creating AI-based frameworks that can gain from precipitation and environment records and tried with flood reproductions, which can anticipate floods better compared to the customary frameworks. Then again, AI can likewise be utilized to screen metropolitan flooding. Specialists at the University of Dundee in the United Kingdom are observing metropolitan flooding by gathering publicly supported information with Twitter and other versatile applications. The information contains pictures and data about the area and circumstances in a territory, which is perceived by the AI. Such frameworks can be utilized to screen and anticipate the harm done by floods alongside different techniques. Similarly, applications dependent on computerized reasoning and profound learning are valuable for disaster the board.

3.3 Volcanic Eruptions

Analysts have consistently battled with discovering techniques to successfully foresee catastrophic events like volcanic ejections. Be that as it may, presently, researchers are preparing AI to perceive minuscule debris particles from volcanoes. The state of the debris particles can be utilized to recognize the sort of well of lava. Such advancements can

help in anticipating ejections and making volcanic danger alleviation methods.

IBM is creating Watson that will anticipate volcanic emissions utilizing seismic sensors and land information. IBM is planning to estimate the areas and the power of emissions with the assistance of Watson. Such applications can assist with forestalling the death toll in regions encompassing dynamic volcanoes.

3.4 Hurricanes

Consistently storms cost property harm worth a huge number of dollars. Consequently, meteorological offices are searching for better procedures to foresee cataclysmic events like tropical storms and twisters, and track their way and power. With more compelling expectation strategies, the concerned specialists can save more lives and decrease property harm. As of late, NASA and Development Seed followed Hurricane Harvey utilizing satellite pictures and AI. The strategy ends up being multiple times better compared to the standard procedures, as the storm can be followed each hour rather than like clockwork with the conventional techniques. Subsequently, the improvements in innovation are helping in observing storms and predicting the way of typhoons, which can aid relief endeavors.

The reception of AI to foresee cataclysmic events will save a great many lives. Moreover, the datasets dissected by the AI-controlled frameworks will help in understanding the greatness and the examples of catastrophic events like floods, quakes, and torrents, which can help in better arranging of foundation in disaster-inclined regions. In this manner, government associations need to convey AI to foresee catastrophic events and screen them precisely to guarantee the security of their residents.

The capability of AI isn't simply in anticipating that a disaster will happen however in foreseeing where it will hit hardest, which protective frameworks are probably going to fizzle, and which networks are in the most peril. This data can be utilized to further develop dynamics with regards to the giving of building grants and protection.

Particularly with cataclysmic events like tropical storms, floods, tidal waves, and quakes, cataclysmic events frequently hit helpless networks the hardest. Man-made disasters like oil slicks do too, a reality exemplified by the Flint water emergency. One of the difficulties that Vulgate refers to is in preparing AI with datasets that don't add to eradicating and harming helpless networks. In all disasters, there are such countless factors that are continually moving, AI might have the option to reach resolutions that people miss. For instance,

[8]https://www.forbes.com/sites/cognitiveworld/2019/03/15/how-ai-can-and-will-predict-disasters/?sh=259782ba5be2

representing the impacts of occasional mosquito populaces while arranging infections like Zika has been an issue of conflict. There are conflicts about its grouping by the World Health Organization (WHO), which pronounced a finish to the infection's status as a worldwide wellbeing crisis, however, a few investigators are stressed the renaming might have been too early. Artificial intelligence could demonstrate the importance of following and arrangement endeavors, just as the refreshing and support of basic gear and safeguards. Lately, when cataclysmic events struck, individuals on the ground have regularly gone to web-based media and impromptu volunteer gatherings notwithstanding, and some of the time as opposed to, depending on help from the public authority or conventional magnanimous associations. Networks have demonstrated that they're equipped for banding together even with disasters and help that doesn't come rapidly enough. The Mexico City earthquake of 2017[9] was one example of the ubiquitous use of social media for the organization of citizen volunteers to save lives. People used social media to effectively crowdsource rescue operations, putting up requests for items and assistance, which were then distributed by volunteer groups, and then social media was used to coordinate meetings and deliveries. Most online media stages as of now depend on AI calculations, however extra AI usefulness could be of incredible help during disasters, helping both common individuals and people on call stay up with the latest and coordinated. Natural hazards can cause calamitous harm and huge financial misfortune. The real harm and misfortune saw in the new many years have shown an expanding pattern. Subsequently, disaster chiefs need to assume a developing liability to proactively ensure their networks by creating effective administration procedures. Various exploration studies apply man-made reasoning (AI) procedures to deal with disaster-related information for supporting educated disaster executives. Conveyed correctly, existing timetable calculations could be utilized to convey and appropriate data where it's generally required. Or then again, AI could be utilized to scratch data from a great many online media posts and enlighten salvage laborers to the hardest-hit regions and individuals in the most need.

The coronavirus pandemic has revealed a lack of disaster preparedness on a global scale. This is even though COVID-19 is not the first pandemic we've faced in recent years—between 2011 and 2018, the World Health Organization tracked 1,483 epidemics and pandemics.[10] Nor will the current pandemic be the last. As indicated by a 2019 report from the Global Preparedness Monitoring Board, pandemic occasions are on the ascent. However by and large the worldwide reaction is hazardously receptive, inadequately planned, and subverted by an "absence of proceeded with political will." These equivalent issues are clear in our reaction to other serious disasters—regardless of whether at the neighborhood, public or worldwide scale. Models incorporate enormous scope climate or seismic occasions or international strains. Luckily, we have instruments available to us that we can use for our potential benefit. Among them is AI, which you can execute to help and expand the abilities to existing frameworks and faculty at each stage in the disaster life cycle. A worldwide disaster frequently starts at a hyperlocal problem area. Artificial intelligence models that search for a spike of notices or occasions across a bunch of recognized areas and afterward cross-reference these against related information focuses can tell us about expected disasters before they strike. For instance, in our pandemic situation, AI can mine online media information, news reports, general wellbeing information, or web search tool contributions to follow reports of diseases or expanded questions identifying with manifestations. These, along with data, for example, medical clinic affirmations information, might be utilized to screen the spread of an illness, raising the alert when a specific thickness is reached or when geolocation information shows that people from an influenced district are going into another area. Truth be told, an AI framework was among quick to perceive the novel Covid episode—it simply required natural eyes to comprehend the importance.

Simulated intelligence additionally has esteem in featuring potential natural disasters like quakes. A new neural net venture identified multiple times a greater number of quakes than conventional techniques, assisting researchers with building more precise models around seismic movement. Man-made intelligence models can likewise recognize cyberattacks, blackouts, and supply issues, and that's only the tip of the iceberg, permitting both nearby and worldwide substances to get ready on the off chance that these early admonition signs form into something else. For disaster help, we need the best answer for doing a salvage reaction and crisis get away from course arranging, just as astute property conveyance. To do this, we first need to sort out precise harm data, like the area of harmed structures, harmed streets, and overwhelmed regions, and so on The entirety of this harm data can be given by harm planning innovation. We put harm data on a guide so it can give dynamic help to people and governments.

Beforehand, disaster alleviation work depended vigorously on directing field studies by individuals. In this way, if completely programmed harm planning innovation is accomplished, individuals may stress over losing their positions.

---

[9] https://becominghuman.ai/the-life-saving-potential-of-ai-in-disaster-relief-c0129135b6ce

[10] https://www.forbes.com/sites/forbestechcouncil/2020/05/26/how-ai-can-be-used-as-a-disaster-preparedness-and-support-system/?sh=1a8c5a421c72

Yet, that probably won't occur – because we need individuals to accomplish more refined help work. We should change the job of these individuals as we improve the effectiveness of disaster alleviation. Another moral issue is "knowledge idiocy." Artificial insight depends on AI. On the off chance that a particular harm situation has not been learned by a machine, it is feasible for that machine to commit errors. Subsequently, AI innovation isn't yet totally dependable. Misinterpretations may defer the salvages and lifesaving. A machine can commit errors. Yet, when the innovation is all around created, in specific situations, it can work shockingly better than a human. We are exploiting AI to upgrade our capacity to react to disasters, not to cause individuals to lose their positions. The mix of AI and the contribution of individuals can speed up our speed toward a truly disaster-versatile society.

REFERENCE

1. https://safetymanagement.eku.edu/blog/the-benefits-challenges-of-using-artificial-intelligence-for-emergency-management/

2. https://www.itu.int/en/myitu/News/2021/03/24/08/49/AI-natural-hazards-disasters

3. https://safetymanagement.eku.edu/blog/the-benefits-challenges-of-using-artificial-intelligence-for-emergency-management/

4. https://development.asia/insight/how-ai-can-boost-disaster-response-and-recovery

5. https://azure.microsoft.com/es-es/blog/using-ai-and-iot-for-disaster-management/

6. https://azure.microsoft.com/es-es/blog/using-ai-and-iot-for-disaster-management/

7. https://www.forbes.com/sites/cognitiveworld/2019/03/15/how-ai-can-and-will-predict-disasters/?sh=259782ba5be2

8. https://www.forbes.com/sites/cognitiveworld/2019/03/15/how-ai-can-and-will-predict-disasters/?sh=259782ba5be2

9. https://becominghuman.ai/the-life-saving-potential-of-ai-in-disaster-relief-c0129135b6ce

10. https://www.forbes.com/sites/forbestechcouncil/2020/05/26/how-ai-can-be-used-as-a-disaster-preparedness-and-support-system/?sh=1a8c5a421c72

CHAPTER 18

Application of Artificial Intelligence for Managing Risks of Disasters

Akanksha Jain

Student of BBALLB Program,
School of Law, Galgotias University, Greater Noida, UP, India.
akanksha_jain.gsolllb@galgotiasuniversity.edu.in.

Mudit Saxena

Student of BBALLB Program,
School of Law, Galgotias University, Greater Noida, UP, India.
mudit_saxena.gsolllb@galgotiasuniversity.edu.in.

Abstract

Over the past few decades, various kinds of disasters have been occurring all over the world each and every day among which they can be natural, technological and man-made. With the disastrous calamities striking all the more regularly as of late due to which there is a rise in emphasis on studying and putting forth strategies of disaster management and establishing the state-of-art advancements to minimize the losses.

In disaster planning, artificial intelligence can do what human brain may neglect or fail to do in the midst of emergencies. This research paper is divided into 3 parts: In the first part of the paper, the research background is established and it particularly examines different existing strategies of disaster management followed in our nation & its opportunities and challenges. An enormous sum is spent by our administration as well as aid agencies in relief and rehabilitation gauges each year. As the famous proverb says "better safe than sorry". The authors in this part highlight how it has now become progressively apparent that an investment in a fiasco preparedness can spare a large number of lives, essential financial resources, occupations and lessen the expense of overall relief assistance, and the increasing need for inculcating the field of Artificial Intelligence (AI) into development of the existing mechanisms.

Furthermore, in the second part of this research paper, the authors further explore and discuss ways and methodology in which AI can be applied and adopted in the disaster management practices, and also find out the systems prevailing in the world involving use of basic AI mechanisms presenting an in- depth analysis of the same, thereby providing a theoretical analysis in addition to an empirical comparison of each country in order to promote a knowhow of their trends, mechanisms while also simultaneously highlighting the policies followed by these countries. In this part the authors also study and put forth the progress made until now in the field of artificial intelligence and how using AI in the data analysis can identify risk areas and determine future needs. Such software algorithms that imitate human intelligence can help in generating conclusions from natural phenomena presented by spatial data.

The last part of this paper presents the author's recommendations and suggestions which shall aid in the development of a splendid model or mechanism inculcating the ideas utilized by the countries with best disaster management frameworks. This part of the research paper also recommends the changes that should be incorporated in order to address & alleviate the related technological and social challenges that may arise with the application of this modern-day technology. Furthermore, the authors in this part also present certain exhortations to the legislature relating to several other adjustments that could be made to existing laws in our nation or presenting new structure which shall aid easy and proper implementation, management, application and adoption of this new design which in turn shall help benefit masses.

Keywords: Artificial Intelligence, Disaster Management, Technological advancements, Machine Learning, Information Technology

1. Introduction

Cataclysmic events are not really uncommon occasions and happen from one side of the planet to the other causing a ton of material harm and, sadly, once in a while loss of living souls. In managing such undesirable occasions, the main thing is presence of various types of information, which are these days accessible like never before previously. With the improvement of innovation and sensors, today information are gotten from various sources. To react rapidly to a fiasco, and to make sufficient clearing, and later on recuperation plans, precise and state-of-the-art spatial information are required. Know the area, just as to follow and break down aloof and dynamic dangers all together recognize and distinguish the potential risks and perils on schedule. Once in a while it is important to consolidate and incorporate information from various information sources. For instance, it could be expected to examine coupled satellite symbolism, drone symbolism and seismic sensor information. Also, in a debacle the executives, information examination is regularly required continuously or close to ongoing, which is anything but a simple errand when performed physically. Such and comparable issues can be tended to by applying strategies for man-made brainpower. Man-made brainpower calculations, that emulate human insight, have gotten exceptionally well known among explores managing various errands in misfortune the executives. The initial segment of the paper characterizes and portrays the idea of man-made consciousness, just as its sorts and most significant subfields. The second piece of the paper gives an outline of the utilization of AI in geospatial examination in a debacle the board through the outline of the contextual analyses.

2. Artificial Intelligence

To tackle social issues, Indian new businesses are developing a lot AI arrangements in training, wellbeing, monetary administrations, and different fields.

Man-made consciousness or Artificial Intelligence (AI) is acquiring a sensational shift the universe of innovation where it tends to be applied for greater efficiency and achievement to improve on the framework. From simply your wireless to the finding of illnesses, AI is currently being utilized in many fields, offering superior and exact gadget activity with quality. In each space and not simply innovation, it has demonstrated to be a way breaking innovation.

As the quickest developing economy with the world's second-biggest populace, India has a major stake in the AI upheaval. The main innovation organizations in the country, like IITs, NITs, and IIITs, can be the support of AI analysts and new businesses. To take care of social issues, Indian new businesses are developing a lot AI arrangements in schooling, wellbeing, monetary administrations, and different fields.

For example, the Deccan Article noticed that the primary Community Center for Artificial Intelligence was dispatched in Hyderabad. They additionally referenced that The Heart Institute is a drive of the Hexagon Capability Center India (HCCI), the best item advancement focus of the innovation significant Hexagon AB. It perceives this foundation as a drive of opportune cultural obligation. The middle will prepare more than 350 understudies in a few clumps each year.

A portion of the AI's principle possibilities in India are:

- Digital colleagues to be utilized by a few profoundly progressed associations to speak with clients, saving the requirement for HR.
- Together with different developments, associations can utilize AI to settle on machines take choices quicker than an individual and perform activities quicker.
- In pretty much every region, AI controls a few developments that will assist people with beating most of intricate issues.
- Trade and Development consent to work together to use the force of state of the art innovation to improve and grow exchange, like AI and blockchain.

Moreover, organizations like Google, Microsoft, and Amazon are attempting to accomplish the public authority's requirements of distributed computing and AI. Privately owned businesses will race to win large agreements, add to the surge of assets to make inventive innovation, and set up new AI and information logical new companies as the Indian government pushes for advanced change and presents more AI drives.

Be that as it may, a portion of AI's significant reception challenges are:

- India has a relatively modest number of analysts in the field of AI and exploration creation.
- India has next to no neighbourhood attention to the most recent information that is being produced by others every day.
- Given the current and likely potential outcomes, Indian organizations have been hesitant to acknowledge AI.
- Despite the quantity of accessible standard bundles, India doesn't have adequate qualified faculty to apply AI to its own difficulties and information.
- In its ability to deal with difficulties, current AI methodologies are insignificant, and they should create to manage the intricacy of life in India.

As a general rule, India's computerized impression has seen huge development. The public authority is likewise pushing various projects toward the target of specialized framework. Various offices and man- made reasoning establishments including areas are creating strategy designs and projects that ingrain such abilities. With somewhat more drive towards assets and systems that support its turn of events, the Indian man-made consciousness market, which is as yet viewed as arising, can surely take a jump.

Human existence is in peril because of human exercises and catastrophic event. Debacle is a one kind of occasion which impacts human existence as far as life and abundance like 6500 individuals passed on in 2017 in Asian mainland because of 200 catastrophe and furthermore billion dollars financial loses not to fail to remember the current pandemic and loss of lives. Yet, nobody can stay away from catastrophe until we live on the lap of nature. We can just limit the death toll and financial misfortunes by utilizing logical based appropriate arrangement with the assistance of PC, Information Communication Technology (ICT) and Artificial Intelligence. All most all private and government organizations like Indian Meteorological division (IMD), National remote sensing agency (NRSA), The Central water commission (CWC) and so forth utilizing web, Geographical Information System (GIS) and Remote Sensing (RS) like part of data correspondence innovation in calamity the executives interaction. It isn't sufficient to utilize ICT just in a fiasco the board cycle since present and future time of designing is Artificial Intelligence. Thus, it is important to utilize man-made brainpower in a debacle the executives cycle to limit loses of human existence and furthermore salvage activity time by utilizing advanced mechanics, drone, and sensors and so on.

Disaster word is the blend of two word "DES" and "star" signifying "terrible" and "star" separately thus, a Disaster is a genuinely interruptions in local area or a general public material loses ,financial loses, social loses, ecological loses and so forth.

The executives implies interaction of constantly or managing individuals or thing. Disaster the Management can be characterized as the getting sorted out and dealing with the asset and reaction to bargain philanthropic effect in crisis.

Disaster risk management manages in three stages[1]:

1. *Pre-Disaster* (before a Disaster): Action assumed to diminish human misfortune &prefer loses.
2. *Disaster occurrence* (during a Disaster): action taken to limit the need of casualties i.e. emergency reactions

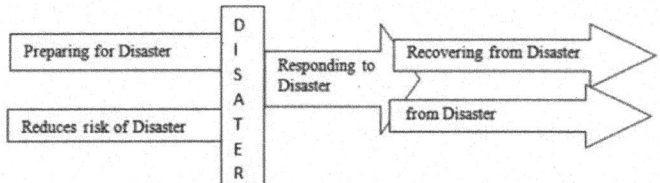

Fig. 18.1 Disaster Management

Source: Adapted from *Artificial Intelligence in Disaster Management* by Shiv Kumar & Shrawan kumar Shrama, IOSR Journal of Computer Engineering (IOSR-JCE), 2019, p.63, available at *https://iosrjournals. org/iosr-jce/papers/Vol21-issue3/Series-1/I2103016369.pdf*

3. *Post Disaster* (after Disaster): activity taken for recuperate and unwavering quality taken of offered local area. The principle objectives of calamity the executives are:
   - Reduces or stay away from, loses from dangers
   - Assure brief help to casualties
   - Achieve and compelling recuperating.

These are four phase of Disaster management[2], But they can overlap:

1. *Mitigation:* Mitigation exercises really wipe out Disaster exactness or limit the impact of Disaster for example Government funded training weakness examination and so on
2. *Preparedness:* making arrangements for reacting for example crisis preparing cautioning framework. Man-made consciousness in Disaster Management
3. *Responses:* activity to limit the peril causes by a Disaster for example crisis alleviation, search and salvage
4. *Recovery:* standardization of local area for example transitory lodging, awards, clinical consideration and so forth

Hazard is a dangerous condition causing loss of life or property basically there two type of hazards[3]

1. *Natural hazards:* land slide, floods, drought, fires etc.
2. *Manmade hazards:* explosion, pollution, war, dam failure etc.

3. II. Artificial Intelligence

Computerized reasoning means counterfeit gadget having insight that implies artificial gadget which can obtain information, get information and apply the information. Yet, according to father of AI, John McCarthy AI is "the science

[1] http://www.habitat.org/lc/TheForum/english/pdf/Forum_Vol19_1.pdf
[2] http://restoreyoureconomy.org/disaster-overview/phases-of-disaster/
[3] http://www.undp.org/content/dam/india/docs/hazaras_disasters_and_your_community_a_primer_for_parliamentarians.pdf

and designing of making insight machine".151% financial misfortunes is because of climate related loses. Simulated intelligence has the chance for the climate likewise[4]:

1. Climate change
2. Bio variety and environmental change
3. Clear air
4. Weather and Disaster flexibility

Man-made brainpower in Disaster Management Artificial intelligence Applications

- Predication and anticipating
- Early cautioning framework
- Resilience framework
- Resilience arranging

Artificial intelligence part utilized by Disaster the executives

- Satellite
- Crowd sourcing
- Sensor and IoT
- Mobile GPS
- Simulation
- Combination of variations IOT's
- Amend flying

Cataclysmic events are on the ascent because of environmental change. Man-made consciousness can further develop fiasco reaction, from diminishing an opportunity to evaluate harm to checking online media to all the more rapidly and successfully convey help.

Be wary with regards to the impediments of AI, and more coordinated effort is vital to augment its advantages.

In excess of 160 million individuals a year are undermined by floods, typhoons, fires and other catastrophic events. Furthermore, the circumstance will probably deteriorate.

As of now, catastrophic events happen multiple times as frequently as they did in 1970. As per gauges, such occasions could fill in recurrence and savagery with the impacts of environmental change.

Man-made brainpower can possibly mitigate the harm by marshalling alleviation assets all the more productively and adequately. It can speed up the conveyance of help and hone the choices of alleviation laborers on the cutting edges.

Computer based intelligence IN GEOSPATIAL ANALYSIS IN DISASTER MANAGEMENT

Computer based intelligence strategies and calculations have discovered their use in all main subject areas, thus did in the field of calamity the executives. Analysts are right now putting forth extraordinary attempts to foster frameworks that can distinguish, and possibly one day anticipate ,quakes, which will be conceivably empowered with the execution of AI. Instances of utilizing AI in calamity the board can likewise be found in weakness and openness appraisals. Moreover, AI is being utilized for handling data, (for example, satellite photographs) and speeding up reaction when a debacle happens. These applications require spatial information. Geospatial investigation is a significant piece of catastrophe the executives that can be found in the entirety of its stages, from relief to recuperation. Because of the need for spatial information, there is countless ventures that apply AI techniques in spatial information investigation in catastrophe the board.[5]

Catastrophe flexibility endeavours might look totally different tomorrow from how they show up today. When a propelling twister or tropical storm is recognized, for instance, geo-spatial, climate and past catastrophe information could be utilized to foresee the number of individuals will be dislodged from their homes and where they will probably move. Such bits of knowledge could help crisis work force recognize how much guide (water, food, and clinical consideration) will be required and where to send it. Man-made intelligence calculations could promptly evaluate flooding, building and street harm dependent on satellite pictures and climate figures, permitting rescuers to circulate crisis help all the more successfully and distinguish those still in harm's way and confined from get away from courses.

Debacle the board is by all accounts a main impetus for India's growing architects, with understudies at one more part of IIT thinking of a modest checking and cautioning framework for avalanches, which kill handfuls in India every year. Four understudies of the Indian Institute of Technology-Madras have assembled drones that can distinguish individuals caught in misfortune hit regions and impart the data to alleviation teams for activity. The 'Eye in the Sky' drones are man-made reasoning and PC vision empowered and can recognize people to some degree covered in garbage utilizing swarm knowledge modules. The innovation was created dependent on the experience of past information on catastrophe the

---

[4]http://www3.weforum.org/docs/Harnessing_Artificial_Intelligence_for_the_Earth_report_2018.pdf

[5](PDF) ARTIFICIAL INTELLIGENCE AND GEOSPATIAL ANALYSIS IN DISASTER MANAGEMENT. Available from: https://www.researchgate.net/publication/335447930_ARTIFICIAL_INTELLIGENCE_AND_GEOSPATIAL_ANALYS IS_IN_DISASTER_MANAGEMENT [accessed Aug 31 2021].

board. The group won the finals of Indian Innovation Growth Program University Challenge held at IIT-Bombay as of late and was among the main 18 creative new companies from the nation over. It will get ₹10 lakh as value less subsidizing. It has additionally won the Microsoft AI for Earth award.

Lt. Gen. (retd) P.R. Shankar, the group's staff counsel and Professor of Practice, Department of Aerospace Engineering, IIT-Madras, said the advancement depended on "modern problematic advances. It will be an amazing asset for saving lives and giving aid during catastrophe alleviation and philanthropic guide tasks". As per him, with additional minor improvement it very well may be broadly utilized in reconnaissance tasks. "The advancement group is working with NDMA and Armed Forces to create and convey native innovations for absolutely Indian answers for Indian issues," he said.

In another case, scientists at IIT-Bombay have fostered an AI calculation that can assist with following catastrophic events on the ground, screen urban communities from the skies, and help security powers recognize extremists in the dark. The calculation, collaborated with an innovation that guarantees checking insusceptible to environmental eccentricities, can assist with saving critical time for salvage activities during calamities. Customarily, climate and calamities have been observed through information from satellites that take constant pictures and pillar them to the ground. In any case, actual squares in the air, for example, substantial brown haze or overcast cover, can make issues in this strategy for perception. This is a significant obstacle during the rainstorm, when an enormous piece of India is inclined to flooding. As radar can penetrate through overcast cover, radar satellites have arisen as another option.

At the point when radar skips off surfaces, its appearance makes a picture of the surface. Nonetheless, while a few radar satellites have been conveyed to screen the climate in the course of recent years — like Sentinel-1, RadarSAT-2, and the forthcoming NISAR — radar pictures are famously difficult to decipher.

The assignment regularly requires profoundly talented manual work by individuals prepared in the physical science of radar dissipating — how radar signals are redirected by surfaces — which is incredibly costly. Metropolitan scenes, where various shapes hurl confounded pictures, make the assignment seriously overwhelming.

The calculation contrived by Shaunak De and Avik Bhattacharya, specialists at IIT-Bombay's Microwave Remote Sensing Laboratory, can precisely decipher these pictures like a human would. To pull this off, the specialists depended on profound learning, a technique where a PC is

over and again took care of huge volumes of comparable information of the sort that should be recognized later.

For instance, a calculation can more than once be taken care of a great many feline pictures from everywhere the world with the goal that it sees how a feline's face is organized. Then, at that point, when it takes a gander at an image of an alternate feline, it can promptly distinguish the creature thusly.

The IIT-Bombay calculation has been taken care of gigantic measures of information on metropolitan scenes and their subsequent radar pictures. Subsequently, it can take a gander at the consequence of a radar-dispersing and distinguish the kind of building or construction that caused it. The PC calculation was basically prepared very much like a human would have been. "The calculation has been shown to beat cutting edge methods and has human-like objective recognizable proof exactness," said De. "Albeit the preparation is a tedious cycle, when the model is made it tends to be applied to countless radar pictures in a moment or two. Subsequently we can effectively, efficiently and precisely map metropolitan focuses in enormous areas of radar information."

The calculation vows to be an opportune mediation. In 2017, the United Nations assessed that more than 54% of the total populace – over 3.8 billion individuals – lived in metropolitan regions, a number that keeps on developing hazardously quick. Worryingly, a great deal of this development is spontaneous and involves wild extension, frequently at the expense of successful administration, metropolitan plan, ideal use of normal assets, and ecological wellbeing.

Accordingly, a great deal of metropolitan regions are inclined to misleadingly disturbed catastrophic events like flooding, and unfit for compelling debacle the executives. In the event of catastrophic events, the calculation can expeditiously make a guide of all settlements in an area and, inside only hours, a legitimate relief or departure plan can be established and surprisingly took care of into Google guides to help local people. On other days, the framework can likewise be utilized to screen unlawful developments or by security powers to spot dugouts or guerrilla development as it can adequately "see" in obscurity.

One more forward leap at another IIT

Avalanches are set off by quakes or rains, or even changes in groundwater pressure. They are irritated by human exercises like deforestation and development.

Understudies of software engineering and structural designing at IIT-Mandi, situated in avalanche inclined Himachal Pradesh, have made a framework that screens climate and soil development. At whatever point any of the sensors distinguishes a huge soil shift, it sets off a notice through signals close by streets, alarming vehicular traffic. Every one of the sensors is additionally equipped for sending mass SMSes to local people, a shelter for times that require brief clearing. IIT-Mandi restricted with the nearby organization to send their hardware at 10 areas around, making the biggest avalanche cautioning framework in India's set of experiences.

The group that fostered this framework is known as the iIoTs (Intelligent IoT Solutions) and has petitioned for patent and the framework purportedly just expenses around Rs 20,000.

Catastrophe hazard decrease, readiness, reaction, recuperation, alleviation and recovery. These are the structure squares of calamity the board. Drones help build up and enhance the effect of every one of these squares by 3x, 10x or even 25x. Catastrophe reaction, specifically, has seen significant steps and improvement with these Unmanned Aerial Vehicles (UAVs) or drones.

The name, "drone" is—pretty much—normal name of the automated flying frameworks; its truncation is UAS. Much of the time we can discover other appearance like UAV (Unmanned Aerial Vehicle) however in Europe the Re-motely Piloted Aircraft Systems (RPAS) is likewise regularly utilized name. Creator is certain, the name "drone" reasonable for everyone anyway numerous specialists wish to communicate it more modern with UAV, UAS or RPAS. There are numerous approach to scale various debacles. Fiascos can be scaled from restricted to heightened, by the affected region or populace, from the ejection to gradually spreading when it creates, or from multiple points of view contingent upon the condition we consider. This paper utilizes specifically a few fiascos like floods, earth-shakes, atomic mishaps and woodland fires, anyway illustratively communicates that point is so colossal, all introduced work is simply contacting the surface. Before the ejection as a pre-debacle action drone application can uphold the anticipation or have the option to supply the early location. If there should arise an occurrence of man-made fiascos like a substance mishap during illicit vehicle the drone street perception has a place with counteraction, following a harmful smoke spreading has a place with early identification, while staying away from the a heightened woods fire by drone flight watch can have a place with both avoidance and early location. After the ejection drone can uphold the administration with continuous checking that implies for the most part the speedy and significant data in regards to the mediation or alleviation. In light of the by drone provided data the impact of the debacle can be moderated all the more adequately and all of important data can uphold settling on better choice. Completing fundamental mediations, regularly it implies after calamity, drone can uphold the fast harm appraisal and furthermore help recuperation. This drone application is

named as post-fiasco action. This application is the nearest to the common life.

Contingent upon the kind of calamity, the influenced region, seriousness, and so on the above exercises can be very surprising from one another's. The reaction at emitted atomic mishap demands distinctive drone action than the gradually raised flood. Opposite side drone applications can rely additionally upon the degree of overseeing catastrophe. At the settle the executives require strategically data however end-clients' needs data promptly about the circumstance. Thusly drone applications in overseeing level can be isolated into 3 gatherings like strategical, functional and strategic levels.

We should get some setting before we move to the drone-sway in misfortune reaction, search and salvage.

Occasion skyline for a calamity – How drones help to enhance fiasco reaction

Does the word 'debacle the executives' mean the very that it did in 2019 (or previously)? Coronavirus has made us mindful of the one truth that we never truly contemplated: 'It COULD happen to me!'

Considering this, the earnestness for legitimate Disaster Risk Reduction (DRR), mindfulness and readiness has taken centerstage. Drones have been a 'deliverer' no matter how you look at it inside catastrophe readiness.

In any case, the inborn characterizing point of a debacle is that it's an occasion. Like any occasion, it has an occasion skyline – a timetable of potential causes finishing into the catastrophe (occasion) trailed by potential activities, impacts or repercussions.

One can use drones from various perspectives:

Pre-DRR (looking over and planning hazard profiling and distinguishing proof) Also, DRR (hazard moderation and calamity readiness).

In any case, when there is a looming calamity, the crisis catastrophe reaction' 'activities' become undeniably more effective. Drones help to advance the reaction time as well as lift the adequacy of these activities. We should take a gander at a portion of these drone-applications and their effect in misfortune reaction.

Drone-further developed crisis reaction time

Everything's with regards to the response or reaction time. One can additionally isolate this debacle reaction time into recognition, examination and activity.

Discovery – Drone-drove reconnaissance assists with fast irregularity or change recognition. These drones can adjust their flight-way mid-air to research a dubious event. This fundamentally decreases the time taken to 'recognize' a potential or evident fiasco.

Investigation – Drone-fuelled surveillance gives a direct examination of the fiasco point. You can peruse more on this at a later point.

Activity – Drones instigate brief on-ground activity, a lot quicker than manual identification + investigation and activity.

Drones decrease the general catastrophe reaction time by (up to) 44.46%. This time decreases the degree of a possible fiasco. Most importantly, it helps save lives.

Drone-empowered situational mindfulness – arranging and procedure

Envision a drone arriving at the occasion site – say a fire 'problem area'. The drone rapidly directs a high-goal visual/warm study – radiated back live to the ground group. The firemen would know precisely how to design their activities to appropriately use their assets (water, gear, staff, and so on) and get the ideal outcome.

Such drone-drove situational mindfulness would mean the contrast between a contained blast and a crazy fierce blaze. You saw this point above when we talked about the 'examination' some portion of reaction time.

Basically, one should capitalize on the restricted reaction time. Drones help rapidly investigate the whole region, delineating every expected bottleneck, flare focuses, exits, vulnerable sides, and so forth One doesn't get various opportunities to settle on the best decision. Drones help crisis catastrophe groups settle on the ideal choice at the ideal time.

On-point and quick clinical and basics supply-drop with drones

Drones should be lightweight yet strong. They ought to be effectively perform supply-drop runs with clinical and fundamental bundles. Such bundles are basic to the prosperity of abandoned survivors (floods, tornadoes, seismic tremors, and so on)

The drones are likewise valuable in health related crises. In India's capital, New Delhi, there is 1 rescue vehicle accessible (dynamic) for each 1, 44,736 arrangement of residents. This is 30.9% dissimilar from the World Health Organization's 'normal rescue vehicle accessibility' proportion. Also, an examination showed that of the relative multitude of fatalities to formally dressed staff since 1994, 25% might have been stayed away from with legitimate 'on the way' care.

Drones can arrive at these health related crises on schedule and convey hardware like Automated External Defibrillators (AED) to save lives and help in ground groups. The speed and productivity of drone-drove reaction can overcome any barrier among assets and genuine need.

Drone-drove Search and Rescue (SAR)

Presently to the genuine salvage part of catastrophe reaction. This is the place where drones have the best substantial effect. For instance, idea Forge has been a consistently present accomplice for the National Disaster Relief Force (NDRF). These drones have been quintessential in different Search and Rescue activities.

The likelihood of discovering survivors is most noteworthy inside the prompt 72 hours following a debacle. Past the likelihood decreases quickly. It's fundamental to be quick and solid in these salvage tasks.

The drone's direct high-res visual and warm imaging to give an unmistakable image of survivors, considerably under rubble or inside distant fissure. The drones cover various sections of land rapidly giving an itemized standpoint of the landscape. This aides the in ground group see all passageways and way towards the survivors. It additionally assists them with understanding the current circumstance as far as correspondence or transport disturbance.

One illustration of such inquiry and salvage is from the Uttarakhand surges of 2015. The calamity had left numerous survivors flung over the precarious landscape. In ground calamity reaction groups worked nonstop to save individuals. In any case, their (manual) visual arrive at confined them. The rugged geology further emphasized the issue.

Here, NDRF conveyed idea Forge drones across the beset region to search for survivors, even in distant areas. Serendipitously, the drones assist with discovering numerous such survivors who were in the end carried out. Idea Forge drones have been essential for some such SAR tasks the nation over. Drones support calamity reaction, search and salvage.

How AI can further develop fiasco versatility and aid projects

As another model, different associations are utilizing AI procedures to decipher online media takes care of following calamities. This kind of examination could give crucial on-the-scene data about foundation harm and aid being given to casualties by hailing pictures from covers where individuals are without covers or waiting outside in the roads.

However even as numerous public area associations and private area information players, for example, Mastercard, Microsoft and Google add to the improvement of calamity alleviation, the effect of the endeavours is as yet kept down by a few difficulties.

One is restricted extension. Numerous private-area drives include one or a couple of government or NGO accomplices, and spotlight on explicit use cases, frequently in relative confinement from the bigger fiasco alleviation local area and without reconciliation into set up calamity help conventions. This prompts discontinuity of endeavours and may bring about AI-inferred bits of knowledge and algorithmic apparatuses being given to associations that can't maintain them or consolidate them adequately into their choice cycles.

Second, while much information exists that could help catastrophe alleviation – satellite, geo-spatial, telecom, and online media, monetary – it's not generally available when it's required. Likewise, datasets are once in a while joined in manners that could open extra knowledge, both with other large datasets yet additionally with information from experienced agents on the ground. This ground view can be significantly more important than bits of knowledge from large information yet is frequently not caught and investigated in a methodical manner.

At last, in calamity circumstances where, by definition, living souls are in question, be mindful with regards to AI's limits. Information examination doesn't generally convey what defenders claim, making it trying to survey such claims without a set up cycle to thoroughly audit calculation strategies and suppositions. For instance, AI models intended to survey private harm have been utilized on business structures even through these structures depend on various materials, development strategies and guidelines. In reality as we know it where the morals of AI are progressively examined, there are no principles to which engineers and clients have consented to follow.

How might we boost the advantages of AI in cataclysmic event situations? There are three freedoms:

In the first place, improve joint effort between current drives, zeroed in on explicit use cases between a couples of accomplices, into a more effect centred organization of AI-driven calamity support. The consideration as of now dedicated to creating calculations ought to be adjusted with basically as much energy and assets to ensure these instruments are generally available and utilized on the forefront of calamity help. As a rule, that implies greater capacity building. We additionally see duplication of endeavours, with the information science local area chipping away at comparative use cases, which could be smoothed out. One alternative may be to build up a domain-explicit association or alliance across which industry and worldwide offices would facilitate centred advancement groups, as only one model.[6]

Second, in the close to term, foster more fundamental information catch and coordination instruments across various organizations on the ground, as opposed to zeroing in most of venture on profoundly progressed AI. This could give the data "fuel" for new lifesaving calculations in future. Consequently, it is helpful to spend an equivalent measure of advancement exertion on these essential apparatuses while more refined calculations are likewise being created.

At long last, there is a dire requirement for more domain-explicit concessions to moral AI standards. Numerous drives have been begun by worldwide organizations, including the United Nations and the European Union, to foster standards to direct gainful employments of AI by and large. Yet, given the wide extension, this is probably going to set aside time. In the meantime, it is helpful to adjust partners all the more barely in explicit domains, like calamity reaction. This may incorporate setting a calculation audit cycle to guarantee AI arrangements fulfil determined guidelines before they are broadly delivered.

The chance for AI to help in the fiasco versatility field is tremendous – directing aid projects, guaranteeing better clearings, conveying aid that could help tens if not a huge number of individuals each year. While there are difficulties to survive, with the right degree of coordination and organization, this more promising time to come could be a bit more reachable.

3. Conclusion

With clear direction on prescribed procedures, AI will improve and better as far as openness, interoperability, and reusability. Artificial intelligence devices for moderation, readiness, Response, recuperation of dry season offers useful assets for dry spell the board framework. The innovation AI can be utilized to tackle the issue of moderation stage. While innovation of advanced mechanics and multi specialist framework can be utilized for reaction and recuperation period of dry spell the executives framework .advanced mechanics and multi specialist can likewise be helpful for emergency the board framework .automated can be utilized for looking and salvage to save the existences of salvage laborers and difficulties looked by them. Because of the way that about 80% of the information that are produced and utilized in various fields of life and science are geospatial in nature, viable use of AI is profoundly attached with the geospatial world (Dasgupta 2017)[7]. Among the spaces of utilization of AI is additionally geospatial investigation in misfortune the

[6]Adeel A, Gogate M, Farooq S, Ieracitano C, Dashtipour K, Larijani H, Hussain A (2018) A survey on the role of wireless sensor networks and IoT in disaster management. In: Geological disaster monitoring based on sensor networks. Springer, pp 57–66
[7]Dasgupta, A., 2017. How AI is disrupting everything and where geospatial fits in? https://www.geospatialworld.net/article/ai-is-disrupting-where-geospatial-fit/[accessed Aug 31 2021].

executives. As innovation develops and progresses, there is a more extensive range of sensors that give spatial information. For speedier and upgraded incorporation and examination of those information, and to get investigation results in close to continuous and hence speed up catastrophe reaction, AI calculations are by and large progressively utilized. As well as securing responses when the fiasco happens, these calculations can help in distinguishing hazard regions and settling on better choices later on. In light of the enormous number of logical exploration projects, one might say that this point is truly exceptional and it will be intriguing to perceive how these strategies will develop later on.

REFERENCES

1. Sara Saravi, Roy Kalawsky, Use of Artificial Intelligence to Improve Resilience and Preparedness Against Adverse Flood Events, May 2019.
2. Muhammad Arslan, Ana-Maria Roxin, Christophe Cruz, A Review on Applications of Big Data for Disaster Management, January 2018.
3. Khaled M. Khalil, M. Abdel-Aziz, Taymour T. Nazmy, The Role of Artificial Intelligence Technologies in Crisis Response.
4. Muhammad Imran, Carlos Castillo, Patrick Meier, AIDR: Artificial Intelligence for Disaster Response, April 2014.
5. Disruptive Technologies and their Use in Disaster Risk Reduction And Management, ITUGET 2019

CHAPTER 19

Scalable IOT solutions with the Amazon Echo Flex Model for 3P Integrations

Anil Kumar Bheemaiah

UMN Twin Cities,
psychEDU@yopmail.com

Abstract

IaC is also CaC, Circuits as Code, we introduce a uniform framework for IOT based sensor fusion and automated persistence to AWS S3 using the per-observer design pattern defined in reactive streams. A uniform scalable IoT architecture is in the automated code generation of Alexa Skills with both AlexaPi and the flex echo. We introduce CaC using the TOMU board, an open source ARM v7 based architecture.

Keywords: IaC, CloudFormation, CaC, Circuits as Code, AWS, stack, SaaS, AIaaS, IoT, ARM

What:

The Amazon Echo Flex, retailing at $24.99 is presented as an attractive scalable IOT platform for use with grid compatible IOT solutions, in conjunction with the open source Tomu and Fomu platforms for multi sensor integrated IOT with Alexa skills and AWS Lambda cloud functions. We compare this with the AlexPi solution, enabling IOT with inexpensive hardware like the raspberry pi zero W or orange pi, or any scalable browser based device, as an IOT solution with Alexa. The marketing pitch for the echo flex, remains as a power source for all the hardware supported by AlexaPi or any other computing needing a 5v USB-A bus and thus supplements the AlexaPi. A case study of flooding in the Lilydale Regional Park in St Paul is presented where a scalable network of Tomu based water level indicators is hypothesized to predict flooding for closure of the park.

How:

Simple resistive water level monitoring sensors are integrated with Tomu and Echo Flex boards using the Alexa Gadget API, USB function for an Rx formulation of Alexa IOT interactions. This allows periodic uploading of water level information to AWS S3 for data mining and predictive analytics.

A hypothetical model to compute the operations of such a 'N' node grid is presented with a case study of lilydale park and the Mississippi river.

Why:

Simplicity, robustness and cost effective solutions, lead to the evolution of the IOT or things network, while Lora or SigFox are touted as solutions we present a simpler approach using WiFi and VUI based echo flex units for IOT.

Applications:

IoT for AI for Earth series, starring Early Bird Warning for Flood Prediction Analytics, an AIaaS data mining Lambda of S3 data from a network of IoT nodes with river level sensors.

1. Introduction

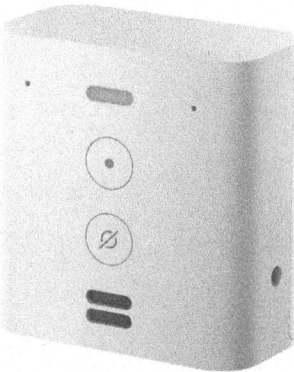

Fig. 19.1 The Echo Flex from Amazon, an e-literacy solution and a new era in alternative computing models? (im-tomu n.d.; Krol 2019)

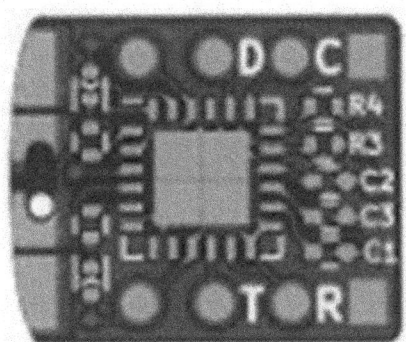

Fig. 19.2 I Am Tomu, the New Open Source Arm M3 Based Iot Architecture For Alexa Integration. (im-tomu n.d.)

2. Problem Definition

Defining a reactive stream based interface for an Alexa based IOT solution. As directives and events, with handlers for event programming with lambda functions. We describe the creation of a USB based IOT input for multi sensor fusion based on AlexaPi or Flex based USB input for automated S3 based persistence using the per-observer design pattern.

3. Background

<original-contribution>

CaC or circuit as Code is the machine genome representation for template driven code generation as JSON or YAML specifications for the automated creation of circuits and PCB layout from schematics using AI driven routing software like Adobe Eagle. Here we represent the use of AlexaPi with the TOMU board.

When we use a CaC representation, we define the code C = [c] as a directed graph with an AIML like pattern-template markup language enabling both scripting and genomic representation as JSON for C.

Let TOMU represent the graph with the nodes and vertices of the TOMU circuit, then we have the set V of variables in TOMU that can be substituted with templates. We also define behavioural, creational and functional design patterns for circuits, allowing symbolic circuit analysis and genesis from circuit generators as code generators in CaC.

V = [A0, A1, A2, A3, A4] for five sensor inputs to TOMU, and also the templates of two port design patterns, TP, we define a library of TP templates, amplification as current mirrors are a needed template for addition to IOT designs for multi sensor fusion IOT boards with AlexaPi.

USB substitution with Qi is another template to consider which we call the FP or four port design patterns with Qi built in.

With this we have a parametric genome of [TOMU, [TP], [Se]] for the design of a multi sensor for sensors [Se] with a parametric model Mp for each Se, for the code generation of a mapping from Se to TP, for integration in isomorphism to the resultant circuit.

The resulting circuit can be readily converted to a layout using an automated program like Autocad Eagle. Mouser or Arrow has the tools for the purchase of the components needed and the PCB services.

Created a schematic

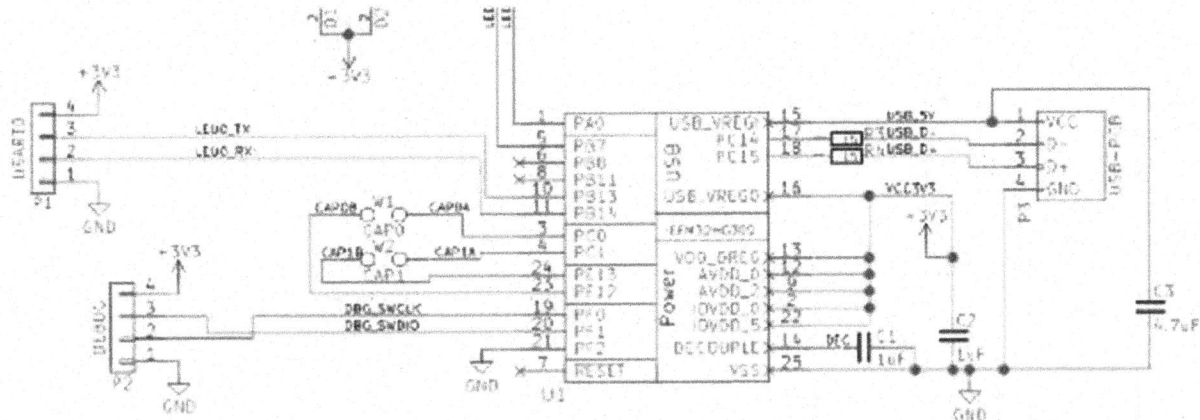

Fig. 19.3 The Circuit Diagram for the Tomu. ("Tomu - A ARM Microprocessor Which Fits in Your USB Port" n.d.)

3.1 Walkthrough: of Main.py:(alexa-pi n.d.)

Class:

1. Player
2. Token

Need to add more classes as needed, the AlexaPi code has the player class, with additional APL code functionality to be integrated and the token class for authentication and AVS interface, using the AVS SDK specifications, see (alexa n.d.).

AlexaPi can be integrated into an AWS IaC, with the authoring of an Alexa Skill from a template for the IoT skill required for the IOT gadget integrated.

```
# from https://github.com/respeaker/Alexa/
blob/mas ter/alexa.py

def alexa_speech_recognizer_generate_
data(audio, boundary):

def alexa_speech_recognizer(audio_stream):

#

https://developer.amazon.com/public/solutio
ns/alexa/alexa-voice-service/rest/speechrec
ognizer-requests

url =

'https://access-alexa-na.amazon.com/v1/avs/
speechrecognizer/recognize'

def alexa_getnextitem(navigationToken): #

https://developer.amazon.com/public/solutio
ns/alexa/alexa-voice-service/rest/audioplay
er-getnextitem-request

def alexa_playback_progress_report_
request(requ estType, playerActivity, stream_
id):

#

https://developer.amazon.com/public/solutio
ns/alexa/alexa-voice-service/rest/audioplay
er-events-requests

def process_response(response):

def trigger_callback(trigger):

def trigger_process(trigger):

def cleanup(signal, frame):
```

AVS urls and details are at : ("Alexa Voice Service v20160207 | Alexa Voice Service" n.d.)

4. Per-Observer for Automated Persistence To S3

The IaC for a Lambda to automate in the use of AVS API for the per-observer pattern to version and persist to S3.

Needed data structures are:

[IAM, path]

Event stream PO = [[Delta], TimeStamp, [DS]] for [DS] where DS are the data structures to be persisted and [Delta] are snapshots of each DS in an isomorphism.

```
{

"AWSTemplateFormatVersion" : "2010-09-09",
```

"Description" : "AWS CloudFormation Sample Template S3_Website_Bucket_With_Retain_On_Delete: Sample template showing how to create a publicly accessible S3 bucket configured for website access with a deletion policy of retain on delete.

WARNING This template creates an S3 bucket that will NOT be deleted when the stack is deleted. You will be billed for the AWS resources used if you create a stack from this template.",

```
"Resources" : {
 "S3Bucket" : {
  "Type" : "AWS::S3::Bucket",
  "Properties" : {
   "AccessControl" : "PublicRead",
   "WebsiteConfiguration" : {
   "IndexDocument" : "index.html",
   "ErrorDocument" : "error.html"
   }
  },
  "DeletionPolicy" : "Retain"
 }
},


"Outputs" : {
 "WebsiteURL" : {
  "Value" : { "Fn::GetAtt" : [ "S3Bucket",
"WebsiteURL" ] },
  "Description" : "URL for website hosted on
S3"
},
```

```
"S3BucketSecureURL" : {

  "Value" : { "Fn::Join" : [ "", [
"https://", { "Fn::GetAtt" : [ "S3Bucket",
"DomainName" ] } ] ] },

    "Description" : "Name of S3 bucket to hold
website content"

    "Handler" : String,
    "KmsKeyArn" : String,
    "Layers" : [ String, ... ],
    "MemorySize" : Integer,
    "ReservedConcurrentExecutions"
: Integer,
    "Role" : String,
    "Runtime" : String,
    "Tags" : [ Tag, ... ],
    "Timeout" : Integer,
    "TracingConfig" :
TracingConfig,
    "VpcConfig" : VpcConfig
  }
}
```
("[No Title]" n.d.)

The code is stored on a code url access resource on S3 as previously described in this publication.

Deployment uses an SDK in python/JS for deployment with security on Alexa hosting, with an associated arn for the lambda.("[No Title]" n.d.)

```
  }

  }

}("[No Title]" n.d.)
```

"AWS CloudFormation provides a common language for you to model and provision AWS and third party application resources in your cloud environment. AWS CloudFormation allows you to use programming languages or a simple text file to model and provision, in an automated and secure manner, all the resources needed for your applications across all regions and accounts. This gives you a single source of truth for your AWS and third party resources."("AWS CloudFormation - Infrastructure as Code & AWS Resource Provisioning" n.d.)

```
{
  "Type" : "AWS::Lambda::Function",
  "Properties" : {
    "Code" : Code,
    "DeadLetterConfig" :
DeadLetterConfig,
```

```
    "Description" : String,
    "Environment" : Environment,
    "FunctionName" : String,
```

5. Security Features

JISON parser for url evaluation is by a filter for malware in uniform resources, in a reactive framework it iterates all resources with a filter to evaluate the threat for black listing such resources as malware and sandboxing them. ("Jison" n.d.)

6. Case Study

River Mississippi floods at Lilydale Regional Park, St Paul. MN, USA.

AI For Earth Series.

We consider a network of simple conductive level and flow sensors(Contributors to Wikimedia projects 2006) with pi based hardware , using the grid point for networking, using AlexaPi and Flex hardware.

Flood Impacts

13.3 feet: Water encroaches on Water Street

14 feet: Minor Flood Stage

14 feet: Lilydale Park area begins to become submerged

15 feet: Moderate Flood Stage

17 feet: Major Flood Stage

17.5 feet: Harriet Island begins to become submerged

18 feet: Shepard / Warner Road may become impassable ("Flood Information" 2015)

("Flood Information" 2015) *National Weather Service website. Including a network of Earth Cams.*

Level Flow sensor integration and the early bird warning system, form another hypothetical AIaaS for any river in the world. For robust data prediction the minimum number of nodes is determined by the confidence intervals of the prediction accuracy and a model of submergence from the GIS of that region of the river. This forms the flood impact data to be broadcasted on an early bird warning system. The threshold needs to be determined on an average level indicator, averaged from many sensors for fault tolerance. There are many cams for flood detection at St Paul, MN with an amateur network on Earthcam website. Predictive analytics, forms a datamining AIaaS, migratable with AWS to any river in the world including the HoH river in Olympic National Park Seattle, where predictive analytics is required. (admin 2011)

The above framework can be easily applied to any river in the world using a FaaS framework as part of the AI for Earth, AIaaS service, saving human lives and flora and fauna by predictive analytics.

</original-contribution>

7. Discussion

A grid based approach to AIaaS using WIFI and power, with an amateur IoT infrastructure that is reliable, fault tolerant and cost effective is presented. The flip classroom for alternative learning, combined with CoderDojo, make this publication accessible even to citizens of the indigenous planet , even without a GED degree.

CaC is proven useful to much of the planet, needing AIaaS services for IoT fabrication, the TOMU is used as an example of AlexaPi based VUI in the design of IoT for predictive analytics and data mining, proving that technology can be useful in a "peace Tribe" approach to disaster casualty and damage mitigation by careful planning.

AI for Earth and IoT, lead to informed planning towards better living with the elements.

8. Future Work

In future work, we prove with the case study of Mike Dodge in The Olympic Peninsula, the use of AIaaS, for grid based PID systems and poacher detection by gunshot detection and DAS systems. This PID system can alert Mike Dodge and the wildlife, thus reducing lethality and conserving fauna and flora. IoT and AIaaS are thus proven useful in conservation monitoring and casualty prevention, the road to veganism.

REFERENCES

1. admin. 2011. "Hoh Indian Tribe Safe Homelands Act." Hoh Tribe. Hoh Tribe. March 13, 2011. http://hohtribe-nsn.org/our-history/testimony-of-chair man-walter-ward-hoh-indian-tribe/.
2. alexa. n.d. "Alexa/avs-Device-Sdk." GitHub. Accessed December 31, 2019. https://github.com/alexa/avs-device-sdk.
3. alexa-pi. n.d. "Alexa-pi/AlexaPi." GitHub. Accessed December 31, 2019. https://github.com/alexa-pi/AlexaPi.
4. "Alexa Voice Service v20160207 | Alexa Voice Service." n.d. Accessed December 31, 2019. https://developer.amazon.com/en-US/docs/alexa/alexa-voice-service/api-overview.html.
5. "AWS CloudFormation - Infrastructure as Code & AWS Resource Provisioning." n.d. Amazon Web Services, Inc. Accessed December 31, 2019. https://aws.amazon.com/cloudformation/.
6. Contributors to Wikimedia projects. 2006. "Level Sensor - Wikipedia." Wikimedia Foundation, Inc. February 10, 2006. https://en.wikipedia.org/wiki/Level_sensor.
7. "Flood Information." 2015. Saint Paul, Minnesota. October 26, 2015. https://www.stpaul.gov/departments/emergency-management/flood-preparations.
8. im-tomu. n.d. "Im-Tomu/tomu-Hardware." GitHub. Accessed December 29, 2019. https://github.com/im-tomu/tomu-hardware.
9. "Jison." n.d. Accessed December 31, 2019. https://zaa.ch/jison/.
10. Krol, Jacob. 2019. "The Echo Flex Is a Compact Alexa Device Designed for Utility." CNN Underscored. CNN Underscored. November 29, 2019. https://www.cnn.com/2019/11/29/cnn-undersco red/amazon-echo-flex-review/index.html.
11. "[No Title]." n.d. Accessed December 31, 2019a. https://docs.aws.amazon.com/AWSCloudForma tion/latest/UserGuide/sample-templates-services-us-west-2.html#w2ab1c28c58c13c35.
12. ———. n.d. Accessed December 31, 2019b. https://docs.aws.amazon.com/AWSCloudForma tion/latest/UserGuide/aws-resource-lambda-fun ction.html.
13. ———. n.d. Accessed December 31, 2019c. https://docs.aws.amazon.com/lambda/latest/dg/n odejs-create-deployment-pkg.html.
14. "Tomu - A ARM Microprocessor Which Fits in Your USB Port." n.d. I'm Tomu - A Tiny ARM Microprocessor Which Fits in Your USB Port. Accessed December 31, 2019. https://tomu.im/tomu.html.
15. "Volunteering." 2015. Saint Paul, Minnesota. October 26, 2015. https://www.stpaul.gov/departments/emergency-management/volunteering.
16. "World's Oldest Ritual Discovered. Worshipped the Python 70,000 Years Ago - Apollon." n.d. Accessed December 31, 2019. https://www.apollon.uio.no/english/articles/200 6/python-english.html.

CHAPTER 20

Internet of Things Applications Towards Mapping of Technologies in Areas of Diagnostics, Testing, Healthcare Delivery Solutions and Equipment Supplies: Challenges and Opportunities in India

Ashok G. Matani

Professor- Department of Mechanical Engineering,
Government College of Engineering,
Jalgaon - 425001 [MS] India,
dragmatani@gmail.com, ashokgm333@rediffmail.com

Abstract

The Internet of Things, or IoT, is a scalable and automated solution that has seen explosive growth in other industries such as automated manufacturing, wearable consumer electronics, and asset management. IoT consists of several functional components: data collection, transfer, analytics, and storage. Data is collected by sensors installed on mobile, end-user hardware like phones, robots, or health monitors. Then, the mobile data is sent to the central cloud server for analytics and decision-making, such as if a machine requires proactive maintenance to prevent unexpected breakdown or if a patient needs to come in for a check-up. The primary challenge is to integrate and streamline digital infrastructure at various stages of the public health response.

This paper highlights the latest developments in internet of things applications towards mapping of technologies in areas of diagnostics, testing, healthcare delivery solutions and equipment supplies and its potential challenges and opportunities in India.

Keywords: Integrate and streamline digital infrastructure, public health response, electronic medical records, deep learning and block chain technology, cryptographic protocols

1. Introduction

In the midst of the current virus outbreak, a dramatic boost in the use of digital and remote technologies is observed. Videoconferencing is now ubiquitous, which helps with social distancing while keeping businesses running. This has often triggered organizations to adapt new technologies faster than they had planned – schools are changing to video-classes, and even religious gatherings are conducted online. [12] The usage of personal remote monitoring devices or apps – Hong Kong has issued wrist bands for arriving passenger with a high-risk profile, while Singapore has a monitoring app for those on Stay Home Notice. In Singapore, temperature measurements at the entrances of almost all public buildings since weeks – connected and report their data into a central instance for real time analysis.[1]

Connecting health systems together can reduce a huge amount of manual admin tasks by consolidating EMRs (electronic medical records), scheduling systems, and patient monitoring into one place. As all hospital resources are being stretched, having a tool to monitor patients all around the hospital and ensure that medication is delivered effectively will be a massive help. Apart from the many cases of corona virus sectioning off parts of hospitals and taking up a huge proportion of hospital staff's time and attention, other high-risk patients still require the same levels of care. Devices that monitor glucose levels for diabetic patients keep track of blood pressure and heart rate levels and alert to issues can allow hospital staff to take care of these patients remotely while in another section of the hospital.[9] Devices for patients at home can also connect to EMRs (electronic medical records) so that chronically ill patients do not necessarily have to visit

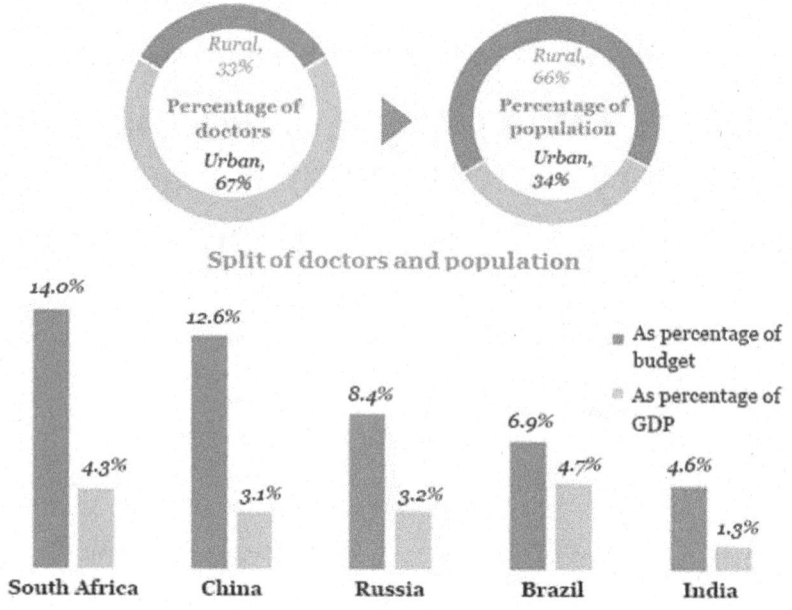

Fig. 20.1   Split of doctors and population

Source: https://www.pwc.in/industries/healthcare/

the hospital or medical center while still being attended by medical staff. [2]

2. Government of India Taking Special Efforts for Mapping of Technologies

The Department of Science and Technology (DST) a department under the Ministry of Science and Technology, Government of India has set up a Covid-19 task force for mapping of technologies to fund nearly market-ready solutions in the area of diagnostics, testing, healthcare delivery solutions and equipment supplies. [10] The task force will map technologies from research and development labs, academic institutions, start-ups, and Micro, Small and Medium Enterprises (MSMEs). Some of these solutions are masks and other protective gear, sanitizers and affordable kits for screening for the corona virus. [3] Ventilators, oxygenators, data analytics for tracking, monitoring and controlling the spread of the virus through artificial intelligence are also being mapped. The capacity mapping group consists of representatives from DST, Department of Biotechnology (DBT), Indian Council for Medical Research (ICMR), Ministry of Electronics and Information Technology, and Council for Scientific and Industrial Research (CSIR). It also has representative from the Atal Innovation Mission (AIM), Ministry of Micro, Small and Medium Enterprises (MSME), Startup India and All India Council for Technical Education

(AICTE). The task force will identify the most promising start-ups that are close to scale up their production in these areas.[4]

3. Latest Innovations in Utilizing Artificial Intelligence Techniques in COVID-19 Treatment and Research

The Indian Institute of Information Technology (IIIT), Bhagalpur, has developed a software that can read chest X-ray films or plates and diagnose whether a patient has contracted the Covid-19 virus or not. The software works based on X-Ray/CT Scan digital inputs and capable for detecting COVID-19 within a very short time. [5] The proposed software can read scanned chest X-ray film or plate scanned and uploaded in a computer in less than one second. Chest X-rays of more than 20 persons were uploaded in the computer and the software gave 100% result and matched with the conventional microbiological swab tests. Software analysis accuracy is expected to be around 95-96%, with only 4-5% of error or less dependent on other factors.[8] The software has been developed by utilizing artificial intelligence techniques t6o develop such model a large number of input data is required. In current scenario there is no indigenous biomedical database available in view of the medical database of few foreign Universities have been utilizing to develop this AI based model for COVID-19 detection. [6]

The Indian Institute of Information Technology and Management-Kerala (IIITM-K) has developed an artificial intelligence semantic search engine to enable researchers to get deeper insights into scientific studies. Named *www.vilokana.in*, which in Sanskrit means 'finding out', the search engine was developed by Centre for Artificial General Intelligence and Neuromorphic Systems (neuroAGI), IIITM-K. [11] The search engine makes easy the contextual search of information from the vast domain of scientific literature, which is a difficult problem faced by scientists and people to get deeper insights into scientific studies. This is a good initiative in the fight against COVID-19 as such AI tools can help extract contextual insights from research articles. The user can supply keyword-based queries, the meaning of which the search engine will be able to understand, and find the relevant text from the scientific papers.[7]

4. Conclusions

It is now the moment for countries to fast-track the construction of new digital infrastructure, such as IoT along with AI, in addition to the hastening of vital projects and major infrastructure construction that's already included in countries' financial stimulus plans. The year 2020 should have been the start of an exciting decade in medicine and science, with the development and maturation of several digital technologies that can be applied to tackle major clinical problems and diseases. These digital technologies include the internet of things (IoT) with next-generation telecommunication networks such as 5G, big-data analytics, artificial intelligence (AI) that uses deep learning and block chain technology.

REFERENCES

1. Eremia, M., L. Toma, and M. Sanduleac. 2017. The smart city concept in the 21st century. *Procedia Engineering* 181: 12–19. doi:https://doi.org/10.1016/j.proeng.2017.02.357.

2. Elhayatmy, G., Dey, N., Ashour, A.S. (2018). Internet of Things Based Wireless Body Area Network in Healthcare. In: Dey, N., Hassanien, A., Bhatt, C., Ashour, A., Satapathy, S. (eds) Internet of Things and Big Data Analytics Toward Next-Generation Intelligence. Studies in Big Data, vol 30. Springer, Cham. https://doi.org/10.1007/978-3-319-60435-0_1

3. Humayun, M., N. Z. Jhanjhi, M. Z. Alamri, and A. Khan. 2020. Smart cities and digital governance. In *Employing Recent Technologies for Improved Digital Governance*, ed. by V. Ponnusamy, K. Rafique, and N. Zaman. IGI Global. doi:https://doi.org/10.4018/978-1-7998-1851-9. [Crossref], [Google Scholar]

4. Kirimtat, A., O. Krejcar, A. Kertesz, and M. Fatih Tasgetiren. 2020. Future trends and current state of smart city concepts: A survey. *IEEE Access* 8:86448–67. doi:https://doi.org/10.1109/ACCESS.2020.2992441.

5. Shahzad, G., H. Yang, A. Waheed Ahmad, and C. Lee. 2016. Energy-efficient intelligent street lighting system using traffic-adaptive control. *IEEE Sensors Journal* 16 (13):5397–405. doi:https://doi.org/10.1109/JSEN.2016.2557345.

6. Sundhari, R. P. M., and K. Jaikumar. 2020. IoT assisted Hierarchical Computation Strategic Making (HCSM) and Dynamic Stochastic Optimization Technique (DSOT) for energy optimization in wireless sensor networks for smart city monitoring. *Computer Communications* 150:226–34. doi:https://doi.org/10.1016/j.comcom.2019.11.032. [

7. S. Kumar, O. Kaiwartya, M. Rathee, N. Kumar and J. Lloret, "Toward Energy-Oriented Optimization for Green Communication in Sensor Enabled IoT Environments," in IEEE Systems Journal, vol. 14, no. 4, pp. 4663-4673, Dec. 2020, doi: 10.1109/JSYST.2020.2975823.

8. Talal, M., Zaidan, A.A., Zaidan, B.B. *et al.* Smart Home-based IoT for Real-time and Secure Remote Health Monitoring of Triage and Priority System using Body Sensors: Multi-driven Systematic Review. *J Med Syst* 43, 42 (2019). https://doi.org/10.1007/s10916-019-1158-z

9. Trencher, G. 2019. Towards the smart city 2.0: Empirical evidence of using smartness as a tool for tackling social challenges. *Technological Forecasting and Social Change* 142: 117–28. doi:https://doi.org/10.1016/j.techfore.2018.07.033.

10. U. S. Shanthamallu, A. Spanias, C. Tepedelenlioglu and M. Stanley, "A brief survey of machine learning methods and their sensor and IoT applications," 2017 8th International Conference on Information, Intelligence, Systems & Applications (IISA), 2017, pp. 1-8, doi: 10.1109/IISA.2017.8316459.

11. Zhang, H., M. Babar, M. Usman Tariq, M. Ahmad Jan, V. G. Menon, and L. Xingwang. 2020. SafeCity: Toward safe and secured data management design for IoT-enabled smart city planning. *IEEE Access* 8:145256–67. doi:https://doi.org/10.1109/ACCESS.2020.3014622.

12. https://irena.org/publications/2021/Aug/Renewable-energy-statistics-2021

13. https://www.pwc.in/industries/healthcare/

Latest Advancements in IoT and Sensors Applications in Renewable Energy Systems Optimization

Ashok G. Matani

Professor Mechanical Engineering
Government College of Engineering,
Amravati – 444 604 [M.S.] India
ashokgm333@rediffmail.com, dragmatani@gmail.com

Abstract

The geographic data and business data is used to develop Geographic Information Systems (GIS) enabled solutions. This digitized data of infrastructure components is used for analytics and real-time monitoring of assets. These solutions are implemented for policy makers, power plant companies, and distribution companies. Geographic Information Systems (GIS) in addition to Remote Sensing (RS) helps in mapping on spatial and temporal scales of the resources and demand. The spatial database of resource availability and the demand assists in the regional energy planning for energy companies. Since 2010,, global investment in renewable energy capacity has touched the USD 200 billion mark every year achieving USD 282 billion in 2019. Dollar investment in new renewable power capacity including all hydropower far exceeded investment in natural gas, coal and nuclear power capacity in 2019, approximately 75% of the total committed to new power generating capacity.

Keywords: Sensor-based technology and data science, efficiency and automation of wind farms and solar fields

1. Introduction

The wind, solar, and geothermal resources are normally installed in interior remote places whereas majority of power demand is in urban areas. Hence an electric superhighway providing infrastructure for electricity to get easily and efficiently is needed. The smart grid is making effective utilization of these energy resources by giving grid operators new tools to reduce power demand quickly when wind or solar power dips, and have more energy storage capabilities to absorb excess wind and solar power when not required, then to release that energy when the wind and solar power dips. In effect, energy storage will help to smooth out the variability in wind and solar resources, making them easier to use. Building an electric superhighway can also help solve the problem, as it will help to ship the power to where it is needed. In this way, connecting wind resources from a diversity of geographic locations assists to balance fluctuations in wind power. Having such geographically diverse wind resources on a single electric superhighway will result in a more steady supply of wind power to the national power grid towards optimizing grid resources.

Investments in renewable energy systems had increased on wind and solar power, with wind power preferring over solar PV since 2010. Developing and emerging economies outweighed developed countries in renewable energy capacity investment for the fifth year running, reaching USD 152 billion. Capacity investment reduced in China and India, outside these two countries rose 17% in developing countries to a record USD 59.5 billion as compared to renewable energy capacity investments in developed countries increased 2% to USD 130 billion.

Renewable energy is now-a-days utilizing the smart grid, due to utility curtailments at the residential, commercial and industrial, and utility levels. After wind energy, now solar energy installations are to a computer-based IoT. The information is integrated and analyzed to reduce losses, maximize power resources, minimize costs, increase system reliability, and enhance electric power efficiency.

In addition to power utilities, solar aggregators, such as SolarCity, are using data centers to interact with the smart grid and perfect operations and maintenance functions. Distributed power networks are integrated with power

Table 21.1 Renewable energy capacity (GW) – for the year 2018

	BRICS	EU-28	China	US	Germany	India	Japan	UK	World total
Geotechnical power	0.1	0.9	0.0	2.5	0.0	0.0	0.5	0.0	13.3
Bio Power	44	42	17.8	16.2	8.4	10.2	4.0	7.7	130
Hydro power	519	130	322	80	5.6	45	22	1.9	1132
Solar power	214	115	176	62	45	33	56	13	505
Ocean power	0.0	0.0	0.2	0.0	0.0	0.0	0.0	0.0	0.5
Wind power	262	179	210	96	59	35	3.7	21	591
Concentrating solar thermal power	0.8	2.3	0.2	1.7	0.0	0.2	0.0	0.0	5.5
Total renewable energy capacity	1040	469	727	250	119	124	86	44	2378
Per capita capacity	0.2	0.7	0.3	0.6	1.4	0.05	0.5	0.6	0.2

** BRICS countries includes Brazil, Russian Federation, India, China, South Africa
Source: https://irena.org/publications

generation, power transmission, and power distribution, with power meters and home appliances, such as refrigerators, TV sets, washing machines, and personal computers also considered part of the network. Residential systems are made of copper and WiFi based whereas energy utilities made of fiber optics to shield noise from other electrical sources. This information flow benefits both the generator and the utility, saving money for both in the process.

2. IoT Applications Areas in Renewable Energy

2.1 Automation to Improve Overall Production

Solar and wind energy are the most popular renewable energy sources due to abundance availability and reliability as compared to any other renewable energy sources. In 2019, Germany sufficed a quarter of its energy demands from its windmill farms. The cost associated with energy production through these resources has also decreased significantly. From the year 1977 onwards, the cost of solar panels has reduced by 99%. Japan, Germany and China are the global leaders in using solar energy.

The assimilation of Artificial Intelligence (AI) and Internet of Things (IoT) systems along with sensors in solar and wind energy systems application had increased their reliability. In order to maximize energy production, most of the solar panels use dual-axis trackers. These tracking systems calibrate the angle of solar panels and assist to receive the maximum solar radiation throughout the day.

Artificial Intelligence (AI) and Internet of Things (IoT) systems can be used to remotely regulate and control these tracking systems to ensure maximum energy production efficiency. By using analytics solutions, the movement of the sun and solar radiation is tracked which is used to automatically adjust the angle of solar panels. Also Artificial Intelligence (AI) and Internet of Things (IoT) systems in wind energy systems are used to monitor operating parameters affecting power generation.

2.2 Smart grids for Elevated Renewable Implementation

The growth of renewable energy is restricted due to less reliability of transmission & distribution systems. The traditional energy grids were built to support the one-way transmission of uniform energy from power plants and bill the customers once a month. Hence now-a-days these grids are not applied to support the varying electricity supply from renewable sources. Artificial Intelligence (AI) and Internet of Things (IoT) systems has enabled the creation of smart grids supporting manual switching between renewable and long-established power plants to ensure an uninterrupted power supply. This switching in smart grids is supporting the varying nature of renewable energy and facilitates non-stop energy supply to the consumers.

2.3 IoT Increasing the Adoption of Renewable Systems

Development of smart grids through Artificial Intelligence (AI) and Internet of Things (IoT) systems has escalated the growth of renewable energy sources. Because they offer benefits of power consumption monitoring and real-time alerting which allows energy utilities to include renewable sources for energy distribution.

Below are some of these benefits:

Contribution from end Consumers

Even the end-consumers are now utilizing renewable energy sources to reduce their electricity bills and become self-dependent. Many countries and India are providing solar subsidies to citizens to increase the adoption of renewable energy systems. Countries are assisting the renewable enegy users to develop solar stations on their rooftop and use them for personal electricity needs. Moreover, consumers can also discharge the excess electricity into the smart grids in exchange for money. This is helping countries to increase the overall adoption of renewables and create a greener environment for citizens to live in.

Balancing Supply and Demand

Smart grids allow energy utilities to provide consumers with a consistent power supply. The integration of Artificial Intelligence (AI) and Internet of Things (IoT) systems in renewable energy assists the energy suppliers to accommodate electricity from renewable sources and suffice the end-consumer demands. The use of smart energy meters on a commercial level gives real-time consumption data to electricity suppliers. By using analytics and data processing solutions, they can also develop trends and patterns related to peak load conditions. Therefore, by using manual switching techniques, energy utilities have reduced the use of power plants during normal off-peak timings and run them when the electricity demand is extreme, resulting in synchronizing the demand and supply conditions in addition to reducing the emission limits of toxic substances in the environment.

Cost-Effectiveness

As per estimates, the global energy demands can be fulfilled by harnessing 1.2% of solar energy from the Sahara desert (around 110400 km^2) thereby reducing losses linked with the transmission and distribution of electricity from such a remote location. Power losses in transmission lines can reach up to 10% for long distances thereby creating complications and challenges which are preventing the escalated growth of solar and renewable energy as a whole. Moreover, implementation of Artificial Intelligence (AI) and Internet of Things (IoT) systems in solar energy will also reduce the cost of building and managing solar stations significantly. Real-time monitoring and predictive analytics features of Artificial Intelligence (AI) and Internet of Things (IoT) systems are used to monitor parameters that can reduce the efficiency of the power station or result in unexpected breakdowns. Hence, utilities can cut some cost related to inspection and repairs; and improve their efficiency.

3. Remote Asset Monitoring and Management Improving Reliability

Affixing Artificial Intelligence (AI) and Internet of Things (IoT) systems sensors to generation, transmission and distribution equipments enables energy companies to monitor it remotely. These sensors measure parameters such as vibration, temperature and wear to optimize maintenance schedules. This preventative maintenance approach can significantly improve reliability by keeping equipment in optimal equipment and providing the opportunity to make repairs before it fails.

4. A more Distributed Grid

The energy grid is becoming more distributed thanks to the rise of residential solar and other technologies. Homeowners and businesses can now generate their own electricity by placing solar panels on their rooftops or even building small wind turbines on their properties is increasingly distributed power system represents a major change for energy companies. In addition to managing a few large generators, they must also now manage a growing number of small generation resources located across the grid. Smart grid technology powered by IoT is helping to enable this distributed energy transformation. A smart grid uses IoT technology to detect changes in electricity supply and demand.

5. More Informed Customers thereby Identifying Waste Areas

Artificial Intelligence (AI) and Internet of Things (IoT) systems technology helps energy customers to be more informed about their energy usage. Internet-connected smart meters collect usage data and send it to both utilities and customers remotely. Because of smart meter technology, many energy companies are now sending customers detailed reports about their energy usage. Customers can also install smart devices in their homes or commercial buildings that measure the power consumed by each appliance and device. They can use this information to identify waste and especially power-hungry appliances to save on their energy bills. Other IoT devices, such as thermostats, can automatically optimize their operation to reduce energy use. Residential customers could potentially benefit the most from these technologies, as the U.S. residential sector representing 37% of energy usage. The commercial using 35% and industrial sectors using 27 % could benefit substantially as well.

6. Improved Grid Management to Build New Infrastructure

Artificial Intelligence (AI) and Internet of Things (IoT) systems technology enables the integration of more distributed resources into the grid thereby improving grid management. Placing sensors at substations and along distribution lines provides real-time power consumption data that energy companies are using to make decisions about voltage control, load switching, network configuration and more which are automated. Sensors located on the grid alerts operators to outages, allowing them to turn off power to damaged lines to prevent electrocution, wildfires and other hazards. Smart switches can isolate problem areas automatically and reroute power to get the lights back on sooner.

Power usage data can also serve as the basis for load forecasting resulting in managing congestion along transmission and distribution lines and ensures that all of the connected generation plants meet requirements related to frequency and voltage control. This power consumption data can also help companies decide where to build new infrastructure and make infrastructure upgrades. The Artificial Intelligence (AI) and Internet of Things (IoT) systems is transforming nearly every sector of our economy, including the one that powers — the energy sector. In the near future, the energy industry will be becoming smarter, more efficient, more distributed and more reliable, due to effective utilization of the Artificial Intelligence (AI) and Internet of Things (IoT) systems.

6. Flying Robots Traveling Dozens of Kilometres without Stopping Planned for Utilization by Power Companies

Energy generating and transmission companies in Europe and other developed economies are utilizing drones used for surveillance of long-distance grids for identification of damage and leaks to avoid network failures to avoid losses of billions of dollars being incurred per year. Italy's Snam-one of , biggest gas utility in Europe is utilizing BVLOS drones in the Apennine hills around Genoa for scouting a 20 km stretch of pipeline because they fly beyond the visual line of sight of operators. France's RTE - a subsidiary of Snam and EDF's network have tested prototypes of long-distance drones which are flying at low altitudes over pipelines and power lines. The company also tested a long-distance drone inspecting 50 km range of transmission lines and sent data to virtually model a section of the grid. For the coming two years, on drone technology, the company has planned a budget for investing 4.8 million Euros ($5.6 million). France's RTE - a subsidiary of Snam and EDF's network have recently tested prototypes of long-distance drones flying at low altitudes for surveillance of pipelines and power lines.

According to Navigant Research reports, various power grid companies are planning to spend from about $2 billion in the year 2020 to more than $13 billion/year on drones and robotics by 2026 globally. At present due to network failures and forced shutdowns, the energy sector incurs a loss of about $170 billion every year. For controlling these losses, flying robots travelling dozens of Kilometers without stopping are now utilized by power companies. New advanced technology drones which are 100 times faster than manual measurement, more accurate than helicopters and with artificial intelligence devices on board are now utilized by renewable energy companies in various sectors to monitor and link solar and wind parks to grids.

7. Conclusions

Artificial Intelligence (AI) and Internet of Things (IoT) sensors to generation, transmission and distribution equipments enables energy companies to monitor it remotely. These sensors measure various parameters namely - vibrations, temperature and wear to optimize maintenance schedules. This preventative maintenance approach had resulted in significantly improving reliability by keeping equipment in optimal equipment and providing the opportunity to make repairs before it fails. In digital twin technology, Artificial Intelligence (AI) and Internet of Things (IoT) sensors attached to the physical unit collect data about its performance are providing significant results. Apart from supporting preventative maintenance programs, this digital twin technology enables virtual troubleshooting and support from remote locations. Artificial Intelligence (AI) and Internet of Things (IoT) sensors also helps to improve safety. Data analytics and machine learning is assisting in making data-driven decisions for predicting weather conditions, increasing affordability and improving shortcomings maintaining the supply chain, thereby enhancing productivity.

REFERENCES

1. Aras Ahmadi, Ligia Tiruta-Barna, Enrico Benetto, Florin Capitanescu, Antonino Marvuglia, On the importance of integrating alternative renewable energy resources and their life cycle networks in the eco-design of conventional drinking water plants, Journal of Cleaner Production, 135 (11) (2016), pp. 872–883.
2. Abraham Debebe Woldeyohannes, Dereje Engida Woldemichael, Aklilu Tesfamichael Baheta, Sustainable renewable energy resources utilization in rural areas, Renewable and Sustainable Energy Reviews, 66 (12.) (2016), pp. 1-9.
3. Aksoezen, M., Daniel, M., Hassler, U., Kohler, N., 2015. Building age as an indicator for energy consumption. Energy and Buildings 87, 74–86.
4. Freitas, S., Catita, C., Redweik, P., Brito, M.C., 2015. Modelling solar potential in the urban environment: State-of-the-art review. Renewable and Sustainable Energy Reviews 41, 915–931.

5. Fumo, N., Biswas, M.R., 2015. Regression analysis for prediction of residential energy consumption. Renewable and Sustainable Energy Reviews 47, 332–343.

6. Hassaan, M.A., 2015. A GIS-based suitability analysis for siting a solid waste incineration power plant in an urban area case study: Alexandria Governorate, Egypt. Journal of Geographic Information System 7 (6), 643.

7. Jianli Pan, Raj Jain Subharthi Paul, Tam Vu, Abusayeed Saifullah, Mo Sha, An Internet of Things Framework for Smart Energy in Buildings: Designs, Prototype and Experiments, IEEE Internet of Things Journal, 2 (6) (2015), pp. 527–537.

8. Mattinen, M.K., Heljo, J., Vihola, J., Kurvinen, A., Lehtoranta, S., Nissinen, A., 2014. Modeling and visualization of residential sector energy consumption and greenhouse gas emissions. Journal of Cleaner Production 81, 70–80.

9. Morano, P., Locurcio, M., Tajani, F., 2015. Energy production through roof-top wind turbines A GIS-based decision support model for planning investments in the City of Bari (Italy). International Conference on Computational Science and Its Applications, Springer, New York, NY, pp. 104–119.

10. S. Surender Reddy, P.R. Bijwe, Day-Ahead and Real Time Optimal Power Flow considering Renewable Energy Resources, International Journal of Electrical Power & Energy Systems, 82 (11) (2016), pp. 400–408.

11. Steven E. Collier, the Emerging Enernet: Convergence of the Smart Grid with the Internet of Things, IEEE Rural Electric Power Conference, 2015: p. 65–68.

12. T. Adefarati, R.C. Bansal, Integration of renewable distributed generators into the distribution system: a review, IET Renewable Power Generation, 10 (7) (2016), pp. 873–884.

13. Qie Sun, Hailong Li, Zhanyu Ma, Chao Wang, Javier Campillo, Qi Zhang, Fredrik Wallin, Jun Guo, A Comprehensive Review of Smart Energy Meters in Intelligent Energy Networks, IEEE Internet of Things Journal, 3 (4) (2015), pp. 464–479

14. Wencong Su, Jianhui Wang, Jaehyung Roh, Stochastic Energy Scheduling in Microgrids with Intermittent Renewable Energy Resources, IEEE Transactions on Smart Grid, 5 (4) (2014), pp. 1876–1883.

15. Various reports published in The Times of India Mumbai edition, 2020.

16. Various reports published in The Times of India Mumbai edition, 2020.

17. Various reports of Zee News T V channel, 2020.

18. Various reports of ABP News T V channel, 2020.

19. Various reports of Government of India , 2020.

20. Various reports of Government of Maharashtra, 2020.

21. https://www.ren21.net/gsr-2019/

22. https://www.smartgrid.gov

23. https://www.softwebsolutions.com

24. https://energycentral.com

25. https://www.renewableenergymagazine.com

Part 4

APPLICATION OF REMOTE SENSING, GIS, DRONE AND UAV FOR DISASTER RISK MANAGEMENT

Chapter 22   GIS, Remote Sensing and Drones for Disaster Risk Management

Chapter 23   Integrating Weather Model & Remote Sensing Indices for Wheat Yield Prediction in Haryana, India

Chapter 24   Floods, Sandbar Dynamics, and its Impact on Communities: GIS Based Case Studies from Assam, India

Chapter 25   GIS Based Hazard Mapping and Vulnerability Assessment of Natural Hazards: A Case Study of Rudraprayag, Uttarakhand

Chapter 26   Preparedness and Damage Assessment using UAVs for Management of Flood in India

Chapter 27   Cyclone Preparedness, Rescue Operations and Damage Assessment using UAVs

GIS, Remote Sensing and Drones for Disaster Risk Management

Venkata Rajgopala Gunturu

Geologist, USDMA-UDRP Worldbank,
Deharadun

Abstract

Concerns of Disaster Management is very serious issue in these days. Disaster activity accelerated by both Geo-genic and anthropogenic factors. GIS, Remote sensing and utilization of drones mostly called UAV very useful to meet the challenges of Disaster Management. It facilitates to acquire and analyze the data even for in accebile areas. The human endeavor can be useful and productive with wise use of these technologies to the betterment to improve in acquiring good Quality of data in Disaster and Risk assessment. It facilitates the existing governing process make more alert and made early response to save life and properties. Loss of Life and wealth can be mitigated at higher margins with the help of these tools. The capabilities of these technologies in full utilization in mitigating loss of life threatening and economic aspects. This includes 3d surface model analysis and visualization of Terrain of high altitudes and rainfall, run off and water drainage behavior in large scale and its effects on Mass movements, Mass wasting, Liquefaction area and landslide inventories.. This can be a huge help in an early stage of interpretation to derive good result. In the last decades along with the space born plat forms drones and Synthetic aperture radars, Unmanned vehicles. It facilitates to know high-resolution images to interpret slope stability analysis with high precision rates. The UAV is in early stage and very useful in future to improve in data inventory and acquisition in Disaster and Risk Management. GIS Enables efficient use of disaster inventory databases and visualize the real picture to make decisions. Using simulation and visualization give broad picture to better understanding real world problem and reduce cognition efforts at greater extent. Open source GIS Emergency Management: (1) GIS Remote sensing and Drones in Preparedness Phase. (2) GIS Remote sensing and Drones in responsive phase. (3) GIS Remote sensing and Drones in recovery phase. (4) GIS and Remote sensing Drones in the mitigation phase. (5) GIS in Disaster data inventory data interpretation and deterministic models and visulvalization. (6) GIS remote sensing in long term and short term surveillance tool.

Keywords: GIS, Remote sensing and Drones for Disaster Risk Management. (Session serial number 9 Technical Session).

1. General Picture of Disaster Management Cycle

1.1 Basic Definitions

- *Prevention*—relates to activities that will either prevent an incident occurring or minimize the impact of a potential incident;
- *Mitigation*—in a similar manner to prevention, seeks to reduce the likelihood and impact of a hazard or an event on a community.

1.2 General Definitions of Standard References of OSHA

- *Preparedness*—relates to activities to ensure that communities are better placed to Mnd to and cope with the impact of an incident;
- *Response*—relates to activities that allow a community to control, respond to and reduce the impact of an incident;
- *Recovery*—relates to returning the community to a state of preparedness and to recover from the impact of an incident and move toward rehabilitation. Activity to understand Immediate response, Deployment, Sustained Reponses, Situation awareness.

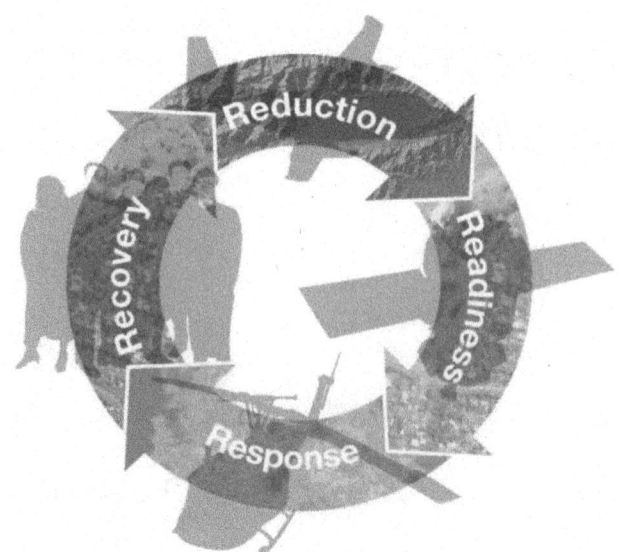

Fig. 22.1

2. Methods

2.1 GIS Remote Sensing and Drones in Preparedness Phase

Prevention and Preplanning

Planning

- Preparation of development plans for cities, dams, roads, and other development works
- General purpose master plans and land use plans.
- Discouraging new development in hazard prone areas.
- Selection of best activity pattern based on risk zones.
- Quick decision making in rescue and relief operations
- Identifying subsidence and uplifted areas
- Identifying Hazard probability. Which area most likely to hit
- A coastal surge, River flooding and River bank protection
- Wind blown hot deserts and dust storms
- Seismically active Hazard zoning maps
- Hazard Severity: Which areas most likely to happened
- Affected population: Where vulnerable people likely to impacted.

Prepardness Phase

Reduction and Readiness

Administrative and Technical Controls

- Identifying parcel grids
- (1) Hazard score per affected parcel: (2) Hazard score per usng cell: Assign a hazard score for each USNG Cell Score is calculated as the sum HPS of all parcels.

- Depth grids
- Surge
- Wind speed area.
- Data acquisition
- National level
- State level
- District level
- Block level
- Ward or village level
- Site investigation scale

Techniques based on revisiting ground-based benchmarks, such as optical leveling or Global Positioning System (GPS), generally offer precise measurements, well recognized by the authorities in charge of the risk management. Nevertheless, the following shortcomings could appear.

Landslides in Preparedness Stage

Landslides are General phenomenon in Elevated Mountian chains Like Himalayas,Alps. Even though landslide don't always occur as a cluster but the sporadic distributions is very isolated events. Landslides generally effect the human life at a great pace and frequent during monsoon. Depending on the type of movements we address like slide, topple, flow, fall, spread. The pace of the movement meter to many metes per years depending upon the Geological and Topographical, climate, Morphometiric entities. Depending upon the root cause and nature they have divided into Geogenic, Biogenic, Anthropogenic related aspects where intensity may change place to place depends on the above conditions. Landslide inventory can be generated by using GIS and Remote Sensing methods along with drones. High resolutions images like DEM, Radar borne Imaging can give reliable information's during pre and post monsoon images with settle to huge difference in their morphometry by analyzing different parameter. The images acquired by ca Ground resolution of the remote sensing data up to 20*20 pixels which can be visualized by Lithological, morphological and structural geological analysis like lineaments, faults, folds and vegetative index, slope angel, aspect, debris movements on meter and kilometer wise calculations which can help in evacuation of vulnerable areas prior to the slip events. Robust technologies like multi spectral analysis and SPOT or IRS images, or using airborne or space borne in SAR techniques Landslide hazard zone mapping involves a detailed assessment and analysis of the past occurrences of landslides in conditions of their location, size and incidence with respect to various geo-environmental factors that cause landslides and mass movements. Landslide hazard zonation map included a map separating the draw out varying degrees of predictable slope stability. The map has an inbuilt factor of forecasting and hence is of probabilistic nature. Depending upon the methodology adopted and the comprehensiveness of the input data used, a landslide hazard zonation map is able to provide help concerning some or all the following individual factor maps:

- Landslide location
- Slope steepness
- Land use/ land cover
- Geology or litho logy
- Density of drainages
- Rainfall

Individual landslides are generally small but they are very frequent in certain mountain regions. Landslides occur in a large variety, depending on the type of movement (slide, topple, flow, fall, spread), the speed of movement (mm/year - m/sec), the material involved (rock, debris, soil), and the triggering mechanism (earthquake, rainfall, human interaction). In the phase of disaster prevention satellite imagery can be used for two purposes: landslide inventory and the mapping of factors related to the occurrence of landslides, such as litho logy, geomorphologic setting, faults, land use, vegetation and slope angels. For landslide inventory mapping the size of the landslide features in relation to th e ground resolution of the remote sensing data is very important. A typical landslide of 40000 m2, for example, corresponds with 20 x 20 pixels on a SPOT Pan GPS, Radar interferometer. Warning systems for landslides are only operational in a few places in the world, with a very high density of information (landslide dates as well as daily rainfall should be known in order to establish rainfall thresholds. Very High Resolution (VHR) imagery, such as from IKONOS-2, might be used successfully for landslide inventory for many cases.

Use of Remo sensing and GIS in Geo-matic, Geodetic survey for Assessing Earthquake monitoring and surveillance

National Seismic Telemetry network is Analyzing past Hundred years of data from different Historical and ongoing records to evaluated epicenters which can cause severe damage. High resolution maps can acquired centimeter variance to establish building codes in these area to built Earthquake proof resistant structures. Unvaco and some Geomatic,Geodetic research centers rigorously working in these areas to save the human lives and properties. Time to time Management and dissipating data using high resolutions remote sensing maps.

Use of remote sensing in Volcanic Hazards

The major applications of remote sensing in volcanic hazard assessment are:

- monitoring volcanic activity & detecting volcanic eruptions,

- identification of potentially dangerous volcanoes, especially in remote areas and
- mapping volcanic landforms and deposits

Capacity Building in the Focussed Areas with Known Data Analysis

- Shelter
  - Safe sheltering, Reolcation in emergency. Alternative routes for Safe and Emergency Transit during Trivial Situations. Analysis of alternative nearest neighbor hoods through satellite images and remote sensing help.
- Food
  - Stocking the food in the Emergency area and food supply chain in the right time. Communications
  - Satellites communication and prepare for the best Infrastructure arrangement during floods, landslides, volcanic eruptions, Desert Storms in which communication is severely effected and prepared to contact for isolated communities. Time to time enquiry through different channels like Command control rooms, live telecasts and broadcasting methods and other sources of information that can help the peoples lives at its best.
- Clearance and access
  - Accebility and clearance during mass transits and obstructive roads due to floods and landslides.
- Water and power supplies
  - Utility arrangements forecast and shrewd management of Essential services during Emergency and Disaster prone areas.
- Temporary subsistence supplies
- Health and sanitation
  - Avoidance of epidemics and diligent efforts in the right time that can cause disaster.
- Public information
- Making aware of the public giving prior calls and use of crowd sourcing at its best.
- Security
  - Providing good security and enforce statutory, Legal obligations. Enforcement of people rights and shun the cause detrimental social elements that can jeopardize the peoples interest like loonies due to bad situations, Prevaricating and avoid creating unnecessary propaganda during bad situation.
  - Construction requirements.
  - Temporary construction of Shelters for the Dislodge and disrupted people and providing confidence amongst the communities to avoid any tensions.

• Techniques like satellite imagery and GIS help to identify areas that are disaster prone, zoning them according to risk magnitudes, inventory populations and assets at risk, and simulating damage scenarios. These tools are even useful in managing disasters as they provide instant access to information required in management decisions. Modern communication systems have also proved very useful, particularly in search and rescue operations. They not only help in providing warnings before the disaster, but also help in creating awareness which helps in reducing panic, confusion and mental stress. A communication network system helps in establishing contacts between relief teams which, with better central coordination, can work more efficiently

Table 22.1 Methods and List of Data Aqusitions

Type of Information	Data Required	Sensor Example	Application Examples
1. Location of fault zones and rupture zones	High Resolution DEM	Airborne Radar and SAR Example	Use of land use planning around active fault to reduce risk from future development in fault hazard location
2. Fault displacement	Interferometric SAR	ERSI/2, ?ENVISAT, ASAR, ALOS, PLASAR,	Knowledge of Fault displacement rates used in Numerical modeling to forecast possible Earthquakes
3. Flood plain mapping	DEM	Airborne LIDAR, ESRI, ENVISAT, ASAR, ALOS, PALSAR	Identification of flood plain can help in inform change and identification development of protective measures
4. Land cover and land use	Optical and Polar metric SAR	SPOT ASTER RADSAT-2	Use to know catchment Management and flood risk Management
5. Vegetation change	Consistent time series data	SPOT ASTER RADSAT-2	Determining Drought Zones, Inform Fire Hazard.
6. Determining Lahar and Lava Flow	DEM High Resolution optical Imagery	SAR Airborne LIDAR SPOT SPOT AVNIR -2, ASTER	Hazard zoning, Public Awareness, Determining Safety shelters
7. Locating potential and actual unstable slopes	DEM Interoferometric, SAR, High Resolution Stereo optical Imagery	Airborne LIDAR, ERSI, ENVISAT, ASAR, ALOS, PLASAR, Aerial Photography.	Hazard mapping for Infrastructure planning
8. Earthquake Management	Chemical Sensors, Radio Repeaters	FLIR, LiDAR, VIIRS, SAR	Allows development of baseline data, Provides near real-time information on incident, Autonomous or remotely piloted flight to position and patrol, Rapid mapping of incident.
9. Base line Infrastructure Map	Very High Resolution optical Imagery	Aerial photography, Quick birds, Iknos, World view	Assist Hazard mapping to iidentify key infrastructure at risk can then be addressed through mitigation or built in redundancy Can also be used for later damage assessment post disaster
10. Base line Topographic Data	Moderate to high resolution optical Imagery	SPOT, ANVIR-2, Aerial Photography Quick Bird, IKNOOS, World View	Hazard Modeling
11. Fire Management	High Resolution Thematic Maps	EO, FLIR, LiDAR, VIIRS, Chemical Sensors, SAR, Radio Repeaters, AIRDAS, AMS-Wildfire	Allows development of baseline data and pre-incident risk assessment, Rapid detection of fire, Provides near real-time information on incident, Autonomous or remotely piloted flight to position and patrol, Rapid mapping of incident scene and identification of hazards for manned aircraft, Identifies and assesses water storage points, Ongoing monitoring of fire and fire behaviour, 3-dimensional plume mapping and monitoring, Provides communications support
12. Locating potential and actual unstable slopes	DEM Interoferometric, SAR, High Resolution Stereo optical Imagery	Airborne LIDAR, ERSI, ENVISAT, ASAR, ALOS, PLASAR, Aerial Photography.	Hazard mapping for Infrastructure planning

Reference: ISPRS - International Archives of the Photogrammetry Remote Sensing and Spatial Information Sciences

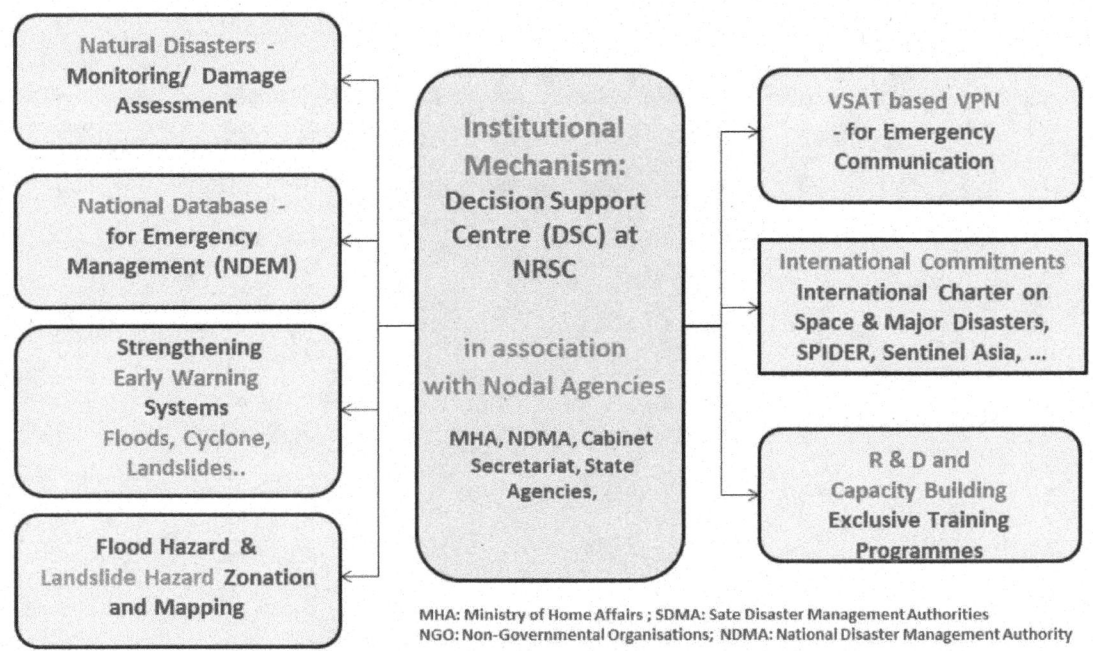

Fig. 22.2 GIS in Disaster Management Indian context

Courtesy: Ministry of Home affairs.

Pre-disaster Mapping using there information sensors and analyze the data to the extent that it facilitates the full pictures to make alerts and prepared for the next post planning stage and readiness review with minimal loss. Some useful application described below. These can facilitate Assess the temporal evolution of Geological criticality. Measure deformation events.

Assess the Residual Risk at a Critical event landslides. The principle of InSAR is briefly introduced in this paper. And DEM measurements are compared with the 1:50,000 China DEM to validate the method. The good coherence between these two DEMs indicates that InSAR is potential in DEM measuring with low cost and high accuracy.

In the second part of this paper, DEM derived with an external low-accuracy DEM (SRTM: Shuttle Radar Topographic Mapping) is compared with the one without an external DEM. The results show that the latter is more unstable than the former, besides it has an overall offset. DEM is significant topography information. With the launch of high accuracy SAR satellite, InSAR will provide a cost-effective way to produce DEM

Historical prospective and philosophical outlook

Disasters always occasion surprise and shock; they are unwanted by those affected by them, although not always unpredictable. Disasters also generate narratives and media representations of the heroism, failures, and losses of those who are affected and respond.

2.2 Role of GIS, Remote Sensing, UAV in Public Domain for Preparedness and Responsive Stage

Disaster definition

Disasters always occasion surprise and shock; they are unwanted by those affected by them, although not always unpredictable. Disasters also generate narratives and media representations of the heroism, failures, and losses of those who are affected and respond.

Physical and Medical Catastrophes, where a healthcare system collapses, and (4) Mega-Pandemics, requiring planning ahead for measures such as social distancing, i.e. large-scale isolation of people in order to prevent the disease from spreading. They are also in part geographical. Thus,

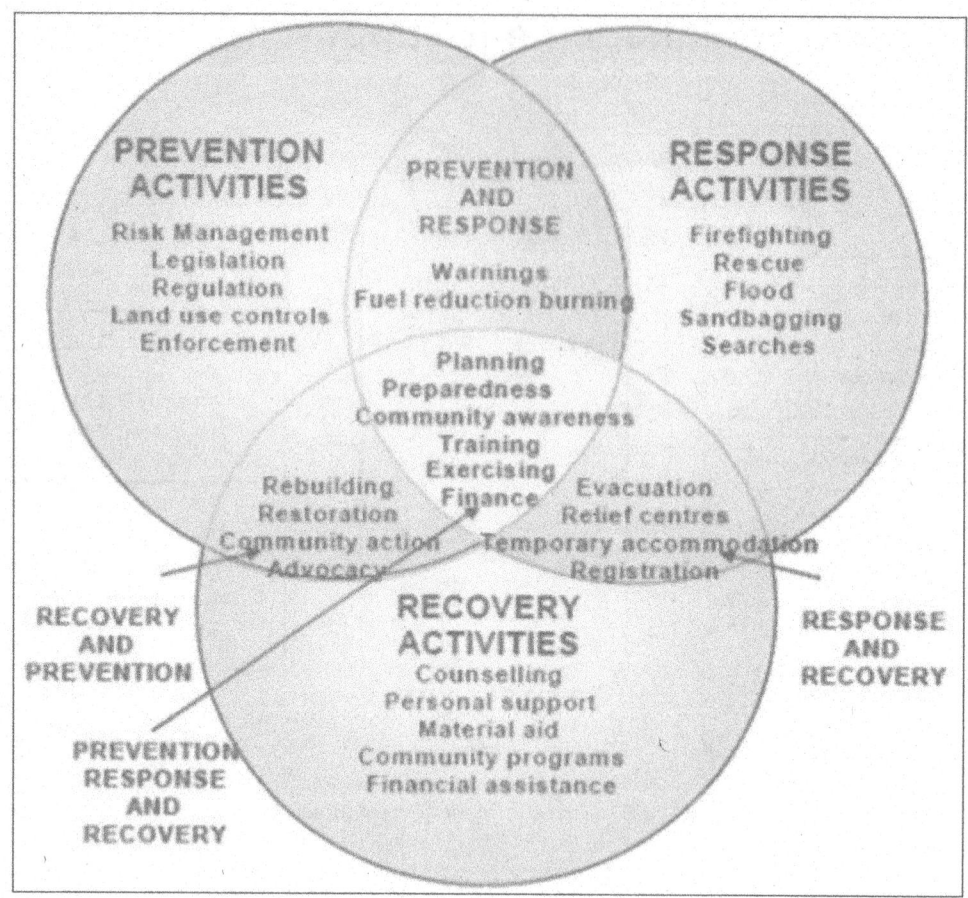

Fig. 22.3 General picture of Disaster Recovery

he writes, a disaster in his terminology is 'a large-scale disruptor that creates a burden of patient need that exceeds the *region's* clinical carrying capacity and '"catastrophe" refers narrowly to the collapse of a previously functional healthcare institution'.

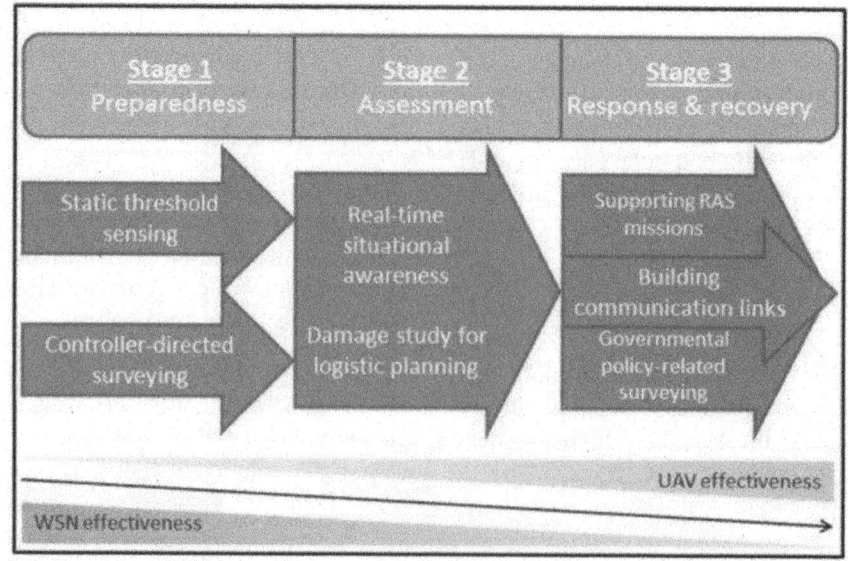

Fig. 22.4

Mobile Aerial Communication Infrastructure

Smart City Sensing

One fundamental aspect of a smart city is its sensing capability, provided through a large number of sensors deployed. But the deployment of these sensors is only part of the required infrastructure, as the generated data has to be collected and aggregated to support informed decision making. UAVs can play an essential role in providing a mobile wireless sensor network [network relay connectivity and situational They are expected to communicate with many different smart objects, such as sensors and embedded devices Their mobility the ability to provide real-time data and the potential to carry hardware for on-board decision making make UAVs the ideal candidate. Indeed, as projected by in UAVs are expected to play a critical role in smart cities and city-wide IoT (Internet-of-Things) infrastructure.

Intelligence Gathering using Drone-UAV (Unmanned Aerial Vehicle).

Drone-Unmanned Aerial Vehicle.An unmanned aerial vehicle (UAV), commonly known as a Drone, is an aircraft without a human pilot on board. UAVs can be remote controlled aircraft (e.g. flown by a pilot at a ground control station) or can fly autonomously based on pre-programmed flight plans or more complex dynamism

UAV are very useful in civil defence and other relief related inputs because of it cost effectiveness and big data generation with high intelligence information use. It is very useful in in-acceile areas where human intervention is less and data gathering is very useful. Multiple UAVs can be useful for commercial and industrial disaster where public life is seriously involved. Because of high sensing capabilities these can so reliable and deployed easily to generate for immediate actions which is important in responsive and rehabilitation phase. When a build up of debris or sediment is located, this material can be scheduled for removal as part of an ongoing risk management plan. UAVs have the potential to provide a significant enhancement to existing capabilities, as they can be pre-programmed to fly specific flight paths over key river courses, levee banks and infrastructure to capture imagery for examination and evaluation. After an event, baseline data can be used to support damage assessments and to assist in the prioritization of recovery activity, for example debris removal or reconstruction of key roads and bridges. Before an incident, UAVs have the potential to help develop our understanding of the microphysics and properties of clouds. This intern provides a better understanding of rainfall and energy release from cloud formations and helps to improve weather forecasting and planning. It can also useful by these utilities like Public Safety and Civil Security

- Emergency/Disaster Monitoring and Control
- Traffic and Crowd Management
- Security for Public Events
- Environmental Management
- (Big) Data Generation
- Surveying, Coordination between heterogeneous systems

UAV use in fold Management

Flood hazard maps are used to develop mitigation plans against the damage caused by flood waters, for example, the construction of dams and levee banks. During a flood, excessive build-up of debris and sediment at bridges, culverts and drains can lead to the failure of that infrastructure, so it is essential that regular inspections of these locations are conducted before, during and after a flood event. When a build up of debris or sediment is located, this material can be scheduled for removal as part of an ongoing risk management plan. UAVs have the potential to provide a significant enhancement to existing capabilities, as they can be pre-programmed to fly specific flight paths over key river courses, levee banks and infrastructure to capture imagery for examination and evaluation. After an event, baseline data can be used to support damage assessments and to assist in the prioritization of recovery activity, for example debris removal or reconstruction of key roads and bridges. Before an incident, UAVs have the potential to help develop our understanding of the microphysics and properties of clouds. This intern provides a better understanding of rainfall and energy release from cloud formations and helps to improve weather forecasting and planning.

Monitoring

UAV can be useful in monitoring of industrial hazards and gas oil spill monitoring where hazard monitoring and surveillance. Potential Gas leakages can be detected with vigilant approach using UAV. Industrial corridors are using effectively to do day to day monitoring using UAV in preparedness and responsive phases.

Synthetic aperture Radars and Inferrograms

1. Inteferograms and SAR(Synthetic aperture radars) Interferograms using synthetic aperture radars useful in subsidence rates especially in Krast Toptographic areas of Himiliyan frontal thrust where high rainfall and tectonic activities are prevailed and can be intense during rainy seasons. Pre and post monsoonal with temporal variation related picture that can be depictable small scale to large scale variation in subsidence levels. This can be detected by Interferograms of hyperspectral and synthetic aperture radar images which

can be useful to detect large scale subsidence and cost-effective in detecting less instrumental deployments. By analyzing and visualizing big scientific image data's where subsidence rate and its precession can be achieved by taking image processing and visulvalization. Visible Infrared Imager Radiometer Suite (VIIRS can be useful in this context with big data generation in preparedness and responsive phases. Visible Infrared Imager Radiometer Suite (VIIRS)—these types of sensors provide advanced imaging and radiometric capabilities and are used extensively in weather mapping and forecasting;

2. *Chemical Detectors*—these sensors can be used to measure a range of particular chemicals that can be explosive, dangerous, or indicative of drug cultivation or manufacture; and

   Synthetic Aperture Radar (SAR)—these types of sensors can detect and map the earth and identify particular features on the earth.

Groudwater pumping rates in industrical areas where scarcity of water and alarming subsidence studies due to high drawdown rates in many urbanization and river delta fronts.

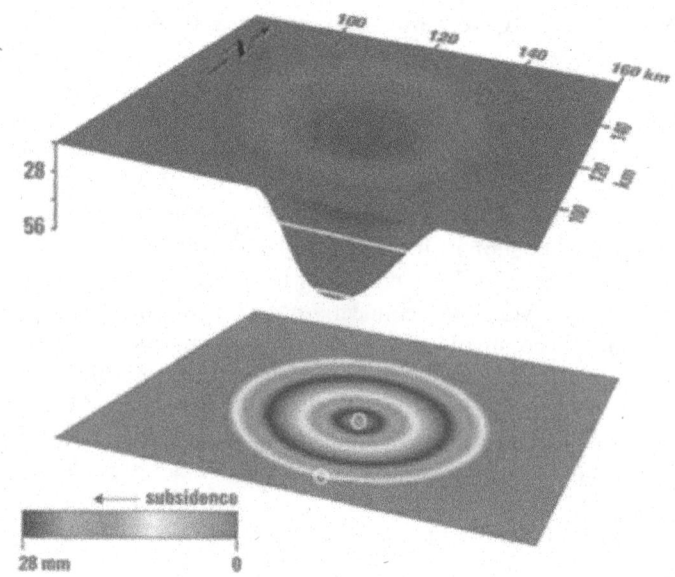

Fig. 22.5

Picture depicting Mapping InSAR displacement. In this illustration, two InSAR fringes nad deformation studies. Lowering the bowl is infers a subsidence.

2.3 GIS Remote Sensing and Drones in Responsive Phase

Landslides in Responsive and Recovery Stage

Situational context	Visibility range	Sensors	Operational analysis	Responsive	End user and potential use of space inputs
GIS and remote sensing Satellites	<100meter visible	Hyper spectral and Gama	Time to time monitoring to take decision support	Monitoring of landslide prone areas by high reolusion maps a	State relief commissioner/ Disaster collector/Hazard zone maps and landlide potential area
Manned and Aerial photography	<50 meters visible	SAR			
Drones and unmanned vehicles	Less than 6 to 10 meters	Close vicinity			

Floods in Responsive and Recovery Stage

Situational context	Visbility range	Sensors	Operational analysis	Responsive	End user and potential use of space inputs
GIS and remote sensing Satellites	<100meter visbile	Hyper spectral and Gama	Time to time monitoring to take decision support	Flood maps of river and flood indurate area	State relief commissioner/ Disaster collector/Hazard zone maps and Flood indurate potential area
Manned and Aerial photography	<50 meters visible	SAR			
Drones and un manned vehicles	Less than 6 to 10 meters	Close vicinity			

2.4 Economic Recovery Health and Social Services

Response to lowest community like panchayt and block level information through crowd sourcing and other mobile communications. Priority fund releases on emergency basis depending on severity of the situation. Immediate restoration measure using Satellite images and aerial photographs and air based monitoring for acquisition of latest position in the ground level situation. Identification of safe area for flood protection measures.

- Search and life rescue
- Food supply chain.
- Medical care during emergency tracking through satellite navigation.
- Fuel, patient movement
- Power, water communication utilities
- Public health emergency forest fire monitoring
- Medical supply chain.
- Housing
- Infrastructure systems
- Natural and cultural resources
- Initial damage Assessment
- Declaration
- Recovery and financial assistance from Governments
- Repair and rehabilitation in a systematic way

point-cloud data (LIDAR, photogrammetric) Document dimensions of damaged facilities; change detection (e.g. Calculate volume of fill to repair a road). cost of damage (e.g. estimate the volume of debris in an area) Drones Observe specific sites at high resolution using various sensors; monitor repairs (e.g. monitor debris removal operations) Infrared/thermograph Feature extraction; observe electrification; monitor repairs

2.5 GIS and Remote Sensing Drones in the Mitigation Phase

Here, we provide a critical review of drone-based remote sensing of natural hazard-related disasters to highlight research trends, biases, and expose new opportunities. We performed a systematic literature search using the Preferred Reporting Items for Systematic Reviews and Meta-Analyses methodology, resulting in 635 relevant articles from which we derived statistics relating to geography, drone hardware, disaster management application, and drone remote sensing data type and analysis method. Key findings include a bias towards: (i) mass movement hazards (38%); (ii) small (< 1 km²) (76%) and rural (79%) study areas in high-income countries and territories (64%); (iii) image-based observations of features from the natural environment (77%); and

(iv) support of mitigation-related vulnerability assessment and risk modeling (54%) and environmental recovery (23%). We recommend that future studies focus on: (i) earthquakes, floods, and cyclones and other windstorms due to higher loss of life and economic impacts; (ii) larger and urban study areas in low, lower-middle, and upper-middle income countries and territories to support vulnerable populations; (iii) under-demonstrated (and especially response-related) disaster management activities, which generally require observations of built features from urban environments; and (iv) data standards for integrating drone-based remote sensing with international disaster management methodologies.

Annexure

Our Experiences

Poornagiri Case. Review and Alternate Design (Shri Purnagiri Temple Protection Work and Approach in District Champawat, Uttarakhand) Contract No.: 208/UDRP/AF/IC/1

Location: Poornagiri Uttrakhandh(lat 29° 8'15.54"N Long: 80°11'54.22"E).

Nature of the work: Slope protection in hilly pilgrim area where crowd management and slope slip events due to heavy rains and natural calamities in Himalyan Frontal thrust Zone of Siesmic zone 5. Seismic coefficients: Horizontal seismic coefficient: 0.12 Vertical seismic coefficient: 0.08 Factor of safety The recommended factor of safety in static condition is 1.30 (IRC HRB SP – 15). As per the report 'IITK-GSDMA Guidelines for Seismic Design of Earth Dams and Embankments Provisions with Commentary And Explanatory Examples (August 2005; Revised May 2007), a limit equilibrium factor of safety of 1.0 shall be considered acceptable in the equivalent-static seismic slope stability assessment. .0 Codal Provisions Seismicity as per IS 1893 part-1 (2016), Purnagiri falls under seismic zone IV. Figure 19: Seismic zonation of map of Utharakhand Seismic coefficients: Horizontal seismic coefficient: 0.12 Vertical seismic coefficient: 0.08 Factor of safety The recommended factor of safety in static condition is 1.30 (IRC HRB SP – 15). As per the report 'IITK-GSDMA Guidelines for Seismic Design of Earth Dams and Embankments Provisions with Commentary And Explanatory Examples (August 2005; Revised May 2007), a limit equilibrium factor of safety of 1.0 shall be considered acceptable in the equivalent-static seismic slope stability assessment. 5.0 Design Methodology After identification of critical locations, design approaches are as under:

- Anchoring large blocks/overhangs
- Consolidation of small blocks which are vulnerable to detachment

- Revetment of surface with mesh
- Limit equilibrium method and finite element method are adopted.

Fig. 22.6 Location map

Fig. 22.7 Google earth image of the study area

Nature of work: Slope stability investigation:

Method used: Drone survey

Fig. 22.8 Aerial view of the location

Fig. 22.9

Fig. 22.10 Valley on the return path side

Identifying hanging and detached blocks which can aggravate slip event in extreme climatic conditions along with seismicity. Close observations time to time to avoid any loose contact and provide rock fall protection using drone survey. This is the preparedness for future program. The area was a sandstone hosted Siwalik age and structurally controlled limb of a tight over tuned syncline and anticline loose core subjected to water erosion.3D model generated using drone images on a slope to analyze vulnerable locations with two different flight modes from NW and NE. The above locations identified meticulously with vigilant observations to esess the vulnerable slope due to rotational block detachment in folded syncline of disturbed zone of in accessible are. The objective of this project to avoid slippages and mass movement for safe transit of piligrams during heavy rains. We are at prevention stage and design a safe slope stabilization programs funded by udrp-world bank. We are using drones in this context of inaccessible areas to explored of highly fractured sandstone detached blocks. Our project is using drones for prevention stage and investing colossal amount of money in the interest of public safety. we are ensuring the following vital points in the above context Public Safety and Civil Security

- Emergency/Disaster Monitoring and Control
- Traffic and Crowd Management
- Security for Public Events
- Environmental Management

We are engaging Wapcos along the individual consultants to analyze effective support systems and built safe transit.

3. Limitations

Despite the capabilities of remote sensing technologies in natural and human disaster management, there are still some limitations in its deployment due to the divide between developed and developing countries, data accessibility (especially high resolution imagery) and technological limitations. This paper examines the recent developments in the application of remote sensing in disaster management such as the proliferation of data through unprecedented sources (Google Earth, crowd sourcing, Global Land Cover) and improvement in data resolutions and integration of technologies).

4. Conclusions

Disaster Mangement concerns are vital in public domain that can be addressed using Remote sensing and UAV techniques is the need of the hour. This can be genrally a big data scientific generation using inputs from various source. All the developing and developed countries widely using to address their problem at par excellence. This can be useful in always despite of its limitations.

5. Acknowledgement

I am thankful to my colleagues and friends of UDRP-World Bank Unit

REFERENCES

1. National Alliance for Public Safety GIS (NAPSG) Foundation, FEMA, General edition for public
2. NRSA, Open source
3. ISRO, Open source
4. India wris version 4.00, Open source
5. cornices, Open source
6. NASA, ESRI, Open source, Data archives and thematic mapping
7. Springer.com, Open source, Earth science magazines
8. NIDM Delhi and CBRI Roorke,USDMA, Open source, Ear science magazines
9. ISPRS - International Archives of the Photogrammetry Remote Sensing and Spatial Information Sciences

Integrating Weather Model & Remote Sensing Indices for Wheat Yield Prediction in Haryana, India

Manjeet

Department of Agricultural Meteorology,
CCS HAU Hisar

manjeetk703@gmail.com

Anurag

Department of Agricultural Meteorology,
CCS HAU Hisar

Ram Niwas

Department of Agricultural Meteorology,
CCS HAU Hisar

Rajeev

Department of Agricultural Meteorology,
CCS HAU Hisar

Dinesh Tomar

Department of Soil Science,
CCS HAU Hisar

Ram Niwas

Computer Section, College of Basic Sciences,
Ccs Hau Hisar

S. K. Bansal

Department of Geography, MDU Rohtak

Abstract

Wheat is a major food grain crop of main agricultural region *i.e.* northern plain of India. Haryana state holds a premium position in wheat production (*Rabi* Season) in the country. Pre-harvest yield estimation of wheat has key role in policy framing. In Haryana, Agriculture is a big support to its economy which continues to occupy a prominent position in State GDP. In present research, Agromet-Spectrals models have been developed for this purpose *i.e.* yield estimation in Haryana with the help of input data such as meteorological indices and satellite based NDVI (NASA's-MODIS) from 2000-2017. Empirical models were developed for predicting wheat yield for Hisar and Karnal districts representation the two agro-climatic zone of state in Haryana, India. The models were developed used weather variable (Temperature (Minimum and Maximum), Relative Humidity (Morning and Evening) and Rainfall) and spectral indices Normalized Difference Vegetative Index viz. Agromet-model (weather model) and Agromet-spectral model (MODIS-NDVI). Weather or Agromet model was integrated with NDVI values for both location to enhanced the accuracy of models. Regression models were developed using significant weather variables and NDVI data for wheat yield prediction at both location. The result revealed that the models when integrated with remote sensing data (NDVI) gave better prediction as compared to agromet model that depends only on weather variables. Agromet-models (adjusted R2 = 0.38 to 0.78) whereas satellite data based NDVI i.e. MODIS-NDVI for both station gave best result (Adjusted R2 = 0.61-0.86) as compared to weather models. MODIS-NDVI pixel based values observed to be more effective for wheat yield predication in integrated with weather parameters. This study could help the provincial government of Haryana as well as in northern plains in estimation of yield prior harvest at first week of April by using weather spectral (NDVI-MODIS) models.

Keywords: Agromet-Spectral model, MODIS, NDVI, Remote sensing, Weather parameter

1. Introduction

Wheat (*Triticum aestivum* L.) is a major Cereal crop of the world in terms of production. In India, wheat is the second important food crop being next to rice (Ranjan *et al.*, 2012) and contributes to the total food grain production of the country to the extent of about 35 per cent. (Anonymous, 2019). Yield prediction is a major step for various policy decisions related to distribution and export-import of food grain. In Haryana, Agriculture is a big support to its economy which continues to occupy a prominent position in State GDP. Despite the decline in the share of agriculture sector in the Gross State Domestic Product to 18 percent (2017-18) about two third population of the state still depends upon agriculture for their livelihood. The growing population in agrarian countries like India posing a great pressure on food-grain production. Therefore, for proper planning and management of products, various models and techniques have been developed for accurately prediction of production especially in wheat being main food grain. Earthworm helps in soil sustainable development and increases the yield of crop (Kumar et al., 2020) Mostly, all models use meteorological parameters as input for yield prediction. The NDVI values of wheat during different phonological stages. was observed 0.3 to 0.35 at emergence stage, 0.40 to 0.50 at tillering stage, 0.55 to 0.65 at milking stage, 0.35 to 0.45 at maturity and 0.25 to 0.30 at harvesting stage (Parida and Ranjan, 2019).

Besides meteorological data, remote sensing data have also proved helpful to increase accuracy and timely forecast of yield. A prominent crop weather model was developed by Fisher et al., (1924) and further some modified by Hendricks et al., (1943) and experimentally applied by Agarwal et al., (2007) on the basis of different weather parameter combination for forecasting yield. Weather plays a dominated role on growth and overall condition of a crop. Different weather parameters affect differently on different stages of crop growth. The present study is an effort to find out the weather element or their combination that are responsible for crop yield prediction. Correlation and regression analysis was carried out using Excel spread sheet and SPSS package. A regression correlation analysis was carried out between weather parameters and yield of wheat crop. To carry out this task, sum and sum product values (Agarwal et al., 2007) were taken as input independent factor and yield data as dependent factor in SPSS software to find out those parameters or their combination which were most affecting wheat yield. Sisodia et al., (2014) developed agromet statistical regression models based on meteorological parameter i.e minimum and maximum temperature, relative humidity, wind-velocity and sunshine hours using 20 years data from (1990-91 to 2009-10), to predict wheat yield two month prior to harvest. Saeed et al., (2017) developed agromet-spectral model to forecast wheat yield before harvest with root mean square errors (RMSEs) less than 5%. The NDVI shows strong relationship with crop physiological attributes and high value of NDVI is associated with faster growth rate and higher biomass accumulation during the vegetative stage, and a longer grain filling period by delaying leaf senescence during the ripening phase thereby increasing yield (Babar et al., 2006). Remotely sensed imagery give the information of crop quality and development at different growth stages but some uncertainty

in soil, climatic condition, management and other input data will decrease the prediction accuracy (Jin et al., 2018).

He also used minimum and maximum temperature, rainfall and sunshine hours with MODIS derived NDVI values, that gave better performance in forecasting wheat yield three weeks before harvest in Punjab province of Pakistan. A robust yield model was exercised for estimating and forecasting wheat yield in Hungary at country level in the period of 2003–2015 using MODIS-NDVI data (P. Bognar et al., 2017). Keeping in view these efforts worldwide, this study was designed with the objective to develop an integrated model for yield prediction of wheat by taking meteorological data in corporation with Remote Sensing data derived from two sources IRS and MODIS-NDVI for two locations of different Agro-climatic zones of Haryana state in India.

2. Material and Methods

2.1 Study Area

The present study was conducted for Haryana state by taking two locations i.e. Hisar and Karnal that represent the two agro-climatic zone of the state. Hisar and Karnal districts are located between of 290 09' N, 750 43' E and 29° 43' N latitude, 76° 58' E longitude of western and eastern part of Haryana respectively (Fig.1). The climatic region lies between semi-arid to humid condition.

2.2 Data Collection

Satellite based NDVI values taken from NASA's Moderate Resolution Imaging Spectroradiometer (MODIS, 16 days composite imageries of 250 m resolution) were used from 2000-2017. Rabi season MODIS imagery of path 147 and row 41 were downloaded for whole of growing season on fortnight basis. These composite images were spanning from first-November to April (Rabi Season) were obtained for the time period of 2000 to 2017, covering the entire wheat crop cycle at Hisar and Karnal district of Haryana. Meteorlogical parameters viz. Temperature (Maximum and Minimum), Relative Humidity (Morning and Evening) and Rainfall data were collected from Department of Agricultural Meteorological, Chaudhary Charan Singh, Haryana Agricultural University, Hisar (Haryana) and Central Soil Salinity Research Centre, Sirsa (Haryana) from 2000 to 2017. These models integrated with NDVI values from both of sources for corresponding location for above said time period (2000-2017) to enhance the accuracy of models. The statistics of the wheat yield (Kg/ha) from 2000 to 2017 for Hisar and Karnal (Haryana) were collected from the Haryana Statistical Abstract published on annual basis by Department of Economic and Statistical Analysis, Govt. of Haryana.

Correlation of different combination of yield and weather parameter and then sum products (Agarwal *et al.* (2007) were derived using M S Excel.

2.3 Coefficient of Determination

R-squared also known as the coefficient of determination-is a statistical analysis tool used to predict the future output and how closely it aligns to a single measured model. The adjusted R-squared compares the descriptive power of regression models two or more variables that include a diverse number of independent variables known as a predictor. The validation of these Agromet model equations were execute for the next two consecutive years 2015-16 &2016-17. Different models were prepared viz. Agomet model, Agromet Spectral Model (IARI-NDVI) and Agromet Spectral Model (MODIS NDVI) for wheat yield estimation at regional level in Haryana and described on Table 23.1.

2.3 Normalized Vegetation Index (NDVI)

Normalized vegetation index (NDVI) is calculated as (Rouse Jr *et al.*, 1974):

$$NDVI = (NIR - RED)/(NIR + RED)$$

Where, NIR and RED are the reflectance in the near-infrared and red spectral channels, respectively.

2.4 Selection of Region of Interest (ROIs):

The FCC (False Colour Composite) image of Rabi season of Hisar and Karnal districts were analyzed in different location for identification of wheat crop and polygon (region of interest) were generated. Three locations were chosen Fig. 23.1 for both district to minimize of chance of error that may occurred to mixing of pixels with other crops. These polygons were used as a mask to obtain NDVI values of each season.

Table 23.1 Weather and spectral indices used in models using composite weather variables

	Simple Weather Indices						Weighted Weather Indices					
	TMAX	TMIN	RH 1	RH II	Rf	NDVI	TMAX	TMIN	RH 1	RH II	Rf	NDVI
TMAX	Z10						Z11					
TMIN	Z120	Z20					Z121	Z21				
RH 1	Z130	Z230	Z30				Z131	Z231	Z31			
RH II	Z140	Z240	Z340	Z40			Z141	Z241	Z341	Z41		
Rf	Z150	Z250	Z350	Z450	Z50		Z151	Z251	Z351	Z451	Z51	
NDVI	Z160	Z260	Z360	Z460	Z560	Z60	Z161	Z261	Z361	Z461	Z561	Z61

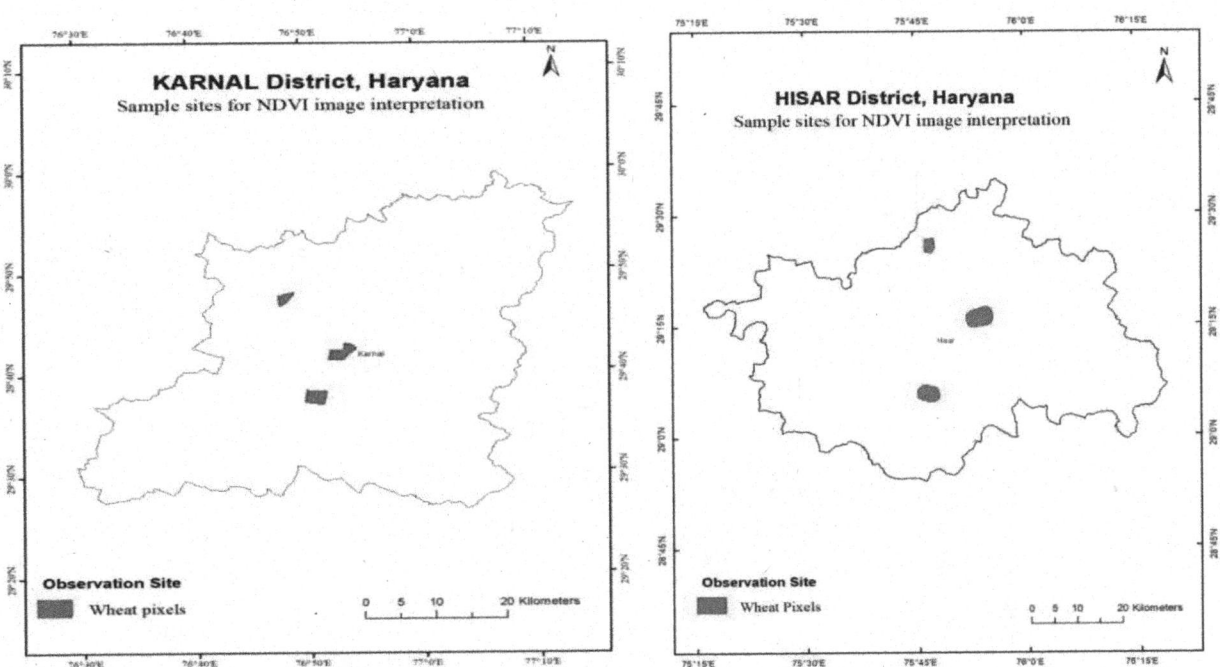

Fig. 23.1 Wheat growing sites for NDVI image interpretation in Karnal and Hisar district

Table 23.2 Effective weather parameters for Hisar and Karnal district (Sum products-correlation)

Location	Year	2000-01	2001-02	2002-03	2003-04	2004-05	2005-06	2006-07	2007-08	2008-09	2009-10	2010-11	2011-12	2012-13	2013-14	2014-15	2015-16	2016-17
	Time	1	2	3	4	5	6	7	8	9	10	11	12	13	14	15	16	17
Hisar	Yield	4447	4283	4182	4062	4135	4162	3704	4392	3920	4829	4139	4600	5098	4477	4180	4310	4758
	Z131	-1934.95	-2363.81	-2167.82	-2282.69	-2067.37	-2791.21	-2614.77	-1770.12	-2466.38	-2039.63	-2522.52	-1940.19	-1946.65	-2120.04	-2693.18	-2018.48	-2696.4
	NDVImax (MODIS)	0.76	0.78	0.73	0.78	0.77	0.77	0.76	0.76	0.80	0.82	0.82	0.79	0.83	0.84	0.83	0.83	0.84
Karnal	Yield	4395	4635	4580	4363	4138	4183	4367	4423	4629	4601	4518	4670	5670	4912	4046	4543	5212
	Z41	9.71	8.57	34.04	10.85	-14.22	-1.05	4.02	-12.25	7.73	10.39	12.08	5.12	36.32	4.55	-11.45	-17.03	-3.80
	Z230	1605 / 3.73	1784 / 7.26	1911 / 6.87	1995 / 8.49	2036 / 9.28	1807 / 6.10	2001 / 0.13	1710 / 8.26	1989 / 4.71	1884 / 8.47	1885 / 5.91	1775 / 8.99	1792 / 5.56	1808 / 3.11	1918 / 5.72	1936 / 7.65	1848 / 0.04
	Z451	-225.09	1586.86	208.84	-341.22	-243.17	-1158.36	877.09	-322.05	486.46	225.44	-183.06	-119.54	6385.68	1413.93	-5144.58	-382.51	-1013.38
	NDVmax (MODIS)	0.82	0.84	0.84	0.83	0.82	0.83	0.8	0.8	0.86	0.82	0.85	0.83	0.86	0.85	0.85	0.85	0.86

2.5 Generation of NDVI Values

Average NDVIs of each polygon was calculated through masking the field by overlaying the ROIs with MODIS-NDVI images using Overlay option of ENVI ("Environment for Visualizing Images"). Average NDVI of each polygon was obtained and so obtained 3 NDVI values corresponding to each polygon were further analyzed to get final NDVI value of a season for a station. NDVI, which is measurement of vigour of crop plant, was calculated using following equation:

3. Result and Discussion

Regression analysis gave summary output that included partial regression coefficient of effective parameter and intercept value to form equation in which yield as dependent and other significant parameters are independent. Table 23.2 details the variables derived based on sum product-correlation of significant weather variables for developing regression models for Hisar and Karnal districts.

Where, Z131 = sum of product of maximum temperature and morning relative humidity, Z41 = Sum of product of evening relative humidity, Z230 = sum of minimum temperature and morning relative humidity, Z451 = sum of product of evening relative humidity and rainfall.

3.1 Agromet Model

The Agromet model worked better for Karnal station with adjusted R2 value of 0.78. The reason may be climatic variability which is less at Karanl as compared to Hisar where the model could not show better results (Adjusted R2 0.38). Agromet yield model equation for Hisar and Karnal districts is present in Table 23.3.

Table 23.3 Agromet regression model equation for Hisar and Karnal districts

Location	Regression Equation	Adjusted R2	R2
Hisar	Y = 5942.17 + 0.73(Z131)	0.38	0.42
Karnal	Y = 5237.23 + 6.44(Z41) − 0.04(Z230) + 0.12(Z451)	0.78	0.83

Further the Agromet Yield models were validated for 2015-16 & 2016-17 for wheat yield estimation for districts Hisar and Karnal as shown in Table 23.4.

The validation of Agromet models revealed that result were better for first year 2015-16 as compared to 2016-17. The post validation test is done for the fitted model using (Percentage deviation) test. This measure the deviation (in percentage) of forecast yield from the observed yield. For the year 2015-16, percentage deviation is comes out to be 3.80%. there is only one dependent variable in the given model along with

Table 23.4   Validation of Agromet models

Location	Observed Yield (Kg/hac.)		Regression Equation	Predicted Yield (Kg/ha)			
	2015-2016	2016-2017		2015-2016	% Deviation	2016-2017	% Deviation
Hisar	4310	4758	Y = 5942.17 + 0.73(Z131)	4474.30	3.80	3973.79	-16.48
Karnal	4543	5212	Y = 5237.23 + 6.44(Z41) − 0.04(Z230) + 0.12(Z451)	4283.46	-5.70	4351.97	-16.50

intercept term. Validity test based on a single year can't be considered since it can't be because of the changes in the trend of observed value. In order to select a good model, the model validation for multiple years. It is very clear from the 2016-17 (%deviation 16.48) data that the model is not so good to explain the forecasting. The wheat yield was higher in 2016-17 from normal, that's why the errors are on higher side.

3.2 Agromet-Spectral Model (MODIS-NDVI)

In this model the Agromet models were integrated with crop specific NDVI values or real ground/pixel based NDVI (MODIS satellite data). The regression yield model developed for Hisar and Karnal districts showed considerable

improvements over previous checked models. Again the model worked better for Karnal region as compared to Hisar and this time the adjusted R2 value express its applicability for Hisar region also.

Table 23.5   Regression yield model equation developed with addition of NDVI (MODIS) for Hisar and Karnal district

Location	Regression Equation	Adjusted R^2	R^2
Hisar	Y = 1850.72 + 0.77 (Z131) + 5318.85 (NDVImax)	0.61	0.66
Karnal	Y = 354.78 + 1.99(Z41) − 0.05(Z230) + 0.13 (Z451) + 6155.59(NDVImax)	0.86	0.90

Table 23.6   Validation of Agromet-spectral (MODIS-NDVI) Yield models for wheat yield estimation for districts Hisar and Karnal during 2015-16& 2016-17

Location	Observed Yield (Kg/ha)		Regression Equation	Predicted Yield (Kg/ha)			
	2015-16	2016-17		2015-16	% Deviation	2016-17	% Deviation
Hisar	4310	4758	Y = 1850.72 + 0.77(Z131) + 5318.85(NDVImax)	4701.5	8.32	4242.3	10.84
Karnal	4543	5212	Y = 354.78 + 1.99 (Z41) − 0.05(Z230) + 0.13 (Z451) + 6155.59(NDVImax)	4479.2	1.42	4590.4	11.93

MODIS-NDVI (wheat pixel based) satellite data considerably improved the accuracy of agromet models for both of the regions as this NDVI values is pixel based or wheat grown area. Agromet models with integration of satellite based NDVI (MODIS) data can help in predicting wheat yield before two month of harvest upto 90% accuracy. The validation of model shows that prediction of yield was within acceptable limits for 2015-16. The production was exceptionally high in 2016-17 as compared to recent past due to supporting weather condition, which increase the validation errors. But in normal year the prediction were very close to real values. The R2 values were 0.66 & 0.90 for Hisar and Karnal respectively This is due to more homogeneity of wheat cropped area in Karnal as compared to Hisar. Similar result found by Singh *et al.,* (2002) estimated the wheat yield in small areas in India using IRS-NDVI and obtained very low error in the range of 1.6-6.7%. Also Nagy *et al.,* (2018) also estimated the

wheat and maize yield 6-8 weeks befroe harvest at regional level in Hungary using MODIS-NDVI. Wang *et al.,* (2019) estimation the winter wheat yield with a realtive of about 6% for selected regions of China.

4. Conclusion

The main objective of the study was to develop a best fit regression model for early wheat yield forecasting during wheat growing season using weather parameters (viz. max. and min. temperature, morning and evening relative humidity and rainfall).

The agromet models were developed on the basis of correlations of wheat yield and weather parameters of *rabi* season (October to March) for the period of fifteen years (2000-2015). The results revealed that weather model alone worked (forecast) well for yield prediction for both Hisar and Karnal regions. Further, to increase the accuracy of models remote sensing data (NDVI) was integrated in weather models that gave high coefficient of determination. The result were better for Karnal as compared to Hisar due to different climatic condition or continuous wheat growing area and high soil moisture retentation capacity. MODIS derived NDVI (exact wheat pixels in field) was tested by integrated with Agromet model. It was found that the weather model integrated with MODIS-NDVI gave more accurate model for wheat yield estimation. The result revealed that maximum temperature and morning RH are determining factors for prediction of wheat yield at Hisar. By inclusion of NDVI as another variable the model accuracy was highest (Adjusted R2=0.61) and error were 8% & 10% for (2015-16 &2016-17). Similarly, minimum temperature & RH (morning and evening) were determining factor for yield prediction at Karnal. By Integration of NDVI, the model accuracy reached to highest among all previous models (Adjusted R2=0.86). The errors were 1.4% and 11.9% for the two year *i.e.* 2015-16 & 2016-17 for validation of wheat yield. The results also emphasis that NDVI values can be a good estimator of crop yield and used for yield estimation and prediction. Agromet models with integration of satellite based NDVI (MODIS) data can help to predict wheat yield with highest accuracy in comparison to Agromet. This study could help the provincial government of Haryana as well as in northern plains in estimation of yield prior harvest at first week of April by using weather spectral (NDVI-MODIS) models.

5. Conflict of Interest

The authors declare that they have no conflict of interest.

REFERENCES

1. Agrawal, R. and Mehta, S. C. Weather based forecasting of crop yields, pests and diseases-IASRI Models. Journal of Indian Society Agriculture statistics., (2007), **61**(2): 255–263.
2. Anonymous, (2019) www.business-standard.com, news article dt. February 28, 2019.
3. Babar, M. A., Reynolds, M. P., Van Ginkel, M., Klatt, A. R., Raun, W. R. and Stone, M. L., 2006. Spectral reflectance indices as a potential indirect selection criteria for wheat yield under irrigation. Crop Science, **46**(2): 578–588.
4. Bognar, P., Kern, A., Pásztor, S., Lichtenberger, J., Koronczay, D. and Ferencz, C., Yield estimation and forecasting for winter wheat in Hungary using time series of MODIS data. *International journal of remote sensing*, (2017), **38**(11): 3394–3414
5. Hendrick, W.A. and Scholl, J.C.,. Technique in measuring joint relationship. The joint effects of temperature and precipitation on crop yield. *N. Carolina Agriculture Exp. Statistics Technology Bulletin*, (1943), **74**.
6. Jin, X., Kumar, L., Li, Z., Feng, H., Xu, X., Yang, G. and Wang, J., 2018. A review of data assimilation of remote sensing and crop models.European Journal of Agronomy, 92: 141–152.
7. Kumar, R., Sharma, P., Gupta, R. K., Kumar, S., Sharma, M.M.M., Singh, S. and Pradhan, G., 2020. Earthworms for Eco-friendly Resource Efficient Agriculture. In *Resources Use Efficiency in Agriculture* 47–84.
8. Nagy, A., Fehér, J. and Tamás, J., 2018. Wheat and maize yield forecasting for the Tisza river catchment using MODIS NDVI time series and reported crop statistics. Computers and Electronics in Agriculture, 151, pp. 41–49.
9. Parida, B. R. and Ranjan, A. K., 2019. Wheat Acreage Mapping and Yield Prediction Using Landsat-8 OLI Satellite Data: a Case Study in Sahibganj Province, Jharkhand (India). Remote Sensing in Earth Systems Sciences, 2(2-3): 96–107.
10. Ranjan, R., Nain, A.S. and Panwar, R. Predicting yield of wheat with remote sensing and weather data. Journal of Agrometeorology., (2012), **9**(2): 158–166.
11. Rouse Jr, J., Haas, R. H., Schell, J. A., & Deering, D. W. 'Monitoring vegetation systems in the Great Plains with ERTS' *NASA. Goddard Space Flight Center 3d ERTS-1 Symposium,* (1974), **1**: 309–317.
12. Saeed, U., Dempewolf, J., Becker-Reshef, I., Khan, A., Ahmad, A., & Wajid, S. A. 'Forecasting wheat yield from weather data and MODIS NDVI using Random Forests for Punjab province, Pakistan', *International journal of remote sensing.* (2017), **38**(17): 4831–4854.
13. Singh, R. A. N. D. H. I. R., Semwal, D. P., Rai, A. and Chhikara, R.S., 2002. Small area estimation of crop yield using remote sensing satellite data. International Journal of Remote Sensing, 23(1), pp. 49–56.
14. Sisodia, B. V. S., Yadav, R. R., Kumar, S., & Sharma, M. K 'Forecasting of pre-harvest crop yield using discriminant function analysis of meteorological parameters', *Journal of Agrometeorology.* (2014), **16**(1): 121–125.
15. Wang, Y., Xu, X., Huang, L., Yang, G., Fan, L., Wei, P. and Chen, G., 2019. An Improved CASA Model for Estimating Winter Wheat Yield from Remote Sensing Images. Remote Sensing, **11**(9): 1–19.

CHAPTER 24

Floods, Sandbar Dynamics, and its Impact on Communities: GIS Based Case Studies from Assam, India

Pulak Das

School of Human Ecology, Ambedkar University Delhi,
Kashmere Gate, Lothian Road, Delhi-110006
pulak@aud.ac.in; pulakdas.ecology@gmail.com

Abstract

Present paper intends to understand the impacts of spatio-temporal dynamicity of sandbars on the people who live on these 'land pieces', in Brahmaputra river system in Assam. The work uses a geospatial approach to calculate the morphometry of sandbars and river banks, and socio-economic studies such as questionnaire surveys and field observations. It is observed that the inhabited sandbar decreases from 3.1 to 1.2 km^2 in 10 years, while the uninhabited sandbar increases from 3.2 to 6.3 km^2 during the same period. Farming and wage labouring are two important livelihood options in one of the study areas. The family size here ranged between 2 and 8 with a mean of 4.7. It is observed that from an agricultural land of one bigha, the watermelon cropping can earn over Rs. 70000 annually. From the second site, it is observed that change in sandbar geometry may cause change in dwelling place in the same region resulting into change in livelihood from farming to fishing. Catching of fishes such as 'Bolihara' (*Cabdio morar*), 'Nara' (*Labeo bata*), 'Aari' (*Sperata seenghala*), 'Hilsa' (*Tenualosa ilisha*), 'Bhorali' (*Wallago attu*), 'Bahu' (*Labeo catla*) and 'Kuhri' (*Labeo gonius*) helps the community earn around Rs. 50000 to Rs. 200000 annually.

Keywords: Farming; Fishing; Geospatial; Livelihood; Sandbar

1. Introduction

Sandbars in rivers are dynamic entities that change shape and size over time (Bhowmik and Demissie, 2001). Sandbars develop under specific hydraulic conditions in channel evolution stages, as the channel widens from an initially straight channel, with erodible bed and banks (Jang and Shimizu, 2005). Channel-bed configurations generally include forms such as 'bars' and 'bedforms'; bedforms include ripples, dunes, and anti-dunes, and remain submerged, except during droughts or in ephemeral streams. Bars refer to large bedform configurations that are often exposed during low flows. They are usually submerged at least once a year in order to prevent vegetation growth. Bars can be viewed as alluvial bed deposits that are transported under high flow conditions. During channel bar development process bars are stabilized by native vegetation if they remain emerged from water for quite a long period of time which leads to the reduction of active channel width and in process

the islands develop (Julien, 2002). Examples of bars are point bars, side bars and mid-channel bars. Channel bars are caused by the changes in river gradient. When a river flowing on erodible bed and bank is straightened within the upper reach for any purpose, the normal reaction of the river is to erode the straightened reach due to its increased gradient and deposit the eroded materials within immediate downstream non-channelized reach of the river (Bhowmik and Demissie, 2001). The dumping of sediments can occur because of the weight of the sediment load itself, when the load becomes excessive for the river to carry it along (Brierley and Fryirs, 2004) and sand gets deposited owing to a sudden loss of velocity of the river as it descends onto the flat lands from the hilly terrain (Lahiri-Dutt, 2014). The silt accumulation from erosion process led to increase in height of sand deposit in the region of higher land between channels; consequently, there is a bifurcation of river with oblique flow. The oblique flow causes river-bank erosion when it is resisted by river bank. The eroded sediment is again transported away by the flow and gets deposited to form a new channel deposit. This causes a cyclical event of river bank-erosion and formation of channel deposit/bar (Mukherjee, 2011). Vegetation succession on channel bars can increase the stability of these semi-stable lands (Coulthard, 2005) and take the form of a riverine island. The river island mostly experience erosion on its upstream side and deposition on its downstream side leading to migration of islands towards downstream direction (Coleman, 1969). Brice (1964) differentiates between channel bars and river islands based on the height, that is, whether or not they rise over water continually. In his plan of classification, channel bars are unvegetated and submerged at a bankfull stage (when the entire river channel is filled with water from one bank to the other), whereas river islands are vegetated and rise above the surface of the water. In middle Ganga plains of eastern Uttar Pradesh and Bihar states of India, these sandbars are known as 'Diaras' and are made of coarser sands and gravels (Lahiri-Dutt, 2014). Diaras are spread all over the Ganga plains; Sharma (2010) estimates that they cover nearly 0.9 million hectares in the state of Bihar alone. In the Indus plains in Pakistan, these lands are described as 'Kuchha' (wet and fragile, as opposed to 'Pucca', or more permanent lands) and 'Baet' (rising like mounds between the two branches of rivers). In Bengal, north eastern states of Assam, and Tripura, and in Bangladesh these are called as 'Chars' or 'Char-Chapori' ('Chapori' is used for sandbars attached to banks, as opposed to 'Chars' which are floating or island sandbars).

The unstable nature of the sandbars and islands create vulnerable conditions for the people who use and depend on these 'pieces of land' for various socio-economic activities. The spatial and temporal instability creates conditions in which these lands can be used for a limited period of time in a year which although sometimes synchronize with the normal cycle of emergence and submergence but remains largely at the mercy of various other factors like changing climatic conditions, socio-political situations, changes in land use and land cover pattern at the upstream, and fluvial geomorphological episodes. This results into various social impacts on people and communities living along and using these bars and islands. The impacts may be such as changes in and effect on livelihood conditions, loss of land, loss of property, human displacement, and impact on health and education (Baviskar, 2011; National Dalit Watch, 2010). Das et al. (2014) while discussing about socio-economic impact of river bank erosion mentioned that the overall scenario of river bank erosions and their impacts are very depressing. As a result of river bank erosion and their displacement, forced migrants are at the risk of insecurities in different form. The uncertainties that they face are economic insecurity, social insecurity, and health insecurity due to unemployment, deprivation of civic rights, and basic infrastructure

issues respectively. Insecurities caused by involuntary migration leads to deprivation, destitute, fragility and more vulnerability. In the northeastern part of India, the two main rivers, Brahmaputra and Barak are joined by numerous small and large tributaries. Banks of the river Brahmaputra are said to be extremely unstable because of frequent changing flows influenced by the southwest monsoon. The most striking feature of the change in channel configuration of the Brahmaputra is the continuous shift of the thalweg from one location to another within the bank lines of the river, the movement is high during May to June and drops during the peak flood season of July to August. Braided characteristic features of this river form numerous big and small sandbars differing in size and permanency (Ullah et al., 2010). Thousands of people are affected due to inundation and instability of channel bars in and along River Brahmaputra and impacted severely (Das et al., 2009). Frequent shifts and relocations create landlessness, acute poverty, epidemic diseases, and lawlessness. All these factors affect the livelihood and wellbeing of the life of people of char area (Mahamud, 2011). There are around 2000 chars in the state of Assam, covering over 3 lakhs hectares of geographical area and supporting a population of around 25 lakhs (As per the Directorate of Char Areas Development, Government of Assam 2002-2003). As per a survey done during 2002-2003, more than 80% of people are illiterate in sandbar areas in Assam. The chars account for about 5 percent of the total area of the state spreading across 14 districts, 55 blocks and around 2,300 villages. The Char areas bring in a lot of vulnerabilities requiring the inhabitants to shift their homes at frequent intervals (OKD Institute of Social Change and Development, 2014).

Present study intends to understand the impact on people due to the vulnerable situations created by appearance and disappearance of sandbars in Brahmaputra river system in Assam. The work is based on a mixed approach of socioeconomic and geospatial methods. The research question is how does unstable sandbars affect the quality of life of people, who lives there. Application of geospatial techniques for mapping of these fluvial hazard conditions (due to accretion and erosion) is one of the affective steps in managing them. Mapping of the spatial distribution of vulnerability of the people residing along the river bank is also very much required to understand the severity of the problem (Kienberger et al., 2009).

2. Materials and Methods

2.1 Study Site

Two areas in the Brahmaputra river system are selected for the study (Fig. 24.1). These places are Nepalpara in Chirang

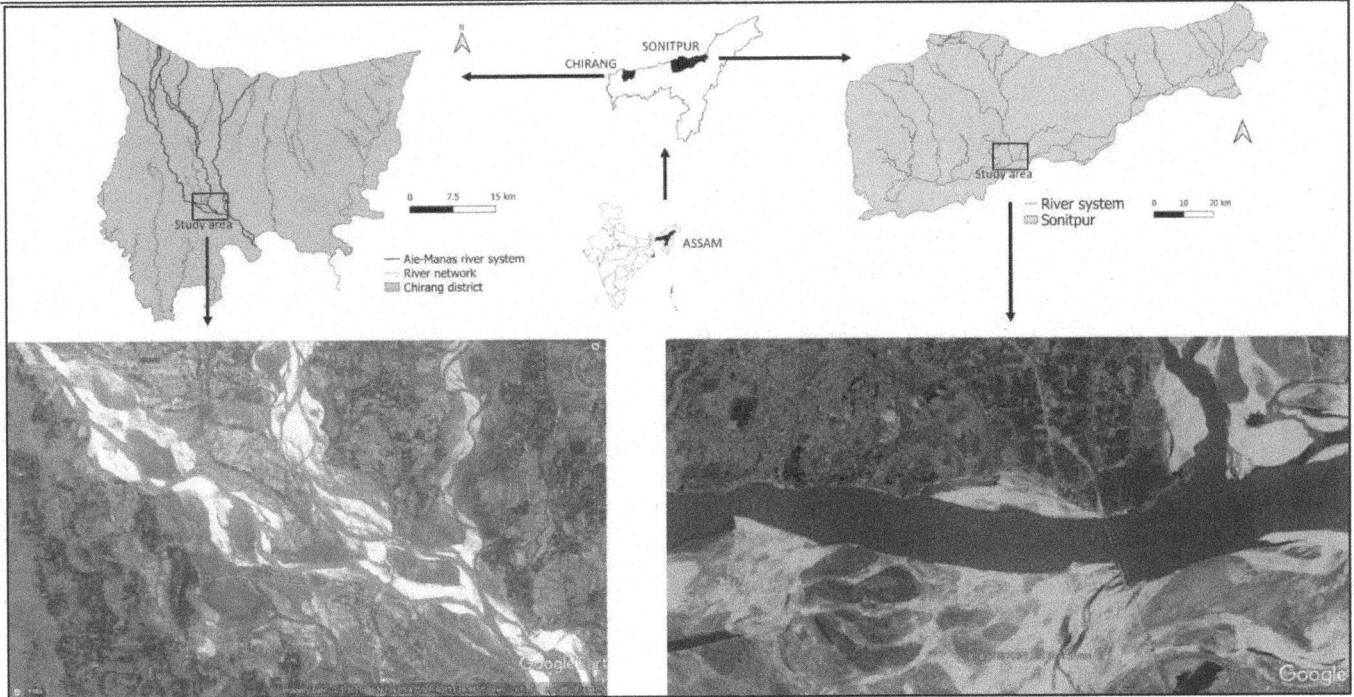

Fig. 24.1 Study sites in Chirang and Sonitpur district, Assam, India

district and Bhomoragudi in Sonitpur district, in state of Assam, India. Nepalpara is situated in Aie-Manas system of larger Brahmaputra riverine system. The Chirang district shares an international boundary with Bhutan on the North. Aie river originates from the Black mountains of Bhutan which flows through the district and falls into the mighty river Brahmaputra. The soil type of this area is basically sandy to sandy loam with alluvial deposits. The climate of this region is sub-tropical warm and humid during summers and dry to cool during the winter. The average annual rainfall of this area is 1900 mm of which it is in the monsoon that accounts 75% of the rainfall. Aie river is one of the major perennial rivers of this area forming one of the northern tributaries of river Brahmaputra. The river is fairly wide and has a braided course forming large islands of sandbars on its bed including deposition of silts and debris that is carried from the upstream. During the monsoon, sudden flood flow from the hills cause havoc to the people dwelling in and around the river. According to the Census of India 2011, the village Nepalpara comes under Sidli Tehsil of district Chirang. The total population of the village is around 1006 people which consists of around 195 households. Bhomodagudi is situated in the northern bank of mighty Brahmaputra in the foothills of eastern Himalaya.

2.2 Geospatial Approach

In order to understand the spatio-temporal dynamics, the schematic methodology is given below (Fig. 24.2). High resolution Google earth imageries are used for both the study areas. Four images between years 2010 and 2020 are used for site 1 (Nepalpara). Three images between years 2003 and 2020 are used for the site 2 (Bhomoragudi). The open source software QGIS Desktop 3.4.15 is used for image processing. The images were georeferenced with UTM projection and digitization is performed for geodatabase creation. Sandbars and rivers banks across different years are created as vector file with attributes.

2.3 Socioeconomic Study

Both primary and secondary data have been used for conducting this research which included qualitative and quantitative approach. There was use of mixed methods which included semi-structured interviews based on the questionnaire. The survey was open to respondents of all sex and also included people of all age groups. The questionnaire included both closed ended as well as open-ended. The interviews continued with people approaching themselves to the spot out of curiosity and then taking a form of group discussions along with interview. This further took the shape of snow ball sampling where the interviewed people introduced to the other similar people of their village. A considerable number of people associated with fishing were interviewed using snowball Sampling. Boat was hired to observe the char that people use for fishing. Fishermen were distinguished on the bases of professional, seasonal, and subsistence along with full-time, seasonal and part-time. Group discussion

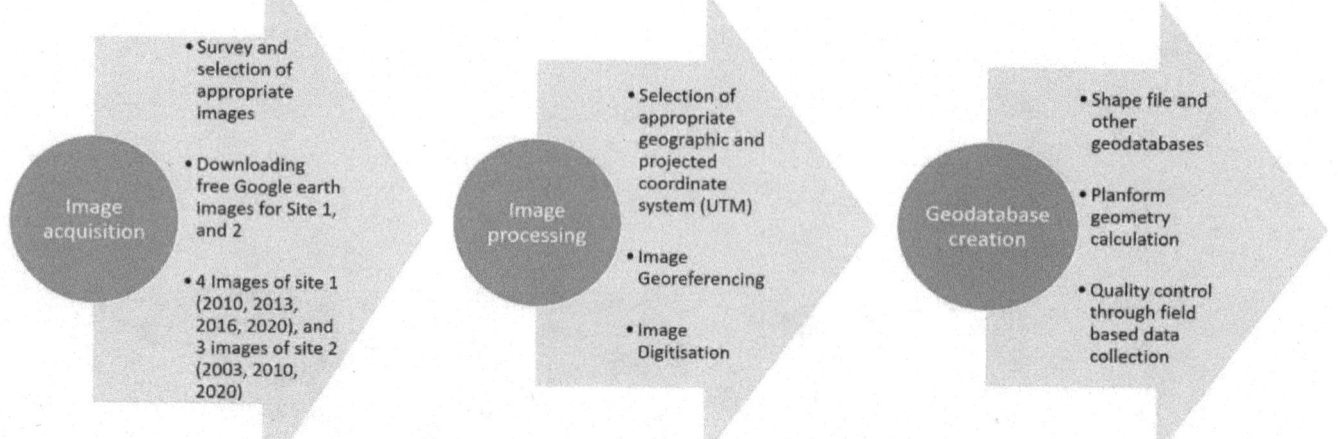

Fig. 24.2 Schematic diagram of the geospatial approach.

with the fishermen and members of the households of fishers were conducted twice during the field visit to understand loss of land, fear of displacement, government initiatives, and topics related to their life and livelihood. The secondary data included already available data such as journal articles, book chapters etc.

3. Results

It is observed (Fig. 24.3, and 24.4) that the Nepalpara village land area decreases from 3.1 km^2 in 2010 to 1.2 km^2 in 2020. Simultaneously, we can see that the sandbars surrounding the village increases from km^2 in 2010 to 6.3 km^2 in 2020. A little stability in the morphology of the river can be observed after the year 2016 to 2020 as there has been a slight decline in the area of the sandbar and a much lower decrease in the village area in comparison to the other years.

The sex ratio of the village showed that female percentage is slightly higher (51%) than male (49%) (Fig. 24.5). When we look at the size of the households surveyed, maximum number of the families (40.9%) had a family size of 3 to 4 members, followed by family size between 5 and 6 members (31.8%), followed by family size with less than or equal to 2 (27.3%). It is observed that around 95% of the households surveyed were involved in farming as their main source of income followed by 5% as boatman. The other sources of income of the households in Nepalpara village include wage labors (only) (86%), followed by wage labour (with small shop) (9%), and as boatman (5%). In order to estimate the income of the households from watermelon cultivation the cost of inputs have been calculated according to the size of the sandbars cultivated. The inputs include cost of 50 g of seed

for one bigha i.e. Rs. 1300/- which accounts for 250 holes in one bigha. The other inputs include bamboos or nets for fencing the cultivated land which costs around Rs. 800/- per bigha followed by cow dung which in this case was fulfilled by their cattle without any expense and followed by the use of fertilizers like urea which cost for around Rs. 2000/- per bigha of land. The estimated input cost for 1 bigha of land thus cost up to Rs. 4100/- and the maximum in this case Rs. 24000/- for 6 bighas of land. The estimated output income of the households accounted for Rs. 75000/- for 1 bigha of land which involved the factors like number of fruits produced in one plant i.e., around 4-5 fruits, the selling price of watermelon costs about Rs 10/- per kg to Rs 60/- per fruit, if we see the average weight of a watermelon. It should be noted that it is the estimated income from watermelon harvest earned after 6 months of continuous work. The profit earned from the watermelon harvest is estimated by deducting the input cost from the output income of the cultivation. This accounts for a profit of Rs. 70900/- for one bigha of watermelon cultivation. The main crop include watermelon as the major crop along with other crops like bitter melon, cucumber, bottle gourd etc. grown in less quantities. The people from this village do continuous hard work for 6 months from October to May and are thus seasonal farmers and the rest of the monsoonal period because of flood they are forced to stay in their village. Their income is received at the time of harvest and differs on who plants how much. These also depends very much on the climate, as mentioned by one of the villagers how on 2018 their crops were damaged because of hailstorm and resulted in heavy loss. Thus, seasonality plays an important role in this case. While one can't assume the same returns for the same person the next year or so, as like their complex habitat, their area of farmland may increase or decrease with personal

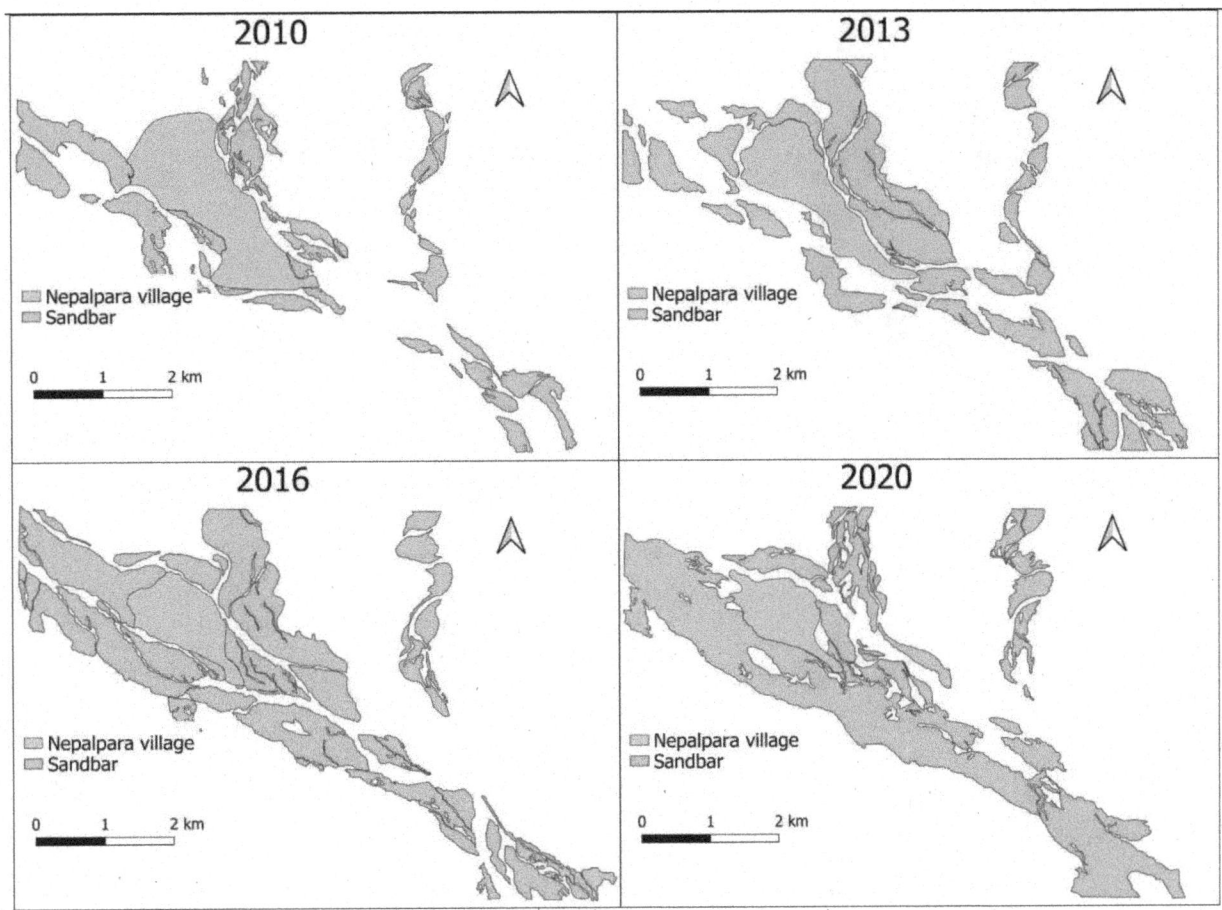

Fig. 24.3   Planform geometry of uninhabited and inhabited sandbars in study site 1.

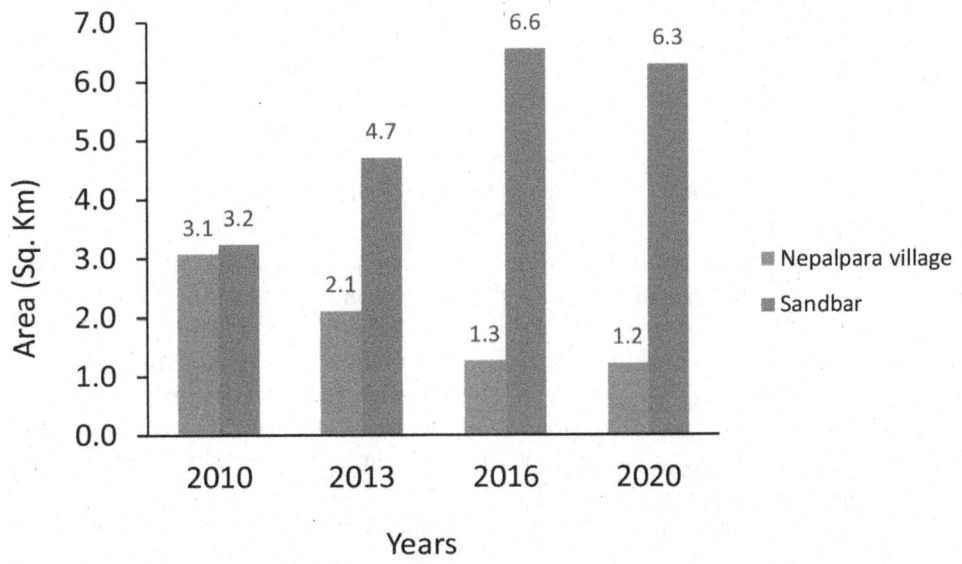

Fig. 24.4   Changes in area of uninhabited and inhabited sandbars.

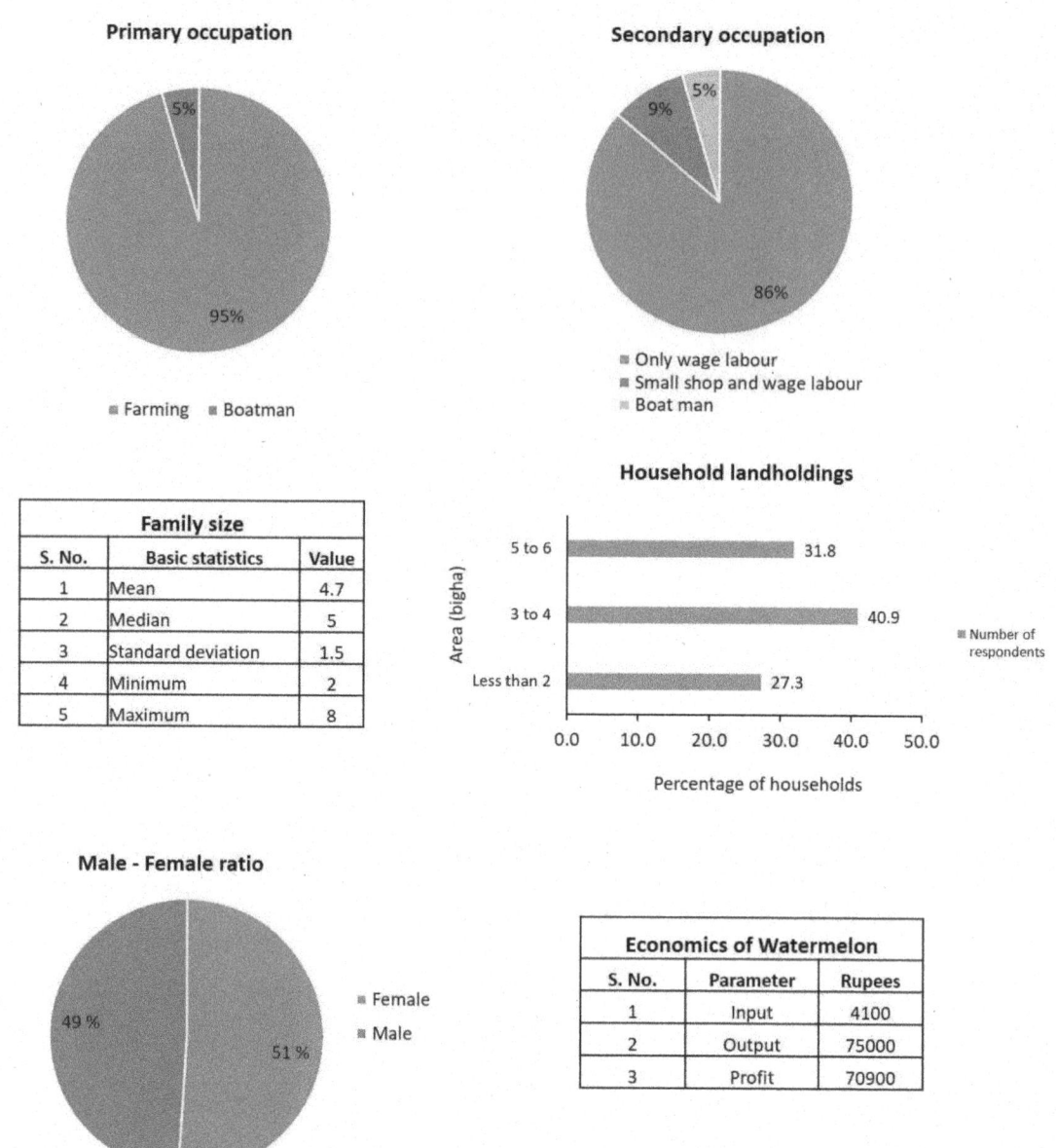

Fig. 24.5 Socioeconomic variables in study site 1.

or seasonal circumstances and simultaneously so does their incomes. Some of the other activities that take place in these chars are cattle grazing and fishing whereas, these are only done on a subsistence level. Their cattle are mostly used for manure and daily milk intake. Some of the vegetation that were found on the charlands were *Neyraudia reynaudiana* (local name – 'Nangdor' in Bodo, 'Boronga' in Bengali, *Pennisetum purpureum* (Elephant grass), and 'Jhao bon'. The Elephant grass had multiple uses like in the making of fences around the farm lands as well as fodder for their cattle.

It is observed in the second site (Fig. 24.6) that the habitation is bound to shift from middle of the sandbar in year 2003 to the river bank in the year 2020. It explains the dynamicity of the river and resultant shifts of char dwellers. The river also provides them the land to sustain their life by carrying out agricultural activity with fertile sandy soil which is good for cultivating various crops like groundnut, corn, mustard, rice, watermelon and many more. Eventually, this sandbar shows a change in morphology due to erosional processes and floods over the period since 2003 which led to the shift of the char as well as the people living and dependent on it. Formation of another sandbar can be seen due to depositional activity near the river bank. There seem to be a shift of income sources, where fishing turned into their primary source of living in 2020, partly because of the loss they faced during

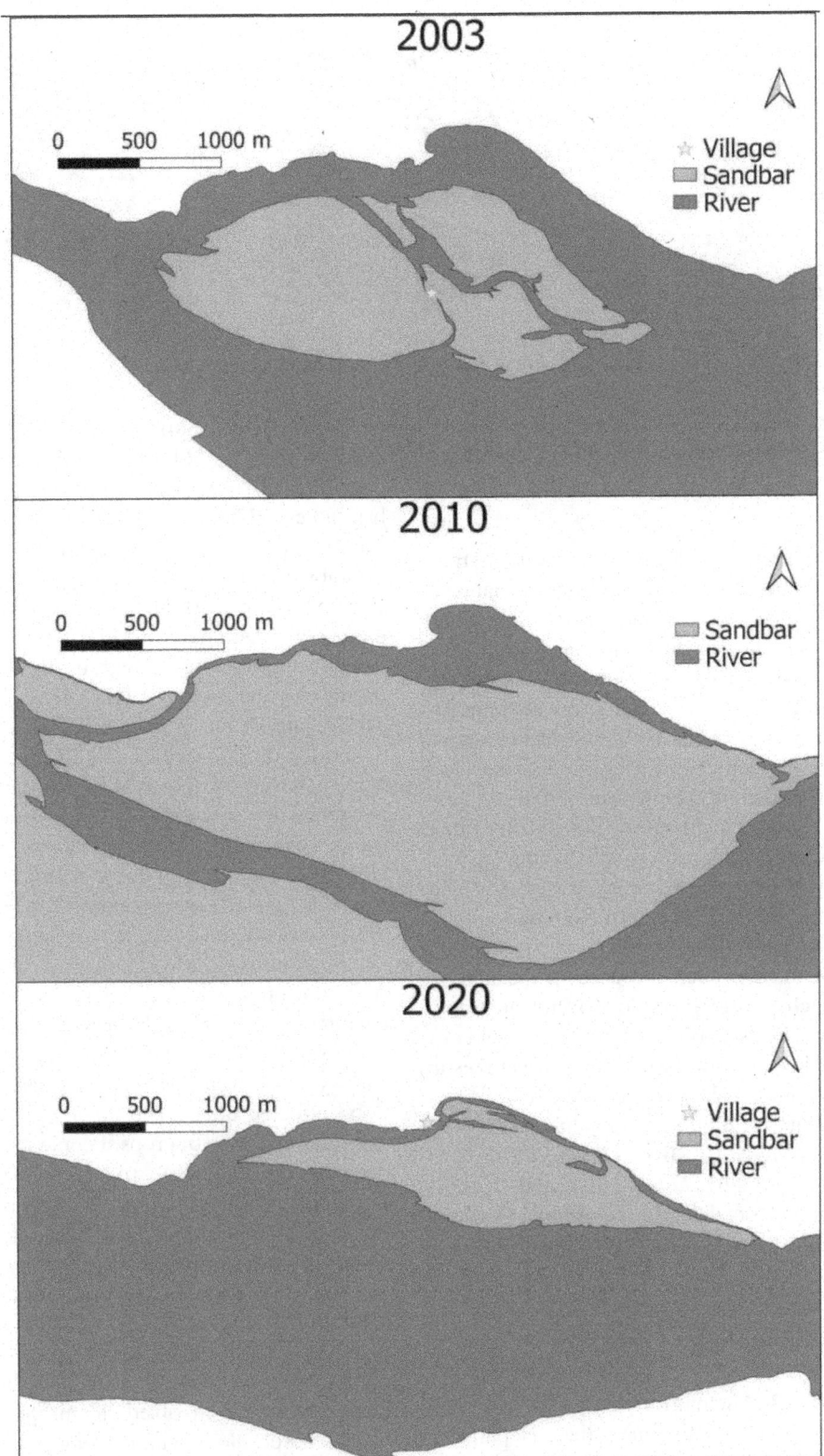

Fig. 24.6   Planform geometry of sandbars in study site 2

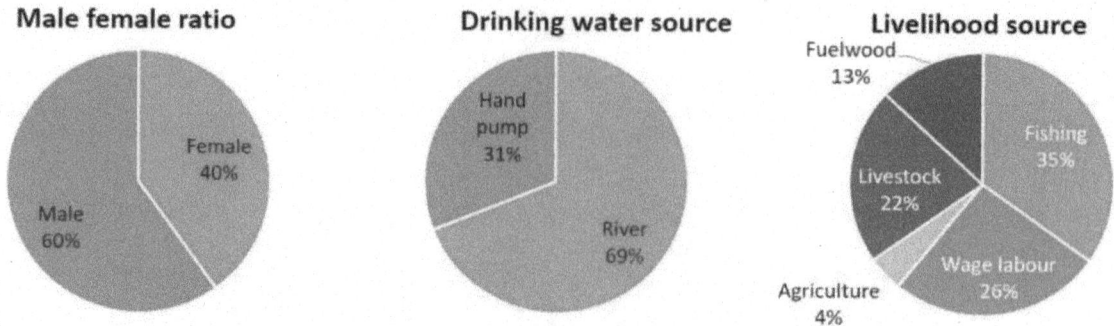

Fig. 24.7 Socioeconomic variables in study site 2

the lockdown where they had to throw away crops under 4-5 bighas of land and also mainly due to the shift of the chars that they decided upon carrying out fishing as their primary source of income.

From the following figure (Fig. 24.7) it is observed that around 60% of the population is male and the remaining 40% are female. It is observed that females use the river to avail water supply which they directly bring filling in a bucket which says 69 percent of the household uses it. It becomes difficult for the members to access to water supply which is the essential part of one's livelihood. Handpumps are available to those who can afford it and it accounts for 31 percent of the total household being surveyed. The main source of income that they are involved in after shifting from the char of 2003 to the current location is now fishing (35%). Around 26% respondents are involved in wage labour which is also important for the survival. The shift from agriculture is prominent as it shows only 1 person is carrying out agriculture near his land. Livestock are used in the urgent need for earning, which is after flood or to buy anything important and fuelwood are used as sustenance or are sold off to earn some penny. Thus, the source of income becomes a crucial aspect in determining their socio-economic condition. Fishes such as, 'Bolihara' *(Cabdio morar)*, 'Nara' *(Labeo bata)*, 'Aari' *(Sperata seenghala)*, 'Hilsa' *(Tenualosa ilisha)*, 'Bhorali' *(Wallago attu)*, 'Bahu' *(Labeo catla)* and 'Kuhri' *(Labeo gonius)* are found on daily basis. Annual income of fishermen may range from less than Rs. 50000 to over Rs. 200,000.

4. Discussion

The sandbars of the Aie-Brahmaputra river system are very dynamic in nature. Many villages like the village Nepalpara have been affected by the erosion of the river resulting in loss of their initial lands and being pushed back, also leading to circumstances where there are people now living in their neighbor's lands. Sarmah and Sarma (2017) observed in a sandbar area of Manas-Beki-Brahmaputra River system that in last over four decades, although the sand deposition has increased by over 10%, around a dozen of villages over sandbars have undergone severe erosion. These could have a relation with the construction of dams upstream like the Kurichhu dam in Bhutan with a capacity of 60 MW in the upper part of Aie river resulting in the reduction of flow in the river during the winters and flashfloods during the monsoon because of the sudden release of water from the floodgates. This results in the inundation of areas in western Assam, of which Chirang is one of the affected districts. While flood control is one of the reasons for dams, these have further worsened the situation and the people continue suffering every year. Some of the techniques that the villagers of Nepalpara practiced in order to stop their land from eroding was use of traditional bamboo fences which couldn't stop the flow of the river during monsoon. Sandbars differ from one another as well as, human use of these lands also differ from area to area, and from one river system to another (Lahiri-Dutt, 2014). Talukdar et al. (2009) delineated three sub-agroecosystems in Char areas of Nalbari, Assam. These sub systems were occasionally, annually, and frequently flood affected areas. The latter was observed to be less or not suitable for Rabi crops. People of Nepalpara are majorly dependent on charland farming which seems to have changed in the year 2020 as before that majority of the people were involved in different types of wage labors works like lifting stones in quarry mines, work in nearby towns, labor in oil and gas refinery nearby in the town (Khan and Bhuyan, 2019). Literature suggests that this change has occurred because of the profit that others saw coming from these crops while earlier hesitant whereas, it is to be remembered that even those who were involved in this practice were occasional wage laborers along with farming. These sandbars often show the existence of complex powerplays (Lahiri-Dutt, 2014) resulting in ownership and dispute over lands in some of the cases where the richer ones are mostly better off and get control over these lands. Whereas, in the case of Nepalpara, in order to understand this class differentiation comprising of the capitalist farmer, middle farmer, and the poor farmers as mentioned by Bernstein (2010), the villagers that were surveyed were found to own small landholdings and used family labor and thus alternated between working as wage labors as well as petty commodity producers. Along with this, even the land holdings as mentioned earlier might change each year. Along with their incomes as like the complex unstable habitats, their conditions keep changing. The Char dwellers have always found out new ways of building their assets and livelihoods. Study in Bhomoragudi saw a shift from agriculture to fishing since past few years after the sandbar people shifted from the char to the river bank. Additionally, the household sell their livestock in times of need. Hoque and Hazarika (2020) in a study in five sandbar villages in Mandia Development Block in Assam observed that 65% of people are dependent on farming. They also observed that only around 20 families earn between 10 thousand and 20 thousand rupees from fishing monthly. Literacy rate ranged between 17.63 and 18.36% in the same study area. More than 20% of households has annual income less than 20000 rupees. Less than 20% of people has income between 60 thousand and 3 Lakhs of rupees. Further, they noticed that more than 60% of families in each of the five villages are very poor (below poverty level). Thus, the result of the study showed that the sandbar dwellers are involved in more than one livelihood option (Alam et al., 2018). The fishermen in the present study prefer to fish near the edge of the sandbars. Ahmed et al. (2013) states that subsistence fishing is carried out by almost all households in rural areas that are near to a water body which in this study is the river Brahmaputra. There are more of seasonal (April to July) and subsistence farming (throughout the year). Very poor communication system made the lives of fishermen dependent on the chars more vulnerable (Ullah et al., 2010). Government rations and housing are some incentives given to the fishermen household, but availing the housing intervention is not very easy by the lower rank fishermen as they cannot afford to pay to the 'middleman'.

In a study in Bangladesh, Sarker et al. (2003) have observed that satellite imageries, in combination with social surveys, provides a good understanding of the interaction between the physical environment and the livelihoods of the Sandbar dwellers. Ullah et al. (2010) also studied the geometry of sandbars in Bangladesh and observed that the sandbars have increased significantly between 1983 and 2004. They have observed that sandbars are characterised by vulnerable and difficult living conditions and excessive constraints of resources. Kumar and Das (2019) in a study in Brahmaputra observed that sandbar dwellers, which constitute around 10% of Assam's population, live a precarious life in

backwardness and poverty. River Brahmaputra is a highly braiding river with intensive erosion and deposition leading to continuous change in geometry and land use and land cover (Saikia et al., 2019). Interestingly between 1994 and 2014 increase in agricultural practice is observed in sandbars in River Brahmaputra (Saikia et al., 2019). Kumar and Das (2019) observed that land holding, land lost due to erosion, household size and education are some of the factors which play a key role in this regard. They also argued that location of a char is important; some chars are more migration prone than others. Interestingly they found that larger households have greater probability to migrate. They have argued that livelihood diversification is a better way to keep them away from distress caused by migration. OKD Institute of Social Change and Development (2014) in a detailed study of people living on sandbars in Assam noticed that education, in terms of mean years of schooling across spatial diversity categories is lowest in sandbars in Assam, (lower than 5). Literacy rates among the age group of 7 + and 15 + years is lowest in char areas. 33% of children (highest among the spatial diversity groups) have never been enrolled in school. The percentage of non-electrified households is high in char areas; 47.1% as compared to 32% in state of Assam. Over 84% of houses in char areas in Assam lack improved sanitation facilities. Percentage of married woman between 15- and 19-years age group is significantly higher (25.3 %) in chars of Assam as compared to general regions (13.5 %), and other groups also. Unemployment rate in sandbar areas is the lowest of all spatial diversity categories in Assam where the numbers of casual workers are also one of the highest. In terms of incidences of multidimensional poverty, sandbar areas have the highest numbers as compared to all other categories of spatial regions. Especially the asset poverty is acute in char areas. Sandbar inhabitants displaced by sandbar erosion have no other alternative than to settle on accreting sandbar elsewhere, creating a typical social and economic sandbar environment. The economics of the sandbars are largely based on agriculture, fishing and livestock-rearing. Education, health and extension services and support to cope with the calamities of flood and erosion are minimal. This not only results in individual misery, but also in unrealized potential of resources on the chars (Sarker et al., 2003).

5. Conclusion

From the two studies in Brahmaputra river system we can conclude that the sandbars are highly dynamic both spatially and temporally. The area of sandbars both inhabited and uninhabited may change differently across time and space. This dynamicity directly impacts the inhabitants of sandbars in many ways. They may have to move from one place to other in search of a land for their homes. Their primary livelihood options may get converted from one form to other such as from farming to fishing. It is observed that the sandbars also provide fertile lands for farming watermelons and other crops. These add on to the overall income of the households. The sandbars and river banks also provide opportunity for fishing number of locally available fishes with high demands in the surrounding markets. Owing to their low socio-economic condition, the inhabitants are also vulnerable to power politics which can prevent them from getting the benefits provided by various government agencies.

6. Acknowledgement

The author would like to acknowledge Ms. Aditi Ramchiary, Ms. Sanjukta Mondal, and respondents of the two study sites for participating in the study.

REFERENCES

1. Ahmed, N., Rahman, S., Bunting, S.W., & Brugere, C. (2013). Small-scale fishing and management strategies, Bangladesh. *Singapore Journal of Tropical Geography, 34*, 86–102.

2. Alam, Md. R., Malak, Md., A., & Quader, M. A. (2018). Livelihood vulnerability of Char land people in Brahmaputra-Jamuna River system, *Jagannath University Journal of Life and Earth Sciences, 4*(1), 54–64.

3. Baviskar, A. (2011). What the Eye Does Not See: The Yamuna in the Imagination of Delhi, *Economic & Political Weekly, XLVI* (50), 45–53.

4. Bernstein, H. (2010). *Class Dynamics of Agrarian Change (Agrarian Change and Peasant Studies)*, Lynne Rienner, 1st edition, 160 p.

5. Bhowmik, N. G., & Demissie, M. (2001). *River Geometry, Bank Erosion, and Sand Bars within the main stem of the Kankakee River in Illinois and Indiana*, Contract Report 2001-09, Illinois Department of Natural Resources, Office of Realty and Environmental Planning.

6. Brice, J.C. (1964). Planform Properties of Meandering Rivers. In C.M. Elliot (Ed.), *River Meandering*, New York: ASCE, 1–15.

7. Brierley, G. J., & Fryirs, K. A. (2004). *Geomorphology and river management: applications of the river styles framework*. Blackwell Publishing, Oxford.

8. Coleman, J.M. (1969). Brahmaputra River channel processes and sedimentation. *Sedimentary Geology 3*, 129–239.

9. Coulthard, T. J. (2005). Effects of Vegetation on Braided Stream Pattern and Dynamics, *Water Resources Research, 41* (4), W04003.

10. Das, P., Chutiya, D., Hazarika, N., & International Centre For Integrated Mountain Development. (2009). *Adjusting to Floods on the Brahmaputra Plains, Assam, India*, Kathmandu, International Centre for Integrated Mountain Development. [Pdf] Retrieved from the Library of Congress, https://www.loc.gov/item/2013332917/.

11. Das, T. K., Haldar, S. K., Gupta, I. D., & Sen, S. (2014). River Bank Erosion Induced Human Displacement and Its Consequences, *Living Reviews in Landscape Research, 8*(3).

12. Hoque, D., & Hazarika, C. (2020). An Empirical Analysis of Income and Livelihood Pattern in Sandbar Areas along the River Brahmaputra in Assam, *International Journal of Social Science and Humanity, 10* (2), 35–41.

13. Jang, C-L., & Shimizu, Y. (2005). Numerical Simulation of Relatively Wide, Shallow Channels with Erodible Banks, *Journal of Hydraulic Engineering, ASCE, 131* (7), 565–575.

14. Julien, P.Y. (2002). *River Mechanics*, Cambridge University Press.

15. Khan, A., & Bhuyan, M. J. (2019). Quarrying and Livelihood Issues Of A Himalayan Foothill Village In Lakhimpur District, Assam, *International Journal of Scientific & Technology Research, 8*(10), 1052–1061.

16. Kienberger, S., Amoaka J, F., Zeil, P., Hutton, C., Lang, S., & Clark, M. (2009). *Modelling socio-economic vulnerability to floods: Comparison of Methods Developed for European and Asian Case Studies, Sustainable Development: A challenge for European research*, 26–28 May 2009, Brussels, conference paper.

17. Kumar, B., & Das, D. (2019). Livelihood of the Char Dwellers of Western Assam, *Indian Journal of Human Development, 13*(1), 90–101.

18. Lahiri-Dutt, K. (2014). Chars: Islands that float within rivers, *Shima: The International Journal of Research into Island Cultures, 8*(2), 22–38.

19. Mahamud, Md. S. (2011). *Intervention of Char development and settlement project: does it make a difference in people's livelihood at Boyer Char in Bangladesh.* Master in Public Policy and Governance Program, Department of General and Continuing Education North South University, Bangladesh, pp 104.

20. Mukherjee, J. (2011). *No Voice, No Choice: Riverine Changes and Human Vulnerability in the 'Chars' of Malda and Murshidabad*, Occasional Paper, 28, Salt Lake City (Institute of Development Studies Kolkata).

21. National Dalit Watch. (2010). *The uncertainties of life, living through waters of dejection*, National Campaign on Dalit Human Rights, New Delhi, www.ncdhr.org.in

22. OKD Institute of Social Change and Development. (2014). *Assam Human Development Report-2014, Managing diversities, Achieving human development*, Planning and development Department, Government of Assam.

23. Saikia, L., Mahanta, C., Mukherjee, A., & Borah, S. B. (2019). Erosion–deposition and land use/land cover of the Brahmaputra river in Assam, India, *Journal of Earth System Science, 128* (8), 211.

24. Sarker, M. H., Huque, I., Alam, M., & Koudstaal, R. (2003). Rivers, chars and char dwellers of Bangladesh, *International Journal of River Basin Management, 1*(1), 61–80.

25. Sarmah, R. K., & Sarma, U. (2017). Temporal changes of Fluvio-Morphological scenario and its impact on Settlement: A GIS based study for Mandia block, Barpeta District, Assam, *ADBU- Journal of Engineering Technology, 2*, 00602627.

26. Sharma, M. (2010). 'Diara Diary'. In M. Rangarajan (Ed.), *Environmental Issues in India, A Reader,* (pp. 275–287): Pearson New Delhi.

27. Talukdar, M. C., Kandali, G. G., Basumatary, A., & Das, A. K. (2009). Crop suitability for Char areas of Nalbari District, Assam, *Agropedology, 19*(1), 41–46.

28. Ullah, H., Islam, Md. N., & Malak, Md. A. (2010). Charland Dynamics of the Brahmaputra- Jamuna River in Bangladesh, *The Jahangirnagar Review, Part II: Social Sciences, XXXIV*, 165–182.

CHAPTER 25

GIS Based Hazard Mapping and Vulnerability Assessment of Natural Hazards: A Case Study of Rudraprayag, Uttarakhand

Vaibhav Pundir
Student, Center for Disaster Management,
Jamia Millia Islamia

Abstract

Rudraprayag district is one of the 13 districts of Uttarakhand, established on 16th September 1997 and is bounded by Uttarkashi on the north, Chamoli on east, Pauri Garhwal on south and Tehri Garhwal on the west. It covers an area of 1984 sq. km. and lies between 30°19'00" and 30° 49' North and longitude 78° 49' and 79° 21' 13" East. The district has faced many natural hazards in past years, Kedarnath Floods 2013 being the worst of them. These natural hazards are the most common in state of Uttarakhand which lies in seismic zone V and receives immense rainfall. The present study shows user-friendly GIS maps to determine district vulnerability assessment to earthquake, landslides, and floods. Hazard and Social Vulnerability maps have been prepared with the help of ArcGIS 10.2.2. Secondary data from Census 2011 has been used to analyze vulnerability of population to the mentioned hazards. Three types of hazard maps have been presented in this paper. First Landslide Susceptibility Map with the help of Digital Elevation Map, slope and aspect showing the areas prone to landslide using GIS. Secondly, Flood Zonation Map has been prepared to identify flood hazard zones and categorize them from very low to very high. Lastly, an Earthquake Zonation Map for the year 2017 is prepared showing magnitude, its impact on settlement. The paper shows that people are most vulnerable by floods as most of the settlement is at low level where flood zonation shows high risk followed by landslides and at last earthquake which is unpredictable. Thus, this study will help the Government, NGOs and other stakeholders to prepare for these natural hazards in a better way and mitigate accordingly to create resilience among the communities that are vulnerable to such hazards. This study will also help in updating the present District Disaster Management Plan of Rudraprayag and create a disaster resilient environment.

Keywords: Hazard, Vulnerability, Disaster, GIS (Geographic Information System), Floods, Landslides, Earthquakes, Social Vulnerability

1. Introduction

An increase in frequency and intensity of natural hazards is resulting in heavy socio-economic losses. Effective disaster management can be the key to minimize these losses. However, the identification of appropriate tools and techniques can aid effective disaster mitigation and risk reduction. plays a significant role in assessment and response planning hazards in anticipation. One such way is mapping through Arc GIS. Individuals, businesses, and communities make decisions daily that affect their vulnerability to natural hazards. If prudent judgments are to be taken, decision-makers must be aware that risk and hazard information exists and that it is easily available in a clear and useable format.

(The National Academies of Sciences, 1991). Arc GIS can be an effective tool to map, assess and inform the way forward for different stakeholders exposed to disaster risks.

2. Hazard Assessment

Hazard assessments are simply a method of detecting hazards, assessing the risks posed by those hazards, and controlling the risks of the experiment's hazards by adding suitable hazard controls into the experimental design process. There are many different types of hazard assessment techniques available, ranging from simple qualitative to complicated quantitative reviews.

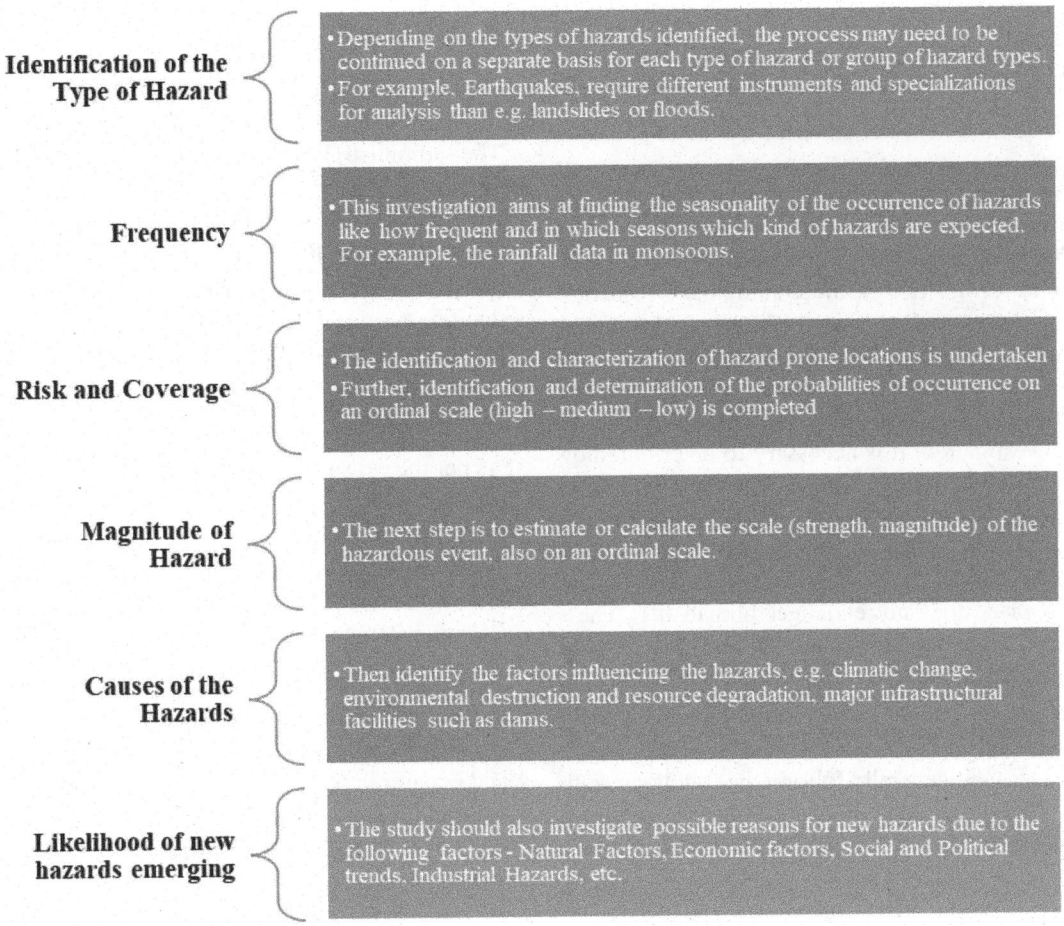

Identification of the Type of Hazard
- Depending on the types of hazards identified, the process may need to be continued on a separate basis for each type of hazard or group of hazard types.
- For example, Earthquakes, require different instruments and specializations for analysis than e.g. landslides or floods.

Frequency
- This investigation aims at finding the seasonality of the occurrence of hazards like how frequent and in which seasons which kind of hazards are expected. For example, the rainfall data in monsoons.

Risk and Coverage
- The identification and characterization of hazard prone locations is undertaken
- Further, identification and determination of the probabilities of occurrence on an ordinal scale (high – medium – low) is completed

Magnitude of Hazard
- The next step is to estimate or calculate the scale (strength, magnitude) of the hazardous event, also on an ordinal scale.

Causes of the Hazards
- Then identify the factors influencing the hazards, e.g. climatic change, environmental destruction and resource degradation, major infrastructural facilities such as dams.

Likelihood of new hazards emerging
- The study should also investigate possible reasons for new hazards due to the following factors - Natural Factors, Economic factors, Social and Political trends, Industrial Hazards, etc.

Fig. 25.1   Steps in Hazard Assessment

A hazard assessment can take the form of a checklist or a simple inspection of the work environment. Even if the work environment is the same, daily hazard assessments should be performed. The goal of performing daily danger assessments is to avoid growing complacent or simply not noticing your surroundings. Hazard evaluations allow workers to evaluate the work environment each day and decide which safety measures to implement based on the existing risk. Workers can use daily assessments to perceive safety measures as situational and adjust them as the environment and hazards change. Field level hazard assessments (FLHA) or risk assessments are other names for them. (The National Academies of Sciences 1991)

Hazard assessments determine where an event of natural hazards is likely to occur, how regularly it is likely to happen, and the severity of its physical and/or economic effects. Even though the precision of scientific understanding varies as per various hazards, the frequency of large floods and major forest fires in a specific area is comprehended than the date and location.

The extent to which local hazards and risks can be assessed is determined by the amount of data available. Access to data can be improved by conducting studies on the physical aspects of disasters that occur in the local context (Du et al. 2015). Some of the socioeconomic factors that govern data availability and thus the response to natural disasters.

The use of tools such as information and communication technology and geographic information system along with data analytics has been an important part of performing hazard assessments for effective results. The advancement of multi-hazard geographic information system (GIS) for all regional and local contexts allows data to be retrieved, evaluated, and presented in two- and three-dimensional maps to be used by a broader range of recipients.

The risk assessments process should begin with determining what natural hazards can be anticipated and how they may change in the short to medium term due to climate change. First and foremost, all potential hazards are identified. The areas that may be affected by the hazard are then marked; a process known as Hazard Mapping. The hazards' severity, intensity, and frequency are ascertained, and the hazards' causes are investigated. Earthquakes, volcanic activity, floods, drought, storms, and epidemics are all potential hazards.

To assess the degree of risk, as well as the attributes and scale of potential loss from extreme weather events, it is necessary to investigate not only the likelihood of occurrence but also the force and timeframe of the event. It is possible to do so by utilizing historical data that is available in written form as well as in the recollection of the community's residents. Furthermore, climatological, geological, hydrological, agricultural, environmental, and epidemiological data can be gathered from appropriate sources and government agencies for detailed analysis. However, before conducting this in-depth investigation, it is necessary to determine how susceptible population groups are to the event and how susceptible people are to this hazard. There is no need for hazard analysis if there are no vulnerable people or elements at the site of the hazard. It is because the extreme natural hazard, in this case, does not endanger human life. These are the first steps in vulnerability analysis, and they must be completed before proceeding to a detailed hazard assessment.

2.1 Steps in Hazard Assessment

The Hazard assessment generally follows the following steps depending on the type of natural hazard. The approach may differ as per the nature of the hazard, as a unified approach cannot be applied comprehensively.

3. Study Area

The area selected for the study is the district of Rudraprayag in Uttarakhand, which falls in Garhwal Himalayan region. The administrative boundaries of the district fall under 78o48'46" E and 79o21'45" E longitude and 30o10'36" N and 30o48'50" N latitude. Two of the major rivers, Mandakini and Alaknanda flow through the district, with Mandakini river being the major stream draining the Rudraprayag district. A major Hindu pilgrim destination, Kedarnath, is a Nagar panchayat located nearer to the origin of the river Alaknanda. (Disaster Mitigation and Management Centre (DMMC) 2014)

As per the census of India 2011, the population of the district is 2.42 lakhs, which had a percentage increase of 6.53 from the population of 2.27 lakhs as per Census of India 2001. The area of Rudraprayag district in total is around 1,984 sq. km. with a population density of 122 persons per sq.km. (Khanduri et al. 2018)

As per the seismic zoning map of India, The Rudraprayag district is categorized under Zone V. There have been several incidences of landslides and earthquakes, causing human and economic losses, which makes the district vulnerable to natural disasters, majorly floods, landslides and earthquakes. (Disaster Mitigation and Management Centre (DMMC) 2014)

Location Map of Study Area

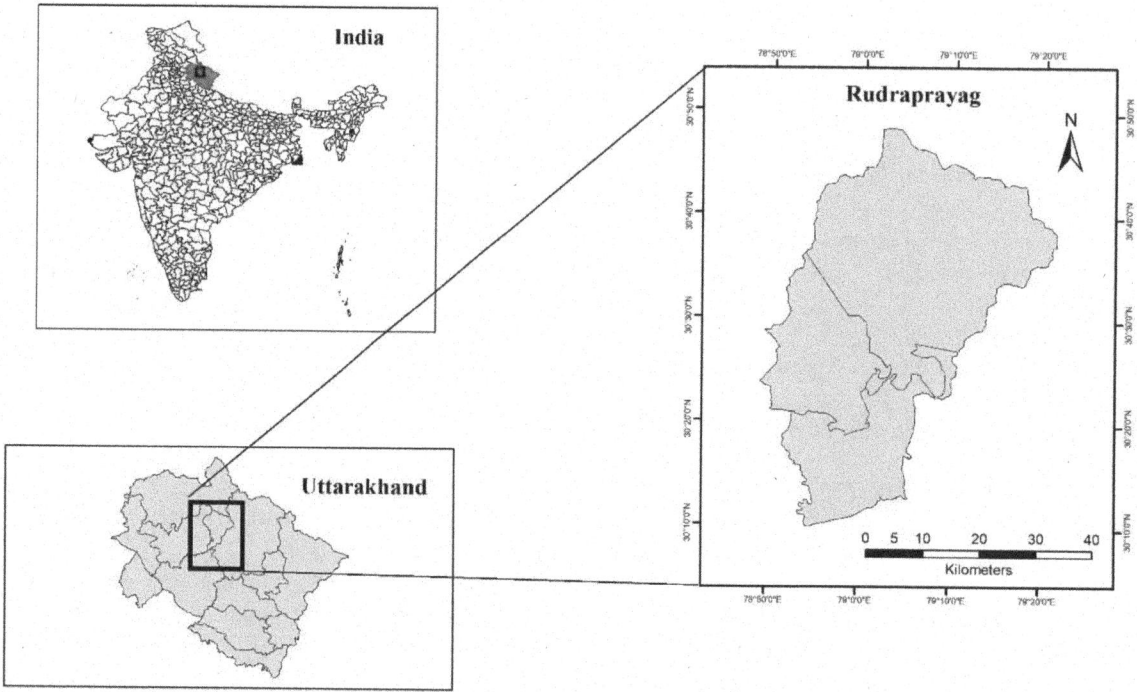

Map 25.1 Location map of Study Area - Rudraprayag District in Uttarakhand State, India

4. Hazard Vulnerability

4.1 Methodology

Table 25.1 describes the material used for the hazard vulnerability assessment for the purpose of this study. The materials and methods adapted for the study are explained further in Fig. 25.2.

Map 25.2 shows the administrative area of the Rudraprayag District. The maps delineate the study area and forms a basis for mapping of hazard vulnerability for landslides, floods and earthquakes in the area.

4.2 Landslide Susceptibility

Landslides, defined as the mass movement of rock, debris, or downslope (Cruden, 1991), can be caused by a wide variety of external factors. It includes heavy rainfall, seismic activity, variations in water level, storm waves, or rapid stream erosion, which together cause a sudden increase in shear stress or decrease in strength properties of slope-forming materials. Landslides are one of the most dangerous natural hazards, claiming people's lives almost every year and causing massive damage to property in mountainous regions (Hansen, 1984; Chung and Fabbri, 1995).

In recent times, landslide hazard analysis has played an essential role in the advancement of land use regulations aimed at minimizing the loss of life and property damage (Huabin et al. 2005). Landslide assessment has used various approaches, that can be classified as qualitative factor overlay, simulation approaches, geotechnical process models, and so on.

To prepare a landslide susceptibility map the first step is to prepare a digital elevation model (DEM). Using DEM data downloaded from SRTM, slope angle, slope aspect, slope elevation was prepared in ArcGIS 10.2.2 software. These factors were evaluated by assigning weights to each causative factor and finally, a landslide susceptibility map was prepared.

Table 25.1   Details of Data Source

Data Layers	Data Format	Sources of Data	Scale/Resolution
Slope Angle, Slope Aspect, Slope Elevation	Raster Grid	SRTM DEM, (USGS)	1 arc second global 30*30 m spatial resolution
Earthquake Data	Spreadsheet	IMD	—

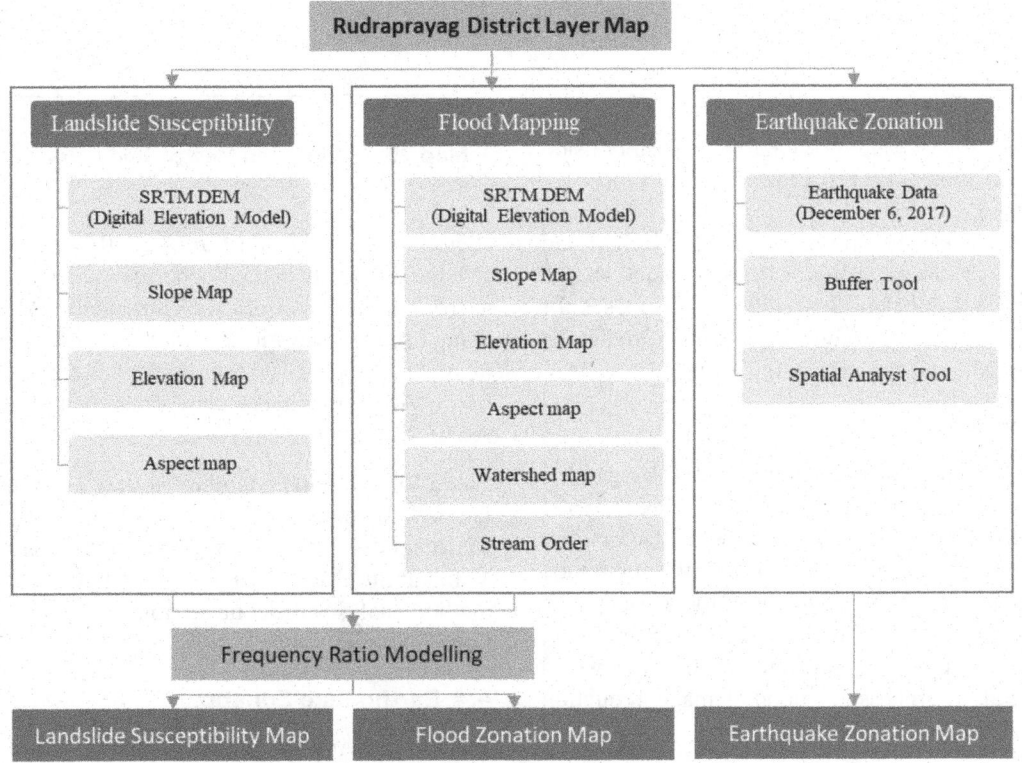

Fig. 25.2   Methodology for Hazard Vulnerability Mapping

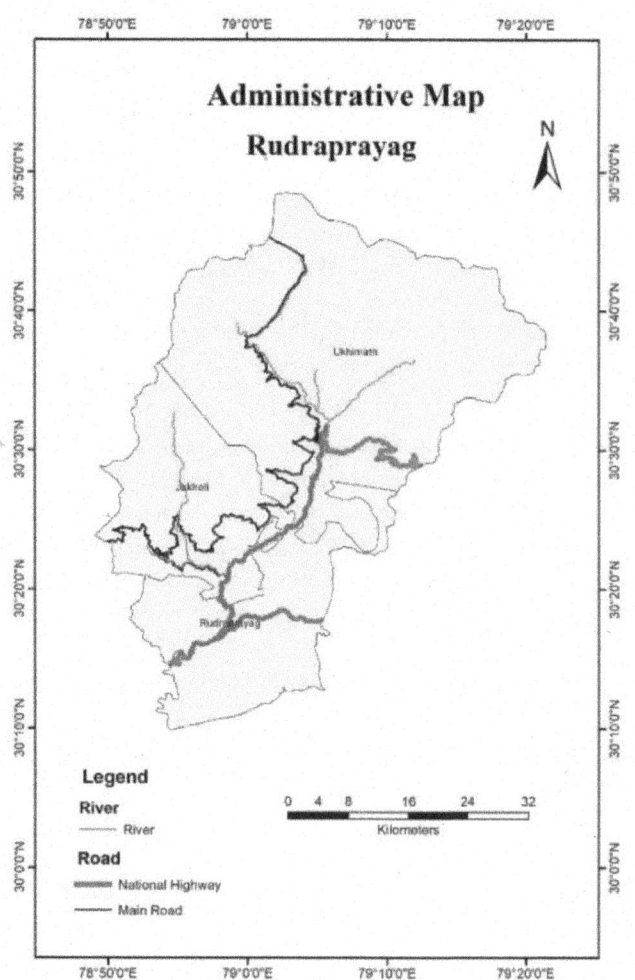

Map 25.2 Administrative Map of Rudraprayag District using ArcGIS

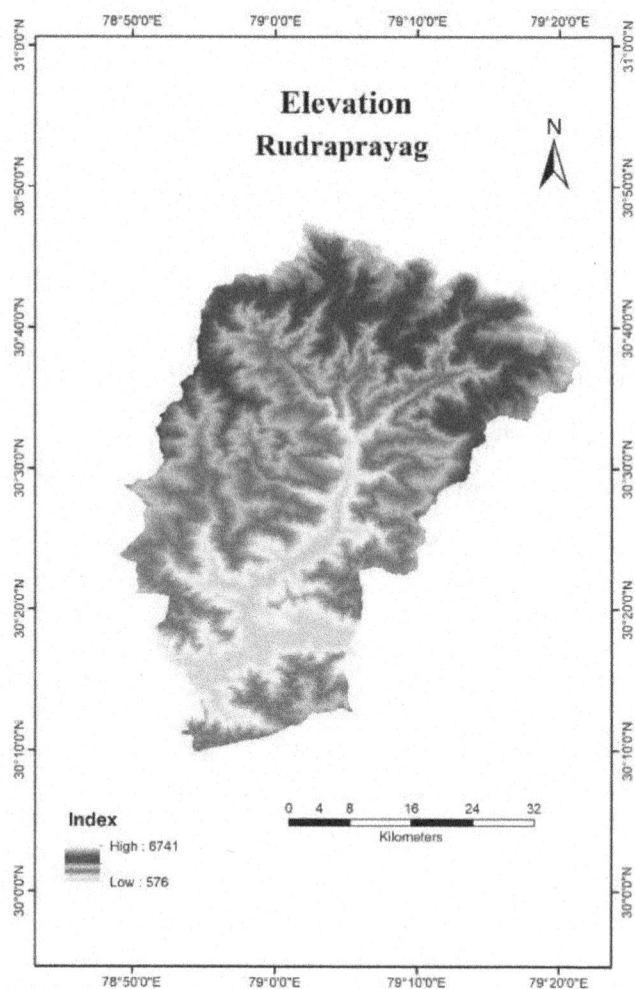

Map 25.3 Elevation Map of Study Area from DEM-SRTM

All factors were converted to raster maps and overlaid and then with the help of raster calculator in ArcGIS and spatial analyst tool was used to calculate weights of all classes for Frequency Ratio (FR). These weights will help to predict the probability of landslide occurrence in the area.

4.3 Flood Mapping

Floods are amongst the most devastating natural disasters. Floods are a major threat in India. Floods are caused by the irregular coincidence of extreme meteorological factors, but anthropogenic activities also have an impact on the magnitude and implications of the events (Samuels, Borga, Baltas, & Casale, 1997). The observed increase in the magnitude, frequency, and intensity of flood events around the world has raised general awareness of flood damage reduction measurements (Hall et al., 2014).

The characterization of flood-prone areas is a critical element of sound urban planning and disaster management policy

(Feloni, Mousadis, and Baltas 2020). This is useful for risk reduction, for which the flood vulnerability assessments form a very important part. Flood Vulnerability Mapping was done using Frequency Ratio Model in which five parameters were taken i.e., Slope, Elevation, Aspect, Stream Order, and Water basin. All these layers were constructed and combined in ArcGIS.

Flood Vulnerability Mapping is very essential in identifying factors affecting floods. In this present study, the Frequency Ratio model (FR) has been used to construct the Flood Vulnerability Map of Rudraprayag District, Uttarakhand. FR method analyses the contribution of various factors related to flood mapping.

4.4 Earthquake Zonation

India's growing population and widespread unscientific constructions, such as multi-story luxury apartments, massive factory buildings, massive malls, superstores,

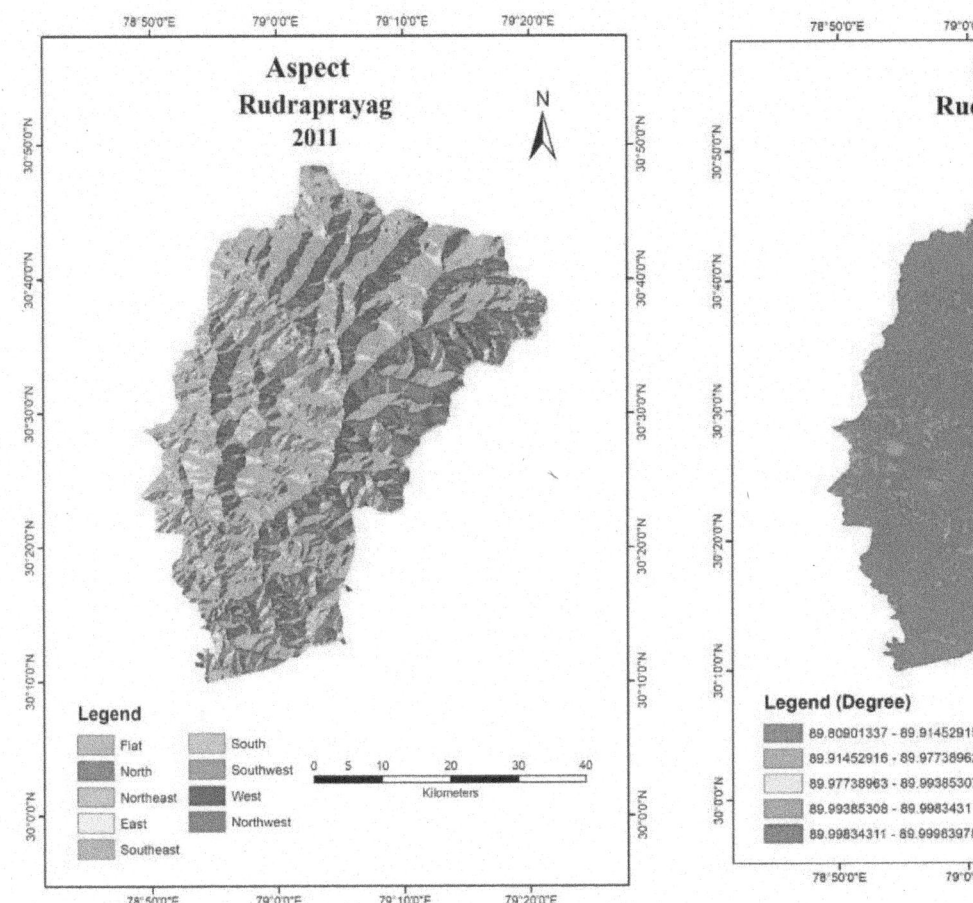

Map 25.4   Aspect map of Study Area using DEM-SRTM

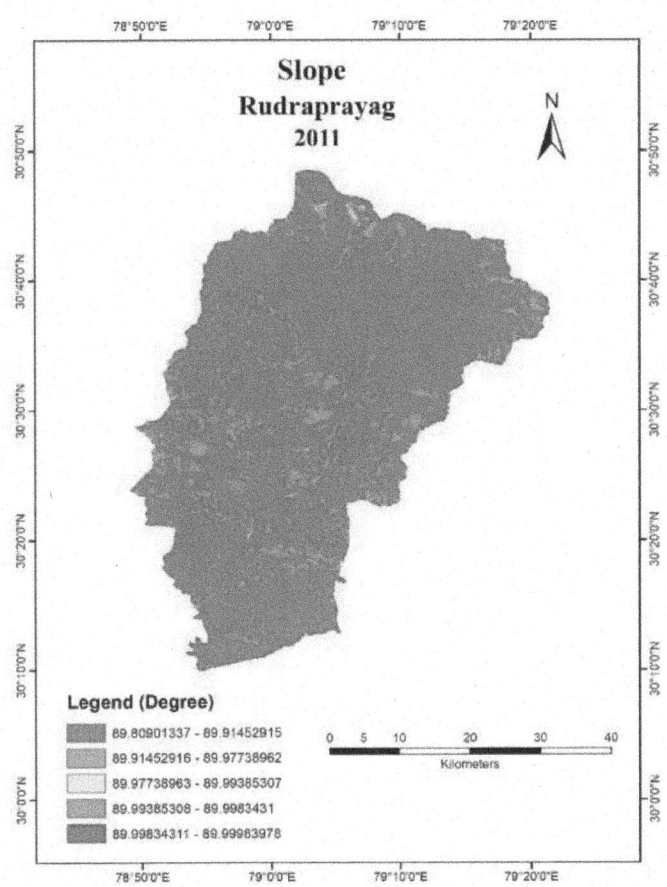

Map 25.5   Slope Map of Study Area using DEM-SRTM

storage facilities, and masonry buildings, put the country at risk. The National Disaster Management Authority of India defines an earthquake as a natural disaster that takes place without warning and causes violent shaking of the ground or everything above it. It is caused by the release of cumulative stress caused by moving lithospheric or crustal plates.

The earthquake risk or harm potential of a region is caused by a mixture of seismic hazards and the vulnerability and exposure of the physical environment. The devastation caused by recent earthquakes around the world has highlighted the need for seismic risk assessment in disaster management applications. (Sinha, Aditya, and Gupta 2008)

Earthquake zonation is a technique to determine the level of risk of an earthquake within a region (Sekac et al. 2016). Earthquake is one of the natural hazards which causes huge loss and destruction all over the world.

In this paper, earthquake zonation is done of Rudraprayag district, Uttarakhand. The earthquake zonation in the Map 8: Earthquake Zonation Map of Study Area shows the epicenter

is in Ukhimath Tehsil of Rudraprayag District of December 6, 2017, of magnitude 5.1. The depth of this earthquake was 10m and the horizontal distance was 8.1 km. For the present paper, the seismic data was collected from IMD 2019 in a excel spreadsheet and then exported to ArcGIS format and then with help of ArcGIS Analyst tool, buffer zone was created for the earthquake epicentre. From earthquake depth and magnitude, we can classify the level of hazard. The shallower the depth of earthquake the greater the hazard while deeper the depth of earthquake less the hazard. Similarly, higher the magnitude stronger the hazard and lower the magnitude weaker the hazard (Sekac et al. 2016). The horizontal distance shows the impact of earthquake in the region.

5. Social Vulnerability

Another important task under this research was to assess the vulnerability of Rudraprayag district based on social parameters. Social Vulnerability refers to the socioeconomic

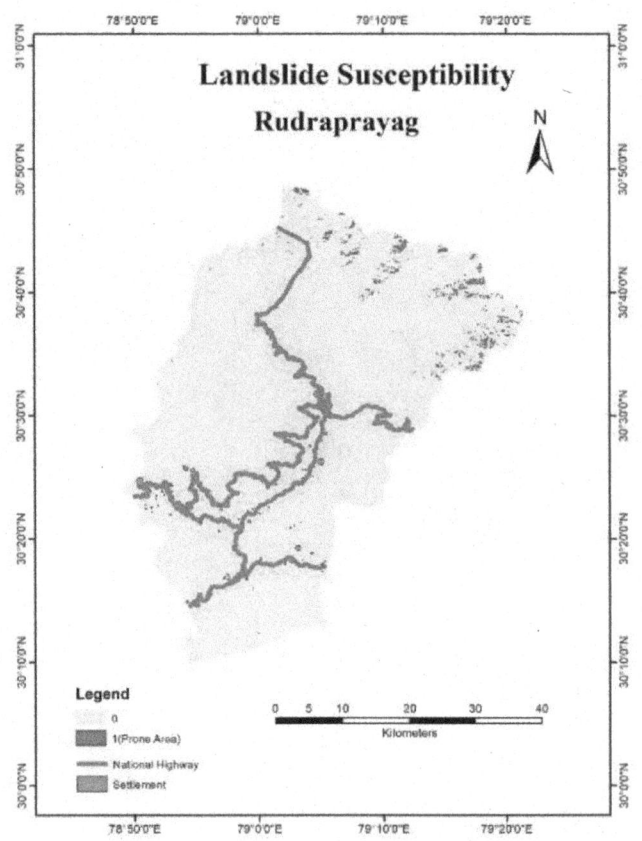

Map 25.6 Landslide Susceptibility Map of Study Area using Frequency Ratio

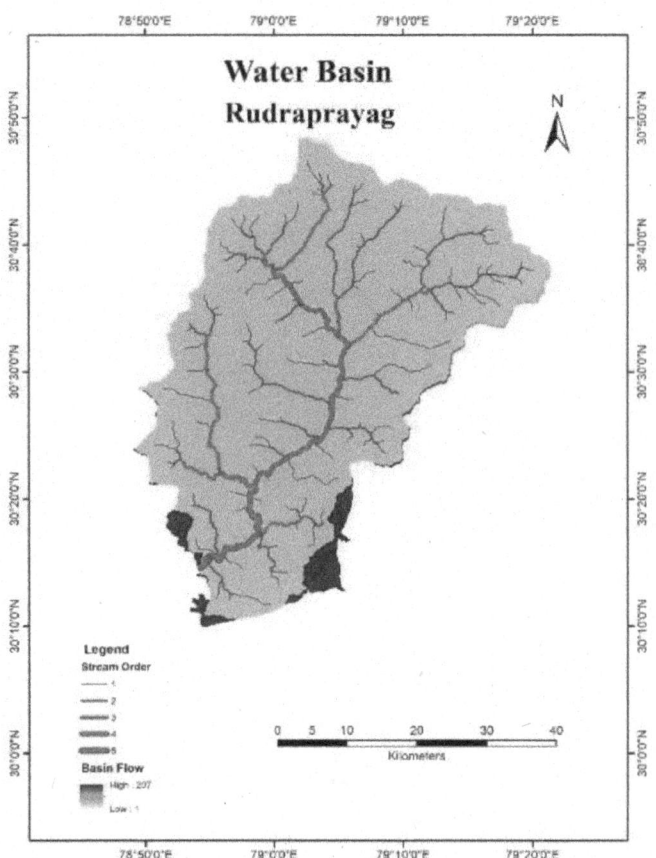

Map 25.7 Water Basin Map of Study Area using DEM-SRTM

and demographic factors that affect the resilience of communities. Effective addressing of the social vulnerability decreases both human suffering and economic loss after a disaster.

The district map of Rudraprayag was created and data on various social parameters was obtained through census 2011. Multi criteria analysis was done to obtain the results. The social parameters used were total population, male population, female population, total household, housing density, population density and literacy. All the blocks were ranked according to these individual parameters. Ranking was done from 1 to 3 and blocks assigned as rank 1 was most vulnerable to disasters and the vulnerability decreased from 1 to 3. Thus, block with rank 3 was least vulnerable. The rank sum was calculated for each block and based on it a vulnerability map was created classifying Rudraprayag district into high, medium and low vulnerable areas.

The maps were made using ArcGIS and Erdas software. The step-wise approach followed for the assessing the vulnerability is discussed in Fig. 25.3.

The method used to carry out the research is rank sum method statistics, the Mann–Whitney U test also called

Wilcoxon rank-sum test is a nonparametric test of the null hypothesis that it is equally likely that a randomly selected value from one sample will be less than or greater than a randomly selected value from a second sample. This test can be used to determine whether two independent samples were selected from populations having the same distribution; a similar nonparametric test used on dependent samples is the rank sum test. Here, we use the smallest planning unit, a municipal ward to carry out our research.

The comparative vulnerability of each district was based on specific indicators. Following are the selected indicators used to develop a composite index of vulnerability:

1. **Total population:** Population concentration is an important factor affecting vulnerability of an area. The area with high population will be more vulnerable to any disaster whereas an area with low or no population will not be affected so much by disaster because for a hazard to turn into disaster, there should be a considerable population that is to be affected.

2. **Male population:** High male population leads to decreased vulnerability in comparison to the female population. Males have more physical strength that

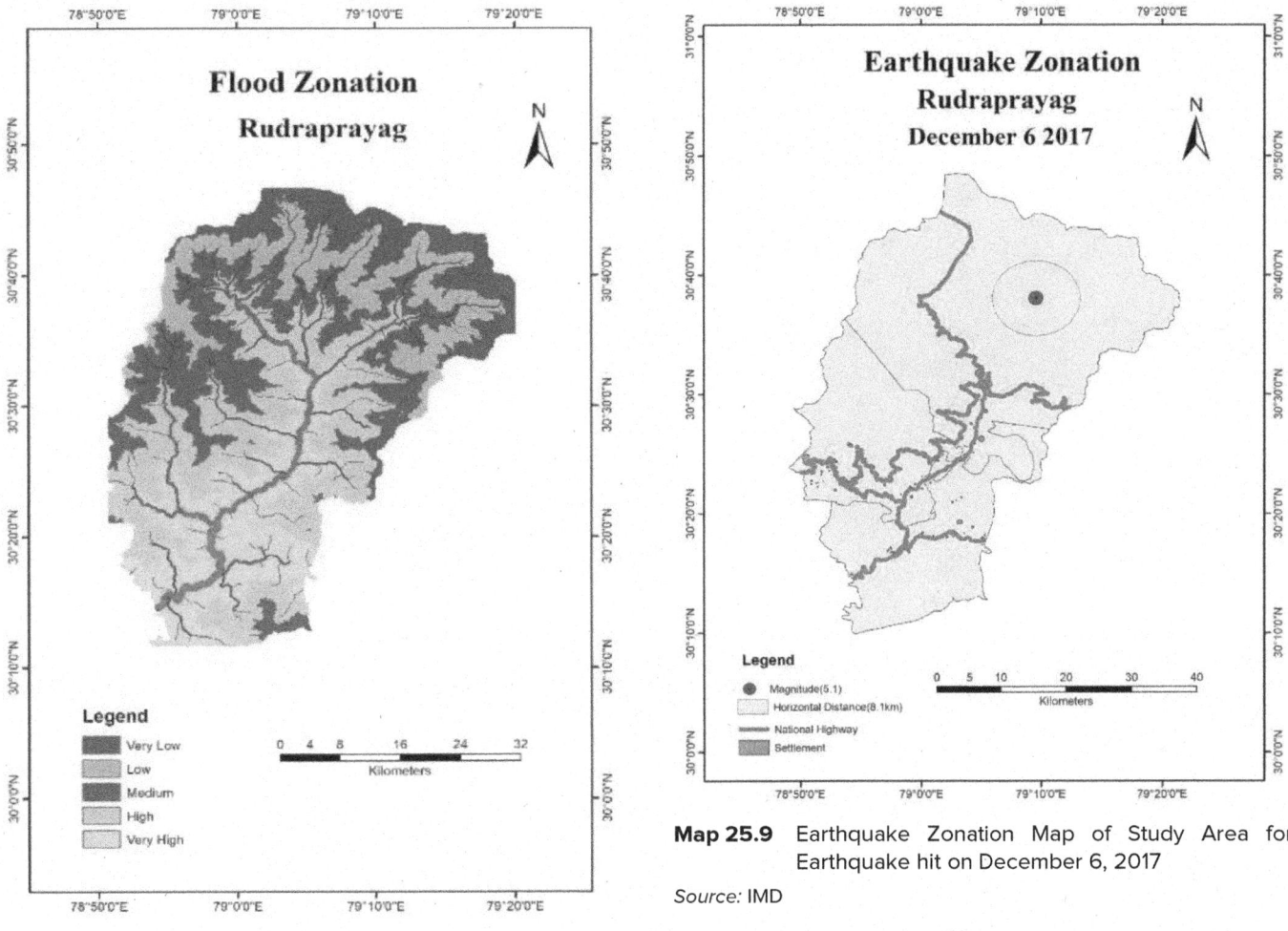

Map 25.9 Earthquake Zonation Map of Study Area for Earthquake hit on December 6, 2017

Source: IMD

Map 25.8 Flood Zonation Map of Study Area classifying flood zones

Table 25.2 Secondary Data for Social Vulnerability Assessment

Block Name	Total Population	Population Density	Male Population	Female Population	Households	Literacy Rate
Ukhimath	87,024	77	42,614	44,410	18,524	83.26
Rudraprayag	91,859	259	42,976	48,883	21,497	82.18
Jakholi	63,402	126	28,999	34,403	13,521	77.27

Source: Census of India, 2011

makes them more resilient and are easily able to cope with the effects of disaster.

3. *Female population:* Women have mobility constraints during an extreme event especially during pregnancy and inherent limited physical flexibility than men. Moreover, women take more time to recover than men due to various reasons such as employment, low wage and family responsibilities (Cutter et al., 2003)

4. *Total household:* A house and its occupants regarded as a unit is referred to the household. Areas with high households are more vulnerable as there are more occupants in a single house leading to high risk. Response mechanisms are also difficult to carry out in such situations.

5. *Population Density:* Population density has long been viewed as one of the main contributing factors to the

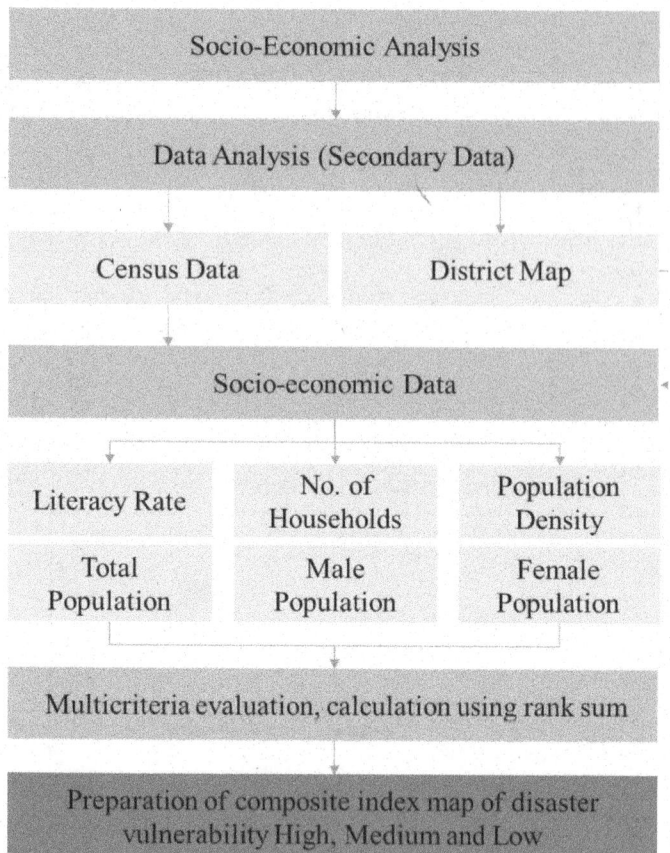

Fig. 25.3   Methodology for Social Vulnerability Assessment

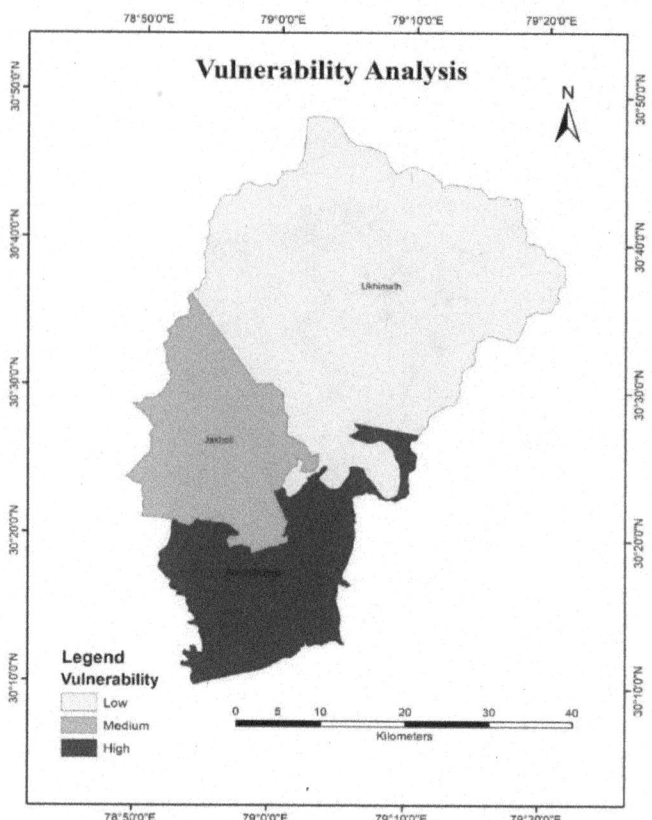

Map 25.10   Vulnerability Map of Rudraprayag District

6. Results

6.1 Landslide Susceptibility

From the Map 25.6 it is clear that the Ukhimath region is the most unstable and vulnerable and is at constant threat from landslides, especially during and after an intense spell of rainfall. This is mainly because of the steep slopes in the area with loose and unconsolidated materials and we can also find evidence of active or past landslips. Besides the zone is also located near faults and tectonically weak zones. It further includes areas where mountain cutting for roads and other human activities are intense. Also because of high altitude, rugged terrain, less agriculture land and extreme environments conditions it restricts the economy of the area to flourish to its full extent.

6.2 Flood Zonation

From the Map 25.8 Rudraprayag block is the most vulnerable to the flood. The main reason behind this high prone flooding area is due to presence of two prominent rivers Alaknanda

vulnerability status of communities, both in developed and underdeveloped nations. High housing density, crowding index and population density and high number of socially deprived population with low living standards/ quality is vulnerable to hazards (Akhtar Alam et el., 2017).

6. *Literacy:* An educated person is always less vulnerable than an uneducated person as literate people are aware of the risk their locality possesses and they develop local coping mechanisms to deal with the local disasters. He/she explores and tries to find out other suitable means to be safe.

After evaluation of all the parameters mentioned above, the overall vulnerability of each block was obtained, and it was found to be highly variable. The Rudraprayag block was found to be highly vulnerable as these compose of old central business district where people are, less literate and high household density reside. The other districts were found to be comparatively less vulnerable.

and Mandakini flowing throughout the block and meeting at Rudraprayag. This area vulnerability can be seen as it was one of the most affected regions during 2013 Uttarakhand Flood. With high annual average rainfall of 1229 mm (IMD), this leads to overflow of embankments and preach of river channels leading to flooding in the low-lying areas. The given figure shows five classes of vulnerability of flood prone areas from very low to very high where Rudraprayag block is very high prone to floods and Ukhimath block least prone.

6.3 Social Vulnerability

From the Map 25.10 it is clear that Rudraprayag block is highly vulnerable followed by Jakholi block and Ukhimath block as the least vulnerable block. By adopting certain policies at the local level, it is possible to lessen the vulnerability of the region. The Table 25.3: Social Vulnerability of Study Area shows the vulnerability classes and all the social factors resulting in the block vulnerability.

Table 25.3   Social Vulnerability of Study Area

Sr. No	Vulnerability Class	Total population likely to be affected (Persons)	Number of male population likely to be affected	Number of female population likely to be affected	No. of households likely to be affected
1	High	91,859	42,976	48,883	21,497
2	Medium	63,402	28,999	34,403	35,863
3	Low	87,024	42,614	44,410	18,524

Source: Census of India, 2011

7. Conclusion

In this study, the focus was on three main natural hazards in Rudraprayag District i.e., Floods, Landslide and Earthquake. The earthquake zonation for the earthquake of December 6, 2017 of magnitude 5.1 was mapped using GIS. The flood map was prepared using FR model with various factors and district was divided into five prone areas starting from very low to very high. Landslide Susceptibility map was also prepared using FR model showing landslide prone areas. Finally, a social vulnerability map was prepared using social parameters such as total population, male population, female population, total household, housing density, population density and literacy. These social parameters were then using weighted rank were arranged and a map was prepared showing Rudraprayag as the most vulnerable block in the whole district.

The paper will help in deducing the overall vulnerability of the people and different areas of the study area prone to hazards which will help in scheming of policies and plans for further development of the region with the aim of increasing the social status of people which will in turn help to decrease the vulnerability of the region. This study will also help in updating the present District Disaster Management Plan of Rudraprayag and create a disaster resilient environment.

Advance scientific technologies like drones, AI, and GIS are nowadays helpful in disaster management and helps to better understand the disaster risk. It also helps to better prepare in the future, as planning for areas that are at high risk will be given importance and new ways will be sought to mitigate the effects of the disasters.

REFERENCES

1. Chung, C.F. and Fabbri, A.G. 1995: Multivariate regression analysis for landslide hazard zonation. In Carrara, A. and Guzzetti, F., editors, Geographical Information Systems in assessing natural hazards, Dordrecht: Kluwer, 107–42.
2. Cruden, D.M. 1991: A simple definition of a landslide. Bulletin International Association of Engineering Geology 43, 27–29.
3. Disaster Mitigation and Management Centre (DMMC). 2014. *Geological Investigations in Rudraprayag District with Special Reference to Mass Instability.* Dehradun.
4. Du, Yan, Yibo Ding, Zixiong Li, and Guangwen Cao. 2015. "The Role of Hazard Vulnerability Assessments in Disaster Preparedness and Prevention in China." *Military Medical Research* 2(1):1–23. DOI: 10.1186/s40779-015-0059-9.
5. Feloni, Elissavet, Ioannis Mousadis, and Evangelos Baltas. 2020. "Flood Vulnerability Assessment Using a GIS-Based Multi-Criteria Approach—The Case of Attica Region." *Journal of Flood Risk Management* 13(S1):1–15. DOI: 10.1111/jfr3.12563.
6. Hall, J., Arheimer, B., Borga, M., Brázdil, R., Claps, P., Kiss, A., … Llasat, M. C. 2014. Understanding flood regime changes in Europe: A state of the art assessment. Hydrology and Earth System Sciences, 18(7), 2735–2772.
7. Hansen, A. 1984: Landslide hazard analysis. In Brunsden, D. and Prior, D.B., editors, Slope instability, New York: Wiley, 523–602.
8. Huabin, Wang, Liu Gangjun, Xu Weiya, and Wang Gonghui. 2005. "GIS-Based Landslide Hazard Assessment: An Overview." *Progress in Physical Geography* 29(4):548–67. DOI: 10.1191/0309133305pp462ra.
9. Khanduri, S., KS Sajwan, A. Rawat, C. Dhyani, and S. Kapoor. 2018. "Disaster in Rudraprayag District of Uttarakhand Himalaya: A Special Emphasis on Geomorphic Changes and

Slope Instability." *Journal of Geography & Natural Disasters* 08(01). DOI: 10.4172/2167-0587.1000218.

10. Samuels, P. G., Borga, M., Baltas, E., & Casale, R. 1997. Introductory chapter. In R. Casale, B. Pedroli, & P. Samuels (Eds.), River Basin modeling, management and flood mitigation. Proceeding of the workshop/expert meeting (pp. 25–26). Monselice, Italy.

11. Sekac, Tingneyuc, Sujoy Kumar Jana, Indrajit Pal, and Dilip Kumar Pal. 2016. "GIS Based Evaluation in Earthquake Hazard Micro-Zonation - A Case Study of Madang and Morobe Province, Papua New Guinea." *International Journal of Advanced Engineering Research and Science* 3(8):95–104. DOI: 10.22161/ijaers.3.8.2.

12. Sinha, Ravi, K. S. P. Aditya, and Achin Gupta. 2008. "GIS-Based Urban Seismic Risk Assessment Using RISK.Iitb." *ISET Journal of Earthquake Technology* 45(3–4):41.

13. The National Academies of Sciences. 1991. "Hazard and Risk Assessment." in *A Safer Future: Reducing the Impacts of Natural Disasters*. The National Academies Press.

CHAPTER 26

Preparedness and Damage Assessment using UAVs for Management of Flood in India

Rudrashis Majumder

Ph.D. Student, Department of Aerospace Engineering,
Indian Institute of Science, Bangalore
rudrashism@iisc.ac.in

Shuvrangshu Jana

Post-doctoral Fellow, Department of Aerospace
Engineering,
Indian Institute of Science, Bangalore
shuvrangshuj@iisc.ac.in

Prathyush P. Menon

Associate Professor, College of Engineering,
Mathematics and Physical Sciences, University of
Exeter, UK
p.m.prathyush@exeter.ac.uk

Debasish Ghose

Professor, Department of Aerospace Engineering,
Indian Institute of Science, Bangalore
dghose@iisc.ac.in

N. M. Prusty

Humanitarian Aid International, India
nmprusty51@gmail.com

Bipasha Mukherjee

Humanitarian Aid International, India
bipasha@hai-india.org

Aditi Ghosh

Humanitarian Aid International, India
adghosh@gmail.com

Abstract

The casualties and infrastructure damage caused by natural disasters necessitate efficient disaster management. The era of fast-paced development in Unmanned Aerial Vehicles (UAVs) technology and their use in various domains have opened a new paradigm on their use in natural disaster management. In this paper, a two-stage operational lifecycle for flood management using UAVs is envisaged. First, the pre-disaster preparedness, concerning surveying-related events that precede the flood, setting up Early Warning Systems (EWS), and requirements of UAVs for rapid and efficient deployment during the flood, is decided. Next, the damage assessment phase, which provides post-disaster logistics planning to initiate the reconstruction of infrastructure, is executed. Each stage with varying priority levels lasts for a different time span and imposes a different set of task demands on the UAVs. Our present work focuses on the detailed study of how UAVs can be deployed in these two phases of flood management in the Indian context.

Keywords: Disaster management; Preparedness; Damage Assessment; Unmanned Aerial Vehicle (UAV)

1. Introduction

The occurrence of natural or man-made disasters imposes a high threat to humanity in terms of casualties and economic losses. The last few decades of disaster research have shown an increasing interest in involving recent technology tools to reduce the effect of the disaster. Disaster management, or, in general, emergency management, involves policy-making and administrative decisions, different operational jobs, and the use of relevant technologies with the aim of controlling the adverse scenario caused by a disaster. There are four stages of activities in disaster management. First, mitigation, which includes the activities to reduce the possibility of a disaster occurring. Secondly, in the preparedness phase, essential measures are taken in the disaster-prone area to reduce the damage for an unavoidable disaster by building up resilience. The third phase involves the immediate response activities to minimize the damage caused. In the fourth phase, recovery activities are carried out to regain normalcy in the disaster-affected area. The preparedness activities before the occurrence of disaster immensely help in planning the emergency response system to save human and animal lives. It also increases situational awareness of both the government and residents of the disaster-prone area by sending warning messages. However, once the disaster takes place, the response and recovery activities need to be carried out efficiently in order to minimize the effect of the devastation. Therefore, post-disaster damage assessment also deserves significant attention to strengthen the actions taken in response and recovery phases. In this paper, we mainly focus on the preparedness activities and damage assessment involving Unmanned Aerial Vehicle (UAV) technology.

The preparedness phase of disaster management comprises proper planning and execution of spreading awareness, early warning systems (EWS), resource identification and management, and other necessary pre-disaster activities. Despite getting worldwide acknowledgment, this field still lacks attention from disaster researchers. In literature like (Gillespie and Streeter, 1987; Sutton and Tierney, 2006), the authors try to conceptualize the idea of disaster preparedness. In the review work (Dekens, 2007), the author suggests the integration of local knowledge and practices to facilitate disaster preparedness. The paper (Ryan et al., 2020) presents a detailed literature review on the effect of community communication and engagement techniques to improve hazard preparedness.

A detailed survey on pre-disaster preparedness and planning for flood is given in (Raikes et al., 2019). The paper (Saravi et al., 2019) focuses on the development and evaluation of machine learning-based models to build resilience and preparedness against adverse flood scenarios. (Girons Lopez et al., 2017) describes the efficiency of flood early warning systems. Algorithms from (Menon et al., 2014) can be adapted for faster determination of hot spots, which are areas of higher probability of being affected in the case of flooding, and for demarcating such areas. Drone technology is evolving continuously, and after being heavily used in commercial applications, the technology is now being introduced in disaster management and rescue operations (Kim and Davidson, 2015; Velev et al., 2019; Bravo and Leiras, 2015; Qadir et al., 2021; Gkotsis et al., 2017). In (Griffin, 2014), a systematic analysis of how UAVs can be useful in disaster management has been addressed. In the papers (Luo et al., 2019; Quaritsch et al., 2010), the UAV-assisted network systems for disaster management have been studied. The paper (Adams and Friedland, 2011) presents a survey of UAV imagery collection in disaster management. In (Erdelj and Natalizio, 2016; Erdelj et al., 2017), the potential applications of UAVs in disaster management are highlighted with a detailed review of related literature. These papers also present the open challenges to use UAVs in this area. The work in (Petrides et al., 2017) focuses on the advantages of using UAVs in emergency preparedness and response operations.

In (Kamilaris and Prenafeta-Boldú, 2018), a deep learning technique is used on the images collected from the UAVs to predict disasters. The research in (Gautam et al., 2020) uses UAVs to capture high-resolution images for planning disaster risk management in the future. In (Casado and Leinster, 2020), a UAV-based decision-making framework has been proposed to build resilience towards flood. (Salmoral et al., 2020) evaluates how UAVs can be used in the preparedness and response phase of floods in both England and India.

In order to start the reconstruction phase to regain normalcy, it is important to do a proper damage assessment for the disaster-affected locations. Capturing the images of the emergency locations from unmanned vehicles can provide a clear picture of the devastation caused by a flood. The paper (Yamazaki and Matsuoka, 2007) uses remote sensing techniques for post-disaster damage assessment. In (Myint et al., 2008), satellite-dependent geospatial techniques are used. In (Inoguchi et al., 2021), time-cost per unit area is used as one of the evaluation criteria to understand or estimate damage after a disaster.

(Romali et al., 2015) use stage–damage functions for the assessment of flood damages and presents a review of the methods used to construct stage–damage function curves for residential, agricultural, and other similar categories. Luino et al. (2009) present the evaluation of damage produced by a flood using a geographic information system (GIS). The paper (König et al., 2002) focuses on the damage caused by urban flooding and the generation of flooding-damage relations with statistical surveys about historical flood events. Several other papers like (Merz et al., 2013; Sieg et al., 2017) use a tree-based modeling approach for flood damage assessment.

The authors in (Ezequiel et al., 2014) discuss the use of a low-cost UAV-based remote sensing system to collect aerial imagery of the disaster-affected area and the required data processing for post-disaster assessment. In the paper (Adsanver et al., 2021), drones are considered for post-disaster damage assessment operations. Specifically, this paper solves the problem of damage assessment using mixed-integer linear programming (MILP) when a set of drones are used to evaluate damages in a limited time. Anders et al. (2020) focus on damage analysis using low altitude aerial photography with a UAS and demonstrate the impact of flight altitude and direction on the quality of surface models and orthophotos. The paper (Gebrehiwot et al., 2019) presents a deep convolutional network for flood mapping using UAVs. Jiménez-Jiménez et al. (2020) propose damage assessment for urban flood using high-resolution remote sensing data and an object-based approach. Munawar et al. (2021) present a review of the recent developments in flood management based on image processing, artificial intelligence, and UAVs with a focus on post-disaster. The paper (Pi et al., 2021) presents a fully annotated dataset including object classes, people, flooded areas, and damaged buildings, vegetation, road, etc. and uses convolutional neural network (CNN) models for detecting and segmenting critical objects in the aerial footage of disaster sites collected by UAVs. Valentijn et al. (2020) also introduce CNN-based classification of building damage in remote sensing images collected by UAVs. Kakooei and Baleghi (2017) use an integrated approach of disaster damage assessment using satellites, aircraft, and UAVs. (Gebrehiwot and Hashemi-Beni, 2021) create three-dimensional inundation mapping using UAV image segmentation and digital surface model (DSM).

UAV technology is not only more affordable and accessible nowadays, but it's also often more efficient at managing disasters than other methods currently in use. The article by Rajan et al. (2021) highlights different potential uses of UAVs in disaster management applications. In the present study, we focus on the usage of UAVs in order to facilitate efficient preparedness and damage assessment of floods in the Indian context. Despite much attention in disaster management research, only a few literature is available on which modern technologies are integrated into unmanned vehicles for disaster management in India. This paper indicates the need for UAVs in various applications to strengthen disaster response activities. A real-life case study based on the flood in the Jajpur district of Odisha in India is given here.

The remaining part of this paper is organized as follows. Section 2 focuses on the preparedness aspects for flood using UAVs. In Section 3, usage of UAVs in flood damage assessment is considered. Section 4 presents the case studies in the Indian context. In Section 5, the main challenges encountered in the operations using drones are discussed. Section 6 concludes this study.

2. Flood Preparedness with UAVs

Being prepared for the extremities of a natural disaster can help individuals and communities to cope with the consequences of the disaster. Once the risks associated with a disaster are assessed, making decisions about appropriate countermeasures to minimize the impact becomes easier. The preparedness for flood includes a set of jobs in order to gain resilience for fighting against the severity caused by a flood. In general, structural preparedness, accumulation of resources, proper planning for resource distribution, land-water boundary monitoring, etc., are a few examples of preparedness activities. Successful execution of these activities improves social resilience towards floods. A subset of these activities can be carried out using unmanned aerial systems, which is more advantageous than manual operations as the latter is time-taking and sometimes lacks accuracy. Customized drones with functionalities such as cameras, sensors, GPS and navigation systems, etc., can provide quicker and more accurate solutions for pre-disaster preparedness activities in order to protect infrastructure and reduce casualties.

In the preparedness phase, mapping the land-water boundary and preparing the digital elevation model (DEM) of the area is performed using UAVs. Real-time monitoring of land-water boundary provides dynamic information about the extent of the spread of floodwater. Residents staying in the areas more prone to the severity of flood (e.g., low lands, locations near dams, etc.) can be alerted based on the spatial and temporal status of the land-water boundary. The creation of DEM before flood helps after a disaster as it can be used to compare with the DEM captured after the flood to get an estimation of the level of severity. Planned mitigation activities can be able to prevent or minimize the intensity of floods in that area. The paper (Tripathi, 2015) is an analysis of the trend and preparedness of floods in India.

During the preparedness stage, the desired specifications of UAVs to be deployed during the flood are determined. The choice of UAV fleets with their payload and endurance capabilities, sensor needs, communication requirements, and operating scalability are the major concerns for deploying UAVs in flood scenarios. The UAV fleet could include both fixed-wing and rotary-wing aircraft. For large-area surveys, fixed-wing UAVs are favored, but rotary-wing UAVs will assist in accurately deploying cargo to the desired place. Commercial UAVs should be preferred because they can easily be scaled up during the emergency response phase. Algorithm requirements for speedy and efficient deployment of UAVs for the mission are among the advanced concerns. Onboard algorithms for vision-based landing on a platform, survivor detection, tracking, payload delivery, etc., should be handled by the UAV autopilot. The overall system architecture should be robust and scalable. Using drones for disaster relief also helps to handle communication between different agencies and individuals. The following basic specification should be considered for UAVs to be operated in flood relief/rescue operations.

1. UAVs should be designed so that they can operate in light rain.
2. UAVs should be stable in the presence of wind gust.
3. UAVs which are used for the rescue operation should be able to detect humans and communicate the information to the base station.
4. UAVs should be able to carry the payload and release the payload at the desired location and come back to the base station. The payload could be a lifeboat, medical packet, food items, communication equipments, etc.

5. The provision for the operation of UAV in manual or autonomous mode through a mobile app.

6. Drones should able to follow geo-fence boundaries regulated by government authorities.

7. UAVs should be well-equipped to form a communication network in case the cellular towers are damaged or malfunctioning.

2.1 Awareness

Situational awareness is very important in building resilience towards any kind of disaster. In general, floods can take from a few hours to a few days to develop to the maximum extent. Hourly updates about the status of the flood, as for example, water depth, the spread of flood, etc., in an area can help residents to take required measures to save their lives. Also, an inspection of the real-time status of floodwater can help government disaster management authorities to plan the evacuation of the residents in advance. This situational awareness can be obtained by the usage of drones in a cost-effective manner. Specifically, in a disaster situation, actions need to be initiated within a short response time frame. Drones assist in quick coverage of the total area of concern, mapping all the potential danger zones, available road networks for a safe evacuation, etc. The time-bound change in land-water boundary and DEM can be helpful in creating awareness about the flood situation. An early warning system (EWS) can be developed for flood, which can alert people by sending SMS or broadcasting in local radio or television channels. Flood in India occurs either slowly or suddenly due to various reasons like excessive rainfall, overflowing of a river, collapsed dams, etc. Hourly monitoring of the flood-prone area can be helpful to develop awareness about the situation, and necessary steps to evacuate people from the disaster-affected region can be initiated.

2.2 Resource Delivery Planning

Once the flood takes place, allocation and distribution of different critical and general resources become the priority. However, a few parts of the existing road network may become inundated with floodwater or damaged. Hence, pre-planning resource distribution can help the authority in assisting the residents in the post-disaster situation. Usage of UAVs can help in mapping the area more prone to flood. Then, depending on the DEM, multiple resource stations can be set up so that the problem caused by the damaged road network can be minimized. UAVs also can help in sending critical resources like medicines, etc., to stranded people. In India, because of a flood (or accompanying landslides), places can be inaccessible for disaster workers. Also, it is very common for the roads to get damaged so as to restrict the transportation of resources. Therefore, the disaster

management authority in India can use customized drones beforehand to plan the best locations for the resource stations for easy resource transport. Also, planning and design of a self-sufficient team of these specially designed drones are a part of the preparedness activity.

2.3 Surveillance Preparation

The main functionality of unmanned aerial systems, which has been mostly exploited in disaster management, is the surveillance operation (Neto et al., 2012; Abdallah et al., 2019; Guo et al., 2020; Ravichandran et al., 2019). Surveillance is important both before and after the occurrence of a flood. Before the flood occurs, the team of UAVs can do a monitoring job for the flood-prone area to predict potential danger. After the flood takes place, surveillance of UAVs in a timely manner can provide the update about the disaster-affected area, the hourly change in the water level, and survivors stranded in water-logged buildings. UAVs can also help to find elevated lands in the flooded area to shift people as well as domestic animals for safety. Different machine learning and image processing-based algorithms have been tested so far in the surveillance work of UAVs (Sharma, 2017; Dong et al., 2020). In (Ramasamy and Ghose, 2016, 2017), learning-based surveillance algorithms are proposed to increase the probability of target detection. A few other papers like (Ravichandran et al., 2019; Shetty and Ghose, 2020; Shetty et al., 2021) present various sophisticated algorithms for survivor detection during floods. Many districts of the Indian states are flood-prone because of their proximity to rivers or coastal areas. In order to conduct smooth monitoring of flood situation in an Indian context, a surveillance setup is to be made with a team of drones equipped with wi-fi sensors, camera, lidar, GPS systems, etc., that can be deployed before and after the occurrence of flood to collect dynamic information about the affected areas. For example, the authors in (Salmoral et al., 2020) developed a deployment analysis matrix of existing UAS applications. An online survey was carried out in England to assess how the technology could be further developed to meet flood emergency response needs. The deployment analysis matrix has the potential to be translated into an Indian context and other countries.

3. Damage Assessment with UAVs

Natural disasters potentially cause significant loss of life, injuries, and damages. The ability of emergency management professionals to observe damaged infrastructure, vegetation, etc., and perform timely initial assessments is critical. Evaluation of damage sets the idea of response and recovery steps after the disaster. Usually, the losses and damages that occur after a disaster can be in terms of structural damages, agricultural losses, damages of road networks, etc. Disaster can also cause an interruption in communication networks due to the damages of mobile phone towers. Manual information gathering by the disaster response workers to get an accurate picture of the disaster is a non-trivial job since getting to all the disaster locations may not be easy due to flood water or debris. UAVs make this situation comfortable for the authorities by quickly scanning a vast area and gathering real-time data and high-resolution images for post-disaster analysis. Aerial images captured from the UAVs are used to determine the magnitude of damage. Manned aircraft or helicopters are often too expensive to use in this context. Satellite mapping sometimes does not meet high-resolution needs, and it provides only vertical images. The use of UAVs for disaster mapping is more cost-effective and takes less response times when compared to traditional methods. Hence, drones not only save the workers from injuries and further casualties but also make the relevant data available to the authority in a shorter response time. The skeleton of damage assessment activities includes a comparison between the land-water boundary between pre and post-disaster scenarios, digital elevation maps (DEM), road network topology, and the area's structural topology.

3.1 Land-water Segmentation

The hourly monitoring of the land-water boundary is important to understand the extent of the flood and the localities affected by it. Land-water segmentation is not only important for the purpose of damage assessment, it also plays a significant role in preparedness operations. A pre-flood mapping of this boundary helps in building awareness among the authority and the inhabitants. Based on the above, the early-warning system may send sufficient forecast about the possible extent of the flood. This can be followed by evacuation and other pre-disaster operations. In post-flood environment, this mapping can help to understand the extent of the flood and the consequent damages of crops, road networks, etc. The paper (Hashemi-Beni and Gebrehiwot, 2021) uses convolutional neural network and region growing method on UAV data to identify the flood extent. Similar setup and use of technologies can be implemented by the disaster management authority of India in case of flood.

3.2 Structural Damages

Besides casualties, buildings and other physical structures also get affected by the occurrence of flood. Before initiating the recovery actions, it is important for the disaster management authority of the government to identify the structural damages in a flood-affected area. Only after that, proper planning for reconstruction and budget allocation are possible. However, the inundated lands may pose a challenge to the disaster workers to reach every corner physically and figure out the level of structural damages. The unmanned aerial vehicles make this job easy. The high-resolution images captured by the drones can help in identifying the damages in the houses, bridges, boundary walls, etc. Once these images are collected for a large area, they have to be analyzed by various computer software and algorithms to locate structural damages. The precise information about the devastation based on the studied images can help the assessors to estimate the financial loss. This also makes the budget allocation possible for the central or state government so that the recovery may start soon after the flood water goes away. There are a few papers published on the usage of UAVs in detecting structural damages. In (Kerle et al., 2020), UAV-based damage analysis is reviewed with more sophisticated texture and segmentation-based approaches using advanced deep learning. Fernandez Galarreta et al. (2015) focus on the damage feature extraction of oblique UAV images. A few other papers like (Chowdhury et al., 2020; Yamazaki et al., 2015; Sui et al., 2014) also provide information on the UAV-based structural damage analysis of different types of disasters. There are a few flood-prone Indian states like Bihar, Odisha, Maharashtra, West Bengal, etc., where a large number of people suffer due to damage of dwellings. UAVs can make life easier for the authority to detect the extent of structural damages in those places.

3.3 Crop Damages

Since flood is a major threat to vegetation and agricultural production, analysing the impact of flood on the agricultural production is of paramount importance. Flood water causes enormous damage to the agricultural produce in the affected area. The inundated agricultural land causes the damage of different seasonal crops. Also the sedimentation from the flood water changes the property of the lands to disturb the agriculture of that place for a long-term. While the assessment of crop damage is vital, the conventional manual methods can take months to finish and also suffer from inaccuracies and subjective bias. The delay and inaccuracies may result in depriving the farmers from getting government aid and they have to wait for another plantating season for income to be generated. The captured imagery from the UAVs can make this process quick and easy for the experts to estimate the loss and declare economic help to the farmers. Very few available literature talk about the technicality of crop damage analysis. In (Tapia-Silva et al., 2011), authors have developed remote sensing methods for the evaluation of crop damage due to flood. Garcia Millan et al. (2020) focus on crop loss estimation using various digital surface models. Needless to say, Indian agriculture suffers a lot because of flood. Planned use of a UAVs to collect images of the inundated agricultural land can make the job of the authority easy in making future plans for compensating crop damages and the financial losses of the farmers.

3.4 Road Network Damage

Knowing the status of the road network is an essential factor to carry on disaster response activities. This is important to plan rescue operations, relief allocation, and resource distribution. Also, since flood causes enormous damage of infrastructure, road networks also get affected because of damage. Roads can become inaccessible by the resource vehicles or even the disaster response personnel. Also, this makes finding an evacuation route difficult in the disaster locations. Hence, after the occurrence of flood, the importance of having a track of the road network damages can not be ignored by the authorities. It also helps in making the financial budget for the reconstruction of roads. However, needless to say that a manual survey of the road network may be impossible or critical to conduct. A quick assessment of damages of the road can be performed by planning a UAV missions along with the existing road network. The coordinates of the existing road network can be fed to the UAV as waypoints for the mission. UAVs need to be equipped with a downward-facing camera for capturing images. From the images acquired by the UAVs, the conditions of the roads in the post-disaster situation can be analyzed. The high-resolution images can give a fair indication about the damaged roads. The damaged roads should be avoided as much as possible during the response activities. The monetary budget released for the reconstruction of the roads also need to be updated according to the images. In (Kashyap et al., 2019), a dynamic routing method for resource transportation is proposed based on the data on road network and traffic flow captured by a team of UAVs. Several other papers like (Schnebele et al., 2014; Saad and Tahar, 2019; Ybañez et al., 2021) also explain the deployment of UAVs to update the information about the accessible road network after a disaster. Being a populated country, India needs a planned response phase after flood to support a large number of flood victims. Efficient use of drones can assist in mapping the accessible road network for resource tranportation.

4. Case Study

Our case study is modeled on the flood incident that occurred in the Jajpur district of Odisha in India in the year 2020. Due to unprecedented rainfall, a total number of around 1.4 Million people in 20 districts (Angul, Balasore, Bhadrak, Bargarh, Jajpur, Cuttack, and others) have been affected due to the flood situation in Odisha. Around 340 villages and a population of around 0.2 Million have been marooned by the flood. While 17 human casualties have been reported, around 10,000 houses have been damaged, and 1,68,904 hectares of crop area have been affected due to this incident. Both urban and rural infrastructure (like power supply, water, roads, communication) were heavily damaged. Social infrastructure like schools, colleges, health centers, and shops, were also severely affected. Huge crop areas, as well as fishing ponds, were submerged. Embankment breaches were seen at several locations.

Pre-Disaster exhaustive micro-drone surveillance and mapping were conducted to identify zones susceptible to breaches, erosion, flooding, and waterlogging. The main idea behind these operations was to provide data that would help develop preparedness by the civic authorities and residents. Once the flood occurred, drones were used to collect image-based data from the affected areas and determine the extent of damage and loss. The flood occurred on August 30, 2020 and drones were deployed on September 3, 2020 in 23 of the most affected villages of Jajpur district for the post-flood damage assessment.

Data capturing and mapping exercises in the villages were started within a week of the flood. Most parts of the villages were seen to be submerged at the time of drone mapping activity. Through the drone-mapping exercise and interaction with the local residents, it was clear that the houses, agricultural lands, trees, and other infrastructures were either submerged or damaged. Consequently, many villagers had to move to safer places, while some had to take shelter in open spaces.

The mapping was done using a 4k HD vision camera stationed on the drone. Types of data captured through drones were the images of the buildings collapsed and damaged, submerged agriculture lands, and other infrastructure damages. The total area covered for mapping was almost 2 sq. kms. Initially, 4k HD vision data captured the affected area using one drone, and then the mapping of those areas was done using another drone having mapping capability onboard. The captured images were processed on Artificial Intelligence (AI) and Machine Learning (ML)-powered cloud-based photogrammetry engine to generate the outputs. The ortho-elevation was also generated through DEM software. The use of AI/ML-based algorithms was used to fine-tune the DEM, which further assisted in generating a true ortho-model with perfect vertical height. The crop health analysis of the damaged areas was done by capturing images with the specialized multi-spectral camera and analyzing the images with the AI/ML tool.

Drones were No permission-No take-off (NPNT) compliant, with an array of features ranging from tracking a single object to semi-autonomous flights. The drones currently have camera resolution of 64 MP. Video Resolution was set to 4K:3840×2160 24/25/30p and FHD: 1920×1080 24/25/30/48/50/60/120p. The flight time was 25 to 30 minutes in a single flight with an elevation of 50 to 60 meters depending upon terrain and towers in specific areas.

Figure 26.1 shows a DEM for Dihapal village of Jajpur district in Odisha obtained from the drone imagery and further analysis. This DEM can be used for preparedness activities by identifying more flood-prone areas. The idea derived from the DEM can help in the awareness of the local authority. The evacuation work or locating the resource stations also can be facilitated from the information acquired from the DEM.

Figure 26.2 shows a few damaged houses in a particular area captured by UAVs. The same analysis can be done in the other disaster locations also to get an estimation of structural damages. This is very helpful for the government to announce the compensation packages and rehabilitation schemes.

Figure 26.3 shows a few submerged agricultural lands from which the damage of crops and the loss of the farmers can be estimated. In Fig. 26.4, an analysis is shown about the crop damage. It shows that the area bounded by a yellow-colored border suffers more from crop damages while the green-bordered areas are less affected in this term.

Figure 26.5 shows a road fully submerged in floodwater. This gives an idea about how the UAVs can be used to update the status of the road network after the flood occurs.

Figures 26.1-26.5 give a clear indication that using UAVs for disaster management can give a much clear idea about the devastation caused by floods. It is not difficult to understand that the manual-mode analysis of the same will take a much longer time, and the interpretation from the manual data will not have a comparable clarity that would be adequate to understand the situation.

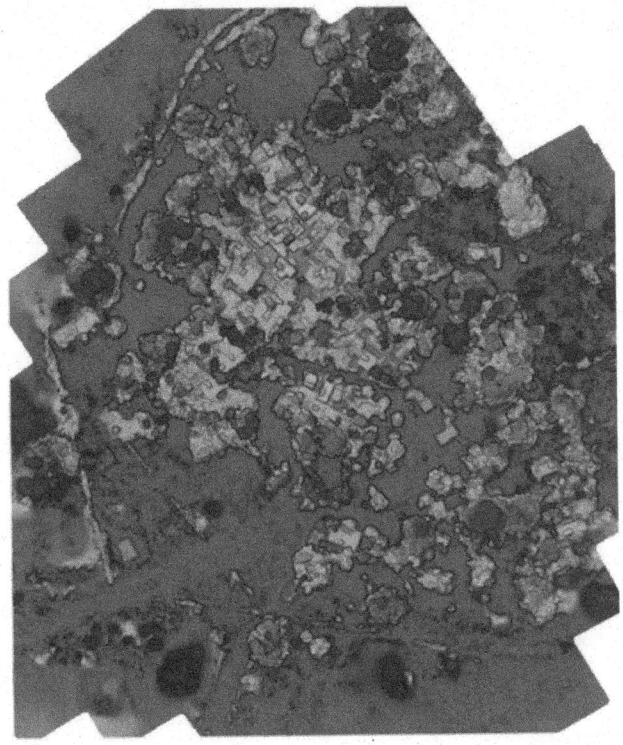

Fig. 26.1 Digital elevation map (DEM) in Dihapal, Odisha, India

Fig. 26.2 Indication of structural damages from UAV images

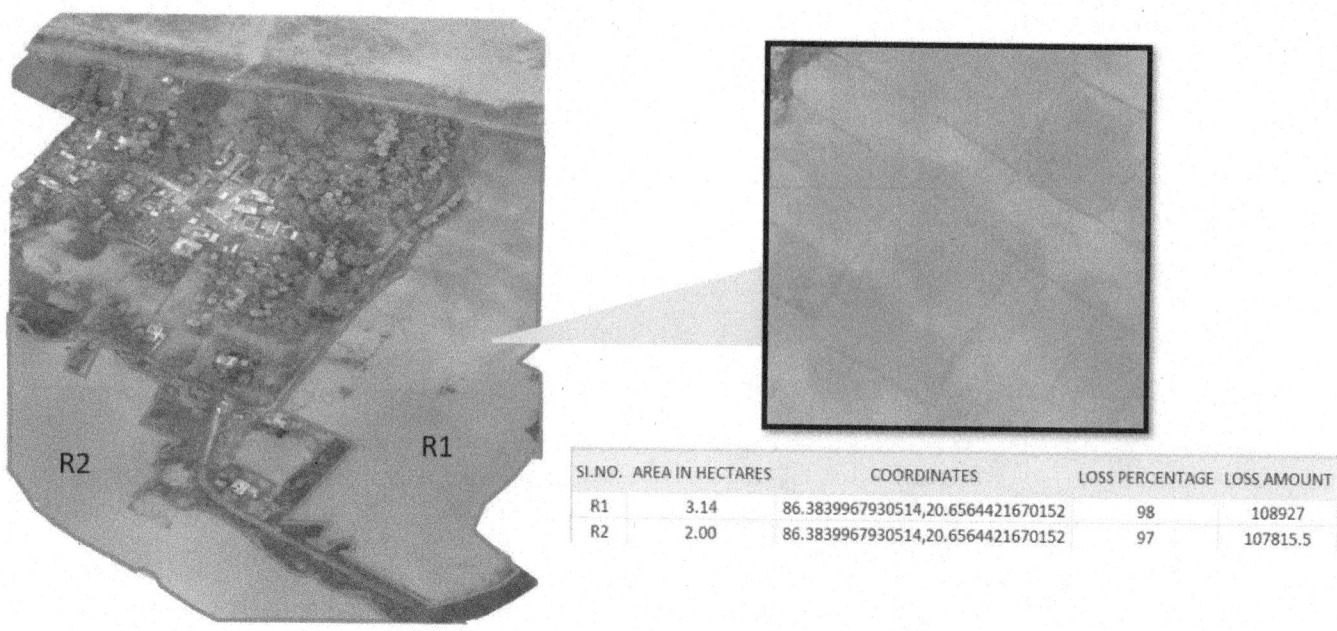

SI.NO.	AREA IN HECTARES	COORDINATES	LOSS PERCENTAGE	LOSS AMOUNT
R1	3.14	86.3839967930514,20.6564421670152	98	108927
R2	2.00	86.3839967930514,20.6564421670152	97	107815.5

Fig. 26.3 Submerged agricultural land captured from UAVs

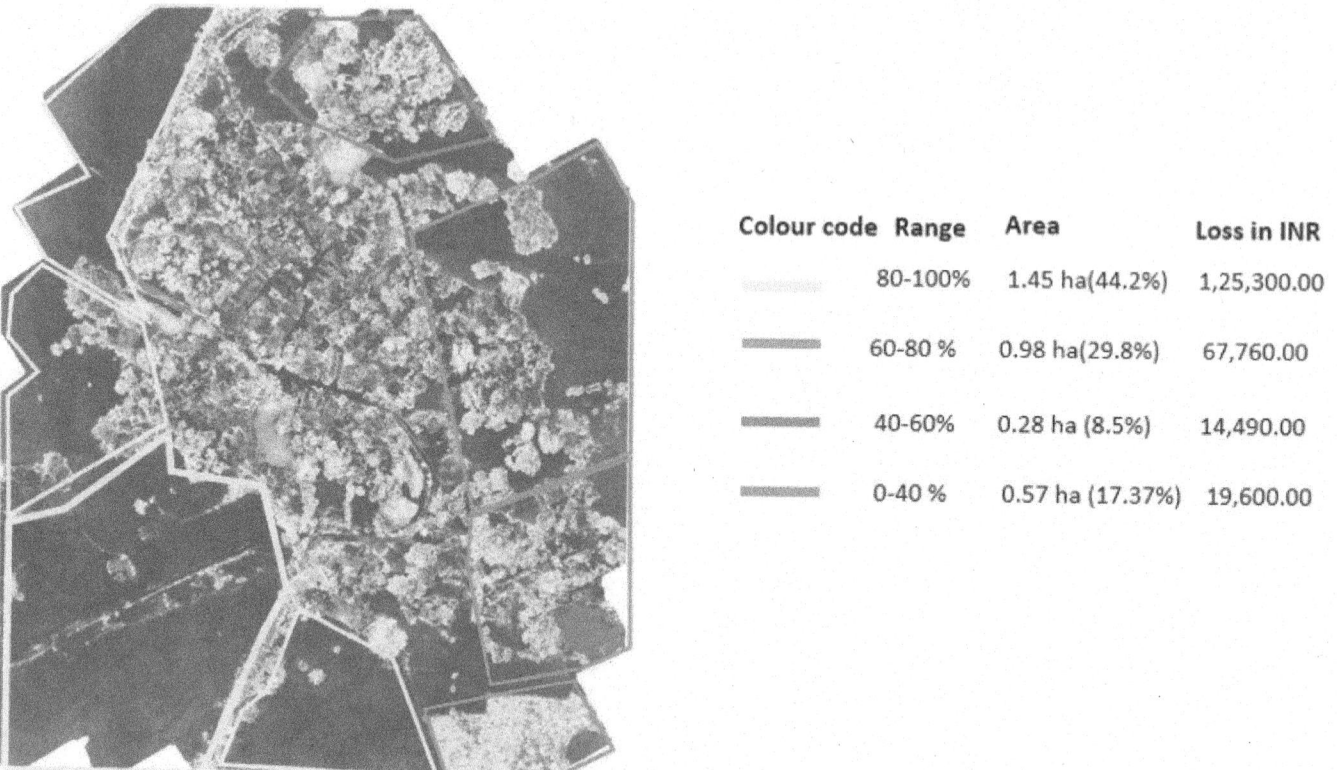

Colour code	Range	Area	Loss in INR
	80-100%	1.45 ha(44.2%)	1,25,300.00
	60-80 %	0.98 ha(29.8%)	67,760.00
	40-60%	0.28 ha (8.5%)	14,490.00
	0-40 %	0.57 ha (17.37%)	19,600.00

Fig. 26.4 Crop damage analysis in Dihapal, Odisha, India

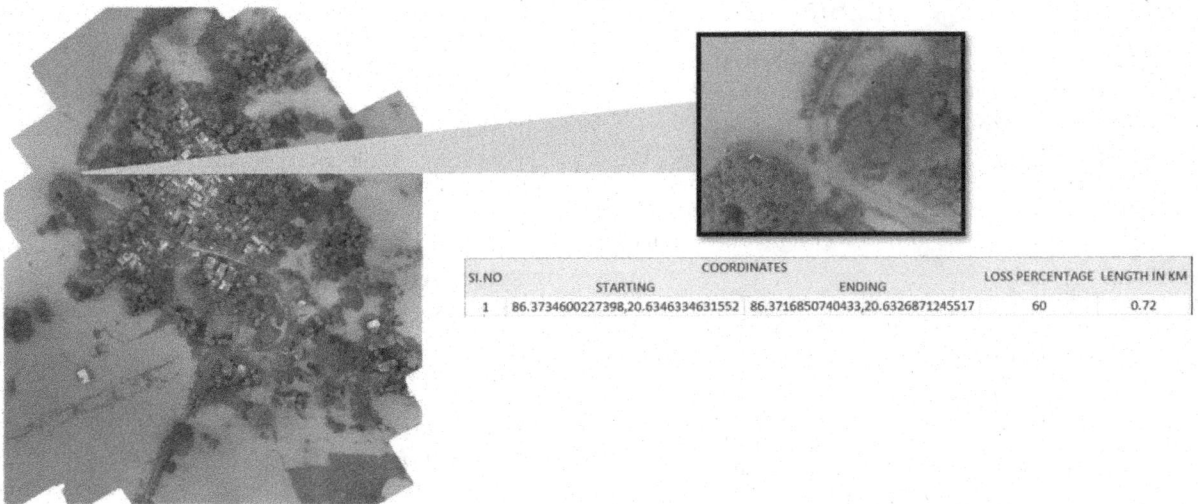

SI.NO	COORDINATES		LOSS PERCENTAGE	LENGTH IN KM
	STARTING	ENDING		
1	86.3734600227398,20.6346334631552	86.3716850740433,20.6326871245517	60	0.72

Fig. 26.5   Submerged roads in Dihapal, Odisha, India

5. Challenges

Although it is advantageous to use drone imagery for the analysis of the impact of a flood, using drones for preparedness and damage assessment also needs to overcome a set of challenges related to drone operation. First, the endurance of the drone needs to be increased for large-scale operations as the base station might be far away from the remote flood locations. Secondly, it is difficult to operate drones in a rainy environment. In dense fog, the field of view is not adequate. Also, the water droplets due to fog can cause malfunction of the drones. In addition, flying drones in windy weather are difficult with commercial drones. For all these reasons, flying window time was drastically reduced, which delayed the overall drone operation. Another significant challenge was the poor network connectivity, which caused communication interruption between the drones and the base station.

6. Conclusions

In summary, this paper focuses on the pre-disaster preparedness and post-disaster damage analysis for flood situations. The preparedness activities are important to mitigate the effect of floods in both rural and urban environments. In this paper, as a part of the preparedness activity, we focus on making a self-sufficient set of unmanned aerial vehicles which can work together in a difficult environment in order to collect real-time information both before and after a disaster. Response and recovery activities have to be initiated after the occurrence of a flood. However, to initiate such activities, a thorough analysis of loss and damage caused by the flood towards buildings, vegetations, or other infrastructures has to be done.

Using UAVs for this purpose is cost-effective, less risky, and more efficient in terms of response time. The case study shows the usage of UAVs for the coverage and damage assessment of the Jajpur flood in India. There are numerous potential technologies like machine learning, image processing, computer vision, etc., that can be integrated with the UAVs to make them as autonomous as possible. Our future work will include engaging these cutting-edge technologies with more efficient drones to analyze floods in India, overcoming the present challenges. There is considerable potential in using some of the technologies developed for the purpose of drone based flood management activities for other applications on water bodies such as oil spill detection in oceans and saving of marine lives by controlling pollution caused by such spillages.

7. Acknowledgmemt

The researchers from the Indian Institute of Science and University of Exeter acknowledge partial funding support from the EPSRC-GCRF project "Emergency flood planning and management using unmanned aerial systems" (EP/P20839X/1).

Humanitarian Aid International (HAI) acknowledges the Center for Youth and Social Development (CYSD), Odisha, for funding and logistics support during the project work. The data collection using drones has been carried out in partnership with Invent Grid Pvt. Ltd., based in Bhubaneswar, India, under the direction of HAI. Invent Grid has also provided their expertise in data processing, output generation, DEM, and presentation of the outcome.

REFERENCES

1. Abdallah, A., Ali, M. Z., Mišić, J., and Mišić, V. B. (2019). Efficient security scheme for disaster surveillance UAV communication networks. *Information*, 10(2): 43.

2. Adams, S. M. and Friedland, C. J. (2011). A survey of unmanned aerial vehicle (UAV) usage for imagery collection in disaster research and management. In *9th International Workshop on Remote Sensing for Disaster Response*, volume 8, pages 1–8.

3. Adsanver, B., Coban, E., Balcik, B., et al. (2021). Drone routing for post-disaster damage assessment. *Dynamics of Disasters: Impact, Risk, Resilience, and Solutions*, pages 1–29.

4. Anders, N., Smith, M., Suomalainen, J., Cammeraat, E., Valente, J., and Keesstra, S. (2020). Impact of flight altitude and cover orientation on digital surface model (DSM) accuracy for flood damage assessment in murcia (spain) using a fixed-wing uav. *Earth Science Informatics*, pages 1–14.

5. Bravo, R. and Leiras, A. (2015). Literature review of the application of UAVs in humanitarian relief. *Proceedings of the XXXV Encontro Nacional de Engenharia de Producao, Fortaleza, Brazil*, pages 13–16.

6. Casado, M. R. and Leinster, P. (2020). Towards more effective strategies to reduce property level flood risk: standardising the use of unmanned aerial vehicles. *Journal of Water Supply: Research and Technology-Aqua*, 69(8): 807–818.

7. Chowdhury, T., Rahnemoonfar, M., Murphy, R., and Fernandes, O. (2020). Comprehensive semantic segmentation on high resolution UAV imagery for natural disaster damage assessment. In *2020 IEEE International Conference on Big Data (Big Data)*, pages 3904–3913. IEEE.

8. Dekens, J. (2007). *Local Knowledge for Disaster Preparedness: A Literature Review*. International Centre for Integrated Mountain Development (ICIMOD), Lalitpur, Nepal.

9. Dong, J., Ota, K., and Dong, M. (2020). Real-time survivor detection in UAV thermal imagery based on deep learning. In *2020 16th International Conference on Mobility, Sensing and Networking (MSN)*, pages 352–359. IEEE.

10. Erdelj, M. and Natalizio, E. (2016). UAV-assisted disaster management: Applications and open issues. In *2016 International Conference on Computing, Networking and Communications (ICNC)*, pages 1–5. IEEE.

11. Erdelj, M., Natalizio, E., Chowdhury, K. R., and Akyildiz, I. F. (2017). Help from the sky: Leveraging UAVs for disaster management. *IEEE Pervasive Computing*, 16(1): 24–32.

12. Ezequiel, C. A. F., Cua, M., Libatique, N. C., Tangonan, G. L., Alampay, R., Labuguen, R. T., Favila, C. M., Honrado, J. L. E., Canos, V., Devaney, C., et al. (2014). UAV aerial imaging applications for post-disaster assessment, environmental management and infrastructure development. In *2014 International Conference on Unmanned Aircraft Systems (ICUAS)*, pages 274–283. IEEE.

13. Fernandez Galarreta, J., Kerle, N., and Gerke, M. (2015). UAV-based urban structural damage assessment using object-based image analysis and semantic reasoning. *Natural Hazards and Earth System Sciences*, 15(6): 1087–1101.

14. Garcia Millan, V. E., Rankine, C., and Sanchez-Azofeifa, G. A. (2020). Crop loss evaluation using digital surface models from unmanned aerial vehicles data. *Remote Sensing*, 12(6): 981.

15. Gautam, S., Pudasaini, U., Adhikari, B., Phuyal, S., and Chapagain, S. (2020). Enabling the implementation of UAV into local resource mapping and disaster preparedness. In *AGU Fall Meeting Abstracts*, volume 2020, pages NH026–07.

16. Gebrehiwot, A., Hashemi-Beni, L., Thompson, G., Kordjamshidi, P., and Langan, T. E. (2019). Deep convolutional neural network for flood extent mapping using unmanned aerial vehicles data. *Sensors*, 19(7): 1486.

17. Gebrehiwot, A. A. and Hashemi-Beni, L. (2021). Three-dimensional inundation mapping using UAV image segmentation and digital surface model. *ISPRS International Journal of Geo-Information*, 10(3): 144.

18. Gillespie, D. F. and Streeter, C. L. (1987). Conceptualizing and measuring disaster preparedness. *International Journal of Mass Emergencies and Disasters*, 5(2): 155–176.

19. Girons Lopez, M., Di Baldassarre, G., and Seibert, J. (2017). Impact of social preparedness on flood early warning systems. *Water Resources Research*, 53(1): 522–534.

20. Gkotsis, I., Eftychidis, G., and Kolios, P. (2017). The use of UAS in disaster response operations. In *Fifth International Conference on Remote Sensing and Geoinformation of the Environment (RSCy2017)*, volume 10444, page 104440W. International Society for Optics and Photonics.

21. Griffin, G. F. (2014). The use of unmanned aerial vehicles for disaster management. *Geomatica*, 68(4): 265–281.

22. Guo, Q., Peng, J., Xu, W., Liang, W., Jia, X., Xu, Z., Yang, Y., and Wang, M. (2020). Minimizing the longest tour time among a fleet of UAVs for disaster area surveillance. *IEEE Transactions on Mobile Computing*, pages 1–1.

23. Hashemi-Beni, L. and Gebrehiwot, A. A. (2021). Flood extent mapping: an integrated method using deep learning and region growing using UAV optical data. *IEEE Journal of Selected Topics in Applied Earth Observations and Remote Sensing*, 14: 2127–2135.

24. Inoguchi, M., Tamura, K., Uo, K., Kobayashi, M., and Morishima, A. (2021). Time-cost estimation for early disaster damage assessment methods, depending on affected area. *Journal of Disaster Research*, 16(4): 733–746.

25. Jiménez-Jiménez, S. I., Ojeda-Bustamante, W., Ontiveros-Capurata, R. E., and Marcial-Pablo,

26. M. d. J. (2020). Rapid urban flood damage assessment using high resolution remote sensing data and an object-based approach. *Geomatics, Natural Hazards and Risk*, 11(1): 906–927.

27. Kakooei, M. and Baleghi, Y. (2017). Fusion of satellite, aircraft, and UAV data for automatic disaster damage assessment. *International Journal of Remote Sensing*, 38(8-10):2511–2534.

28. Kamilaris, A. and Prenafeta-Boldú, F. X. (2018). Disaster monitoring using unmanned aerial vehicles and deep learning. *arXiv preprint arXiv:1807.11805*.

29. Kashyap, A., Ghose, D., Menon, P. P., Sujit, P., and Das, K. (2019). UAV aided dynamic routing of resources in a flood

scenario. In *2019 International Conference on Unmanned Aircraft Systems (ICUAS)*, pages 328–335. IEEE.

30. Kerle, N., Nex, F., Gerke, M., Duarte, D., and Vetrivel, A. (2020). UAV-based structural damage mapping: A review. *ISPRS International Journal of Geo-Information*, 9(1): 14.

31. Kim, K. and Davidson, J. (2015). Unmanned aircraft systems used for disaster management. *Transportation Research Record*, 2532(1): 83–90.

32. König, A., Sægrov, S., and Schilling, W. (2002). Damage assessment for urban flooding. In *Global Solutions for Urban Drainage*, pages 1–11. ASCE.

33. Luino, F., Cirio, C. G., Biddoccu, M., Agangi, A., Giulietto, W., Godone, F., and Nigrelli, G. (2009). Application of a model to the evaluation of flood damage. *Geoinformatica*, 13(3): 339–353.

34. Luo, C., Miao, W., Ullah, H., McClean, S., Parr, G., and Min, G. (2019). Unmanned aerial vehicles for disaster management. In : Durrani T., Wang W., Forbes S. (eds), editor, *Geological Disaster Monitoring based on Sensor Networks*. Springer Natural Hazards, pages 83–107. Springer, Singapore.

35. Menon, P. P., Edwards, C., Shtessel, Y. B., Ghose, D., and Haywood, J. (2014). Boundary tracking using a suboptimal sliding mode algorithm. In *53rd IEEE Conference on Decision and Control*, pages 5518–5523. IEEE.

36. Merz, B., Kreibich, H., and Lall, U. (2013). Multi-variate flood damage assessment: a tree-based data-mining approach. *Natural Hazards and Earth System Sciences*, 13(1): 53–64.

37. Munawar, H. S., Hammad, A. W., Waller, S. T., Thaheem, M. J., and Shrestha, A. (2021). An integrated approach for post-disaster flood management via the use of cutting-edge technologies and UAVs: A review. *Sustainability*, 13(14): 7925.

38. Myint, S., Yuan, M., Cerveny, R., and Giri, C. (2008). Categorizing natural disaster damage assessment using satellite-based geospatial techniques. *Natural Hazards and Earth System Sciences*, 8(4): 707–719.

39. Neto, J. M. M., da Paixao, R. A., Rodrigues, L. R. L., Moreira, E. M., dos Santos, J. C. J., and Rosa, P. F. F. (2012). A surveillance task for a UAV in a natural disaster scenario. In *2012 IEEE International Symposium on Industrial Electronics*, pages 1516–1522. IEEE.

40. Petrides, P., Kolios, P., Kyrkou, C., Theocharides, T., and Panayiotou, C. (2017). Disaster prevention and emergency response using unmanned aerial systems. In *Smart Cities in the Mediterranean*, pages 379–403. Springer.

41. Pi, Y., Nath, N. D., and Behzadan, A. H. (2021). Detection and semantic segmentation of disaster damage in UAV footage. *Journal of Computing in Civil Engineering*, 35(2): 04020063.

42. Qadir, Z., Ullah, F., Munawar, H. S., and Al-Turjman, F. (2021). Addressing disasters in smart cities through UAVs path planning and 5g communications: A systematic review. *Computer Communications*, 168: 114–135.

43. Quaritsch, M., Kruggl, K., Wischounig-Strucl, D., Bhattacharya, S., Shah, M., and Rinner, B. (2010). Networked UAVs as aerial sensor network for disaster management applications. *Elektrotechnik und Informationstechnik*, 127(3): 56–63.

44. Raikes, J., Smith, T. F., Jacobson, C., and Baldwin, C. (2019). Pre-disaster planning and preparedness for floods and droughts: A systematic review. *International Journal of Disaster Risk Reduction*, 38:101207.

45. Rajan, J., Shriwastav, S., Kashyap, A., Ratnoo, A., and Ghose, D. (2021). Disaster management using unmanned aerial vehicles. In *Unmanned Aerial Systems*, pages 129–155. Elsevier.

46. Ramasamy, M. and Ghose, D. (2016). Learning-based preferential surveillance algorithm for persistent surveillance by unmanned aerial vehicles. In *2016 International Conference on Unmanned Aircraft Systems (ICUAS)*, pages 1032–1040. IEEE.

47. Ramasamy, M. and Ghose, D. (2017). A heuristic learning algorithm for preferential area surveillance by unmanned aerial vehicles. *Journal of Intelligent & Robotic Systems*, 88(2-4): 655.

48. Ravichandran, R., Ghose, D., and Das, K. (2019). UAV based survivor search during floods. In *2019 International Conference on Unmanned Aircraft Systems (ICUAS)*, pages 1407–1415. IEEE.

49. Romali, N. S., Yusop, Z., Ismail, Z., et al. (2015). Flood damage assessment: A review of flood stage–damage function curve. *ISFRAM 2014*, pages 147–159.

50. Ryan, B., Johnston, K. A., Taylor, M., and McAndrew, R. (2020). Community engagement for disaster preparedness: A systematic literature review. *International journal of disaster risk reduction*, 49: 101655.

51. Saad, A. M. and Tahar, K. N. (2019). Identification of rut and pothole by using multirotor unmanned aerial vehicle (UAV). *Measurement*, 137: 647–654.

52. Salmoral, G., Rivas Casado, M., Muthusamy, M., Butler, D., Menon, P. P., and Leinster, P. (2020). Guidelines for the use of unmanned aerial systems in flood emergency response. *Water*, 12(2): 521.

53. Saravi, S., Kalawsky, R., Joannou, D., Rivas Casado, M., Fu, G., and Meng, F. (2019). Use of artificial intelligence to improve resilience and preparedness against adverse flood events. *Water*, 11(5): 973.

54. Schnebele, E., Cervone, G., and Waters, N. (2014). Road assessment after flood events using non-authoritative data. *Natural Hazards and Earth System Sciences*, 14(4): 1007–1015.

55. Sharma, S. (2017). Flood-survivors detection using IR imagery on an autonomous drone. Stanford University: Stanford, CA, USA. pages 8–12.

56. Shetty, S. J. and Ghose, D. (2020). Weight-based exploration for unmanned aerial teams searching for multiple survivors. *arXiv preprint arXiv:2012.11131*.

57. Shetty, S. J., Ravichandran, R., Tony, L. A., Abhinay, N. S., Das, K., and Ghose, D. (2021). Implementation of survivor detection strategies using drones. In *Unmanned Aerial Systems*, pages 417–438. Elsevier.

58. Sieg, T., Vogel, K., Merz, B., and Kreibich, H. (2017). Tree-based flood damage modeling of companies: Damage processes and model performance. *Water Resources Research*, 53(7): 6050–6068.

59. Sui, H., Tu, J., Song, Z., Chen, G., and Li, Q. (2014). A novel 3D building damage detection method using multiple overlapping UAV images. *The International Archives of Photogrammetry, Remote Sensing and Spatial Information Sciences*, 40(7): 173.

60. Sutton, J. and Tierney, K. (2006). Disaster preparedness: Concepts, guidance, and research. *Colorado: University of Colorado*, 3: 1–41.

61. Tapia-Silva, F.-O., Itzerott, S., Foerster, S., Kuhlmann, B., and Kreibich, H. (2011). Estimation of flood losses to agricultural crops using remote sensing. *Physics and Chemistry of the Earth, Parts A/B/C*, 36(7-8): 253–265.

62. Tripathi, P. (2015). Flood disaster in india: an analysis of trend and preparedness. *Interdisciplinary Journal of Contemporary Research*, 2(4): 91–98.

63. Valentijn, T., Margutti, J., van den Homberg, M., and Laaksonen, J. (2020). Multi-hazard and spatial transferability of a CNN for automated building damage assessment. *Remote Sensing*, 12(17): 2839.

64. Velev, D., Zlateva, P., Steshina, L., and Petukhov, I. (2019). Challenges of using drones and virtual/augmented reality for disaster risk management. *International Archives of the Photogrammetry, Remote Sensing and Spatial Information Sciences*, 42(3/W8).

65. Yamazaki, F., Matsuda, T., Denda, S., and Liu, W. (2015). Construction of 3D models of buildings damaged by earthquakes using UAV aerial images. In *Proceedings of The 10th Pacific Conference Earthquake Engineering Building an Earthquake-Resilient Pacific*, volume 204.

66. Yamazaki, F. and Matsuoka, M. (2007). Remote sensing technologies in post-disaster damage assessment. *Journal of Earthquake and Tsunami*, 1(03): 193–210.

67. Ybañez, R. L., Ybañez, A. A. B., Lagmay, A. M. F. A., and Aurelio, M. A. (2021). Imaging ground surface deformations in post-disaster settings via small UAVs. *Geoscience Letters*, 8(1): 1–14.

CHAPTER 27

Cyclone Preparedness, Rescue Operations and Damage Assessment using UAVs

Rudrashis Majumder
Ph.D. Student, Department of Aerospace Engineering,
Indian Institute of Science, Bangalore
rudrashism@iisc.ac.in

Shuvrangshu Jana
Post-doctoral Fellow, Department of Aerospace
Engineering, Indian Institute of Science, Bangalore
shuvrangshuj@iisc.ac.in

Prathyush P. Menon
3Associate Professor, College of Engineering,
Mathematics and Physical Sciences,
University of Exeter, UK
p.m.prathyush@exeter.ac.uk

Debasish Ghose
Professor, Department of Aerospace Engineering,
Indian Institute of Science, Bangalore
dghose@iisc.ac.in

N. M. Prusty
Humanitarian Aid International, India
nmprusty51@gmail.com

Bipasha Mukherjee
Humanitarian Aid International, India
bipasha@hai-india.org

Aditi Ghosh
Humanitarian Aid International, India
adghosh@gmail.com

Abstract

UAV's capability to access remote and inaccessible areas within a quick time can be utilized for effective cyclone management. This paper presents the possible application of UAVs at different stages of cyclone mitigation. The overall system architecture necessary for preparedness, rescue operation, resource allocation, and damage assessment using UAVs during cyclones is described. Although general commercial UAVs are reported to be used in cyclone operations, UAV systems should be planned specifically for cyclone operations to improve efficiency. Here, the specification required for effective and safe UAV operations in the post-cyclone scenario is presented. Mission planning required for various rescue, relief, and damage assessment missions related to cyclone management is discussed. A case study of deploying UAV in Amphan cyclone operation in West Bengal is also presented. This paper can help disaster management authorities to develop UAV systems specifically to cater to cyclone operations.

Keywords: Disaster response; Cyclone management; Unmanned Aerial Vehicle

1. Introduction

The frequency of natural disasters like cyclones will increase due to climate change, and the government authorities need to prepare a mitigation plan for different stages of disaster. UAVs can be utilized for situational awareness, rescue operation, communication system, and damage assessment in a disaster scenario. UAVs pose the advantages of quick deployment, remote accessibility, and the capability of providing high spatial and temporal images and communicating with ground IOTs. Nowadays, quick deployment of UAVs in remote disaster-affected areas is possible due to the rapid advancement of miniaturized UAVs along with the availability of open-source autopilot software such as Ardupilot/ Px4. Application of UAVs in a disaster-related scenario is reported in various literature such as Erdelj et al. (2017a); Panda et al. (2019); Malandrino et al. (2019); Kashyap et al. (2019). A robust communication platform is required in just the aftermath of the disaster in order to maintain communication with various stakeholders. UAVs can provide communication in case of damage to communication infrastructure. UAV-based IOT platform for disaster management is reported in Ejaz et al. (2019).

In particular, UAVs can be used in the pre-cyclone stage to spread awareness among people in remote locations to provide evacuation instructions on short notice. UAVs can be deployed for survivor detection (Ravichandran et al. (2019)), weak coast spot detection, coverage mission (Allen and Mazumder (2020)), and detailed damage assessment (Fernandez Galarreta et al. (2015)) for effective resource allocation and rehabilitation plans in the post-cyclone period. UAVs can be equipped for emergency payload transfer to critical areas like hospitals, as access to the area can be blocked for multiple days after a cyclone. Application of UAVs in cyclone is reported in hurricane Harvey (Yeom et al. (2019)), hurricane Maria (Schaefer et al. (2020)).

Damage assessment of cyclones is reported in various literature such as Haq et al. (2012); Mallick et al. (2017); Nandi et al. (2020); Shamsuzzoha et al. (2021); Erdelj et al. (2017b). Damage assessment of Mangrove forests due to Typhoon Yolanda in Calauit island through manual surveying is reported in Malabrigo Jr et al. (2016); Primavera et al. (2016). The use of unmanned aerial vehicles (UAVs) for mapping and artificial intelligence (AI) to undertake various types of analysis in the areas of disaster management has made its beginning in post-disaster damage, loss, and needs assessment (PDNA) (Calantropio et al., 2021; Yuan and Liu, 2018; Wu et al., 2020). UAVs are able to generate high-resolution micro-level maps that can show features like buildings, roads, embankments, crop areas, plantations, mangroves, etc., with greater accuracy. AI application is able to create a qualitative and quantitative analysis of the damage and losses to the features mentioned above (Lüthi, 2019; Syifa et al., 2019). After hurricane Harvey, structural damage assessment using DJI Phantom 4 pro is performed after capturing the images at height of 80 m and at an overlap of 80 % Yeom et al. (2019). Damage assessment of roads with the captured images from UAV using convolution neural networks is discussed in (Bocanegra and Haddad (2021)). In this case, CNN is used on the images of roads captured from DJI Matrice 600 Pro after the natural disasters, and AlexNet is reported to be the best network with an average value of 74.07 %. In Kakooei and Baleghi (2017), the fusion of oblique images from UAV and vertical images from a satellite is proposed for post-disaster assessment. Damage assessment using neural network involving captured images from UAV is reported in Duarte et al. (2017); Xu et al. (2018); Vetrivel et al. (2018); Nex et al. (2019).

This paper describes how the advancement in the UAV and associated technological development could be utilized in the different phases of cyclone management at varying levels of authority. Although UAV is used in cyclone management; however, UAVs are not designed for cyclone-specific operations. In most cases, an additional sensor like a camera or lidar is fitted with the commercial drones and used in disaster operations. Commercial drones lack the efficiency to operate quickly in cyclone-affected areas due to wind disturbances. Most importantly, these are not equipped with the advanced algorithms required to perform survivor detection and precise payload delivery. This paper describes the UAV specifications required to operate safely and effectively in a multi-UAV post-cyclone scenario. The trade-off of the selection of the type of UAVs for different missions related to cyclones is addressed. The planning required for coverage, search and rescue, and payload delivery related to cyclone operations are presented. The software framework required for multi-UAV operations by multiple authorities in the immediate aftermath of the cyclone is also discussed. We have presented a case study of deploying UAV locally in Cyclone Amphan.

The rest of the paper is described as follows: Section 2 describes the scope and advantages of UAV in cyclone management. The technical specification required for UAV system design and multi-UAV system to deploy in cyclone operations is discussed in Section 4. Planning required to perform UAV operations for specific cyclone-related missions is presented in 5. Section 6 describes the UAV planning for damage assessment mission. A case study of the deployment of the cyclone is presented in 7.

2. Applications of UAV in Cyclone Management

There is no standard literature available for the various stages of disaster management. Alexander (2002) classified disaster cycle into four phases of prevention, preparedness, response, and recovery; whereas, Erdelj et al. (2017b), classified disaster into three stages: preparedness, assessment, response, and recovery. In general, disaster management is performed at different hierarchical levels of Government with varying disaster mitigation plans. We have considered four stages of cyclone management to reflect the varying needs and applications of UAVs at different stages. The four stages are preparedness, rescue operations, resource allocation, and damage assessment. Considering the various application of UAVs, the tasks associated with the UAV at different stages of cyclone management is presented in Fig. 27.1. In this case, the three-level hierarchy is considered considering the Indian scenario where the cyclone is managed through a hierarchical level consisting of center, state, and district authorities. The actors are the people affected in cyclone and might need evacuation/relief assistance.

At the preparedness stage of the cyclone, the major task involves the prediction of the path of the cyclone, evacuation planning, creating situational awareness, and planning to

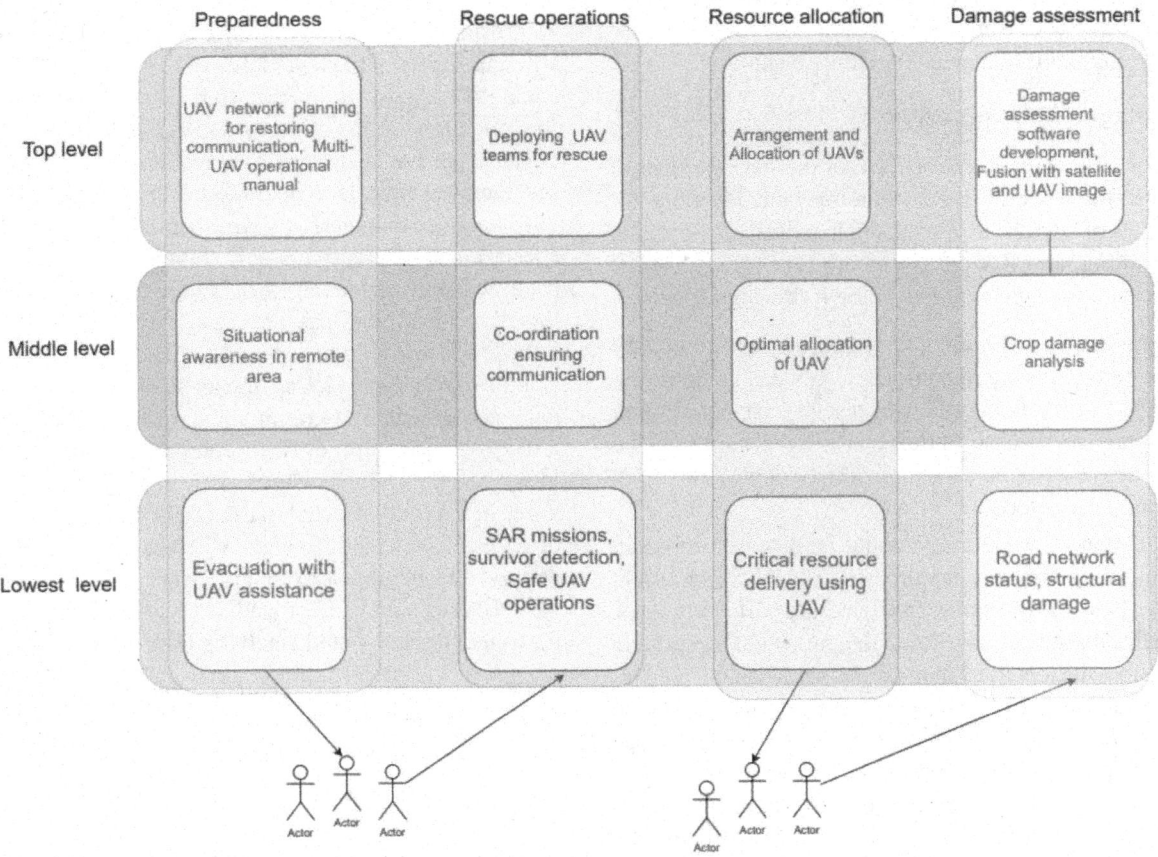

Fig. 27.1   Application of UAV in cyclone management

handle the power and communication interruption. At this stage, UAVs can be used for situational awareness and evacuation from coastal and remote areas. UAVs can help create a communication network with the ground IOTs in just the aftermath of a cyclone in case the major communication infrastructure is damaged. However, the creation of this network will require extensive planning from top-level authorities. Due to UAVs' easy access and operation, nowadays multiple local authorities independently operate UAVs to get a quick picture immediately after a disaster. At the preparedness stage, the Government at the topmost level also needs to develop a framework to accommodate the multiple drones by multiple authorities for the safe operation of UAVs in just the aftermath of a cyclone.

In the rescue operation, important tasks are the deployment of rescue personnel, coordination and maintaining communication among the multiple stakeholders, and planning search and rescue missions. At this stage, UAVs could be used for survivor detection and restoring network connectivity. Generally, the roads are blocked due to uprooted trees in just the aftermath of the cyclone; therefore, UAVs can

be deployed rapidly to access the areas not accessible through traditional means. Some areas like island might be cut-off from the mainland, and deployment of a network of UAVs could help restore communication.

In the resource allocation stage, major tasks are the computation of demands, allocation of resources, and distribution of resources. UAVs could be useful to supply relief material to survivors in remote areas. A coverage mission by UAVs along the coastal line or covering the cyclone's path might help quickly assess the level of damage and corresponding requirement of relief materials. Critical resources like oxygen and medicine could be supplied to remote areas using specially designed UAVs.

In the damage assessment stage, the important tasks are analysis of structural damages, agricultural crop damages, infrastructure damages, and help in government authorities in the policy-making decision. Currently, most damage analysis is performed using satellite images and manual surveying of the affected areas. UAVs fitted with a camera can capture spatial and high-resolution damages of the affected areas at the desired frequency, which could be used for damage analysis using image processing and machine learning techniques. Images captured from UAVs also could be used to fuse with the satellite images for damage analysis.

2.1 Advantages of Using UAVs

Inclusion of any technology/software in the management of disaster operation should be safe and reliable, flexible for varying levels of operation, quickly deployable on the ground, ease in handling, and low cost in nature. The advantages of UAV in disaster management lies in the following aspects.

1. For any disaster, the initial few hours are very crucial for survival and rescue operations. UAVs can be deployed in a short time for search and rescue missions. Proper planning of the base station considering the predicted path of the cyclone can immediately deploy the UAV for survivor detection.

2. The extent of the damage could be assessed in detail from oblique images captured from UAV which might not be possible to capture from satellite or radar images. Satellite-based damage mapping may not accurately describe the detailed damage of an affected area as fine spatial and high temporal resolution data could be unavailable. For example, the damage due to a surge in water level will happen along the coastal lines so that a UAV survey will capture accurate information rather than satellite image. The images captured from the satellite are costlier and also not readily available. Also, sometimes information from satellite data is of limited use because of cloud cover.

3. With the rapid advancement in miniaturization of avionics, lightweight structural materials, and open-source drone software, the cost of UAV operations is relatively cheaper than other methods.

4. The operation with drones is reliable and does not depend on the existing ground infrastructures that could have been damaged by the cyclone.

5. With the advent of various low-cost read-to-fly drones available in the market, drone operation is easy for local authorities with little knowledge of drone technology.

6. Mission operational with drones provides flexibility in terms of duration, frequency, time, and scale of operation.

7. Operation with UAVs ensures the accessibility to remote areas.

2.2 Selection of UAV

During pre and post-cyclone operations, the primary tasks are coverage, search and rescue, and payload delivery. In the case of a cyclone, both the fixed-wing and rotary-wing should be deployed based on the mission requirement. A coverage mission will require a long-endurance UAV, whereas a critical payload delivery mission requires hovering capability. Apart from the specific mission requirement, the selection of the type of UAV needs to be performed considering payload carrying capability, the requirement of the landing area, and operational cost. Fixed-wing UAVs will have advantages in terms of long endurance, high-speed coverage, aerodynamic efficiency; whereas, multi-rotor will have advantages of precise payload delivery and lesser take-off/landing area requirement. The technical knowledge required to operate a fixed-wing is higher than a multi-rotor. Considering the obstacles of uprooted trees, damaged power, and communication lines, the operation of a fixed-wing is more difficult compared to a multi-rotor at a lower height. The main bottleneck in deployability of fixed-wing in cyclone-affected areas could be of non-availability of take-off and landing area, whereas multi-rotor could be deployed from almost from any location. Hand launch fixed-wing UAVs could be deployed; however, this required skilled personnel to launch and catch the UAV during landing.

Coverage missions will require long endurance and high-speed UAV for quick coverage of the damaged area. Search and rescue missions also require long endurance and high-speed UAVs; however, SAR missions need to be planned at a lower height, and it requires hovering around the survivor to gather detailed information. Payload delivery mission of general items requires a UAV with high payload capability; however, delivering a critical item to a survivor/hospital might require precise delivery. Situational awareness/ evacuation planning with UAV might require the hovering capability of UAV along with high speed. In the case of structural damage assessment, UAVs need to operate at low altitudes in cluttered environments with uncertain obstacles; however, agriculture damage assessment could be performed at higher altitudes with high speed to cater to larger areas. Considering all the above facts, it is recommended that coverage mission and general relief mission could be planned using fixed-wing UAVs, whereas SAR mission and critical payload delivery mission with multi-rotor UAV. However, an initial coarse SAR mission could be planned with fixed-wing UAV quickly, and after assessment of initial damage, a finer SAR mission using multi-rotor UAV could be planned for specific areas. In the case of evacuation missions and damage assessment missions, the selection should be made considering the specific evacuation requirement. Therefore, a UAV fleet deployed in cyclones should consist of both the fixed-wing and multi-rotor wings to optimally cater to the requirement of different missions. Specifically, a UAV fleet with only a fixed-wing should not be considered to avoid a long time of deployment in case of extensive damage to the take-off area.

3. Specification of UAV Systems

UAVs with desired hardware and software capability and detailed mission planning are required for efficient cyclone management. UAVs need to be designed/procured considering the specific operational requirement of autopilot functionalities, payload-carrying capability, and sensor requirement for cyclone management. The important basic technical specification of UAVs for cyclone operation are listed as follows:

1. UAVs should be able to capture images/videos while performing autonomous waypoint missions. It should be equipped with a minimal sensor suite of IMU, altimeter, GPS, and camera.
2. UAVs used for precise payload delivery and survivor detection should have the capability of processing images on board in real-time.
3. Generally, the wind speed is high a few days before and after the cyclone; UAVs should withstand high wind and gust to be operational during the critical evacuation and rescue operation period.
4. UAVs should be equipped with the Inter-agent collision avoidance algorithm and obstacle avoidance algorithm for safe operations in a complex multi-drone mission by multiple authorities.
5. The UAV should have an algorithm to restrict inside the Geofence area to remain in the designated corridor without violating the statutory regulations.

Apart from the basic specifications, UAVs could be equipped with thermal imaging sensors for the detection of survivors. The capability to transmit the imagery to the ground station in real-time would be better for survivor detection. The UAVs used for a longer coverage mission should have sufficient capacity of storage for the images/ videos. The efficient operation of multiple UAVs requires coordination among UAVs, optimal task allocation to individual UAVs, and collision avoidance. Multiple UAVs should be operated in a centralized architecture for optimal use; however, communication with the base station/leader UAV should be kept at a minimal. The multi-UAV software architecture should have the following specifications for safe and efficient operations.

1. It should be scalable to handle missions with few UAVs to missions with a large number of UAVs.
2. It should be flexible to accommodate the different types of UAVs.

Additionally, some of the UAV fleets should also be capable of operating at night. UAVs should be deployed with the area's topology in mind, as some UAVs may struggle to perform well in high-altitude environments.

4. Preparedness Stage

At the preparedness stage, apart from situational awareness and evacuation planning using UAV, the UAV specific tasks are UAV system design and development of regulatory framework required for UAV operations during the disaster.

4.1 UAV System Design

UAVs should be designed keeping in mind the specification listed in Section 3. The UAV can be designed in a specific configuration such as hexacopter to improve wind resistance capability. A robust and adaptive controller should be used to handle the high disturbances from wind gusts (Fernández et al. (2017); Jana and Bhat (2017)). The main autopilot, along with the vision processing module, should have the capability of human detection, survivor tracking, and payload delivery.

In case of a UAV fleet designed with commercial UAVs, the vehicle needs to be reconfigured for the advanced mission as commercial UAVs are mostly equipped only for autonomous waypoint mission. These types of UAVs need to be equipped with a vision processing module for onboard image processing required for SAR and payload delivery missions. The vision processing module should have the computation capability to process the image in real-time for SAR missions. The mission algorithm should be developed considering the compatibility with the existing code of commercial autopilot. The software architecture should be designed to incorporate the commercial UAVs with little modification. Software architecture proposed by Agnel Tony et al. (2021) for multi-drone mission could be used for integration of autopilot of commercial UAV. This will also help in scaling the UAV operations with different UAV systems.

4.2 UAV Opereations

The disaster control room should have a dedicated unit to handle the complex operation of multiple drones by multiple authorities. It should clearly mention the geo-fence restrictions for each drone and local station to avoid collision among the drones. If the UAV operation is planned beforehand, then the UAV decision support system (DSS) framework should be able to deploy the drones in the overall resource and task allocation framework. DSS framework for resource and task allocation proposed by Jana et al. (2021) could be used in this purpose. The overall software framework should be able to assign the drones dynamically in the desired area. The DSS should include GUI to monitor the location of drones and analysis of live footage.

It might not be possible to plan UAV operations in advance using a central base station in many cases. In many cases, local pilots might be flying manually to assess the ground situation. Flying drones by multiple people can create chaos and also risk the chance of collision avoidance. So, a software framework is required for coordination among multiple pilots, providing permission from the government authority and addressing the local people's concerns due to UAV operations. The software framework should include the pilot information and desired flight plan for the permission of the disaster management authority.

5. Rescue Operations and Resource Allocation

In the rescue operation stage, deployment of UAV needs to be planned for coverage missions, SAR missions, payload delivery, and damage assessment. The planning related to UAV design, and algorithm requirements are discussed in this section. The overall UAV operations can be handled in different hierarchical operation layers through the main base station and multiple local base stations.

5.1 Coverage Mission

Total UAVs should be distributed into the different base stations instead of a single base station for better coverage. The expected disaster-affected areas should be classified into different zones based on the expected spread of the cyclone affected areas, available UAVs, the endurance of UAVs, topology of the area, and various other local factors such as logistics road network, availability of the suitable site. A dynamic partitioning algorithm could also be considered to balance the load on UAVs with continuous assessment of each area's coverage requirement. Each base station should be assigned a particular area. The area under a base station should be further divided based on the number of UAVs for coverage missions under that station. Voronoi partitioning algorithm based on endurance could be considered for allocation. Overall mission planning for each UAV to be designed considering endurance of UAV, speed of UAV and desired overlap in captured images. The area under each base station is to be allocated to UAVs through optimal task allocation, and the corresponding waypoints are to be loaded in the autopilot of each UAV. The images captured from the UAV could be stored or transmitted to the base station.

5.2 SAR Mission

Application of UAV in search and rescue operation after the disaster could help in rapid detection of survivors and deployment of relief in a short time. The search and rescue mission will be planned as a coverage mission; however, a UAV will be assigned once an object of interest is detected. Onboard vision processing module to be equipped with human detection or any specific object detection. Machine Learning-based algorithms could be used for the detection of

humans after training with available images from a similar disaster location.

5.3 Relief Distribution

Generally, post-cyclone relief distribution involves providing dry food packets and medicines to an area; however, in some cases, payload needs to be dropped precisely near a survivor standing on a boat, roof, or a critical medical item like blood/ oxygen to a hospital in a remote area. General payload delivery could be arranged through fixed-wing and multi-rotor to be used for precise delivery. For delivery using a fixed-wing, it should be fitted with a mechanism to trigger the release of payload based on the GPS location. The error in GPS location could be around 1-2 m, and payload to be planned to be dropped over an area. In case of precise delivery with a multi-rotor wing, it should have the capability to detect the specific target (survivor/landing pad) and then release the payload or land at the desired location. The UAVs are to be designed to carry the desired payload and the controller to be designed considering the possible variation of mass and inertia over the flight regime. Apart from direct payload delivery, the mission needs to be designed over the pre-cyclone road network to assess the current road status for relief delivery through conventional transport.

6. Damage Assessment

In the case of a cyclone, damage assessment include agricultural damage, structural damage, mangroves damage. The damage assessment mission needs to be planned at different layers from coarser to finer coverage based on the assessment after each layer. The altitude of the operations should also be decided based on the camera specifications and terrain characteristics. Damage assessment is mostly performed from the captured images from the camera; however, other sensors such as lidar/radar could be used for specific requirements. Locally damage analysis could be performed using visual cues after generating the orthomosaic images; however, for a large region, an automated software integrated with machine learning techniques has to be used for quick assessment. For advanced analysis, the mission needs to be planned carefully considering the illumination, the incident angle of the camera, the field of view of the camera, and desired overlap. Cameras need to be calibrated properly as the analysis results are sensitive to the camera calibration parameters. Generally, a mission is to be planned as a straight and level flight; however, it will be difficult to maintain throughout the flight duration due to disturbances such as wind gusts. So, the vehicle states parameters also need to be stored at the desired frequency to obtain the exact location and orientation of the captured images. Vehicle state parameters include its position, velocity, Euler angles, and angular rates. Currently, most commercial UAVs allow to store these parameters at a ground station; however, the flight logs are sometimes unavailable due to communication failure. To obtain high accuracy in damage analysis, the flight parameters need to be stored onboard at the desired frequency. The captured images need to be geo-tagged for better analysis. Although a few images from disaster locations are available, authorities might need to create training databases after ground survey aftermath of a disaster for future applications.

7. Case Study

In order to implement the large-scale deployment of UAVs in cyclone situations, we have deployed UAVs locally during cyclone Phani (2019), Bulbul(2019), and Amphan (2020) to understand the ground complexities involved in UAV operation during the cyclone. We performed preliminary damage analysis from the captured images and augmented the training dataset to be used for future cyclones.

Cyclone Amphan, the most powerful storm in the Bay of Bengal in over a decade, ripped through West Bengal (Kolkata, North 24 Parganas, South 24 Parganas Hooghly, Howrah, and East Medinipur) as well as Bangladesh. Amphan's landfall process commenced from the afternoon (20th May 2020) to early morning (21st May 2020), causing enormous damage to people's lives, infrastructure, agriculture, and property. We have deployed drones in 30 locations covering 11-gram panchayats of district South-24 Pargana in state WestBengal of India. The UAV operation is performed at the height of 80 m. The endurance of the vehicle was around 25-30 minutes. UAV is fitted with 4k HD vision camera. Sample images captured by the UAV is shown in Fig. 27.2. Visual analysis of these raw images could provide a quick assessment of the urgent relief/rescue operations.

Fig. 27.2 Damages captured by UAVs in West Bengal: damaged building, damaged Jetty, uprooted trees, damaged embankment (anti-clockwise from top corner)

Fig. 27.3 Sagar Island, West Bengal

The images are further processed in Invent Grid's photogrammetry engine. Images are further stitched to obtain an orthomosaic view to obtain a better idea of a large area. Fig. 27.3 shows an orthomosaic view of Sagar island after stitching the images captured from the UAV. A preliminary report on crop damage analysis is shown in Fig. 27.4. The Colour code shows the boundary colors of the patches of the agricultural field. The following lesson is learned for future deployment of UAVs in cyclone operation.

| | | | Total 3.28 Hectare |
Colour code	Range	Area	Loss in INR
	80-100%	1.45 ha(44.2%)	1,25,300.00
	60-80 %	0.98 ha(29.8%)	67,760.00
	40-60%	0.28 ha (8.5%)	14,490.00
	0-40 %	0.57 ha (17.37%)	19,600.00

Fig. 27.4 Analysis of crop damage at Ganga Sagar in West Bengal

1. Sufficient datasets of cyclone-affected images are required to improve the accuracy of ML algorithms.

2. Wind is the crucial factor to be taken into the design. Currently, we could operate only at some specific duration of the day.

3. A great detail of logistical planning (Battery Charging, base station, etc.) is required to deploy drones in remote cyclone-affected areas as existing infrastructure is damaged.

4. Privacy issues and government regulations for deploying drones in cyclone-affected civilian areas need to be addressed.

5. Collaboration for humanitarian actors and experts from drone operations need to be enhanced for better efficiency.

8. Conclusions

This paper presents a planning framework for the application of UAVs in cyclone management. Details of planning related to the UAV design stage to the UAV deployment stage at various stages of cyclone operation are addressed. Different hardware and software specifications of UAV systems for deployment in cyclone management are listed. Cyclone-specific coverage mission, search and rescue mission, damage assessment mission is presented. Initial experiences of deployment of UAV in cyclone situation shows that UAV can be utilized to accurately map the cyclone-affected areas.

9. Acknowledgement

The researchers from the Indian Institute of Science and University of Exeter acknowledge partial funding support from the EPSRC-GCRF project "Emergency flood planning and management using unmanned aerial systems" (EP/P20839X/1).

Humanitarian Aid International (HAI) acknowledges the HCL Foundation, India for funding and Sabuj Sangh for logistics support during the project work. The data collection using drones has been carried out in partnership with Invent Grid Pvt. Ltd., based in Bhubaneswar, India, under the direction of HAI. Invent Grid has also provided their expertise in data processing, output generation, DEM, and presentation of the outcome.

REFERENCES

1. Agnel Tony, L., Jana, S., Varun V, P., Bhise, A. A., Mozhi Varman S, A., Vidyadhara B, V., Gadde, M. S., Krishnapuram, R., and Ghose, D. (2021). Autonomous cooperative multi-vehicle system for interception of aerial and stationary targets in unknown environments. *arXiv e-prints*, pages arXiv–2109.

2. Alexander, D. E. (2002). *Principles of emergency planning and management.* Oxford University Press on Demand.

3. Allen, R. and Mazumder, M. (2020). Toward an autonomous aerial survey and planning system for humanitarian aid and disaster response. In *2020 IEEE Aerospace Conference*, pages 1–11. IEEE.

4. Bocanegra, M. G. and Haddad, R. J. (2021). Convolutional neural network-based disaster assessment using unmanned aerial vehicles. In *SoutheastCon 2021*, pages 1–6. IEEE.

5. Calantropio, A., Chiabrando, F., Codastefano, M., and Bourke, E. (2021). Deep learning for automatic building damage assessment: Application in post-disaster scenarios using uav data. *ISPRS Annals of the Photogrammetry, Remote Sensing and Spatial Information Sciences*, 1: 113–120.

6. Duarte, D., Nex, F., Kerle, N., and Vosselman, G. (2017). Towards a more efficient detection of earthquake induced facade damages using oblique uav imagery. *The International Archives of Photogrammetry, Remote Sensing and Spatial Information Sciences*, 42: 93.

7. Ejaz, W., Azam, M. A., Saadat, S., Iqbal, F., and Hanan, A. (2019). Unmanned aerial vehicles enabled iot platform for disaster management. *Energies*, 12(14): 2706.

8. Erdelj, M., Król, M., and Natalizio, E. (2017a). Wireless sensor networks and multi-uav systems for natural disaster management. *Computer Networks*, 124: 72–86.

9. Erdelj, M., Natalizio, E., Chowdhury, K. R., and Akyildiz, I. F. (2017b). Help from the sky: Leveraging UAVs for disaster management. *IEEE Pervasive Computing*, 16(1): 24–32.

10. Fernández, R. A. S., Dominguez, S., and Campoy, P. (2017). L 1 adaptive control for wind gust rejection in quad-rotor uav wind turbine inspection. In *2017 International Conference on Unmanned Aircraft Systems (ICUAS)*, pages 1840–1849. IEEE.

11. Fernandez Galarreta, J., Kerle, N., and Gerke, M. (2015). UAV-based urban structural damage assessment using object-based image analysis and semantic reasoning. *Natural Hazards and Earth System Sciences*, 15(6): 1087–1101.

12. Haq, M. Z., Robbani, M., Ali, M., Hasan, M. M., Hasan, M. M., Uddin, M. J., Begum, M., Da Silva, J. A. T., Pan, X.-Y., and Karim, M. R. (2012). Damage and management of cyclone sidr-affected homestead tree plantations: a case study from patuakhali, bangladesh. *Natural Hazards*, 64(2): 1305–1322.

13. Jana, S. and Bhat, M. S. (2017). Composite adaptive control using output feedback and application to micro air vehicle. In *2017 SICE International Symposium on Control Systems (SICE ISCS)*, pages 1–8. IEEE.

14. Jana, S., Majumder, R., Menon, P. P., and Ghose, D. (2021). Decision support system (DSS) for hierarchical allocation of resources and tasks for disaster management. Presented at *5th International Conference on Dynamics Of Disasters (DOD)*, Athens, Greece.

15. Kakooei, M. and Baleghi, Y. (2017). Fusion of satellite, aircraft, and UAV data for automatic disaster damage

assessment. *International Journal of Remote Sensing*, 38(8-10): 2511–2534.

16. Kashyap, A., Ghose, D., Menon, P. P., Sujit, P., and Das, K. (2019). UAV aided dynamic routing of resources in a flood scenario. In *2019 International Conference on Unmanned Aircraft Systems (ICUAS)*, pages 328–335. IEEE.

17. Lüthi, S. (2019). Applying machine learning methods to the assessment of tropical cyclone impacts. Master's thesis, ETH Zurich.

18. Malabrigo Jr, P., Umali, A. G., Replan, E., et al. (2016). Damage assessment and recovery monitoring of the mangrove forests in calauit island affected by typhoon yolanda (haiyan). *Journal of Environmental Science and Management*, (2).

19. Malandrino, F., Chiasserini, C.-F., Casetti, C., Chiaraviglio, L., and Senacheribbe, A. (2019). Planning uav activities for efficient user coverage in disaster areas. *Ad Hoc Networks*, 89: 177–185.

20. Mallick, B., Ahmed, B., and Vogt, J. (2017). Living with the risks of cyclone disasters in the south-western coastal region of bangladesh. *Environments*, 4(1): 13.

21. Nandi, G., Neogy, S., Roy, A. K., and Datta, D. (2020). Immediate disturbances induced by tropical cyclone fani on the coastal forest landscape of eastern india: A geospatial analysis. *Remote Sensing Applications: Society and Environment*, 20: 100407.

22. Nex, F., Duarte, D., Steenbeek, A., and Kerle, N. (2019). Towards real-time building damage mapping with low-cost uav solutions. *Remote sensing*, 11(3): 287.

23. Panda, K. G., Das, S., Sen, D., and Arif, W. (2019). Design and deployment of uav-aided post-disaster emergency network. *IEEE Access*, 7: 102985–102999.

24. Primavera, J., Dela Cruz, M., Montilijao, C., Consunji, H., Dela Paz, M., Rollon, R., Maranan, K., Samson, M., and Blanco, A. (2016). Preliminary assessment of post-haiyan mangrove damage and short-term recovery in eastern samar, central philippines. *Marine pollution bulletin*, 109(2): 744–750.

25. Ravichandran, R., Ghose, D., and Das, K. (2019). UAV based survivor search during floods. In *2019 International Conference on Unmanned Aircraft Systems (ICUAS)*, pages 1407–1415. IEEE.

26. Schaefer, M., Teeuw, R., Day, S., Zekkos, D., Weber, P., Meredith, T., and Van Westen, C. J. (2020). Low-cost uav surveys of hurricane damage in dominica: automated processing with co-registration of pre-hurricane imagery for change analysis. *Natural Hazards*, 101(3): 755–784.

27. Shamsuzzoha, M., Noguchi, R., and Ahamed, T. (2021). Damaged area assessment of cultivated agricultural lands affected by cyclone bulbul in coastal region of bangladesh using landsat 8 oli and tirs datasets. *Remote Sensing Applications: Society and Environment*, 23: 100523.

28. Syifa, M., Kadavi, P. R., and Lee, C.-W. (2019). An artificial intelligence application for post-earthquake damage mapping in palu, central sulawesi, indonesia. *Sensors*, 19(3): 542.

29. Vetrivel, A., Gerke, M., Kerle, N., Nex, F., and Vosselman, G. (2018). Disaster damage detection through synergistic use of deep learning and 3d point cloud features derived from very high resolution oblique aerial images, and multiple-kernel-learning. *ISPRS journal of photogrammetry and remote sensing*, 140: 45–59.

30. Wu, K.-S., He, Y.-r., Chen, Q.-j., and Zheng, Y.-m. (2020). Analysis on the damage and recovery of typhoon disaster based on uav orthograph. *Microelectronics Reliability*, 107: 113337.

31. Xu, Z., Wu, L., and Zhang, Z. (2018). Use of active learning for earthquake damage mapping from uav photogrammetric point clouds. *International journal of remote sensing*, 39(15-16): 5568–5595.

32. Yeom, J., Han, Y., Chang, A., and Jung, J. (2019). Hurricane building damage assessment using post-disaster uav data. In *IGARSS 2019-2019 IEEE International Geoscience and Remote Sensing Symposium*, pages 9867–9870. IEEE.

33. Yuan, F. and Liu, R. (2018). Integration of social media and unmanned aerial vehicles (uavs) for rapid damage assessment in hurricane matthew. In *Construction Research Congress 2018*, pages 513–523.

Part 5

APPLICATION OF REMOTE SENSING, GIS, DRONE AND UAV FOR DISASTER RISK MANAGEMENT

Chapter 28 Analysis of Compensatory Citizen Services from the Disaster Management Institutional Set Up in India

Chapter 29 Assessment for Efficient Achievement of Disaster Resilience in India

Chapter 30 Multi-player Game-based Algorithm Using Set Partitioning for Resource Allocation during Natural Disaster Response

Chapter 31 Comparing priorities of Providers and Users with respect to Disaster Management Strategies

Chapter 32 Law and Disaster Management: A Critical Understanding

Chapter 33 Governance of Disaster Management: Lessons Learnt and a Roadmap to Avert a Future Chamoli Like Disaster

Chapter 34 Disaster Risks and Management in India: A Critical Analysis of the Disaster Management Act

Chapter 35 Democratizing Disaster Risk Reduction: A Local Governance Approach to Contextual Knowledge Production for Flood Planning in Kuttanad, India

Chapter 36 Sustainable Operation & Maintenance (O&M) of Multi-purpose Disaster Shelters (MPDS) in Bangladesh

Chapter 37 Disaster Management in India: A Systematic Approach

Analysis of Compensatory Citizen Services from the Disaster Management Institutional Set Up in India

Devashish De

Independent Researcher

M.Sc. (Disaster Management) from Jamsetji Tata School of Disaster Studies,
Tata Institute of Social Sciences, Deonar, Bombay, India -400088
devashishde@gmail.com

Abstract

This paper is a relook at the way the disaster management institutional set up has grown in India and looks at the efficacy of compensation mode of receipt either through a government declaration of relief or receipts from insurance sector. The findings are that due to poor record of citizen services rendered by existing insurance firms, the infusion of liquid capital in the insurance sector will remain circumspect. Now that the economic revival after Lockdown 4.0 has become imminent there is a requirement to reduce dependency on foreign products and services and the call of 'Atmanirbhar' or self-sufficiency can only be achieved if the insurance giants at multinational level are forced to cough out their share of humongous profits. The existing government treasury is stretched and may not be in a position to fulfil declared political obligation. The article also marks a number of legislations which become limitations in accumulating large Disaster Relief corpus at national and state level. It concludes that group insurance is a innovative concept to meet all ends as it is a promise to share the load of Government announced relief as it empowers the people and shifts the liability on insurance funds. The gain on vote banks could also be the reason as to why the government of the day may just adopt it.

Keywords: Group Insurance, Compensation, Disaster Hierarchy in India.

1. Introduction

The Disaster Management set up in India has been institutionalised right from the village level up through block, district, state and national level. In the cities the Panchayat system of governance as in villages has been equated along with Urban Local Bodies. Presently the Village Disaster Management Plan has remained the focus of completion by state governments in the year 2018-20 until the COVID19 pandemic struck[1] in the first quarter of 2020 and thereafter it has been felt that the Smart City arrangements[2] will require a look, denovo. The role of state as seen in everyday lives dwells upon early warning, transport and evacuation during the onset of Disaster, food and medicine inventory management, sanitation set up, community management in camps meant for them etc as the Disaster strikes.

The paper is in two parts. In the first part the Disaster management institutional set-up has been charted. In the second part the compensation mechanism has been documented in isolation so that multiple data on relief, rehabilitation, prevention, mitigation and other agendas spelled by Disaster Management conceptual education to include the Hyogo & Sendai frameworks and the honourable Prime Minister's 10 point agenda is not addressed concurrently thus infusing possible incoherence .

2. Methodology

To arrive at the results the data has been collated through recent and of past journalistic enterprise which has been collecting inputs in bits on the Disaster support mechanism in

[1]http://theshillongtimes.com/2020/05/14/we-the-people-have-failed-in-disaster-management/ accessed on 31 May2020.
[2]https://economictimes.indiatimes.com/news/politics-and-nation/45-smart-city-command-and-control-centres-turn-into-covid-19-war-rooms/articleshow/74904329.cms?from=mdr accessed on 31 May 2020.

India. Once overlaid the strengths and weaknesses of policy has been clear which has also helped assess the best route or solution to the problem.

3. Literature Review: The Disaster Management Set Up in India

Apart from the nodal agencies of NDMA, SDMA & DDMA as enshrined in the Disaster Management Act of 2005, the line directorates at the level of administration at district, state and national level namely as PWD, PDS, Electric and Water boards, Industrial Safety, agriculture, health, earth sciences are suitability integrated for evaluation and prevention measures against known risk pattern in administrative jurisdictions. For example, monitoring of COVID19 pandemic has been delegated to Ministry of Health and Family welfare whereas the incidence related to Vishakhapatnam Gas leak was taken control of by Ministry of Environment. To a large extent the judiciary at the apex level and high courts have been monitoring environmental damage and a separate National Green Tribunal oversees the legal compliance. The Environment Impact Assessment of upcoming and existing projects have been under study for optimum results and a definitive policy is yet to be framed in the field.

At the State level, Relief Commissioners & at the District Level, the DDMO and the District Collector and Magistrate have been holding the incident command mechanism. At places the Secretary, Revenue has been resolving these duties at the state level again. Routine monitoring at NDMA level is being facilitated by Indian Meteorological Department (IMD), Ministry of Urban Affairs, DGFASLI, Ministry of Earth sciences and many other ministries and research agencies. Thus, besides NDMA at the national level, SDMA

at the state level and the scores of DDMA set ups there has been adequate integration from local and national agencies as stated above. Besides this a number of UN agencies, International and National NGOs have been efficient service providers.

Critical action plans have been initiated by the High-powered committee mechanism to formulate policies in green field areas -COVID19 is one such challenge. In addition, there has been a spurt and thrust in innovation and start up culture. Formulation of Development report and revision of State, District & Department Disaster Management plans have been successful in documenting the capacity building achieved for meeting Disaster Management goals. Areas as mental health and cattle and animal protection have been grey areas due to shortage of trained manpower and priority for human lives at the onset of Disasters has thus relegated these fields. But now custom missions have taken off to name a few which are catering for these shortcomings. Some noteworthy missions and projects are listed subsequently, which form part of the prevention and mitigation cycle in Disaster Management.

Tehsildar at Taluka level, BDO at circle level, Gram Sevak / Talathi/ VDO in consultation with the Sarpanch of the village are important functionaries who carry out government orders. At the city or town level for multi-storey buildings, ward members, society secretary, revenue collectors and municipal officers and functionaries are instrumental in similar action. For human resource development NIDM has been instituted under the Disaster Management Act of 2005.

Government of India gazette serial number 326 dated 30May2019 has declared that Corporate Social Responsibility (CSR) under the Companies Act will now include Disaster Management Activities to include relief, rehabilitation and reconstruction activities. Before the ordinance was floated

Table 28.1 Reference to select projects and missions that are integrated in Disaster Management

Projects[3]						
National Cyclone Risk Mitigation Project	India Disaster Resource Network (MHA)	National Communication Emergency Plan	Mobile radiation Detection System	National Disaster Response Reserve	Aapda Mitra Scheme	*See Reference s for complete list*
Missions						
National Initiative on Climate Resilient Agriculture	Mission Milk	National Solar Mission	Total Sanitation Campaign	Jawaharlal Nehru National Urban Renewal Mission	Providing Urban Amenities to Rural Areas	*See Reference s for complete list*
Atal Innovation Mission (AIM)	AMRUT	Ayushman Bharat	Digital India	Make In India	Pradhan Mantri Awas yojana	
Skill India	Fasal Bima Yojana	Sansad Adarsh Gram Yojana	PAHAL	Jan Dhan Yojana	MUDRA	

[3] https://www.ndmindia.nic.in/programs accessed on 31 May 2020.

key CSR activities have included earmarking of specialist staffers for Disaster Management activities, activation of 'Lifeline Express', an accident relief train; placement of VSAT apparatus, creation of medical aid shelters, mobile phone link up arrangements, work from home internet services, mobile ATMs for cash by banks, school support mechanisms, setting up of relief camps by provision of tents, DG sets, cranes, water trawlers, ready to eat meal packets, blankets, clothing and sleeping arrangements etc . In addition, post disaster needs assessment(PDNA) has been facilitated by various UN organisations through provision of software loaded tablets .Provision of mental health workers support over a decade of rehabilitation effort by academic institutions as TISS, preservation of livelihood and culturally transmitted skills as well as reviving livelihood by NGOs in field, micro level initiatives as provision of small machines as flour grinder, sewing machines, construction material & community cooking arrangements etc have been the conspicuous elements of effective Disaster Management in India. Some of the noteworthy names in the field are OXFAM India, CARE, SEEDS, Save the Children, IFRC & Indian Red Cross etc.

There have been some areas in the institutional set-up of Disaster Management in India for which concerned policy have been non-negotiable to date.

India has in principle foreign policy of not accepting foreign aid since these come with preconditions and hidden agendas and is therefore refrained from. The issues were cleared during the onset of Kerala Floods of 2018. In the same vein participation by foreign armies in Disaster Management activities is circumspect. However, India endeavours to help out all nations in lieu. For example, during the Wuhan air evacuation in January-February of 2020 there were no embargo on getting back US and Maldivian nationals[4] on Airforce & Air India flights.

India has offered aid to Pakistan during the set of Disasters that struck in 2015 but the same was not accepted.

Cattle and animal management becomes a critical management task during Disasters in India. The compensation for milch animals, drought animals, Sheep, goats, pigs and poultry are the only figures which have been documented. The loss of fishing due to ocean acidification has yet not been documented and saving of wild life from forest fires etc may still require consolidation of policy.

4. Results and Analysis: Procedure for Compensation of Disaster Victims

India is a disaster-prone state. While the compensation packages that are being announced have a politically inclined intent, the capacity of the exchequer is generally not being accounted for before declaration of relief[5]. These days the deficit of compensation and reconstruction effort is being contested between the Chief ministers and the Centre and more often than not the Chief Ministers of Indian states have remained vocal for receipt of monies from Donors by an appeal of help. This can be seen on television as West Bengal continues to seek monetary help to overcome the reconstruction challenge posed by Cyclone Amphan. Public across the board have scant understanding of the degree to which their regions are prone to Disasters and while insurance is the only ready way out, but purchase of the same doesn't match the need for such covers. Since the compensation slabs are less in terms of ex-gratia declared for release after an incidence has been declared as Disaster the Government of India has been pursing a follow up in fulfilment through Insurance as COVID 19 was declared as Disaster[6] for release of insurance[7]. Similarly, the Fasal Bima Yojana are new age policy upgrades to meet compensation requirements as desired. Somehow the scores of Rural Development Institutes and Community Development Training Institutions have rarely come up with solutions to the village communities with suited reply to their problems. This may have been because the institutional set-up of village headman has been to a large extent political. So his or her focus has been politics and development support concurrently. When the author visited Toramba in Latur tehsil of Osmanabad in the year 2018 he had witnessed the mindless punching of borewells without a scientific support system in place. The sugarcane and onion produce suffered from lack of electric supply in villages and other infrastructure. So, while CSR support in terms of machinery etc may look very good but at the end it doesn't assure the sustainable development concept of life. Migrations follow up in generations.

Select Charts are reflected for assimilation.

[4]https://www.indiatoday.in/india/story/iaf-air-india-flights-evacuate-indians-foreigners-wuhan-japan-ship-1650379-2020-02-27 accessed on 31 May 2020

[5]https://www.financialexpress.com/money/insurance/check-how-victims-can-be-compensated-at-time-of-natural-or-man-made-disasters/1711684/ accessed on 01 June 2020.

[6]https://www.freepressjournal.in/india/india-declares-coronavirus-outbreak-a-notified-disaster-announces-compensation-for-families-of-deceased accessed on 01 June 2020.

[7]https://www.latestlaws.com/latest-news/insurance-regulatory-body-irdai-mandates-inclusion-of-covid-19-in-all-medical-policies/ accessed on 01 June 2020.

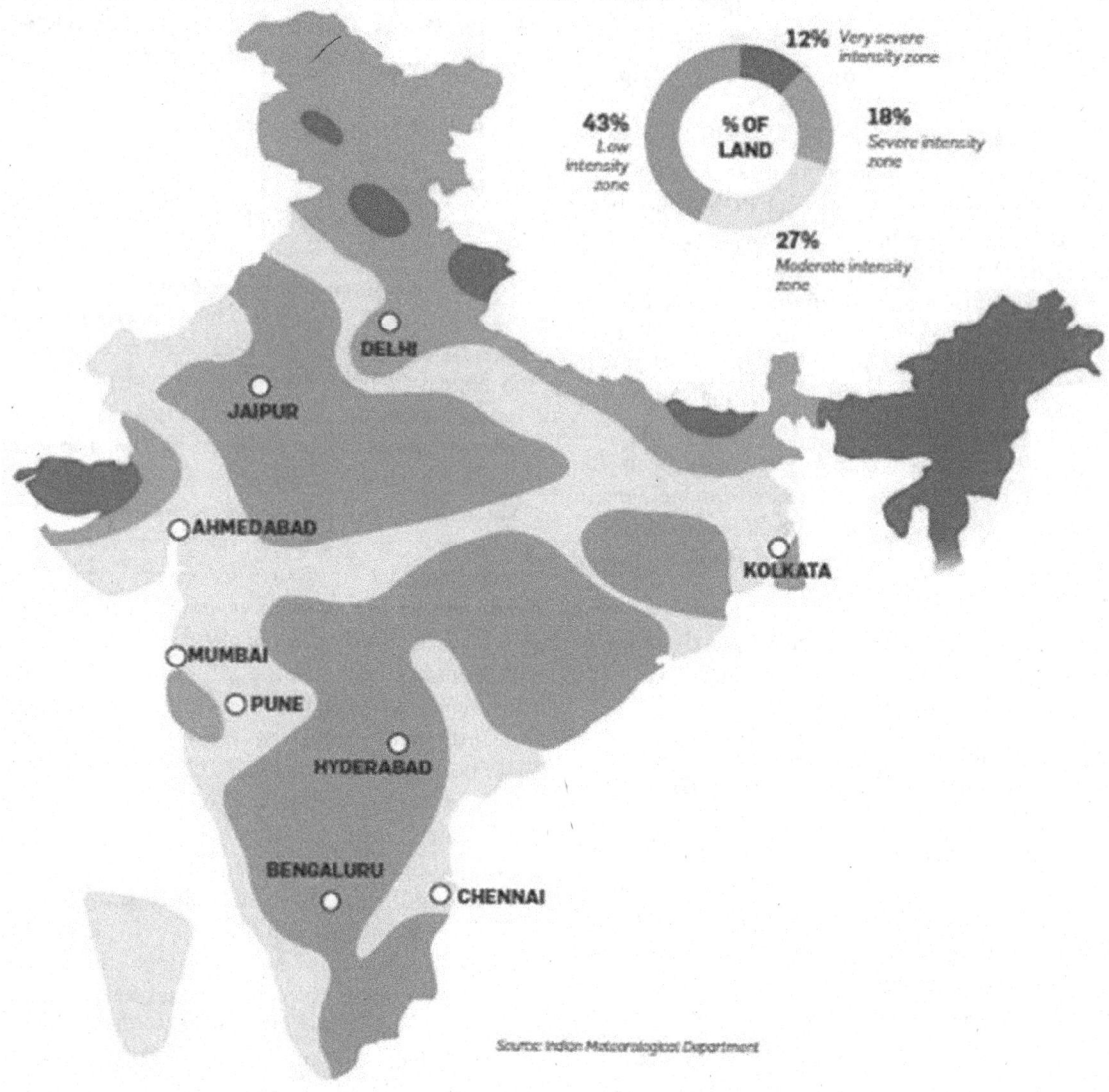

Fig. 28.1 Representational image of Earthquake Prone regions in India

Source: https://economictimes.indiatimes.com/spotlight/how-to-protect-your-assets-from-natural-disasters/tomorrowmakersshow/69426428.cms accessed on 01June 2020

Table 28.2 India Disaster Vulnerability in %ages[8]-Rough Estimates.

S. No.	Disaster	%age
1	Earthquake/ Moderate Earthquake	30/27
2	Flood	27
3	Cyclone/Tsunami over 7516 km coastline	76
	Safe Zone	43

[8]https://economictimes.indiatimes.com/spotlight/how-to-protect-your-assets-from-natural-disasters/tomorrowmakersshow/69426428.cms accessed on 01June2020.

Table 28.3 Compensation/ Insurance package[9]

S. No.	Package Base	Insurance	Cost$/Compensation #	Source
1	1500 sq.ft Flat	50 Lakhs	₹1700/-$	*Less than 1% of those who can afford Home insurance subscribe to it *Only 10% of Disaster Losses covered by insurance in Asia.
2	Contents of Flat worth 10 lakhs (*Cash, documents, Share Certificates, Debit/Credit card losses not covered*)	Total 50 + 10 = 60 lakhs	₹1700 + ₹400 = ₹2100/-$	
3	Ex-Gracia (to include relief workers)		₹4 lakhs #	
4	40-60% Disability		₹59,100/-#	
5	More than 60% Disability		₹2 Lakhs #	
6	Hospitalisation Cost per Week		₹12700/-#	
7	Hospitalisation Cost less than a Week		₹4300/-#	
8	Desilting of Agricultural land/hectare		₹2200/-#	
9	Land Loss due to Landslide/Avalanche/ Change of Course of River(per hectare)		₹37500/-#	
10	Crop loss at 33% and beyond (Earlier 50%) per hectare		₹9000/-# (Rainfed areas) ₹13500/-# (Irrigated Land) ₹18000/- (Perennial Crops)	
Offers (Reasons: Global warming & Climate Change, Dent to Government Treasury is a reality consideration by government functionaries, Victims not getting their due despite declaration as common occurrence)				
11	Group Insurance Schemes from Insurance Firms	₹50 lakhs (20-25% discount per flat amounting to a cost less than ₹500/- per flat per year)		Individual seeking all around is avoided. A group of beneficiaries can fight their rights cases better.
12	Pradhan Mantri Fasal Bima Yojana	On agricultural produce. (optional)	Intends to release the farmer from the debt cycle. Introduced but effectiveness yet to be settled .	It doesn't offer group insurance compensation to include loanee farmers, non-loanee farmers, share croppers & tenant farmers.
				Additional infrastructure for support could be airconditione d granaries, subsidised truck, few nights stay arrangements in remote out of state market, online ticket for sale of market produce .

5. Discussion

In the absence of a Catastrophe Bond in India, it is worthwhile to look at the historical precedence of compensation mechanisms those which have been notified by government from time to time. Their practices have been contradictory and such is still continuing. One of them has been Calamity Relief Fund[10] . The 90 days period earmarked for the Next of kin for claiming the insurance[11] by IRDAI has been marked in the mourning period of the loss of bread earner. When people advise you to look out for a firm with good record of payment made to claimants, this anomaly or inadvertent formalised process defects gets established. The claimant who is a poor lady in all probability is less knowledgeable since she is not the investor ab initio and she may not be literate enough to quote the insurance policy number in the first place. So, some

---

[9] https://www.thehindu.com/news/national/karnataka/compensation-for-natural-disaster-victims-increased/article7111471.ece accessed on 01June2020
[10] https://www.thehindu.com/books/disaster-insurance/article2037568.ece accessed on 01 June 2020.
[11] https://economictimes.indiatimes.com/wealth/insure/90-day-limit-no-basis-to-deny-insurance-claim/canararobecoshowsp_dp/62859399.cms accessed on 01 June 2020.

security will have to be tied during the investment stage itself so that neither it becomes the headache of the courts due to an administrative procedural deformity infused in connivance with commercial insurance firms in all probability nor it becomes a weapon in the hands of the opposition of the ruling party. This fact has to be given credence for the fact that Kautilya in Arthashastra which has been the backbone of our Indian identity has defined Disaster as loss of a bread winner only and this must govern our disbursement of relief packages. Even at the cost of insurance firms being exposed to stringency of administration they still get to gain heavily from the investment of premiums gained over a long period of time . The policy limitations on the state with respect to receipt borrowings is governed by Fiscal Responsibility and Budget Management Act[12]. Article 293(1) also prohibits the state from borrowing from outside the territory of Indian state. The invocation of a disaster cess is marred by very many differentials. So, it is but obvious that the state treasury will feel the pinch in disbursements of politically oriented relief declarations.

Digitisation of compensation documents is another grey area. In a visit to the DDMO office in Jagatsinghpur district of Odisha state, it was seen that the place was store house of old compensation applications and marred the very requirement of it being an incident command centre. The officer is also one on special duty and is not qualified in Disaster Management profile but meets the contingent requirement on adhoc basis. Digitisation of paper records could have been a better step to arrive at better functional efficiency. With such tender understanding on compensations and relief, people at large are likely to be cheated and corruption could accrue which is avoidable in an age where the honourable Prime Minister is advocating all digital evaluation of damage, identification of beneficiary and disbursal of benefits.

6. Conclusion

Over a period of 15 years the Disaster Management framework in India has consolidated. Yet the outlook of a nation has been progressive and case studies have helped in research and learnings. On the first day of Lockdown 5.0 due to the inflicted miseries from the Corona pandemic the shackles of governance at the Panchayat and the ward level has been tested and found responsive. The migrant crisis was an administrative void yet alert Ward members, Mukhiyas & Sarpanches saw to it that their village folks who had once ventured to the cities found adequate relief on their return to their homes. The Bihar government set an example by provision of free masks, sanitisers and soaps to each returning and existing member. The paper sets out the holistic ambition of governance on a positive note, yet in an isolated study on compensations the derivations are stark and needs to be refigured. The paper sees the group insurance as a weapon in the hands of the common man and insists on its implementation as a empowerment of the masses. This can be integrated with the Pradhan Mantri Fasal Bima Yojana as well to enable its conversion as a successful model, thereby reducing the weight of litigation thrust by insurance firms on a record of deviations.

7. Acknowledgements

The author would like to thank the villagers of Toramba who facilitated an intrinsic understanding of Disasters in Marathwada while he was on post-graduation in field.

REFERENCES

1. Capacity Building of Panchayats: Tasks Ahead Author(s): Mahi Pal Source: Economic and Political Weekly, Vol. 38, No. 6 (Feb. 8-14, 2003), pp. 507-510 Published by: Economic and Political Weekly Stable URL: https://www.jstor.org/stable/4413181 Accessed: 29-05-2020 11:40 UTC
2. Ridhi Kale, Looking ahead: What will smart cities look like? | India Today InsightSmart cities could help protect people against the pandemics of the future https://www.indiatoday.in/india-today-insight/story/looking-ahead-what-will-smart-cities-look-like-1683042-2020-05-28 accessed on 31 May 2020.
3. State & District administration, 2009, DARPG accessed on 31May2020. www.darpg.gov.in › sites › default › files › sdadmin15
4. https://ndma.gov.in/en/ongoing-project.html accessed on 31 May 2020.
5. http://www.indiascienceandtechnology.gov.in/st-vision/national-missions accessed on 31 May 2020.
6. https://www.narendramodi.in/narendra-modi-s-missions-211393 accessed on 31 May 2020.
7. https://www.financialexpress.com/india-news/narendra-modis-top-10-signature-infrastructure-projects-to-power-new-india/613121/ accessed on 31 May 2020.
8. https://www.indiatoday.in/education-today/gk-current-affairs/story/8-missions-govt-napcc-1375346-2018-10-25 accessed on 31 May 2020.
9. https://www.thehindu.com/news/national/karnataka/compensation-for-natural-disaster-victims-increased/article7111471.ece accessed on 01 June 2020.
10. https://www.financialexpress.com/industry/banking-finance/financial-planning-tips-5-important-disclosures-to-your-

---

[12]https://www.livemint.com/opinion/columns/opinion-a-sustainable-option-for-funding-disaster-management-in-india-1561626888086.html accessed on 01June2020.

spouse-to-deal-with-untimely-demise/278265/ accessed on 01 Jun 2020.

11. https://www.livemint.com/opinion/columns/opinion-a-sustainable-option-for-funding-disaster-management-in-india-1561626888086.html accessed on 01June2020

12. https://www.epw.in/journal/2019/25/special-articles/financing-disaster-management.html accessed on 01 June 2020.

13. https://www.orfonline.org/research/pradhan-mantri-fasal-bima-yojana-an-assessment-of-indias-crop-insurance-scheme-51370/ accessed on 01 June 2020.

CHAPTER 29

Assessment for Efficient Achievement of Disaster Resilience in India

Gargaei M. Chakravarthy

Consultant Engineer, G Infra, Andhra Pradesh, India
Pgmc92.se@gmail.com,
+917013749149

Abstract

India is a country where the development is flourishing from Physical, Social, Environmental areas to Technology, Governance, And Fiscal Sustainability. But Disaster Risk (DR)[1] is a negative indicator and reducing that, requires furtherance of SDGs. Because a country's preparedness and proneness are the reasons for a hazard to be transformed into a disaster. India is engaged with UNDP[2] and US for building the capacity to DRR[3]. India has in-house capacity, however because of incomplete-inconsistent data gaps it isn't effective. In this paper, the ranks of India in global platform for DRR is observed. Thus, the challenges and their countermeasures required to achieve greater good results at different stages are provided. Meanwhile, it is observed that a state's income plays a vital role in governance, sustaining vulnerabilities and acquire resilience to DR. Consequently, the leading factors and underlying drives of risk which create exacerbate[4] conditions and their causes are also discussed. Hence, it is concluded by furnishing additional identified elements to overcome the road blocks for putting DRR plans into operation, also various available opportunities to exercise for encouraging investments into infrastructural needs, find funding resources and how to less exertion on spending national or local budget on DR are confronted.

Keywords: 1: The potential loss of life or damaged assets which could occur to a system or society, 2: United nations development program, 3: Disaster Risk Reduction, 4: make a problem worse.

1. Introduction

India has always stood unique through various aspects such as Geographical features, Economic progress, Technology acquaintance, Industrial advancement, Socio-Cultural adoption, Population growth and more. India continues to be under the Lower-middle-income group. However, there are few contributing factors among these which led the country to be still developing, and few many give the title as a developed nation. In case of innovation sector, India is well ahead of most emerging economies and on par with several advanced economies. India is the 6th largest economy with 6th rank in nominal GDP, with a growth rate of 12.546 among the other countries though the world thought it has been knocked off course a bit through the impact of the pandemic as per world GDP rankings 2021. With the emerging investments and development in various sectors, India's GDP for 2019 is 5.54% increase from 2018-2.28% rise from 2017-15.6% shoot up from 2016-9.09% surge from 2015. The sector wise GDP in India is, Agriculture (Agriculture, forestry & fishing) is 20.19%, Industrial sector (Mining & Quarrying) is 25.92% i.e.,1.63, Manufacturing-14.43%, Electricity, gas, water supply & other utility services are 2.7%, Services (53.89%)-Public administration, Defense & other services is 15.42%, Financial, real estate & professional services is 22.05% and Trade, Hotels, Transport, communications & services related to broadcasting is 16.42%. Also, India is given 29th rank in INFORM Risk, among 195 countries in the world with a score of 14 for Hazard & Exposure, 56 for Vulnerability, and 98 for lack of coping capacity.

Between 2000-2019, India ranked 3rd for Avg. Fatalities in the world, 2nd for Avg. Losses in Million US$ PPP. By the end of 2020, India is at 131/188 countries in Human Development Index, 89/181 in World Risk Index with overall 6.62 score i.e., with Medium Exposure (12.51), High-Susceptibility (32.08), Lack of Adaptive Capacities (78.15), Vulnerability (52.94) and Lack of Coping Capacities (48.60) with infrastructure profile (Transportation, telecommunications, energy, power, healthcare, water and sanitation). And

Indian rank in WRI with its indicators are shown here in Fig. 29.1. For Quality of infrastructure ranked 66/137 in Global Competitiveness Index, with the indicator pillars such as Institutional, Infrastructure, Macroeconomic Stability (43rd), Health, Primary-higher Education, Training, Goods & Labor market efficiency, Financial market development (40th), Technology readiness, Market size (3rd), Business sophistication, Innovation (35th). Among these, India ranked 100th place for 5 pillars with mixed results on various aspects of Governance (59th), Transport (28th), Electricity (103rd) although improved significantly in past few years. Also, in FM Global resilience Index 2021, India is at 62/130 scoring 52 estimated under Economy, Risk quality and Supply chain as core factors. And 24th rank in Macroeconomic Resilience index (MRI) 2021, where it is observed that the advanced economies with higher levels of macro and health insurance resilience before pandemic were more resilient to subsequent global downturn than the emerging markets like India. This shows the need to improve importance of insurance among people in India. The components of MRI are Fiscal space, Monetary policy space, Banking Industry backdrop, Labor market efficiency, Financial market development, Economic complexity, Income inequality insurance penetration, Human capital, low carbon economy. Furthermore, India stands at 31st with 5% index and 2.6 billion USD protection gap with below 25% resilience index score in NatCat-RI.

2. Observations

From the above data, it is recognized that building resilience starts with understanding the disaster risk which is to be faced at occurrence of a disaster. In India (2000-2019)-79,732 people have lost their lives, 108 crore people were affected in 321 natural disaster events by the end of Feb-2021, as per UNDRR. For the past 50 years (1970-2019), a total or more than 7,063 extreme weather events (EWEs) with at least one death have occurred causing more than 1,41,308 deaths on an average of 20 deaths per disaster event in the world. In Fig. 29.2, the occurrence of disasters by its type in comparison between 1980's and 2000's is shown as a reference of how large the disaster occurrences increased in the world along with the development. And India is 3rd in disaster ranking, with worldwide losses of $3trillion by the end of 2020 claiming 1.23 million lives on an average of 60,000 per annum affecting 4 billion people with $2.97 trillion in economic losses over the last two decades (2000-2020). Besides US, China and India have taken the hardest hit from natural disasters due to massive population around 70% of global total i.e., 280 crores.

High income countries have accounted for most total economic losses (67%) with a total of US$1.99trillion despite accounted for lower deaths for less than 10% of total population between 2000-2019, as shown in the Fig. 29.3. On contrary, the countries within other income groups, such as Low-income countries which are 23%, have reported significantly lower total economic losses but had highest average no. of deaths per disaster event appr. 284 deaths per event then followed by Low-Middle income country's having an appr.255 deaths per event. As shown in the Fig. 29.4. Overall losses from natural disasters (ND) in 2019 is US$150bn which is at the same level as in 2013 US$140bn. And around US$52bn insured losses made-up

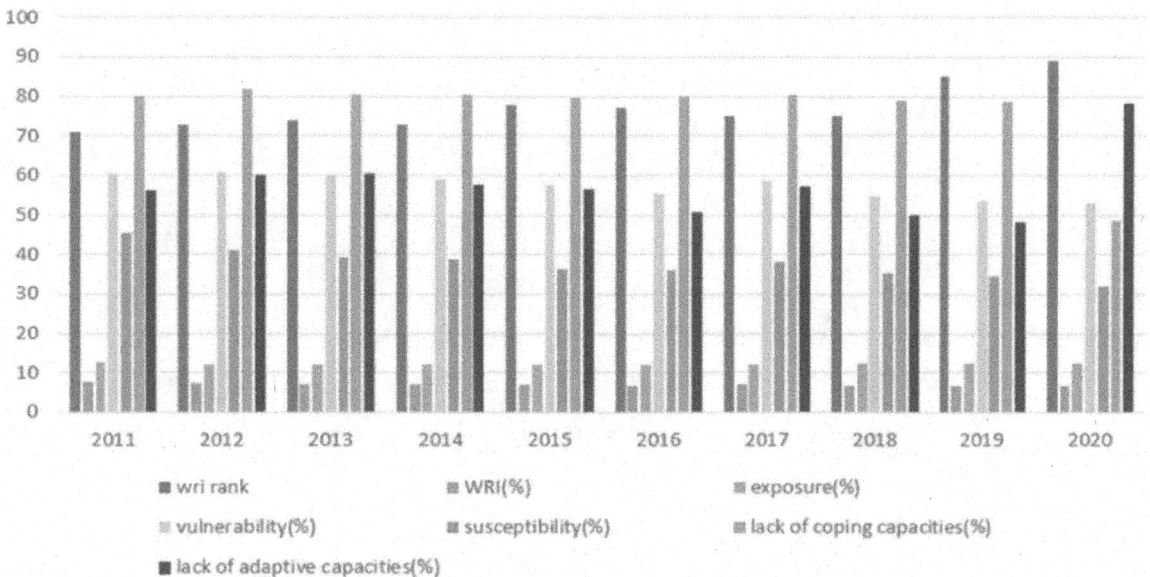

Fig. 29.1   World Risk Index-Indicators of India

Source: Data obtained from "Global Risk Index Reports from 2011–2020" and Explored into a single chart

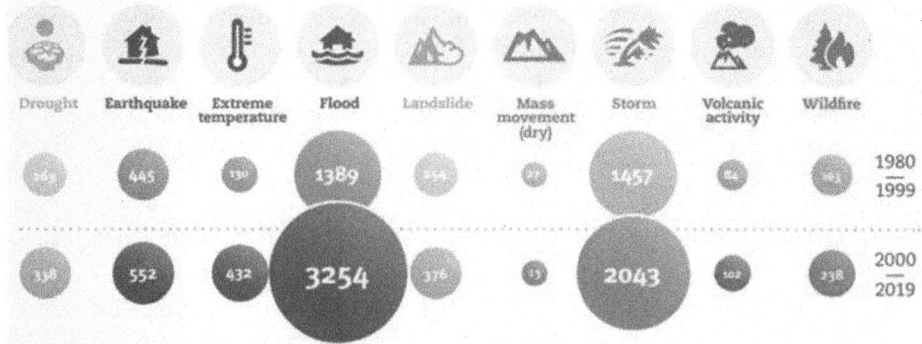

Fig. 29.2 Total disaster events by type: 1980–1999 vs. 2000–2019

Source: "Human Cost of Disasters 2000–2019 Report from UNDRR"

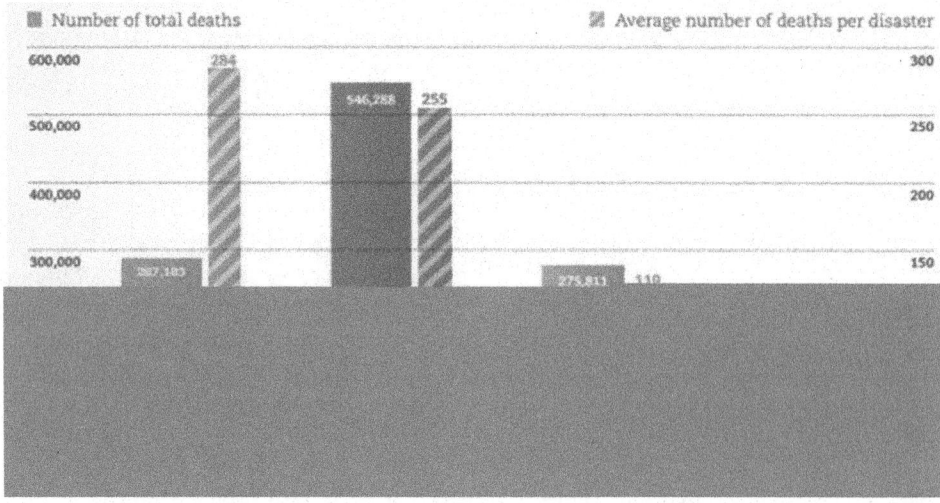

Fig. 29.3 Total numbers of deaths compared to the average number of deaths per disaster by income group (2000–2019)

Source: "Human Cost of Disasters 2000–2019 Report from UNDRR"

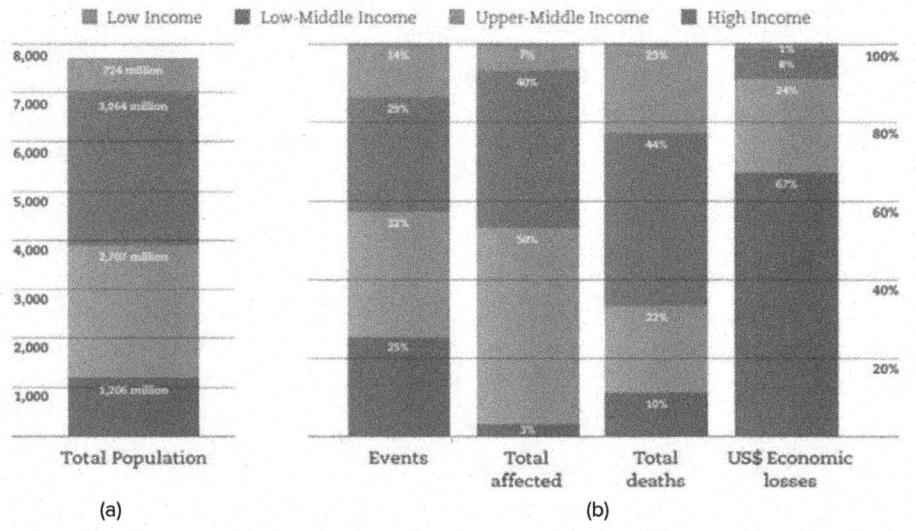

Fig. 29.4 (a) Global population distribution by income group (millions), (b) Population various types of impacts on countries/territories by income group (2000-2019)

Source: "Human Cost of Disasters 2000–2019 Report from UNDRR"

1/3rd of overall losses as that of the year 2016. This signifies the role of insurance at different segments in post disaster. The Economic losses when compared to GDP results, there's a stark difference between income groups. Despite accounting for most of the world's economic losses, high-income countries have lowest level of losses as a GDP% and contrastingly, low-income countries had highest level of losses as a GDP% and is 3 times higher than High-income countries. From the Fig. 29.5, it is shown how the EWEs increase cause the losses and compared to countries GDP of different income groups between 1998-2017. And the similar principles are followed, when the Indian states are observed. But, there remains a gap in data of economic losses from disasters worldwide, particularly incomplete from Africa and South Asian countries. And these gaps are of concern since economic data is often used to establish policy priorities. Despite the substantial amounts of missing data, low-income and Low-middle income countries still report higher relative economic losses due to impact of disasters. From this, it is clear that, better risk governance, infrastructure, surveillance systems, insured property rate and reduced exposure to natural hazards are likely responsible for the improved protection in countries as income levels increase.

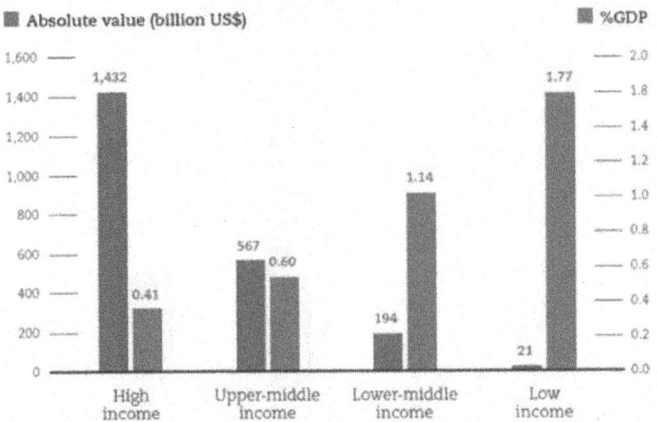

Fig. 29.5 Recorded climate-related disaster losses per income group compared to GDP losses 1998–2017

Source: "Economic Losses, Poverty & Disasters, 1998–2017 by UNISDR report"

Hence, better data collection would improve our under-standing of disaster risks and impacts and improve analysis. More in-depth data collection such as damage of infrastructure, dis-aggregated demographic data, and impacts on local economy would help decision makers prioritize and target new measures more effectively. This determines the importance of development of national disaster loss database in India, which is vital for implementing DRR strategies aligned with Sendai framework at all levels. And also, reporting the economic losses should be improved like prioritizing development of realistic and standard operational methods by reviewing existing methodologies for estimating losses.

3. Theory of Observations

Natural hazards are the leading cause of large-scale damage to infrastructures worldwide, as we discussed in the "Observations". The majority of India's natural disasters are annual occurrences such as floods, cyclones and related events. Climate change is becoming paramount to disaster impacts causing the poor often to lose their habitat, and mitigation measures are insufficient forcing them to return to vulnerable areas in India. From Fig. 29.6, the percentage of population below poverty line in all Indian states between various time spans are shown which highlights the point of need to put greater efforts in mitigation measures. Thus, the Indian government capacities, managing risks and sustainable development are challenged, about taking appropriate actions and effective response by implementing the priories such as understanding risk, strengthening governance, managing DR, investing in DRR for resilience, enhancing disaster preparedness for effective response to build back better in recovery, rehabilitation and reconstruction phases.

India is a part of the "Coalition for Disaster Resilient Infrastructures (CDRI)" working with every single needed effort and has been concreting the initiative works with interaction of Sendai framework-SDGs-Climate change adoption with furthermore focus on enhancing DM capabilities for minimizing multi-hazard-oriented disaster loss through improving Human resources and technology. The overrated preparation mightn't be enough in a catastrophe and the disasters erode development gains leading to deficits in development and that creating new risks. Here comes the point of question about, where does the Technology-Finance-Capacity Development of India, stand for!

4. Factors of Observations

The 10-point agenda by the Indian prime minister, is proposed in such a way that all the sectors must imbibe the principles of disaster risk management (DRM) to address several critical issues ranging from mainstream DRR in development of sectors, risk coverage, women empowerment, risk mapping, use of modern technology, the role of academic institutions furtherance, local capacity building and cohesion in the international response. With the adoption and enhancement of Techno-Legal Enforcement of DM act in India including the modification of existing laws, develop control rules and bylaws which can ensure safer infrastructure and that highlights the political environment such that the multilevel stakeholder coordination can be strengthened. But the knowledge spread and awareness among Officials/Stakeholders and developing capacities with cutting edge level must be reinforced and to be enhanced. There is a need to widely circulate the concepts-issues-challenges-approaches for DRR prepared in

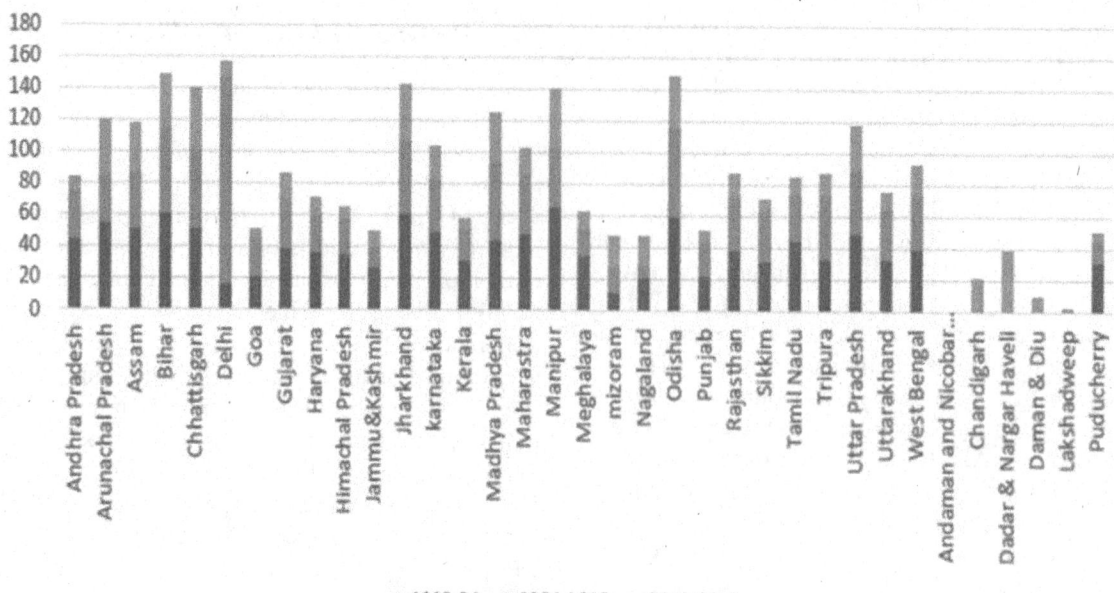

■ 1993-94 ▨ 2004-2005 ▨ 2011-2012

Fig. 29.6 % of population below poverty lie in Indian states

Source: Annual reports of states, from niti.gov.in- NITI Aayog reports- explored into single chart"

Vernacular languages to increase awareness at the community level. Thus, strengthening DR governance with clear vision, competence, plans, guidelines and coordination across sectors with public & private investments in DR prevention/ reduction through Structural and Non-structural measures needs to be stepped up until disaster resilient societies are formed.

As per "Investing in Urban Resilience" report by 2030, without significant investment into making cities more resilient, natural disasters may cost cities worldwide around $314billion each year. That is, the development projects we work on these years must meet the world standards and contribute to the resilience of all level communities with disaster safety and is a smart strategy which plays off in the long term in India, which have been started but has to penetrated into every sector of infrastructure development. The action plan might be as shown in Fig. 29.7 here.

While improvements made in terms of Early warnings, Preparedness and Responsive Mechanisms that can lead in reduction of losses in a single hazard scenario, but it is clear from past experiences that the overlap of events and interplay between risk drivers such as poverty, climate change, pollution, population growth in vulnerable areas, uncontrollable urbanizations, unknown migrated population, loss of biodiversity, requires greater strengthening of disaster risk governance.

Here comes the roles of successful achievement of SDGs. India has higher rate of growth but major challenges. The underdevelopment pockets need rapid improvement in

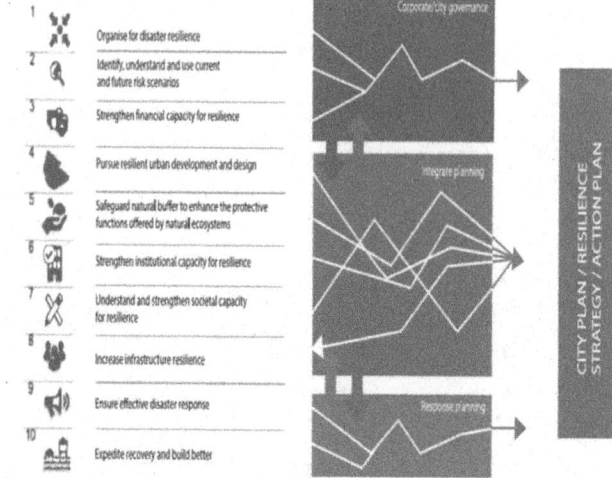

Fig. 29.7 Action plan

Source: "Making Cities Resilient report from UNDRR, also mcr2030. undrr.org"

inclusive growth, sustaining 8% or higher GDP growth and meet SDG commitments i.e., to make New India by 2022 and the performance of India in SDG achievement is shown in Fig. 29.8, which explains the goal wise performance as Achievers-Front runners -Performers- Aspirants of that respective goal. And when compared to 2019, India has become front runner in various achievement of SDGs by 2020 with an overall score of 66/100. There are various successful strategies implemented with special focus on Infrastructure, Skill development and financial institution.

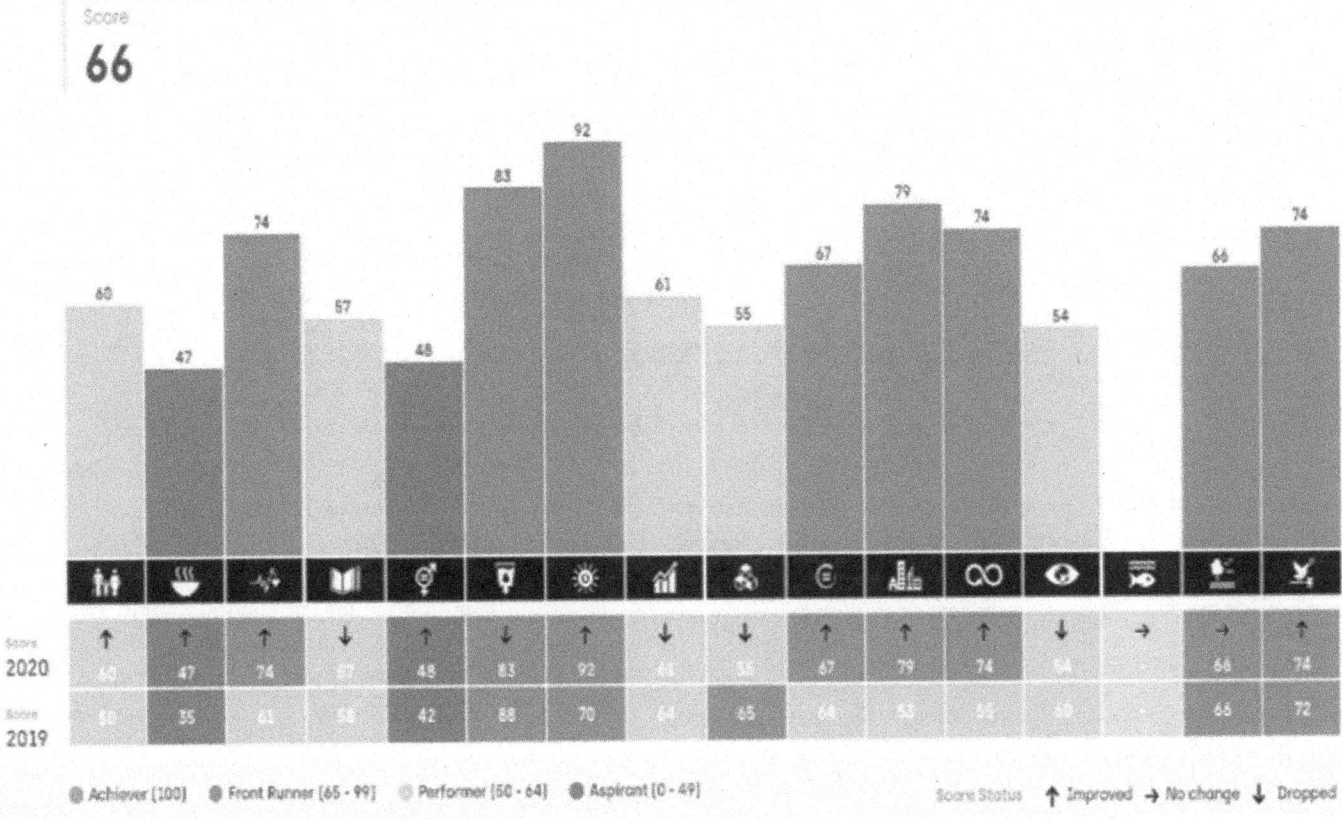

Fig. 29.8 Goal-wise performance

Source: "SDG India Index and Dashboard 2019–2020" by niti.gov.in-NITI Aayog, govt. of India"

And there are several SDGs and targets set in contribution of reducing the DR, build resilience even where DR reduction is not explicit. For reference, targets related to promoting education-SDG4(upgrading and building hospitals and schools), SDG9-building resilient infrastructures, SDG11-Cities, among other cited goals reaffirm the interrelationship between DRR & SD. These SDGs are interconnected, for explanation SDG1(no poverty) +SDG2(Zero hunger by 2030) gives the role of diversification in strategies to improve production, productivity, employment, income growth and sustainability as well as reduce the risks associated with market volatility, climate change and natural disasters. Also, SDG2+SDG17(Global partnership) lists the important enablers for implementing the entire SDG framework under 5 sub-categories- Finance, Technology, Capacity Building, Trade, Systematic issues (Including policy & institutional coherence, multi-stakeholder partnerships, data, Monitoring and accountability). In India, the data on SDG17-parteneship for the goals not yet formalized to understand the efforts put to establish the resilience and build back better. In addition, SDG3(Good health & Well-being) +SDG11(Sustainable cities & Communities) associates between inadequate, unsafe & unaffordable housing and poor health outcomes are clear although further research is needed to understand the

exposure responses, to improve quality, safety procedures. To achieve these requirements, the low-income countries like ours are facing specific disaster risk challenges that need adequate sustainable and timely provisions of support through finance, technology transfer, capacity building from developed counties and partners which are tailored to their needs and priorities as identified in them. Then, the time remains closely left to deliver effectively on hopes and aspirations raised by the adoption of Sendai framework for DRR-the SDGs-Paris-Agreement. Resilient infrastructure is an essential part of this drive and there are 5 points to be considered for investing in new or replacing existing infrastructure as a core element of recovery and beyond. They are, the states which are to be encouraged to incorporate infrastructure resilience in their local DRR strategies, strengthen the infrastructure regulations, the exposure of infrastructure investments to risk should be measured and monitored with discloser should be made mandatory, actively engage and create incentives for private sector to participate in the quest of building sustainable-resilient infrastructure reaching in all levels, and Enhancement of knowledge and capacity building development. From Fig. 29.9, it is shown how the public-private partnership for development in India has been working from 1991 to 2017. In general terms, most

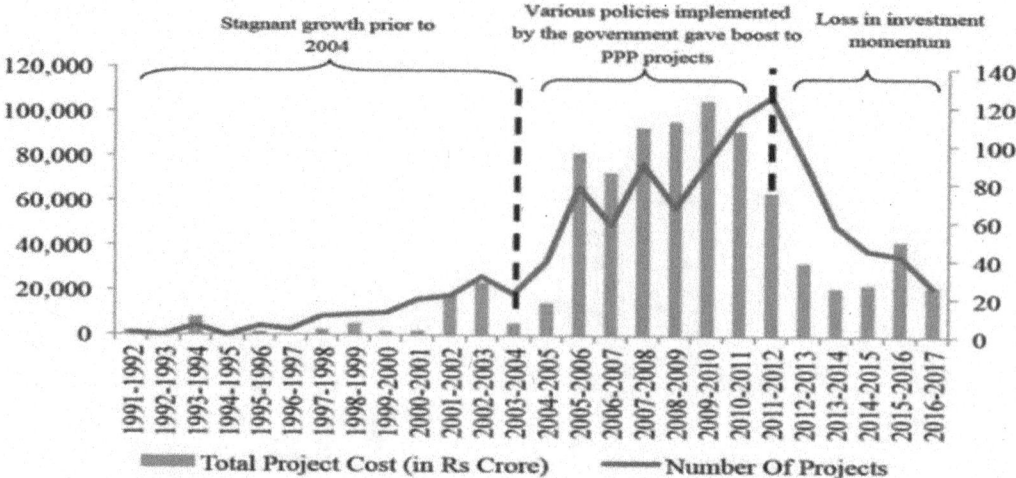

Fig. 29.9   Development of the Public Private Partnership landscape in India through different phases

Source: "infrastructureindia.gov.in, filtered for cost pf projects > 5crores and development available by 2016

of the capacity development projects are being developed by the private sectors.

It is known fact that, the quality of governance brings the investment, growth, sustainability, resilience and infrastructure's inclusivity. Thus, the tools required to see through the information, policy and fiscal gaps across different levels of government are to be bind with regulatory approaches. India have been concentrating on the adoption of mechanisms that access losses, estimate needs and channeling adequate funds to disaster affected areas through timely manner to this date from RRR phases to provide resilient community and infra through integrated DRR measures into restoration of various systems. But, the mobilization of required services and rapid technical support in post disaster phase must be improvised to lead the concept of build-back-better. Here, the biggest challenge is the conflict between the need to get back normal VS time taken to build back for and by the people as investing has challenges and public resources alone mayn't be sufficient and it is more difficult to mobilize additional funds in post disaster phase. And also with present data availability scenario, devising the suitable indicators to monitor, implement, measure and report the progress related to a course of action immediately is a tough deal.

5. Challenges and Counter Measures

There are numerous challenges that hinder effective implementation of policies as envisaged at national level. For example, lack of comprehensive and contextualized disaster information available to planners and disaster managers at all levels of governance makes prioritization impossible. Also, lack of administrative capacities at local levels may contribute to situations where intended impact is not reached

same as of environmental protection. Similarly multi-utilization of funds, poor working conditions, low motivation may contribute to challenges and to mitigate these concerns would be by support in the form of adequate funding-comprehensive monitoring-evaluation of plans-programmes-initiatives even at lower levels. But, lack of public finance and funding for DRR at local levels as local govt continues to struggle with their local budgets and that brings more gaps between funding needs and available revenue for taxation and loans. With observation of recent multiple events, the high exposure of many Indian cities to flooding, rise of sea level, potential scale of droughts, decreasing water availability should be prioritized in integrating of DRR to minimize adverse economic and human impacts through resilient urban planning. And without addressing capacity gaps, though respective funds are established, the intended DRM infrastructure mightn't be achieved. Training, education, research and awareness are considered as vital components of the capacity development to have a strategic approach and can be effectively addressed only with active participation of the stakeholders. But there seems a wide gap in the available knowledge, skill, attitude of disaster mangers for effective managing of the emergency situations practically at local levels showing capacity-risk ratio remarkably low as per NIDM study.

It is observed that risk financing and risk transfer like insurance can cover and reduce the residual economic risk however in India low levels of insurance may give larger declination in economic output and are considered fiscal losses than the countries with higher insurance rate (like high income countries). Also, Post disaster financial needs are often defined in 3 phases. i.e., the immediate relief & rescue response operations (funds for urgent rescue, food, medicine, clean water, shelter), early recovery (funds to restore livelihoods & community within weeks) and reconstruction (substantial funds for rebuilding damaged infrastructure). Hence, delay in funding in these phases bring negative economical and communal impacts. And, the capacity development in context of DRR is categorized as risk management cycle(Prevention, preparedness, response & recovery), structural capacity(Structural/non-structural buildings), targeted holistic approach(human built/technical, natural environmental), built environmental prospective(planning-construction-technical systems with in a building), natural & phycological mechanisms(Coping, adopting), institutional capacity(administrative, technical, financial), element of risk (hazard/exposure/vulnerability), element if impact (human, economic, environmental, political, social). Though the DM in India have undergone substantive changes over past decades, there are specific gaps and challenges identified in 5 main areas. They are Governance (Organizational, legal, policy frameworks), Risk Identification, Assessment-Monitoring-Early warning, Knowledge management-education-reducing underlying risk factors, Preparedness for effective response and recovery.

India standing as most populated country, the impact and outcome of a disaster also sticks out in every aspect following the need to rebuild resilient structures. For reference, when the Indian states are grouped together by income levels, there are notable difference in disaster impacts across the groups. In brief, the role of central govt has been supportive to states in terms of physical and financial resources and complementary measures in sectors such as transport, warning, inter-state movement of food grains. As part of mitigation process the 6 critical factors namely event prediction, dissemination of warning, risk avoidance action, necessary hardware, emergency response plan and its prompt activation should be planned and implemented in disaster prone areas, and given the states ability to mobilize financial resources has been much

less in comparison to that of center, it is not logical to expect the states to take major financial burden for the crucial disaster management tasks. There are 4 identified types for effective-credible-strong DRR governance system development. They are Functional capacity (support planning, leadership, resource management, monitoring, evaluation), Technical capacity (technical expertise, Knowledge), hard capacities (technical and functional, explicit and tacit knowledge and methodologies, organizational, structures, systems, procedure or policies), soft capabilities (social or relational skills, organizational culture, leadership, knowledge and experience, analysis, organizational adaptability, flexibility).

The national statistical systems of different countries similar to India are facing significant challenges. These challenges arise form increasing demands for high quality and trustworthy data to guide decision making coupled with data revolution. The world bank has developed improved statistical performance indicators (SPI) which will replace statistical capacity index (SCI) to monitor and help such countries to create a mechanism which focuses on key dimensions of a country's statistical performance. The Fig. 29.10, shows the SPI of India from 2016 to 2019 for each pillar considered.

The key pillars of a country's statistical performance to be considered are Data Use-80/100-(legislature, executive branch, civil society, academia and international bodies), Data Services-88/100-(quality of data releases, online access openness, effectiveness of advisory & analytical services related to statistics and availability of secure microdata access), Data Products-60/100-(social, economic, environmental, institutional dimensions using SDGs to support the 2030 agenda achievements enabling the country's emphasis to reflect user needs), Data sources-68.9/100-(censuses & surveys, administrative data, geospatial data, private sector data and citizenship generated data, this can help in highlighting the areas of investment required in

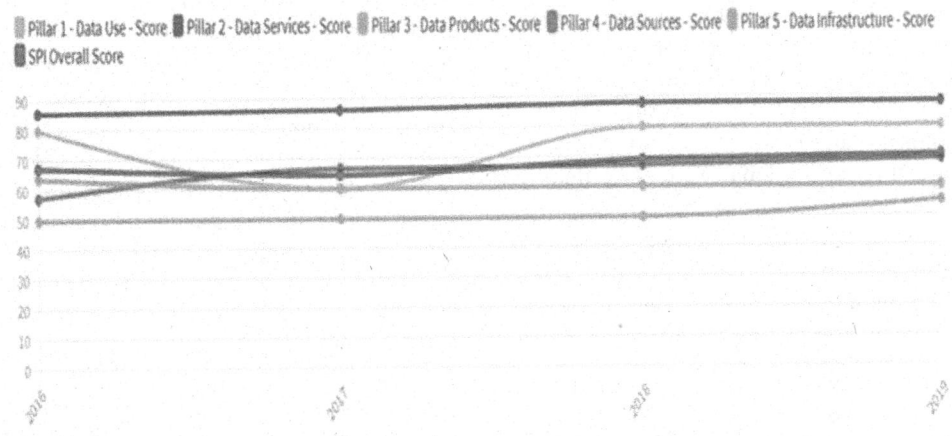

Fig. 29.10   SPI of India 2016–2019

Source: "worldbank.org, Statistical performance indicators- India"

country), Data infrastructure-55/100-(law, governance & institutional framework for statistical system, standards, methods & concepts of frameworks for compliance, statistical literacy, partnerships needs for statistical systems and finance mobilizing). The SPI is composed of more than 50 indicators and contain data of 174 countries by which it covers 99.2% of the world population. India scored 70.4/100 on world bank's SPI overall score for 2019. These are 51 indicators covering 14 out of 22 dimensions have been compiled in India. Though these indicators provide data for 5 pillars, yet there are major gaps in several pillar because there are still need to be developed to access where in some cases data coverage is limited. And to understand the emerging need to collect all kinds of data and its utilization in India in managing data and adoption of successful strategies, we need to develop this index in local standards. The significant data gaps are due to under reported disasters which often misses the risks of smaller and repeatedly occurred and in sum equally damaging events. This can result in poor understanding of the impacts of disasters. It can be difficult to obtain data on risks, hazards, exposure, vulnerability ad consequential severity as changes and improvements tend to be happening in a developing country like India.

The NDM plan is an important step towards taking risk transfer and insurance agenda to a higher level of commitment and improvement. For the maintaining relief funds monitored by MHA, India have been a self-insurer. However, it is still under expedition to reach risk informed investments. But, mandatory property insurance solution in respect to property tax payers in hazardous areas can be good beginning for risk transfer. In India, there is need to put strong effort in risk transfer mechanisms and create awareness and establish suitable environment so that risk bearers such as banks and insurance agencies get motivated to invest more in this agenda. Also working with various international organizations following these indicator principles might bring rapid results, such as. Use of publicly assessable data, transparent methodology, easy replicability, time series data to track performances, clear portrayal of outcomes and their supporting elements, being reflective to SDGs and also enable a glance comparison on the global scale. And compared to direct physical effects, indirect economic losses are more difficult to measure. In addition, there are limited available sources of data for measuring the indirect losses. Whereas some disasters are notoriously hard to measure, such as droughts particularly in context of growing global warming impact and the climate change emergencies including the improvement of disaster epidemiology deplanement after facing the latest pandemic.

For managing the development funds and to strengthen financial resilience, scaling up of existing financial instruments is necessary. And also, India has strict regulations to control unplanned development in vulnerable areas, what is lacking is the enforcement of such regulations. Furthermore, lack of technical manpower, lack of capacity of the local self govt's, lack of political will at local level are some of the reasons behind non-compliance of various regulations. Thus, creating risk analysis framework that gives more quantitative, scientific and technical scenarios that are important for policy makers to interpret, demonstrate and understanding the risk and probability and get engaged in risk management decisions with more transparent decision making.

6. Analysis and Comparisons

India is home to 14 of the 20 high-risk cities in the world. And organizing the city and stakeholders understanding the risk through-risk assessments, assessing state of resilience and establishing the resilience plan-of action and financing -implementing the action plan while monitoring & follow-up of devaluation in DRR indicators may help in achieving long standing resilience. There's also need to strengthen the inter-country coordination and cooperation mechanisms in data sharing-early warning, because we can estimate the damage caused due to an event but we might need more information to understand about how well we can manage communities if the disastrous events occur. And if there's no information regarding the infrastructure maintenance and failure indicators, even if a relatively identical disaster event occurs, that can cause more damage due to growth in population, wealthier property, population density, unplanned growth with infrastructures and the potential loss maybe more than just scaling historical loss and there's is no way to get full detailed loss data.

Furthermore, despite several breakthrough innovations, adoption of new science and technology in facing unprecedented challenges of disasters, their upscale adoption in practice is limited in Indian states. In general terms, the integrated research, monitoring and data analysis will be needed in combination with targeted capacity development to fill the existing knowledge gaps in local level. Focused studies on disaster risk communication would help local residents to understand and interpret warnings which would aid in steering communication strategies is the most effective achievement. In addition, the effective deployment of early warning systems supported by increasingly accurate weather forecasts of various kinds have the potential to protect vulnerable populations worldwide and save many lives. Strengthening Hydromet division of IMD that monitors rainfall, Hydromet forecasting (QPF), design, national-international cooperation and public awareness in all states and UT's since there are only 13 participating states in India are involved through world bank assisted hydrological project to improve hydrological information system in India, it's a challenge to consider local data and aid information in order to account the small-scale vulnerable issues. Therefore, expanding tax base by the govt. should be considered for the national calamity contingency duty in the budget. From the Fig. 29.11, the contingency fund of all states released by central govt. is shown. And it is understood that, the fund varies with disaster occurrences and provided for restoration.

As shown in Fig. 29.12, There is vast variation in performance of Indian states GDP growth, which is not healthy for country's overall development. Haryana, Gujarat, Karnataka and Telangana emerged as states with highest GDP growth surpassing National GDP while some state grow lower, when the performance in terms of financial, infrastructure, basic welfare indicators, social parameters such as human development index, physical infra, Fiscal deficit, improvement, management, expenditure, commitments, and development indices range but it is burden to other states at the same time when other small or medium range of events occurs and those states might be in need of equal attention and help. Given the wide gap between the funds sought, it is suggested that suitable changes are to be made to DM act for various recommendations made by the standing committee for autoschediasm financial arrangements of states. And Fig. 29.14, shows the NDRF releases, when compard to SDRF i.e. Fig. 29.13, it is understood that, how the distribution is diverted in the immediate rescue and relief operations scenario between the states.

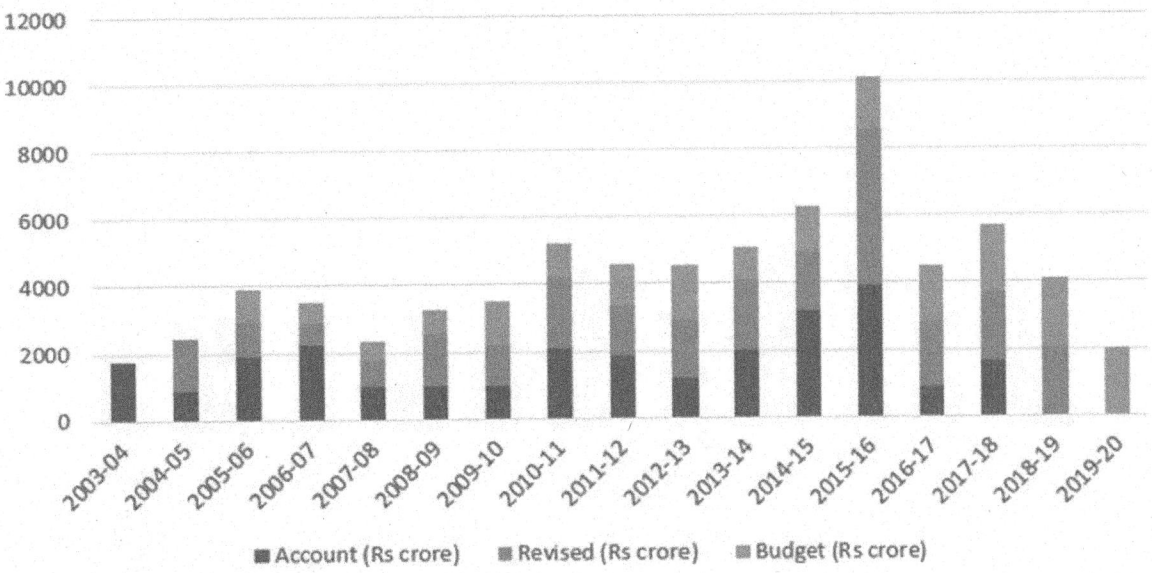

Fig. 29.11   Contingency Fund of all States

Source: Annual Budget Data Reports b/w 2003–2020 from Ministry of Home Affairs India-explored into a single chart"

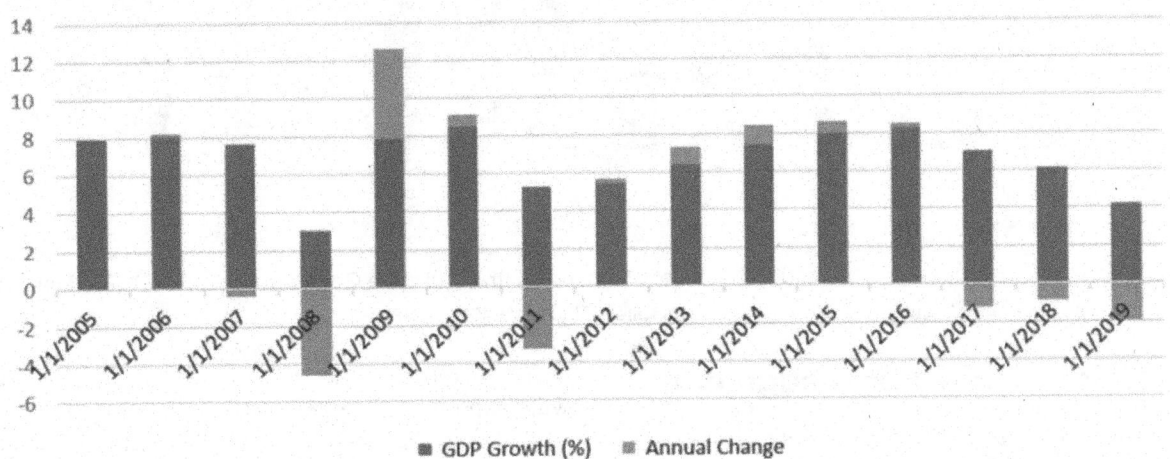

Fig. 29.12   India GDP Growth Rate 2005–2020, Macrotrends

Source: "Data Reports obtained from Macrotrends-India GDP Growth Rate b/w 2005–2020, explored into a single chart"

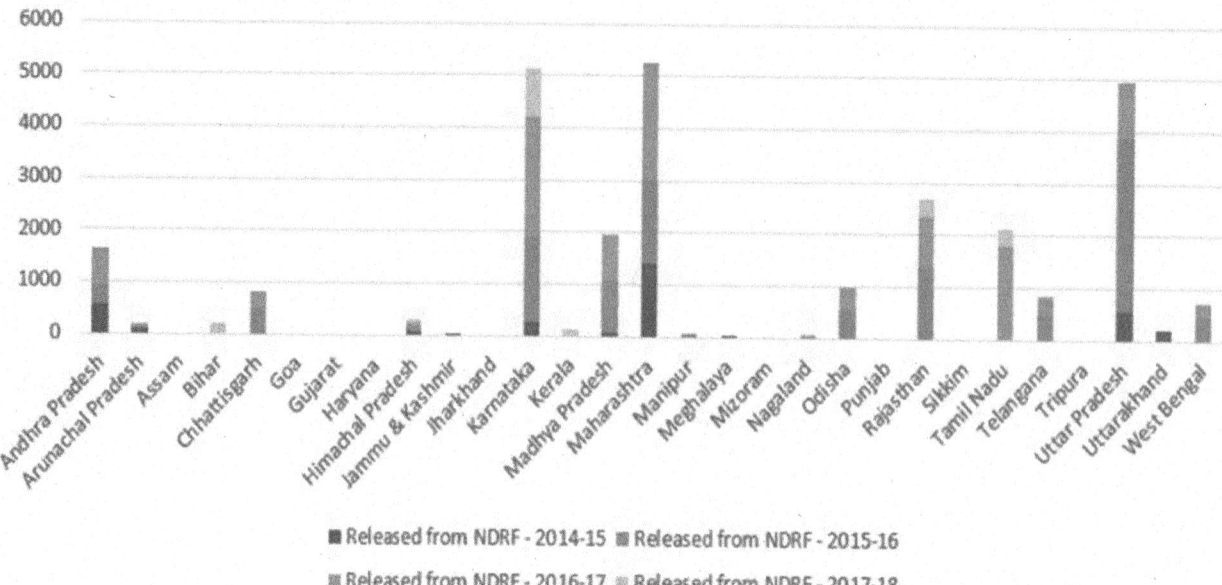

Fig. 29.13   State wise releases of SDRF from 2014–15 to 2017–18 from MHA

Source: "Annual Budget Data Reports b/w 2014–2018 From Ministry of Home Affairs and explored into single chart"

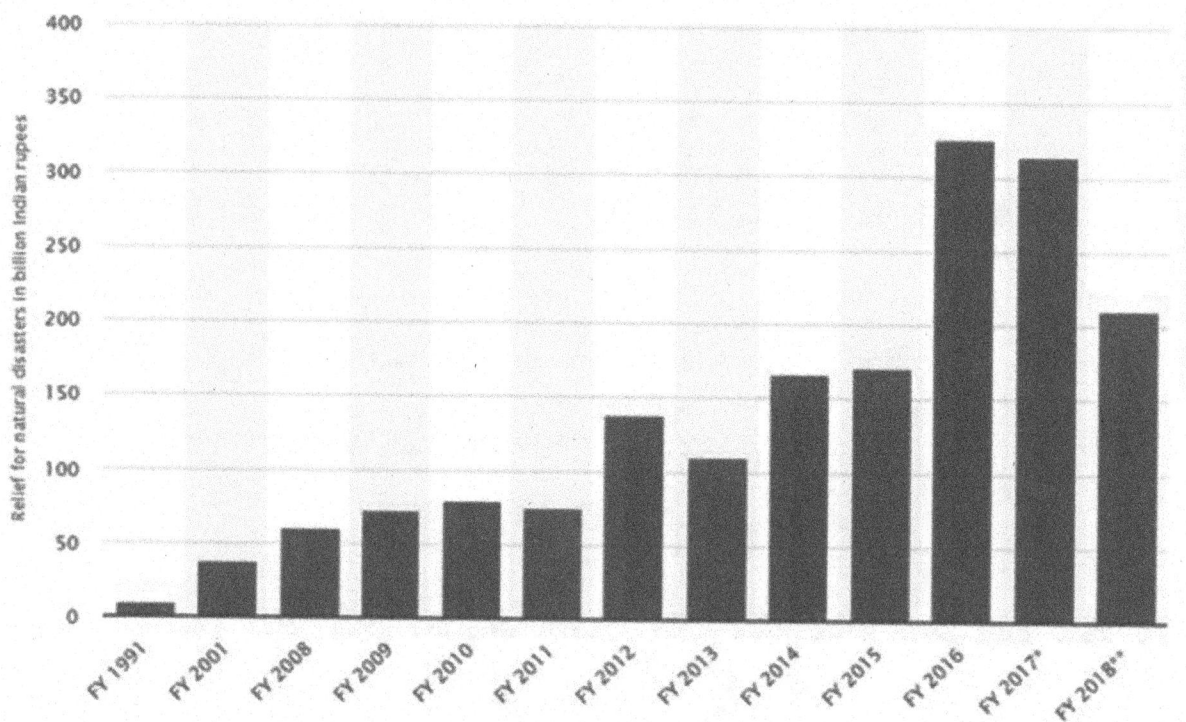

Fig. 29.14   Revenue Expenditure on Natural disaster relief of India's Central and state Governments FY 1991–2018 (in Billion INR)

Source: "Statista.com- Revenue Expenditure on Natural Disasters relief of India b/w 1991–2018" available data"

7. Discussion and Acknowledgment

India is at rapidly urbanizing phase, that requires substantial and well-planned infrastructure investments to meet growing resource demands and also tend to increase the overall exposure and addressing vulnerability together with exposure represent the gateway for risk reduction. Considering the environmental risk factors, future growth trajectories, patterns of development to support resilience planning, connect cities with necessary technical expertise and tools thus improving the states standards. But, the non-availability of data, periodicity issues and incomplete coverage of administrative data at local state levels have made measuring the progress virtually impossible. And the states with high populations also had high morality rate due to EWEs in the last two decades (as shown in the Fig. 29.15) despite a decrease in humanitarian and economic losses with better DM and adoption of upgraded technology. Although few states in India might have robust systems but many states don't and the SDM agencies can harness the data to devise specific strategies so the insights on prioritizing and improving action plans can be provided as there's a trend of sharp rise in EWEs. Thus, enhancing the radar observational network development particularly over the regions with large data gaps in the country and development of an advanced operational forecast system for multi-hazard early warning systems, improvement of integrated metrological services under the MoES scheme, also effectively incorporated ocean data both surface and sub-surface in operational cyclone

forecasting system in view of increasing global warning effect of rise of sea levels. However, an early weather warning awareness may save losses to human life but future climate predictions may help policymakers to plan risk mitigation infrastructure, planning land use, better infrastructure coverage for vulnerable populations.

Also, there are limitations observed in some states such as non-inclusion of indirect and delayed morality due to extreme weather, underreporting of deaths and low level of death registration and low density of observation network. In keeping with the discourse on mitigation for achievement of SDG13- Climate action, the 15th finance commission (XVFC) for 2021-2026 recommended setting up disaster mitigation funds at central and state levels, and from the Fig. 29.16, the performance of states to achievement of SDGs is understood with their score. In a departure from expenditure-based approach to assessing state wise allocation for the state disaster response and management fund XVFC introduces a

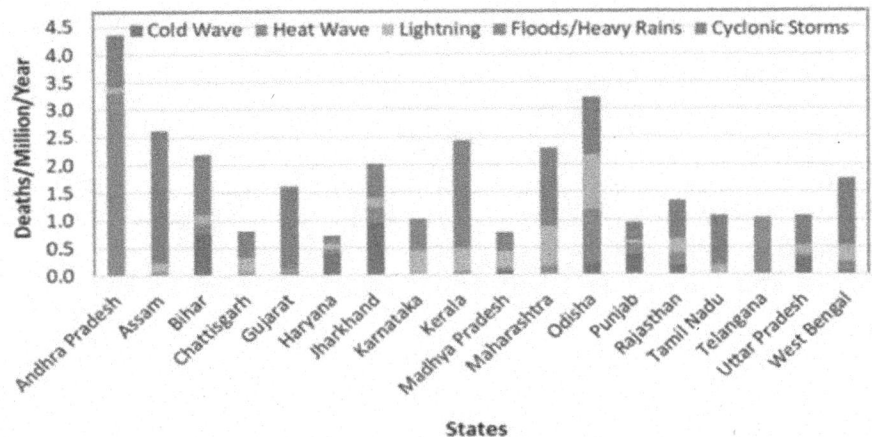

Fig. 29.15 State wise and EWE wise distribution of morality rates (Deaths/year/million population) during 2000–2019 with state more than 15 million population

Source: "An assessment of long-term changes in mortalities due to expreme weather events in India: A study of 50 years' data, 1970–2019 by M Rajeevan, the former secretary of the Ministry of Earth Sciences, and senor meteorologists Kamaljit Ray, R.K. Giri, S.S. Ray and A.P. Dimiri"

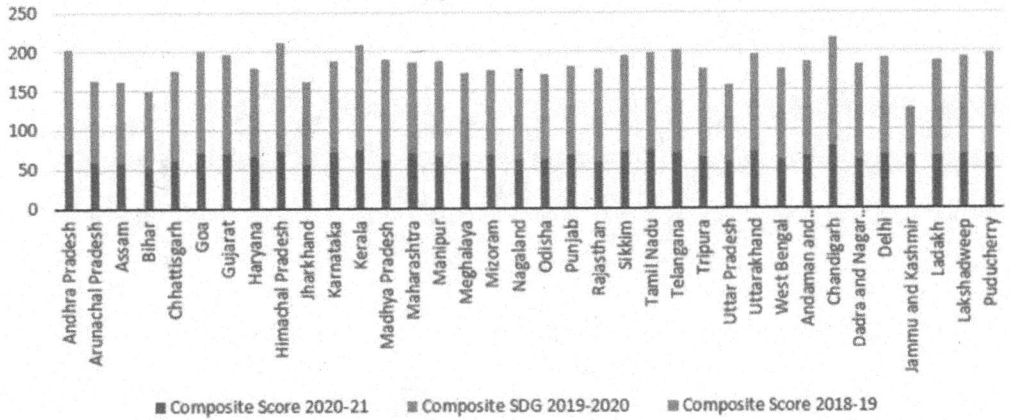

Fig. 29.16 SDG Data Index, performance of Indian States

Source: "SDG Data Index of India reports from 2018–2021- and explore into single chart"

methodology that reflects the risk and vulnerability profile for each state and recommended the corpus of ₹1,60,153 crore for State DM in which union share is ₹1,22,601 crores and states share is ₹37,552 crores. Out of the total given to states, 20% of that has to be segregated as state disaster mitigation and the rest to be spent as per guidelines to developed by MHA such that the fund will bolster the states ongoing efforts to scaleup climate resilient infrastructure. And by observing the Fig. 29.17, it is estimated that, each state expenditure varies with type of projects implemented and related and that leading to high differences each year. By the end of 2020, 15 states were Front runners and 13 states were performers and the aspirants are completely transformed with new Indian strategies.

A state economic growth can be estimated through variables like infrastructure development, social sector expenditure-Financial inclusion (which seems to be important drives of growth) and urbanization (seems to have negative effect of growth). While investment data at the state level are not available to examine the influence of growth at state level. The analysis of determines of interstate GSDP growth has been under research area in India.

But, the development sector (Social, capital outlay) and non-development sectors (pensions, loans, etc.,) are compared among the states revenues, it is clear that the development brings sustainability of the state but also exposes and creates unidentified vulnerabilities which leads to create more unknown risk in the society. Fig. 29.18, gives the total outlook of the states that spent for developmet of their standards. Wihtin the year 2017 to 2020, the expenditure increaased annually in all the respective states. But the point to be observed are, are there improvement in standards of public too. For example, the unemployment rate, awareness in societies, no.of sustainable industries increase, growth of different sectors, decrease inindustrial and administration accidents, mortality rate, data usage, enterpenuership, etc. similarily, when the development expenditure of states with their GSDP

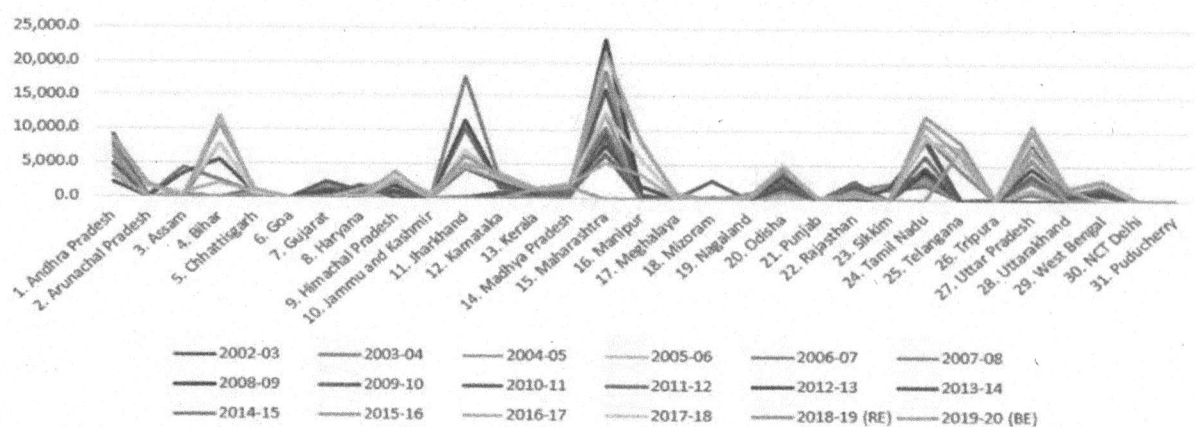

Fig. 29.17 Expenditure on Operations and maintenance of states, 2002–2020

Source: "Annual Budget reports of Indian states from Ministry of Home affairs, Gov. of India, explored into single chart"

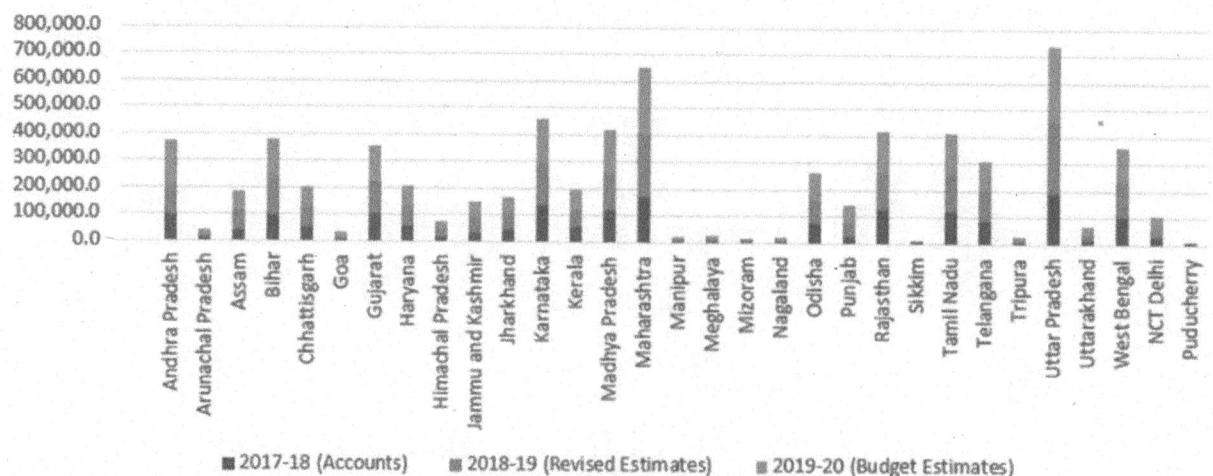

Fig. 29.18 Development Expenditure of the states

Source: "Annual Budget reports of Indian states from Ministry of Home affairs, Gov. of India, explored into single chart"

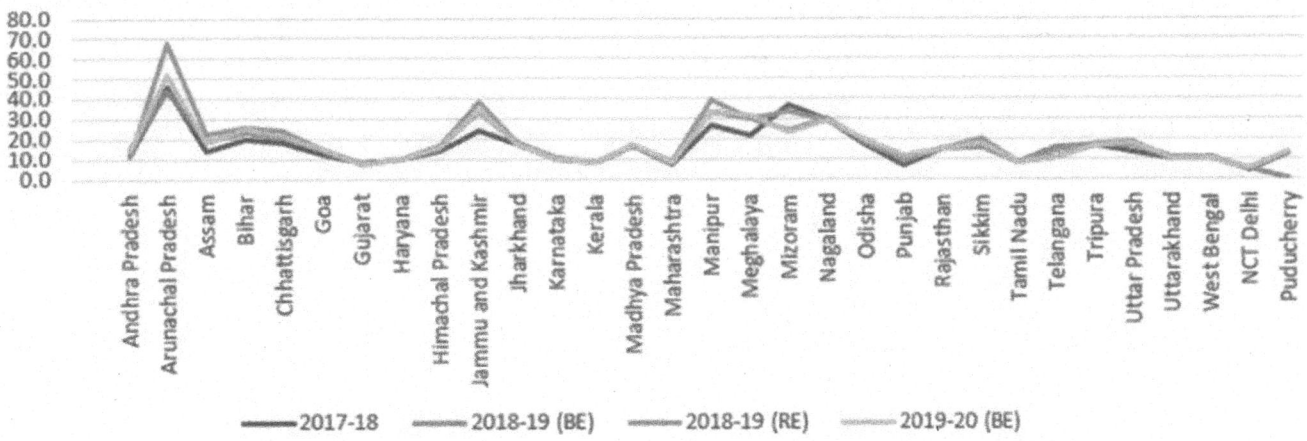

Fig. 29.19 Development Expenditure of states with % of GSDP, 2017–2020

are compared and observed, as in the Fig. 29.19, it is understood that the pandamic has caused lot of distress in society but, the rate of distress caused isn't to be bothersome as the overall development between 2017-2020 has led to the financial sustainbility seen through acheivemnt of SDGs as most of the Indian states are best performers. And then, when the Non-developmetn sectors of indian states are compared, that is Fig. 29.20, we can find that the loans payment, pension given for various reasons, taxation etc have increased drastically in comparision to 2017-2020.

There are notable vacancies in key depatments such as, health, schools, agriculture extensions, skilled workers ect,. That is low developmet cycle that create a under development tag of the respective area are to be worked out well. And when the Fig. 29.21 is prepared, the social sector (expenditure of stares

compared to percentage of GSDP, these were interconnected to the above mentionaed factors to development criteria. And from Fig. 29.22, the comparisionis made between capital outlay with GSDP, a similar pattern is found same as that of in overall Development expenditure of a state acheiveed to outrun its position among other states and improvise in all segments. And, from the analysis of both development and non-development sectors of states, it is concluded that, the unplanned and sustandard infrastructure combined with poor implementation of planning, relief and rehaibitation measures increase the human, physical and economic losses sustained after a disaster. While economically stronger sections of society will have more resileince in bouncing back to near normalcy while taking care of weaker section in the society to recover fast.

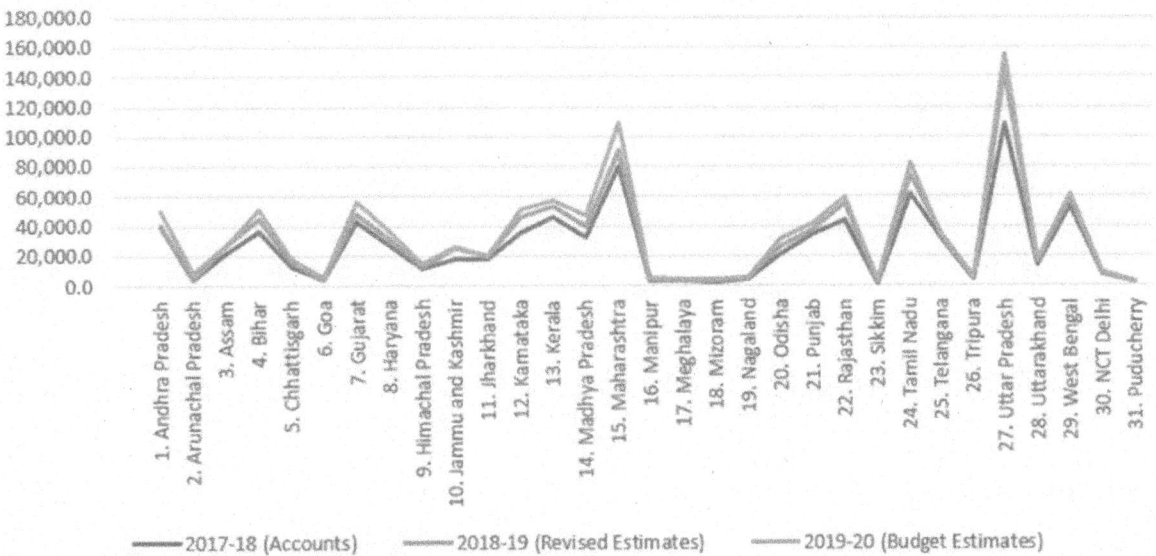

Fig. 29.20 Non-Development Expenditure of State, 2017–2020

Source: "Annual Budget reports of Indian states from Ministry of Home affairs, Gov. of India, explored into single chart"

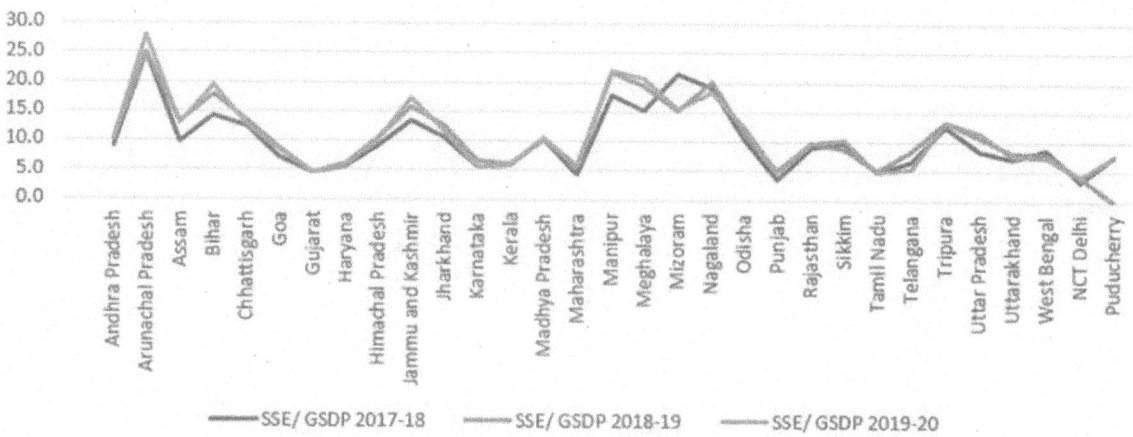

Fig. 29.21 Development expenditure-Social Sector Expenditure with % of GSDP

Source: "Annual Budget reports of Indian states from Ministry of Home affairs, Gov. of India, explored into single chart"

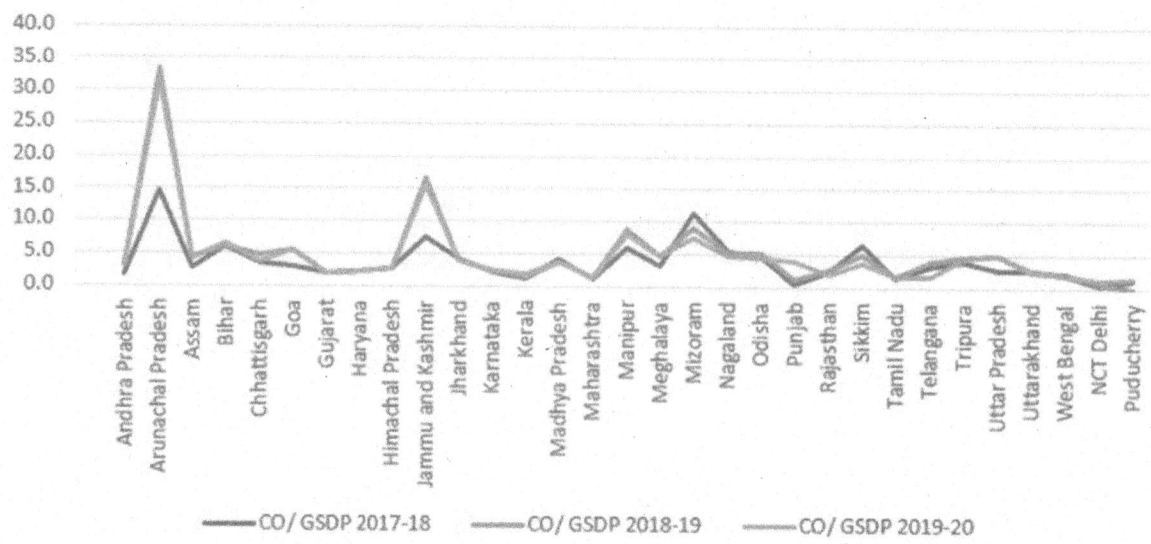

Fig. 29.22 Development Expenditure-Capital Outlay with % of GSDP

Source: "Annual Budget reports of Indian states from Ministry of Home affairs, Gov. of India, explored into single chart"

From various observations made in this paper, India has covered 13 goals- 39 Targets- 62 Indicators in the year 2018-19 and by the year 2019-20, 17 SD goals- 54 Targets- 100 Indicators and by the year 2020-21 the SDG reached to 17 goals-70 targets and 115 indicators from the NITI Aayog efforts which has intensive collaborations with UN & UNDP agencies, MoSPI, State govt's and also other ministries. With this index, it is understood how well India has put its efforts in achieving the SDGs. Such that the economy, infrastructure, agriculture, education, health care, law & order, inclusive development, governance, Entrepreneurship, tourism, environment, cleanliness which are the observed factors to rank the state's development and competitive growth. Also Smart cities are one source to build India as a resilient country and is achieved by following the measures for resilience, such as organize for disaster resilience, identify, understand and use current and future risk scenarios,

by strengthening financial capacity, by pursuing the resilient urban development and design, also safeguard the natural buffers to enhance the protective functions offered by natural ecosystems, strengthening institutional capacity, increase infrastructure, ensure effective preparedness and disaster response, also expedite the recovery and build back better. The point to be considered is that identifying the risks and emphasizing strategies for future climate change scenarios will help in gaining investors by also providing the clear picture of the costs and benefits of the investment decision making. It is understood that, investing in more resilient infrastructure can provided net benefit in low- and middle-income countries of $4.2trillion with $4 in benefit for each $1 invested. From life lines report, though not discussed in this paper, the investments as said above can improve the quality of essential services and thus contributing to more resilient and prosperous societies. However, being a developing nation- India lack the expertise, tools & instrument to factor the potential impacts of disasters into their investment's decisions. As discussed in above topics, the management of local budget is to be favored firstly such that it can help in maintain the central funds regarding providing the right help at right time. But, the local govt has always focused on addressing immediate issues, spend money on political favorable schemes than the overall development schemes. Same goes with central governance. Though various considerable steps been taken by center govt, for example developing a national database for various elements including the portal for collecting information on migrant and other kinds of workers/labor, skilled and unskilled people in detail in various sectors. Also produced various initiatives for increasing the entrepreneurship in the country, encouraging different innovations, visions and missions for furthermore gaining in all constituents. This can be seen from the development and non-development figures.

And when a country rebuilds stronger, faster, and more inclusively after disasters, they can reduce the impact on people livelihood and wellbeing as much as potential cutting global average losses, though the impacts of EWEs are unequal in different parts of the country due to variation in vulnerability which has to followed up to local levels. As discussed here, as a measure, in India the natural ecosystems are under stress and declined, around 10% wildlife threatened with extinction-agriculture biodiversity declined over 90%, around half the water bodies are polluted beyond drinking and even agriculture use, also 2/3rd land is degraded to various levels of sub optimal productivity, and air pollution in several cities is among the world's worst and modern wastes such as chemical, electrical are being produced beyond our capacity to manage and recycle. In other terms, the reduction measure to control the impact of an uncontrollable event are still in developing stage and are to be identified though the development steps can be seen from afar.

8. Conclusion

Thus, when Indian ranks in global platform are verified, the overall development of the country in respective factors or observation are understood. This giving the precise image where and what required to be concentrated in the future to standout in our mark. Further, the challenges that are observed in various stages for achieving our goals are discussed with their countermeasures. Also, by detailed observations of states progress in several indicators, underlying driver of risk are compared, remarked and explained about suitable and unrequired matters of concern and how the states income interconnected with the attainment of resilience to DR. also, how can the funding increased, obtain investments in various sectors can be acquired is discussed relatively with the topic

verified along with needs and functionality and about the need of additional focus in different elements and if attained what can be procured. Also, how the development of private sector can facilitate investments and how multilateral grants available for climate change related activities. The scope of development of India has high potential for achieving rapid boost to support overall development as the work age population outweighs the dependents with 68.5% of the total population and through this the associated investment in economy is gained and the availability of employment opportunities can be increased bringing the economic benefits such that the trajectory formed represents a significant challenge of the country to Surpass other nations is all segments in the upcoming decades. But, the levels of investment in both public and private sectors are falling short annually, as the availability of working people are also decreased as the government are feeding the needy in the name of effortless reduction of poverty instead of putting efforts in improving employment for all who can work to earn. This non-availability of worker class may lead to disruption in the growth and at one extent this balance might collapse giving greater impact which are hard to observe.

REFERENCES

1. Global risk index reports from 2011 to 2020, weforum.org
2. Human cost of disasters 2000-2019, report from UNDRR
3. Economic losses, poverty & disaster, 1998-2017 report by UNISDR
4. Making cities resilient report from UNDRR i.e., mcr2030.undrr.org
5. SDG index and dashboard reports from 2015 to 2020 of India, from niti.gov.in i.e., NITI Aayog, govt. of India
6. Infrastructureindia.gov.in for project development reports on India in various categories
7. Worldbank.org, for statistical reports of India for Statistical performance indicators as shown in fig:10 between 2016 to 2019
8. Annual budget reports of Indian states from 2000 to 2019, by Ministry of Home Affairs and also Planning commission of India for Data Reports, from Govt. of India, mha.gov.in
9. Macrotrends.net-economy-GDP growth and countries ranks under World bank reports for GDP growth rate of India between 2005 to 2020
10. Statista.com for the reports on Expenditure on natural disaster relief of India, by Indian govt.
11. An assessment of long-term changes in mortalities due to extreme weather events in India: A study of 50 years' data, 1970–2019 by M Rajeevan, the former secretary of the Ministry of Earth Sciences, and senior meteorologists Kamaljit Ray, R.K. Giri, S.S. Ray and A.P. Dimri
12. Economic survey reports from 2016 to 2020 by Ministry of Finance, Dept of Economic Affairs, Govt. of India, indiabudget.gov.in

13. INFORM Severity index of all counties and India of 2019 & 2020

14. The Global competitiveness reports from 2017 to 2020, weforum.org

15. How to make cities more resilient, A handbook for Local Government Leaders for Global Campaign 2010-2020, UNISDR

16. Strategic approach to capacity development for implementation of Sendai Framework for Disaster Risk Reduction, A Concise Guide

17. Local government powers for disaster risk reduction, a study on local level authority and capacity for resilience,2017, UNISDR

18. Country profile of India, CDRI

19. Promoting disaster risk resilience technologies and innovations in India, by Intellecap

20. Community resilience: The heart of climate action, India Climate collaborative, by Suranjana Gupta, 2020

21. Disaster risk reduction in India, status reports, UNDRR & ADPC

22. India VNR 2020 report, Decade of action, taking SDGs from global to local by NITI Aayog, 2020

23. Disaster risk management status report, towards identifying national and local priorities for the implementation of Sendai framework for DRR, Ministry of home affairs, Govt. of India

24. A study 'Measuring disaster risks and resilience at sub-national level in India, by Dr. P. G. Dhar Chakraborthy" etc.,

Multi-player Game-based Algorithm Using Set Partitioning for Resource Allocation During Natural Disaster Response

Rudrashis Majumder

Ph.D. Student, Department of Aerospace Engineering,
Indian Institute of Science, Bangalore
rudrashism@iisc.ac.in

Debasish Ghose

Professor, Department of Aerospace Engineering,
Indian Institute of Science, Bangalore
dghose@iisc.ac.in

Abstract

In the event of multiple emergencies co-occurring due to a natural disaster, it is crucial to allocate different necessary resources to the emergency locations. Resource allocation becomes a non-trivial job for the disaster management authority, especially when the available resources are insufficient to satisfy all the emergency locations at a time. In our present work, a multi-event crisis management system to be used by the authority is proposed based on a two-player non-cooperative, strategic game model. In the proposed system, each emergency event occurring in separate locations is treated as a player in the game, which is assumed to compete with other disaster-affected locations for multiple resources available in limited quantities. Based on a general cost function model, each player incurs a non-monetary cost for obtaining resources from the resource locations. The solution of the resource allocation problem is derived using the Nash equilibrium-based optimization methodology. The existence of multiple Nash equilibria can be handled by using the concept of payoff dominance. If there are more than two players in need of resources, the set of players are partitioned into subsets such that no subset contains more than two players, and then the basic two-player game is used to find the allocation within each subset. A numerical example is presented to show the applicability of the algorithm.

Keywords: Disaster response; Resource allocation; Decision Support System; Game theory; Nash equilibrium; Multiplayer game

1. Introduction

Natural disasters like floods, cyclones, etc., cause huge destruction and casualties. In the post-disaster phase, various response activities are to be initiated to minimize the impact of the disaster and regain normalcy. These include allocation of critical resources, survivor detection, and rescue, reconstruction of the damaged infrastructures, etc. However, a lack of efficient decision-making in the response phase may delay the recovery of the disaster-affected locations. To automate the decision-making process after a disaster, an intelligent decision support system (DSS) is of utmost importance. Past literature indicates the interest of the disaster-research communities in building effective DSS. An intelligent DSS tool to deal with imperfect information after a disaster is discussed in (Vitoriano et al., 2015). An elaborated overview of emergency DSS and the construction of DSS are given in (Zhou et al., 2018). The paper (Newman et al., 2017) provides a detailed review of DSS natural hazard risk reduction. In (Aifadopoulou et al., 2018), a web-based DSS is developed based on geographical information systems (GIS) to manage transport networks and infrastructures. Zamanifar and Hartmann (2021) present a systematic case study to suggest decision attributes for disaster recovery and planning of transportation networks. Several other papers like (Wallace and De Balogh, 1985; Horita and de Albuquerque, 2013; Sati, 2015; Liashenko et al., 2019; Brooks et al., 2016; Cavdur and Sebatli, 2019) can be referred to get insights about disaster DSS. Decision-making associated with all the phases of disaster management, i.e., prevention, preparedness, response, and recovery, can be integrated into DSS software. However, in this paper, we mainly focus on developing DSS systems dedicated to the response stages of disaster management, especially for resource allocation activity.

Once the post-disaster situation is recognized as a potential crisis, disaster management authority starts allocation and distribution of resources using the concept of supply chain management (Wang et al., 2016; Dubey et al., 2019). Using optimization concepts in supply chain networks has become an interesting topic of concern in disaster research (Huang et al., 2015; Hu and Sheng, 2015; Bayram, 2016; Xu et al., 2019). In (Özdamar et al., 2004), a mathematical model integrates multi-commodity network flow and vehicle routing problems. Solving resource allocation and scheduling problems with a set of various heuristic algorithms is given in (Wex et al., 2014). In (Ferrer et al., 2018), multi-criteria optimization for last-mile resource distributions is discussed. Allocation of resources to mitigate simultaneous disaster is done using stochastic optimization in (Doan and Shaw, 2019). (Burkart et al., 2017) talk about the multi-object location-routing problem to reduce the unserved demand of the crisis locations. In (Baidya and Bera, 2019) introduces a multi-object multistage transportation network in a fuzzy-stochastic environment. The authors in (Zheng et al., 2015) introduce an application of evolutionary optimization for disaster relief operations.

Interaction between multiple government and private stakeholders is required for the successful implementation of disaster responses. This makes the game theory a useful tool for disaster management. The use of game-based models in disaster management is reported in many pieces of literature like (Eid et al., 2015; Gao et al., 2018; Lai et al., 2015). (Usta et al., 2018; Ergün et al., 2019) use cooperative game for various emergency logistic planning. More articles are available in the detailed review (Seaberg et al., 2017). (Fragkos et al., 2019) introduce multi-agent disaster management for UAV-based public safety systems. This non-cooperative game, being a potential game, ensures the existence of the pure strategy Nash equilibrium (PSNE) system. In (Yang and Xu, 2012), a sequential game is formulated between the decision-maker and emergency locations. In (Gupta and Ranganathan, 2006; Ranganathan et al., 2007), resource scheduling problems are expressed as a non-cooperative game, and the Nash

equilibrium of the game is approximated by a combinatorial algorithm. (Wang et al., 2009) use ant-colony optimization (ACO) to solve a similar problem. The paper (Nagurney et al., 2016) also uses the concept of Nash equilibrium in post-disaster relief work.

In (Majumder et al., 2019a), the preliminary formulation of a resource allocation problem to allocate indivisible resources among disaster locations is discussed using a basic non-cooperative game. Authors of that paper extend their work in (Majumder et al., 2019b) to prove the existence of PSNEs in that game model proposed for indivisible resource allocation. However, both of these papers focus on a two-player game where each player incurs a non-monetary cost for possible allocations of resources, and Nash equilibria provide a socially acceptable solution to the game. In this paper, the previous work in (Majumder et al., 2019a,b) is further extended to address the resource allocation problem for a general n-player situation. The main contribution of the present paper is that here we use set partitioning to divide all players into subgroups, each containing two players. We consider a numerical example where indivisible resources are needed by multiple disaster locations at the same time instant. Based on the demand of the players and the availability of the required resources, the final allocation is decided by the authority according to the Nash equilibrium of the non-cooperative game. This method provides a valuable insight into a fair and efficient strategy for the distribution of resources among the players in a resource-constrained environment.

The rest of this paper is organized as follows. Section 2 describes the importance of an automated DSS for resource allocation. The game-theoretic formulation is explained in Section 3. In Section 4, the extension of the game-theoretic model is described for multi-player $n > 2$ involvement. A detailed example is presented in Section 5 with numerical results. In Section 6, we discuss our findings briefly. Section 7 concludes the paper.

2. Resource Allocation Problem

The geographical properties of an area make it prone to different natural disasters like floods, cyclones, earthquakes, etc. The occurrence of a natural disaster creates a long-term impact on humanity, society, and the economy of the place. To mitigate the devastation caused by any disaster, immediate measures are to be adopted by the disaster management authority. Resource allocation stands as one of the primary post-disaster activities to reduce casualties and damage. In this phase, inhabitants of the disaster-affected area are supported by providing various general and critical resources. Ample availability of resources helps the authority to satisfy all the disaster locations fully. However, in a realistic scenario, resources can be insufficient to fulfill the demands of the locations at the same time. In such situations, an automated, fair, and efficient resource allocation methodology should be devised to nullify the effect of possible bias in manual decision-making.

After a natural disaster occurs, strategic relation between multiple government and private agencies is essential for achieving effective disaster response. Since game-theoretic concepts focus on the strategic interactions between rational agents, the application of game theory to build disaster response models is justified. The development of game-theoretic models to facilitate resource allocation mainly construct a game-like situation, where different agents are players with their respective payoff or cost structures. Analyzing such an algorithm helps in a detailed understanding of optimal resource allocation strategies in a limited resource condition. The use of the game algorithm by the authority helps to generate an automated decision-making framework for resource allocation, which removes the bias associated with decisions made by human beings.

3. Game Formulation and Nash Solution

3.1 Non-cooperative Game

Game theory is the analysis of strategic exchanges between a number of rational and intelligent decision-makers. In the case of non-cooperative games, players will try to improve their utility or payoff (or reduce the cost incurred by them) individually. In this paper, we use a non-cooperative, strategic form game model for two players. These types of games are also called matrix games, and we represent these types of games through the use of payoff or cost matrices.

A strategic game can be represented as $G = N, (S_i)_{\forall i \in N}, (U_i)_{\forall i \in N}$ where

1. $N = \{1, 2, ..., n\}$ is a set of players
2. $S_1, S_2, ..., S_n$ are the strategy sets of the players $i = \{1, 2, ..., n\}$ respectively
3. $U_i : S_1 \times S_2 \times ... \times S_n \to \mathbb{R}$ for $i = 1, 2, ..., n$ are called the utility functions or cost functions of the players.

3.2 Pure Strategy Nash Equilibrium (PSNE)

Given a strategic game $G = \langle N, (S_i), (C_i) \rangle$, a strategy profile $s^* = (s_1{}^*, s_2{}^*, ..., s_n{}^*)$ is called a pure startegy Nash equilibrium (PSNE) of game G if unilateral deviation from the strategy s^* is not beneficial for player i. Mathematically,

$$C_i(s_i{}^*, s_{-i}^*) \le C_i(s_i, s_{-i}^*), \ \forall s_i \in S_i, \ \forall i \in N \qquad (1)$$

where the actions of the players other than the ith player are denoted as s_{-i}. In (1), the function C denotes the cost function and the players want to minimize the cost incurred by them.

3.3 Game Model for Resource Allocation

In our present resource allocation framework, the disaster management authority uses the proposed algorithm assuming the disaster locations as players. With a set of n players or locations, limited indivisible resources are to be distributed in a fair approach. The possible number of resource units allocated to the players are treated as the set of strategies of the game. The cost function of the game C is defined as the sum of four additive components which capture the cost charged on the players in different situations.

Let A be the availability of the required resources. After getting hit by the natural disaster, each player or location raises a demand d_i (where $i \in N$) of that particular resource. In general, the demand is obtained from various ground parameters associated with the locations and the severity of the disaster. The players convey their demands to the authority. In a resource-constrained environment, $A < \sum_{i=1}^{n} d_i$. The amount of resource units allocated to the ith player P_i is denoted as a_i. Since an insufficient resource can not satisfy all the players together, a non-cooperative game-like setup is created by the authority treating different a_i as the possible strategies of the players. The required resource being indivisible, there is a discrete set of allocation strategies for each player where $0 \le a_i \le d_i$. Based on the results given by the game-theoretic algorithm, the authority distributes the resources among the players.

In our present setup, we use the cost function for a simple two-player game explained in our previous work (Majumder et al., 2019a). In another work (Majumder et al., 2019b), we have shown that the cost function defined in (2) has a nice property of existence of pure strategy Nash equilibrium (PSNE).

$$\frac{d_i - a_i}{d_i} + \frac{d_i - a_i}{d_i} + \frac{g(d_{-i}, A, a_i)}{d_{-i}} + h(A, a_i, a_{-i}) \frac{\dfrac{a_i}{d_i}}{\dfrac{ai}{d_i} + \dfrac{a_{-i}}{d_{-i}}} \qquad (2)$$

where, the functions $f(.)$, $g(.)$, and $h(.)$ are defined as follows:

$$f(x, y, z) = \begin{cases} x - y - z & \text{if } x - y - z \ge 0 \\ 0 & \text{otherwise} \end{cases} \qquad (3)$$

$$g(x, y, z) = \begin{cases} x - y + z & \text{if } x - y + z \ge 0 \\ 0 & \text{otherwise} \end{cases} \qquad (4)$$

$$h(x, y, z) = \begin{cases} y + z - x & \text{if } x - y - z \le 0 \\ 0 & \text{otherwise} \end{cases} \qquad (5)$$

When the final allocation leaves behind a set of unused resources even during emergencies, the cost function (2) imposes an under-utilization cost on the players. This penalty is denoted by the first component of (2) which is nonzero whenever the total number of resource units allocated to the players is less than the availability. The second term corresponds to the dissatisfaction due to the player's own choice, which penalizes the player when the allocation a_i is less than d_i. The third term indicates how much restriction one player puts on the other player. This cost is nonzero when the allocation to P_i does not restrict the other player P_{-i} to satisfy its demand d_{-i}. The fourth term penalizes the conflict situation on the resource availability created by two players. This term becomes nonzero if the total number of units requested by the players exceeds the availability. The fourth term tries to fairly allocate the responsibility of conflict between players. The cost function provides the elements of the game matrices for the non-cooperative game. The Nash equilibrium, being a socially agreeable outcome for non-cooperative games, serves here as the solution for the resource allocation problem. This solution $a^* = (a_i^*, a_{-i}^*)$ is implemented by the authority on the two players, and resources are distributed accordingly. The existence of PSNE for the game using (2) is ensured in case of indivisible resource and two-players scenario by (Majumder et al., 2019b). Getting the PSNEs in this kind of problem makes the implementation of the solution straight-forward compared to mixed strategy Nash equilibrium. However, existence of more than one PSNE may be tricky to handle. There are several selection criteria which can be used to select a particular PSNE from a set of multiple PSNEs. In the following subsection 3.4, we introduce an importance concept to avoid the situation of multiple PSNEs.

Note that the cost defined by (2) is for a two-player game. The extension of this framework to a generalized n-player game is explained in Section 4.

3.4 Payoff Dominance: Selection of Nash Equilibria

In the case of non-cooperative games, PSNE is an action profile which has the feature that no single player can obtain a higher payoff (or smaller cost) by unilateral deviation from this profile. If solving this game leads to multiple PSNEs, then we have to choose one PSNE out of the set for implementing as the allocation vector. We use the property of payoff dominance to select a unique PSNE. The matrix below shows a two player-two strategy game matrix whose elements represents the costs charged on the players. Player P_1 is the row player who chooses between rows or strategies S_{11} and S_{12}. Similarly, P_2 is the column player choosing strategies S_{21} and S_{22}.

	S_{21}	S_{22}
S_{11}	**W, w**	Y, x
S_{12}	X, y	**Z, z**

Let us assume that the above game has two PSNE: (S_{11}, S_{21}) and (S_{12}, S_{22}). Their corresponding costs are (W, w) and (Z, z). If $W \leq Z$ and $w \leq z$ and at least one equality is strict then we say that the PSNE (S_{11}, S_{21}) is payoff dominant (Harsanyi and Selten, 1988). Otherwise, (S_{12}, S_{22}) is payoff dominant.

4. Multiplayer Game Solution from Two-Player Game Solution

The previous section explains the two-player game model for resource allocation. When there are only two disaster locations, the strategic game with cost function (2) is capable of distributing resources among the players. However, when there are more than two players, the problem becomes more complicated. In general, multi-player games are not easy to handle, and the optimal solution is not assured to exist always. To tackle this issue, we extend the two-player game to a multi-player game by using the concept of set partitioning.

If the set of players be $N = 1, ..., n$ and $n > 2$, then the set is partitioned into two groups of players and considered as two different players in (2). In the first stage, the game algorithm is executed on these two groups, and primary allocation vectors are derived. If these groups contain more than two players, then again, in the second stage, the partitioning is done to find the subgroups, and the primary allocation is taken as the availability to the primary groups. In this way, the partitioning and allocation are done at different stages of smaller subgroups recursively and continues until each subgroup contains only two players.

Figure 30.1 explains the procedure. As an example, if $n = 5$, then in the first stage of partitioning, two groups are created. Let us assume that one group G_1 has two players while the other group G_2 has three players. The first stage allocation to group G_j, $(j = 1, 2)$ becomes the availability of resources for the players of the group in the second stage allocation. Clearly, in the second stage, G_1 contains only two players, and the allocation can be done straight-ways. In the case of G_2, another partitioning is required where the first subgroup SG_1 gets two players and the second subgroup SG_2 has only one player. Again the allocation is carried out in the subgroups.

The partitioning of the players can be done based on various ground parameters of concern. As an example, emergency sites situated at the same province can be taken together in one subgroup. Other factors like the severity of the disasters, different geographical identities (near river banks or coastal area) can also help in deciding the approach for partitioning. However, any arbitrary partitioning is also good for this algorithm to be executed. Since the areas affected by disaster are countable, the complexity issues are not significant for this extension of two-player game to n-player cases. The applicability of the algorithm is explained numerically in the

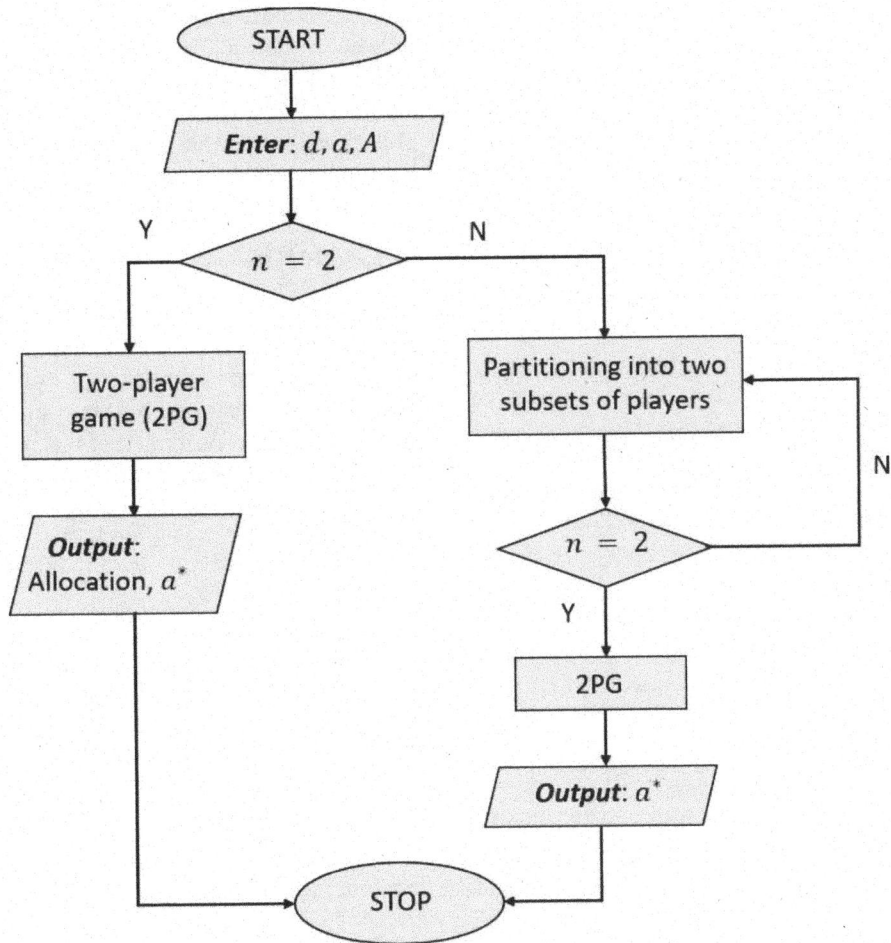

Fig. 30.1 Flowchart for multi-player game

next section. It should, however, be noted that the solution so obtained may not be the same as in the case if the game has been solved as an *n*-player game directly. Hence, the solutions obtained are locally two-player optimal solutions but not necessarily n-player optimal. One must also keep in mind that the overall *n*-player game many not have a pure strategy Nash equilibrium solution or even if it does have a solution, it may be computationally intractable. On the other hand, the two-player game always provides a solution.

5. Numerical Results

In this section, we take an example with numerical values to describe the application of the extended game-theoretic algorithm in order to solve a resource allocation problem. We consider $n = 5$, and a limited amount of indivisible resources are to be distributed among these five disaster locations. Let the demand of the locations be $d = [3, 4, 6, 7, 10]$ with the total demand being $\sum_i d_i = 30$, raised simultaneously. If the

availability $A = \sum_i d_i$, then all the disaster locations or players can be fully satisfied with respect to their demand. However, in a realistic scenario, the availability can be less than the total demand of the players making the allocation of resources a non-trivial problem. In this situation, first, the set of players is partitioned in the approach mentioned in Section 4. Here we assume that $A = 27$. Table 30.1 explains the allocation of resources with the mentioned demand vector and availability.

Table 30.1 Resource allocation using set partitioning

Sl. No.	Players	d	P_I	d_I	A_I	P_{II}	A_{II}	A_{III}	a^*
1	L_1	3	L_1			L_1		3	3
2	L_2	4	L_2	13	13	L_2	7	4	4
3	L_3	6	L_3			L_3	6		6
4	L_4	7	L_4	17	14	L_4	7		7
5	L_5	10	L_5			L_5	7		7

In Table 30.1, the players are enlisted serially based on the time when they raise demands for resources. In the first phase of partitioning P_I, players L_1, L_2, and L_3 are taken in the first group G_1. Similarly, L_4 and L_5 are taken in the second group G_2. Now, G_1 and G_2 are considered as two players with total demands of 13 and 17, respectively, and the total availability is $A = 27$. In the first phase of allocation A_I using the two-players game, the group G_1 gets 13 units of the required resource while G_2 gets 14 units of resource. Now, there are only two players in G_2 and 14 resources are available for them. Hence, our two-player game model can be implemented in it to find the final allocations of L_4 and L_5 without further partitioning of group G_2. By doing this, both L_4 and L_5 gets 7 resource units in the second phase allocation A_{II}. However, since G_1 contains three players, it needs further partitioning into subgroup SG_1 having L_1 and L_2, and subgroup SG_2 contains only one player, L_3. Available resources for G_1 be 13 in number. In A_{II}, SG_1 gets 7 resource units whereas L_3 (or SG_2) gets 6. Now, in the third phase allocation A_{III} in SG_1, L_1 and L_2 get 3 and 4 units, respectively. Hence the final allocation becomes $a^* = [3, 4, 6, 7, 7]$ and $\sum_i a_i^* = A$. However, it can be clearly understood that different partitioning policy may give rise to different a^*.

6. Discussions

The main objective of the paper is to allocate indivisible resources among several disaster locations when the total availability of resources does not suffice the demand of the disaster locations together at a time. In our previous work, we proposed a non-cooperative game-based framework for allocating resources among two players. However, in reality, there can be any finite number of disaster locations for which a two-player game model is not sufficient. In our present work, we try to extrapolate our work for a general scenario. Section 4 and 5 demonstrates how the cost function (2) for a two-player game can be extended to find the solutions for a general n-player ($n > 2$) situation. The Nash equilibrium is the best strategy for each player when the other players are also taking their best strategies. The existence of multiple Nash equilibria can be handled by the concept of payoff dominance, as explained in (Majumder et al., 2019a,b). The solutions considered in Section 5 are payoff dominant on the other possible solutions.

However, one important point to note is that the set partitioning concept used to extend the two-player game for multiplayer scenarios provides only a sub-optimal solution. A different policy involved in set partitioning will lead to different final allocations a^*. However, in any of the partitioning choices, the solution obtained will be bound by the cost components, e.g., under-utilization, dissatisfaction,

restriction on the other player, and the availability constraint. Hence, in the final allocation, there will be neither under-utilization and nor conflict, and all the resources available at the time of allocation will be distributed among the players. This research can be further improved to identify the best partitioning rule in terms of fairness and optimality.

7. Conclusions

In a post-disaster environment, the resources can be available in a limited quantity. Hence, one player's choice has a direct impact on the choices made by the other players. The players compete for a near-optimal and fair allocation of resource units. The main contribution of this paper is to find a solution to a resource allocation problem using multiplayer game. From a two-player game-based solution proposed earlier, we extend our work to solve multiplayer games by partitioning the set of players. This partitioning is continued until each subset of the players contains no more than two players. Then we use the two-player game model on all the subsets to find the final allocation of limited individual resources. The Nash equilibrium-based optimization is implemented as it provides a socially agreeable allocation to all the players. The entire idea has been explained by using an example where indivisible resources are distributed among several disaster locations. The results produced in this paper show that in a resource-constrained situation, the proposed game-theoretic algorithm for n-players can provide a potential and efficient solution for resource allocation. In the future, we plan to extend our research further to find a set partitioning rule which can provide a better solution to optimize the final allocations. The possible ways to implement multiplayer games for resource allocation other than set partitioning will also be investigated.

References

1. Aifadopoulou, G., Chaniotakis, E., Stamos, I., Mamarikas, S., and Mitsakis, E. (2018). An intelligent decision support system for managing natural and man-made disasters. *International Journal of Decision Support Systems*, 3(1–2): 91–105.
2. Baidya, A. and Bera, U. K. (2019). New model for addressing supply chain and transport safety for disaster relief operations. *Annals of Operations Research*, 283(1–2): 33–69.
3. Bayram, V. (2016). Optimization models for large scale network evacuation planning and management: A literature review. *Surveys in Operations Research and Management Science*, 21(2): 63–84.
4. Brooks, B., Curnin, S., and Bearman, C. (2016). An assessment of the opportunities to improve strategic decision-making in emergency and disaster management. *Australian Journal of Emergency Management*, 31(4): 38–43.
5. Burkart, C., Nolz, P. C., and Gutjahr, W. J. (2017). Modelling

beneficiaries' choice in disaster relief logistics. *Annals of Operations Research*, 256(1): 41–61.

6. Cavdur, F. and Sebatli, A. (2019). A decision support tool for allocating temporary-disaster-response facilities. *Decision Support Systems*, 127: 113145.

7. Doan, X. V. and Shaw, D. (2019). Resource allocation when planning for simultaneous disasters. *European Journal of Operational Research*, 274(2): 687–709.

8. Dubey, R., Gunasekaran, A., and Papadopoulos, T. (2019). Disaster relief operations: Past, present and future. *Annals of Operations Research*, 283(1–2): 1–8.

9. Eid, M. S., El-Adaway, I. H., and Coatney, K. T. (2015). Evolutionary stable strategy for postdisaster insurance: Game theory approach. *Journal of Management in Engineering*, 31(6): 04015005.

10. Ergün, S., Usta, P., Gök, S. Z. A., and Weber, G. W. (2019). A game theoretical approach to emergency logistics planning in natural disasters. *Annals of Operations Research*, 283(1–2): 1–14.

11. Ferrer, J. M., Martín-Campo, F. J., Ortuño, M. T., Pedraza-Martínez, A. J., Tirado, G., and Vitoriano, B. (2018). Multi-criteria optimization for last mile distribution of disaster relief aid: Test cases and applications. *European Journal of Operational Research*, 269(2): 501–515.

12. Fragkos, G., Tsiropoulou, E. E., and Papavassiliou, S. (2019). Disaster management and information transmission decision-making in public safety systems. In *2019 IEEE Global Communications Conference (GLOBECOM)*, pages 1–6. IEEE.

13. Gao, Y., Li, Z., Wang, F., Wang, F., Tan, R. R., Bi, J., and Jia, X. (2018). A game theory approach for corporate environmental risk mitigation. *Resources, Conservation and Recycling*, 130: 240–247.

14. Gupta, U. and Ranganathan, N. (2006). Social fairness in multi-emergency resource management. In *IEEE International Symposium on Technology and Society (ISTAS)*, NY, USA, pages 1–9.

15. Harsanyi, J. C. and Selten, R. (1988). *A general theory of equilibrium selection in games*, volume 1. The MIT Press.

16. Horita, F. E. and de Albuquerque, J. P. (2013). An approach to support decision-making in disaster management based on volunteer geographic information (vgi) and spatial decision support systems (sdss). In *ISCRAM*. Citeseer.

17. Hu, Z.-H. and Sheng, Z.-H. (2015). Disaster spread simulation and rescue time optimization in a resource network. *Information Sciences*, 298: 118–135.

18. Huang, K., Jiang, Y., Yuan, Y., and Zhao, L. (2015). Modeling multiple humanitarian objectives in emergency response to large-scale disasters. *Transportation Research Part E: Logistics and Transportation Review*, 75: 1–17.

19. Lai, C., Chen, X., Chen, X., Wang, Z., Wu, X., and Zhao, S. (2015). A fuzzy comprehensive evaluation model for flood risk based on the combination weight of game theory. *Natural Hazards*, 77(2): 1243–1259.

20. Liashenko, O., Kyryichuk, D., Krugla, N., and Lozhkin, R. (2019). Development of a decision support system for mitigation and elimination the consequences of natural disasters in ukraine. *International Multidisciplinary Scientific GeoConference: SGEM*, 19(2.1): 825–832.

21. Majumder, R., Warier, R. R., and Ghose, D. (2019a). Game-theoretic model based resource allocation during floods. In Presented at *4th World Congress on Disaster Management*, Mumbai, India.

22. Majumder, R., Warier, R. R., and Ghose, D. (2019b). Game theory-based allocation of critical resources during natural disasters. In *2019 Sixth Indian Control Conference (ICC)*, pages 514–519.

23. Nagurney, A., Flores, E. A., and Soylu, C. (2016). A generalized nash equilibrium network model for post-disaster humanitarian relief. *Transportation research part E: logistics and transportation review*, 95: 1–18.

24. Newman, J. P., Maier, H. R., Riddell, G. A., Zecchin, A. C., Daniell, J. E., Schaefer, A. M., van Delden, H., Khazai, B., O'Flaherty, M. J., and Newland, C. P. (2017). Review of literature on decision support systems for natural hazard risk reduction: Current status and future research directions. *Environmental Modelling & Software*, 96: 378–409.

25. Özdamar, L., Ekinci, E., and Küçükyazici, B. (2004). Emergency logistics planning in natural disasters. *Annals of Operations Research*, 129(1–4): 217–245.

26. Ranganathan, N., Gupta, U., Shetty, R., and Murugavel, A. (2007). An automated decision support system based on game theoretic optimization for emergency management in urban environments. *Journal of Homeland Security and Emergency Management*, 4(2): 1–25.

27. Sati, S. (2015). Scalable framework for emergency response decision support systems. In *2015 IEEE International Symposium on Technologies for Homeland Security (HST)*, pages 1–6. IEEE.

28. Seaberg, D., Devine, L., and Zhuang, J. (2017). A review of game theory applications in natural disaster management research. *Natural Hazards*, 89(3): 1461–1483.

29. Usta, P., Ergün, S., and Alparslan-Gok, S. Z. (2018). A cooperative game theory approach to post-disaster housing problem. In *Handbook of Research on Emergent Applications of Optimization Algorithms*, pages 314–325. IGI Global.

30. Vitoriano, B., Rodríguez, J. T., Tirado, G., Martín-Campo, F. J., Ortuño, M. T., and Montero, J. (2015). Intelligent decision-making models for disaster management. *Human and Ecological Risk Assessment: An International Journal*, 21(5): 1341–1360.

31. Wallace, W. A. and De Balogh, F. (1985). Decision support systems for disaster management. *Public Administration Review*, pages 134–146.

32. Wang, X., Wu, Y., Liang, L., and Huang, Z. (2016). Service outsourcing and disaster response methods in a relief supply chain. *Annals of Operations Research*, 240(2):471–487.

33. Wang, Z., Xu, W., Yang, J., and Peng, J. (2009). A game theoretic approach for resource allocation based on ant colony optimization in emergency management. In *International Conference on Information Engineering and Computer Science (ICIECS)*, Wuhan, China, pages 1–4.

34. Wex, F., Schryen, G., Feuerriegel, S., and Neumann, D. (2014). Emergency response in natural disaster management:

Allocation and scheduling of rescue units. *European Journal of Operational Research*, 235(3): 697–708.

35. Xu, N., Zhang, Q., Zhang, H., Hong, M., Akerkar, R., and Liang, Y. (2019). Global optimization for multi-stage construction of rescue units in disaster response. *Sustainable Cities and Society*, 51: 101768.

36. Yang, J. J. and Xu, C. H. (2012). Emergency decision engineering model based on sequential games. *Systems Engineering Procedia*, 5: 276–282.

37. Zamanifar, M. and Hartmann, T. (2021). Decision attributes for disaster recovery planning of transportation networks; a case study. *Transportation Research Part D: Transport and Environment*, 93: 102771.

38. Zheng, Y.-J., Chen, S.-Y., and Ling, H.-F. (2015). Evolutionary optimization for disaster relief operations: A survey. *Applied Soft Computing*, 27: 553–566.

39. Zhou, L., Wu, X., Xu, Z., and Fujita, H. (2018). Emergency decision making for natural disasters: An overview. *International journal of disaster risk reduction*, 27: 567–576.

CHAPTER 31

Comparing priorities of Providers and Users with Respect to Disaster Management Strategies

Rajat Agrawal

Professor, Department of Management Studies and Associated Faculty
Centre of Excellence in Disaster Mitigation and Management,
Indian Institute of Technology Roorkee

Div Jyot Singh

JRF, DPIITIPR Chair,
Indian Institute of Technology Roorkee

Abstract

As population continue to rise and climate changes continue to occur, natural and other disasters are seeing a rise in severity. Various disasters such as floods, fires, storms, earthquakes, and pandemics etc., cause havoc resulting in loss of life, resources and assets (Bahinipati, 2016). It is estimated that about 90% percent of disasters are caused by natural hazards and are inevitable in most cases. The impact of these disaster is worst experienced by developing countries like India due the presence of largely dense populations (Slettebak, 2013). A 2013 United Nations Development Programme report suggests that poorer minorities and people belonging to low income groups are far more vulnerable to disasters. Depending on the type of disaster, there are various mitigation strategies that a government can implement to encourage timely response to disasters and can significantly reduce the impact of disasters. These strategies, if implemented systematically, can help in enhancing resilience, timely evacuation, and support and recovery operations in disaster prone areas. Different types of disasters mitigation process involve different approaches and therefore it is important for the government to clearly identify which disaster mitigation and management strategy to be prioritised. For this study, a brainstorming session was organised with the experts in the field of disaster management to understand the various required strategies that can be implemented for disaster management and mitigation in developing countries like India. Some of the identified strategies are increasing public awareness, mitigation infrastructure development, human capacity development for locals, better equipment, developing standard operating procedures in disaster relief, coordination between various agencies, etc. After these strategies were identified, a survey was conducted where two group, comprising of 27 experts or people related to disaster management (providers) and 34 people from general public (users) living in a vulnerable environment and with the potential of being affected by disasters were chosen. These groups were provided with the identified strategies to be prioritized and all the responders were asked to set the identified strategies in a decreasing order of priority to identify which strategy needed maximum attention according to the respective responders' perspective. Based on the result of the survey, rank correlation was calculated to understand the similarities and dissimilarities in priorities set by the two identified groups and a significant similarity was observed between the priorities set by the experts and users. Hence, this study provides a milestone to understand the point of view of potential disaster victims and will assist the government in preparation of strategies for disaster management. This study comprised of only 61 respondents and therefore it is difficult to generalize the result with accuracy and thus provides future opportunity for similar study on a larger scale.

Keywords: Disaster management, mitigation strategies, rank correlation

1. Introduction

Almost every part of the world gets affected by disasters. In case of India, various disasters such as floods, drought and cyclones often occur due to varying seasons and a diverse geography. Apart from these, other major disasters such as earthquakes, landslides and hailstorms pose a great threat to the northern regions on the India territory (Tirthankar, 2012). Timely response for disaster management and disaster mitigation is possible only when the authorities are prepared and have action plans placed ahead of the events. Hence, a set of strategies designed to assist with disaster management and mitigation measures has the potential to significantly reduce the impact of disasters on human, their habitats and to other resources (Bahinipati, 2016). This study first identifies a set of strategies for disaster management and later finds a correlation between how providers (experts) and users (general public) rank the identified strategies. The correlation between the ranking of the two groups helped in understanding the similarities and dissimilarities in the priorities set by the two identified groups. Hence, this study helps to identify the strategies that the government should focus on for further development and implementation.

2. Purpose of Study

During a disaster, different types of disasters mitigation process involve different approaches. Depending on how the emergency response is made, the outcome in the form of impact to human life and resources varies significantly. Apart from human lives an estimated 2% of the India's GDP is lost to natural disasters (Kumar, 2012). This study is aimed at helping the government to clearly identify which disaster mitigation and management strategy to be prioritised. During an onset of a disaster, various mitigation strategies from a government can be implemented to encourage timely response to disasters and using the correct set of strategies can significantly reduce the impact of disasters. For the purpose of this study, various scholarly articles and papers from year 2000 to 2020 were reviewed for understanding disaster management studies in developed countries. Keywords such as "disaster management", "mitigations strategies", "prevention of natural disasters in developed countries", "risk reduction and mitigation", "post disaster strategies", etc., were used to conduct the literature review. Scholars, Government officials, agencies and policy makers, who decide and provide infrastructure or services have been identified as "providers". General public from all walks of life, who represent the impacted have been identified as "users".

3. Literature Review

The purpose of the literature review is to prepare an inventory of various strategies for disaster management. Disaster management is the skilful method of minimizing the impact of a disaster and includes various aspects such as understanding the hazards, planning and preparing for disasters, prevention and mitigation, etc. (Qureshi et al., 2006). A disaster management cycle is comprised of four stages, i.e. preparedness, response, recovery and mitigation. Some of the critical tasks involved throughout these cycles for disaster management are capacity building, preparation

for a disaster, emergency response during a disaster and recovery and mitigation steps. Hence it becomes important to identify various strategies from within these four cycle of disaster management.

Disaster management is primarily dependent on the preparedness of the national agencies and this may require development of various systems to predict or identify the occurrence of a disaster (for example: cyclone, earthquake, etc.) and reporting of the incident to the authorities and general public by use of alarm systems, media, social media and other response mechanisms (Saito, 2007). Nations such as Japan and China, who identify their vulnerabilities and prepare themselves ahead of a disaster are far more effective at managing the impact of natural hazards and disasters (Shaw, 2009). Also, in order for disaster management systems and techniques to be effective, it is very important that the public is able to responds appropriately in the event of onset of a disaster which required the public to be prepared and well informed (Alcántara-Ayala, 2002). A public that is aware of their responsibilities during a disaster can greatly contribute in mitigating the disaster outcomes (Qureshi et al., 2006). Therefore, "preparedness by public awareness" can be identified as one of the important strategy from preparedness and response stage of a disaster management cycle.

During and before a disaster, the timely response of authorities is dependent on inputs from various services and equipment. One example of a technique which most developed nations have deployed is a system of advance early warning systems that enable timely alarm and evacuation which in turn helps the response teams by buying some time for preparing a better organised emergency response (Saito, 2007). Therefore development and acquiring of various systems and equipment that record or warn against various disasters becomes essential for a timely response. Along with various equipment, in order to support post disaster operations, a solid mitigation infrastructure is also required for monitoring the severity and accessing the situations of various region during and after a disaster occurs (Qureshi et al., 2006). One such example is a network of beacons or unmanned vehicles or the use of Geographic information systems (GIS). Therefore, "development of better equipment and disaster mitigation infrastructure" can be identified as another strategy for the preparedness stage of disaster management, with the potential of greatly affecting the outcomes of various disaster management operations.

Another strategy for responding to disasters efficiently is training of man force. It is important that the task forces be appropriately trained to deal with a disaster during and post a disaster. Preparing teams for mitigation processes requires human capacity development on both organisational and individual level (Shaw, 2009). Developing standard operating procedures and practicing dry runs to evaluate the effectiveness of the response is one way to ensure that teams are well prepared for disaster mitigation processes. Hence, "human capacity development" and "development of standard operating procedures" are another set of important strategies from the mitigation and response stage, respectively, of the disaster management cycle for aiding with disaster relief.

Another factor that influences the outcome of a disaster is the coordination of various agencies and organisations such as NGOs, privately funded organisations and government authorities. Coordination in disaster management is highly dependent on the economy of the country. Unlike low-income economies that are unable to invest significantly, developed countries display better coordination among the various agencies due to abundance of funds and other resources (Ishiwatari and Surjan, 2019). Thus developed countries are far better at responding and managing disasters when compared to developing countries (Qureshi et al., 2006). Hence a good "coordination between agencies" can be identified as another strategy from the response stage of disaster management cycle.

It is important to understand that sustainable disaster management does not solely depend on technological solutions provided by engineering devices, but it is a product of development through knowledge, land management, social regulations and economical improvement (Souheil and Graham, 2002). Sustainable Disaster Planning is possible by preventive urban planning that is based on considering the natural disasters that are prevailing in the respective regions (Alcántara-Ayala, 2002). Disaster planning highly incorporates engineering solutions such as disaster proof housing by considering engineering constraints and criteria, appropriate material selections, creating and implementing designs by testing on scale models (Kaiser, 2015). For example, countries like Japan implement urban planning for risk reduction thereby greatly reducing the vulnerability and risk to the population (Wamsler, 2004). Hence "safe housing" can be identified as another preventive strategy from the preparedness stage of disaster management cycle.

Disasters can cause various financial crunches for people and government due to loss of property, assets or other resources. One lesser followed strategy in developing countries like India is the use of insurance disaster mechanism for disaster mitigation. Insurance against disasters can prove to be a valuable tool for encouraging loss reduction by providing recovery funds against various disasters or other hazards (Kunreuther, 1996). Therefore, providing affordable and practical investments options in the form of "insurance mechanism" can be identified as a disaster mitigation strategy

for the users. Hence, on the basis of literature review, 8 important strategies and their respective disaster management stage for further studies are identified as shown in Table 31.1.

Table 31.1 Identified disaster management strategies

	Disaster Management Strategies	Disaster Management Cycle/Stage
1.	increasing public awareness by use of social media	Preparedness and Response
2.	better infrastructure development	Preparedness
3.	human capacity development for locals through training	Mitigation
4.	developing standard operating procedures for disaster relief	Response
5.	coordination between various agencies	Response
6.	development of knowledge about disaster mitigation	Preparedness
7.	safe housing	Preparedness
8.	insurance mechanism for disasters	Recovery

4. Methodology

A quantitative study was conducted by collecting survey responses from two groups. Two separate groups were identified as "user group" (general public) and "expert group" (provider) respectively. Audience from all walks of life were selected as members of the general public group. The expert group included mostly researchers with expertise or relation to disaster, civil, environment or other forms of management. A set of eight strategies were identified by review of literature and two set of identical surveys were distributed amongst the two groups to rank for prioritising the eight disaster mitigation strategies that were identified earlier. The ranked responses from the two identical surveys were used to compute the average ranking (scores) for all the identified strategies. Spearman's rank correlation was then computed between the two set of average ranks of all the strategies. Figure 31.1 shows the steps used for conducting this study.

5. Data Collection

Survey results were collected using the online tool "survey monkey" and an average ranking was calculated for all the 8 identified strategies. The average ranking for each strategy is given by

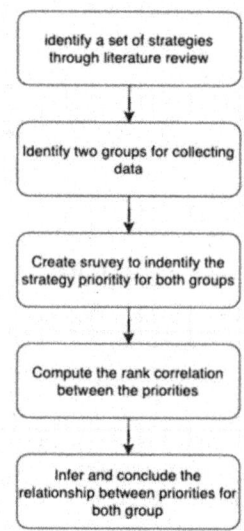

Fig. 31.1 Steps for comparing priorities of providers and users

Table 31.2 Average ranking for disaster management strategies

	Disaster Management Strategies	Average Rank(Expert)	Average Rank (Public)
1.	increasing public awareness by use of social media	3.07	3.03
2.	better infrastructure development	6.04	5.68
3.	human capacity development for locals through training	4.30	4.29
4.	developing standard operating procedures for disaster relief	4.22	4.91
5.	coordination between various agencies	5.63	4.32
6.	development of knowledge about disaster mitigation	6.15	6.53
7.	safe housing	3.67	4.24
8.	insurance mechanism for disasters	2.93	3.00

$$\frac{(x_1 w_1 + x_2 w_2 + \ldots + x_n w_n)}{\text{total responses}} \tag{1}$$

Where w is the weight of ranked position and "x" is the response count for answer choice.

Weights were assigned on the basis of ranking given by the responders. Highest weight was given to the most preferred choice and least weight was given to the least preferred choice. For example, the strategy that was assigned the rank #1 by the responder was assigned a weight of 8 whereas the strategy that was assigned the rank #8 was assigned a weight of 1. The average rankings obtained for all the strategies for the both groups are as shown in Table 31.2 and Fig. 31.2.

6. Analysis of Results

Rank correlation was used to develop and understand the relation between the obtained results. Spearman's Rank Correlation Coefficient is a statistical measure of the relationship between two sets of data. The relationship between the average rankings obtained for both the groups was calculated using:

$$R_s = 1 - \left(\frac{6 \Sigma d^2}{n(n^2 - 1)} \right) \tag{2}$$

Where R_s is the spearman's rank correlation coefficient and Σd^2 is the sum of square of difference of the two average rankings

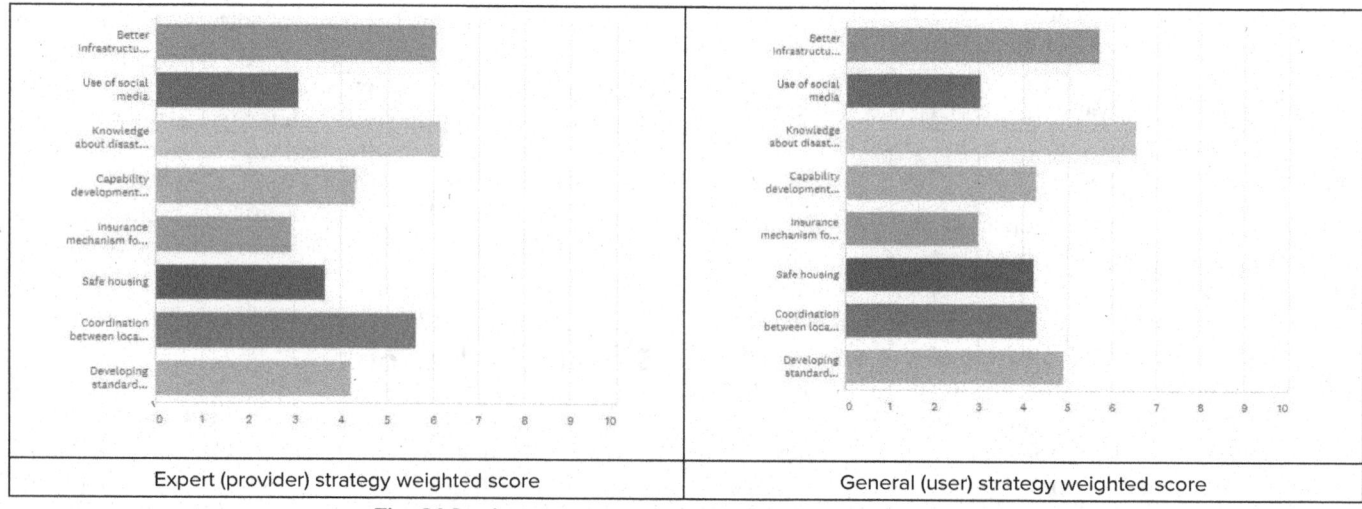

Expert (provider) strategy weighted score	General (user) strategy weighted score

Fig. 31.2 Average score for the strategies for both groups

The average scores obtained in table 2 were used to calculate the coefficient Rs (spearnam's rank correlation coefficient). "R" programming language for statistical computing was used for computing Rs and the correlation between the variables was estimated to be 0.8743131 (t= 4.4124, p=0.0045, df = 6). The "t" statistic associated with the correlation coefficient was significant (t greater than 1.96) at 95% confidence level (interval 0.4418917 : 0.977320).

7. Discussion and Implications

Since the correlation between the variables is significant (0.8743) and the "t" statistic associated with the correlation coefficient is also significant at a confidence level of 95%, it is safe to imply that there exists a strong correlation between the average scores of the individual strategies for the two groups. It can therefore be inferred that the priorities of providers and users with regards to disaster management strategies are quite well aligned.

As shown in Fig. 31.2, "Development of knowledge about disaster mitigation" and "development of better infrastructures" have been identified as the most important strategies by both the group with similar average scores and it can be inferred that people have rated the preparedness stage as the most important stage when it comes to disaster management. Apart from these strategies, the expert group has also identified "coordination between various agencies and organisations" as third most important strategy for disaster management whereas the users have identified "developing standard operating procedures for disaster relief" as the third most important strategy.

It is also important to notice the "users" group has ranked three strategies, i.e. safe housing, coordination between various agencies and human capacity development for locals through training in a very similar manner. The average scores by participants for "users" group have similar numbers, which means that these strategies are of almost similar importance to an average person of the society. The experts identified human capacity development for locals through training as the fourth most important strategy. The other remaining four identified strategies, that is, increasing public awareness by use of social media, human capacity development for locals through training, safe housing and insurance mechanism for disasters, have also received quite similar average scores from both the groups, however, Insurance mechanism for disasters and increasing public awareness by use of social media received the least scores from both the groups.

Despite there being a strong correlation between the thoughts of both the groups, during the process of data collection, we have realised that there is a gap between the though process and the implementation of the strategies with respect to disaster management. It is clear, that the experts or providers are well aware of the disaster management strategies but despite these strategies being correctly identified, users are not very satisfied with the implementation of these strategies as of now. This calls for scrutiny from the government's end as far as implementation efforts towards these strategies are concerned.

8. Conclusion

With the help of this study, a strong correlation between the priorities set by two groups (experts and users) was identifed. It was discovered that some of the strategies falling under the "Preparedness" stage for disaster management received the highest scores from both groups. Strategies from "Response" stage also received significant high scores followed by the "Mitigation" stage. Recovery stage, despite receiving similar scores, was ranked very low by both the groups. Therefore, it is clear that both the users and providers are on the same page as far as identifying and prioritising of disaster management strategies is concerned. Preparedness and response stages are significantly important for minimising the losses to an exemplary level during disasters and countries like India should learn from the experience of countries like Japan to implement disaster management measures. By preparing before a disaster and by responding efficiently during and after the disaster, with the help of local government, public corporations and private citizens, the severity of the disaster can be minimised significantly (Saito, 2007).

During the course of this study, it was identified that there was a mutual understanding about the priorities for the strategies for disaster management amongst both the groups of experts and users. However, despite this alignment in the priorities of both the groups (providers and users), in order to achieve improvements in the disaster management and mitigation efforts, there is an urgent need for putting more thoughts and efforts in the implementation process of the identified strategies. Hence, for future recommendations, another strategy would be to develop a mechanism to monitor, audit and inspect the progress on the implementation of the disaster management strategies identified in this study. Both, providers and users would appreciate if the Government of India and other responsible agencies could keep a check and show significant future focus towards four of the most important identified strategies, that are; development of knowledge about disaster mitigation, development of better infrastructure, coordination between various agencies and developing standard operating procedures for disaster relief, respectively.

REFERENCES

1. Alcántara-Ayala, I., 2002 "Geomorphology, natural hazards, vulnerability and prevention of natural disasters in developing countries," Geomorphology, vol. 47, no. 2–4, pp. 107–124

2. Bahinipati, C. S., Patnaik U., and Viswanathan P. K., 2016 "What Causes Economic Losses from Natural Disasters in India?," in Advances in Environmental Engineering and Green Technologies, IGI Global, pp. 157–175.

3. Ishiwatari, M. and Surjan, A., 2019. Good enough today is not enough tomorrow: Challenges of increasing investments in disaster risk reduction and climate change adaptation. Progress in Disaster Science, 1, p.100007.

3. Kaiser, M.A.D., 2015 *"L.L.C., Building a Better World: Engineering Disaster Proof Housing". age, 18, p.1.*

4. Kumar, T., 2012. *Managing Disasters In India.* [online] Insightsonindia.com. Available at: <https://www.insightsonindia.com/wp-content/uploads/2013/09/managing-disasters-in-india.pdf> [Accessed 22 January 2021].

5. Kunreuther, H., 1996. "Mitigating disaster losses through insurance". *Journal of risk and Uncertainty, 12*(2), pp.171-187.

6. Saito, T., 2007, August. Disaster management of local government in Japan. In *National Workshop, organized by UNCRD and Japan-Peru Center for Seismic Research and Disaster Mitigation (CISMID)/Peru National University of Engineering (UNI).*

7. Shaw, R., Takeuchi, Y. and Rouhban, B., 2009. *"Education, capacity building and public awareness for disaster reduction".* In Landslides–Disaster Risk Reduction (pp. 499–515). Springer, Berlin, Heidelberg.

8. Slettebak, R. T., 2013 "Climate Change, Natural Disasters, and Post-Disaster Unrest in India," India Review, vol. 12, no. 4, pp. 260–279

9. Souheil El-Masri & Graham Tipple (2002) Natural Disaster, Mitigation and Sustainability: The Case of Developing Countries, International Planning Studies, 7: 2, 157–175

10. Tirthankar, Roy, 2012 "Natural Disasters and Indian History: Oxford India Short Introductions," OUP Catalogue, Oxford University Press, number 9780198075370

11. Wamsler, C., 2004. *"Managing urban risk: perceptions of housing and planning as a tool for reducing disaster risk".* National Emergency Training Center

12. Qureshi, A. M., Butt, M. and Khan, O. M., *"The Role of GIS and Public Awareness for Disaster Management,"* 2006 International Conference on Advances in Space Technologies, Islamabad, 2006, pp. 37–42, doi: 10.1109/ICAST.2006.313794.

CHAPTER 32

Law and Disaster Management: A Critical Understanding

Awekta Verma
Associate Professor, Faculty of Law (LC-I),
University of Delhi

Abstract

The geographical location of India makes it a disaster prone country and over a period of time these disasters have caused immense loss of life, property and environment. Natural hazards do happen and we may not be able to stop them from happening but an appropriate legal framework and its implementation in letter and spirit can determine the extent of death and destruction caused by it. There are many laws for ensuring safety of life and property in India but it is The Disaster Management Act, 2005 which provides for a comprehensive legal and institutional framework for disaster management in a holistic manner in India. To minimize loss of life and property disaster management is imperative. It needs to cover and be operative in all phases i.e. pre-disaster phase, during disaster and post disaster. Moreover, India has signed the declaration on the 2030 Agenda for Sustainable Development which comprised of seventeen Sustainable Development Goals at the Sustainable Development Summit of the United Nations in September 2015. The SDGs focus on five Ps i.e. people, planet, prosperity, peace and partnership. Ten of the seventeen SDGs relate to disaster risk reduction and form the core of any development strategy. Laws need to be framed and implemented to realize the SDGs. This paper is an attempt to critically understand the role that law, especially the Disaster Management Act, 2005 is playing to manage disasters in India. A sincere attempt has been made to suggest the way forward after weighing the merits and demerits of the current laws and their implementation.

Keywords: Disaster, disaster management, sustainable development, disaster risk reduction.

1. Introduction

As per Disaster Management Act 'disaster' means a catastrophe, mishap, calamity or grave occurrence in any area, arising from natural or man made causes, or by accident or negligence which results in substantial loss of life or human suffering or damage to, and destruction of, property, or damage to, or degradation of, environment, and is of such a nature or magnitude as to be beyond the coping capacity of the community of the affected area.[1] India has witnessed many disasters - natural as well as man-made, since time immemorial. They cause immense loss to life, property, environment, economy, social life and society. Whether a natural hazard will become a disaster or not depends on the level of development, preparation, planning and population of a particular State. Countries which invest in disaster resilient infrastructure, urban planning, early warning system, capacity building of the communities and ensure proper implementation of laws suffer the least in term of loss of life

and property. Whereas densely populated, unplanned cities and urban areas suffer the most when disaster strikes. Thus, disaster management is a governance issue. Better laws, their implementation and good governance leads to fewer losses whenever disaster occurs. It ensures safer communities and makes building back, resettlement and rehabilitation easier. So, law plays an important role at all times- pre-disaster, disaster and post-disaster. All actions with respect to disaster management and planning i.e. prevention, preparedness, reduction, rescue, relief, response, recovery and rehabilitation, are guided, regulated and steered by law. Rules, regulations and proper regulatory mechanism are needed for successful handling of disasters. Especially we need them for sustainable approach to disaster management and disaster risk reduction. In fact the approach of the whole world has now shifted from being response and relief centric to focusing on prevention, risk reduction and developing resilience. This paradigm shift has taken place because of the new norms being recognized by the international community and laws are needed to give effect to the mandate of the various international frameworks developed for ensuring sustainable disaster management. So, better laws reduce vulnerability, impact; ensure better response and efficient management of disasters.

2. Impact of Disasters

Man cannot stop natural hazards from occurring but enacting appropriate legal framework and ensuring its proper implementation for dealing with all pre-disaster, disaster and post-disaster scenario will go a long way in minimizing the death and destruction caused by disasters. According to the vulnerability Atlas of India, the Indian Subcontinent is one of the most disaster prone areas in the world.[2] As per the study done by the UN office for Disaster Risk Reduction (UNISDR) during the period from 1998-2017 i.e. almost 20 years, the economic losses suffered by India amount to about 79.5 billion US$.[3] The ongoing COVID pandemic- a natural disaster has impacted India and the whole world adversely. Globally the economic growth reduced to an annualised rate of −3.4% to −7.6% in the year 2020.[4] In India, according to the ministry of statistics and program implementation, the economy contracted by 7.3% in the April-June quarter of 2021.[5] The pandemic has upended the lives of the people all over the world. In fact it has emerged as one of the biggest natural disaster in human history. As per WHO worldwide it has killed 4,470,969 people and impacted 214, 468,601 people worldwide.[6] In India as per the data released by the Ministry of Health and Family Welfare there have been 3,26,95,030 confirmed cases,4,37,830 deaths and a total of 63,09,17,927 have been vaccinated.[7] World faced a great humanitarian crisis as nobody was prepared for a natural disaster in the form of COVID-19 pandemic. India is still reeling under its impact and devising many strategies like vaccination, social distancing, economic stimulus etc to minimize its socio-economic impact. Without a comprehensive legal framework it is difficult to handle such pandemics or disasters which have enormous impact on human lives.

Thus, though disasters are inevitable but their impact on human life and assets can be minimized with proper planning and implementation of laws. It's stated that prevention is better than cure and the same applies to disasters. For formulating appropriate laws, policies, measures, strategies and response it becomes important to understand the problems and challenges faced by the victims of disaster. The inequities prevalent in Indian society make it doubly challenging as these get further manifested during disasters and need to be addressed by the law by incorporating an inclusive approach. Post disaster the victims face many problems and are vulnerable to many wrongs. The problem is further compounded by illiteracy, lack of knowledge and

awareness of - laws, redressal mechanisms, agencies or authorities involved in relief and rehabilitation work etc. The main issues faced by people during and in the aftermath of disaster are listed below:

- *Lack of Basic Necessities of Life:* Loss of property, home, displacement etc. during disasters lead to inability of survivors to meet the basic necessities of life like food, shelter, clothing etc. The poor are impacted more and this leads to loss of human dignity. Women, children, disabled and elderly are the worst affected. Rise in prices put the goods beyond the buying capacity of the people. According to the Poverty and Shared Prosperity Report 2020(PSPR2020), at the world level COVID-19 will probably drive between 88 and 115 million people into extreme poverty i.e. earning under $1.90 a day in 2020 .[8]

- *Livelihood Loss:* Many people lose their jobs and livelihood because of adverse effects of disasters. This pushes them into a cycle of poverty from which they can't emerge without proper support and rehabilitation. In India millions of people have lost their job during the pandemic. According to International labor Organisation(ILO) about 400 million workers in informal economy in India are at risk of being pushed into poverty. And as per Centre for Monitoring Indian Economy, since April 2020, more than 18.9 million salaried people have lost their jobs and about 5 million lost it in just one month i.e. July 2020.[9]

- *Crime:* Crime against women, children and other vulnerable sections increase during disasters as they are more exposed and vulnerable due to loss of secure shelter, family etc. Moreover, loss of job, employment, poverty also pushes some into a life of crime. Trafficking in women and children increases as they are extremely vulnerable during disasters and more opportunities to commit such crimes are present because of lax law and order during these times.

- *Mental Health:* Loss of family members, way of life, loved ones, job, assets and property creates mental trauma to many people. Lack of proper rehabilitation measures and access to resources, health professionals and counselors further exacerbate the matters. Many survivors take to alcohol or drugs and develop suicidal tendencies as they fail to cope up with the harsh realities and lose all hope of building their lives all over again.

- *Loss of Important Documents:* People lose their important documents in floods, fire, earthquake and other disasters and find it difficult to claim relief announced by the authorities. Illiteracy and lack of any knowledge about the proper forums to be approached in such cases makes the matter worse for poor people.

- *Dearth of Medical Facilities:* Disasters lead to damage to infrastructure and deterioration of the hygienic standards. This can lead to outbreak of diseases. Shortage of medicines, doctors and health professionals increases the risk and number of fatalities. During the pandemic the shortfall and difficulty in accessing healthcare facilities was amply visible and the Supreme Court had to direct that COVID-19 tests should be done free of cost in government hospitals. Also, that COVID-19 patients should be given proper treatment and dead bodies should be handled in a dignified manner in the hospitals.[10]

- *Miscellaneous:* Disasters have many adverse effects like it leads to break in education for many children. During the current pandemic many children have dropped out of school and the number is rising continuously. This in turn will lead to rise in child labour and drag the families deep into the circle of poverty.

The COVID-19 created a humanitarian crisis in India as lakhs of migrant laborers were stranded at various places and yearned to go to their homes. The Supreme Court of India had to intervene and it directed that transportation be provided by the government to these labourers to go to their homes. Further directions were given to withdraw cases of violation of lockdown norms against them.[11]

As far as India is concerned we have many legislations dealing with different kinds of hazards or emergencies but the main central legislation enacted for the specific purpose of dealing with disasters is the Disaster Management Act, 2005. Initiative at international level like declaring 1990s as an International Decade for Natural Disaster Reduction (IDNDR), 1994 Yokohama Strategy and Plan of Action for a Safer World, adoption of International Strategy for Disaster Reduction (ISDR) and creation of Secretariat of the ISDR (UNISDR) in the year 1999, adoption of Hyogo Framework for Action 205-2015 and national events like 1999 odisha super cyclone, 2001 Gujarat earthquake, 2004 Asian Tsunami; all of these subsequently led to the enactment of the Disaster Management Act,2005 (hereinafter referred as DMA)on December 23, 2005.[12]

3. Legislative Matrix

The Government of India enacted DMA for undertaking a holistic, coordinated and prompt response to any disaster situation so as to effectively manage disasters and related matters. The DMA emphasizes on prevention, preparedness and mitigation in disaster management and provides for requisite institutional mechanisms for drawing up and monitoring the implementation of the disaster management plans, ensuring measures by different departments and

ministries of the Government. Thus, it provides for institutional, legal, financial co-ordination mechanisms at four levels i.e. the Centre, state, district and local levels. At the level of Government of India, Ministry of Home Affairs is the nodal ministry for disaster management since 2002 and has to co-ordinate the actions of various Ministries/ Departments of Government of India, State Governments, the NDMA, SDMAs, governmental and non-governmental organisations.

At the institutional level the DM Act envisages a three tier structure whereby National Disaster Management Authority, State Disaster Management Authority and District Disaster Management Authority have been set up at national, state and district level under the Chairmanship of the Prime Minister, Chief Ministers and District Magistrates respectively. All three authorities have to work in co-ordination to give relief to victims of disasters. At the national level it establishes four important entities and lays down their structure, role, powers and functions:

- *The National Disaster Management Authority (NDMA):* It has the responsibility for laying down policies, plans and guidelines for disaster management so as to ensure timely and effective response to disasters.

- *The National Executive Committee (NEC):* It has to assist the National Authority and is comprised of secretary level officers of the Government of India

- *The National Institute of Disaster Management(NIDM):* It has to function within the broad policies and guidelines laid down by NDMA. It is responsible for planning and promoting training and research programmes in the area of disaster management for stakeholders, documentation and development of a national level information base with respect to disaster management policies, prevention mechanisms and mitigation measures.

- *The National Disaster Response Force(NDRF):* Section 44DM Act 2005, provides for its establishment for specialist response to threatening disaster situation or disaster. It consists of trained professionals units and is under general superintendence, direction and control of NDMA. The objective is to have a force with specialized skills and capabilities for rescue operations in case of disasters. The Central Government appoints the Director General of NDRF.

In fact the DM Act mandates that every Ministry or the Department of the Government of India has the responsibility to take measures for disaster management. Financing is an important element in disaster management and the DM Act envisages financing arrangements for both response and mitigation activities. So at national level, two funds are provided for: The National Disaster Response Fund (NDRF) and The National Disaster Mitigation Fund (NDMF). Similar funds are provided for at the state and district levels.

Disaster Management has been defined in a comprehensive manner in Section 2(e), though it needs to be amended post-Sendai to make resilience also a part of it.

Presently, disaster management means a continuous and integrated process of planning, organizing, co-coordinating and implementing measures which are necessary or expedient for-

(i) Prevention of danger or threat of any danger;

(ii) Mitigation or reduction of risk of any disaster or its severity or consequences;

(iii) Capacity-building;

(iv) Preparedness to deal with any disaster;

(v) Prompt response to any threatening disaster situation or disaster;

(vi) Evacuation, rescue and relief;

(vii) Rehabilitation and reconstruction

All the above measures focusing on prevention, mitigation or reduction of risk, capacity building, preparedness, prompt response, evacuation, recue and relief, rehabilitation and reconstruction show a victim centric approach. But these are mere guidelines as no accountability is fixed on any one if there is poor performance on these scores. There is no clear demarcation of responsibilities as to who will be held responsible in case these measures are not taken.

A noteworthy feature of the DM Act is that it provides for the development of National Policy which shall be guiding the framing of National Plan for Disaster Management for the whole country. As per the DM Act, it is mandatory for NEC to make a National Plan. The annual review and update of the plan is also provided for in the DM Act. However, no mechanism has been provided for whereby consistency of all the plans could be ensured. The National Policy on Disaster Management was framed in 2009. It envisioned to build a safe and disaster resilient India by developing a holistic, proactive, multi-disaster oriented and technology driven strategy through a culture of prevention, mitigation, preparedness and response. The objectives being to focus on prevention, preparedness and resilience at all levels, adopting mitigation measures, early warning, linking disaster management and development, and ensuring efficient response and relief. However, it's only after over ten years from the enactment of the DM Act that National Plan was made. On 1st June2016 Prime Minister Shri Narendra Modi released the National Disaster Management Plan. It's the first ever such plan for the country and aims to make India disaster resilient and significantly reduce the loss of lives and assets.

The plan was based on the four main themes of the "Sendai Framework", i.e. understanding disaster risk, improving disaster risk governance, investing in disaster risk reduction (through structural and non-structural measures) and disaster preparedness, early warning and building back better in the aftermath of a disaster. Keeping up with the new development the National Plan was again revised in the year 2019 whereby it was improved upon and given a new dimension in the light of adoption of three landmark international instruments by the GOI in the year 2015 which greatly impact the global approach towards disaster management. They are – Sendai Framework for Disaster Reduction(SFDRR), Sustainable Development Goals(SDGs) and Paris Agreement on Climate Change at the 21st Conference of Parties(COP21) under the United Nations Framework Convention on Climate Change in December 2015.[13] The new plan seeks to establish coherence between the three international agreements with special emphasis on Ten Point Agenda on DRR pronounced by the Prime Minister during Asian Ministerial Conference on DRR(AMCDRR) in November 2016 in New Delhi. It also makes social inclusion and mainstreaming of DRR as its integral features. In the context of social inclusion the plan focuses on gender based vulnerabilities, scheduled castes and scheduled tribes, elderly, children and persons with disabilities. The purpose is to help all stakeholders in achieving national goals.

The plan envisages three time frames – short, medium and long term ending by 2022, 2027 and 2030 for different activities to be undertaken under it. The long term period is similar to the ending year of all post-15 global frameworks. However, there is no mention of fixing accountability for the lapses in the plan. In its absence the victims of disaster remain at the mercy of the officials who may or may not act according to the laudable policies and plans laid down by the government.

Another remarkable development has been the adoption of Ten-point agenda by The Prime Minister, Shri Narendra Modi, in his inaugural speech at the Asian Ministerial Conference on Disaster Risk Reducon 2016, held in New Delhi during November 2016 (AMCDRR), which has also been incorporated in the NDMP. The ten key features are as follows:

1. All development sectors must imbibe the principles of disaster risk management

2. Risk coverage must include all, starting from poor households to SMEs to multi-national corporations to nation states

3. Women's leadership and greater involvement should be central to disaster risk management

4. Invest in risk mapping globally to improve global understanding of Nature and disaster risks

5. Leverage technology to enhance the efficiency of disaster risk management efforts

6. Develop a network of universities to work on disaster-related issues

7. Utilise the opportunities provided by social media and mobile technologies for disaster risk reduction

8. Build on local capacity and initiatives to enhance disaster risk reduction

9. Make use of every opportunity to learn from disasters and, to achieve that, there must be studies on the lessons after every disaster

10. Bring about greater cohesion in international response to disasters"[14]

The AMCDRR is action oriented and many initiatives like Jan Dhan Yojna, Suraksha Bima Yojana and Fasal Bima Yojana have been launched to benefit millions of people in India. It aims to make DRR all pervasive in disaster management. Community participation, inclusion and use of technology for better planning, response and reconstruction has been emphasized. But the lack of accountability for ensuring that these guidelines are followed in letter and spirit takes the steam out of the whole initiative. Infrastructure projects have been marred by low quality and bad designing in India which results in huge economic losses. To ensure that they are disaster resilient is easier said than done because of lack of accountability mechanisms.

4. National Plan for Disaster Management

The National Plan for disaster management 2016 provided for eighteen broad activities to serve as a checklist while responding to the disasters and the same continues in the 2019 plan. It prioritizes and takes care of the basic needs and requirements of the survivors. The checklist mentions the following victim centric measures:

- Early Warning, Maps, Satellite inputs, Information Dissemination
- Search, Rescue and Evacuation of People and Animals
- Medical Care
- Drinking Water/Dewatering Pumps/Sanitation Facilities/ Public Health
- Food & Essential Supplies
- Communication
- Housing and Temporary Shelters
- Power and Fuel

- Transportation Relief Logistics and Supply Chain Management
- Disposal of Animal Carcasses
- Fodder for livestock in scarcity-hit areas
- Rehabilitation and Ensuring Safety of Livestock and other Animals, Veterinary Care
- Relief Employment

These response and recovery activities are also supported by the statutory measure provided under Section 12 of the DM Act which mandates the National Disaster Management Authority to lay down guidelines for the minimum standards of relief to be provided to persons affected by disaster. It gives a very wide power to the National Authority so as to include whatever it thinks necessary to be provided to the survivors, though some things like shelter, food, drinking water, medical cover, sanitation, special provision for widows and orphans, ex gratia payment for loss of life and assistance because of damage to houses have been specifically mentioned. Accordingly, the National Disaster Management Authority has laid down guidelines for minimum standard of relief to be provided to victims of disaster.[15] The States too under Section 19 DM Act are mandated to frame the guidelines for providing relief to persons affected by disaster in the State and these guidelines have to be in tandem with the guidelines laid down by the national authority and in no case less than the minimum standards specified therein.

So as per the mandate of DM Act and the DMP the Governemnt needs to provide and a victim can ask for following reliefs:

- *Temporary Shelter:* Survivors too have a right to live with dignity and disasters do not vanquish this fundamental right. It is very important to have a safe and secure shelter for survival in the beginning or aftermath of the disaster. For enduring the disaster as well as for a disease free, healthy, safe and secure life availability of temporary shelters is a necessity which has to be provided by the Government under the DMP. The DMP mandates that temporary relief camps and shelters be established with provision for basic necessities like sufficient number of toilets, water supply, generators with fuel for power back up. Hygiene has to be maintained at community and camp kitchen. It commands that 3liters per day per person of drinking water should be made available. The drinking water supply has not be more than 500 mtrs from the camp. Also, one toilet per 30 persons, with separate facilities for women and children is to be provided. A minimum 3.5 Sq.m .of covered area per person is to be provided. Safety and security of inmates especially women, widows and children. Special arrangements should be made for old people, differently abled and those with serious medical condition.

The livestock of farmers need shelter too but this has not been provided for the guidelines. It has an important bearing on the reconstruction and rebuilding the lives of the villagers.

- *Essential items:* Survivors need items of daily needs to live a life of dignity. Food, clothes, blankets, bed sheets, basic kitchen items, hygienic products etc need to be supplied and should be culturally appropriate. DMP provides for giving dignity kits to women which should have sanitary napkins and disposable bags. It mandates that children and lactating mothers should be given milk and dairy products. Minimum 2,400Kcal per day of food product should be given to men and women. Children should be provided 1,700Kcal per day.

- *Medical Facilities:* As per the guidelines mobile medical teams have to visit camps. Necessary basic arrangements are to be made for safe delivery. Those needing urgent medical attention and hospitalization need to be provided with transportation to hospitals. Steps are to be taken to prevent spread of communicable diseases.

- *Search, Rescue and Reunion:* Disasters lead to separation of family members and it is a very traumatic experience for the family members. The guidelines mandate keeping a separate record of all widows and orphaned children. Women who have lost their husband are to be provided the certificate within 15 days by the concerned authorities. All necessary measures in connection with widows and children need to be done within a period of 45 days of the disaster. Though it is not specifically laid down in the guideline but the DMP mentions earnest efforts be made in the direction of search, recue and later reunion of the survivors to their respective families. Its taken up as a matter of great humanitarian concern.

- *Psychosocial Support, ex-gratia payment:* The guidelines provide for giving psychosocial support to the needy in the aftermath of the disasters. The victims need empathy and compassion from the professionals as well as society so as to heal their wounds and be able to rebuild their lives. The shock and pain that the disasters bring lead to psychological problems in the survivors and psychological counseling helps them in facing the reality and taking control of their lives in a positive manner. The ex gratia payment for loss of life, damage to house and rebuilding ones life is to be made according to the norms set by the Ministry of Home Affairs for assistance from SDRF.

The States may not be in a position to provide all the things listed therein and the national authority provides for the course to be followed in such a scenario. So during the first three days they may focus on providing the basic norms, from fourth day onwards till 10th day efforts should be made to follow majority of the norms prescribed by NDMA and after 11 days all the norms prescribed by NDMA should be followed. These guidelines have not been incorporated in the statute so as to make them justiciable. As they are minimum guidelines so authorities are not accountable and the victims can't demand the relief mentioned therein as a matter of right. Neglect and deliberate inaction on the part of authorities in this regard can't be called into question in the court of law. There is no provision for grievance redressal and victims get further victimized due to state apathy in many circumstances. Rights without remedies remain meaningless and the same is the scenario with the minimum standard of relief provided in the guidelines.

No discrimination is to be made on the basis of sex, caste, community, descent or origin while providing compensation and relief to the victims of disaster. However, the redressal mechanism in case of violation has not been provided for in the Act.

5. Offences and Penalties

Chapter X of the DM Act, 2005 makes causing of obstruction to any official engaged in discharging his functions under the Act or refusing to comply with directions of such official an offence. Making false claim or misappropriating the money or material meant for disaster relief is also an offense. But no prosecution can be initiated against the government official without the prior sanction of the government and no court can take cognizance of an offence under this Act except on a complaint made by the authorities or officers recognized under section 60 of DM Act or unless the any person has given prior notice of 30 days to the authorities designated under the DM Act. So no quick remedial action or redressal of grievance is provided for in the DM Act for the victims of disasters. Everything is dependent on the goodwill and discretion of the concerned officials. In Swaraj Abhiyan v Union of India[16] the Supreme Court had to give directions to the States i.e. Bihar, Gujarat and Haryana to consider whether conditions for declaring drought exist in their States as the farmers were a distressed lot and were denied basic humanitarian assistance because of non-declaration of drought.

6. Challenges and Lessons Learnt

The DM Act has proved deficient to deal with situations like the current pandemic. Though COVID 19 pandemic was declared a disaster under it and NDMA, SDMA continue to promulgate orders, guidelines etc under it, but we need separate comprehensive legislation to deal with health emergencies and pandemics. A lack of co-ordination between different departments, ministries, the centre and states was quite visible during the pandemic. In the ensuing confusion it is the general public which suffered the most. Almost every issue of governance from providing food, shelter, transport, free medical treatment and testing to poor, availability of PPE kits to doctors landed up at the Supreme Court which gave ample orders and directions and gave relief to the citizenry. Learning from this experience we have to enact better laws and formulate rules and regulations with minutest details and fixing responsibility at every level from centre, state, district to local authorities while ensuring proper co-ordination between them.

- Because of lack of proper legal framework and coordination many issues came to the fore like the oxygen tankers could not reach Delhi as they were struck at borders due to lack of clearance given to them from transit state.

- There is lack of coordination and integration between various ministries while responding to disasters.

- With the onset of the pandemic lack of essential PPE kits, testing kits etc which were not manufactured in India put the focus on need for manufacturing equipment and becoming self reliant. The momentum should not be lost as self reliance becomes the new mantra.

- There is lack of capacity building and training to handle disasters like the current pandemic, nuclear disasters, chemical disasters etc. We need special task force for such disasters.

- Need to implement laws relating to environment protection, building regulations etc in normal times as climate change has increased the frequency and severity of disasters and flouting of these laws with impunity only aggravates the risk. Urban planning and ensuring proper implementation of it needs to be done on a priority basis.

- Capacity building of the community, all the stakeholders, along with accountability of the responsible authorities is the need of the hour for ensuring better disaster management.

To conclude, Justice Madan Lokur, aptly stated in Swaraj Abhiyan v Union of India, " The problem is not lack of resources or capabilities, but lack of will"[17]

REFERENCES

1. Section 2(d), Disaster Management Act,2005
2. Government of India, (2017). An Introduction to the Vulnerability Atlas of India First Revision, 2006. Building Materials and Technology Promotion Council, Ministry of Housing and Poverty Alleviation. *First Revision*, 2006 Retrieved from https://www.bmtpc.org/admin/ PublisherAttachement/An%20Introduction%20to%20the%20 Vulnerability%20Atlas%20of%201. According to it 59% of land is vulnerable to earthquakes,8.5% of land is vulnerable to cyclones, 5% of land is vulnerable to floods and around one mllion houses are damaged annually.
3. UNISDR (2017) , *Economic Losses, Poverty and Disasters* Centre for Research on the Epidemiology of Disasters CRED, , P.4 Retrieved from https://www.unisdr.org/2016/iddr/ IDDR2018_Economic%20Losses.pdf
   India is ranked *amongst* world top five countries in terms of economic losses suffered due to disasters.
4. CRS Report.(2021). Global Economic Effects of COVID 19, Retrieved from https://sgp.fas.org/crs/row/R46270.pdf
5. Shreyansh Mangla, (2021, July 11). Impact of COVID on Indian Economy. Times of India. Retrieved from https:// timesofindia.indiatimes.com/readersblog/shreyansh-mangla/ impact-of-covid-19-on-indian-economy-2-35042/
6. Retrieved from https://covid19.who.int/
7. Retrieved from https://mygov.in/covid19
8. World Bank, World Economic Forum, Retrieved from https:// www.weforum.org/agenda/2020/11/covid-19-global-poverty- inequality-un-economics-coronavirus-pandemic/
9. Kamdar,Bansai.(2020,September 10) .India's Rich Prosper During the Pandemic While Its Poor Stand Precariously at the Edge. *The Diplomat* Retrieved from https://thediplomat. com/2020/09/indias-rich-prosper-during-the-pandemic- while-its-poor-stand-precariously-at-the-edge/
10. In re proper treatment of COVID-19 patients and dignified handling of dead bodies in hospitals etc 2020 SCC OnLine SC 530
11. Problems and Miseries of Migrant labourers, In re 2020 SCC OnLine SC 490, 492
12. Earlier, some states had enacted their own disaster management legislation like The Gujarat State Disaster Management Act, 2003; the Bihar Disaster Management Act, 2004; the Uttar Pradesh Disaster Management Act,2005; and the Uttaranchal Disaster Management and Prevention Act, 2005.
13. See, National Disaster Management Plan, 2019, National Disaster Management Authority, Government of India November 2019, new Delhi. available at https://ndma.gov. in/images/policyplan/dmplan/ndmp-2019.pdf (last seen Oct 29,2020)
14. Id.
15. See https://ndma.gov.in/images/guidelines/guideline-on- minimum-standard-of-relief.pdf
16. Swaraj Abhiyan v. Union of India AIR 2016 SC 2929
17. Id.

CHAPTER 33

Governance of Disaster Management: Lessons Learnt and a Roadmap to Avert a Future Chamoli Like Disaster

Gopal Vasudeo Wamane

Doctoral Fellow, Jamsetji Tata School of Disaster Studies,
TISS, Mumbai
mp2020dss001@stud.tiss.edu
8766982075

Abstract

The Chamoli disaster due to avalanche in Uttarkhand's Chamoli district in Garhwal Himalayas on 07 Feb 2021, and the subsequent destruction to life and property was a reminder of the Kedarnath tragedy of 2013. Large mass of snow, ice and rock avalanche along with a hanging mass of rock crashed into the Raunthi Garh valley floor (Correspondent, 2021), near Raini village in Chamoli district of Uttarakhand. A swollen water level in the tributaries washed away 13.2MW Rishiganga hydropower project near Joshimath and considerably damaged 520MW Tapovan-Vishnugad hydropower project.

This paper explores lessons learnt and aims to present its thoughts on disaster governance and developing resilient infrastructure by leveraging the application of science and developing governance models which employs 'Janbhagidari' as its key principle. Paper will discuss use of a system akin to Tsunami Warning System, Railway Crossing Relay System and a series of Signalling System across the river valley in order to minimise the damage. Apart from the techniques mentioned, the paper also discusses the use of field measurements to measure abrupt changes in surface air pressure due to sudden avalanches/snowpack accelerations or landslides.

The paper proposes for geo-mapping of debris deposited on hill slopes along the river-basin project, to prepare a 'River Basin Disaster Risk Assessment' (RBDRA) plan with the help of locals and training under the 'District Disaster Management Action Plan' with support of civil society organisations and institutions working in areas of disaster resilience in consonance with objectives laid in the Sendai Framework and the Sustainable Development Goals.

Keywords: Governance, Disaster Management, Glacial outburst, Flood, Janbhagidari, Geo-mapping.

1. Introduction

Uttarakhand, also commonly known as the "Dev Bhumi or Land of the Gods" for its spiritual identity. Once, the spiritual land of India has been started to transform into the land of dams and jungle of concretes, due to the rapid infrastructural and economic development, the environment of Uttarakhand has been degraded up to extreme limit. The purity and spirituality of this holy land has been polluted with ruthless economic desire. Understanding the frequent disasters we can certainly think of the Newtons third law "For every action, there is an equal and opposite reaction", the nature is reacting with extreme events cloudburst, associated flash floods, landslide or the glacial lake outburst flood (GLOF) as the adverse effects of the so called development activities. The logo of CoP-11 Convention on Biological Diversity has a beautiful message ""Nature Protects if She is Protected" (COP-11, 2012), however, the excessive human interference to the natural environment leads to not only a quasi-natural hazard but also a remarkable disaster with societal costs.

Contextualising the region in the larger context human life and Himalayan ecosystem, it contains all the water that drains the three large river systems namely Ganga, Indus and Brahmaputra, this is a hydrosphere of glaciers outside the artic region in the world's tallest mountains, the melting of snow and precipitation forms the vibrant and sometimes wicked flows of rivers, and of intimately connected river and cultural life ways. The 5,000 or more glaciers that make up this hydrosphere are the 'Third Pole,' the largest glacial field outside the North and South Poles (Bahadur, 1993)

Given the unique status of river Ganga, Brahmaputra, and Meghna along with its tributaries and the water it holds, has granted them a revered position in cultural narratives and practices. The river Ganga is the most revered and she is worshipped as a Mother Goddess and eternal purifier. The tributaries to the Brahmaputra are worshipped by Tibetan Buddhists and Hindus and the main stems of the Brahmaputra and Barak rivers are considered sacred by indigenous peoples. With the growing population and quest for more water, we find water entering a new phase of global commodification, putting at stake its sacredness, its tributaries and the human populations that depend upon them.

The paper combines a historical analysis of the developmental politics and activism on dams as agents of development with an ethnography of the experiences of the recent debate on hydropower projects in the Himalayan region. The Tehri dam at the meeting point of the Bhagirathi and Bhilangana rivers, comes at a cost of the submergence of old Tehri village. With its 260-metre-high wall of water in the Garhwal range of the Himalaya, lays in the highly vulnerable seismic activity zone. The new Tehri town sits on a higher ground but falls short of reflecting the confusion and madness of an organically grown township and the spirit that comes from centuries of living history and culture.

2. Brief Historical Overview

A lot has water has passed through the turbines and over spillways (McCully, 2001), the rapidly expanding emphasis on hydropower development in areas prone to geological and hydro-climatic hazards has called into question the risks posed to multiple environmental, ecological and societal cost. But this has received inadequate attention in hydropower planning processes, and even in the campaigns of most citizen initiatives contesting these dams. Using a political ecology framework to analyze the paper explores the reasons why dam safety and hazard potential are often marginal topics in hydropower governance and suggests measures to avert any future incident. The unequal risk of hazardousness of hydropower infrastructure can be seen with a blind-eye to environmental consequence, effect on communities with accelerating processes of social marginalization on one hand and the appropriation of economic benefits by powerful interest groups.

The paper brings into analytical focus to explore the challenges and opportunities that influence the production of knowledge that can create a fertile terrain for contesting hazardous hydropower projects and promoting alternative popular conceptions of risk. The findings will contribute to an emerging body of technological development and research about the implications of hydropower expansionism in the Himalayan hazardscape (Kelly D. Alley & and Mitra, 2014)

The region calls for sustainable development with its ecosystem and water flows necessary for all life, we find this region is damaged with a model of development that is not in sink with sustainable development, while the rivers are progressively dammed to meet the energy demands of growing populations. The emerging hydro-complexity poses a serious risk for the residents living in the river basin area or the river-valley. The increase in climate-induced extreme events, incessant rains, cloudburst and associated flooding shatter against the obstructions and diversions created by the hydropower industry (Khan, 2010). Thus, a greater public participation and awareness of these concrete structures, their pathways, and its implications for river flows needs to be understood.

In 2002, the Government of India announced a plan of 50,000-megawatt initiative to reduce the gap between supply and the growing demand for power. The hydropower initiative is active in the Indian Himalayas where the steep valleys of tributaries to the Indus, Ganga, and Brahmaputra rivers can generate larger power output. This infrastructural growth may not improve access to energy for people living in Himalayan cities and towns; generally citizens living near these facilities get the end of the trickle down effects of a power supply that is directed to high end consumers such as industries and urban blocks (Sreekumar, 2010). These high end users consume this increase in energy while also withdrawing water and returning wastewater to the river system.

3. Temples of the New Age (Nehru, 1958) or Temples of Doom (McCully, 2001)

Concerned with the construction of large dams in the environmentally fragile and seismically active region in Himalayas and the developmental politics in India. It deals with the ideological designs that shapes the implementation of dams in India and juxtaposes it with alternative visions. Reflections on the use of political language on the idea of dams, the study reveals the logic of the discourse, in how it restricts or enables the critique of large dams. The larger consensus is embedded as they are within an overwhelming and seemingly common-sense developmental imagination in the postcolonial world. There are several case examples, which show that the critique of large projects can be formulated based on the historical contingency of developmental perspectives and societal visions. (Werner, 2015)

The 2018 Kerala deluge, where state received heavy monsoon rainfall resulting in dams filling to capacity, causing widespread devastation and loss of lives. By August 15, shutters of the state's 34 out of 42 dams had to be opened following incessant rains in catchment areas. The water discharge from the reservoirs soon led to flooding of other areas. The Kerala High Court appointed Jacob P Alex as the amicus curiae to assist the court in flood-related cases. Mr.Alex informed the court that the Sudden release of water simultaneously from different reservoirs during the heavy rain had aggravated the damage during the floods. He also said that dams in the State did not have an effective flood control zone and flood cushions. Heavy precipitation, poor dam management and weak Early Warning and Response system can be stated as underlying reasons for the damages caused by the worst flood of the century in Kerala.

With the commitment to reduce our dependence on coal and find new ways for electricity generation, we find large dams at the heart of developmental discourse in India. But we need to ask an important question on livelihood, development, environment, and alternative vision to achieve the same, it is not restricted to politicians/ activists, but also to academic and intellectual concerned with questions of vision for modern India.

4. Disaster Governance & Localisation

The critical approach to governance, should pivot the roles citizen monitoring, judicial review vis-à-vis the functions of the state. But what we find is government agencies are waiving environmental protocols under the neoliberal demands for industry incentives (Rajshekhar, 2013). As we find state regulatory functions weaken, citizens are taking up monitoring exercises and are pushing judiciary to enforce appropriate environmental policies and laws.

We find the government has opened the sector for private investments to boost up the hydroelectricity capacity with luring by incentives for open access and the freedom to sell power on a merchant basis. Thereby transferring the hydrological risks to the public, trading in Clean Development Mechanism (CDM) carbon credits, and speculation on 'memoranda of understanding' and clearances (Dharmadhikary, 2005) (Yumnam, 2012). We find 'hollowing out" (Milward, 2000) of regulatory mechanism, in the current phase of government administration in India. This has led to shifting of responsibility to the courts to take stricter actions against government agencies and industry agents.

Comparing it with countries like Nepal, Bhutan, and Bangladesh, the regulatory agencies are even weaker but citizen action is slowly pushing for accountability and monitoring. While in China, any push for information on the construction and functioning of dams is severely constrained. The study finds that citizens in democratic countries enjoy more freedom in anti-dam protest mobilization than those in authoritarian polity, thus pointing towards political structures having significant impact on anti-dam protest mobilization. (Khatun, 2013)

5. Dam and its Functions

With the use of hydropower technology, the water source and availability are modified in time and space in an attempt to meet year-round demand. Also, the hydropower is attractive for contemporary societies, for generating the 'peaking power.' The large storage dams can hold a massive amount of water behind a barrage and facilitate far-reaching water redistribution and reallocation schemes. Water is then released through a head race tunnel to generate power on demand. With run of the river projects, the downstream flow regime alternates between diminished flow at some hours of the day and rushes of water at others. During the monsoon, flooding can occur during a heavy or extreme rain event or by sudden releases of water from the dam reservoir to relieve water pressure. This puts residents downstream at significant risk from changes in stream flow and also from changes and increases in sediment deposition, especially when sediment includes the muck or debris of a dam construction site. This means that residents living downstream from one or many dams and diversions are constantly responding to these changes in the river's rate, direction and volume of flow, and all these create cumulative challenges to human adaptation and resilience (Programme, 2010) (Lahiri-Dutt, 2012). River flows that are altered by hydroelectric dams and canals and diverted to needy urban centers are also affecting the groundwater recharge rate. In Bangladesh surface water is and will remain in high demand to offset the inability to use arsenic-contaminated groundwater for human consumption.

6. Hydropower Development & Impact on River Basin

Hydropower is an important energy strategy that reshapes the hydrosphere as it becomes a functioning part of it. Large dams were built just after Indian Independence as part of national development and despite major oppositions to them, projects grew in number over the following three decades (Chellaney, 2011). Large hydropower projects have received criticism across the world for their debilitating consequences: the massive displacement of people, the redirection of water in ways that create new forms of scarcity, and the hydrologically and ecologically destructive interventions in river and terrestrial systems (McCully, 2001) (Dams, 2000). The current wave of dam investment in India is motivated by interests in powering industrial growth and urban expansion in the face of dwindling gas reserves and problems with coal block development.

In the State of Uttarakhand, along the tributaries of the Ganga River, the Tehri dam and several run of the river dams were completed in the first decade of the twenty-first century to provide energy and water supply to the northwestern states of Uttar Pradesh, Delhi and Rajasthan. In Sikkim, a series of dams is under construction along the Teesta River and along the Rangit that flows into it. In the state of Arunachal Pradesh, the government has sketched up a series of projects along the main tributaries of the Brahmaputra, the Siang, Subansiri, Lohit, and Dibang rivers, while the tributaries of river manas like river Tawang and Nyamjang Chhu is also dotted with many proposed projects.

The state of Arunachal Pradesh is midst of a "Hydroelectricity Megawatt" transformation poised to outpace the states of Himachal Pradesh and Uttarakhand in terms of its production. However, the state lacks the roads, bridges, transmission lines, and supporting infrastructure needed for private sector participation. This has slowed the destruction of the hydrosphere to some extent but enabled a lively game of speculation through 'Memoranda of Agreement' or 'Memoranda of Understanding' between politicians, government officials and specific investor companies. Since projects listed by the Central Electricity Authority are allocated to private companies through preliminary memoranda of understanding or agreement, there is ample opportunity for private deals, covert decision-making and corruption (Rajshekhar, 2013). These are agreements that entail a particular channeling of private capital through individuals holding specific government and private company posts; this capital may not be invested in local economies. As many have recently noted, the process creates an unofficial protocol and pricing system, and while following government rules and procedures to some extent, adds the incentive of profit making from paper clearances and permits, a remaking of the license raj that plagued the early years of India's infrastructure development. The long gestation period in the hydropower industry is the riskiest part, followed with procurement memoranda and clearances (Rajshekhar, 2013).

The media and informed observers have known about China's plan to develop four run of the river projects along the Yarlung Tsangpo for several years and their push forced the Chinese government's recent announcement in its energy development plan for 2015 (Watts, 2010). One dam has been completed at Zangmu and three more are under construction at Dagu, Jiacha, and Jiexu. There are also basic infrastructure projects near Motuo at the Great bend, indicating that a dam larger than the Three Gorges dam could be constructed there in the future.

The state of Kerala experienced unprecedentedly severe flooding, various experts held the dams responsible for aggravating the floods, but a report by the Central Water Commission (CWC) absolved the dams and their operators from any blame (Thakkar, 2018). Such acts put light on some often-neglected facts, large dams are risk-laden artifacts-exposed to earthquakes, floods, extreme rainfall, avalanches and landslides.

Humans will strive for excellence, but a slightest error, it is able to cause an equal number of environmental hazards, functioning instability ultimately. As these catastrophes and numerous others in the past remind us, dams do sometimes fail or otherwise produce large-scale hazards. The history of the modern large dam includes a long list of dam-related disasters with a substantial human death toll (McCully, 2001). This fact is often forgotten or negated, partly owing to "hydro hubris" (Pearce, 1992)—with unwavering faith in the godlike power and virtuosity of modern hydraulic engineering and the large dams infallible to human errors. We find attempts to ignore or negate the fallibility of dams due to associated economic and political reasons behind, to an extent to erase such "accidents" from collective memory (Armiero, 2011).

The dominant pro-dam discourse celebrates hydropower as sustainable renewable source of energy indispensable to development objectives, in the backdrop of 'green growth', 'climate change mitigation', and poverty alleviation (Schneider, 2013). While the dam lobby readily discusses mitigation strategies for contentious "externalities" like social displacement or ecological impacts, but the important question of environmental and technological risks emanating from hydropower infrastructure rarely figures in public narratives. As we observe, the global hydropower frontier is expanding into many highly hazard-prone river basins, risk management emerges as a major challenge of environmental governance (Mukerjee, 2015).

With private and public corporations eyeing to tap world's remaining unexploited rivers, located in ecologically sensitive forest and mountain areas where climate change increasingly destabilizes precarious local environmental equilibria (Kelly-Richards, 2017). The question of relevance is how new hydro infrastructure interacts with environmental hazards, and how decision-makers act to mitigate and adapt the associated risks is acutely relevant.

7. Design/Methodology/Approach

The paper proposes a framework for disaster management planning with its 'River Basin Disaster Risk Assessment' (RBDRA) plan. A plan incorporates principles of disaster governance with appropriate legislation, localisation-*Janbhagidari*-community participation by 'reinforcement of local capacities', leveraging technology for the unique 'River Basin Risk Management System' ['RBRMS'] on lines of Tsunami Warning System, Railway Crossing Relay System and employing field measurements to measure abrupt changes in surface air pressure.

The paper engenders the dialectical water-society understandings with the notions of hydro-social cycle. The widespread engineering of river systems and developing a public database that bring the hydropower infrastructure to the center of the water-society discussion. The water basin is mapped not only with the dams, spillways, tunnels and power houses, but also human settlements who have made the river valleys their home and all this is carved out of the terrain that is interfering with the hydrosphere of the region. Developing a "bottom-up resistance to energy infrastructure" will only stifle the growth as energy consumption do marks important indicator of the growth of a nation. We propose identification of this material infrastructures with community participation and a disaster governance legislative treatment. Thus leveraging the principles of political ecology (Wikipedia, 2021) to democratizing the economy with a means of creating more social control over the market from the bottom up approach, so that the demands of people and environment provide a counterweight to the dictates of profit for few.

8. 'River Basin Risk Management System' ['RBRMS']

The 'River Basin Risk Management System' ['RBRMS'] is based on the integrated principle which deploys a series of measures to achieve a minimised impact of any disaster with a River Basin Approach. The measures included—

1. Disaster Governance & Participation
   (a) Regulatory-Governance Approach
   (b) Agenda for Localisation with reinforcement of local capacities
2. Technological intervention—
   (a) Tsunami Warning System,
   (b) Railway Crossing Relay System and employing field measurements to measure abrupt changes in surface air pressure.

Regulatory-Governance Approach

The paper proposes a Risk Impact Assessment ['RIA'] framework as against the Environmental Impact Assessment ['EIA'] as a tool used to identify the environmental, social and economic impacts of a project prior to decision-making (CBD, 2021). The EIA tool aims to predict the environmental impacts at an early stage in project planning and design, thereby reducing adverse impacts of projects to suit the local environment and present the predictions and options to decision-makers, we have seen its limitations and pitfalls. While the Risk Impact Assessment framework at the river basin level will help to assess the probability of a disaster and estimating the cost in the event of a disaster. The RIA at the river basin level will be a guiding framework to provide a holistic view of its development and adhering to its principles the EIA can be prepared at individual project level.

At a macrolevel river basin specific indicators like classification of topography like those based on nature rock strata or earthquake proneness etc; identification of risk to encompass individual perception, social representation and objective assessment; risk reduction strategy to for prevention and mitigation, disaster management for response and recovery, and the governance and financial protection for institutionalization and risk transfer (Martha Liliana Carreno, 2007). A matrix for the EIA can be prepared based on the broader principles laid out by the Risk Impact Assessment framework to manage or mitigate the realization of high probability/high consequence risk events.

Agenda for Localisation with reinforcement of local capacities

India a continent size country is prone to a variety of disasters and hence it is necessary to build capacity and reduce disaster losses by evolving a workable methodology for community-based disaster risk management. The World Humanitarian Summit (2016) discussions on making the humanitarian system more effective and relevant, by ensuring humanitarian preparedness and response capacity with those nearest to the crisis affected-populations as they are best placed to respond quickly and appropriately. The Grand Bargain Commitments agreed at the Summit are a landmark attempt at reforming the international humanitarian system (Practice, 2018). There are varying factors which influences progress towards a 'participation revolution' and 'reinforcement of local capacities' in different contexts. A proactive plan with necessary socio-economic, scientific and technical considerations along with implementation, monitoring and review strategies for effective disaster risk management will help in delivering self-initiatives and actions on the part of local communities to eliminate / reduce losses or threats from potential disasters.

With the Chamoli disaster, Bhagirathi and Alaknanda have shown us a trailer, Uttarakhand is yet to witness an array of devastations bring to forefront the calls by Chandi Prasad Bhatt and the Chipko movement which started in Reni the very place affected the most. The unabated approvals for the hydropower plants and blasting in the fragile Himalayas points towards vulnerability to cause natural disasters. May it be to stop construction of these hydropower plants, including Tehri dam, Tapovan-Vishnugad, Pancheshwar, Roopali Gadh and Kishau dams. We need to understand the hydro-social cycle as a means of theorizing and analyzing the water-society relations (Jamie Linton, 2014). The Chamoli disaster brings us to understanding that disasters are not only linked to hazardous events but also to the vulnerabilities of the exposed elements and capacities within the society to cope with them due to anthropogenic interventions.

The disaster struck Raini village, the cradle of the Chipko Movement, initiated by villagers in Uttarakhand in the 1970s. It is necessary to employ traditional knowledge and know-how, to act against these risks and ensure support for necessary knowledge, technologies, resources, and skills for managing these risks by active participation/partnership of the public with support from professionals, administrators and other stakeholders.

It should be ensured that in designing, implementing, and reviewing crisis responses, there should be active empowering for affected populations. People must have an early say in the design and planning phase of response, communication and feedback mechanisms to set up participation with the community and should regularly test with the disaster affected populations to involve in reviews and evaluations. It should be endured people are treated with dignity, standards of staff behaviour and the collaborating agencies to demonstrate practical competency in working with conflict-sensitivity, community survivor for the plan of adaptation.

Data and information on land use changes, riverbed and flow regime changes, and actual stages of hydropower project construction should be available to all river basin residents, scientists, civil society, and governments through online resources. Also the use of satellite imagery and aerial photography will facilitate the most conscientious use of these shared hydrological resources.

The Janbhagidari will contributes to the aim of citizen groups to limit, monitor and regulate the practices of hydropower companies and the management of their infrastructure in the river basis of their immediate dependence. These motivated citizen with knowledge exchanges through online portals and social media, can push for better transnational instruments for formal governmental data sharing.

The Sustainable Development Goals (SDG-9) calls for building resilient infrastructure, to promote inclusive and sustainable industrialization and to foster innovation. The experience of anti-dam or the environmental movement calls for develop models of governance which ingrains principles of "Janbhagidari".

Leveraging the underlying theme : Tsunami Warning System (TWS)

The TWS is made up of a network of seismic monitoring stations and sea level gauges. It relies on measuring the movement of dart buoys – which record changes in the sea level—or assessing the bottom pressure of the propagating tsunami. The TWS uses geospatial data and GIS analysis techniques to build an accurate tsunami forecasting system at the specified Tsunami Warning Centers. Thus the resulting forecast can be integrated into applications and visualizations to assess hazard risk and provide mitigation for the coastal communities and urban centers.

Here we discuss how, we can leverage the available TWS and geospatial technologies to address issues in 'River Basin Risk Management System' ['RBRMS'] hazard mitigation and emergency management models. Additionally, with the prototype developed can be scaled and coupled with other vulnerable river basins to develop evacuation models, visualization, mapping for the use of communities-private entities-government.

Leveraging the underlying theme: Railway Crossing Relay System

The Geological Survey of India (GSI) in a report states large mass of snow, ice and rock avalanche along with a hanging mass of rock crashing into the Raunthi Garh valley floor. The impact pulverised the combination of rock, snow and ice causing a rapid flow downstream of Raunthi Garh and into the Rishiganga valley leading to the deluge (Correspondent, 2021).

Understanding the kind of disasters and leveraging the underlying theme of railway crossing relay system to ensure the accidents are minimised, a similar "relay system" can be thought of for the river basin. The river basin be mapped with a series of signalling devices which can picked any unfortunate incident and correspondingly alert the residents living in the areas.

Such series of relay stations can be established along the length of river valley, which will be beneficial for the people living and working in the region. The deluge destroyed the 13.2 MW Rishiganga power plant and damaged the 520 MW Tapovan-Vishnugadh hydel power project, along with workers in tunnels been fatally trapped.

Field measurements to measure abrupt changes in surface air pressure

In all areas of the basin the warming climate will induce faster glacial melt and bring more water into the river system at some times of the year. This can lead to flash floods especially at times when heavy rainfall combines with glacial lake outbursts or GLOFs within the glacial formations (Correspondent, 2021). The dams are dis-embedding the river from their ecological and hydrological systems and are subjecting the river's flow to nested infrastructures with engineering control. When additional water enters the system from a glacial lake outburst, the pressure on the reservoirs quickly increases. At those moments of crisis, water has to be released suddenly from reservoirs by opening the barrage gates and this puts everyone and everything downstream at greater risk of flooding. Increased rainfall and glacial melt may help to recharge groundwater and dilute pollution in the river stream but both can lead to dangerous and even deadly hydro-hazards.

Measurement of surface air pressure and snowpack accelerations by employing the field measurement instruments to measure the abrupt changes in surface air pressure will help in a developing a response to any such event (Stephan Simioni, 2015).

9. Conclusion

A study by National Remote Sensing Centre (NRSC) indicated that, "the time taken from the initiation of the avalanche and its disastrous impact up to Tapovan barrage site near Joshimath was barely 50 minutes, which indicates availability of a very low lead time for raising any warning for the downstream areas." The threat of climate change is real, it is causing higher temperatures in the upper reaches of the Himalaya and apart from this the constant freezing and thawing of ice made parts of rocks weak making them vulnerable to collapse. The Geological Survey of India report noted that "Areas having risks posed by smaller mountain glaciers were also becoming important sites where such hazards formed. The steep higher order streams and the narrow river valleys in the high-altitude areas of Himalayas remain extremely hazard prone, which are not only vulnerable to Glacial Lake Outburst Flood (GLOF)/ Landslide Lake Outburst Flood (LLOF) hazards but have also become locale for a major disaster caused due to the domino effect of large/mega landslide and avalanche".

The ruthless human desire for rapid development has increased and accelerated the impact of the disaster. There should be emphasis on groups training with the early warning

system, effective evacuation plans and responsive disaster management group be prepared with the assistance with National Disaster Management Authority (NDMA) and these groups can be deployed block wise with active participation of local inhabitants.

The state of Uttarakhand falls in seismic zone V, and thus efforts should be to avoid construction of big dams on highly seismic areas, even though its technical feasibility is proven but any negative impact should be kept in mind. Due care be taken that proposed dam won't submerge the important holy confluences, otherwise the river morphology and ecology will be disturbed.

The dams construction in the vulnerable high terrain areas with weak lithology be avoided for big dams, instead small dams in upper catchment areas be considered according to the stream order and distribution of contours. It is also important to maintain enough distance between two dams so that the natural flow of the rivers won't be interrupted. This type of dams can also play a vital role in village electrification generating the hydro power as well as can provide irrigational water.

An accelerated efforts for plantation of Oak in high mountain areas with social forestry be undertaken with the cooperation of local governing bodies and local inhabitants. The oaks has proven capability to compaction the lithology with organic matters than pine or other gymnosperms. In the Eco-sensitive zones, there should be restriction on mass tourism especially in the Char Dhams, Valley of Flowers and several glaciers and snouts areas. Environmental Tax must be collected from the tourists and vehicles to regulate the influx of vehicular movement in high terrain areas.

Apart from this the construction of buildings on unstable hill slopes and young flood pains should be restricted. While due attention be paid to sanitation and sewerage systems as it has a detrimental impact in the environment.

> "Earth provides enough to satisfy every man's need,
> But not every man's greed"
>
> —*Mahatma Gandhi*

10. Acknowledgement

The author is grateful to Prof. Janki Andharia, Dean -Jamsetji Tata School of Disaster Studies, Professor TISS, Mumbai campus, for the kind support and encouragement.

REFERENCES

1. Alley, K. D., Hile, R., & Mitra, C. (2014). Visualizing Hydropower Across the Himalayas:Mapping in a time of

Regulatory Decline. *Himalaya, the Journal of the Association for Nepal and Himalayan Studies*, Vol. 34: No. 2, Article 9.

2. Armiero, M. (2011). *A Rugged Nation: Mountains and the Making of Modern Italy*. The Whitehorse Press: Cambridge, UK.

3. Bahadur, J. (1993). The Himalayas: A Third Polar Region. Snow and Glacier Hydrology. *International Associaltion of Hydrological Sciences* (pp. 181-190). Proceedings of the Kathmandu Symposium.

4. CBD. (2021). *EIA*. Retrieved from www.cbd.int: https://www.cbd.int/impact/whatis.shtml Chellaney, B. (2011). *Water: Asia's New Battleground*. Georgetown: Georgetown University Press. COP-11. (2012). *COP-11*. Retrieved from Convention on Biodiversity: https://www.cbd.int/cop11/

5. Correspondent, S. (2021, June 29). Retrieved from www.thehindu.com: https://www.thehindu.com/news/national/chamoli-disaster-due-to-avalanche-says-geological-survey-of-india/article35031786.ece

6. Dams, W. C. (2000). *Dams and Development: A New Framework for Decision-Making*. The Report of the World Commission on Dams. Earthscan.

7. Dharmadhikary, S. (2005). *Unravelling Bhakra: Assessing the Temple of Resurgent India.* . Report of a Study. Badwani: Manthan Adhyayan Kendra.

8. Jamie Linton, J. B. (2014). The hydrosocial cycle: Defining and mobilizing a relational-dialectical approach to water. *http://dx.doi.org/10.1016/j.geoforum.2013.10.008*, 170–180.

9. Kelly D. Alley, H. R., & and Mitra, C. (2014). Visualizing Hydropower Across the Himalayas: Mapping in a time of Regulatory Decline. *Himalaya, the Journal of the Association for Nepal and Himalayan Studies*, Vol. 34: No. 2, Article 9.

10. Kelly-Richards, S. S.-C. (2017). *Governing the transition to renewable energy: A review of impacts and policy issues in the small hydropower boom.* https://doi.org/10.1016/j.enpol.2016.11.035.

11. Khan, S. H. (2010). Hydrocomplexity: New Tools for Solving Wicked Water Problems. *IAHS Proceedings*, Reports No. 338.

12. Khatun, K. R. (2013). *Political Structure and Anti-dam Protest Movements: Comparing Cases of India and China;*. Uppsala: Department of Earth Sciences, Geotryckeriet, Uppsala University.

13. Lahiri-Dutt, K. (2012). Large Dams and Changes in an Agrarian Society: Gendering the Impacts of Damodar Valley Corporation in Eastern India. *Water Alternatives*, 529–542.

14. Martha Liliana Carreno, O. D. (2007). A disaster risk management performance index. *Nat Hazards*, 1–20.

15. McCully, P. (2001). *Silenced River: The Ecology and Politics of Large Dams*. London and New York: Zed Book Ltd.

16. Milward, H. B. (2000). Governing the Hollow State. *Journal of Public Administration, Research and Theory 10 (2): 359–379.*

17. Mukerjee, M. (2015). *The Impending Dam Disaster in the Himalayas.* Retrieved from www.scientificamerican.com: https://www.scientificamerican.com/article/the-impending-dam-disaster-in-the-himalayas/

18. Nehru, J. (1958). *Jahawarlal Nehru Speeches-Vol 3*. New Delhi: Publication Division Ministry of Information and Broadcasting GOI.

19. Pearce, F. (1992). *The Dammed: Rivers, Dams and the Coming World Water Crisis;*. London: Bodley Head: London, UK.

20. Practice, L. i. (2018). *Disaster and Emergences Preparedness Program.* https://reliefweb.int/sites/reliefweb.int/files/resources/Localisation-In-Practice-Full-Report-v4.pdf.

21. Programme, C. D. (2010). The Waters of the Third Pole: Sources of Threat, Sources of Survival. *London: Aon Benfield UCL Hazard Research Centre*.

22. Rajshekhar, M. (2013, May 5). *Hydelgate: Dam Frenzy Fails to Notice Environmental Concerns.*

23. Retrieved from The Hindu: http://m.economictimes.com/news/news-by-industry/energy/power/hydelgate-dam-frenzy-fails-to-noticeenvironmental-concerns/articleshow/19902212.cms>

24. Schneider, H. (2013). *World Bank Turns to Hydropower to Square Development with Climate Change*. Retrieved from www.washingtonpost.com: https://www.washingtonpost.com/business/economy/world-bank-turnsto-hydropower-to-square-development-with-climate-change/2013/05/08/b9d60332-b1bd-11e2-9a98-4be1688d7d84_story.html

25. Sreekumar, N. A. (2010). Electricity for All. India Together.

26. Stephan Simioni, R. S. (2015). Field measurements of snowpack response to explosive loading. *https://doi.org/10.1016/j.coldregions.2015.06.011*, 179-190.

27. Thakkar, H.. (2018). Role of dams in Kerala's flood disaster. *Econ. Polit. Wkly. LIII*, pp. 20-23. Watts, J. (2010, May 24). *Chinese Engineers Propose World's Biggest Hydro-Electric Project in Tibet Mega-Dam on Yarlung Tsangpo River Would Save 200m Tonnes*. Retrieved from The Guardian: http://www.theguardian.com/environment/2010/may/24/chinese-ydroengineerspropose-tibet-dam

28. Werner, H. (2015). *The Politics of Dams Developmental Perspectives and Social Critique in Modern India*. OUP.

29. Wikipedia. (2021). *Political_ecology*. Retrieved from https://en.wikipedia.org/wiki/Political_ecology: https://en.wikipedia.org/wiki/Political_ecology

30. Yumnam, J. (2012). *An Assessment of Dams in India's North East Seeking Carbon Credits from Clean Development Mechanism of the United Nations Framework Convention on Climate Change*. Manipur: Citizens' Concern for Dams and Development.

CHAPTER 34

Disaster Risks and Management In India: A Critical Analysis of the Disaster Management Act

Akash Kumar Patel

Centre of Excellence in Disaster Mitigation & Management
Indian Institute of Technology, Roorkee, India
akashnitb19@gmail.com

Divya Jain

Department of Urban Planning
School of Planning and Architecture, New Delhi, India
divya.jain11@gmail.com

Abstract

The manifestations of nature are boundless—what nurtures life and beauty, is perhaps the greatest source of destruction as well, when it unleashes its wrath in the form of natural disasters. The evolution of the human race, particularly progress in science and technology has resulted in frequent occurrences of natural as well as 'man-made' disasters-ranging from a disaster affecting smaller regions to a global pandemic. It is now more than ever that the concept of 'disaster management' has assumed significance worldwide owing to the global pandemic of COVID-19. It is the need of the hour to formulate advanced policies and adopt best practices to reduce the risk of disasters, and the best possible way to reduce such risks is to ensure effective integration of Disaster Risk Reduction (DRR) policies with available cutting-edge technology in the field of disaster management. Many nations have accordingly formulated disaster management acts for effective management of disasters in their countries, Indian Government enacted Disaster Management Act, 2005 for the same. India is one of the ten most disaster-prone countries in the world. Due to its vast territory, large population and adverse geo-climatic conditions, environmental degradation, and non-scientific development practices, it is frequently exposed to nature as well as man-made disasters. Disaster Management (DM) Act, 2005 caused a paradigm shift in the conventional regime of disaster management and ushered in a new approach for effective disaster management. This act proved to be a distinct move from the earlier approach of post-disaster relief to pre-disaster preparedness, mitigation, and risk reduction. It is an important watershed in the evolution of a legal framework for disaster management in India. Amidst of COVID-19 pandemic, the need to review this act in its techno-financial aspect becomes more significant. This study will critically analyze the DM act and will put forward its merits and shortcomings in the techno-financial aspect. This study will critically analyze the effectiveness of the DM act in terms of managing disasters in the country. Also, the study will refer to some best practices of Disaster Management Acts around the globe and propose future strategies for the effective management of disasters.

Keywords: Disasters, Disaster Management Act, Disaster Risk Reduction, Techno-Financial Aspect

1. Introduction

India is prone to various types of disasters such as earthquakes, floods, tsunami, cyclones, landslides, etc. and it is susceptible to such disasters because of several natural and anthropogenic factors, such as adverse geo-climatic conditions, population growth, topographic features, degradation of the environment, rural-urban migration, industrial growth, unplanned developmental practices, etc.

These factors are mainly responsible for multiplying the frequency and aggravating the impact of disasters that cause heavy socio-economic as well as biodiversity loss. (NDMA, 2018)

In the wake of the Bhuj earthquake and the tsunami of 2004, the Government of India enforced the National disaster management act, 2005. The National Disaster Management Act provides for a detailed framework from the Union and state

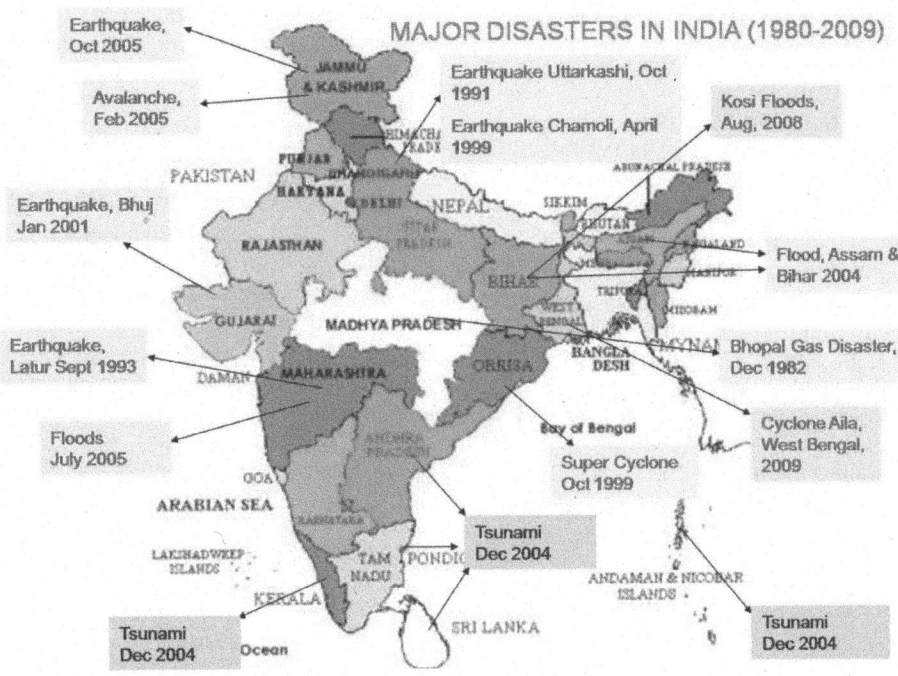

Fig. 34.1   Major Disasters in India Source: Wikimedia Commons

Source: Wikimedia Commons

government to the district and local levels to prepare, execute and implement disaster management plans in the country. India's National Disaster Manager Authority (NDMA) is the apex agency to initiate processes to alleviate suffering arising out of various disasters such as natural, man-made, biological, chemical, and hydrological disasters. It was created under the framework of the National Disaster Management (DM) Act 2005, which provides in it superseding powers to make rules and regulations for the prevention, containment, evacuation, providing relief to victims in unfortunate situations of disaster. (NDMA, 2019)

2. Institutional Arrangements Before the DM Act, 2005

Earlier, the responsibility of the management of natural as well as man-made disasters vests with the state governments concerned. The Government of India had played an enabling and supportive role. At times of disasters, the Government of India supported the concerned State governments in terms of financial and human resources. Post-independence, the Ministry of Agriculture acted as the nodal ministry for disaster management in the country. The Natural Disaster Management (NDM) Division of the Ministry of Agriculture, chaired by a Joint Secretary, assisted the Central Relief Commissioner had the responsibility of managing disasters. According to types and nature of disasters, the different ministry was provided with nodal role and responsibility. For example, the Ministry of Civil Aviation was provided a nodal role for air accidents; the Ministry of Railways was provided a nodal role for rail accidents, etc.

National Crisis Management Committee (NCMC) was the apex organization, headed by the Cabinet Secretary, with Secretaries of the different government Departments and Secretary to the Prime Minister as Members. NCMC guided and establish coordination among various departments of the Government of India in the situation of crisis. (Planning Commission, 2012)

In 2001, after the Gujarat earthquake, the subject of disaster management was transferred from the Ministry of Agriculture to the Ministry of Home Affairs (MHA). The Ministry of Agriculture continued to be in charge of the management of incidents related to agriculture such as drought, pest attack, cold waves, frost, and hailstorms. (NDMA, 2019)

High powered committee (HPC) created by the Union government in 1999 recommends the establishment of a separate Ministry of Disaster Management. It had also recommended the formation of the National Council on Disaster Management. At the central level, the central idea behind the formation of a National Emergency Management Authority (NEMA) is to facilitate coordination and take measures for preparedness, prevention, mitigation, response, recovery, and relief to people. (NDMA, 2016)

3. National Disaster Management Act, 2005

The super-cyclone of 1999, which occurred in the Orissa region, was a watershed event in the development of disaster legislation in the country. It forced the Government of Orissa to take proactive steps towards strengthening its disaster management framework and the formation of the Orissa State Disaster Management Authority (OSDMA), the first authority solely dedicated to disaster management established in India. The framework provided within the OSDMA act later acted as a role model for the National Disaster Management Act of 2005 and helped the policymakers in its enactment. (Sarkar & Sarma, 2006)

The National disaster management Act, 2005, provides the framework for institutional structures at the national, state, and district levels. It contains 11 chapters, which have 79 sections. It contains detailed provisions for NDMA, SDMA, DDMA, measures by the government for DM, etc. (GoI, 2005)

Table 34.1 NDMA and Important Sections

Chapter I	Preliminary (01-02)
Chapter II	The National Disaster Management Authority (03-13)
Chapter III	State Disaster Management Authority (14-24)
Chapter IV	District Disaster Management Authority (25-34)
Chapter V	Measures by the Government for Disaster Management (35-40)
Chapter VI	Local Authorities (41)
Chapter VII	National Institute of Disaster Management (42-43)
Chapter VIII	National Disaster Response Force (44-45)
Chapter IX	Finance, Accounts and Audit (46-50)
Chapter X	Offences And Penalties (51-60)
Chapter XI	Miscellaneous (61-79)

Source: Adopted from NDMA Act,2005

3.1 Purpose of the Act

Disaster management has not been mentioned 7th schedule of the Indian Constitution, where subjects are listed in the union, state, concurrent list. Powers are divided between central and state governments, they can make laws within their respective domain. Due to the absence of a constitutional list of subjects, disaster management had been controlled by state governments within the competence as adopted in the colonial period. The basic responsibility for disaster management is vested with the concerned State Government. At times of disasters, the Government of India supported the concerned State governments in terms of financial and human resources. Central government facilitated other services such as inter-state movement, transport, warning, and food grains in the affected areas.

The main purpose behind the act was to create an apex-level body for the management of disasters in the country. For this purpose, National Disaster Management Authority (NDMA) was created, and a regulatory framework was given for the creation of State Disaster Management Authorities (SDMA) at the state level and District Disaster Management Authorities (DDMA) at the district level. This act changed the approach of government from providing relief in the post-disaster period to take proactive steps for preparedness, mitigation, and risk reduction in the pre-disaster period. NDMA act has well served its purpose to some extent that after enactment of the act there have been several advancements in the field of Disaster Management in the country. The act also helped in generating awareness of Disasters among different stakeholders. (Paul & Rajib, 2018)

3.2 Defining Disaster

The NDMA Act defines a disaster as *"a catastrophe, mishap, calamity or grave occurrence in any area, arising from natural or man-made causes, or by accident or negligence which results in substantial loss of life or human suffering or damage to, and destruction of, property, or damage to, or degradation of, environment, and is of such a nature or magnitude as to be beyond the coping capacity of the community of the affected area"*. (GoI, 2005)

3.3 Legal Institutional Framework

India's National Disaster Manager Authority (NDMA) is the apex agency to initiate processes to alleviate suffering arising out of various disasters such as natural, man-made, biological, chemical, and hydrological disasters. It was formed under the framework of the National Disaster Management (DM) Act 2005, which provides it extensive powers to make rules and regulations for the prevention, evacuation, providing relief, and various other disaster relief measures in the interest of the affected people.

The Act provides for setting up of a National Disaster Management Authority (NDMA), which is headed by the Prime Minister, State Disaster Management Authorities (SDMAs), which is headed by the Chief Ministers, District Disaster Management Authorities (DDMAs), which is headed by Collectors/District Magistrates/Deputy Commissioners. The Act further contains provisions for the formation of the different executive as well as advisory committees at national and state levels. The National Authority has powers for the formation of the advisory committee consisting of experts of different domains. Central Government can fix the number of members from time to time basis after consultation with the national disaster management authority. (Das, 2012)

Following the provisions enumerated in the DM act, 2005, the National Institute of Disaster Management (NIDM) for capacity building and training of personnel and the National Disaster Response Force (NDRF) for emergency operation

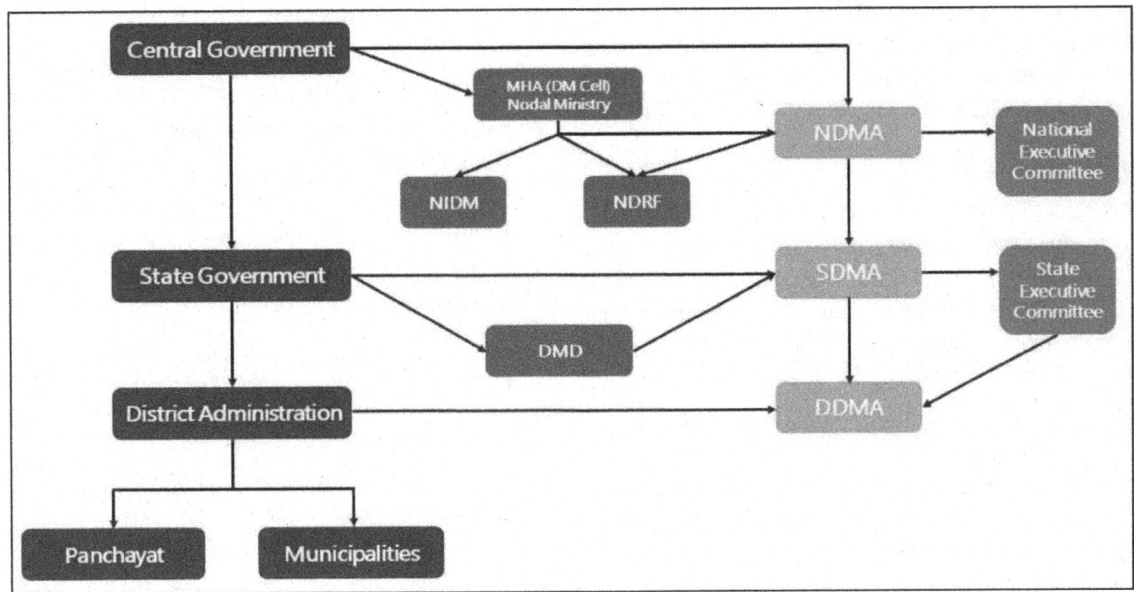

Fig. 34.2 Institutional Framework for DM

Source: Adopted from NDMA Act,2005

have been established. It also gives directions to the Ministry and Departments concerned in the preparation of their disaster management plans aligned with the National disaster management plan for disaster management. The act also mentions the Disaster Management Department (DMD) at the state level that will be linked up with SDMA for managing affairs and decisions related to disasters at the state level. The act also contains provisions regarding financial mechanisms such as the formation of the National Disaster Mitigation Fund and National Disaster Response Fund at the national, state, and district levels for disaster risk management.

National Executive Committee (NEC) and State Executive Committee (SEC) were created under the framework of DM Act, 2005 to assist the National disaster management authority (NDMA) in the execution of its duties and functions. NEC is headed by the Home Secretary, who act as *ex-officio* Chairperson with other Secretaries under Ministries or Departments of Union government under Ministry of Agriculture, Environment Forest and climate change, Jal Shakti, Power, Finance, Health, Rural Development, Urban Development, Science and technology, atomic energy, Defense, Space, Telecommunication and Chief of defense staff are its ex-officio Members. Similarly, SEC is headed by the Chief Secretary who will act as *ex-officio* Chairperson with four other Secretaries of State Government as it may think fit.

After the implementation of the 73rd and 74th constitutional amendment acts to the constitution and the emergence of independent, rural and urban governments, as key administrative units, the role of local authorities is now increased in administration. The National Disaster

Management Act, 2005 has provisions for local bodies that what role they will play in disaster risk management. The Act also endows certain responsibilities and functions to local Government (urban and rural) in disaster risk management. (GoI, 2005)

3.4 Financial Arrangements

After independence, the financing mechanism for disaster management has been decided according to successive finance commission's recommendations. The (9th FC) ninth finance commission introduced the calamity Relief fund. In addition, (10th FC) The Tenth finance commission proposed a national fund for calamity relief. The (11th FC) eleventh finance commission made a recommendation for the creation of the national calamity contingency fund instead of the national fund for calamity relief. (Delhi & Dhar Chakrabarti, 2009)

The Act contains provisions for the creation of two Funds, namely, the **National Disaster Response Fund (NDRF)** and the **National Disaster Mitigation Fund (NDMF)** at the national level. The Act enumerates that the Response Fund will be provided to the NEC for rehabilitation, response, relief, and recovery operations. As per guidelines formulated by the Union government after consultation with the NDMA. The NDMF has been dedicated for mitigation purposes while other fund NDRF has to be used for response and recovery purposes. (Delhi & Dhar Chakrabarti, 2009)

The Act contains provisions for the creation of mitigation and response funds at the state and district levels. The SDRF be provided to the SEC for rehabilitation, response, relief, and recovery operations, and SDMF shall be made provided to the SDMA for dedicated mitigation purposes. However, similar fund at district level has not been created by the State Governments, which is a major criticism. (NIDM, 2009)

3.5 Other Provisions

The act also has miscellaneous provisions which act as directives to central Government, State Governments, Local Governments, media, etc. These enumerate certain provisions which have to be followed by the central Government while compensation (such as discrimination, rescue operations). Some of these are briefly mentioned below:

- NDMA Act mandates the National disaster management authority to prepare an Annual plan, in the specified format and at a specific time as given by the central government and present its annual report to the central government mentioning its activities and accounts of the previous financial year.

- It also contains provisions regarding power to make laws by central as well as state government and delegation of powers.

- NDMA Act provides immunity to officials and employees of the central and state government from legal processes concerning a decision taken for disaster management within their respective jurisdiction.

- This act provides overriding powers to the Central government in case of a disaster in the country.

- The act also provides penal provisions for different offenses committed during the disaster mentioning actions by different stakeholders, which will be considered as offenses and penalties will be charged based on the law. (GoI, 2005)

4. Case Studies

4.1 South Africa: Disaster Management Act

The South African disaster management act has been proved to be the most effective among all disaster management acts for disaster management. Consultation with various stakeholders has been done while drafting this act. Through an amendment of the Constitution, the subject of disaster management was added to the concurrent list, in which the national and provisional government's role was clearly defined.

The South African disaster management act envisages a three-layer legal-institutional framework for effective management of disaster at the national, regional, and local levels. At the apex level, the Intergovernmental Committee on Disaster Management (ICDM) has been created. The ICDM is headed by a Cabinet Member appointed by the President.

- Through an amendment of the Constitution, the subject of disaster management was added to the concurrent list, in which the national and provisional government's role was clearly defined.

- The act contains provisions for volunteers to ensure their participation and their role has been appreciated.

- The act classifies disasters in different types, declaration of disaster after its occurrence vests within the competent authority.

- The Act talks rigorously about risk assessment and makes compulsory for competent authorities to update risk profile for the region.

- The act emphasizes generating public awareness, research, and new ideas for effective disaster management.

- Ensures that decisions are taken after consensus and coordination between various stakeholders and committees and by integrating of government's agencies dealing in the field of disaster management. (Van Niekerk, 2015)

4.2 The Philippines: Disaster Risk Reduction and Management Act

As the Philippines is susceptible to a variety type of disasters as the region falls within the "Pacific ring of fire belt". The Philippines has always taken prior steps towards disaster mitigation and management. The legal-institutional framework envisaged in the act also talks about disasters that are dynamic in structure. It also talks about the social, economic, and environmental impact of climate change on communities. The policies framed by the Philippines are focused on the adaptation of climate change and disaster risk reduction. The definition of vulnerable communities has been mentioned in the act which is **people, who are highly exposed to poverty due to disasters it includes children, women, the elderly, differently-abled, and ethnic minorities**. It holistically covers all types of disasters and defines vulnerable communities. (Brower & Magno, 2011)

- To review National framework and policies after five years.

- Integration of all government departments engaged in the management of disaster for effective management of disaster.

- The National Disaster Risk Reduction and Management Council, apart from government departments, has representatives from cities, civil society organizations, non-governmental organizations, and private sectors to ensure stakeholder participation.

- Act provides powers to penalize for offenses mentioned in the act.
- It contains provisions for the registration of volunteers for disaster management. (Coppola, 2006)

4.3 Queensland, Australia Disaster Management Act

Queensland is an excellent example of a State which initiated a proactive step towards framing holistic legislation for disaster management and enacted legislation that helped in managing disasters in the country. In 1975, Queensland enacted the State Counter Disaster Organization Act. The highlight of Queensland's disaster legislation is local governments have been endowed with powers to manage disasters within their jurisdiction. The body which is responsible for the management of disasters in the state is the "Department of Emergency Services". The Act envisages a multi-layered structure for the management of disasters at the state, district, and local government levels.

- Local governments have been endowed with powers to manage disasters within their jurisdiction.
- The Act has provisions, which helps competent authority to declare a disaster at local, district and state level.
- It contains provisions for the registration of volunteers for disaster management with the state emergency services to help authorities in rescue and relief operations.
- The act clearly defines the vulnerable groups and communities as infants, preschoolers, pregnant women, and nursing mothers, differently-abled, and the elderly.

- The act contains provisions for insurance, catastrophe bonds, and public-private partnership. (Bajracharya et al., 2011)

4.4 Case Study of Using NDMA Act in Managing COVID 19 Outbreak

The National disaster management act divides powers to manage disasters at the center, state, and district levels. Disaster management cells and working committees are present at each level to handle the disasters effectively. In the absence of a dedicated public health act, the Union government relied on the National disaster management act to control the spread of COVID 19, which is more relevant for disasters other than biological disasters.

COVID-19 was the first pan India biological disaster that was handled using the National disaster management act, 2005. At the beginning of the pandemic, the central government taken the charge to handle the pandemic and imposed a nationwide lockdown to control the spread of COVID-19. After this nation was unlocked in a phase-wise manner. It was partially successful as cases reduced significantly in the first wave of COVID-19. Later, the central Government realized that state and local governments are more aware of ground-level situations that encounter disasters. So, in the second phase, it was left on the state government to take decisions regarding lockdown and supply of goods and services.

COVID-19, popularly known as the Novel Corona Virus originated in Wuhan in 2019, affects the respiratory system

Table 34.2 Comparative Analysis of DM Act of India, South Africa, Philippines, and Australia

Parameters	India	South Africa	Philippines	Australia
Constitutional Backing	No	Yes (Concurrent Subject)	No	No
Definition	Covers Mainly Natural Disasters	Covers All Kind of Disaster	Covers All Kind of Disaster	Covers All Kind of Disaster
Vulnerable Sections	Not Clearly Defined	Defined	Defined	Defined
Powers	Vertical and Horizontal Integration	Vertical and Horizontal Integration	Vertical and Horizontal Integration	Vertical and Horizontal Integration
Financial Provisions	2 Funds (NDRF & NDMF)	Yes	Yes	Yes
Insurance	No	Yes	Yes	Yes
Parameters	India	South Africa	Philippines	Australia
Role Of Private Sector	No	Yes	Yes	Yes
Other Finance Instruments	No	Yes (Catastrophe Bonds)	Yes (Catastrophe Bonds)	Yes (Catastrophe Bonds)
Public Health	No	Yes	Yes	Yes
Review Of Policy	No Such Provisions	Yes	Yes (In 5 Years)	No
Responsibility	Central Govt.	Local Govt.	Local Govt.	Local Govt.
Model	Top-Down	Bottom-Up	Bottom-Up	Bottom-Up
Awareness and Training	Yes (NIDM)	Yes	Yes	Yes

Source: Adopted from analysis of Disaster Management Acts of India, South Africa, Philippines and Australia

which was declared as a global pandemic in the year 2020 by the World Health Organization (WHO).

The Disaster Management Act, 2005 mentions non-discrimination in compensation and relief based on sex, caste, age, religion, or descent among vulnerable communities. The central government used different sections of the act to penalize people for spreading fake claims regarding the COVID pandemic. (Dhuria et al., 2020)

Another Important Act used along with NDMA Act

- Epidemic disease Act,1897—It helps in the prevention and control of an outbreak of disease within any particular area.
- Essential Commodities Act,1955—It helps control the supply of important and necessary commodities in unforeseen conditions.
- Food Safety Act, 2006—It aims to ensure that safe food is consumed by people, standards have been provided by FSSAI. (Dhuria et al., 2020)

Approach Adopted to Control the Spread of COVID 19 by India

- **Social distancing:** As social distancing is a must to control the spread of COVID 19, for this purpose complete lockdown was imposed.
- **Proactive Approach:** India was among those who took proactive action by imposing a ban on international travel to control the spread of COVID 19.
- **People Management:** COVID can impact people's health physically and psychologically. People should support each other to prevent incidents of suicide. For this purpose, Government took initiatives like "Manodarpan" to help people.
- **Partnership:** Partnership with all the stakeholders engaged in disaster management is necessary to mitigate the effect of disasters. During the pandemic India engaged in SAARC and other multilateral groups to handle the pandemic.
- **Preparation and Collaboration:** To control the spread of COVID, the Government dedicated several hospitals for COVID 19 to ensure the availability of beds, ventilators, and PPE kits. To handle the spread, Government divided the districts into red, yellow, and green zones according to no of cases in the area. For contact tracing, the Government launched the "AarogyaSetu" app to control the spread of COVID 19.

5. Assessment of Impact of Disaster Before and After Act

The assessment with the help of GIS tools has been performed to understand the effectiveness of the DM Act been in terms of managing the incidents of disasters countrywide. For this purpose, two parameters have been taken for the assessment, and weightage is assigned to them in the GIS Application. Parameters considered for assessment are as follows:

- Fatalities (85%)
- Affected people (15%) due to ambiguity and unavailability of data.

Datasets for this purpose have been collected from various sources (disaster datasets and newspapers for the recent incident). Political Map of India (Survey of India) has been used for this purpose. ArcGIS has been used to map state-wise disasters and their impacts as per the assigned weightage of fatalities and affected people.

Two maps represent the impact of disasters that occurred before and after the enactment of the disaster management act. For this analysis, the overlay function has been used on the political map of India with the preparation of an inventory of disaster databases. As result, maps depicting the impact of state-wise disasters have been obtained as per assigned weightage.

The Figure 34.3 indicates that the impact of disasters has been significantly reduced after the enactment of the National Disaster Management Act, 2005. So, it can be deduced that the DM act has proved to be effective in the management of disasters in the country. It has provided better preparedness through coordination among different stakeholders and organizations working to ensure disaster risk reduction. Disaster Management Act with its full potential has tried to bridge the gap between governmental and other stakeholders involved in managing disasters in the country. However, more steps are required in this regard to handling man-made disasters, biological disasters, and disasters of progressive nature.

6. Critical Analysis

The Disaster Management Act mentions the functions and responsibilities of the Union Government, State Governments, departments of central as well as state Governments. DM act has made it compulsory that every Ministry or Department of the central government to formulate a Disaster Management Plan with subjects enumerated in the DM Act. The act makes

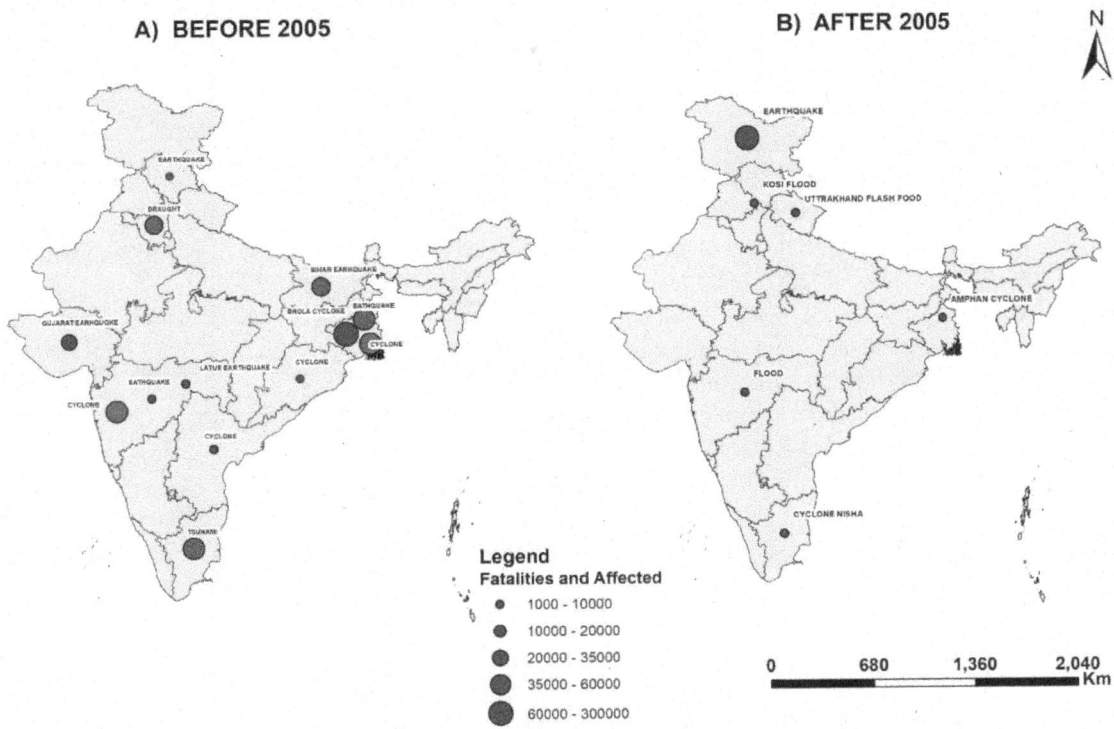

Fig. 34.3 Comparison of Impact of Disasters Before and After 2005

Source: Generated through ArcGis based on major disasters datasets along with political map of India(SOl)

it compulsory for every Ministry or Department of Union government should take appropriate steps to finance activities mentioned in its disaster Management Plan.

These steps effectively increase the pre-planning and post-planning measures that need to be taken for disaster management in the country. The act also highlights the departmental functions and responsibilities which are intended to be performed disaster management process that directly increases the accountability of measures for the preparedness, prevention, and mitigation of disaster. The act has positively impacted the awareness among the stakeholders and authorities regarding disaster management and capacity building.

The act mandates the Union government to take appropriate steps to coordinate with the United Nations bodies, sovereign governments of other countries, international non-governmental organizations for the achievement of objectives of the act. India has been effectively coordinating to attain the goals set under the Hyogo Framework of Action and Sendai Framework for Disaster Risk Reduction through sustained and coordinated steps for DRR. This ensures the proper formulation and implementation of measures mentioned in the act and also collaborating with renowned global agencies for the promotion of research and sharing of knowledge, ideas, experiences, and technological interventions in the fields of disaster risk reduction and disaster-resilient infrastructure.

The establishment of NIDM fosters the training of DM professionals, promoting awareness among people. It helped in generating new ideas and research for the effective management of disasters. The formation of NDRF is a remarkable step to carry out response and recovery operations during a disaster or post-disaster situation. The NDRF has shown its performance in saving lives of people during major disasters such as Bihar Floods (2008), Cyclone in West Bengal (2009), Uttarakhand Glacial Outburst (2021), etc. which subsequently magnified its necessity and importance to a country like India which experiences frequent hazards.

Although the act provides a certain course of actions and provisions that will help in accelerating the disaster management process in the country still there are some major concerns that need to be addressed as it's been almost 15 years of the enactment of the DM act. It's high time to review the efficacy of the act, in today's context to make the act more effective and efficient.

For an instance, the definition of disaster doesn't holistically cover all types of disasters. It doesn't visualize a situation when disaster can be caused because of international migration and spread through human contact via viral contaminations spreading across the border as well as within the country. The view that disaster occurs in any particular area by using the word *"any area"* in the definition of "disaster" makes it short-sighted. The Act defines those disasters are sudden but in reality, they can be sudden or/and progressive. For example, epidemics cannot be treated as disasters given the definition provided in the act, as it doesn't cause substantial loss of life in the beginning but in a later phase, its impacts are severe on the community. Epidemics of tuberculosis, covid-19, and HIV has caused substantial loss to life but still, no effective mechanism is available to handle such disasters. The Act also doesn't mention radioactive disasters and there is a lack of provisions concerning radioactive disasters.

The Act makes it mandatory for the State Government to take appropriate steps for the establishment of adequate early warning systems up to the level of vulnerable communities. But there is no clear mention of vulnerable communities. The act doesn't specify that which communities are considered as vulnerable pre-or-post disaster period which makes it ambiguous.

The act contains provisions regarding devolution of powers from union Govt-State Govt-District Administration. The act has created a "top-down model" for disaster management in the country by providing the overriding powers to the central government in the formulation and execution of the disaster management policies and plans in the country which rarely involve community and stakeholder participation. Thus, the devolution of power is still questionable.

The Disaster Management Act 2005 contains guidelines for the creation of two different funds at national, state, and district levels as Disaster Response Fund (DRF) and Disaster Mitigation Fund (DMF). At the national level, the Act contains provisions for the creation of the **National Disaster Response Fund (NDRF)** and the **National Disaster Mitigation Fund (NDMF)**.

Mitigation measures are mainly in the form of development works, which are generally funded from the planned budget of the Ministries and Government departments. However, there is a lack of consensus among various stakeholders on the composition, nature, scope, and corpus of the Mitigation Fund that will be formed at the National, State, and District levels.

However, such funds have not been created by the state government at district levels as mentioned in the act. Even after the act the earlier funds such as the national crisis management fund still existed.

It is not mentioned how much money will be provided in the funds for different purposes, which creates lots of ambiguities and brings it under bureaucratic discretion. There are no provisions for insurance and other means of finance in the act. The Act doesn't mention public-private partnership that how the private sector can be engaged in Disaster management?

Table 34.3 Strengths and Weaknesses of DM Act

Strengths	Weaknesses
Provides legal backing for Disaster Management	Doesn't cover all types of Disaster
Provides a legal-institutional framework of agencies	Doesn't define vulnerable communities
Coordinate with the United Nations agencies, international organizations, and sovereign Government	The top-down model approach has been considered
Provides immunity to officers engaged in Disaster Management	Central Govt has been endowed with more responsibilities
Arrangement of funding through NDRF and NDMF	No defined mechanism for funding. (Majorly based on successive FC recommendations)
Mentions measures for Disaster Management by providing authorities with certain functions to perform	At the central level powers has been concentrated
Facilitating training and guidance in Disaster Management through establishing NIDM	No mention of insurance and private sector
Executive and advisory body at national and state level	
Constituting National Disaster Response Force	

7. Suggestions and Recommendations

After rigorously analyzing the Disaster Management act and comparing it with disaster management acts of few countries, these are some major concerns found in the DM act. These concerns need to address as in the wake of the COVID-19 pandemic, NDMA Act was invoked in the whole country. Policymakers and other stakeholders should coordinate at a common platform to take a holistic and robust policy for Disaster Management.

- **Definition of disaster:** The definition given in the act should be more inclusive and able to cover all types of disasters (man-made and biological disasters). The act should be able to able to handle disasters, which are not sudden (climate change, environmental degradation, etc.). Definition in the Act should be amended as per present need.
- **Disaster-prone zones:** India is prone to various types of disasters. Based on past evidence, the whole country can be divided into disaster-prone zones. It will help in better coordination and utilization of resources.

- **Vulnerable communities:** The act should clearly define vulnerable communities. Currently, it is left for the discretion of DM officials and in the absence of such provisions, victims of disasters are left behind.
- **Review provisions:** There have to be review provisions mentioned in DM act after five years and consultation should take place among stakeholders and DM professionals. Such consultation will lead to an effective Disaster management act, which will be able to handle disasters of varying nature.
- **Funding mechanism:** The funding mechanism as envisaged in the DM act needs to be followed strictly and should be given adequate funds to tackle the situation of disaster. State Government should take the required steps for the creation of District disaster management authority and respective funds at the district level.
- **Decentralization of Powers:** The primary responsibility to handle the disaster should vest with local government and should be provided with adequate funds, functions, and functionaries to deal with the disasters. This will help in the effective management of disasters through a bottom-up approach.
- **Insurance and other financial instruments:** Insurance provisions and other financial instruments (catastrophe bonds, weather derivates) should be included in the DM act. It will reduce the burden from public authorities and generate more funds for the effective management of disasters. Such insurance instruments (Pradhanmantri Fasal Bima Yojna) are being used in the agricultural sector through Government intervention.
- **Public-private partnership:** Public-private partnership is widely being used in developed countries in the field of disaster management. It also helps in reducing the burden from public authorities, having resource constraints. It should be integrated with the DM act.
- **Public health:** In the wake of the current COVID-19 pandemic, which exposed our public health system, the need of situation is to integrate public health in disaster management. It will help in the effective utilization of available resources and managing disasters.
- **Inclusion of rights and duties:** The responsibilities, rights, and duties of people and the communities should be mentioned in the act. Community participation and disaster preparedness at the community level should be incorporated into the act. These can be integrated with the role of local government.
- **Risk transfer mechanism:** The Act should incorporate risk-transfer mechanisms, inter-governmental risk pool, and cost-sharing with the private sector to reduce the financial burden from the government.

- **Private sector participation:** The responsibilities, rights, and duties of the private sector should be incorporated in the act. It will help in regulating the activities of the private sector engaged in disaster management.
- **Grievance redressal:** The act should incorporate grievance redressal for effective implementation of relief, rehabilitation and reconstruction measures taken by the government. It will ensure that no victims are left behind.
- **Volunteer participation:** As incorporated in the disaster management act of South Africa and the Philippines, the National disaster management act should contain the provisions for the registration of volunteers. It will enhance the volunteers' participation in disaster management.

By incorporating above mentioned suggestions and recommendations, the National Disaster Management Act can be made more effective and robust. It can be effectively used in the management of all kinds of disasters.

8. Conclusion

In recent times, due to climate change and anthropogenic activities, incidences of disasters have gone manifold. Such a situation poses a threat as well as provides an opportunity to manage the disaster effectively. For such a herculean task, a robust Disaster Management Act becomes essential. This will help different officials, authorities, and institutions to effectively manage the disasters at ground level. National Disaster Management Act, 2005 has helped authorities and institutions in managing disasters throughout the country but has certain limitations. After 15 years of its enactment and in the wake of COVID 19 pandemic, it is need of hour to amend it as per current situation. Our policymakers are having deliberate discussions for the amendment of the act. It is expected that above-mentioned points will be incorporated in the act and DM authorities and institutions will be strengthened after the amendment.

REFERENCES

1. Bajracharya, B., Childs, I., & Hastings, P. (2011). Climate change adaptation through land use planning and disaster management: Local government perspectives from Queensland Climate change adaptation through land use planning and disaster management: Local government perspectives from Queensland. *17th Pacific Rim Real Estate Society Conference Climate Change and Property: Its Impact Now and Later 16-19 January 2011, Gold Coast, January,* 1–16. http://www.prres.net/papers/Bajracharya_Childs_Hastings_Climate_change_disaster_managemen t_and_land_use_planning.pdf

2. Brower, R. S., & Magno, F. A. (2011). A "third way" in the philippines: Voluntary organizing for a new disaster management paradigm. *International Review of Public Administration, 16*(1), 31–50. https://doi.org/10.1080/122644 31.2011.10805184

3. Coppola, D. (2006). Introduction to International Disaster Management. In *Introduction to International Disaster Management*. https://doi.org/10.1016/C2009-0-64027-7

4. Das, P. (2012). Disaster Management in India : Policy Review and Institutional Structure. *Asia-Pacific Journal of Sciences, IV*(1), 37–52.

5. Dhuria, M., Ayub, A., Kumar, A., Ahmad, S., & Kumar, P. (2020). Is India Ready to Address COVID-19 Like Pandemics: A Perspective From Existing Public Health Acts. *Indian Journal of Public Health Research & Development, 11*(11). https://doi.org/10.37506/ijphrd.v11i11.11358

6. GoI. (2005). *DM_act2005.pdf* (pp. 1–28).

7. NDMA. (2016). National Disaster Management Plan (NDMP). *Government Policy*, 1–192. http://ndma.gov.in/ images/policyplan/dmplan/National Disaster Management Plan May 2016.pdf

8. NDMA. (2018). *Annual Report*.

9. NDMA. (2019). National Disaster Management Plan (2019). *National Disaster Management Authority, Government of India. November, November*, 384. https://ndma.gov.in/sites/ default/files/PDF/ndmp-2019.pdf Accessed on 29.06.2021

10. NIDM. (2009). *FINANCING DISASTER MANAGEMENT IN INDIA A Study for the National Institute of Disaster management* (Issue August).

11. Paul, I., & Rajib, S. (2018). *Disaster Risk Governance in India and Cross Cutting Issues.*

12. Planning Commission. (2012). *Twelfth Five Year Plan (2012–2017): Faster, More Inclusive and Sustainable Growth* (Vol. 1). SAGE Publications.

13. Sarkar, S., & Sarma, A. (2006). Disaster Management Act, 2005: A Disaster in Waiting? *Economic and Political Weekly, 41*(35), 3760–3763. https://doi.org/10.2307/4418643

14. Van Niekerk, D. (2015). Disaster risk governance in Africa: A retrospective assessment of progress in against the hyogo framework for action (2000-2012). *Disaster Prevention and Management, 24*(3), 397–416. https://doi.org/10.1108/DPM-08-2014-0168

15. Dhar Chakrabarty, P.G., 2009. Financing Disaster Management in India, a Study for the Thirteenth Finance Commission, New Delhi: National Institute of Disaster Management.

CHAPTER 35

Democratizing Disaster Risk Reduction: A Local Governance Approach to Contextual Knowledge Production for Flood Planning in Kuttanad, India

Kaniska Singh

Ph.D. Candidate, Centre for Policy Studies,
IIT Bombay, Mumbai-400076

Fathima Nidha

M.Tech. CTARA, IIT Bombay, Mumbai-400076

Rohit Joseph

M.Tech. CTARA, IIT Bombay, Mumbai-400076

N. C. Narayanan

Professor, CTARA, IIT Bombay, Mumbai-400076.
Tel : +91 22 2576 7842/7870

Abstract

During the 2018 Kerala floods, the Kuttanad region was one of the worst-hit because of its peculiar topography. Large engineering structures for water control were built after the 1950s to facilitate rice cultivation, and later development interventions like roads altered the hydrology and seriously affected the system's ability to cope with flash floods. The local adaptation knowledge has been slowly replaced by knowledge borne out of top-down, managerial, and command and control-driven approaches to managing floods. With the help of an empirical study, the paper demonstrates the possibility of localizing scientific knowledge and integrating it with local knowledge through deliberative platforms for flood risk planning at the Panchayat level. Local and participatory exploration of perceptions about floods and vulnerability integrated with scientific techniques of remote sensing, GIS, and flood zone mapping, was undertaken. The bottom-up knowledge creation through community participation in the flood risk planning at the Panchayat level paves the way to integrate complex and contested realities of privileged and marginal epistemic groups and knowledge systems.

Keywords: Contextual Knowledge; Disaster Risk Reduction; Integrated Methodology; Local Flood Risk planning, Contested Knowledge

1. Introduction

The Indian subcontinent is biophysically vulnerable to a range of disasters like flooding, drought, cyclones, heat waves, nuclear disasters (NDMP, 2019). Different kinds of flooding like urban and riverine flooding have become one of the most common hazards in the Indian subcontinent. Approximately 12 % of the lands in India are prone to flooding and river erosion (NDMP,2019). Flooding has always existed as a natural process in and around riverine settlements. Regions like Kuttanad in Kerala, the *diaries* of Gandak, Kosi in Bihar, the Sunderbans in West Bengal, and the Brahmaputra basin in Assam experience recurrent flooding every year. In many regions where flooding has always been a part of riverine, and floodplain ecosystems, controlling floods can simultaneously affect the ecosystems and livelihoods of the dependent populations (McCully, 2008; Blaikie et al., 1994). Non-structural measures that facilitate 'living with floods' have emerged as a policy suggestion for better flood and ecosystem management.

Historically, floods have always been part of people's lives in Kuttanad. Kuttanad, the lowest-lying region of India, is waterlogged for most of the year and subject to prolonged floods and inundation during the monsoon season (Vishnu et al., 2018). It is characterized by the Vembanad wetland system, resulting from the convergence of the four principal rivers of Kerala that drain into the Arabian Sea (Kumar & Devadas, 2015). It forms a bowl-like structure making it more susceptible to waterlogging. The region itself is reclaimed from various fragmented landmass in the Vembanad lake. Issues like soil salinity and soil degradation have increased due to seawater intrusion and frequent flooding (Parameswaran, 1987), respectively. With time, the frequency of the floods and losses have increased, with a higher probability of such extremes in flood plains and low-lying coastal areas (UNEP, 2020).

Nevertheless, communities residing in hazard-prone areas like floodplains develop distinctive ways of dealing with the hazards and reducing disaster risk and losses (Shaw et al., 2008). These adaptation techniques are rarely included in disaster and flood planning at the national, state, or district level. While the local adaptation strategies can or cannot be the most effective way of dealing with hazards, people's knowledge and inclusion of different epistemic communities in Disaster Risk Reduction (DRR) governance are valuable additions (Faas, 2016). Besides, it refrains from portraying hazard-impacted communities as hapless victims of hazard (Gaillard and Mercer, 2013) and acknowledges people's agency, coping capacity, and strategies.

When informed by multiple stakeholders' disaster perceptions, the more grounded adaptation strategies deployed by communities can initiate significant improvement in the DRR plan. The perception of stakeholders, especially the affected community, and their adaptation strategies are best understood through participatory programs (López-Marrero, 2011; Allen, 2006; and Mulligan & Vahanvati, 2017). Participatory disaster and flood risk planning possible at the local level open up spaces to deconstruct & counter official and limited discourses and new ways of imagining the reality based on otherwise subjugated forms of knowledge (Baghel, 2014).

This paper argues that the inclusion of impacted communities, local adaptation strategies & knowledge in DRR planning, specifically flood risk planning is essential to devising ways of 'living with floods.' Participatory methods representing different groups can open spaces for integrating technical

expertise and local knowledge and provide a deliberative platform. The representation of different epistemic groups (marginal and privileged) and the contested knowledge within communities add another layer of nuance and complexity in local flood risk planning. Such nuanced planning based on a layered understanding of realities on the ground can be best achieved by bottom-up disaster and flood risk planning at the local government level with representation by different epistemic communities. It further shows how flood risk planning can be contextualized through planning at the Panchayat level.

The paper is divided into five sections. The first section includes the introduction of the paper, followed by the literature review in the next section. The following section deals with the methodological details of the study, including a brief description of the study area. The fourth section includes findings of the research and analysis around those findings. The last section involves a discussion around the findings and conclusion.

2. Approaches and Knowledge Systems in Flood Risk Planning

2.1 The dominance of Technical Knowledge in Flood Risk Planning in India

Disaster Risk Reduction policies and Practices across multiple scales primarily revolve around scientific approaches and knowledge systems and are considered a primary source of credible knowledge within DRR (Spiekermann et al., 2015). Scientific communities and policymakers often affiliate to the notion of 'objective rationality' hardly questioning the meaning of rationality, objectivity (Alexander and Davis, 2012), the role of the subjectivity of experts' knowledge (Baghel, 2014), and embedded-ness of any kind of knowledge, in larger power structures, cultural differences, and context (Spiekermann et al. 2015). It is also contested that scientific knowledge alone can address the complexity involved with DRR (Spiekermann et al. 2015) as science has been abused to justify injustices instead of reducing them (Alexander and Davis, 2012). Gaillard (2010) claims that the Hazard Paradigm of DRR has been informing DRR policies and policymakers. The Hazard paradigm, rightly called the 'dominant paradigm' by Hewitt (1983), is generally coupled with the command-and-control approach and top-bottom framework (Gaillard and Mercer, 2013) with a focus on scientific knowledge for dealing with disasters and evoking interventions at the national level (IFRC, 2011). It is coupled with the inferior status given to local knowledge by policymakers and development experts with labels like 'non-knowledge, `primitive' and 'maladaptive' and kept in the realm by 'skepticism,' 'mysticism' and 'superstition' by western scientists (Hiwasaki, 2017). The local knowledge, experience, and disaster memory are often dismissed as knowledge, are grossly undervalued (Blaikie et al., 1995; Mercer, 2012), and underappreciated (Spiekermann et al. 2012).). The local knowledge has also undergone erosion owing to the altered flood ecosystem that outpaces the development of local knowledge in its response (Baghel, 2014). The tacit and traditional knowledge systems, like a weather prediction, have become redundant at the face of climate change (Rai & Khawas, 2019), roots of which are often found in more distant and scalar processes and factors.

There has been more interest in including indigenous and traditional local community knowledge in DRR (Shaw et al. 2008). It gained momentum after the 2004 Indian Ocean Tsunami, where traditional prediction systems of Simeulue Island communities demonstrated their effectiveness (Rai & Khawas, 2019; Gaillard & Mercer,2013; Hiwasaki, 2017. A growing body of literature around knowledge systems, DRR, and Climate change has been arguing for the integration of scientific and local knowledge systems in DRR (Gaillard and Mercer, 2013; Pathirage et al. 2014; Spiekermann et al. 2015) while simultaneously vouching for the insufficiency of either of this knowledge in addressing Disaster Risk. The non-inclusion of traditional knowledge results from the lack of connection between local people and state officials and engineers (Hilhorst et al., 2015). The poor integration of scientific and local knowledge in DRR policies also increases the frequency of disasters (Gaillard and Mercer, 2013). Interestingly, the non-appreciation of different knowledge systems is mutual (Spiekermann et a. 2012), which can only be addressed when different knowledge systems are integrated (Gaillard and Mercer, 2013) and appreciate each other's unique contribution and relevance in DRR practice and policy. The fragmentation of knowledge within DRR (Spiekermann et al., 2015) can be addressed through hybrid methods and interdisciplinary approaches (Baghel, 2014). Elsewhere, Mehta (2003) argues that understanding the local dynamics can enrich policymakers' sensitivity to local people's coping strategies. However, scholars maintain that there is also a need to question local knowledge alike (Mercer, 2012) and assess its effectiveness in addressing people's vulnerability (Hiwasaki, 2017) and stay away from over-romanticization of this knowledge (Gaillard and Mercer, 2013).

Technical approaches and knowledge also dominate Flood risk planning practice in many countries like Pakistan, Bangladesh, and India(Abbas et al.2016). Flood risk planning in India has focused on structural and non-structural solutions in India. (Gupta, Javed, and Datta, 2003). Structural flood control planning aims to stop floodwater from reaching different locations through tangible interventions. Embankments, dams, reservoirs, drainage channels (Gupta

et al., 2003), guide dams, bunds, and spurs are the most commonly used structural measures in India and worldwide. Historically, embankments, bunds had pre-existed in many flood-prone areas in India, even before the Indian State came into being (Abbas et al., 2016).

On the other hand, non-structural measures attempt to address the intangible aspects of vulnerability and reduce the negative impacts of the flood (Mohanty, Mudgil, and Karmakar, 2020). Many non-structural measures like flood plain zoning, land use remote sensing, GIS tools, climate modeling, climate forecasting, flood flow modeling, and flood extent modeling have been part of flood management practice and research. Lately, non-structural solutions have been emphasized in India's disaster policy frameworks. National Water Policy executed in 2012 emphasized flood plain zonation. However, the approach remains marginal in practice (Ashraf et al., 2017).

Flood management in India is still trapped in imaginations of the structural measures to 'control' or 'resist' floods. The reliance on structural measures to control floods remains one of the dominant but inadequate approaches for flood management(Abbas et al., 2016). It remains the '*Symbolic icon of flood management* (p. 155) after many decades of adopting the first flood control policy in 1954(Das and Das, 2017). Scholars like Mishra (1997), Dixit (2003) working on Kosi floods have also incessantly argued against the centrality of structural solutions in flood management and their long-term cascading flooding effects. D'Souza (2003) argued that these solutions have undesirable consequences on people and the ecosystem(Baghel, 2014).

One reason for this overemphasis can be found in the State List, which only mentions structural measures for flood management (Mohanty et al., 2020). Baghel (2014) argued that the unquestioned status of structures like embankments and dams for controlling floods is one example of governmental rationality within projects on the river. While for Lahiri-Dutt(2000), it was the validation of the expert knowledge and post-colonial India sought from scientific and technical knowledge that led to such choices. This knowledge produced through the imperial rules is assumed to be perfectly able to qualify as context-independent, translocate and replicate without compromising the effectiveness of such knowledge (Lahiri-Dutt,2000). The dominance of technical knowledge is often a result of unquestioned reliance on experts, western knowledge, and hegemony.

2.2 Community Engagement and Local Governance in Flood Risk Planning

The body of literature advocating for more engagement with local communities and local government bodies has been developing in the last few decades. This literature relies on empirical evidence across different parts of the world engaging in local disaster planning and involving local communities in the process. (Ganapati & Ganapati, 2008) argue for the inclusion of multiple stakeholders in disaster-prone areas in disaster adaptation projects. They demonstrate that Agencies like World Bank, which had only limited knowledge and proximity with the local life and capacities, only selected the direct beneficiaries (Ganapati & Ganapati, 2008). Iglesias et al. (2008) make a similar argument in the paper that DRR is everyone's business from the residents, business community, government institutions, and private sector. The household and community level preparedness is central to reducing disaster losses in terms of lives and livelihood. López-Marrero & Tschakert (2011) showed the failure of the traditional top-down approach in controlling the hazard and used participatory methods for building more resilient communities in flood-prone areas by analyzing the case of the northeastern part of Puerto Rico. Mulligan & Vahanvati(2017) studied the success of Owner driven reconstruction (ODR) in the 2008 Kosi flood-affected areas of Bihar, which required stakeholder participation to construct climate-resilient houses to promote sustainability and resilience skills training, construction supervision, and construction itself.

The role of communities affected in flood adaptation is vital in understanding their perception and implementing effective adaptation methods. Mondal et al. (2018) added that the perception of the affected people and the official of institutions (i.e., PRI) is a definitive indicator of the ground situation or facts essential for managing natural disasters in the study areas. Gupta et al. (2003) argue that better community participation in flood management through training and maintenance of flood protection structures by communities can improve flood preparedness manifold. While overviewing flood management in India, Mohanty, Mudgil, and Karmakar (2020) also opined that India's current flood management system falls short of acknowledging the importance of community participation as non-structural measures for flood-impacted communities. Allen (2006) added that understanding local knowledge is an essential strategy. However, community-based activities could entrust a significant responsibility to the community without assessing their capacity or training them to adapt. Therefore, practical community-government cooperation in disaster preparedness is imperative. The familiarity with the local community makes the local government an essential player in all the phases of disaster (Kusumari et al., 2010).

Even though the critical role of local government is acknowledged, the dearth of resource capabilities and knowledge deficit at this level is a less explored area (Kusumari et al., 2010). Bang (2013) hypothesizes that

centralized national governance has led to a non-empowered local government to carry out DRR functions. At the same time, Mondal et al. (2018) state that the engagement of government and critical stakeholders with local communities is also warranted where unknown factors of disaster risk like climate variability manifest in the local context.

Researchers have also argued for the engagement of local-level government in disaster and flood risk planning. Our first Disaster Management Act, 2005 of India, has specified three tiers of planning at the National, State, and District level, warranting a top-down policymaking and governance process. Local authorities like Panchayati Raj institutions are mentioned in the act, but their role is limited to the consultation and implementation of district disaster plans. In chapter 6, DM act, 2005, the local authorities have limited autonomy to take measures for disaster management.

3. Flood Risk Planning at Local Governance Level in Kuttanad

3.1 Study Area

The selected study area is Kainakary Panchayat, one of the worst flood-hit villages in the Kuttanad region, consisting of 15 wards and covering 36.6 square kilometers. The ward map of Kainakary is shown in Fig. 35.1. As per the data of the Panchayat census of 2021, Kainakary has a total population of 25922 with 5240 households (Kainakary Gram Panchayat, 2021). Kainakary is considered a collection of islands characterized by many polders and *Kaayalnilams* surrounded by rivers running through the Panchayat. Polders are the paddy cultivation lands reclaimed from low-lying areas crisscrossed by backwaters, rivers, and streams,

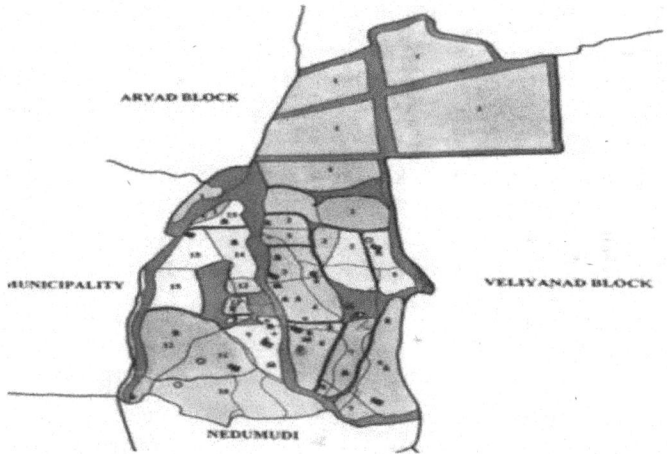

Fig. 35.1 Ward Map of Kainakary (Kainakary Gram Panchayat, 2021)

protected by embankments (Kranenburg, 2001). The polders and *Kaayalnilams* are characterized by solid and wide embankments locally known as 'bunds' where most of the population is housed (Kainakary Gram Panchayat, 1996).

Life with constant contact with floodwater affects the quality of life in various aspects. So, understanding the nature and pattern of local flooding is a critical aspect physically in understanding vulnerabilities. The heterogeneous nature of the terrain is also influential to the nature of floods. The polders form a base for understanding the flood risks here, and the varying characteristics of the landforms add to the more profound understanding of the different issues faced by the community.

Kerala allocates 44 % of the budget to Panchayati Raj Institutes(PRIs) as a 'plan fund' where different mandatory working groups operate in different sectors. Currently, these plans display the meaning of vulnerability which is vaguely equated with 'supposedly' socially and economically vulnerable groups, namely poor, children, women, elderly, and SC/STs population. On the one hand, socioeconomic factors shaping vulnerability are acknowledged through these mandatory working groups. However, vulnerability is reified (Faas, 2011) and limitedly defined. On the other hand, it displays a lack of understanding of the socio-spatiality of vulnerability, the contestations around adaptive and coping strategies of different populations towards hazards like flood, both of which are this study's focus.

3.2 Nature of Study and Methods

Wisner et al.(2004) defined disaster risk as 'Compound function of natural hazard and differential vulnerability of population' (p.45). The IPCC Fifth Assessment Report (AR5) defines risk as the potential for consequences where something of value is at stake and where the outcome is uncertain, recognizing the diversity of value (Pachauri & Meyer, 2014). Later, 'risk' was identified as the compound effect of hazard, exposure, and vulnerability (Slovic, 1987, Kron, 2002). DasGupta & Shaw (2017) added another layer of coping capacity, the absence of which can be detrimental for risk reduction, unlike the other components where their presence elevates the risk.

$$\text{Disaster Risk} = \frac{\text{Hazard} \times \text{Exposure} \times \text{Vulnerability}}{\text{Coping capacity}}$$

The mathematic equation signifies the relation effect of these dimensions of disaster risk and is not essentially mathematical (Karmakar, 2020). This study is focusing on the aspects of vulnerability and coping strategies.

Gaillard and Jigyasu's (2016) delineation of three major approaches (Economic reductionism/Quantitative,

Anthropological pluralism/Qualitative, and, Participatory pluralism/Participatory) to understanding resilience or vulnerability informs the paper's methodological considerations. This approach also partially addresses the need to integrate local and scientific knowledge systems in DRR (Gaillard and Mercer, 2013), taking socio-economic/ biophysical vulnerability and coping strategies (Gaillard and Jigyasu, 2016) to inform flood risk planning at the Panchayat level.

The study has twin motivations. First, it attempts to understand the socio-spatial nature of vulnerability towards floods in Kainakary using the integration of technical approaches (GIS, Remote Sensing, DEM), Quantitative (surveys), Qualitative (In-depth interviews, FGDs), and participatory methods (PRA, Panchayat members, residents, and students). Then it moves on to analyze socio-spatial vulnerability and contestations around coping strategies related to perennial flooding through engagement with Panchayat members. The choice of hybrid methodology helps integrate different kinds of knowledge, and representative participants ensure that various epistemic communities are included. The paper demonstrates how local people's perspectives and contextual knowledge systems can be integrated into understanding people's vulnerability through semi-formal platforms like Gram Sabhas at the ward level. The scientific knowledge assessing physical and social vulnerability is shared with the community at these platforms. Additionally, the Indigenous Technology Knowledge is collected and integrated with the findings of scientific approaches, especially the coping strategies at the Gram Panchayat(GP) level. This planning and the integration can go beyond the GP to form a basis of bottom-up flood risk planning.

The research approach adopted for the study was a mixed-method that systematically integrates both quantitative and qualitative data within a single investigation and is interdisciplinary in approach. With the help of Participatory Rural Appraisal techniques of transect walk, resource mapping, and livelihood mapping, the initial exploration of the field was undertaken. It was followed by a household (HH) survey designed in the Open Data Kit (ODK), and flood mapping was undertaken to understand local people's perception of the recurrent flood and the differential impact the floods had on their houses and their livelihood. The data collection methods were Household surveys, In-depth Interviews, GIS, Remote Sensing, and Focussed Group Discussions (See Fig. 35.2).

The primary data was collected through household surveys using mobile apps (ODK and OSM tracker), semi-structured interviews, and Focused Group Discussions (FGDs). Digital elevation modeling (DEM) under Topography analysis has been used to reclassify the regions based on flood vulnerability.

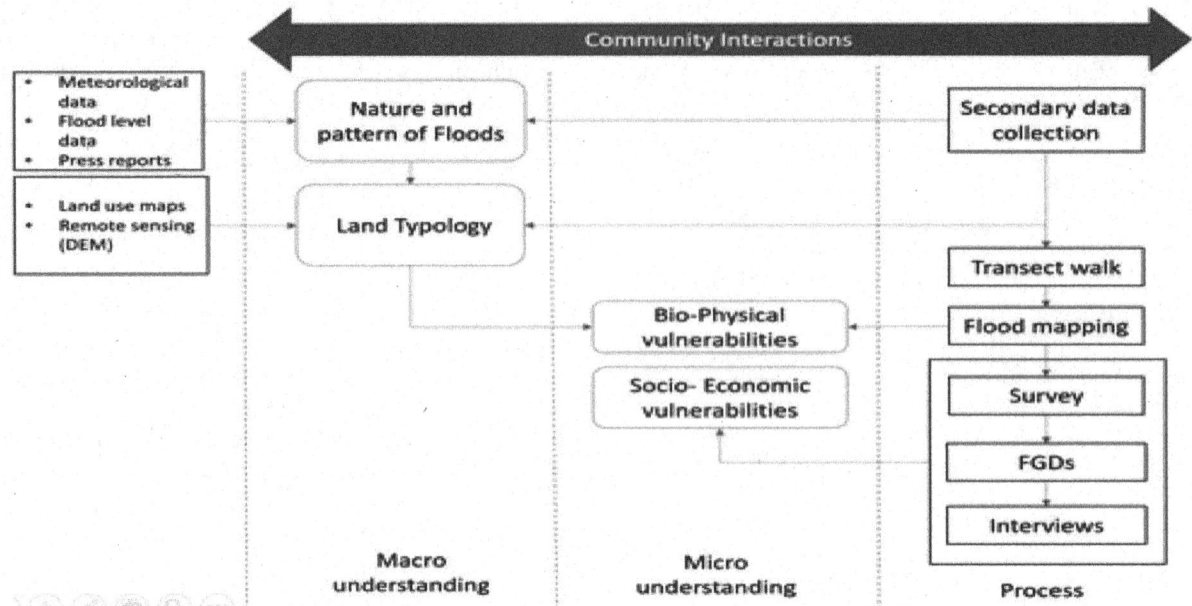

Fig. 35.2 Methodological Choices And Disaster Risk Components.

The methods for topographical vulnerability analysis include three steps. The primary step is the development of a base map. As the region's central land-use portion covers paddy fields and water bodies, the land area needed to be separated for better analysis. The land area was separated from the paddy and water bodies and maintained as a base map for the analysis. A multispectral heat map was developed based on elevations and correlated against the landforms.

Next, a household survey was undertaken to assess social and economic vulnerability dimensions like caste, land ownership, flood levels, gender, and the effect of their interaction. The samples were 606, covering 11.5 % of the 5689 households in the Panchayat (Census, 2011). Cluster sampling ensured people from all geographical areas, land typologies, and different socio-economic sectors.

Interviews and Focus Group Discussions were conducted to understand the coping strategies of the cultivators as well as residents within the polders. The participants were chosen purposively from the representatives of the *Padashekharam* committee, farmers, Gram Panchayat officials, ward Councilors, and residents. The interviews were transcribed and analyzed thematically. The *Padasekharam committees* have a significant role in the decision-making in the locality in terms of agricultural practices, management of outer bounds above which the houses situate, and further on, the flood control and management. A detailed understanding of different aspects of agriculture – like challenges, sustenance, flooding, and coping strategies-was understood through the Focus Group Discussions (FGDs) carried out with 10 group farming committees.

Moreover, 30 in-depth interviews were conducted with farmers of five *Padashekharams* selected based on their flood vulnerability. Quantitative data collected through household surveys were analyzed using numerical methods. The tools used for quantitative data analysis included MS Excel, QGIS, and rwh advisor. The qualitative data collected through field notes, FGDs, and semi-structured interviews were transcribed to thick descriptions, and thematic analysis was performed.

4. Findings and Analysis

4.1 Mapping Physical Vulnerability

The land use map prepared by the State Land Use Board contains 21 land use classifications for Kuttanad. Different land typologies emerged from the triangulated data generated in the process. The paddy fields in Kuttanad are mostly human-made reclamations from shallow portions and flood plains of Vembanad Lake. The major land typologies identified in the region are bunds, islands inside paddy fields, and reclaimed paddy lands. The biophysical properties such as elevation, soil properties of these land typologies vary. Ground-truthing was conducted to verify how the nature and pattern of floods vary in each of these typologies. Based on DEM, Land-use mapping, and interaction with Panchayat members, the flood level and inundation period were high in islands inside the paddy fields compared to the other land typologies. Therefore, the areas inside the paddy fields are physically more vulnerable on counts of lower elevation, and the households residing in those areas have higher flood risk than other land typologies. The relation between elevations

Table 35.1 Mean Flood Level In Different Land Typologies, Compiled From The Survey And Spatial Mapping.

Land Typology	Nature of Land	Median of maximum flood level (In meters)	Physical Vulnerability ranking
Land Typology I	Reclaimed and Lake lands	1.2	Least Vulnerable
Land Typology II	Island between Paddy fields	1.7	Most Vulnerable
Land Typology III	Bunds and Marshy land	1.4	Medium Vulnerable

and vulnerability to floods was found through the survey, which shows the maximum flood level in the households (during floods of 2018) in different land types. It shows that the households located in the island paddies were the worst affected, with the median maximum flood level around 1.7 meters, followed by bunds and marshes with 1.4 meters. The reclaimed paddies have comparatively lesser impacts, with the median maximum flood level being 1.2 meters. Based on spatial mapping as well as survey findings, the physical vulnerability was found to be in the following order:

Land Typology II > Land Typology III > Land Typology I (See Table 35.1)

The nature of knowledge produced in the process is technical and takes an important place in disaster planning by deepening spatial understanding at the macro and micro levels. These approaches are beneficial to understand biophysical and geographical dimensions at the macro scale. However, knowledge about the manifestations of both micro and macro aspects of vulnerability is most approximately produced in the day-to-day life of affected communities. The communities and the local governance actors are both first responders as well as first knowledge producers. From documenting the mundane information about the details of floods to understanding the experiences of living and responding to floods, warrants inclusion of lived knowledge of the local population.

4.2 Socio-economic Dimensions of Vulnerability

Findings from the survey show the concentration of marginal socioeconomic groups in more vulnerable land typologies. For example, 54.4 % of the population inhabiting the least vulnerable typology is the General caste. Other Backward Caste(OBC) is 34.5%, and Schedule Caste(SC) is only 8% of the total population inland typology I. The most vulnerable areas are majorly inhabited by OBCs, followed by General and SC populations. However, on analyzing the land typologies disaggregation within each caste group, it was found that 27 % of the overall Schedule Caste participants inhabit land typology II followed by 11 % of OBC and 8 % General Caste participants. It was also found that around 46 % of the participants residing inland typology II owned paddy fields with an average of 91.1 cents and a median value

of 100 cents, wherein 54 % of the participants did not have paddy land ownership. It also found that only 2 % of the total female-headed households lived in the most protective regions, followed by 9 % in the most vulnerable regions. In contrast, the majority live in bunds and marshy lands. When intersected with caste data, it was found that none of the Upper caste female-headed households was located in the most vulnerable areas, which was inhabited disproportionately by SC female-headed households followed by OBC households.

Figure 35.3 shows the class distribution of people inhabited in these different land typologies. It shows that people belonging to weaker economic classes are majorly inhibited in paddy islands and marshes, followed by bunds. We can see that the people belonging to comparatively higher economic classes are predominant in the safer reclaimed paddy lands.

The data displays heterogeneity and disaggregation at the level of communities, local power relations, and within this caste, gender groups are considered homogeneous. In the OBC category, for example, the distribution of risk and vulnerability within the category greatly varies where some OBC participants seem to be enjoying land ownership and inhabitation of less vulnerable areas, a similar number of OBC respondents are also burdening the risk and vulnerability towards floods disproportionately. The above findings show that caste, gender, land ownership, and class shape differential vulnerabilities. However, the relation can only be known through a more grounded and in-depth understanding of the caste system at the research site. In the next section, the coping strategies of different participants would be explored in-depth.

4.3 Cropping Pattern as Adaptive Strategies

Owing to the historical nature of the perennial flooding in the polders and residence inside the polders, people have developed coping and adaptive strategies to safeguard their livelihood and houses. The cropping pattern was found as one of the region's main coping and adaptive strategies concerning safeguarding agricultural fields and houses inside the paddy fields. Participants reminisced the earlier single cropping pattern, which some of them also opined was better for flood cushioning as it gave more space and time for river water to flow. The economy of Kuttanad is mainly dependent

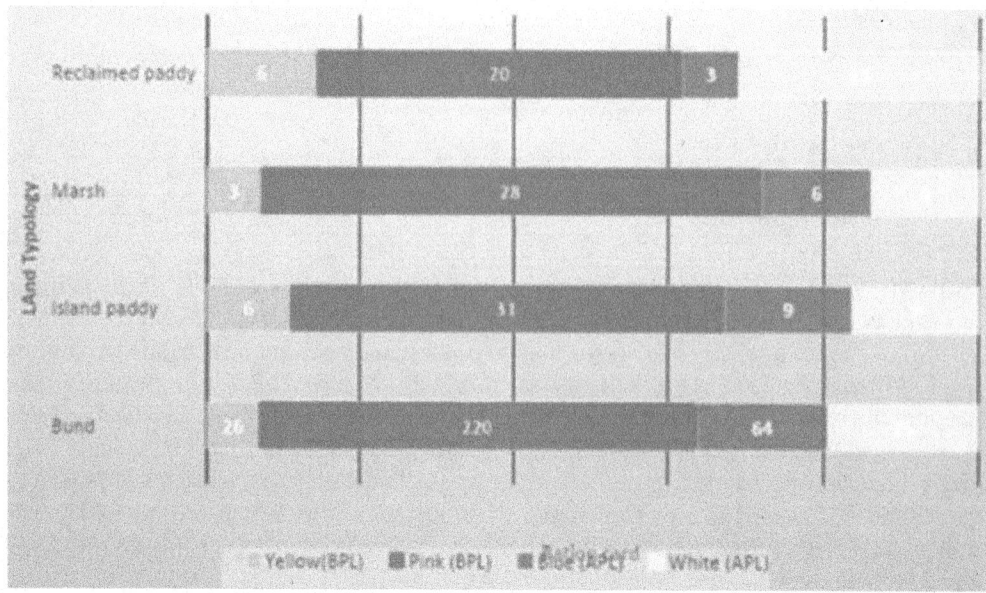

Fig. 35.3 Class Distribution Within Different Land Typologies, Compiled From The Survey.

on paddy cultivation. The double-cropping prompted by the green revolution era warranted interventions like *Thottapally Spillway* to divert floodwaters to the Arabian sea and *Thanneermukkom Bund* to regulate saltwater intrusion. The second crop became popular with time due to various factors like more minor pests and diseases and the possibility of higher productivity. In contrast, in earlier times, polders were essentially left as floodplains to accommodate the monsoons after the summer crop (Padmakumar, 2013). It is also argued that the structures built for doubling cropping intensity have failed to fulfill the promises on which their existence was premised (Parameswaran, 1987; Vallikappen, 2020).

Engagement with different participants from different *Padashekaram* revealed two dominant rationales for second cropping: a flood adaptation strategy and a livelihood strategy. One group of participant cultivators were in support of double cropping as it promised more profit from cultivation. These participants added that stronger bunds could also lead to multiple cropping patterns, best described as 'the more, the merrier. For these participants, second cropping has been a livelihood strategy. While some opined that second cropping is not done essentially for for-profit purposes but as a flood adaptation strategy wherein it provides flood protection to the houses inside the paddy fields.

Additionally, participants favoring second and even multiple cropping in Kainakary also maintained that the flooding in the region is 'hydraulic events' exacerbated by extreme rainfall. It also supports the livelihoods of the landless laborers too. These variations in perceptions regarding the cropping patterns uncover the contested knowledge and differential

interests existing in the community about the flood risks and mitigation strategies in the local context.

It is evident that second cropping as a strategy for the entire Panchayat, irrespective of differential vulnerability and nature of bunds, indirectly leads to less and less room for water to navigate, ultimately leading to fewer lands for flood cushioning. The interplay of physical (elevation of the land) and infrastructural vulnerability (nature of bunds) at the polder level makes some polders more vulnerable to flooding than others. Nevertheless, more importantly, these patterns of vulnerability are relational. For example, some lands at a higher elevation than others and protected by bunds would eventually refrain from acting as cushions. In comparison, the polders, which are poorly protected by bunds at a lower elevation, would act as flood cushions for the entire region resulting in increased pressure on the bunds, crop loss, and a threat for those living inside the paddy fields. This reveals the unequal distribution of flood risks and vulnerability.

On the other hand, structural solutions increased the region's vulnerability because of pseudo security and disruption of the complex and fragile ecosystem of the area(Parameswaran, 1987). A single cropping pattern, known as a better strategy for reducing flood risk, was replaced by a less adaptive strategy of double cropping. In effect, the policy solutions proposed during the Kuttanad Development plan during 1954 made the second cropping famous in the region responsible for environmental degradation and increasing future flood risk. Development as well as agricultural processes coerced this shift. As a result, the Kuttanad Development Plan in 1954 emerged as one of the fundamental drivers in exacerbating the long-term risk for short-term agricultural productivity for the least vulnerable paddy cultivators. The burden of these disaster risks is borne by the most vulnerable paddy cultivators and residents within the community.

Hence, the strategy of double cropping is considered counterproductive at two levels. At the level of structural solutions, it has resulted in long-term flood risk for the entire region. In the short run, it protects some fields at the cost of others with inequitable outcomes. The benefits of double-cropping for dominant farmers and protection through permanent bunds and structural solutions against flooding in Kainakary Panchayat are subsidized by people living in the most susceptible land typology II with the lowest elevation. Permanent bunds in these polders leave even less room for water, which flows to polders with weaker and porous bunds and is less elevated. When analyzed at the scale of the Panchayat, the preconditions of the second cropping are the very causal factors associated with an increase in flood hazard frequencies and impacts in the long run. The replacement of a more effective traditional single cropping pattern replaced by a flood risk-inducing second cropping pattern is an example of withering traditional knowledge being outsmarted by external interventions as discussed by Baghel (2014) and Rai & Khawas (2019).

5. Discussion and Conclusion

The findings show that the socio-economically marginal communities like landless people or female-headed households are concentrated around more vulnerable land typologies, which are susceptible to higher hazard risk. Both spatial and social vulnerabilities also overlap for some communities like SC female-headed households. While the spatial vulnerability is created mainly through structural solutions and the Vembanad wetland ecosystems, the concentration of marginal and privileged communities around most and least vulnerable areas, respectively, is a function of power relations. The latter is beyond the scope of the paper. Nevertheless, the impact of structural solutions on different kinds of social groups unraveled insightfully in the study.

The coping and adaptation strategy employed by the most vulnerable socio-spatial communities living in the paddy fields is second cropping facilitated by structural solutions like *Thanneermukkom* bund and *Thottapally Spillway*. However, these gradually exacerbated disaster risk in the Kuttanad region. The second cropping has different meanings and impacts for people who were socio-spatially differently located. The second copping pattern also emerged to boost the agricultural productivity for the group of farmers benefitting from double cropping. For farmers and people living within those fields, and did not benefit from the pattern still had to cultivate twice to safeguard their houses from floods. The agricultural benefits and the flood risk related to double cropping and structural solutions are inequitably distributed across the community.

A non-localized disaster planning coupled with a dearth of contextual and contested knowledge is often less equipped to take cognizance of the complex nature of reality and dialectic between the most and least vulnerable people within the community. The dominance of scientific knowledge foregrounding technical approaches and structural solutions in flood mitigation further adds unwanted risks in the future. This brings us to our primary question of the sole credibility of 'scientific knowledge' borne out of technical expertise. It can be shown that this knowledge which only delves into the imageries of rivers and flood control, can easily slip into the unjust outcomes for marginal epistemic communities. This crucial lack of understanding within both development and disaster planning can only be bridged through the representation of these epistemic communities, their world view, experiences, and the humility to acknowledge the failure of the heterogeneous and hegemonic discourses and narratives within scientific and local communities. This research attempted to generate contextual knowledge production with the help of a technical and participatory approach. Technical approaches like GIS, Remote sensing were used to understand the local and micro-level peculiarities of the physiography and thus physical vulnerability. The qualitative and quantitative methods were crucial in understanding the correlation between flood plain zonation, socioeconomic factors, and overall vulnerability for different groups at a granular level. Similarly, the differential vulnerability of different social groups and households was demonstrated through survey findings.

Such processes also create spaces of participatory and democratic deliberation of multiple epistemic groups and stakeholders at the local government level. The flood risk planning at the semi-formal platforms below constitutionally empowered Gram Sabhas opens ways for accountable, transparent, and adaptive governance. The co-production of knowledge in such deliberative spaces while including local and contextual knowledge can also facilitate documentation of Indigenous Technology knowledge (ITK). Thus, we argue not only for integrating ITK (NPDM, 2009) but also for making scientific knowledge more accessible and democratic through deliberative institutional mechanisms of dialogue at the local level. A local disaster plan built on contestations within local people's knowledge & values, technical expertise, and knowledge wherever required widens the possibilities of better adaptation. While a more grounded flood risk planning with integration of both technical and people's knowledge surely does open the possibilities of robust & inclusive DRR plans. The task is far from over if the exogenous factors and processes which create vulnerabilities and flood risk are left unaddressed.

6. Acknowledgement

We would like to thank Kerala Institute of Local Administration (KILA) and Kerala State Disaster Management Authority (KSDMA), Nedumudy Panchayat members, Kainakary Panchayat members, Duleep Mathal Nature Conservation Trust, CANALPY, students & professors from IIT Bombay and the residents of Kainakary Panchayat who extended their unwavering support throughout the research study.

REFERENCES

1. Abbas, A., Amjath-Babu,T.S., Kächele, H., Usman M., & Müller, K. (2016). An overview of flood mitigation strategy and research support in South Asia: implications for sustainable flood risk management, *International Journal of Sustainable Development & World Ecology*, 23: 1, 98–111, DOI: 10.1080/13504509.2015.1111954

2. Ashraf, S., & Luqman, Md., & Iftikhar, Md., & Ashraf, I. & Hassan, Z. (2017). Understanding Flood Risk Management in Asia: Concepts and Challenges. 10.5772/intechopen.69139.

3. Alexander, D. & Davis, I. (2012). Disaster Risk Reduction: An Alternative Viewpoint. International Journal of Disaster Risk Reduction. 2. 1–5. 10.1016/j.ijdrr.2012.10.002.

4. Allen, K. M. (2006). Community-based disaster preparedness and climate adaptation: local capacity-building in the Philippines. *Disasters*, 30(1), 81–101.

5. Baghel, R. (2014). *River Control in India*.

6. Bang, H. N. (2013). Governance of disaster risk reduction in Cameroon: The need to empower local government. Journal of Disaster Risk Studies 5(2), 77–87.

7. Blaikie, P., Cannon, T., Davis, I., & Wisner, B. (1994). At risk. *Natural hazards, people's vulnerability and disasters*.

8. Census of India (2011). Office of the Registrar General & Census Commissioner, New Delhi, 27-12-2013.

9. CSE (1991). *Floods, Flood Plains and Environment Myths*, State of India's Environment A Citizen's Report, Centre for Science and Environment, New Delhi

10. Das, A., & Das, P. (2017). Local Solutions to Local Disasters: Governance in Flood Management in Assam

11. DasGupta, R., & Shaw, R. (2017). Disaster Risk Reduction: A Critical Approach. In I. Kelman,

12. J. Mercer, & J. Gaillard, *The Routledge Handbook of Disaster Risk Reduction Including Climate Change Adaptation* (pp. 12-23). England: Routledge

13. D'Souza, R. (2020). Event, process and pulse: resituating floods in environmental histories of South Asia. *Environment and History*, 26(1), 31–49.

14. Dekens, J. (2007). *Local knowledge for disaster preparedness: A literature review*. International Centre for Integrated Mountain Development (ICIMOD).

15. Dixit, A. (2003). Floods and vulnerability: need to rethink flood management. *Flood problem and management in South Asia*, 155–179.

16. Faas, A. J. (2016). Disaster vulnerability in anthropological perspective. Annals of Anthropological Practice, 40(1), 14–27.

17. Gaillard, J. C., & Jigyasu, R. (2016). Measurement and evidence: whose resilience for whom? *Resilience Development Initiative*, *11*, 1–15.

18. Gaillard, J.C., and J. Mercer. (2013). From knowledge to action: Bridging gaps in disaster risk reduction. *Progress in Human Geography* 37(1): 93–114.

19. Ganapati, N. E., & Ganapati, S. (2008). Enabling participatory planning after disasters: A case study of the World Bank's housing reconstruction in Turkey. *Journal of the American Planning Association*, 75(1), 41–59.

20. Gupta S., Javed A., Datt D. (2003) Economics of Flood Protection in India. In: Mirza M.M.Q., Dixit A., Nishat A. (eds) Flood Problem and Management in South Asia. Springer, Dordrecht. https://doi.org/10.1007/978-94-017-0137-2_10

21. Hiwasaki, L. (2017). Local Knowledge for Disaster Risk Reduction Including Climate Change Adaptation. In *The Routledge Handbook of Disaster Risk Reduction Including Climate Change Adaptation* (pp. 227–237). Routledge.

22. Hilhorst D., Baart J., Haar G. & Leeftink F.M, (2015). 'Is disaster "normal" for indigenous people? Indigenous knowledge and coping practices', *Disaster Prevention and Management* 24(4), 506–522. 10.1108/DPM-02-2015-0027

23. Iglesias, G., Arambepola, N., & Rattakul, D. (2008). Mainstreaming Disaster Risk Reduction into Local Governance. Asian Disaster Preparedness Center.

24. International Federation of Red Cross and Red Crescent Societies (IFRC), (2011). Desk Review on Trends in the Promotion of Community-Based Disaster Risk Reduction Through Legislation. Geneva: International Federation of Red Cross and Red Crescent Societies.

25. Kainakari Gram Panchayat. (1996). Kainakari Gram Panchayat Development Report. Alappuzha: Kainakari Gram Panchayat.

26. Kainakari Gram Panchayat. (2021). Kainakari Gram Panchayat Development Report. Alappuzha: Kainakari Gram Panchayat.

27. Kranenburg, R. (2001). Compact Geography of the Netherlands. Utrecht: KNAG.

28. Kron, W. (2002). Keynote lecture: Flood risk= hazard× exposure× vulnerability. *Flood defence*, 82–97.

29. Kumar, S., & Devadas, V. (2015). Integrated Planning for Sustainable Development of Kuttanad Wetland Region, Kerala State. International Conference on Emerging Trends in Engineering, Science and Technology (ICETEST) (pp. 1660–1667). Procedia Technology.

30. Kusumasari, B., Alam, Q., & Siddiqui, K. (2010). Resource capability for local government in managing disaster. *Disaster Prevention and Management: An International Journal*.

31. Lahiri-Dutt, K. (2000). Imagining rivers. *Economic and Political Weekly*, 2395–2400.

32. López-Marrero, T., & Tschakert, P. (2011). From theory to practice: building more resilient communities in flood-prone areas. *Environment and Urbanization, 23*(1), 229–249.

33. Manyena, B., O'Brien, G., O'Keefe, P. and Rose, J. (2011) Disaster resilience: a bounce back or bounce forward ability? Local Environment: The International Journal of Justice and Sustainability, 16 (5). pp. 417–424. ISSN 1354–9839.

34. McCully,P. (2007) "Before the Deluge: Coping with Floods in a Changing Climate," IRN Dams, Rivers and People Report 2007, International Rivers Network, Berkeley, CA.

35. Mehta, Lyla. (2003). Contexts and constructions of water scarcity. Economic and Political Weekly. 38. 10.2307/4414344.

36. Mercer, J., (2012) Knowledge and disaster risk reduction. In *Handbook of Hazards and Disaster Risk Reduction* (pp. 89–100). Routledge.

37. Mishra, D. K., (1997). The Bihar flood story, *Economic and Political Weekly* **XXXII**(35), 2206–2217.

38. Mondal, D., Chowdhury, S., & Basu, D. (2018). Role of panchayat (Local self-government) in managing disaster in terms of reconstruction, crop protection, livestock management and health and sanitation measures. *Natural Hazards, 94*(1), 371–383.

39. Mohanty, M. P., Mudgil, S., & Karmakar, S. (2020). Flood management in India: a focussed review on the current status and future challenges. *International Journal of Disaster Risk Reduction, 49*, 101660.

40. National Disaster Management Authority. (2009). National Policy on Disaster Management - 2009. 1– 56.

41. National Disaster Management Authority. (2019). National Disaster Management Plan - 2019. 1–384

42. Pachauri, R., & Meyer, L. (2014). *Climate change 2014: synthesis report. Contribution of Working Groups I, II and III to the fifth assessment report of the Intergovernmental Panel on Climate Change*. IPCC.

43. Padmakumar, D. K. (2013). Kuttanad-Global Agricultural Heritage: Promoting Uniqueness. *Proceedings of the Kerala Environment Congress - 2013* (pp. 62–74). Thiruvananthapuram: Centre for Environment and Development.

44. Parameswaran M.P., (1987). Eco-degradation at Kuttanad-a review, Environmental Services Group.

45. Parasuraman, S., & Sengupta, S. (2001). World commission on Dams: Democratic means for sustainable ends. *Economic and Political Weekly*, 1881–1891.

46. Pathirage, C., Seneviratne, K., Amaratunga, D., & Haigh, R. (2014). Knowledge factors and associated challenges for successful disaster knowledge sharing. *Prepared for the Global Assessment Report on Disaster Risk Reduction, 2015*, 1–30.

47. Rai, P. & Khawas, V., (2019). 'Traditional knowledge system in disaster risk reduction: Exploration, acknowledgement and proposition', *Jàmbá: Journal of Disaster Risk Studies* 11(1), a484. https://doi.org/10.4102/jamba.v11i1.484

48. Renn, O. (2017). *Risk governance: coping with uncertainty in a complex world*. Routledge.

49. Shaw R., Uy N., and Baumwoll J. (eds) (2008). Indigenous Knowledge for Disaster Risk Reduction: Good Practices and Lessons Learnt from the Asia-Pacific Region. Bangkok: UNISDR

50. Spiekermann, R., S. Kienberger, J. Norton, F. Briones, and J. Weichselgartner. (2015). The disaster-knowledge matrix: Reframing and evaluating the knowledge challenges in disaster risk reduction. *International Journal of Disaster Risk Reduction* 13: 96–108.

51. Slovic, P. (1987). Perception of risk. *Science*, 280–285.

52. Tobin, G. A. (1999). Sustainability and community resilience: the holy grail of hazards planning?. *Global Environmental Change Part B: Environmental Hazards, 1*(1), 13–25.

53. UNEP. (2020, March 03). How climate change is making record-breaking floods the new normal. Retrieved September 2020, from United Nations Environment programme: https://www.unenvironment.org/news-and-stories/story/how-climate-change-making record-breaking-floods-new-normal

54. UNISDR, 2005. Hyogo Framework for Action 2005–2015: Building the Resilience of Nations and Communities to Disasters. Extract from the final report of the World Conference on Disaster Reduction (A/CONF.206/6)

55. UNISDR (United Nations International Strategy for Disaster Reduction). 2015. Sendai framework for disaster risk reduction 2015–2030.

56. Vahanvati, M., & Mulligan, M. (2017). A new model for effective post-disaster housing reconstruction: Lessons from Gujarat and Bihar in India. *International Journal of Project Management, 35*(5), 802–817.

57. Vallikappen, T. (2020). The Making and Unmaking of Kuttanad : Development and Transformations Below Sea Level. Norway: University of Bergen.

58. Vishnu, C. L., Sajinkumar, K. S., Oommen, T., Coffman, R. A., Thrivikramji, K. P., Rani, V. R., & Keerthy, S. (2019). Satellite-based assessment of the August 2018 flood in parts of Kerala, India. *Geomatics, Natural Hazards and Risk, 10*(1), 758–767.

CHAPTER 36

Sustainable Operation & Maintenance (O&M) of Multi-purpose Disaster Shelters (MPDS) in Bangladesh

Mohammad Shariful Islam

Professor, Dept. of Civil Engineering,
Bangladesh University of Engineering and Technology,
Dhaka-1000, Bangladesh
msharifulbd@gmail.com; msharifulislam@ce.buet.ac.bd

Samira Tasnim Progga

Postgraduate Student, Dept. of Civil Engineering,
Bangladesh University of Engineering and Technology,
Dhaka-1000, Bangladesh
stprogga@gmail.com; 1018042226@ce.buet.ac.bd

Tahsin Reza Hossain

Professor, Dept. of Civil Engineering,
Bangladesh University of Engineering and Technology,
Dhaka-1000, Bangladesh,
tahsin.hossain@gmail.com; tahsin@ce.buet.ac.bd

Abstract

After one of the most notable cyclones, *Gorky,* the Government of Bangladesh prepared a master plan for the construction of cyclone shelters along the coastal belt. To provide shelter during cyclones, around 4,000 Multi-purpose Disaster Shelter (MPDS) have been built across the country. The Cyclone Shelter Construction, Maintenance and Management Policy 2011 outlines the standards and guidelines for shelters including the facilities to be ensured for all its users. But there are some gaps in the O&M schemes that are being practiced. All the facilities that must be ensured are sometimes missing. Based on the available literature review it can be said that the current O&M scheme must be improved. The school schedule may be updated as well, based on the time cycle of the cyclone. Because of the recent Covid-19 situation, shelter space cannot be utilized to its full capacity. Necessary steps to fight against this situation is also paramount. Some previous studies and projects aimed to find out the condition of the existing MPDSs. But a proper, comprehensive and broad study on the existing O&M practices, building health, the satisfaction of the users is a must to develop a sustainable O&M protocol for the MPDSs.

Keywords: Multi-purpose shelter, disaster management, operation and maintenance (O&M), COVID-19.

1. Introduction

The coastline of Bangladesh is about 710 km long and the continental shelf extends over an area of about 24,800 sq. Miles (Ahsan, 2013). Due to geographic location and geophysical conditions, Bangladesh is one of the most disaster-prone countries in the world. The location of the off-shore islands and the triangular funnel shape of the Bay of Bengal have made the coastal areas susceptible to cyclone and tidal surges (Cyclone shelter construction, management and maintenance policy, 2011). These catastrophic natural disasters cause casualties and damage to houses, infrastructures, agriculture, etc., washing away hard-earned development of years in a minute. Among the natural disasters, the cyclone is the most devastating one in the coastal zone. Bangladesh is the world's third most vulnerable country to sea-level rise in terms of the number of people, and among the top ten countries in terms of percentage of people living in low-lying coastal zones

(Pender, 2008). On average, a severe tropical cyclone hits Bangladesh every 3 years and the country has been hit by 16 major cyclones with a loss of nearly 500,000 lives since the 1960s (Karim and Mimura, 2008).

In the year 1991, one of the most notable cyclones, *Gorky* claimed almost 140,000 lives, as many as 10 million people lost their homes and overall property damage was in the billions of dollars (https://www.britannica.com). This incident triggered the Government of Bangladesh (GoB) to prepare a master plan for the construction of cyclone shelters along the coastal belt. In recent years, Bangladesh has faced some other disastrous cyclones e.g., cyclone *Sidr* of 2007, *Aila* of 2009, *Bulbul* of 2019 and *Amphan* of 2020 (https://www.dhakatribune.com). Total damages and loss of BDT 115.6 billion (US$ 1.7 billion) were estimated during *Sidr* 2007 (https://reliefweb.int). To protect the people of the coastal zone and their properties from devastating cyclones like *Sidr*, *Aila*, *Amphan* etc., an initiative of constructing cyclone shelters has been taken by the Government of Bangladesh and the non-government organizations, different development partner countries and organizations. Around 4000 Multi-Purpose Cyclone Shelters (MPCS) or Multi-Purpose Disaster Shelter (MPDS) have already been built across the country (Miyaji, Okazaki and Chiho, 2017) which can accommodate 500-2500 people each in case of cyclones (Paul, 2008). However, the cyclone-affected areas of Bangladesh can be divided into different levels of risk zones as shown in Fig. 36.1.

From the map, we can see that areas like Chattogram, Cox's Bazar, Bhola are in high-risk zone where the surge height can be as high as 1m or more. Patuakhali, Noakhali etc. are in risk areas with a surge height of less than 1m. On the other hand, Khulna, Bagerhat, Barishal, etc are in high wind areas with no surge. Depending on the risk level, each MPDS must have a different design, facilities, preparedness etc.

MPDSs basically have dual usage, i.e., during normal time and during emergency time. Normally, throughout the year, MPDSs are used as educational institutes, religious centers, office space etc. (Cyclone Shelter Policy, 2011). But during the emergency time, the structure is used as a disaster shelter. The primary problems with the existing cyclone shelters are the gaps in the existing O&M schemes. A national policy entitled 'Cyclone Shelter Construction, Maintenance and Management Policy 2011' (DMB, 2011) outline the standards and guidelines of construction, maintenance and management of the shelters. However, people who are directly responsible of the O&M of the MPDS and those who are the first-hand users, do not have easy access to it. As a result, most of the shelters are managed by different

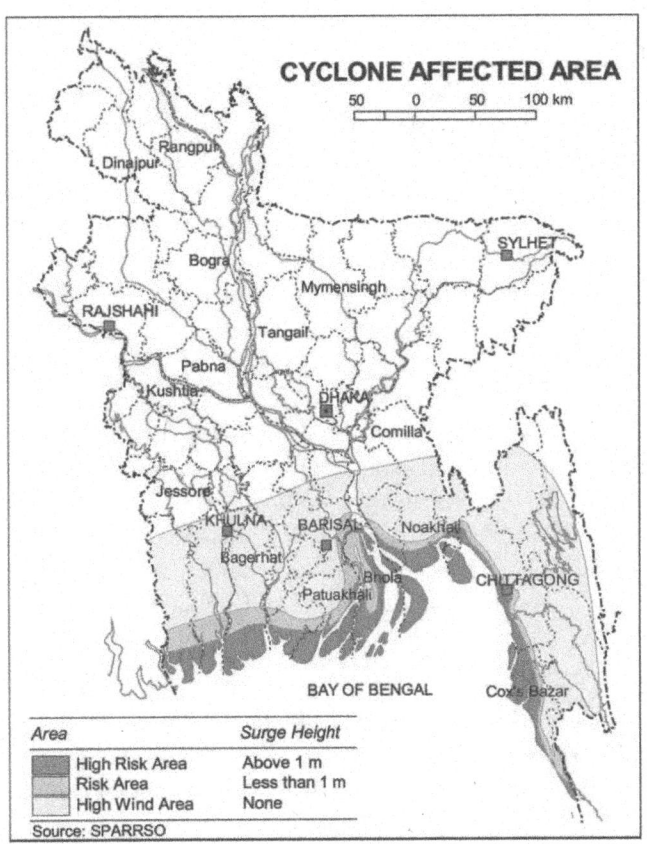

Fig. 36.1   Different level of risk zone of Bangladesh
Source: SPARRSO

authorities (Care Bangladesh, and C3ER, n.d.). And a huge number of shelters are currently out of use.

Different studies and projects have been undertaken to improve the current condition of the existing MPDS of the coastal zones of Bangladesh. The Multipurpose Disaster Shelter Project (MDSP) by the Government of Bangladesh mainly focused on reducing the lives of affected local people and their domestic animals and increasing the targeted population to be covered by accessible MPDS (LGED, 2014). To achieve the target, they planned to improve the existing structures, construct new ones and improve the connecting road. Another ADB project named 'Bangladesh: Emergency Assistance Project', targets to construct 3 MPDS in Ukhiya that will be used as school during the normal time (ADB, 2014). The project also aims at working on areas with road access, water and sanitation, energy supply and disaster risk mitigation. A project of Care Bangladesh conducted through the Center for Climate Change and Environmental Research (C3ER), BRAC University aimed to assess the existing MPDS and outline measures to improve communities' disaster resilience (Care Bangladesh, C3ER, n.d.). A wide ranged survey was also undertaken on 164 MPDSs in the Cox's Bazar Sadar, Ramu and Moheshkhali. Another study carried out by Miyaji et al. (2017) in Padmapukur Union, Shyamnagar Upazila, Khulna and Hatiya Island, Hatiya Upazila, Noakhali showed the behavior of the local people towards evacuation, their preparedness for the disaster and for a long-term stay in the MPDS (Miyaji, Okazaki and Chiho, 2017). Other than these, several other studies and projects on the national, private or international level have been conducted. A few of them are not directly related to MPDS but other shelters or low-cost safe housing such as a study based on cyclone resilient shelter for displaced citizens of Myanmar (Islam and Hossain, 2018), vulnerability reduction of the local building (Moles, Islam, Hossain and Poddar, 2013) and vernacular housing for disaster-prone areas in Bangladesh (Moles, Islam, Hossain and Poddar, 2013). But a complete picture covering O&M practice, maintenance and building health monitoring, repair and retrofitting scheme of the existing situation is yet to be drawn.

This paper focuses on the gaps in the existing O&M schemes of the MPDS based on literature, reports, guidelines and existing practices. The Government of Bangladesh, humanitarian actors and donor community are looking for a sustainable solution on operation and maintenance of existing and newly constructed MPDSs. An integrated approach is needed for a more sustainable O&M of the existing MPSDs of this country.

2. Present State of MPDS

A cyclone shelter is usually an elevated solid construction that provides safety and security from the cyclones and associated storm surges (Rahman and Islam, n.d.). But a cyclone or disaster shelter is called MPDS when the structure is used for another purpose during normal time. Usually, an MPDS can be used as school, college, madrasa, mosque, temple, monastery, church, community center, community clinic, office space etc. (Cyclone Shelter Policy, 2011).

To ensure disaster risk reduction and preparedness during the emergency time, the Ministry of Disaster Management and Relief has formulated 'Cyclone Shelter Construction, Maintenance and Management Policy 2011'. This policy states the factors to consider during choosing the location and design of shelter, essential facilities to ensure, management and maintenance schemes to follow, its dual usage during regular time and emergency time, formation of the disaster management committee and its responsibility etc. in a very detailed manner. According to the Cyclone Shelter Policy of 2011, 3 standard designs for the construction of cyclone shelters are suggested based on mainly plinth area and capacity. The basic details of the 3 designs are presented in Table 36.1.

Table 36.1 Basic details of the 3 standard designs of cyclone shelters (Cyclone Shelter Policy, 2011)

Design Category	Purpose	Plinth Area (sq. m)	Approximate Land Area	Approximate Capacity
1	College/Higher Secondary School/Madrasa-cum-Multi-purpose Shelter	275-300	12 decimal of an acre	1000 persons per floor from second floor
2	Primary School-cum-Multi-purpose Shelter	220-230	10 decimal of an acre	800 persons per floor from second floor
3	Multi-purpose Shelter	200	10 decimal of an acre	750 persons per floor from second floor

Some basic requirements of a cyclone shelter as per the Cyclone Shelter Policy (2011) are:

(i) Foundation for at least three stories

(ii) Ramp facilities up to first floor

(iii) A reasonable sized room reserved for helpless and disabled people

(iv) Rest of the first floor for domestic animals

Some factors that need to be considered during choosing the location according to the Cyclone Shelter Policy (2011) are:

(i) The shelter must be within 1.5 km distance of the community.

(ii) The approach road must be user-friendly and linked to the main road.

(iii) The shelter should not be standalone unless absolutely necessary. Multi-purpose use must be ensured.

(iv) It cannot be constructed in the headquarters of districts, upazila and municipality. Priority should be given to open spaces of school, college and madrasas.

Essential facilities/requirements to be ensured according to the Cyclone Shelter Policy (2011) are:

(i) Ramp up to first floor for children, women, elderly people, people with severe illness and special needs and cattle must be ensured.

(ii) Separate toilet facilities for women and a separate room for pregnant and lactating mothers must be ensured.

(iii) Shelters should have three stories with first floor for cattle.

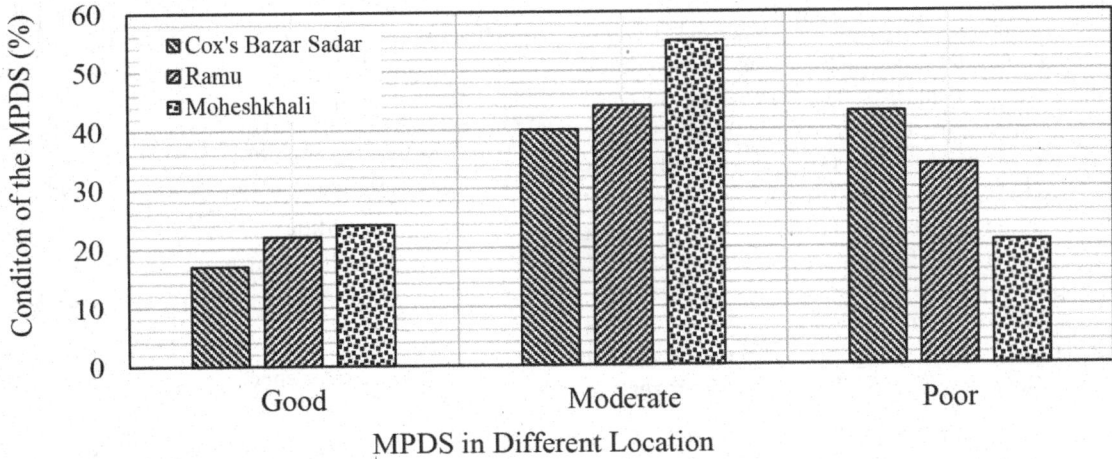

Fig. 36.2   Condition of the existing MPDS in different location (Care Bangladesh and C3ER, n.d.)

(iv) Sufficient light, especially on top of the roof must be ensured for visibility during an emergency time like storm and heavy rain during night.

(v) Arrangement of solar panel for emergency electricity and rain water harvesting for safe drinking water is a must.

At present, there are almost 4000 shelters all over the country (Paul, 2009). According to the study conducted by Care Bangladesh and C3ER, these are being used as schools, health care center, community buildings and so on in Cox's Bazar Sadar, Ramu and Moheshkhali, (Care Bangladesh and C3ER, n.d.).

But unfortunately, at present 1,576 out of 3,976 shelters are not in use due to poor O&M scheme (Paul, 2009). The study of Care Bangladesh and C3ER as presented in Fig. 36.2, shows an overall condition of the MPDS situated in the study areas. From the graph, we can see that most of the MPDSs in Cox's Bazar Sadar are in poor condition, while in Ramu and Moheshkhali most of them are in moderate condition. However, condition of a lot of shelters in total is poor, which is a big concern.

According to Miyaji et al. (2017), the survey conducted in Padmapukur Union and Hatiya Union showed that 80% of respondent said the main issue for them is the physical capacity of the shelters. It is difficult to maintain hygiene, adequate water and sanitation facilities, and privacy. As most of the MPDSs are used as educational institutes, most of the rooms are usually assigned as teachers' room, classroom or storage rooms. So, some rooms were found locked during emergency times. The toilet issue is a big problem in the shelters as well. First of all, there is not enough toilet present in the shelters. Most of them are outside the structure. So, it becomes very difficult to use them during the cyclone when

the surroundings are inundated. In situations like this, the emergency toilets on the rooftop become the only option for both men and women staying in the shelter.

A lot of the existing structures are vulnerable to the major natural calamities that are very common in coastal zones, e.g. earthquake, cyclone, tsunami etc. From Fig. 36.3, it can be seen that most of the shelters are vulnerable against Earthquake that is 86% of the data points, 10% are vulnerable against cyclone and the remaining are vulnerable against tsunami. So, while designing the MPDS in cyclone or Earthquake-prone areas, wind velocity, EQ load and other considerations must be incorporated into the design according to the current BNBC, 2020 for a more stable and safe structure.

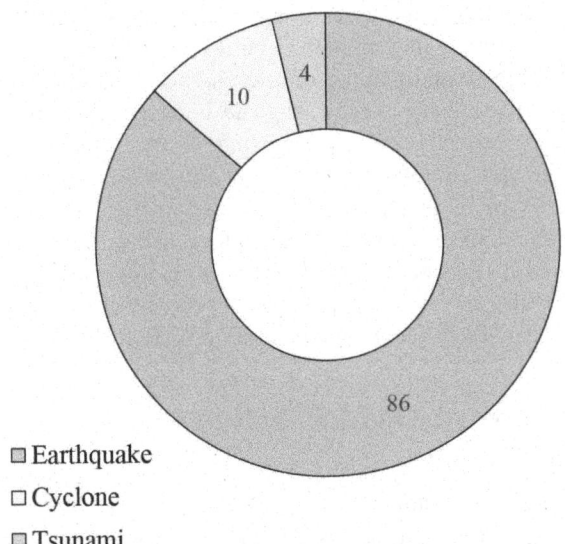

Fig. 36.3   Vulnerability (%) of existing MPDS against different disaster (Mahmood, Dhakal and Kamruzzaman, 2013)

Currently, the world is facing another serious issue of the Covid-19 pandemic. This present situation is posing challenges in all sectors and disaster management and preparedness issue is no different than that. As the Coronavirus Disease or Covid-19 is a contagious disease, a lot of people staying together in an overcrowded shelter poses double threat for them. People have to make a difficult choice of either staying home during the emergency time to avoid Covid-19 or going to a congested shelter and facing the chances of getting infected with the deadly disease. Moreover, the shelters now need extra preparedness for this pandemic situation such as separate room for Covid-19 patients, Personal Protection Equipment (PPE), hand washing facilities, hand sanitizer etc.

To address this situation, recently the Ministry of Disaster Management and Relief (MoDMR), International Federation of Red Cross and Red Crescent Societies (IFRC), Bangladesh Red Crescent Societies (BDRCS) and Cyclone Preparedness Programme (CPP) revised the cyclone preparedness and early action plan in both 2020 and 2021 (CPP, 2021). A National Lesson Learned Programme Workshop was also arranged where several recommendations were made to ensure safety against Covid-19 during emergency time. According to the workshop, volunteers' personal safety must be ensured through the use of face masks, face shields, hand washing soap, hand sanitizers etc. Use of social media, like Facebook can be used involving the volunteers to raise awareness among the community people. To ensure the physical distance between volunteers and to make easy wearing face mask all the time during house visits, small groups of volunteers can be assigned. As a result, they can easily reach the community with early warning messages. To ensure proper physical distance among the users in the shelter, a lesser number of affected people in each MPDS must be maintained. To attain this, an increased number of safe and prepared shelters with an adequate water source, hygiene items, first aid facilities etc. are needed. Awareness-raising is also very important among the community people to educate them about the severity of the situation and the need to maintain personal hygiene, physical distance and other necessary measures. More meetings before the disasters are also suggested either physically or virtually to ensure better preparedness and service delivery for the community in need.

3. Current O&M Practice

By definition, Operation and Maintenance or O&M means the functions, duties and labor associated with the daily operation and normal repairs, replacement of parts and structural components, and other activities needed to preserve an asset so that it continues to provide acceptable services and achieves its expected life (https://www.lawinsider.com).

The Cyclone Shelter Policy (2011) states in details the construction, maintenance and management scheme of the MPDS of Bangladesh. The following factors are discussed in the policy in details:

(i) Selection of location
(ii) Design for construction of cyclone shelters
(iii) Essential facilities
(iv) Cyclone shelter management
(v) Responsibility of local disaster management committee
(vi) Maintenance of the list of cyclone shelters
(vii) Repair, maintenance, abandoning and sale of cyclone shelters
(viii) Use of cyclone shelters during the normal time
(ix) Cyclone shelter management committee
(x) Scope of work for the cyclone shelter management committee

So, the policy provides instructions about the O&M of an MPDS from the beginning of its construction. But there are a few factors that are not described or prescribed in detail about an MPDS; such as, the policy states that an MPDS needs a separate room or toilet for women, but it does not specify the required number of separate rooms/toilets. According to the policy, solar panel or rainwater harvesting facilities are a must, but the maintenance procedure for such facilities are not specified. The policy suggests a catchment area of 1.5 km for each shelter. But it does not state the justification or basis of it. Moreover, population, level of risk, surrounding environment, connectivity etc. are not the same for all the shelters. So, a specific catchment area may not be suitable for all the areas.

Another problem with the existing Cyclone Shelter Policy, 2011 is the inaccessibility. The document is mostly available on the internet and in English Language. Even if a Bangla version of the document exists, it is very hard to find. So, the English version, in spite of being comparatively more available, is not very suitable for the community people of the targeted areas because of the language barrier. A pocketbook containing the main points of the policy in Bangla may be useful for the efficient management.

Even though, the Cyclone Shelter Policy (2011) has recommended a specific design for all the MPDS of Bangladesh, but, because of the unavailability and language barrier of the policy, it may not be always possible to follow the design. Moreover, different MPDSs are funded and constructed by different constructing and funding authorities as shown in Fig. 36.4, e.g. Bangladesh Govt., local or private funding, NGOs, INGOs etc. So, a similar design is not always followed.

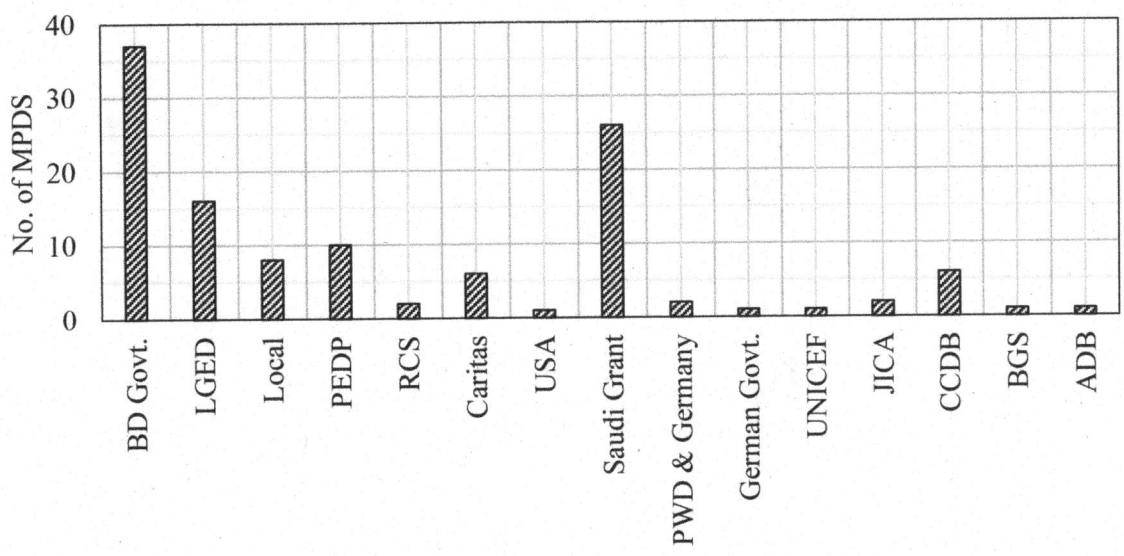

Fig. 36.4 Different constructing authorities of MPDS in Bangladesh (Care Bangladesh and C3ER, n.d.)

In the Cyclone Shelter Policy (2011), different management authorities are for the different situations are specified. In Table 36.2, the responsible authorities are mentioned with the respective situation.

The Cyclone Shelter Policy (2011) also specifies a 7-member 'Cyclone Shelter Management Committee' for shelters that are not being used as school, college, madrasa, mosque, temple or any other organization such as standalone shelters.

But according to the study by Care Bangladesh and C3ER, different authorities, such as, Disaster Management Committee (DMC), School Management Committee (SMC), Project Implementation officer (PIO), Disaster Shelter Management Committee (DSMC), local people etc. are overseeing the O&M of different MPDS situated in Cox's Bazar Sadar, Ramu, Moheshkhali as shown in Fig. 36.5. From the graph, it can be seen that, even though most of the structures are managed by the SMC, other authorities are also overseeing the O&M schemes of some shelters. So, it creates an inconsistency in the current O&M practice.

Generally, tropical cyclones strike Bangladesh in two seasons; during March to July and during September to December (https://bd.usembassy.gov). And from the study a 50 years occurrence history (1960-2010), as presented in Fig. 36.6 we can see that the majority of it occurs in May and November (https://en.banglapedia.org). As a result, educational activities get hampered in the MPDSs that are being used as educational institutes. The current O&M scheme may include special consideration or provision addressing this issue. A detailed plan can be introduced to make an efficient time management cycle all year round. A location-based education plan especially for cyclone-prone areas may provide a solution to this. The structure can be used from January to April and June to October for normal time use and for preparation of emergency time use. A maintenance protocol can be followed to prepare the structure for the emergency situation at the peak time. The schedule may be prepared in a manner so that the peak time does not have any examination or such important event. And during December, the structure can undergo repair works.

Table 36.2 Responsible authority for MPDS management in different situation (Cyclone Shelter Policy, 2011)

Sl. No	Responsible Authority	Relevant Situation
1	Community people	Must be involved during construction as they are the targeted user
2	Constricting organization	If they are the targeted user
3	Relevant management committee of educational institute	If the MPDS is supposed to be used as an educational institute during the normal time
4	Ministry Disaster Management and Relief	If a previous organization surrenders the ownership

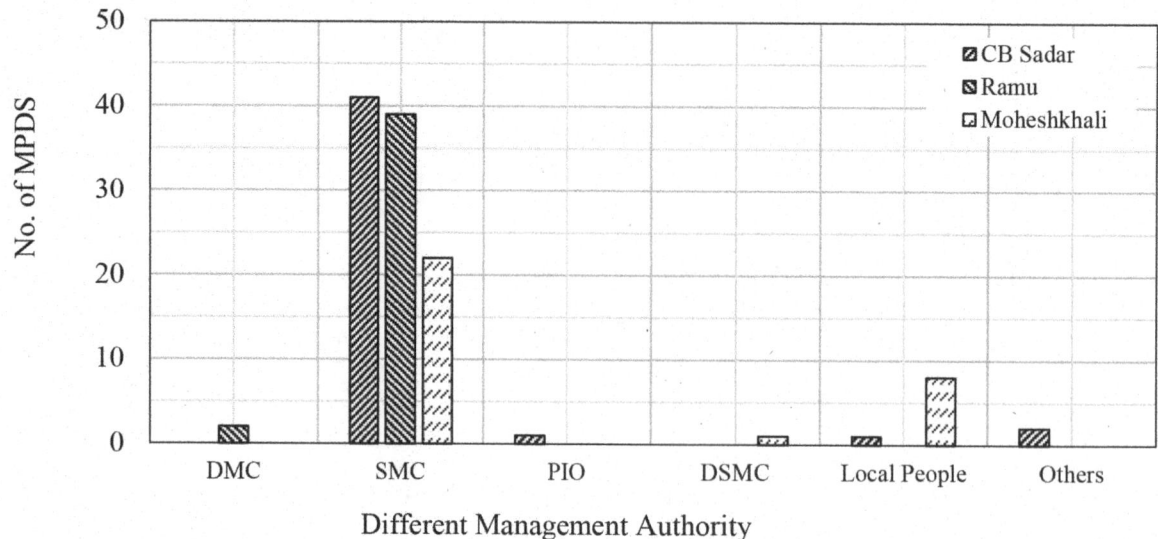

Fig. 36.5 Different management authorities of MPDS (Care Bangladesh and C3ER, n.d.)

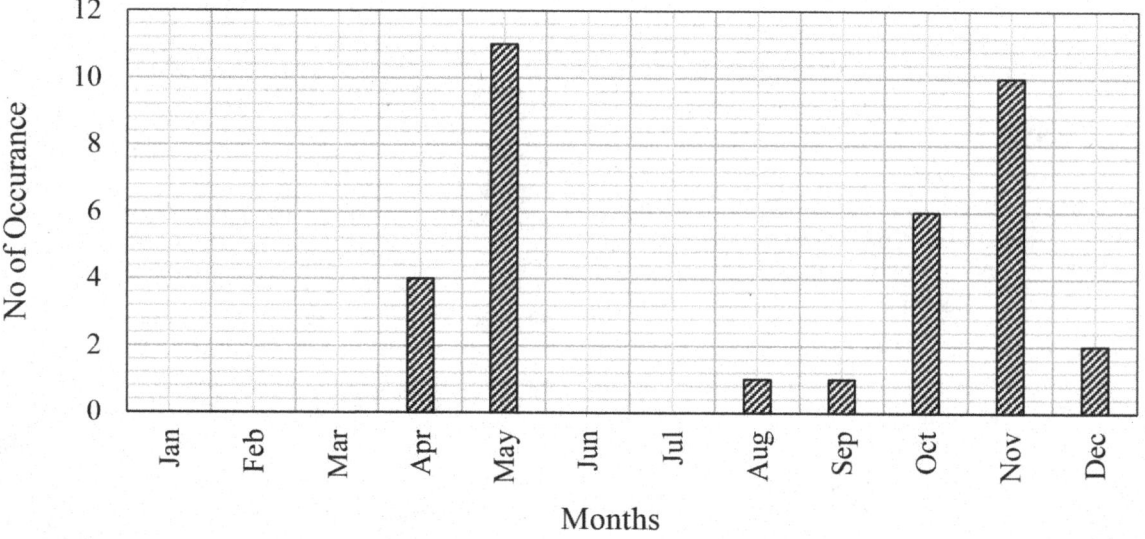

Fig. 36.6 No of occurrence of cyclone on different months from 1960-2010 (https://en.banglapedia.org).

4. Gaps in Previous Studies

In previous years several surveys have been conducted to collect information about the existing MPDS and the behavior and experience of the users in affected areas. Miyaji et al. (2007) conducted a questionnaire survey to understand the evacuation behavior of the local people of Padmapukur Union, and Hatiya Island. This survey mostly focused on how the community people of those areas react after a warning, their preparedness for sudden evacuation and long-term stay at the shelter. The survey conducted by Care Bangladesh and C3ER aimed to assess the condition of the existing shelters in terms of building health, available facilities etc. Based on the result of this survey, it can be said that the survey was very wide-ranging and conducted on a huge number of MPDS. The survey focused on the building health, facilities such as toilet, staircase, pathway, water availability, electricity, solar panel, RWH system etc., shelter specifications such as length, the width of walls, beams, columns, room numbers etc.

But an overall and comprehensive survey must be conducted. These studies did not cover the O&M practice, fund availability, user satisfaction etc. To understand where the gaps are in the O&M of the existing shelters, survey questionnaires need to focus on the O&M schemes, current practices, funds for O&M and responsible authority for this task. Direct interaction with the users are also needed to know about their point of view, previous experience, suggestion etc.

5. Development of Survey Tool

To identify the gaps properly in the existing O&M scheme of the MPDS of Bangladesh, a detailed and comprehensive survey must be conducted. The focus should be on a few specific items, such as previous performance history of the structure, topography of the area, existing mechanism of maintenance including the management of MPDS, who are responsible for the scheme and the source of the fund to carry it out, current building health condition and experience of the users.

The survey tool can have two parts; one is the assessment of the O&M of the MPDS and another is the assessment of the satisfaction of the users, both regular time users and emergency time users.

The O&M assessment survey format can be divided into different sections focusing on different desired information, such as, general information and topography, available facilities, existing O&M schemes and building health conditions. The general information, previous performance history, topography of the area, if the structure is situated in a risk zone etc. will be the focus of this section. The information gathers about the available facilities e.g., availability of separate room, toilet for women, water facilities, RWH and solar panel, staircase, emergency exit, waste management system, drainage system, storage room, emergency tools, first aid box etc. of the respective MPDS will be in the section facilities. Information regarding the existing O&M practices, who are responsible for the task, fund availability, source of fund, and how the fund is utilized will be collected in a separate section. And the section about building health conditions will focus on the cracks, spalling or any other damages on the structural elements such as, beams, columns, slabs, floors, etc. Overall condition of roof, toilets, retaining walls on the surrounding areas, waste management system, drainage system, staircases, emergency exits, front yards, connecting roads etc. will be also noted down.

The satisfaction survey should mainly focus on the overall experience of both regular and emergency users and their recommendations. It must be kept in mind during preparing the questionnaire that the questions must be applicable for all types of respondents. So, very limited and open questions need to be included in the satisfaction survey questionnaire. Hopefully, this type of satisfaction survey can provide a different scenario from their point of view.

For a fruitful and thorough survey result, the different respondent groups must be targeted. For example, for knowledge about the existing O&M scheme of an MPDS, the members of the management committee are the ideal respondent. And for an efficient satisfaction survey officials of the administration of that area, local Govt. representatives, respective Project Implementation Officer (PIO), officials from Local Government Engineering Department (LGED), Thana Education Officer (TEO), Assistant Thana Education Officer (ATEO), member of school management committee, shelter management committee, normal time users like teachers, student, parents of students, emergency time users, community people, members of BDRCS, CPP and other volunteer organization etc. Contact information of the surveyor and respondent must be collected so that they can be contacted later if needed. A complete assessment survey must be conducted for each type of MPDS.

The following flowchart in Fig. 36.7 can be used to prepare a smart and complete survey questionnaire and carry out the survey successfully for the gap analysis in the current O&M practice of the MPDS of Bangladesh.

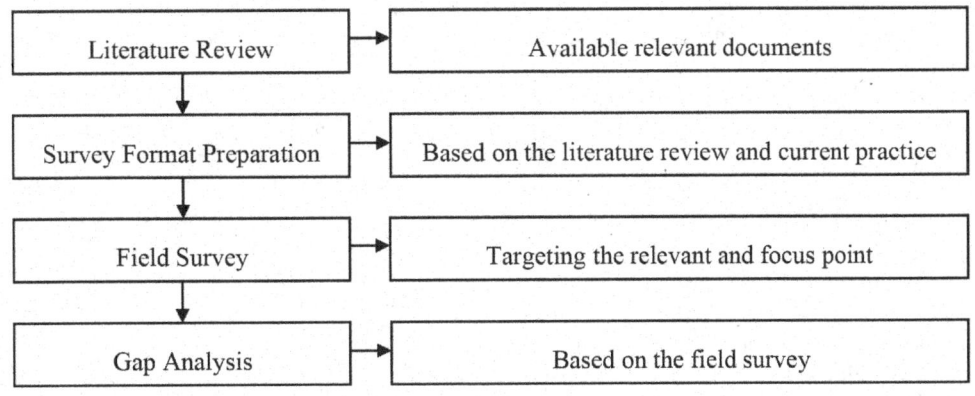

Fig. 36.7 Flowchart showing the steps of survey

6. Conclusions and Recommendations

To provide safety against one of the major disasters, Cyclone, to the people living in the coastal zone of Bangladesh there are around 4000 cyclone shelters. These shelters are being used as cyclone shelters during disaster times and school, college, madrasa, mosque, temple, church, monastery, office space, community clinic, community center etc. during normal times. Since the beginning of the MPDS use, overall casualties and damages have drastically reduced. But, even the existing shelters are not enough. Moreover, due to reasons like gaps in the present O&M practices, coordination and policy, accessibility of a standard policy etc., almost 40% of the existing shelters are currently out of use. So, to increase the population covered by MPDS, more working, safe and prepared shelters are required. For this purpose, budgets must be allocated to improve, renovate, retrofit and upgrade the existing MPDS to prevent asset, resource and land waste.

Most of the MPDS are used as educational institutes, so, the structures have heavy furniture like almirahs, file cabinets, desks, benches, tables, chairs etc. During the emergency time, moving these heavy furniture can hinder the process of instant transfer of a shelter. So, consideration can be given to this issue. Movable furniture with wheels underneath can be a good option in this regard. More toilet facilities must be ensured for the users with accessible water facilities. Moreover, extra safety precautions measures like handwashing facilities, hand sanitizers, PPE, separate room for Covid-19 patients must be ensured for the current pandemic situation. The academic program of the coastal zone or cyclone-affected areas may also be consistent with the occurrence period of disaster in those areas. . Also, the time during April and September can be utilized to achieve more preparedness against the cyclones and December can be used for necessary upgradation, repair works and retrofitting etc.

For proper availability and inflow of O&M fund, revenue generation is a must. The standalone structures can be rented as office space, community center, community clinic etc. depending on the need of the area. And if the area already has enough of these types of facilities, the standalone shelters can be used as a youth club, library, office scape for volunteers etc. This practice will not only ensure an all-year-round O&M practice but also will prevent illegal activities concerning the structure.

The main focus of this paper was to shed light on the gaps in O&M of the MPDS of Bangladesh. All the studies have been conducted based on the available literatures such as some national guidelines, policies, technical reports, research papers etc. But to have a complete and all-inclusive picture of the current situation, a smart and thorough field survey is needed to be conducted with a proper and complete survey questionnaire.

7. Acknowledgment

The authors would like to thank Bangladesh University of Engineering and Technology, (BUET), Dhaka for supporting this work.

REFERENCES

1. Ahsan, M. E. (2013). Coastal zone of Bangladesh: fisheries resources and its potentials. Lambert Academic Publishing. DOI: 10.13140/2.1.1253.7928.
2. Asian Development Bank (ADB), (2014). Emergency Assistance Project, Initial Environment Examination.
3. Bangladesh Cyclone of 1991. Retrieved from https://www.britannica.com/event/Bangladesh-cyclone-of-1991
4. Center for Climate Change and Environmental Research (C3ER), BRAC University, commissioned by Care Bangladesh (n.d.). Scoping and structural assessment of the state of multi-purpose cyclone shelters and landslide shelters in Cox's Bazar.
5. Cyclone. (n.d.). Retrieved from https://en.banglapedia.org/index.php/Cyclone
6. Cyclone Preparedness Programme (CPP), (2021). Combating cyclone in Covid-19 environment: Modified Cyclone Preparedness & Early Action Plan
7. Cyclone Sidr in Bangladesh: damage, loss, and needs assessment for disaster recovery and reconstruction. (20/04/2008). Retrieved from https://reliefweb.int/report/bangladesh/cyclone-sidr-bangladesh-damage-loss-and-needs-assessment-disaster-recovery-and
8. Islam, M. S. and Hossain, T. R. (2018). Cyclone resilience of mid-term shelter for displaced citizens of Myanmar, Cox's Bazar: Pilot study (Analytical Results for Option-2). Seminar Organised by Caritas Bangladesh, Cox's Bazar, Bangladesh.
9. Karim, M. F. and Mimura, N. (2008). Impacts of climate change and sea-level rise on cyclonic storm surge floods, *Global Environmental Change, 18: 490-500.*
10. Local Government Engineering Department (LGED), Government of the People's Republic of Bangladesh, (2014), Multi-Purpose Disaster Shelter Project (MDSP), Environmental & social management framework (ESMF) and tribal development framework (TDF).
11. Mahmood, M. N., Dhakal, S. and Kamruzzaman, M. (2013). Should the disaster management strategies in Bangladesh be Just about constructing new shelter?, Proceedings in 19th CIB World Building Congress, Brisbane, 5-9 May, 2013.
12. –(2021). Major Cyclones in the History of Bangladesh, *Dhaka Tribune,* Retrieved from https://www.dhakatribune.com/bangladesh/2021/05/24/major-cyclones-in-the-history-of-bangladesh
13. Ministry of Disaster Management and Relief (MoDMR), Government of the People's Republic of Bangladesh, (2011). Cyclone Shelter Construction, maintenance and Management Policy.

14. Ministry of Housing and Public Works, Government of the People's Republic of Bangladesh, (2021). Bangladesh National Building Code

15. Miyaji, M., Okazaki, K. and Chiho, O. (2017). A study on the use of cyclone shelters in Bangladesh. *Journal of Architecture and Planning*, DOI: 10.3130/aija.82.1871.

16. Moles, O., Caimi, A., Islam, M.S., Hossain, T.R. and Podder, R.K. (2014). From local building practices to vulnerability reduction: building resilience through existing resources, knowledge and know-how. Procedia Economics and Finance. Elsevier, Vol. 18, *pp. 932-939*, DOI:10.1016/S2212-5671 (14)01020-X).hal-01159948 (www.sciencedirect.com).

17. Moles, O., Islam, M. S., Hossain, T. R. and Podder, R. K. (2013). Improvement of vernacular housing for disaster prone areas in Bangladesh: a six year experience. Proceeding of Vernacular Heritage and Earthen Architecture: contributions for sustainable development, Correia, Carlos & Rocha (Eds), pp. 683–688.

18. Operation and Maintenance. (n.d.) Retrieved from https://www.lawinsider.com/dictionary/operations-maintenance-om

19. Paul, B. (2009). Why relatively fewer people died? The case of Bangladesh's Cyclone Sidr, Natural *Hazards: Journal of the International Society for the Prevention and Mitigation of Natural Hazards*, Springer, vol. 50(2), *pp 289-304*

20. Pender, J. (2008). Community-led adaptation in Bangladesh. Retrieved from http://www.fmreview.org/FMRpdfs/FMR31/FMR31.pdf

21. Rahman, A. and Islam, R. (n.d.). Adopting to cyclonic storm surges: Bangladesh. Climate of Coastal Cooperation.

22. Tropical Cyclones. (n.d.). Retrieved from https://bd.usembassy.gov/u-s-citizen-services/local-resources-of-u-s-citizens/living-in-bangladesh/tropical-cyclones/

CHAPTER 37

Disaster Management in India: A Systematic Approach

Sunil Kumar Chaudhary

Executive Engineer, Road Construction Department,
Vaishali Road Division, Hazipur

Abstract

India has been traditionally vulnerable to natural disaster on account of its unique geo-climate conditions. Floods, droughts, cyclones, earthquakes, and landslides have been a recurrent phenomena. About 60% of the landmass is prone to earthquake of various intensities; over 40 million hectares is prone to floods; about 8 % of total area is prone to cyclones and 68% of the areas is susceptible to drought[1]. In the decade 1990-2000, an average of about 4344 people lost their lives about about 30 million people were affected by disaster every year[10]. The loss in terms of private, community and public assets has been astronomical. The Government of India have adopted mitigation and prevention as essential components of their development strategies. The plan emphasizes the fact that development cannot be sustainable without mitigation being built into development process. Each State is supposed to prepare a plan scheme for disaster mitigation in accordance with the approach outlined in the plan. In brief, mitigation is being institutionalized into development planning. The Finance Commission makes recommendation with regard to devolution of funds between Central Government and State Government as also outlays for relief and rehabilitation. In the present paper authors have made an attempt to highlight the measures, shortcoming, measures taken for the mitigation of the disaster.

Keywords: Disaster, Management, Mitigation, Rehabilitation, Prevention, Relief

1. Introduction

It is really an unfortunate and undesirable situation that in our country where more than 6 crore people are affected by disasters every year. Statistics is shown in Fig. 37.1[10]

We have no policy on systematic disaster Management[2]. It is only after a disaster strikes that the wheels of the government, both at the centre and at the states, move and that too slowly. Despite the need to build up capabilities to meet the challenges of disasters, the thrust has unfortunately been

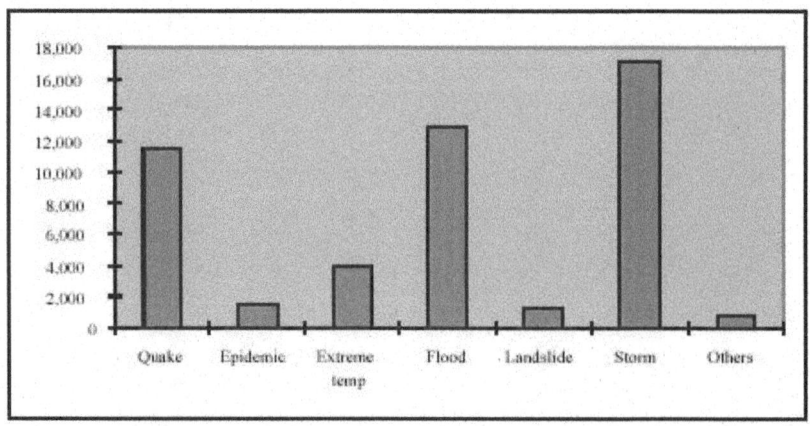

Fig. 37.1 Mortality due to natural hazards (1990-2000)

on alleviation and relief. Even the relief has not been quick and adequate, as few disasters such as Orissa super cyclone, Tsunami of 2004, Gujarat earthquake etc experiences has shown. India's response to and tackling of this two major disasters has thrown up the following weakness in our disaster management efforts :[13]

(a) Inadequate Early Warning System[5]

Though, the forecasting, monitoring and warning mechanisms are beautifully articulated on paper in practice, the warnings are not early enough and they do not reach all those likely to be affected. In case of Tsunami, 2004; Bhuj earthquake etc for example, communication facilities which we have no policy on systematic disaster Management.

(b) Lack of Pre-disaster Preparedness

With disasters striking India with increased regularity, there should be a plan in place to tackle the disaster and reduce its

Fig. 37.2   Tsunami of 2004

(http://upload.wikimedia.org/wikipedia/commons/2/2d/200 4-tsunami. jpg)

Fig. 37.3   Bhuj(2001) earthquake

(http://proxied.changemakers.net/journal/300510/dis8.jpg)

Fig. 37.4   Orissa super cyclone

(http://www.lwsi.org/images/cs-disas_prepared.jpg)

Fig. 37.5   Bihar Flood 2009

(http://1.bp.blogspot.com/_fabeCWoNzTg/SLfTDs6JtII/ AAAAAAAAAjw/Wlm2avBtNIM/s400/bihar_flood14.jpg)

impact. On the contrary, people are caught unaware time and again. There is not planned information system as to what needs to be done when faced with a calamity. For example, during Tsunami, 2004, dead body laid floating in the water for many days due to the unavailability or lack of required equipment to meet the need of the time/emergency.

(c) Inadequate and Slow Relief

Relief is an important aspect of the disaster management to provide help to the affected people. The relief operations are often handled in ad hoc and haphazard manner. How efficiently to provide food, medicine, to reduce the suffering of the affected people etc are addressed and met improperly. Even days after the Bhuj earthquake, and Tsunami, 2004,, many people could not be provided with safe drinking water, temporary shelter, and medicines. Such a scenario gives rise to law and order problem- looting of the relief materials and outbreak of the epidemic due to rotting dead bodies on the other hand.

(d) Lack of Co-ordination

Disaster management requires concerted efforts from Central Government, State Government, NGOs, International agencies and private sectors etc. Because of the lack of the co-ordination, relief material is not property distributed among the people. Even worst happens when they are mis-utilized and are not distributed uniformly.

(e) Slow Rehabilitation and Reconstruction

While immediately after a disaster strikes, there is hectic relief and rescue mission, mainly aimed at feeding the people and stalling the outbreak of an epidemic, relief and rescue cannot go on endlessly and rehabilitation and reconstruction should be given proper attention. However, this is an area which is often ignored and progressed is slow once the initial attention fades away. Restoration of infrastructure, hospitals, schools, houses, and sources of living of the people needs to be given proper attention.

(f) Proper Administration

A quick assessment of the extent of the damage is necessary so that relief and rehabilitation work can be properly planned. However, it was seen that even many months after the Bhuj earthquake and Tsunami of 2004, the government was yet to finish the preliminary survey of assessing the total impact of the damage. Apart from this, poor administration frustrated the best intentions and efforts of private initiatives. After the quake, Gujarat government was too slow and indecisive on some of the best rehabilitation plans proposed by the NGOs and Corporate.

(g) Poor Management of Finances for Post-disaster Relief

Mostly relief and rehabilitation work suffers from the lack of co-ordination, proper management, and supervision at all levels and indicated the absence of adequate planning and preparedness to meet any emergency. Consequently, the funds are mis-utilized and relief measures were tardy and inadequate, providing scope for pilferage of relief and rehabilitation remained unutilized and there is huge shortfall in distribution of emergency relief, shelter material cloths, house building assistance etc. There have also been reports of relief and rehabilitation funds being utilized for paying salary arrears of the state government employees.

(h) Symbolism Rather than Relief

It has been a recurrent experience that rather than making a serious effort at planning and management for tackling frequent disasters, our government adopts symbolic gestures like helicopter survey of disaster affected areas. The politics of relief works in a manner that tall claims are made by the Government other than the affected state to help the affected districts and by sending huge financial help but these claims prove hollow once the calamity recedes.

(i) No Instruction for Pre-seismic Period

There is no instruction for the pre-seismic period. Unfortunately, in the present administrative set up, no official will visit the people during pre-seismic period to tell them about an eminent earthquake. But, during the post-seismic period, a large number of officials will visit the affected people with food, tents, medicine, cloths and compensation funding to the relatives of the dead.

2. Measures/Facts Taken to Improve Disaster Management in India[13,14]

2.1 Central Level

At the central or national level, Ministry of Home affairs is entrusted with the nodal responsibility of managing disaster. At the apex level, there are two cabinet committees' viz. cabinet committee on national calamity and cabinet committee on security. All the major issues concerning natural disasters are placed before cabinet committee on natural calamity whereas calamities which can affect internal security or which may be caused due to use of nuclear, biological or chemical weapons etch are placed before cabinet committee on security. The NCMC (National Crisis Management Committee) is the next important functionary. The cabinet secretary heads it. It includes secretaries of concerned department/ministers. Its main function is to give direction to Crisis Management Group (CMG) and any minister/department for specific action needed for meeting the crisis situation. CMG lies below the NCMC. The Central Relief Commissioner is its chairman. His primary function is to coordinate all the relief operations for natural disaster. Apart from coordinating the relief operations, it reviews the contingency plans formulated by Central Ministers/Department and measures required for dealing with natural disaster. CMG meets every six months however in event of any disaster it frequently meets to review the relief operation and explore all possibilities to render all possible help to the affected region.

2.2 State and District Level[15,16,17]

At the state level, there are state relief commissioners who are in charge of the relief measures in wake of natural disaster in the perspective states. The chief secretary is the overall in charge of the relief operations in the state. The relief commissioner and additional relief commissioner work under his direction and control. In addition, there are number of secretaries, head of various departments who also work under the overall direction of chief secretary. At the district level, districts are headed by District Collector or district magistrate who is responsible for the overall supervision and monitoring of relief measures and preparation of disaster management plans. At the tehsil level DSO/SDM take care of the disaster management. Despite there being a general tardiness about the manner in which we respond to disasters, there has been significance progress in this area and there have been many experiments and success stories worth emulating,

(i) Learning from the Latur earthquake calamity, Maharastra has launched India's first disaster management infor-network. Soon after this quake, state government launched the Maharastra Emergency Earthquake Rehabilitation programme. The programme aimed at achieving preparedness through an information-network so that unpredictable and uncontrolled disaster impacts could be offset with planned and manageable disaster mitigation efforts. This info-network links the state government machinery with all its tehsils and districts along with other strategically and economically important agencies based in the state.The Multi-hazards Disaster Mitigation Plan will create disaster management information at emergency operation centre at state government headquarters. Apart from forewarning of calamities like flood, earthquake, etc; post disaster relief and rehabilitation is another area of use of this network. It will help in co-ordinating among hospitals, voluntary organizations, ambulances, fire brigades and government relief measures.

(ii) Some State Government have got their acts together, learning from past experiences. In 1991, A.P. Government was able to implement previously planned programme to evacuate 6 lakh people from the path of an approaching cyclone with 52 hours. Fatalities numbered less than on tenth of what could have otherwise been. This was achieved through a planned approach combing both traditional and advanced channels.

(iii) The IMD has set up a National Seismic Telemetry Network to anticipate threats from seismic disturbances. After the Gujarat quake, 10 new seismological observation equipped with latest facilities were set up and 14 of the 45 existing observatories were upgraded with state of the art digital seismograph for better monitoring of effects of earthquake in the seismic zones.

(iv) The IMD has set up cyclone warning centres along many coastlines. Information on cyclone warning is furnished to the central control room in the Ministry of Agriculture. Besides, high powered cyclone detection radars are installed at various places on the coastal belt, that can track disturbances within a range of 400 KM. Satellite imagery is another tool used when cyclone are beyond the range of the coastal radars. The ISRO has placed 250 storm warning receivers all along the Indian coast. In a time of crisis, these receivers are switched on via satellite and broadcast siren and local language warnings.

(v) Measures for flood mitigation were taken from 1950 onwards, as against the total of 40 million hectares prone to floods, area of about 15 million hectares have been protected by construction of embankment. The State Government have been assisted to take up mitigation programmed like construction of raised platforms etc. To evolve both short-term and long term strategies for flood management / erosion control, Government of India have recently constituted Central Task Force under the chairmanship of Central Water Commission. The task for will examine causes of the problem of recurring floods and erosion in States and region prone to the flood and erosion; and suggest short term and long term measures.

(vi) Due to erratic behavior of monsoons, both low and medium rainfall regions are vulnerable to periodical drought. Experience has been that almost every third year is a drought. Local communities have devised indigenous safety mechanism and drought oriented farming methods in many parts of the country. From the experience of managing the past droughts particularly severe drought of 1987, a number of programme have been launched by the Government to mitigate the impact of drought in the long run.

(vii) In order to respond effectively to floods, Ministry of Home Affairs have initiated National Disaster Risk Management Programme in all the flood prone States. Assistance is being provided to the States to draw up disaster management plans at the State, District, Block/Taluka and village levels. Awareness generation campaigns to sensitize all the stakeholders on the need for flood preparedness and mitigation measures.

(viii) A Comprehensive programme has been taken up for earthquake risk mitigation. Although, the BIS has laid down the standard for construction in the seismic zones, these are not being followed. The building construction in urban and suburban areas is regulated by the Town and Country Planning Act and Building Regulations. In many cases, Building regulations do not incorporate the BIS codes. In the rural areas, the bulk of the housing is non-engineering construction. A

National Core Group for Earthquake Risk Mitigation has been constituted consisting of experts in earthquake engineering and administrators. The core group has been assigned with the responsibility of drawing up a strategy and plan of action for mitigating the impacts of earthquakes' providing advice and guidance to the States on various aspects of earthquake mitigation; developing/organizing the preparation of handbooks/ pamphlet/types designs for earthquake resistance construction.; working out systems for assisting the States in the seismically vulnerable zone to adopt/ integrate appropriate BIS code in their buildings; evolving systems in the training of municipal engineers as also practicing architects and engineers in the private sectors in the salient features of BIS codes; evolving systems for training of masons and carry out intensive awareness generation campaigns.

(ix) Hospital preparedness is crucial to any disaster response system. Each hospital should have an emergency preparedness plan to deal with mass casualty incidents and the hospital administration/ doctor trained for the emergency. The curriculum for medical doctors does not include hospitals preparedness for emergencies. Therefore, capacity building through in service training of the current health managers and medical personnel in hospitals preparedness for emergencies or mass casualty's incidents management is essential.

(x) While above mitigation measures will take care of the new constructions, the problem of unsafe existing building stock would still remain. It will not be possible to address the whole existing building; therefore, the most important buildings such as hospitals, schoold, cinema halls, muti-storied apartment are being focused on. The States have been instructed and advices to have such buildings assessed and where necessary retrofitted. The ministry of Civil Aviatioin, Railways, Telecommunication, Power and Heath and Family Welfare have been instructed to take up necessary action for detailed evaluation and retrofitting of lifeline buildings located in seismically vulnerable zones so as to ensure that they comply with the BIS norms.

Accordingly, the Finance Ministry had advised RBI to issue suitable instructions to tall the banks and financial institutions to see that BIS codes laws are scrupulously followed while financing/refinancing construction activities in seismically prone zones. .

Ministry of Rural Development are carrying out an exercise for this purpose. This initiative is expected to go along way in popularization of seismically safe construction at village/block levels.

(xi) A project for cyclone mitigation has been drawn up in consultation with the cyclone prone states. This projects envisages construction of cyclone shelters, costal shelters belt plantation in areas which are prone to storm surges,strengthening of warning system, training and education etc. This project has also been given in principle clearance by the Planning Commission and is being taken up with World Bank assistance.

(xii) A national core group has been constituted under the chairmanship of secretary, Border Management and comprising of Secretary, DST; Road Transport &Highways, and the heads of GSI and NRSA for drawing up a strategy and plan of action for mitigating the impact of landslide, provide advise and guidance to the State Government on various aspects of landslide mitigation,monitor the activities relating to landslide mitigation including landslide hazard zonation and to evolve early warning system and protocol for landslide/ landslide risk reduction..

(xiii) A disaster risk management programme has been taken up in 169 districts iin 17 multi-hazard prone states with the assistance of UNDP, USAID and EU. Under this project, the States are being assisted to draw up State,District, Block level disaster management plans; village disaster management plans are being developed in conjunction with the Panchayati Raj institutions and disaster management team consisting of village volunteers are being trained in various preparedness and response functions such as search and rescue, first aid, relief coordination, shelter management etc. Equipment needs for district and state emergency operation centers have been identified by the state nodal agencies and equipment is being provided to equip them.

(xiv) The Government has initiated a national wide awareness generation compaign as part of its overall disaster risk management strategy. In order to devise an effective and holistic campaign, a steering committee for mass media campaign has been constituted at the national level with due representation of experts from diverse stream of communication.

(xv) Disaster management as a subject in Social Sciences has been introduced in the school curriculum for class VIII &IX. The CBSE which has introduced the curriculum runs a very large number of schools throughout the country. The teachers are being trained to teach disaster management for class X.

(xvi) In order to assist the State Government in capacity building and awareness generation activities and to learn from the past experiences including sharing of best practices, the Ministry of Home Affairs has compiled/prepared a set of resource material developed by various organization/institutions to be replicated and disseminated by State Government based on their vulnerability after translating it into the local languages.

3. Development of Response System

Mitigation and preparedness measures go hand in hand for vulnerability reduction and rapid response to disaster. Several inadequacies of response were noted in the aftermath of Bhuj earthquake, 2001. The govt. decided to remove the inadequacies to maintain preparedness at all times. Major response initiatives include:

(i) **Preparation of Special Response Teams:** The central Govt. is now in the process of training and equipping specialist and rescue teams. Each team includes doctors, paramedics, structural engineers etc. These teams will be stationed in different parts of the country.

(ii) **Incident Command System:** In order to professionalize the response system, it is proposed to develop incident command system. It is a very effective system in which the most experienced and knowledgeable person at a disaster site is designated as incident commander who is charged with the responsibility of inter agency coordination and management of the incident.

(iii) **Standard Operating Procedure:** Standard operating procedure are being laid down to ensure that all step need to be taken for disaster management are put in place. Each department/sector will have their own SOP's for each level of functionaries.

(iv) **Trigger Mechanism:** The high powered committee on disaster management has incorporated trigger mechanism as an emergency quick response mechanism. It has been envisaged as a preparedness plan whereby the receipt of a signal of an impending disaster would simultaneously energize and activate the mechanism for response and mitigation without loss of crucial time.

(v) **Emergency Operation Centre:** It has also been recommended for setting up of emergency operation centers at the national capitals, state capitals and district headquarters. EOC will function as nerve centres for integrated command and control structure. Technological Developments Technological innovations are vital for effective disaster management, the DST, Govt. of India is taking several measure to upgrade technological inputs. The important developments include:

(a) *India Disaster Resource Network:* This is a web enabled centralized data base which will ensure quick access to resources to minimize response time tune in emergencies.

(b) *Development of GIS based National Database for Disaster Management:* The GIS is an effective tool for emergency responders to access information in terms of crucial parameters for the disaster affected areas. This includes location of public facilities, communication links, transport network etc.

(c) *Installation of Early Warning and Hazard Detection Equipment:* Early warning system has already been installed for cyclones and floods in the country by IMD and CWC. There is a well established organizational set up for detecting, tackling and forecasting cyclones. Now, govt. has also succeeded in acquiring and installing the Tsunami warning and detection system in the aftermath of Tsunami disaster of 2004.

4. What India Needs

In the view of the frequency of disaster striking India, there is a need for continued vigilance, preparedness and conscious efforts to reduce the occurrence and for mitigation of impact of natural disaster. What is requires is a planned approach to disaster management; its management is a fundamental component of sustainable development because the reduction of disaster equivalent to increased development. The following suggestions can be offered for effective disaster management system in India:

(i) There should be a proper multi-tier organizational structure in a focussed and co-ordinated manner responsible for the overall management at national, state, districts and village levels.

(ii) The basic design of disaster management should consist of planned co-ordinated efforts in following important areas:

   – Identification and prediction
   – Early warning system
   – Evacuation
   – Relief
   – Rescue
   – Rehabilitation
   – Compensation
   – Reconstruction
   – Preparedness

(iii) There is a need to share the expertise and experiences so that states can learn from each other. There is also a need for training personnel likely to face natural disaster and those who deal with the relief operations.

5. Conclusions

India in the recent years has made significant development in the area of disaster management. A new culture of preparedness, quick response, strategic thinking and prevention is being ushered. The administrative framework is being streamlined to deal with the various disasters. Effort are also being made to make disaster management a community movement wherein where is greater participation of the people. However, a lot more need to be done to make disaster management a mass movement in near future.

REFERENCES

1. D. E. Tallman, G. G. Wallace, Synth. Met. 90 (1997) 13.
2. H. W. Kroto, J. E. Fischer, D. E. Cox, The Fullerenes, Pergamon, Oxford, 1993.
3. A. G. MacDiarmid, A. J. Epstein, in W. R. Salaneck, D. T. Clark, E. J. Samuelson, (eds.), Science and Applications of Conducting Polymers, Adam Hilger, Bristol, 1991, p. 117.
4. D. I. Eaton, Porous glass support material, US Patent No. 3 904 422 (1975).
5. http://upload.wikimedia.org/wikipedia/commons/2/2d/2004-tsunami.jpg
6. http://proxied.changemakers.net/journal/300510/dis8.jpg
7. http://www.lwsi.org/images/cs-disas_prepared.jpg
8. http://1..bp.blogspot.com/_fabeCWoNzTg/SLfTDs6JtII/AAAAAAAAAjw/Wlm2avBtNIM/s400/bihar_flood14.jpg
9. IFRC and WPNS, Well Prepared National Society Self Assessment, 2003
10. ISDR, ADB, AU, NEPAD, Guidelines for Mainstreaming Disaster Risk Reduction into Development, 2004, www.unisdr.org/eng/risk-reduction/sustainabledevelopment/cca-undaf/cca-undaf.htm
11. ISDR, Words into Action: A Guide For Implementing the Hyogo Framework for Action, United Nations, 2007, www.unisdr.org
12. ISDR, Living with Risk, 2004, www.unisdr.org
13. Govt. of India (2001), "High Powered Committee on Disaster Management-Report", Department of Agriculture &Cooperation, Ministry of Agriculture, New Delhi
14. Govt. of India (2003), "Disaster Risk Reduction—The Indian Model", Ministry of Home Affairs, Govt of India, New Delhi.
15. Govt. of India (2004), Disaster Management Status Report 2004, Ministry of Home Affairs, Govt of India, New Delhi.
16. Sarkar Subhradipta, Sarma Archana (2006)," Disaster Management Act 2005", Economic and Political Weekly, Mumbai, pp 3760–3763, 2nd September 2006 Sharma Vinod (2001), "Disaster Management", Indian Institute of Public Administration, New Delhi
17. Ravindra K. Pande, Participation in practice and disaster management: experience of Uttaranchal (India), Disaster Prevention and Management, Vol. 14, 3, 2006

Part 6

RISK GOVERNANCE IN THE AGE OF PANDEMICS

Chapter 38   Existing Resilience Framework for Disaster Risk Management in India

Chapter 39   System Dynamics Approach for Covid-19 Disaster Management

Chapter 40   Global Pandemic: Need for a Legal Framework

Chapter 41   Governance for COVID-19 in Bangladesh

Chapter 42   Atmanirbharta–The Journey from disaster to human resilience

Chapter 43   Development of Decision Support System for Effective COVID-19 Management

Chapter 44   Disaster Management Law in the Context of Covid-19

Chapter 45   Accelerating Action on SFDRR Targets D, E and G and Related SDGs in this Decade of Implementation

Existing Resilience Framework for Disaster Risk Management in India

Manish Sharma

Manipal University Jaipur,
School of Architecture and Design, Jaipur, India
manishsharma.ar@gmail.com

Nand Kumar

Malaviya National Institute of Technology,
Department of Architecture and Planning, Jaipur, India
nkumar.arch@mnit.ac.in

Ashwani Kumar

Malaviya National Institute of Technology,
Department of Architecture and Planning, Jaipur, India
akumar.arch@mnit.ac.in

Abstract

Resilient cities have the physical, social, institutional, and economic capacity to withstand and absorb the impacts of disasters and climate change. Cities in India, despite evolving as the engines of economic growth for the nation, are still grappling with urban issues like inadequacy of basic services like electricity, infrastructure deficit, futile urban planning process and unchecked organic growth of the cities. In India, the policies guiding the urban development generally do not take into account the ideology to make cities resilient to disaster risks, since the prime focus of the development is still on meeting basic physical infrastructure requirements like transport, housing, services and health infrastructure amidst the rapid urbanization. India accounts for 24 per cent of the deaths due to disasters in Asia, on account of its size of the vulnerable population and the developmental planning with negligence on the resilience front (Ministry of Finance, n.d.). This paper presents the existing institutional structure in place at different levels of administration and the status of key emergency infrastructure linked the disaster management in India. It identifies the key areas of concerns associated with the existing framework in the country and put forth suggestions to improve upon the present state of concerned disaster management mechanism.

Keywords: Resilience, disaster management, institutional framework

1. Introduction

The concepts of resilience, vulnerability, adaptive capacity are gaining popularity among the policy makers, organizations and individuals working in the field of planning and risk reduction, to enable better understanding and to produce more proactive responses to disasters. United Nations International Strategy for Disaster Reduction (UNISDR) defines resilience as "The ability of a system, community, or society exposed to hazards to resist, absorb, accommodate to, and recover from the effects of a hazard in a timely and efficient manner, including through the preservation and restoration of its essential basic structures and functions."

As centers of concentrated human population and varied economic activity, cities are vulnerable to various risks (Pelling, 2003). This is especially true about climate change and natural disasters. As Hewitt (1997) states, firstly, the increasing scales and the proximity of energy or energy transportation routes concentration leads to the vulnerability of urban areas. Second, conditions of congestion increase disease transmission risk and constrain relief works. Thirdly, cities being complex systems are less predictable to prepare for lurking risks. Also, during political unrest, urban populations can be exploited and repressed. Also, as Puente (1999) argues growing contribution of urban areas to GDP and high concentration of development in a small number of large urban places has challenged the state's capacity to respond to demands for urban services, which are critical to the functioning of a city.

The potential of a hazard to become a disaster depends on the degree of exposure of its population and its physical and economic assets. High vulnerability in low exposure conditions, for example, case of sand storms in desserts, and comparatively low vulnerability conditions with a high number of exposed populations and assets translate to less damages. Hence, disasters can be assessed as a function of exposure and vulnerability. The concentration of exposed assets in vulnerable environment increase the disaster risk. Unplanned and unregulated urbanization, evident in the developing countries, increase the urban vulnerability by straining the existing resources, thereby falling short in providing basic services to all. Urbanization, migration, population growth and economic development all increase the concentration of people and assets in high-risk areas. (Dickson, et al., 2012). Very rapid urban population growth during the last few decades due to economic factors such as a decrease in economic opportunities in rural areas and consequent migration to the urban areas. The rapid urbanization has led to a proliferation of slums and has severely strained the resources in our urban areas (Sinha & Goyal, 2012).

As synthesized in IPCC Fifth Assessment Report (IPCC, 2014), the climatic findings forecast more frequent disasters, and an accelerated rate of sea level rise, with disproportionately high impacts on urban areas. With negligence on environment front, deforestation and urban industrial growth the human induced disasters have also increased. The loses due to disasters can accredit to the geographical attribute of a place, like a coastline vulnerable to cyclones and hurricanes on the one hand, and the coping mechanism in place on the other hand which defines the preparedness and absorption capacity of the community. While amending the geographical qualities of a place is beyond the purview of the human race, the latter aspect defines the magnitude of the damage caused by a disaster. It involves the community as the main component, with the governance, infrastructure, resource availability, organizational preparedness from all the stakeholders. Since this varies with country to country, and community to community, some are touted to be more resilient than the other, or in other words, some are more prone to disaster induced damage than others. Disaster management priorities vary between developed and developing countries (Table 38.1). According to Emergency Events Dataset (EM-DAT), amongst the top ten countries in terms of loss of lives due

Table 38.1 Disaster Management Action Priorities in developed and developing regions

Disaster Management Priorities	
Developed Regions	**Developing Regions**
Prediction	Rescue
Preparedness	Recovery
Prevention	Relief
Participation	Rehabilitation
Publicity through media	Reconstruction

Source: (Singh, 2017)

to natural disasters during the past two decades (1997-2017 period), roughly all are amongst the most populous countries of the world (amongst the top one-third contributors to the world population) (Table 38.2). India is amongst the most vulnerable nations amongst them. This can be attributed to its geology, geographical setting and climate. In the Indian context, it's ripe to involve resilience considerations into urban planning, policies and governance setup since only a few cities have developed master plan, city development plan documents, and the planning exercise needs to be executed for the majority of the towns and disaster resilience considerations can be embedded in the planning stage itself. Also, the colossal number of exposed vulnerable population in urban locations in India and their marginalized subsistence that often lacks safe and secure access to essential services and depends on fragile urban systems which makes them vulnerable to system failures in the wake of disaster and climate related stress.

Table 38.2 Countries with highest numbers of deaths due to natural disasters during the period 1997-2017 and their respective populations for 2017.

Sr. No.	Country	No. of deaths	Population
1	Haiti	237382	10,983,274
2	Indonesia	185051	263,510,146
3	Myanmar	139715	54,836,483
4	China	120100	1,389,351,025
5	India	98700	1,342,512,706
6	Pakistan	85904	196,744,376
7	Russian Federation (the)	58571	143,375,006
8	Sri Lanka	37574	20,905,335
9	Iran (Islamic Republic of)	32248	80,945,718
10	Venezuela (Bolivarian Republic of)	30319	31,925,705

Source: Extracted from EM-DAT: The Emergency Events Database - Université catholique de Louvain (UCL) - CRED, D. Guha-Sapir - www.emdat.be, Brussels, Belgium and Worldometers (www.Worldometers.info): Elaboration of data by United Nations, Department of Economic and Social Affairs, Population Division. World Population Prospects: The 2015 Revision. (Medium-fertility variant).

2. Indian Scenario

2.1 Disaster Scenario

Indian sub-continent is considered to be amongst the world's most disaster prone areas due to the high frequency of natural hazards, the large size of the exposed population with little protection of the safety nets, poor infrastructure and severely tight finances translating into weak coping capabilities. Floods, droughts, cyclones, earthquakes and landslides have been a recurrent phenomenon. About 60% of the landmass is prone to earthquakes of various intensities; over 40 million hectares is prone to floods; about 8% of the total area is prone to cyclones and 68% of the area is susceptible to drought (Mondal). India, especially the urban areas, is witnessing exponential population growth. It is estimated that of the nearly 30% of India's population or about 300 million people live in towns and cities. This population is estimated to reach 534 million by 2026 (HUP; USAID, n.d.). Along with rapid urbanization, there has been a more rapid growth in the population residing in slums. Poor are more vulnerable to disaster risk due to limited resources at their disposal (Ministry of Home Affairs, 2011). It is estimated that nearly one-third of India's urban population or nearly 100 million live in slums characterized by overcrowding, poor hygiene and sanitation and the absence of civic services. The UNHABITAT estimates that the slum population in India will double to 200 million by 2020, thereby increasing the quantum of a vulnerable population, if requisite efforts to strengthen disaster risk resilience are not taken.

As per the Global Assessment Report, 2015 by UNISDR, 42 million human life years were lost world over in disasters every year between 1980 and 2012 with over 80 per cent of the total life years lost in disasters falling over low and middle-income countries. India accounts for 24 per cent of the deaths due to disasters in Asia, on account of its size of the vulnerable population and the developmental planning with negligence on the resilience front (Ministry of Finance, n.d.). On the economic side too, India, on account of its varied topography ranging from mountainous regions in the north, flood plains in the east, desert and arid lands in the west and a vast coastline in the southern peninsula which is susceptible to various natural disasters, loses about 2 per cent of its Gross Domestic Product on an average due to these disasters (Ministry of Home Affairs, 2011). Some of the major disaster event occurrences in the country are listed in Table 38.3.

Table 38.3 Some of the major the disaster events in India during the period 1999-2014.

Sr. No.	Name of Event	Year	State & Area	Fatalities
1	Floods	Oct-14	Jammu & Kashmir	
2	Cyclone Hud Hud	Sep-14	Andhra Pradesh & Odisha	
3	Odisha Floods	Oct-13	Odisha	21
4	Andhra Floods	Oct-13	Andhra Pradesh	53
5	Cyclone Phailin	Oct-13	Odisha and Andhra Pradesh	23
6	Floods/Landslides	Jun-13	Uttarakhand and Himachal Pradesh	4,094
7	Cyclone Mahasen	May-13	Tamil Nadu	8
8	Cyclone Nilam	Oct-12	Tamil Nadu	65
9	Uttarakhand Floods	Aug – Sep 2012	Uttarkashi, Rudraprayag and Bageshwar	52
10	Assam Floods	July – Aug 2012	Assam	—
11	Cyclone Thane	Dec-11	Tamil Nadu, Puducherry	47
12	Sikkim Earthquake	Sep-11	Sikkim, West Bengal, Bihar	60
13	Odisha Floods	Sep-11	19 Districts of Odisha	45
14	Sikkim Earthquake	2011	North Eastern India with epicenter near Nepal Border and Sikkim	97 people died (75 in Sikkim)
15	Cloudburst	2010	Leh, Ladakh in J&K	257 people died
16	Drought	2009	252 Districts in 10 States	—
17	Krishna Floods	2009	Andhra Pradesh, Karnataka	300 people died
18	Kosi Floods	2008	North Bihar	527 deaths, 19,323 livestock perished, 2,23,000 houses damaged, 3.3 million persons affected

Sr. No.	Name of Event	Year	State & Area	Fatalities
19	Cyclone Nisha	2008	Tamil Nadu	204 deaths
20	Maharashtra Floods	Jul-05	Maharashtra State	1094 deaths, 167 injured, 54 missing
21	Kashmir	2005	Mostly Pakistan, Partially Kashmir	1400 deaths in Kashmir (86,000 deaths in total)
22	Tsunami	2004	Coastline of Tamil Nadu, Kerala, Andhra Pradesh, Pondicherry and Andaman and Nicobar Islands of India	10,749 deaths, 5,640 persons missing, 2.79 million people affected, 11,827 hectares of crops damaged, 300,000 fisher folk lost their livelihood
23	Gujarat Earthquake	2001	Rapar, Bhuj, Bhachau, Anjar, Ahmedabad and Surat in Gujarat State	13,805 deaths, 6.3 million people affected
24	Orissa Super Cyclone	1999	Orissa	Over 10,000 deaths

Source: National Disaster Management Authority Website (http://www.ndma.gov.in/en/disaster-data- statistics.html)

Table 38.4 Damage due to natural disasters in India.

Damage Due to Natural Disasters in India			
Year	People Affected (million)	Houses and Buildings or Property Damaged	Amount of Damage or Loss (Rs. Crore)
1990	31.7	1,019,930	10.71
1991	342.7	1,190,109	10.9
1992	190.9	570,969	20.05
1993	262.4	1,529,916	50.8
1994	235.3	1,051,223	10.83
1995	543.5	2,088,355	40.73
1996	549.9	2,376,693	50.43
1997	443.8	1,103,549	NA
1998	521.7	1,563,405	0.72
1999	501.7	3,104,064	1020.97
2000	594.34	2,736,355	800
2001	788.19	846,878	12000

Source: (Singh, 2017)

Changing landscape: A contrast in approach of authorities during the last decade of 20th century and the beginning of the 21st century

The International Decade for Natural Disaster Reduction (1990- '00) promoted the Yokohama message of 1994, stressing the need for a drastic change in the need for disaster mitigation, focused on disaster prevention, mitigation, preparedness and relief as the four elements to be incorporated in the development plans, inter-relating with sustainable development and environment protection and ensure their follow-up. Yokohama Strategy also supported that disaster response yields short-term results with high input resources while prevention and mitigation strategies help in achieving long-term safety improvements, proving vital for integrated disaster management.

During the 1990's, India was grappling with a number of issues, and with the country's economy in tatters. A little heed was given to disaster management, which had the conventional approach of reactive relief as the response. One important reason for this state was the fact that there had not been many disaster events in urban areas in the post-independence fifty year period and this had created a sense of complacence in the system. Hence devoid of safety nets, robust coping mechanism, efficient disaster preparedness and weak economic condition of the masses in general, the number of people affected and lives lost had been on a constant rise (Table 38.4, Fig. 38.1 and Fig. 38.2) for both natural and technological disasters; hence it was imperative to check the approach the of disaster planning and management and plan resource investment accordingly, since the studies world over have suggested that a part investment in the disaster preparedness and capacity development can reduce the disaster losses to a great extent (UNISDR, 2015).

Though India is experiencing natural and man-made disasters since the very past, but since there had not been many instances of large scale natural disasters like earthquakes in urban areas in the post-independence 50 years period (this might be due to limited urbanization and consequently few cities and towns), which kept the attention of the authorities away from the topic and brought a sense of complacence in the system (Jain, 2004). 1993 Latur earthquake was amongst the worst since independence, but it failed to garner much impact in terms of disaster awareness since it broadly affected the rural regions. It was only after the 2001 Gujarat earthquake that the vulnerability of the built stock in urban areas was exposed. The 2001 Gujarat earthquake has been a major turning point in India towards agenda of seismic risk reduction (Jain, 2004). After the Gujarat earthquake of 2001 and the damaging tsunami in 2004 on the eastern

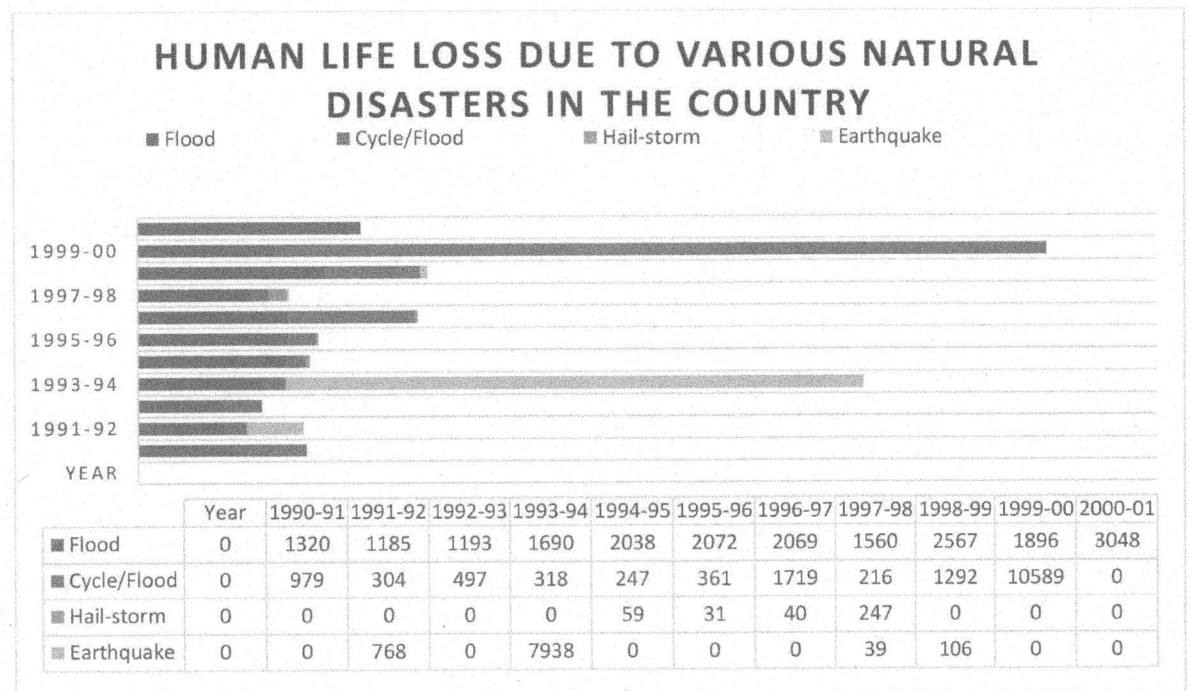

HUMAN LIFE LOSS DUE TO VARIOUS NATURAL DISASTERS IN THE COUNTRY

Year	1990-91	1991-92	1992-93	1993-94	1994-95	1995-96	1996-97	1997-98	1998-99	1999-00	2000-01
Flood	0	1320	1185	1193	1690	2038	2072	2069	1560	2567	1896	3048
Cycle/Flood	0	979	304	497	318	247	361	1719	216	1292	10589	0
Hail-storm	0	0	0	0	0	59	31	40	247	0	0	0
Earthquake	0	0	768	0	7938	0	0	0	39	106	0	0

Fig. 38.1   No. of deaths due to various natural disasters in India.

Source: (Singh, 2017)

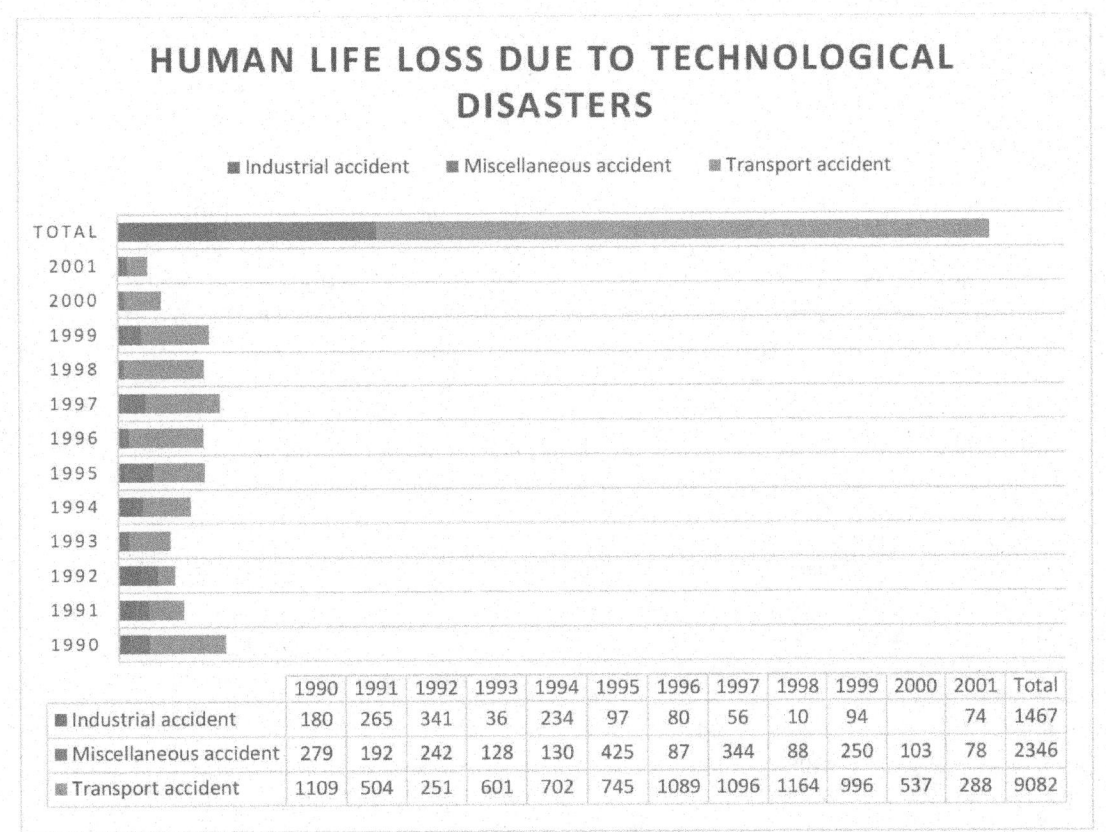

HUMAN LIFE LOSS DUE TO TECHNOLOGICAL DISASTERS

	1990	1991	1992	1993	1994	1995	1996	1997	1998	1999	2000	2001	Total
Industrial accident	180	265	341	36	234	97	80	56	10	94		74	1467
Miscellaneous accident	279	192	242	128	130	425	87	344	88	250	103	78	2346
Transport accident	1109	504	251	601	702	745	1089	1096	1164	996	537	288	9082

Fig. 38.2   No. of people deaths due to various technological disasters in India.

Source: EM-DAT: The Emergency Events Database - Université catholique de Louvain (UCL) - CRED, D. Guha-Sapir - www.emdat.be, Brussels, Belgium

coast of India, the authorities have radically changed their stance on disasters. Initially, the focus had been entirely on post disaster response and relief measures and rehabilitation of the displaced with very little consideration to mitigation and preparedness strategies. It was in the 10th Five Year Plan (2002-2007) that an independent chapter was added titled 'Disaster Management: The Development Perspective' institutionalizing the agenda in the country, emphasizing the importance for integrating mitigation in developmental process for sustainable development. Though Indian authorities had been trying to develop and build capacities through a variety of enabling mechanisms for disaster risk reduction, including creating awareness amongst the vulnerable communities and developmental initiatives, but they had not shown very positive results. A paradigm shift is realized in the approach of the Government of India towards disaster management. An ardent need to inculcate disaster resilience framework into the developmental planning and process to build and sustain a sustainable environment is felt. It has also been widely accepted that building disaster resilience is a multi-disciplinary process, crossing all sectors of development (Ministry of Home Affairs, 2011). Since studies and experiences globally have proved that planning for mitigation and preparedness strategies and frameworks with investments towards building disaster resilience are more resource and cost effective than spending colossal amounts on relief and rehabilitation process. After the recognition of the importance of a framework for disaster risk resilience on international front through world conferences under UNISDR and rising frequent disaster knocks on its soil, the Government of India has placed disaster management amongst the important tiers of Indian policy framework.

The disaster scenario on the national front is evolving from managing disasters to managing risks in line with the International levels. In line with the Hyogo Framework of Action (2005-2015), the Government of India had identified the need of capacity building at various levels, since disaster risk reduction demands the involvement of various sectors and stakeholders, and particularly the individuals. With the Sendai Framework for Disaster Risk Reduction (2015-2030), which advocates implementation of integrated measures to reduce disaster exposure and vulnerability and increase preparedness with an overall goal to strengthen resilience, and understanding the disaster risk and investments resilience building as the priority areas, there is a need for the identification of risk drivers at various levels and then prioritize investments for resilience building, while keeping track of the existing environment, infrastructure and community in focus. The role of Government of India has also been to facilitate the various state governments to align the disaster risk resilience efforts, as disaster is a state subject according to the Constitution of India, through various institutional bodies, human resource development

and structural mitigation measures, though the more focused approach is needed at various levels of governance, including Panchayati Raj Institutions level.

3. Institutional Framework

In the event of a disaster, according to the federal setup of India, the State Government has the prime responsibility for undertaking rescue, relief and rehabilitation. Supplementing the actions and roles of State Governments, the Central Government provides financial and logistic support in the event of a disaster. At the State level, response, relief and rehabilitation are handled by Disaster Management and Relief Department. District administration is the key level for disaster management and rehabilitations. The district disaster management plans are formulated, directed, supervised and monitored at the district level during calamity relief. The critical segment of coordination and liaising with the State Government as well as the nearest units of Relief forces and other Central Government organizations like Ministry of Communication, Ministries of Water Resources and Surface Transport etc. occurs at the ground level, which could complement the works of the district administration in the rescue and relief actions. Hence a holistic response is expected at the district level by the coordination of various stakeholders.

3.1 Role of Government at Various Levels

Central Government

At the national level, the Ministry of Home Affairs (MHA) is the nodal Ministry for all matters concerning disaster management except drought, which continues to be handled by the Ministry of Agriculture even after 2002, since after the major earthquake of Gujarat which shook the nation in 2001, disaster risk management garnered attention on a pan India level. Other ministries provide emergency support as per the activities falling under their purview (Table 38.5).

Table 38.5 Supporting ministries for different disasters in India.

Disaster	Nodal Ministry
Draught Relief	Ministry of Agriculture
Other Natural Disaster Management	Ministry of Home Affairs
Railway Accidents	Ministry of Railways
Chemical Disasters	Ministry of Environment and Forests
Biological Disasters	Ministry of Health
Nuclear Disasters	Department of Atomic Energy

Source: Ministry of Home Affairs, 2011

Technical support regarding the issue of early warnings, preparedness, etc. are taken care by organizations like Central Water Commission (floods), Indian Meteorological Department (earthquake/ cyclone), Bureau of Indian Standards (building and project norms), etc. National Disaster Management Authority (NDMA) has been established by the Ministry of Home Affairs as the apex dedicated organization within the government for capacity building, to establish, mobilize and strengthen response and rescue teams in states, provide support to frame disaster management plans, etc. Concerning specific disasters, National core groups comprising of experts have been constituted to draw a strategy plan to mitigate the impacts of specific disaster, like an earthquake. The United Nations through its programs like UNDP (United Nations Development Programme) and UNISDR (United Nations International Strategy for Disaster Reduction) in association with MHA engage the state governments and the concerned local officials in promoting disaster mitigation.

State Government

The main responsibility to manage disaster risks is essentially vested in respective State Governments, where the Central Government has only supporting the role of being only the resource provider of physical and financial nature. The State Disaster Management Authority (SDMA) coordinates the multidisciplinary activities for disaster management amongst various state departments and ministries. But only a few states have constituted the respective SDMA. Also, since the requirement of different states varies in terms of their susceptibility to specific disasters, specialized rescue forces are needed. On a broader level, disbursal of responsibilities to certain departments like the fire department, officials like the district magistrate, etc. are given disaster management responsibilities in addition to their original duties. This results in deviated focus and average efforts especially in line with mitigation and preparedness.

Though every hazard prone district requires a specific hazard mitigation plan, and need to maintain an online inventory of resources available in the private and public sector for quick and efficient mobilization of resources, it seems a long shot when the internet connectivity in some district is abysmal. Also, the time taken to rebuild, reinstate the infrastructure is fairly long, as many of the hazard prone areas lie in a difficult geological strata where the ground infrastructure is poor. Also, rural areas, which due to poor infrastructure, overlooking of safety norms, and cash crunch are more vulnerable to disaster risks. Awareness campaigns amongst the inhabitants and special focused groups in forms of professionals like engineers, architects and amongst students by inculcating engineering aspects of disaster mitigation into educational courses are there, but mostly focused in urban areas.

District and local level

District administration is the focal point to implement and execute various government plans. The administration and accounting of relief work are maintained at the local level. As per the 73rd and 74th Constitutional amendments, Panchayati Raj Institutions have been recognized as the Institutions of self- government and can be empowered to be effective instruments in managing the disaster preparedness, relief and response activities. Other stakeholders at the institutional level like the fire department, civil defense and home guards, police and paramilitary force, NGO's, etc. have key duties to perform.

New approach

The disaster risk management in India is perceived with a novel objective of mitigation and preparedness from the earlier approach which focused on relief and rehabilitation, as was the case with the majority of the developing countries facing fund crunch. In the post-independence era, the government focused on developing infrastructure and fight wide-spread poverty. And the technology regarding early warning systems still at nascent stage, the government mostly focused on after-math of disasters, rather than preparedness. After the globalization and liberalization during early 1990's, the status of Indian economy improved. Huge investments have been made in for the establishment of infrastructure and development of both the consumer and manufacturing sector. It was after the Gujarat earthquake of 2001, which caused heavy loss of life and property in the entire state, that the government was forced to revisit its long standing strategy involving a reactive attitude of relief and rehab. As an aftermath of the event, a need was felt for the establishment of institutions with a holistic approach towards disaster management. In congruence with the new ideology, the National Policy on Disaster Management had proposed to integrate disaster mitigation into developmental planning documents, though the extent to which it is incorporated and executed on the ground is highly skeptical in regards to the poor implementation of original planning strategies in place.

Vulnerability reduction, or providing protection from natural calamities is subject involving multiple disciplines. It requires integrated efforts to achieve the holistic goal of making the communities resilient to disasters as laid down in the Sendai Framework for Disaster Risk Reduction 2015-2030. In the new regime and organizational structure too, the role of Central Government is supportive, defined only through the provision of financial and logistic help whereas the prime responsibility of conducting rescue and relief operations, carrying out rehabilitation activities lies with the State Government in the event of natural disasters.

Emergency and Healthcare

The local bodies, which form the 3rd tier of governance in India, are responsible for addressing specific emergencies for e.g. fire outburst, flooding, etc. through the dedicated departments like Fire Department. In some cities, where flooding is not a regular concern, a temporary control room is established to attend to any emergencies arising during the monsoon season like in Jaipur city. But in the landscape of growing concern over urban flooding cases in many cities and towns of India, owing to an insufficient storm water drainage system and poor maintenance, a dedicated department is the need of the hour. Also, fire departments in many Indian cities are ill-equipped to respond effectively in case of a big fire hazard, as evident from the fire incident at an oil depot in the Jaipur city where the authorities struggled to manage the outburst (Gupta, 2010).

In a disaster response mechanism, hospital preparedness occupies a crucial place. In comparison to developed countries of the world, India seems to lag far behind in provision of hospitals, physicians, and health staff (Fig. 38.3). According to the Govt. of India (2005) and National Health Profile (2015) statistics, the number of PHCs (Primary Health Centre) in India was 23,236, which is far below the required number of more than 38,000 for the population in excess of 114 crore in 2005, which increased to 24,049 in 2012 and 25,020 in 2014 falling short than the required PHC's by more

than 15,000 according to the erstwhile Planning Commission of India standards of one PHC for 20,000-30,000 population. Similarly shortage of health infrastructure can be assessed in terms of provision of Sub- Centres, Community Health Centres, etc., which along with the PHCs form the three tier health infra setup in India (GOI, 2014) (Planning Commission of India, n.d.)(Table 38.6). In terms of medical staff too, a dire need is felt to supplement the numbers to bring them at par with the required numbers (Table 38.7).

The ability of hospitals to function largely depends on lifelines and other basic services such as electrical power, water and sanitation, communications, and waste management and disposal. Hospital authorities, cognizant of the facts outlined above frequently produce emergency response plans-but such plans often fail to incorporate prevention and mitigation measures or to strengthen the role of hospital disaster committees in risk management (Manivelan, n.d.). According to the National Health Profile (2015) compiled by Central Bureau of Health Insurance, only about 21.6 crore people, less than one-fifth of the total population, are covered under health insurance. The government of India runs many programs to provide health insurance covers to the down-trodden and the needy, for e.g., about 15.5 crore people are covered under the three central govt. funded health schemes, namely Employees State Insurance Scheme, Rashtriya Swasthya Bima Yojna and Central Government Health Scheme apart from the standard health insurance.

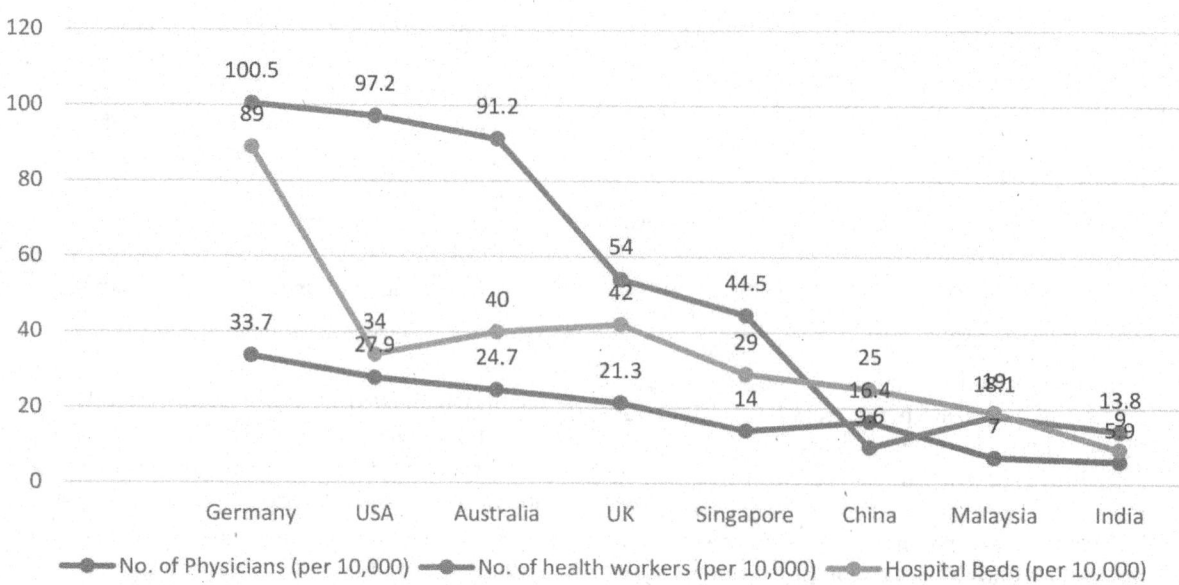

Fig. 38.3 Comparison of Health infrastructure in various countries of the world.

Source: World Health Statistics, 2005, WHO

Table 38.6 Status of Health Centres in India in 2005 and 2012.

State/Uts/All India	Sub Centre 2005	Primary Health Centres (PHCs) 2005	Community Health Centres (CHCs) 2005	Sub Centre 2012	Primary Health Centres (PHCs) 2012	Community Health Centres (CHCs) 2012
Andhra Pradesh	12522	1570	164	12522	1624	281
Arunachal Pradesh #	379	85	31	286	97	48
Assam 5	5109	610	100	4604	975	109
Bihar 4#	10337	1648	101	9696	1863	70
Chhattisgarh	3818	517	116	5111	755	149
Goa	172	19	5	205	19	5
Gujarat	7274	1070	272	7274	1158	318
Haryana	2433	408	72	2520	447	109
Himachal Pradesh	2068	439	66	2065	472	76
Jammu and Kashmir	1879	334	70	1907	396	84
Jharkhand4	4462	561	47	3958	330	188
Karnataka	8143	1681	254	8871	2310	180
Kerala *1	5094	911	106	4575	809	217
Madhya Pradesh 4	8874	1192	229	8869	1156	333
Maharashtra	10453	1780	382	10580	1811	363
Manipur	420	72	16	420	80	16
Meghalaya	401	101	24	397	109	29
Mizoram	366	57	9	370	57	9
Nagaland	394	87	21	396	126	21
Odisha 6	5927	1282	231	6688	1226	377
Punjab	2858	484	116	2951	449	132
Rajasthan	10512	1713	326	11487	1528	382
Sikkim	147	24	4	147	24	2
Tamil Nadu 2	8682	1380	35	8706	1227	385
Tripura	539	73	10	719	79	12
Uttarakhand	1576	225	44	1848	257	59
Uttar Pradesh	20521	3660	386	20521	3692	515
West Bengal 3	10356	1173	95	10356	909	348
Andaman & Nicobar Islands	107	20	4	119	22	4
Chandigarh	13	0	1	16	0	2
Dadra and Nagar Haveli	38	6	1	50	6	1
Daman and Diu	21	3	1	26	3	2
Delhi	41	8	0	41	5	0
Lakshadweep	14	4	3	14	4	3
Puducherry	76	39	4	51	24	4
All India	146026	23236	3346	148366	24049	4833

Source: (GOI, 2014)

Table 38.7 Healthcare staff status in India.

S. No.	Staff details	Required	Available	Shortage
1	Doctors at Primary Health Centres	25,724	22,842	2,882
2	Specialists	12,172	4,124	8,048
3	Pediatricians	3,043	440	2,603
4	Physicians	3,043	704	2,339
5	Surgeons	3,043	781	2,262
6	Health Assistant (M)	22,842	19,927	2,915
7	Health Assistant (F)	22,842	19,855	2,987
8	Health Worker (M)	137,311	71,053	66,258
9	Pharmacists	25,885	21,118	4,767
10	Lab Technicians	25,885	13,262	12,623
11	Nurses	44,143	27,336	16,807

Source: Health Information of India, 2004, Central Bureau of Health Intelligence

4. Cloud of Existing Instruments

4.1 Building By-Laws and Codes: Legal instruments

Before the earthquake of Gujarat in 2001, seismic codes were not mandatory in most of the country (Jain, 2004). While the government projects followed the codes, the private players generally overlooked them. In the post 2004 earthquake era, seismic codes garnered attention and were made mandatory. Many building bylaws have been reviewed and revised to incorporate the Bureau of Indian Standards (BIS) seismic codes of construction and the National Building Code (NBC), according to the specific seismic zones. NBC details out the best practices and the minimum standards to be ensured for constructing a safe built environment. Technical implementation for improving the strength of existing structures and safety aspects for new construction have been encompassed in the Model Building Bylaws which provide the local bodies and planning authorities with baseline conditions to develop building bylaws in the country. The BIS codes need regular revision to embrace the changing technology and the changing safety scenarios in the wake of climate change and disaster concerns. But the ground conditions are grim when, according to UNHABITAT (2008), much urban expansion in developing cities takes place outside the official and legal frameworks of building codes, land use regulations, and land transactions.Also, the concern is regarding the sincerity and the mechanism to enforce the codes.

Hazard Safety Cells have been inducted in state/Union Territory to review government buildings, lifeline infrastructure and assisting the local bodies in reviewing the structural and safety competency of the new designs undergoing the building plan approval channel.

4.2 Capacity Building and Training Programs

Built environment involves the roles of many service providers, of which engineers and architects form the technical team, masons and laborers form the execution team, while the review team comprising of the competent officials of the local bodies, agencies like PCB (Pollution Control Board), NGT (National Green Tribunal), Fire Department, etc. which respond in both pre-execution and post-execution stage. Two National Programmes directed at capacity building for earthquake mitigation for engineers and architects are in place. Engineering and architectural colleges too are being assisted to build capacities to aide state governments in assessment and retrofitting of built infrastructure (NDMA, n.d.). Faculty members of the selected state institutes are also trained through workshops under National Programme on Earthquake Engineering Education (NPEEE), the first phase of which was concluded in 2007. Ministry of Home Affairs, along with All India Council of Technical Education (AICTE) and Council of Architecture (COA) which are the governing bodies for technical and architecture education respectively, have worked to integrate earthquake engineering aspects in technical education curricula for engineering and architectural undergraduate courses.

4.3 Safety Cover

Provision of protection in the form of insurance cover and other safety nets are in the process of gaining a foothold in India. According to the Insurance Regulatory and Development Authority (IRDA), insurance penetration in the country reached 3.4 per cent mark in the Financial Year 2015-16 and is expected to breach 4 per cent in FY 17. In the Union Budget 2017, the government under the Pradhan Mantri Fasal Bima Yojna (PMFBY), increased the crop insurance coverage from 30 per cent to 40 per cent and the beneficiaries are expected to increase from the current level of 20 per cent to 50 per cent in the next two years. An allocation of Rs 9,000 crore has been made under PMFBY for crop insurance in 2017-18 (Foundation, 2017).

Having a large chunk of population as economically weaker section, who are the most vulnerable of all (Wisner, et al., 2004), it becomes more important since these are the people who are worst affected, and devoid of any safety nets. In terms of quantum, the losses incurred by the weaker section might be less, but since a disaster has the potential to wipe off their overall life savings, safety cover is of vital importance.

4.4 Emergency Force

National Emergency Response Force (NERF) under the Central Government supplements the existing setup in case of emergency. The States have their specialist teams for responding to disasters. Apart from these, other reserve force battalions are trained for basic search and rescue operations.

Also, fire services are trained and developed as a multi-hazard response force, to support the capacity for emergency response.

5. Funding Mechanism

Central Government is the authority disbursing funds for all activities related to disaster management, including mitigation plans, preparedness, rescue, relief and rehabilitation. Though traditionally it has not been addressed in the Five Year Plan documents although funds have been deployed to mitigate natural disasters. The Government of India appointed Finance Commission reviews the expenditure of funds after every five years. It is on the recommendation of Finance Commission that the division of tax and non-tax revenues between the Central and the State Governments is done and also various provisions of relief actions and the share of expenditure are laid. Earlier, the Finance Commissions were mandated to be a concern with relief and rehab works. The Eleventh Finance Commission had put in place a Calamity Relief Fund (CRF) in each state in which the Central Government contributes 75% of the amount of the Calamity Relief Fund in each State. 25% is contributed by the State and this fund takes care of the finances during response and relief measures during an event of a disaster. It was in the Twelfth Finance Commission, where the terms of reference have been revised and the Commission is mandated to look into mitigation and prevention aspects too, apart from relief and rehab (NDMA, n.d.). At the Central Government level, a National Calamity Contingency Fund (NCCF) is provisioned to take care of situations where further assistance is required on account of the vast effects of disasters. Though in the existing arrangements, mitigation and capacity building occupies the central focus in the framework for disaster risk resilience, it is equally important to strengthen the post disaster preparedness too. Response teams to act in an emergency situation of a disaster event has been in place, along with the National Emergency Response Force acts as reserve force to the response teams at the state level, which can provide assistance to the local efforts.

6. Causes of Concern

Though there has been a significant change in the institutional arrangement and approach towards disaster management, certain issues still lurk in the current setup. Firstly, the Central Govt. through NDMA has directed the States to prepare a Disaster Management Plan, which is still pending for a few states like Andhra Pradesh (The Economic Times, 2017). Apart from this, many state governments are yet to form state advisory committees as laid down under the Section 17 of the Disaster Management Act (DMA). With the limited efforts to check the efficiency of these state disaster management plans, as evident from the notices served to the states of Uttarakhand, Tamil Nadu, Odisha, Andhra Pradesh, Maharashtra, West Bengal and Gujarat on failure in implementing DMA, the sincerity of the authorities and their efforts is under question.

Secondly, it has been realized that an integrated effort is needed from all the stakeholders and concerned departments to achieve the goal of disaster risk resilience. Due to the highly connected nature of the disaster risks, urban policies corresponding to the resilience essentially need to be multi-dimensional, catering to various sectors (Nijkamp and Finco, 2000). The multi-sectoral approach for multi-hazard prevention requires professionals of specific nature. Hence, focus on professional training is of utmost importance. Also, the provision of specialized team amongst the development authorities or infrastructure development ministries, with objectives to align the developmental process with disaster resilience goals is still averted. This increases the vulnerability quotient of the settlements in the wake of negligence and can prove resource draining in the long run by requiring emergency corrections in forms of evacuation planning strategies etc. In the absence of digital databases and maps, land-use plans, GIS based city maps, certain tasks of disaster mitigation become tedious and resource intensive, which is a case with India as the digitization is underway but limited to a few departments and locations, and is still at a nascent stage in the rural areas.

Departments directly connected with an emergency like the fire department faces a shortage in terms of staff and equipment. Also, the existing equipment are not in line with the current time technology in terms of extinguishers, fire tenders, fire ladder etc. A CAG report from 2016 also highlighted that 78% funds earmarked for the purchase of fire safety appliances were unused in many cities like Mumbai, Pune, Nashik etc. (Online, 2017).

Another aspect is the hospital preparedness in the wake of disaster events, which is very crucial. The public expenditure on health in India during 2012-13 was 1.08 per cent of GDP, which has remained unchanged since 2009-10 and is the lowest among BRICS nations and more than only Myanmar in the South-East Asian region (Dey, 2015). Though health centers at the city and district levels are to have an emergency preparedness plan, but the existing situation shows the healthcare infrastructure is already reeling under huge population pressure. Only a few hospitals are well-equipped to manage large numbers of trauma patients. Not only there is a shortage of staff and hospital beds, the Centralized Accident and Trauma Services are struggling with shortage of ambulances too. Only a few big hospitals have mass casualty management plan, and of that too, only some practice mock drills (Satapathy, n.d.). Apart from this, the traffic congestion on the roads hinders the swift movement of lifeline service vehicles such as ambulances and fire brigades.

Another major challenge lies in the monitoring of the implementation of codes and laws which in regards to weak enforcement framework are often flouted. Though at the time of building plan approvals, all necessary requirements stated in the National Building Code and local bylaws are met, but in the absence of efficient monitoring, in many cases, the provisions remain in paper. Also, many local authorities do away with the formality of taking the structural safety certificate, also limited to buildings with height more than 15m, rather than requiring structural drawing set. In the absence of accountability, responsible persons like engineers, regardless of whether building conforms to the codes, have no difficulty in giving the structural certificate. On the one hand, there is no mechanism to check the competency of an engineer/ other professionals and on the other side, there is no fear in professionals of their licenses being revoked in case of sub-standard services (Jain, 2004). In the current scenario of relentless development, where the cities are now going vertical (Fig. 38.4) due to the lack of ground space, compact development, and skyrocketing land prices, it is very critical to procure and check all the safety norms of building proposals, especially in Tier II and Tier III cities where the local bodies have limited resources to keep a check on unauthorized development.

While discussing safety, there is an emphasis on 'retrofitting' of existing infrastructure, but in a scenario of the limited

Fig. 38.4   Mid and high rise development are on the rise in the current developmental scenario.

Source: Author

availability of resources, many such proposals fail to take off. In many cities and towns of India, prime lands are occupied by old inhabited dilapidated structures, in the heart of the city, which in the absence of proper maintenance and retrofitting are susceptible to damage due to natural and human activities like in case of heavy rainfall or vibrations due to construction activity posing accessibility challenge in narrow, encroached and congested streets to emergency services (Fig. 38.5a, b, c). In terms of other mandatory provisions, fire norms are greatly flouted. An audit by Nagpur Municipal Corporation's fire department found that out of 1596 buildings, which are 15 meters or higher, only 282 had complied with fire safety norms which shows the abysmal condition of enforcement of fire norms (Online, 2017).

(a)   (b)   (c)

Fig. 38.5   (a). (b) and (c) Old city cores, characterized by narrow, congested streets, have some old inhabited buildings in dilapidated conditions,

Source: Author

At present, there are no clear legal responsibilities of different stakeholders in the construction process. This paints a picture of low accountability, making the concept of professional liability insurance difficult to work in India (Jain, 2004). Furthermore, the insurance sector has a limited penetration till date in the country. In rural areas, the government provides crop insurance at subsidized premiums and under various schemes. A tendency of granting loan waiver by the government to farmers of the draught hit region sometimes provides favor to the safe, financially strong farmers as well, and the resultant expenditure is borne by the calamity fund as a relief measure, which otherwise could have been used in order to prevent reoccurrence of specific calamity through measures like strengthening the irrigation networks etc. The hurdles faced in getting the claim approved is seen as another challenge in the insurance sector, which is plagued by heavy legal paperwork.

7. Conclusion and Way Forward

Due to its variable geographical and geological conditions, India is susceptible to damages incurred due to various disasters. The changed approach to counter disaster risk in India has induced a policy and strategic shift from concentrating on relief measures to disaster mitigation and management measures. This paradigm shift would require huge investments in building the new infrastructure and strengthening the existing one, in technological advancement to improve the early warning systems, ensuring adequate disaster preparedness measures etc. Though this has been ensured through the allocation of funds in the five-year plans on the recommendation of Twelfth Finance Commission through Disaster Mitigation Fund to enable states to take mitigation measures, its effects are yet to be seen on the ground. Moreover, transparency in relief operations is ardently sought to ensure the relief funds reach the rightful hands. A revision in the strategy to provide relief to actual needy is necessary so that resources are not wasted and are allocated proportionately and are not underutilized.

In regards to the incessant urbanization and accompanied population explosion, there is a need to plan, regulate and monitor the city expansion, especially in the fringe and dense areas as the latter is more vulnerable due to increasing number of exposed population and over exploitation of resources, pressure on infrastructure and non-compliance of the building codes. Hence the developmental guidelines in the form of official documents such as Master Plans and City Development Plans should be coherent with the Disaster Management Plans for the area, which is currently at a nascent stage in the developmental planning structure of the country and at the same time ensuring adherence to the building code.

After the disastrous earthquake of Gujarat, special focus has been laid on earthquake mitigation by inculcating the seismic structural codes from Bureau of Indian Standards into the building bye-laws and developmental codes. But in the absence of strict enforcement and unawareness of the practicing professionals in the field like engineers and architects, even the new built stock piles up the vulnerable inventory list. Hence training programs for concerned professionals and the authorities in the regulatory bodies to generate awareness about the use and supervision of relevant codes becomes indispensable. The focus should be on putting in place a system for code compliance of new constructions and thereafter, a systematic and well-debated approach to retrofitting should be adopted, otherwise, a huge volume of the unsafe built stick will be added each day, which will be required to be retrofitted in future.

Though the fire department is being nurtured as the multi-hazard response units, the absence of elementary and adequate equipment in accordance with the local ground needs make the department vulnerable to carrying out its basic services. For example, increasing the building height norms beyond the existing capacity of the concerned fire department of the city compromises the safety concerns of the users, which might, unfortunately, result into loses of life and property in the absence of timely action. Hence the departments responding to the emergency situations need to be well resourced and technologically full proof. On the disaster preparedness front, after the constitution of relief forces, there is a need to strengthen the existing healthcare infrastructure to respond to the emergency needs and a robust network of hospitals, clinics and nursery staff is to be developed.

Institutional framework forms key component of the disaster response and resilience strategy. Despite having no dearth of human resource, there is a need to strengthen the institutional framework to make it more robust and effective. Though the resources already exist, the challenge lies in streamlining and integrating them. In today's time when hazards are inevitable, societies should be prepared to cope with them effectively. Efforts are to be undertaken to integrate disaster mitigation efforts at the local level combined with developmental planning exercise, and supportive environment for initiatives managing disasters at national, state, district and local levels.

REFERENCES

1. Census Department of India, 2011. *District Census Handbook 2011*, s.l.: s.n.
2. Dey, S., 2015. *Times of India*. [Online] Available at: http://m.timesofindia.com/india/Less-than-20-of-population-under-health-insurance-cover-Report/articleshow/49082784.cms [Accessed 23 09 2017].

3. Dickson, E., Baker, J. L., Hoornweg, D. & Tiwari, A., 2012. *Urban Risk Assessments.* Washington D.C.: The World Bank.

4. Foundation, I. B. E., 2017. *Indian Insurance Industry Overview & Market Development Analysis.* [Online] Available at: https://www.ibef.org/industry/insurance-sector-india.aspx [Accessed 23 09 2017].

5. GOI, 2014. *Open Government Data (OGD) Platform India.* [Online] Available at: https://data.gov.in/sites/default/files/datafile/facilitiesfunctioning2005-2012.csv [Accessed 23 09 2017].

6. Gupta, K., 2010. Design of district emergency operations centres, and the case study of Indian Oil Corporation of Jaipur depot explosion. *International Journal of Emergency Management,* 7(3-4), pp. 221–232.

7. Hewitt, K., 1997. Regions of Risk: A Geographical Introduction to Disasters. First ed. s.l.:Routledge.

8. HUP; USAID, n.d. *Urban Health and Corporate Social Responsibiity in India: A factsheet.* [Online] Available at: http://hupindia.org/resources/Factsheets/CSR%20Factsheets%20on%20Health%20and%20WASH/Urban%20Health%20and%20CSR.pdf [Accessed 2017].

9. IPCC, 2014. *Climate change 2014: Fifth Assessment Report: Impacts, Assessment and vulnerability. Intergovernmental Panel on Climate Change (IPCC),* Cambridge, UK and New York, NY, USA: Cambridge University Press.

10. Jain, S. K., 2004. *Implications of 2001 Bhuj Earthquake for Seismic Risk Reduction In India.* Vancouver, s.n.

11. Manivelan, D. R., n.d. *Abstracts: Thematic Session – Disaster Health Management.* [Online] Available at: http://nidm.gov.in/idmc/IDMC_Abstract/E1-Health.pdf [Accessed 18 06 2017].

12. Ministry of Finance, G. o. I., n.d. *Tenth Five-Year Plan (2002-07),* New Delhi: Govt. of India.

13. Ministry of Home Affairs, G. o. I., 2011. *Disaster Management in India.* New Delhi: s.n.

14. Mondal, P., n.d. *Disaster Management in India: Classification, Policies and other Details.* [Online] Available at: http://www.yourarticlelibrary.com/essay/disaster-management-in-india-classification-policies-and-other-details/25006/

15. NDMA, I., n.d. *Mitigation.* [Online] Available at: http://ndmindia.nic.in/Mitigation/index.htm [Accessed 12 04 2017].

16. Nijkamp, P. & Finco, A., 2000. Evaluation of Complex Resilience Strategies for Sustainable Cities. *CeSET,* pp. 119–141.

17. Online, F., 2017. *London fire: How safe are highrises in Indian cities like Delhi, Mumbai and Bengaluru.* [Online] Available at: http://www.financialexpress.com/india-news/london-fire-how-safe-are-indian-highrises-in-cities-like-mumbai-delhi-and-bengaluru/717344/

18. Pelling, M., 2003. The Vulnerability of Cities. New York: Taylor and Francis.

19. Planning Commission of India, n.d. *Planning Commission of India.* [Online] Available at: http://planningcommission.nic.in/reports/peoreport/peo/peo_chc.pdf [Accessed 23 09 2017].

20. Puente, S., 1999. Social vulnerability to disasters in Mexico City: An assessment method. In: J. K. Mitchell, ed. *Crucibles of hazard: Mega-cities and disasters in transition.* Tokyo, Japan: United Nations University Press, pp. 295–334.

21. Satapathy, S., n.d. *Abstracts: Thematic Session- Disaster Health Management.* [Online] Available at: http://nidm.gov.in/idmc/IDMC_Abstract/E1-Health.pdf [Accessed 18 06 2017].

22. Singh, R. B., 2017. Introduction to Natural Hazards and Disasters. In: R. B. Singh, ed. *Natural Hazards and Disaster Management.* Jaipur: Rawat Publications, pp. 3–40.

23. Sinha, R. & Goyal, A., 2012. *A National Policy for Seismic Vulnerability Assessment of Buildings and Procedure for Rapid Visual Screening of Buildings for Potential Seismic Vulnerability,* Bombay: IIT Bombay.

24. The Economic Times, 2017. *Politics and Nation.* [Online] Available at: https://www.google.co.in/amp/m.economictmes.com/news/politics-and-nation/supreme-court-raps-centre-on-implementation-of-disaster-management-law/amp_articleshow/58417172.cms [Accessed 24 09 2017].

25. UNISDR, 2009. *United Nations International Strategy for Disaster Reduction,* Geneva: United Nations.

26. UNISDR, 2015. *Making Development Sustainable: The Future of Disaster Risk Management. Global Assessment Report in Disaster Risk Reduction 2015,* Geneva, Switzerland: United Nations Office for Disaster Risk Reduction (UNISDR).

27. Wisner, B., Blaikie, P., Cannon, T. & Davis, I., 2004. *At Risk: Natural Hazards, People's Vulnerability and Disasters.* Second edition ed. London: Routledge.

CHAPTER 39

System Dynamics Approach for COVID-19 Disaster Management

Anjali Saraswat

Malaviya National Institute of Technology Jaipur

anjalisaraswat7@gmail.com

8802707584

Satish Pipralia

Malaviya National Institute of Technology Jaipur

spipralia.arch@mnit.ac.in

9549658126

Abstract

The infectious disease of Coronavirus (Covid-19) materialized first in the Chinese megacity Wuhan and ever since it has become a pandemic disaster striking 220 countries with a mortality rate of 3.4%. Catastrophically affecting cities' environments, economy, transportation, along with particularly crumbling health as well as social lives of citizens, Covid-19 collapsed the cities spine and altered people's way of living drastically. The paper begins with exploring the scenarios of Covid-19 disaster in Indian cities and understands the mitigation strategies opted by the Indian government to combat the pandemic. The spread of Covid-19 disaster in Indian states reveals that nearly 65% mortality share of the covid patients is bestowed in four states of Maharashtra, Tamil Nadu, Delhi and Karnataka. The concerns towards the disaster management of this pandemic arises with the megacities of the country becoming the covid epicentre. Further a causal loop diagram is prepared, using the system dynamics modelling technique which articulates the interconnections between various variables of urban functions during the Covid-19 pandemic. The dynamics between social, economic, environment and infrastructure subsystems reveal how the various covid management strategies adopted have affected urban dwellers. The results gauged from system dynamics modelling are further utilized to suggest recommendations for managing Covid-19 disaster in mega cities. Exploring disaster management strategies, using the system dynamics modelling technique for Covid-19 pandemic raises high hope for surviving this disaster in the context of Indian cities.

Keywords: Covid-19, coronavirus, mega cities, pandemics, India

1. Introduction

Coronavirus disease popularly known as COVID-19 is a contagious disease originated due to the corona virus identified in the city of Wuhan, Hubei Province, China (Li et al., 2021). Establishing itself through its first confirmed cases in the year 2019, COVID-19 by the year 2021 has become a behemoth pandemic taking the life of nearly 4 million people across the globe (Haq, 2020). The ordeal of enduring this epidemic has tampered the human psyche substantially. Nevertheless, with the surging modernity and globalisation we stand with the persuading circumstances to reanalyse and evaluate our current ongoing infrastructures expansion, administrative systems and susceptibilities the urban centres are exposed to. Cities and urban centres are the engines of economic growth accommodating an enormous population which makes them exposed to many disasters especially the low paid and marginalized groups in the society (Aslam, 2020; Mallya & D'Silva, 2020). Megalopolis of the nation's face colossal threat accounting to nearly half of covid cases share, thus it becomes imperative for the city planners and decision makers to make necessary amendments in the urban planning principles and propositions. The health complications that arose for the whole nation are such that the absolute economy has come to standstill. The pressing priority is to be able to bounce back from this trounce and pursue building buoyant city development models. Being a distinctive disaster occurring in the cities across the world, the pandemic constitutes numerous challenges for societies and their administrative structures. Thus, it becomes imperative to explore various requisite planning, recovery and adaptation initiatives to overcome the pandemic. Strategizing such combined efforts to deal with this pandemic would lead into making our urban landscapes more sustainable and certainly resilient.

2. COVID-19 Scenario in Indian Cities

The response mechanism of the Indian cities to the COVID-19 pandemic has been conscientious, expansive and magnificently calibrated by the consolidated efforts of the local, central and state governments accompanying the private sector and zealous citizens participation. Being an unprecedented, one of its kind disasters the combating strategies were explored from the lessons learned globally, reciprocating to the discrete challenges faced in each phase of the pandemic and evolved across the context of each city

(Mehta, 2021; The Research Unit for Political Economy, 2020). The start points of the recovery mechanism involved attempts to break off the link with the outside via closing the borders, testing people on the move, follow up surveillance and tracing the contacts so as to dwindle the arising Covid-19 cases numbers.

Subsequently as the covid situations aggravated, a series of lockdowns was imposed in the country consecrated by the central government under the Disaster Management Act of 2005 to prevent further spread of the virus. Lockdown 1 began from 25 March 2020 and lasted 21 days, later lockdown 2 occurred from 15 April 2020 to 3 May 2020 (19 days) and lockdown 3 & 4 both lasted 14 days from 4 May 2020 to 17 May 2020 and 18 May 2020 to 31 May 2020. The extent of all the durations of lockdown was accompanied with a diversified character based on the circumstances in each urban area ("Covid-19: Collateral Damage of Lockdown in India," 2020; Narayanan & Saha, n.d.; Singh et al., 2021; Tak et al., n.d.). The count of confirmed covid positive cases at the start of the lockdown was 500 and soon after the lockdown was initiated the rate of doubling of covid cases came down to six days by April 6 2020 and further to eight days by 18 April 2020. The collaborative efforts of

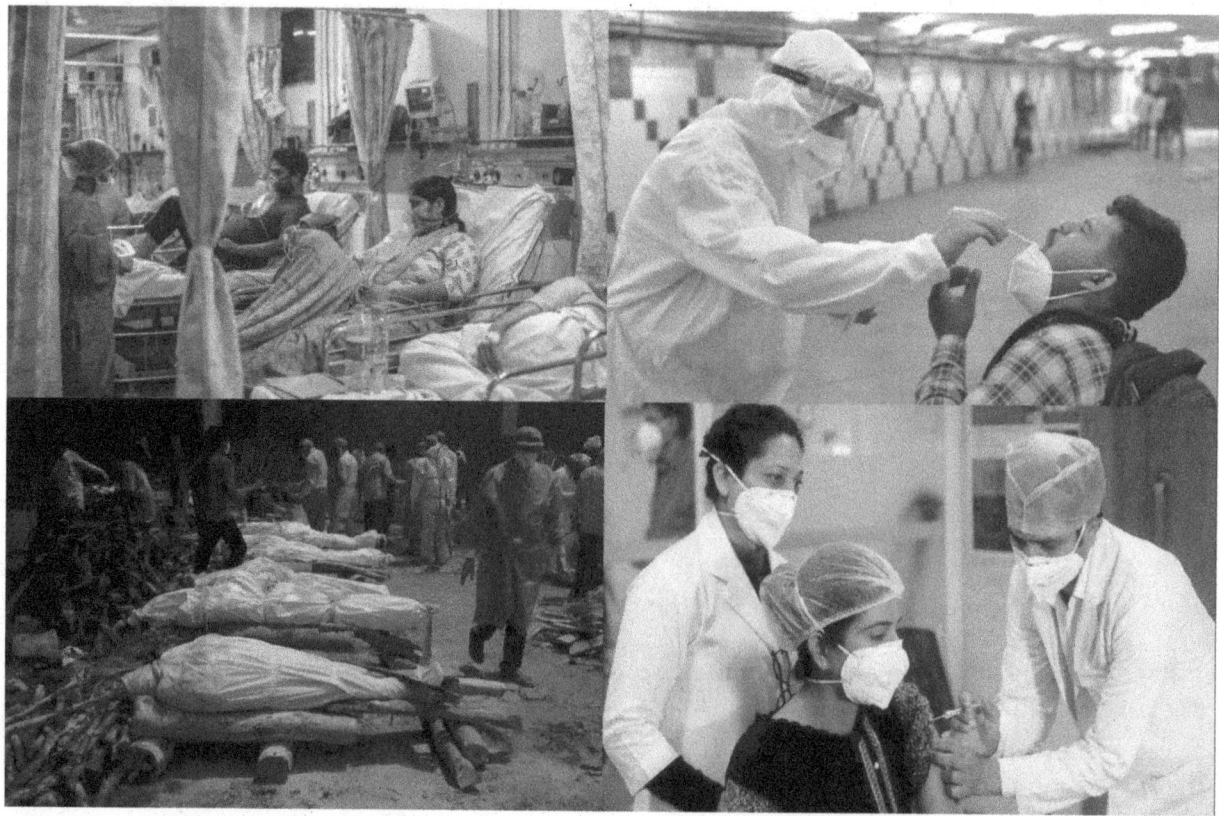

Fig. 39.1 Rinsing Covid cases in India; Rapid antigen covid tests; Increasing mortality rate; Vaccination against coronavirus
Source: 1,2,3,4

the central and state governments in the country assisted the burgeoning of finer strategies and guided the association of plenty of stakeholders' interpretations to counter multiple challenges. In order to assess the coverage of COVID-19 in urban centres, the districts were classified into 3 zones based on the intensity of the active cases as green, red and orange zones. Contemplated with the rise of covid positive cases, the majority of the districts in the nation constituted under the red and orange zones, with a scant few under green zones (see Fig. 39.2).

Majority of districts under the green zone were set up in the North East and a handful in Himachal Pradesh, Bihar, Chhattisgarh, Jharkhand, Odisha and West Bengal. The central India had most districts with orange zones, together with districts from North east, Odisha, West Bengal and others dissipated across several states. The districts largely hit by the coronavirus were in the state of Maharashtra, Haryana, Punjab, Rajasthan, Gujrat and southern states of Kerala, Tamil Nadu and Andhra Pradesh represented by the red zones.

Further exploration of the spread of covid cases at the end of the year 2020 reveals that over 83.64 lakh people were tested positive, engendering second rank to India across the globe after USA in COVID- 19 counts. The mortality and recovery count of individuals amongst the 83,64,086 people who tested positive for coronavirus was 1,24,315 and

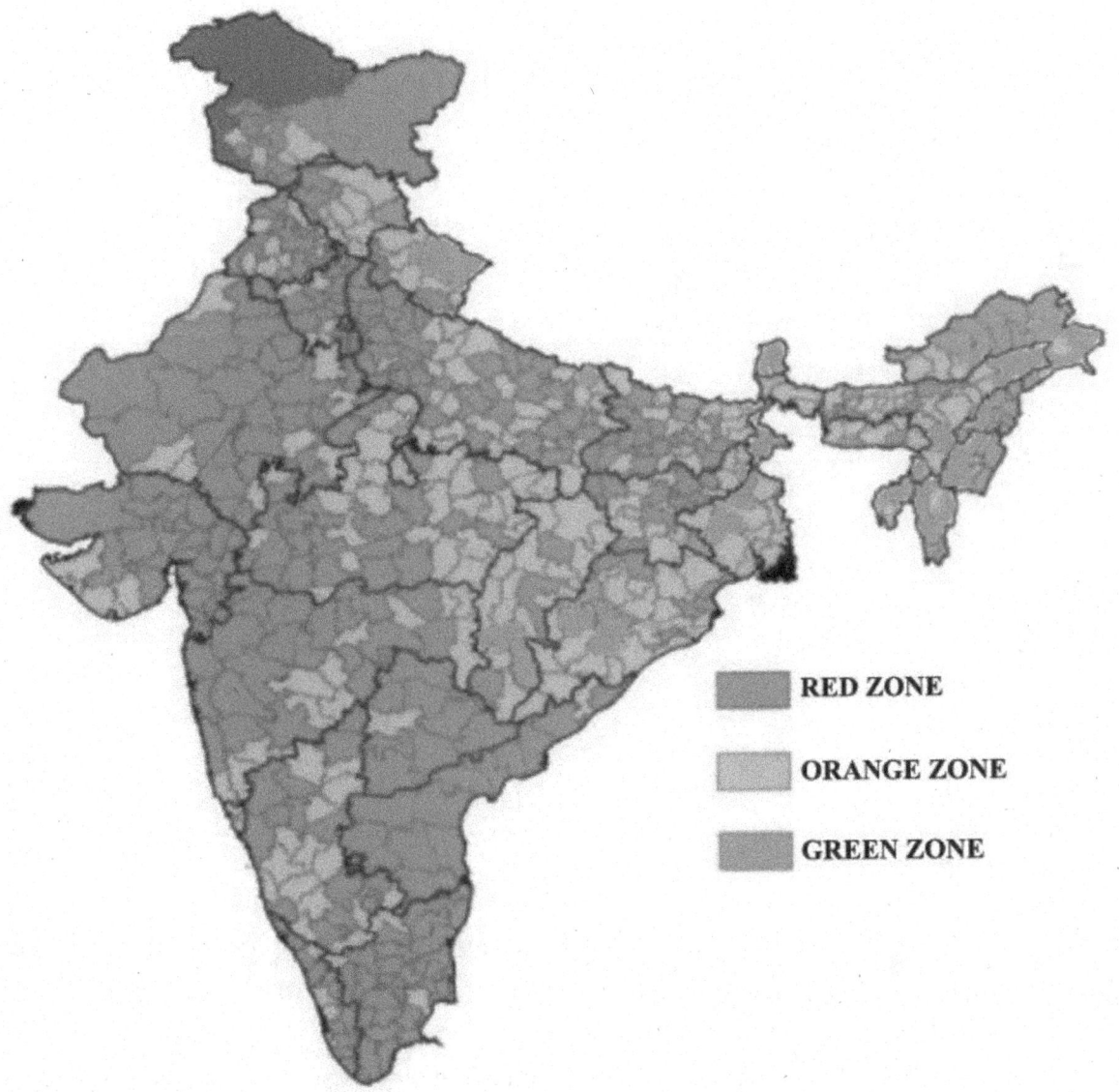

Fig. 39.2   Red, orange and green zones classification in Indian districts

Source: www.covid19india.org (Covid data as in May 2020)

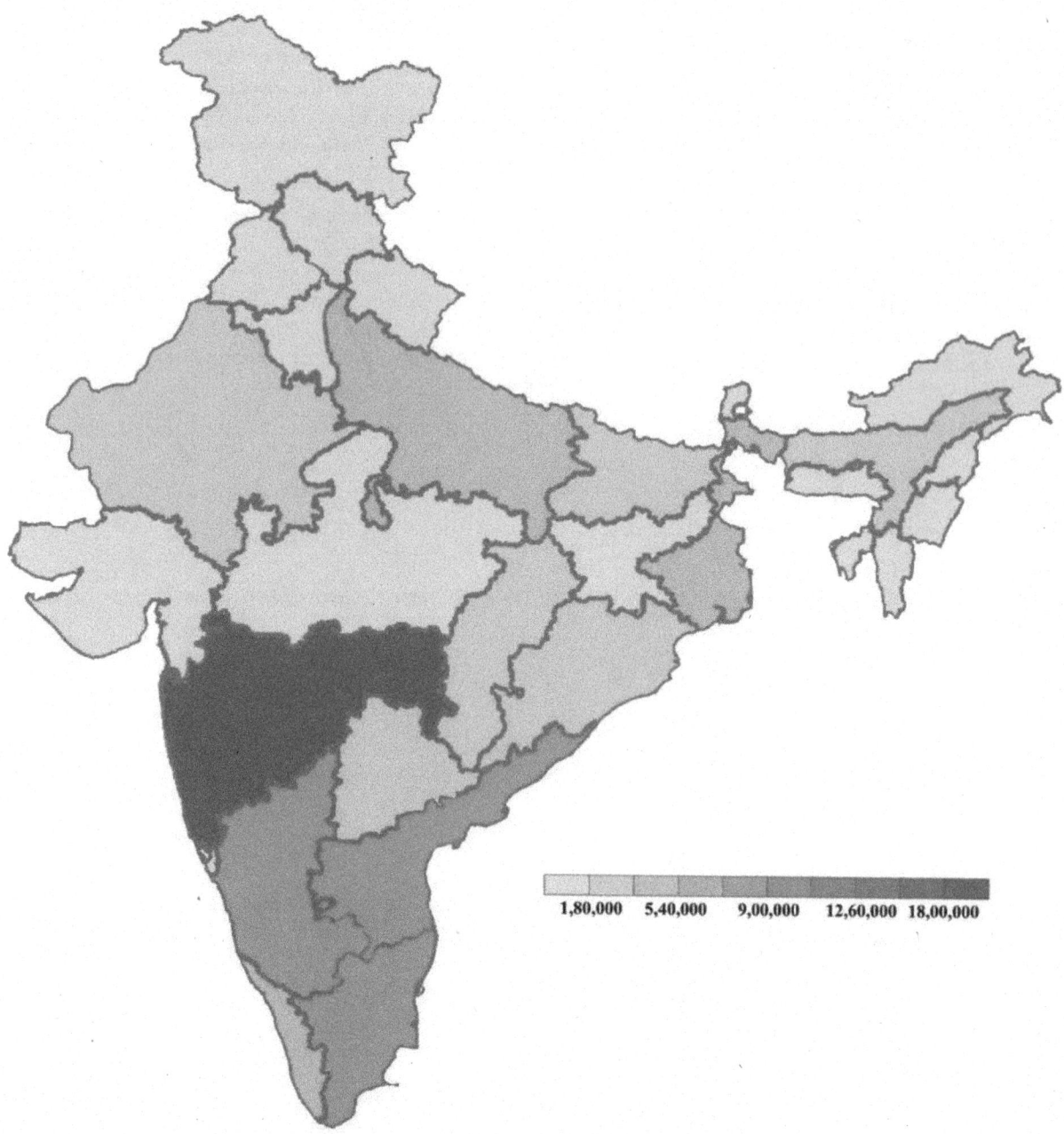

Fig. 39.3 Total covid cases in Indian states

Source: Ministry of Health and Family Welfare (Covid data at the end of 2020)

77,11,809. The states of Maharashtra, Karnataka, Andhra Pradesh and Tamil Nadu became the Covid-19 hotspots in the country with 16.98 lakh, 8.35 lakh, 8.33 lakh and 7.34 lakh covid positive individuals (see figure below) accounting for almost half the share in the country. Nearly 65% mortality share of the covid patients was bestowed by just four states of Maharashtra, Tamil Nadu, Delhi and Karnataka.

3. System Dynamics Assessment of COVID-19 Pandemic

System dynamics is a modelling technique that uses integrated forecast and multiple scenario simulations to support decision making based on real world problems. The feedback control theory applied using causal loop diagrams

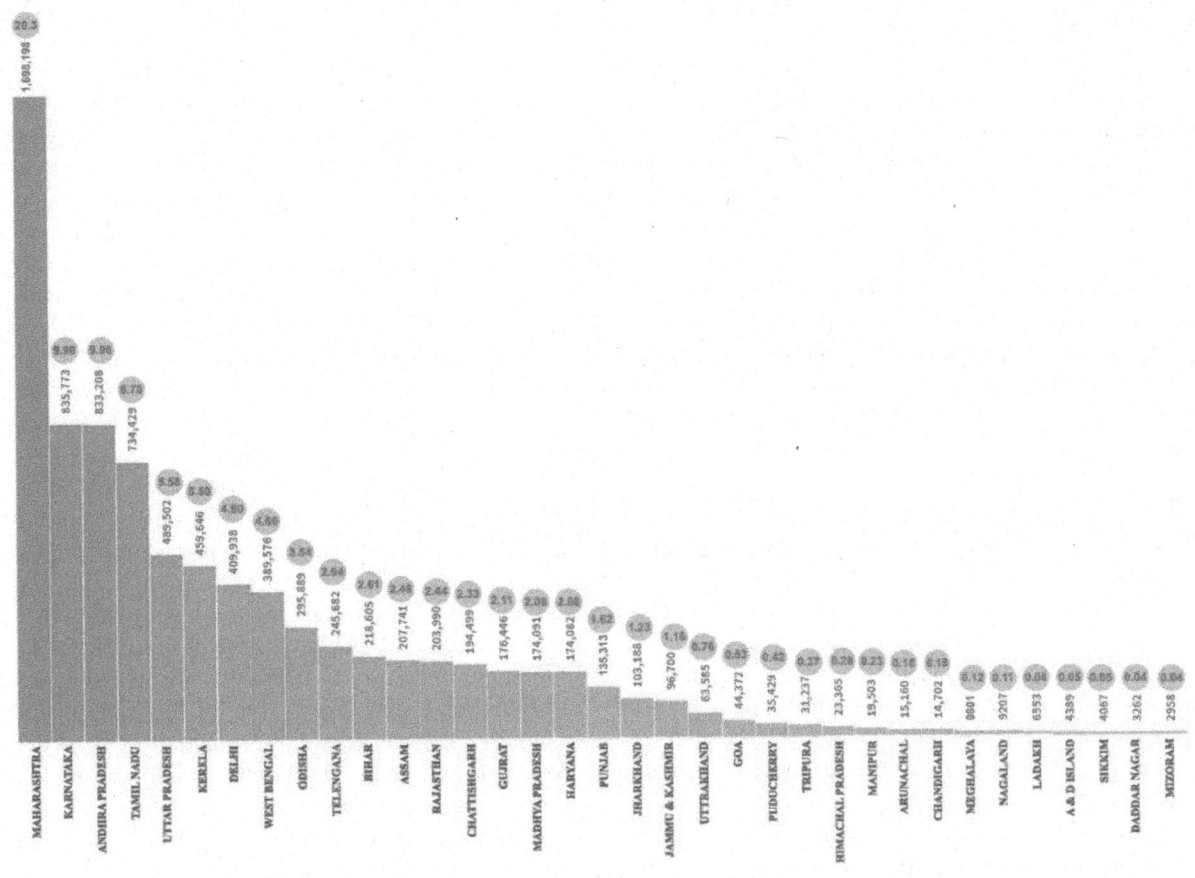

Fig. 39.4 Distribution and share of covid cases in Indian states

Source: Ministry of Health and Family Welfare (Covid data at the end of 2020)

in system dynamics modelling enables studying of complex systems which are non- linear in nature (Coyle, 1996; Mohapatra et al., 1994). It acknowledges systems function as a whole while interacting with several other subsystems. The systems-based approach enables us to interpret real world problems by investigating individual components of a system which are interconnected and interdependent on each other. The concerns of any subsystem can be clearly visualized over the entire system through a period of time. System Dynamics modelling technique is widely used in many research areas such as urban planning, industrial, health, biology, social sciences, software engineering, tourism, environmental and demographic systems. In current times the use of System Dynamics approach is widely being promoted throughout various public and private sectors as it assists in depth policy analysis and supports decision making.

System dynamics assessment of covid-19 pandemic intends to assess the various scenarios generated by the various covid-19 management strategies employed by the government (Jia et al., 2021; Tutsoy & Polat, 2021; Zhang et al., 2021).

The various after effects of these plans of actions materialized in social, economic, environment and health infrastructure sub systems. Understanding the various complexity between the several variables of these subsystems would enable us to functionally manage this pandemic. Evolving a causal loop diagram to understand these changing dynamics would enable us to connect the feedback loops and work towards suitable solutions. There exist certain variables that direct or indirectly affect the COVID-19 situation in an urban area.

Amidst the Covid-19 pandemic, there are a series of measures taken by the governments in order to reduce the spread of the covid virus and also to safeguard the life of the citizens. These measures are on accounts of certain restrictions and major enactments to effectively fight the battle of this epidemic. Restrictions measures occurred in terms of movement curtailments of goods and facilities across international, national, regional, state and local borders; commerce diminution happened in terms of pausing the manoeuvring of non-essential goods and services; halting the social mobilization of people especially by law enforcement officers and the imposition of series of country lockdowns. Extensive enactments involved the various incentive policies launched as per government schemes to benefit the citizens suffering from the illness as well as the consequences of lockdown and information campaigns aimed at making the general public aware of the infection, its prevention measures as well as updating them about the various administrative initiatives. Moreover, establishing large scale covid-19 testing centres was a predominant step in order to identify the source issue and then seek the intended solutions. The entire medical infrastructure is what has enabled the capacity to deal with this pandemic, thus it is exceedingly crucial to strengthen it by providing financial aid and more equipment. Imposing lockdowns across the country has been one of the elementary steps taken by the governments all over the world as soon as the covid case curve has elevated. Such a state of isolation generated for the masses has resulted in bringing down the transmission events. The rising count of covid positive individuals has laid a massive load on the social health infrastructure, generating burden on medical professionals with long working hours in perilous circumstances. With this amount of pressure, the various medical facilities' capacity is not being fully utilized. Ensuring to meet the rising demands of several resources in the hospitals would fulfill the medical facility capacity and result in reducing the burdens on medical professionals as well as fabricate facile accessibility to hospitals which in turn would minimize the vulnerable citizens. Exposed to the possibility of acquiring covid, the vulnerable citizens add to the covid positive individuals.

The measures of lockdown require most people to stay isolated, which reduces the availability of people and resources to work on the vaccines supply chain. With large government and private organisations working on, first finding vaccines and now producing the volumes required for every individual requires creating vast vaccine supply chains which makes the vaccines available. Utilization of vaccines by applying to the individuals is only made possible with their availability in desired amounts and the more they are used the less their quantity becomes. Only by giving citizens the covid vaccine doses can their immunity to oppose the virus be put in, which ultimately supports the campaign happening to support and manufacture more vaccines and thus eventually the citizens immunity will ascent. The campaigns for vaccines reduce the exposure of people to transmission risks and in turn more the transmission risks the impacts of vaccine campaigns will reduce. Non covid infected citizens are benefited with good psychological health and well being by practicing habits of hygiene as well as limiting themselves from social mobilization. Restricting the social mobilization of people at public places is a chief covid management strategy to prevent the spread of the virus. Though social mobilization

allows people to interact and communicate, largely uplifting their psychological health, in order for citizens to remain non-infected from the covid virus restrictions on social interactions have to be maintained. With more people breaking the social distance norms the vulnerable population would increase. Additionally, as the number of covid positive individuals rises, their movements restrict and so does social mobilization. The pandemic has not just attacked the physical well being of people but also mental health with undetermined lockdowns and mightily changing lifestyles, thus instigating distress and anxiety in the minds of many which eventually forces individuals to practice additional hygiene measures and collapses their psychological health. Appropriate execution of all the covid management strategies necessitates administrative efficiency, which not just averts laws violation and spreading of misleading information as well as lessens the distress and anxiety among individuals. Spread of wrong or incorrect information by the masses puts an interruption in the effectiveness of how administration works. Conducting relevant information campaigns on the do's and don'ts in the covid crisis helps the people to make better judgement in the time of crisis as well as aids not spreading misleading information. If the momentum of misleading information is large at a place as well as violation of laws the distress and anxiety amongst the people would elevate. Numerous incentive policies offered by the government to the sufferers of the epidemic in terms of economic reforms and programs or even rebates and concessions helps them overcome the setbacks of the pandemic as well as lessens their distress and anxiety. Further effort to prevent the spread of the covid-19 virus is in terms of setting up several commerce diminutions to halt the movement of non-essential goods and services. Such a step would enable several drawbacks to business owners and thus invite for more incentive policies by the government. Moreover, with such restrictions placed on business, a large number of commerce cessations would occur which would result in diminishing the economy. Attempts of various incentive policies by the government would reduce the number of business cessation. Solidity of the several logistics utilized in commercial setups improves the degree of amenities and commodities which would in turn reduce the distress and anxiety of business owners and the end users of facilities. Better the logistics solidity in a business more will be the productivity hence lesser commerce cessation events would occur. Better economy would prevent businesses from shutting down thus lowering the rates of business cessation. Restrictions measures occurred in terms of movement curtailments of goods and facilities across international, national, regional, state and local borders Sealing the international, national, regional, state and local borders would curtail the movement of goods and facilities, consequently shrinking the market largely for the same. Impacts of better

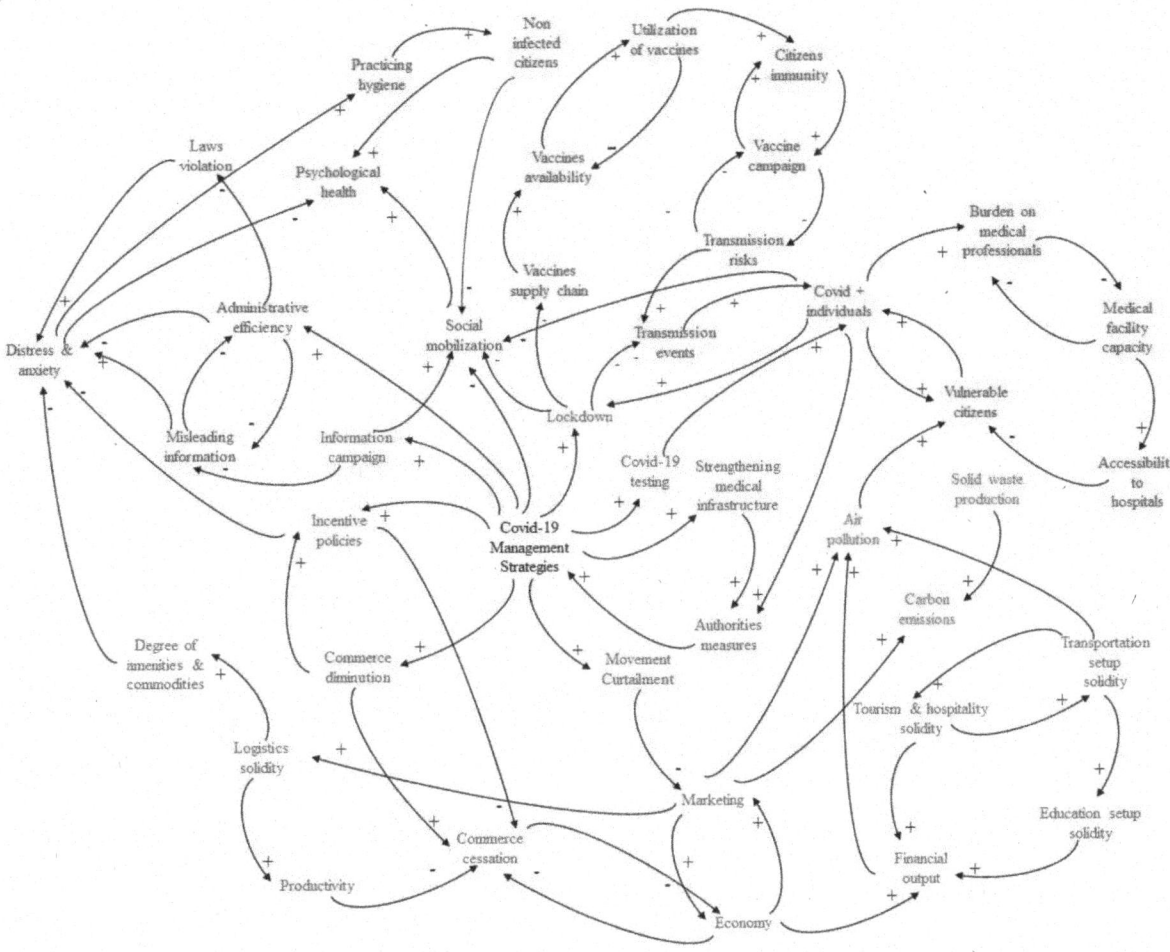

Fig. 39.5   Causal loop diagram for Covid-19 assessment

Source: Generated by author

markets can be observed in terms of boosting the economy and vice versa. The economy of a place mainly determines the financial outputs of the region, predominantly amplified by the education, tourism and hospitality industry solidarity. Additionally, marketing efforts and financial output of a place contribute to increased air pollution levels due to transport usage and fumes initiated in various processes. Solidity of the transportation system strengthens the tourism, hospitality and education setups as it provides the means of connection and communication from one place to another. Also, in tourism and hospitality setups, the individuals are required to make movements from one place to another which in turn assists the transportation setup. Large quantities of smoke generated by the vehicles in transportation setups is a huge contributor to air pollution levels. Marketing processes also accord with the city's carbon emissions levels. Solid waste produced during various processes is also a significant carbon emissions contributor. Strengthening the medical infrastructure in terms

of providing various equipment needed for patients and doctors such as beds, ventilations, masks, sanitizers and PPE kits is an indispensable covid management strategy which also helps strengthens the various attempts made by the authorities as several measures and in turn also supports the covid management. Setting up covid testing centres assists in identifying the covid positive individuals which in turn supports the authorities measures. Urban area air pollution levels add to the city's vulnerable population.

4. Recommendations

The study of the Covid -19 scenario in Indian cities as well as understanding the impacts this pandemic has created on various social, economic, environment and infrastructure subsystems through developing causal loop diagrams reveals how intensely the urban areas are affected. With a series of lockdowns happening and movements curtailed, jobs,

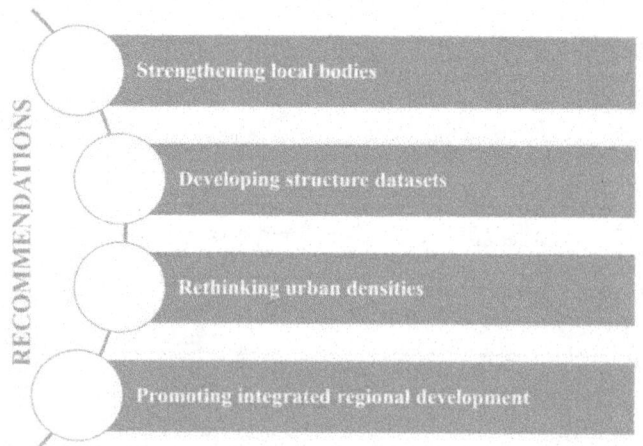

Fig. 39.6 Recommendations for Covid-19 management
Source: Generated by author

services, economy and people's physical and mental health are substantially tumbling. Unpreparedness of the people, especially the economically weaker sections and labour class reveals the social disparity that exists in urban centres. Questions are also raised on the tightly compacted cities having high densities as it leads to rapid spread of the virus. Therefore, we suggest some recommendations in order to ameliorate the covid pandemic disaster management process for our urban centres.

4.1 Strengthening Local Bodies

In order to have effective management of the covid-19 disaster it is extremely crucial to strengthen our local government bodies as they are first hand organisations in power to manage all the resources needed to mitigate the pandemic aftereffects (Afonso, 2021; Chaudhary, n.d.; Shringare & Fernandes, 2020). The incapability of the cities across the globe to deploy assets and execute policies can be reflected by the expeditious spread of the coronavirus and swiftly rising covid positive patients' numbers. Covid largely impacts our health infrastructure, social existence, regions economy and surrounding environments. The swift urbanisation of various services and equipments in the hospitals such as the PPE kits, gloves, medicines and availability of beds requires immediate addressing by the local governments in order to meet those demands. Arranging additional number of beds and scare medicines of covid can be best and timely deliver by the communications of local governments. Even the measures of patrolling for monitoring that the rules of lockdown and movement curtailment are followed is superbly managed by the local government. Municipal bodies being the lowest at the hierarchy are finely aware of the on-ground situations and thus can take effective measures for identifying the vulnerable groups to be catered for incentives programmes.

After the second wave of covid hitting our country, our prime focus is onto making the vaccines available to all our citizens, which requires reaching the best ends of the city and falls into the responsible hands of local governments. A considerate approach needs to be followed with support from the state and central governments, devoting administrative, fiscal and functional power to urban local bodies.

4.2 Developing Structure Datasets

The initial combating techniques, while the covid positive curve was rising in the country involved locating and tracing the covid positive patients by maintaining their datasets. Throughout the first and second wave of coronavirus in the country, it is these datasets which enables us to compute covid cases, recovered and death rates (Azeroual & Schöpfel, 2021). Only with the availability of this data were we able to classify the districts in our country as red, orange and green zones and enforce the movement restrictions accordingly. With the help of these datasets, the coronavirus status amongst distinct administrative wards and zones was recognized and responsive containment plans and strategies were prepared. With the third wave predicted to hit the country in future, vaccination accessibility to all is the critical focus and to decide on the outspreads of it properly digital spatial data of the cities come to astounding use. To improve the capacities of our cities it is crucial to examine digital technologies and their indispensable role in disaster management. Integrated command and control centres, developed under the smart city mission by Government of India were being used during covid times for real time data monitoring which helped us mitigate the covid disaster very well.

4.3 Rethinking Urban Densities

One of the main mitigation measures of covid disaster is social distancing and is widely propagated by the country's administration as 'Do gaz duri, mask hai zaroori' meaning 'two yards distance, mask is important'. The city urban centres have become the epicentres of the Covid-19 disaster, with nearly 65% mortality share of the covid patients is contributed by just four megacities of Maharashtra, Tamil Nadu, Delhi and Karnataka. Characterised by massive densities, commonly rupturing their mass, these cities onset colossal social, economic and environmental damage (Cerami et al., 2021; Kartha & Pathan, n.d.). A catastrophic disaster such as the covid-19 pandemic extends a sizable threat to the people living in their tightly packed mega cities, offering a consummate environment for infections to spread. Thus, it's the appropriate time for us to rethink these urban densities in terms of practising 'optimum population projection' for developing our city development plans. When we plan our city's infrastructure based on current population projection, after the plan period the population continues to outgrow causing excessive densities to settle in urban areas with less facilities available. Efforts to readdress Urban and Regional Development Plans Formulation and Implementation guidelines needs to be made to develop cities with urban densities that are less vulnerable to catastrophes and are more functional, self-contained with integrated land use policies. A well distributed economy leads to equitable sharing of resources and opportunities as well as lessens the burden on the blooming megacities densities attempted policies such as Integrated Development of Small and Medium Towns.

4.4 Promoting Integrated Regional Development

With the rise in covid positive cases in the country an uninformed lockdown was imposed on the country, restricting people's movement and forcing them to stay indoors. Several industries and markets were shut down for months, leaving daily wage workers and migrant labourers helpless. With almost no savings and earnings, they were compelled to leave the megacities back to their homes and with no means of communication people proceeded on foot (Fan, 2021; Gunn et al., 2021; Misra & Gupta, 2021). This largely reflects the existing regional disparity, with economic centres held at megacities and supreme exploitation of rural counterparts. Developing coordination and overcoming complex administrative boundaries requires regionally integrated plans which would bring together several administrative bodies.

5. Conclusion

The covid-19 pandemic has divested cities across the globe and so has it in India. With megacities becoming the epicentre of the spread of the infection and a third wave of coronavirus predicted, it became vital for disaster management authorities and policy makers to work towards making circumstances preferable. System dynamics analysis of the covid-19 reveals the interrelationship between social, economic, environment and infrastructure subsystems and the varied role played by each variable in covid-19 dynamics in cities. Based on this understanding we suggest certain recommendations to reinforce covid-19 disaster management in our cities which largely involve strengthening our local bodies, developing structure datasets, rethinking urban densities and promoting overall integrated regional development. Therefore, we need to reflect upon how well prepared our cities are to confront pandemics of such nature and take the essential steps to prepare our cities in those directions.

References

1. Dhruv Khullar (2021, May 4) 'Inside India's COVID-19 Surge'. https://www.newyorker.com/science/medical-dispatch/inside-indias-covid-19-surge

2. Sharangee Dutta (2021, JUL 19) 'India records 38,164 fresh Covid-19 cases; 499 deaths reported'. https://www.hindustantimes.com/india-news/india-records-38-164-fresh-covid-19- cases-499-deaths-reported-101626665416062.html

3. Antonia Noori Farzan and Claire Parker (2021, April 28) 'How did the covid-19 outbreak in India get so bad?'.https://www.washingtonpost.com/world/2021/04/27/india-covid-surge-faq/

4. FE Online (2021, January 14) 'Covid-19 Vaccine India Update: Arvind Kejriwal's Delhi govt aims to vaccinate 1 lakh people per day'. https://www.financialexpress.com/lifestyle/health/covid-19-vaccine-india-update- coronavirus-vaccine-delhi-update/2170664/

5. Afonso, W. (2021). Planning for the Unknown: Local Government Strategies from the Fiscal Year 2021 Budget Season in Response to the COVID-19 Pandemic. In State and Local Government Review (p. 0160323X2110327). https://doi.org/10.1177/0160323x211032728

6. Aslam, M. K. (2020). INFLUENCE OF COVID-19 AT GLOBAL LEVEL. In COVID-19 Pandemic update 2020 (pp. 192–198). https://doi.org/10.26524/royal.3718

7. Azeroual, O., & Schöpfel, J. (2021). Trustworthy or not? Research data on COVID-19 in data repositories. In Libraries, Digital Information, and COVID (pp. 169–182). https://doi.org/10.1016/b978-0-323-88493-8.00027-6

8. Cerami, C., Popkin-Hall, Z. R., Rapp, T., Tompkins, K., Zhang, H., Muller, M. S., Basham, C., Whittelsey, M., Chhetri, S. B., Smith, J., Litel, C., Lin, K. D., Churiwal, M., Khan, S., Rubinstein, R., Claman, F., Mollan, K., Wohl, D., Premkumar, L., ... Lin, J. T. (2021). Household transmission of SARS-CoV-2 in the United States: living density, viral load, and disproportionate impact on communities of color. Clinical Infectious Diseases: An Official Publication of the Infectious Diseases Society of America. https://doi.org/10.1093/cid/ciab701

9. Chaudhary, D. (n.d.). Post COVID-19 Local Government Under the Federalism in Nepal (Local Government's Experience from Nepal). In SSRN Electronic Journal. https://doi.org/10.2139/ssrn.3853462

10. Covid-19: collateral damage of lockdown in India. (2020). In BMJ (p. m1797). https://doi.org/10.1136/bmj.m1797

11. Coyle, R. G. (1996). Optimization in system dynamics. In System Dynamics Modelling (pp. 236–248). https://doi.org/10.1007/978-1-4899-2935-8_8

12. Fan, B. E. (2021). Migrant workers with COVID-19: Recognizing the crucial role non- governmental organizations perform. The Lancet Regional Health. Western Pacific, 9, 100145.

13. Gunn, V., Somani, R., & Muntaner, C. (2021). Health care workers and migrant health: Pre- and post-COVID-19 considerations for reviewing and expanding the research agenda. Journal of Migration and Health, 4, 100048.

14. Haq, M. N. ul. (2020). IMPACT OF COVID 19 ON THE GLOBAL ECONOMY. In COVID- 19 Pandemic update 2020 (pp. 208–213). https://doi.org/10.26524/royal.37.20

15. Jia, S., Li, Y., & Fang, T. (2021). System dynamics analysis of COVID-19 prevention and control strategies. Environmental

Science and Pollution Research International. https://doi.org/10.1007/s11356-021-15902-2

16. Kartha, M., & Pathan, H. (n.d.). Simulation Study on Effect of Lockdown and Recovery Time on Spread of COVID-19 in High and Low-Density Areas. In SSRN Electronic Journal. https://doi.org/10.2139/ssrn.3572697

17. Li, Y., Luan, S., Li, Y., & Hertwig, R. (2021). Changing emotions in the COVID-19 pandemic: A four-wave longitudinal study in the United States and China. Social Science & Medicine, 285, 114222.

18. Mallya, P. D., & D'Silva, R. (2020). Impact Of Covid – 19 Crisis On The Global Economy And Other Sectors Worldwide. Idea Publishing.

19. Mehta, F. (2021). Covid Chronicles of India. Blue Rose Publishers.

20. Misra, P., & Gupta, J. (2021). Impact of COVID 19 on Indian Migrant Workers: Decoding Twitter Data by Text Mining. The Indian Journal of Labour Economics : The Quarterly Journal of the Indian Society of Labour Economics, 1–17.

21. Mohapatra, P. K. J., Mandal, P., & Bora, M. C. (1994). Introduction to System Dynamics Modeling. Orient Blackswan.

22. Narayanan, S., & Saha, S. (n.d.). Urban food markets and the COVID-19 lockdown in India. https://doi.org/10.31235/osf.io/fdgky

23. Shringare, A., & Fernandes, S. (2020). COVID-19 Pandemic in India Points to Need for a Decentralized Response. In State and Local Government Review (Vol. 52, Issue 3, pp. 195–199). https://doi.org/10.1177/0160323x20984524

24. Singh, G., Professor, A., Department of Chemistry, DDU Gorakhpur University, Gorakhpur, Pradesh, U., & India. (2021). Declining COVID-19 Mortality with the Lockdown in India. In Journal of Communicable Diseases (Vol. 53, Issue 02, pp. 76–81). https://doi.org/10.24321/0019.5138.202129

25. Tak, A., Das, B., & Gahlot, S. (n.d.). COVID-19 and Lockdown in India: Evaluation using Analysis of Covariance. https://doi.org/10.21203/rs.3.rs-170123/v1

26. The Research Unit for Political Economy. (2020). Crisis and Predation: India, COVID-19, and Global Finance. Monthly Review Press.

27. Tutsoy, O., & Polat, A. (2021). Linear and non-linear dynamics of the epidemics: System identification based parametric prediction models for the pandemic outbreaks. ISA Transactions. https://doi.org/10.1016/j.isatra.2021.08,008

28. Zhang, Z., Kong, L., Lin, H., & Zhu, G. (2021). Modeling coupling dynamics between the transmission, intervention of COVID-19 and economic development. Results in Physics, 28, 104632.

CHAPTER 40

Global Pandemic: Need for a Legal Framework

N. Nabila Hoque
Bar-at-Law
Nabila.hoque411@gmail.com

Abstract

The primary objectives of this paper is to present a notion in favour of the need for a legal framework with two important prepositions. Firstly, that unprecedented Global Pandemic can't be measured by the conventional sophistication that goes in the socio-economic system of sovereign nation and secondly the roots of a pandemic expansion & impact cannot be reduced if international disparity exists in the process. The present COVID-19 is not the first, the world witnessed pandemics in past, nations had to deal with them within their own territorial arrangements, without any global legal framework. A global pandemic effects the public health, economy and society of the infected nations without any discrimination however, disparity exists in approach taken to deal with such crises by the nations in lack of international agreements. WHO created, among others, the International Sanitary Regulations-1969 and International Health Regulations-1969 (updated in 2005). However, these or any other legal standings have almost nothing about a pandemic's impact on economy or sharing international responsibility in reducing such economic vulnerability. The novel coronavirus has infected more the 200 counties, the mortality rate is soaring globally placing an huge challenge on existing health care facilities, it has disrupted the global economy, inter and intra-country supply chain is distorted causing stocks to crashed, trades to shrink. People (inland and migrant) around the globe are losing their lost jobs and the world stands at point blank to face, what might be, the worst recession. Infected countries are trying to manage this ugly situation by offering stimulus packages but there exists a glaring disparity. A national policy in not enough to tackle a global pandemic, what the world needs is a uniform global policy, a legal framework. A legal framework that will provide international agreement to prevent, regulate, control, monitor and reduce impacts of global pandemic on human health and economy. The legal framework may framed following the footsteps of other international conventions (e.g. Basel Convention) along with supportive national legislations. The COVID-19 pandemic is presently raging throughout the world creating multidimensional crisis for the society at large, thus it is high time for the international community to come forward to reach an agreement. The same will be structured to: reduce the virus at source and prevent cross boarder spreading; promote & ensure sound health management facilities to face the challenge of pandemic; advocate for workers to obtain subsistence benefit during the crisis period and re-employment in new normal time; make countries diligent to oblige with aid/investment financing; create pressure on importer/exporter, buyer/seller to forgo force majeure during such times and most importantly ensure research & development. Concerned activists groups/agencies should come forward and take initiative to influence the global leaders by raising their voice for such a legal framework.

Keywords: Pandemic, Public Health, Disparity, Uniform Global Policy, Legal Framework

1. Introduction

1.1 Meaning of Global Pandemic

Merriam-Webster dictionary defines pandemic[1] as outbreak of a disease occurring over a wide geographic area and affecting an exceptionally high proportion of the population. Meaning pandemic is the worldwide spread of any disease such as influenza virus or the novel coronavirus disease of 2019 (COVID-19). Dan Epstein, a spokesman for the Pan American Health Organization, a regional office of the World Health Organization went on to mention "A pandemic is basically a global epidemic—an epidemic that spreads to more than one continent". The World Health Organization (WHO) is responsible for declaring as disease as global

---

[1]Martin Downs, MPH, "What Is a Pandemic?", WebMD, https://www.webmd.com/cold-and-flu/features/what-is-pandemic

pandemic occurs. The WHO does this by monitoring outbreaks of a disease and obtaining advice and information from various international health experts[2].

1.2 Brief History of Global Pandemic

Contagious infectious diseases have been a threat to humans from prehistoric days. Any disease taking the form of a pandemic is the vilest of all scenarios. The following are few among the many Pandemics[3] that the world battled till date:

Antonine Plague (165 AD): Also known as the Plague of Galen, this ancient pandemic the spread across Asia Minor, Egypt, Greece, and Italy. Though the actual cause is till date unknown, it is presumed to have been either Smallpox or Measles. The disease spread from the soldiers returning to Rome from Mesopotamia which caused the death of over 5 million people and destroying the Roman army.

Plague of Justinian (541–542): The disease that perhaps lead to the death of half the population of Europe, up to 25 million people, over a mere span of one year. This was the first recorded incident of the Bubonic Plague outbreak, it affected the Byzantine Empire and Mediterranean port cities. It completely destroyed Constantinople, with a mortality rate of an estimated 5,000 people per day.

The Black Death (1346-1353): This plague outbreak devastated Europe, Africa, and Asia killing about 200 million people (estimated). It was presumed to have emerged from Asia, which probably spread across the continents through fleas and rats that were often found in merchant ships. In order resist this wide spread disease sailors were placed in isolation or a *"quarantino"* i.e. origin of the word quarantine.

Third Cholera Pandemic (1852–1860): Often described as the deadliest of all cholera pandemics. Just like the previous ones, this too emerged from India, spreading through the river Ganges across Asia, Europe, North America and Africa taking millions of lives.

Influenza Pandemic (1918): The lethal outbreak of influenza spread across the world, contaminating over 33 percent of the global population and killing 20 – 50 million people. Of the 500 million people infected in the 1918 pandemic, the mortality rate was estimated at 10 to 20 percent with up to 25 million deaths in the first 25 weeks alone.

Coronavirus Pandemic (December 2019-till date): The coronavirus pandemic is the most defining global health crisis of the twenty first century, often consider as the worst challenge for the world since World War- II. The virus that causes COVID is from the family of viruses called "Coronaviridae". In Wuhan, China, an extremely coronavirus began to spread among the people from December 2019, while initially considered as an epidemic in China, the virus has since spread to every continent except Antarctica, the WHO declared Covid-19 a global pandemic in March 2020. COVID-19 is so much more than just a health crisis, it created a devastating social, economic, political and humanitarian crises that is leaving deep scars on the world.

1.3 Learning from Pandemic

Along with the wounds and scars of the pandemics comes few great lessons from pandemics[4] for humans. A list containing the principals and steps that have been picked up from the pandemics. There are four key principles that pandemics taught us:

(a) Roles and responsibilities of health workers. Health workers and caregivers are inevitably on the front line in a pandemic. While they have an ethical obligation to provide safe care, they do so with the knowledge that they bear a high personal risk of infection.

(b) Consequences on trade among nations. The international spread of disease or the threat of its spread reduces commerce with affected areas. Governments must, therefore, attempt to balance two competing goals to prevent infectious disease from crossing their borders while simultaneously minimizing the economic impacts of disease-related restrictions on travel and trade.

(c) Ensuring impartial access to health-care resources. The Constitution of the WHO-1946 defines health as "a state of complete physical, mental and social well-being and not merely the absence of disease or infirmity", it also states that "the enjoyment of the highest attainable standard of health is one of the fundamental rights of every human being without distinction of race, religion, political belief, economic or social condition." Often few epidemics are recurring in nature because the infected population do not have access to adequate vaccines and drugs. Polio was of the similar nature however, Rotary International, the Centers for Disease Control and Prevention (CDC), UNICEF, WHO and international financial partners worked together to change that. They established an example of impartial access to health-care resources by ensuring that Polio vaccine is made readily available for children throughout the globe.

---

[2]Health Direct (2021), "What is a pandemic?" https://www.healthdirect.gov.au/what-is-a-pandemic

[3]MPH Online, "Outbreak: 10 of The Worst Pandemics In History" https://www.mphonline.org/worst-pandemics-in-history/

[4]Institute of Medicine (2007), "Ethical and Legal Considerations in Mitigating Pandemic Disease: Workshop Summary", Washington, DC: The National Academies Press, https://doi.org/10.17226/11917.

(d) Individual rights versus public welfare. Today due to COVID-19, in all public places there it is mandatory to wear masks and people often need to take thermal scans. Individuals with fevers or no masks are taken aside, examined and, at times, prevented from entering said public places. These are examples of instances in which individual rights have been sacrificed in the interest of protecting the public from infectious diseases. Such choices often curb individual rights but are an effective measure for the greater good of public welfare.

Beside the four principles in general the following four key steps are also to be taken during a pandemic situation;

(a) Acknowledgement. Members of a community begin to acknowledge the increasing number of cases and/ or deaths resulting from the outbreak of a particular contagious disease.

(b) Managing Unpredictability. It involves the society creating an intellectual framework to understand the pandemics pattern, rate of infection etc. and marginalizing the threshold of the disease's unpredictability

(c) Public Response. After recognition of a pandemic, the people generally demand collective measure. The history reflects on the importance of developing a resilient consensus among the public, taking into account the different cultures, approach, socio-economic status and political views.

(d) Preparedness. Once a pandemic subdues, life begins to return to its normal patterns, and healthy people begin to place the epidemic in the past. However, it is of crucial importance for the community or government to maintain integrity in its warning methods, preparation and planning, while keeping the general people alert but not alarmed or completely disengaged.

A global pandemic effects the public health, economy and society of the infected nations without any discrimination. Public health comes first consideration for a nation to find the way of saving life. Preparedness is the key to addressing any health crisis so far. Individual nations may try to mitigate the situation with coordinated efforts form the citizens and country's health care experts and professional. But however, disparity exists in approach taken to deal with such crises by the nations in lack of international legal framework.

1.4 Objectives and Methodology

The objectives of the paper is to explore the overall situation and impact of global pandemic and its mitigation measures without having an acceptable legal framework; to identify the global pandemic associated elements either inheritance or exploitation that hampers life and livelihood, international trade business growth and development and wellbeing of the global people; investigate the major challenges of governance associated with mitigating the risks and misery of global pandemic; and finally farming a proposed legal framework for handling pandemic globally in an equal scale. Comprehensive desk-based research has been done mainly on the basis of published literature to understand the global pandemic and the governance in pursing potential public health. However, this is a concept paper inspired and guided, in terms of structure and language, by the Pandemic Influenza Preparedness Framework 2011 (WHO) and The Coronavirus Act 2020 (UK).

2. Impact of a Global Pandemic

Every pandemic has a wide scaled and lasting detrimental socio-economic effect on life and livelihood of the people and COVID-19 has no exception. However, irrespective of nations most effected sectors due to COVID-19 outbreak are:

2.1 Health Care

COVID-19 has led to a histrionic fatality rate around the globe and illustrates an unmatched challenge to public health[5]. The Healthcare sector all over the globe is struggling to cope with the massive blow of imbalance in supply and demand caused by COVID-19. At the initial stage the medical supply chains over the world were in a brittle stage. The closure of the manufacturing sector led to scarcity of medicines, testing kits, and other necessary commodities. The healthcare sector, consisting of numerous doctors, nurses, and all other healthcare workers are risking their lives to fulfil their duty to save lives under these traitorous circumstances. As an addition to their burden, the frontline heroes have also been battling with emotional and physiological distress along accusation of the people[6]. Governments and organizations need to reprioritize long-term healthcare plans at a macro level.

The pandemic has also highlighted the deep rooted structural problems affecting healthcare systems in many countries.

---

[5]Infosys BPM (2020), "The COVID-19 era: A new learning curve for global healthcare", https://www.infosysbpm.com/blogs/healthcare/the- covid-19-era-a-new-learning-curve-for-global-healthcare.html

[6]Hossain, M. J. (2020), "Impact of COVID-19 Pandemic among Health Care Providers in Bangladesh: A Systematic Review", Bangladesh Journal of Infectious Diseases, 7(00), S8-S15. https://doi.org/10.3329/bjid.v7i00.50156

A part of the healthcare system is proper distribution of the vaccine. COVID has the capability of infecting 100 percent of the people however till date only 32.5 percent of the world's population has been fully vaccinated. More than 6.06 billion doses have been administered across 184 countries[7]. The developed countries have vaccinated their population and brought back some sense of normality in their lifestyle. On the other hand there are regions is African countries where vaccine is yet to reach. Covax forecasts that the originally estimated vaccine supply for remaining of 2021 and beginning 2022 has reduced due to[8]: (i) export bans (e.g. India); (ii) challenges in scaling up production (e.g. Johnson & Johnson and AstraZeneca vaccines) and; (iii) delays for other vaccines.

2.2 Human Rights

Almost last 2 years have been disastrous year for human rights worldwide. The pandemic has overturned the society in the same way any other significant any disaster consisting of mass killing would, and to an extent even more[9]. It has given many governments the perfect ploy to take advantage of the vulnerable situation to restrict citizens' rights and authorize emergency legislation with lasting consequences in the long-run. The society does not consider all people as equal, equality in human race is a mere concept, people were not equal before the pandemic, and we have not been equal in the face of it. Everyone might have been stuck in the same storm named COVID-19 but everyone did not have the same boat to survive, while some people had luxurious yachts, many struggled to keep their broken raft from sinking. Those who were poor before it have become poorer; those who were disadvantaged now face even greater disadvantages. The senior citizens have become more vulnerable, not just because of their health risks associated with age, more so due to their social circumstances. Senior citizens living on their own have been further detached from their loved ones and the rest of the community due to the lockdown, national and international travel restrictions etc[10]. As a result of this pandemic the staggering gender inequality was once again brought to everyone's attention. For millions of female employees in various sized economies, in addition to long of earning, unpaid care, domestic work and domestic violence has detonated like a bomb. The society as a whole is facing challenges in these unchartered territory and time, the female population has been dealing with the wrath of this pandemic. It has been predicted that about 11 million girls may never return to school, taking us back to a much increased gender gap in basic education, which in turn will push these girls towards child marriage, teen pregnancy and a steep increase in gender based violence[11].

2.3 Economy

This pandemic has caused detrimental effect on people's income source as a result of untimely deaths, nonattendance of work, reduced productivity leading to negative supply shock, because of worldwide supply chain disruptions and shutdown of factories[12]. On top of the shortage of supply the expenditure pattern of consumers have taken a drastic shift due to lower income. The hardest blow was taken by industries such as tourism, hospitality, transportation and entertainment. The overall financial impact of the pandemic varies between the type of workers, e.g. office workers have shifted to working from home, while in many other sectors workers have such as tourism, retail, transport etc. suffered a substantial decrease in work and income. The continuously spreading disease is likely to continue having negative impact on the aforesaid industries, specifically in developing countries, the financial situation is not likely to gain back its pace in recent future. A developing country like Bangladesh is one of the major remittance recipients, the pandemic has drowned the Bangladeshi migrant workers into uncertainty due to the following: (i) Migrants who lost their jobs abroad and are unable to come home; (ii) Migrants who have been appointed but are unable to travel abroad for the job and;(ii) Migrants who came home but are unable to go back to resume their job. 2020-21 has had enormous negative impact in the world economy, the overall globalization and inter-dependent economies, made it extremely hard and expensive to control spreading of the virus. As history has taught us pandemics are not likely to disappear, they keep cycling back thus proactive

---

[7]Bloomberg (2021), "More Than 6.06 Billion Shots Given: Covid-19 Tracker", https://www.bloomberg.com/graphics/covid-vaccine-tracker- global-distribution/

[8]Mwai, Peter (2021), "Covid-19 Africa: What is happening with vaccine supplies?", BBC, https://www.bbc.com/news/56100076

[9]Mijatović, Dunja (2020), "Human Rights Talk: Covid-19 and Human Rights – Lessons learned from the pandemic", Vienna, Council of Europe Commissioner for Human Rights, https://www.coe.int/en/web/commissioner/-/the-impact-of-covid-19-on-human-rights-and-how-to-move- forward

[10]Mijatović, Dunja (2020), "Human Rights Talk: Covid-19 and Human Rights – Lessons learned from the pandemic", Vienna, Council of Europe Commissioner for Human Rights, https://www.coe.int/en/web/commissioner/-/the-impact-of-covid-19-on-human-rights-and-how-to- move-forward

[11]UN Women (2020), "COVID-19 and its economic toll on women: The story behind the numbers", https://www.unwomen.org/en/news/stories/2020/9/feature-covid-19-economic-impacts-on-women?gclid=CjwKCAjwy7CKBhBMEiwA0Eb7aq9ty6pMT6FNF7bjLXzGi4PZ67QQzTa8_TUH5lhruoZ4d_K2kaq6fxoCLisQAvD_BwE

[12]Pak A, Adegboye OA, Adekunle AI, Rahman KM, McBryde ES and Eisen DP (2020), "Economic Consequences of the COVID-19 Outbreak: the Need for Epidemic Preparedness. Front. Public Health", 8:241. doi: 10.3389/fpubh.2020.00241, https://www.frontiersin.org/articles/10.3389/fpubh.2020.00241/full

international actions are required not only for protection of human lives but also to conserve the economy and thus livelihood of people.

3. Legal Framework

Need for a Legal Framework: The roots of a pandemic expansion & impact cannot be reduced if international disparity exists in the process. It observed that COVID-19 outbreak has broken traditional cohesiveness among the nations as because there is legal framework binding upon. Thus for a Legal Framework can be thought by the international community to re-build the cohesiveness among nations as well to reduce disparity on socio-economic measures that seen in reducing and mitigating global pandemic. A legal Framework[13] will be transparent, in the public domain, binding and enforceable. The mere enactment of a legal framework will not itself lead to an actual response towards the pandemic, nevertheless, it is the stepping stone for ensuring global compliance and a guide for actions to be taken in such unprecedented scenarios. An international legal framework to deal with pandemics will not only hold nations accountable for both the acts and omissions, it will allow the public to be aware of their rights and to some extent responsibilities under such circumstances. All member states willing to participate will be encouraged to plan for pandemics within a legal framework, the principle of sovereignty means that each state will have the absolute discretion to devise its own national legal approach within the broad parameters of the international one. As pandemic governance even by description is alarmed with the administration of cross-border pressures, it is rather imperative that the proposed legal framework supporting governance measures are coherent across all member states for assurance of an effective response. Once a new legal framework come into effect, evaluation its implementation and actual impact on preparedness and response performance can direct further practice and propose required amendments. All these functions require valid data capturing the key attributes of national legislation in a form that can be used by academics, lawyers, health practitioners, policymakers and the general public.

3.2 Proposed Structure of Legal Framework

The following is a proposed international policy for pandemic, prepared in light of the structure and language demonstrated by the Pandemic Influenza Preparedness Framework 2011[14]

and The Coronavirus Act 2020[15]. The concept being that interested countries will sign an international policy that was designed to outline obligations and rights of Member States during a pandemic.

International Pandemic Policy, 2021 (1st Draft)

I. Objective

Thus international policy was designed to outline obligations and rights of Member States for handling pandemic. The Policy will be governed by the Secretariat consisting of one representative from WHO, UN organizations (including Human Rights Council) and Member State. This Policy is also intended to assist the Member States in minimizing the rate and toxicity of the viruses with human pandemic potential and ensure a sound management as closely as possible to its origin Member State.

II. General

1. Member States, through their National Hospitals and Other authorized laboratories, should in a rapid, systematic and timely manner provide biological materials from all cases of contagious viruses with human pandemic potential, as feasible, to the Secretariat approved Reference Laboratory (Laboratory) of the originating Member State.

2. The Laboratory will share genetic sequence data, and analyses arising from that data, relating to contagious viruses with human pandemic potential with all Member States in a rapid, timely and systematic manner.

3. Member States can them request the Secretariat for consultation on the best process for further discussion and resolution of issues relating to viruses with pandemic potential as part of this International Pandemic Policy (Policy).

4. The Secretariat with help of the Member States will put in place in a timely manner a transparent traceability mechanism that uses an electronic system in order to track in real time the movement of virus.

III. Risk assessment and Risk response

1. To ensure that rapid, systematic and timely feedback is provided to originating laboratories and Member States, the Secretariat will also include in the traceability

---

[13]Speakmana, Elizabeth M, Burris, Scott, Coker, Richard (2017), "Pandemic legislation in the European Union: Fit for purpose? The need for a systematic comparison of national laws", Health Policy, https://researchonline.lshtm.ac.uk/id/eprint/4433709/1/Pandemic%20legislation%20in%20the%20European%20 Union_GOLD%20VoR.pdf

14 Pandemic Influenza Preparedness Framework 2011, WHO, https://apps.who.int/gb/pip/pdf_files/pandemic- influenza-preparedness-en.pdf

15 Coronavirus Act 2020, United Kingdom https://www.legislation.gov.uk/ukpga/2020/7/contents

mechanism and associated electronic reporting systems in the summary report of laboratory analyses. Member States will have the option to request any other available information required by the originating laboratory regarding biological materials of the virus.

2. Member States should, working with the Secretariat, contribute to a the pandemic benefit- sharing system and call upon relevant institutions, organizations, and entities, vaccines, diagnostics and pharmaceutical manufacturers and public health researchers to also make appropriate contribution to this system.

3. The Secretariat will coordinate influenza pandemic preparedness and response in accordance with applicable national & international health regulations provisions and this Policy. As regards the benefits outlined in this Policy, the Secretariat should pay particular attention to policies and practices that promote the fair, equitable and transparent allocation of scarce medical resources (including, but not limited to, vaccines, antivirals and diagnostic materials) during pandemics based on public health risk and needs, including the epidemiology of the pandemic. During inter-pandemic periods, the Member State representative in the Secretariat will work with Member States and relevant stakeholders to prepare for the aforementioned role.

IV. Diagnostic reagents and test kits

1. The Laboratories, working with the Secretariat and Member State government, will continue to make available to National Hospitals and Other authorized laboratories, without charge, supplies of noncommercial diagnostic reagents and test kits for the identification and characterization of clinical specimens.

2. The diagnostic manufacturers will be subsidized by the government for concessional and/or preferential rates, supplies of diagnostic reagents and test kits for the identification and characterization of clinical specimens of the virus, if circumstances warrant.

V. Provision for vaccination

1. Pharmaceuticals from each member state will be encouraged to submit a proposal for making an adequate vaccine. The selected pharmaceuticals from each Member State will then complete to prepare the vaccine. The first pharmaceutical to prepare an effective vaccine (authorized by the WHO) will sell the formula to the Member State that have the capacity to purchase and produce the vaccine.

2. All Member States will be able to quote the number of vaccines required for their individual countries, when quoting all immigrant workers, foreign students and tourists (unable to go back home due to the pandemic) will be taken into account along with the citizens.

3. The pharmaceutical companies will prepare vaccine for their home state and also sell to other member state who require them. Member states will have the option to buy the vaccine from any other pharmaceuticals preparing the vaccine, if the locally produced vaccine is not enough or if vaccine is not being locally produced. As all vaccine will be following the same formula and components they will be uniformly priced, within an option for a further concession for under developed/ developing Member States.

4. The vaccine will be distributed to all Member States within the same timeframe, ensuring that adequate quantities of vaccines are made available to developing countries at the same time as to developed countries, on the basis of public health risk and needs. Ideally each member state will receive vaccine for 25% of its quote in phase 1, with the whole distribution process broken down into 4 phases (i.e. 25% of the quote) for ease of distribution and vaccination, unless the situation demands access to more vaccine at the time. The Member States will be encouraged to being a synchronized vaccination campaign for the people in their individual countries.

VI. Capacity building and Stockpiles

1. Upon request, Member States with advanced regulatory capacity should improve and strengthen the work that has been undertaken by Member States with the Secretariat, particularly in developing countries, to strengthen the capacity of regulatory authorities to carry out the necessary measures for the rapid approval of safe and effective vaccines, diagnostics and pharmaceutical products, including products developed from the use biological materials, especially those derived from new subtypes viruses.

2. Member States should make publicly available information on the notification of health regulatory approval of vaccines, diagnostics and pharmaceutical products for viruses with human pandemic potential, including those developed from the use of the biological materials.

3. The Secretariat will continue to work with other multilateral agencies, donors, international philanthropic organizations/entities, private foundations, and other potential partners, including institutions, organizations and entities and in particular influenza vaccine, diagnostic and pharmaceutical manufacturers, to seek commitments for contributions, maintain and further develop a stockpile of antiviral

medicines and associated equipment for use in containment of outbreaks of viruses with human pandemic potential.

4. The Member State Representative from the Secretariat will continue to coordinate with Member States, institutions, organizations and other entities and encourage them to maintain and further develop stockpiles of antiviral medicines and associated equipment for use in containment of outbreaks

5. The WHO members in the Secretariat will continue to seek the guidance of expert advice in determining the size, composition, replenishment, operational use and deployment procedures for use of the antivirals stockpile.

VII. Financing Mechanisms

1. The vaccine, diagnostic and pharmaceutical manufacturers, using the Secretariat, will make an annual partnership contribution to WHO for improving global pandemic response. It is decided that the sum of the annual contributions shall be further defined with specific amounts to be contributed by each company as well as the mechanism for implementation

2. Member States and other stakeholders are encouraged to consider making donations and in-kind contributions to Secretariat for improving global pandemic preparedness and response.

3. The contribution acquired under shall be used for improving pandemic preparedness and response, inter alia, for conducting disease burden studies, strengthening laboratory and surveillance capacity, access and effective deployment of pandemic vaccines and antiviral medicines.

4. The Member States are urged to continue and increase their support to strengthen laboratory and surveillance capacity particularly in developing/under developed Member States by providing adequate financial and technical support.

VIII. Other Obligations of Member States during a Pandemic:

1. Member State shall incorporate this Policy by passing national legislation that gives effect to this Policy in the national legal system.

2. Member States shall ensure that the spreading of virus is reduced to a minimum, taking all required safety measures including but not limited to quarantining infected or potentially infected people, prohibition of events and gatherings, making mask mandatory. The Member State will have the option to fine citizens if for not following the safety measures without a valid reason.

3. Member States will have the option to reappointment of retired health-care workers and recruit volunteers from final year medical and/or nursing school (only for ground and paper work) during a pandemic to tackle the crisis. Member State will provide free treatment and medicines to any all patients, infected by the virus, under the age of 05 and above the age of 50 throughout the tenure of their treatment. If patients suffer from long term medical condition directly as a result of being infected by the virus, Member State will provide subsided medicine and treatment for the patients within the age limit.

4. New measures will be taken by Member State to ensure that the food supply chain is closely monitored to avoid sudden flux in pricing or scarcity of food in rural areas. The member state will also have the option to set up state monitored food markets to ensure the community has access to food and groceries at a controlled price.

5. Trans-boundary movement of goods and commodities (not luxury products) within Member States will be completely export and/or import tax free during the duration of the Pandemic. The Member State exporting said goods and commodities will ensure that all required precaution are taken as per the importing Member States standard for minimum probability of virus transmission, including virus test of the people involved in transportation and/or authenticity of vaccine card with the date base. If the standards are not matched the company exporting will be reprimanded based of the severity of the error, the same will vary from official notification till cancelation of export license.

6. Member State will be encouraged to introduce a 03 months' rent period for all commercial tenants. This option provides a three months' grace period to struggling businesses. For residential rent landlords will not have the right to evict tenants (tenants will retain their right to discontinue tenancy) during a complete lockdown scenario however, the provision does not waive a tenant's liability to pay rent.

7. If any employee is laid-off in the Member State during a pandemic, it will be mandatory for the employer to pay, the said employee 60 (sixty) day's basic wages, in addition to any other payment due as per the national law and employment agreement. If employer intends to employ again any employee, in the same position, within a period of 1 year of such lay-off, the employer shall send a notice the laid-off employee asking him to apply for his old employment, and if he does then he shall be given first preference, and if more than one such retrenched employee apply, preference shall be given on the basis of their merit.

8. If an immigrant employee from a Member State is laid-off another Member State during a pandemic, it will be mandatory for the employer to pay, the said employee 120 (one hundred and twenty) day's basic wages, in addition to any other payment due as per the national law and employment agreement. If the worker is unable to find another job and wants to return to their own country within this 04 months from being laid, the immigrant employee will be sent home free of cost by the Member State. After the expiry of the 04 months period the Member State will be able to charge for their travel expense at 30% (thirty percent) concession.

9. Member State will set up booths for eligible unemployed people i.e. citizens after 02 (two) months of unemployment and legal immigrants after 04 (four) months of unemployment. These booths will register the unemployed workers using the unique number in their identification document e.g. NID, Passport, PAN card etc. and finger print. The Member State will provide them pandemic unemployment allowance every month. The allowance will stop once the unemployed worker gets a job or WHO declares the cessation of the pandemic whichever is earlier. The onus will be on the employer to cross-check the worker national identification number (or other identification number) with the Member States data base and update them as employed once they join said employer. If the employer fails to do the same the Member State will have the authority to retrieve the unemployment benefit paid to the employee during his/her term of being employed from the employer and make employer sign a bond and take note in the database to ensure that the employee is not be laid-off for the same. However, if the employee registered with a fake number or got the job with a forfeited identification document he/she will be barred from receiving pandemic benefit.

10. All educational institutions in the Member State shall remain closed, with option for online learning, till the Laboratory confirms enough people have been vaccinated to ensure heard immunity. In order to encourage parents from urban areas to send their children back to school after the pandemic, to control child labor and child marriage, weekly food & grocery coupons, that can be used in state food markets, will be provided to all students with a minimum of 90% (ninety percent) attendance, save for absence due to illness, in the previous month.

11. National Legislations will be amended in Member States to allow the use of video/audio- enabled hearings without the need for a physical courtroom with all parties taking part in the hearings using telephone or video conferencing facilities.

12. Member state shall have a separate fund in their annual budget for pandemic. The money allocated every fiscal year will be considered as a fixed deposit in the National Bank only to be used during a pandemic for vaccine, state food markets, travel expenses of immigrant workers, pandemic allowance etc.

IX. Miscellaneous

1. *Research and Development:* Each Member State shall invest at least the minimum amount set by the Secretariat, based on the said Member State's last year's GDP, for research and development on a national scale. The goal is to obtain new knowledge that it might use to create new vaccines, medicines, treatment, cure, services, systems etc. for viruses with human pandemic potential while maintaining transparency and access to information among Member States and Secretariat. In addition Secretariat shall actively seek the participation of scientists from virus originating Member States in scientific projects associated with research on clinical specimens and/or viruses from their countries and actively engage them in preparation of manuscripts for presentation and publication for all.

2. *Revision and Amendment:* This Policy sets out the entire and complete understanding between the Member States hereto in relation to the pandemic and supersedes any previous discussions, verbal promises, written or unwritten documents. The policy will be revised every two years within the first quarter. Notwithstanding anything herein, no variation or amendment of this Policy shall be effective unless made in writing and signed by the all the full Secretariat.

X. Dispute Resolution

In the event of any dispute, claim or controversy arising under or relating to this Policy, including any dispute concerning the existence or enforceability hereof ("Dispute"), the Member States shall attempt in the first instance to resolve such Dispute through friendly consultations. If the Dispute is not resolved within 90 (ninety) days of notification of the Dispute by one party to the other, then either party may refer the Dispute to arbitration to be conducted by the Secretariat. The arbitration tribunal shall comprise 3 (three) arbitrators. Member States in dispute shall each appoint 1 (one) arbitrator, and the 2 (two) arbitrators so appointed shall then appoint the third arbitrator, who shall be the chairman of the arbitral tribunal. Decision of the arbitral tribunal shall be final and binding on the parties. The language of the arbitration shall be English. Unless otherwise stated in the decision of the arbitral tribunal, the Member States shall pay the fees of their respective legal counsels and appointed arbitrator and equally share the common costs of the arbitration including venue charges and fees of the third arbitrator.

4. Conclusion

The present COVID-19 is not the first, the world witnessed pandemics in past, nations had to deal with them within their own territorial arrangements, without any global legal framework. A global pandemic effects the public health, economy and society of the infected nations without any discrimination however, disparity exists in approach taken to deal with such crises by the nations in lack of international agreements. Presently the novel coronavirus has been infected more the 200 counties, the mortality rate is soaring globally placing an huge challenge on existing health care facilities, it has disrupted the global economy, inter and intra-country supply chain is distorted causing stocks to crashed, trades to shrink. People around the globe are losing their lost jobs. Infected countries has been trying to manage this ugly situation by offering stimulus packages but there exists a glaring disparity. A national policy in not enough to tackle a global pandemic, what the world needs is a uniform global policy, a legal framework. A legal framework that will provide international agreement to prevent, regulate, control, monitor and reduce impacts of global pandemic on human health and economy. The COVID-19 pandemic is presently raging throughout the world creating multidimensional crisis for the society at large, thus it is high time for the international community to come forward to reach an agreement. The same may be structured to: reduce the virus at source and prevent cross boarder spreading; promote & ensure sound health management facilities to face the challenge of pandemic; advocate for workers to obtain subsistence benefit during the crisis period and re-employment in new normal time; make countries diligent to oblige with aid/investment financing; create pressure on importer/exporter, buyer/seller to forgo force majeure during such times and most importantly ensure research & development. Concerned activists groups/agencies should come forward and take initiative to influence the global leaders by raising their voice for such a legal framework.

REFERENCES

1. Bloomberg (2021), "More Than 6.06 Billion Shots Given: Covid-19 Tracker", https://www.bloomberg.com/graphics/covid-vaccine-tracker-global-distribution/

2. Coronavirus Act 2020, United Kingdom https://www.legislation.gov.uk/ukpga/2020/7/contents

3. Health Direct (2021), "What is a pandemic?" https://www.healthdirect.gov.au/what-is-a- pandemic

4. Hossain, M. J. (2020), "Impact of COVID-19 Pandemic among Health Care Providers in Bangladesh: A Systematic Review", Bangladesh Journal of Infectious Diseases, 7(00), S8- S15. https://doi.org/10.3329/bjid.v7i00.50156

5. Infosys BPM (2020), "The COVID-19 era: A new learning curve for global healthcare", https://www.infosysbpm.com/blogs/healthcare/the-covid-19-era-a-new-learning-curve- for-global-healthcare.html

6. Institute of Medicine (2007), "Ethical and Legal Considerations in Mitigating Pandemic Disease: Workshop Summary", Washington, DC: The National Academies Press, https://doi.org/10.17226/11917.

7. Martin Downs, MPH, "What Is a Pandemic?", WebMD, https://www.webmd.com/cold- and-flu/features/what-is-pandemic

8. Mijatović, Dunja (2020), "Human Rights Talk: Covid-19 and Human Rights – Lessons learned from the pandemic", Vienna, Council of Europe Commissioner for Human Rights, https://www.coe.int/en/web/commissioner/-/the-impact-of-covid-19-on-human-rights- and-how-to-move-forward

9. MPH Online, "Outbreak: 10 of The Worst Pandemics In History" https://www.mphonline.org/worst-pandemics-in-history/

10. Mwai, Peter (2021), "Covid-19 Africa: What is happening with vaccine supplies?", BBC, https://www.bbc.com/news/56100076

11. Pak A, Adegboye OA, Adekunle AI, Rahman KM, McBryde ES and Eisen DP (2020), "Economic Consequences of the COVID-19 Outbreak: the Need for Epidemic Preparedness. Front. Public Health", 8:241. doi: 10.3389/fpubh.2020.00241, https://www.frontiersin.org/articles/10.3389/fpubh.2020.00241/full

12. Pandemic Influenza Preparedness Framework 2011, WHO, https://apps.who.int/gb/pip/pdf_files/pandemic-influenza-preparedness-en.pdf

13. Speakmana, Elizabeth M, Burris, Scott, Coker, Richard (2017), "Pandemic legislation in the European Union: Fit for purpose? The need for a systematic comparison of national laws", Health Policy, https://researchonline.lshtm.ac.uk/id/eprint/4433709/1/Pandemic%20legislation%20in%20the%20European%20Union_GOLD%20VoR.pdf

14. WHO (2021), "International Health Regulations", https://www.who.int/health- topics/international-health-regulations#tab=tab_1

15. UN Women (2020), "COVID-19 and its economic toll on women: The story behind the numbers", https://www.unwomen.org/en/news/stories/2020/9/feature-covid-19-economic-impacts-on-women?gclid=CjwKCAjwy7CKBhBMEiwA0Eb7aq9ty6pMT6FNF7bjLXzGi4PZ67QQzTa8_TUH5lhruoZ4d_K2kaq6fxoCLisQAvD_BwE

CHAPTER 41

Governance for COVID-19 in Bangladesh

Nasim Banu
Pro-Vice Chancellor
Bangladesh Open University
nasimbanu411@yahoo.com

Abstract

Bangladesh is recognised a disaster prone country with high population density. Natural disasters are being intensified in Bangladesh due to global climate change with affecting economic growth and upsetting macro-economic balances. Managing natural disasters, given priority to risk reduction and adaptation, the country has an increasing growing and stable economy with basic healthcare opportunities but however, lack of western standard hospital facilities for all. Bangladesh is now facing un pretended global pandemic COVID-19 from March 2020. This paper presents brief of governance and challenges in combating COVID-19 in Bangladesh in all indicators that pose threat to public health and economy. On the outbreak of COVID-19 in Bangladesh, government has been taken steps like: brought back its citizens from COVID-19 infected countries and quarantined them for 14 days; restricted travel and entry in Bangladesh; suspended on-arrival visa and stopped all international flight; started corona versus testing and confirmed its presence in Bangladesh in 08 March 2020; closed all formal and informal educational institutions from March 17 to 06 August 2020; declared nationwide holiday from 26 march to 30 May 2020 and thus all public and private offices were closed except emergency services; closed public transports, shops, shopping malls, labour ripened works in both formal and informal sectors up to May 2020 except green market, grocery and medicine shops; banned public gathering; asked people to stay home, maintain social distancing and health instructions; emphasised to increase the testing capacity, hospital facilities with more testing kits, ventilator and better oxygen system; earmarked a few hospitals for COVID patient only and expanded other hospitals with COVID unit; imposed sector wise lockdown for a period of 14-21 days. The socio-economic impact of COVID-19 is strongly felt by Bangladesh which caused death of its citizens, shrink the merchandise trade, loss of job of migrant workers that effects the remittance flow and, unemployed huge inland workforce. Under the unprecedented disruption to economy to regain economic activities and minimise sufferings of people government has announced around $11.90 billion, 3.6 per cent of total GDP, stimulus packages for providing capital to the industry, farming, business and trade; payment of wages to RMG workers and; distribution of cash and food grain to the targeted communities etc. The COVID-19 has also broken the classic inter-personal relationships, out of fear in most cases COVID patients are avoided by their near and dear to facilitate care and even in funeral. Experts opine that presence of COVID-19 may prolong in Bangladesh and about 20 million occupational people will lose their source of income. Thus, finding a solution to address the threat of disaster like COVID-19 for socioeconomic risk of recession should have national objective of strategic planning of Bangladesh to ensure that resources used and operations launched to counter pandemic produce best possible results. However, nothing will be enough until people follow the thumb rule of social distancing in combating the situation. So, there should be a comprehensive governance and management program to build the capacity of the country to meet the challenges of COVID-19 situation through saving life and livelihoods; ensuring that existing infrastructure are well maintained and fit-to-purpose; awareness building among the people at large on the consequence of COVID 19; capacity building and strengthening health institutions to enhance treatment facilities and; research and development to ensure the global development thinking on COVID-19.

Keywords: Covid 19, Pandemic, Social distancing, lockdown, Stimulus package, Bangladesh

1. Introduction

Few natural tragedies in the world history have apprehended the global concern as is Covid-19, Novel Coronavirus.

The world had experienced pandemics earlier but no one has occupied international response equal to Covid-19 mobilisation of the World Health Organisation(WHO). China on 31 December 2019, reported to the WHO about a disease of pneumonia with unknown causes that has outbreak in a cluster of people in its Wuhan City of Hubei Province. On 12 January 2020, WHO confirmed that a Novel Coronavirus, the cause of respiratory illness. Within March 2020 the Covid-19, Novel Coronavirus has been transmitted and infected most of the nations of the world with remarkable death toll. The Coronavirus was confirmed that spreading to Bangladesh on 8 March 2020. Bangladesh was born in 1971 through the war of liberation with inadequate health facilities both in quality and quantity. At that time, more than 50 percent of the population was suffering from protein caloric malnutrition which makes people easily vulnerable to infectious diseases like Malaria, Tuberculosis, Small-pox, Cholera etc (GoB, First FYP,1973). Bangladesh is recognised a disaster prone country with high population density. Natural disasters are being intensified in Bangladesh due to global climate change with affecting economic growth and upsetting macro-economic balances. Managing natural disasters, given priority to risk reduction and adaptation, the country has an increasing growing and stable economy with basic opportunities of live and livelihood. Over the time, Bangladesh has made good progress in combating infectious diseases that concerned with MDG-6. Presently 85 percent Bangladeshi people have standard nutritional food and longevity of the people has increased to 70 years (GoB, 7th FYP, 2015). However, Bangladesh has now been facing unprecedented global pandemic Covid-19 with governance challenges in combating Covid-19 which in all indicators pose threat to public health and economy of the country.

Objective and Methodology. The major objectives of the paper is to explore the overall situation of Global Pandemic Covid-19 and their governance issues in Bangladesh. The detailed objectives are to identify the Covid-19 associated health risk of the citizens of the country; its impact of the country's socio-economy; investigate the major challenges of governance associated preparedness and humanitarian measures mitigating Covid-19 risks and misery of the citizen's livelihood and; provided with concluding remarks for sustainable preparedness programs to take in new normal life. Comprehensive desk-based research has been done mainly on the basis of published literature and public policy/strategy actions to understand the Bangladesh stands on Covid-19 governance. Besides this, researcher' day to monitoring and observation of the country's Covid-19 situation has been helped to accomplish this paper.

2. Covid-19 in Bangladesh

2.1. The data is changing every day with adding the number of infected persons as well death toll. Initially, Covid-19 infection was mostly limited within the cities of Bangladesh.

Subsequently, infection was transmitted all over the country particularly in May-June 2021 when Indian type Delta variant migrated to Bangladesh. Covid-19 caused inconveniences and sufferings and become great public health and governance concern for Bangladesh. Government of Bangladesh (GoB) took prompt measures to control the speed of coronavirus by imposing restrictions on movement and shut down all non-essential businesses with very first detection of coronavirus cases on March 2020. But however, this put millions out ofjob.

Bangladesh is hosting more than 01 million Myanmar Rohingya Refugees. They are residing in the camp in a very close proximity i.e. more than 46000 in per sq km, considered one of the densest inhabitation in the earth (UNHCR,2020). Covid regulations particularly social distancing is not at all possible to maintain in the Rohingya camps as they have to share common kitchen, toilets, and corridors; thus their heath have become great concern during Covid-19. In fact, enforcing social distancing and social isolation in thickly populated country like Bangladesh is very difficult. Government took all possible preventive measures in the refugees camp but however, first covid patients was detected in the camp on14 May 2020 (TBS Report, 2020). Like other parts of the country the Rohingya camps were also under the coverage of lockdown and directed prohibitions, but arrival of Myanmar Rohingya refugees could not stoped, still they are arriving in Bangladesh (Kuddus, et.al, 2020).

3. Impact Analysis

In Bangladesh, Covid-19 has spread its adverse effects on public health, economy, education and public behaviour and social relationship. Covid-19 destroyed/disordered the health system of the country; increased Covid-19 infection and mortality; increased poverty, unemployment and food insecurity with less economic activity and loss of livelihood. Covid-19 has triggered mass panic among citizens of Bangladesh and broken the classic inter-personal relationships. In early stage of Covid 19 outbreak in Bangladesh, it was observed that; patients and medical staff fled from hospital after admitting an immigrant patient with flu-like symptom even before the identification of first Covid-19 patient. Out of fear of infection family doctors, clinics and hospitals in residential and remote areas were shut down. In most cases Covid-19 patients were avoided by their near and dear to facilitate care and even in funeral. Panic buying, terror, social stigma and mistrust was highly visible during the lockdown period. Before Covid-19 situation the poverty rate of Bangladesh was 20.5 percent which has raised to 42.0 percent during Covid-19 period; income has decreased of 56.0 percent families who are at marginal level of poverty and they are maintaining their life with earlier savings and decreasing food expenditure; many children of poor families has already been engaged in child labour; drop out rate of students apprehended to raise by 8.0 percent; during corona there happened 13,886 child marriage in 21 districts of Bangladesh among them 50.6 percent are 16-17 years old; 47.7 percent are13-15 years old and 1.7 percent are 10-12 years old (Daily Kalerkantho 2021).

Public Health: Bangladesh is a thickly populated county with about 170 million people.On an average, the country spends less than 5 % of its GDP on health sector. Bangladesh has basic health care opportunities with success story of immunisation program. But on the event of Covid-19 in March 2020 health sector of Bangladesh was adversely effected due to lack of proper information and professional knowledge on global pandemic Covid-19, Coronavirus and; unavailability of proper personnel protective equipment (PPE), masks and hand gloves etc. that required for the health service provider in Covid-19. pandemic situation. Bangladesh experienced 4 percent mortality rate in case of doctors for pandemic Covid-19 when the global statistics was 2.5 percent. According to experts opinion, improper and low quality PPE was the primary cause for such a high mortality rate of doctors in Bangladesh (Corraya, 2020). In March 2020 while Covid-19 attacked Bangladesh had only 6 physicians for every 10,000 people with shortage of about 50.000 health care staff including doctors against sectioned post, 1,169 Intensive Care Unit (ICU) beds among which 432 in public and 737 in private hospitals and 94 laboratories to perform Covid-19 tests in the country.

Table 41.1 The Shortage of Bangladesh Health Care Personnel in March 2020

Name of the Posts	Sanctioned Posts	Held in	Vacancies/ Shortage
Physicians	29,320	17,956	11,364
Nurses & Midwives	42,974	37,106	5,868
DGHS Officials/Staff include Medical Technicians & Pharmacies	111,907	80,354	31,553
Others	1,556	1,236	320
Total	185,757	136,652	49,105

Source: Ministry of Health, GoB

GoB has been in the right process of filling the vacancies of health sector and improving the inadequate infrastructural facilities of the country priority basis to provide service to the nation in prevailing Covid-19 situation.

As on 18 April 2020, the per million covid tests rate was in the country only 124 and thus many were out of tested which caused transmission of Coronavirus in the society. Private hospitals in Bangladesh have larger share that provide services to the patients. But, at early stage of Covid-19, most of the private hospitals were hesitant to treat covid patients for safety of their regular noncovid patients and lack of trained personnel to deal with Covid-19 (Tajmim, 2020). However, GoB had urged and took strong stand for treating covid patients in private hospitals of the country and then well known private hospitals came forward to treat covid patients establishing separate covid unit in their domain.

Economy: Bangladesh has been enjoying stable economy over the years with impressive Gross Domestic Product (GDP) growth. Over the Seventh Five Year Plan period (FY 2016-2020) the expected GDP growth was estimated 7.40 percent and in the first 4 years the average GDP grew by 7.60 percent. In March 2020 global pandemic Covid-19 attacked Bangladesh effecting human lives, health and economic growth and thus, GDP growth pulled down to 7.13 percent (GoB, 8th FYP 2000). Pandemic Covid -19 has swept globe with impact on output and trade because of closing international borders, the scarcity of raw material sources and cancellation of orders which has led to Bangladesh economy at risk. Through trade and financial flows, Bangladesh economy is far more integrated with global economy; thus with slowdown of global economy due to Covid-19, Bangladesh will have greater effect on its export, remittance, GDP growth and employment etc.after the global financial crisis of 2008-09 (GoB, 8th FYP, 2020).

Readymade Garments Industry (RMG) of Bangladesh is the sector where work about 4 million low income people includes 85 percent women and almost similar number of people indirectly depend on RMG value chain (Dhaka Tribune 2020a). RMG products alone cover 83 percent of the country's export. Nearly USD 3 billion worth of work-orders have been cancelled during Covid-19 that affected about 4 million people directly involved in this industry (Paul, 2020). Many RMG workers have lost their jobs and did not get their previous month salary. A study found that Bangladesh RMG sector has experienced: (i) order cancellations and re-negotiations by buyers during the early stage Pandemic Covid-19; (ii) In compared to 2019, On average, almost 17.4 percent revenue has declined of BGMEA member factories in 2020; (iii) In to pre-Covid-19 levels, 7.4 percent employment has declined by in the second half of 2020; (iv) Covid-19 caused some factories to delay or to decrease planned investment, including in increasing automation; (v) in case of health, On average, the workers of 3.6 percent RMG factories experienced with symptoms of or tested of Covid-19 positive in-between late 2020 to early 2021 (Laura et al., 2021). During lockdown for Covid-19, agricultural farming of Bangladesh has greatly affected as because access to agricultural products, materials, markets and advisory services was restricted. The prices of basic commodities has increased at a noticeable rate because of hampering production and distortion of supply chain. The agricultural products in the urban areas were sold at a high price, while the marginal farmers deprived of getting the fair price in the areas where the product grow. Due to lockdown transport of animal, poultry and fish feed were hampered and value chain of perishable items are disrupted which has led the producers to shut down production in many cases. Lockdown with quarantine measures led to slowdown agricultural processing, trade and impaired production activities and lowered consumer demand, particularly for limited hotel, restaurant and coffee shop operations (Assaubayeva et al., 2020). Moreover, he country's fish and dairy farmers are now bearing their brunt. Crab, shrimp, and fish farmers faced export restrictions caused major economic losses. Exports from Bangladesh constitute more than 70% of crabs in the Chinese market. The export ban in China is a big setback for the crab industry (Roy, 2020). All this was the likely cause of hampering food production and crop supply chain and landing the country in a famine situation. To protect the country from probable famine and save farmers' economy, GoB has announced a few stimulus packages for them with 2 percent agricultural loan for continuing agricultural production and cropping. The Covid-19 intensifies numerous socio-economic crises like joblessness, consumption of reserve funds, and shrinking of the country!s remittance inflow. There are 13 million Bangladeshi migrants workers play significant role in Bangladesh economy through remitting about 15 million USD in a year. Due to Covid-19 Bangladeshi migrants workers affected along with their 30 million dependants at home. Covid-19 caused for unemployment of Bangladeshi migrant workers, short working hours which led them to poor quality life and limited their cash flow to their families (Karim et al., 2020). On the other hand, remittance is one of the greatest sources of economy of this country. Most of the migrant Bangladeshi workers have to return from abroad and thus their source of income has already reduced to a great extent. In Covid-19 situation except few top, pharmaceuticals companies of the country have been struggling as most drugs, other than few clod and fever related drugs, export and internal selling is reduced (Noyon AU, 2020). Due to global restriction and nationwide lockdown the airline industry has made considerable loss with cancellation of international and domestic flight. According to the International Air Transport Association (IATA), revenue loss of this sector may become USD 252,000,000 due to the outbreak of Covid-19 (Deb et al., 20120). According to Tour Operators Association of

Bangladesh (TOAB) its members incurred losses of Tk 57 billion within the sixth months of global pandemic Covid 19 outbreak while Pacific Asia Travel Association (PATA) has recorded losses of almost TK 180 billion (Dhaka Tribune 2020) this year due to the pandemic. The members of the association have been supporting each other in different ways since the pandemic broke out. Due to the economic setback, it may likely, the poverty rate in Bangladesh will increase from 20.5 percent to 40.9 percent if Covid-19 leads to a 25 percent decrease in family income. Consequently, the successes over the past two decades in alleviating poverty can fizzle out (Ahmed, 2020).

To save life, according WHO prescription, Bangladesh has also been followed the path of lockdown and social distancing measures to restrict the expansion of coronavirus infections in the country. Thus, the wheel of economy has turned into almost still, livelihood is hampered. The product and services of the manufacturing industries, poultry and dairy farm, markets, shopping centres, etc are seriously affected under the governance measures like lockdown and social distancing. However, to reshape economy of the country and to ensure livelihood means for the citizens government has declared stimulus packages for various sectors of economy including supply food and other essentials to the citizens of need particularly under privileged citizens. Recently, the government has relaxed lockdown to some extend and allowed manufacturing industries, poultry and dairy farm, markets, shopping centres, etc to run their business but however, maintaining social and physical distancing along with all other rules and restrictions of health and sanitation to stop coronavirus transmission in the community. It is not so easy, rather too difficult to monitor and control people's behaviour in case of following imposed covid instructions and restrictions. So there is a great challenge continuously running most of the mills, factories shop and markets unless or until the Covid-19 situation is over. However, the GoB is trying to keep running the economy of the country.

Education: Government of Bangladesh has declared close both formal and informal all educational institutions without any exception Bangladesh in 17 March 2020 as part of preventive measures to restrict the spread of coronavirus Covid-19. Since then, students of all levels are being compelled to stay at home to maintain social distancing and keeping them safe form coronavirus. The closure of educational institutions has observed as an effective strategy for breaking the critical transmission chain during the pandemic like Covid-19 (Luca at el., 2018) However, it has negative impact on student's, specially underprivileged/disadvantaged students, academic study include interruption in learning and disruption in assessment (UNSECO, 2020a). Over 60 percent of the student form world are adversely affected with nationwide closure of educational institutions on the event of Covid-19 (UNESCO, 2020b). Covid-19 situation is not still under control in Bangladesh thus, considering the health issue the educational institutions can not be reopened. Therefore, many schedule internal and public assessments related examinations have to postponed or canceled. The delay in re-opening educational institutions may have negatively affect student's mental state and academic growth (Chandasiri, 2020); forced them long-time quarantine at home caused disturbance and deterioration in study habits and performance of work, that eventually resulted in growing stress and dysfunctional learning behaviour (Men et al., 2020). A study revealed that at undergraduate level 57.5 percent students are mentally stressed; 30.2 percent are having anxiety, and 58.8 percent are suffering from depression (Banna, et.al, 2020). The tertiary-level students are heavily affected, by pandemic Covid-19. They become: socially aloof as no meeting with friends and relatives (Cao et al., 2020) ; financially harder condition as losing of part-time jobs; emotionally sick as increasing frustration, anxiety and boredom (Brooks et al., 2020) and; academically uncertain situation as growing worried about future education and career (Cao et al., 2020). In Bangladesh, there are over 5000 tertiary educational institutions having four million students (Ahmed, 2020). With an aim to diminish the disruptions in tertiary education of the country, government has taken program to vaccinate the all the students of above 18 on priority basis but due to shortage of enough vaccine the program is still yet to be completed. As a measure to keep the student in touch with educational learning process government announced on-line classes and assignment basis assessment. The University Grant Commission (UGC) has provided with loan to university students to buy laptop/smart phone as helping staff for on-line classes. Even though due to lack of resources, low speed internet and some of their mental instability could not avail the facility/opportunity of on-line classes (Islam, et.al, 2020). However, research finding is that students are uncomfortable and distressed by online learning strategy (Al-Tammemi et al., 2020). Students faced challenges in switching to online lectures, adjusting in new online assessment methods and workloads, communicating with teachers, and dealing with many online education issues like unavailability of electronic devices, weak or no internet access, high cost of internet, etc. (Owusu-Fordjour et al., 2020). In a word, Bangladesh's education sector has really been passing through a long term disaster. UNISEF in its report mentioned that more than 40 million students of Bangladesh from primary to higher education are adversely effected due to prolong Covid-19 situation and thus urged for immediate re-opening of educational institutions of the country. UNISEF also opined that so long the children will be out of school, the risk of child labour, child marriage and violence among children will increase and the possibility of returning school will decrease (Kalerkantho, 2021). However Government of Bangladesh has re-opened the educational institutions for classes I-XII on 12 September 2021 and asked the universities to take decisions accordingly at their convenience. The Universities have decided to re-open from 5 October 2021.

Children: All the educational institutions of Bangladesh was closed from 17 March 2020 to 11 September 2021 with an intension save the educational children from the averse effect of Covid-19 and its transmission as well. More so, government has declared time to time nationwide/area wise lockdown and followed social distancing as a tool to curve infection of Covid-19 in the country. Thus, the children had to stay at home and the educational children was touched with online academic activities. In this situation the children had less opportunity to interact with their peers and physical activities. (Jiao et al., 2020) and hence, they had been suffering from anxiety, sleeping disorder, stress and depression like health hazards (Ramchandani 2020; Rawstrone 2020 104). A study found that among the Bangladeshi children 30.5 percent had mild, 19.3 percent moderate, and 7.2 percent severe level of mental disturbances during Covid-19 (Yeasmin et al., 2020). Due to Covid-19, the children of Bangladesh are in a sort of traumatic condition for which they need proper behaviour and mental treatment, suitable opportunities for physical and academic activities in order to grow up as fit citizen to led Bangladesh in future.

Household Income: The COVID-19 has had an adverse impact on different sectors of Bangladesh putting millions of working people out of job with declined the average household income by 20 percent. However, the unemployment rate bring down with the resumption of economic activities in new normal situation. According to a survey of Bangladesh Bureau of Statistics: (i) the average monthly income of each household was BDT 19,425 in March 2020 that came down to BDT 15,492 in August 2020 (ii) the average expenditures of a family were Tk 15,403 in March 2020 that came down to Tk 14,119 in August 2020 i.e. household expenditure come down by 6.14 percent during the period (iii) some 68.39 percent of the families went through financial crisis among which 21.33 percent with monthly income BDT 20,000 or less received government reliefs and assistance during April -July 2020 (iv) the country had 08 percent day labourers in March 2020 that came down to 4 percent in July 2020 but, again raised to 7.5 percent in September 2020 (v) there were 17 percent businessmen in the country in March 2020 that came down to 10 percent in July 2020 but, again raised to 17 percent in September 2020 in the new normal situation (vi) the agriculture sector of the country had not been much affected in between March-July 2020, due to the outbreak of Covid-19 but, the agriculture-dependent households remained unchanged at 10 percent (Prathom Also 2020).

Fraudulent: Covid-19 outbreak and its spreading effected almost all crucial sectors of Bangladesh including public health, economy education social values. To provide covid test services few health organisations have emerged in the country who issued false results. This fraudulent activity put the victims in danger both in getting proper treatment and going abroad for business and works as many counties imposed journey restriction of Bangladeshi citizens because unreliability of covid tests. Due to Covid-19 there created a huge demand for coronavirus certificate among the Bangladeshi migrant workers to get back their host countries. In this situation a hospital owner of Bangladesh sold huge number of certificates with negative Covid-19 test results without performing any tests of the concerned. However this hospital owner was arrested for his unholy business. In another case two doctors were engaged in selling fake corona test results from their labs; they are also arrested by law enforcing agency of the country. On the other hand, few ecommerce business organisations grew up during period and attracted people to deliver goods at home in a chipper prize but ultimately betrayed with customer taking advance money. However, all of them are in custody for being judicial trail. All these fraudulent activities were huge blow to the image of Bangladesh.

Bangladesh is a disaster resilient country. Taking proper governance measure to curb the spread of Covid-19 with lifting restrictions on movement and withdrawn lockdown for free choice of livelihood in the new normal condition, Bangladesh will be able to overcome the shocks of Covid-19 within its limited scope and financial capacity but however with international community support/assistance.

4. Governance Issues

The population density of Bangladesh is very high in comparison to other developed countries. Thus, Covid-19 pandemic has posed great threat to the life and livelihood of the citizens of Bangladesh, its economy and development. Covid-19 transmission in the community and death tolls are the burning issues of Bangladesh like other countries of the world. In this situation GoB has been working as part of governance strategies to: increase response and recovery plan/program to strengthen health facilities; improve resource allocation for relief and stimulus package; promote agriculture and manufacturing industry to ensure food security and livelihood; ensure positive and effective risk communication towards citizens of the country and; liaison with international community for financial/technical/information sharing to boost economy and development

targets. GoB, as its governance strategies, has been taken many initiatives with its ability and capacity to curb and control coronavirus transmission in the community at the very early stage when it was emerged in Wuhan city in China. The initiatives are: (i) evacuation of Bangladeshi citizens form Covid-19 affected countries (ii) imposing travel and entry restrictions (iii) taking social distancing measures (iv) fighting disinformation (v) shutting down of educational institutions (vi) restrictions and stopping the movement of mass vehicles (vii) imposing lockdown (viii) ensuring Covid-19 testing facilities (ix) arranging Covid-19 treatment (x) creating nationwide awareness building about Covid-19 symptoms (xi) tracing of returnees from abroad to ensure their home quarantine (xii) deploying of army in aid to cvil administration to enforce lockdown (xiii) providing reliefs goods to needy and jobless due to lockdown (xix) announcing stimulus package for the various sectors of economy (xx) providing food items to the citizens with reduced price (xxi) driving mobile court to maintain the stability of market price (xxii) asking the moneyed/riches men to help the poor in Covid-19 crisis (Islam et al., 2020).

Imposed Measures: In line with said initiatives Government of Bangladesh (GoB): (i) cautioned the airport authorities on 22 January 2020 for screening travellers from China; (ii) evacuated and brought back of its 312 citizens from Wuhan, China in special flight attending with physicians, nurse and medical equipment 01 February 2020 and they were quarantined for 14 days at Haji Camp very near to Dhaka airport but, none of them were tested covid-19 positive; (iii) instructed Dhaka airport (Hazrat Shahjalal International Airport) authority to introduce thermal scanner tarting on 22 January 2020 to scan the passengers coming form China to detect corona infections; (iv) suspended on-arrival visa for Chinese visitors on 2 February 2020 (35) and, asked Chittagong Port Authority to examine all the sailors of the ships coming from East Asian countries as a preventive measure to the spread of coronavirus; (v) closed all the educational institutions of the country on 17 March 2020 for reminder period of the month while confirmed 8 Covid-19 patients in the country; (vi) declared on 23 March 2020 a ten-day nationwide public holiday from 26 March to 4 April 2020, while 33 Covid-19 patients were confirmed in the country, with closing public and private offices excepting public emergency services, pharmacy and green markets to curve the community transmission of coronavirus asking people to stay at home and maintain social distancing; (vii) imposed a complete lockdown until the situation improves over the Cox's Bazar District on 9 April 2020 where the majority of the Myanmar Rohingya refuge camps are located. With the announcement of nation wide holiday sparked by Covid-19 led to left Dhaka about 10 million people includes rickshaw pullers, day labourers, factory workers, maids and others for their village home which immediately threatened millions of livelihoods in the country. Army was deployed as an aid to civil administration in addition to regular law enforcing agency to enforce social distancing as well as awareness building among the people. Maintain social distancing in a thickly populated country like Bangladesh is a great challenge and almost impossible where most people live in a close proximity sharing common kitchen, toilets, and corridors (Ahmed et al., 2020). It has been found a significant obstacle against social distancing while the garments industry (RMG) that earned USD 29 billion in 2017 (BGMEA, 2020) was partially kept outside from lockdown for livelihood of particular class of people and export earning. However, there are challenges in implementation of the WHO recommended social distancing in congested regions, especially in marginal communities (Topader, 2020).

Stimulus Package: Government of Bangladesh (GoB) has so far allocated 15.4 billion USD under stimulus packages for various sectors of the country to rebound the economic activities and productions and; minimise the suffering of citizens that arises out of Covid-19 impact. Among which 166 million USD has disbursed so far to 4.4 million beneficiaries, including poor elderly, widows, disabled persons, and informal sector workers. The total package was 3.6 percent of country's GDP that aimed for: (i) providing working capital facility to the affected industries and services sector organisations; (ii) supplying working capital to the cottage, small and medium industrial enterprises; (iii) providing special fund for the export-oriented industries; (iv) expanding the facilities of Export Development Fund (EDF) that introduced by Bangladesh Bank; (v)incentive packages for Pre-Shipment Credit Refinance Scheme; (vi) special honourarium for doctors, nurses and health worker's; (vii) health and life insurance of medical services personnel; (viii) agriculture refinancing scheme and agriculture subsidy; (ix) refinancing scheme for the low-income professional farmers and small businessmen; (x) selling rice at BDT 10 per kg to the poor and low income group citizens; (xi) distributing cash among the target-based communities; (xii)incentive packages for expanding the coverage of allowance programme; (xiii) building houses for the homeless people; (xiv) purchase operation of 200,000 metric tonnes Boro rice/paddy and; (xv) mechanisation of agriculture works; (xvi) free distribution of food materials; (xvii) financial assistance to the qaumi madrasa students and teachers in two phases and imams and muazzin of the mosques; (xviii) allocation to Palli Sanchay Bank, Probsahi Kalyan Bank and Palli Karma Sahayak Foundation to help the youths and expatriates who has lost jobs due to Pandemic Covid-19 (xix) making arrangements for supplying combined harvesters and reapers at subsidised prices (xx) providing loan for the farmers at 4 percent interest

to offset the agriculture fallout of COVID-19. Prime Minister of Bangladesh Sheikh Hasina has made an announcement that all the government launched programmes to help the people affected badly in the wake of the COVID-19 outbreak will continue until the present crisis is over.

Health Care: GoB has expanded to 800 laboratories where Covid test facilities are available now and 53 approved RT-PCR Laboratories. There are 12,347 general and 1,092 ICU beds available in pubic hospitals for Covid-19 patients (Dhaka Tribune Report, 2021). To met the demand and serve the nation in Covid-19 crisis, GoB appointed 2,000 assistant surgeons (doctors) and 5,054 nurses on emergency basis. But still there were about shortage of 50.000 physicians, nurses, medical technicians, and other relevant health workers (Mamun, 2020). GoB made arrangement for Covid-19 patients treatment in all public hospitals of the country and earmarked 3 hospitals, established a new hospital and a filed hospital at Dhaka for exclusive treatment of Covid patients.

Vaccination: Pandemic Covid-19 has caused a devastating impact worldwide as there was no vaccine against coronavirus or limited drugs available to combat this pandemic. However the vaccines have invented and approved by WHO like Oxford-AstraZeneca, Moderna, Phizer and, Sionphram etc. Serum Institute of India has come forward as in one of the producer and merchandiser of Oxford-AstraZeneca vaccine. At the first opportunity Government of Bangladesh through Beximco Pharma a renowned pharmaceuticals manufacturing of Bangladesh, came to agreement on 5 November 2020 with Serum Institute of India to import 30 million doses AstraZeneca vaccine. Bangladesh paid in advance for 15 million doses (The Daily Star, 2021). On 25 January Bangladesh received 5 million doses vaccine from Serum Institute of India under contract and 2 million doses as gift from Indian government (Dhaka Tribune, 202 1).Receiving these 7 million doses vaccine from India, Bangladesh initiated nation-wide vaccination activities from 7 February 2021 targeting 80% population to be vaccinated within 6 months (Reuters, 2021). Bangladesh was to supposed get 5 million doses vaccine per month from Serum Institute of India but however, as yet they supplied only 7 million doses and another 3.2 million was received by Bangladesh as a gift from Indian government before March 2021. As India stoped exporting AstraZeneca vaccine, Bangladesh had to suspended its first dosing vaccination program form 26 April 2021 and looked for alternative sources. But uncertainty was there for second dose to 1.3 million people who had AstraZeneca vaccine as first dose. Later the uncertainty has mitigated receiving AstraZeneca vaccine from Japan under COVAX. Bangladesh also received Moderna, and Pfizer–BioNTech vaccine from USA and Sionpharm from China. As on 21 September 2021, Bangladesh administered 37,400,947 vaccine which about 11.5 percent of the country's population.As a part of vaccine governance GoB had launched an online registration portal prior to initiated vaccination activities inviting the citizens of age 55 or above using their NID number. Eventually registration was open for the citizens of age 40, then 35, then 30 in-between from 5-19 July 2021. Now registration age is lower-down to 18. Now the government has a plan to vaccinate the school going children of 12-17 years very soon with Pfizer–BioNTech.

The success of vaccination governance in Bangladesh is entirely depend on import-supply, in the present situation which seems not very smooth. On 16 August 2021 The government has signed a trilateral memorandum of understanding (MoU) for bottling, labelling and dispensing Sinopharm's Covid-19 vaccine in Bangladesh. Under the MoU, local vaccine producer, Incepta Vaccines Ltd, will dispense five million doses of Sinopharm vaccine each month from its plant in Dhaka. GoB will purchase necessary vaccine doses produced here at a cheaper rate, hopefully within 3-4 months Incepta Vaccines Ltd, will be able to marketing vaccines and thus administering of vaccine in Bangladesh will get desired shape. On 23 September2021, the Prime Minister Sheik Hasina made the call in her prerecorded speech for the "White House Global Covid-19 Summit" that "For effective global vaccination, Covid-19 vaccines need to be declared as 'global public good'. To guarantee universal access, local production of vaccines by the developing countries and LDCs that have the capacity must be allowed,"

Digitalisation: Virtual technology is considered one of the most effective governance tool to control coronavirus transmission in the community. GoB has been pursuing virtual technology with its limited digital capacity since March 2020 when the Covid-19 outbreak in Bangladesh. Virtual technology has been extending critical role against fighting Covid-19. It is found beneficial for exploring telemedicine, planning, treatment and curving coronavirus infections in the community particularly of remote areas of the country with awareness building to the citizens and; helping to improve surveillance systems in Covid-19 crisis situation through live video streaming. Telemedicine, video streaming, virtual conference, virtual court, virtual class room, online educating etc are being used in Bangladesh to maintain social and physical distancing to control Covid-18 transmission across the country (Islam et al., 2000). Using virtual technology GoB and social media of the country has been creating awareness among the citizens regarding the effect and impact of Covid-19; measures that need to be followed for controlling coronavirus transmission and; social responsibility. GoB produced some videos for the country men on activities that citizens should do and or avoid to be safe from Covid-19 transmission. Almost all of the government and even NGOs have been commencing their business with virtual technology with increase of Covid-19 transmission.

Judiciary of Bangladesh arranged virtual court; Ministry of Education has encouraged the educational institution with logistic support to continue to their academic activities and; Heath Directorate and IEDCR, Ministry Health and Except the, above, with the increasing of corona virus (COVID-19) has been regularly meeting the press with Covid-19 update, research and development through virtual means. Through often video conference with local level administration and other responsible persons/organisations Honourable Prime Minister of Bangladesh Sheikh Hasina is closely observing the Covid-19 pandemic situation and the exception status of measures and initiatives taken by government to get rid of Covid-19. Bangladesh is digitally increasing but still there are short of technological infrastructure and financial constraint; many migrant slum dwellers and marginal level people have lack of skill to operate and affordability to get virtual device.

Supporting Governance: The Government of Bangladesh (GoB) responded fast with its limited resource and technical ability to curb the spreading of Covid-19 with taking public health measures; helping programs to poor and vulnerable households with cash and food and; providing stimulus package for firms to sustain employment in key sectors of economy of the country. Private sector of the country and World Bank has come forward to support GoB for strengthening its national arrangements for public health emergency services and livelihood. Some NGOs, businessmen, politicians as well as social workers in Bangladesh have come forward to provide foods and other aids to the poor and workless people during the lockdown. A business hub Bashundhara Group was built 200 bedded field hospital at their coast and provided mask and PPE for health workers, doctors dealing Covid-19 patient's treatment in collaboration with GoB. Besides many other businessmen, private financial and non-financial organisations were also found to provide donation to Prime Minister's special fund for Covid-19 management in Bangladesh

The World Bank has come forward (World Bank 2020), within 21 days of first detection of covid-19 patient in Bangladesh, with a project titled "Covid-19 Emergency Response and Pandemic Preparedness Project" amounting 100 million USD to help Bangladesh in detecting, managing and treating suspected and confirmed Covid-19 cases includes: benefiting Bangladeshi people with medical and testing facilities and national health system; equipping designated laboratories with equipments, testing kits, reagents and trained staff; (iii) delivering medical support for meeting increase demanding services required to handle and curve Covid-19 pandemic; mobilising services to ensure faster procurement action to buy critical items for Covid-19 detection, prevention and recovery and; supporting screening designated health facilities and entry points in Bangladesh.

The world bank has also approved another few projects amounting 1.745 billion USD for Bangladesh to help create quality employment, services and immediate economic recovery form global Pandemic like Covid-19 with building national resilience for future. The projects include: to help Bangladesh to come back from the impact of Covid-19 with attracting 2 billion USD direct private investment and creating 1,50,000 jobs; to support GoB response to Covid-19 crisis with helping recovery and building resiliency of economy as well as workers and vulnerable populations; to establish an integrated cloud computing digital platform that enable the government to operate virtually and deliver critical public services to citizens and businesses and; to help recover from the economic impacts of COVID 19 with providing immediate social protection and livelihoods support to the rural poor by engaging them in labor-intensive civil works.

More so, on 14 April 2021 the World Bank and GoB signed three financial agreements amounting 1.04 million USD to build resilience to future crises, including vaccination against COVID-19 and acceleration economic recovery of Bangladesh

5. Concluding Remarks

Covid-19 situation in Bangladesh is rapidly evolving, most nations in this situation prefer for a total lockdown to save life first with high financial costs. But the country like Bangladesh can not effort such lockdown as its huge population lives on hand to mouth with no savings and unsecure livelihood. Thus. GoB need to be consider the issue of life and livelihood both equally in taking measures like complete lockdown to curve the community transmission of coronavirus. Lockdown is no doubt one of the effective measure to restrict/control community transmission of Covid-19 but not the effective therapy to mitigate Covid-19. Under the present knowledge and understanding vaccination is so far the best measures to safe life and GoB should give priority to vaccinate its citizens along with children as per WHO's guideline. Along with vaccination program, the preventive measures for Covid-19, like tracing of cases and contacts with immediate expansion of testing labs and ensuring enough testing kits; awareness building among the citizens to promote good hand hygiene practices, and follow strict quarantine. As health care staffs are proportionately inadequate for serving about 170 million population of the country thus, students of life science departments of universities may be be trained to carry out Covid-19 test immediately transforming their labs fit to covid-19 test labs. GoB should come forward to ensure the access of marginal population to proper hygiene facilities as well as vaccination program; supply of PPE for doctors and related health care worker.

Ethnic community, low-income/no-income families, people with disabilities, returnee migrant workers, informal and low wage earners such as daily women headed household, transgender and sex worker and tea plantation workers of the country has been at risk due the Covid-19 outbreak and thus they need extensive humanitarian aid. GoB should strengthen its aid program and world community may asked to come forward in helping them. About 7 percent Bangladeshi population are senior citizens (UN 2020) vulnerable to Covid-19. It is seen that these senior citizens require hospitalisation and intensive care while contracting Covid-19, they may require. So GoB should arrange ICU beds ventilation supports at least in every public hospitals in the country. As a riverine country, Bangladesh may think to arrange for mobile healthcare facilities for covid tests using water vehicles for the people of remote areas. Fear and anxiety about the pandemic are causing overwhelming stress for everyone (Xaio et al., 2020). mixed messages piles up the stress while the real facts and understanding reduces the stress. GoB should use political leaders, social activists, print and electronic media and religious leaders particularly Imam of Mosques to dissemination of factual scientific information on Covid-19 among the mass population of Bangladesh in the crisis situation like Covid-19. Dissemination of Covid-19-related basic knowledge among marginal people would be the key to controlling the spread of the coronavirus (Zhong et al., 2020).

Bangladesh need definite source of fund for restoration of livelihood that effected by Covid-19 as well as to help its marginal people, and hosted Rohingya refugees. The World Bank has come forward to support Bangladesh with projects, in mitigating the Covid-19 effect. Individuals, business houses effort of the country and government stimulus package has supported citizens in fighting Covid-19 crisis situation. But these are not enough to the actual need (Dhaka Tribune 2020 ; World Bank 2020). So, immediate international help is required for Bangladesh to rebuilt livelihood for the citizens and resilience. However, GoB may think to save money for fighting with Covid-19 crisis, postponing the less important development works and projects for the time being swell as making effort through diplomatic channel to fid foreign source of fund as for its national interest.

Covid-19 pandemics cause public health, economic, and social impute in Bangladesh. Thus, to fight with this pandemic crisis requires national tasks and global partnership. Awareness need to be build up among the public to protect themselves by abiding health guideline, maintaining hygiene and social distancing and avoiding with crowded places and gathering. From GoB side coordinated and effective planning and strategies are required for both the ongoing preparedness and afterwards recovery program to manage this pandemic

Covid-19 and take into new normal life. However there is no alternative except but, strengthen the health care facilities and preparedness for the humanitarian support to be reached the targeted vulnerable communities which immediately need to be outlined. Considering economic implications of Covid-19 based on the vulnerabilities GoB should incorporated in mid term Five Year Plan and long term Perspective Plan. Without strong national strategic planning and multi-sectoral collaboration including supports from the private sectors of the country and international community, sustainable recovery from global pandemic likeCovid-19 may not be possible.

REFERENCES

1. Ahmed HU. Economic ramifications of Covid-19 in Bangladesh. The Financial Express, 2020 May07.
2. Ahmed N, Rony RJ, Zaman KT. Social Distancing Challenges for Marginal Communities during COVID-19 Pandemic in Bangladesh. J of Biomed Analytics. 2020 May 21;3(2): 5–14. https://doi.org/10.30577/jba.v3i2.45
3. Ahmed, M. (2020). Tertiary Education during Covid-19 and Beyond. The Daily Star. https:// www.thedailystar.net/opinion/news/tertiary-education-during-covid-19-and-beyond-1897321
4. Al-Tammemi, A. B., Akour, A., & Alfalah, L. (2020). Is It Just about Physical Health? An Internet-Based Cross-Sectional Study Exploring the Psychological Impacts of COVID-19 Pandemic on University Students in Jordan Using Kessler Psychological Distress Scale. https:// doi.org/10.1101/2020.05.14.20102343
5. Assaubayeva D and Bi Yi PW. Response to Covid-19 for sustainable agriculture transformation. The Financial Express. 2020 May 30.
6. BGMEA. [11]Bangladesh Garments Manufacturers and Exporters Association,"URL http:// www.bgmea.com.bd/home/pages/TradeInformation; 2020. [Accessed]
7. Brooks SK, Webster RK, Smith LE, Woodland L, Wessely S, Greenberg N, Rubin GJ. The psychological impact of quarantine and how to reduce it: rapid review of the evidence. The lancet. 2020 Mar 14;395(1 0227):9 12–20. https://doi.org/10.1016/S0140-6736(20)30460-8. 199 www.bsmiab.org/jabet Rahman et al., JAdv Biotechnol Exp Ther. 2021 May; 4(2): 187–199
8. Brooks, S. K., Webster, R. K., Smith, L. E., Woodland, L., Wessely, S., Greenberg, N., & Rubin, G. J. (2020). The Psychological Impact of Quarantine and How to Reduce It: Rapid Review of the Evidence. The Lancet, 395, 912–920. https://doi.org/10.1016/ S0140-6736(20)30460-8
9. Cao, W., Fang, Z., Hou, G., Han, M., Xu, X., Dong, J., & Zheng, J. (2020). The Psychological Impact of the COVID-19 Epidemic on College Students in China. Psychiatry Research, 287, Article ID: 112934. https://doi.org/10.1016/j.psychres.2020.112934
10. Chandasiri, O. (2020). The COVID-19: Impact on Education. Journal of Asian and African Social Science and Humanities, 6, 37–42. https://www.aarcentre.com/ojs3/index.php/aarcentre/ article/view/207/472
11. Daily Prothom Alo, English Desk (2020), Household incomes fell by 20pc due to COVID-19: BBS survey, 6 October 2020, Dhaka
12. Daily Star Report (2020)"Painful jabs: Bangladesh's Covid-19 immunisation fiasco". The Daily Star. 28 April 2020. Retrieved 30 April 2021
13. Deb SK, Nafi SM. Impact of COVID-19 Pandemic on Tourism: Perceptions from Bangladesh. Available at SSRN 3632798. 2020 Jun 22. https://ssrn.com/abstract=3632798 or http:// dx.doi.org/10.2139/ssrn.3632798.
14. Dhaka Tribune (2020b), Tackling Covid-19: Bangladesh Will Need $378 Million Fund, Available online at: https://www.dhakatribune.com/bangladesh/foreign-affairs/2020/03/29/bangladesh-will-require-378mn-fund-for-covid-19-preparedness
15. Dhaka Tribune Report (2021), Dhaka Tribune Report, 16 September,2021, Dhaka
16. Dhaka Tribune. (2020a). Coronavirus: BGMEA says orders worth $3.15 billion cancelled so far. Retrieved April 20, 2020, from https://www.dhakatribune.com/bangladesh/2020/04/12/coronavirus-bgmea-reports-3-15-billion-in-order-cancellations.
17. Islam Kariul M, Ali Shukur M, Akanda Rahman Z, Rahman Shahnaz, Sharif Kamruzzaman AHM, Pavel Kader A and Baki Jannatul (2020), COVID-19 Pandemic and Level of Responses in Bangladesh, https://clinmedjournals.org/author-guidelines.php
18. Jiao WY, Wang LN, Liu J, Fang SF, Jiao FY, PettoelloMantovani M, Somekh E. Behavioral and emotional disorders in children during the COVID-19 epidemic. The journal of Pediatrics. 2020 Jun; 221:264. https://doi.org/10.1016/j. jpeds.2020.03.013.
19. Kalerkantho Report, (2021), That Daily Kalerkantho (Bangl News Paper),5 September, 2021, Dhaka, Bangladesh.
20. Laura Boudreau and Farria Naeem (2021), The Economic Effects of COVID-19 on Readymade Garment Factories in Bangladesh, Published on 23 July 2021,Search https://pedl.cepr.org/ user/ login
21. Luca, G. D., Kerckhove, K. V., Coletti, P., Poletto, C., Bossuyt, N., Hens, N., & Colizza, V. (2018). The Impact of Regular School Closure on Seasonal Influenza Epidemics: A DataDriven Spatial Transmission Model for Belgium. BMC Infectious Diseases, 18, 29. https:// doi.org/ 10.1186/s1 2879-017-2934-3
22. Meo, S. A., Abukhalaf, A. A., Alomar, A. A., Sattar, K., & Klonoff, D. C. (2020). COVID-19 Pandemic: Impact of Quarantine on Medical Students!# Mental Wellbeing and Learning Behaviors. Pakistan Journal of Medical Sciences, 36, S43-S48. https://doi.org/10.12669/ pjms.36.COVID19-S4.2809
23. Noyon AU. A virus that even eats into pharma sector. TBS News. 2020 May 13.

24. Paul TC. COVID-19 and its impact on Bangladesh economy. The Financial Express. 2020 June 19.

25. Prothom Alo (2020), Household incomes fell by 20pc due to COVID-19: BBS survey, Prothom Alo, 06 October, 2020, Dhaka, Bangladesh

26. Ramchandani P. Covid-19: We can ward off some of the negative impacts on children. News Scientist. 2020 April 8.

27. Rawstrone A. Survey reveals impact of lockdown on children. Nursery World, 01 May 2020.

28. Reuters.$The wait is over!: Bangladesh begins COVID-19 vaccinations. Arab News, 7 February, 2021.

29. Review Article l Ope Access, Covid-19 Pandemic and Level of Responses in Bangladesh

30. Roy R. Covid-1 9: Increasing economic resilience of the agriculture sector. The Business Standard.2020 May 05.

31. The World Bank (2020) World Bank Fast-Tracks $100 Million COVID-19 (Coronavirus) Support for Bangladesh. (2020). Available online at: https://www.worldbank.org/en/news/pressrelease/2020/04/03/world-bank-fast-tracks-100-million-covid-19-coronavirus-supportforbangladesh (accessed April 11, 2020).

32. Topader RA. COVID-19 threatens to cause a humanitarian crisis. Bangla-mirror-news. 2020 April 10.

33. Tribune Report. 5 million Covid-19 vaccine doses arrive in Dhaka. Dhaka Tribune, 25 January, 202.

34. UNESCO (2020a). Adverse Consequences of School Closures. UNESCO. https:// en.unesco.org/covid19/educationresponse/ consequences [Paper reference 1]

35. UNESCO (2020b). Education: From Disruption to Recovery. UNESCO. https://en.unesco.org/ covid1 9/educationresponse

26. United Nations Department of Economic and Social Affairs (2020),World Population Prospects - The 2010 Revision, (2011), Available online at: https://web.archive.org/web/20110506065230/ http://esa.un.org/unpd/wpp/index.htm (accessed March 23, 2020).

27. World Bank (2020), bankhttps ://documents.worldbank.org/curated/en/92609 1585406468147/ Proj ect-Information-Document-Bangladesh-COVID-19-Emergency-Response-andPandemicPreparedness-Project-P173757

28. Xiao H, Zhang Y, Kong D, Li S, Yang N (2020) Social capital and sleep quality in individuals who self-isolated for 14 days during the coronavirus disease 2019 (COVID-19) outbreak in January 2020 in China. Med Sci Monit. 26:e923921. doi: 10.12659/MSM.923921

29. Yeasmin S, Banik R, Hossain S, Hossain MN, Mahmud R, Salma N, Hossain MM. Impact of COVID-19 pandemic on the mental health of children in Bangladesh: A cross sectional study, Children and youth services review, 01 October 2020;117: 105277. https://doi.org/10.1016/ j.childyouth.2020.105277.

30. Zhong B L, Luo W, Li H M, Zhang Q Q, Liu X G, Li W T, et al. (2020), Knowledge, attitudes, and practices towards COVID-19 among Chinese residents during the rapid rise period of the COVID-19 outbreak: a quick online cross-sectional survey. Int J Biol Sci. (2020) 16:1745–52. doi: 10.7150/ijbs.45221

CHAPTER 42

Atmanirbharta—The Journey from Disaster to Human Resilience

Falguni Garg

B.Arch, Faculty of Architecture,
Class of 2017-22, Sri Sri University,
Corresponding author: falguni.g2017barch@srisriuniveristy.edu.in

Lakhan Dhameja

B.Arch, Faculty of Architecture,
Class of 2017-22, Sri Sri University,
lakhan.d2017barch@srisriuniveristy.edu.in

Abstract

Around 2.3 million people become homeless every year in India due to disasters. This paper will speak of empowerment on the basis of human resilience and the need to design sustainable buildings and settlements that can cope with natural and anthropogenic disasters. The site for the design is a 5.27 acre land located in Mouza Bhoinagar, Bayababa slum in ward no. 35, Bhubaneshwar. Design considerations at the site level allow for natural surveillance, a major aspect of Oscar Newman's Defensible Space Theory and design considerations at the Unit level looks at multi-functionality, day- lighting, and ventilation of the dwelling unit, a modular approach of planning, incrementality of dwellings, prevention of overcrowding and proper site planning. Disaster resilient strategies are adopted by doing a Hazard Vulnerability Capacity Assessment, taking into consideration cyclones, earthquakes, heat waves, and floods. The focus is on marginalized sections of the society, where the user is empowered to have a key role in decisions related to his/her built environment extending control over the nature of spaces with the option for incremental expansion.

Keywords: Sustainable-housing, resilient-architecture, cost-effective, energy-efficient design, user-centric

1. Introduction

It is said that time heals everything. Or maybe, it just prepares us for the worst. With the adverse effects of climate change, the sad reality for the people living in informal settlements today is that by the time they are able to recover from the previous disaster, a new one is already knocking on their door. Around 2.3 million people become homeless every year in India due to disasters (Suliman, 2017). They end up losing their single largest asset owned, in one stroke of fate. This paper focuses on building the adaptive capacity of these people and will speak of empowerment on the basis of human resilience on the outside, and a very practical and detailed plan of action for the same, on the inside.

The dire need to design sustainable buildings and settlements, which are resilient and can cope with natural and anthropogenic disasters is addressed. Ready-to-build designs for socially inclusive, cost- effective housing are proposed that are a part of a liveable neighbourhood, directly contributing to sustainable cities and communities that can be further replicated and scaled. Quoting the Danish architect, Bjarke Ingels (Jordan, 2018), *"Architects have to become more than just designers of two- dimensional facades or three-dimensional architectural objects. We have to become designers of ecosystems, systems of both ecology and economy. We channel not only the flow of people throughout things and buildings, but also the flow of resources, like heat, energy, waste, and water. Sustainability can't be a moral sacrifice or a political dilemma. It has to be a design challenge."* Rising to this challenge during a Design Hackathon, conducted jointly by Sri Sri University and Taru Leading edge for a slum rehabilitation project in Bhubaneswar, the design discussed in this paper was proposed.

2. Innovations for Disaster Resilient Design

A literature review was conducted to understand (1) how to determine disaster risk (2) urban design principles like defensible space theory (3) affordable housing solutions (4) sustainable village model and (5) Government Schemes.

2.1 Understanding Hazard, Vulnerability and Capacity Assessment (HVCA)

In order to assess disaster risks, a Hazard Vulnerability Capacity Assessment (HVCA) is a useful assessment tool, Table 42.1 (Taru Leading Edge, 2020). This is a crucial step in Disaster Risk Reduction (DRR) planning. An important component of the disaster risk reduction programme, it helps appropriate authorities to prepare for emergency situations. Disaster risk may be reduced by lowering a society's susceptibility by increasing its ability to withstand shocks and stressors. In order to address vulnerabilities and prepare for response and recovery from hazard occurrences, HVCA's goal is to assist communities in making risk-based decisions. The inter-relationship of hazards, vulnerability and disaster risk is shown in the equation below (Taru Leading Edge, 2020):

$$\text{Disaster Risk } (R) = \frac{\text{Hazard } (H) \times \text{Vulnerability } (V)}{\text{Capacity } (C)}$$

Table 42.1   Risk Assessment Matrix (From TARU Leading Edge, 2020)

Risk Assessment	Very unlikely to happen	Unlikely to happen	Possibility could happen	Likely to happen	Very likely to happen
Catastrophic	Moderate	Moderate	High	Critical	Critical
Major	Low	Moderate	Moderate	High	Critical
Moderate	Low	Moderate	Moderate	Moderate	High
Minor	Very Low	Low	Moderate	Moderate	Moderate
Superficial	Very Low	Very Low	Low	Low	Moderate

2.2 Defensible Space Theory by Oscar Newman

Oscar Newman (Newman, 1996) initially introduced the notion of "defensible space" in his book of the same name published in 1972. In the 1970s, as urban crime issues grew, the idea gained popularity, combining parts of a criminal theory with a set of urban design principles. According to Newman, the concept of defensible space is an effective crime prevention strategy in residential areas. All of the Defensible Space initiatives share a common goal: they reorganise communities' physical layouts so that individuals have more control over the spaces around their houses. This covers the streets and grounds around their buildings, as well as the lobbies and hallways within (Fig. 42.1). The initiatives aid people in preserving the locations where they may live out the beliefs and lifestyles that they hold dear. As a result, the architect can play an important role by providing sensitive design solutions.

Defensible Space relies on self-help rather than government involvement and is thus one method of enhancing community capacity. Residents must become involved if crime is to be

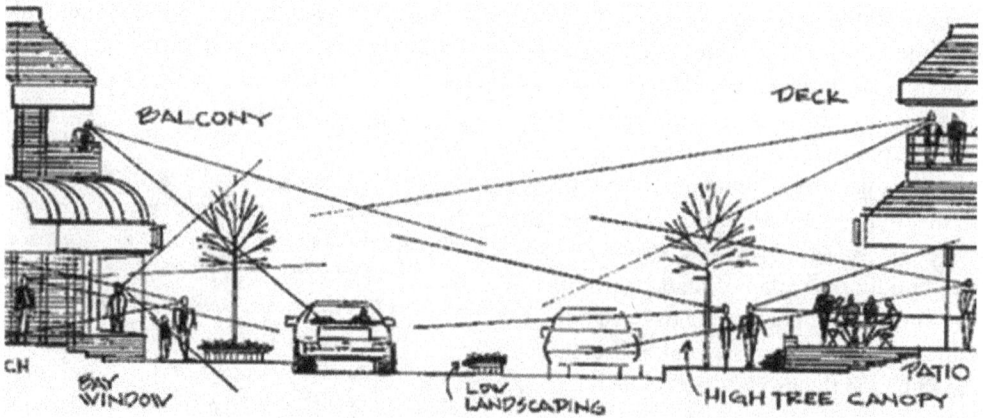

Fig. 42.1   Diagram depicting natural surveillance

reduced and criminals are to be eliminated. It has the power to unite people of all backgrounds and socioeconomic statuses in a mutually beneficial alliance. Defensible Space may introduce low-income individuals to the advantages of mainstream life and provide them with a chance to observe how their own activities can improve the world and lead to upward mobility.

2.3 Affordable Housing Case Studies

Aranya Low-Cost Housing (Sharma & Metha, 2007): Aranya, 6 kilometres from Indore, was planned to house 60,000 people in 6500 houses on an 85-hectare net planning area. The Vastu-Shilpa Foundation, spearheaded by Architect B.V Doshi, created the master-plan in 1983. The Master-plan is organised around a central spine that includes housing as well as the business centre. Six sectors, each with a population of 7000-12,000 people, are located to the east and west of the spine and are divided diagonally by linear parks. A cluster of ten houses, each with a courtyard at the rear, opens onto a street. The internal streets and squares have been paved. Each group of twenty dwellings is equipped with a septic tank, and power and water are accessible throughout. The neighbourhood was planned in such a manner that all of the amenities are fairly dispersed and a connection to the town centre is preserved. Pedestrian access was simplified.

The concept for this slum development proposal came from existing slum settlements, where a tiny neighbourhood is established with dwellings extending to the outdoors. Trees were planted in public locations, and streets with space for social, economic, and household activity were planned. The majority of the plots are tiny and grouped in low-rise blocks with longer side façades angled north- south to decrease solar radiation on the building. In order to clearly separate automobile and pedestrian traffic, informal interconnected open areas were established that were solely used by walkers. Vehicle access was restricted to 15-meter-wide rectilinear and official roadways.

Belapur Housing (Mendes, Beirão, Duarte, & Celani, 2013): Charles Correa created the Belapur Housing in the years 1983-1986 with a home typology ranging from 45 sq.m.-70 sq.m. to accommodate more than 90% of Bombay's low-income population. The proposal exhibits high densities - 500 people per hectare, including outdoor areas, schools, and so on. Located on six hectares of ground within one kilometre from New Bombay's core, the development had to cater to the needs of low- and middle-income residents alike. This design uses a fractal structure to show the hierarchy of community areas, with seven dwelling units arranged around an 8m x 8m courtyard. The houses were designed as an evolutionary module, where "units are packed close enough to provide the benefits of high density, yet separate enough to allow for

individual identity and growth" – this strategy enables growth from "a single lean-to roof to urban town-houses" because each dwelling is freestanding and does not share any wall or land with its neighbours, allowing a family to expound.

Inferences: Key lessons from these case studies, to be incorporated into the design solution being proposed are summarised below.

Natural surveillance—One major issue in affordable housing projects is the increased crime rates because of negative spaces and blind spots which are created at the corners and the rear parts of the building. Providing houses in a linear arrangement and also along the boundary instead will reduce blind spots, which attracts crime and dump. This is also useful in ensuring that one is vigilant to mitigate possible disasters.

Increased sense of ownership—Another problem is, a common courtyard shared between 5 to 6 units ends up in a bad condition due to decreased sense of ownership amongst the residents. Instead of a common courtyard, providing a personal courtyard to every unit will not only give the users their personal outdoor space but will also help them in running small businesses. This space can also double as a multipurpose space that could serve well in disasters such as the current COVID-19 Pandemic.

Incremental approach—Engaging the local residents in the construction process and giving them an incremental model allows families to build according to their perceived needs in the near future. Modular planning of units will further help in creating rental and commercial opportunities for the families. Such an approach could ensure disaster-resistant construction processes through quality control and additionally the build capacity of the home-owner in understanding how his house has been built.

Traffic management—Dividing the vehicular and pedestrian access by separating their routes plays a vital role in traffic management throughout the site. Also introducing intersections or chowks at various junctions will help in easy navigation and effective supervision. Integrating emergency evacuation and disaster mitigation measures (such as fire brigade routes) also becomes an important site planning measure.

2.4 Concept of a Self Sustained Village Model

Economic development, environmental conservation, and social justice are the three pillars of sustainable development. (Fig. 42.2).

While pursuing new economic development models, long-term sustainable development should not be overlooked in favour of short-term individual gains. Instead of abusing environmental resources, economic development should

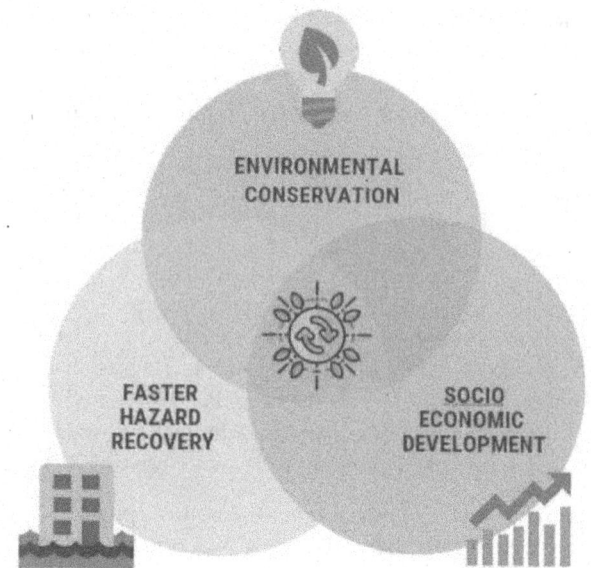

Fig. 42.2 Venn diagram showing the concept of a self-sustained model

balance and buffer the environmental load, and the natural resources and environments required by humans should be well protected.

Development should be accompanied by societal contributions; hence, a balanced model of sustainable development based on the economy, environment, and society is required to achieve sustainable development in human civilization. (Abazi, Chaushi, Chaushi, & Tanevska, 2017)

The design proposed in this paper attempts to create housing as an asset for the community, while at the same time the process of building opens out variety of job opportunities for the workers by strengthening the local craftsmanship using vernacular materials and construction techniques. Using renewable energy like solar to create a self sustaining village model ensures economic development with minimal environmental damage.

Being Environmentally Responsive

Some eco-friendly measures that will be taken up in the design are:

(a) Using materials like hollow concrete blocks, fly ash bricks, terracotta for construction, which are available within a 15 km radius of the site to minimize carbon emissions caused due to transport

(b) Harvesting rainwater at the site level and unit level which can be further used for various activities like cleaning, washing and in case of fire emergencies

(c) Managing the site and construction waste by creating terrazzo tiles for flooring and debris walls for small compound walls and sitting areas

(d) Separating dry and wet waste at the unit level for effective site waste management

(e) Reusing and recycling at the site itself for creating a closed loop within the society

Faster Recovery from Hazards

Measures to enable disaster resilience include:

(a) *Joy Pumps* to alleviate water scarcity issues, particularly when there is no clean surface water source, no electricity, and limited financial resources.

(b) *Cycle Run Water Pumps* a saver of time, electricity/fuel. Lifts water from streams, ponds, canals, and wells using human power generated by pedalling a bicycle.

(c) *Concrete Hollow Blocks* are easy to install due to their uniform size and shape. They are also lighter, which allows for faster construction and better earthquake resistance. Even unskilled labourers can easily work with hollow blocks.

(d) Using renewable energy sources such as solar energy to meet basic electrical needs on a daily basis

Strengthening Socio-Economic Aspects

Measures to enhance the community capacity include:

(a) Building with local material and construction techniques like filler slabs and terracotta jali walls that support the local craftsmen and generates revenue within the community

(b) Multifunctional spaces like courtyards and terraces encourage small business setups run by the women and offers communal spaces in times like the COVID 19 pandemic

(c) Chowk system encourages community interaction and acts as a small commercial hub providing multiple opportunities for sellers, vendors. etc. enhancing skill development through self-help groups

(d) Conducting workshops, encouraging the people living there to start their own business and become self-sustained

2.6 Government Schemes Applicable

Two schemes that are applicable were studied and are summarized below.

Pradhan Mantri Awas Yojana (PMAY): The Pradhan Mantri Awas Yojana (PMAY) is a Central Government Credit Linked Subsidy Scheme (CLSS). It is a first-of-its-kind programme aimed at providing 'Housing For All' to the urban society's Economically Weaker Section (EWS), Low Income

Group (LIG), Middle Income Group-I (MIG-I), and Middle-Income Group-II (MIG-II) by the end of 2022. Home-owners would receive a home loan interest subsidy under this Pradhan Mantri Yojana when they buy, build, extend, or upgrade their house. Two government nodal organisations, the Housing and Urban Development Corporation (HUDCO) and the National Housing Bank (NHB) would route subsidy to lending institutions, which will then assist qualifying applicants in obtaining the subsidy (Indiabulls Home Loans, n.d.).

Valmiki Ambedkar Awas Yojana (VAMBAY) – The Valmiki Ambedkar Awas Yojana (VAMBAY) is a government-sponsored programme for slum dwellers. The scheme's primary goal is to alleviate housing difficulties for slum dwellers living below the poverty line in many towns and cities around the state. The primary purpose of VAMBAY is to provide or improve existing housing for those living below the poverty line in urban slums, in order to realise the goal of "Shelter for All." The VAMBAY will target slum residents in urban areas who are below the poverty line, including members of the EWS who do not have appropriate housing. People with disabilities, on the other hand, will be given precedence (Watsan).

3. Context of the Project-Slum Rehabilitation Site: Bhoi Nagar Bhubaneswar

Bhubaneswar, the state capital of Odisha, is also known as the "Temple City of India." It lies on the west bank of river Kuakhai, which is a tributary of River Mahanadi that flows about 30 km southeast of Cuttack. The city has a spatial spread of 135 sq. km with 67 Census wards and a population of more than 8 Lakhs. It has a population density of 6,228 people/ sq km.

The site for the slum rehabilitation is located in the heart of the city and is well connected to the neighbourhood areas. The majority of the important places, like a bus station, a government school, public park, community centre, mall and public toilets are located within a 2 km radius around the site. The site for the design is a 5.27 acre land located in Mouza Bhoinagar, Bayababa slum in ward no. 35, Bhubaneshwar.

The site is well connected through a road network and its prime location allows for easy accessibility to the neighbourhood commercial, residential and public areas. It is adjacent to a canal and lacks a proper drainage system which makes it susceptible to seasonal flooding. The prime location of the site creates ample job opportunities for the residents and makes it an ideal place for starting their own businesses. The site possesses a huge threat of loss of life and property due to multi-hazard risks of cyclones, heatwaves, flooding. There is also an increased chance of spreading water-borne diseases due to contaminated conditions of the canal. Figure 42.3 below shows the site along with the surrounding area.

3.1 Hazard Analysis

City level: Unplanned growth of the city has resulted in floods and waterlogging in the low- lying areas of the city. Due to various flood control measures in upstream areas, the

Fig. 42.3 Satellite image of the site

overall flood risk for the city of Bhubaneswar is very low. Yet, during times of sudden downpours, due to lack of pervious surfaces and poor stormwater management systems, urban floods are experienced.

Heatwave is becoming a common phenomenon in cities and is exacerbated due to the heat island effect caused by an increase in built-up structures. Extremely high monthly mean maximum temperature, between the months of April and August and continuous increase in the number of hot days is a sure sign of heat resilience being an important design consideration. This becomes important while designing affordable housing as passive features for reduction in heat gain play a key role to reduce user comfort.

Cyclones are a common occurrence in Odisha and Bhubaneswar (one of the cities of Khordha district) is located about 45 km from the coast, has felt the brunt of at least two severe super-cyclones, the most recent one being Fani in May 2019. During Fani, Bhubaneswar suffered significant property and infrastructure damage, and the entire Smart City network was disrupted, in addition to significant environmental damage.

Earthquakes are less of a risk in Bhubaneswar. According to the Bureau of Indian Standards (BIS) on a scale ranging from I to V, in order of increasing susceptibility to earthquakes, Bhubaneswar lies in seismic zone III, which is a moderate seismic risk zone.

Site level: The site is well connected throughout its boundary. Its prime location allows for easy accessibility to the neighbourhood commercial, residential and public areas.

Being adjacent to a canal makes the site susceptible to urban floods. Currently, there is a lack of proper drainage systems and health care facilities and there is no proper arrangement of basic amenities like electricity and water. A common threat is the loss of life and property due to severe cyclones and heatwaves in the summer. The outbreak of water-borne diseases is also likely due to the contaminated condition of the canal.

Using the HVCA Risk assessment matrix (Table 42.1) an analysis was carried out, to assess the disaster risk, so that design measures can be implemented to mitigate and reduce it.

Through this assessment of the project site, it is evident that the overall risk of floods and cyclones is the highest considering their frequency and catastrophic nature. With the site abutting a canal, it is at a big risk for floods. To reduce the overall risk, design solutions have to be provided at both the unit and site levels. With Odisha lying in a high damage risk zone, wind hazard is a major risk and the planning and designing strategies should follow the guidelines of wind hazard.

The region being vulnerable to really high temperatures during the summer months, heatwaves create a moderate risk to the site. This risk can be reduced by using several construction techniques and using the building orientation to create mutual shading.

Even though the site lies in a moderate seismic risk zone, simple structural strategies can substantially reduce the overall risk of earthquakes.

Table 42.2 Risk assessment matrix for Bhoi nagar, Bayababa slum site in Bhubaneswar, Odisha

HAZARDS	FREQUENCY	ASSESSMENT	NO.	VULNERABILITY	ASSESSMENT	NO.	CAPACITY ASSESSMENT	NO.	RISK
Cyclones	Very likely to happen	Catastrophic	5	High damage risk zone, Vb = 50m/s	Likely to happen	4	Sturdy roof, Framed RCC structure, Uninterrupted wind movement due to linear cluster orientation	4	5
Flood	Likely to happen	Major	4	Site is located in an area liable to floods	Very likely to happen	5	Unit level- Raised plinth levels; Site level - provision of swales, effective sewer system, porous pathways	3.5	5.71
Heat wave	Possibly could happen	Major	3	Heat island effect, High monthly mean maximum temperature from April to August	Likely to happen	4	Hollow concrete blocks, Filler slabs, Mud plastering, Courtyard planning, Mutual shading	3	4
Earthquake	Possibly could happen	Moderate	3	Site lies in moderate damage risk zone i.e. zone III	Possibly could happen	3	Simple rectangular forms, Low rise structure, Tied framed structure, Damping foundation	4	2.25

HIGH   MODERATE   LOW

4. Designing for Disaster Resilience

The slum rehabilitation project was designed at two levels, the site level where connectivity with the city and the urban linkages are detailed out, and the unit level where the user comfort is the key driver. Units are combined into clusters that then get integrated into a community on the site. Design features at each of these two levels, site and unit, are discussed below.

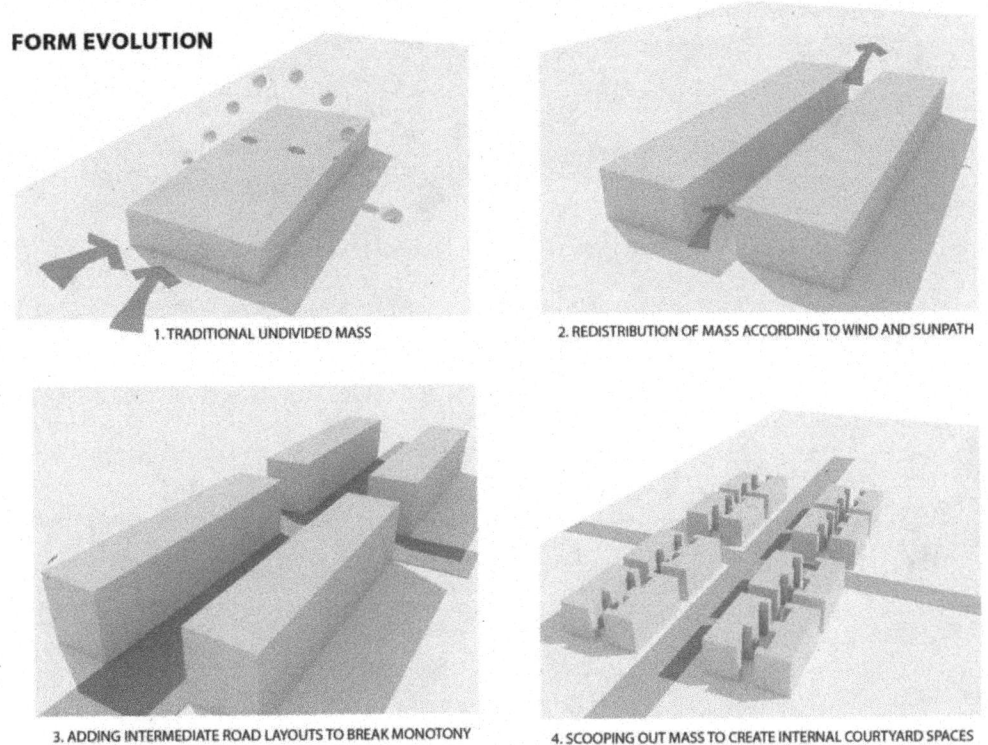

FORM EVOLUTION

1. TRADITIONAL UNDIVIDED MASS

2. REDISTRIBUTION OF MASS ACCORDING TO WIND AND SUNPATH

3. ADDING INTERMEDIATE ROAD LAYOUTS TO BREAK MONOTONY

4. SCOOPING OUT MASS TO CREATE INTERNAL COURTYARD SPACES

Fig. 42.4   Different stages of form evolution

The form was developed by keeping in mind several factors like the sun and the wind. The building mass was divided along the north-south axis which helped in the undisturbed flow of winds and hence made it a step closer to being cyclone resilient. For safety reasons and to break the monotony, the building mass was further divided in the east-west axis by secondary roads. These masses were further divided into smaller units so that common courtyard spaces would evolve, creating a sense of ownership and encouraging small businesses to grow (Fig. 42.4).

4.1 Design Considerations at Site Level

After removing 0.9 acres of ancillary amenities from the total site area, the remaining 4.37 acres of land was designed keeping the neighbourhood context in mind. The 200 units on the ground floor are arranged along the north-south axis so that the longer sides of the clusters are not exposed to the prevailing southerly wind, generating resilience.

The site has multiple entry and exit points, which helps through-and-through commute, preventing the chances of traffic congestion. The 6 m spine road runs along both ends of the site fulfil the fire safety norms and create *chowks* at every junction. Instead of a long continuous row of houses, there are breaks after every two to three clusters, creating opportunities for mixed-use units to have small shops throughout the length (Figure 42.5). The houses in the lower portion of the site are Ground +1 clusters with a flat roof. The owner can increase their unit to another floor if needed keeping in view the future growth in the family. For an interesting commute and easier allocation of houses, the street has houses with various contrasting facades. Colour theory also plays a role in user psychology, generating a happier feeling further reducing the crime rates and generating a safer living experience.

One major issue that informal settlements face is the high crime rates because of negative spaces and blind spots. The linear row housing pattern in the site allows for natural

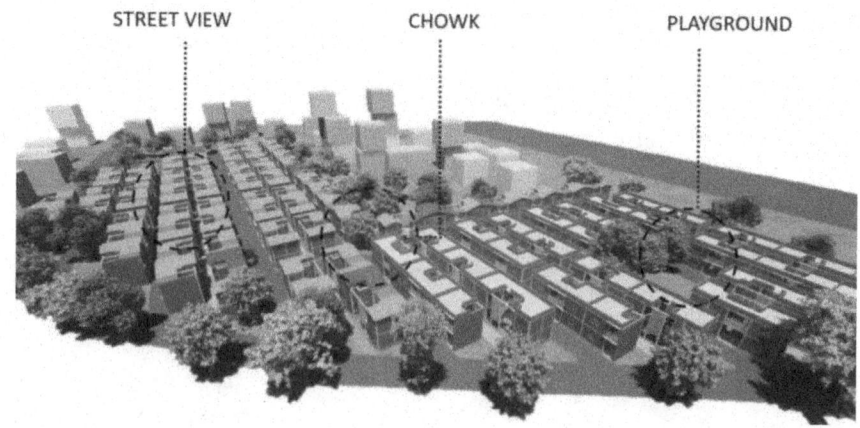

Fig. 42.5 Bird's eye view of the site highlighting various regions

Fig. 42.6 Site plan indicating area coverage

surveillance which is a major aspect of Oscar Newman's Defensible Space Theory (Newman, 1996). To induce a safer living experience, site planning is done in a way that there are no blind spots. The roads are not adjacent to the boundary walls avoiding unclaimed spaced turning into a dumping ground. Introducing *chowks* at certain distances also allows for easy traffic management and effective supervision (Fig. 42.7).

Concept of Services: How They Enhance Disaster Resilience

Certain pockets created along the proposed road are used to harvest rainwater for any emergency need in the future. The site is vulnerable to flooding at the point where the canal takes a turn and in order to prevent that an embankment is created. In case of excessive flooding, the water will go to the pond which is created beyond the embankment area. This public park serves as a multi-purpose recreational space, a space to conduct meetings for the various official decisions, etc. and

is built in a way without imposing any foreign element in context to the site surroundings

An area of 200 sq.m. is allotted on the site for rainwater harvesting. This patch can harvest almost 30,000 Litres of water, given that the average rainfall in Bhubaneswar is 1500 mm. This is in addition to the rainwater harvesting at the cluster level over an area of 54 sq.m., where up to 80,000 litres can be annually harvested. Swales are provided on the site to enhance percolation and reduce erosion. This is a cost-effective and resilient approach for stormwater management that also reduces the load on the municipal sewer systems. The stormwater drains on site have a grille to reduce the chance of blockage from plastic and other debris. The grilles are topped with pebbles, which allows effective drainage and easy installation.

The design separates the waste water, using the greywater into planters. This reduces the load on the Sewage Treatment Plant, whether it is on site or at the municipal level. Only

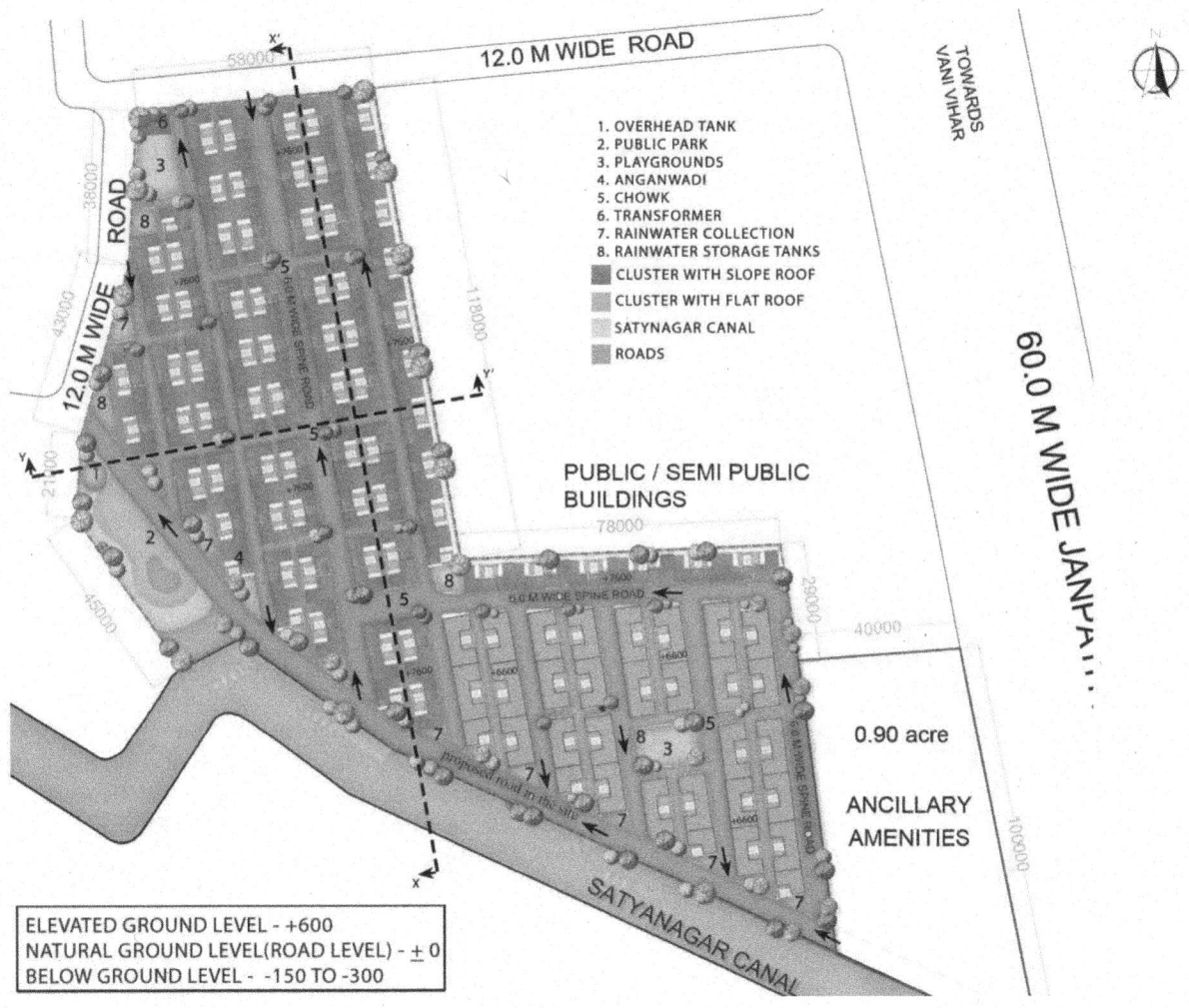

Fig. 42.7 Site plan

Table 42.3 Area Statement

SITE: 5.27 acres (21328 sq.m)	
Ancillary area: 0.9 acres (3642 sq.m); **Available site:** 4.37 acres (17685 sq.m); **Existing road:** 1387 sq.m (8% of site)	
Suggested DU/Acre: 100 **Proposed DU/acre:** Min. 91.5 Max. 104.5	**Dwelling units on site:** 437 DU **Dwelling units on site:** Min - 400, Max - 456
Residential cover proposed: 3.059 acres12,380 sq.m	**Residential ground covered:** 1.5 acres (5900 sq.m)
FAR allowed: 1.75	**FAR achieved:** Min. 0.7, Max. 0.78
Built up area (BUA) allowed: 30,949 sq.m	**BUA proposed:** Min. 11,800 sq.m, Max. 13,562 sq.m
DWELLING UNITS	
Cluster Type 1: Two (2) Dwelling Units: 60 sq.m	Type 1: 29 sq.m, Type 2: 31Sqm
No. of Cluster Type 1: Min. 72, Max. 83	Total Area: Min. 4,320 sq.m, Max. 4,980 sq.m
Cluster Type 2: 2 Dwelling Units: 58 sq.m	Type 1: 29 sq.m
No. of Clusters: Min. 128, Max. 147	Total Area: Min. 7,424 sq.m, Max. 8,506 sq.m
Dwelling Units	**Total: 400, Incremental up to 456**
Ground Floor: 200, First Floor: 200, Second Floor (Incremental): 56	

the sewage is transported into the STP or municipal sewers, and this is done by sharing common sewage lines running between two (2) rows of houses, and not on the main road, to make it easy for maintenance, without disrupting the general vehicular movement.

A key design feature of the community is *atmanirbharta* or self-sufficiency and this is attempted at all levels, including self-reliance with respect to energy for the housing. The RESCO model is proposed for solar energy provision. In Odisha, the Renewable Energy Service Company (RESCO) Model has been implemented. Both the Central and State Government agencies give liberal and favourable rules for RESCO solar developers in order to reach their target of 40GW of rooftop solar by 2022. Key features of the RESCO model is that there is no upfront investment, continuous operations and maintenance support is provided. This allows better monitoring of load and consumption and reduces the load of paying back on the users, as it is distributed over a time period and collected as rent for services provided. (Renewable Energy Service Company (RESCO), n.d.)

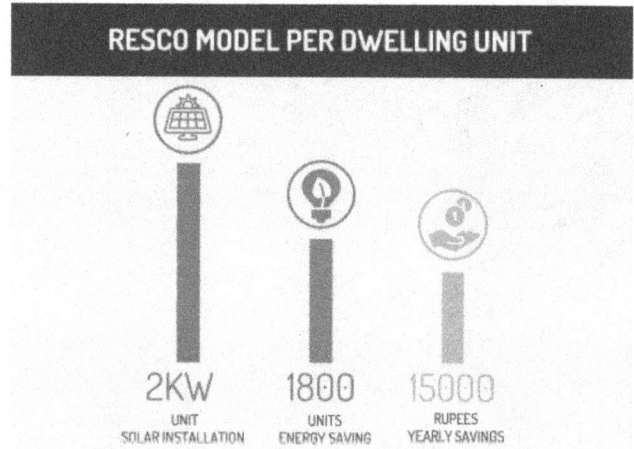

Fig. 42.8   Bar chart showing the savings obtained per dwelling unit by using RESCO

The Solar Energy system on the site not only provides a decentralized power generation model that is linked to housing but additionally offsets dependence on grid power, which most often is from coal- based thermal power plants. The energy-saving can be as much as Rs. 1200-1400 per cluster per month which amounts to a yearly saving of Rs 13-15,000 per cluster. The electricity demand of 6 to 6.5 kWh per dwelling unit adds up to almost 25kWh per cluster. The size of the unit for each cluster would be 5kW, assuming that a 1kW panel produces 4 to 4.5kWh/day (Patel, n.d.).

4.2 Design Considerations at Unit Level

To meet the community's future demands, a modular approach to planning was used. This assists the owner in generating

rental and commercial opportunities. Incrementality of dwellings is also considered for easy vertical extension of their houses. Different aspects of human scale and interaction have been incorporated as design elements for a humane-people-friendly architecture of the clusters. The cluster opens to a common area between the 2 units which can be used for parking hence preventing crowded parked roads. The units with 2 bedrooms can be easily used for mixed-use or renting purposes.

A back entry allows for a separate fire exit and also opens up to the personal courtyard space. A utility balcony on the upper floor is provided for washing utensils, clothes etc. Provision of niches, lofts and storage systems for maximum space utilisation are proposed to cater to the daily needs of storage. One major issue with a common courtyard between 5 to 6 units is no one maintains it. A personal courtyard not only ensures day-lighting and ventilation of the dwelling unit but at the same time also creates a multi-functional space for the people living there.

When 2 clusters face each other in this way, it creates a space with 4 courtyards on the same side, creating a private space for pedestrian use and even small communal gatherings, where women can meet and work on small business ideas. The 2.5 m wide pathway between the units is lined with drainage lines which allow for common sewer lines coming from the units on both sides. The main roads have a stormwater drainage system so that there is no flooding on the main roads during heavy rains (Fig. 42.10, Fig. 42.11). This creates a win-win situation for everyone. The owner gets to have the comfort of his or her own courtyard but still keep the communication and interaction with the neighbours intact.

4.3 Disaster Resilient Features

Each unit has been designed to be able to cope with the three major hazards, cyclones, heatwave and floods (Fig. 42.12). In addition to this basic precaution has also been taken to make the structure earthquake resistant. To resist cyclones, a framed structure with Reinforced Cement Concrete (R.C.C) roof slab has been proposed, which creates a solid form preventing any damage in case of severe cyclonic winds. Cycle-run water pumps and joy pumps help mitigate water scarcity problems in case of no electricity due to power outages caused by disruptions during cyclones. Solar energy systems also provide backup for water pumping and basic electricity.

A heatwave can be mitigated by the courtyard space in every house that maintains ventilation through the stack effect. The street maintains a lower temperature than the ambient due to the mutual shading of the surrounding units. Filler slab lowers the inside temperature and walling made of hollow concrete blocks creates a cavity wall with air acting as an added insulation.

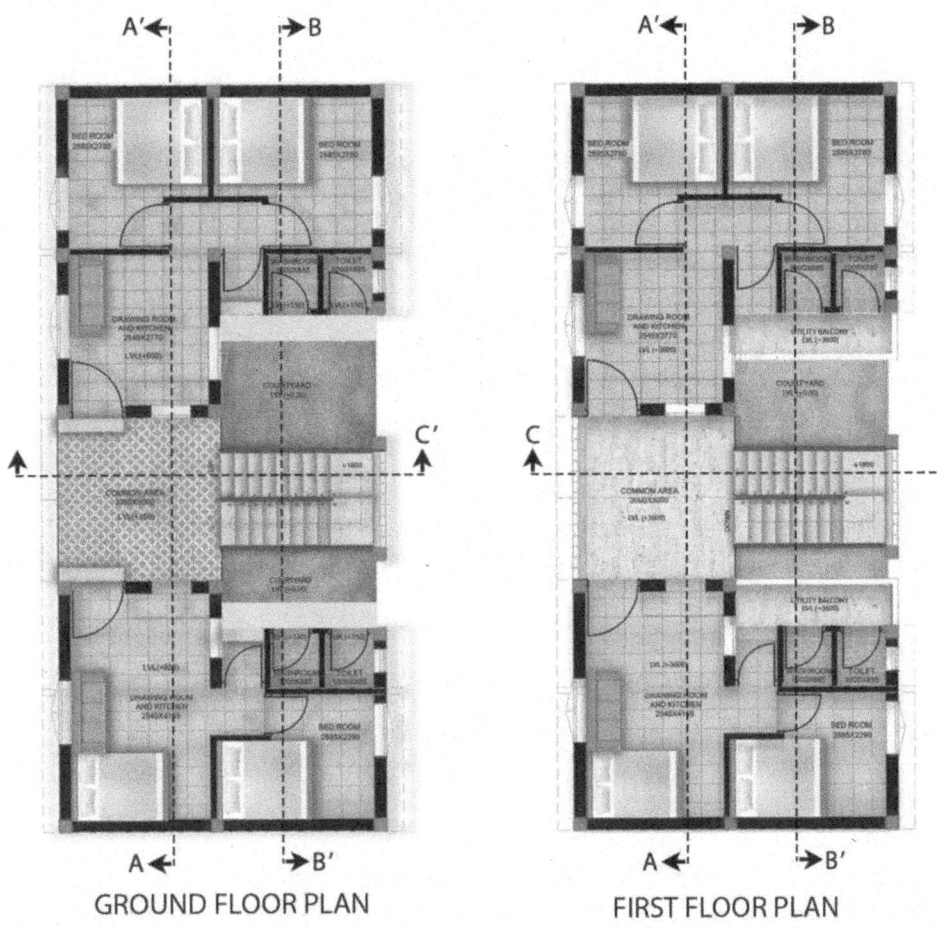

GROUND FLOOR PLAN   FIRST FLOOR PLAN

Fig. 42.9 Floor plans of cluster type 1 (Area – 60 sq.m.)

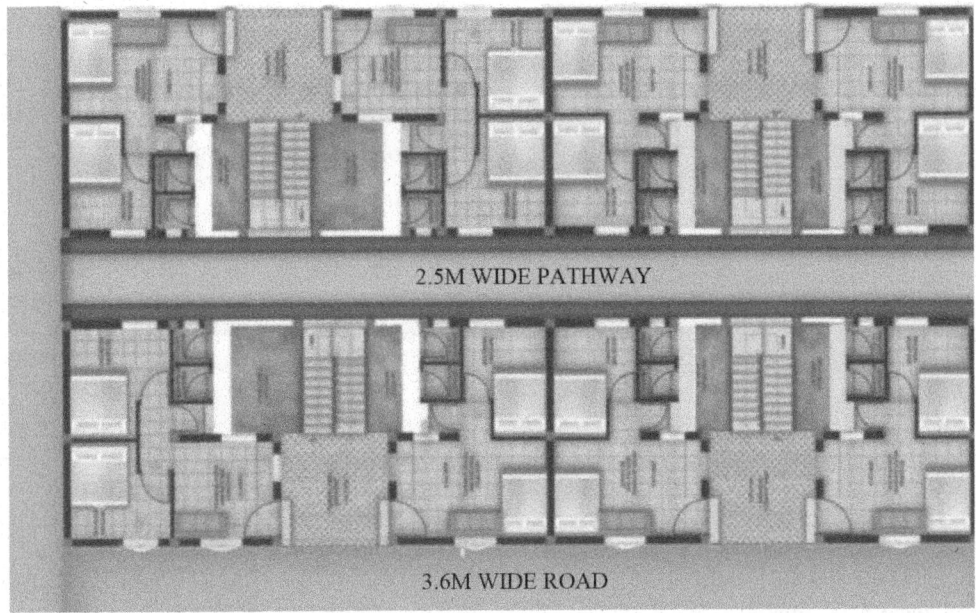

Fig. 42.10 Cluster plan showing the unit connectivity with the courtyard and roads

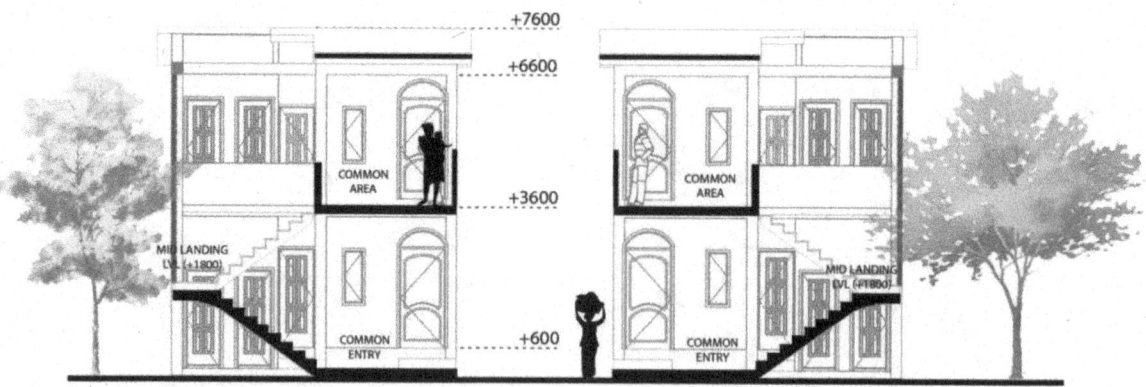

Fig. 42.11 Section across the cluster

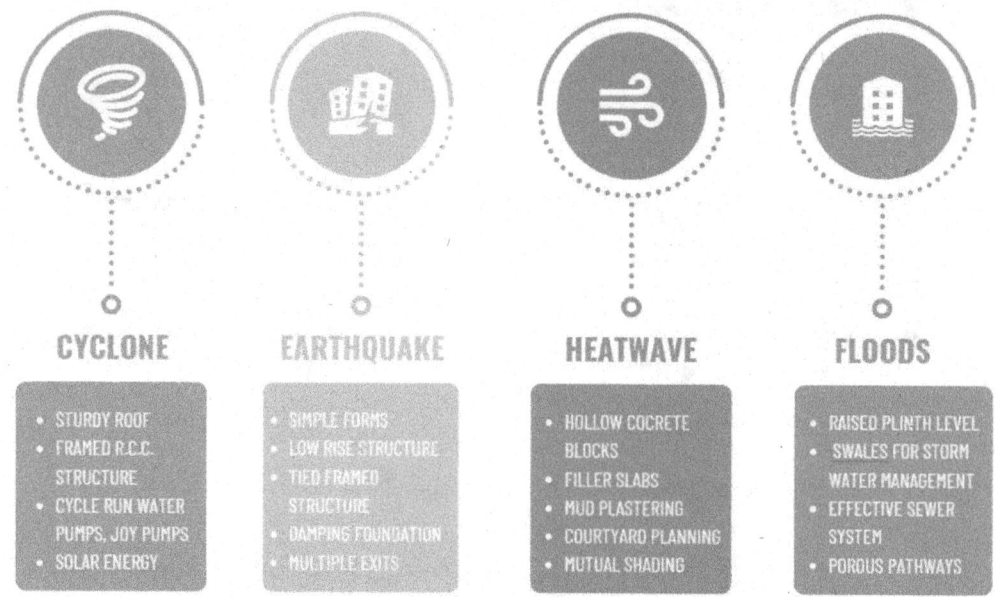

Fig. 42.12 Diagram showing various disaster resilient features

Raised plinth levels reduce the risk of flooding. Swales on the main roads allow for effective stormwater management. Separation of sewer lines allows for effective drainage and minimized mixing of stormwater and sewage water which will reduce the chances of flooding and spreading of water-borne diseases. The porous pathways allow for rainwater to recharge the groundwater table. A personal rain reservoir for every unit is provided under the staircase, where the harvested rainwater from the roof can be stored. This water can be used for activities like washing, gardening, etc. saving the virgin water that is provided/purchased from the Municipal authorities.

Though the risk of earthquakes is not high, a low rise, tied framed structure with simple forms gives stability to the structure during earthquake vibrations.

4.4 Construction Details

The construction techniques used are simple and easy to maintain. In addition, it is expected that the house owners will be in a position to do minor repairs on their own, using a local tradesperson. The walls are constructed with hollow concrete blocks and fly ash bricks.

The roofing is mainly reinforced concrete slab variation, using filler slabs to reduce the materials and therefore the costs. Terracotta tiles, indigenous to Odisha are also used to generate local employment and align the houses to the local vernacular style. The external walls are plastered with cement plaster, and the interior walls are plastered with a mud-based plaster to give it an earthy and cool effect and to reduce the use of cement. It also has a cooling effect and can be

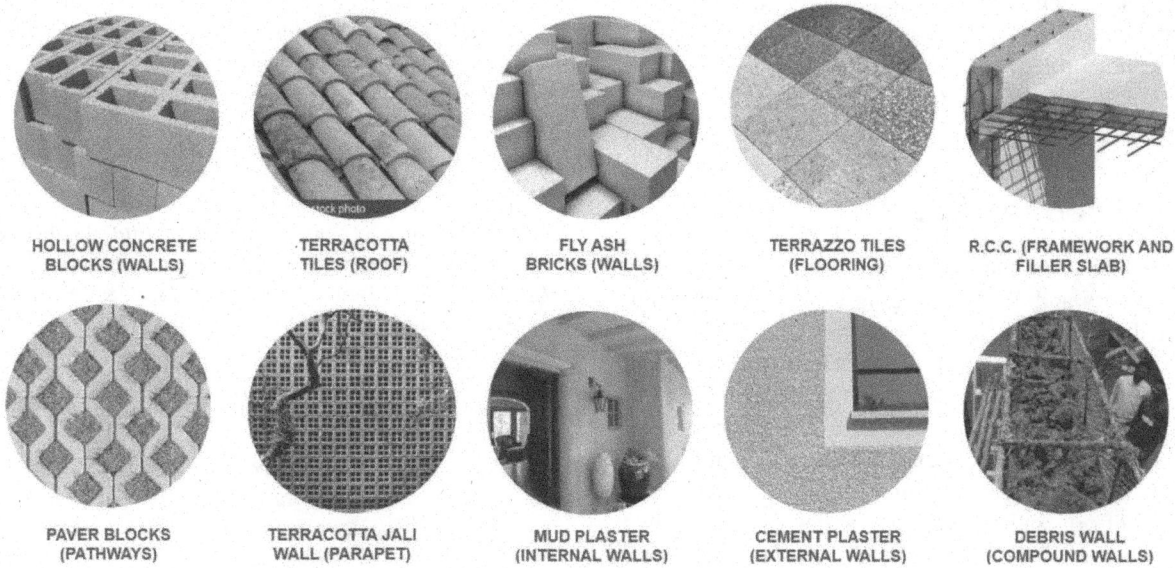

HOLLOW CONCRETE BLOCKS (WALLS)	TERRACOTTA TILES (ROOF)	FLY ASH BRICKS (WALLS)	TERRAZZO TILES (FLOORING)	R.C.C. (FRAMEWORK AND FILLER SLAB)
PAVER BLOCKS (PATHWAYS)	TERRACOTTA JALI WALL (PARAPET)	MUD PLASTER (INTERNAL WALLS)	CEMENT PLASTER (EXTERNAL WALLS)	DEBRIS WALL (COMPOUND WALLS)

Fig. 42.13   Diagram showing the various construction materials used

used either as-is or whitewashed where light and brightness is needed. Terrazzo tiles form a rugged flooring and when locally produced, create avenues for employment and local enterprises. Paver blocks are used for external surfaces, in a way that will enable the percolation of rainwater (Fig. 42.13).

Overall, the design has a sensitivity to the local culture and surroundings and wherever possible, a sustainable solution that enhances the local architectural tradition, in which locally sourced renewable resources are used is provided. Almost all the materials used are available within a 15 km radius of the site, decreasing the carbon footprint because of reduced transportation. The focus is on marginalised sections of the society, with the intention of promoting a participatory approach to housing, where the user is empowered to have a key role in decisions related to his/her built environment extending control over the nature of spaces with the option for incremental expansion.

5. Conclusion

The primary objective of this paper was to create a sustainable community based on the concept of human resilience. This allows the user to play a vital role in the design process making the design more disaster resilient. Various problems were addressed and rectified at the root level to create a more user-centric design:

- Crime prevention using defensible space theory and natural surveillance using clusters arranged in a linear pattern

- Ensuring proper daylight and ventilation for all the units by providing personal courtyard spaces to every dwelling unit

- Harvesting rainwater at the site level and unit level and investing in solar energy which will further help in daily needs and also in case of disaster-related emergencies

- Providing user-friendly solutions like cycle run water pumps, joy pumps, RESCO models etc. for faster recovery from hazards

- Separating dry and wet waste at the unit level to provide optimal waste management on the job site. Reusing and recycling on-site to create a complete loop within the society

- Building with local materials and construction techniques will not only support the local craftsmen but generate revenue within the community

- Modular planning of units to create rental and commercial opportunities for the families

- Proper vehicular and pedestrian traffic segregation through the establishment of a road hierarchy

- Chowk system encourages community interaction and acts as a small commercial hub providing multiple opportunities for sellers, vendors. etc.

- Creating multi-functional spaces like courtyards and terraces which encourages small business setups run by the women

Architects play a key role in building disaster resilience and should believe in the empowerment of permanence, which means, that they provide communities not with just a product but a process, which in turn could lead to the solution. Empowering communities with knowledge and the ability to adapt and respond to any adverse situations such as disasters reduces risk and enhances resilience. Thus Atmanirbharta is the key to human resilience.

6. Acknowledgement

Our sincere thanks to the Faculty of Architecture (FOA), Sri Sri University and TARU: Leading Edge for the Design Hackathon that provided us opportunities to work on this exciting slum rehabilitation project. The various online webinars and workshops conducted by TARU helped us in achieving the final outcome we arrived at. This was a group submission, so we would like to cite our fellow team members Pooshan Mataji Vardhineedi, Abhinash Sethi and Sathabdhi Penta whose efforts and dedication was key in making this project a success. We would like to thank our faculties, Ar. Anisa Azharunnisa and Ar. Sarit Sekhar Mukherjee for guiding us during the Design Hackathon. We would like to express our gratitude to Prof. (Dr). Geeta Vaidyanathan for her constant support and guidance in writing this paper.

REFERENCES

1. Abazi, H., Chaushi, B. A., Chaushi, A., & Tanevska, H. A. (2017, December). Identifying factors that influence sustainable development: the case of Macedonia. *ResearchGate*.
2. Donnelly, P. G. (2010). Newman, Oscar: Defensible Space Theory. Thousand oaks, CA: Sage Publishing.
3. Garg, Falguni; Dhameja, Lakhan; Vardhineedi, Pooshan mataji; Sethi, Abhinash; Penta, Sathabdhi. (2020). *ATMANIRBHARTA - The journey from disaster to human resilience*. Bhubaneswar: Sri Sri University TARU Leading Edge collaborative.
4. *Home loan pradhan mantri awas yojana*. (n.d.). Retrieved from Bajaj Finserv: https://www.bajajfinserv.in/home-loan-pradhan-mantri-awas-yojana
5. *Indiabulls Home Loans*. (n.d.). Retrieved from Pradhan Mantri Awas Yojana Pmay Clss: https://www.indiabullshomeloans.com/pradhan-mantri-awas-yojana-pmay-clss
6. Jordan, E. (2018, July 18). *Bjarke Ingels on Achieving Sustainability Through Info-Driven Design*. Retrieved from Whitewall: https://whitewall.art/design/bjarke-ingels-achieving- sustainability-info-driven-design
7. Mendes, L. T., Beirão, J. N., Duarte, J. P., & Celani, G. (2013). A Bottom-Up Social Housing System Described with. In R. Stouffs, & S. Sariyildiz, *eCAADe 2013 Computation and Performance Volume 2* (pp. 705-714). Netherlands: eCAADe.
8. Newman, O. (1996). *Creating Defensible Space*. Washington, D.C.: U.S. Department of Housing and Urban Development, Office of Policy Development and Research.
9. Patel, J. (n.d.). *How Much Electricity Does One Solar Panel Produce in a Day?* Retrieved from Let's save electricity: https://letsavelectricity.com/how-much-electricity-does- one-solar-panel-produce-in-a-day/
10. *Renewable Energy Service Company (RESCO)*. (n.d.). Retrieved from CleanMax: https://www.cleanmax.com/solar-solutions-in-india/resco-model.php
11. Sharma, U., & Metha, B. (2007). Aranya Township, Indore - India, An experiment on sustainable human habitat. In *Journal of Architecture and Planning, Vol 6, 2007 - Urban Design: Case based theory and practice (Part II)* (pp. 15-32). Karachi: Department of Architecture and Planning, NED University of Engineering and Technology, Karachi, Pakistan.
12. Suliman, A. (2017, October 13). *Disasters make 14 million people homeless each year: U.N.* Retrieved from Reuters: https://www.reuters.com/article/us-un-disaster-displacement-idUSKBN1CH35D
13. Taru Leading Edge. (2020). *Understanding Hazard, Vulnerability and Capacity Assessment (HVCA)*. Watsan. (n.d.). Retrieved from SaciWATERs: http://www.saciwaters.org/watsan/pdfs/vambay.pdf

CHAPTER 43

Development of Decision Support System for Effective COVID-19 Management

Shuvrangshu Jana
Post-doctoral Fellow, Department of
Aerospace Engineering,
Indian Institute of Science, Bangalore
shuvrangshuj@iisc.ac.in

Rudrashis Majumder
Ph.D. Student, Department of Aerospace Engineering,
Indian Institute of Science, Bangalore
rudrashism@iisc.ac.in

Aashay Bhise
Project Associate, Department of
Aerospace Engineering,
Indian Institute of Science, Bangalore
meetaashay3@gmail.com

Nobin Paul
Ph.D. Student, Department of Aerospace Engineering,
Indian Institute of Science, Bangalore
nobinpaul@iisc.ac.in

Stuti Garg
Project Assistant, Department of
Aerospace Engineering,
Indian Institute of Science, Bangalore
stutigarg9@gmail.com

Debasish Ghose
Professor, Department of Aerospace Engineering,
Indian Institute of Science, Bangalore
dghose@iisc.ac.in

Abstract

This paper discusses a Decision Support System (DSS) for cases prediction, allocation of resources, and lockdown management for managing COVID-19 at different levels of a government authority. Algorithms incorporated in the DSS are based on a data-driven modeling approach and independent of physical parameters of the region, and hence the proposed DSS is applicable to any area. Based on predicted active cases, the demand of lower-level units and total availability, allocation, and lockdown decision is made. A MATLAB-based GUI is developed based on the proposed DSS and could be implemented by the local authority.

Keywords: COVID-19; Decision Support System; GUI; Resource allocation; Lock-down management; Prediction

1. Introduction

Management of COVID-19 involves optimal lockdown planning, estimation and arrangement of critical medical resources, and allocation of resources among the units in an optimal manner. The human intervention for this set of activities is sometimes not optimal because of bias and other inaccuracies. Hence, building an autonomous decision support system (DSS) to handle all the activities related to disaster management can address the problems arising from the situation more effectively.

In the past, developing DSS has been given much importance by disaster researchers. Some early works of literature mainly focus on designing the decision support system for the influenza pandemic response. Jenvald et al. (2007) propose a simulation framework to simulate the pandemic environment and relate it to the decision support system (DSS) for influenza preparedness and response. (Fair et al., 2007) developed another simulation setup to model the time-dependent evolution of influenza.(Arora et al., 2012) focus on the complexities associated with the decision-making during the outbreak of influenza pandemic. (Araz et al., 2013) design a DSS to take decisions on the closure and reopening of schools to minimize influenza infection. (Araz, 2013) present a general multi-criteria decision-making framework to make preparedness plans with DSS in order to integrate the estimation of important epidemiological parameters.

(Fogli and Guida, 2013) develops a decision system for emergency response during a pandemic. (Shearer et al., 2020) incorporates dynamic information about the pandemic from the situational awareness framework and integrates it into the broader DSS for pandemic response. Authors in (Phillips-Wren et al., 2020) mainly focus on decision-making during the stressful outbreak of COVID-19. (Currion et al., 2007) talk about the significance of an open-source software model for disaster management. A brief introduction to Sahana software is also given in this paper. (Iyer and Mastorakis, 2006) discuss the important elements of disaster management and the development of a software tool to facilitate disaster DSS. Several other papers like (Li et al., 2013; Shukla and Asundi, 2012) also focus on the software modeling for emergency and disaster management.

Researchers of different fields focused on developing DSS to mitigate the effect of the COVID-19 pandemic outbreak in 2020. (Güler and Geçici, 2020) find the solution for the problem of shift scheduling of the physicians by using mixed-integer programming and then using it in a DSS. In (Sharma et al., 2020), a multi-agent intelligent system is developed for decision-making to assist the patients. (Hashemkhani Zolfani et al., 2020) address hospital location selection problem for COVID-19 patients using gray-based DSS. The paper (Govindan et al., 2020) develops a practical decision support system depending on the health-practitioners' knowledge and fuzzy information system to break the chain of COVID infection. (Marques et al., 2021) uses AI-based prediction model for decision making in COVID-19 situation.

The DSS related to COVID-19 reported in the literature is mostly focused on specific activities related to resource management by medical personnel in a hospital environment. However, an integrated DSS covering estimation, allocation, and lockdown management for government authority will help efficient disaster management. This paper describes autonomous DSS that addresses prediction, allocation, and optimal lockdown management for efficient management of COVID-19 in India. The algorithms incorporated in DSS are scalable and flexible, and thus it applies to any level of a government authority. The algorithms are based on a short-term prediction of COVID-19 cases using the time series data of reported cases. A graphical GUI is developed for decision making and the GUI inputs are demand/availability of critical items and total cases, recovered cases, and deceased cases. The proposed DSS could help the authorities to take crucial allocation and lockdown decisions in an optimal manner.

The rest of the paper is described as follows: Section 2 describes the current status of the decision-making process in COVID-19 and the requirement of DSS. The overview of the algorithms incorporated in DSS is presented in Section 3. The description of the GUI of DSS is shown in Section 4.

2. COVID-19 management

The important tasks of a COVID management authority are the prediction of COVID-19, computation of demand, allocation and distribution of critical items, and decision making for the level of lockdown. In general, COVID-19 is managed through different hierarchical levels of authorities, and each level has different responsibilities. COVID-19 management structure in the context of India is shown in Fig. 43.1. In this case, COVID management is performed through centre, state, district, and block hierarchy. Different responsibilities at each level are also mentioned. At centre level critical resources like oxygen and ventilator are allocated to different states, and those items are further distributed to district authorities to be distributed to the hospital. Clearly, the allocation of critical resources is performed at different levels, and the allocation factor is not the same at each level. The allocation should generally depend on the parameters related to active cases, total cases, test positive ratio, and existing resources. At the initial stages of the pandemic, the decision for the lockdown was taken only at the top level; however, at later stages, the local authorities also took the drastic decision of lockdown. The primary factors behind the resource allocation and lockdown decision are the prediction of total cases and active cases. Currently, different physical models are adopted by different authorities; however, there is no standardized model approved by the government authority. Also, modeling the dynamics of the pandemic is complex, and its parameter needs to be calibrated for each new area. Therefore, sometimes the factors behind the allocation are not justifiable in a quantitative sense.

2.1 Decision Support System for COVID-19

COVID-19 management at the government level is a complex task to ensure proper estimation of demand, optimal allocation of resources, and optimal lockdown management. The critical decision needs to be taken considering economic, medical, and complex social factors. Also, the decision-making criteria need to be formulated using quantitative tools rather than qualitative factors for fair and optimal allocation. As decision-making has to be performed at each level, it might not be possible for each allocation authority to model these factors quantitatively. Currently, a COVID management authority has no standard tool to ensure optimal allocation and lockdown. Clearly, it is not easy to always make optimal decisions by a COVID-19 management authority without access to high-level technical expertise. A DSS for taking the decision of allocation and lockdown could help the government authorities in the optimal decision and avoid catastrophic failure.

In general, a decision support software should be able to integrate the information from the multiple layers of spatial

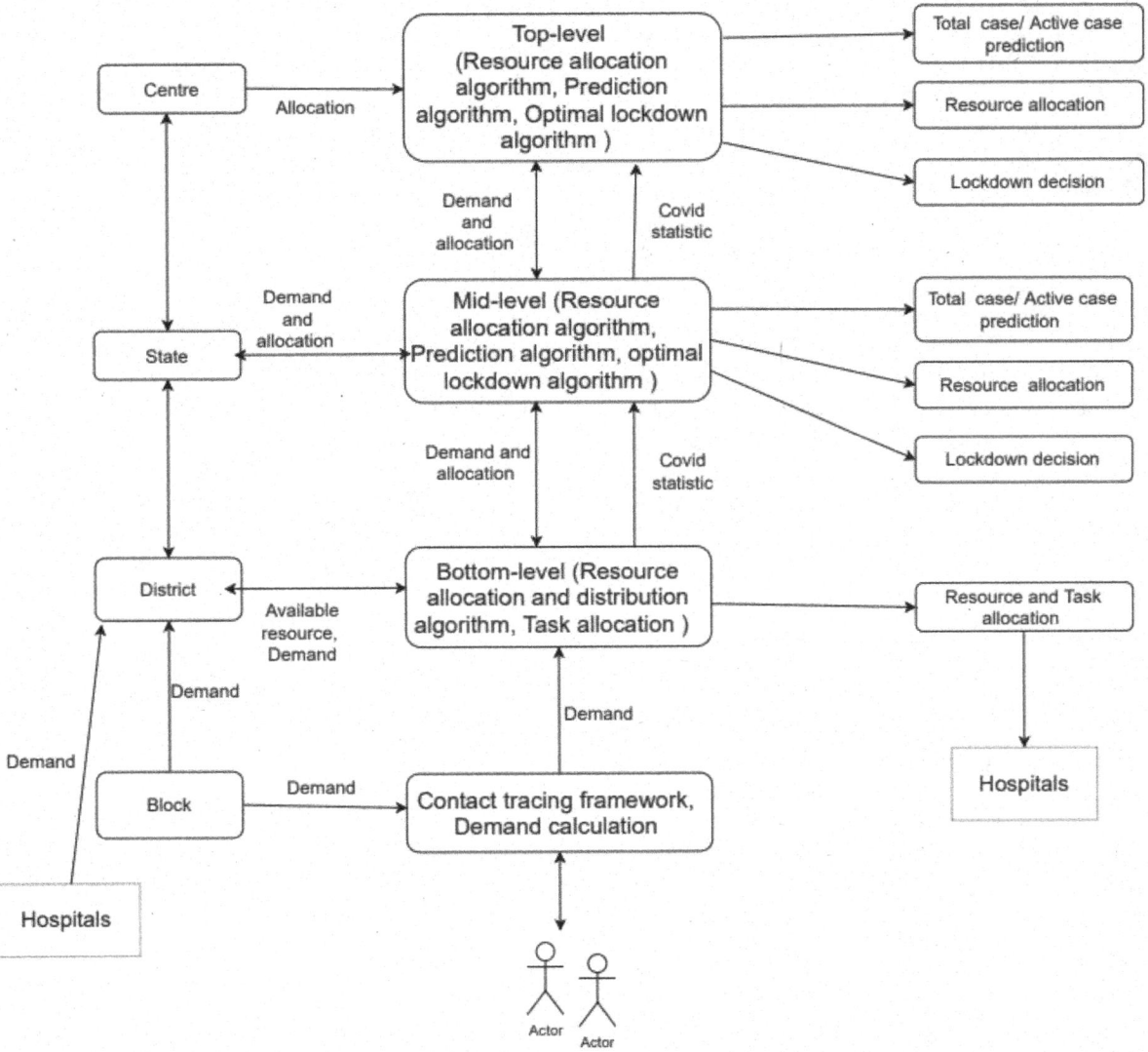

Fig. 43.1 COVID management at different level

and statistical databases and aid in decision making. In the case of COVID-19 management, DSS should be designed such that it could take the decision of estimation, allocation, and lockdown management from the observed cases of total cases recovered cases and deceased cases without the requirement of complex algorithm parameters. Apart from allocation and lockdown analysis, the prediction of COVID-19 should be available to authorities for decision-making. The prediction module should be integrated into suitable external information sources for the early prediction of disaster.

3. Algorithms

In this section, the overview of algorithms for decision-making is discussed. Algorithms need to be designed,

keeping in mind that they should be scalable and flexible. The scalability is required to ensure that DSS is applicable at lower levels consisting of the population in millions to higher-level consist of the population in tens of millions. Flexibility is required so that the algorithms are mostly independent of the region. The three important algorithms for prediction, allocation, and lockdown management is discussed.

3.1 COVID-19 Prediction

The various COVID-19 prediction models are available in literature based on physical modeling, data-driven modeling, and a hybrid approach that combines physical and data-driven modeling. The physical and hybrid models will require transmission parameters for each region; however, the data-driven model will need only the observed values of total cases, recovered cases, and deceased cases. Physical modeling tries to model the actual dynamics of the pandemic, but most of the pandemic-related government decisions are taken based on the reported cases. Public perception of COVID management is mostly based on the reported cases rather than the actual COVID cases. The data-driven model will satisfy the flexible criteria and also be simple for lower-level authorities. We have considered a data-driven adaptive short-term model reported by Jana and Ghose (2020) for the development of DSS. In this case, case prediction is developed using time series data of previous observations. The prediction function is adaptively updated based on weighted least square functions to track the current dynamics of COVID-19. The total cases, active cases, deceased cases, and active cases could be predicted using the previous observations, and the prediction is found to be reasonable up to 2-3 weeks. As the function is adaptive and the decision frequency of administration will not be generally higher than two weeks, this algorithm could be integrated into DSS.

3.2 Allocation

Disaster management authorities allocate the lower units based on resources available from the upper administrative level and the demand requirement for the lower administrative level. The resource allocation module should be able to allocate optimally among the lower level using their demand and severity (Jana et al., 2021a). The allocation mechanism in COVID-19 is complex as the unit demand of each critical item might vary from region to region based on region-specific medical and social factors. For example, the amount of oxygen to be provided to the patient could differ depending on the medical protocol developed by the individual region. So, the demand for medical items of low-level units is difficult to compare because of variation in protocol and unavailability of data of existing resources. So, for this, algorithms need to be selected which can incor-porate those uncertain factors. In this case, we have considered an optimization model which considers the demand of lower units and demand based on their active cases (Jana et al. (2021b)). For allocation of each item, the inputs are the demand of each item and the maximum value of the active cases over the next seven days. This prediction of active cases is performed using the prediction algorithm described earlier. This algorithm provides a closed-form solution, and it is scalable for any number of units.

3.3 Lockdown Management

The decision for lockdown allows less medical load, but it has a detrimental effect on the economy and various social factors. However, it is difficult to incorporate all these factors accurately in the decision-making process as modeling of this factor is not possible at each level. To develop a simple DSS, it should be independent of those factors. Since ensuring the availability of the medical items is the main criteria for

lockdown, we have adopted a lockdown algorithm for DSS, proposed by Jana and Ghose (2021) to ensure that there is no scarcity of medical items. In this algorithm, the demand of each item over the next 14 days is checked, and lockdown is recommended if the availability of any of the critical items is lower than the demand at any point. The demand for the next 14 days of each item is calculated as a function of predicted active cases.

4. Graphical User Interface Design

Graphical user interface to be designed so that it is easily implementable at lowest lower level of authorities with limited access to technical resources. Tentative input and output of the DSS is shown in Fig. 43.2. Clearly, user needs to enter the COVID statistic and the demand of critical items for decision making process and no specific parameter related to a particular area is needed.

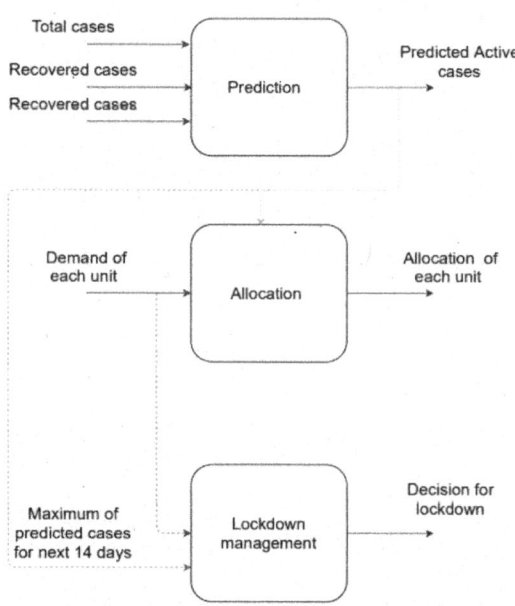

Fig. 43.2   Input-output block diagram of GUI

Generally, statistics of COVID cases are available in a specific format, and GUI has to be designed so that the output is obtained with limited manual intervention. The input data could be linked with the database of COVID-19 to reflect the automatic change in the status. Currently, We have developed the DSS in MATLAB specific to the Indian context; however, it is easily adaptable for different countries. The snapshots of the different tabs of GUI are shown in Figs. 43.3–43.8. GUI has three tabs: prediction, allocation, and lockdown. GUI is currently developed for the central government of India, and few states are considered for demonstration of GUI. The

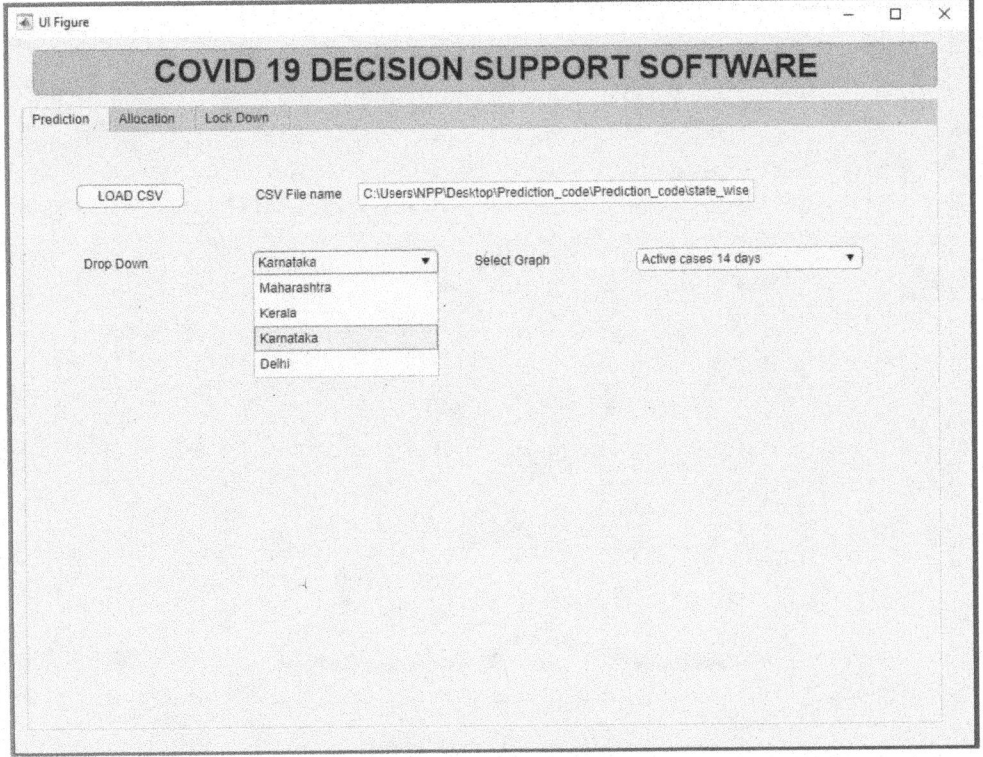

Fig. 43.3 Prediction Tab (a)

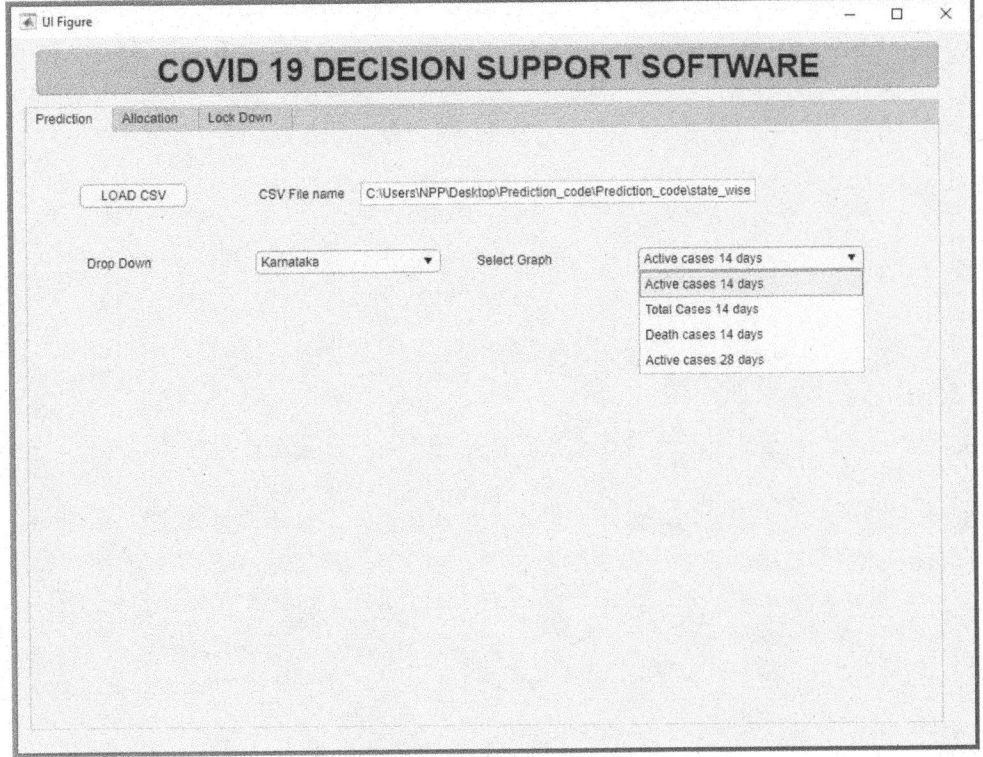

Fig. 43.4 Prediction Tab (b)

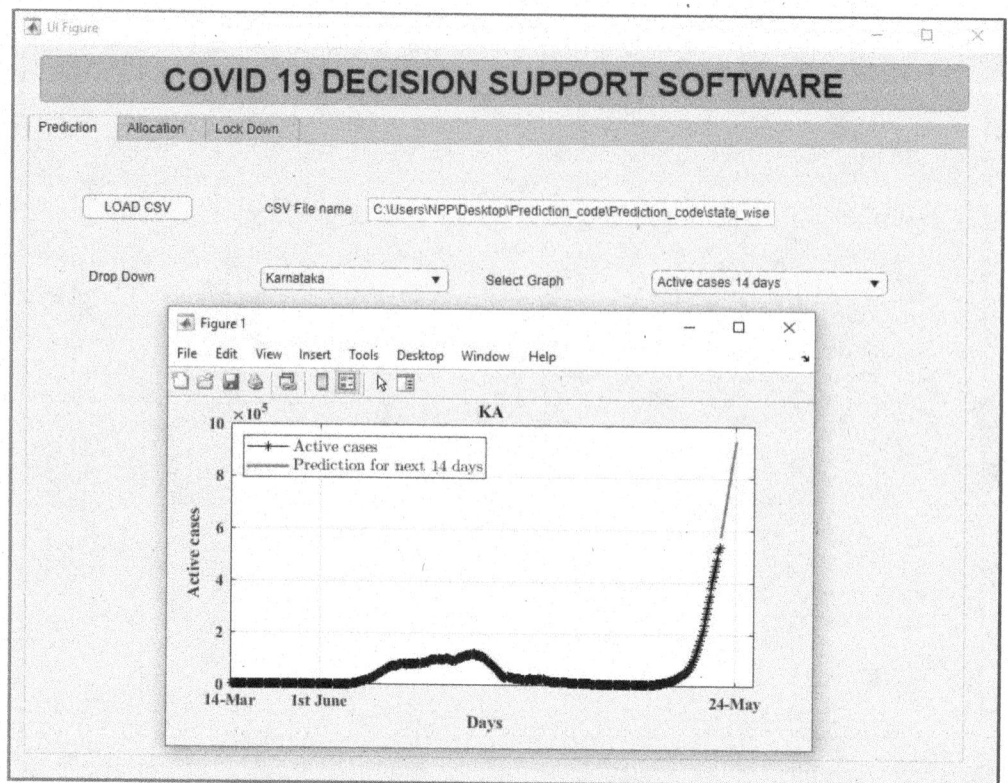

Fig. 43.5   Prediction Tab (c)

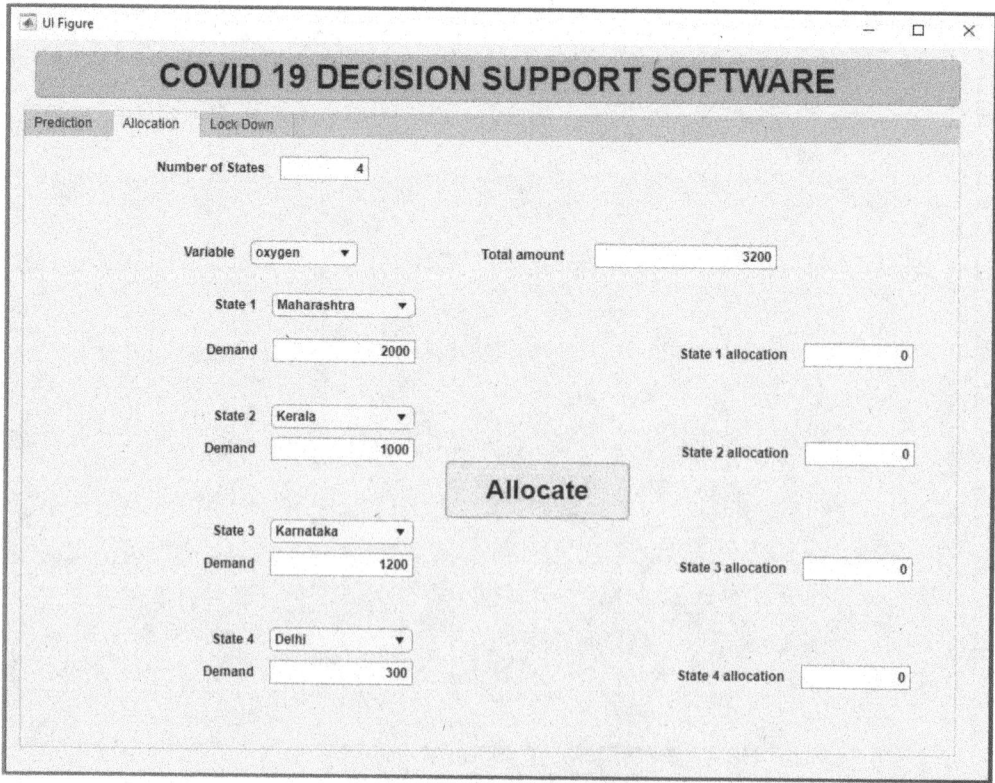

Fig. 43.6   Allocation Tab (a)

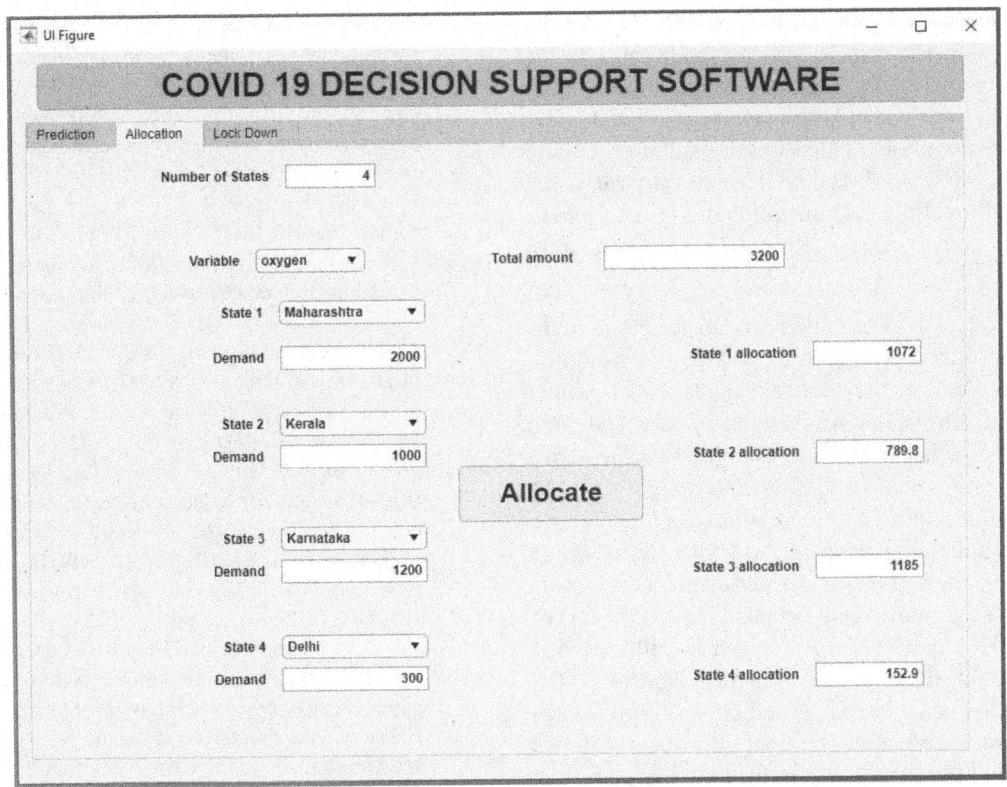

Fig. 43.7   Allocation Tab (b)

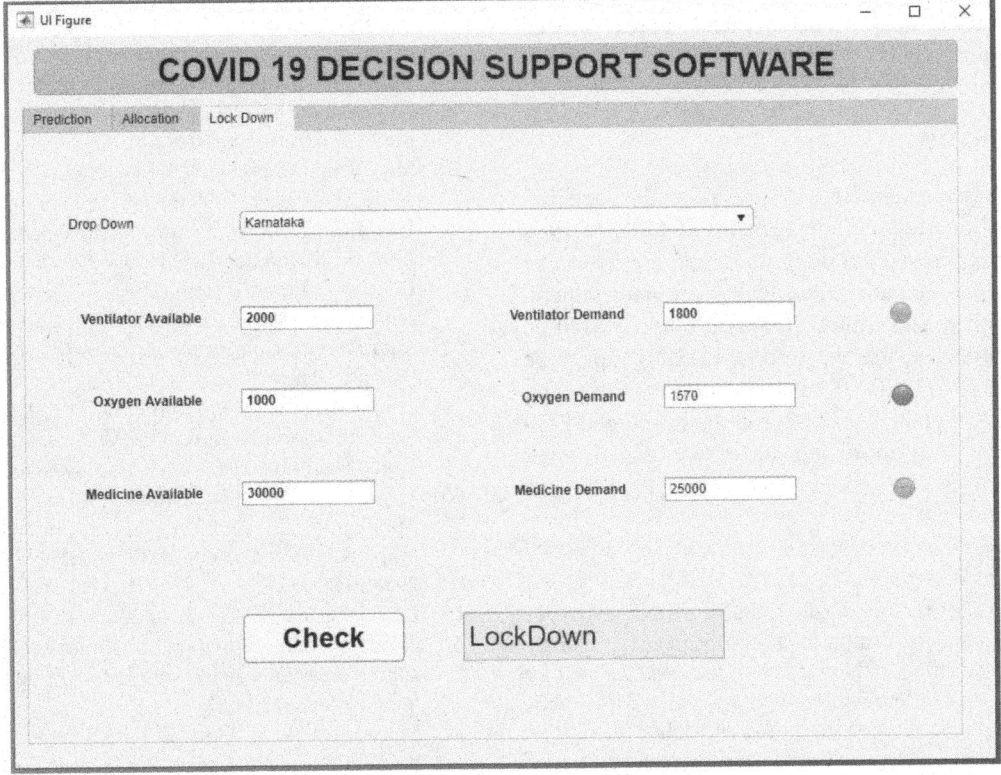

Fig. 43.8   Lockdown Tab

prediction tab selects cases history from the CSV file, and the prediction graph is generated. In the case of India, this file is directly available from the "https://api.covid19india.org/". Based on the states and type of graph tab, the predicted graph is generated. The snapshots related to the prediction tab are shown in Fig. 43.3 -Fig. 43.5. The GUI is currently run using the data up to 10 May 2021, and the graph in Fig. 43.5 shows the prediction of active cases of Karnataka for the next 14 days.

In the allocation tab (Fig. 43.6), the user can select the items to be allocated and the corresponding units for allocation. In this case, we have demonstrated for four states. The user only needs to enter the corresponding demand of each state and the total amount. The back-end algorithm predicts the active cases and incorporates that in the allocation algorithm. An allocation scenario is considered to demonstrate the effective integration of the allocation algorithm with GUI. As shown in Fig. 43.6, the allocation of oxygen is performed considering four states, and their individual demands are 2000, 1000, 1200, 300 MT. The total available oxygen for allocation is 3200 MT. The final allocation is shown in Fig. 43.7. The allocation algorithm considered the prediction of active cases of states on the back-end side. The final allocation is shown to be 1072, 789.8, 1185, 152.9 MT. In the lockdown tab (Fig. 43.7) user only needs to enter the available values of the critical items.

The back-end checks using predicted demand and recommend the lockdown requirement.

5. Conclusions

In this paper, a decision support system to aid in the decision-making of authorities for the management of COVID-19 is presented. The proposed DSS consists of the prediction of COVID-19, optimal allocation, and lockdown management. The backend algorithms for the DSS are developed based on a data-driven approach so that the proposed DSS is applicable for any region. A MATLAB GUI is developed incorporating the proposed DSS. Authorities could use the developed DSS for managing the allocation and lockdown-related tasks related to COVID-19.

REFERENCES

1. Araz, O. M. (2013). Integrating complex system dynamics of pandemic influenza with a multi-criteria decision making model for evaluating public health strategies. *Journal of Systems Science and Systems Engineering*, 22(3): 319–339.
2. Araz, O. M., Lant, T., Fowler, J. W., and Jehn, M. (2013). Simulation modeling for pandemic decision making: A case study with bi-criteria analysis on school closures. *Decision Support Systems*, 55(2): 564–575.
3. Arora, H., Raghu, T., and Vinze, A. (2012). Decision support for containing pandemic propagation. *ACM Transactions on Management Information Systems (TMIS)*, 2(4): 1– 25.
4. Currion, P., Silva, C. d., and Van de Walle, B. (2007). Open source software for disaster management. *Communications of the ACM*, 50(3): 61–65.
5. Fair, J. M., LeClaire, R. J., Wilson, M. L., Turk, A. L., DeLand, S. M., Powell, D. R., Klare, P. C., Ewers, M., Dauelsberg, L., and Izraelevitz, D. (2007). An integrated simulation of pandemic influenza evolution, mitigation and infrastructure response. In *2007 IEEE Conference on Technologies for Homeland Security*, pages 240–245. IEEE.
6. Fogli, D. and Guida, G. (2013). Knowledge-centered design of decision support systems for emergency management. *Decision Support Systems*, 55(1): 336–347.
7. Govindan, K., Mina, H., and Alavi, B. (2020). A decision support system for demand management in healthcare supply chains considering the epidemic outbreaks: A case study of coronavirus disease 2019 (COVID-19). *Transportation Research Part E: Logistics and Transportation Review*, 138: 101967.
8. Güler, M. G. and Geçici, E. (2020). A decision support system for scheduling the shifts of physicians during COVID-19 pandemic. *Computers & Industrial Engineering*, 150: 106874.
9. Hashemkhani Zolfani, S., Yazdani, M., Ebadi Torkayesh, A., and Derakhti, A. (2020). Application of a gray-based decision support framework for location selection of a temporary hospital during COVID-19 pandemic. *Symmetry*, 12(6): 886.
10. Iyer, V. and Mastorakis, N. E. (2006). Important elements of disaster management and mitigation and design and development of a software tool. *WSEAS Transactions on Environment and Development*, 2(4):263–282.
11. Jana, S. and Ghose, D. (2020). Adaptive short term COVID-19 prediction for india. *MedRxiv*.
12. Jana, S. and Ghose, D. (2021). Optimal lockdown management using short term COVID-19 prediction model (submitted). *World Congress on Disaster Management (WCDM)*.
13. Jana, S., Majumder, R., Menon, P. P., and Ghose, D. (2021a). Decision support system (DSS) for hierarchical allocation of resources and tasks for disaster management. Presented at *5th International Conference on Dynamics Of Disasters (DOD)*, Athens, Greece.
14. Jana, S., Rudrashis, M., and Ghose, D. (2021b). Critical medical resource allocation during COVID-19 pandemic (submitted). *World Congress on Disaster Management(WCDM)*.
15. Jenvald, J., Morin, M., Timpka, T., and Eriksson, H. (2007). Simulation as decision support in pandemic influenza preparedness and response. *Proceedings ISCRAM2007*, pages 295–304.
16. Li, J. P., Chen, R., Lee, J., and Rao, H. R. (2013). A case study of private–public collaboration for humanitarian free and open source disaster management software deployment. *Decision Support Systems*, 55(1): 1–11.
17. Marques, J. A. L., Gois, F. N. B., Xavier-Neto, J., and Fong, S. J. (2021). Prediction for decision support during the COVID-19 pandemic. In *Predictive Models for Decision Support in the COVID-19 Crisis*, pages 1–13. Springer.

18. Phillips-Wren, G., Pomerol, J.-C., Neville, K., and Adam, F. (2020). Supporting decision making during a pandemic: Influence of stress, analytics, experts, and decision aids. *The Business of Pandemics: The COVID-19 Story*, page 183.

19. Sharma, A., Bahl, S., Bagha, A. K., Javaid, M., Shukla, D. K., Haleem, A., et al. (2020). Multi-agent system applications to fight COVID-19 pandemic. *Apollo Medicine*, 17(5): 41.

20. Shearer, F. M., Moss, R., McVernon, J., Ross, J. V., and McCaw, J. M. (2020). Infectious disease pandemic planning and response: Incorporating decision analysis. *PLoS medicine*, 17(1): e1003018.

21. Shukla, M. M. and Asundi, J. (2012). Considering emergency and disaster management systems from a software architecture perspective. *International Journal of System of Systems Engineering 4*, 3(2): 129–141.

CHAPTER 44

Disaster Management Law in the Context of Covid 19

Priya A Sondhi
Associate Professor, School of Law,
Bennett University, Greater Noida

Abstract

Covid 19 is the first pan India disaster after 2005, when the Disaster Management Act was enacted. It is the true test of the machinery for disaster management in general and law in particular. Covid 19 brought into picture a century old law Epidemic Diseases Act and an unknown important law Disaster Management Act 2005 (hereinafter referred to as DM Act). Suddenly, people became aware of the Disaster Management Act and questions were raised about its status of implementation and effectiveness. Besides, questions were raised about the governmental mechanism relating to Covid 19 and the DM Act.

It also resulted into active involvement of both executive by way of delegated legislation and judiciary; both Supreme Court of India and the High Courts in different States, to protect the rights of people by way of suo-moto petitions and writ petitions. This resulted into generation of a credible body of disaster management law jurisprudence.

This article looks forward to evaluation of this recently evolved jurisprudence in Disaster Management Law

Keywords: delegated legislation, Supreme Court, High Court, judgement, Disaster Management Act 2005

1. Introduction

Covid 19 is the first pan India disaster after 2005, when the Disaster Management Act was enacted and proved out to be the true test of the machinery for disaster management evolved by the Statute. It also resulted into people becoming aware of a hitherto unknown Disaster Management Act and questions were raised about its status of implementation and effectiveness. Besides, questions were raised about the governmental mechanism relating to Covid 19 and the DM Act.

Covid 19 also brought unprecedented challenges. New challenges in the form of misbehavior with doctors and nurses were also handled by way of an ordinance.

The lockdown was very difficult phase for the present generation, which is born and brought up in an atmosphere of fundamental rights bestowed to us by the Constitution of India and evolving concept of unremunerated rights. Thus, forming the basis for the challenge to the constitutional validity of lockdown and social distancing. The lockdown also led to certain economic and legal reforms which were essential to give relief the masses of India who faced economic and other pressures due to lockdown for example extension of limitation.

It also resulted into active involvement of judiciary; both Supreme Court of India and the High Courts in different States, to protect the rights of people by way of suo-moto petitions and writ petitions. This resulted into generation of a credible body of disaster management law jurisprudence.

2. Methods

The research is essentially doctrinal in nature. The research design is descriptive and diagnostic in nature because it suits the need to study and evaluate the judgments of Supreme Courts and various High Courts relating to challenges placed by COVID 19. The author is conscious of and has prior knowledge of the main issues and challenges to be investigated.

The author has studied the original judgments from library and online resources to understand judicial perspectives.

The primary source of information is the bare acts. Judicial precedents and other print or online sources are secondary in nature.

The focus of the study as stated were reflected in the following objectives:

1. To study the law applicable to the scenario created by COVID 19
2. To evaluate the immediate legal reforms
3. To evaluate the judicial precedents relating to core issues and challenges posed by COVID 19

with the above methodology in mind the research results into the following discussion—

3. Discussion

In order to understand the entire façade of legal regime during Covid, this article will have a three-pronged approach. This article is divided into Part 1—Law at normative level—wherein the author has examined the law applicable, the Disaster Management machinery and constitutional validity of lockdown and social distancing, in Part II—Judicial responses, wherein the author has analyzed the judicial response to Covid 19 followed by conclusions and suggestions

3.1 Part 1—Law at Normative Level

In this part the author has focused on law applicable, the Disaster Management machinery and constitutional validity of lockdown and social distancing.

A. Applicable Law

In case of the pandemic, orders for lockdown and social distancing were imposed invoking the powers under Epidemic Diseases Act, 1897 and Disaster Management Act 2005. District Magistrates also imposed prohibitory orders under Section 144 of the Code of Criminal Procedure in several districts. This part is divided into following subparts – Epidemic diseases Act 1897, Disaster Management Act 2005 and penal provisions

Epidemic Diseases Act 1897

On March 11, 2019, Karnataka was the first state which implemented this legislation to prevent the spread of Covid 19. At that time around 29 people were tested positive in Karnataka for COVID-19, followed by Haryana which declared COVID-19 as an epidemic under this Act on March 12. This brought into picture a 124 year old legislation, which helped in handing bubonic plague in Mumbai way back in 1896. Hence the preamble—"better prevention of the spread of dangerous epidemic disease".

The Act does not have any definition of epidemic diseases and provides for regulation by state governments, inspection and segregation of persons.

On 22nd April 2020, the Government took the "Ordinance route" to amend the Epidemic Diseases Act, 1897. Unfortunately, there were several stray acts of violence against frontline health care service personnel as well as destruction of property. The Disaster Management Act, (Act 53 of 2005), is of recent origin, the punitive provisions thereof are found to be grossly inadequate and wanting. Therefore, provisions were made for protection of the "healthcare service personnel" and damage or loss to any "property" against acts of violence. Section 2A which now empowers the Centre to inspect and detain any bus or train or goods vehicle or aircraft, or of any person intending to travel therein, besides the pre-existing similar power in regard to any ship or vessel.

In addition to this, in, In Re Distribution of Essential Supplies and Services During Pandemic(2021), directions were given for the welfare of health professionals.

Disaster Management Act 2005

In so far as applicability of the Disaster Management Act 2005 is concerned, Sec 3 provides for establishment of National Disaster Management Authority, Sec 6 (2) (i) provides for powers and functions of the NDMA to take measures for the prevention of disaster, or its mitigation, or preparedness and capacity building for dealing with a disaster situation or threatening disaster situation. As per Section 8, a National Executive Committee is constituted to assist the National Authority in performance of its duty. The Secretary to the government of India, who is in charge of the Ministry or Department of the Central Government having administrative control of the disaster management is the Chairperson, ex officio. Here, it is important to note that "Central Government" means the Ministry or Department of the Government of India having administrative control of disaster management. Currently the Home Ministry is the ministry having administrative control of disaster management. Thus, we receive instructions for Secretary, Home ministry.

It may be noted here that section 36 provides for responsibilities of Ministries or Departments of Government of India. It is the responsibility of every Ministry or Department of the Government of India to take measures necessary for prevention of disasters, mitigation, preparedness and capacity-building in accordance with the guidelines laid down by the National Authority. Hence the ministry for Health and family affairs comes into picture. Similarly, section 39 provides for responsibilities of departments of the State Government. It is the responsibility of every department of the Government of a State to take measures necessary for prevention of disasters, mitigation, preparedness and capacity-building in accordance with the guidelines laid down by the National Authority and the State Authority.

Penal Provisions. Under this subhead we need to study Sec 188, 269, 270, 271 IPC and Sec 144 Cr PC

Section 188 of IPC: This section is relevant because Section 3 of the Epidemic Diseases Act 1897 states that violation of regulations issued under the Act will be an offence under Section 188 IPC. In so far as the pandemic is concerned, the second limb of the offence is relevant, which deals with . . . disobedience causing or tending to cause "danger to human life, health or safety. . . ".

Section 269 of IPC: This provision deals with the offence of "Negligent act likely to spread infection of disease dangerous to life".

Section 270 of IPC: This provision deals with malignant act likely to spread infection of disease dangerous to life.

Section 271 of IPC: This provision deals with disobedience to quarantine rule.

Sec 144 of CrPC: This provision deals with power to issue order in urgent cases of nuisance of apprehended danger.

This law empowers the magistrate of any state or union territory in India to pass an order prohibiting the gathering of four or more people in a specified area. It is often used to clamp down on telecommunication services and order Internet shutdowns.

Hence, we have sufficient law at normative level.

B. **Constitutional Validity of lockdown and social distancing**

In so far as constitutional validity of lockdown and social distancing are concerned, to begin with, the right to life is most sacrosanct and takes precedence over all other rights. The lockdown has raised two essential questions-

1. Whether the lockdown is constitutionally valid?
2. Whether the method of operation of lockdown is constitutionally valid?

From the perspective of fundamental rights, in so far as lockdown is concerned, it is constitutionally valid. Two fundamental rights enshrined in Article 19 of the Constitution of Indian are getting affected. Art. 19 states as under:

Protection of certain rights regarding freedom of speech, etc.

1. All citizens shall have the right-

  (a) to freedom of speech and expression;

  (b) to assemble peaceably and without arms;

  (c) to form associations or unions;

  (d) to move freely throughout the territory of India;

  (e) to reside and settle in any part of the territory of India;[and]

  (g) to practise any profession, or to carry on any occupation, trade or business.

Here, the two fundamental rights getting affected are stated as under:

Art. 19 (1) (d) to move freely throughout the territory of India;

Art. 19 (1) (g) to practise any profession, or to carry on any occupation, trade or business.

Here, it is pertinent to note that both the abovementioned rights are subject to reasonable restrictions under Art 19(5) and Art 19(6) respectively.

Art. 19 (5) states as under:

Nothing in [sub-clauses (d) and (e)] of the said clause shall affect the operation of any existing law in so far as it imposes, or prevent the State from making any law imposing, reasonable restrictions on the exercise of any of the rights conferred by the said sub-clauses either in the interests of the general public or for the protection of the interests of any Scheduled Tribe.

Art 19(6) states as under:

(6) Nothing in sub-clause (g) of the said clause shall affect the operation of any existing law in so far as it imposes, or prevent the State from making any law imposing, in the interests of the general public, reasonable restrictions on the exercise of the right conferred by the said sub-clause, and, in particular, _18[nothing in the said sub-clause shall affect the operation of any existing law in so far as it relates to, or prevent the State from making any law relating to,-

(i) the professional or technical qualifications necessary for practising any profession or carrying on any occupation, trade or business, or

(ii) the carrying on by the State, or by a corporation owned or controlled by the State, of any trade, business, industry or service, whether to the exclusion, complete or partial, of citizens or otherwise].

Thus, both the fundamental rights are subject to reasonable restrictions 'in the interest of public at large'

In Narendra Kumar vs Union of India (1960), the Hon'ble Supreme Court held that to determine the reasonableness of a restriction, among other factors, it must consider the background of the circumstances in which the order is issued and "whether the restraint caused by the law is more than necessary in the interest of the general public."

Thus, Centre can impose a lockdown in the entire country considering the rapid spread of Covid 19. This challenge is not possible since both the fundamental rights are subject to reasonable restrictions in the interest of public at large.

In Bannari Amman Sugars Ltd. V. CTO, (2005) the Hon'ble Supreme Court observed that reasonableness of restriction is to be determined in an objective manner and from the standpoint of interest of the general public and not from the standpoint of the interests of persons upon whom the restrictions have been imposed or upon abstract consideration. A restriction cannot be said to be unreasonable merely because in a given case, it operates harshly.

One more important case to be considered here is Rai Sahib Ram Jawaya Kapur vs The State Of Punjab AIR (1955), wherein the Hon'ble Supreme Court had to deal with the extent of executive power and executive function in a situation where the executive was alleged to have violated the fundamental rights of the citizen vested in them by the Constitution of India without a legislative sanction. This landmark judgement delivered by our apex court in the wake of our independence is now acting as a touchstone for understanding the federal feature of the Indian Constitution through separation of powers.

It was observed by the Hon'ble Supreme Court even if the acts of the executive are illegal in the sense that they are not warranted by law, but no fundamental rights of the petitioners have been infringed thereby, the latter would obviously have no right to complain under Article 32 of the Constitution though they may have remedies elsewhere if other heads of rights are infringed. The material question for consideration therefore here is: What fundamental rights of the petitioners, if any, have been violated by the delegated legislation of MHA and MoHFA in furtherance of their policy of managing the Covid 10 Scenario?

The essential answer to it is no fundamental right is getting affected. Right to life being the most sacrosanct fundamental right; takes precedence in a scenario like this.

Here, it is relevant to quote recent judgement dated 20.05.20 of the High Court of Telangana, Ganta Jai Kumar vs State of Telangana, (2020), wherein the order dated 11.04.20 of the District Medical and Health Officer, Hyderabad excluding private hospitals from treating Covid 19 patients was challenged.

It was observed by the Hon'ble High Court that Right to health is integral part of the Right to life and is a facet of Art 21, restriction thereupon must be reasonable, fair and just. The state cannot incapacitate a person by restricting his choice particularly when it comes to a disease which affects life or health of a person's kin. The order was held as violative of Art.14 and Art.21 of the Constitution of India and also the principles of natural justice (for not giving any reasons) and is set aside.

The following judgments were relied upon in the case-

In Assn. of Medical Super specialty Aspirants & Residents v. Union of India (2019), recently, the Supreme Court of India emphasized the primary duty of the State to 'provide all facilities' to make meaningful the right of a citizen to secure his health.

In State of Punjab v. Ram Lubhaya Bagga (1998), it was observed that it is for the State to secure health to its citizens as its primary duty. No doubt the Government is rendering this obligation by opening government hospitals and health centers, but in order to make it meaningful, it has to be within the reach of its people, as far as possible, to reduce the queue of waiting lists, and it has to provide all facilities to employ best of talents and tone up its administration to give effective contribution, which is also the duty of the Government

In State of Punjab v. Mohinder Singh Chawla (1997) it was observed that right to health is integral to the right to life. Government has a constitutional obligation to provide health facilities.

3.2 Part II—Judicial Responses

In this part the author has analyzed the important judicial responses to Covid 19. The researcher has considered ten important areas where relevant judicial pronouncements have been made.

1. Migrant Labour: In, Alakh Alok Srivastava vs UOI directions were given to shift the migrants to shelter as per the directions of MHA dated 29 March 2020. In, Suo moto petition, In re problems and miseries of migrant labourers – directions were made for immediate provision for adequate transport arrangement, food and shelters are to be provided by the Centre and State Governments free of costs. It was observed that though the Government of India and the State Governments have taken measures yet there have been inadequacies and certain lapses. In, Suo moto petition, In re problems and miseries of migrant laborer's, later, amongst others, directions were given to all States and UTs to identify stranded migrants and transport them back to native places within 15 days. States were directed to consider withdrawal of all cases filed against migrants under Disaster Management Act for lockdown violations, for attempting to walk to native places, crowding at stations etc In event of demand of Shramiktrains, the railways were directed to provide trains within 24 hours. In, In-Re Inhuman Condition At Quarantine Centres And For Providing Better Treatment To Corona Positive (2021), the Allahabad High Court observed that even though the Uttar Pradesh Government has taken satisfactory steps to enhance medical infrastructure in the state and subdue the pandemic, its efforts will not show result unless the public adheres to the Covid-19 protocol. The observation was made as the Bench noted several media reports regarding overcrowding in tourist places, especially hill stations.

2. Covid tests: In Shashank Deo Sudhi vs Union of India (2020), initially in Aril 2020, the supreme court gave directions for free covid tests. The Court directed that free testing will be available to persons eligible under Ayushman Bharat Pradhan Mantri Jan Aarogya Yojana as already implemented by the Government of India, and any other category of economically weaker sections of the society as notified by the Government for free testing for COVID-19.

In, Suo Motu vs State of Gujarat (2020), The Gujarat High Court observed that Gujarat Government should not restrict the number of COVID-19 tests on the fear that more tests would lead to 70% of the population testing positive. It was further observed that the argument that 'more number of tests will lead to 70% of the population testing positive for covid, thereby leading to fear psychosis' should not be a ground to refuse or restrict the testing. In, Suo Motu vs State of Gujarat (2020), the Gujarat High Court further held that private doctors and hospitals need not wait for approval from the government authorities for carrying out COVID-19 tests on those categories of patients mentioned in the testing guidelines laid down by the Indian Council of Medical Research (ICMR). It was observed that the requirement of prior approval for COVID-19 testing by private doctors and hospitals was delaying the process. In, Ganta Jai Kumar vs State of Telangana (2020), The Telangana High Court observed that a medical emergency is not an excuse to trample on the fundamental rights of a citizen under Article 21 of the Constitution. Thus, the Court quashed a government order which compelled citizens to get testing and treatment for COVID-19 from designated government hospitals and prevented them from approaching private hospitals and laboratories for such purposes even though they have requisite approval from the ICMR

3. Vaccine policy: In, In Re Distribution of Essential Supplies and Services During Pandemic (2021), it was observed that the manner in which Centre's current vaccine policy has been framed would prima facie result in a detriment to the right to public health which is an integral element of Article 21 of the Constitution, thus Central Government was directed to consider revisiting its current vaccine policy to ensure that it withstands the scrutiny of Articles 14 and 21

of the Constitution of India. It was observed that it is likely that compelling the State Governments to negotiate with manufacturers on the ground of promoting competition and making it attractive for new vaccine manufactures will result in a serious detriment to those in the age group of 18 to 44years, who will be vaccinated by the State Governments.

4. Oxygen Supply: After various orders came from High Court of Delhi, Allahabad, Jharkhad and others, In, In Re Distribution of Essential Supplies and Services During Pandemic (2021), directions were given for maintaining proper oxygen supply. In Union of India vs Rakesh Malhotra (2021), the Supreme Court directed an audit of the supplies of liquid medical oxygen made by the Centre to all States and Union Territories. It observed that the purpose is to ensure that the supplies which have been allocated are reaching their destination; that they are being made available through the distribution network to the hospitals or, as the case may be, the end users efficiently and on a transparent basis; and to identify bottlenecks or issues in regard to the utilization of oxygen. The Court also directed that the audit will be conducted by sub-groups which are to be formed by the 12-member National Task Force constituted by the Court to formulate the methodology to allocate oxygen to states.

5. Education and exams: In Amit Bathla vs CBSE (2020), CBSE propounded a scheme of assessment for board exams. In, Mamta Sharma vs CBSE (2021), the Supreme Court refused to interfere with schemes propounded by CBSE and ICSE for evaluation of Class XII students, noting that there are other set of students who are supporting and do not want any interference their way. Further, the Bench observed that it finds that the schemes "fair and reasonable", which take into consideration concerns of all students and are in larger public interest.

The Central Board of Secondary Education later on, informed the Supreme Court that results of Class XII Board Examination 2021 for CBSE will be declared by 31st July 2021, and dispute regarding computation of results done in accordance to its assessment policy for Class XII students will be referred to a Committee constituted by CBSE

6. Covid patients: In, In Re Distribution of Essential Supplies and Services During Pandemic (2021), it was directed that admissions to hospital must be based on need. The Central Government, in consultation with the respective State Governments, must formulate guidelines on the stage at which hospitalization is required so as to ensure that scarce hospital beds are not occupied by persons who do not need hospitalization. This aspect should be based on the advice of medical experts and can be suitably altered given the needs of each State (or regions within the State) and in the course of the experiences gained during the pandemic.

Days after the Supreme Court directed the Central Government to frame a uniform national policy on hospital admissions, the Union Ministry of Health and Family Welfare revised the National Policy for Admission of COVID Patients to various categories of COVID facilities. The Health Ministry has called this move a 'patient-centric measure', which aims to ensure a prompt, effective, and comprehensive treatment of patients suffering from COVID19.

In Abhinav Thapar vs Union of India (2021), the Supreme Court issued notice to the UOI on a plea seeking directions to the Centre and the state governments to set up a mechanism for scrutinising and auditing the bills of Covid-19 patients who have complaints of being overcharged.

7. Masks: In, Vishal S Awtani vs State of Gujarat (2020), directed the Gujarat government to come out with a policy or order, directing that all those caught not wearing face cover/mask shall be compulsorily sent to COVID-19 care centres for community service. The Supreme Court later on stayed the Gujarat High Court order which had directed the State of Gujarat to come up with a policy or order that would direct for those caught without a face cover/mask to be compulsorily sent to COVID-19 care centres for community service. While staying the order, the Supreme Court remarked that the Gujarat High Court direction was disproportionate and may lead to health problems. The top court however asserted that masks are compulsory & violators should be penalized as per law.

In Saurabh Sharma vs SDM (2021), Delhi High Court dismissed writ petitions challenging the imposition of fines by the Delhi government on persons not wearing masks while travelling alone in personal vehicles. The Court said that the mask is like a "suraksha kavach" protecting both the person wearing it and those around.

8. Parole: In, In Re: Contagion Of Covid 19 Virus In Prisons(2020), expressing concern over the overcrowding of prisons, the top court had said that there are 1,339 prisons in the country housing approximately 4,66,084 inmates. Quoting a report of the National Crime Records Bureau (NCRB), it had said the occupancy rate of Indian prisons is at 117.6 per cent, and in states such as Uttar Pradesh and Sikkim, the occupancy rate is as high as 176.5 per cent and 157.3 per cent respectively. prisoners convicted of or charged with offences having jail term of up to seven years can be given parole to decongest jails.

In the same case on 7-5-2021, the authorities are directed to ensure that proper medical facilities are provided to all prisoners who are imprisoned. The spread of Covid19 virus should be controlled in the prisons by regular testing being done of the prisoners but also the jail staff and immediate

treatment should be made available to the inmates and the staff.

9. Black fungus: Concerns about drug supply were raised by Delhi High Court, Bombay High Court, Telangana High Court, M.P High Court among others.

10. Religion: In the case of Odisha Vihash Parishad vs Union of India, the Supreme Court allowed the Rath Yatra at Puri in the year 2020, observing the strict restrictions and regulations of the Centre and the State Government. In the year 2021, in the case of Ratha Yatra Committee, Bhatli and Ors. v. Government of Odisha, the Supreme Court dismissed a batch of petitions seeking permission to hold Rath Yatras in other temples in the State of Odisha at par with with Rath Yatra at the iconic Puri Jagannath Temple. It held that given the country is only recovering from second wave of Covid-19.

4. Conclusions

To begin with, there is a distinction between constitutional validity of Lockdown and measures. Lockdown or social distancing may be constitutionally valid, but the measures adapted to achieve the goals can be challenged. The contribution of judiciary has resulted into evolving of a reliable body of jurisprudence. This can be a part of formative work for many researches in near and distant future.

The process of operationalisation of law and policy relating to Covid 19 is a continuous process and as the pandemic reaches its end, we will have a considerable body of jurisprudence to study.

REFERENCES

1. Disaster Management Act 2005
2. The Epidemic Diseases Act 1897
3. The Epidemic diseases (Amendment) Act 2020
4. Indian Penal Code 1860
5. Criminal Procedure Code 1973
6. Abhinav Thapar vs Union of India 8-10-2021 (Supreme Court)
7. Amit Bathla vs CBSE, (2020)7 SCC 233
8. Mamta Sharma vs CBSE, 22-6-2021 (Supreme Court)
9. Narendra Kumar vs Union of India 1960 AIR 430
10. Bannari Amman Sugars Ltd. V. CTO, (2005) 1 SCC 625
11. Rai Sahib Ram Jawaya Kapur vs The State Of Punjab AIR 1955 SC 549, 1955 2 SCR 225
12. Assn. of Medical Super speciality Aspirants & Residents v. Union of India (2019) 8 SCC
13. State of Punjab v. Ram Lubhaya Bagga (1998) 4 SCC 117
14. State of Punjab v. Mohinder Singh Chawla (1997) 2 SCC 83
15. In-Re Inhuman Condition At Quarantine Centres And For Providing Better Treatment To Corona Positive, 8-7-2021 (Allahabad High Court)

16. In Re : Contagion Of Covid 19 Virus In Prisons(2020)

17. Suo Motu vs State of Gujarat, 22-5-2020 (Gujarat High Court)

18. Suo Motu vs State of Gujarat, 29-5-2020 (Gujarat High Court)

19. Ganta Jai Kumar vs State of Telangana, 20-5-2020 (Telangana High Court),

20. Odisha Vihash Parishad vs Union of India, 22-06-2020 (Supreme Court)

21. Ratha Yatra Committee, Bhatli and Ors. v. Government of Odisha, 06-06-2020 (Supreme Court)

22. Alakh Alok Srivastava vs UOI, 31 March 2020 (Supreme Court)

23. Suo moto 6/20 In re problems and miseries of migrant labourers, 26 May 2020 (Supreme Court)

24. Suo moto 6/20 In re problems and miseries of migrant labourers – 9 June 2020 (Supreme Court)

25. In Re Distribution of Essential Supplies and Services During Pandemic, Suo Moto Writ Petition(Civil) No. 3/2021, LL 2021 SC 236

26. Vishal S Awtani vs State of Gujarat, 2-12-2020 (Gujarat High Court)

27. Saurabh Sharma vs SDM, 7-4-2021, (Delhi High Court)

CHAPTER 45

Accelerating Action on SFDRR Targets D, E and G and Related SDGs in this Decade of Implementation

Aloysius Rego

Mainstreaming RSA Practitioners Network MPN 2012 onwards,
former Dy Executive Director, Asian Disaster Preparedness Center ADPC
(1996-2011, Joint Director, National Safety Council of India (1986-96)
regoloy@gmail.com; +917506361554 (India); +201093219110 (Egypt)

Abstract

The Sendai Framework (SFDRR) has three specific system development targets. Target E focusses on building national and 'local' DRR strategies that were to have been achieved by 2020, to be implemented during the "decade of action" 2021-2030. Two other related system building targets were Target G 'increasing availability and access to multi-hazard early warning systems' (MHEWS) and disaster risk information/ assessments and target D 'reducing direct damage to critical infrastructure and basic services disruption'.

The paper reviews the progress made and continuing gaps on DPRR in context of SDGs and Climate Change Adaptation, the progress made on each of these three targets, gives specific examples from different regions worldwide, suggests specific strategies to accelerate action on these targets, recommends formulating and monitoring interim targets to be achieved by 2023 during the SFDRR mid-term review.

The paper welcomes innovative approaches such as modifying agendas in case of slower than expected progress (E.g. Target E); supplementary regional targets such as in Africa and linking DPRR and CCA as in the Pacific, promoting disaster resilience in critical infrastructure and proposes approaches to accelerate implementation of Targets E, G, and D in the second half of the implementation decade to make significant progress by 2030.

Keywords: SFDRR Targets, SDGs, Accelerating action, Implementation

1. Introduction

Reducing unacceptable disaster impacts; by active national and local strategies, enhanced assessment, early warning and reduced damage to critical infrastructure

Twenty years into this new century, disaster risks are taking new shapes and scales with every passing year. From 2000-2019, "7,348 climatological and geophysical disasters killed **1.23 million people,** an average of **60,000** per annum and affected over **4 billion:** injured, homeless, displaced or needing **assistance** leading to approximately US$ 2.97 trillion in economic losses worldwide highlighted by SRSG Ms Mizutori and CRED's Dr Guha-Sapir in their report on the Human Cost of Disasters **(CRED and UNDRR, 2020)**, overviewing the first 20 years of the 21st century. "A majority

of fatalities from 2000-19 were from earthquakes and tsunamis; but over 90%events were floods, storms, droughts, heatwaves and extreme weather events. 6,681 climate-related disasters from 200-2019 caused 510,837 deaths, 3.9 billion people affected, compares with 3,656 climate-related events in 1980-1999 accounted for 995,330 deaths (47% by drought/ famine) and 3.2 billion affected in 1980-1999. **(CRED and UNDRR, 2020)**

Disasters negatively impact development gains, weaken resilience, increase vulnerabilities and impact peoples' lives irreversibly. According to World Bank report of 2016 which studied 117 countries, the **real cost** to global economy is an impact on well being equivalent to consumption losses of **US$ 520 billion per annum**, with **disaster** pushing **26 million people into poverty every year**" **(World Bank,**

2020). For example, Myanmar's 2008 Cyclone Nargis, forced half of its poor farmers to sell off assets including land, to relieve debt, whose economic/social repercussions will be felt for generations The report assesses benefits of resilience-building interventions including early warning systems, improved access to personal banking, insurance policies, social protection, cash transfers and public works programs to help people better respond to and recover. These measures combined help countries save $100 billion a year and reduce disaster's impact on well-being by 20 percent. For example, Kenya's social protection system provided additional resources to vulnerable farmers to help prepare for and mitigate impacts well before the 2015 drought, In Pakistan 2010's floods, the government rapid-response cash grant program supported recovery of 8 million people, lifting many from near-certain poverty. The report showed building poor people's resilience is gaining ground (**World Bank, 2020**).

Climate change, poverty, and inequality are defining challenges of our time—and it is crucial that we tackle them together, recognizing the interconnections between people, the planet, and the economy. The COVID-19 pandemic and economic crisis have been devastating; as countries get through the crisis and start to build back, we need to support them in pursuing green, resilient, and inclusive development. The WBG's Climate Change Action Plan 2021–2025 aims to advance Green, Resilient, and Inclusive Development (GRID) which pursues poverty eradication and shared prosperity with a sustainability lens.

2. Methodology

The paper focusses on

(a) International and national frameworks on DPRR and CCA, their links and connection to development agendas

(b) The seven global targets of SFDRR, with special focus on three targets,

(c) Target E to be achieved by 2020: focussing on national and "local" DRR Strategies, to be actively implemented by 2030

(d) Target G on Disaster risk assessment and early warning systems;

(e) Target D on building resilient critical infrastructure and preventing disruption of basic services

(f) Making 2021-2030 a more effective decade of action

The paper addresses key priorities in each area and the three selected targets, discusses work done so far with examples drawn from specific countries and regions, identifies key

challenges and recommends more effective actions to be taken in the rest of the decade. It serves as an input to the ongoing mid-term review of the SFDRR and identifies approaches and strategies to link it more effectively to the Paris agreement on CCAM and Sustainable Development Goals (SDGs).

Key frameworks for action on disaster risk and climate change (in the context of sustainable development)

The International Decade for Natural Disaster Reduction (IDNDR) from 1990-1999 at its mid-term conference adopted the Yokohama Strategy for a Safer World (YSSW) in May 1994. In 2000, a dedicated UN agency was created for action on Disaster Reduction. The second international conference in Kobe adopted the Hyogo Framework for Action (HFA 2005-2015). Ten years later, on the fourth anniversary of the devastating triple disaster in March 2011, the third World Conference on Disaster Reduction in March 2015 adopted the Sendai Framework on **Disaster Risk Reduction** (SF**DRR**). Building on YSSW and HFA focussed on disaster losses, SFDRR expanded DRR's scope to 'natural', man-made, environmental, technological and biological hazards and risks; emphasised DRM as opposed to DM; defined SFDRR **outcome** as reduction of disaster risk; **goals preventing new** risk, **reducing existing risk** and **strengthening resilience**; articulating guiding principles of state's responsibility to prevent/reduce DR, and engage all-of-society, all-of-State institutions (**UNDRR, 2015**).

The United Nations Framework Convention on Climate Change (UNFCCC) an international treaty adopted at the "Rio Earth Summit" in 1992 entered into force on 21 March 1994, and has near-universal membership (**UNFCCC, 1992**). It is a framework for international cooperation to combat climate change by limiting average global temperature increases and the resulting climate change, and coping with impacts that were, by then, inevitable, with its ultimate aim focussed on preventing "dangerous" human interference with the climate system. 197 countries who ratified the Convention are called Parties to the Convention. The UNFCCC has two sister Rio Conventions, UN Convention on Biological Diversity (**UNCBD, 1992**) and UN Convention to Combat Desertification (**UN CCD, 1992**). By 1995, countries launched negotiations to strengthen the global response to climate change, and, two years later, adopted the Kyoto Protocol that legally binds developed country Parties to emission reduction targets. There are now 192 Parties to the Kyoto Protocol. The Protocol's first commitment period started in 2008 and ended in 2012. (**UN FCCC Kyoto Protocol, 1998**) The second commitment period began on 1 January 2013 and ended in 2020.

The 2015 Paris Agreement, adopted on 12 December 2015, builds on work undertaken under the Convention and charts a new course seeking to accelerate the actions and investment needed for a sustainable low carbon future. Its central aim is to strengthen the global response by keeping a global temperature rise this century well below 2 degrees Celsius above pre-industrial levels and to pursue efforts to limit the temperature increase even further to 1.5 degrees Celsius, and aims to strengthen the ability of countries to deal with climate change impacts (**UNFCCC Paris Agreement, 2015**).

To reach these ambitious goals, appropriate financial flows, including before 2025, setting a new goal on provision of finance from USD 100 billion floor, and an enhanced capacity building framework, and Initiative, will be put in place: supporting action by developing countries and those most vulnerable, aligned to their national objectives, enhancing transparency of action through a more robust transparency framework.

Overall six frameworks were adopted in 2015-2016: the SFDRR, the **Sustainable Development Goals (UN SDGs, 2015)**, Paris **Climate Agreement (UNFCCC Paris Agreement, 2015)**, and Addis Ababa Action Agenda (**UN AAAA, 2015**) in 2015; and World Humanitarian Summit's Istanbul 'Agenda for Humanity' (**UN AFH, 2016**) and **New Urban Agenda** (NUA) in Quito in 2016 (**UN Habitat 3, 2016**); significantly shifted and aligned the international development agenda. Like its predecessors SFDRR catalysed action on resilience globally, aligned with other constituent international agendas, shaped overall by SDGs and Paris Agreement.

Five year since 2015's adoption of six agendas, 2021-2030 was endorsed by UN General Assembly as the '**Decade for Action**' Seven years since **SFDRR**'s adoption, with less than a decade left for implementation, this **paper** focuses on the substantive targets E, G and D, recognises Target E's **slow progress of implementation** and recommends a **revised deadline**, consolidation nationally and 'locally, and **accelerated implementation of these three targets**.

YSSD and HFA **shifted disaster management practice from emergency response** to **more systemic approaches, cementing** global norms of **disaster preparedness, mitigation** and **prevention**. Selected achievements are given in Table 45.1

Sendai yielded **mixed results. Positively,** SFDRR's **global DRR targets** until 2030, reinforced **preparedness** and **prevention, vulnerability reduction** and **building resilience. Negatively politicized negotiation** curtailed inclusion of ambitious, concrete indicators to track progress toward its goals, and **prevented inclusion** of **institutions** to **monitor SFDRR implementation. Goals** were lacking in HFA and sought to include in initial new framework drafts. SFDRR **improved** compared to **predecessor. Firstly,** SFDRR better **understood resilience** and strengthens its application in DRR strategy-. **SFDRR** highlights **limitations** on global cooperation in **international disaster relief.** strongly focussing on **prevention** and **preparedness. Secondly,** SFDRR includes **public health**, role of **women in DRR,** and **local-level actions,** all **known to** strongly **influence vulnerability** and **resilience. Thirdly,** SFDRR sought to overcome HFA deficiencies on **monitoring** and **reporting,** establishing substantive **commitments** to be reached by 2030, 1) **Reducing** the number of **people killed** or otherwise **affected** by disasters, 2) **Lowering damage** to critical **infrastructures,** 3) **Scaling up international partnerships** that support developing countries' DRR efforts, 4) **Setting up** National and local **institutions** by **2020,** 5) Improving **DRIA** and **MHEWS (CSS, 2020).**

DRR, is seen as primary responsibility of **local** or regional, not **national authorities.** in many countries DM Agendas **lack of binding implications, enabling** policy-makers pay **lip service without** having to fear **real commitments.** DRR became clearer under HFA and SFDRR, but remained a **side issue** in **global development politics and development agendas.** The **link** between **economic growth** and disaster **vulnerability** gained little attention and the high-profile

Table 45.1   Selected achievements and challenges of international DRR Governance under HFA.

Field of Action	Achievements	Observed Challenges
DRR as a **political priority**	• normative pressure • new institutions and legislations	• global governance n binding implementation for development and environmental protection
Risk identification, assessment and monitoring	• multi-hazard • early warning	• social and economic vulnerabilities within societies
Culture of safety and resilience	• consensus on resilience and knowledge management	• integration of local knowledge • systematic scientific advisory mechanisms
Reduction of risk factors	• little achieved, inadequate resources	• local reach, social n economic vulnerability within societies
Disaster preparedness DP	• DP capacity-development	• inclusion of all relevant stakeholders

Source: CSS, 2020

agenda, **both MDGs and SDGs. Global environmental politics**, especially climate change effects developed separately from DM agendas, leading to **policy duplication nationally** and **internationally**.

For example, aligning the **Cancun A**daptation Framework agreed at 2010 UN **COP 16** and **Warsaw** International Mechanism for **Loss** and **Damage** from Climate Change Impacts agreed at 2013 **COP 19** (UN FCCC 2010; 2013) If it had been better linked with HFA could have facilitated interdisciplinary knowledge and collaboration (**CSS, 2020, UNFCCC Paris Agreement, 2015**).

Action on DPRR, Response and Recovery and CC Adaptation and Mitigation must link across all SDGs, and work with agencies taking lead on each agenda, UNDRR, UNDP, UNOCHA, UN Habitat, UNFCCC, other UN Agencies, Development Banks, National Development Agencies, Regional Country Associations, Private sector, INGOs, National and local NGOs and Academic Institutions.

At each national level, DPRR and CCAM must be mainstreamed into development in each sector: social, environmental and economic, at multiple levels, national to local and in between, and across multiple institutions. **Isolated working does not help.**

3. SFDRR's Seven Global Targets

For the first time, SFDRR adopted seven global **targets** (para 18), for global **progress assessment. Four** targets focussed on **decreasing:** disaster mortality (Target **a**); people affected (Target **b**), direct disaster economic loss (Target **c**), direct

damage to **critical infrastructure** and **service** disruption (Target **d**); while last **three** aim to **increase** countries **national** and '**local**' DRR **strategies**, (Target **e**), enhance international cooperation and sustainable support to complement national actions (Target **f**), and increase availability and access to multi-hazard early **warning** systems (MHEWS) and disaster **risk** information/ **assessments** (Target **g**) (**UNDRR 2015**).

Six of seven targets were to be achieved by 2030, but **Target E** was **to be achieved by 2020**, serving as **base** and **instrumental** to achieving **other targets.**

The following Fig. 45.1 shows linkages **between relevant SDGs** and the **seven SFDRR targets**. In addition, **target G** is related to **SDG 3 (health)** and **SDG 4 (education)**.

4. Words into Action Guidelines (UN Disaster Risk Reduction 2017 b)

Words into Action (WiA) is a series of guidelines, based on global expertise, communities of practice, and networks of DRR practitioners provide practical, specific advice on implementing a people-centred approach to DRR in line with SFDRR 2015-2030. Most guides have a length of 10 - 60 pages with complementary information: online packages, wiki-type platforms, etc. They are reviewed and updated every few years, or more frequently. They provide a) **Guidance** on **how to implement** SFDRR; b) Worldwide **access to expertise, communities of practice, professional networks and platforms,** c) Support **training, national programs** and capacity building.

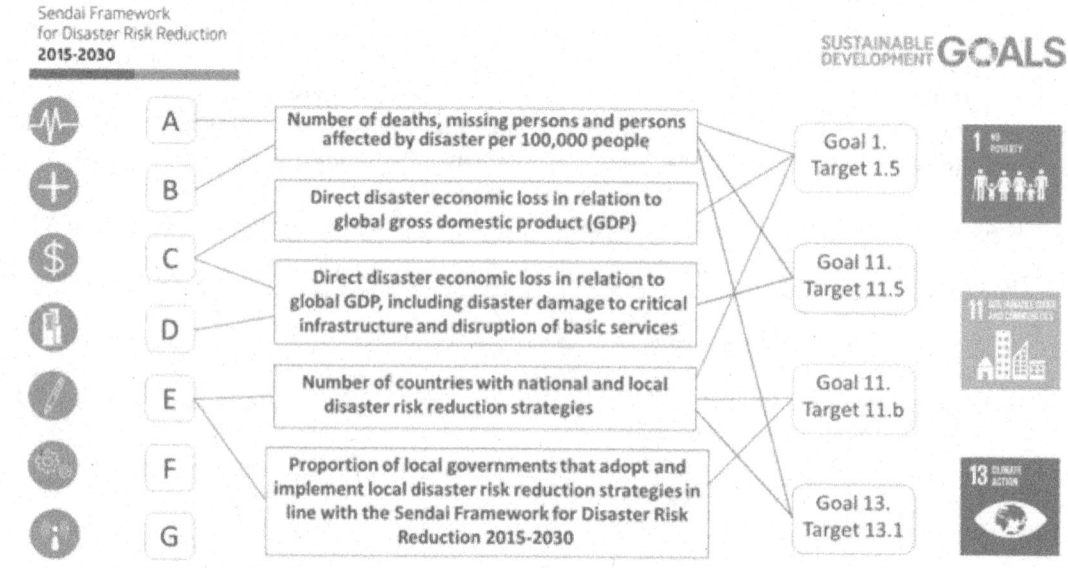

Fig. 45.1 Reducing direct damage to critical infrastructure and basic services disruption

Table 45.2 Ministerial Distribution of Official Sendai Focal Points in OECD Countries.

Interior (16)	PM or Cabinet (5)	Environment (4)	Foreign Affairs (4)	Justice (4)	Defence (2)	Others(2)
Australia, Chile, Estonia, Finland, Germany, Greece, Hungary, Latvia(HFA), Lithuania, Luxembourg, Mexico, Portugal, Slovakia, South Korea, Spain, USA	Colombia, Italy, Japan, Turkey, United Kingdom.	Czech Republic, France, Poland, Switzerland.	Belgium, Ireland, Israel, New Zealand	Iceland (NDMO), Netherlands, Norway, Sweden.	Denmark, Slovenia.	Austria (Education), Canada (Public Safety).

Source: CSS, 2020

Five guides were prepared by the summer of 2017. As of mid- 2022, twelve guides have been prepared and some more are in the pipeline. They are available on Prevention Web and printed version.

WIA 4 and **WIA 6** for **Targets E 1** and **E 2**

Two guides focus on targets E1 and E2.

WIA

4, 2019 Guidelines: Developing national DRR strategies **(UNDRR 2019 a)**.

WIA 6, 2019 Guidelines: Implementation guide for local disaster risk reduction and resilience strategies **(UNDRR 2019 b)**

An earlier version was published for consultation as WIA 2017 Guidelines: National focal points for DRR, National Platforms for DRR and Local Platforms for DRR **(UNDRR 2017 d)**.

These should also be read along with WIA 2017 Guidelines on National disaster risk assessment (NDRA) **(UNDRR 2017 c)**.

WIA 2017 Guidelines: Build back better in recovery, rehabilitation and reconstruction (Consultative Version) **(UNDRR 2017 e)**.

WIA 08 2020: Guidelines on Enhancing disaster preparedness for effective response **(UNDRR 2020)**.

A number of other guides are prepared on other topics but so far no guides have been published on targets d and G.

5. SFDRR National Implementation

SFDRR's national **implementation** and progress reporting is led by **Sendai Focal Points (SFP)** and country administrator for reporting. By **January 2020**, **131 countries** had a registered SFP **(UNDRR, 2017a)**.

Within **OECD, 35 countries designated SFPs** and remaining two designated HFA FPs or National Disaster Management Organization (NDMO). Over two-thirds of 35 OECD countries with SFPs allocated implementation and reporting to NDMO **(CSS, 2020)**.

Table 45.2 shows the Ministries assigned in OECD Countries.

Ministry of Interior is most common Ministry of OECD Countries SFPs, but some assign PM's or **Cabinet Office**, the **Ministry** of **Environment, Foreign Affairs, Justice** or **Defense**, while almost all have **NDMOs. Eleven** countries chose their Focal Point **outside** the main **civil protection** organization, **four** to Ministry of **Environment, four** to **Foreign Affairs, one** to **Education** (Austria), **one** to the **Cabinet Office** (Japan) and **one** to Department of the **Interior** (USA). The **two** groups that **split** the **impl**ementation and **report**ing duties from the operational civil protection organization appear to perceive Sendai through an **environmental** or a **development aid** angle. **A very useful paper provides Country Profiles for 6 states (Austria, France, Germany, New Zealand, Sweden, Switzerland covering their NDMO & Focal Point, National Platform, National Strategy, Implementation challenges reported by country and next steps**

The online **Sendai Framework Monitoring Tool (SFMT)** has **four roles** in SFMT: a) *Coordinator* usually the SFP, can only be created by UNDRR. Other roles assigned by coordinator; also responsible for adding country's basic demographic and socio-economic data (population, GDP, etc); b) *Contributors* relevant government ministry responsible for reporting data on assigned indicators, c) *Validators* checks assigned indicators correctly entered, not in conflict with government's dataset. Do not have to review empirical evidence and verify reported data, d) *Observers* to see activity and data, not public and not yet validated, e.g. Red Cross observer to cross-check data, or Prime Minister's Office to observe reporting progress.

SFMT uses data from previous year for **Targets A** to **E** due on 31 March, while Targets **F** and **G** are due by **1 October**. **87 countries** reported data readiness in **2017**. **Data** collection **more established** for people affected or killed and **physical destruction of buildings**, and **less common** for economic

Table 45.3

	Coordinator	Contributors,	Validators	Observers.
OVERALL average	1.3	3.4	1.5	1.2
New Zealand	1	1	1	
Germany	1	17	1	
Chile (highest)	2	41	31	58

(Source: UNDRR reports and commentaries)

losses, disruptions to **basic services** and damage to specific assets. Targets A and B have highest availability w indicators ranging from **66** per cent (**B.5**) to **83** per cent (**A.2**). More than half countries can compare to baselines from 2005 to 2015. Data availability for other targets more limited. **Lowest availability** indicator on **internatl support (F) (UN Disaster Risk Reduction, 2017 a)**.

On **1 Oct 2019**, UNDRR had **152 countries** w SFMT access.

By **2020, 104 countries** started reporting at least one target for 2018, with **48 validating** at **least one target**. "SFM Data not yet comprehensive enough to derive meaningful national, regional or global trends" (**UNDRR**). UNDRR used EM-DAT data on trends on human cost of disasters for IDDR Day 13 October 2020. "those countries that do not have a well-managed national disaster loss database (DLDB) and systematic methods of data collection, are disadvantaged in reporting. UNDRR adapted DesInventar DLDB software, for countries to record required DLD data in line with **Targets A to D**.

Achievements and **challenges in Target E** by end 2020: A cup half empty or half full

Target E *aimed to 'Substantially increase number of countries with national and local disaster risk reduction strategies by 2020'*.

- E-1 Number of countries adopting and implementing national DRR strategies aligned with SFDRR 2015-2030.
- E-2 %age of local governments adopting and implementing local DRR strategies aligned with national strategies.

This was the first targets to be achieved; a base for other targets. 101 of 195 countries prepared national strategies by end 2020 (Target E1); only 72 had 'local' strategies in place. Progress was slow; and needs accelerate action, at least achieving target E1 and at least 60 %of all local targets E2 by 2022 and use the remaining 8 years to implement the agreed target

3.1 Progress of National Strategies (Target E1) 2015–2020

By end-2020, 101 countries reported national DRR strategies (Table 45.4).

Four regions had a DRR strategy in over 50% countries in Dec 2020, Arab States and Asia Pacific each report 59 %, ECA 53% and Americas 51%. Two key elements of National DRR strategies: coherence and accountability show progress, with 85 countries reporting positively on coherence and compliance, with SDGs and Paris Agreement. There is Progress but much needs to be done by 2022

Table 45.4 Progress on National DRR Strategies by region

Sr No	Regions	Countries per region	National DRR strategies (% age in region)	
			2015	2020
1	Africa	44	10 (23%)	18 (41%)
2	Americas and the Caribbean	35	6 (17%)	18 (51 %)
3	Arab States	22	6 (27%)	13 (59%)
4	Europe and Central Asia	55	12 (22%)	29 (53%)
5	Asia and Pacific	39	10 (26%)	23 (59%)
	Total World	**195**	**44 (23%)**	**101 (52%)**

(Source: UNDRR Target E Report, Table 2 Fig-4 SFM, Aug 2020, pg 19 (UNDRR,2020 a) and Map in UNDRR Annual report Dec 2020, pg 35) (UNDRR,2020 b), Extracted and adapted from Table 4 of paper by Rego A, 2021)

Table 45.5 Progress on 'Local' DRR Strategies by region

Sr No	Regions	Countries per region	'Local' DRR Strategies (% age in region)	
			2015	2019
1	Africa	44	10 (23%)	16 (36%)
2	Americas and the Caribbean	35	7 (20%)	9 (26%)
3	Arab States	22	5 (23%)	9 (26%)
4	Europe and Central Asia	55	10 (18%)	24 (44%)
5	Asia and Pacific	39	7 (18%)	14 (36%)
	Total	195	39 (20%)	72 (37%)

(Source: UNDRR Target E Report, Table 5 SFM, Aug 2020, pg 19 (UNDRR,2020 a) and Map in UNDRR Annual report Dec 2020, pg 35) (UNDRR,2020 b), Extracted and adapted from paper by Rego A,2021)

3.2 Progress of Local Strategies (Target E2) 2015–2019

Risk governance was strengthened locally with 72 countries having local Governments with DRR strategies in 2019, up from 39 countries in 2015. 69 countries reported having both national and local DRR strategies in 2019, a rise from 35 countries in 2015. 96 countries reported either national or local DRR strategies or both, a rise from 48 countries in 2015. There is progress but much more needs to be done to reach our proposed target of 60 % 'local' DRR strategies by 2022.

4. SFDRR Target E Action Sub-regionally

Regional/sub-regional strategies and legally binding DRR frameworks incentivise national DRR strategy. The Caribbean, Disaster Management Strategy boosted country DRR work programmes; the ASEAN Agreement on Disaster Management and Emergency Response (AADMER) activated 10 South East Asian country programs and in the Pacific, most SIDS developed Joint National Action Plans (JNAPs) for DRR and CC under the Pacific Resilience Framework. Regional institutions must play a special role, given common geography and hazard risks in SIDS (**Rego A, 2021**).

4.1 National and Local Strategies (Target E) Chile and Ecuador (*Source:* Greiving S, 2021)

E2: **Chile**an Association of **Municipalities** (AMUCH,) assessed municipal capacities for Disaster and Management in **247** municipalities, (**70%** of all **local governments**). **87.2% municipalities** surveyed have DRM unit, great differences in capacities in each municipality. Using a commune development typology from SUBDERE ("Natural Hazard Analysis Guide for Land-Use Planning"), between **large metropolitan** communes with high n/or medium development, **28%** have a Risk Management **Directorate** (with own resources) and **45%** an **Office** or Department. Semi-urban and rural communes with low development, **48%**

Table 45.6 Similarities and differences between Chile and Ecuador

Issue and Indicator	Chile	Ecuador
Past disasters	Earthquakes and tsunamis greatest damage, droughts, intense rainfall, floods landslides	Earthquake, tsunami, volcano ,heavy rain, drought, landslides; multi-hazard events
Population, total	19.0 million (2019)	17.4 million (2019)
Urban population % of total	88% (2019)	64% (2019)
Urban population growth (annual %)	1.27% (2019)	1.93% (2019)
Informal settlements	741 informal settlements, populated by 43,000 families (2018)	88% municipalities w informal settlements 2.9 mn inhabitants (20% of population)
Indicator E-1: Did Chile and Ecuador adopt national DRR strategies in line with DRR 2015–2030?	Adopted national DRR strategy. Official version not in line w SFDRR, but new version, used internally will be adopted soon	Adopted national DRR strategy. In line with Sendai Framework
Indicator E-2: Percentage of local governments with local DRR strategies in line w natl strategies.	About 40% local governments local DRR strategies. Not linked to Sendai targets	Exact numbers not available. Not linked to Sendai targets

Table 45.7   Disasters and losses, by African Regional Economic Community (REC), 2015–2018 (Van Niekerk, 2019)

Regional Economic Community	No. of recorded disaster events		Death (SFDRR Target (a) per 100000 Population		No affected Target (b) per 100,000 Population		Direct economic loss 1000 US$) (Target c)	
	2015-16	2017-18	2015–16	2017–18	2015–16	2017–18	2015–16	2017–18
IGAD/EAC	39	40	0.57	1.3	7967.78	373.84	1,873 700	483,600
ECCAS	45	68	9.8	8.09	1647.59	2885.96	379,798	280,833
North Africa	112	258	2.3	4.29	394.85	3132.33	20,017	36,000
SADC	84	80	4.06	5.22	7513.25	2579.98	492,515	2,536,612
ECOWAS	31	28	0.54	0.63	905.73	1377.39	69,100	4,807,094
Total	311	474	2.36	2.7	4380.83	1712.56	2,835,130	8,144,139

have **Office** or **Department**, while **36%** have only **one DM person in charge**. **41.8%** municipalities have a Community **Plan** for Civil Protection and Emergencies in force, **31.2%** consider **DRM** in their **Community Regulatory Plans**, **24.9%** have **management plan** and **48.3%** have an **exclusive budget** for disaster/emergency risk reduction.

"In **Ecuador, SNGRE, Association of Municipalities, INEC, and Association of Risk Professionals**" developed a "**Risk Management Index**" adjusted to GADs' competencies, monitored within GADM's institutional setup and budget. The "Guidelines for including DRM in PDOT" refer to SFDRR but not linked to targets A, B and C. For D, the PEEGRD is the National Strategy. Several strategies from both PEEGRD and "Guidelines for including DRM into PDOT" are reflected in response preparedness simulacrum and public awareness campaigns.

4.2 SFDRR Implementation in Africa Targets E

Progress in Program for implementing **SFDRR 2015-2030** and **Africa Strategy for DRR** from 2015-2018 has one Continental and six Regional Reports. for East African Community (**EAC**); Economic Community for Central African States (**ECCAS**); Eco Community of West Africa States (**ECOWAS**); Inter-governmental Authority for Development (**IGAD**); Southern African Development Community (**SADC**) and Union du Maghreb Arabe (**UMA**) and North Africa (including Egypt and Saharawi Republic).

The region had an increase in Disasters from **311** in 2015-16 to **474** for 2017-18. **Droughts, floods, storms** and **epidemics** caused most loss in lives, livelihoods, critical infrastructure, and greatest economic impact **and affected highest** number of **people**. Heightened reporting on extensive risks by MS, with **transportation** and **industrial accidents increasing** over the two periods under investigation (**African Union, 2019**).

Sendai Target E: Increase the number of **countries** with **DRR strategies:**

Few countries have DM policies before 1990s Since HFA, **MS** made **strides** in **developing strategies, promulgating laws** and **revisiting existing plans, strategies** and **legislation.** Most post-2000 policies and strategies aligned with HFA, wand SFDRR. Although there is increase in national DRR policies, strategies, and plans, actual implementation throughout levels of government remains problematic. Only **4.55%** MS reported full implementation of national DRR strategies address all SFDRR objectives/priority areas, **77.27%** MS reported partial implementation and **18.18%** reported no implementation. (Table 45.8). African Countries with DRR strategies **increased** by **22%** since **2015**. Countries

Table 45.8   African member states' progress: Sendai Framework Target (E)

Disaster risk governance aspect	Percentage of countries (%)
Countries with national DRR/DRM **policy or legislation**	88
Countries with national DRR **Strategy/Plan**	65
Countries with **legislation/policies** that seek to address global and continental -- DRR target to **reduce disaster mortality**	79
--to reduce the number of people affected by disasters	80
--DRR target to incorporate DRR in country's educational systems at all levels	74
--DRR target to reduce economic loss due to disasters	65
--DRR target to increase funding for DRR	71
Presence of government institution(s) responsible for DRR/DRM	94
Countries with national DRR/DRM Platform	81
Countries with parliamentary subcommittee dealing with DRR issues	62

Source: Countries reporting on the Sendai Framework and the African Programme of Action

reported strategies aligned with SFDRR and PoA., and in many cases, most are being revised. **Djibouti, Democratic Republic of the Congo, Somalia, Sudan, Guinea-Bissau, Liberia, Niger, Senegal, Cameroon, Congo, Equatorial Guinea, and Gabon** do **not currently have any DRR strategies in place. Only 38% of subnational level** entities reported existence of DRR strategies and plans, mostly **in urban centers,** with **rural municipalities lagging** behind.. This figure relates to 21 countries that reported on this target **(Van Niekerk, 2019).**

For **Target (e),** lack of implementation of national policies and strategies at national (cross-sectoral coordination and buy-in) and subnational levels, and funding support for their implementation, greatly affects achievement of this target. RECs should support countries that do not have national policies and laws in place, and create funding streams for tracking funds allocated for implementation at all levels of government, reported annually.

5. Challenges and Ongoing Actions Till 2022 End (UNDRR, 2020b)

COVID-19 pandemic slowed Governments in developing national DRR strategies, but triggered awareness to adopt all risk DRR strategies, including biological hazards / pandemics / health emergencies. Improved access and analysis of disaster risk and climate data at various scales must reorient Governments' to risk-informed development using the SDGs, SFDRR and the Paris agreement with communications and advocacy by stakeholders'.

Target E is being accelerated nationally by UNDRR, and 20 partners from 2020-2022 in 40 SIDS, LDCs and LLDCs: **19** in **2020** (in bold) and 21 in 2021-22, selected for their special needs, high exposure and vulnerability to hazards: **12** in **Africa** (Benin, Burkina Faso, Chad, Ethiopia, Guinea-Bissau, Lesotho, **Malawi**, Mozambique, Niger, Sao Tomé and Principe, **Uganda,** Tanzania); **9** in **Americas and Caribbean** (Bahamas, **Belize, Cuba, Dominica**, Grenada, **Haiti**, Saint Kitts and Nevis, Suriname, Trinidad and Tobago); **4 Arab** states (**Comoros, Djibouti, Mauritania, Sudan**) and **15** in **Asia-Pacific** (Afghanistan, **Bangladesh, Cambodia**, Fiji, **Kiribati, Lao PDR,** Marshall Islands, Micronesia, Nauru, Palau, **Solomon Islands, Timor-Leste,** Tuvalu, Vanuatu). Planning and action in **remaining 45 countries** by end 2022, so we have strategies in all 195 countries and focus on **implementing** in **next 8 years.**

5.1 Target G on EWS in Relation to Overall SFDRR, SDGs and Paris

Early warning **(Target G)** is one of **seven global targets** reflecting need for paradigm shift in the way risk information is developed, assessed and **utilized** in multi-hazard early warning systems, DRR strategies and government policies.

Early warning contributes to **sustainable development** especially goals on **food security, healthy lives, resilient cities, environmental management** and **climate change adaptation**

The **Paris Agreement** stipulates early warning systems as a major focus area to enhance adaptive capacity, strengthen resilience, reduce vulnerability and minimize loss and damages associated with adverse effects of climate change.

Target G *Substantially increase **availability of** and **access to** the people by 2030 of **multi-hazard early warning systems (MHEWS)** and **disaster risk information** and **assessments** to.*

- G-1 Countries with multi-hazard early warning systems (**MHEWS**). (Compound G2 - G5)
- G-2 Countries with multi-hazard **monitoring** and **forecasting** systems.
- G-3 People per 100,000 covered by **early warning information** thru **local governments** or **national dissemination mechanisms**.
- G-4 Percentage of **local governments** having a **plan to act on EWS**.
- G-5 Countries with **accessible, understandable, usable** and **relevant** disaster **risk information** and **assessment** available to people at national and local levels.
- G-6 %age of population exposed to or at risk from disasters **protected** thru **pre-emptive evacuation** following EW

*Member State (able to do so) are **encouraged** to provide information on number of **evacuated people***

5.2 MHEWS (G1 to G4 and G 6)

Checklist is key outcome of May 2017 Conference organised by International Network for Multi-Hazard Early Warning Systems (IN-MHEWS) updating original document, *Developing EW Systems: A Checklist*, outcome of 3rd International Conference on EW: from Concept to Action, in **March 2006** in Bonn, Germany (**WMO UNISDR UNESCO Mexico 2017**).

Four elements of **efficient, people-centred** early warning systems **EWS** are:

(i) **Disaster risk (DR) knowledge** based on systematic DR data **collection** and **assessments**;

(ii) **Detection, monitoring, analysis** and **forecasting** of hazards consequences;

(iii) **Dissemination** and **communication**, by official source, of **authoritative, timely, accurate** and **actionable** warnings and information on **likelihood** and **impact**; and

(iv) **Preparedness** at all levels to respond to warnings received.

"**Multi-Hazard**" includes multiple major hazards that a country faces, and (2) specific contexts where hazardous events occur simultaneously, cascadingly or cumulatively over time, considering potential interrelated effects. Hazards include **biological, environmental, geological, hydro-meteorological** and **technological** processes and phenomena. **Main actors** involved, their roles, responsibilities and **cross-cutting** issues including governance and institutional arrangements, a multi-hazard approach to early warning, involvement of local communities and consideration of gender, age and disability and cultural diversity.

People-centred MHEWS empowers communities threatened by hazards to act in advance appropriately to reduce personal injury, illness, life loss and damage to property, assets and environment. Stakeholders must work together ensuring MHEWS operates as expected, enables benefit from traditional indigenous knowledge on hazards; geospatial technologies to ensure information on exposed elements is up to date; latest information communication technologies facilitate communication among all stakeholders to ensure warnings reach those at risk. Periodic system improvements must incorporate lessons learned from routine operations, taking advantage of regional and global capacities /support mechanisms. The system must have an enabling environment, good governance, adequate operational capacities, clear roles and responsibilities for all stakeholders and be adequately resourced with effective operational plans **Standard operating procedures** SOPs outlining tasks as routine system operation, defining different stakeholders roles at different times facilitating decision-making and delegation of authority to decision makers on short notice when nominated decision-makers cannot be reached in sudden-onset events. There should be regular testing and feedback for continuous system improvement.

Key elements of MHEWS not adequately covered are

- Forecasting
- Warning Dissemination and communication
- • Detailed Preparedness and Anticipatory Action
- Adequate emphasis on role of Local, National Governments, NGOs, Media, Private sector, Academic and Research Communities

Disaster Risk Information and Assessments (DRIA) (WMO UNISDR UNESCO Mexico 2017)

DRIA is aligned to component 1 of **MHEWS : i) disaster risk knowledge** using systematic data collection and disaster risk **assessments**.

Risks arise from **hazards, exposure** of people and assets to hazards, their **vulnerabilities** and coping **capacities** at particular location. **Risk Assessments** require systematic data **collection** and **analysis** and **dynamics** and **compounding impacts** of hazards with vulnerabilities from **unplanned urbanization**, changes in **rural land use**, environmental **degradation** and climate **change**. **Risk level** changes depending on actual impacts and consequences and must **include** assessment of **community's coping** and **adaptive capacities** and gauging **perception** of **level of risk** faced by those **vulnerable**.

The **purpose of DRIA** studies are to assess human reactions to warnings, provides insights to **improve EWS performance identify** the **location of vulnerable groups, critical infrastructure** and **assets**, to design **evacuation** strategies including evacuation **routes** and **safe areas**, and **expand warning messages** to include possible **impacts.**

Key questions to ask

Are key hazards and related threats identified? Are exposure, vulnerabilities, capacities and risks assessed? Are roles and responsibilities of stakeholders identified? Is risk information consolidated?

Progress made on **National Loss Data bases** in six states **(Center for Security Studies (CSS), ETH, 2020)**

Austria, France, Germany, New Zealand, Sweden, Switzerland

National Disaster Loss Database, Data sources, Data Readiness, Coordinator, Contributors, Validator, Observers

Challenges and **Limitations:**

1) Patchy data availability; 2) Difficult data aggregation; 3) Private sector data owners (especially for Target D); 4) Cross-country comparability; 5) Indirect economic costs, 6) Tail Risks.

Recommended Actions

a) Utilise existing knowledge in civil society and academia; b) "Good" institutions for good data c) Thinking beyond Sendai.

Chile and Ecuador: National and **Local Strategies, DRIA** and **MHEWS from Multi-Risk Assessment and Management MH RA M (target G) (Greiving S, 2021).**

Chile and Ecuador share **similar hazard profiles**, and **risk assessment** approaches, **specialized technical institutions** for monitoring at national level. From a **political-administrative** perspective, both countries have **centralized**

Table 45.9   Similarities n differences between global input indicator G from **Chile** and **Ecuador**

Indicator G	Chile	Ecuador
Indicator G-2: Do Chile and Ecuador have MH monitoring and forecasting systems in place?	Extensive hazard monitoring and forecasting systems exist, but only for various single hazards (managed by diff authorities).	Extensive hazard monitoring and fore-casting systems exist, but only for single hazards (managed by various different authorities).
Indicator G-3: No of people per 100,000 covered by EW information thru local government or thru natl disseminat mechanisms.	25% of population has comprehensive early warning center which delivers infrmtn thru mobile phone network	No quantitative information available. Early warning information delivered for different hazards by various different agencies
Indicator G-4: Percentage of local governments having a plan to act on early warnings.	68% of municipalities have a Communal Emergency Plan	18% municipalities have action plan on tsunami EW system (only coastal regions), 3–5% municipalities hv plan on volcano EW system volcanic regions
Indicator G-5: Do Chile and Ecuador hv accessible, understandable, usable and relevant DR information and assessment available to people at national and local levels?	Systematic information is openly available.	Accessible, understandable, usable and relevant information available. Most of the data on threats is not open access.
Indicator G-6: %age popn exposed to or at risk from disasters protected thru pre-emptive evacuation following early warning	No quantitative information available.	No quantitative information available.

governments. **Local level does not possess self-governed rights.** Both countries have instructions to ensure inclusion of DRR in local plans, in line with national strategies. Only existence of guidelines to include DRR is insufficient, considering technical and financial limitations that most local-level administrations face. **Specific local institutional arrangements** between municipal councils and institutional actors at other governance levels, **regional governments, ministries,** and **NGOs,** shape quality of risk management. Both countries **widely disregard public participation** and risk communication highly acknowledged as key elements of risk assessment and management and **key root cause** for given vulnerability. Another key vulnerability is **informal settlements** in hazard prone areas and consequent inattention of national government's spending to resettlement schemes. Cascading effects of disruption of infrastructure services is becoming **relevant**, especially after disasters like 2010 earthquake in Chile or Rio Coca Erosion vis a vis the Central Hidroeléctrica Coca Codo Sinclair + oleoductos in Ecuador

5.3 SFDRR Implementation in Africa Targets G and D (Van Niekerk, 2019)

Programme of Action for implementation of Sendai Framework 2015-2030 and Africa Strategy for DRR 2015-2018.

Target G substantially **increases availability** of and **access** to **multi-hazard early warning systems (MHEWS)** and disaster **risk information and assessments** to people **by 2030.**

Five additional African targets were agreed by countries to develop data by 2020 to measure progress in achieving additional targets:

- Substantially increase no of countries with **DRR** in their **educational systems** at all levels, both stand-alone **curriculum** and integrated into different curricula;
- Increase no of countries with **risk-informed preparedness** plans, periodically tested and, response/post-disaster recovery and reconstruction mechanisms;
- Increase **integration** of **DRR** in **regional** and **national sustainable development,** and **climate change adaptation** frameworks, **mechanisms** and processes;
- Substantially expand scope and increase no of **domestic financing sources** in DRR;
- Substantially **increase regional networks** or **partnerships** for knowledge management and capacity development, including specialized regional centres and networks.

Three are related to **selected targets**

Progress

Sendai Target G increase availability of and access to MHEWS:

Data indicates **no significant increase in EWS amongst Member States since 2015,** but some reported refining their systems over last five years. **Eighty-two** percent countries reported **some form** of **MHEWS** in place. **Challenges** are **lack of** systems integration, multiple early warning

systems at various levels and in different sectors that are not coordinated, and national sovereignty issues in cross-border early warning systems. Countries' meteorological and hydrological services are greatest sources of early warning information. Most countries have a **number of single-hazard focused warning systems**, which are **very sector specific** with very little integration. Countries reported increase in MHEWS development and implementation but most countries are concerned on **lack of integration** of these systems. Most countries believed RECs need to play a leading role in ensuring synergies in MHEWS and regional warnings. The main challenge for this indicator is poor coordination at national and regional level. The lack of meteorological data capture platforms or networks also contribute to less effective early warning systems at national levels. Data on the accessibility of these systems by the broader public is limited. Communication processes must be put in place to adequately communicate EW information to those most in need. In achieving Target (g), countries will need to substantially increase the availability of and access to MHEWS and **disaster risk information by 2030**. It is suggested that the **Africa Union Commission**, through the **RECs** and **sharing of information between states**, implementing measures aimed at **better** use and **integration** of EWS and **promoting**, assisting, and enhancing **regional MHEWS** among countries, cognizant of the necessity of sovereign national warnings.

PoA Additional Target 1: Increase **number of countries** with DRR in their **educational systems at all levels**:

- **MS made significant progress in** including **DRR in Education Systems at all levels. At** both primary and secondary level all MS made moderate to substantial progress. **Uptake of DRR within primary and secondary school curriculum has been limited.**
- **Most progress made at tertiary education level** where MS reported substantial achievement of target. More attention to tertiary education, more at post-graduate level than undergraduate, largely due to current need within market and nature of disaster studies.

PoA Additional Target 2: Increase **integration of DRR** in regional and national **sustainable development**, and **climate change adaptation** frameworks, **mechanisms** and processes

- MS made **moderate - substantial progress in integrating DRR, development** and CC **plans.**
- There is **improvement in integrating DRR into environmental policies, insurance sector and other development frameworks and processes** by MS.

PoA Additional Target 4: **Increase** number of **countries** with, and **periodically test**, risk-informed **preparedness**

plans, response, and **post-disaster recovery**/reconstruction mechanisms.

- Most MS reported existence of preparedness and recovery plans and **increase in plans** especially in **south** and **eastern regions**.

EWS in Caribbean National Assessments and Road Maps (Gazole C 2019)

Caribbean Comprehensive Disaster Management (CDM) Strategy 2014 – 2024 prioritizes integrated, improved and expanded community Early Warning Systems.

EWS National Assessments and **South-South Cooperation** - using **MHEWS Checklist**, national *EWS Gap Report*, national *EWS Roadmap* a blueprint for further improvement and investment in EWS and DRR efforts.

Five country case studies Antigua and Barbuda, Dominica, Dominican Republic, Saint Lucia and Saint Vincent and the **Grenadines (SVG)**.

Convener: National Office of Disaster Services (**NODS**), **Antigua** and Barbuda, Office of Disaster Management (**ODM**) **Dominica**, Centre for Emergency Operations (**COE**) in **Dominican Republic**, and National Emergency Management Organizations (**NEMO**) in both **St. Lucia** and Saint **Vincent** and the Grenadines.

Identification of Actors:

- **Central Government Agencies**: DM authority; civil protection (fire departments, ambulance services); police departments; meteorological, seismological and geological services; health, education, environment, agriculture, planning, housing and urban works, energy and telecommunications, air and port authorities, water and sanitation management agencies, and in a few instances, local government departments;
- *District Disaster Coordinators:* Umbrella bodies through which Community DM Committees liaise between communities and national disaster management authorities;
- *International and national NGOs' and entities:* National Red Cross, Caritas, OXFAM, Plan International, Doctors of the World, and Adventist Development and Relief Agency, in addition to UNDP, CDEMA and IFRC;
- *Other stakeholder groups:* Chambers of commerce, radio stations, Councils for persons with disabilities, youth and for older persons, and newspapers, among others.

All Roadmaps contain

(a) Actions linked to the identified priorities;

Table 45.10 Sections and Information in the Gap Reports

DOMINICA	DOMINICAN REPUBLIC	ST. LUCIA
• Disaster History Inventory • EWS Capacities and Assets: National Emergency Planning Organisation structure mandates & HR, DRR Document Inventory Alert Level Actions, EWS Tools and Equipment Inventory - Regional EWS Support by Hazard • Organizational Culture and Readiness Survey	• Disaster History Inventory • Mapping of Disaster Mechanisms and Structures • Mapping of EWS Policy Documents, Protocols, Procedures and Studies	• Current status of EWS tables detailing locations and amount of equipment, range coverage, operational status, funds specific existing policies and systems

Source: Gazole C, 2019

(b) General Timeframe

(c) Responsible lead agency/supporting agencies for each action

Some Roadmaps are costed, specifically by Antigua and Barbuda, Saint Vincent & Grenadines.

Lessons are **learned** in each of the following **areas**, which can guide similar locations

- Launch and Coordination of EWS Gaps report
- Awareness Raising, Preparation and Training of Participants
- Application of Checklist, Verification of Sources and Supporting Evidence
- Formulation and Measurability of the Road Map
- Integration Harmonisation and Alignment
- Engagement of Actors, Participation Consultation and Validation, Dissemination of Road Map
- Conclusions, Upscaling and replication of processes to strengthen EWS

Sendai Target D: Reduce disaster damage to critical infrastructure and disruption of basic services (African Union 2019; UNDRR, 2020; UNDP 2020, World Bank, 2020).

Target D of SFDRR is *"Substantially* **reduce** *disaster* **damage** *to* **critical infrastructure** *and* **disruption of basic services**, *among them* **health** *and* **educational facilities**, *including through* **developing their resilience** *by 2030."*

- D-1 (**Compound**) **Damage** to **critical infrastructure** attributed to disasters. (D2-D4)
- D-2 Number of **destroyed** or **damaged health facilities** attributed to disasters.
- D-3 Number of destroyed or damaged **educational facilities** attributed to disasters.
- D-4 Number of **other** destroyed or damaged **critical infrastructure units** and **facilities** including

transportation units and infrastructures) attributed to disasters. *Protective and green infrastructure should be included where relevant.*

- D-5 (**Compound**) **Disruptions** to **basic services** attributed to disasters. (D6 - D8).
- D-6 Number of **disruptions** to **educational services** attributed to disasters.
- D-7 Number of disruptions to **health** and security service structures and electricity plants and transmission towers and attributed to disasters.
- D-8 Number of **disruptions** to other **basic services** attributed to disasters.

Importance of target (d) of SFDRR, seeks reduction in damage to critical infrastructure by 2030 highlighted on IDDR (13 October), 2019.

SFDRR was launched in 2015. The scale of insured economic losses over three years 2015-2018 are in the top five for insured losses over **last thirty years**, including record-breaking year of **2017** which came to **$135 billion** bookmarked by **$50 billion** in insured losses in **2016** and **$80 billion** in **2018**. Overall insurance industry estimates of direct economic losses during those three years comes to **$665 billion**. A considerable proportion of those losses comes from **infrastructure** failures in high-income countries. These years have coincided with new records on **global warming**; and the last five years being the hottest on record globally. According to UN Office for DRR, an estimated **US$90 trillion will be invested in infrastructure by 2030.** Hence, if infrastructures **built to last**, this is a **great opportunity** to **avoid the creation of new risk** and to **adapt** to extreme weather events, increase possibility of eradicating poverty in low- and middle-income countries by reducing economic losses. (**UNDRR, 2019 and 2020**),

Indicators terminologies in SFDRR Target (d) n SDG Goal 11, Target 11.5.2 'Direct disaster economic loss in relation to global GDP, including disaster damage to critical

Table 45.11 Data disaggregation and statistical processing - SDG 11.5.2 and SFDRR Target(d)

Terminologies	Duration	Assessment Process	Scale
Damage	Physical harm, not structural or architectural, may continue to be habitable, although regarding repair or cleaning within hours after event	Assessed soon after the event to estimate recovery cost and claim insurance payments	These are tangible and relatively easy to measure.
Critical infrastructure	Physical structures, facilities, networks and assets support services economically socially, or operationally essential to functioning society/community	Number of times interruption or damage occurs per population and sector	By country, event, hazard type, sub-national administrative unit, asset
Disruption	Disturbance/ interruption of services, activities, or process affect different segments of population with different degrees of severity, including cases where service delivery continues	Disruptions of services can be measured in smaller units of time, e.g. hours or minutes or seconds	Disruption of services may occur at irregular periods of time (or) can due to lower levels of quality
Basic services	Services needed for all of society to function effectively: water supply, sanitation, health care, education, housing, food supply services by critical infra electricity, telecom, transport, finance, waste management for all of society to function	Duration of service disruption and number of people who did not receive basic services	By destroyed/damaged, transportation mode, service sector (duration: short, medium and long; an affected scale in terms of household numbers)

infrastructure and disruption of basic services'. Gaps in data losses caused by cascading effects due to infrastructure interdependencies are identified as a key challenge for critical infrastructure protection and must be addressed.

A **Preparedness Framework** reflecting **Anticipatory action** with integration of Habitat III's model, is needed as a tool to fill gaps and accommodate dynamics of hazards n resilience in measuring SDGs and SFDRR indicators.

On average, **11% increase in loss of critical infrastructure is** reported by member states (MS 2015-18). Damage to **critical infrastructure and disruption of basic services** significantly **under reported**. MS experience difficulties in reporting damage on critical infrastructure and disruption of basic services.

Data is mostly available or quantified only at national levels, while most losses are sustained at local levels. With available data, countries reported a significant increase in damage from 2015-16 (128%). 9.3 decrease of 24% in 2016-17 and a 58% increase from 2017-18 (UNDRR 2019). Despite

increase in damage reported, losses are less between the comparative periods 2015–16 to 2017–18. Data by countries is only related to number of facilities destroyed or damaged. Very little data on losses are recorded, eg: number of school days lost; impact on supply chains and other business opportunities; or additional deaths and affected people through the loss of health facilities. Although useful to record critical infrastructure losses, it is recommended that countries draw correlations with the direct and indirect economic losses related to Target (c) of the SFDRR (**African Union 2019**).

Targets E G and D in countries

All three are key targets in our seven SFDRR targets, the most specific in terms of action, which need firm action. The challenges faced are reflected in the following Table 45.12.

SFDRR Mid-term Review 2022–Recommendations

SFDRR is coming to its mid-point mark and is doing a mid-term review to assess progress and make adjustments in its broad direction and focus. Clearer linkages with the SDGs

Table 45.12 Number of countries at a specific stage of reporting SFDRR indicators for year 2018 as of Oct 2020. (UNDRR,)

	Not started	In progress	Ready for validation	Validated	Total
Target E	115	21	24	37	197
Target G	130	40	4	23	197
Target D	140	18	10	16	184

Source: UNDRR, 2019 and 2020

and the value of resilience in building sustainability is part of the UNDRR advocacy and repositioning. Attention to the areas of progress committed to by the seven SFDRR targets especially these three will be important, but of most relevance will be their contributions to advancing the SDGs.

Conclusions and Recommendations

We needs to take action to make the implementation decade 2021-2030 more effective in achieving the SDG Targets.

We must first focus on **making progress** and systems in **achieving targets E, G** and **D**. We must progress on achieving our earliest **Target E** set for 2020 at both national and local levels, **speed up progress** and implementation, and achieve the target **by** the SFDRR midpoint, **June 2023 at latest**. We must measure progress on **Target G** Disaster Risk Impact assessment (**DRIA**) and Multi hazard Early Warning System (**MHEWS**). Though targeted for 2030, we must identify **mid-term targets** both of substance and numbers of countries and achieve these **by 2025** latest. Critical infrastructure, the focus of **Target D** should be assessed and progress focussed on ensuring **ongoing** and **new infrastructure** being **built differently** and **better**, looking ahead at the huge volume being planned and implemented. We must work closely with the Coalition on Disaster Resilient Infrastructure (**CDRI**) which has 31 member countries as on mid May 2022. We must reflect on and assess the status of **existing infrastructure** and take up at least 10 % which is **oldest** and **worst off**, to **retrofit or replace**, and then take up the balance in a structured and phased manner. We must document progress and assess SFDRR implementation over last 7 years since 2015 and then set targets for coming every 3 years, 2021-2023, 2024 2026, and 2027-2029, with pending actions taken up in 2030 n rolling forward into expanded agendas.

We must map out the national, state and local level DM institutions and plans in each country, strengthen them and start up institutions and plans where none exist

We must haveDPRR action plans at each level, within and across sectors, using existing sectoral budgets and expand actions with national budgets.

We must routinize action for preparedness and resilience across organisations at each level, and link to development plans at that level. We must implement DM action plans at subnational, district and city levels, continue work with communities, both under projects, with national and local development budgets and through volunteers, using a high volume of local capacity. We must accelerate using the AAPDA Mitra Program and have other countries establish similar schemes and collaborate where they already exist

We must look at SDG targets in country, and ensure that these are implemented through well-resourced action plans. We must integrate our SFDRR/DPRR work into national plans for SDG 2030 and Climate action.

REFERENCES

1. African Union (2019) *Biennial Report on the Programme of Action for the Implementation of the Sendai Framework for Disaster Risk Reduction 2015-2030 in Africa 2015-2018*, Kenya, pp 23
2. Cabinet Office Japan (2018) *Japan: White paper on disaster management, 2018,* Tokyo, Japan, pp 35
3. CADRi Partnership: Capacity for Disaster Reduction Initiative (2020) *Annual Report 2020*, Geneva, Pgs 40
4. Centre for Research on Epidemiology of Disasters-CRED and UN Disaster Risk Reduction (2020), *Human Cost of Disasters– An overview of the last 20 years 2000-2019*, Geneva, Pgs 30
5. Center for Security Studies (CSS), ETH (2020) *Monitoring and Reporting under the Sendai Framework for Disaster Risk Reduction* commissioned by the Federal Office for Civil Protection (FOCP), Zurich, pgs 29 http://www.css.ethz.ch/en/publications/risk-and-resilience-reports.html
6. China National Platform (2010) Department of International Cooperation and Rescue Ministry of Emergency Management; Ministry of Civil Affairs, Government of China, Deputy Director General China National Committee for International Disaster Reduction, (CNCIDR) URL http://www.mca.gov.cn
7. Etinay, N, Egbu, C and Murray V (2018), *Building Urban Resilience for Disaster Risk Management and Reduction*, ISSN 1877-7058 Procedia Engineering 212 https://doi.org/10.1016/j.proe ng.2018.01.074 pp 575-582
8. Gazole C (2019) CDEMA EU IFRC UNDP *Strengthening EWS in the Caribbean – National Assessments and Road Maps*, Jamaica, pp 23
9. Global Facility for Disaster Reduction and Recovery GFDRR and World Bank (2020), *Annual Report 2020 GFDRR: Bringing Resilience to Scale*, Washington DC, Pgs 168 https://reliefweb.int/report/world/gfdrr-annual-report-2020-bringing-resilience-scale
10. Greiving S, et al *Multi-Risk Assessment and Management—A Comparative Study of the Current State of Affairs in Chile and Ecuador* Dortmund, Germany *Sustainability* **2021**, *13*(3), 1366; https://doi.org/10.3390/su13031366 https://www.mdpi.com/journal/sustainability
11. Human Development Report (HDR) 2020 UNDP (2020) *The Next Frontier: Human Development and the Anthropocene*, New York, pgs 412
12. Hardoy J. (IIED – América Latina) and Filippi M.E (PhD candidate, UCL), with Johnson C.(Dr) (UCL), Gencer E.(CUDRR+R), Morera B. (100 Resilient Cities) and Satterthwaite D.(IIED) (2019) and UN Disaster Risk Reduction (2019) *Developing Local Disaster Risk Reduction Strategies: Words into Action*, Geneva, Pgs 59

13. India National Platform (2011) Ministry of Home Affairs (MHA) Government of India URL http://mha.gov.in

14. Japan National Platform (2009) Cabinet Office, Government of Japan Director for Disaster Preparedness, Disaster Management Bureau URL http://www.cao.go.jp

15. Johnson C. (Dr.) (2019) *Challenges in developing an integrative resilient strategy in Kampala, Uganda*, in UNDRR's WIA *Local DRR and Resilience Strategies*, London, pp 84-85

16. Korea National Platform (2013) Ministry of the Interior and Safety (MOIS), Government of Korea, Deputy Director URL http://www.mois.go.kr/eng/a01/engMain.do

17. National Disaster Management Authority, Govt of India URL https://ndma.gov.in

18. Nyandiko Nicodemus, Department of Disaster Management and Sustainable Development, Masinde Muliro, University of Science and Technology, Kenya (2020) *Achieving Sendai Framework in Africa: Progress and challenges toward Target E*, Kakamega, Kenya pp 25

19. Peters K., ODI (2018) *Accelerating Sendai Framework implementation in Asia: Disaster risk reduction in contexts of violence, conflict and fragility*, London, Pgs 40

20. Poljanšek K., Marin-Ferrer M., Vernaccini L., Marzi S., Messina L.(2019), *Review of the Sendai Framework Monitor and Sustainable Development Goals indicators for inclusion in the INFORM Global Risk Index*, Brussels,(EUR 29753 EN, ISBN 978-92-76-03850-4, doi:10.2760/54937), pgs 110

21. ONEMI, (2018) *Chilean National Platform and Action Plan for DRR* (November 2018) Santiago, Chile https://www.researchgate.net/publication/329912607_CHILEAN_NATIONAL_PLATFORM_AND_ACTION_PLAN_FOR_DRR

22. Rego A (2021) *Chapter 11 Target E of Sendai Framework: Current Status and How to complete it by 2022 end*, Bangkok Pgs 18,

23. UN AAAA (2015) *Addis Ababa Action Agenda of the 3rd International Conference on Financing for Development July 2015*, Ethiopia Pgs 68

24. UN AFH (2016) *Agenda for Humanity Annex to Report of the UNSG for the World Humanitarian Summit*, Istanbul, Turkey, Pgs 16

25. UN CBD (1992) *UN Convention on Biological Diversity*, Rio de Janeiro Pp 28

26. UN CCD (1992) *UN Convention to Combat Desertification*, Rio de Janeiro Pp 54

27. UN Development Programme (2020) *Annual Report 2020*, New York, Pgs 48

28. UN Disaster Risk Reduction (2015) *Sendai Framework for Disaster Risk Reduction, 2015-2030*, Geneva, Pgs 38 https://www.undrr.org/publication/sendai-framework-disaster-risk-reduction-2015-2030

29. UN Disaster Risk Reduction (2016) *Report of the Open-ended Intergovernmental Expert Working Group on Indicators and Terminology relating to Disaster Risk Reduction*, Geneva, Pgs 41 https://www.preventionweb.net/publication/report-open-ended-intergovernmental-expert-working-group-indicators-and-terminology

30. UN Disaster Risk Reduction (2017 a) *Sendai Framework Data readiness review*, Geneva, Pgs 77 https://www.undrr.org/publication/sendai-framework-data-readiness-review-2017-global-summary-report

31. UN Disaster Risk Reduction (2017 b) *Words into Action Guidelines:*

32. UN Disaster Risk Reduction (2017 c) *National Disaster Risk Assessment: Words into Action*, Geneva, Pgs 77

33. UN Disaster Risk Reduction (2017 d) *: National focal points for disaster risk reduction, national platforms for disaster risk reduction, local platforms for disaster risk reduction: Words into Action*, Geneva, Pgs 76

34. UNDRR Words Into Action WIA (2017e) Guidelines: Build back better in recovery, rehabilitation and reconstruction (Consultative Version)

35. UN Disaster Risk Reduction (2019 a) *Developing National Disaster Risk Reduction Strategies: Words into Action*, Geneva, Pgs 45 https://www.undrr.org/publication/words-action-guidelines-developing-national-disaster-risk-reduction-strategies

36. UN Disaster Risk Reduction (2019 b) *Developing Local Disaster Risk Reduction Strategies: Words into Action*, WIA 6 Geneva, Pgs 59 https://www.undrr.org/publication/words-action-guidelines-implementation-guide-local-disaster-risk-reduction-and

37. UN Disaster Risk Reduction (2019 c) *UNDRR Work Programme2020-2021*, Geneva, Pgs 64

38. UN Disaster Risk Reduction (2020 a) *Annual Report 2019*, Geneva, Pgs 76 https://www.undrr.org/publication/undrr-annual-report-2019

39. UN Disaster Risk Reduction (2020 b) *Status Report on Target E Implementation*, Geneva, Pgs 54 https://www.undrr.org/publication/status-report-target-e-implementation-2020

40. UN Disaster Risk Reduction (2020 c) *Annual Report 2020*, Geneva, Pgs 88

41. UN Disaster Risk Reduction (2020 d) *ARISE annual report 2020 – Resilient Business, Sustainable World, Geneva/ Deer Park(US)*, Pgs 42

42. UNDRR Words Into Action WIA 4,(2020 e) Guidelines: *Developing national DRR strategies*

43. UNDRR Words Into Action WIA 08 (2020 f): Guidelines on Enhancing disaster preparedness for effective response

44. UN Disaster Risk Reduction (2021) *Nature-based solutions for disaster risk reduction: Words into Action*, Geneva, Pgs 259

45. UN FCCC (1992) *UN Framework Convention on Climate Change*, Rio De Janeiro, pp 9

46. UNFCCC (1998) *Kyoto Protocol to the UN Framework Convention on Climate Change*, Kyoto, Japan, pp 21

47. UNFCCC (2015) *Paris Agreement on Climate Change*, Paris, France, pp 25

48. UN Habitat 3 (2016) *New Urban Agenda*, Quito, Ecuador pp 66 www.habitat3.org

49. UN SDGs (2015) *Transforming our World- The 2030 Agenda for Sustainable Development*, New York, Pp 41 https://www.sustainabledevelopment.un.org

50. Van Niekerk et al. (2019) *Implementing the Sendai Framework in Africa,* International Journal of Disaster Risk Science, Johannesburg Pgs 184–187

51. World Bank (2020) *Global Economic Prospects – Chapter 3,- June 2020*, Washington D C, pp 151–157

52. World Bank, IFC and MIGA (2021) *Climate Change Action Plan 2021- 2025 -Supporting Green, Resilient, and Inclusive Development*, Washington DC, Pgs 62

53. WMO UNISDR UNESCO Mexico (2017) *Multi Hazard Early Warning Systems: A Checklist Outcome of 1st MHEWS Conference in Cancun, Mexico May 2017* (WMO Publication)